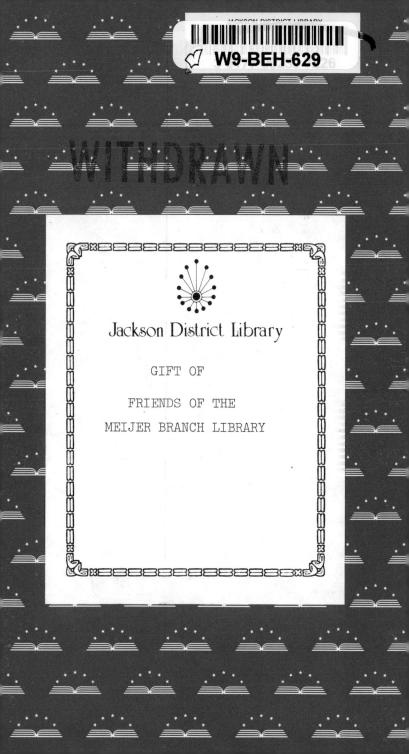

WILLIAM JAMES

WILLIAM JAMES

WRITINGS 1878–1899

Psychology: Briefer Course

*The Will to Believe
and Other Essays in Popular Philosophy*

*Talks to Teachers on Psychology
and to Students on Some of Life's Ideals*

Selected Essays

THE LIBRARY OF AMERICA

Reprinted by permission of the publisher from *Psychology: Briefer Course*;
The Will to Believe and Other Essays in Popular Philosophy; *Talks to Teachers
on Psychology*; *Essays in Philosophy*; *Essays in Psychology*; *Essays in Radical
Empiricism*; *Pragmatism*; and *Essays in Religion and Morality* by William
James; Frederick H. Burkhardt, General Editor, Cambridge, Mass.: Harvard
University Press, Copyright © 1984, 1979, 1983, 1978, 1983, 1976, 1975, 1982
by the President and Fellows of Harvard College.

The paper used in this publication meets the
minimum requirements of the American National Standard for
Information Sciences—Permanence of Paper for Printed
Library Materials, ANSI z39.48—1984.

Distributed to the trade in the United States
and Canada by the Viking Press.

Library of Congress Catalog Number: 91–58225
For cataloging information, see end of Notes.
ISBN 0-940450-72-0.

First Printing
The Library of America—58

Manufactured in the United States of America

GERALD E. MYERS
WROTE THE NOTES AND SELECTED
THE ESSAYS FOR THIS VOLUME

Grateful acknowledgment is made to the National Endowment for the Humanities, the Ford Foundation, and the Andrew W. Mellon Foundation for their generous support of this series.

Contents

Psychology: Briefer Course   1

The Will to Believe and Other Essays
    in Popular Philosophy 445

Talks to Teachers on Psychology
    and to Students on Some of Life's Ideals 705

Selected Essays 889

Chronology 1139

Note on the Texts 1168

Notes 1178

PSYCHOLOGY: BRIEFER COURSE

Preface

IN PREPARING the following abridgment of my larger work, the *Principles of Psychology*, my chief aim has been to make it more directly available for class-room use. For this purpose I have omitted several whole chapters and rewritten others. I have left out all the polemical and historical matter, all the metaphysical discussions and purely speculative passages, most of the quotations, all the book-references, and (I trust) all the impertinences, of the larger work, leaving to the teacher the choice of orally restoring as much of this material as may seem to him good, along with his own remarks on the topics successively studied. Knowing how ignorant the average student is of physiology, I have added brief chapters on the various senses. In this shorter work the general point of view, which I have adopted as that of 'natural science,' has, I imagine, gained in clearness by its extrication from so much critical matter and its more simple and dogmatic statement. About two fifths of the volume is either new or rewritten, the rest is 'scissors and paste.' I regret to have been unable to supply chapters on pleasure and pain, æsthetics, and the moral sense. Possibly the defect may be made up in a later edition, if such a thing should ever be demanded.

I cannot forbear taking advantage of this preface to make a statement about the composition of the *Principles of Psychology*. My critics in the main have been so indulgent that I must cordially thank them; but they have been unanimous in one reproach, namely, that my order of chapters is planless and unnatural; and in one charitable excuse for this, namely, that the work, being largely a collection of review-articles, could not be expected to show as much system as a treatise cast in a single mould. Both the reproach and the excuse misapprehend the facts of the case. The order of composition is doubtless unshapely, or it would not be found so by so many. But planless it is not, for I deliberately followed what seemed to me a good pedagogic order, in proceeding from the more concrete mental aspects with which we are best acquainted to the so-called elements which we naturally come to know later by way of abstraction. The opposite order, of 'building-up' the mind out of its 'units of composition,' has the merit of expository elegance, and gives a neatly subdivided table of contents; but it often purchases these advantages at the cost of reality and truth. I admit that my 'analytic' order was stumblingly carried out; but this again was in consequence of what I thought were pedagogic necessities. On the whole, in spite of my critics, I venture still to think that the 'unsystematic' form charged upon the book is more apparent than profound, and that we really gain a more living understanding of the mind by keeping our attention as long as possible upon our entire conscious states as they are concretely given to us, than by the *post-mortem* study of their comminuted 'elements.' This last is the study of artificial abstractions, not of natural things.[1]

But whether the critics are right, or I am, on this first point, the critics are wrong about the relation of the magazine-articles to the book. With a single exception all the chapters were written for the book; and then by an afterthought some of them were sent to magazines, because the completion of the whole work seemed so distant. My lack of capacity has doubtless been great, but the charge of not having taken the utmost pains, according to my lights, in the composition of the volumes, cannot justly be laid at my door.

[1]In the present volume I have given so much extension to the details of 'Sensation' that I have obeyed custom and put that subject first, although by no means persuaded that such order intrinsically is the best. I feel now (when it is too late for the change to be made) that the chapters on the Production of Motion, on Instinct, and on Emotion ought, for purposes of teaching, to follow immediately upon that on Habit, and that the chapter on Reasoning ought to come in very early, perhaps immediately after that upon the Self. I advise teachers to adopt this modified order, in spite of the fact that with the change of place of 'Reasoning' there ought properly to go a slight amount of re-writing.

Contents

CHAPTER I

Introductory 11
*Psychology defined; psychology as a natural science, its data.
The human mind and its environment. The postulate that
all consciousness has cerebral activity for its condition.*

CHAPTER II

Sensation in General. 18
*Incoming nerve-currents. Terminal organs. 'Specific ener-
gies.' Sensations cognize qualities. Knowledge of acquaintance and knowledge-about. Objects of sensation appear in
space. The intensity of sensations. Weber's law. Fechner's
law. Sensations are not psychic compounds. The 'law of relativity.' Effects of contrast.*

CHAPTER III

Sight 35
*The eye. Accommodation. Convergence, binocular vision.
Double images. Distance. Size, color. After-images. Intensity
of luminous objects.*

CHAPTER IV

Hearing 54
*The ear. The qualities of sound. Pitch. 'Timbre.' Analysis of
compound air-waves. No fusion of elementary sensations of
sound. Harmony and discord. Discrimination by the ear.*

CHAPTER V

Touch, the Temperature Sense, the Muscular Sense,
and Pain 67
*End-organs in the skin. Touch, sense of pressure. Localiza-
tion. Sensibility to temperature. The muscular sense. Pain.*

CHAPTER VI

SENSATIONS OF MOTION   77
*The feeling of motion over surfaces. Feelings in joints. The
sense of translation, the sensibility of the semicircular canals.*

CHAPTER VII

THE STRUCTURE OF THE BRAIN.   84
Embryological sketch. Practical dissection of the sheep's brain.

CHAPTER VIII

THE FUNCTIONS OF THE BRAIN.   98
*General idea of nervous function. The frog's nerve-centres.
The pigeon's nerve-centres. What the hemispheres do. The
automaton-theory. The localization of functions. Brain and
mind have analogous 'elements,' sensory and motor. The
motor zone. Aphasia. The visual region. Mental blindness.
The auditory region, mental deafness. Other centres.*

CHAPTER IX

SOME GENERAL CONDITIONS OF NEURAL ACTIVITY   124
*The nervous discharge. Reaction-time. Simple reactions.
Complicated reactions. The summation of stimuli. Cerebral
blood-supply. Brain-thermometry. Phosphorus and thought.*

CHAPTER X

HABIT   137
*Its importance, and its physical basis. Due to pathways
formed in the centres. Its practical uses. Concatenated acts.
Necessity for guiding sensations in secondarily automatic
performances. Pedagogical maxims concerning the formation
of habits.*

CHAPTER XI

THE STREAM OF CONSCIOUSNESS   152
*Analytic order of our study. Every state of mind forms part
of a personal consciousness. The same state of mind is never
had twice. Permanently recurring ideas are a fiction. Every
personal consciousness is continuous. Substantive and
transitive states. Every object appears with a 'fringe' of
relations. The 'topic' of the thought. Thought may be*

rational in any sort of imagery. Consciousness is always especially interested in some one part of its object.

CHAPTER XII

THE SELF 174

The Me and the I. The material Me. The social Me. The spiritual Me. Self-appreciation. Self-seeking, bodily, social, and spiritual. Rivalry of the Mes. Their hierarchy. Teleology of self-interest. The I, or 'pure ego.' Thoughts are not compounded of 'fused' sensations. The 'soul' as a combining medium. The sense of personal identity. Explained by identity of function in successive passing thoughts. Mutations of the self. Insane delusions. Alternating personalities. Mediumships or possessions. Who is the Thinker.

CHAPTER XIII

ATTENTION 210

The narrowness of the field of consciousness. Dispersed attention. To how much can we attend at once? The varieties of attention. Voluntary attention, its momentary character. To keep our attention, an object must change. Genius and attention. Attention's physiological conditions. The sense-organ must be adapted. The idea of the object must be aroused. Pedagogic remarks. Attention and free-will.

CHAPTER XIV

CONCEPTION 229

Different states of mind can mean the same. Conceptions of abstract, of universal, and of problematic objects. The thought of 'the same' is not the same thought over again.

CHAPTER XV

DISCRIMINATION 234

Discrimination and association; definition of discrimination. Conditions which favor it. The sensation of difference. Differences inferred. The analysis of compound objects. To be easily singled out, a quality should already be separately known. Dissociation by varying concomitants. Practice improves discrimination.

CHAPTER XVI

ASSOCIATION   242

*The order of our ideas. It is determined by cerebral laws.
The ultimate cause of association is habit. The elementary
law in association. Indeterminateness of its results. Total
recall. Partial recall, and the law of interest. Frequency,
recency, vividness, and emotional congruity tend to determine the object recalled. Focalized recall, or 'association by
similarity.' Voluntary trains of thought. The solution of
problems. Similarity no elementary law; summary and
conclusion.*

CHAPTER XVII

THE SENSE OF TIME   266

*The sensible present has duration. We have no sense for
absolutely empty time. We measure duration by the events
which succeed in it. The feeling of past time is a present
feeling. Due to a constant cerebral condition.*

CHAPTER XVIII

MEMORY.   272

*What it is. It involves both retention and recall. Both ele-
ments explained by paths formed by habit in the brain. Two
conditions of a good memory, persistence and numerousness
of paths. Cramming. One's native retentiveness is unchangeable. Improvement of the memory. Recognition.
Forgetting. Pathological conditions.*

CHAPTER XIX

IMAGINATION   286

*What it is. Imaginations differ from man to man; Galton's
statistics of visual imagery. Images of sounds. Images of
movement. Images of touch. Loss of images in aphasia. The
neural process in imagination.*

CHAPTER XX

PERCEPTION   295

*Perception and sensation compared. The perceptive state of
mind is not a compound. Perception is of definite things.
Illusions. First type: inference of the more usual object.*

Second type: inference of the object of which our mind is full. 'Apperception.' Genius and old-fogyism. The physiological process in perception. Hallucinations.

CHAPTER XXI

THE PERCEPTION OF SPACE 316
The attribute of extensity belongs to all objects of sensation. The construction of real space. The processes which it involves: 1) Subdivision; 2) Coalescence of different sensible data into one 'thing'; 3) Location in an environment; 4) Place in a series of positions; 5) Measurement. Objects which are signs, and objects which are realities. The 'third dimension,' Berkeley's theory of distance. The part played by the intellect in space-perception.

CHAPTER XXII

REASONING. 330
What it is. It involves the use of abstract characters. What is meant by an 'essential' character. The 'essence' varies with the subjective interest. The two great points in reasoning, 'sagacity' and 'wisdom.' Sagacity. The help given by association by similarity. The reasoning powers of brutes.

CHAPTER XXIII

CONSCIOUSNESS AND MOVEMENT 347
All consciousness is motor. Three classes of movement to which it leads.

CHAPTER XXIV

EMOTION 350
Emotions compared with instincts. The varieties of emotion are innumerable. The cause of their varieties. The feeling, in the coarser emotions, results from the bodily expression. This view must not be called materialistic. This view explains the great variability of emotion. A corollary verified. An objection replied to. The subtler emotions. Description of fear. Genesis of the emotional reactions.

CHAPTER XXV

INSTINCT. 366

*Its definition. Every instinct is an impulse. Instincts are not
always blind or invariable. Two principles of non-uniformity.
Enumeration of instincts in man. Description of fear.*

CHAPTER XXVI

WILL 387

*Voluntary acts. They are secondary performances. No third
kind of idea is called for. The motor-cue. Ideo-motor action.
Action after deliberation. Five chief types of decision. The
feeling of effort. Healthiness of will. Unhealthiness of will.
The explosive will: 1) from defective inhibition; 2) from exaggerated impulsion. The obstructed will. Effort feels like an
original force. Pleasure and pain as springs of action. What
holds attention determines action. Will is a relation between
the mind and its 'ideas.' Volitional effort is effort of attention. The question of free-will. Ethical importance of the
phenomenon of effort.*

EPILOGUE

PSYCHOLOGY AND PHILOSOPHY. 427

*What the word metaphysics means. Relation of consciousness
to the brain. The relation of states of mind to their 'objects.'
The changing character of consciousness. States of consciousness themselves are not verifiable facts.*

INDEX 435

CHAPTER I

INTRODUCTORY

The definition of Psychology may be best given in the words of Professor Ladd, as the *description and explanation of states of consciousness as such*. By states of consciousness are meant such things as sensations, desires, emotions, cognitions, reasonings, decisions, volitions, and the like. Their 'explanation' must of course include the study of their causes, conditions, and immediate consequences, so far as these can be ascertained.

Psychology is to be treated as a natural science in this book. This requires a word of commentary. Most thinkers have a faith that at bottom there is but one Science of all things, and that until all is known, no one thing can be completely known. Such a science, if realized, would be Philosophy. Meanwhile it is far from being realized; and instead of it, we have a lot of beginnings of knowledge made in different places, and kept separate from each other merely for practical convenience' sake, until with later growth they may run into one body of Truth. These provisional beginnings of learning we call 'the Sciences' in the plural. In order not to be unwieldy, every such science has to stick to its own arbitrarily-selected problems, and to ignore all others. Every science thus accepts certain data unquestioningly, leaving it to the other parts of Philosophy to scrutinize their significance and truth. All the natural sciences, for example, in spite of the fact that farther reflection leads to Idealism, assume that a world of matter exists altogether independently of the perceiving mind. Mechanical Science assumes this matter to have 'mass' and to exert 'force,' defining these terms merely phenomenally, and not troubling itself about certain unintelligibilities which they present on nearer reflection. Motion similarly is assumed by mechanical science to exist independently of the mind, in spite of the difficulties involved in the assumption. So Physics assumes atoms, action at a distance, etc., uncritically; Chemistry uncritically adopts all the data of Physics; and Physiology adopts those of Chemistry. Psychology as a natural science deals with things in the same partial and provisional way. In addition to the 'material world' with all its determinations, which the other sciences of nature assume, she assumes additional data peculiarly her own, and leaves it to more developed parts of Philosophy to test their ulterior significance and truth. These data are—

1. *Thoughts and feelings*, or whatever other names transitory *states of consciousness* may be known by.

2. *Knowledge*, by these states of consciousness, of other facts. These things may be material objects and events, or other states of mind. The material objects may be either near or distant in time and space, and the states of mind may be those of other people, or of the thinker himself at some other time.

How one thing *can* know another is the problem of what is called the Theory of Knowledge. How such a thing as a 'state of mind' can be at all is the problem of what has been called Rational, as distinguished from Empirical, Psychology. The *full* truth about states of mind cannot be known until both Theory of Knowledge and Rational Psychology have said their say. Meanwhile an immense amount of provisional truth about them can be got together, which will work in with the larger truth and be interpreted by it when the proper time arrives. Such a provisional body of propositions about states of mind, and about the cognitions which they enjoy, is what I mean by Psychology considered as a natural science. On any ulterior theory of matter, mind, and knowledge, the facts and laws of Psychology thus understood will have their value. If critics find that this natural-science point of view cuts things too arbitrarily short, they must not blame the book which confines itself to that point of view; rather must they go on themselves to complete it by their deeper thought. Incomplete statements are often practically necessary. To go beyond the usual 'scientific' assumptions in the present case, would require, not a volume, but a shelfful of volumes, and by the present author such a shelfful could not be written at all.

Let it also be added that **the human mind is all that can be touched upon** in this book. Although the mental life of lower creatures has been examined into of late years with some success, we have no space for its consideration here, and can only allude to its manifestations incidentally when they throw light upon our own.

Mental facts cannot be properly studied apart from the physical environment of which they take cognizance. The great fault of the older rational psychology was to set up the soul as an absolute spiritual being with certain faculties of its own by which the several activities of remembering, imagining, reasoning, willing, etc., were explained, almost without reference to the peculiarities of the world with which these activities deal. But the richer insight of modern days perceives that our inner faculties are *adapted* in advance to the features of the world in which we dwell, adapted, I mean, so as to secure our safety and prosperity in its midst. Not only are our capacities for forming new habits, for remembering sequences, and for abstracting general properties from things and associating their usual consequences with them, exactly the faculties needed for steering us in this world of mixed variety and uniformity, but our emotions and instincts are adapted to very special features of that world. In the main, if a phenomenon is important for our welfare, it interests and excites us the first time we come into its presence. Dangerous things fill us with involuntary fear; poisonous things with distaste; indispensable things with appetite. Mind and world in short have been evolved together, and in consequence are something of a mutual fit. The special interactions between the outer order and the order of consciousness, by which this harmony, such as it is, may in the course of time have come about, have been made the subject of many evolutionary speculations, which, though they cannot so far be said to be conclusive, have at least refreshed and enriched the whole subject, and brought all sorts of new questions to the light.

The chief result of all this more modern view is the gradually growing conviction that **mental life is primarily teleological**; that is to say, that our various ways of feeling and thinking have grown to be what they are because of their utility in shaping our *reactions* on the outer world. On the whole, few recent formulas have done more service in psychology than the Spencerian one that the essence of mental life and bodily life are one, namely, 'the adjustment of inner to outer relations.' The adjustment is to immediately present objects in lower animals and in infants. It is to objects more and more remote in time and space, and inferred by means of more and more complex and exact processes of reasoning, when the grade of mental development grows more advanced.

Primarily then, and fundamentally, the mental life is for the sake of action of a preservative sort. Secondarily and incidentally it does many other things, and may even, when ill 'adapted,' lead to its possessor's destruction. Psychology, taken in the widest way, ought to study every sort of mental activity, the useless and harmful sorts as well as that which is 'adapted.' But the study of the harmful in mental life has been made the subject of a special branch called 'Psychiatry'—the science of insanity—and the study of the useless is made over to 'Æsthetics.' Æsthetics and Psychiatry will receive no special notice in this book.

All mental states (no matter what their character as regards utility may be) **are followed by bodily activity of some sort.** They lead to inconspicuous changes in breathing, circulation, general muscular tension, and glandular or other visceral activity, even if they do not lead to conspicuous movements of the muscles of voluntary life. Not only certain particular states of mind, then (such as those called volitions, for example), but states of mind as such, *all* states of mind, even mere thoughts and feelings, are *motor* in their consequences. This will be made manifest in detail as our study advances. Meanwhile let it be set down as one of the fundamental facts of the science with which we are engaged.

It was said above that the 'conditions' of states of consciousness must be studied. **The immediate condition of a state of consciousness is an activity of some sort in the cerebral hemispheres.** This proposition is supported by so many pathological facts, and laid by physiologists at the base of so many of their reasonings, that to the medically educated mind it seems almost axiomatic. It would be hard, however, to give any short and peremptory proof of the unconditional dependence of mental action upon neural change. That a general and usual amount of dependence exists cannot possibly be ignored. One has only to consider how quickly consciousness may be (so far as we know) abolished by a blow on the head, by rapid loss of blood, by an epileptic discharge, by a full dose of alcohol, opium, ether, or nitrous oxide—or how easily it may be altered in quality by a smaller dose of any of these agents or of others, or by a fever,—to see how at the mercy of bodily happenings our spirit is. A little stoppage of the gall-duct, a swallow of cathartic medicine, a cup of strong coffee at the proper moment, will entirely overturn for the time a man's views of life. Our moods and resolutions are more determined by the condition of our circulation than by our logical grounds. Whether a man shall be a hero or a coward is a matter of his temporary 'nerves.' In many kinds of insanity, though by no means in all, distinct alterations of the brain-tissue have been found. Destruction of certain definite portions of the cerebral hemispheres involves losses of memory and of acquired motor faculty of quite determinate sorts, to which we shall revert again under the title of *aphasias.* Taking all such facts together, the simple and radical conception dawns upon the mind that mental action may be uniformly and absolutely a function of brain-action, varying as the latter varies, and being to the brain-action as effect to cause.

This conception is the 'working hypothesis' which underlies all the 'physiological psychology' of recent years, and it will be the working hypothesis of this book. Taken thus absolutely, it may possibly be too sweeping a statement of what in reality is only a partial truth. But the only way to make sure of its unsatisfactoriness is to apply it seriously to every possible case that can turn up. To work an hypothesis 'for all it is worth' is the real, and often the only, way to prove its insufficiency. I shall therefore assume without scruple at the outset that the uniform correlation of brain-states with mind-states is a law of nature. The interpretation of the law in detail will best show where its facilities and where its difficulties lie. To some readers such an assumption will seem like the most unjustifiable *a priori* materialism. In one sense it doubtless is materialism: it puts the Higher at the mercy of the Lower. But although we affirm that the *coming to pass* of thought is a consequence of mechanical laws,—for, according to another 'working hypothesis,' that namely of physiology, the laws of brain-action are at bottom mechanical laws,—we do not in the least explain the *nature* of thought by affirming this dependence, and in that latter sense our proposition is

not materialism. The authors who most unconditionally affirm the dependence of our thoughts on our brain to be a fact
are often the loudest to insist that the fact is inexplicable, and
that the intimate essence of consciousness can never be rationally accounted for by any material cause. It will doubtless
take several generations of psychologists to test the hypothesis
of dependence with anything like minuteness. The books
which postulate it will be to some extent on conjectural
ground. But the student will remember that the Sciences constantly have to take these risks, and habitually advance by zig-
zagging from one absolute formula to another which corrects
it by going too far the other way. At present Psychology is on
the materialistic tack, and ought in the interests of ultimate
success to be allowed full headway even by those who are
certain she will never fetch the port without putting down the
helm once more. The only thing that is perfectly certain is
that when taken up into the total body of Philosophy, the
formulas of Psychology will appear with a very different
meaning from that which they suggest so long as they are
studied from the point of view of an abstract and truncated
'natural science,' however practically necessary and indispensable their study from such a provisional point of view may be.

The Divisions of Psychology.—So far as possible, then,
we are to study states of consciousness in correlation with
their probable neural conditions. Now the nervous system is
well understood to-day to be nothing but a machine for receiving impressions and discharging reactions preservative to
the individual and his kind—so much of physiology the
reader will surely know. Anatomically, therefore, the nervous
system falls into three main divisions, comprising—

1) The fibres which carry currents in;
2) The organs of central redirection of them; and
3) The fibres which carry them out.

Functionally, we have sensation, central reflection, and motion, to correspond to these anatomical divisions. In Psychology we may divide our work according to a similar scheme,
and treat successively of three fundamental conscious processes and their conditions. The first will be Sensation; the
second will be Cerebration or Intellection; the third will be

the Tendency to Action. Much vagueness results from this division, but it has practical conveniences for such a book as this, and they may be allowed to prevail over whatever objections may be urged.

CHAPTER II

SENSATION IN GENERAL

Incoming nerve-currents are the only agents which normally affect the brain. The human nerve-centres are surrounded by many dense wrappings of which the effect is to protect them from the direct action of the forces of the outer world. The hair, the thick skin of the scalp, the skull, and two membranes at least, one of them a tough one, surround the brain; and this organ moreover, like the spinal cord, is bathed by a serous fluid in which it floats suspended. Under these circumstances the only things that can *happen* to the brain are:

1) The dullest and feeblest mechanical jars;

2) Changes in the quantity and quality of the blood-supply; and

3) Currents running in through the so-called afferent or centripetal nerves.

The mechanical jars are usually ineffective; the effects of the blood-changes are usually transient; the nerve-currents, on the contrary, produce consequences of the most vital sort, both at the moment of their arrival, and later, through the invisible paths of escape which they plough in the substance of the organ and which, as we believe, remain as more or less permanent features of its structure, modifying its action throughout all future time.

Each afferent nerve comes from a determinate part of the periphery and is played upon and excited to its inward activity by a particular force of the outer world. Usually it is insensible to other forces: thus the optic nerves are not impressible by air-waves, nor those of the skin by light-waves. The lingual nerve is not excited by aromatic effluvia, the auditory nerve is unaffected by heat. Each selects from the vibrations of the outer world some one rate to which it responds exclusively. The result is that our sensations form a discontinuous series, broken by enormous gaps. There is no reason to suppose that the order of vibrations in the outer world is anything like as interrupted as the order of our sensations. Between the quickest audible air-waves (40,000 vibrations a second at the outside) and the slowest sensible heat-waves (which number probably billions), Nature must somewhere have realized innumerable intermediary rates which we have no nerves for perceiving. The process in the nerve-fibres themselves is very likely the same, or much the same, in all the different nerves. It is the so-called 'current'; but the current is *started* by one order of outer vibrations in the retina, and in the ear, for example, by another. This is due to the different *terminal organs* with which the several afferent nerves are armed. Just as we arm ourselves with a spoon to pick up soup, and with a fork to pick up meat, so our nerve-fibres arm themselves with one sort of end-apparatus to pick up air-waves, with another to pick up ether-waves. The terminal apparatus always consists of modified epithelial cells with which the fibre is continuous. The fibre itself is not directly excitable by the outer agent which impresses the terminal organ. The optic fibres are unmoved by the direct rays of the sun; a cutaneous nerve-trunk may be touched with ice without feeling cold.[1] The fibres are mere transmitters; the terminal organs are so many imperfect telephones into which the material world speaks, and each of which takes up but a portion of what it says; the brain-cells at the fibres' central end are as many others at which the mind listens to the far-off call.

The 'Specific Energies' of the Various Parts of the Brain.—To a certain extent anatomists have traced definitely the paths which the sensory nerve-fibres follow after their entrance into the centres, as far as their termination in the gray matter of the cerebral convolutions.[2] It will be shown on a later page that the consciousness which accompanies the excitement of this gray matter varies from one portion of it to another. It is consciousness of things seen, when the occipital lobes, and of things heard, when the upper part of the tem-

[1] The subject may feel *pain*, however, in this experiment; and it must be admitted that nerve-fibres of every description, terminal organs as well, are to some degree excitable by mechanical violence and by the electric current.

[2] Thus the optic nerve-fibres are traced to the occipital lobes, the olfactory tracts go to the lower part of the temporal lobe (hippocampal convolution), the auditory nerve-fibres pass first to the cerebellum, and probably from thence to the upper part of the temporal lobe. These anatomical terms used in this chapter will be explained later. The *cortex* is the gray surface of the convolutions.

poral lobes, share in the excitement. Each region of the cerebral cortex responds to the stimulation which its afferent
fibres bring to it, in a manner with which a peculiar quality of
feeling seems invariably correlated. This is what has been
called the law of 'specific energies' in the nervous system. Of
course we are without even a conjectural explanation of the
ground of such a law. Psychologists (as Lewes, Wundt,
Rosenthal, Goldscheider, etc.) have debated a good deal as to
whether the specific quality of the feeling depends solely on
the *place* stimulated in the cortex, or on the *sort of current*
which the nerve pours in. Doubtless the sort of outer force
habitually impinging on the end-organ gradually modifies the
end-organ, the sort of commotion received from the end-
organ modifies the fibre, and the sort of current a so-modified
fibre pours into the cortical centre modifies the centre. The
modification of the centre in turn (though no man can guess
how or why) seems to modify the resultant consciousness.
But these adaptive modifications must be excessively slow;
and as matters actually stand in any adult individual, it is safe
to say that, more than anything else, the *place* excited in his
cortex decides what kind of thing he shall feel. Whether we
press the retina, or prick, cut, pinch, or galvanize the living
optic nerve, the Subject always feels flashes of light, since the
ultimate result of our operations is to stimulate the cortex of
his occipital region. Our habitual ways of feeling outer things
thus depend on which convolutions happen to be connected
with the particular end-organs which those things impress.
We *see* the sunshine and the fire, simply because the only peripheral end-organ susceptible of taking up the ether-waves
which these objects radiate excites those particular fibres
which run to the centres of sight. If we could interchange the
inward connections, we should feel the world in altogether
new ways. If, for instance, we could splice the outer extremity
of our optic nerves to our ears, and that of our auditory
nerves to our eyes, we should hear the lightning and see the
thunder, see the symphony and hear the conductor's movements. Such hypotheses as these form a good training for
neophytes in the idealistic philosophy!

Sensation distinguished from Perception.—It is impossible rigorously to *define* a sensation; and in the actual life of

consciousness sensations, popularly so called, and perceptions merge into each other by insensible degrees. All we can say is that *what we mean by sensations are* FIRST *things in the way of consciousness*. They are the *immediate* results upon consciousness of nerve-currents as they enter the brain, and before they have awakened any suggestions or associations with past experience. But it is obvious that *such immediate sensations can only be realized in the earliest days of life*. They are all but impossible to adults with memories and stores of associations acquired. Prior to all impressions on sense-organs, the brain is plunged in deep sleep and consciousness is practically nonexistent. Even the first weeks after birth are passed in almost unbroken sleep by human infants. It takes a strong message from the sense-organs to break this slumber. In a new-born brain this gives rise to an absolutely pure sensation. But the experience leaves its 'unimaginable touch' on the matter of the convolutions, and the next impression which a sense-organ transmits produces a cerebral reaction in which the awakened vestige of the last impression plays its part. Another sort of feeling and a higher grade of cognition are the consequence. 'Ideas' *about* the object mingle with the awareness of its mere sensible presence, we name it, class it, compare it, utter propositions concerning it, and the complication of the possible consciousness which an incoming current may arouse, goes on increasing to the end of life. In general, this higher consciousness about things is called Perception, the mere inarticulate feeling of their presence is Sensation, so far as we have it at all. To some degree we seem able to lapse into this inarticulate feeling at moments when our attention is entirely dispersed.

Sensations are cognitive. A sensation is thus an abstraction seldom realized by itself; and the object which a sensation knows is an abstract object which cannot exist alone. *'Sensible qualities' are the objects of sensation*. The sensations of the eye are aware of the *colors* of things, those of the ear are acquainted with their *sounds*; those of the skin feel their tangible *heaviness, sharpness, warmth* or *coldness*, etc., etc. From all the organs of the body currents may come which reveal to us the quality of *pain*, and to a certain extent that of *pleasure*.

Such qualities as *stickiness, roughness*, etc., are supposed to be felt through the coöperation of muscular sensations with those of the skin. The geometrical qualities of things, on the other hand, their *shapes, bignesses, distances,* etc. (so far as we discriminate and identify them), are by most psychologists supposed to be impossible without the evocation of memories from the past; and the cognition of these attributes is thus considered to exceed the power of sensation pure and simple.

'Knowledge of Acquaintance' and 'Knowledge-about.' —Sensation, thus considered, differs from perception only in the extreme simplicity of its object or content. Its object, being a simple quality, is sensibly *homogeneous*; and its function is that of mere *acquaintance* with this homogeneous seeming fact. Perception's function, on the other hand, is that of knowing something *about* the fact. But we must know *what* and *which* fact we mean, all the while, and the various *whats* and *whiches* are what sensations give. Our earliest thoughts are almost exclusively sensational. They give us a set of *whats*, or *thats*, or *its*; of subjects of discourse in other words, with their relations not yet brought out. The first time we see *light*, in Condillac's phrase we *are* it rather than see it. But all our later optical knowledge is about what this experience gives. And though we were struck blind from that first moment, our scholarship in the subject would lack no essential feature so long as our memory remained. In training-institutions for the blind they teach the pupils as much *about* light as in ordinary schools. Reflection, refraction, the spectrum, the ether-theory, etc., are all studied. But the best taught born-blind pupil of such an establishment yet lacks a knowledge which the least instructed seeing baby has. They can never show him *what* light is in its 'first intention'; and the loss of that sensible knowledge no book-learning can replace. All this is so obvious that we usually find sensation 'postulated' as an element of experience, even by those philosophers who are least inclined to make much of its importance, or to pay respect to the knowledge which it brings.

Sensations distinguished from Images.—Both sensation and perception, for all their difference, are yet alike in that their objects appear *vivid, lively,* and *present.* Objects merely *thought of, recollected,* or *imagined,* on the contrary, are relatively faint and devoid of this pungency, or tang, this quality of *real presence* which the objects of sensation possess. Now the cortical brain-processes to which sensations are attached are due to incoming currents from the periphery of the body—an external object must excite the eye, ear, etc., before the sensation comes. Those cortical processes, on the other hand, to which mere ideas or images are attached are due in all probability to currents from other convolutions. It would seem, then, that the currents from the periphery normally awaken a kind of brain-activity which the currents from other convolutions are inadequate to arouse. To this sort of activity—a profounder degree of disintegration, perhaps—the quality of vividness, presence, or reality in the object of the resultant consciousness seems correlated.

The Exteriority of Objects of Sensation.—Every thing or quality felt is felt in outer space. It is impossible to conceive a brightness or a color otherwise than as extended and outside of the mind. Sounds also appear in space. Contacts are against the body's surface; and pains always occupy some organ. An opinion which has had much currency in psychology is that sensible qualities are first apprehended as *in the mind itself*, and then 'projected' from it, or 'extradited,' by a secondary intellectual or super-sensational mental act. There is no ground whatever for this opinion. The only facts which even seem to make for it can be much better explained in another way, as we shall see later on. The very first sensation which an infant gets *is* for him the outer universe. And the universe which he comes to know in later life is nothing but an amplification of that first simple germ which, by accretion on the one hand and intussusception on the other, has grown so big and complex and articulate that its first estate is unrememberable. In his dumb awakening to the consciousness of *something there*, a mere *this* as yet (or something for which even the term *this* would perhaps be too discriminative, and the intellectual acknowledgment of which would be better expressed by the bare interjection 'lo!'), the infant encounters an object in which (though it be given in a pure sensation) all the 'categories of the understanding' are contained. *It has externality, objectivity, unity, substantiality, causality, in the full sense in which any later object or system of objects has these things.* Here the young knower meets and greets his world; and the miracle of knowledge bursts forth, as Voltaire says, as much in the infant's lowest sensation as in the highest achievement of a Newton's brain.

The physiological condition of this first sensible experience is probably many nerve-currents coming in from various peripheral organs at once; but this multitude of organic conditions does not prevent the consciousness from being one consciousness. We shall see as we go on that it can be one consciousness, even though it be due to the coöperation of numerous organs and be a consciousness of many things together. The Object which the numerous inpouring currents of the baby bring to his consciousness is one big blooming buzzing Confusion. That Confusion is the baby's universe; and the universe of all of us is still to a great extent such a Confusion, potentially resolvable, and demanding to be resolved, but not yet actually resolved, into parts. It appears from first to last as a space-occupying thing. So far as it is unanalyzed and unresolved we may be said to know it sensationally; but as fast as parts are distinguished in it and we become aware of their relations, our knowledge becomes perceptual or even conceptual, and as such need not concern us in the present chapter.

The Intensity of Sensations.—A light may be so weak as not sensibly to dispel the darkness, a sound so low as not to be heard, a contact so faint that we fail to notice it. In other words, a certain finite amount of the outward stimulus is required to produce any sensation of its presence at all. This is called by Fechner the law of the *threshold*—something must be stepped over before the object can gain entrance to the mind. An impression just above the threshold is called the *minimum visibile, audibile*, etc. From this point onwards, as the impressing force increases, the sensation increases also, though at a slower rate, until at least an *acme* of the sensation is reached which no increase in the stimulus can make sensibly more great. Usually, before the acme, *pain* begins to mix with the specific character of the sensation. This is definitely observable in the cases of great pressure, intense heat, cold, light, and sound; and in those of smell and taste less definitely so only from the fact that we can less easily increase the force of the stimuli here. On the other hand, all sensations, how-

ever unpleasant when more intense, are rather agreeable than
otherwise in their very lowest degrees. A faintly bitter taste,
or putrid smell, may at least be *interesting*.

Weber's Law.—I said that the intensity of the sensation
increases by slower steps than those by which its exciting
cause increases. If there were no threshold, and if every equal
increment in the outer stimulus produced an equal increment
in the sensation's intensity, a simple straight line would represent graphically the 'curve' of the relation between the two
things. Let the horizontal line stand for the scale of intensities
of the objective stimulus, so that at o it has no intensity, at 1
intensity 1, and so forth. Let the verticals dropped from the
slanting line stand for the sensations aroused. At o there will
be no sensation; at 1 there will be a sensation represented by
the length of the vertical S^1—1, at 2 the sensation will be
represented by S^2—2, and so on. The line of S's will rise
evenly because by the hypothesis the verticals (or sensations)
increase at the same rate as the horizontals (or stimuli) to
which they severally correspond. But in Nature, as aforesaid,
they increase at a slower rate. If each step forwards in the
horizontal direction be equal to the last, then each step upwards in the vertical direction will have to be somewhat
shorter than the last; the line of sensations will be convex on
top instead of straight.

Fig. 2 represents this actual state of things, o being the
zero-point of the stimulus, and conscious sensation, represented by the curved line, not beginning until the 'threshold'

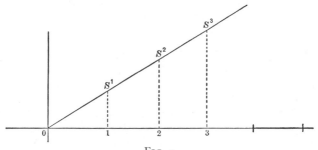

FIG. 1.

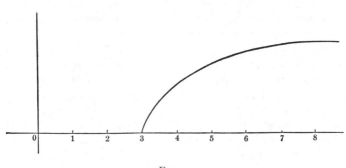

FIG. 2.

is reached, at which the stimulus has the value 3. From here onwards the sensation increases, but it increases less at each step, until at last, the 'acme' being reached, the sensation-line grows flat. The exact law of retardation is called *Weber's law*, from the fact that he first observed it in the case of weights. I will quote Wundt's account of the law and of the facts on which it is based.

"Everyone knows that in the stilly night we hear things unnoticed in the noise of day. The gentle ticking of the clock, the air circulating through the chimney, the cracking of the chairs in the room, and a thousand other slight noises, impress themselves upon our ear. It is equally well known that in the confused hubbub of the streets, or the clamor of a railway, we may lose not only what our neighbor says to us, but even not hear the sound of our own voice. The stars which are brightest at night are invisible by day; and although we see the moon then, she is far paler than at night. Everyone who has had to deal with weights knows that if to a pound in the hand a second pound be added, the difference is immediately felt; whilst if it be added to a hundredweight, we are not aware of the difference at all. . . .

"The sound of the clock, the light of the stars, the pressure of the pound, these are all *stimuli* to our senses, and stimuli whose outward amount remains the same. What then do these experiences teach? Evidently nothing but this, that one and the same stimulus, according to the circumstances under which it operates, will be felt either more or less intensely, or not felt at all. Of what sort now is the alteration in the circumstances upon which this alteration in the feeling may depend? On considering the matter closely we see that it is everywhere of one and the same kind. The tick of the clock is a feeble stimulus for our auditory nerve, which we hear plainly when it is alone, but not when it is added to the strong stimulus of the carriage-wheels and other noises of the day. The light of the stars is a stimulus to the eye. But if the stimulation which this light exerts be added to the strong stimulus of daylight, we feel nothing of it, although we feel it distinctly when it unites itself with the feebler stimulation of the twilight. The poundweight is a stimulus to our skin, which we feel when it joins itself to a preceding stimulus of equal strength, but which vanishes when it is combined with a stimulus a thousand times greater in amount.

"We may therefore lay it down as a general rule that a stimulus, in order to be felt, may be so much the smaller if the already preëxisting stimulation of the organ is small, but must be so much the larger, the greater the preëxisting stimulation is. . . . The simplest relation would obviously be that the sensation should increase in identically the same ratio as the stimulus. . . . But if this simplest of all relations prevailed, . . . the light of the stars, e.g., ought to make as great an addition to the daylight as it does to the darkness of the nocturnal sky, and this we know to be not the case. . . . So it is clear that the strength of the sensations does not increase in proportion to the amount of the stimuli, but more slowly. And now comes the question, in what proportion does the increase of the sensation grow less as the increase of the stimulus grows greater? To answer this question, every-day experiences do not suffice. We need exact measurements, both of the amounts of the various stimuli, and of the intensity of the sensations themselves.

"How to execute these measurements, however, is something which daily experience suggests. To measure the strength of sensations is, as we saw, impossible; we can only measure the difference of sensations. Experience showed us what very unequal differences of sensation might come from equal differences of outward stimulus. But all these experiences expressed themselves in one kind of fact, that the same difference of stimulus could in one case be felt, and in another case not felt at all—a pound felt if added to another pound, but not if added to a hundredweight. . . . We can quickest reach a result with our observations if we start with an arbitrary strength of stimulus, notice what sensation it gives us, and then *see how much we can increase the stimulus without making the sensation seem to change.* If we carry out such observations with stimuli of varying absolute amounts, we shall be forced to choose in an equally varying way the amounts of addition to the stimulus which are capable of giving us a just barely perceptible feeling of *more*. A light to be just perceptible in the twilight need not be near as bright as the starlight; it must be far brighter to be just perceived during the day. If now we institute such observations for all possible strengths of the various stimuli, and note for each strength the amount of addition of the latter required to produce a barely perceptible alteration of sensation, we shall have a series of figures in which is immediately expressed the law according to which the sensation alters when the stimulation is increased. . . ."

Observations according to this method are particularly easy to make in the spheres of light, sound, and pressure. Beginning with the latter case,

"We find a surprisingly simple result. *The barely sensible addition to the original weight must stand exactly in the same proportion to it*, be the *same fraction* of it, no matter what the absolute value may be of the weights on which the experiment is made. . . . As the average of a number of experiments, this fraction is found to be about ⅓; that is, no matter what pressure there may already be made upon the skin, an increase or a diminution of the pressure will be *felt*, as soon as the added or subtracted weight amounts to one third of the weight originally there."

Wundt then describes how differences may be observed in the muscular feelings, in the feelings of heat, in those of light, and in those of sound; and he concludes thus:

"So we have found that all the senses whose stimuli we are enabled to measure accurately, obey a uniform law. However various may be their several delicacies of discrimination, *this* holds true of all, that *the increase of the stimulus necessary to produce an increase of the sensation bears a constant ratio to the total stimulus*. The figures which express this ratio in the several senses may be shown thus in tabular form:

$$
\begin{array}{lll}
\text{Sensation of light} & \ .\ \ .\ \ .\ \ . & \frac{1}{100} \\
\text{Muscular sensation} & \ .\ \ .\ \ .\ \ . & \frac{1}{17} \\
\left.\begin{array}{l}\text{Feeling of pressure,}\\ \quad''\quad\ ''\ \text{ warmth,}\\ \quad''\quad\ ''\ \text{ sound,}\end{array}\right\} & \ .\ \ .\ \ .\ \ . & \frac{1}{8}
\end{array}
$$

"These figures are far from giving as accurate a measure as might be desired. But at least they are fit to convey a general notion of the relative discriminative susceptibility of the different senses. . . . The important law which gives in so simple a form the relation of the sensation to the stimulus that calls it forth was first discovered by the physiologist Ernst Heinrich Weber to obtain in special cases."[3]

Fechner's Law. — Another way of expressing Weber's law is to say that to get equal positive additions to the sensation, one must make equal *relative* additions to the stimulus. Professor Fechner of Leipzig founded upon Weber's law a theory of the numerical measurement of sensations, over which much metaphysical discussion has raged. Each just perceptible addition to the sensation, as we gradually let the stimulus increase, was supposed by him to be a *unit* of sensation, and all these units were treated by him as equal, in spite of the fact that *equally perceptible* increments need by no means appear *equally big* when they once are perceived. The many pounds which form the just perceptible addition to a hundredweight feel bigger when added than the few ounces which form the just perceptible addition to a pound. Fechner ignored this fact. He considered that if *n* distinct perceptible steps of increase might be passed through in gradually increasing a stimulus from the threshold-value till the intensity *s* was felt, then the sensation of *s* was composed of *n* units, which were of the same value all along the line.[4] Sensations once represented by numbers, psychology may become, according to Fechner, an 'exact' science, susceptible of mathematical treatment. His general formula for getting at the number of units in any sensation is $S = C \log R$, where S stands for the sensation, R for the stimulus numerically estimated, and C for a constant that must be separately determined by experiment in each particular order of sensibility. The sensation is proportional to the logarithm of the stimulus; and the absolute values, in units, of any series of sensations might be got from the ordinates of the curve in Fig. 2, if

---

[3] *Vorlesungen über die Menschen- und Thierseele*, Lecture VII.

[4] In other words, S standing for the sensation in general, and Δ for its noticeable increment, we have the equation $\Delta S = $ const. The increment of stimulus which produces ΔS (call it ΔR) meanwhile varies. Fechner calls it the 'differential threshold'; and as its *relative* value to R is always the same, we have the equation $\Delta R / R = $ const.

it were a correctly drawn logarithmic curve, with the thresholds rightly plotted out from experiments.

Fechner's psycho-physic formula, as he called it, has been attacked on every hand; and as absolutely nothing practical has come of it, it need receive no farther notice here. The main outcome of his book has been to stir up experimental investigation into the validity of Weber's law (which concerns itself merely with the just perceptible increase, and says nothing about the measurement of the sensation as a whole) and to promote discussion of statistical methods. Weber's law, as will appear when we take the senses, *seriatim*, is only approximately verified. The discussion of statistical methods is necessitated by the extraordinary fluctuations of our sensibility from one moment to the next. It is found, namely, when the difference of two sensations approaches the limit of discernibility, that at one moment we discern it and at the next we do not. Our incessant accidental inner alterations make it impossible to tell just what the least discernible increment of the sensation is without taking the average of a large number of appreciations. These *accidental errors* are as likely to increase as to diminish our sensibility, and are eliminated in such an average, for those above and those below the line then neutralize each other in the sum, and the normal sensibility, if there be one (that is, the sensibility due to constant causes as distinguished from these accidental ones), stands revealed. The methods of getting the average all have their difficulties and their snares, and controversy over them has become very subtle indeed. As an instance of how laborious some of the statistical methods are, and how patient German investigators can be, I may say that Fechner himself, in testing Weber's law for weights by the so-called 'method of true and false cases,' tabulated and computed no less than 24,576 separate judgments.

Sensations are not compounds. The fundamental objection to Fechner's whole attempt seems to be this, that although the outer *causes* of our sensations may have many parts, every distinguishable degree, as well as every distinguishable quality, of the *sensation itself* appears to be a unique fact of consciousness. Each sensation is a complete integer. "A strong one," as Dr. Münsterberg says, "is not the multiple of a weak one, or a compound of many weak ones, but rather something entirely new, and as it were incomparable, so that to seek a measurable difference between strong and weak sonorous, luminous, or thermic sensations would seem at first sight as senseless as to try to compute mathematically the difference between salt and sour, or between headache and toothache. It is clear that if in the stronger sensation of light the weaker sensation is not *contained*, it is unpsychological to say that the former differs from the latter by a certain *increment*."[5] Surely our feeling of scarlet is not a feeling of pink with a lot more pink added; it is something quite other than pink. Similarly with our sensation of an electric arc-light: it does not contain that of many smoky tallow candles in itself. Every sensation presents itself as an indivisible unit; and it is quite impossible to read any clear meaning into the notion that they are masses of units combined.

There is no inconsistency between this statement and the fact that, starting with a weak sensation and increasing it, we feel 'more,' 'more,' 'more,' as the increase goes on. It is not more of the same *stuff* added, so to speak; but it is more and more *difference*, more and more *distance*, which we feel between the sensation we start from and the one we compare with it, each being a unit. In the chapter on Discrimination we shall see that Difference can be perceived between simple things. We shall see, too, that *differences themselves differ*— there are *various directions of difference*; and along any one of them a series of things may be arranged so as to increase steadily in that direction. In any such series the end differs more from the beginning than the middle does. Differences of 'intensity' form one such direction of possible increase—so our judgments of more intensity can be expressed without the hypothesis that more units have been added to a growing sum.

The so-called 'Law of Relativity.'—Weber's law seems only one case of the still wider law that the more we have to attend to the less capable we are of noticing any one detail. The law is obvious where the things differ in kind. How easily do we forget a bodily discomfort when conversation waxes hot; how little do we notice the noises in the room so long as

[5]*Beiträge zur experimentellen Psychologie*, Heft 3, p. 3.

our work absorbs us! *Ad plura intentus minus est ad singula sensus*, as the old proverb says. One might now add that the homogeneity of what we have to attend to does not alter the result; but that a mind with two strong sensations of the same sort already before it is incapacitated by their amount from noticing the detail of a difference between them which it would immediately be struck by, were the sensations themselves weaker and consequently endowed with less distracting power.

This particular idea may be taken for what it is worth.[6] Meanwhile it is an undoubted general fact that the psychical effect of incoming currents does depend on what other currents may be simultaneously pouring in. Not only the *perceptibility* of the object which the current brings before the mind, but the *quality* of it, is changed by the other currents. "Simultaneous[7] sensations modify each other" is a brief expression for this law. "We feel all things in relation to each other" is Wundt's vaguer formula for this general 'law of relativity,' which in one shape or other has had vogue since Hobbes's time in psychology. Much mystery has been made of it, but although we are of course ignorant of the more intimate processes involved, there seems no ground to doubt that they are physiological, and come from the interference of one current with another. A current interfered with might naturally give rise to a modified sensation.

Examples of the modification in question are easy to find.[8] Notes make each other sweeter in a chord, and so do colors when harmoniously combined. A certain amount of skin dipped in hot water gives the perception of a certain heat. More skin immersed makes the heat much more intense, although of course the water's heat is the same. Similarly there is a *chromatic minimum* of size in objects. The image they cast

[6] I borrow it from Ziehen: *Leitfaden der physiologischen Psychologie*, 1891, p. 36, who quotes Hering's version of it.

[7] Successive ones also; but I consider simultaneous ones only, for simplicity's sake.

[8] The extreme case is where green light and red, *e.g.*, falling simultaneously on the retina, give a sensation of yellow. But I abstract from this because it is not certain that the incoming currents here affect different fibres of the optic nerve.

on the retina must needs excite a sufficient number of fibres, or it will give no sensation of color at all. Weber observed that a thaler laid on the skin of the forehead feels heavier when cold than when warm. Urbantschitsch has found that all our sense-organs influence each other's sensations. The hue of patches of color so distant as not to be recognized was immediately, in his patients, perceived when a tuning-fork was sounded close to the ear. Letters too far off to be read could be read when the tuning-fork was heard, etc., etc. The most familiar examples of this sort of thing seem to be the increase of *pain* by noise or light, and the increase of *nausea* by all concomitant sensations.

Effects of Contrast.—The best-known examples of the way in which one nerve-current modifies another are the phenomena of what is known as 'simultaneous color-contrast.' Take a number of sheets of brightly and differently colored papers, lay on each of them a bit of one and the same kind of gray paper, then cover each sheet with some transparent white paper, which softens the look of both the gray paper and the colored ground. The gray patch will appear in each case tinged by the color *complementary* to the ground; and so different will the several pieces appear that no observer, before raising the transparent paper, will believe them all cut out of the same gray. Helmholtz has interpreted these results as being due to a false application of an inveterate habit—that, namely, of making allowance for the color of the medium through which things are seen. The same *thing*, in the blue light of a clear sky, in the reddish-yellow light of a candle, in the dark brown light of a polished mahogany table which may reflect its image, is always judged of its own proper color, which the mind *adds* out of its own knowledge to the appearance, thereby correcting the falsifying medium. In the cases of the papers, according to Helmholtz, the mind believes the color of the ground, subdued by the transparent paper, to be faintly spread *over* the gray patch. But a patch to *look* gray through such a colored film would have really to *be* of the complementary color to the film. Therefore it *is* of the complementary color, we think, and proceed to *see* it of that color.

This theory has been shown to be untenable by Hering. The discussion of the facts is too minute for recapitulation here, but suffice it to say that it proves the phenomenon to be physiological—a case of the way in which, when sensory nerve-currents run in together, the effect of each on consciousness is different from that which it would be if they ran in separately.

'*Successive contrast*' differs from simultaneous contrast and is supposed to be due to fatigue. The facts will be noticed under the head of 'after-images,' in the section on Vision. It must be borne in mind, however, that after-images from previous sensations may coexist with present sensations, and the two may modify each other just as coexisting sensational processes do.

Other senses than sight show phenomena of contrast, but they are much less obvious, so I will not notice them here. We can now pass to a very brief survey of the various senses in detail.

CHAPTER III

SIGHT

The **Eye's Structure** is described in all the books on anatomy. I will only mention the few points which concern the psychologist.[1] It is a flattish sphere formed by a tough white membrane (the sclerotic), which encloses a nervous surface and certain refracting media (lens and 'humors') which cast a picture of the outer world thereon. It is in fact a little camera obscura, the essential part of which is the sensitive plate.

[1]The student can easily verify the coarser features of the eye's anatomy upon a bullock's eye, which any butcher will furnish. Clean it first from fat and muscles and study its shape, etc., and then (following Golding Bird's method) make an incision with a pointed scalpel into the sclerotic half an inch from the edge of the cornea, so that the black choroid membrane comes into view. Next with one blade of a pair of scissors inserted into this aperture, cut through sclerotic, choroid, and retina (avoid wounding the membrane of the vitreous body!) all round the eyeball parallel to the cornea's edge.

The eyeball is thus divided into two parts, the anterior one containing the iris, lens, vitreous body, etc., whilst the posterior one contains most of the retina. The two parts can be separated by immersing the eyeball in water, cornea downwards, and simply pulling off the portion to which the optic nerve is attached. Floating this detached posterior cap in water, the delicate retina will be seen spread out over the choroid (which is partly iridescent in the ox tribe); and by turning the cup inside out, and working under water with a camel's-hair brush, the vessels and nerves of the eyeball may be detected.

The anterior part of the eyeball can then be attacked. Seize with forceps on each side the edge of the sclerotic and choroid (not including the retina), raise the eye with the forceps thus applied and shake it gently till the vitreous body, lens, capsule, ligament, etc., drop out by their weight, and separate from the iris, ciliary processes, cornea, and sclerotic, which remains in the forceps. Examine these latter parts, and get a view of the ciliary muscle which appears as a white line, when with camel's-hair brush and scalpel the choroid membrane is detached from the sclerotic as far forwards as it will go. Turning to the parts that cling to the vitreous body observe the clear ring around the lens, and radiating outside of it the marks made by the ciliary processes before they were torn away from its suspensory ligament. A fine capillary tube may now be used to insufflate the clear ring, just below the letter *p* in Fig. 3, and thus to reveal the suspensory ligament itself.

All these parts can be seen in section in a frozen eye or one hardened in alcohol.

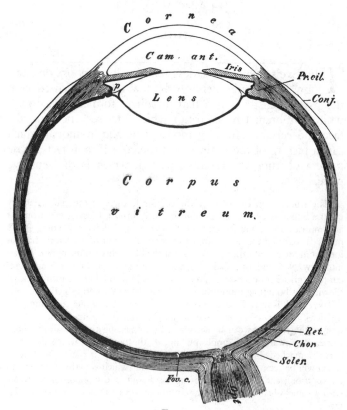

FIG. 3.

The retina is what corresponds to this plate. The optic nerve pierces the sclerotic shell and spreads its fibres radially in every direction over its inside, forming a thin translucent film (see Fig. 3, *Ret.*). The fibres pass into a complicated apparatus of cells, granules, and branches (Fig. 4), and finally end in the so-called rods and cones (Fig. 4,—9), which are the specific organs for taking up the influence of the waves of light. Strange to say, these end-organs are not pointed forwards towards the light as it streams through the pupil, but backwards towards the sclerotic membrane itself, so that the light-waves traverse the translucent nerve-fibres, and the

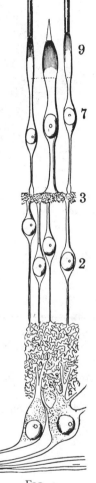

FIG. 4.

cellular and granular layers of the retina, before they touch
the rods and cones themselves. (See Fig. 5.)

The Blind Spot.—The optic nerve-fibres must thus be un-
impressible by light directly. The place where the nerve enters
is in fact entirely blind, because nothing but fibres exist there,

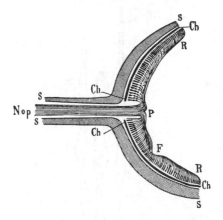

FIG. 5.—Scheme of retinal fibres, after Küss. *Nop*, optic nerve; *S*, sclerotic; *Ch*, choroid; *R*, retina; *P*, papilla (blind spot); *F*, fovea.

the other layers of the retina only beginning round about the entrance. Nothing is easier than to prove the existence of this blind spot. Close the right eye and look steadily with the left at the cross in Fig. 6, holding the book vertically in front of the face, and moving it to and fro. It will be found that at about a foot off the black disk disappears; but when the page is nearer or farther, it is seen. During the experiment the gaze must be kept fixed on the cross. It is easy to show by measurement that this blind spot lies where the optic nerve enters.

The Fovea.—Outside of the blind spot the sensibility of the retina varies. It is greatest at the *fovea*, a little pit lying

FIG. 6.

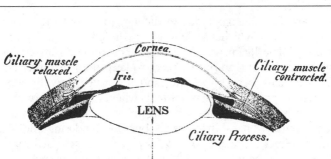

F<small>IG</small>. 7.

outwardly from the entrance of the optic nerve, and round which the radiating nerve-fibres bend without passing over it. The other layers also disappear at the fovea, leaving the cones alone to represent the retina there. The sensibility of the retina grows progressively less towards its periphery, by means of which neither colors, shapes, nor number of impressions can be well discriminated.

In the normal use of our two eyes, the eyeballs are rotated so as to cause the two images of any object which catches the attention to fall on the two foveæ, as the spots of acutest vision. This happens involuntarily, as anyone may observe. In fact, it is almost impossible *not* to 'turn the eyes,' the moment any peripherally lying object does catch our attention, the turning of the eyes being only another name for such rotation of the eyeballs as will bring the foveæ under the object's image.

Accommodation.—The *focussing* or *sharpening* of the image is performed by a special apparatus. In every camera, the farther the object is from the eye the farther forwards, and the nearer the object is to the eye the farther backwards, is its image thrown. In photographers' cameras the back is made to slide, and can be drawn away from the lens when the object that casts the picture is near, and pushed forwards when it is far. The picture is thus kept always sharp. But no such change of length is possible in the eyeball; and the same result is reached in another way. The lens, namely, grows more convex when a near object is looked at, and flatter when the object recedes. This change is due to the antagonism of the circular 'ligament' in which the lens is suspended, and the 'ciliary muscle.' The ligament, when the ciliary muscle is at rest, assumes such a spread-out shape as to keep the lens rather flat. But the lens is highly elastic; and it springs into the more convex form which is natural to it whenever the ciliary muscle, by contracting, causes the ligament to relax its pressure. The contraction of the muscle, by thus rendering the lens more refractive, adapts the eye for near objects ('accommodates' it for them, as we say); and its relaxation, by rendering the lens less refractive, adapts the eye for distant vision. Accommodation for the near is thus the more *active* change, since it involves contraction of the ciliary muscle. When we look far off, we simply let our eyes go passive. We feel this difference in the effort when we compare the two sensations of change.

Convergence accompanies accommodation. The two eyes act as one organ; that is, when an object catches the attention, both eyeballs turn so that its images may fall on the foveæ. When the object is near, this naturally requires them to turn inwards, or converge; and as accommodation then also occurs, the two movements of convergence and accommodation form a naturally associated couple, of which it is difficult to execute either singly. Contraction of the pupil also accompanies the accommodative act. When we come to stereoscopic vision, it will appear that by much practice one can learn to converge with relaxed accommodation, and to accommodate with parallel axes of vision. These are accomplishments which the student of psychological optics will find most useful.

Single Vision by the two Retinæ.—We hear single with two ears, and smell single with two nostrils, and we also see single with two eyes. The difference is that we also *can* see double under certain conditions, whereas under no conditions can we hear or smell double. The main conditions of single vision can be simply expressed.

In the first place, impressions on the two foveæ always appear in the same place. By no artifice can they be made to appear alongside of each other. The result is that one object, casting its images on the foveæ of the two converging eyeballs will necessarily always appear as what it is, namely,

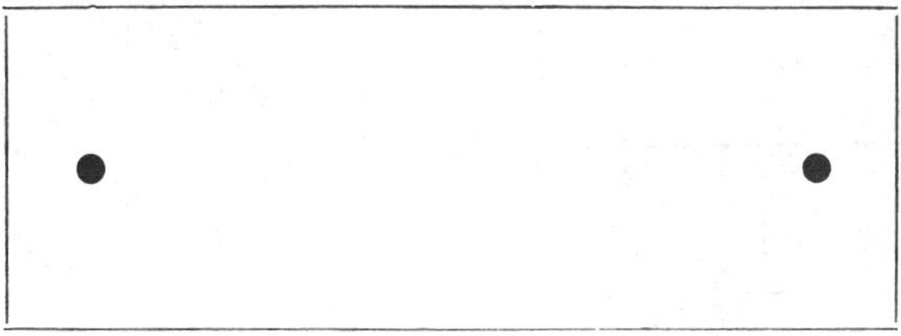

Fig. 8.

one object. Furthermore, if the eyeballs, instead of converging, are kept parallel, and two similar objects, one in front
of each, cast their respective images on the foveæ, the two
will also appear as one, or (in common parlance) 'their images
will fuse.' To verify this, let the reader stare fixedly before
him as if through the paper at infinite distance, with the
black spots in Fig. 8 in front of his respective eyes. He will
then see the two black spots swim together, as it were, and
combine into one, which appears situated between their
original two positions and as if opposite the root of his
nose. This combined spot is the result of the spots opposite
both eyes being seen in the same place. But in addition to the
combined spot, each eye sees also the spot opposite the *other*
eye. To the right eye this appears to the left of the combined
spot, to the left eye it appears to the right of it; so that
what is seen is *three* spots, of which the middle one is seen by
both eyes, and is flanked by two others, each seen by one.
That such are the facts can be tested by interposing some
small opaque object so as to cut off the vision of either
of the spots in the figure from the *other* eye. A vertical partition in the median plane, going from the paper to the nose,
will effectually confine each eye's vision to the spot in front
of it, and then the single combined spot will be all that
appears.[2]

If, instead of two identical spots, we use two different figures, or two differently colored spots, as objects for the two
foveæ to look at, they still are seen in the *same place*; but since

[2]This vertical partition is introduced into stereoscopes, which otherwise
would give us three pictures instead of one.

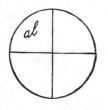

FIG. 9.

they cannot appear as a single object, they appear there *alternately* displacing each other from the view. This is the phenomenon called *retinal rivalry*.

As regards the parts of the retinæ round about the foveæ, a similar correspondence obtains. Any impression on the upper half of either retina makes us see an object as below, on the lower half as above, the horizon; and on the right half of either retina, an impression makes us see an object to the left, on the left half one to the right, of the median line. Thus each quadrant of one retina corresponds as a whole to the geometrically *similar* quadrant of the other; and within two similar quadrants, *al* and *ar* for example, there should, if the correspondence were carried out in detail, be geometrically similar points which, if impressed at the same time by light emitted from the same object, should cause that object to appear in the same direction to either eye. Experiment verifies this surmise. If we look at the starry vault with parallel eyes, the stars all seem single; and the laws of perspective show that under the circumstances the parallel light-rays coming from each star must impinge on points within either retina which *are* geometrically similar to each other. Similarly, a pair of spectacles held an inch or so from the eyes seem like one large median glass. Or we may make an experiment like that with the spots. If we take two exactly similar pictures, no larger than those on an ordinary stereoscopic slide, and if we look at one with each eye (a median partition confining the view) we shall see but one flat picture, all of whose parts appear single. 'Identical retinal points' being impressed, both eyes see their object in the same direction, and the two objects consequently coalesce into one.

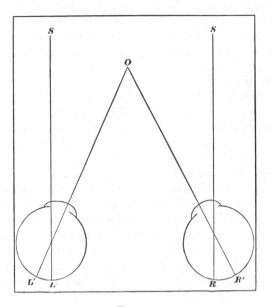

FIG. 10.

Here again retinal rivalry occurs if the pictures differ. And it must be noted that when the experiment is performed for the first time the combined picture is always far from sharp. This is due to the difficulty mentioned on p. 39, of accommodating for anything as near as the surface of the paper, whilst at the same time the convergence is relaxed so that each eye sees the picture in front of itself.

Double Images.—Now it is an immediate consequence of the law of identical location of images falling on geometrically similar points that *images which fall upon geometrically* DIS-PARATE *points of the two retinæ should be seen in* DISPARATE *directions, and that their objects should consequently appear in* TWO *places, or* LOOK DOUBLE. Take the parallel rays from a star falling upon two eyes which converge upon a near object, *O*, instead of being parallel as in the previously instanced case. The two foveæ will receive the images of *O*, which therefore will look single. If then *SL* and *SR* in Fig. 10 be the parallel rays, each of them will fall upon the nasal half of the retina which it strikes. But the two nasal halves are disparate, geo-metrically *symmetrical*, not geometrically *similar*. The star's image on the left eye will therefore appear as if lying to the left of *O*; its image on the right eye will appear to the right of this point. The star will, in short, be seen double—'homony-mously' double.

Conversely, if the star be looked at directly with parallel axes, any near object like *O* will be seen double, because its images will affect the outer or cheek halves of the two retinæ, instead of one outer and one nasal half. The position of the images will here be reversed from that of the previous case. The right eye's image will now appear to the left, the left eye's to the right; the double images will be 'heteronymous.'

The same reasoning and the same result ought to apply where the object's place with respect to the direction of the two optic axes is such as to make its images fall not on non-similar retinal halves, but on non-similar parts of similar halves. Here, of course, the positions seen will be less widely disparate than in the other case, and the double images will appear to lie less widely apart.

Careful experiments made by many observers according to the so-called haploscopic method confirm this law, and show that *corresponding points, of single visual direction*, exist upon the two retinæ. For the detail of these one must consult the spe-cial treatises.

Vision of Solidity.—This description of binocular vision follows what is called the theory of identical points. On the whole it formulates the facts correctly. The only odd thing is that we should be so little troubled by the innumerable dou-ble images which objects nearer and farther than the point looked at must be constantly producing. The answer to this is that *we have trained ourselves to habits of inattention* in regard to double images. So far as things interest us we turn our foveæ upon them, and they are necessarily seen single; so that if an object impresses disparate points, that may be taken as proof that it is so unimportant for us that we needn't notice whether it appears in one place or in two. By long practice one may acquire great expertness in detecting double images, though, as someone says, it is an art which is not to be learned completely either in one year or in two.

FIG. II

Where the disparity of the images is but slight it is almost impossible to see them as if double. They give rather the perception of a solid object being there. To fix our ideas, take Fig. 11. Suppose we look at the dots in the middle of the lines *a* and *b* just as we looked at the spots in Fig. 8. We shall get the same result—i.e., they will coalesce in the median line. But the entire lines will not coalesce, for, owing to their inclination, their tops fall on the temporal, and their bottoms on the nasal, retinal halves. What we see will be two lines crossed in the middle, thus (Fig. 12):

FIG. 12.   FIG. 13.   FIG. 14.

The moment we attend to the tops of these lines, however, our foveæ tend to abandon the dots and to move upwards, and in doing so, to converge somewhat, following the lines, which then appear coalescing at the top as in Fig. 13.

If we think of the bottom, the eyes descend and diverge, and what we see is Fig. 14.

Running our eyes up and down the lines makes them con-

verge and diverge just as they would were they running up
and down some single line whose top was nearer to us than
its bottom. Now, if the inclination of the lines be moderate,
we may not see them double at all, but single throughout
their length, when we look at the dots. Under these conditions their top does look nearer than their bottom—in other
words, we see them stereoscopically; and we see them so even
when our eyes are rigorously motionless. In other words, the
slight disparity in the bottom-ends which *would* draw the
foveæ divergently apart makes us see those ends farther, the
slight disparity in the top ends which *would* draw them con-
vergently together makes us see these ends nearer, than the
point at which we look. The disparities, in short, affect our
perception as the actual movements would.[3]

The Perception of Distance.—When we look about us at
things, our eyes are incessantly moving, converging, diverging, accommodating, relaxing, and sweeping over the field.
The field appears extended in three dimensions, with some of
its parts more distant and some more near.

"With one eye our perception of distance is very imperfect, as
illustrated by the common trick of holding a ring suspended by a
string in front of a person's face, and telling him to shut one eye and
pass a rod from one side through the ring. If a penholder be held
erect before one eye, while the other is closed, and an attempt be
made to touch it with a finger moved across towards it, an error will
nearly always be made. . . . In such cases we get the only clue from
the amount of effort needed to 'accommodate' the eye to see the
object distinctly. When we use both eyes our perception of distance
is much better; when we look at an object with two eyes the visual
axes are converged on it, and the nearer the object the greater the
convergence. We have a pretty accurate knowledge of the degree of
muscular effort required to converge the eyes on all tolerably near
points. When objects are farther off, their apparent size, and the
modifications their retinal images experience by aërial perspective,

---

[3]The simplest form of stereoscope is two tin tubes about one and one-half
inches calibre, dead black inside and (for normal eyes) ten inches long. Close
each end with paper not too opaque, on which an inch-long thick black line
is drawn. The tubes can be looked through, one by each eye, and held either
parallel or with their farther ends converging. When properly rotated, their
images will show every variety of fusion and non-fusion, and stereoscopic
effect.

come in to help. The relative distance of objects is easiest determined by moving the eyes; all stationary objects then appear displaced in the opposite direction (as for example when we look out of the window of a railway car) and those nearest most rapidly; from the different apparent rates of movement we can tell which are farther and which nearer."[4]

Subjectively considered, distance is an altogether peculiar content of consciousness. Convergence, accommodation, binocular disparity, size, degree of brightness, parallax, etc., all give us special feelings which are *signs* of the distance feeling, but not it. They simply suggest it to us. The best way to get it strongly is to go upon some hill-top and invert one's head. The horizon then looks very distant, and draws near as the head erects itself again.

The Perception of Size.—"The dimensions of the retinal image determine primarily the sensations on which conclusions as to size are based; and the larger the visual angle the larger the retinal image: since the visual angle depends on the distance of an object the correct perception of size depends largely upon a correct perception of distance; having formed a judgment, conscious or unconscious, as to that, we conclude as to size from the extent of the retinal region affected. Most people have been surprised now and then to find that what appeared a large bird in the clouds was only a small insect close to the eye; the large apparent size being due to the previous incorrect judgment as to the distance of the object. The presence of an object of tolerably well-known height, as a man, also assists in forming conceptions (by comparison) as to size; artists for this purpose frequently introduce human figures to assist in giving an idea of the size of other objects represented."[5]

Sensations of Color.—The system of colors is a very complex thing. If one take any color, say green, one can pass away from it in more than one direction, through a series of greens more and more yellowish, let us say, towards yellow, or through another series more and more bluish towards blue. The result would be that if we seek to plot out on paper the various distinguishable tints, the arrangement cannot be

[4] H. Newell Martin: *The Human Body*, p. 530.
[5] *Ibid.*, p. 531.

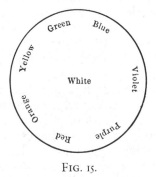

FIG. 15.

that of a line, but has to cover a surface. With the tints arranged on a surface we can pass from any one of them to any other by various lines of gradually changing intermediaries. Such an arrangement is represented in Fig. 15. It is a merely classificatory diagram based on degrees of difference simply felt, and has no physical significance. Black is a color, but does not figure on the plane of the diagram. We cannot place it anywhere alongside of the other colors because we need both to represent the straight gradation from untinted white to black, and that from each pure color towards black as well as towards white. The best way is to put black into the third dimension, beneath the paper, *e.g.*, as is shown perspectively in Fig. 16, then all the transitions can be schematically shown. One can pass straight from black to white, or one can pass round by way of olive, green, and pale green; or one can change from dark blue to yellow through green, or by way of sky-blue, white and straw color; etc., etc. In any case the changes are continuous; and the color system thus forms what Wundt calls a tri-dimensional continuum.

Color-mixture. — Physiologically considered, the colors have this peculiarity, that many pairs of them, when they impress the retina together, produce the sensation of white. The colors which do this are called *complementaries*. Such are spectral red and green-blue, spectral yellow and indigo-blue. Green and purple, again, are complementaries. All the spectral colors added together also make white light, such as we daily

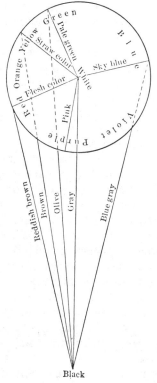

Green
Pale green
Straw color
Yellow
Blue
Orange
Sky blue
White
Red
Flesh color
Pink
Violet
Purple
Reddish brown
Brown
Olive
Gray
Blue gray
Black

FIG. 16 (after Ziehen).

experience in the sunshine. Furthermore, both homogeneous ether-waves and heterogeneous ones may make us feel the same color, when they fall on our retina. Thus yellow, which is a simple spectral color, is also felt when green light is added to red; blue is felt when violet and green lights are mixed. Purple, which is not a spectral color at all, results when the waves either of red and of violet or those of blue and of orange are superposed.[6]

---

[6]The ordinary mixing of *pigments* is not an addition, but rather, as Helmholtz has shown, a subtraction, of lights. To *add* one color to another we must either by appropriate glasses throw differently colored beams upon the same reflecting surface; or we must let the eye look at one color through an inclined plate of glass beneath which it lies, whilst the upper surface of the

From all this it follows that there is no particular congruence between our system of color-sensations and the physical
stimuli which excite them. Each color-feeling is a 'specific
energy' (p. 19) which many different physical causes may
arouse. Helmholtz, Hering, and others have sought to simplify the tangle of the facts, by physiological hypotheses
which, differing much in detail, agree in principle, since they
all postulate a limited number of elementary retinal processes
to which, when excited singly, certain 'fundamental' colors
severally correspond. When excited in combination, as they
may be by the most various physical stimuli, other colors,
called 'secondary,' are felt. The secondary color-sensations are
often spoken of as if they were compounded of the primary
sensations. This is a great mistake. The *sensations as such* are
not compounded—yellow, for example, a secondary on
Helmholtz's theory, is as unique a quality of feeling as the
primaries red and green, which are said to 'compose' it. What
are compounded are merely the elementary retinal processes.
These, according to their combination, produce diverse results on the brain, and thence the secondary colors result
immediately in consciousness. The 'color-theories' are thus
physiological, not psychological, hypotheses, and for more
information concerning them the reader must consult the
physiological books.

The Duration of Luminous Sensations.—"This is
greater than that of the stimulus, a fact taken advantage of in
making fireworks: an ascending rocket produces the sensation
of a trail of light extending far behind the position of the
bright part of the rocket itself at the moment, because the
sensation aroused by it in a lower part of its course still persists. So, shooting stars appear to have luminous tails behind
them. By rotating rapidly before the eye a disk with alternate
white and black sectors we get for each point of the retina
alternate stimulation (due to the passage of white sector) and

---

glass reflects into the same eye another color placed alongside—the two
lights then mix on the retina; or, finally, we must let the differently
colored lights fall in succession upon the retina, so fast that the second is
there before the impression made by the first has died away. This is best done
by looking at a rapidly rotating disk whose sectors are of the several colors to
be mixed.

rest (when a black sector is passing). If the rotation be rapid enough the sensation aroused is that of a uniform gray, such as would be produced if the white and black were mixed and spread evenly over the disk. In each revolution the eye gets as much light as if that were the case, and is unable to distinguish that this light is made up of separate portions reaching it at intervals: the stimulation due to each lasts until the next begins and so all are fused together. If one turns out suddenly the gas in a room containing no other light, the image of the flame persists a short time after the flame itself is extinguished."[7] If we open our eyes instantaneously upon a scene, and then shroud them in complete darkness, it will be as if we saw the scene in ghostly light through the dark screen. We can read off details in it which were unnoticed whilst the eyes were open. This is the primary positive after-image, so called. According to Helmholtz, one third of a second is the most favorable length of exposure to the light for producing it.

Negative after-images are due to more complex conditions, in which fatigue of the retina is usually supposed to play the chief part.

"The nervous visual apparatus is easily fatigued. Usually we do not observe this because its restoration is also rapid, and in ordinary life our eyes, when open, are never at rest; we move them to and fro, so that parts of the retina receive light alternately from brighter and darker objects and are alternately excited and rested. How constant and habitual the movement of the eyes is can be readily observed by trying to 'fix' for a short time a small spot without deviating the glance; to do so for even a few seconds is impossible without practice. If any small object is steadily 'fixed' for twenty or thirty seconds it will be found that the whole field of vision becomes grayish and obscure, because the parts of the retina receiving most light get fatigued, and arouse no more sensation than those less fatigued and stimulated by light from less illuminated objects. Or look steadily at a black object, say a blot on a white page, for twenty seconds, and then turn the eye on a white wall; the latter will seem dark gray, with a white patch on it; an effect due to the greater excitability of the retinal parts previously rested by the black, when compared with the sensation aroused elsewhere by light from the white wall acting on

[7]Martin: *op. cit.*, p. 516.

the previously stimulated parts of the visual surface. All persons will recall many instances of such phenomena, which are especially noticeable soon after rising in the morning. Similar things may be noticed with colors; after looking at a red patch the eye turned on a white wall sees a blue-green patch; the elements causing red sensations having been fatigued, the white mixed light from the wall now excites on that region of the retina only the other primary color sensations. The blending of colors so as to secure their greatest effect depends on this fact; red and green go well together because each rests the parts of the visual apparatus most excited by the other, and so each appears bright and vivid as the eye wanders to and fro; while red and orange together, each exciting and exhausting mainly the same visual elements, render dull, or in popular phrase 'kill,' one another. . . .

"If we fix steadily for thirty seconds a point between two white squares about 4 mm. (⅙ inch) apart on a large black sheet, and then close and cover our eyes, we get a negative after-image in which are seen two dark squares on a brighter surface; this surface is brighter close around the negative after-image of each square, and brightest of all between them. This luminous boundary is called the *corona*, and is explained usually as an effect of simultaneous contrast; the dark after-image of the square it is said makes us mentally err in judgment and think the clear surface close to it brighter than elsewhere; and it is brightest between the two dark squares, just as a middle-sized man between two tall ones looks shorter than if alongside one only. If, however, the after-image be watched it will often be noticed not only that the light band between the squares is intensely white, much more so than the normal idio-retinal light [see below], but, as the image fades away, often the two dark after-images of the squares disappear entirely with all of the corona, except that part between them which is still seen as a bright band on a uniform grayish field. Here there is no *contrast* to produce the error of judgment, and from this and other experiments Hering concludes that light acting on one part of the retina produces inverse changes in all the rest, and that this plays an important part in producing the phenomena of contrasts. Similar phenomena may be observed with colored objects; in their negative after-images each tint is represented by its complementary, as black is by white in colorless vision."[8]

This is one of the facts referred to on p. 33 which have made Hering reject the psychological explanation of simultaneous contrast.

[8]Martin, pp. 524–7.

The Intensity of Luminous Objects.—Black is an optical sensation. We have no black except in the field of view; we do not, for instance, see black out of our stomach or out of the palm of our hand. *Pure* black is, however, only an 'abstract idea,' for the retina itself (even in complete objective darkness) seems to be always the seat of internal changes which give some luminous sensation. This is what is meant by the 'idio-retinal light,' spoken of a few lines back. It plays its part in the determination of all after-images with closed eyes. Any objective luminous stimulus, to be perceived, must be strong enough to give a sensible increment of sensation over and above the idio-retinal light. As the objective stimulus increases the perception is of an intenser luminosity; but the perception changes, as we saw on p. 25, more slowly than the stimulus. The latest numerical determinations, by König and Brodhun, were applied to six different colors and ran from an intensity arbitrarily called 1 to one which was 100,000 times as great. From intensity 2000 to 20,000 Weber's law held good; below and above this range discriminative sensibility declined. The relative increment discriminated here was the same for all colors of light, and lay (according to the tables) between 1 and 2 per cent of the stimulus. Previous observers have got different results.

A certain amount of luminous intensity must exist in an object for its color to be discriminated at all. "In the dark all cats are gray." But the colors rapidly become distincter as the light increases, first the blues and last the reds and yellows, up to a certain point of intensity, when they grow indistinct again through the fact that each takes a turn towards white. At the highest bearable intensity of the light all colors are lost in the blinding white dazzle. This again is usually spoken of as a 'mixing' of the sensation white with the original color-sensation. It is no mixing of two sensations, but the replacement of one sensation by another, in consequence of a changed neural process.

CHAPTER IV

The Ear.—"The auditory organ in man consists of three portions, known respectively as the *external ear*, the *middle ear* or *tympanum*, and the *internal ear* or *labyrinth*; the latter contains the end organs of the auditory nerve. The external ear consists of the expansion seen on the exterior of the head, called the *concha*, M, Fig. 17, and a passage leading in from it, the *external auditory meatus*, G. This passage is closed at its inner end by the *tympanic* or *drum membrane*, T. It is lined by skin, through which numerous small glands, secreting the *wax* of the ear, open.

"*The Tympanum* (P, Fig. 17) is an irregular cavity in the temporal bone, closed externally by the drum membrane. From its inner side the *Eustachian tube* (R) proceeds and opens into the pharynx. The inner wall of the tympanum is bony except for two small apertures, the *oval* and *round foramens*, o and r, which lead into the labyrinth. During life the round aperture is closed by the lining mucous membrane, and the oval by the stirrup-bones. The *tympanic membrane*, T, stretched across the outer side of the tympanum, forms a shallow funnel with its concavity outwards. It is pressed by the external air on its exterior, and by air entering the tympanic cavity through the Eustachian tube on its inner side. If the tympanum were closed these pressures would not be always equal when barometric pressure varied, and the membrane would be bulged in or out according as the external or internal pressure on it were the greater. On the other hand, were the Eustachian tube always open the sounds of our own voices would be loud and disconcerting, so it is usually closed; but every time we swallow it is opened, and thus the air-pressure in the cavity is kept equal to that in the external auditory meatus. On making a balloon ascent or going rapidly

---

*In teaching the anatomy of the ear, great assistance will be yielded by the admirable model made by Dr. Auzoux, 56 Rue de Vaugirard, Paris, described in the catalogue of the firm as "No. 21—*Oreille, temporal de* 60 cm., nouvelle édition," etc.

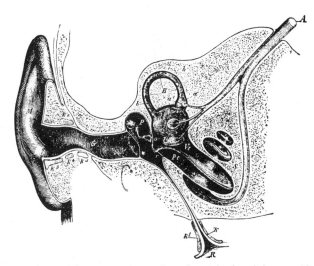

FIG. 17.—Semidiagrammatic section through the right ear (Czermak). *M*, concha; *G*, external auditory meatus; *T*, tympanic membrane; *P*, tympanic cavity; *o*, oval foramen; *r*, round foramen; *R*, pharyngeal opening of Eustachian tube; *V*, vestibule; *B*, a semicircular canal; *S*, the cochlea; *Vt*, scala vestibuli; *Pt*, scala tympani; *A*, auditory nerve.

down a deep mine, the sudden and great change of aërial pressure outside frequently causes painful tension of the drum membrane, which may be greatly alleviated by frequent swallowing.

The Auditory Ossicles.—"Three small bones lie in the tympanum forming a chain from the drum membrane to the oval foramen. The external bone is the *malleus* or *hammer*; the middle one, the *incus* or *anvil*; and the internal one, the *stapes* or *stirrup.*" They are represented in Fig. 18.[1]

Accommodation is provided for in the ear as well as in the eye. One muscle an inch long, the *tensor tympani*, arises in the petrous portion of the temporal bone (running in a canal parallel to the Eustachian tube) and is inserted into the malleus below its head. When it contracts, it makes the membrane of the tympanum more tense. Another smaller muscle, the *stape-*

[1]This description is abridged from Martin's *Human Body*, pp. 535–36.

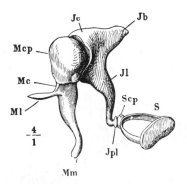

FIG. 18.—*Mcp, Mc, Ml,* and *Mm* stand for different parts of the malleus; *Jc, Jb, Jl, Jpl,* for different parts of the incus. *S* is the stapes.

dius, goes to the head of the stirrup-bone. These muscles are by many persons felt distinctly contracting when certain notes are heard, and some can make them contract at will. In spite of this, uncertainty still reigns as to their exact use in hearing, though it is highly probable that they give to the membranes which they influence the degree of tension best suited to take up whatever rates of vibration may fall upon them at the time. In listening, the head and ears in lower animals, and the head alone in man, are turned so as best to receive the sound. This also is a part of the reaction called 'adaptation' of the organ (see the chapter on Attention).

The Internal Ear.—"The labyrinth consists primarily of chambers and tubes hollowed out in the temporal bone and inclosed by it on all sides, except for the oval and round foramens on its exterior, and certain apertures for blood-vessels and the auditory nerve; during life all these are closed water-tight in one way or another. Lying in the *bony labyrinth* thus constituted, are membranous parts, of the same general form but smaller, so that between the two a space is left; this is filled with a watery fluid, called the *perilymph*; and the *membranous internal ear* is filled by a similar liquid, the *endolymph.*

The Bony Labyrinth.—"The bony labyrinth is described in three portions, the *vestibule,* the *semicircular canals,* and the

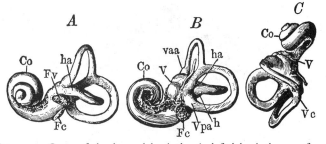

FIG. 19.—Casts of the bony labyrinth. *A*, left labyrinth seen from the outer side; *B*, right labyrinth from the inner side; *C*, left labyrinth from above; *Co*, cochlea; *V*, vestibule; *Fc*, round foramen; *Fv*, oval foramen; *h*, horizontal semicircular canal; *ha*, its ampulla; *vaa*, ampulla of anterior vertical semicircular canal; *vpa*, ampulla of posterior vertical semicircular canal; *vc*, conjoined portion of the two vertical canals.

cochlea; casts of its interior are represented from different aspects in Fig. 19. The vestibule is the central part and has on its exterior the oval foramen (*Fv*) into which the base of the stirrup-bone fits. Behind the vestibule are three bony semicircular canals, communicating with the back of the vestibule at each end, and dilated near one end to form an *ampulla*. . . . The bony cochlea is a tube coiled on itself somewhat like a snail's shell, and lying in front of the vestibule.

The Membranous Labyrinth.—"The membranous vestibule, lying in the bony, consists of two sacs communicating by a narrow aperture. The posterior is called the *utriculus*, and into it the membranous semicircular canals open. The anterior, called the *sacculus*, communicates by a tube with the membranous cochlea. The membranous semicircular canals much resemble the bony, and each has an ampulla; . . . in the ampulla one side of the membranous tube is closely adherent to its bony protector; at this point nerves enter the former. The relations of the membranous to the bony cochlea are more complicated. A section through this part of the auditory apparatus (Fig. 20) shows that its osseous portion consists of a tube wound two and a half times around a central bony axis, the *modiolus*. From the axis a shelf, the *lamina spiralis*,

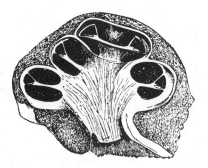

FIG. 20.—A section through the
cochlea in the line of its axis.

projects and partially subdivides the tube, extending farthest
across in its lower coils. Attached to the outer edge of this
bony plate is the membranous cochlea (*scala media*), a tube
triangular in cross-section and attached by its base to the
outer side of the bony cochlear spiral. The spiral lamina and
the membranous cochlea thus subdivide the cavity of the
bony tube (Fig. 21) into an upper portion, the *scala vestibuli*,
SV, and a lower, the *scala tympani*, *ST*. Between these lie the
lamina spiralis (*lso*) and the membranous cochlea (*CC*), the
latter being bounded above by the membrane of Reissner (*R*)
and below by the basilar membrane (*b*)."[2]

The membranous cochlea does not extend to the tip of the
bony cochlea; above its apex the scala vestibuli and scala tympani communicate. Both are filled with perilymph, so that
when the stapes is pushed into the oval foramen, *o*, in Fig. 17,
by the impact of an air-wave on the tympanic membrane, a
wave of perilymph runs up the scala vestibuli to the top,
where it turns into the scala tympani, down whose whorls it
runs and pushes out the round foramen, *r*, ruffling probably
the membrane of Reissner and the basilar membrane on its
way up and down.

The Terminal Organs.—"The membranous cochlea contains certain solid structures seated on the basilar membrane

[2]Martin: *op. cit.*, pp. 538–40.

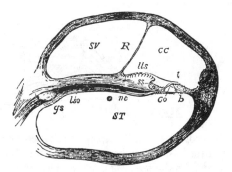

FIG. 21.—Section of one coil of the cochlea, magnified. *SV*, *scala vestibuli*; *R*, membrane of Reissner; *CC*, membranous cochlea (*scala media*); *lls*, *limbus laminæ spiralis*; *t*, tectorial membrane; *ST*, scala tympani; *lso*, spiral lamina; *Co*, rods of Corti; *b*, basilar membrane.

and forming the *organ of Corti*. . . . This contains the end organs of the cochlear nerves. Lining the sulcus spiralis, a groove in the edge of the bony lamina spiralis, are cuboidal cells; on the inner margin of the basilar membrane they become columnar, and then are succeeded by a row which bear on their upper ends a set of short stiff hairs, and constitute the *inner hair-cells*, which are fixed below by a narrow apex to the basilar membrane; nerve-fibres enter them. To the inner hair-cells succeed the *rods of Corti* (*Co*, Fig. 21), which are represented highly magnified in Fig. 22. These rods are stiff and arranged side by side in two rows, leaned against one another by their upper ends so as to cover in a tunnel; they are known respectively as the *inner* and *outer rods*, the former being nearer the *lamina spiralis*. . . . The inner rods are more numerous than the outer, the numbers being about 6000 and 4500 respectively. Attached to the external sides of the heads of the outer rods is the *reticular membrane* (*r*, Fig. 22), which is stiff and perforated by holes. External to the outer rods come four rows of *outer hair-cells*, connected like the inner row with nerve-fibres; their bristles project into the holes of the reticular membrane. Beyond the outer hair-cells is ordinary columnar epithelium, which passes gradually into

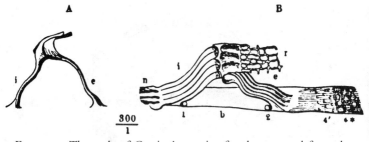

FIG. 22.—The rods of Corti. *A*, a pair of rods separated from the rest; *B*, a bit of the basilar membrane with several rods on it, showing how they cover in the *tunnel of Corti*; *i*, inner, and *e*, outer rods; *b*, basilar membrane; *r*, reticular membrane.

cuboidal cells lining most of the membranous cochlea. From the upper lip of the sulcus spiralis projects the *tectorial membrane* (*t*, Fig. 21) which extends over the rods of Corti and the hair-cells."[3]

The hair-cells would thus seem to be the terminal organs for 'picking up' the vibrations which the air-waves communicate through all the intervening apparatus, solid and liquid, to the basilar membrane. Analogous hair-cells receive the terminal nerve-filaments in the walls of the saccule, utricle, and ampullæ (see Fig. 23).

The Various Qualities of Sound.—Physically, sounds consist of vibrations, and these are, generally speaking, *aërial waves*. When the waves are non-periodic the result is a *noise*; when periodic it is what is nowadays called a *tone*, or *note*. The *loudness* of a sound depends on the *force* of the waves. When they recur periodically a peculiar quality called *pitch* is the effect of their *frequency*. In addition to loudness and pitch tones have each their *voice* or *timbre*, which may differ widely in different instruments giving equally loud tones of the same pitch. This voice depends on the *form* of the aërial wave.

Pitch.—A single puff of air, set in motion by no matter what cause, will give a sensation of sound, but it takes at least four or five puffs, or more, to convey a sensation of pitch.

[3]Martin: *op. cit.*, pp. 540–42.

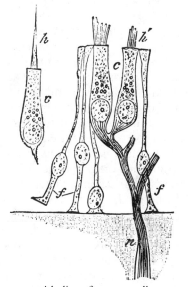

FIG. 23.—Sensory epithelium from ampulla or semicircular canal, and saccule. At *n* a nerve-fibre pierces the wall, and after
branching enters the two hair-cells, *c*. At *h* a 'columnar cell'
with a long hair is shown, the nerve-fibre being broken away
from its base. The slender cells at *f* seem unconnected with
nerves.

The pitch of the note *c*, for instance, is due to 132 vibrations a
second, that of its octave *c′* is produced by twice as many, or
264 vibrations; but in neither case is it necessary for the vibrations to go on during a full second for the pitch to be discerned. "Sound vibrations may be too rapid or too slow in
succession to produce sonorous sensations, just as the ultra-
violet and ultra-red rays of the solar spectrum fail to excite the
retina. The highest-pitched audible note answers to about
38,016 vibrations in a second, but it differs in individuals;
many persons cannot hear the cry of a bat nor the chirp of a
cricket, which lie near this upper audible limit. On the other
hand, sounds of vibrational rate about 40 per second are not
well heard, and a little below this . . . they produce rather a
'hum' than a true tone sensation, and are only used along

with notes of higher octaves to which they give a character of greater depth."[4]

The entire system of pitches forms *a continuum of one dimension*; that is to say, you can pass from one pitch to another only by one set of intermediaries, instead of by more than one, as in the case of colors. (See p. 47.) The whole series of pitches is embraced in and between the terms of what is called the musical scale. The adoption of certain arbitrary points in this scale as 'notes' has an explanation partly historic and partly æsthetic, but too complex for exposition here.

The 'timbre' of a note is due to its *wave-form*. Waves are either simple ('pendular') or compound. Thus if a tuning-fork (which gives waves nearly simple) vibrate 132 times a second, we shall hear the note *c*. If simultaneously a fork of 264 vibrations be struck, giving the next higher octave, *c'*, the aërial movement at any time will be the algebraic sum of the movements due to both forks; whenever both drive the air one way they reinforce one another; when on the contrary the recoil of one fork coincides with the forward stroke of another, they detract from each other's effect. The result is a movement which is still periodic, repeating itself at equal intervals of time, but no longer *pendular*, since it is not alike on the ascending and descending limbs of the curves. We thus get at the fact that non-pendular vibrations may be produced by the fusion of pendular, or, in technical phrase, by their *composition*.

Suppose several musical instruments, as those of an orchestra, to be sounded together. Each produces its own effect on the air-particles, whose movements, being an algebraical sum, must at any given instant be very complex; yet the ear can pick out at will and follow the tones of any one instrument. Now in most musical instruments it is susceptible of physical proof that with every single note that is sounded many upper octaves and other 'harmonics' sound simultaneously in fainter form. On the relative strength of this or that one or more of these Helmholtz has shown that the instrument's peculiar voice depends. The several vowel-sounds in the human voice also depend on the predominance of diverse upper harmonics

[4]Martin: *op. cit.*, pp. 543–44.

accompanying the note on which the vowel is sung. When
the two tuning-forks of the last paragraph are sounded together the new form of vibration has the same *period* as the
lower-pitched fork; yet the ear can clearly distinguish the resultant sound from that of the lower fork alone, as a note of
the same pitch but of different timbre; and within the compound sound the two components can by a trained ear be
severally heard. Now how can one resultant wave-form make
us hear so many sounds at once?

The analysis of compound wave-forms is supposed (after
Helmholtz) to be effected through the different rates of sympathetic resonance of the different parts of the membranous
cochlea. The basilar membrane is some twelve times broader
at the apex of the cochlea than at the base where it begins,
and is largely composed of radiating fibres which may be likened to stretched strings. Now the physical principle of sympathetic resonance says that when stretched strings are near a
source of vibration those whose own rate agrees with that of
the source also vibrate, the others remaining at rest. On this
principle, waves of perilymph running down the scala tympani at a certain rate of frequency ought to set certain particular fibres of the basilar membrane vibrating, and ought to
leave others unaffected. If then each vibrating fibre stimulated
the hair-cell above it, and no others, and each such hair-cell,
sending a current to the auditory brain-centre, awakened
therein a specific process to which the sensation of one particular pitch was correlated, the physiological condition of our
several pitch-sensations would be explained. Suppose now a
chord to be struck in which perhaps twenty different physical
rates of vibration are found: at least twenty different hair-cells
or end-organs will receive the jar; and if the power of mental
discrimination be at its maximum, twenty different 'objects' of
hearing, in the shape of as many distinct pitches of sound,
may appear before the mind.

The rods of Corti are supposed to be *dampers* of the fibres
of the basilar membrane, just as the malleus, incus, and stapes
are dampers of the tympanic membrane, as well as transmitters of its oscillations to the inner ear. There must be, in fact,
an instantaneous *damping* of the physiological vibrations, for
there are no such positive after-images, and no such blendings

of rapidly successive tones, as the retina shows us in the case of light. Helmholtz's theory of the analysis of sounds is plausible and ingenious. One objection to it is that the keyboard of the cochlea does not seem extensive enough for the number of distinct resonances required. We can discriminate many more degrees of pitch than the 20,000 hair-cells, more or less, will allow for.

The so-called Fusion of Sensations in Hearing.—A very common way of explaining the fact that waves which singly give no feeling of pitch give one when recurrent, is to say that their several sensations *fuse into a compound sensation.* A preferable explanation is that which follows the analogy of muscular contraction. If electric shocks are sent into a frog's sciatic nerve at slow intervals, the muscle which the nerve supplies will give a series of distinct twitches, one for each shock. But if they follow each other at the rate of as many as thirty a second, no distinct twitches are observed, but a steady state of contraction instead. This steady contraction is known as *tetanus.* The experiment proves that there is a physiological cumulation or overlapping of processes in the muscular tissue. It takes a twentieth of a second or more for the latter to relax after the twitch due to the first shock. But the second shock comes in before the relaxation can occur, then the third again, and so on; so that continuous tetanus takes the place of discrete twitching. Similarly in the auditory nerve. One shock of air starts in it a current to the auditory brain-centre, and affects the latter, so that a dry stroke of sound is heard. If other shocks follow slowly, the brain-centre recovers its equilibrium after each, to be again upset in the same way by the next, and the result is that for each shock of air a distinct sensation of sound occurs. But if the shock comes in too quick succession, the later ones reach the brain before the effects of the earlier ones on that organ have died away. There is thus an overlapping of processes in the auditory centre, a physiological condition analogous to the muscle's tetanus, to which new condition a new quality of feeling, that of pitch, directly corresponds. This latter feeling is a new kind of sensation altogether, not a mere 'appearance' due to many sensations of dry stroke being compounded into one. No sensations of dry stroke can exist under these circumstances, for their physiological conditions have been replaced by others. What 'compounding' there is has already taken place in the brain-cells before the threshold of sensation was reached. Just so red light and green light beating on the retina in rapid enough alternation, arouse the central process to which the sensation *yellow* directly corresponds. The sensations of red and of green get no chance, under such conditions, to be born. Just so if the muscle could feel, it would have a certain sort of feeling when it gave a single twitch, but it would undoubtedly have a distinct sort of feeling altogether, when it contracted tetanically; and this feeling of the tetanic contraction would by no means be identical with a multitude of the feelings of twitching.

Harmony and Discord.—When several tones sound together we may get peculiar feelings of pleasure or displeasure designated as consonance and dissonance respectively. A note sounds most consonant with its octave. When with the octave the 'third' and the 'fifth' of the note are sounded, for instance c—e—g—c', we get the 'full chord' or maximum of consonance. The ratios of vibration here are as 4:5:6:8, so that one might think simple ratios were the ground of harmony. But the interval c—d is discordant, with the comparatively simple ratio 8:9. Helmholtz explains discord by the overtones making 'beats' together. This gives a subtle grating which is unpleasant. Where the overtones make no 'beats,' or beats too rapid for their effect to be perceptible, there is consonance, according to Helmholtz, which is thus a negative rather than a positive thing. Wundt explains consonance by the presence of strong identical overtones in the notes which harmonize. No one of these explanations of musical harmony can be called quite satisfactory; and the subject is too intricate to be treated farther in this place.

Discriminative Sensibility of the Ear.—Weber's law holds fairly well for the intensity of sounds. If ivory or metal balls are dropped on an ebony or iron plate, they make a sound which is the louder as they are heavier or dropped from a greater height. Experimenting in this way (after others) Merkel found that the just perceptible increment of loudness required an increase of $\frac{3}{10}$ of the original stimulus everywhere between the intensities marked 20 and 5000 of his arbitrary scale. Below this the fractional increment of stimulus must be larger; above it, no measurements were made.

Discrimination of differences of *pitch* varies in different parts of the scale. Between 200 and 1000 vibrations per second, one fifth of a vibration more or less can make the sound sharp or flat for a good ear. It takes a much greater *relative* alteration to sound sharp or flat elsewhere on the scale. The chromatic scale itself has been used as an illustration of Weber's law. The notes seem to differ equally from each other, yet their vibration-numbers form a series of which each is a certain multiple of the last. This, however, has nothing to do with intensities or just perceptible differences; so the peculiar parallelism between the sensation series and the outer-stimulus series forms here a case all by itself, rather than an instance under Weber's more general law.

CHAPTER V

TOUCH, THE TEMPERATURE SENSE, THE MUSCULAR SENSE, AND PAIN

Nerve-endings in the Skin. — "Many of the afferent skin-nerves end in connection with hair-bulbs; the fine hairs over most of the cutaneous surface, projecting from the skin, transmit any movement impressed on them, with increased force, to the nerve-fibres at their fixed ends. . . . Fine branches of axis cylinders have also been described as penetrating between epidermic cells and ending there without terminal organs. In or immediately beneath the skin several peculiar forms of nerve end organs have also been described; they are known as (1) *Touch-cells*; (2) *Pacinian corpuscles*; (3) *Tactile corpuscles*; (4) *End-bulbs*."[1]

These bodies all consist essentially of granules formed of connective tissue, in which or round about which one or more sensory nerve-fibres terminate. They probably magnify impressions just as a grain of sand does in a shoe, or a crumb does in a finger of a glove.

Touch, or the Pressure Sense. — "Through the skin we get several kinds of sensation; touch proper, heat and cold, and pain; and we can with more or less accuracy localize them on the surface of the Body. The interior of the mouth possesses also three sensibilities. Through touch proper we recognize pressure or traction exerted on the skin, and the force of the pressure; the softness or hardness, roughness or smoothness, of the body producing it; and the form of this, when not too large to be felt all over. When to learn the form of an object we move the hand over it, muscular sensations are combined with proper tactile, and such a combination of the two sensations is frequent; moreover, we rarely touch anything without at the same time getting temperature sensations; therefore pure tactile feelings are rare. From an evolution point of view, touch is probably the first distinctly

[1]Martin: *op. cit.*, p. 556.

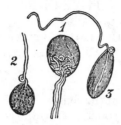

FIG. 24.—End-bulbs
from the conjunctiva
of the human eye,
magnified.

differentiated sensation, and this primary position it still largely holds in our mental life."[2]

Objects are most important to us when in direct contact. The chief function of our eyes and ears is to enable us to prepare ourselves for contact with approaching bodies, or to ward such contact off. They have accordingly been characterized as organs of anticipatory touch.

"The delicacy of the tactile sense varies on different parts of the skin; it is greatest on the forehead, temples, and back of the forearm, where a weight of 2 milligr. pressing on an area of 9 sq. millim. can be felt. . . .

"In order that the sense of touch may be excited neighboring skin areas must be differently pressed. . . . When the hand is immersed in a liquid, as mercury, which fits into all its inequalities and presses with practically the same weight on all neighboring immersed areas, the sense of pressure is only felt at a line along the surface, where the immersed and non-immersed parts of the skin meet. . . .

The Localizing Power of the Skin.—"When the eyes are closed and a point of the skin is touched we can with some accuracy indicate the region stimulated; although tactile feelings are in general characters alike, they differ in something besides intensity by which we can distinguish them; some sub-sensation quality not rising definitely into prominence in

[2]Martin: *op. cit.*, p. 558.

consciousness must be present, comparable to the upper par-
tials determining the timbre of a tone. The accuracy of the
localizing power varies widely in different skin regions and is
measured by observing the least distance which must separate
two objects (as the blunted points of a pair of compasses) in
order that they may be felt as two. The following table illustrates some of the differences observed—

Tongue-tip.	1.1 mm.	(.04 inch)
Palm side of last phalanx		
of finger.	2.2 mm.	(.08 inch)
Red part of lips	4.4 mm.	(.16 inch)
Tip of nose	6.6 mm.	(.24 inch)
Back of second phalanx		
of finger.	11.0 mm.	(.44 inch)
Heel	22.0 mm.	(.88 inch)
Back of hand.	30.8 mm.	(1.23 inches)
Forearm.	39.6 mm.	(1.58 inches)
Sternum.	44.0 mm.	(1.76 inches)
Back of neck	52.8 mm.	(2.11 inches)
Middle of back	66.0 mm.	(2.64 inches)

The localizing power is a little more acute across the long axis
of a limb than in it; and is better when the pressure is only
strong enough to just cause a distinct tactile sensation, than
when it is more powerful; it is also very readily and rapidly
improvable by practice." It seems to be naturally delicate in
proportion as the skin which possesses it covers a more movable part of the body.

"It might be thought that this localizing power depended
directly on nerve distribution; that each touch-nerve had connection with a special brain-centre at one end (the excitation
of which caused a sensation with a characteristic local sign),
and at the other end was distributed over a certain skin area,
and that the larger this area the farther apart might two
points be and still give rise to only one sensation. If this were
so, however, the peripheral tactile areas (each being determined by the anatomical distribution of a nerve-fibre) must
have definite unchangeable limits, which experiment shows
that they do not possess. Suppose the small areas in Fig. 25 to
each represent a peripheral area of nerve-distribution. If any

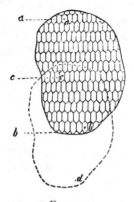

FIG. 25.

two points in *c* were touched we would according to the theory get but a single sensation; but if, while the compass points remained the same distance apart, or were even approximated, one were placed in *c* and the other on a contiguous area, two fibres would be stimulated and we ought to get two sensations; but such is not the case; on the same skin region the points must be always the same distance apart, no matter how they be shifted, in order to give rise to two just distinguishable sensations.

"It is probable that the nerve areas are much smaller than the tactile; and that several unstimulated must intervene between the excited, in order to produce sensations which shall be distinct. If we suppose twelve unexcited nerve areas must intervene, then, in Fig. 25, *a* and *b* will be just on the limits of a single tactile area; and no matter how the points are moved, so long as eleven, or fewer, unexcited areas come between, we would get a single tactile sensation; in this way we can explain the fact that tactile areas have no fixed boundaries in the skin, although the nerve distribution in any part must be constant. We also see why the back of a knife laid on the surface causes a continuous linear sensation, although it touches many distinct nerve areas; if we could discriminate the excitations of each of these from that of its immediate neighbors we would get the sensation of a series of points touching us, one for each nerve region excited; but in the absence of intervening unexcited nerve areas the sensations are fused together. . . .

The Temperature-sense. Its Terminal Organs.—"By this we mean our faculty of perceiving cold and warmth; and, with the help of these sensations, of perceiving temperature differences in external objects. Its organ is the whole skin, the mucous membrane of mouth and fauces, pharynx and gullet, and the entry of the nares. Direct heating or cooling of a sensory nerve may stimulate it and cause pain, but not a true temperature sensation; . . . hence we assume the presence of temperature end organs. [These have not yet been ascertained anatomically. Physiologically, however, the demonstration of special spots in the skin for feeling heat and cold is one of the most interesting discoveries of recent years. If one draw a pencil-point over the palm or cheek one will notice certain spots of sudden coolness. These are the cold-spots; the heat-spots are less easy to single out. Goldscheider, Blix, and Don-aldson have made minute exploration of determinate tracts of skin and found the heat- and cold-spots thickset and perma-nently distinct. Between them no temperature-sensation is ex-cited by contact with a pointed cold or hot object. Mechanical and faradic irritation also excites in these points their specific feelings respectively.]

The feeling of temperature is relative to the state of the skin. "In a comfortable room we feel at no part of the Body either heat or cold, although different parts of its surface are at different temperatures; the fingers and nose being cooler than the trunk which is covered by clothes, and this, in turn, cooler than the interior of the mouth. The temperature which a given region of the temperature organ has (as measured by a thermometer) when it feels neither heat nor cold is its *temperature-sensation zero*, and is not associated with any one objective temperature; for not only, as we have just seen, does it vary in different parts of the organ, but also on the same part from time to time. Whenever a skin region has a temper-ature above its sensation zero we feel warmth and *vice versa*; the sensation is more marked the greater the difference, and the more suddenly it is produced; touching a metallic body, which conducts heat rapidly to or from the skin, causes a

FIG. 26.—The figure marked C P
shows the cold-spots, that marked
H P the heat-spots, and the middle one the hairs on a certain
patch of skin on one of Goldscheider's fingers.

more marked hot or cold sensation than touching a worse
conductor, as a piece of wood, of the same temperature.

"The change of temperature in the organ may be brought
about by changes in the circulatory apparatus (more blood
flowing through the skin warms it and less leads to its cooling), or by temperature changes in gases, liquids, or solids in
contact with it. Sometimes we fail to distinguish clearly
whether the cause is external or internal; a person coming in
from a windy walk often feels a room uncomfortably warm
which is not really so; the exercise has accelerated his circulation and tended to warm his skin, but the moving outer air
has rapidly conducted off the extra heat; on entering the
house the stationary air there does this less quickly, the skin
gets hot, and the cause is supposed to be oppressive heat of
the room. Hence, frequently, opening of windows and sitting
in a draught, with its concomitant risks; whereas keeping
quiet for five or ten minutes, until the circulation has returned
to its normal rate, would attain the same end without danger.

"The acuteness of the temperature sense is greatest at temperatures within a few degrees of 30° C. (86° F.); at these differences of less than 0.1° C. can be discriminated. As a means
of measuring absolute temperatures, however, the skin is very
unreliable, on account of the changeability of its sensation
zero. We can localize temperature sensations much as tactile,
but not so accurately."[3]

Muscular Sensation.—The sensation in the muscle itself
cannot well be distinguished from that in the tendon or in its

[3]Martin: *op. cit.*, pp. 558–63, with omissions.

insertion. In muscular fatigue the insertions are the places most painfully felt. In muscular rheumatism, however, the whole muscle grows painful; and violent contraction such as that caused by the faradic current, or known as cramp, produces a severe and peculiar pain felt in the whole mass of muscle affected. Sachs also thought that he had demonstrated, both experimentally and anatomically, the existence of special sensory nerve-fibres, distinct from the motor fibres, in the frog's muscle. The latter end in the 'terminal plates,' the former in a network.

Great importance has been attached to the muscular sense as a factor in our perceptions, not only of weight and pressure, but of the space-relations between things generally. Our eyes and our hands, in their explorations of space, move over it and through it. It is usually supposed that without this sense of an intervening motion performed we should not perceive two seen points or two touched points to be separated by an extended interval. I am far from denying the immense participation of experiences of motion in the construction of our space-perceptions. But it is still an open question *how* our muscles help us in these experiences, whether by their own sensations, or by awakening sensations of motion on our skin, retina, and articular surfaces. The latter seems to me the more probable view, and the reader may be of the same opinion after reading Chapter VI.

Sensibility to Weight.—When we wish to estimate accurately the weight of an object we always, when possible, lift it, and so combine muscular and articular with tactile sensations. By this means we can form much better judgments.

Weber found that whereas ⅓ must be added to a weight resting on the hand for the increase to be felt, the same hand actively 'hefting' the weight could feel an addition of as little as ¹⁄₁₇. Merkel's recent and very careful experiments, in which the finger pressed down the beam of a balance counterweighted by from 25 to 8020 grams, showed that between 200 and 2000 grams a constant fractional increase of about ¹⁄₁₃ was felt when there was no movement of the finger, and of about ¹⁄₁₉ when there was movement. Above and below these limits the discriminative power grew less.

Pain.—The physiology of pain is still an enigma. One might suppose separate afferent fibres with their own end-organs to carry painful impressions to a specific pain-centre. Or one might suppose such a specific centre to be reached by currents of overflow from the other sensory centres when the violence of their inner excitement should have reached a certain pitch. Or again one might suppose a certain extreme degree of inner excitement to produce the feeling of pain in all the centres. It is certain that sensations of every order, which in moderate degrees are rather pleasant than otherwise, become painful when their intensity grows strong. The rate at which the agreeableness and disagreeableness vary with the intensity of a sensation is roughly represented by the dotted curve in Fig. 27. The horizontal line represents the threshold both of sensational and of agreeable sensibility. Below the line is the disagreeable. The continuous curve is that of Weber's law which we learned to know in Fig. 2, p. 26. With the minimal sensation the agreeableness is *nil*, as the dotted curve shows. It rises at first more slowly than the sensational intensity, then faster; and reaches its maximum before the sensation is near its acme. After its maximum of agreeableness the dotted line rapidly sinks, and soon tumbles below the horizontal into the realm of the disagreeable or painful in which it

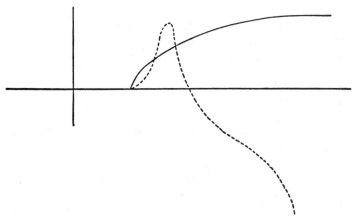

FIG. 27 (after Wundt).

declines. That all sensations are painful when too strong is a piece of familiar knowledge. Light, sound, odors, the taste of sweet even, cold, heat, and all the skin-sensations, must be moderate to be enjoyed.

The quality of the sensation complicates the question, however, for in some sensations, as bitter, sour, salt, and certain smells, the turning point of the dotted curve must be drawn very near indeed to the beginning of the scale. In the skin the painful quality soon becomes so intense as entirely to overpower the specific quality of the sort of stimulus. Heat, cold, and pressure are indistinguishable when extreme—we only feel the pain. The hypothesis of separate end-organs in the skin receives some corroboration from recent experiments, for both Blix and Goldscheider have found, along with their special heat- and cold-spots, also special 'pain-spots' on the skin. Mixed in with these are spots which are quite feelingless. However it may stand with the terminal pain-spots, separate paths of *conduction* to the brain, for painful and for merely tactile stimulations of the skin, are made probable by certain facts. In the condition termed *analgesia*, a touch is felt, but the most violent pinch, burn, or electric spark destructive of the tissue will awaken no sensation. This may occur in disease of the cord, by suggestion in hypnotism, or in certain stages of ether and chloroform intoxication. "In rabbits a similar state of things was produced by Schiff, by dividing the gray matter of the cord, leaving the posterior white columns intact. If, on the contrary, the latter were divided and the gray substance left, there was increased sensitiveness to pain, and possibly touch proper was lost. Such experiments make it pretty certain that when afferent impulses reach the spinal cord at any level and there enter its gray matter with the posterior root-fibres, they travel on in different tracks to conscious centres; the tactile ones coming soon out of the gray network and coursing on in a readily conducting white fibre, while the painful ones first travel on farther in the gray substance. It is still uncertain if both impulses reach the cord in the same fibres. The gray network conducts nerve impulses, but not easily; they tend soon to be blocked in it. A feeble (tactile) impulse reaching it by an afferent fibre might only spread a short way and then pass out into a single good conducting fibre in a white column, and proceed to the brain; while a stronger (painful) impulse would radiate farther in the gray matter, and perhaps break out of it by many fibres leading to the brain through the white columns, and so give rise to an inco-ordinate and ill localized sensation. That pains are badly localized, and worse the more intense they are, is a well-known fact, which would thus receive an explanation."[4]

Pain also gives rise to ill-coördinated movements of defence. The stronger the pain the more violent the start. Doubtless in low animals pain is almost the only stimulus; and we have preserved the peculiarity in so far that to-day it is the stimulus of our most energetic, though not of our most discriminating, reactions.

Taste, smell, as well as hunger, thirst, nausea, and other so-called 'common' sensations need not be touched on in this book, as almost nothing of psychological interest is known concerning them.

[4]Martin: *op. cit.*, p. 568.

CHAPTER VI

SENSATIONS OF MOTION

I treat of these in a separate chapter in order to give them the emphasis which their importance deserves. They are of two orders:

1) Sensations of objects moving over our sensory surfaces; and

2) Sensations of our whole person's translation through space.

1) **The Sensation of Motion over Surfaces.**—This has generally been assumed by physiologists to be impossible until the positions of *terminus a quo* and *terminus ad quem* are severally cognized, and the successive occupancies of these positions by the moving body are perceived to be separated by a distinct interval of time. As a matter of fact, however, we cognize only the very slowest motions in this way. Seeing the hand of a clock at XII and afterwards at VI, I judge that it has moved through the interval. Seeing the sun now in the east and again in the west, I infer it to have passed over my head. But we can only *infer* that which we already generically know in some more direct fashion, and it is experimentally certain that we have the feeling of motion given us as a direct and simple *sensation*. Czermak long ago pointed out the difference between *seeing the motion* of the second-hand of a watch, when we look directly at it, and noticing the fact that it has *altered its position*, whilst our gaze is fixed upon some other point of the dial-plate. In the first case we have a specific quality of sensation which is absent in the second. If the reader will find a portion of his skin—the arm, for example—where a pair of compass-points an inch apart are felt as one impression, and if he will then trace lines a tenth of an inch long on that spot with a pencil-point, he will be distinctly aware of the point's motion and vaguely aware of the direction of the motion. The perception of the motion here is certainly not derived from a preëxisting knowledge that its starting and ending points are separate positions in space, because positions in space ten times wider apart fail to be discriminated as

such when excited by the compass-points. It is the same with the retina. One's fingers when cast upon its peripheral portions cannot be counted—that is to say, the five retinal tracts which they occupy are not distinctly apprehended by the mind as five separate positions in space—and yet the slightest *movement* of the fingers is most vividly perceived as movement and nothing else. It is thus certain that our sense of movement, being so much more delicate than our sense of position, cannot possibly be derived from it.

Vierordt, at almost the same time, called attention to certain persistent illusions, amongst which are these: If another person gently trace a line across our wrist or finger, the latter being stationary, it will feel to us as if the member were moving in the opposite direction to the tracing point. If, on the contrary, we move our limb across a fixed point, it will seem as if the point were moving as well. If the reader will touch his forehead with his forefinger kept motionless, and then rotate the head so that the skin of the forehead passes beneath the finger's tip, he will have an irresistible sensation of the latter being itself in motion in the opposite direction to the head. So in abducting the fingers from each other; some may move and the rest be still, but the still ones will feel as if they were actively separating from the rest. These illusions, according to Vierordt, are survivals of a primitive form of perception, when motion was felt as such, but ascribed to the whole 'content' of consciousness, and not yet distinguished as belonging exclusively to one of its parts. When our perception is fully developed we go beyond the mere relative motion of thing and ground, and can ascribe absolute motion to one of these components of our total object, and absolute rest to another. When, in vision for example, the whole field of view seems to move together, we think it is ourselves or our eyes which are moving; and any object in the foreground which may seem to move relatively to the background is judged by us to be really still. But primitively this discrimination is not perfectly made. The sensation of the motion spreads over all that we see and infects it. Any relative motion of object and retina both makes the object seem to move, and makes us feel ourselves in motion. Even now when our whole field of view really does move we get giddy, and feel as if we too were moving; and we still see an apparent motion of the entire field of view whenever we suddenly jerk our head and eyes or shake them quickly to and fro. Pushing our eyeballs gives the same illusion. We *know* in all these cases what really happens, but the conditions are unusual, so our primitive sensation persists unchecked. So it does when clouds float by the moon. We *know* the moon is still; but we *see* it move faster than the clouds. Even when we slowly move our eyes the primitive sensation persists under the victorious conception. If we notice closely the experience, we find that any object towards which we look appears moving to meet our eye.

But the most valuable contribution to the subject is the paper of G. H. Schneider,[1] who takes up the matter zoölogically, and shows by examples from every branch of the animal kingdom that movement is the quality by which animals most easily attract each other's attention. The instinct of 'shamming death' is no shamming of death at all, but rather a paralysis through fear, which saves the insect, crustacean, or other creature from being *noticed at all* by his enemy. It is paralleled in the human race by the breath-holding stillness of the boy playing 'I spy,' to whom the seeker is near; and its obverse side is shown in our involuntary waving of arms, jumping up and down, and so forth, when we wish to attract someone's attention at a distance. Creatures 'stalking' their prey and creatures hiding from their pursuers alike show how immobility diminishes conspicuity. In the woods, if we are quiet, the squirrels and birds will actually touch us. Flies will light on stuffed birds and stationary frogs. On the other hand, the tremendous shock of feeling the thing we are sitting on begin to move, the exaggerated start it gives us to have an insect unexpectedly pass over our skin, or a cat noiselessly come and snuffle about our hand, the excessive reflex effects of tickling, etc., show how exciting the sensation of motion is *per se*. A kitten cannot help pursuing a moving ball. Impressions too faint to be cognized at all are immediately felt if they move. A fly sitting is unnoticed,—we feel it the moment it crawls. A shadow may be too faint to be perceived. If we hold a finger between our closed eyelid and the sunshine we

[1] *Vierteljahrsschrift für wissenschaftliche Philosophie*, ii, 377.

do not notice its presence. The moment we move it to and fro, however, we discern it. Such visual perception as this reproduces the conditions of sight among the radiates.

In ourselves, the main function of the peripheral parts of the retina is that of sentinels, which, when beams of light move over them, cry 'Who goes there?' and call the fovea to the spot. Most parts of the skin do but perform the same office for the finger-tips. Of course *movement of surface under object is (for purposes of stimulation) equivalent to movement of object over surface*. In exploring the shapes and sizes of things by either eye or skin the movements of these organs are incessant and unrestrainable. Every such movement draws the points and lines of the object across the surface, imprints them a hundred times more sharply, and drives them home to the attention. The immense part thus played by movements in our perceptive activity is held by many psychologists to prove that the muscles are themselves the space-perceiving organ. Not surface-sensibility, but 'the muscular sense,' is for these writers the original and only revealer of objective extension. But they have all failed to notice with what peculiar intensity muscular movements call surface-sensibilities into play, and how largely the mere discernment of impressions depends on the mobility of the surfaces upon which they fall.

Our *articular surfaces are tactile organs* which become intensely painful when inflamed. Besides pressure, *the only stimulus they receive is their motion upon each other*. To the sensation of this motion more than anything else seems due the perception of the position which our limbs may have assumed. Patients cutaneously and muscularly anæsthetic in one leg can often prove that their articular sensibility remains, by showing (by movements of their well leg) the positions in which the surgeon may place their insensible one. Goldscheider in Berlin caused fingers, arms, and legs to be passively rotated upon their various joints in a mechanical apparatus which registered both the velocity of movement impressed and the amount of angular rotation. The minimal felt amounts of rotation were much less than a single angular degree in all the joints except those of the fingers. Such displacements as these, Goldscheider says, can hardly be detected by the eye. Anæsthesia of the skin produced by induction-currents had no disturbing effect on the perception, nor did the various degrees of pressure of the moving force upon the skin affect it. It became, in fact, all the more distinct in proportion as the concomitant pressure-feelings were eliminated by artificial anæsthesia. When the joints themselves, however, were made artificially anæsthetic, the perception of the movement grew obtuse and the angular rotations had to be much increased before they were perceptible. All these facts prove, according to Herr Goldscheider, that *the joint-surfaces and these alone are the seat of the impressions by which the movements of our members are immediately perceived.*

2) **Sensations of Movement through Space.**—These may be divided into feelings of rotation and feelings of translation. As was stated at the end of the chapter on the ear, the labyrinth (semicircular canals, utricle and saccule) seems to have nothing to do with hearing. It is conclusively established to-day that the semicircular canals are the organs of a sixth special sense, that namely of rotation. When subjectively excited, this sensation is known as *dizziness* or *vertigo*, and rapidly engenders the farther feeling of nausea. Irritative disease of the inner ear causes intense vertigo (Ménière's disease). Traumatic irritation of the canals in birds and mammals makes the animals tumble and throw themselves about in a way best explained by supposing them to suffer from false sensations of falling, etc., which they compensate by reflex muscular acts that throw them the other way. Galvanic irritation of the membranous canals in pigeons causes just the same compensatory movements of head and eye which actual rotations impressed on the creatures produce. Deaf and dumb persons (amongst whom many must have had their auditory nerves or labyrinths destroyed by the same disease which took away their hearing) are in a very large percentage of cases found quite insusceptible of being made dizzy by rotation. Purkinje and Mach have shown that, whatever the organ of the sense of rotation may be, it must have its seat in the head. The body is excluded by Mach's elaborate experiments.

The semicircular canals, being, as it were, six little spirit-levels in three rectangular planes, seem admirably adapted to be organs of a sense of rotation. We need only suppose that when the head turns in the plane of any one of them, the relative inertia of the endolymph momentarily increases its pressure on the nerve-termini in the appropriate ampulla, which pressure starts a current towards the central organ for feeling vertigo. This organ seems to be the cerebellum, and the teleology of the whole business would appear to be the maintenance of the upright position. If a man stand with shut eyes and attend to his body, he will find that he is hardly for a moment in equilibrium. Incipient fallings towards every side in succession are incessantly repaired by muscular contractions which restore the balance; and although impressions on the tendons, ligaments, foot-soles, joints, etc., doubtless are among the causes of the compensatory contractions, yet the strongest and most special reflex arc would seem to be that which has the sensation of incipient vertigo for its afferent member. This is experimentally proved to be much more easily excited than the other sensations referred to. When the cerebellum is disorganized the reflex response fails to occur properly and loss of equilibrium is the result. Irritation of the cerebellum produces vertigo, loss of balance, and nausea; and galvanic currents through the head produce various forms of vertigo correlated with their direction. It seems probable that direct excitement of the cerebellar centre is responsible for these feelings. In addition to these corporeal reflexes the sense of rotation causes compensatory rollings of the eyeballs in the opposite direction, to which some of the subjective phenomena of *optical vertigo* are due. Steady rotation gives no sensation; it is only starting or stopping, or, more generally speaking, acceleration (positive or negative), which impresses the end-organs in the ampullæ. The sensation always has a little duration, however; and the feeling of reversed movement after whirling violently may last for nearly a minute, slowly fading out.

The cause of the *sense of translation* (movement forwards or backwards) is more open to dispute. The seat of this sensation has been assigned to the semicircular canals when compounding their currents to the brain; and also to the utricle. The latest experimenter, M. Delage, considers that it cannot possibly be in the head, and assigns it rather to the entire body, so far as its parts (blood-vessels, viscera, etc.) are movable against each other and suffer friction or pressure from their relative inertia when a movement of translation begins. M. Delage's exclusion of the labyrinth from this form of sensibility cannot, however, yet be considered definitively established, so the matter may rest with this mention.

CHAPTER VII

THE STRUCTURE OF THE BRAIN*

Embryological Sketch.—The brain is a sort of *pons asino-rum* in anatomy until one gets a certain general conception of it as a clue. Then it becomes a comparatively simple affair. The clue is given by comparative anatomy and especially by embryology. At a certain moment in the development of all the higher vertebrates the cerebro-spinal axis is formed by a hollow tube containing fluid and terminated in front by an enlargement separated by transverse constrictions into three 'cerebral vesicles,' so called (see Fig. 28). The walls of these vesicles thicken in most places, change in others into a thin vascular tissue, and in others again send out processes which produce an appearance of farther subdivision. The middle vesicle or mid-brain (*M-b* in the figures) is the least affected by change. Its upper walls thicken into the optic lobes, or *corpora quadrigemina* as they are named in man; its lower walls become the so-called peduncles or *crura* of the brain; and its cavity dwindles into the aqueduct of Silvius. A section through the adult human mid-brain is shown in Fig. 31.

The anterior and posterior vesicles undergo much more considerable change. The walls of the posterior vesicle thicken enormously in their foremost portion and form the *cerebellum* on top (*Cb* in all the figures) and the *pons Varolii* below (*P.V.* in Fig. 33). In its hindmost portions the posterior vesicle thickens below into the medulla oblongata (*Mo* in all the figures), whilst on top its walls thin out and melt, so that one can pass a probe into the cavity without breaking through any truly nervous tissue. The cavity which one thus enters from

*This chapter will be understood as a mere sketch for beginners. Models will be found of assistance. The best is the 'Cerveau de Texture de Grande Dimension,' made by Auzoux, 56 Rue de Vaugirard, Paris. It is a wonderful work of art, and costs 300 francs. M. Jules Talrich of No. 97 Boulevard Saint-Germain, Paris, makes a series of five large plaster models, which I have found very useful for class-room purposes. They cost 350 francs, and are far better than any German models which I have seen.

without is named the *fourth ventricle* (4 in Figs. 32 and 33).
One can run the probe forwards through it, passing first under the cerebellum and then under a thin sheet of nervous
tissue (the *valve of Vieussens*) just anterior thereto, as far as the
aqueduct of Silvius. Passing through this, the probe emerges
forwards into what was once the cavity of the anterior vesicle.
But the covering has melted away at this place, and the cavity
now forms a deep compressed pit or groove between the two
walls of the vesicle, and is called the *third ventricle* (3 in Figs.
32 and 33). The 'aqueduct of Sylvius' is in consequence of this
connection often called the *iter a tertio ad quartum ventricu-
lum*. The walls of the vesicle form the *optic thalami* (*Th* in all
the figures).

From the anterior vesicle just in front of the thalami there
buds out on either side an enlargement, into which the cavity
of the vesicle continues, and which becomes the *hemisphere* of
that side. In man its walls thicken enormously and form folds,
the so-called *convolutions*, on their surface. At the same time
they grow backwards rather than forwards of their starting-
point just in front of the thalamus, arching over the latter;
and growing fastest along their top circumference, they end
by bending downwards and forwards again when they have
passed the rear end of the thalamus. When fully developed in
man, they overlay and cover in all the other parts of the brain.
Their cavities form the *lateral ventricles*, easier to understand

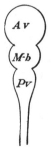

FIG. 28.   FIG. 29.

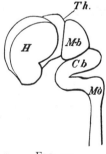

FIG. 30.

(All after Huguenin.)

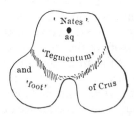

FIG. 31.—The 'nates' are the anterior corpora quadrigemina, the spot above *aq* is a section of the sylvian aqueduct, and the tegmentum and two 'feet' together make the Crura. These are marked *C.C.*, in Fig. 33, and a cross (+) marks the aqueduct, in Fig. 32.

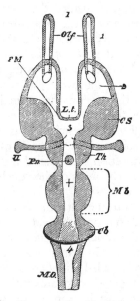

FIG. 32 (after Huxley).

by a dissection than by a description. A probe can be passed into either of them from the third ventricle at its anterior end; and like the third ventricle, their wall is melted down along a certain line, forming a long cleft through which they can be entered without rupturing the nervous tissue. This cleft, on account of the growth of the hemisphere outwards, backwards, and then downwards from its starting point, has got rolled in and tucked away beneath the apparent surface.[1]

At first the two hemispheres are connected only with their respective thalami. But during the fourth and fifth months of embryonic life they become connected with each other above the thalami through the growth between them of a massive system of transverse fibres which crosses the median line like a great bridge and is called the *corpus callosum*. These fibres radiate in the walls of both hemispheres and form a direct con-

---

[1] All the places in the brain at which the cavities come through are filled in during life by prolongations of the membrane called *pia mater*, carrying rich plexuses of blood-vessels in their folds.

nection between the convolutions of the right and of the left side. Beneath the corpus callosum another system of fibres called the *fornix* is formed, between which and the corpus callosum there is a peculiar connection. Just in front of the thalami, where the hemispheres begin their growth, a ganglionic mass called the *corpus striatum* (*C.S.*, Figs. 32 and 33) is formed in their wall. It is complex in structure, consisting of two main parts, called *nucleus lenticularis* and *nucleus caudatus* respectively. The figures, with their respective explanations, will give a better idea of the farther details of structure than any verbal description; so, after some practical directions for dissecting the organ, I will pass to a brief account of the physiological relations of its different parts to each other.

Dissection of Sheep's Brain.—The way really to understand the brain is to dissect it. The brains of mammals differ only in their proportions, and from the sheep's one can learn all that is essential in man's. The student is therefore strongly urged to dissect a sheep's brain. Full directions of the order of procedure are given in the human dissecting books, e.g., Holden's *Practical Anatomy* (Churchill), Morrell's *Student's Manual of Comparative Anatomy, and Guide to Dissection* (Longmans), and Foster and Langley's *Practical Physiology* (Macmillan). For the use of classes who cannot procure these books I subjoin a few practical notes. The instruments needed are a small saw, a chisel with a shoulder, and a hammer with a hook on its handle, all three of which form part of the regular medical autopsy-kit and can be had of surgical-instrument-makers. In addition a scalpel, a pair of scissors, a pair of

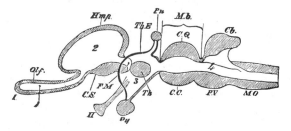

FIG. 33 (after Huxley).

dissecting-forceps, and a silver probe are required. The solitary student can find home-made substitutes for all these things but the forceps, which he ought to buy.

The first thing is to get off the skull-cap. Make two sawcuts, through the prominent portion of each condyle (or articular surface bounding the hole at the back of the skull, where the spinal cord enters) and passing forwards to the temples of the animal. Then make two cuts, one on each side, which cross these and meet in an angle on the frontal bone. By actual trial, one will find the best direction for the sawcuts. It is hard to saw entirely through the skull-bone without in some places also sawing into the brain. Here is where the chisel comes in—one can break by a smart blow on it with the hammer any parts of the skull not quite sawn through. When the skull-cap is ready to come off one will feel it 'wobble.' Insert then the hook under its forward end and pull firmly. The bony skull-cap alone will come away, leaving the periosteum of the inner surface adhering to that of the base of the skull, enveloping the brain, and forming the so-called *dura mater* or outer one of its 'meninges.' This dura mater should be slit open round the margins, when the brain will be exposed wrapped in its nearest membrane, the *pia mater*, full of blood-vessels whose branches penetrate the tissues.

The brain in its pia mater should now be carefully 'shelled out.' Usually it is best to begin at the forward end, turning it up there and gradually working backwards. The *olfactory lobes* are liable to be torn; they must be carefully scooped from the pits in the base of the skull to which they adhere by the branches which they send through the bone into the nose-cavity. It is well to have a little blunt curved instrument expressly for this purpose. Next the *optic nerves* tie the brain down, and must be cut through—close to the chiasma is easiest. After that comes the *pituitary body*, which has to be left behind. It is attached by a neck, the so-called *infundibulum*, into the upper part of which the cavity of the third ventricle is prolonged downwards for a short distance. It has no known function and is probably a 'rudimentary organ.' Other nerves, into the detail of which I shall not go, must be cut successively. Their places in the human brain are shown in Fig. 34. When they are divided, and the portion of dura mater (tento-

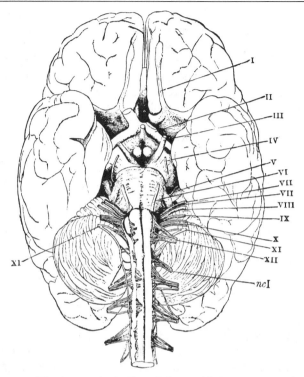

FIG. 34.—The human brain from below, with its nerves numbered (after Henle). I, olfactory; II, optic; III, oculo-motorius; IV, trochlearis; V, trifacial; VI, abducens oculi; VII, facial; VIII, auditory; IX, glosso-pharyngeal; X, pneumogastric; XI, spinal accessory; XII, hypoglossal; *nc*I, first cervical, etc.

rium) which projects between the hemispheres and the cerebellum is cut through at its edges, the brain comes readily out.

It is best examined fresh. If numbers of brains have to be prepared and kept, I have found it a good plan to put them first in a solution of chloride of zinc, just dense enough at first to float them, and to leave them for a fortnight or less. This softens the pia mater, which can then be removed in large shreds, after which it is enough to place them in quite weak alcohol to preserve them indefinitely, tough, elastic, and in their natural shape, though bleached to a uniform white color. Before immersion in the chloride all the more superficial adhesions of the parts must be broken through, to bring the fluid into contact with a maximum of surface. If the brain is used fresh, the pia mater had better be removed carefully in most places with the forceps, scalpel, and scissors. Over the grooves between the cerebellum and hemispheres, and between the cerebellum and medulla oblongata, thin cobwebby moist transparent vestiges of the *arachnoid* membrane will be found.

The subdivisions may now be examined in due order. For the convolutions, blood-vessels, and nerves the more special books must be consulted.

First, looked at from above, with the deep *longitudinal fissure* between them, the hemispheres are seen partly overlapping the intricately wrinkled *cerebellum*, which juts out behind, and covers in turn almost all the medulla oblongata. Drawing the hemispheres apart, the brilliant white *corpus callosum* is revealed, some half an inch below their surface. There is no median partition in the cerebellum, but a median elevation instead.

Looking at the brain from below, one still sees the longitudinal fissure in the median line in front, and on either side of it the *olfactory lobes*, much larger than in man; the *optic tracts* and *commissure* or *'chiasma'*; the *infundibulum* cut through just behind them; and behind that the single *corpus albicans* or *mamillare*, whose function is unknown and which is double in man. Next the *crura* appear, converging upon the pons as if carrying fibres back from either side. The *pons* itself succeeds, much less prominent than in man; and finally behind it comes the medulla oblongata, broad and flat and relatively large. The pons looks like a sort of collar uniting the two halves of the cerebellum, and surrounding the medulla, whose fibres by the time they have emerged anteriorly from beneath the collar have divided into the two crura. The inner relations are, however, somewhat less simple than what this description may suggest.

Now turn forwards the cerebellum; pull out the vascular *choroid plexuses* of the pia, which fill the fourth ventricle; and bring the upper surface of the *medulla oblongata* into view.

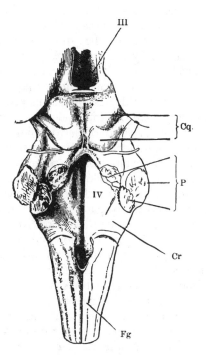

FIG. 35.—Fourth ventricle, etc. (Henle). *III*, third ventricle; *IV*, fourth ventricle; *P*, anterior, middle, and posterior peduncles of cerebellum cut through; *Cr*, restiform body; *Fg*, funiculus gracilis; *Cq*, corpora quadrigemina.

The *fourth ventricle* is a triangular depression terminating in a posterior point called the *calamus scriptorius*. (Here a very fine probe may pass into the central canal of the spinal cord.) The lateral boundary of the ventricle on either side is formed by the *restiform body* or *column*, which runs into the cerebellum, forming its *inferior* or *posterior peduncle* on that side. Including the calamus scriptorius by their divergence, the posterior columns of the spinal cord continue into the medulla as the *fasciculi graciles*. These are at first separated from the broad restiform bodies by a slight groove. But this disappears anteriorly, and the 'slender' and 'ropelike' strands soon become outwardly indistinguishable.

Turn next to the ventral surface of the medulla, and note the *anterior pyramids*, two roundish cords, one on either side of the slight *median groove*. The pyramids are crossed and closed over anteriorly by the *pons Varolii*, a broad transverse band which surrounds them like a collar, and runs up into the cerebellum on either side, forming its *middle peduncles*. The pons has a slight median depression and its posterior edge is formed by the *trapezium* on either side. The trapezium consists of fibres which, instead of surrounding the pyramid, seem to start from alongside of it. It is not visible in man. The *olivary bodies* are small eminences on the medulla lying just laterally of the pyramids and below the trapezium.

Now cut through the peduncles of the cerebellum, close to their entrance into that organ. They give one surface of section on each side, though they receive contributions from three directions. The posterior and middle portions we have seen: the *anterior peduncles* pass forwards to the *corpora quadrigemina*. The thin white layer of nerve-tissue between them and continuous with them is called the *valve of Vieussens*. It covers part of the canal from the fourth ventricle to the third. The cerebellum being removed, examine it, and cut sections to show the peculiar distribution of white and gray matter, forming an appearance called the *arbor vitæ* in the books.

Now bend up the posterior edge of the hemispheres, exposing the corpora quadrigemina (of which the anterior pair are dubbed the *nates* and the posterior the *testes*), and noticing the *pineal gland*, a small median organ situated just in front of them and probably, like the pituitary body, a vestige of something useful in premammalian times. The rounded posterior edge of the corpus callosum is visible now passing from one hemisphere to the other. Turn it still farther up, letting the medulla, etc., hang down as much as possible and trace the under surface from this edge forwards. It is broad behind but narrows forwards, becoming continuous with the *fornix*. The anterior stem, so to speak, of this organ plunges down just in front of the *optic thalami*, which now appear with the fornix arching over them, and the median *third ventricle* between them. The margins of the fornix, as they pass backwards, diverge laterally farther than the margins of the corpus callo-

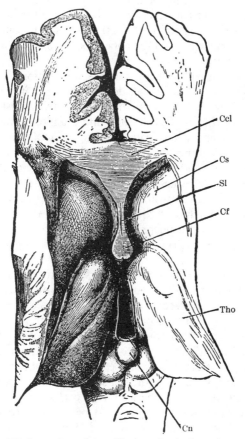

FIG. 36.—Horizontal section of human brain just above the thalami.—*Ccl*, corpus callosum in section; *Cs*, corpus striatum; *Sl*, septum lucidum; *Cf*, columns of the fornix; *Tho*, optic thalami; *Cn*, pineal gland. (After Henle.)

sum, and under the name of *corpora fimbriata* are carried into the lateral ventricles, as will be seen again.

It takes a good topographical mind to understand these ventricles clearly, even when they are followed with eye and hand. A verbal description is absolutely useless. The essential thing to remember is that they are offshoots from the original cavity (now the third ventricle) of the anterior vesicle, and that a great split has occurred in the walls of the hemispheres so that they (the lateral ventricles) now communicate with the exterior along a cleft which appears sickle-shaped, as it were, and folded in.

The student will probably examine the relations of the parts in various ways. But he will do well to begin in any case by cutting horizontal slices off the hemispheres almost down to the level of the corpus callosum, and examining the distribution of gray and white matter on the surfaces of section, any one of which is the so-called *centrum ovale*. Then let him cut down in a fore-and-aft direction along the edge of the corpus callosum, till he comes 'through' and draw the hemispherical margin of the cut outwards—he will see a space which is the ventricle, and which farther cutting along the side and removing of its hemisphere-roof will lay more bare. The most conspicuous object on its floor is the *nucleus caudatus* of the *corpus striatum*.

Cut the corpus callosum transversely through near its posterior edge and bend the anterior portion of it forwards and sideways. The rear edge (*splenium*) left *in situ* bends round and downwards and becomes continuous with the *fornix*. The anterior part is also continuous with the fornix, but more along the median line, where a thinnish membrane, the *septum lucidum*, triangular in shape, reaching from the one body to the other, practically forms a sort of partition between the contiguous portion of the lateral ventricles on the two sides. Break through the *septum* if need be and expose the upper surface of the fornix, broad behind and narrow in front where its *anterior pillars* plunge down in front of the third ventricle (from a thickening in whose anterior walls they were originally formed), and finally penetrate the corpus albicans. Cut these pillars through and fold them back, exposing the thalamic portion of the brain, and noting the under surface of the fornix. Its diverging *posterior pillars* run backwards, downwards, and then forwards again, forming with their sharp edges the *corpora fimbriata*, which bound the cleft by which the ventricle lies open. The semi-cylindrical welts behind the *corpora fimbriata* and parallel thereto in the wall of the ventricle are the *hippocampi*. Imagine the fornix and corpus callosum shortened in the fore-and-aft direction to a transverse cord; imagine the hemispheres not having grown backwards and downwards round the thalamus; and the corpus fimbriatum on either side would then be the upper or anterior margin of a split in the wall of the hemispheric ventricle of which the lower and posterior margin would be the posterior border of the corpus striatum where it grows out of the thalamus.

The little notches just behind the anterior pillar of the fornix and between them and the thalami are the so-called *foramina of Monro* through which the plexus of vessels, etc., passes from the median to the lateral ventricles.

See the thick *middle commissure* joining the two thalami, just as the corpus callosum and fornix join the hemispheres. These are all embryological aftergrowths. Seek also the *anterior commissure* crossing just in front of the anterior pillars of the fornix, as well as the *posterior commissure* with its lateral prolongations along the thalami, just below the pineal gland.

On a median section, note the thinnish *anterior wall* of the third ventricle and its prolongation downwards into the *infundibulum*.

Turn up or cut off the rear end of one hemisphere so as to see clearly the optic tracts turning upwards towards the rear corner of the thalamus. The *corpora geniculata* to which they also go, distinct in man, are less so in the sheep. The lower ones are visible between the optic-tract band and the 'testes,' however.

The brain's principal parts are thus passed in review. A longitudinal section of the whole organ through the median line will be found most instructive (Fig. 37). The student should also (on a *fresh* brain, or one hardened in bichromate of potash or ammonia to save the contrast of color between white and gray matter) make transverse sections through the *nates* and *crura*, and through the hemispheres just in front of the corpus albicans. The latter section shows on each side the *nucleus lenticularis* of the corpus striatum, and also the *inner capsule* (see Fig. 38, *Nl*, and *Ic*).

When all is said and done, the fact remains that, for the

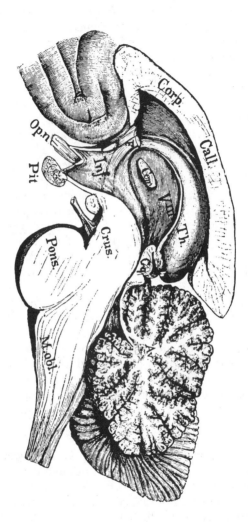

FIG. 37.—Median section of human brain below the hemispheres.
Th., thalamus; *Cq*, corpora quadrigemina; *V*III, third ventricle; *Com*,
middle commissure; *F*, columns of fornix; *Inf.*, infundibulum; *Op.n*,
optic nerve; *Pit*, pituitary body; *Av.*, arbor vitæ. (After Obersteiner.)

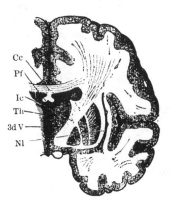

FIG. 38.—Transverse section through right hemisphere (after Gegen-baur). *Cc*, corpus callosum; *Pf*, pillars of fornix; *Ic*, internal capsule; *V*, third ventricle; *Nl*, nucleus lenticularis.

beginner, the understanding of the brain's structure is not an easy thing. It must be gone over and forgotten and learned again many times before it is definitively assimilated by the mind. But patience and repetition, here as elsewhere, will bear their perfect fruit.

CHAPTER VIII

THE FUNCTIONS OF THE BRAIN

General Idea of Nervous Function.—If I begin chopping the foot of a tree, its branches are unmoved by my act, and its leaves murmur as peacefully as ever in the wind. If, on the contrary, I do violence to the foot of a fellow-man, the rest of his body instantly responds to the aggression by movements of alarm or defence. The reason of this difference is that the man has a nervous system, whilst the tree has none; and the function of the nervous system is to bring each part into harmonious coöperation with every other. The afferent nerves, when excited by some physical irritant, be this as gross in its mode of operation as a chopping axe or as subtle as the waves of light, convey the excitement to the nervous centres. The commotion set up in the centres does not stop there, but discharges through the efferent nerves, exciting movements which vary with the animal and with the irritant applied. These acts of response have usually the common character of being of service. They ward off the noxious stimulus and support the beneficial one; whilst if, in itself indifferent, the stimulus be a sign of some distant circumstance of practical importance, the animal's acts are addressed to this circumstance so as to avoid its perils or secure its benefits, as the case may be. To take a common example, if I hear the conductor calling 'All aboard!' as I enter the station, my heart first stops, then palpitates, and my legs respond to the air-waves falling on my tympanum by quickening their movements. If I stumble as I run, the sensation of falling provokes a movement of the hands towards the direction of the fall, the effect of which is to shield the body from too sudden a shock. If a cinder enter my eye, its lids close forcibly and a copious flow of tears tends to wash it out.

These three responses to a sensational stimulus differ, however, in many respects. The closure of the eye and the lachrymation are quite involuntary, and so is the disturbance of the heart. Such involuntary responses we know as 'reflex' acts. The motion of the arms to break the shock of falling may also be called reflex, since it occurs too quickly to be deliberately intended. It is, at any rate, less automatic than the previous acts, for a man might by conscious effort learn to perform it more skilfully, or even to suppress it altogether. Actions of this kind, into which instinct and volition enter upon equal terms, have been called 'semi-reflex.' The act of running towards the train, on the other hand, has no instinctive element about it. It is purely the result of education, and is preceded by a consciousness of the purpose to be attained and a distinct mandate of the will. It is a 'voluntary act.' Thus the animal's reflex and voluntary performances shade into each other gradually, being connected by acts which may often occur automatically, but may also be modified by conscious intelligence.

The Frog's Nerve-centres.—Let us now look a little more closely at what goes on.

The best way to enter the subject will be to take a lower creature, like a frog, and study by the vivisectional method the functions of his different nerve-centres. The frog's nerve-centres are figured in the diagram over the page, which needs no further explanation. I shall first proceed to state what happens when various amounts of the anterior parts are removed, in different frogs, in the way in which an ordinary student removes them—that is, with no extreme precautions as to the purity of the operation.

If, then, we reduce the frog's nervous system to the spinal cord alone, by making a section behind the base of the skull, between the spinal cord and the medulla oblongata, thereby cutting off the brain from all connection with the rest of the body, the frog will still continue to live, but with a very peculiarly modified activity. It ceases to breathe or swallow; it lies flat on its belly, and does not, like a normal frog, sit up on its fore-paws, though its hind-legs are kept, as usual, folded against its body and immediately resume this position if drawn out. If thrown on its back it lies there quietly, without turning over like a normal frog. Locomotion and voice seem entirely abolished. If we suspend it by the nose, and irritate different portions of its skin by acid, it performs a set of remarkable 'defensive' movements calculated to wipe away the irritant. Thus, if the breast be touched, both fore-paws will rub it vigorously; if we touch the outer side of the elbow, the

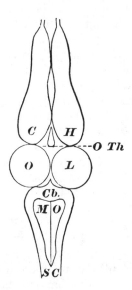

FIG. 39.—*C H*, cerebral hemispheres; *O Th*, optic thalami; *O L*, optic lobes; *Cb.*, cerebellum; *M O*, medulla oblongata; *S C*, spinal cord.

hind-foot of the same side will rise directly to the spot and wipe it. The back of the foot will rub the knee if that be attacked, whilst if the foot be cut away, the stump will make ineffectual movements, and then, in many frogs, a pause will come, as if for deliberation, succeeded by a rapid passage of the opposite unmutilated foot to the acidulated spot.

The most striking character of all these movements, after their teleological appropriateness, is their precision. They vary, in sensitive frogs and with a proper amount of irritation, so little as almost to resemble in their machine-like regularity the performances of a jumping-jack, whose legs must twitch whenever you pull the string. The spinal cord of the frog thus contains arrangements of cells and fibres fitted to convert skin-irritations into movements of defence. We may call it the *centre for defensive movements* in this animal. We may indeed go farther than this, and by cutting the spinal cord in various places find that its separate segments are independent mechanisms, for appropriate activities of the head and of the arms and legs respectively. The segment governing the arms is especially active, in male frogs, in the breeding season; and these members alone, with the breast and back appertaining to them, and everything else cut away, will actively grasp a finger placed between them and remain hanging to it for a considerable time.

Similarly of the medulla oblongata, optic lobes, and other centres between the spinal cord and the hemispheres of the frog. Each of them is proved by experiment to contain a mechanism for the accurate execution, in response to definite stimuli, of certain special acts. Thus with the medulla the animal swallows; with the medulla and cerebellum together he jumps, swims, and turns over from his back; with his optic lobes he croaks when pinched; etc. *A frog which has lost his cerebral hemispheres alone is by an unpractised observer indistinguishable from a normal animal.*

Not only is he capable, on proper instigation, of all the acts already mentioned, but he guides himself by sight, so that if an obstacle be set up between him and the light, and he be forced to move forwards, he either jumps over it or swerves to one side. He manifests sexual passion at the proper season, and, unlike an altogether brainless frog, which embraces anything placed between his arms, postpones this reflex act until a female of his own species is provided. Thus far, as aforesaid, a person unfamiliar with frogs might not suspect a mutilation; but even such a person would soon remark the almost entire absence of spontaneous motion—that is, motion unprovoked by any present incitation of sense. The continued movements of swimming, performed by the creature in the water, seem to be the fatal result of the contact of that fluid with its skin. They cease when a stick, for example, touches his hands. This is a sensible irritant towards which the feet are automatically drawn by reflex action, and on which the animal remains sitting. He manifests no hunger, and will suffer a fly to crawl over his nose unsnapped at. Fear, too, seems to have deserted him. In a word, he is an extremely complex machine whose actions, so far as they go, tend to self-preservation; but still a *machine*, in this sense—that it seems to contain no incalculable element. By applying the right sensory stimulus to him we are almost as certain of getting a fixed response as an organist is of hearing a certain tone when he pulls out a certain stop.

But now if to the lower centres we add the cerebral hemispheres, or if, in other words, we make an intact animal the subject of our observations, all this is changed. In addition to the previous responses to present incitements of sense, our frog now goes through long and complex acts of locomotion *spontaneously*, or as if moved by what in ourselves we should call an idea. His reactions to outward stimuli vary their form, too. Instead of making simple defensive movements with his hind-legs, like a headless frog, if touched; or of giving one or two leaps and then sitting still like a hemisphereless one, he makes persistent and varied efforts of escape, as if, not the mere contact of the physiologist's hand, but the notion of danger suggested by it were now his spur. Led by the feeling of hunger, too, he goes in search of insects, fish, or smaller frogs, and varies his procedure with each species of victim. The physiologist cannot by manipulating him elicit croaking, crawling up a board, swimming or stopping, at will. His conduct has become incalculable—we can no longer foretell it exactly. Effort to escape is his dominant reaction, but he *may* do anything else, even swell up and become perfectly passive in our hands.

Such are the phenomena commonly observed, and such the impressions which one naturally receives. Certain general conclusions follow irresistibly. First of all the following:

The acts of all the centres involve the use of the same muscles. When a brainless frog's hind-leg wipes the acid, he calls into play all the leg-muscles which a frog with his full medulla oblongata and cerebellum uses when he turns from his back to his belly. Their contractions are, however, *combined* differently in the two cases, so that the results vary widely. We must consequently conclude that specific arrangements of cells and fibres exist in the cord for wiping, in the medulla for turning over, etc. Similarly they exist in the thalami for jumping over seen obstacles and for balancing the moved body; in the optic lobes for creeping backwards, or what not. But in the hemispheres, since the presence of these organs *brings no new elementary form of movement* with it, but only *determines differently the occasions* on which the movements shall occur, making the usual stimuli less fatal and machine-like, we need suppose no such machinery *directly* coördinative of muscular contractions to exist. We may rather assume, when the mandate for a wiping-movement is sent forth by the hemispheres, that a current goes straight to the wiping-arrangement in the spinal cord, exciting this arrangement as a whole. Similarly, if an intact frog wishes to jump, all he need do is to excite from the hemispheres the jumping-centre in the thalami or wherever it may be, and the latter will provide for the details of the execution. It is like a general ordering a colonel to make a certain movement, but not telling him how it shall be done.

The same muscle, then, is repeatedly represented at different heights; and at each it enters into a different combination with other muscles to coöperate in some special form of concerted movement. At each height the movement is discharged by some particular form of sensorial stimulus, whilst the stimuli which discharge the hemispheres would seem not so much to be elementary sorts of sensation, as groups of sensations forming determinate *objects* or *things*.

The Pigeon's Lower Centres.—The results are just the same if, instead of a frog, we take a pigeon, cut out his hemispheres carefully and wait till he recovers from the operation. There is not a movement natural to him which this brainless bird cannot execute; he seems, too, after some days to execute movements from some inner irritation, for he moves spontaneously. But his emotions and instincts exist no longer. In Schrader's striking words:

"The hemisphereless animal moves in a world of bodies which . . . are all of equal value for him. . . . He is, to use Goltz's apt expression, *impersonal*. . . . Every object is for him only a space-occupying mass, he turns out of his path for an ordinary pigeon no otherwise than for a stone. He may try to climb over both. All authors agree that they never found any difference, whether it was an inanimate body, a cat, a dog, or a bird of prey which came in their pigeon's way. The creature knows neither friends nor enemies, in the thickest company it lives like a hermit. The languishing cooing of the male awakens no more impression than the rattling of the peas, or the call-whistle which in the days before the injury used to make the birds hasten to be fed. Quite as little as the earlier observers have I seen hemisphereless she-birds answer the courting of the male. A hemisphereless male will coo all day long and show distinct signs of sexual excitement, but his activity is without any object, it is entirely indifferent to him whether the she-bird be there or not. If one is placed near him, he leaves her unnoticed. . . . As the male pays no attention to the female, so she pays none to her young. The brood may follow the mother ceaselessly calling for food, but they might as well ask it from a stone. . . . The hemisphereless pigeon is in the highest degree tame, and fears man as little as cat or bird of prey."

General Notion of Hemispheres.—All these facts lead us, when we try to formulate them broadly, to some such conception as this: *The lower centres act from present sensational stimuli alone; the hemispheres act from considerations,* the sensations which they may receive serving only as suggesters of these. But what are considerations but expectations, in the fancy, of sensations which will be felt one way or another according as action takes this course or that? If I step aside on seeing a rattlesnake, from considering how dangerous an animal he is, the mental materials which constitute my prudential reflection are images more or less vivid of the movement of his head, of a sudden pain in my leg, of a state of terror, a swelling of the limb, a chill, delirium, death, etc., etc., and the ruin of my hopes. But all these images are constructed out of my past experiences. They are *reproductions* of what I have felt or witnessed. They are, in short, *remote* sensations; and the main difference between the hemisphereless animal and the whole one may be concisely expressed by saying that *the one obeys absent, the other only present, objects.*

The hemispheres would then seem to be the chief seat of memory. Vestiges of past experience must in some way be stored up in them, and must, when aroused by present stimuli, first appear as representations of distant goods and evils; and then must discharge into the appropriate motor channels for warding off the evil and securing the benefits of the good. If we liken the nervous currents to electric currents, we can compare the nervous system, C, below the hemispheres to a direct circuit from sense-organ to muscle along the line S . . . C . . . M of

Fig. 40. The hemisphere, *H*, adds the long circuit or loop-line through which the current may pass when for any reason the direct line is not used.

Thus, a tired wayfarer on a hot day throws himself on the damp earth beneath a maple-tree. The sensations of delicious rest and coolness pouring themselves through the direct line would naturally discharge into the muscles of complete extension: he would abandon himself to the dangerous repose. But the loop-line being open, part of the current is drafted along it, and awakens rheumatic or catarrhal reminiscences, which prevail over the instigations of sense, and make the man arise and pursue his way to where he may enjoy his rest more safely. Presently we shall examine the manner in which the hemispheric loop-line may be supposed to serve as a reservoir for such reminiscences as these. Meanwhile I will ask the reader to notice some corollaries of its being such a reservoir.

First, no animal without it can deliberate, pause, postpone, nicely weigh one motive against another, or compare. Prudence, in a word, is for such a creature an impossible virtue. Accordingly we see that nature removes those functions in the exercise of which prudence is a virtue from the lower centres and hands them over to the cerebrum. Wherever a creature has to deal with complex features of the environment, prudence is a virtue. The higher animals have so to deal; and the more complex the features, the higher we call the animals. The fewer of his acts, then, can *such* an animal perform with-

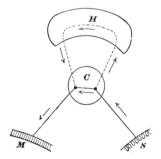

FIG. 40.

out the help of the organs in question. In the frog many acts
devolve wholly on the lower centres; in the bird fewer; in the
rodent fewer still; in the dog very few indeed; and in apes and
men hardly any at all.

The advantages of this are obvious. Take the prehension of
food as an example and suppose it to be a reflex performance
of the lower centres. The animal will be condemned fatally
and irresistibly to snap at it whenever presented, no matter
what the circumstances may be; he can no more disobey this
prompting than water can refuse to boil when a fire is kindled
under the pot. His life will again and again pay the forfeit of
his gluttony. Exposure to retaliation, to other enemies, to
traps, to poisons, to the dangers of repletion, must be regular
parts of his existence. His lack of all thought by which to
weigh the danger against the attractiveness of the bait, and of
all volition to remain hungry a little while longer, is the direct
measure of his lowness in the mental scale. And those fishes
which, like our cunners and sculpins, are no sooner thrown
back from the hook into the water than they automatically
seize the hook again, would soon expiate the degradation of
their intelligence by the extinction of their type, did not their
extraordinary fecundity atone for their imprudence. Appetite
and the acts it prompts have consequently become in all
higher vertebrates functions of the cerebrum. They disappear
when the physiologist's knife has left the subordinate centres
alone in place. The brainless pigeon will starve though left on
a corn-heap.

Take again the sexual function. In birds this devolves exclusively upon the hemispheres. When these are shorn away the
pigeon pays no attention to the billings and cooings of its
mate. And Goltz found that a bitch in heat would excite no
emotion in male dogs who had suffered large loss of cerebral
tissue. Those who have read Darwin's *Descent of Man* know
what immense importance in the amelioration of the breed in
birds this author ascribes to the fact of sexual selection. The
sexual act is not performed until every condition of circumstance and sentiment is fulfilled, until time, place, and partner
all are fit. But in frogs and toads this passion devolves on the
lower centres. They show consequently a machine-like obedience to the present incitement of sense, and an almost total

exclusion of the power of choice. Copulation occurs *per fas aut nefas*, occasionally between males, often with dead females, in puddles exposed on the highway, and the male may be cut in two without letting go his hold. Every spring an immense sacrifice of batrachian life takes place from these causes alone.

No one need be told how dependent all human social elevation is upon the prevalence of chastity. Hardly any factor measures more than this the difference between civilization and barbarism. Physiologically interpreted, chastity means nothing more than the fact that present solicitations of sense are overpowered by suggestions of æsthetic and moral fitness which the circumstances awaken in the cerebrum; and that upon the inhibitory or permissive influence of these alone action directly depends.

Within the psychic life due to the cerebrum itself the same general distinction obtains, between considerations of the more immediate and considerations of the more remote. In all ages the man whose determinations are swayed by reference to the most distant ends has been held to possess the highest intelligence. The tramp who lives from hour to hour; the bohemian whose engagements are from day to day; the bachelor who builds but for a single life; the father who acts for another generation; the patriot who thinks of a whole community and many generations; and, finally, the philosopher and saint whose cares are for humanity and for eternity,—these range themselves in an unbroken hierarchy, wherein each successive grade results from an increased manifestation of the special form of action by which the cerebral centres are distinguished from all below them.

The Automaton-Theory.—In the 'loop-line' along which the memories and ideas of the distant are supposed to lie, the action, so far as it is a physical process, must be interpreted after the type of the action in the lower centres. If regarded here as a reflex process, it must be reflex there as well. The current in both places runs out into the muscles only after it has first run in; but whilst the path by which it runs out is determined in the lower centres by reflections few and fixed amongst the cell-arrangements, in the hemispheres the reflections are many and instable. This, it will be seen, is only a difference of degree and not of kind, and does not change the reflex type. The conception of *all* action as conforming to this type is the fundamental conception of modern nerve-physiology. This conception, now, has led to two quite opposite theories about the relation to consciousness of the nervous functions. Some authors, finding that the higher voluntary functions seem to require the guidance of feeling, conclude that over the lowest reflexes some such feeling also presides, though it may be a feeling connected with the spinal cord, of which the higher conscious self connected with the hemispheres remains unconscious. Others, finding that reflex and semi-automatic acts may, notwithstanding their appropriateness, take place with an unconsciousness apparently complete, fly to the opposite extreme and maintain that the appropriateness even of the higher voluntary actions connected with the hemispheres owes nothing to the fact that consciousness attends them. They are, according to these writers, results of physiological mechanism pure and simple.

To comprehend completely this latter doctrine one should apply it to examples. The movements of our tongues and pens, the flashings of our eyes in conversation, are of course events of a physiological order, and as such their causal antecedents may be exclusively mechanical. If we knew thoroughly the nervous system of Shakespeare, and as thoroughly all his environing conditions, we should be able, according to the theory of automatism, to show why at a given period of his life his hand came to trace on certain sheets of paper those crabbed little black marks which we for shortness' sake call the manuscript of *Hamlet*. We should understand the rationale of every erasure and alteration therein, and we should understand all this without in the slightest degree acknowledging the existence of the thoughts in Shakespeare's mind. The words and sentences would be taken, not as signs of anything beyond themselves, but as little outward facts, pure and simple. In like manner, the automaton-theory affirms, we might exhaustively write the biography of those two hundred pounds, more or less, of warmish albuminoid matter called Martin Luther, without ever implying that it felt.

But, on the other hand, nothing in all this could prevent us from giving an equally complete account of either Luther's or

Shakespeare's spiritual history, an account in which every gleam of thought and emotion should find its place. The mind-history would run alongside of the body-history of each man, and each point in the one would correspond to, but not react upon, a point in the other. So the melody floats from the harp-string, but neither checks nor quickens its vibrations; so the shadow runs alongside the pedestrian, but in no way influences his steps.

As a mere *conception*, and so long as we confine our view to the nervous centres themselves, few things are more seductive than this radically mechanical theory of their action. And yet our consciousness *is there*, and has in all probability been evolved, like all other functions, for a use — it is to the highest degree improbable *a priori* that it should have no use. Its use *seems* to be that of *selection*; but to select, it must be efficacious. States of consciousness which feel right are held fast to; those which feel wrong are checked. If the 'holding' and the 'checking' of the conscious states severally mean also the efficacious reinforcing or inhibiting of the correlated neural processes, then it would seem as if the presence of the states of mind might help to steer the nervous system and keep it in the path which to the consciousness seemed best. Now on the average what seems best to consciousness is really best for the creature. It is a well-known fact that pleasures are generally associated with beneficial, pains with detrimental, experiences. All the fundamental vital processes illustrate this law. Starvation; suffocation; privation of food, drink, and sleep; work when exhausted; burns, wounds, inflammation; the effects of poison, are as disagreeable as filling the hungry stomach, enjoying rest and sleep after fatigue, exercise after rest, and a sound skin and unbroken bones at all times, are pleasant. Mr. Spencer and others have suggested that these coincidences are due, not to any preëstablished harmony, but to the mere action of natural selection, which would certainly kill off in the long-run any breed of creatures to whom the fundamentally noxious experience seemed enjoyable. An animal that should take pleasure in a feeling of suffocation would, if that pleasure were efficacious enough to make him keep his head under water, enjoy a longevity of four or five minutes. But if conscious pleasure does not reinforce, and conscious pain does not inhibit anything, one does not see (without some such *a priori* rational harmony as would be scouted by the 'scientific' champions of the automaton-theory) why the most noxious acts, such as burning, might not with perfect impunity give thrills of delight, and the most necessary ones, such as breathing, cause agony. The only considerable attempt that has been made to explain the *distribution* of our feelings is that of Mr. Grant Allen in his suggestive little work, *Physiological Æsthetics*; and his reasoning is based exclusively on that causal efficacy of pleasures and pains which the partisans of pure automatism so strenuously deny.

Probability and circumstantial evidence thus run dead against the theory that our actions are *purely* mechanical in their causation. From the point of view of descriptive Psychology (even though we be bound to assume, as on p. 15, that all our feelings have brain-processes for their condition of existence, and can be remotely traced in every instance to currents coming from the outer world) we have no clear reason to doubt that the feelings may react so as to further or to dampen the processes to which they are due. I shall therefore not hesitate in the course of this book to use the language of common-sense. I shall talk as if consciousness kept actively pressing the nerve-centres in the direction of its own ends, and was no mere impotent and paralytic spectator of life's game.

The Localization of Functions in the Hemispheres.— The hemispheres, we lately said, must be the organ of memory, and in some way retain vestiges of former currents, by means of which mental considerations drawn from the past may be aroused before action takes place. The vivisections of physiologists and the observations of physicians have of late years given a concrete confirmation to this notion which the first rough appearances suggest. The various convolutions have had special functions assigned to them in relation to this and that sense-organ, as well as to this or that portion of the muscular system. This book is no place for going over the evidence in detail, so I will simply indicate the conclusions which are most probable at the date of writing.

Mental and Cerebral Elements.—In the first place, there is a very neat parallelism between the analysis of brain-functions by the physiologists and that of mental functions by the 'analytic' psychologists.

The phrenological brain-doctrine divided the brain into 'organs,' each of which stood for the man in a certain partial attitude. The organ of 'Philoprogenitiveness,' with its concomitant consciousness, is an entire man so far as he loves children, that of 'Reverence' is an entire man worshipping, etc. The spiritualistic psychology, in turn, divided the Mind into 'faculties,' which were also entire mental men in certain limited attitudes. But 'faculties' are not mental *elements* any more than 'organs' are brain-elements. Analysis breaks both into more elementary constituents.

Brain and mind alike consist of simple elements, sensory and motor. "All nervous centres," says Dr. J. Hughlings Jackson, "from the lowest to the very highest (the substrata of consciousness), are made up of nothing else than nervous arrangements representing impressions and movements. . . . I do not see of what other 'materials' the rest of the brain *can* be made." Meynert represents the matter similarly when he calls the cortex of the hemispheres the surface of projection for every muscle and every sensitive point of the body. The muscles and the sensitive points are *represented* each by a cortical point, and the Brain is little more than the sum of all these cortical points, to which, on the mental side, as many sensations and *ideas* correspond. The sensations and ideas of sensation and of motion are, in turn, the elements out of which the Mind is built according to the analytic school of psychology. The relations between objects are explained by 'associations' between the ideas; and the emotional and instinctive tendencies, by associations between ideas and movements. The same diagram can symbolize both the inner and the outer world; dots or circles standing indifferently for cells or ideas, and lines joining them, for fibres or associations. The associationist doctrine of 'ideas' may be doubted to be a literal expression of the truth, but it probably will always retain a didactic usefulness. At all events, it is interesting to see how well physiological analysis plays into its hands. To proceed to details.

The Motor Region.—The one thing which is *perfectly* well established is this, that the 'central' convolutions, on either side of the fissure of Rolando, and (at least in the monkey) the calloso-marginal convolution (which is continuous with them on the mesial surface where one hemisphere is applied against the other), form the region by which all the motor incitations which leave the cortex pass out, on their way to those executive centres in the region of the pons, medulla, and spinal cord from which the muscular contractions are discharged in the last resort. The existence of this so-called 'motor zone' is established by anatomical as well as vivisectional and pathological evidence.

The accompanying figures (Figs. 41 and 42), from Schäfer and Horsley, show the topographical arrangement of the monkey's motor zone more clearly than any description.

Fig. 43, after Starr, shows how the fibres run downwards. All sensory currents entering the hemispheres run out from the Rolandic region, which may thus be regarded as a sort of funnel of escape, which narrows still more as it plunges beneath the surface, traversing the inner capsule, pons, and parts below. The dark ellipses on the left half of the diagram stand for hemorrhages or tumors, and the reader can easily trace, by

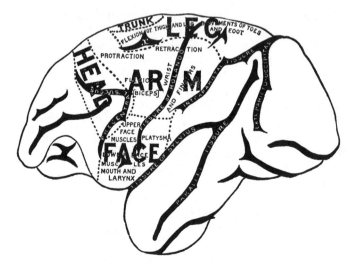

FIG. 41.—Left hemisphere of monkey's brain. Outer surface.

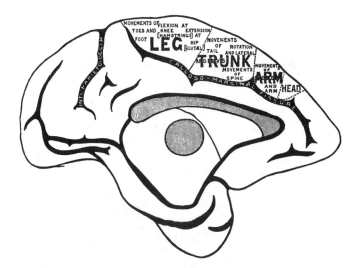

FIG. 42.—Left hemisphere of monkey's brain. Mesial surface.

following the course of the fibres, what the effect of them in interrupting motor currents may be.

One of the most instructive proofs of motor localization in the cortex is that furnished by the disease now called aphemia, or *motor aphasia*. Motor aphasia is neither loss of voice nor paralysis of the tongue or lips. The patient's voice is as strong as ever, and all the innervations of his hypoglossal and facial nerves, except those necessary for speaking, may go on perfectly well. He can laugh and cry, and even sing; but he either is unable to utter any words at all; or a few meaningless stock phrases form his only speech; or else he speaks incoherently and confusedly, mispronouncing, misplacing, and misusing his words in various degrees. Sometimes his speech is a mere broth of unintelligible syllables. In cases of pure motor aphasia the patient recognizes his mistakes and suffers acutely from them. Now whenever a patient dies in such a condition as this, and an examination of his brain is permitted, it is found that the lowest frontal gyrus (see Fig. 44) is the seat of injury. Broca first noticed this fact in 1861, and since then the gyrus has gone by the name of Broca's convolution. The injury in right-handed people is found on the left hemisphere, and in left-handed people on the right hemisphere. Most people, in fact, are left-brained, that is, all their delicate and specialized movements are handed over to the charge of the left hemisphere. The ordinary right-handedness for such movements is only a consequence of that fact, a consequence which shows outwardly on account of that extensive crossing of the fibres from the left hemisphere to the right half of the body only, which is shown in Fig. 43, below the letter *M*. But the left-brainedness might exist and *not* show outwardly. This would happen wherever organs on *both* sides of the body could be governed by the left hemisphere; and just such a case seems

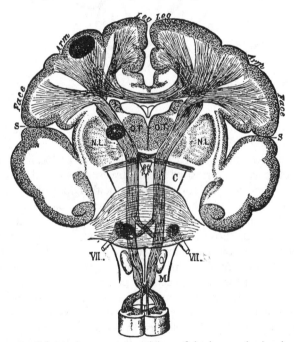

FIG. 43. — Schematic transverse section of the human brain, through the rolandic region. *S*, fissure of Sylvius; *N.C.*, *nucleus caudatus*, and *N.L.*, *nucleus lenticularis*, of the corpus striatum; *O.T.*, thalamus; *C*, crus; *M*, medulla oblongata; *VII.*, the facial nerves passing out from their nucleus in the region of the *pons*. The fibres passing between *O.T.* and *N.L.* constitute the so-called internal capsule.

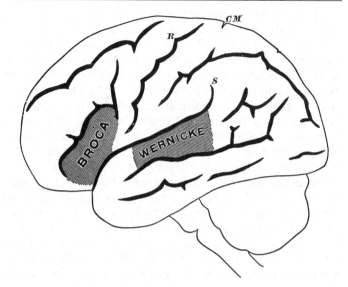

Fig. 44.—Schematic profile of left hemisphere, with the parts shaded whose destruction causes motor ('Broca') and sensory ('Wernicke') aphasia.

offered by the vocal organs, in that highly delicate and special motor service which we call speech. Either hemisphere *can* innervate them bilaterally, just as either seems able to innervate bilaterally the muscles of the trunk, ribs, and diaphragm. Of the special movements of speech, however, it would appear (from these very facts of aphasia) that the left hemisphere in most persons habitually takes exclusive charge. With that hemisphere thrown out of gear, speech is undone; even though the opposite hemisphere still be there for the performance of less specialized acts, such as the various movements required in eating.

The visual centre is in the *occipital lobes*. This also is proved by all the three kinds of possible evidence. It seems that the fibres from the *left* halves of *both* retinæ go to the *left* hemisphere, those from the right half to the right hemisphere. The consequence is that when the right occipital lobe, for example, is injured, 'hemianopsia' resluts in both eyes, that is, both retinæ grow blind as to their right halves, and the patient loses the leftward half of his field of view. The diagram on p. 117 will make this matter clear (see Fig. 45).

Quite recently, both Schäfer and Munk, in studying the movements of the eyeball produced by galvanizing the visual cortex in monkeys and dogs, have found reason to plot out an analogous correspondence between the upper and lower portions of the retinæ and certain parts of the visual cortex. If both occipital lobes were destroyed, we should have double hemiopia, or, in other words, total blindness. In human hemiopic blindness there is insensibility to light on one half of the field of view, but mental images of visible things remain. In *double* hemiopia there is every reason to believe that not only the sensation of light must go, but that all memories and images of a visual order must be annihilated also. The man loses his visual 'ideas.' Only 'cortical' blindness can produce this effect on the ideas. Destruction of the retinæ or of the visual tracts anywhere between the cortex and the eyes impairs the retinal sensibility to light, but not the power of visual imagination.

Mental Blindness.—A most interesting effect of cortical disorder is *mental blindness*. This consists not so much in insensibility to optical impressions, as in *inability to understand them*. Psychologically it is interpretable as *loss of associations* between optical sensations and what they signify; and any interruption of the paths between the optic centres and the centres for other ideas ought to bring it about. Thus, printed letters of the alphabet, or words, signify both certain sounds and certain articulatory movements. But the connection between the articulating or auditory centres and those for sight being ruptured, we ought *a priori* to expect that the sight of words would fail to awaken the idea of their sound, or of the movement for pronouncing them. We ought, in short, to have *alexia*, or inability to read; and this is just what we do have as a complication of *aphasic* disease in many cases of extensive injury about the fronto-temporal regions.

Where an object fails to be recognized by sight, it often happens that the patient will recognize and name it as soon as he touches it with his hand. This shows in an interesting way how numerous are the incoming paths which all end by running out of the brain through the channel of speech. The

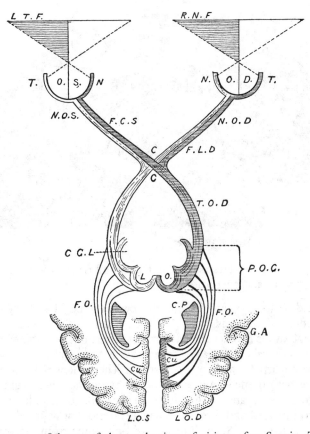

FIG. 45.—Scheme of the mechanism of vision, after Seguin. The *cuneus* convolution (*Cu*) of the right occipital lobe is supposed to be injured, and all the parts which lead to it are darkly shaded to show that they fail to exert their function. *F.O.* are the intra-hemispheric optical fibres. *P.O.C.* is the region of the lower optic centres (corpora geniculata and quadrigemina). *T.O.D.* is the right optic tract; *C.*, the chiasma; *F.L.D.* are the fibres going to the lateral or temporal half *T.* of the right retina, and *F.C.S.* are those going to the central or nasal half of the left retina. *O.D.* is the right, and *O.S.* the left, eyeball. The rightward half of each is therefore blind; in other words, the right nasal field, *R.N.F.*, and the left temporal field, *L.T.F.*, have become invisible to the subject with the lesion at *Cu.*

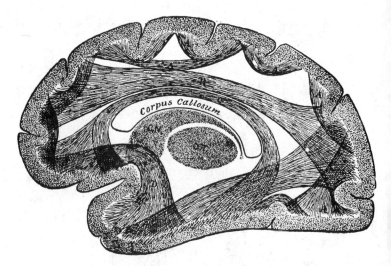

FIG. 46.—Fibres associating the cortical centres together. (Schematic, after Starr.)

hand-path is open, though the eye-path be closed. When mental blindness is most complete, neither sight, touch, nor sound avails to steer the patient, and a sort of dementia which has been called *asymbolia* or *apraxia* is the result. The commonest articles are not understood. The patient will put his breeches on one shoulder and his hat upon the other, will bite into the soap and lay his shoes on the table, or take his food into his hand and throw it down again, not knowing what to do with it, etc. Such disorder can only come from extensive brain-injury.

The centre for hearing is situated in man in the upper convolution of the temporal lobe (see the part marked 'Wernicke' in Fig. 44). The phenomena of aphasia show this. We studied motor aphasia a few pages back; we must now consider *sensory aphasia*. Our knowledge of aphasia has had three stages: we may talk of the period of Broca, the period of Wernicke, and the period of Charcot. What Broca's discovery was we have seen. Wernicke was the first to discriminate those cases in which the patient can *not even understand* speech from those in which he can understand, only not talk; and to ascribe the former condition to lesion of the temporal lobe. The condition in question is *word-deafness*, and the disease is *auditory aphasia*. The latest statistical survey of the subject is that by Dr. M. Allen Starr. In the seven cases of *pure* word-deafness which he has collected (cases in which the patient could read, talk, and write, but not understand what was said to him), the lesion was limited to the first and second temporal convolutions in their posterior two thirds. The lesion (in right-handed, i.e., left-brained, persons) is always on the left side, like the lesion in motor aphasia. Crude hearing would not be abolished even were the left centre for it utterly destroyed; the right centre would still provide for that. But the *linguistic use* of hearing appears bound up with the integrity of the left centre more or less exclusively. Here it must be that words heard enter into association with the things which they represent, on the one hand, and with the movements necessary for pronouncing them, on the other. In most of us (as Wernicke said) speech must go on from auditory cues; that is, our visual, tactile, and other ideas probably do not innervate our motor centres directly, but only after first arousing the mental sound of the words. This is the immediate stimulus to articulation; and where the possibility of this is abolished by the destruction of its usual channel in the left temporal lobe, the articulation must suffer. In the few cases in which the channel is abolished with no bad effect on speech we must suppose an idiosyncrasy. The patient must innervate his speech-organs either from the corresponding portion of the other hemisphere or directly from the centres of vision, touch, etc., without leaning on the auditory region. It is the minuter analysis of such individual differences as these which constitutes Charcot's contribution towards clearing up the subject.

Every namable thing has numerous properties, qualities, or aspects. In our minds the properties together with the name form an associated group. If different parts of the brain are severally concerned with the several properties, and a farther part with the hearing, and still another with the uttering, of the name, there must inevitably be brought about (through the law of association which we shall later study) such a connection amongst all these brain-parts that the activity of any one of them will be likely to awaken the activity of all the rest. When we are talking whilst we think, the *ultimate* process is utterance. If the brain-part for *that* be injured, speech is impossible or disorderly, even though all the other brain-parts be intact: and this is just the condition of things which, on p. 113, we found to be brought about by lesion of the convolution of Broca. But back of that last act various orders of succession are possible in the associations of a talking man's ideas. The more usual order is, as aforesaid, from the tactile, visual, or other properties of the things thought-about to the sound of their names, and then to the latter's utterance. But if in a certain individual's mind the *look* of an object or the *look* of its name be what habitually precedes articulation, then the loss of the *hearing* centre will *pro tanto* not affect that individual's speech or reading. He will be mentally deaf, i.e., his *understanding* of the human voice will suffer, but he will not be aphasic. In this way it is possible to explain the seven cases of word-deafness without motor aphasia which figure in Dr. Starr's table.

If this order of association be ingrained and habitual in that individual, injury to his *visual* centres will make him not only word-blind, but aphasic as well. His speech will become confused in consequence of an occipital lesion. Naunyn, consequently, plotting out on a diagram of the hemisphere the 71 irreproachably reported cases of aphasia which he was able to collect, finds that the lesions concentrate themselves in three places: first, on Broca's centre; second, on Wernicke's; third, on the supra-marginal and angular convolutions under which those fibres pass which connect the visual centres with the rest of the brain (see Fig. 47). With this result Dr. Starr's analysis of purely sensory cases agrees.

In the chapter on Imagination we shall return to these differences in the sensory spheres of different individuals. Meanwhile few things show more beautifully than the history of our knowledge of aphasia how the sagacity and patience of many banded workers are in time certain to analyze the darkest confusion into an orderly display. There is no 'organ' of Speech in the brain any more than there is a 'faculty' of Speech in the mind. The entire mind and the entire brain are

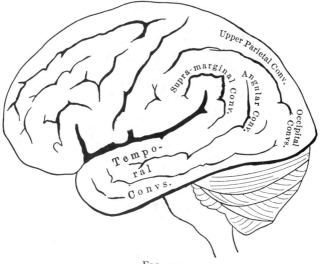

FIG. 47.

more or less at work in a man who uses language. The sub-joined diagram, from Ross, shows the four parts most vitally concerned, and, in the light of our text, needs no farther explanation (see Fig. 48, p. 122).

Centres for Smell, Taste, and Touch.—The other sensory centres are less definitely made out. Of smell and taste I will say nothing; and of muscular and cutaneous feeling only this, that it seems most probably seated in the motor zone, and possibly in the convolutions immediately backwards and midwards thereof. The incoming tactile currents must enter the cells of this region by one set of fibres, and the discharges leave them by another, but of these refinements of anatomy we at present know nothing.

Conclusion.—We thus see the postulate of Meynert and Jackson, with which we started on p. III, to be on the whole most satisfactorily corroborated by objective research. *The highest centres do probably contain nothing but arrangements for representing impressions and movements, and other arrangements for coupling the activity of these arrangements together.* Currents pouring in from the sense-organs first excite some

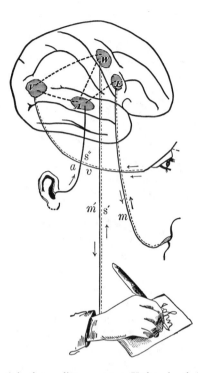

FIG. 48.—*A* is the auditory centre, *V* the visual, *W* the writing, and *E* that for speech.

arrangements, which in turn excite others, until at last a discharge downwards of some sort occurs. When this is once clearly grasped there remains little ground for asking whether the motor zone is exclusively motor, or sensitive as well. The whole cortex, inasmuch as currents run through it, is both. All the currents probably have feelings going with them, and sooner or later bring movements about. In one aspect, then, every centre is afferent, in another efferent, even the motor cells of the spinal cord having these two aspects inseparably conjoined. Marique, and Exner and Paneth have shown that by cutting *round* a 'motor' centre and so separating it from the influence of the rest of the cortex, the same disorders are produced as by cutting it out, so that it is really just what I

called it, only the funnel through which the stream of innervation, starting from elsewhere, escapes; *consciousness accompanying the stream, and being mainly of things seen if the stream is
strongest occipitally, of things heard if it is strongest temporally, of
things felt, etc., if the stream occupies most intensely the 'motor
zone.'* It seems to me that some broad and vague formulation
like this is as much as we can safely venture on in the present
state of science—so much at least is not likely to be overturned. But it is obvious how little this tells us of the detail of
what goes on in the brain when a certain thought is before
the mind. The general forms of relation perceived between
things, as their identities, likenesses, or contrasts; the forms of
the consciousness itself, as effortless or perplexed, attentive or
inattentive, pleasant or disagreeable; the phenomena of interest and selection, etc., etc., are all lumped together as effects
correlated with the currents that connect one centre with another. Nothing can be more vague than such a formula.
Moreover certain portions of the brain, as the lower frontal
lobes, escape formulation altogether. Their destruction gives
rise to no local trouble of either motion or sensibility in dogs,
and in monkeys neither stimulation nor excision of these
lobes produces any symptoms whatever. One monkey of
Horsley and Schäfer's was as tame, and did certain tricks as
well, after as before the operation.

It is in short obvious that our knowledge of our mental
states infinitely exceeds our knowledge of their concomitant
cerebral conditions. Without introspective analysis of the
mental elements of speech, the doctrine of Aphasia, for instance, which is the most brilliant jewel in Physiology, would
have been utterly impossible. Our assumption, therefore
(p. 14), that mind-states are absolutely dependent on brain-
conditions, must still be understood as a mere postulate. We
may have a general faith that it must be true, but any exact
insight as to *how* it is true lags wofully behind.

Before taking up the study of conscious states properly so
called, I will in a separate chapter speak of two or three aspects of brain-function which have a general importance and
which coöperate in the production of all our mental states.

CHAPTER IX

SOME GENERAL CONDITIONS OF NEURAL ACTIVITY

The Nervous Discharge.—The word discharge is constantly used, and must be used in this book, to designate the escape of a current downwards into muscles or other internal organs. The reader must not understand the word figuratively. From the point of view of dynamics the passage of a current out of a motor cell is probably altogether analogous to the explosion of a gun. The matter of the cell is in a state of internal tension, which the incoming current resolves, tumbling the molecules into a more stable equilibrium and liberating an amount of energy which starts the current of the outgoing fibre. This current is stronger than that of the incoming fibre. When it reaches the muscle it produces an analogous disintegration of pent-up molecules and the result is a stronger effect still. Matteuci found that the work done by a muscle's contraction was 27,000 times greater than that done by the galvanic current which stimulated its motor nerve. When a frog's leg-muscle is made to contract, first directly, by stimulation of its motor nerve, and second reflexly, by stimulation of a sensory nerve, it is found that the reflex way requires a stronger current and is more tardy, but that the contraction is stronger when it does occur. These facts prove that the cells in the spinal cord through which the reflex takes place offer a resistance which has first to be overcome, but that a relatively violent outward current outwards then escapes from them. What is this but an explosive discharge on a minute scale?

Reaction-time.—The measurement of the time required for the discharge is one of the lines of experimental investigation most diligently followed of late years. Helmholtz led the way by discovering the rapidity of the outgoing current in the sciatic nerve of the frog. The methods he used were soon applied to sensory reactions, and the results caused much popular admiration when described as measurements of the 'velocity of thought.' The phrase 'quick as thought' had from time immemorial signified all that was wonderful and elusive of determination in the line of speed; and the way in which Science laid her doomful hand upon this mystery reminded people of the day when Franklin first '*eripuit cœlo fulmen*,' foreshadowing the reign of a newer and colder race of gods. I may say, however, immediately, that the phrase 'velocity of *thought*' is misleading, for it is by no means clear in any of the cases what particular act of thought occurs during the time which is measured. What the times in question really represent is the total duration of certain *reactions upon stimuli*. Certain of the conditions of the reaction are prepared beforehand; they consist in the assumption of those motor and sensory tensions which we name the expectant state. Just what happens during the actual time occupied by the re-action (in other words, just what is added to the preëxistent tensions to produce the actual discharge) is not made out at present, either from the neural or from the mental point of view.

The method is essentially the same in all these investigations. A signal of some sort is communicated to the subject, and at the same instant records itself on a time-registering apparatus. The subject then makes a muscular movement of some sort, which is the 'reaction,' and which also records it-self automatically. The time found to have elapsed between the two records is the total time of that reaction. The time-registering instruments are of various types. One type is that of the revolving drum covered with smoked paper, on which one electric pen traces a line which the signal breaks and the 'reaction' draws again; whilst another electric pen (connected with a rod of metal vibrating at a known rate) traces alongside of the former line a 'time-line' of which each undulation or link stands for a certain fraction of a second, and against which the break in the reaction-line can be measured. Compare Fig. 49, where the line is broken by the signal at the first arrow, and continued again by the reaction at the second. The machine most often used is Hipp's chronoscopic clock. The hands are placed at zero, the signal starts them (by an electric connection), and the reaction stops them. The duration of their movement, down to 1000ths of a second, is then read off from the dial-plates.

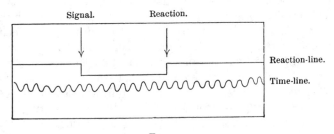

Fig. 49.

Simple Reactions. — It is found that the reaction-time differs in the same person according to the direction of his expectant attention. If he thinks as little as possible of the movement which he is to make, and concentrates his mind upon the signal to be received, it is longer; if, on the contrary, he bends his mind exclusively upon the muscular response, it is shorter. Lange, who first noticed this fact when working in Wundt's laboratory, found his own 'muscular' reaction-time to average 0″.123, whilst his 'sensorial' reaction-time averaged as much as 0″.230. It is obvious that experiments, to have any *comparative* value, must always be made according to the 'muscular' method, which reduces the figure to its minimum and makes it more constant. In general it lies between one and two tenths of a second. It seems to me that under these circumstances the reaction is essentially a reflex act. The preliminary *making-ready* of the muscles for the movement means the excitement of the paths of discharge to a point just short of actual discharge before the signal comes in. In other words, it means the temporary formation of a real 'reflex-arc' in the centres, through which the incoming current instantly can pour out again. But when, on the other hand, the expectant attention is exclusively addressed to the signal, the excitement of the motor tracts can only begin after this latter has come in, and under this condition the reaction takes more time. In the hair-trigger condition in which we stand when making reactions by the 'muscular' method, we sometimes respond to a wrong signal, especially if it be of the same *kind* with the one we expect. The signal is but the spark which touches off a train already laid. There is no thought in the matter; the hand jerks by an involuntary start.

These experiments are thus in no sense measurements of the swiftness of *thought*. Only when we complicate them is there a chance for anything like an intellectual operation to occur. They may be complicated in various ways. The reaction may be withheld until the signal has consciously awakened a distinct idea (Wundt's discrimination-time, association-time), and may then be performed. Or there may be a variety of possible signals, each with a different reaction assigned to it, and the reacter may be uncertain which one he is about to receive. The reaction would then hardly seem to occur without a preliminary recognition and choice. Even here, however, the discrimination and choice are widely different from the intellectual operations of which we are ordinarily conscious under those names. Meanwhile the simple reaction-time remains as the starting point of all these super-induced complications, and its own variations must be briefly passed in review.

The reaction-time varies with the *individual* and his *age*. Old and uncultivated people have it long (nearly a second, in an old pauper observed by Exner). Children have it long (half a second, according to Herzen).

Practice shortens it to a quantity which is for each individual a minimum beyond which no farther reduction can be made. The aforesaid old pauper's time was, after much practice, reduced to 0.1866 sec.

Fatigue lengthens it, and *concentration of attention* shortens it. The *nature of the signal* makes it vary. I here bring together the averages which have been obtained by some observers:

	Hirsch.	Hankel.	Exner.	Wundt.
Sound	0.149	0.1505	0.1360	0.167
Light	0.200	0.2246	0.1506	0.222
Touch	0.182	0.1546	0.1337	0.213

It will be observed that *sound* is more promptly reacted on than either *sight* or *touch*. *Taste* and *smell* are slower than either. The *intensity of the signal* makes a difference. The intenser the stimulus the shorter the time. Herzen compared the reaction from a *corn* on the toe with that from the skin of the hand of the same subject. The two places were stimulated simultaneously, and the subject tried to react simultaneously with both hand and foot, but the foot always went quickest. When the sound skin of the foot was touched instead of the corn, it was the hand which always reacted first. *Intoxicants* on the whole lengthen the time, but much depends on the dose.

Complicated Reactions.—These occur when some kind of intellectual operation accompanies the reaction. The rational place in which to report of them would be under the head of the various intellectual operations concerned. But certain persons prefer to see all these measurements bunched together regardless of context; so, to meet their views, I give the complicated reactions here.

When we have to think before reacting it is obvious that there is no definite reaction-time of which we can talk—it all depends on how long we think. The only times we can measure are the *minimum* times of certain determinate and very simple intellectual operations. The *time required for discrimination* has thus been made a subject of experimental measurement. Wundt calls it *Unterscheidungszeit*. His subjects (whose simple reaction-time had previously been determined) were required to make a movement, always the same, the instant they discerned *which* of two or more signals they received. The *excess* of time occupied by these reactions *over the simple reaction-time*, in which only one signal was used and known in advance, measured, according to Wundt, the time required for the act of discrimination. It was found longer when four different signals were irregularly used than when only two were used. When two were used (the signals being the sudden appearance of a black or of a white object), the average times of three observers were respectively (in seconds)

$$0.050 \qquad 0.047 \qquad 0.079.$$

When four signals were used, a red and a green light being added to the others, it became, for the same observers,

$$0.157 \qquad 0.073 \qquad 0.132.$$

Prof. Cattell found he could get no results by this method, and reverted to one used by observers previous to Wundt and which Wundt had rejected. This is the *einfache Wahlmethode*, as Wundt calls it. The reacter awaits the signal and reacts if it is of one sort, but omits to act if it is of another sort. The reaction thus occurs after discrimination; the motor impulse cannot be sent to the hand until the subject knows what the signal is. Reacting in this way, Prof. Cattell found the increment of time required for distinguishing a white signal from no signal to be, in two observers,

0.030   and   0.050;

that for distinguishing one color from another was similarly,

0.100   and   0.110;

that for distinguishing a certain color from ten other colors,

0.105   and   0.117;

that for distinguishing the letter A in ordinary print from the letter Z,

0.142   and   0.137;

that for distinguishing a given letter from all the rest of the alphabet (not reacting until that letter appeared),

0.119   and   0.116;

that for distinguishing a word from any of twenty-five other words, from

0.118   to   0.158 sec.

—the difference depending on the length of the words and the familiarity of the language to which they belonged.

Prof. Cattell calls attention to the fact that the time for distinguishing a word is often but little more than that for distinguishing a letter: "We do not therefore," he says, "perceive separately the letters of which a word is composed, but the word as a whole. The application of this to teaching children to read is evident."

He also finds a great difference in the time with which various letters are distinguished, E being particularly bad.

The time required for association of one idea with another has been measured. Galton, using a very simple apparatus, found that the sight of an unforeseen word would awaken an associated 'idea' in about ⅚ of a second. Wundt next made determinations in which the 'cue' was given by single-syllabled words called out by an assistant. The person experimented on had to press a key as soon as the sound of the word awakened an associated idea. Both word and reaction were chronographically registered, and the total time-interval between the two amounted, in four observers, to 1.009, 0.896,

1.037, and 1.154 seconds respectively. From this the simple reaction-time and the time of merely identifying the word's sound (the 'apperception-time,' as Wundt calls it) must be subtracted, to get the exact time required for the associated idea to arise. These times were separately determined and subtracted. The difference, called by Wundt *association-time*, amounted, in the same four persons, to 706, 723, 752, and 874 thousandths of a second respectively. The length of the last figure is due to the fact that the person reacting was an American, whose associations with German words would naturally be slower than those of natives. The shortest association-time noted was when the word 'Sturm' suggested to Wundt the word 'Wind' in 0.341 second. Prof. Cattell made some interesting observations upon the association-time between the look of letters and their names. "I pasted letters," he says, "on a revolving drum, and determined at what rate they could be read aloud, as they passed by a slit in a screen." He found it to vary according as one, or more than one, letter was visible at a time through the slit, and gives half a second as about the time which it takes to see and name a single letter seen alone. The rapidity of a man's *reading* is of course a measure of that of his associations, since each seen word must call up its name, at least, ere it is read. "I find," says Prof. Cattell, "that it takes about twice as long to read (aloud, as fast as possible) words which have no connexion as words which make sentences, and letters which have no connexion as letters which make words. When the words make sentences and the letters words, not only do the processes of seeing and naming overlap, but by one mental effort the subject can recognise a whole group of words or letters, and by one will-act choose the motions to be made in naming them, so that the rate at which the words and letters are read is really only limited by the maximum rapidity at which the speech-organs can be moved. . . . For example, when reading as fast as possible the writer's rate was, English 138, French 167, German 250, Italian 327, Latin 434 and Greek 484; the figures giving the thousandths of a second taken to read each word. Experiments made on others strikingly confirm these results. The subject does not know that he is reading the foreign language more slowly than his own; this explains why foreigners seem to talk so fast. . . .

"The time required to see and name colours and pictures of objects was determined in the same way. The time was found to be about the same (over ½ sec.) for colours as for pictures, and about twice as long as for words and letters. Other experiments I have made show that we can recognise a single colour or picture in a slightly shorter time than a word or letter, but take longer to name it. This is because in the case of words and letters the association between the idea and name has taken place so often that the process has become automatic, whereas in the case of colours and pictures we must by a voluntary effort choose the name."

Dr. Romanes has found "astonishing differences in the *maximum* rate of reading which is possible to different individuals, all of whom have been accustomed to extensive reading. That is to say, the difference may amount to 4 to 1; or, otherwise stated, in a given time one individual may be able to read four times as much as another. Moreover, it appeared that there was no relationship between slowness of reading and power of assimilation; on the contrary, when all the efforts are directed to assimilating as much as possible in a given time, the rapid readers (as shown by their written notes) usually give a better account of the portions of the paragraph which has been compassed by the slow readers than the latter are able to give; and the most rapid reader whom I have found is also the best at assimilating. I should further say," Dr. R. continues, "that there is no relationship between rapidity of perception as thus tested and intellectual activity as tested by the general results of intellectual work; for I have tried the experiment with several highly distinguished men in science and literature, most of whom I found to be slow readers."

The degree of concentration of the attention has much to do with determining the reaction-time. Anything which baffles or distracts us beforehand, or startles us in the signal, makes the time proportionally long.

The Summation of Stimuli.—Throughout the nerve-centres it is a law that *a stimulus which would be inadequate by* *itself to excite a nerve-centre to effective discharge may, by acting with one or more other stimuli (equally ineffectual by themselves alone), bring the discharge about.* The natural way to consider this is as a summation of tensions which at last overcome a resistance. The first of them produce a 'latent excitement' or a 'heightened irritability'—the phrase is immaterial so far as practical consequences go;—the last is the straw which breaks the camel's back.

This is proved by many physiological experiments which cannot here be detailed; but outside of the laboratory we constantly apply the law of summation in our practical appeals. If a car-horse balks, the final way of starting him is by applying a number of customary incitements at once. If the driver uses reins and voice, if one bystander pulls at his head, another lashes his hind-quarters, the conductor rings the bell, and the dismounted passengers shove the car, all at the same moment, his obstinacy generally yields, and he goes on his way rejoicing. If we are striving to remember a lost name or fact, we think of as many 'cues' as possible, so that by their joint action they may recall what no one of them can recall alone. The sight of a dead prey will often not stimulate a beast to pursuit, but if the sight of movement be added to that of form, pursuit occurs. "Brücke noticed that his brainless hen, which made no attempt to peck at the grain under her very eyes, began pecking if the grain were thrown on the ground with force, so as to produce a rattling sound." "Dr. Allen Thomson . . . hatched out some chickens on a carpet, where he kept them for several days. They showed no inclination to scrape, . . . but when Dr. Thomson sprinkled a little gravel on the carpet, . . . the chickens immediately began their scraping movements." A strange person, and darkness, are both of them stimuli to fear and mistrust in dogs (and for the matter of that, in men). Neither circumstance alone may awaken outward manifestations, but together, i.e., when the strange man is met in the dark, the dog will be excited to violent defiance. Street hawkers well know the efficacy of summation, for they arrange themselves in a line on the sidewalk, and the passer often buys from the last one of them, through the effect of the reiterated solicitation, what he refused to buy from the first in the row.

Cerebral Blood-supply.—All parts of the cortex, when electrically excited, produce alterations both of respiration and circulation. The blood-pressure somewhat rises, as a rule, all over the body, no matter where the cortical irritation is applied, though the motor zone is the most sensitive region for the purpose. Slowing and quickening of the heart are also observed. Mosso, using his 'plethysmograph' as an indicator, discovered that the blood-supply to the arms diminished during intellectual activity, and found furthermore that the arterial tension (as shown by the sphygmograph) was increased in these members (see Fig. 50). So slight an emotion as that produced by the entrance of Professor Ludwig into the laboratory was instantly followed by a shrinkage of the arms. The brain itself is an excessively vascular organ, a sponge full of blood, in fact; and another of Mosso's inventions showed that when less blood went to the legs, more went to the head. The subject to be observed lay on a delicately balanced table which could tip downwards either at the head or at the foot if the weight of either end were increased. The moment emotional or intellectual activity began in the subject, down went the head-end, in consequence of the redistribution of blood in his system. But the best proof of the immediate afflux of blood to the brain during mental activity is due to Mosso's observations on three persons whose brain had been laid bare by lesion of the skull. By means of apparatus described in his book, this physiologist was enabled to let the brain-pulse record itself directly by a tracing. The intra-cranial blood-pressure rose immediately whenever the subject was spoken to, or when he began to think actively, as in solving a problem in mental arithmetic. Mosso gives in his work a large

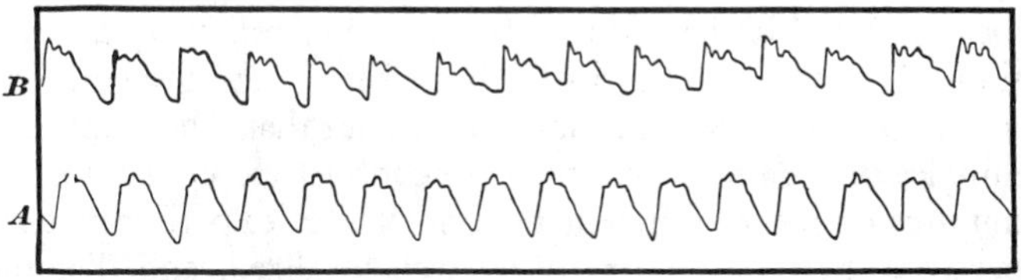

FIG. 50.—Sphygmographic pulse-tracing. *A*, during intellectual repose; *B*, during intellectual activity. (Mosso.)

number of reproductions of tracings which show the instantaneity of the change of blood-supply, whenever the mental activity was quickened by any cause whatever, intellectual or
emotional. He relates of his female subject that one day whilst
tracing her brain-pulse he observed a sudden rise with no apparent outer or inner cause. She however confessed to him
afterwards that at that moment she had caught sight of a *skull*
on top of a piece of furniture in the room, and that this had
given her a slight emotion.

Cerebral Thermometry.—*Brain-activity seems accompanied
by a local disengagement of heat.* The earliest careful work in
this direction was by Dr. J. S. Lombard in 1867. He noted the
changes in delicate thermometers and electric piles placed
against the scalp in human beings, and found that any intellectual effort, such as computing, composing, reciting poetry
silently or aloud, and especially that emotional excitement
such as an angry fit, caused a general rise of temperature,
which rarely exceeded a degree Fahrenheit. In 1870 the inde-
fatigable Schiff took up the subject, experimenting on live
dogs and chickens by plunging thermo-electric needles into
the substance of their brain. After habituation was established, he tested the animals with various sensations, tactile,
optic, olfactory, and auditory. He found very regularly an
abrupt alteration of the intra-cerebral temperature. When, for
instance, he presented an empty roll of paper to the nose of
his dog as it lay motionless, there was a small deflection, but
when a piece of meat was in the paper the deflection was
much greater. Schiff concluded from these and other experiments that sensorial activity heats the brain-tissue, but he did
not try to localize the increment of heat beyond finding that it
was in both hemispheres, whatever might be the sensation
applied. Dr. Amidon in 1880 made a farther step forwards, in
localizing the heat produced by voluntary muscular contractions. Applying a number of delicate surface-thermometers simultaneously against the scalp, he found that when different
muscles of the body were made to contract vigorously for ten
minutes or more, different regions of the scalp rose in temperature, that the regions were well focalized, and that the
rise of temperature was often considerably over a Fahrenheit
degree. To a large extent these regions correspond to the

centres for the same movements assigned by Ferrier and others on other grounds; only they cover more of the skull.

Phosphorus and Thought.—Considering the large amount of popular nonsense which passes current on this subject I may be pardoned for a brief mention of it here. *'Ohne Phosphor, kein Gedanke,'* was a noted war-cry of the 'materialists' during the excitement on that subject which filled Germany in the '60s. The brain, like every other organ of the body, contains phosphorus, and a score of other chemicals besides. Why the phosphorus should be picked out as its essence, no one knows. It would be equally true to say, 'Ohne Wasser, kein Gedanke,' or 'Ohne Kochsalz, kein Gedanke'; for thought would stop as quickly if the brain should dry up or lose its NaCl as if it lost its phosphorus. In America the phosphorus-delusion has twined itself round a saying quoted (rightly or wrongly) from Professor L. Agassiz, to the effect that fishermen are more intelligent than farmers because they eat so much fish, which contains so much phosphorus. All the alleged facts may be doubted.

The only straight way to ascertain the importance of phosphorus to thought would be to find whether more is excreted by the brain during mental activity than during rest. Unfortunately we cannot do this directly, but can only gauge the amount of PO_5 in the urine, and this procedure has been adopted by a variety of observers, some of whom found the phosphates in the urine diminished, whilst others found them increased, by intellectual work. On the whole, it is impossible to trace any constant relation. In maniacal excitement less phosphorus than usual seems to be excreted. More is excreted during sleep. The fact that phosphorus-preparations may do good in nervous exhaustion proves nothing as to the part played by phosphorus in mental activity. Like iron, arsenic, and other remedies it is a stimulant or tonic, of whose intimate workings in the system we know absolutely nothing, and which moreover does good in an extremely small number of the cases in which it is prescribed.

The phosphorus-philosophers have often compared thought to a secretion. "The brain secretes thought, as the kidneys secrete urine, or as the liver secretes bile," are phrases which one sometimes hears. The lame analogy need hardly be pointed out. The materials which the brain *pours into the blood* (cholesterin, creatin, xanthin, or whatever they may be) are the analogues of the urine and the bile, being in fact real material excreta. As far as these matters go, the brain is a ductless gland. But we know of nothing connected with liver- and kidney-activity which can be in the remotest degree compared with the stream of thought that accompanies the brain's material secretions.

CHAPTER X

HABIT

Its Importance for Psychology.—There remains a condition of general neural activity so important as to deserve a chapter by itself—I refer to the aptitude of the nerve-centres, especially of the hemispheres, for acquiring habits. *An acquired habit, from the physiological point of view, is nothing but a new pathway of discharge formed in the brain, by which certain incoming currents ever after tend to escape.* That is the thesis of this chapter; and we shall see in the later and more psychological chapters that such functions as the association of ideas, perception, memory, reasoning, the education of the will, etc. etc., can best be understood as results of the formation *de novo* of just such pathways of discharge.

Habit has a physical basis. The moment one tries to define what habit is, one is led to the fundamental properties of matter. The laws of Nature are nothing but the immutable habits which the different elementary sorts of matter follow in their actions and reactions upon each other. In the organic world, however, the habits are more variable than this. Even instincts vary from one individual to another of a kind; and are modified in the same individual, as we shall later see, to suit the exigencies of the case. On the principles of the atomistic philosophy the habits of an elementary particle of matter cannot change, because the particle is itself an unchangeable thing; but those of a compound mass of matter can change, because they are in the last instance due to the structure of the compound, and either outward forces or inward tensions can, from one hour to another, turn that structure into something different from what it was. That is, they can do so if the body be plastic enough to maintain its integrity, and be not disrupted when its structure yields. The change of structure here spoken of need not involve the outward shape; it may be invisible and molecular, as when a bar of iron becomes magnetic or crystalline through the action of certain outward causes, or india-rubber becomes friable, or plaster 'sets.' All these changes are rather slow; the material in question opposes a certain resistance to the modifying cause, which it takes time to overcome, but the gradual yielding whereof often saves the material from being disintegrated altogether. When the structure has yielded, the same inertia becomes a condition of its comparative permanence in the new form, and of the new habits the body then manifests. *Plasticity*, then, in the wide sense of the word, means the possession of a structure weak enough to yield to an influence, but strong enough not to yield all at once. Each relatively stable phase of equilibrium in such a structure is marked by what we may call a new set of habits. Organic matter, especially nervous tissue, seems endowed with a very extraordinary degree of plasticity of this sort; so that we may without hesitation lay down as our first proposition the following: that *the phenomena of habit in living beings are due to the plasticity of the organic materials of which their bodies are composed.*

The philosophy of habit is thus, in the first instance, a chapter in physics rather than in physiology or psychology. That it is at bottom a physical principle is admitted by all good recent writers on the subject. They call attention to analogues of acquired habits exhibited by dead matter. Thus, M. Léon Dumont writes:

"Everyone knows how a garment, after having been worn a certain time, clings to the shape of the body better than when it was new; there has been a change in the tissue, and this change is a new habit of cohesion. A lock works better after being used some time; at the outset more force was required to overcome certain roughnesses in the mechanism. The overcoming of their resistance is a phenomenon of habituation. It costs less trouble to fold a paper when it has been folded already; . . . and just so the impressions of outer objects fashion for themselves in the nervous system more and more appropriate paths, and these vital phenomena recur under similar excitements from without, when they have been interrupted a certain time."

Not in the nervous system alone. A scar anywhere is a *locus minoris resistentiæ*, more liable to be abraded, inflamed, to suffer pain and cold, than are the neighboring parts. A sprained ankle, a dislocated arm, are in danger of being sprained or dislocated again; joints that have once been attacked by rheumatism or gout, mucous membranes that have been the seat of catarrh, are with each fresh recurrence more prone to a relapse, until often the morbid state chronically substitutes itself for the sound one. And in the nervous system itself it is well known how many so-called functional diseases seem to keep themselves going simply because they happen to have once begun; and how the forcible cutting short by medicine of a few attacks is often sufficient to enable the physiological forces to get possession of the field again, and to bring the organs back to functions of health. Epilepsies, neuralgias, convulsive affections of various sorts, insomnias, are so many cases in point. And, to take what are more obviously habits, the success with which a 'weaning' treatment can often be applied to the victims of unhealthy indulgence of passion, or of mere complaining or irascible disposition, shows us how much the morbid manifestations themselves were due to the mere inertia of the nervous organs, when once launched on a false career.

Habits are due to pathways through the nerve-centres. If habits are due to the plasticity of materials to outward agents, we can immediately see to what outward influences, if to any, the brain-matter is plastic. Not to mechanical pressures, not to thermal changes, not to any of the forces to which all the other organs of our body are exposed; for, as we saw on p. 18, Nature has so blanketed and wrapped the brain about that the only impressions that can be made upon it are through the blood, on the one hand, and the sensory nerve-roots, on the other; and it is to the infinitely attenuated currents that pour in through these latter channels that the hemispherical cortex shows itself to be so peculiarly susceptible. The currents, once in, must find a way out. In getting out they leave their traces in the paths which they take. The only thing they *can* do, in short, is to deepen old paths or to make new ones; and the whole plasticity of the brain sums itself up in two words when we call it an organ in which currents pouring in from the sense-organs make with extreme facility paths which do not easily disappear. For, of course, a simple habit, like every other nervous event—the habit of snuffling, for example, or of putting one's hands into one's pockets, or of biting one's nails—is, mechanically, nothing but a reflex discharge; and its anatomical substratum must be a path in the system. The most complex habits, as we shall presently see more fully, are, from the same point of view, nothing but *concatenated* discharges in the nerve-centres, due to the presence there of systems of reflex paths, so organized as to wake each other up successively—the impression produced by one muscular contraction serving as a stimulus to provoke the next, until a final impression inhibits the process and closes the chain.

It must be noticed that the growth of structural modification in living matter may be more rapid than in any lifeless mass, because the incessant nutritive renovation of which the living matter is the seat tends often to corroborate and fix the impressed modification, rather than to counteract it by renewing the original constitution of the tissue that has been impressed. Thus, we notice after exercising our muscles or our brain in a new way, that we can do so no longer at that time; but after a day or two of rest, when we resume the discipline, our increase in skill not seldom surprises us. I have often noticed this in learning a tune; and it has led a German author to say that we learn to swim during the winter, and to skate during the summer.

Practical Effects of Habit.—First, habit simplifies our movements, makes them accurate, and diminishes fatigue.

Man is born with a tendency to do more things than he has ready-made arrangements for in his nerve-centres. Most of the performances of other animals are automatic. But in him the number of them is so enormous that most of them must be the fruit of painful study. If practice did not make perfect, nor habit economize the expense of nervous and muscular energy, he would be in a sorry plight. As Dr. Maudsley says:[1]

"If an act became no easier after being done several times, if the careful direction of consciousness were necessary to its accomplishment on each occasion, it is evident that the whole activity of a lifetime might be confined to one or two deeds— that no progress could take place in development. A man might be occupied all day in dressing and undressing himself; the attitude of his body would absorb all his attention and

[1] *The Physiology of Mind*, p. 154.

energy; the washing of his hands or the fastening of a button would be as difficult to him on each occasion as to the child on its first trial; and he would furthermore be completely exhausted by his exertions. Think of the pains necessary to teach a child to stand, of the many efforts which it must make, and of the ease with which it at last stands, unconscious even of an effort. For while secondary automatic acts are accomplished with comparatively little weariness—in this regard approaching the organic movements, or the original reflex movements—the conscious efforts of the will soon produce exhaustion. A spinal cord without . . . memory would simply be an idiotic spinal cord. . . . It is impossible for an individual to realise how much he owes to its automatic agency until disease has impaired its functions."

Secondly, *habit diminishes the conscious attention with which our acts are performed.*

One may state this abstractly thus: If an act require for its execution a chain, A, B, C, D, E, F, G, etc., of successive nervous events, then in the first performances of the action the conscious will must choose each of these events from a number of wrong alternatives that tend to present themselves; but habit soon brings it about that each event calls up its own appropriate successor without any alternative offering itself, and without any reference to the conscious will, until at last the whole chain, A, B, C, D, E, F, G, rattles itself off as soon as A occurs, just as if A and the rest of the chain were fused into a continuous stream. Whilst we are learning to walk, to ride, to swim, skate, fence, write, play, or sing, we interrupt ourselves at every step by unnecessary movements and false notes. When we are proficients, on the contrary, the results follow not only with the very minimum of muscular action requisite to bring them forth, but they follow from a single instantaneous 'cue.' The marksman sees the bird, and, before he knows it, he has aimed and shot. A gleam in his adversary's eye, a momentary pressure from his rapier, and the fencer finds that he has instantly made the right parry and return. A glance at the musical hieroglyphics, and the pianist's fingers have rippled through a shower of notes. And not only is it the right thing at the right time that we thus involuntarily do, but the wrong thing also, if it be an habitual thing. Who is there that has never wound up his watch on taking off his waistcoat in the daytime, or taken his latch-key out on arriving at the door-step of a friend? Persons in going to their bedroom to dress for dinner have been known to take off one garment after another and finally to get into bed, merely because that was the habitual issue of the first few movements when performed at a later hour. We all have a definite routine manner of performing certain daily offices connected with the toilet, with the opening and shutting of familiar cupboards, and the like. But our higher thought-centres know hardly anything about the matter. Few men can tell off-hand which sock, shoe, or trousers-leg they put on first. They must first mentally rehearse the act; and even that is often insufficient—the act must be *performed*. So of the questions, Which valve of the shutters opens first? Which way does my door swing? etc. I cannot *tell* the answer; yet my *hand* never makes a mistake. No one can *describe* the order in which he brushes his hair or teeth; yet it is likely that the order is a pretty fixed one in all of us.

These results may be expressed as follows:

In action grown habitual, what instigates each new muscular contraction to take place in its appointed order is not a thought or a perception, but the *sensation occasioned by the muscular contraction just finished*. A strictly voluntary act has to be guided by idea, perception, and volition, throughout its whole course. In habitual action, mere sensation is a sufficient guide, and the upper regions of brain and mind are set comparatively free. A diagram will make the matter clear:

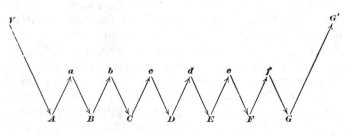

FIG. 51.

Let A, B, C, D, E, F, G represent an habitual chain of muscular contractions, and let a,b,c,d,e,f stand for the several sensations which these contractions excite in us when they are successively performed. Such sensations will usually be in the parts moved, but they may also be effects of the movement upon the eye or the ear. Through them, and through them alone, we are made aware whether or not the contraction has occurred. When the series, A, B, C, D, E, F, G, is being learned, each of these sensations becomes the object of a separate act of attention by the mind. We test each movement intellectually, to see if it have been rightly performed, before advancing to the next. We hesitate, compare, choose, revoke, reject, etc.; and the order by which the next movement is discharged is an express order from the ideational centres after this deliberation has been gone through.

In habitual action, on the contrary, the only impulse which the intellectual centres need send down is that which carries the command to *start*. This is represented in the diagram by V; it may be a thought of the first movement or of the last result, or a mere perception of some of the habitual conditions of the chain, the presence, e.g., of the keyboard near the hand. In the present example, no sooner has this conscious thought or volition instigated movement A, than A, through the sensation a of its own occurrence, awakens B reflexly; B then excites C through b, and so on till the chain is ended, when the intellect generally takes cognizance of the final result. The intellectual perception at the end is indicated in the diagram by the sensible effect of the movement G being represented at G', in the ideational centres above the merely sensational line. The sensational impressions, a,b,c,d,e,f, are all supposed to have their seat below the ideational level.

Habits depend on sensations not attended to. We have called a,b,c,d,e,f by the name of 'sensations.' If sensations, they are sensations to which we are usually inattentive; but that they are more than unconscious nerve-currents seems certain, for they catch our attention if they go wrong. Schneider's account of these sensations deserves to be quoted. In the act of walking, he says, even when our attention is entirely absorbed elsewhere, "it is doubtful whether we could preserve equilibrium if no sensation of our body's attitude were there, and doubtful whether we should advance our leg if we had no sensation of its movement as executed, and not even a minimal feeling of impulse to set it down. Knitting appears altogether mechanical, and the knitter keeps up her knitting even while she reads or is engaged in lively talk. But if we ask her how this is possible, she will hardly reply that the knitting goes on of itself. She will rather say that she has a feeling of it, that she feels in her hands that she knits and how she must knit, and that therefore the movements of knitting are called forth and regulated by the sensations associated therewithal, even when the attention is called away. . . ." Again: "When a pupil begins to play on the violin, to keep him from raising his right elbow in playing a book is placed under his right armpit, which he is ordered to hold fast by keeping the upper arm tight against his body. The muscular feelings, and feelings of contact connected with the book, provoke an impulse to press it tight. But often it happens that the beginner, whose attention gets absorbed in the production of the notes, lets drop the book. Later, however, this never happens; the faintest sensations of contact suffice to awaken the impulse to keep it in its place, and the attention may be wholly absorbed by the notes and the fingering with the left hand. *The simultaneous combination of movements is thus in the first instance conditioned by the facility with which in us, alongside of intellectual processes, processes of inattentive feeling may still go on.*"

Ethical and Pedagogical Importance of the Principle of Habit.—"Habit a second nature! Habit is ten times nature," the Duke of Wellington is said to have exclaimed; and the degree to which this is true no one probably can appreciate as well as one who is a veteran soldier himself. The daily drill and the years of discipline end by fashioning a man completely over again, as to most of the possibilities of his conduct.

"There is a story," says Prof. Huxley, "which is credible enough, though it may not be true, of a practical joker, who, seeing a discharged veteran carrying home his dinner, suddenly called out 'Attention!' whereupon the man instantly brought his hands down, and lost his mutton and potatoes in the gutter. The drill had been thorough, and its effects had become embodied in the man's nervous structure."

Riderless cavalry-horses, at many a battle, have been seen to come together and go through their customary evolutions at the sound of the bugle-call. Most domestic beasts seem machines almost pure and simple, undoubtingly, unhesitatingly doing from minute to minute the duties they have been taught, and giving no sign that the possibility of an alternative ever suggests itself to their mind. Men grown old in prison have asked to be readmitted after being once set free. In a railroad accident a menagerie-tiger, whose cage had broken open, is said to have emerged, but presently crept back again, as if too much bewildered by his new responsibilities, so that he was without difficulty secured.

Habit is thus the enormous fly-wheel of society, its most precious conservative agent. It alone is what keeps us all within the bounds of ordinance, and saves the children of fortune from the envious uprisings of the poor. It alone prevents the hardest and most repulsive walks of life from being deserted by those brought up to tread therein. It keeps the fisherman and the deck-hand at sea through the winter; it holds the miner in his darkness, and nails the countryman to his log-cabin and his lonely farm through all the months of snow; it protects us from invasion by the natives of the desert and the frozen zone. It dooms us all to fight out the battle of life upon the lines of our nurture or our early choice, and to make the best of a pursuit that disagrees, because there is no other for which we are fitted, and it is too late to begin again. It keeps different social strata from mixing. Already at the age of twenty-five you see the professional mannerism settling down on the young commercial traveller, on the young doctor, on the young minister, on the young counsellor-at-law. You see the little lines of cleavage running through the character, the tricks of thought, the prejudices, the ways of the 'shop,' in a word, from which the man can by-and-by no more escape than his coat-sleeve can suddenly fall into a new set of folds. On the whole, it is best he should not escape. It is well for the world that in most of us, by the age of thirty, the character has set like plaster, and will never soften again.

If the period between twenty and thirty is the critical one in the formation of intellectual and professional habits, the period below twenty is more important still for the fixing of *personal* habits, properly so called, such as vocalization and pronunciation, gesture, motion, and address. Hardly ever is a language learned after twenty spoken without a foreign accent; hardly ever can a youth transferred to the society of his betters unlearn the nasality and other vices of speech bred in him by the associations of his growing years. Hardly ever, indeed, no matter how much money there be in his pocket, can he even learn to *dress* like a gentleman-born. The merchants offer their wares as eagerly to him as to the veriest 'swell,' but he simply *cannot* buy the right things. An invisible law, as strong as gravitation, keeps him within his orbit, arrayed this year as he was the last; and how his better-clad acquaintances contrive to get the things they wear will be for him a mystery till his dying day.

The great thing, then, in all education, is to *make our nervous system our ally instead of our enemy*. It is to fund and capitalize our acquisitions, and live at ease upon the interest of the fund. *For this we must make automatic and habitual, as early as possible, as many useful actions as we can*, and guard against the growing into ways that are likely to be disadvantageous to us, as we should guard against the plague. The more of the details of our daily life we can hand over to the effortless custody of automatism, the more our higher powers of mind will be set free for their own proper work. There is no more miserable human being than one in whom nothing is habitual but indecision, and for whom the lighting of every cigar, the drinking of every cup, the time of rising and going to bed every day, and the beginning of every bit of work, are subjects of express volitional deliberation. Full half the time of such a man goes to the deciding, or regretting, of matters which ought to be so ingrained in him as practically not to exist for his consciousness at all. If there be such daily duties not yet ingrained in any one of my readers, let him begin this very hour to set the matter right.

In Professor Bain's chapter on "The Moral Habits" there are some admirable practical remarks laid down. Two great maxims emerge from his treatment. The first is that in the acquisition of a new habit, or the leaving off of an old one, we must take care to *launch ourselves with as strong and decided an initiative as possible*. Accumulate all the possible circum-

stances which shall re-enforce the right motives; put yourself
assiduously in conditions that encourage the new way; make
engagements incompatible with the old; take a public pledge,
if the case allows; in short, envelop your resolution with every
aid you know. This will give your new beginning such a momentum that the temptation to break down will not occur as
soon as it otherwise might; and every day during which a
breakdown is postponed adds to the chances of its not occurring at all.

The second maxim is: *Never suffer an exception to occur till
the new habit is securely rooted in your life.* Each lapse is like the
letting fall of a ball of string which one is carefully winding
up; a single slip undoes more than a great many turns will
wind again. *Continuity* of training is the great means of making the nervous system act infallibly right. As Professor Bain
says:

"The peculiarity of the moral habits, contra-distinguishing
them from the intellectual acquisitions, is the presence of two
hostile powers, one to be gradually raised into the ascendant
over the other. It is necessary, above all things, in such a situation, never to lose a battle. Every gain on the wrong side
undoes the effect of many conquests on the right. The essential precaution, therefore, is, so to regulate the two opposing
powers that the one may have a series of uninterrupted
successes, until repetition has fortified it to such a degree as
to enable it to cope with the opposition, under any circumstances. This is the theoretically best career of mental
progress."

The need of securing success at the *outset* is imperative.
Failure at first is apt to damp the energy of all future attempts, whereas past experiences of success nerve one to future vigor. Goethe says to a man who consulted him about an
enterprise but mistrusted his own powers: "Ach! you need
only blow on your hands!" And the remark illustrates the effect on Goethe's spirits of his own habitually successful career.

The question of 'tapering-off,' in abandoning such habits as
drink and opium-indulgence, comes in here, and is a question
about which experts differ within certain limits, and in regard
to what may be best for an individual case. In the main, however, all expert opinion would agree that abrupt acquisition of

the new habit is the best way, *if there be a real possibility of carrying it out.* We must be careful not to give the will so stiff a task as to insure its defeat at the very outset; but, *provided one can stand it,* a sharp period of suffering, and then a free time, is the best thing to aim at, whether in giving up a habit like that of opium, or in simply changing one's hours of rising or of work. It is surprising how soon a desire will die of ina-nition if it be *never* fed.

"One must first learn, unmoved, looking neither to the right nor left, to walk firmly on the straight and narrow path, before one can begin 'to make one's self over again.' He who every day makes a fresh resolve is like one who, arriving at the edge of the ditch he is to leap, forever stops and returns for a fresh run. Without *unbroken* advance there is no such thing as *accumulation* of the ethical forces possible, and to make this possible, and to exercise us and habituate us in it, is the sov-ereign blessing of regular work."[2]

A third maxim may be added to the preceding pair: *Seize the very first possible opportunity to act on every resolution you make, and on every emotional prompting you may experience in the direction of the habits you aspire to gain.* It is not in the moment of their forming, but in the moment of their pro-ducing *motor effects,* that resolves and aspirations communicate the new 'set' to the brain. As the author last quoted remarks:

"The actual presence of the practical opportunity alone fur-nishes the fulcrum upon which the lever can rest, by means of which the moral will may multiply its strength, and raise itself aloft. He who has no solid ground to press against will never get beyond the stage of empty gesture-making."

No matter how full a reservoir of *maxims* one may possess, and no matter how good one's *sentiments* may be, if one have not taken advantage of every concrete opportunity to *act,* one's character may remain entirely unaffected for the better. With mere good intentions, hell is proverbially paved. And this is an obvious consequence of the principles we have laid down. A 'character,' as J. S. Mill says, 'is a completely fash-ioned will'; and a will, in the sense in which he means it, is an aggregate of tendencies to act in a firm and prompt and

[2] J. Bahnsen: *Beiträge zur Charakterologie* (1867), vol. I, p. 209.

definite way upon all the principal emergencies of life. A tendency to act only becomes effectively ingrained in us in proportion to the uninterrupted frequency with which the actions actually occur, and the brain 'grows' to their use. When a resolve or a fine glow of feeling is allowed to evaporate without bearing practical fruit it is worse than a chance lost; it works so as positively to hinder future resolutions and emotions from taking the normal path of discharge. There is no more contemptible type of human character than that of the nerveless sentimentalist and dreamer, who spends his life in a weltering sea of sensibility and emotion, but who never does a manly concrete deed. Rousseau, inflaming all the mothers of France, by his eloquence, to follow Nature and nurse their babies themselves, while he sends his own children to the foundling hospital, is the classical example of what I mean. But every one of us in his measure, whenever, after glowing for an abstractly formulated Good, he practically ignores some actual case, among the squalid 'other particulars' of which that same Good lurks disguised, treads straight on Rousseau's path. All Goods are disguised by the vulgarity of their concomitants, in this work-a-day world; but woe to him who can only recognize them when he thinks them in their pure and abstract form! The habit of excessive novel-reading and theatre-going will produce true monsters in this line. The weeping of the Russian lady over the fictitious personages in the play, while her coachman is freezing to death on his seat outside, is the sort of thing that everywhere happens on a less glaring scale. Even the habit of excessive indulgence in music, for those who are neither performers themselves nor musically gifted enough to take it in a purely intellectual way, has probably a relaxing effect upon the character. One becomes filled with emotions which habitually pass without prompting to any deed, and so the inertly sentimental condition is kept up. The remedy would be, never to suffer one's self to have an emotion at a concert, without expressing it afterwards in *some* active way. Let the expression be the least thing in the world—speaking genially to one's grandmother, or giving up one's seat in a horse-car, if nothing more heroic offers—but let it not fail to take place.

These latter cases make us aware that it is not simply *partic-*

ular lines of discharge, but also *general forms* of discharge, that seem to be grooved out by habit in the brain. Just as, if we let our emotions evaporate, they get into a way of evaporating; so there is reason to suppose that if we often flinch from making an effort, before we know it the effort-making capacity will be gone; and that, if we suffer the wandering of our attention, presently it will wander all the time. Attention and effort are, as we shall see later, but two names for the same psychic fact. To what brain-processes they correspond we do not know. The strongest reason for believing that they do depend on brain-processes at all, and are not pure acts of the spirit, is just this fact, that they seem in some degree subject to the law of habit, which is a material law. As a final practical maxim, relative to these habits of the will, we may, then, offer something like this: *Keep the faculty of effort alive in you by a little gratuitous exercise every day.* That is, be systematically ascetic or heroic in little unnecessary points, do every day or two something for no other reason than that you would rather not do it, so that when the hour of dire need draws nigh, it may find you not unnerved and untrained to stand the test. Asceticism of this sort is like the insurance which a man pays on his house and goods. The tax does him no good at the time, and possibly may never bring him a return. But if the fire *does* come, his having paid it will be his salvation from ruin. So with the man who has daily inured himself to habits of concentrated attention, energetic volition, and self-denial in unnecessary things. He will stand like a tower when everything rocks around him, and when his softer fellow-mortals are winnowed like chaff in the blast.

The physiological study of mental conditions is thus the most powerful ally of hortatory ethics. The hell to be endured hereafter, of which theology tells, is no worse than the hell we make for ourselves in this world by habitually fashioning our characters in the wrong way. Could the young but realize how soon they will become mere walking bundles of habits, they would give more heed to their conduct while in the plastic state. We are spinning our own fates, good or evil, and never to be undone. Every smallest stroke of virtue or of vice leaves its never so little scar. The drunken Rip Van Winkle, in Jefferson's play, excuses himself for every fresh dereliction by saying, 'I won't count this time!' Well! he may not count it, and a kind Heaven may not count it; but it is being counted none the less. Down among his nerve-cells and fibres the molecules are counting it, registering and storing it up to be used against him when the next temptation comes. Nothing we ever do is, in strict scientific literalness, wiped out. Of course this has its good side as well as its bad one. As we become permanent drunkards by so many separate drinks, so we become saints in the moral, and authorities and experts in the practical and scientific spheres, by so many separate acts and hours of work. Let no youth have any anxiety about the upshot of his education, whatever the line of it may be. If he keep faithfully busy each hour of the working day, he may safely leave the final result to itself. He can with perfect certainty count on waking up some fine morning, to find himself one of the competent ones of his generation, in whatever pursuit he may have singled out. Silently, between all the details of his business, the *power of judging* in all that class of matter will have built itself up within him as a possession that will never pass away. Young people should know this truth in advance. The ignorance of it has probably engendered more discouragement and faint-heartedness in youths embarking on arduous careers than all other causes put together.

CHAPTER XI

The order of our study must be analytic. We are now prepared to begin the introspective study of the adult consciousness itself. Most books adopt the so-called synthetic method. Starting with 'simple ideas of sensation,' and regarding these as so many atoms, they proceed to build up the higher states of mind out of their 'association,' 'integration,' or 'fusion,' as houses are built by the agglutination of bricks. This has the didactic advantages which the synthetic method usually has. But it commits one beforehand to the very questionable theory that our higher states of consciousness are compounds of units; and instead of starting with what the reader directly knows, namely his total concrete states of mind, it starts with a set of supposed 'simple ideas' with which he has no immediate acquaintance at all, and concerning whose alleged interactions he is much at the mercy of any plausible phrase. On every ground, then, the method of advancing from the simple to the compound exposes us to illusion. All pedants and abstractionists will naturally hate to abandon it. But a student who loves the fulness of human nature will prefer to follow the 'analytic' method, and to begin with the most concrete facts, those with which he has a daily acquaintance in his own inner life. The analytic method will discover in due time the elementary parts, if such exist, without danger of precipitate assumption. The reader will bear in mind that our own chapters on sensation have dealt mainly with the physiological conditions thereof. They were put first as a mere matter of convenience, because incoming currents come first. *Psychologically* they might better have come last. Pure sensations were described on page 21 as processes which in adult life are well-nigh unknown, and nothing was said which could for a moment lead the reader to suppose that they were the *elements of composition* of the higher states of mind.

The Fundamental Fact.—The first and foremost concrete fact which everyone will affirm to belong to his inner experience is the fact that *consciousness of some sort goes on*. '*States of mind' succeed each other in him*. If we could say in English 'it thinks,' as we say 'it rains' or 'it blows,' we should be stating the fact most simply and with the minimum of assumption. As we cannot, we must simply say that *thought goes on*.

Four Characters in Consciousness.—How does it go on? We notice immediately four important characters in the process, of which it shall be the duty of the present chapter to treat in a general way:

1) Every 'state' tends to be part of a personal consciousness.

2) Within each personal consciousness states are always changing.

3) Each personal consciousness is sensibly continuous.

4) It is interested in some parts of its object to the exclusion of others, and welcomes or rejects—*chooses* from among them, in a word—all the while.

In considering these four points successively, we shall have to plunge *in medias res* as regards our nomenclature and use psychological terms which can only be adequately defined in later chapters of the book. But everyone knows what the terms mean in a rough way; and it is only in a rough way that we are now to take them. This chapter is like a painter's first charcoal sketch upon his canvas, in which no niceties appear.

When I say *every 'state' or 'thought' is part of a personal consciousness*, 'personal consciousness' is one of the terms in question. Its meaning we know so long as no one asks us to define it, but to give an accurate account of it is the most difficult of philosophic tasks. This task we must confront in the next chapter; here a preliminary word will suffice.

In this room—this lecture-room, say—there are a multitude of thoughts, yours and mine, some of which cohere mutually, and some not. They are as little each-for-itself and reciprocally independent as they are all-belonging-together. They are neither: no one of them is separate, but each belongs with certain others and with none beside. My thought belongs with *my* other thoughts, and your thought with *your* other thoughts. Whether anywhere in the room there be a *mere* thought, which is nobody's thought, we have no means of ascertaining, for we have no experience of its like. The only states of consciousness that we naturally deal with are found in personal consciousnesses, minds, selves, concrete particular I's and you's.

Each of these minds keeps its own thoughts to itself. There is no giving or bartering between them. No thought even comes into direct *sight* of a thought in another personal consciousness than its own. Absolute insulation, irreducible pluralism, is the law. It seems as if the elementary psychic fact were not *thought* or *this thought* or *that thought*, but *my thought*, every thought being *owned*. Neither contemporaneity, nor proximity in space, nor similarity of quality and content are able to fuse thoughts together which are sundered by this barrier of belonging to different personal minds. The breaches between such thoughts are the most absolute breaches in nature. Everyone will recognize this to be true, so long as the existence of *something* corresponding to the term 'personal mind' is all that is insisted on, without any particular view of its nature being implied. On these terms the personal self rather than the thought might be treated as the immediate datum in psychology. The universal conscious fact is not 'feelings and thoughts exist,' but 'I think' and 'I feel.' No psychology, at any rate, can question the *existence* of personal selves. Thoughts connected as we feel them to be connected are *what we mean* by personal selves. The worst a psychology can do is so to interpret the nature of these selves as to rob them of their *worth*.

Consciousness is in constant change. I do not mean by this to say that no one state of mind has any duration—even if true, that would be hard to establish. What I wish to lay stress on is this, that *no state once gone can recur and be identical with what it was before*. Now we are seeing, now hearing; now reasoning, now willing; now recollecting, now expecting; now loving, now hating; and in a hundred other ways we know our minds to be alternately engaged. But all these are complex states, it may be said, produced by combination of simpler ones;—do not the simpler ones follow a different law? Are not the *sensations* which we get from the same object, for example, always the same? Does not the same piano-key, struck with the same force, make us hear in the same way? Does not the same grass give us the same feeling of green, the same sky the same feeling of blue, and do we not get the same olfactory sensation no matter how many times we put our nose to the same flask of cologne? It seems a piece of metaphysical sophistry to suggest that we do not; and yet a close attention to the matter shows that *there is no proof that an incoming current ever gives us just the same bodily sensation twice.*

What is got twice is the same OBJECT. We hear the same *note* over and over again; we see the same *quality* of green, or smell the same objective perfume, or experience the same *species* of pain. The realities, concrete and abstract, physical and ideal, whose permanent existence we believe in, seem to be constantly coming up again before our thought, and lead us, in our carelessness, to suppose that our 'ideas' of them are the same ideas. When we come, some time later, to the chapter on Perception, we shall see how inveterate is our habit of simply using our sensible impressions as stepping-stones to pass over to the recognition of the realities whose presence they reveal. The grass out of the window now looks to me of the same green in the sun as in the shade, and yet a painter would have to paint one part of it dark brown, another part bright yellow, to give its real sensational effect. We take no heed, as a rule, of the different way in which the same things look and sound and smell at different distances and under different circumstances. The sameness of the *things* is what we are concerned to ascertain; and any sensations that assure us of that will probably be considered in a rough way to be the same with each other. This is what makes off-hand testimony about the subjective identity of different sensations well-nigh worthless as a proof of the fact. The entire history of what is called Sensation is a commentary on our inability to tell whether two sensible qualities received apart are exactly alike. What appeals to our attention far more than the absolute quality of an impression is its *ratio* to whatever other impressions we may have at the same time. When everything is dark a somewhat less dark sensation makes us see an object white. Helmholtz calculates that the white marble painted in a picture representing an architectural view by moonlight is, when seen by daylight, from ten to twenty thousand times brighter than the real moonlit marble would be, yet the latter looks white.

Such a difference as this could never have been *sensibly*

learned; it had to be inferred from a series of indirect considerations. These make us believe that our sensibility is altering
all the time, so that the same object cannot easily give us the
same sensation over again. We feel things differently accordingly as we are sleepy or awake, hungry or full, fresh or tired;
differently at night and in the morning, differently in summer
and in winter; and above all, differently in childhood, manhood, and old age. And yet we never doubt that our feelings
reveal the same world, with the same sensible qualities and
the same sensible things occupying it. The difference of the
sensibility is shown best by the difference of our emotion
about the things from one age to another, or when we are in
different organic moods. What was bright and exciting
becomes weary, flat, and unprofitable. The bird's song is
tedious, the breeze is mournful, the sky is sad.

To these indirect presumptions that our sensations, following the mutations of our capacity for feeling, are always
undergoing an essential change, must be added another presumption, based on what must happen in the brain. Every
sensation corresponds to some cerebral action. For an identical sensation to recur it would have to occur the second time
in an unmodified brain. But as this, strictly speaking, is a physiological impossibility, so is an unmodified feeling an impossibility; for to every brain-modification, however small, we
suppose that there must correspond a change of equal amount
in the consciousness which the brain subserves.

But if the assumption of 'simple sensations' recurring in immutable shape is so easily shown to be baseless, how much
more baseless is the assumption of immutability in the larger
masses of our thought!

For there it is obvious and palpable that our state of mind
is never precisely the same. Every thought we have of a given
fact is, strictly speaking, unique, and only bears a resemblance
of kind with our other thoughts of the same fact. When the
identical fact recurs, we *must* think of it in a fresh manner, see
it under a somewhat different angle, apprehend it in different
relations from those in which it last appeared. And the
thought by which we cognize it is the thought of it-in-those-
relations, a thought suffused with the consciousness of all that
dim context. Often we are ourselves struck at the strange dif-

ferences in our successive views of the same thing. We wonder how we ever could have opined as we did last month about a certain matter. We have outgrown the possibility of that state of mind, we know not how. From one year to another we see things in new lights. What was unreal has grown real, and what was exciting is insipid. The friends we used to care the world for are shrunken to shadows; the women once so divine, the stars, the woods, and the waters, how now so dull and common!—the young girls that brought an aura of infinity, at present hardly distinguishable existences; the pictures so empty; and as for the books, what *was* there to find so mysteriously significant in Goethe, or in John Mill so full of weight? Instead of all this, more zestful than ever is the work, the work; and fuller and deeper the import of common duties and of common goods.

I am sure that this concrete and total manner of regarding the mind's changes is the only true manner, difficult as it may be to carry it out in detail. If anything seems obscure about it, it will grow clearer as we advance. Meanwhile, if it be true, it is certainly also true that no two 'ideas' are ever exactly the same, which is the proposition we started to prove. The proposition is more important theoretically than it at first sight seems. For it makes it already impossible for us to follow obediently in the footprints of either the Lockian or the Herbartian school, schools which have had almost unlimited influence in Germany and among ourselves. No doubt it is often *convenient* to formulate the mental facts in an atomistic sort of way, and to treat the higher states of consciousness as if they were all built out of unchanging simple ideas which 'pass and turn again.' It is convenient often to treat curves as if they were composed of small straight lines, and electricity and nerve-force as if they were fluids. But in the one case as in the other we must never forget that we are talking symbolically, and that there is nothing in nature to answer to our words. *A permanently existing 'Idea' which makes its appearance before the footlights of consciousness at periodical intervals is as mythological an entity as the Jack of Spades.*

Within each personal consciousness, thought is sensibly continuous. I can only define 'continuous' as that which is without breach, crack, or division. The only breaches that can well be conceived to occur within the limits of a single mind would either be *interruptions*, *time*-gaps during which the consciousness went out; or they would be breaks in the content of the thought, so abrupt that what followed had no connection whatever with what went before. The proposition that consciousness feels continuous, means two things:

a. That even where there is a time-gap the consciousness after it feels as if it belonged together with the consciousness before it, as another part of the same self;

b. That the changes from one moment to another in the quality of the consciousness are never absolutely abrupt.

The case of the time-gaps, as the simplest, shall be taken first.

a. When Paul and Peter wake up in the same bed, and recognize that they have been asleep, each one of them mentally reaches back and makes connection with but *one* of the two streams of thought which were broken by the sleeping hours. As the current of an electrode buried in the ground unerringly finds its way to its own similarly buried mate, across no matter how much intervening earth; so Peter's present instantly finds out Peter's past, and never by mistake knits itself on to that of Paul. Paul's thought in turn is as little liable to go astray. The past thought of Peter is appropriated by the present Peter alone. He may have a *knowledge*, and a correct one too, of what Paul's last drowsy states of mind were as he sank into sleep, but it is an entirely different sort of knowledge from that which he has of his own last states. He *remembers* his own states, whilst he only *conceives* Paul's. Remembrance is like direct feeling; its object is suffused with a warmth and intimacy to which no object of mere conception ever attains. This quality of warmth and intimacy and immediacy is what Peter's *present* thought also possesses for itself. So sure as this present is me, is mine, it says, so sure is anything else that comes with the same warmth and intimacy and immediacy, me and mine. What the qualities called warmth and intimacy may in themselves be will have to be matter for future consideration. But whatever past states appear with those qualities must be admitted to receive the greeting of the present mental state, to be owned by it, and accepted as belonging together with it in a common self. This community of self is what the time-gap cannot break in twain, and is why a present thought, although not ignorant of the time-gap, can still regard itself as continuous with certain chosen portions of the past.

Consciousness, then, does not appear to itself chopped up in bits. Such words as 'chain' or 'train' do not describe it fitly as it presents itself in the first instance. It is nothing jointed; it flows. A 'river' or a 'stream' are the metaphors by which it is most naturally described. *In talking of it hereafter, let us call it the stream of thought, of consciousness, or of subjective life.*

b. But now there appears, even within the limits of the same self, and between thoughts all of which alike have this same sense of belonging together, a kind of jointing and separateness among the parts, of which this statement seems to take no account. I refer to the breaks that are produced by sudden *contrasts in the quality* of the successive segments of the stream of thought. If the words 'chain' and 'train' had no natural fitness in them, how came such words to be used at all? Does not a loud explosion rend the consciousness upon which it abruptly breaks, in twain? No; for even into our awareness of the thunder the awareness of the previous silence creeps and continues; for what we hear when the thunder crashes is not thunder *pure,* but thunder-breaking-upon-silence-and-contrasting-with-it. Our feeling of the same objective thunder, coming in this way, is quite different from what it would be were the thunder a continuation of previous thunder. The thunder itself we believe to abolish and exclude the silence; but the *feeling* of the thunder is also a feeling of the silence as just gone; and it would be difficult to find in the actual concrete consciousness of man a feeling so limited to the present as not to have an inkling of anything that went before.

'Substantive' and 'Transitive' States of Mind.—When we take a general view of the wonderful stream of our consciousness, what strikes us first is the different pace of its parts. Like a bird's life, it seems to be an alternation of flights and perchings. The rhythm of language expresses this, where every thought is expressed in a sentence, and every sentence closed by a period. The resting-places are usually occupied by sensorial imaginations of some sort, whose peculiarity is that they can be held before the mind for an indefinite time, and contemplated without changing; the places of flight are filled with thoughts of relations, static or dynamic, that for the most part obtain between the matters contemplated in the periods of comparative rest.

Let us call the resting-places the 'substantive parts,' and the places of flight the 'transitive parts,' of the stream of thought. It then appears that our thinking tends at all times towards some other substantive part than the one from which it has just been dislodged. And we may say that the main use of the transitive parts is to lead us from one substantive conclusion to another.

Now it is very difficult, introspectively, to see the transitive parts for what they really are. If they are but flights to a conclusion, stopping them to look at them before the conclusion is reached is really annihilating them. Whilst if we wait till the conclusion *be* reached, it so exceeds them in vigor and stability that it quite eclipses and swallows them up in its glare. Let anyone try to cut a thought across in the middle and get a look at its section, and he will see how difficult the introspective observation of the transitive tracts is. The rush of the thought is so headlong that it almost always brings us up at the conclusion before we can arrest it. Or if our purpose is nimble enough and we do arrest it, it ceases forthwith to be itself. As a snowflake caught in the warm hand is no longer a flake but a drop, so, instead of catching the feeling of relation moving to its term, we find we have caught some substantive thing, usually the last word we were pronouncing, statically taken, and with its function, tendency, and particular meaning in the sentence quite evaporated. The attempt at introspective analysis in these cases is in fact like seizing a spinning top to catch its motion, or trying to turn up the gas quickly enough to see how the darkness looks. And the challenge to *produce* these transitive states of consciousness, which is sure to be thrown by doubting psychologists at anyone who contends for their existence, is as unfair as Zeno's treatment of the advocates of motion, when, asking them to point out in what place an arrow *is* when it moves, he argues the falsity of their thesis from their inability to make to so preposterous a question an immediate reply.

The results of this introspective difficulty are baleful. If to hold fast and observe the transitive parts of thought's stream be so hard, then the great blunder to which all schools are liable must be the failure to register them, and the undue emphasizing of the more substantive parts of the stream. Now the blunder has historically worked in two ways. One set of thinkers have been led by it to *Sensationalism*. Unable to lay their hands on any substantive feelings corresponding to the innumerable relations and forms of connection between the sensible things of the world, finding no *named* mental states mirroring such relations, they have for the most part denied that any such states exist; and many of them, like Hume, have gone on to deny the reality of most relations *out* of the mind as well as in it. Simple substantive 'ideas,' sensations and their copies, juxtaposed like dominoes in a game, but really separate, everything else verbal illusion,—such is the upshot of this view. The *Intellectualists*, on the other hand, unable to give up the reality of relations *extra mentem*, but equally unable to point to any distinct substantive feelings in which they were known, have made the same admission that such feelings do not exist. But they have drawn an opposite conclusion. The relations must be known, they say, in something that is no feeling, no mental 'state,' continuous and consubstantial with the subjective tissue out of which sensations and other substantive conditions of consciousness are made. They must be known by something that lies on an entirely different plane, by an *actus purus* of Thought, Intellect, or Reason, all written with capitals and considered to mean something unutterably superior to any passing perishing fact of sensibility whatever.

But from our point of view both Intellectualists and Sensationalists are wrong. If there be such things as feelings at all, *then so surely as relations between objects exist* in rerum naturâ, *so surely, and more surely, do feelings exist to which these relations are known*. There is not a conjunction or a preposition, and hardly an adverbial phrase, syntactic form, or inflection of voice, in human speech, that does not express some shading or other of relation which we at some moment actually feel to exist between the larger objects of our thought. If we speak objectively, it is the real relations that appear revealed; if we speak subjectively, it is the stream of consciousness that matches each of them by an inward coloring of its own. In either case the relations are numberless, and no existing language is capable of doing justice to all their shades.

We ought to say a feeling of *and*, a feeling of *if*, a feeling of *but*, and a feeling of *by*, quite as readily as we say a feeling of *blue* or a feeling of *cold*. Yet we do not: so inveterate has our habit become of recognizing the existence of the substantive parts alone, that language almost refuses to lend itself to any other use. Consider once again the analogy of the brain. We believe the brain to be an organ whose internal equilibrium is always in a state of change—the change affecting every part. The pulses of change are doubtless more violent in one place than in another, their rhythm more rapid at this time than at that. As in a kaleidoscope revolving at a uniform rate, although the figures are always rearranging themselves, there are instants during which the transformation seems minute and interstitial and almost absent, followed by others when it shoots with magical rapidity, relatively stable forms thus alternating with forms we should not distinguish if seen again; so in the brain the perpetual rearrangement must result in some forms of tension lingering relatively long, whilst others simply come and pass. But if consciousness corresponds to the fact of rearrangement itself, why, if the rearrangement stop not, should the consciousness ever cease? And if a lingering rearrangement brings with it one kind of consciousness, why should not a swift rearrangement bring another kind of consciousness as peculiar as the rearrangement itself?

The object before the mind always has a 'Fringe.' There are other unnamed modifications of consciousness just as important as the transitive states, and just as cognitive as they. Examples will show what I mean.

Suppose three successive persons say to us: 'Wait!' 'Hark!' 'Look!' Our consciousness is thrown into three quite different attitudes of expectancy, although no definite object is before it in any one of the three cases. Probably no one will deny here the existence of a real conscious affection, a sense of the direction from which an impression is about to come, although no positive impression is yet there. Meanwhile we have no names for the psychoses in question but the names hark, look, and wait.

Suppose we try to recall a forgotten name. The state of our consciousness is peculiar. There is a gap therein; but no mere gap. It is a gap that is intensely active. A sort of wraith of the name is in it, beckoning us in a given direction, making us at moments tingle with the sense of our closeness, and then letting us sink back without the longed-for term. If wrong names are proposed to us, this singularly definite gap acts immediately so as to negate them. They do not fit into its mould. And the gap of one word does not feel like the gap of another, all empty of content as both might seem necessarily to be when described as gaps. When I vainly try to recall the name of Spalding, my consciousness is far removed from what it is when I vainly try to recall the name of Bowles. There are innumerable consciousnesses of *want*, no one of which taken in itself has a name, but all different from each other. Such a feeling of want is *toto cœlo* other than a want of feeling: it is an intense feeling. The rhythm of a lost word may be there without a sound to clothe it; or the evanescent sense of something which is the initial vowel or consonant may mock us fitfully, without growing more distinct. Everyone must know the tantalizing effect of the blank rhythm of some forgotten verse, restlessly dancing in one's mind, striving to be filled out with words.

What is that first instantaneous glimpse of someone's meaning which we have, when in vulgar phrase we say we 'twig' it? Surely an altogether specific affection of our mind. And has the reader never asked himself what kind of a mental fact is his *intention of saying a thing* before he has said it? It is an entirely definite intention, distinct from all other intentions, an absolutely distinct state of consciousness, therefore; and yet how much of it consists of definite sensorial images, either of words or of things? Hardly anything! Linger, and the words and things come into the mind; the anticipatory intention, the divination is there no more. But as the words that replace it arrive, it welcomes them successively and calls them right if they agree with it, it rejects them and calls them wrong if they do not. The intention *to-say-so-and-so* is the only name it can receive. One may admit that a good third of our psychic life consists in these rapid premonitory perspective views of schemes of thought not yet articulate. How comes it about that a man reading something aloud for the first time is able immediately to emphasize all his words aright, unless from the very first he have a sense of at least the form of the sentence yet to come, which sense is fused with his consciousness of the present word, and modifies its emphasis in his mind so as to make him give it the proper accent as he utters it? Emphasis of this kind almost altogether depends on grammatical construction. If we read 'no more,' we expect presently a 'than'; if we read 'however,' it is a 'yet,' a 'still,' or a 'nevertheless,' that we expect. And this foreboding of the coming verbal and grammatical scheme is so practically accurate that a reader incapable of understanding four ideas of the book he is reading aloud can nevertheless read it with the most delicately modulated expression of intelligence.

It is, the reader will see, the reinstatement of the vague and inarticulate to its proper place in our mental life which I am so anxious to press on the attention. Mr. Galton and Prof. Huxley have, as we shall see in the chapter on Imagination, made one step in advance in exploding the ridiculous theory of Hume and Berkeley that we can have no images but of perfectly definite things. Another is made if we overthrow the equally ridiculous notion that, whilst simple objective qualities are revealed to our knowledge in 'states of consciousness,' relations are not. But these reforms are not half sweeping and radical enough. What must be admitted is that the definite images of traditional psychology form but the very smallest part of our minds as they actually live. The traditional psychology talks like one who should say a river consists of nothing but pailsful, spoonsful, quartpotsful, barrelsful, and other moulded forms of water. Even were the pails and the pots all actually standing in the stream, still between them the free water would continue to flow. It is just this free water of consciousness that psychologists resolutely overlook. Every definite image in the mind is steeped and dyed in the free water that flows round it. With it goes the sense of its relations, near and remote, the dying echo of whence it came to us, the dawning sense of whither it is to lead. The significance, the value, of the image is all in this halo or penumbra that surrounds and escorts it,—or rather that is fused into one with it and has become bone of its bone and flesh of its flesh; leaving it, it is true, an image of the same *thing* it was before, but making it an image of that thing newly taken and freshly understood.

Let us call the consciousness of this halo of relations around the image by the name of 'psychic overtone' or 'fringe.'

Cerebral Conditions of the 'Fringe.'—Nothing is easier than to symbolize these facts in terms of brain-action. Just as the echo of the *whence*, the sense of the starting point of our thought, is probably due to the dying excitement of processes but a moment since vividly aroused; so the sense of the whither, the foretaste of the terminus, must be due to the waxing excitement of tracts or processes whose psychical correlative will a moment hence be the vividly present feature of our thought. Represented by a curve, the neurosis underlying consciousness must at any moment be like this:

Let the horizontal in Fig. 52 be the line of time, and let the three curves beginning at *a*, *b*, and *c* respectively stand for the neural processes correlated with the thoughts of those three letters. Each process occupies a certain time during which its intensity waxes, culminates, and wanes. The process for *a* has not yet died out, the process for *c* has already begun, when that for *b* is culminating. At the time-instant represented by the vertical line all three processes are *present*, in the intensities shown by the curve. Those before *c*'s apex *were* more intense a moment ago; those after it *will be* more intense a moment hence. If I recite *a,b,c*, then, at the moment of uttering *b*,

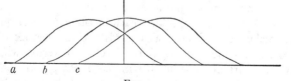

FIG. 52.

neither *a* nor *c* is out of my consciousness altogether, but both, after their respective fashions, 'mix their dim lights' with the stronger *b*, because their processes are both awake in some degree.

It is just like 'overtones' in music: they are not separately heard by the ear; they blend with the fundamental note, and suffuse it, and alter it; and even so do the waxing and waning brain-processes at every moment blend with and suffuse and alter the psychic effect of the processes which are at their culminating point.

The 'Topic' of the Thought.—If we then consider the *cognitive function* of different states of mind, we may feel assured that the difference between those that are mere 'acquaintance' and those that are 'knowledges-*about*' is reducible almost entirely to the absence or presence of psychic fringes or overtones. Knowledge *about* a thing is knowledge of its relations. Acquaintance with it is limitation to the bare impression which it makes. Of most of its relations we are only aware in the penumbral nascent way of a 'fringe' of unarticulated affinities about it. And, before passing to the next topic in order, I must say a little of this sense of affinity, as itself one of the most interesting features of the subjective stream.

Thought may be equally rational in any sort of terms. *In all our voluntary thinking there is some* TOPIC *or* SUBJECT *about* which all the members of the thought revolve. Relation to this topic or interest is constantly felt in the fringe, and particularly the relation of harmony and discord, of furtherance or hindrance of the topic. Any thought the quality of whose fringe lets us feel ourselves 'all right,' may be considered a thought that furthers the topic. Provided we only feel its object to have a place in the scheme of relations in which the topic also lies, that is sufficient to make of it a relevant and appropriate portion of our train of ideas.

Now we may think about our topic mainly in words, or we may think about it mainly in visual or other images, but this need make no difference as regards the furtherance of our knowledge of the topic. If we only feel in the terms, whatever they be, a fringe of affinity with each other and with the topic, and if we are conscious of approaching a conclusion, we feel that our thought is rational and right. The words in every language have contracted by long association fringes of mutual repugnance or affinity with each other and with the conclusion, which run exactly parallel with like fringes in the visual, tactile and other ideas. The most important element of these fringes is, I repeat, the mere feeling of harmony or discord, of a right or wrong direction in the thought.

If we know English and French and begin a sentence in French, all the later words that come are French; we hardly ever drop into English. And this affinity of the French words for each other is not something merely operating mechanically as a brain-law, it is something we feel at the time. Our understanding of a French sentence heard never falls to so low an ebb that we are not aware that the words linguistically belong together. Our attention can hardly so wander that if an English word be suddenly introduced we shall not start at the change. Such a vague sense as this of the words belonging together is the very minimum of fringe that can accompany them, if 'thought' at all. Usually the vague perception that all the words we hear belong to the same language and to the same special vocabulary in that language, and that the grammatical sequence is familiar, is practically equivalent to an admission that what we hear is sense. But if an unusual foreign word be introduced, if the grammar trip, or if a term from an incongruous vocabulary suddenly appear, such as 'rat-trap' or 'plumber's bill' in a philosophical discourse, the sentence detonates as it were, we receive a shock from the incongruity, and the drowsy assent is gone. The feeling of rationality in these cases seems rather a negative than a positive thing, being the mere absence of shock, or sense of discord, between the terms of thought.

Conversely, if words do belong to the same vocabulary, and if the grammatical structure is correct, sentences with absolutely no meaning may be uttered in good faith and pass unchallenged. Discourses at prayer-meetings, reshuffling the same collection of cant phrases, and the whole genus of penny-a-line-isms and newspaper-reporter's flourishes give illustrations of this. "The birds filled the tree-tops with their morning song, making the air moist, cool, and pleasant," is a sentence I remember reading once in a report of some athletic

exercises in Jerome Park. It was probably written unconsciously by the hurried reporter, and read uncritically by many
readers.

We see, then, that it makes little or no difference in what
sort of mind-stuff, in what quality of imagery, our thinking
goes on. The only images *intrinsically* important are the
halting-places, the substantive conclusions, provisional or final, of the thought. Throughout all the rest of the stream, the
feelings of relation are everything, and the terms related almost naught. These feelings of relation, these psychic overtones, halos, suffusions, or fringes about the terms, may be
the same in very different systems of imagery. A diagram may
help to accentuate this indifference of the mental means
where the end is the same. Let A be some experience from
which a number of thinkers start. Let Z be the practical conclusion rationally inferrible from it. One gets to this conclusion by one line, another by another; one follows a course of
English, another of German, verbal imagery. With one, visual
images predominate; with another, tactile. Some trains are
tinged with emotions, others not; some are very abridged,
synthetic and rapid; others, hesitating and broken into many
steps. But when the penultimate terms of all the trains, however differing *inter se*, finally shoot into the same conclusion,
we say, and rightly say, that all the thinkers have had substantially the same thought. It would probably astound each of
them beyond measure to be let into his neighbor's mind and
to find how different the scenery there was from that in his
own.

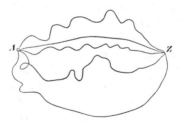

FIG. 53.

The last peculiarity to which attention is to be drawn in this first rough description of thought's stream is that—

Consciousness is always interested more in one part of its object than in another, and welcomes and rejects, or chooses, all the while it thinks.

The phenomena of selective attention and of deliberative will are of course patent examples of this choosing activity. But few of us are aware how incessantly it is at work in operations not ordinarily called by these names. Accentuation and Emphasis are present in every perception we have. We find it quite impossible to disperse our attention impartially over a number of impressions. A monotonous succession of sonorous strokes is broken up into rhythms, now of one sort, now of another, by the different accent which we place on different strokes. The simplest of these rhythms is the double one, tick-tóck, tick-tóck, tick-tóck. Dots dispersed on a surface are perceived in rows and groups. Lines separate into diverse figures. The ubiquity of the distinctions, *this* and *that*, *here* and *there*, *now* and *then*, in our minds is the result of our laying the same selective emphasis on parts of place and time.

But we do far more than emphasize things, and unite some, and keep others apart. We actually *ignore* most of the things before us. Let me briefly show how this goes on.

To begin at the bottom, what are our very senses themselves, as we saw on pp. 18–20, but organs of selection? Out of the infinite chaos of movements, of which physics teaches us that the outer world consists, each sense-organ picks out those which fall within certain limits of velocity. To these it responds, but ignores the rest as completely as if they did not exist. Out of what is in itself an undistinguishable, swarming *continuum*, devoid of distinction or emphasis, our senses make for us, by attending to this motion and ignoring that, a world full of contrasts, of sharp accents, of abrupt changes, of picturesque light and shade.

If the sensations we receive from a given organ have their causes thus picked out for us by the conformation of the organ's termination, Attention, on the other hand, out of all the sensations yielded, picks out certain ones as worthy of its notice and suppresses all the rest. We notice only those sensations which are signs to us of *things* which happen practically or æsthetically to interest us, to which we therefore give substantive names, and which we exalt to this exclusive status of independence and dignity. But in itself, apart from my interest, a particular dust-wreath on a windy day is just as much of an individual *thing*, and just as much or as little deserves an individual name, as my own body does.

And then, among the sensations we get from each separate thing, what happens? The mind selects again. It chooses certain of the sensations to represent the thing most *truly*, and considers the rest as its appearances, modified by the conditions of the moment. Thus my table-top is named *square*, after but one of an infinite number of retinal sensations which it yields, the rest of them being sensations of two acute and two obtuse angles; but I call the latter *perspective* views, and the four right angles the *true* form of the table, and erect the attribute squareness into the table's essence, for æsthetic reasons of my own. In like manner, the real form of the circle is deemed to be the sensation it gives when the line of vision is perpendicular to its centre—all its other sensations are *signs* of this sensation. The real sound of the cannon is the sensation it makes when the ear is close by. The real color of the brick is the sensation it gives when the eye looks squarely at it from a near point, out of the sunshine and yet not in the gloom; under other circumstances it gives us other color-sensations which are but signs of this—we then see it looks pinker or bluer than it really is. The reader knows no object which he does not represent to himself by preference as in some typical attitude, of some normal size, at some characteristic distance, of some standard tint, etc., etc. But all these essential characteristics, which together form for us the genuine objectivity of the thing and are contrasted with what we call the subjective sensations it may yield us at a given moment, are mere sensations like the latter. The mind chooses to suit itself, and decides what particular sensation shall be held more real and valid than all the rest.

Next, in a world of objects thus individualized by our mind's selective industry, what is called our 'experience' is almost entirely determined by our habits of attention. A thing may be present to a man a hundred times, but if he persistently fails to notice it, it cannot be said to enter into his experience. We are all seeing flies, moths, and beetles by the thousand, but to whom, save an entomologist, do they say anything distinct? On the other hand, a thing met only once in a lifetime may leave an indelible experience in the memory. Let four men make a tour in Europe. One will bring home only picturesque impressions—costumes and colors, parks and views and works of architecture, pictures and statues. To another all this will be non-existent; and distances and prices, populations and drainage-arrangements, door- and window-fastenings, and other useful statistics will take their place. A third will give a rich account of the theatres, restaurants, and public balls, and naught beside; whilst the fourth will perhaps have been so wrapped in his own subjective broodings as to be able to tell little more than a few names of places through which he passed. Each has selected, out of the same mass of presented objects, those which suited his private interest and has made his experience thereby.

If now, leaving the empirical combination of objects, we ask how the mind proceeds *rationally* to connect them, we find selection again to be omnipotent. In a future chapter we shall see that all Reasoning depends on the ability of the mind to break up the totality of the phenomenon reasoned about, into parts, and to pick out from among these the particular one which, in the given emergency, may lead to the proper conclusion. The man of genius is he who will always stick in his bill at the right point, and bring it out with the right element—'reason' if the emergency be theoretical, 'means' if it be practical—transfixed upon it.

If now we pass to the æsthetic department, our law is still more obvious. The artist notoriously selects his items, rejecting all tones, colors, shapes, which do not harmonize with each other and with the main purpose of his work. That unity, harmony, 'convergence of characters,' as M. Taine calls it, which gives to works of art their superiority over works of nature, is wholly due to *elimination*. Any natural subject will do, if the artist has wit enough to pounce upon some one feature of it as characteristic, and suppress all merely accidental items which do not harmonize with this.

Ascending still higher, we reach the plane of Ethics, where choice reigns notoriously supreme. An act has no ethical quality whatever unless it be chosen out of several all equally possible. To sustain the arguments for the good course and keep them ever before us, to stifle our longing for more flowery ways, to keep the foot unflinchingly on the arduous path, these are characteristic ethical energies. But more than these; for these but deal with the means of compassing interests already felt by the man to be supreme. The ethical energy *par excellence* has to go farther and choose which *interest* out of several, equally coercive, shall become supreme. The issue here is of the utmost pregnancy, for it decides a man's entire career. When he debates, Shall I commit this crime? choose that profession? accept that office, or marry this fortune?— his choice really lies between one of several equally possible future Characters. What he shall *become* is fixed by the conduct of this moment. Schopenhauer, who enforces his determinism by the argument that with a given fixed character only one reaction is possible under given circumstances, forgets that, in these critical ethical moments, what consciously *seems* to be in question is the complexion of the character itself. The problem with the man is less what act he shall now resolve to do than what being he shall now choose to become.

Taking human experience in a general way, the choosings of different men are to a great extent the same. The race as a whole largely agrees as to what it shall notice and name; and among the noticed parts we select in much the same way for accentuation and preference, or subordination and dislike. There is, however, one entirely extraordinary case in which no two men ever are known to choose alike. One great splitting of the whole universe into two halves is made by each of us; and for each of us almost all of the interest attaches to one of the halves; but we all draw the line of division between them in a different place. When I say that we all call the two halves by the same names, and that those names are '*me*' and '*not-me*' respectively, it will at once be seen what I mean. The altogether unique kind of interest which each human mind feels in those parts of creation which it can call *me* or *mine* may be a moral riddle, but it is a fundamental psychological fact. No mind can take the same interest in his neighbor's *me* as in his own. The neighbor's me falls together with all the rest of things in one foreign mass against which his own *me* stands out in startling relief. Even the trodden worm, as Lotze some-where says, contrasts his own suffering self with the whole remaining universe, though he have no clear conception ei-ther of himself or of what the universe may be. He is for me a mere part of the world; for him it is I who am the mere part. Each of us dichotomizes the Kosmos in a different place.

Descending now to finer work than this first general sketch, let us in the next chapter try to trace the psychology of this fact of self-consciousness to which we have thus once more been led.

CHAPTER XII

THE SELF

The Me and the I.—Whatever I may be thinking of, I am always at the same time more or less aware of *myself*, of my *personal existence*. At the same time it is *I* who am aware; so that the total self of me, being as it were duplex, partly known and partly knower, partly object and partly subject, must have two aspects discriminated in it, of which for shortness we may call one the *Me* and the other the *I*. I call these 'discriminated aspects,' and not separate things, because the identity of *I* with *me*, even in the very act of their discrimination, is perhaps the most ineradicable dictum of commonsense, and must not be undermined by our terminology here at the outset, whatever we may come to think of its validity at our inquiry's end.

I shall therefore treat successively of A) the self as known, or the *me*, the 'empirical ego' as it is sometimes called; and of B) the self as knower, or the I, the 'pure ego' of certain authors.

A) The Self as Known

The Empirical Self or Me.—Between what a man calls *me* and what he simply calls *mine* the line is difficult to draw. We feel and act about certain things that are ours very much as we feel and act about ourselves. Our fame, our children, the work of our hands, may be as dear to us as our bodies are, and arouse the same feelings and the same acts of reprisal if attacked. And our bodies themselves, are they simply ours, or are they *us*? Certainly men have been ready to disown their very bodies and to regard them as mere vestures, or even as prisons of clay from which they should some day be glad to escape.

We see then that we are dealing with a fluctuating material; the same object being sometimes treated as a part of me, at other times as simply mine, and then again as if I had nothing to do with it at all. *In its widest possible sense,* however, *a man's Me is the sum total of all that he* CAN *call his*, not only his body and his psychic powers, but his clothes and his house, his wife and children, his ancestors and friends, his reputation and works, his lands and horses, and yacht and bank-account. All these things give him the same emotions. If they wax and prosper, he feels triumphant; if they dwindle and die away, he feels cast down,—not necessarily in the same degree for each thing, but in much the same way for all. Understanding the Me in this widest sense, we may begin by dividing the history of it into three parts, relating respectively to—

a. Its constituents;

b. The feelings and emotions they arouse,—*self-appre-ciation*;

c. The acts to which they prompt,—*self-seeking and self-preservation*.

a. The constituents of the Me may be divided into three classes, those which make up respectively—

> The material me;
> The social me; and
> The spiritual me.

The Material Me.—The *body* is the innermost part of the material me in each of us; and certain parts of the body seem more intimately ours than the rest. The clothes come next. The old saying that the human person is composed of three parts—soul, body and clothes—is more than a joke. We so appropriate our clothes and identify ourselves with them that there are few of us who, if asked to choose between having a beautiful body clad in raiment perpetually shabby and un-clean, and having an ugly and blemished form always spot-lessly attired, would not hesitate a moment before making a decisive reply. Next, our immediate family is a part of our-selves. Our father and mother, our wife and babes, are bone of our bone and flesh of our flesh. When they die, a part of our very selves is gone. If they do anything wrong, it is our shame. If they are insulted, our anger flashes forth as readily as if we stood in their place. Our home comes next. Its scenes are part of our life; its aspects awaken the tenderest feelings of affection; and we do not easily forgive the stranger who, in visiting it, finds fault with its arrangements or treats it with contempt. All these different things are the objects of instinctive preferences coupled with the most important practical interests of life. We all have a blind impulse to watch over our body, to deck it with clothing of an ornamental sort, to cherish parents, wife and babes, and to find for ourselves a house of our own which we may live in and 'improve.'

An equally instinctive impulse drives us to collect property; and the collections thus made become, with different degrees of intimacy, parts of our empirical selves. The parts of our wealth most intimately ours are those which are saturated with our labor. There are few men who would not feel personally annihilated if a life-long construction of their hands or brains—say an entomological collection or an extensive work in manuscript—were suddenly swept away. The miser feels similarly towards his gold; and although it is true that a part of our depression at the loss of possessions is due to our feeling that we must now go without certain goods that we expected the possessions to bring in their train, yet in every case there remains, over and above this, a sense of the shrinkage of our personality, a partial conversion of ourselves to nothingness, which is a psychological phenomenon by itself. We are all at once assimilated to the tramps and poor devils whom we so despise, and at the same time removed farther than ever away from the happy sons of earth who lord it over land and sea and men in the full-blown lustihood that wealth and power can give, and before whom, stiffen ourselves as we will by appealing to anti-snobbish first principles, we cannot escape an emotion, open or sneaking, of respect and dread.

The Social Me.—A man's social me is the recognition which he gets from his mates. We are not only gregarious animals, liking to be in sight of our fellows, but we have an innate propensity to get ourselves noticed, and noticed favorably, by our kind. No more fiendish punishment could be devised, were such a thing physically possible, than that one should be turned loose in society and remain absolutely unnoticed by all the members thereof. If no one turned round when we entered, answered when we spoke, or minded what we did, but if every person we met 'cut us dead,' and acted as if we were non-existing things, a kind of rage and impotent despair would ere long well up in us, from which the cruellest bodily tortures would be a relief; for these would make us feel that, however bad might be our plight, we had not sunk to such a depth as to be unworthy of attention at all.

Properly speaking, *a man has as many social selves as there are individuals who recognize him* and carry an image of him in their mind. To wound any one of these his images is to wound him. But as the individuals who carry the images fall naturally into classes, we may practically say that he has as many different social selves as there are distinct *groups* of persons about whose opinion he cares. He generally shows a different side of himself to each of these different groups. Many a youth who is demure enough before his parents and teachers, swears and swaggers like a pirate among his 'tough' young friends. We do not show ourselves to our children as to our club-companions, to our customers as to the laborers we employ, to our own masters and employers as to our intimate friends. From this there results what practically is a division of the man into several selves; and this may be a discordant splitting, as where one is afraid to let one set of his acquaintances know him as he is elsewhere; or it may be a perfectly harmonious division of labor, as where one tender to his children is stern to the soldiers or prisoners under his command.

The most peculiar social self which one is apt to have is in the mind of the person one is in love with. The good or bad fortunes of this self cause the most intense elation and dejection—unreasonable enough as measured by every other standard than that of the organic feeling of the individual. To his own consciousness he *is* not, so long as this particular social self fails to get recognition, and when it is recognized his contentment passes all bounds.

A man's *fame*, good or bad, and his *honor* or dishonor, are names for one of his social selves. The particular social self of a man called his honor is usually the result of one of those splittings of which we have spoken. It is his image in the eyes of his own 'set,' which exalts or condemns him as he conforms or not to certain requirements that may not be made of one in another walk of life. Thus a layman may abandon a city infected with cholera; but a priest or a doctor would think such an act incompatible with his honor. A soldier's honor requires him to fight or to die under circumstances where another man can apologize or run away with no stain upon his social self. A judge, a statesman, are in like manner debarred by the honor of their cloth from entering into pecuniary relations perfectly honorable to persons in private life. Nothing is commoner than to hear people discriminate between their different selves of this sort: "As a man I pity you, but as an official I must show you no mercy"; "As a politician I regard him as an ally, but as a moralist I loathe him"; etc., etc. What may be called 'club-opinion' is one of the very strongest forces in life. The thief must not steal from other thieves; the gambler must pay his gambling-debts, though he pay no other debts in the world. The code of honor of fashionable society has throughout history been full of permissions as well as of vetoes, the only reason for following either of which is that so we best serve one of our social selves. You must not lie in general, but you may lie as much as you please if asked about your relations with a lady; you must accept a challenge from an equal, but if challenged by an inferior you may laugh him to scorn: these are examples of what is meant.

The Spiritual Me. — By the 'spiritual me,' so far as it belongs to the empirical self, I mean no one of my passing states of consciousness. I mean rather the entire collection of my states of consciousness, my psychic faculties and dispositions taken concretely. This collection can at any moment become an object to my thought at that moment and awaken emotions like those awakened by any of the other portions of the Me. When we *think of ourselves as thinkers*, all the other ingredients of our Me seem relatively external possessions. Even within the spiritual *Me* some ingredients seem more external than others. Our capacities for sensation, for example, are less intimate possessions, so to speak, than our emotions and desires; our intellectual processes are less intimate than our volitional decisions. The more *active-feeling* states of consciousness are thus the more central portions of the spiritual Me. The very core and nucleus of our self, as we know it, the very sanctuary of our life, is the sense of activity which certain inner states possess. This sense of activity is often held to be a direct revelation of the living substance of our Soul. Whether this be so or not is an ulterior question. I wish now only to lay down the peculiar *internality* of whatever states possess this quality of seeming to be active. It is as if they *went out to meet* all the other elements of our experience. In thus feeling about them probably all men agree.

b. The feelings and emotions of self come after the constituents.

Self-appreciation.—This is of two sorts, *self-complacency* and *self-dissatisfaction*. 'Self-love' more properly belongs under the division *C*, of *acts*, since what men mean by that name is rather a set of motor tendencies than a kind of feeling properly so called.

Language has synonyms enough for both kinds of self-appreciation. Thus pride, conceit, vanity, self-esteem, arrogance, vainglory, on the one hand; and on the other modesty, humility, confusion, diffidence, shame, mortification, contrition, the sense of obloquy, and personal despair. These two opposite classes of affection seem to be direct and elementary endowments of our nature. Associationists would have it that they are, on the other hand, secondary phenomena arising from a rapid computation of the sensible pleasures or pains to which our prosperous or debased personal predicament is likely to lead, the sum of the represented pleasures forming the self-satisfaction, and the sum of the represented pains forming the opposite feeling of shame. No doubt, when we are self-satisfied, we do fondly rehearse all possible rewards for our desert, and when in a fit of self-despair we forebode evil. But the mere expectation of reward *is* not the self-satisfaction, and the mere apprehension of the evil *is* not the self-despair; for there is a certain average tone of self-feeling which each one of us carries about with him, and which is independent of the objective reasons we may have for satisfaction or discontent. That is, a very meanly-conditioned man may abound in unfaltering conceit, and one whose success in life is secure, and who is esteemed by all, may remain diffident of his powers to the end.

One may say, however, that the normal *provocative* of self-feeling is one's actual success or failure, and the good or bad actual position one holds in the world. "He put in his thumb and pulled out a plum, and said, 'What a good boy am I!' " A man with a broadly extended empirical Ego, with powers that have uniformly brought him success, with place and wealth and friends and fame, is not likely to be visited by the morbid diffidences and doubts about himself which he had when he was a boy. "Is not this great Babylon, which I have planted?" Whereas he who has made one blunder after another, and still lies in middle life among the failures at the foot of the hill, is liable to grow all sicklied o'er with self-distrust, and to shrink from trials with which his powers can really cope.

The emotions themselves of self-satisfaction and abasement are of a unique sort, each as worthy to be classed as a primitive emotional species as are, for example, rage or pain. Each has its own peculiar physiognomical expression. In self-satisfaction the extensor muscles are innervated, the eye is strong and glorious, the gait rolling and elastic, the nostril dilated, and a peculiar smile plays upon the lips. This whole complex of symptoms is seen in an exquisite way in lunatic asylums, which always contain some patients who are literally mad with conceit, and whose fatuous expression and absurdly strutting or swaggering gait is in tragic contrast with their lack of any valuable personal quality. It is in these same castles of despair that we find the strongest examples of the opposite physiognomy, in good people who think they have committed 'the unpardonable sin' and are lost forever, who crouch and cringe and slink from notice, and are unable to speak aloud or look us in the eye. Like fear and like anger, in similar morbid conditions, these opposite feelings of Self may be aroused with no adequate exciting cause. And in fact we ourselves know how the barometer of our self-esteem and confidence rises and falls from one day to another through causes that seem to be visceral and organic rather than rational, and which certainly answer to no corresponding variations in the esteem in which we are held by our friends.

c. Self-seeking and self-preservation come next.

These words cover a large number of our fundamental instinctive impulses. We have those of *bodily self-seeking*, those of *social self-seeking*, and those of *spiritual self-seeking*.

Bodily Self-seeking.—All the ordinary useful reflex actions and movements of alimentation and defence are acts of bodily self-preservation. Fear and anger prompt to acts that are useful in the same way. Whilst if by self-seeking we mean the providing for the future as distinguished from maintaining the present, we must class both anger and fear, together with the hunting, the acquisitive, the home-constructing and the tool-constructing instincts, as impulses to self-seeking of the bodily kind. Really, however, these latter instincts, with amativeness, parental fondness, curiosity and emulation, seek not only the development of the bodily Me, but that of the material Me in the widest possible sense of the word.

Our **social self-seeking**, in turn, is carried on directly through our amativeness and friendliness, our desire to please and attract notice and admiration, our emulation and jealousy, our love of glory, influence, and power, and indirectly through whichever of the material self-seeking impulses prove serviceable as means to social ends. That the direct social self-seeking impulses are probably pure instincts is easily seen. The noteworthy thing about the desire to be 'recognized' by others is that its strength has so little to do with the worth of the recognition computed in sensational or rational terms. We are crazy to get a visiting-list which shall be large, to be able to say when anyone is mentioned, "Oh! I know him well," and to be bowed to in the street by half the people we meet. Of course distinguished friends and admiring recognition are the most desirable—Thackeray somewhere asks his readers to confess whether it would not give each of *them* an exquisite pleasure to be met walking down Pall Mall with a duke on either arm. But in default of dukes and envious salutations almost anything will do for some of us; and there is a whole race of beings to-day whose passion is to keep their names in the newspapers, no matter under what heading, 'arrivals and departures,' 'personal paragraphs,' 'interviews,'—gossip, even scandal, will suit them if nothing better is to be had. Guiteau, Garfield's assassin, is an example of the extremity to which this sort of craving for the notoriety of print may go in a pathological case. The newspapers bounded his mental horizon; and in the poor wretch's prayer on the scaffold, one of the most heart-felt expressions was:

"The newspaper press of this land has a big bill to settle with thee, O Lord!"

Not only the people but the places and things I know enlarge my Self in a sort of metaphoric social way. '*Ça me connaît*,' as the French workman says of the implement he can use well. So that it comes about that persons for whose *opinion* we care nothing are nevertheless persons whose notice we woo; and that many a man truly great, many a woman truly fastidious in most respects, will take a deal of trouble to dazzle some insignificant cad whose whole personality they heartily despise.

Under the head of **spiritual self-seeking** ought to be included every impulse towards psychic progress, whether intellectual, moral, or spiritual in the narrow sense of the term. It must be admitted, however, that much that commonly passes for spiritual self-seeking in this narrow sense is only material and social self-seeking beyond the grave. In the Mohammedan desire for paradise and the Christian aspiration not to be damned in hell, the materiality of the goods sought is undisguised. In the more positive and refined view of heaven, many of its goods, the fellowship of the saints and of our dead ones, and the presence of God, are but social goods of the most exalted kind. It is only the search of the redeemed inward nature, the spotlessness from sin, whether here or hereafter, that can count as spiritual self-seeking pure and undefiled.

But this broad external review of the facts of the life of the Me will be incomplete without some account of the

Rivalry and Conflict of the Different Mes. — With most objects of desire, physical nature restricts our choice to but one of many represented goods, and even so it is here. I am often confronted by the necessity of standing by one of my empirical selves and relinquishing the rest. Not that I would not, if I could, be both handsome and fat and well dressed, and a great athlete, and make a million a year, be a wit, a *bon-vivant*, and a lady-killer, as well as a philosopher; a philanthropist, statesman, warrior, and African explorer, as well as a 'tone-poet' and saint. But the thing is simply impossible. The millionaire's work would run counter to the saint's; the *bon-vivant* and the philanthropist would trip each other up; the philosopher and the lady-killer could not well keep house in the same tenement of clay. Such different characters may conceivably at the outset of life be alike *possible* to a man. But to make any one of them actual, the rest must more or less be suppressed. So the seeker of his truest, strongest, deepest self must review the list carefully, and pick out the one on which to stake his salvation. All other selves thereupon become unreal, but the fortunes of this self are real. Its failures are real failures, its triumphs real triumphs, carrying shame and gladness with them. This is as strong an example as there is of that selective industry of the mind on which I insisted some pages back (p. 170 ff.). Our thought, incessantly deciding, among many things of a kind, which ones for it shall be realities, here chooses one of many possible selves or characters, and forthwith reckons it no shame to fail in any of those not adopted expressly as its own.

So we have the paradox of a man shamed to death because he is only the second pugilist or the second oarsman in the world. That he is able to beat the whole population of the globe minus one is nothing; he has 'pitted' himself to beat that one; and as long as he doesn't do that nothing else counts. He is to his own regard as if he were not, indeed he *is* not. Yonder puny fellow, however, whom everyone can beat, suffers no chagrin about it, for he has long ago abandoned the attempt to 'carry that line,' as the merchants say, of self at all. With no attempt there can be no failure; with no failure, no humiliation. So our self-feeling in this world depends entirely on what we *back* ourselves to be and do. It is determined by the ratio of our actualities to our supposed potentialities; a fraction of which our pretensions are the denominator and the numerator our success: thus,

$$\text{Self-esteem} = \frac{\text{Success}}{\text{Pretensions}}.$$

Such a fraction may be increased as well by diminishing the denominator as by increasing the numerator. To give up pretensions is as blessed a relief as to get them gratified; and where disappointment is incessant and the struggle unending, this is what men will always do. The history of evangelical theology, with its conviction of sin, its self-despair, and its abandonment of salvation by works, is the deepest of possible examples, but we meet others in every walk of life. There is the strangest lightness about the heart when one's nothingness in a particular line is once accepted in good faith. *All* is not bitterness in the lot of the lover sent away by the final inexorable 'No.' Many Bostonians, *crede experto* (and inhabitants of other cities, too, I fear), would be happier women and men to-day, if they could once for all abandon the notion of keeping up a Musical Self, and without shame let people hear them call a symphony a nuisance. How pleasant is the day when we give up striving to be young,—or slender! Thank God! we say, *those* illusions are gone. Everything added to the Self is a burden as well as a pride. A certain man who lost every penny during our civil war went and actually rolled in the dust, saying he had not felt so free and happy since he was born.

Once more, then, our self-feeling is in our power. As Carlyle says: "Make thy claim of wages a zero, then; thou hast the world under thy feet. Well did the wisest of our time write: 'It is only with *renunciation* that life, properly speaking, can be said to begin.' "

Neither threats nor pleadings can move a man unless they touch some one of his potential or actual selves. Only thus can we, as a rule, get a 'purchase' on another's will. The first care of diplomatists and monarchs and all who wish to rule or influence is, accordingly, to find out their victim's strongest principle of self-regard, so as to make that the fulcrum of all appeals. But if a man has given up those things which are subject to foreign fate, and ceased to regard them as parts of himself at all, we are well-nigh powerless over him. The Stoic receipt for contentment was to dispossess yourself in advance of all that was out of your own power,—then fortune's shocks might rain down unfelt. Epictetus exhorts us, by thus narrowing and at the same time solidifying our Self to make it invulnerable: "I must die; well, but must I die groaning too? . . . I will speak what appears to be right, and if the despot says, 'Then I will put you to death,' I will reply,

'When did I ever tell you that I was immortal? You will do
your part, and I mine: it is yours to kill and mine to die
intrepid; yours to banish, mine to depart untroubled.' . . .
How do we act in a voyage? We choose the pilot, the sailors,
the hour. Afterwards comes a storm. What have I to care for?
My part is performed. This matter belongs to the pilot. But
the ship is sinking; what then have I to do? That which alone
I can do; submit to being drowned, without fear, without
clamor, or accusing of God; but as one who knows, that what
is born, must likewise die."

This Stoic fashion, though efficacious and heroic enough in
its place and time, is, it must be confessed, only possible as an
habitual mood of the soul to narrow and unsympathetic characters. It proceeds altogether by exclusion. If I am a Stoic, the
goods I cannot appropriate cease to be *my* goods, and the
temptation lies very near to deny that they are goods at all.
We find this mode of protecting the Self by exclusion and
denial very common among people who are in other respects
not Stoics. All narrow people *intrench* their Me, they *retract*
it,—from the region of what they cannot securely possess.
People who don't resemble them, or who treat them with
indifference, people over whom they gain no influence, are
people on whose existence, however meritorious it may
intrinsically be, they look with chill negation, if not with positive hate. Who will not be mine I will exclude from existence
altogether; that is, as far as I can make it so, such people shall
be as if they were not. Thus may a certain absoluteness and
definiteness in the outline of my Me console me for the small-
ness of its content.

Sympathetic people, on the contrary, proceed by the entirely opposite way of expansion and inclusion. The outline of
their self often gets uncertain enough, but for this the spread
of its content more than atones. *Nil humani a me alienum.* Let
them despise this little person of mine, and treat me like a
dog, *I* shall not negate *them* so long as I have a soul in my
body. They are realities as much as I am. What positive good
is in them shall be mine too, etc., etc. The magnanimity of
these expansive natures is often touching indeed. Such persons can feel a sort of delicate rapture in thinking that,
however sick, ill-favored, mean-conditioned, and generally

forsaken they may be, they yet are integral parts of the whole of this brave world, have a fellow's share in the strength of the dray-horses, the happiness of the young people, the wisdom of the wise ones, and are not altogether without part or lot in the good fortunes of the Vanderbilts and the Hohenzollerns themselves. Thus either by negating or by embracing, the Ego may seek to establish itself in reality. He who, with Marcus Aurelius, can truly say, "O Universe, I wish all that thou wishest," has a self from which every trace of negativeness and obstructiveness has been removed—no wind can blow except to fill its sails.

The Hierarchy of the Mes.—A tolerably unanimous opinion ranges the different selves of which a man may be 'seized and possessed,' and the consequent different orders of his self-regard, in an *hierarchical scale, with the bodily me at the bottom, the spiritual me at top, and the extra-corporeal material selves and the various social selves between.* Our merely natural self-seeking would lead us to aggrandize all these selves; we give up deliberately only those among them which we find we cannot keep. Our unselfishness is thus apt to be a 'virtue of necessity'; and it is not without all show of reason that cynics quote the fable of the fox and the grapes in describing our progress therein. But this is the moral education of the race; and if we agree in the result that on the whole the selves we can keep are the intrinsically best, we need not complain of being led to the knowledge of their superior worth in such a tortuous way.

Of course this is not the only way in which we learn to subordinate our lower selves to our higher. A direct ethical judgment unquestionably also plays its part, and last, not least, we apply to our own persons judgments originally called forth by the acts of others. It is one of the strangest laws of our nature that many things which we are well satisfied with in ourselves disgust us when seen in others. With another man's bodily 'hoggishness' hardly anyone has any sympathy; almost as little with his cupidity, his social vanity and eagerness, his jealousy, his despotism, and his pride. Left absolutely to myself I should probably allow all these spontaneous tendencies to luxuriate in me unchecked, and it would be long before I formed a distinct notion of the order of their subordination. But having constantly to pass judgment on my associates, I come ere long to see, as Herr Horwicz says, my own lusts in the mirror of the lusts of others, and to *think* about them in a very different way from that in which I simply *feel*. Of course, the moral generalities which from childhood have been instilled into me accelerate enormously the advent of this reflective judgment on myself.

So it comes to pass that, as aforesaid, men have arranged the various selves which they may seek in an hierarchical scale according to their worth. A certain amount of bodily selfishness is required as a basis for all the other selves. But too much sensuality is despised, or at best condoned on account of the other qualities of the individual. The wider material selves are regarded as higher than the immediate body. He is esteemed a poor creature who is unable to forego a little meat and drink and warmth and sleep for the sake of getting on in the world. The social self as a whole, again, ranks higher than the material self as a whole. We must care more for our honor, our friends, our human ties, than for a sound skin or wealth. And the spiritual self is so supremely precious that, rather than lose it, a man ought to be willing to give up friends and good fame, and property, and life itself.

In each kind of Me, material, social, and spiritual, men distinguish between the immediate and actual, and the remote and potential, between the narrower and the wider view, to the detriment of the former and the advantage of the latter. One must forego a present bodily enjoyment for the sake of one's general health; one must abandon the dollar in the hand for the sake of the hundred dollars to come; one must make an enemy of his present interlocutor if thereby one makes friends of a more valued circle; one must go without learning and grace and wit, the better to compass one's soul's salvation.

Of all these wider, more potential selves, *the potential social Me* is the most interesting, by reason of certain apparent paradoxes to which it leads in conduct, and by reason of its connection with our moral and religious life. When for motives of honor and conscience I brave the condemnation of my own family, club, and 'set'; when, as a Protestant, I turn Catholic; as a Catholic, freethinker; as a 'regular practitioner,' homœopath, or what not, I am always inwardly strengthened in my course and steeled against the loss of my actual social self by the thought of other and better *possible* social judges than those whose verdict goes against me now. The ideal social self which I thus seek in appealing to their decision may be very remote: it may be represented as barely possible. I may not hope for its realization during my lifetime; I may even expect the future generations, which would approve me if they knew me, to know nothing about me when I am dead and gone. Yet still the emotion that beckons me on is indubitably the pursuit of an ideal social self, of a self that is at least *worthy* of approving recognition by the highest *possible* judging companion, if such companion there be. This self is the true, the intimate, the ultimate, the permanent me which I seek. This judge is God, the Absolute Mind, the 'Great Companion.' We hear, in these days of scientific enlightenment, a great deal of discussion about the efficacy of prayer; and many reasons are given us why we should not pray, whilst others are given us why we should. But in all this very little is said of the reason why we *do* pray, which is simply that we cannot help praying. It seems probable that, in spite of all that 'science' may do to the contrary, men will continue to pray to the end of time, unless their mental nature changes in a manner which nothing we know should lead us to expect. The impulse to pray is a necessary consequence of the fact that whilst the innermost of the empirical selves of a man is a Self of the *social* sort, it yet can find its only adequate *Socius* in an ideal world.

All progress in the social Self is the substitution of higher tribunals for lower; this ideal tribunal is the highest; and most men, either continually or occasionally, carry a reference to it in their breast. The humblest outcast on this earth can feel himself to be real and valid by means of this higher recognition. And, on the other hand, for most of us, a world with no such inner refuge when the outer social self failed and dropped from us would be the abyss of horror. I say 'for most of us,' because it is probable that individuals differ a good deal in the degree in which they are haunted by this sense of an ideal spectator. It is a much more essential part of the consciousness of some men than of others. Those who have the most of it are possibly the most *religious* men. But I am sure that even those who say they are altogether without it deceive themselves, and really have it in some degree. Only a non-gregarious animal could be completely without it. Probably no one can make sacrifices for 'right,' without to some degree personifying the principle of right for which the sacrifice is made, and expecting thanks from it. *Complete* social unselfishness, in other words, can hardly exist; *complete* social suicide hardly occur to a man's mind. Even such texts as Job's, "Though He slay me, yet will I trust in Him," or Marcus Aurelius's, "If gods hate me and my children, there is a reason for it," can least of all be cited to prove the contrary. For beyond all doubt Job revelled in the thought of Jehovah's recognition of the worship after the slaying should have been done; and the Roman emperor felt sure the Absolute Reason would not be all indifferent to his acquiescence in the gods' dislike. The old test of piety, "Are you willing to be damned for the glory of God?" was probably never answered in the affirmative except by those who felt sure in their heart of hearts that God would 'credit' them with their willingness, and set more store by them thus than if in His unfathomable scheme He had not damned them at all.

Teleological Uses of Self-interest.—On zoölogical principles it is easy to see why we have been endowed with impulses of self-seeking and with emotions of self-satisfaction and the reverse. Unless our consciousness were something more than cognitive, unless it experienced a partiality for certain of the objects, which, in succession, occupy its ken, it could not long maintain itself in existence; for, by an inscrutable necessity, each human mind's appearance on this earth is conditioned upon the integrity of the body with which it belongs, upon the treatment which that body gets from others, and upon the spiritual dispositions which use it as their tool, and lead it either towards longevity or to destruction. *Its own body, then, first of all, its friends next, and finally its spiritual dispositions,* MUST *be the supremely interesting objects for each human mind.* Each mind, to begin with, must have a certain minimum of selfishness in the shape of instincts of bodily self-seeking in order to exist. This minimum must be there as a basis for all farther conscious acts, whether of self-negation or of a selfishness more subtle still. All minds must have come, by the way of the survival of the fittest, if by no directer path, to take an intense interest in the bodies to which they are yoked, altogether apart from any interest in the pure Ego which they also possess.

And similarly with the images of their person in the minds of others. I should not be extant now had I not become sensitive to looks of approval or disapproval on the faces among which my life is cast. Looks of contempt cast on other persons need affect me in no such peculiar way. My spiritual powers, again, must interest me more than those of other people, and for the same reason. I should not be here at all unless I had cultivated them and kept them from decay. And the same law which made me once care for them makes me care for them still.

All these three things form the *natural Me*. But all these things are *objects*, properly so called, to the thought which at any time may be doing the thinking; and if the zoölogical and evolutionary point of view is the true one, there is no reason why one object *might* not arouse passion and interest as primitively and instinctively as any other. The phenomenon of passion is in origin and essence the same, whatever be the target upon which it is discharged; and what the target actually happens to be is solely a question of fact. I might conceivably be as much fascinated, and as primitively so, by the care of my neighbor's body as by the care of my own. I *am* thus fascinated by the care of my child's body. The only check to such exuberant non-egoistic interests is natural selection, which would weed out such as were very harmful to the individual or to his tribe. Many such interests, however, remain unweeded out—the interest in the opposite sex, for example, which seems in mankind stronger than is called for by its utilitarian need; and alongside of them remain interests, like that in alcoholic intoxication, or in musical sounds, which, for aught we can see, are without any utility whatever. The sympathetic instincts and the egoistic ones are thus coördinate. They arise, so far as we can tell, on the same psychologic level. The only difference between them is that the instincts called egoistic form much the larger mass.

Summary.—The following table may serve for a summary of what has been said thus far. The empirical life of Self is divided, as below, into

	MATERIAL	SOCIAL	SPIRITUAL
SELF-SEEKING	Bodily Appetites and Instincts. Love of Adornment, Foppery, Acquisitiveness, Constructiveness. Love of Home, etc.	Desire to Please, be Noticed, Admired, etc. Sociability, Emulation, Envy, Love, Pursuit of Honor, Ambition, etc.	Intellectual, Moral and Religious Aspirations, Conscientiousness.
SELF-ESTIMATION	Personal Vanity, Modesty, etc. Pride of Wealth, Fear of Poverty.	Social and Family Pride, Vainglory, Snobbery, Humility, Shame, etc.	Sense of Moral or Mental Superiority, Purity, etc. Sense of Inferiority or of Guilt.

B) THE SELF AS KNOWER

The I, or 'pure ego,' is a very much more difficult subject of inquiry than the Me. It is that which at any given moment *is* conscious, whereas the Me is only one of the things which it is conscious *of*. In other words, it is the *Thinker*; and the question immediately comes up, *what* is the thinker? Is it the passing state of consciousness itself, or is it something deeper and less mutable? The passing state we have seen to be the very embodiment of change (see p. 156 ff.). Yet each of us spontaneously considers that by 'I,' he means something always the same. This has led most philosophers to postulate behind the passing state of consciousness a permanent Substance or Agent whose modification or act it is. This Agent is the thinker; the 'state' is only its instrument or means. 'Soul,' 'transcendental Ego,' 'Spirit,' are so many names for this more permanent sort of Thinker. Not discriminating them just yet, let us proceed to define our idea of the passing state of consciousness more clearly.

The Unity of the Passing Thought.—Already, in speaking of 'sensations,' from the point of view of Fechner's idea of measuring them, we saw that there was no ground for calling them compounds. But what is true of sensations cognizing simple qualities is also true of thoughts with complex objects composed of many parts. This proposition unfortunately runs counter to a wide-spread prejudice, and will have to be defended at some length. Common-sense, and psychologists of almost every school, have agreed that whenever an object of thought contains many elements, the thought itself must be made up of just as many ideas, one idea for each element, all fused together in appearance, but really separate.

"There can be no difficulty in admitting that association *does* form the ideas of an indefinite number of individuals into one complex idea," says James Mill, "because it is an acknowledged fact. Have we not the idea of an army? And is not that precisely the ideas of an indefinite number of men formed into one idea?"

Similar quotations might be multiplied, and the reader's own first impressions probably would rally to their support. Suppose, for example, he thinks that "the pack of cards is on the table." If he begins to reflect, he is as likely as not to say: "Well, isn't that a thought of the pack of cards? Isn't it of the cards as included in the pack? Isn't it of the table? And of the legs of the table as well? Hasn't my thought, then, all these parts—one part for the pack and another for the table? And within the pack-part a part for each card, as within the table-part a part for each leg? And isn't each of these parts an idea? And can thought, then, be anything but an assemblage or pack of ideas, each answering to some element of what it knows?"

Plausible as such considerations may seem, it is astonishing how little force they have. In assuming a pack of ideas, each cognizant of some one element of the fact one has assumed, nothing has been assumed which knows the whole fact *at once*. The idea which, on the hypothesis of the pack of ideas, knows, *e.g.*, the ace of spades must be ignorant of the leg of the table, since to account for that knowledge another special idea is by the same hypothesis invoked; and so on with the rest of the ideas, all equally ignorant of each other's objects.

And yet in the actual living human mind what knows the cards also knows the table, its legs, etc., for all these things are known in relation to each other and at once. Our notion of the abstract numbers eight, four, two is as truly one feeling in the mind as our notion of simple unity. Our idea of a couple is not a couple of ideas. "But," the reader may say, "is not the taste of lemonade composed of that of lemon *plus* that of sugar?" No! I reply, this is taking the combining of objects for that of feelings. The physical lemonade contains both the lemon and the sugar, but its taste does not contain their tastes; for if there are any two things which are certainly *not* present in the taste of lemonade, those are the pure lemon-sour on the one hand and the pure sugar-sweet on the other. These tastes are absent utterly. A taste somewhat *like* both of them is there, but that is a distinct state of mind altogether.

Distinct mental states cannot 'fuse.' But not only is the notion that our ideas are combinations of smaller ideas improbable, it is logically unintelligible; it leaves out the essential features of all the 'combinations' which we actually know.

All the 'combinations' which we actually know are EFFECTS, *wrought by the units said to be 'combined,'* UPON SOME ENTITY OTHER THAN THEMSELVES. Without this feature of a medium or vehicle, the notion of combination has no sense.

In other words, no possible number of entities (call them as you like, whether forces, material particles, or mental elements) can sum *themselves* together. Each remains, in the sum, what it always was; and the sum itself exists only *for a by-stander* who happens to overlook the units and to apprehend the sum as such; or else it exists in the shape of some other effect on an entity external to the sum itself. When H_2 and O are said to combine into 'water,' and thenceforward to exhibit new properties, the 'water' is just the old atoms in the new position, $H-O-H$; the 'new properties' are just their combined *effects*, when in this position, upon external media, such as our sense-organs and the various reagents on which water may exert its properties and be known. Just so, the strength of many men may combine when they pull upon one rope, of many muscular fibres when they pull upon one tendon.

In the parallelogram of forces, the 'forces' do not combine *themselves* into the diagonal resultant; a *body* is needed on which they may impinge, to exhibit their resultant effect. No more do musical sounds combine *per se* into concords or discords. Concord and discord are names for their combined effects on that external medium, the *ear*.

Where the elemental units are supposed to be feelings, the case is in no wise altered. Take a hundred of them, shuffle them and pack them as close together as you can (whatever that may mean); still each remains the same feeling it always was, shut in its own skin, windowless, ignorant of what the other feelings are and mean. There would be a hundred-and-first feeling there, if, when a group or series of such feelings were set up, a consciousness *belonging to the group as such* should emerge; and this one hundred and first feeling would be a totally new fact. The one hundred original feelings might, by a curious physical law, be a signal for its *creation*, when they came together—we often have to learn things separately before we know them as a sum—but they would have no substantial identity with the new feeling, nor it with them; and one could never deduce the one from the others, or (in any intelligible sense) say that they *evolved* it out of themselves.

Take a sentence of a dozen words, and take twelve men and tell to each one word. Then stand the men in a row or jam them in a bunch, and let each think of his word as intently as he will: nowhere will there be a consciousness of the whole sentence. We talk, it is true, of the 'spirit of the age,' and the 'sentiment of the people,' and in various ways we hypostatize 'public opinion.' But we know this to be symbolic speech, and never dream that the spirit, opinion, or sentiment constitutes a consciousness other than, and additional to, that of the several individuals whom the words 'age,' 'people,' or 'public' denote. The private minds do not agglomerate into a higher compound mind. This has always been the invincible contention of the spiritualists against the associationists in Psychology. The associationists say the mind is constituted by a multiplicity of distinct 'ideas' *associated* into a unity. There is, they say, an idea of a, and also an idea of b. *Therefore*, they say, there is an idea of $a+b$, or of a and b together. Which is like saying that the mathematical square of a plus that of b is equal to the square of $a+b$, a palpable untruth. Idea of a, plus idea of *b*, are *not* identical with idea of (*a*+*b*). It is one, they are two; in it, what knows *a* also knows *b*; in them, what knows *a* is expressly posited as not knowing *b*; etc. In short, the two separate ideas can never by any logic be made to figure as one idea. If one idea (of *a*+*b*, for example) come as a matter of fact after the two separate ideas (of *a* and of *b*), then we must hold it to be as direct a product of the later conditions as the two separate ideas were of the earlier conditions.

The simplest thing, therefore, if we are to assume the existence of a stream of consciousness at all, would be to suppose that things that are known together are known in single pulses of that stream. The things may be many, and may occasion many currents in the brain. But the psychic phenomenon correlative to these many currents is one integral 'state,' transitive or substantive (see p. 159), to which the many things appear.

The Soul as a Combining Medium.—The spiritualists in philosophy have been prompt to see that things which are known together are known by one *something*, but that something, they say, is no mere passing thought, but a simple and permanent spiritual being on which many ideas combine their effects. It makes no difference in this connection whether this being be called Soul, Ego, or Spirit, in either case its chief function is that of a combining medium. This is a different vehicle of knowledge from that in which we just said that the mystery of knowing things together might be most simply lodged. Which is the real knower, this permanent being, or our passing state? If we had other grounds, not yet considered, for admitting the Soul into our psychology, then getting there on those grounds, she might turn out to be the knower too. But if there be no *other* grounds for admitting the Soul, we had better cling to our passing 'states' as the exclusive agents of knowledge; for we have to assume their existence anyhow in psychology, and the knowing of many things together is just as well accounted for when we call it one of their functions as when we call it a reaction of the Soul. *Explained* it is not by either conception, and has to figure in psychology as a datum that is ultimate.

But there are other alleged grounds for admitting the Soul into psychology, and the chief of them is

The Sense of Personal Identity.—In the last chapter it

was stated (see p. 154) that the thoughts which we actually know to exist do not fly about loose, but seem each to belong to some one thinker and not to another. Each thought, out of a multitude of other thoughts of which it may think, is able to distinguish those which belong to it from those which do not. The former have a warmth and intimacy about them of which the latter are completely devoid, and the result is a Me of yesterday, judged to be in some peculiarly subtle sense the *same* with the I who now make the judgment. As a mere subjective phenomenon the judgment presents no special mystery. It belongs to the great class of judgments of sameness; and there is nothing more remarkable in making a judgment of sameness in the first person than in the second or the third. The intellectual operations seem essentially alike, whether I say 'I am the same as I was,' or whether I say 'the pen is the same as it was, yesterday.' It is as easy to think this as to think the opposite and say 'neither of us is the same.' The only question which we have to consider is whether it be a right judgment. *Is the sameness predicated really there?*

Sameness in the Self as Known.—If in the sentence "I am the same that I was yesterday," we take the 'I' broadly, it is evident that in many ways I am *not* the same. As a concrete Me, I am somewhat different from what I was: then hungry, now full; then walking, now at rest; then poorer, now richer; then younger, now older; etc. And yet in other ways I *am* the same, and we may call these the essential ways. My name and profession and relations to the world are identical, my face, my faculties and store of memories, are practically indistinguishable, now and then. Moreover the Me of now and the Me of then are *continuous*: the alterations were gradual and never affected the whole of me at once. So far, then, my personal identity is just like the sameness predicated of any other aggregate thing. It is a conclusion grounded either on the resemblance in essential respects, or on the continuity of the phenomena compared. And it must not be taken to mean more than these grounds warrant, or treated as a sort of metaphysical or absolute Unity in which all differences are overwhelmed. The past and present selves compared are the same just so far as they *are* the same, and no farther. They are the same in *kind*. But this generic sameness coexists with generic differences just as real; and if from the one point of view I am one self, from another I am quite as truly many. Similarly of the attribute of continuity: it gives to the self the unity of mere connectedness, or unbrokenness, a perfectly definite phenomenal thing—but it gives not a jot or tittle more.

Sameness in the Self as Knower.—But all this is said only of the Me, or Self as known. In the judgment 'I am the same,' etc., the 'I' was taken broadly as the concrete person. Suppose, however, that we take it narrowly, as the *Thinker*, as '*that to which*' all the concrete determinations of the Me belong and are known: does there not then appear an absolute identity at different times? That something which at every moment goes out and knowingly appropriates the *Me* of the past, and discards the non-me as foreign, is it not a permanent abiding principle of spiritual activity identical with itself wherever found?

That it is such a principle is the reigning doctrine both of philosophy and common-sense, and yet reflection finds it difficult to justify the idea. *If there were no passing states of consciousness*, then indeed we might suppose an abiding principle, absolutely one with itself, to be the ceaseless thinker in each one of us. But if the states of consciousness be accorded as realities, no such 'substantial' identity in the thinker need be supposed. Yesterday's and to-day's states of consciousnesses have no *substantial* identity, for when one is here the other is irrevocably dead and gone. But they have a *functional* identity, for both know the same objects, and so far as the by-gone me is one of those objects, they react upon it in an identical way, greeting it and calling it *mine*, and opposing it to all the other things they know. This functional identity seems really the only sort of identity in the thinker which the facts require us to suppose. Successive thinkers, numerically distinct, but all aware of the same past in the same way, form an adequate vehicle for all the experience of personal unity and sameness which we actually have. And just such a train of successive thinkers is the stream of mental states (each with its complex object cognized and emotional and selective reaction thereupon) which psychology treated as a natural science has to assume (see p. 12).

The logical conclusion seems then to be that *the states of*

*consciousness are all that psychology needs to do her work with.
Metaphysics or theology may prove the Soul to exist; but for psychology the hypothesis of such a substantial principle of unity is
superfluous.*

How the I appropriates the Me.—But *why* should each
successive mental state appropriate the same past Me? I spoke
a while ago of my own past experiences appearing to me with
a 'warmth and intimacy' which the experiences thought of by
me as having occurred to other people lack. This leads us to
the answer sought. My present Me is felt with warmth and
intimacy. The heavy warm mass of my body is there, and the
nucleus of the 'spiritual me,' the sense of intimate activity (p.
178), is there. We cannot realize our present self without simultaneously feeling one or other of these two things. Any
other object of thought which brings these two things with it
into consciousness will be thought with a warmth and an intimacy like those which cling to the present me.

Any *distant* object which fulfils this condition will be
thought with such warmth and intimacy. But which distant
objects *do* fulfil the condition, when represented?

Obviously those, and only those, which fulfilled it when
they were alive. *Them* we shall still represent with the animal
warmth upon them; to them may possibly still cling the flavor
of the inner activity taken in the act. And by a natural consequence, we shall assimilate them to each other and to the
warm and intimate self we now feel within us as we think,
and separate them as a collection from whatever objects have
not this mark, much as out of a herd of cattle let loose for the
winter on some wide Western prairie the owner picks out and
sorts together, when the round-up comes in the spring, all the
beasts on which he finds his own particular brand. Well, just
such objects are the past experiences which I now call mine.
Other men's experiences, no matter how much I may know
about them, never bear this vivid, this peculiar brand. This is
why Peter, awakening in the same bed with Paul, and recalling
what both had in mind before they went to sleep, reidentifies
and appropriates the 'warm' ideas as his, and is never
tempted to confuse them with those cold and pale-appearing
ones which he ascribes to Paul. As well might he confound
Paul's body, which he only sees, with his own body, which he

sees but also feels. Each of us when he awakens says, Here's the same old Me again, just as he says, Here's the same old bed, the same old room, the same old world.

And similarly in our waking hours, though each pulse of consciousness dies away and is replaced by another, yet that other, among the things it knows, knows its own predecessor, and finding it 'warm,' in the way we have described, greets it, saying: "Thou art *mine*, and part of the same self with me." Each later thought, knowing and including thus the thoughts that went before, is the final receptacle—and appropriating them is the final owner—of all that they contain and own. As Kant says, it is as if elastic balls were to have not only motion but knowledge of it, and a first ball were to transmit both its motion and its consciousness to a second, which took both up into *its* consciousness and passed them to a third, until the last ball held all that the other balls had held, and realized it as its own. It is this trick which the nascent thought has of immediately taking up the expiring thought and 'adopting' it, which leads to the appropriation of most of the remoter constituents of the self. Who owns the last self owns the self before the last, for what possesses the possessor possesses the possessed. It is impossible to discover any *verifiable* features in personal identity which this sketch does not contain, impossible to imagine how any transcendent principle of Unity (were such a principle there) could shape matters to any other result, or be known by any other fruit, than just this production of a stream of consciousness each successive part of which should know, and knowing, hug to itself and adopt, all those that went before,—thus standing as the *representative* of an entire past stream with which it is in no wise to be identified.

Mutations and Multiplications of the Self.—The Me, like every other aggregate, changes as it grows. The passing states of consciousness, which should preserve in their succession an identical knowledge of its past, wander from their duty, letting large portions drop from out of their ken, and representing other portions wrong. The identity which we recognize as we survey the long procession can only be the relative identity of a slow shifting in which there is always some common ingredient retained. The commonest element of all, the most uniform, is the possession of some common memories. However different the man may be from the youth, both look back on the same childhood and call it their own.

Thus the identity found by the *I* in its *Me* is only a loosely construed thing, an identity 'on the whole,' just like that which any outside observer might find in the same assemblage of facts. We often say of a man 'he is so changed one would not know him'; and so does a man, less often, speak of himself. These changes in the *Me*, recognized by the I, or by outside observers, may be grave or slight. They deserve some notice here.

The mutations of the Self may be divided into two main classes:

a. Alterations of memory; and

b. Alterations in the present bodily and spiritual selves.

a. Of the alterations of memory little need be said—they are so familiar. Losses of memory are a normal incident in life, especially in advancing years, and the person's *me*, as 'realized,' shrinks *pari passu* with the facts that disappear. The memory of dreams and of experiences in the hypnotic trance rarely survives.

False memories, also, are by no means rare occurrences, and whenever they occur they distort our consciousness of our Me. Most people, probably, are in doubt about certain matters ascribed to their past. They may have seen them, may have said them, done them, or they may only have dreamed or imagined they did so. The content of a dream will oftentimes insert itself into the stream of real life in a most perplexing way. The most frequent source of false memory is the accounts we give to others of our experiences. Such accounts we almost always make both more simple and more interesting than the truth. We quote what we should have said or done, rather than what we really said or did; and in the first telling we may be fully aware of the distinction. But ere long the fiction expels the reality from memory and reigns in its stead alone. This is one great source of the fallibility of testimony meant to be quite honest. Especially where the marvellous is concerned, the story takes a tilt that way, and the memory follows the story.

b. When we pass beyond alterations of memory to abnormal *alterations in the present self* we have graver disturbances. These alterations are of three main types, but our knowledge of the elements and causes of these changes of personality is so slight that the division into types must not be regarded as having any profound significance. The types are:

    α. Insane delusions;
    β. Alternating selves;
    γ. Mediumships or possessions.

α. In insanity we often have delusions projected into the past, which are melancholic or sanguine according to the character of the disease. But the worst alterations of the self come from present perversions of sensibility and impulse which leave the past undisturbed, but induce the patient to think that the present *Me* is an altogether new personage. Something of this sort happens normally in the rapid expansion of the whole character, intellectual as well as volitional, which takes place after the time of puberty. The pathological cases are curious enough to merit longer notice.

The basis of our personality, as M. Ribot says, is that feeling of our vitality which, because it is so perpetually present, remains in the background of our consciousness.

"It is the basis because, always present, always acting, without peace or rest, it knows neither sleep nor fainting, and lasts as long as life itself, of which it is one form. It serves as a support to that self-conscious *me* which memory constitutes, it is the medium of association among its other parts. . . . Suppose now that it were possible at once to change our body and put another into its place: skeleton, vessels, viscera, muscles, skin, everything made new, except the nervous system with its stored-up memory of the past. There can be no doubt that in such a case the afflux of unaccustomed vital sensations would produce the gravest disorders. Between the old sense of existence engraved on the nervous system, and the new one acting with all the intensity of its reality and novelty, there would be irreconcilable contradiction."

What the particular perversions of the bodily sensibility may be which give rise to these contradictions is, for the most part, impossible for a sound-minded person to conceive. One patient has another self that repeats all his thoughts for him. Others, amongst whom are some of the first characters in history, have internal dæmons who speak with them and are replied to. Another feels that someone 'makes' his thoughts for him. Another has two bodies, lying in different beds. Some patients feel as if they had lost parts of their bodies, teeth, brain, stomach, etc. In some it is made of wood, glass, butter, etc. In some it does not exist any longer, or is dead, or is a foreign object quite separate from the speaker's self. Occasionally, parts of the body lose their connection for consciousness with the rest, and are treated as belonging to another person and moved by a hostile will. Thus the right hand may fight with the left as with an enemy. Or the cries of the patient himself are assigned to another person with whom the patient expresses sympathy. The literature of insanity is filled with narratives of such illusions as these. M. Taine quotes from a patient of Dr. Krishaber an account of sufferings, from which it will be seen how completely aloof from what is normal a man's experience may suddenly become:

"After the first or second day it was for some weeks impossible to observe or analyze myself. The suffering—angina pectoris—was too overwhelming. It was not till the first days of January that I could give an account to myself of what I experienced. . . . Here is the first thing of which I retain a clear remembrance. I was alone, and already a prey to permanent visual trouble, when I was suddenly seized with a visual trouble infinitely more pronounced. Objects grew small and receded to infinite distances—men and things together. I was myself immeasurably far away. I looked about me with terror and astonishment; *the world was escaping from me*. . . . I remarked at the same time that my voice was extremely far away from me, that it sounded no longer as if mine. I struck the ground with my foot, and perceived its resistance; but this resistance seemed illusory—not that the soil was soft, but that the weight of my body was reduced to almost nothing. . . . I had the feeling of being without weight. . . ." In addition to being so distant, "objects appeared to me *flat*. When I spoke with anyone, I saw him like an image cut out of paper with no relief. . . . This sensation lasted intermittently for two years. . . . Constantly it seemed as if my legs did not belong to me. It was almost as bad with my arms. As for my head, it seemed no longer to exist. . . . I appeared to myself to act automatically, by an impulsion foreign to myself. . . . There was inside of me a new being, and another part of myself, the old being, which took no interest in the newcomer. I distinctly remember saying to myself that the sufferings of this new being were to me indifferent. I was never really dupe of these illusions, but my mind grew often tired of incessantly correcting the new impressions, and I let myself go and live the unhappy life of this new entity. I had an ardent desire to see my old world again, to get back to my old self. This desire kept me from killing myself. . . . I was another, and I hated, I despised this other; he was perfectly odious to me; it was certainly another who had taken my form and assumed my functions."[1]

In cases like this, it is as certain that the *I* is unaltered as that the *Me* is changed. That is to say, the present Thought of the patient is cognitive of both the old Me and the new, so long as its memory holds good. Only, within that objective sphere which formerly lent itself so simply to the judgment of recognition and of egoistic appropriation, strange perplexities have arisen. The present and the past, both seen therein, will not unite. Where is my old Me? What is this new one? Are they the same? Or have I two? Such questions, answered by whatever theory the patient is able to conjure up as plausible, form the beginning of his insane life.

β. The phenomenon of *alternating personality* in its simplest phases seems based on lapses of memory. Any man becomes, as we say, *inconsistent* with himself if he forgets his engagements, pledges, knowledges, and habits; and it is merely a question of degree at what point we shall say that his personality is changed. But in the pathological cases known as those of double or alternate personality the loss of memory is abrupt, and is usually preceded by a period of unconsciousness or syncope lasting a variable length of time. In the hypnotic trance we can easily produce an alteration of the personality, either by telling the subject to forget all that has

[1] *De l'intelligence*, 3me édition (1878), vol. II, p. 461, note.

happened to him since such or such a date, in which case he becomes (it may be) a child again, or by telling him he is another altogether imaginary personage, in which case all facts about himself seem for the time being to lapse from out his mind, and he throws himself into the new character with a vivacity proportionate to the amount of histrionic imagination which he possesses. But in the pathological cases the transformation is spontaneous. The most famous case, perhaps, on record is that of Félida X., reported by Dr. Azam of Bordeaux. At the age of fourteen this woman began to pass into a 'secondary' state characterized by a change in her general disposition and character, as if certain 'inhibitions,' previously existing, were suddenly removed. During the secondary state she remembered the first state, but on emerging from it into the first state she remembered nothing of the second. At the age of forty-four the duration of the secondary state (which was on the whole superior in quality to the original state) had gained upon the latter so much as to occupy most of her time. During it she remembers the events belonging to the original state, but her complete oblivion of the secondary state when the original state recurs is often very distressing to her, as, for example, when the transition takes place in a carriage on her way to a funeral, and she has no idea which one of her friends may be dead. She actually became pregnant during one of her early secondary states, and during her first state had no knowledge of how it had come to pass. Her distress at these blanks of memory is sometimes intense and once drove her to attempt suicide.

M. Pierre Janet describes a still more remarkable case as follows: "Léonie B., whose life sounds more like an improbable romance than a genuine history, has had attacks of natural somnambulism since the age of three years. She has been hypnotized constantly by all sorts of persons from the age of sixteen upwards, and she is now forty-five. Whilst her normal life developed in one way in the midst of her poor country surroundings, her second life was passed in drawing-rooms and doctors' offices, and naturally took an entirely different direction. To-day, when in her normal state, this poor peasant woman is a serious and rather sad person, calm and slow, very mild with everyone, and extremely timid: to look at her one would never suspect the personage which she contains. But hardly is she put to sleep hypnotically when a metamorphosis occurs. Her face is no longer the same. She keeps her eyes closed, it is true, but the acuteness of her other senses supplies their place. She is gay, noisy, restless, sometimes insupportably so. She remains good-natured, but has acquired a singular tendency to irony and sharp jesting. Nothing is more curious than to hear her after a sitting when she has received a visit from strangers who wished to see her asleep. She gives a word-portrait of them, apes their manners, claims to know their little ridiculous aspects and passions, and for each invents a romance. To this character must be added the possession of an enormous number of recollections, whose existence she does not even suspect when awake, for her amnesia is then complete. . . . She refuses the name of Léonie and takes that of Léontine (Léonie 2) to which her first magnetizers had accustomed her. 'That good woman is not myself,' she says, 'she is too stupid!' To herself, Léontine, or Léonie 2, she attributes all the sensations and all the actions, in a word all the conscious experiences, which she has undergone *in somnambulism*, and knits them together to make the history of her already long life. To Léonie 1 [as M. Janet calls the waking woman], on the other hand, she exclusively ascribes the events lived through in waking hours. I was at first struck by an important exception to the rule, and was disposed to think that there might be something arbitrary in this partition of her recollections. In the normal state Léonie has a husband and children; but Léonie 2, the somnambulist, whilst acknowledging the children as her own, attributes the husband to 'the other.' This choice was perhaps explicable, but it followed no rule. It was not till later that I learned that her magnetizers in early days, as audacious as certain hypnotizers of recent date, had somnambulized her for her first *accouchements*, and that she had lapsed into that state spontaneously in the later ones. Léonie 2 was thus quite right in ascribing to herself the children—it was she who had had them, and the rule that her first trance-state forms a different personality was not broken. But it is the same with her second or deepest state of trance. When after the renewed passes, syncope, etc., she reaches the condition which I have called Léonie 3, she is

another person still. Serious and grave, instead of being a
restless child, she speaks slowly and moves but little. Again
she separates herself from the waking Léonie 1. 'A good but
rather stupid woman,' she says, 'and not me.' And she also
separates herself from Léonie 2: 'How can you see anything
of me in that crazy creature?' she says. 'Fortunately I am
nothing for her.' "

γ. In 'mediumships' or 'possessions' the invasion and the passing away of the secondary state are both relatively abrupt, and
the duration of the state is usually short—i.e., from a few
minutes to a few hours. Whenever the secondary state is well
developed, no memory for aught that happened during it remains after the primary consciousness comes back. The subject during the secondary consciousness speaks, writes, or acts
as if animated by a foreign person, and often names this foreign person and gives his history. In old times the foreign
'control' was usually a demon, and is so now in communities
which favor that belief. With us he gives himself out at the
worst for an Indian or other grotesquely speaking but harmless personage. Usually he purports to be the spirit of a dead
person known or unknown to those present, and the subject
is then what we call a 'medium.' Mediumistic possession in all
its grades seems to form a perfectly natural special type of
alternate personality, and the susceptibility to it in some form
is by no means an uncommon gift, in persons who have no
other obvious nervous anomaly. The phenomena are very intricate, and are only just beginning to be studied in a proper
scientific way. The lowest phase of mediumship is automatic
writing, and the lowest grade of that is where the Subject
knows what words are coming, but feels impelled to write
them as if from without. Then comes writing unconsciously,
even whilst engaged in reading or talk. Inspirational speaking,
playing on musical instruments, etc., also belong to the relatively lower phases of possession, in which the normal self is
not excluded from conscious participation in the performance, though their initiative seems to come from elsewhere.
In the highest phase the trance is complete, the voice, language, and everything are changed, and there is no after-
memory whatever until the next trance comes. One curious

thing about trance-utterances is their generic similarity in different individuals. The 'control' here in America is either a grotesque, slangy, and flippant personage ('Indian' controls, calling the ladies 'squaws,' the men 'braves,' the house a 'wigwam,' etc., etc., are excessively common); or, if he ventures on higher intellectual flights, he abounds in a curiously vague optimistic philosophy-and-water, in which phrases about spirit, harmony, beauty, law, progression, development, etc., keep recurring. It seems exactly as if one author composed more than half of the trance-messages, no matter by whom they are uttered. Whether all sub-conscious selves are peculiarly susceptible to a certain stratum of the *Zeitgeist*, and get their inspiration from it, I know not; but this is obviously the case with the secondary selves which become 'developed' in spiritualist circles. There the beginnings of the medium trance are indistinguishable from effects of hypnotic suggestion. The subject assumes the rôle of a medium simply because opinion expects it of him under the conditions which are present; and carries it out with a feebleness or a vivacity proportionate to his histrionic gifts. But the odd thing is that persons unexposed to spiritualist traditions will so often act in the same way when they become entranced, speak in the name of the departed, go through the motions of their several death-agonies, send messages about their happy home in the summer-land, and describe the ailments of those present.

I have no theory to publish of these cases, the actual beginning of several of which I have personally seen. I am, however, persuaded by abundant acquaintance with the trances of one medium that the 'control' may be altogether different from any *actual* waking self of the person. In the case I have in mind, it professes to be a certain departed French doctor; and is, I am convinced, acquainted with facts about the circumstances, and the living and dead relatives and acquaintances, of numberless sitters whom the medium never met before, and of whom she has never heard the names. I record my bare opinion here unsupported by the evidence, not, of course, in order to convert anyone to my view, but because I am persuaded that a serious study of these trance-phenomena is one of the greatest needs of psychology, and think that my personal confession may possibly draw a reader or two into a field which the *soi-disant* 'scientist' usually refuses to explore.[2]

Review, and Psychological Conclusion.—To sum up this long chapter:—The consciousness of Self involves a stream of thought, each part of which as 'I' can remember those which went before, know the things they knew, and care paramountly for certain ones among them as '*Me,*' and *appropriate to these* the rest. This Me is an empirical aggregate of things objectively known. The *I* which knows them cannot itself be an aggregate; neither for psychological purposes need it be an unchanging metaphysical entity like the Soul, or a principle like the transcendental Ego, viewed as 'out of time.' It is a *thought*, at each moment different from that of the last moment, but *appropriative* of the latter, together with all that the latter called its own. All the experiential facts find their place in this description, unencumbered with any hypothesis save that of the existence of passing thoughts or states of mind.

If passing thoughts be the directly verifiable existents which no school has hitherto doubted them to be, then they are the only 'Knower' of which Psychology, treated as a natural science, need take any account. The only pathway that I can discover for bringing in a more transcendental Thinker would be to deny that we have any such *direct* knowledge of the existence of our 'states of consciousness' as common-sense supposes us to possess. The existence of the 'states' in question would then be a mere hypothesis, or one way of asserting that there *must be* a knower correlative to all this known; but the problem *who that knower is* would have become a metaphysical problem. With the question once stated in these terms, the notion either of a Spirit of the world which thinks through us, or that of a set of individual substantial souls, must be considered as *primâ facie* on a par with our own 'psychological' solution, and discussed impartially. I myself believe that room for much future inquiry lies in this direction. The 'states of mind' which every psychologist believes in are by no means clearly apprehensible, if distinguished from their

[2]Some of the evidence for this medium's supernormal powers is given in *The Proceedings of the Society for Psychical Research*, vol. VI, p. 436, and in the first Part of vol. VIII (1892).

objects. But to doubt them lies beyond the scope of our natural-science (see p. 11) point of view. And in this book the provisional solution which we have reached must be the final word: the thoughts themselves are the thinkers.

CHAPTER XIII

ATTENTION

The Narrowness of Consciousness.—One of the most extraordinary facts of our life is that, although we are besieged at every moment by impressions from our whole sensory surface, we notice so very small a part of them. The sum total of our impressions never enters into our *experience*, consciously so called, which runs through this sum total like a tiny rill through a broad flowery mead. Yet the physical impressions which do not count are *there* as much as those which do, and affect our sense-organs just as energetically. Why they fail to pierce the mind is a mystery, which is only named and not explained when we invoke *die Enge des Bewusstseins*, 'the narrowness of consciousness,' as its ground.

Its Physiological Ground.—Our consciousness certainly is narrow, when contrasted with the breadth of our sensory surface and the mass of incoming currents which are at all times pouring in. Evidently no current can be recorded in conscious experience unless it succeed in penetrating to the hemispheres and filling their pathways by the processes set up. When an incoming current thus occupies the hemispheres with its consequences, other currents are for the time kept out. They may show their faces at the door, but are turned back until the actual possessors of the place are tired. Physiologically, then, the narrowness of consciousness seems to depend on the fact that the activity of the hemispheres tends at all times to be a consolidated and unified affair, determinable now by this current and now by that, but determinable only as a whole. The ideas correlative to the reigning system of processes are those which are said to 'interest' us at the time; and thus that selective character of our attention on which so much stress was laid on pp. 170 ff. appears to find a physiological ground. At all times, however, there is a liability to disintegration of the reigning system. The consolidation is seldom quite complete, the excluded currents are not wholly abortive, their presence affects the 'fringe' and margin of our thought.

Dispersed Attention.—Sometimes, indeed, the normal consolidation seems hardly to exist. At such moments it is possible that cerebral activity sinks to a minimum. Most of us probably fall several times a day into a fit somewhat like this: The eyes are fixed on vacancy, the sounds of the world melt into confused unity, the attention is dispersed so that the whole body is felt, as it were, at once, and the foreground of consciousness is filled, if by anything, by a sort of solemn sense of surrender to the empty passing of time. In the dim background of our mind we know meanwhile what we ought to be doing: getting up, dressing ourselves, answering the person who has spoken to us, trying to make the next step in our reasoning. But somehow we cannot *start*; the *pensée de derrière la tête* fails to pierce the shell of lethargy that wraps our state about. Every moment we expect the spell to break, for we know no reason why it should continue. But it does continue, pulse after pulse, and we float with it, until—also without reason that we can discover—an energy is given, something—we know not what—enables us to gather ourselves together, we wink our eyes, we shake our heads, the background-ideas become effective, and the wheels of life go round again.

This is the extreme of what is called dispersed attention. Between this extreme and the extreme of concentrated attention, in which absorption in the interest of the moment is so complete that grave bodily injuries may be unfelt, there are intermediate degrees, and these have been studied experimentally. The problem is known as that of

The Span of Consciousness.—How many objects can we attend to at once when they are not embraced in one conceptual system? Prof. Cattell experimented with combinations of letters exposed to the eye for so short a fraction of a second that attention to them in succession seemed to be ruled out. When the letters formed familiar words, three times as many of them could be named as when their combination was meaningless. If the words formed a sentence, twice as many could be caught as when they had no connection. "The sentence was then apprehended as a whole. If not apprehended thus, almost nothing is apprehended of the several words; but if the sentence as a whole is apprehended, then the words appear very distinct."

A word is a conceptual system in which the letters do not enter consciousness separately, as they do when apprehended alone. A sentence flashed at once upon the eye is such a system relatively to its words. A conceptual system may *mean* many sensible objects, may be translated later into them, but as an actual existent mental state, it does not *consist of* the consciousnesses of these objects. When I think of the word *man* as a whole, for instance, what is in my mind is something different from what is there when I think of the letters *m*, *a*, and *n*, as so many disconnected data.

When data are so disconnected that we have no conception which embraces them together it is much harder to apprehend several of them at once, and the mind tends to let go of one whilst it attends to another. Still, within limits this can be avoided. M. Paulhan has experimented on the matter by declaiming one poem aloud whilst he repeated a different one mentally, or by writing one sentence whilst speaking another, or by performing calculations on paper whilst reciting poetry. He found that "the most favorable condition for the doubling of the mind was its simultaneous application to two easy and heterogeneous operations. Two operations of the same sort, two multiplications, two recitations, or the reciting one poem and writing another, render the process more uncertain and difficult."

M. Paulhan compared the time occupied by the same two operations done simultaneously or in succession, and found that there was often a considerable gain of time from doing them simultaneously. For instance:

"I multiply 421 312 212 by 2; the operation takes 6 seconds; the recitation of four verses also takes 6 seconds. But the two operations done at once only take 6 seconds, so that there is no loss of time from combining them."

If, then, by the original question, how many objects can we attend to at once, be meant how many entirely disconnected systems or processes can go on simultaneously, the answer is, *not easily more than one, unless the processes are very habitual; but then two, or even three*, without very much oscillation of the attention. Where, however, the processes are less automatic, as in the story of Julius Cæsar dictating four letters whilst he writes a fifth, there must be a rapid oscillation of the mind from one to the next, and no consequent gain of time.

When the things to be attended to are minute sensations, and when the effort is to be exact in noting them, it is found that attention to one interferes a good deal with the perception of the other. A good deal of fine work has been done in this field by Professor Wundt. He tried to note the exact position on a dial of a rapidly revolving hand, at the moment when a bell struck. Here were two disparate sensations, one of vision, the other of sound, to be noted together. But it was found that in a long and patient research, the eye-impression could seldom or never be noted at the exact moment when the bell actually struck. An earlier or a later point were all that could be seen.

The Varieties of Attention.—Attention may be divided into kinds in various ways. It is either to

a) Objects of sense (sensorial attention); or to

b) Ideal or represented objects (intellectual attention). It is either

c) Immediate; or

d) Derived: immediate, when the topic or stimulus is interesting in itself, without relation to anything else; derived, when it owes its interest to association with some other immediately interesting thing. What I call derived attention has been named 'apperceptive' attention. Furthermore, Attention may be either

e) Passive, reflex, involuntary, effortless; or

f) Active and voluntary.

Voluntary attention is always derived; we never make an *effort* to attend to an object except for the sake of some *remote* interest which the effort will serve. But both sensorial and intellectual attention may be either passive or voluntary.

In *involuntary attention* of the *immediate sensorial* sort the stimulus is either a sense-impression, very intense, voluminous, or sudden; or it is an *instinctive* stimulus, a perception which, by reason of its nature rather than its mere force, appeals to some one of our congenital impulses and has a directly exciting quality. In the chapter on Instinct we shall see how these stimuli differ from one animal to another, and what most of them are in man: strange things, moving things, wild animals, bright things, pretty things, metallic things, words, blows, blood, etc., etc., etc.

Sensitiveness to immediately exciting sensorial stimuli characterizes the attention of childhood and youth. In mature age we have generally selected those stimuli which are connected with one or more so-called permanent interests, and our attention has grown irresponsive to the rest. But childhood is characterized by great active energy, and has few organized interests by which to meet new impressions and decide whether they are worthy of notice or not, and the consequence is that extreme mobility of the attention with which we are all familiar in children, and which makes of their first lessons such chaotic affairs. Any strong sensation whatever produces accommodation of the organs which perceive it, and absolute oblivion, for the time being, of the task in hand. This reflex and passive character of the attention which, as a French writer says, makes the child seem to belong less to himself than to every object which happens to catch his notice, is the first thing which the teacher must overcome. It never is overcome in some people, whose work, to the end of life, gets done in the interstices of their mind-wandering.

The passive sensorial attention is *derived* when the impression, without being either strong or of an instinctively exciting nature, is connected by previous experience and education with things that are so. These things may be called the *motives* of the attention. The impression draws an interest from them, or perhaps it even fuses into a single complex object with them; the result is that it is brought into the focus of the mind. A faint tap *per se* is not an interesting sound; it may well escape being discriminated from the general rumor of the world. But when it is a signal, as that of a lover on the window-pane, hardly will it go unperceived. Herbart writes:

"How a bit of bad grammar wounds the ear of the purist! How a false note hurts the musician! or an offence against good manners the man of the world! How rapid is progress in a science when its first principles have been so well im-

pressed upon us that we reproduce them mentally with perfect distinctness and ease! How slow and uncertain, on the
other hand, is our learning of the principles themselves, when
familiarity with the still more elementary percepts connected
with the subject has not given us an adequate predis-
position!—Apperceptive attention may be plainly observed in
very small children when, hearing the speech of their elders,
as yet unintelligible to them, they suddenly catch a single
known word here and there, and repeat it to themselves; yes!
even in the dog who looks round at us when we speak of him
and pronounce his name. Not far removed is the talent which
mind-wandering school-boys display during the hours of instruction, of noticing every moment in which the teacher tells
a story. I remember classes in which, instruction being uninteresting, and discipline relaxed, a buzzing murmur was always to be heard, which invariably stopped for as long a time
as an anecdote lasted. How could the boys, since they seemed
to hear nothing, notice when the anecdote began? Doubtless
most of them always heard something of the teacher's talk;
but most of it had no connection with their previous knowledge and occupations, and therefore the separate words no
sooner entered their consciousness than they fell out of it
again; but, on the other hand, no sooner did the words
awaken old thoughts, forming strongly-connected series with
which the new impression easily combined, than out of new
and old together a total interest resulted which drove the
vagrant ideas below the threshold of consciousness, and
brought for a while settled attention into their place."

Involuntary intellectual attention is immediate when we follow in thought a train of images exciting or interesting *per se*;
derived, when the images are interesting only as means to a
remote end, or merely because they are associated with something which makes them dear. The brain-currents may then
form so solidly unified a system, and the absorption in their
object be so deep, as to banish not only ordinary sensations,
but even the severest pain. Pascal, Wesley, Robert Hall, are
said to have had this capacity. Dr. Carpenter says of himself
that "he has frequently begun a lecture, whilst suffering neuralgic pain so severe as to make him apprehend that he would
find it impossible to proceed; yet no sooner has he, by a

determined effort, fairly launched himself into the stream of thought, than he has found himself continuously borne along without the least distraction, until the end has come, and the attention has been released; when the pain has recurred with a force that has over-mastered all resistance, making him wonder how he could have ever ceased to feel it."[1]

Voluntary Attention.—Dr. Carpenter speaks of launching himself by a determined *effort*. This effort characterizes what we called *active or voluntary attention*. It is a feeling which everyone knows, but which most people would call quite indescribable. We get it in the sensorial sphere whenever we seek to catch an impression of extreme *faintness*, be it of sight, hearing, taste, smell, or touch; we get it whenever we seek to *discriminate* a sensation merged in a mass of others that are similar; we get it whenever we *resist the attractions* of more potent stimuli and keep our mind occupied with some object that is naturally unimpressive. We get it in the intellectual sphere under exactly similar conditions: as when we strive to sharpen and make distinct an idea which we but vaguely seem to have; or painfully discriminate a shade of meaning from its similars; or resolutely hold fast to a thought so discordant with our impulses that, if left unaided, it would quickly yield place to images of an exciting and impassioned kind. All forms of attentive effort would be exercised at once by one whom we might suppose at a dinner-party resolutely to listen to a neighbor giving him insipid and unwelcome advice in a low voice, whilst all around the guests were loudly laughing and talking about exciting and interesting things.

There is no such thing as voluntary attention sustained for more than a few seconds at a time. What is called sustained voluntary attention is a repetition of successive efforts which bring back the topic to the mind. The topic once brought back, if a congenial one, *develops*; and if its development is interesting it engages the attention passively for a time. Dr. Carpenter, a moment back, described the stream of thought, once entered, as 'bearing him along.' This passive interest may be short or long. As soon as it flags, the attention is diverted by some

---

[1] *Mental Physiology*, § 124. The oft-cited case of soldiers in battle not perceiving that they are wounded is of an analogous sort.

irrelevant thing, and then a voluntary effort may bring it back to the topic again; and so on, under favorable conditions, for hours together. During all this time, however, note that it is not an identical *object* in the psychological sense, but a succession of mutually related objects forming an identical *topic* only, upon which the attention is fixed. *No one can possibly attend continuously to an object that does not change.*

Now there are always some objects that for the time being *will not develop*. They simply *go out*; and to keep the mind upon anything related to them requires such incessantly renewed effort that the most resolute Will ere long gives out and lets its thoughts follow the more stimulating solicitations after it has withstood them for what length of time it can. There are topics known to every man from which he shies like a frightened horse, and which to get a glimpse of is to shun. Such are his ebbing assets to the spendthrift in full career. But why single out the spendthrift, when to every man actuated by passion the thought of interests which negate the passion can hardly for more than a fleeting instant stay before the mind? It is like 'memento mori' in the heyday of the pride of life. Nature rises at such suggestions, and excludes them from the view:—How long, O healthy reader, can you now continue thinking of your tomb?—In milder instances the difficulty is as great, especially when the brain is fagged. One snatches at any and every passing pretext, no matter how trivial or external, to escape from the odiousness of the matter in hand. I know a person, for example, who will poke the fire, set chairs straight, pick dust-specks from the floor, arrange his table, snatch up the newspaper, take down any book which catches his eye, trim his nails, waste the morning *anyhow*, in short, and all without premeditation,—simply because the only thing he *ought* to attend to is the preparation of a noonday lesson in formal logic which he detests. Anything but *that*!

Once more, the object must change. When it is one of sight, it will actually become invisible; when of hearing, inaudible,—if we attend to it too unmovingly. Helmholtz, who has put his sensorial attention to the severest tests, by using his eyes on objects which in common life are expressly overlooked, makes some interesting remarks on this point in his

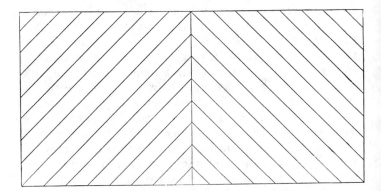

FIG. 54.

section on retinal rivalry. The phenomenon called by that name is this, that if we look with each eye upon a different picture (as in the annexed stereoscopic slide), sometimes one picture, sometimes the other, or parts of both, will come to consciousness, but hardly ever both combined. Helmholtz now says:

"I find that I am able to attend voluntarily, now to one and now to the other system of lines; and that then this system remains visible alone for a certain time, whilst the other completely vanishes. This happens, for example, whenever I try to count the lines first of one and then of the other system. . . . But it is extremely hard to chain the attention down to one of the systems for long, unless we associate with our looking some distinct purpose which keeps the activity of the attention perpetually renewed. Such a one is counting the lines, comparing their intervals, or the like. An equilibrium of the attention, persistent for any length of time, is under no circumstances attainable. The natural tendency of attention when left to itself is to wander to ever new things; and so soon as the interest of its object is over, so soon as nothing new is to be noticed there, it passes, in spite of our will, to something else. *If we wish to keep it upon one and the same object, we must seek constantly to find out something new about the latter*, especially if other powerful impressions are attracting us away."

These words of Helmholtz are of fundamental importance. And if true of sensorial attention, how much more true are they of the intellectual variety! The *conditio sine quâ non* of sustained attention to a given topic of thought is that we should roll it over and over incessantly and consider different aspects and relations of it in turn. Only in pathological states will a fixed and ever monotonously recurring idea possess the mind.

Genius and Attention.—And now we can see why it is that what is called sustained attention is the easier, the richer in acquisitions and the fresher and more original the mind. In such minds, subjects bud and sprout and grow. At every moment, they please by a new consequence and rivet the attention afresh. But an intellect unfurnished with materials, stagnant, unoriginal, will hardly be likely to consider any subject long. A glance exhausts its possibilities of interest. Geniuses are commonly believed to excel other men in their power of sustained attention. In most of them, it is to be feared, the so-called 'power' is of the passive sort. Their ideas coruscate, every subject branches infinitely before their fertile minds, and so for hours they may be rapt. *But it is their genius making them attentive, not their attention making geniuses of them.* And, when we come down to the root of the matter, we see that they differ from ordinary men less in the character of their attention than in the nature of the objects upon which it is successively bestowed. In the genius, these form a concatenated series, suggesting each other mutually by some rational law. Therefore we call the attention 'sustained' and the topic of meditation for hours 'the same.' In the common man the series is for the most part incoherent, the objects have no rational bond, and we call the attention wandering and unfixed.

It is probable that genius tends actually to prevent a man from acquiring habits of voluntary attention, and that moderate intellectual endowments are the soil in which we may best expect, here as elsewhere, the virtues of the will, strictly so called, to thrive. But, whether the attention come by grace of genius or by dint of will, the longer one does attend to a topic the more mastery of it one has. And the faculty of voluntarily bringing back a wandering attention over and over again is the very root of judgment, character, and will. No one is *compos sui* if he have it not. An education which should improve this faculty would be *the* education *par excellence*. But it is easier to define this ideal than to give practical directions for bringing it about. The only general pedagogic maxim bearing on attention is that the more interests the child has in advance in the subject, the better he will attend. Induct him therefore in such a way as to knit each new thing on to some acquisition already there; and if possible awaken curiosity, so that the new thing shall seem to come as an answer, or part of an answer, to a question preëxisting in his mind.

The Physiological Conditions of Attention.—These seem to be the following:

1) *The appropriate cortical centre must be excited ideationally as well as sensorially, before attention to an object can take place.*

2) *The sense-organ must then adapt itself to clearest reception of the object, by the adjustment of its muscular apparatus.*

3) *In all probability a certain afflux of blood to the cortical centre must ensue.*

Of this third condition I will say no more, since we have no proof of it in detail, and I state it on the faith of general analogies. Conditions 1) and 2), however, are verifiable; and the best order will be to take the latter first.

The Adaptation of the Sense-organ.—This occurs not only in sensorial but also in intellectual attention to an object.

That it is present when we attend to *sensible* things is obvious. When we look or listen we accommodate our eyes and ears involuntarily, and we turn our head and body as well; when we taste or smell we adjust the tongue, lips, and respiration to the object; in feeling a surface we move the palpatory organ in a suitable way; in all these acts, besides making involuntary muscular contractions of a positive sort, we inhibit others which might interfere with the result—we close the eyes in tasting, suspend the respiration in listening, etc. The result is a more or less massive organic feeling that attention is going on. This organic feeling we usually treat as part of the sense of our *own activity*, although it comes in to us from our organs after they are accommodated. Any object, then, if *immediately* exciting, causes a reflex accommodation of the sense-organ, which has two results—first, the feeling of activity in question; and second, the object's increase in clearness.

But in *intellectual* attention similar feelings of activity occur. Fechner was the first, I believe, to analyze these feelings, and discriminate them from the stronger ones just named. He writes:

"When we transfer the attention from objects of one sense to those of another, we have an indescribable feeling (though at the same time one perfectly determinate, and reproducible at pleasure), of altered *direction* or differently localized tension (*Spannung*). We feel a strain forwards in the eyes, one directed sidewise in the ears, increasing with the degree of our attention, and changing according as we look at an object carefully, or listen to something attentively; and we speak accordingly of *straining the attention*. The difference is most plainly felt when the attention oscillates rapidly between eye and ear; and the feeling localizes itself with most decided difference in regard to the various sense-organs, according as we wish to discriminate a thing delicately by touch, taste, or smell.

"But now I have, when I try to vividly recall a picture of memory or fancy, a feeling perfectly analogous to that which I experience when I seek to apprehend a thing keenly by eye or ear; and this analogous feeling is very differently localized. While in sharpest possible attention to real objects (as well as to after-images) the strain is plainly forwards, and (when the attention changes from one sense to another) only alters its direction between the several external sense-organs, leaving the rest of the head free from strain, the case is different in memory or fancy, for here the feeling withdraws entirely from the external sense-organs, and seems rather to take refuge in that part of the head which the brain fills. If I wish, for example, to *recall* a place or person, it will arise before me with vividness, not according as I strain my attention forwards, but rather in proportion as I, so to speak, retract it backwards."

In myself the 'backward retraction' which is felt during attention to ideas of memory, etc., seems to be principally constituted by the feeling of an actual rolling outwards and upwards of the eyeballs, such as occurs in sleep, and is the exact opposite of their behavior when we look at a physical thing.

This accommodation of the sense-organ is not, however, the *essential* process, even in sensorial attention. It is a secondary result which may be prevented from occurring, as certain observations show. Usually, it is true that no object lying in the marginal portions of the field of vision can catch our attention without at the same time 'catching our eye'—that is, fatally provoking such movements of rotation and accommodation as will focus its image on the fovea, or point of greatest sensibility. Practice, however, enables us, *with effort*, to attend to a marginal object whilst keeping the eyes immovable. The object under these circumstances never becomes perfectly distinct—the place of its image on the retina makes distinctness impossible—but (as anyone can satisfy himself by trying) we become more vividly conscious of it than we were before the effort was made. Teachers thus notice the acts of children in the school-room at whom they appear not to be looking. Women in general train their peripheral visual attention more than men. Helmholtz states the fact so strikingly that I will quote his observation in full. He was trying to combine in a single solid percept pairs of stereoscopic pictures illuminated instantaneously by the electric spark. The pictures were in a dark box which the spark from time to time lighted up; and, to keep the eyes from wandering betweenwhiles, a pin-hole was pricked through the middle of each picture, through which the light of the room came, so that each eye had presented to it during the dark intervals a single bright point. With parallel optical axes these points combined into a single image; and the slightest movement of the eyeballs was betrayed by this image at once becoming double. Helmholtz now found that simple linear figures could, when the eyes were thus kept immovable, be perceived as solids at a single flash of the spark. But when the figures were complicated photographs, many successive flashes were required to grasp their totality.

"Now it is interesting," he says, "to find that, although we keep steadily fixating the pin-holes and never allow their combined image to break into two, we can nevertheless, before the spark comes, keep our attention voluntarily turned to any particular portion we please of the dark field, so as then, when the spark comes, to receive an impression only from such parts of the picture as lie in this region. In this respect, then, our attention is quite independent of the position and accommodation of the eyes, and of any known alteration in these organs, and free to direct itself by a conscious and voluntary effort upon any selected portion of a dark and undifferenced field of view. This is one of the most important observations for a future theory of attention."[2]

The Ideational Excitement of the Centre.—But if the peripheral part of the picture in this experiment be not physically accommodated for, what is meant by its sharing our attention? What happens when we 'distribute' or 'disperse' the latter upon a thing for which we remain unwilling to 'adjust'? This leads us to that second feature in the process, the *'ideational excitement'* of which we spoke. *The effort to attend to the marginal region of the picture consists in nothing more nor less than the effort to form as clear an* IDEA *as is possible of what is there portrayed*. The idea is to come to the help of the sensation and make it more distinct. It may come with effort, and such a mode of coming is the remaining part of what we know as our attention's 'strain' under the circumstances. Let us show how universally present in our acts of attention is this anticipatory thinking of the thing to which we attend. Mr. Lewes's name of *preperception* seems the best possible designation for this imagining of an experience before it occurs.

It must as a matter of course be present when the attention is of the intellectual variety, for the thing attended to then *is* nothing but an idea, an inward reproduction or conception. If then we prove ideal construction of the object to be present in *sensorial* attention, it will be present everywhere. When, however, sensorial attention is at its height, it is impossible to tell how much of the percept comes from without and how much from within; but if we find that the *preparation* we make for it always partly consists of the creation of an imaginary duplicate of the object in the mind, that will be enough to establish the point in dispute.

[2]*Physiologische Optik*, p. 741.

In reaction-time experiments, keeping our mind intent upon the motion about to be made shortens the time. This shortening we ascribed in Chapter IX to the fact that the signal when it comes finds the motor-centre already charged almost to the explosion-point in advance. Expectant attention to a reaction thus goes with sub-excitement of the centre concerned.

Where the impression to be caught is very weak, the way not to miss it is to sharpen our attention for it by preliminary contact with it in a stronger form. Helmholtz says: "If we wish to begin to observe overtones, it is advisable, just before the sound which is to be analyzed, to sound very softly the note of which we are in search. . . . If you place the resonator which corresponds to a certain overtone, for example g' of the sound c, against your ear, and then make the note c sound, you will hear g' much strengthened by the resonator. . . . This strengthening by the resonator can be used to make the naked ear attentive to the sound which it is to catch. For when the resonator is gradually removed, the g' grows weaker; but the attention, once directed to it, holds it now more easily fast, and the observer hears the tone g' now in the natural unaltered sound of the note with his unaided ear."

Wundt, commenting on experiences of this sort, says that "The same thing is to be noticed in weak or fugitive visual impressions. Illuminate a drawing by electric sparks separated by considerable intervals, and after the first, and often after the second and third spark, hardly anything will be recognized. But the confused image is held fast in memory; each successive illumination completes it; and so at last we attain to a clearer perception. The primary motive to this inward activity proceeds usually from the outer impression itself. We hear a sound in which, from certain associations, we suspect a certain overtone; the next thing is to recall the overtone in memory; and finally we catch it in the sound we hear. Or perhaps we see some mineral substance we have met before; the impression awakens the memory-image, which again more or less completely melts with the impression itself. . . . Different qualities of impression require disparate adaptations. And we remark that our feeling of the *strain* of our inward attentiveness increases with every increase in the strength of the impressions on whose perception we are intent."

The natural way of conceiving all this is under the symbolic form of a brain-cell played upon from two directions. Whilst the object excites it from without, other brain-cells arouse it from within. *The plenary energy of the brain-cell demands the coöperation of both factors:* not when merely present, but when both present and inwardly imagined, is the object fully attended to and perceived.

A few additional experiences will now be perfectly clear. Helmholtz, for instance, adds this observation concerning the stereoscopic pictures lit by the electric spark. "In pictures," he says, "so simple that it is relatively difficult for me to see them double, I can succeed in seeing them double, even when the illumination is only instantaneous, the moment I strive to *imagine in a lively way how they ought then to look*. The influence of attention is here pure; for all eye-movements are shut out."

Again, writing of retinal rivalry, Helmholtz says:

"It is not a trial of strength between two sensations, but depends upon our fixing or failing to fix the attention. Indeed there is scarcely any phenomenon so well fitted for the study of the causes which are capable of determining the attention. It is not enough to form the conscious intention of seeing first with one eye and then with the other; *we must form as clear a notion as possible of what we expect to see. Then it will actually appear*."

In Figs. 55 and 56, where the result is ambiguous, we can make the change from one apparent form to the other by imagining strongly in advance the form we wish to see. Similarly in those puzzles where certain lines in a picture form by their combination an object that has no connection with what the picture obviously represents; or indeed in every case where an object is inconspicuous and hard to discern from the background; we may not be able to see it for a long time; but, having once seen it, we can attend to it again whenever we like, on account of the mental duplicate of it which our imagination now bears. In the meaningless French words '*pas de lieu Rhône que nous*,' who can recognize immediately the

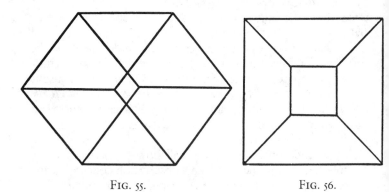

FIG. 55.   FIG. 56.

English 'paddle your own canoe'? But who that has once noticed the identity can fail to have it arrest his attention again?
When watching for the distant clock to strike, our mind is so
filled with its image that at every moment we think we hear
the longed-for or dreaded sound. So of an awaited footstep.
Every stir in the wood is for the hunter his game; for the
fugitive his pursuers. Every bonnet in the street is momentarily taken by the lover to enshroud the head of his idol. The
image in the mind *is* the attention; the preperception is half of
the perception of the looked-for thing.

It is for this reason that men have no eyes but for those
aspects of things which they have already been taught to discern. Any one of us can notice a phenomenon after it has
once been pointed out, which not one in ten thousand could
ever have discovered for himself. Even in poetry and the arts,
someone has to come and tell us what aspects to single out,
and what effects to admire, before our æsthetic nature can
'dilate' to its full extent and never 'with the wrong emotion.'
In kindergarten-instruction one of the exercises is to make the
children see how many features they can point out in such an
object as a flower or a stuffed bird. They readily name the
features they know already, such as leaves, tail, bill, feet. But
they may look for hours without distinguishing nostrils,
claws, scales, etc., until their attention is called to these details; thereafter, however, they see them every time. In short,
the only things which we commonly see are those which we pre-

perceive, and the only things which we preperceive are those which have been labelled for us, and the labels stamped into our mind. If we lost our stock of labels we should be intellectually lost in the midst of the world.

Educational Corollaries.—First, to *strengthen attention in children* who care nothing for the subject they are studying and let their wits go wool-gathering. The interest here must be 'derived' from something that the teacher associates with the task, a reward or a punishment if nothing more internal comes to mind. If a topic awakens no spontaneous attention it must borrow an interest from elsewhere. But the best interest is internal, and we must always try, in teaching a class, to knit our novelties by rational links on to things of which they already have preperceptions. The old and familiar is readily attended to by the mind and helps to hold in turn the new, forming, in Herbartian phraseology, an *'Apperceptionsmasse'* for it. Of course the teacher's talent is best shown by knowing what 'Apperceptionsmasse' to use. Psychology can only lay down the general rule.

Second, take that mind-wandering which at a later age may trouble us *whilst reading or listening to a discourse*. If attention be the reproduction of the sensation from within, the habit of reading not merely with the eye, and of listening not merely with the ear, but of articulating to one's self the words seen or heard, ought to deepen one's attention to the latter. Experience shows that this is the case. I can keep my wandering mind a great deal more closely upon a conversation or a lecture if I actively re-echo to myself the words than if I simply hear them; and I find a number of my students who report benefit from voluntarily adopting a similar course.

Attention and Free-Will.—I have spoken as if our attention were wholly determined by neural conditions. I believe that the array of *things* we can attend to is so determined. No object can *catch* our attention except by the neural machinery. But the *amount* of the attention which an object receives after it has caught our mental eye is another question. It often takes effort to keep the mind upon it. We feel that we can make more or less of the effort as we choose. If this feeling be not deceptive, if our effort be a spiritual force, and an indeterminate one, then of course it contributes coequally with the cerebral conditions to the result. Though it *introduce* no new idea, it will deepen and prolong the stay in consciousness of innumerable ideas which else would fade more quickly away. The delay thus gained might not be more than a second in duration—but that second may be *critical*; for in the constant rising and falling of considerations in the mind, where two associated systems of them are nearly in equilibrium it is often a matter of but a second more or less of attention at the out-set, whether one system shall gain force to occupy the field and develop itself, and exclude the other, or be excluded itself by the other. When developed, it may make us act; and that act may seal our doom. When we come to the chapter on the Will, we shall see that the whole drama of the voluntary life hinges on the amount of attention, slightly more or slightly less, which rival motor ideas may receive. But the whole feeling of reality, the whole sting and excitement of our voluntary life, depends on our sense that in it things are *really being decided* from one moment to another, and that it is not the dull rattling-off of a chain that was forged innumerable ages ago. This appearance, which makes life and history tingle with such a tragic zest, *may* not be an illusion. Effort may be an original force and not a mere effect, and it may be indeterminate in amount. The last word of sober insight here is ignorance, for the forces engaged are too delicate ever to be measured in detail. Psychology, however, as a would-be 'Science,' must, like every other Science, *postulate* complete determinism in its facts, and abstract consequently from the effects of free-will, even if such a force exist. I shall do so in this book like other psychologists; well knowing, however, that such a procedure, although a methodical device justified by the subjective need of arranging the facts in a simple and 'scientific' form, does not settle the ultimate truth of the free-will question one way or the other.

CHAPTER XIV

CONCEPTION

Different states of mind can mean the same. The function by which we mark off, discriminate, draw a line round, and identify a numerically distinct subject of discourse is called *conception*. It is plain that whenever one and the same mental state thinks of many things, it must be the vehicle of many conceptions. If it has such a multiple conceptual function, it may be called a state of compound conception.

We may conceive realities supposed to be extra-mental, as steam-engine; fictions, as mermaid; or mere *entia rationis*, like difference or nonentity. But whatever we do conceive, our conception is of that and nothing else—nothing else, that is, *instead* of that, though it may be of much else *in addition* to that. Each act of conception results from our attention's having singled out some one part of the mass of matter-for-thought which the world presents, and from our holding fast to it, without confusion. Confusion occurs when we do not know whether a certain object proposed to us is *the same* with one of our meanings or not; so that the conceptual function requires, to be complete, that the thought should not only say 'I mean this,' but also say 'I don't mean that.'

Each conception thus eternally remains what it is, and never can become another. The mind may change its states, and its meanings, at different times; may drop one conception and take up another: but the dropped conception itself can in no intelligible sense be said to *change into* its successor. The paper, a moment ago white, I may now see to be scorched black. But my *conception* 'white' does not change into my *conception* 'black.' On the contrary, it stays alongside of the objective blackness, as a different meaning in my mind, and by so doing lets me judge the blackness as the paper's change. Unless it stayed, I should simply say 'blackness' and know no more. Thus, amid the flux of opinions and of physical things, the world of conceptions, or things intended to be thought about, stands stiff and immutable, like Plato's Realm of Ideas.

Some conceptions are of things, some of events, some of

qualities. Any fact, be it thing, event, or quality, may be conceived sufficiently for purposes of identification, if only it be singled out and marked so as to separate it from other things. Simply calling it 'this' or 'that' will suffice. To speak in technical language, a subject may be conceived by its *denotation*, with no *connotation*, or a very minimum of connotation, attached. The essential point is that it should be re-identified by us as that which the talk is about; and no full representation of it is necessary for this, even when it is a fully representable thing.

In this sense, creatures extremely low in the intellectual scale may have conception. All that is required is that they should recognize the same experience again. A polyp would be a conceptual thinker if a feeling of 'Hollo! thingumbob again!' ever flitted through its mind. This sense of sameness is the very keel and backbone of our consciousness. The same matters can be thought of in different states of mind, and some of these states can know that they mean the same matters which the other states meant. In other words, *the mind can always intend, and know when it intends, to think the Same.*

Conceptions of Abstract, of Universal, and of Problematic Objects. — The sense of our meaning is an entirely peculiar element of the thought. It is one of those evanescent and 'transitive' facts of mind which introspection cannot turn round upon, and isolate and hold up for examination, as an entomologist passes round an insect on a pin. In the (somewhat clumsy) terminology I have used, it has to do with the 'fringe' of the object, and is a 'feeling of tendency,' whose neural counterpart is undoubtedly a lot of dawning and dying processes too faint and complex to be traced. (See p. 168.) The geometer, with his one definite figure before him, knows perfectly that his thoughts apply to countless other figures as well, and that although he *sees* lines of a certain special bigness, direction, color, etc., he *means* not one of these details. When I use the word *man* in two different sentences, I may have both times exactly the same sound upon my lips and the same picture in my mental eye, but I may mean, and at the very moment of uttering the word and imagining the picture know that I mean, two entirely different things. Thus when I say: "What a wonderful man Jones is!" I am perfectly aware that I mean by man to exclude Napoleon Bonaparte or Smith. But when I say: "What a wonderful thing Man is!" I am equally well aware that I mean no such exclusion. This added consciousness is an absolutely positive sort of feeling, transforming what would otherwise be mere noise or vision into something *understood*; and determining the sequel of my thinking, the later words and images, in a perfectly definite way.

No matter how definite and concrete the habitual imagery of a given mind may be, the things represented appear always surrounded by their fringe of relations, and this is as integral a part of the mind's object as the things themselves are. We come, by steps with which everyone is sufficiently familiar, to think of whole classes of things as well as of single specimens; and to think of the special qualities or attributes of things as well as of the complete things—in other words, we come to have *universals* and *abstracts*, as the logicians call them, for our objects. We also come to think of objects which are only *problematic*, or not yet definitely representable, as well as of objects imagined in all their details. An object which is problematic is defined by its relations only. We think of a thing *about* which certain facts must obtain. But we do not yet know how the thing will look when realized—that is, although conceiving it we cannot *imagine* it. We have in the relations, however, enough to individualize our topic and distinguish it from all the other meanings of our mind. Thus, for example, we may conceive of a perpetual-motion machine. Such a machine is a *quæsitum* of a perfectly definite kind,—we can tell whether the actual machines offered us do or do not agree with what we mean by it. The natural possibility or impossibility of the thing never touches the question of its conceivability in this problematic way. 'Round-square,' again, or 'black-white-thing,' are absolutely definite conceptions; it is a mere accident, as far as conception goes, that they happen to stand for things which nature never shows us, and of which we consequently can make no picture.

The nominalists and conceptualists carry on a great quarrel over the question whether "the mind can frame abstract or universal ideas." Ideas, it should be said, of abstract or universal objects. But truly in comparison with the wonderful fact that our thoughts, however different otherwise, can still be of *the same*, the question whether that same be a single thing, a whole class of things, an abstract quality or something un-imaginable, is an insignificant matter of detail. Our meanings are of singulars, particulars, indefinites, problematics, and uni-versals, mixed together in every way. A singular individual is as much *conceived* when he is isolated and identified away from the rest of the world in my mind, as is the most rarefied and universally applicable quality he may possess—*being*, for example, when treated in the same way. From every point of view, the overwhelming and portentous character ascribed to universal conceptions is surprising. Why, from Socrates downwards, philosophers should have vied with each other in scorn of the knowledge of the particular, and in adoration of that of the general, is hard to understand, seeing that the more adorable knowledge ought to be that of the more ador-able things, and that the *things* of worth are all concretes and singulars. The only value of universal characters is that they help us, by reasoning, to know new truths about individual things. The restriction of one's meaning, moreover, to an individual thing, probably requires even more complicated brain-processes than its extension to all the instances of a kind; and the mere mystery, as such, of the knowledge, is equally great, whether generals or singulars be the things known. In sum, therefore, the traditional Universal-worship can only be called a bit of perverse sentimentalism, a philo-sophic 'idol of the cave.'

Nothing can be conceived as the same without being conceived in a novel state of mind. It seems hardly necessary to add this, after what was said on p. 156. Thus, my arm-chair is one of the things of which I have a conception; I knew it yesterday and recognized it when I looked at it. But if I think of it to-day as the same arm-chair which I looked at yesterday, it is obvious that the very conception of it *as* the same is an additional complication to the thought, whose in-ward constitution must alter in consequence. In short, it is logically impossible that the same thing should be *known as the same* by two successive copies of the same thought. As a matter of fact, the thoughts by which we know that we mean the same thing are apt to be very different indeed from each other. We think the thing now substantively, now transitively; now in a direct image, now in one symbol, and now in another symbol; but nevertheless we somehow always *do* know which of all possible subjects we have in mind. Introspective psychology must here throw up the sponge; the fluctuations of subjective life are too exquisite to be described by its coarse terms. It must confine itself to bearing witness to the fact that all sorts of different subjective states do form the vehicle by which the same is known; and it must contradict the opposite view.

CHAPTER XV

DISCRIMINATION

Discrimination versus Association.—On p. 23 I spoke of the baby's first object being the germ out of which his whole later universe develops by the addition of new parts from without and the discrimination of others within. Experience, in other words, is trained *both* by association and dissociation, and psychology must be writ *both* in synthetic and in analytic terms. Our original sensible totals are, on the one hand, subdivided by discriminative attention, and, on the other, united with other totals,—either through the agency of our own movements, carrying our senses from one part of space to another, or because new objects come successively and replace those by which we were at first impressed. The 'simple impression' of Hume, the 'simple idea' of Locke are abstractions, never realized in experience. Life, from the very first, presents us with concreted objects, vaguely continuous with the rest of the world which envelops them in space and time, and potentially divisible into inward elements and parts. These objects we break asunder and reunite. We must do both for our knowledge of them to grow; and it is hard to say, on the whole, which we do most. But since the elements with which the traditional associationism performs its constructions—'simple sensations,' namely—are all products of discrimination carried to a high pitch, it seems as if we ought to discuss the subject of analytic attention and discrimination first.

Discrimination defined.—The noticing of any *part* whatever of our object is an act of discrimination. Already on p. 211 I have described the manner in which we often spontaneously lapse into the undiscriminating state, even with regard to objects which we have already learned to distinguish. Such anæsthetics as chloroform, nitrous oxide, etc., sometimes bring about transient lapses even more total, in which numerical discrimination especially seems gone; for one sees light and hears sound, but whether one or many lights and sounds is quite impossible to tell. Where the parts of an object have already been discerned, and each made the object of a special discriminative act, we can with difficulty feel the object again in its pristine unity; and so prominent may our consciousness of its composition be, that we may hardly believe that it ever could have appeared undivided. But this is an erroneous view, the undeniable fact being that *any number of impressions, from any number of sensory sources, falling simultaneously on a mind* WHICH HAS NOT YET EXPERIENCED THEM SEPARATELY, *will yield a single undivided object to that mind.* The law is that all things fuse that *can* fuse, and that nothing separates except what must. What makes impressions separate is what we have to study in this chapter.

Conditions which favor Discrimination.—I will treat successively of differences:

1) So far as they are directly *felt*;
2) So far as they are *inferred*;
3) So far as they are *singled out in compounds*.

Differences directly felt.—The first condition is that *the things to be discriminated must* BE *different,* either in time, place, or quality. In other words, and physiologically speaking, they must awaken neural processes which are *distinct*. But this, as we have just seen, though an indispensable condition, is not a sufficient condition. To begin with, the several neural processes must be distinct *enough*. No one can help singling out a black stripe on a white ground, or feeling the contrast between a bass note and a high one sounded immediately after it. Discrimination is here *involuntary*. But where the objective difference is less, discrimination may require considerable effort of attention to be performed at all.

Secondly, *the sensations excited by the differing objects must not fall simultaneously, but must fall in immediate* SUCCESSION upon the same organ. It is easier to compare successive than simultaneous sounds, easier to compare two weights or two temperatures by testing one after the other with the same hand, than by using both hands and comparing both at once. Similarly it is easier to discriminate shades of light or color by moving the eye from one to the other, so that they successively stimulate the same retinal tract. In testing the local discrimination of the skin, by applying compass-points, it is found that they are felt to touch different spots much more readily when set down one after the other than when both are applied at once. In the latter case they may be two or three inches apart on the back, thighs, etc., and still feel as if they were set down in one spot. Finally, in the case of smell and taste it is well-nigh impossible to compare simultaneous impressions at all. The reason why successive impression so much favors the result seems to be that there is a real *sensation of difference*, aroused by the shock of transition from one perception to another which is unlike the first. This sensation of difference has its own peculiar quality, no matter what the terms may be, between which it obtains. It is, in short, one of those transitive feelings, or feelings of relation, of which I treated in a former place (p. 160); and, when once aroused, its object lingers in the memory along with the substantive terms which precede and follow, and enables our *judgments of comparison* to be made.

Where the difference between the successive sensations is but slight, the transition between them must be made as immediate as possible, and both must be compared *in memory*, in order to get the best results. One cannot judge accurately of the difference between two similar wines whilst the second is still in one's mouth. So of sounds, warmths, etc.—we must get the dying phases of both sensations of the pair we are comparing. Where, however, the difference is strong, this condition is immaterial, and we can then compare a sensation actually felt with another carried in memory only. The longer the interval of time between the sensations, the more uncertain is their discrimination.

The difference, thus immediately felt between two terms, is independent of our ability to say anything *about* either of the terms by itself. I can feel two distinct spots to be touched on my skin, yet not know which is above and which below. I can observe two neighboring musical tones to differ, and still not know which of the two is the higher in pitch. Similarly I may discriminate two neighboring tints, whilst remaining uncertain which is the bluer or the yellower, or *how* either differs from its mate.

I said that in the immediate succession of m upon n the shock of their difference is *felt*. It is felt *repeatedly* when we go back and forth from m to n; and we make a point of getting it thus repeatedly (by alternating our attention at least) whenever the shock is so slight as to be with difficulty perceived. But in addition to being felt at the brief instant of transition, the difference also feels as if incorporated and taken up into the second term, which feels 'different-from-the-first' even while it lasts. It is obvious that the 'second term' of the mind in this case is not bald *n*, but a very complex object; and that the sequence is not simply first '*m*,' then '*difference*,' then '*n*'; but first '*m*,' then '*difference*,' then '*n-different-from-m*.' The first and third states of mind are substantive, the second transitive. As our brains and minds are actually made, it is impossible to get certain *m*'s and *n*'s in immediate sequence and to keep them *pure*. If kept pure, it would mean that they remained uncompared. With us, inevitably, by a mechanism which we as yet fail to understand, the shock of difference is felt between them, and the second object is not *n* pure, but *n-as-different-from-m*. The pure idea of *n* is *never in the mind at all* when *m* has gone before.

Differences inferred.—With such direct perceptions of difference as this, we must not confound those entirely unlike cases in which we *infer* that two things must differ because we know enough *about* each of them taken by itself to warrant our classing them under distinct heads. It often happens, when the interval is long between two experiences, that our judgments are guided, not so much by a positive image or copy of the earlier one, as by our recollection of certain facts about it. Thus I know that the sunshine today is less bright than on a certain day last week, because I then said it was quite dazzling, a remark I should not now care to make. Or I know myself to feel livelier now than I did last summer, because I can now psychologize, and then I could not. We are constantly comparing feelings with whose quality our imagination has no sort of *acquaintance* at the time—pleasures, or pains, for example. It is notoriously hard to conjure up in imagination a lively image of either of these classes of feeling. The associationists may prate of an idea of pleasure being a pleasant idea, of an idea of pain being a painful one, but the unsophisticated sense of mankind is against them, agreeing with Homer that the memory of griefs when past may be a joy, and with Dante that there is no greater sorrow than, in misery, to recollect one's happier time.

The 'Singling out' of Elements in a Compound.—It is safe to lay it down as a fundamental principle that *any total impression made on the mind must be unanalyzable so long as its elements have never been experienced apart or in other combinations elsewhere*. The components of an absolutely changeless group of not-elsewhere-occurring attributes could never be discriminated. If all cold things were wet, and all wet things cold; if all hard things pricked our skin, and no other things did so; is it likely that we should discriminate between coldness and wetness, and hardness and pungency, respectively? If all liquids were transparent and no non-liquid were transparent, it would be long before we had separate names for liquidity and transparency. If heat were a function of position above the earth's surface, so that the higher a thing was the hotter it became, one word would serve for hot and high. We have, in fact, a number of sensations whose concomitants are invariably the same, and we find it, accordingly, impossible to analyze them out from the totals in which they are found. The contraction of the diaphragm and the expansion of the lungs, the shortening of certain muscles and the rotation of certain joints, are examples. We learn that the *causes* of such groups of feelings are multiple, and therefore we frame theories about the composition of the feelings themselves, by 'fusion,' 'integration,' 'synthesis,' or what not. But by direct introspection no analysis of the feelings is ever made. A conspicuous case will come to view when we treat of the emotions. Every emotion has its 'expression,' of quick breathing, palpitating heart, flushed face, or the like. The expression gives rise to bodily feelings; and the emotion is thus necessarily and invariably accompanied by these bodily feelings. The consequence is that it is impossible to apprehend it as a spiritual state by itself, or to analyze it away from the lower feelings in question. It is in fact impossible to prove that it exists as a distinct psychic fact. The present writer strongly doubts that it does so exist.

In general, then, if an object affects us simultaneously in a number of ways, *abcd*, we get a peculiar integral impression, which thereafter characterizes to our mind the individuality of that object, and becomes the sign of its presence; and which is only resolved into *a*, *b*, *c*, and *d*, respectively, by the aid of farther experiences. These we now may turn to consider.

If any single quality or constituent, a, of such an object have previously been known by us isolatedly, or have in any other manner already become an object of separate acquaintance on our part, so that we have an image of it, distinct or vague, in our mind, disconnected with *bcd, then that constituent a may be analyzed out from the total impression.* Analysis of a thing means separate attention to each of its parts. In Chapter XIII we saw that one condition of attending to a thing was the formation from within of a separate image of that thing, which should, as it were, go out to meet the impression received. Attention being the condition of analysis, and separate imagination being the condition of attention, it follows also that separate imagination is the condition of analysis. *Only such elements as we are acquainted with, and can imagine separately, can be discriminated within a total sense-impression.* The image seems to welcome its own mate from out of the compound, and to separate it from the other constituents; and thus the compound becomes broken for our consciousness into parts.

All the facts cited in Chapter XIII to prove that attention involves inward reproduction prove that discrimination involves it as well. In looking for any object in a room, for a book in a library, for example, we detect it the more readily if, in addition to merely knowing its name, etc., we carry in our mind a distinct image of its appearance. The assafœtida in 'Worcestershire sauce' is not obvious to anyone who has not tasted assafœtida *per se.* In a 'cold' color an artist would never be able to analyze out the pervasive presence of *blue*, unless he had previously made acquaintance with the color blue by itself. All the colors we actually experience are mixtures. Even the purest primaries always come to us with some white. Absolutely pure red or green or violet is never experienced, and so can never be discerned in the so-called primaries with which we have to deal: the latter consequently pass for pure.—The reader will remember how an overtone can only be attended to in the midst of its consorts in the voice of a musical instrument, by sounding it previously alone. The imagination, being then full of it, hears the like of it in the compound tone.

Non-isolable elements may be discriminated, provided their concomitants change. Very few elements of reality are experienced by us in absolute isolation. The most that usually happens to a constituent *a* of a compound phenomenon *abcd* is that its *strength* relatively to *bcd* varies from a maximum to a minimum; or that it appears linked with *other* qualities, in other compounds, as *aefg* or *ahik*. Either of these vicissitudes in the mode of our experiencing *a* may, under favorable circumstances, lead us to feel the difference between it and its concomitants, and to single it out—not absolutely, it is true, but approximately—and so to analyze the compound of which it is a part. The act of singling out is then called *abstraction*, and the element disengaged is an *abstract*.

Fluctuation in a quality's intensity is a less efficient aid to our abstracting of it than variety in the combinations in which it appears. *What is associated now with one thing and now with another tends to become dissociated from either, and to grow into an object of abstract contemplation by the mind.* One might call this the *law of dissociation by varying concomitants*. The practical result of this law is that a mind which has once dissociated and abstracted a character by its means can analyze it out of a total whenever it meets with it again.

Dr. Martineau gives a good example of the law: "When a red ivory-ball, seen for the first time, has been withdrawn, it will leave a mental representation of itself, in which all that it simultaneously gave us will indistinguishably co-exist. Let a white ball succeed to it; now, and not before, will an attribute detach itself, and the *color*, by force of contrast, be shaken out into the foreground. Let the white ball be replaced by an egg: and this new difference will bring the *form* into notice from its previous slumber. And thus, that which began by being simply an object, cut out from the surrounding scene, becomes for us first a *red* object, and then a *red round* object; and so on."

Why the repetition of the character in combination with different wholes will cause it thus to break up its adhesion with any one of them, and roll out, as it were, alone upon the table of consciousness, is a little of a mystery, but one which need not be considered here.

Practice improves Discrimination.—Any personal or practical interest in the results to be obtained by distinguishing, makes one's wits amazingly sharp to detect differences. And long training and practice in distinguishing has the same effect as personal interest. Both of these agencies give to small amounts of objective difference the same effectiveness upon the mind that, under other circumstances, only large ones would have.

That 'practice makes perfect' is notorious in the field of motor accomplishments. But motor accomplishments depend in part on sensory discrimination. Billiard-playing, rifle-shooting, tight-rope-dancing demand the most delicate appreciation of minute disparities of sensation, as well as the power to make accurately graduated muscular response thereto. In the purely sensorial field we have the well-known virtuosity displayed by the professional buyers and testers of various kinds of goods. One man will distinguish by taste between the upper and the lower half of a bottle of old Madeira. Another will recognize, by feeling the flour in a barrel, whether the wheat was grown in Iowa or Tennessee. The blind deaf-mute, Laura Bridgman, so improved her touch as to recognize, after a year's interval, the hand of a person who once had shaken hers; and her sister in misfortune, Julia Brace, is said to have been employed in the Hartford Asylum to sort the linen of its multitudinous inmates, after it came from the wash, by her wonderfully educated sense of smell.

CHAPTER XVI

ASSOCIATION

The Order of our Ideas.—After discrimination, association! It is obvious that all advance in knowledge must consist of both operations; for in the course of our education, objects at first appearing as wholes are analyzed into parts, and objects appearing separately are brought together and appear as new compound wholes to the mind. Analysis and synthesis are thus the incessantly alternating mental activities, a stroke of the one preparing the way for a stroke of the other, much as, in walking, a man's two legs are alternately brought into use, both being indispensable for any orderly advance.

The manner in which trains of imagery and consideration follow each other through our thinking, the restless flight of one idea before the next, the transitions our minds make between things wide as the poles asunder, transitions which at first sight startle us by their abruptness, but which, when scrutinized closely, often reveal intermediating links of perfect naturalness and propriety—all this magical, imponderable streaming has from time immemorial excited the admiration of all whose attention happened to be caught by its omnipresent mystery. And it has furthermore challenged the race of philosophers to banish something of the mystery by formulating the process in simpler terms. The problem which the philosophers have set themselves is that of ascertaining, between the thoughts which thus appear to sprout one out of the other, *principles of connection* whereby their peculiar succession or coexistence may be explained.

But immediately an ambiguity arises: which sort of connection is meant? connection *thought-of,* or connection *between the things thought of*? These are two entirely different things, and only in the case of one of them is there any hope of finding 'principles.' The jungle of connections *thought of* can never be formulated simply. Every conceivable connection may be thought of—of coexistence, succession, resemblance, contrast, contradiction, cause and effect, means and end, genus and species, part and whole, substance and property, early and late, large and small, landlord and tenant, master and servant, —Heaven knows what, for the list is literally inexhaustible. The only simplification which could possibly be aimed at would be the reduction of the relations to a small number of *types*, like those which some authors call the 'categories' of the understanding. According as we followed one category or another we should sweep, from any object with our thought, in this way or in that, to others. Were *this* the sort of connection sought between one moment of our thinking and another, our chapter might end here. For the only summary description of these categories is that they are all thinkable relations, and that the mind proceeds from one object to another by some intelligible path.

Is it determined by any laws? But as a matter of fact, What determines the particular path? Why do we at a given time and place proceed to think of b if we have just thought of a, and at another time and place why do we think, not of b, but of c? Why do we spend years straining after a certain scientific or practical problem, but all in vain—our thought unable to evoke the solution we desire? And why, some day, walking in the street with our attention miles away from that quest, does the answer saunter into our minds as carelessly as if it had never been called for—suggested, possibly, by the flowers on the bonnet of the lady in front of us, or possibly by nothing that we can discover?

The truth must be admitted that thought works under strange conditions. Pure 'reason' is only one out of a thousand possibilities in the thinking of each of us. Who can count all the silly fancies, the grotesque suppositions, the utterly irrelevant reflections he makes in the course of a day? Who can swear that his prejudices and irrational opinions constitute a less bulky part of his mental furniture than his clarified beliefs? And yet, the *mode of genesis* of the worthy and the worthless in our thinking seems the same.

The laws are cerebral laws. *There seem to be mechanical conditions on which thought depends, and which, to say the least, determine the order in which the objects for her comparisons and selections are presented.* It is a suggestive fact that Locke, and many more recent Continental psychologists, have found themselves obliged to invoke a mechanical process to account for the *aberrations* of thought, the obstructive prepossessions, the frustrations of reason. This they found in the law of habit, or what we now call association by contiguity. But it never occurred to these writers that a process which could go the length of actually producing some ideas and sequences in the mind might safely be trusted to produce others too; and that those habitual associations which further thought may also come from the same mechanical source as those which hinder it. Hartley accordingly suggested habit as a sufficient explanation of the sequence of our thoughts, and in so doing planted himself squarely upon the properly *causal* aspect of the problem, and sought to treat both rational and irrational associations from a single point of view. How does a man come, after having the thought of A, to have the thought of B the next moment? or how does he come to think A and B always together? These were the phenomena which Hartley undertook to explain by cerebral physiology. I believe that he was, in essential respects, on the right track, and I propose simply to revise his conclusions by the aid of distinctions which he did not make.

Objects are associated, not ideas. We shall avoid confusion if we consistently speak as if *association*, so far as the word stands for an *effect, were between* THINGS THOUGHT OF —*as if it were* THINGS, *not ideas, which are associated in the mind.* We shall talk of the association of *objects*, not of the association of *ideas*. And so far as association stands for a *cause*, it is between *processes in the brain* — it is these which, by being associated in certain ways, determine what successive objects shall be thought.

The Elementary Principle. —I shall now try to show that there is no other *elementary* causal law of association than the law of neural habit. All the *materials* of our thought are due to the way in which one elementary process of the cerebral hemispheres tends to excite whatever other elementary process it may have excited at some former time. The number of elementary processes at work, however, and the nature of those which at any time are fully effective in rousing the others, determine the character of the total brain-action, and, as a consequence of this, they determine the object thought of at the time. According as this resultant object is one thing or another, we call it a product of association by contiguity or of association by similarity, or contrast, or whatever other sorts we may have recognized as ultimate. Its *production*, however, is, in each one of these cases, to be explained by a merely quantitative variation in the elementary brain-processes momentarily at work under the law of habit.

My thesis, stated thus briefly, will soon become more clear; and at the same time certain disturbing factors, which coöperate with the law of neural habit, will come to view.

Let us then assume as the basis of all our subsequent reasoning this law: *When two elementary brain-processes have been active together or in immediate succession, one of them, on reoccurring, tends to propagate its excitement into the other.*

But, as a matter of fact, every elementary process has unavoidably found itself at different times excited in conjunction with *many* other processes. Which of these others it shall awaken now becomes a problem. Shall *b* or *c* be aroused next by the present *a*? To answer this, we must make a further postulate, based on the fact of *tension* in nerve-tissue, and on the fact of summation of excitements, each incomplete or latent in itself, into an open resultant (see p. 132). The process *b*, rather than *c*, will awake, if in addition to the vibrating tract *a* some other tract *d* is in a state of sub-excitement, and formerly was excited with *b* alone and not with *a*. In short, we may say:

The amount of activity at any given point in the brain-cortex is the sum of the tendencies of all other points to discharge into it, such tendencies being proportionate (1) to the number of times the excitement of each other point may have accompanied that of the point in question; (2) to the intensity of such excitements; and (3) to the absence of any rival point functionally disconnected with the first point, into which the discharges might be diverted.

Expressing the fundamental law in this most complicated way leads to the greatest ultimate simplification. Let us, for the present, only treat of spontaneous trains of thought and ideation, such as occur in revery or musing. The case of voluntary thinking towards a certain end shall come up later.

Spontaneous Trains of Thought.—Take, to fix our ideas, the two verses from "Locksley Hall":

"I the heir of all *the ages*, in the foremost files of time,"

and—

"Yet I doubt not through *the ages* one increasing purpose runs."

Why is it that when we recite from memory one of these lines, and get as far as *the ages*, that portion of the *other* line which follows and, so to speak, sprouts out of *the ages* does not also sprout out of our memory and confuse the sense of our words? Simply because the word that follows *the ages* has its brain-process awakened not simply by the brain-process of *the ages* alone, but by it *plus* the brain-processes of all the words preceding *the ages*. The word *ages* at its moment of strongest activity would, *per se*, indifferently discharge into either 'in' or 'one.' So would the previous words (whose tension is momentarily much less strong than that of *ages*) each of them indifferently discharge into either of a large number of other words with which they have been at different times combined. But when the processes of '*I the heir of all the ages*,' simultaneously vibrate in the brain, the last one of them in a maximal, the others in a fading, phase of excitement; then the strongest line of discharge will be that which they *all alike* tend to take. '*In*' and not '*one*' or any other word will be the next to awaken, for its brain-process has previously vibrated in unison not only with that of *ages*, but with that of all those other words whose activity is dying away. It is a good case of the effectiveness over thought of what we called on p. 167 a 'fringe.'

But if some one of these preceding words—'heir,' for example—had an intensely strong association with some brain-tracts entirely disjoined in experience from the poem of "Locksley Hall"—if the reciter, for instance, were tremulously awaiting the opening of a will which might make him a millionaire—it is probable that the path of discharge through the words of the poem would be suddenly interrupted at the word 'heir.' His *emotional interest in that word* would be such that its *own special associations would prevail* over the combined ones of the other words. He would, as we say, be abruptly reminded of his personal situation, and the poem would lapse altogether from his thoughts.

The writer of these pages has every year to learn the names of a large number of students who sit in alphabetical order in a lecture-room. He finally learns to call them by name, as they sit in their accustomed places. On meeting one in the street, however, early in the year, the face hardly ever recalls the name, but it may recall the place of its owner in the lecture-room, his neighbors' faces, and consequently his general alphabetical position; and then, usually as the common associate of all these combined data, the student's name surges up in his mind.

A father wishes to show to some guests the progress of his rather dull child in kindergarten-instruction. Holding the knife upright on the table, he says, "What do you call that, my boy?" "I calls it a *knife*, I does," is the sturdy reply, from which the child cannot be induced to swerve by any alteration in the form of question, until the father, recollecting that in the kindergarten a pencil was used and not a knife, draws a long one from his pocket, holds it in the same way, and then gets the wished-for answer, "I calls it *vertical*." All the concomitants of the kindergarten experience had to recombine their effect before the word 'vertical' could be reawakened.

Total Recall.—The ideal working of the law of compound association, as Prof. Bain calls it, were it unmodified by any extraneous influence, would be such as to keep the mind in a perpetual treadmill of concrete reminiscences from which no detail could be omitted. Suppose, for example, we begin by thinking of a certain dinner-party. The only thing which all the components of the dinner-party could combine to recall would be the first concrete occurrence which ensued upon it. All the details of this occurrence could in turn only combine to awaken the next following occurrence, and so on. If a, b, c, d, e, for instance, be the elementary nerve-tracts excited by the last act of the dinner-party, call this act A, and l, m, n, o, p be those of walking home through the frosty night, which we may call B, then the thought of A must awaken that of B, because a, b, c, d, e will each and all discharge into l through the paths by which their original discharge took place. Similarly they will discharge into m, n, o, and p; and these latter tracts will also each reinforce the other's action because, in the experience B, they have already vibrated in unison. The lines in Fig. 57 symbolize the summation of discharges into each of the components of B, and the consequent strength of the combination of influences by which B in its totality is awakened.

Hamilton first used the word 'redintegration' to designate all association. Such processes as we have just described might in an emphatic sense be termed redintegrations, for they would necessarily lead, if unobstructed, to the reinstatement in thought of the *entire* content of large trains of past experience. From this complete redintegration there could be no escape save through the irruption of some new and strong present impression of the senses, or through the excessive tendency of some one of the elementary brain-tracts to discharge independently into an aberrant quarter of the brain. Such was the tendency of the word 'heir' in the verse from "Locksley Hall," which was our first example. How such tendencies are constituted we shall have soon to inquire with some care. Unless they are present, the panorama of the past, once opened, must unroll itself with fatal literality to the end, unless some outward sound, sight, or touch divert the current of thought.

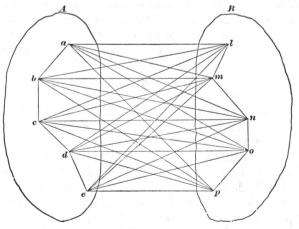

FIG. 57.

Let us call this process *impartial redintegration*, or, still better, *total recall*. Whether it ever occurs in an absolutely complete form is doubtful. We all immediately recognize, however, that in some minds there is a much greater tendency than in others for the flow of thought to take this form. Those insufferably garrulous old women, those dry and fanciless beings who spare you no detail, however petty, of the facts they are recounting, and upon the thread of whose narrative all the irrelevant items cluster as pertinaciously as the essential ones, the slaves of literal fact, the stumblers over the smallest abrupt step in thought, are figures known to all of us. Comic literature has made her profit out of them. Juliet's nurse is a classical example. George Eliot's village characters and some of Dickens's minor personages supply excellent instances.

Perhaps as successful a rendering as any of this mental type is the character of Miss Bates in Miss Austen's *Emma*. Hear how she redintegrates:

" 'But where could *you* hear it?' cried Miss Bates. 'Where could you possibly hear it, Mr. Knightley? For it is not five minutes since I received Mrs. Cole's note—no, it cannot be more than five—or at least ten—for I had got my bonnet and spencer on, just ready to come out—I was only gone down to speak to Patty again about the pork—Jane was standing in the passage—were not you, Jane?—for my mother was so afraid that we had not any salting-pan large enough. So I said, I would go down and see, and Jane said, "Shall I go down instead? for I think you have a little cold, and Patty has been washing the kitchen."—"Oh, my dear," said I—well, and just then came the note. A Miss Hawkins—that's all I know—a Miss Hawkins of Bath. But, Mr. Knightley, how could you possibly have heard it? for the very moment Mr. Cole told Mrs. Cole of it, she sat down and wrote to me. A Miss Hawkins—' "

Partial Recall.—This case helps us to understand why it is that the ordinary spontaneous flow of our ideas does not follow the law of total recall. *In no revival of a past experience are all the items of our thought equally operative in determining what the next thought shall be. Always some ingredient is prepotent over the rest.* Its special suggestions or associations in this case will often be different from those which it has in common with the whole group of items; and its tendency to awaken these outlying associates will deflect the path of our revery. Just as in the original sensible experience our attention focalized itself upon a few of the impressions of the scene before us, so here in the reproduction of those impressions an equal partiality is shown, and some items are emphasized above the rest. What these items shall be is, in most cases of spontaneous revery, hard to determine beforehand. In subjective terms we say that *the prepotent items are those which appeal most to our* INTEREST.

Expressed in brain-terms, the law of interest will be: *some one brain-process is always prepotent above its concomitants in arousing action elsewhere.*

"Two processes," says Mr. Hodgson, "are constantly going on in redintegration, the one a process of corrosion, melting, decay, and the other a process of renewing, arising, becoming . . . no object of representation remains long before consciousness in the same state, but fades, decays, and becomes indistinct. Those parts of the object, however, which possess an interest resist this tendency to gradual decay of the whole object. . . . This inequality in the object, some parts, the uninteresting, submitting to decay, others, the interesting parts, resisting it, when it has continued for a certain time, ends in becoming a new object."

Only where the interest is diffused equally over all the parts is this law departed from. It will be least obeyed by those minds which have the smallest variety and intensity of interests — those who, by the general flatness and poverty of their æsthetic nature, are kept for ever rotating among the literal sequences of their local and personal history.

Most of us, however, are better organized than this, and our musings pursue an erratic course, swerving continually into some new direction traced by the shifting play of interest as it ever falls on some partial item in each complex representation that is evoked. Thus it so often comes about that we find ourselves thinking at two nearly adjacent moments of things separated by the whole diameter of space and time. Not till we carefully recall each step of our cogitation do we see how naturally we came by Hodgson's law to pass from one to the other. Thus, for instance, after looking at my clock just now (1879), I found myself thinking of a recent resolution in the Senate about our legal-tender notes. The clock had called up the image of the man who had repaired its gong. He had suggested the jeweller's shop where I had last seen him; that shop, some shirt-studs which I had bought there; they, the value of gold and its recent decline; the latter, the equal value of greenbacks, and this, naturally, the question of how long they were to last, and of the Bayard proposition. Each of these images offered various points of interest. Those which formed the turning-points of my thought are easily assigned. The gong was momentarily the most interesting part of the clock, because, from having begun with a beautiful tone, it had become discordant and aroused disappointment. But for this the clock might have suggested the friend who gave it to me, or any one of a thousand circumstances connected with clocks. The jeweller's shop suggested the studs, because they alone of all its contents were tinged with the egoistic interest of possession. This interest in the studs, their value, made me single out the material as its chief source, etc., to the end. Every reader who will arrest himself at any moment and say, "How came I to be thinking of just this?" will be sure to trace a train of representations linked together by lines of contiguity and points of interest inextricably combined. This is the ordinary process of the association of ideas as it spontaneously goes on in average minds. *We may call it ordinary, or mixed, association,* or, if we like better, *partial recall.*

Which Associates come up, in Partial Recall?—Can we determine, now, when a certain portion of the going thought has, by dint of its interest, become so prepotent as to make its own exclusive associates the dominant features of the coming thought—can we, I say, determine *which* of its own associates shall be evoked? For they are many. As Hodgson says:

"The interesting parts of the decaying object are free to combine again with any objects, or parts of objects, with which they have at any time been combined before. All the former combinations of these parts may come back into consciousness; one must; but which will?"

Mr. Hodgson replies:

"There can be but one answer; That which has been most *habitually* combined with them before. This new object begins at once to form itself in consciousness, and to group its parts round the part still remaining from the former object; part after part comes out and arranges itself in its old position; but scarcely has the process begun, when the original law of interest begins to operate on this new formation, seizes on the interesting parts and impresses them on the attention to the exclusion of the rest, and the whole process is repeated again with endless variety. I venture to propose this as a complete and true account of the whole process of spontaneous redintegration."

In restricting the discharge from the interesting item into that channel which is simply most *habitual* in the sense of most frequent, Hodgson's account is assuredly imperfect. An image by no means always revives its most frequent associate, although frequency is certainly one of the most potent determinants of revival. If I abruptly utter the word *swallow*, the reader, if by habit an ornithologist, will think of a bird; if a physiologist or a medical specialist in throat-diseases, he will think of deglutition. If I say *date*, he will, if a fruit-merchant or an Arabian traveller, think of the produce of the palm; if an habitual student of history, figures with A.D. or B.C. before them will rise in his mind. If I say *bed, bath, morning*, his own daily toilet will be invincibly suggested by the combined names of three of its habitual associates. But frequent lines of transition are often set at naught. The sight of a certain book has most frequently awakened in me thoughts of the opinions therein propounded. The idea of suicide has never been connected with the volume. But a moment since, as my eye fell upon it, suicide was the thought that flashed into my mind. Why? Because but yesterday I received a letter informing me that the author's recent death was an act of self-destruction. Thoughts tend, then, to awaken their most recent as well as their most habitual associates. This is a matter of notorious experience, too notorious, in fact, to need illustration. If we have seen our friend this morning, the mention of his name now recalls the circumstances of that interview, rather than any more remote details concerning him. If Shakespeare's plays are mentioned, and we were last night reading *Richard II.*, vestiges of that play rather than of *Hamlet* or *Othello* float through our mind. Excitement of peculiar tracts, or peculiar modes of general excitement in the brain, leave a sort of tenderness or exalted sensibility behind them which takes days to die away. As long as it lasts, those tracts or those modes are liable to have their activities awakened by causes which at other times might leave them in repose. Hence, *recency* in experience is a prime factor in determining revival in thought.[1]

Vividness in an original experience may also have the same effect as habit or recency in bringing about likelihood of revival. If we have once witnessed an execution, any subsequent conversation or reading about capital punishment will almost certainly suggest images of that particular scene. Thus it is that events lived through only once, and in youth, may come in after-years, by reason of their exciting quality or emotional intensity, to serve as types or instances used by our mind to illustrate any and every occurring topic whose interest is most remotely pertinent to theirs. If a man in his boyhood once talked with Napoleon, any mention of great men or historical events, battles or thrones, or the whirligig of fortune, or islands in the ocean, will be apt to draw to his lips the incidents of that one memorable interview. If the word *tooth* now suddenly appears on the page before the reader's eye, there are fifty chances out of a hundred that, if he gives it time to awaken any image, it will be an image of some operation of dentistry in which he has been the sufferer. Daily he has touched his teeth and masticated with them; this very morning he brushed, used, and picked them; but the rarer and remoter associations arise more promptly because they were so much more intense.

A fourth factor in tracing the course of reproduction is *congruity in emotional tone* between the reproduced idea and our mood. The same objects do not recall the same associates when we are cheerful as when we are melancholy. Nothing, in fact, is more striking than our inability to keep up trains of joyous imagery when we are depressed in spirits. Storm,

---

[1] I refer to a recency of a few hours. Mr. Galton found that experiences from boyhood and youth were more likely to be suggested by words seen at random than experiences of later years. See his highly interesting account of experiments in his *Inquiries into Human Faculty*, pp. 191–203.

darkness, war, images of disease, poverty, perishing, and dread afflict unremittingly the imaginations of melancholiacs. And those of sanguine temperament, when their spirits are high, find it impossible to give any permanence to evil forebodings or to gloomy thoughts. In an instant the train of association dances off to flowers and sunshine, and images of spring and hope. The records of Arctic or African travel perused in one mood awaken no thoughts but those of horror at the malignity of Nature; read at another time they suggest only enthusiastic reflections on the indomitable power and pluck of man. Few novels so overflow with joyous animal spirits as *The Three Guardsmen* of Dumas. Yet it may awaken in the mind of a reader depressed with sea-sickness (as the writer can personally testify) a most woful consciousness of the cruelty and carnage of which heroes like Athos, Porthos, and Aramis make themselves guilty.

Habit, recency, vividness, and emotional congruity are, then, all reasons why one representation rather than another should be awakened by the interesting portion of a departing thought. We may say with truth that *in the majority of cases the coming representation will have been either habitual, recent, or vivid, and will be congruous.* If all these qualities unite in any one absent associate, we may predict almost infallibly that that associate of the going object will form an important ingredient in the object which comes next. In spite of the fact, however, that the succession of representations is thus redeemed from perfect indeterminism and limited to a few classes whose characteristic quality is fixed by the nature of our past experience, it must still be confessed that an immense number of terms in the linked chain of our representations fall outside of all assignable rule. To take the instance of the clock given on page 251. Why did the jeweller's shop suggest the shirt-studs rather than a chain which I had bought there more recently, which had cost more, and whose sentimental associations were much more interesting? Any reader's experience will easily furnish similar instances. So we must admit that to a certain extent, even in those forms of ordinary mixed association which lie nearest to impartial redintegration, *which* associate of the interesting item shall emerge must be called largely a matter of accident—accident, that is, for our intelligence. No doubt it is determined by cerebral causes, but they are too subtile and shifting for our analysis.

Focalized Recall, or Association by Similarity.—In partial or mixed association we have all along supposed the interesting portion of the disappearing thought to be of considerable extent, and to be sufficiently complex to consti-tute by itself a concrete object. Sir William Hamilton relates, for instance, that after thinking of Ben Lomond he found himself thinking of the Prussian system of education, and dis-covered that the links of association were a German gentle-man whom he had met on Ben Lomond, Germany, etc. The interesting part of Ben Lomond as he had experienced it, the part operative in determining the train of his ideas, was the complex image of a particular man. But now let us suppose that the interested attention refines itself still further and ac-centuates a portion of the passing object, so small as to be no longer the image of a concrete thing, but only of an abstract quality or property. Let us moreover suppose that the part thus accentuated persists in consciousness (or, in cerebral terms, has its brain-process continue) after the other portions of the object have faded. *This small surviving portion will then surround itself with its own associates* after the fashion we have already seen, and the relation between the new thought's ob-ject and the object of the faded thought will be a *relation of similarity*. The pair of thoughts will form an instance of what is called '*association by similarity*.'

The similars which are here associated, or of which the first is followed by the second in the mind, are seen to be *com-pounds*. Experience proves that this is always the case. *There is no tendency on the part of* SIMPLE *'ideas,' attributes, or qualities to remind us of their like*. The thought of one shade of blue does not summon up that of another shade of blue, etc., un-less indeed we have in mind some general purpose of nomen-clature or comparison which requires a review of several blue tints.

Now two compound things are similar when some one quality or group of qualities is shared alike by both, although as regards their other qualities they may have nothing in com-mon. The moon is similar to a gas-jet, it is also similar to a foot-ball; but a gas-jet and a foot-ball are not similar to each other. When we affirm the similarity of two compound things, we should always say *in what respect it obtains*. Moon and gas-jet are similar in respect of luminosity, and nothing else; moon and foot-ball in respect of rotundity, and nothing else. Foot-ball and gas-jet are in no respect similar—that is, they possess no common point, no identical attribute. *Similarity, in compounds, is partial identity*. When the *same* attribute appears in two phenomena, though it be their only common property, the two phenomena are similar in so far forth. To return now to our associated representations. If the thought of the moon is succeeded by the thought of a foot-ball, and that by the thought of one of Mr. X's railroads, it is because the attribute rotundity in the moon broke away from all the rest and surrounded itself with an entirely new set of companions—elasticity, leathery integument, swift mobility in obedience to human caprice, etc.; and because the last-named attribute in the foot-ball in turn broke away from its companions, and, itself persisting, surrounded itself with such new attributes as make up the notions of a 'railroad king,' of a rising and falling stock-market, and the like.

The gradual passage from total to focalized, through what we have called ordinary partial, recall may be symbolized by diagrams. Fig. 58 is total, Fig. 59 is partial, and Fig. 60 focalized, recall. A in each is the passing, B the coming, thought. In 'total recall,' all parts of A are equally operative in calling up B. In 'partial recall,' most parts of A are inert. The part M alone breaks out and awakens B. In similar association or 'focalized recall,' the part M is much smaller than in the previous

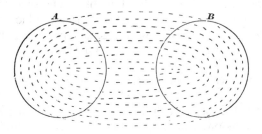

Fig. 58.

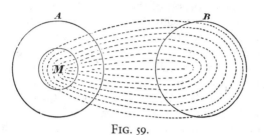

FIG. 59.

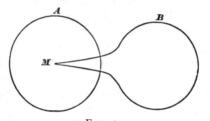

FIG. 60.

case, and after awakening its new set of associates, instead of fading out itself, it continues persistently active along with them, forming an identical part in the two ideas, and making these, *pro tanto*, resemble each other.[2]

[2]Miss M. W. Calkins (*Philosophical Review,* I, 389, 1892) points out that the persistent feature of the going thought, on which the association in cases of similarity hinges, is by no means always so slight as to warrant the term 'focalized.' "If the sight of the whole breakfast-room be followed by the visual image of yesterday's breakfast-table, with the same setting and in the same surroundings, the association is practically total," and yet the case is one of similarity. For Miss Calkins, accordingly, the more important distinction is that between what she calls *desistent* and *persistent* association. In 'desistent' association all parts of the going thought fade out and are replaced. In 'persistent' association some of them remain, and form a bond of similarity between the mind's successive objects; but only where this bond is extremely delicate (as in the case of an abstract relation or quality) is there need to call the persistent process 'focalized.' I must concede the justice of Miss Calkins's criticism, and think her new pair of terms a useful contribution. Wundt's division of associations into the two classes of *external* and *internal* is congruent with Miss Calkins's division. Things associated internally must have some element in common; and Miss Calkins's word 'persistent' suggests how this may cerebrally come to pass. 'Desistent,' on the other hand, suggests the process by which the successive ideas become external to each other or preserve no inner tie.

Why a single portion of the passing thought should break out from its concert with the rest and act, as we say, on its own hook, why the other parts should become inert, are mysteries which we can ascertain but not explain. Possibly a minuter insight into the laws of neural action will some day clear the matter up; possibly neural laws will not suffice, and we shall need to invoke a dynamic reaction of the consciousness itself. But into this we cannot enter now.

Voluntary Trains of Thought.—Hitherto we have assumed the process of suggestion of one object by another to be spontaneous. The train of imagery wanders at its own sweet will, now trudging in sober grooves of habit, now with a hop, skip, and jump, darting across the whole field of time and space. This is revery, or musing; but great segments of the flux of our ideas consist of something very different from this. They are guided by a distinct purpose or conscious interest; and the course of our ideas is then called *voluntary*.

Physiologically considered, we must suppose that a purpose means the persistent activity of certain rather definite brain-processes throughout the whole course of thought. Our most usual cogitations are not pure reveries, absolute driftings, but revolve about some central interest or topic to which most of the images are relevant, and towards which we return promptly after occasional digressions. This interest is subserved by the persistently active brain-tracts we have supposed. In the mixed associations which we have hitherto studied, the parts of each object which form the pivots on which our thoughts successively turn have their interest largely determined by their connection with some *general interest* which for the time has seized upon the mind. If we call Z the brain-tract of general interest, then, if the object abc turns up, and b has more associations with Z than have either a or c, b will become the object's interesting, pivotal portion, and will call up its own associates exclusively. For the energy of b's brain-tract will be augmented by Z's activity,—an activity which, from lack of previous connection between Z and a and Z and c, does not influence a or c. If, for instance, I think of Paris whilst I am *hungry*, I shall not improbably find that its *restaurants* have become the pivot of my thought, etc., etc.

Problems.—But in the theoretic as well as in the practical life there are interests of a more acute sort, taking the form of definite images of some achievement which we desire to effect. The train of ideas arising under the influence of such an interest constitutes usually the thought of the *means* by which the end shall be attained. If the end by its simple presence does not instantaneously suggest the means, the search for the latter becomes a *problem*; and the discovery of the means forms a new sort of end, of an entirely peculiar nature—an end, namely, which we intensely desire before we have attained it, but of the nature of which, even whilst most strongly craving it, we have no distinct imagination whatever (compare p. 231).

The same thing occurs whenever we seek to recall something forgotten, or to state the reason for a judgment which we have made intuitively. The desire strains and presses in a direction which it feels to be right, but towards a point which it is unable to see. In short, the *absence of an item* is a determinant of our representations quite as positive as its presence can ever be. The gap becomes no mere void, but what is called an *aching* void. If we try to explain in terms of brain-action how a thought which only potentially exists can yet be effective, we seem driven to believe that the brain-tract thereof must actually be excited, but only in a minimal and sub-conscious way. Try, for instance, to symbolize what goes on in a man who is racking his brains to remember a thought which occurred to him last week. The associates of the thought are there, many of them at least, but they refuse to awaken the thought itself. We cannot suppose that they do not irradiate *at all* into its brain-tract, because his mind quivers on the very edge of its recovery. Its actual rhythm sounds in his ears; the words seem on the imminent point of following, but fail (see p. 163). Now the only difference between the effort to recall things forgotten and the search after the means to a given end is that the latter have not, whilst the former have, already formed a part of our experience. If we first study *the mode of recalling a thing forgotten*, we can take up with better understanding the voluntary quest of the unknown.

Their Solution.—The forgotten thing is felt by us as a gap in the midst of certain other things. We possess a dim idea of where we were and what we were about when it last occurred to us. We recollect the general subject to which it pertains. But all these details refuse to shoot together into a solid whole, for the lack of the missing thing, so we keep running over them in our mind, dissatisfied, craving something more. From each detail there radiate lines of association forming so many tentative guesses. Many of these are immediately seen to be irrelevant, are therefore void of interest, and lapse immediately from consciousness. Others are associated with the other details present, and with the missing thought as well. When *these* surge up, we have a peculiar feeling that we are 'warm,' as the children say when they play hide and seek; and such associates as these we clutch at and keep before the attention. Thus we recollect successively that when we last were considering the matter in question we were at the dinner-table; then that our friend J. D. was there; then that the subject talked about was so and so; finally, that the thought came *a propos* of a certain anecdote, and then that it had something to do with a French quotation. Now all these added associates *arise independently of the will*, by the spontaneous processes we know so well. *All that the will does is to emphasize and linger over those which seem pertinent, and ignore the rest*. Through this hovering of the attention in the neighborhood of the desired object, the accumulation of associates becomes so great that the combined tensions of their neural processes break through the bar, and the nervous wave pours into the tract which has so long been awaiting its advent. And as the expectant, subconscious itching, so to speak, bursts into the fulness of vivid feeling, the mind finds an inexpressible relief.

The whole process can be rudely symbolized in a diagram. Call the forgotten thing Z, the first facts with which we felt it was related a, b, and c, and the details finally operative in calling it up l, m, and n. Each circle will then stand for the brain-process principally concerned in the thought of the fact lettered within it. The activity in Z will at first be a mere tension; but as the activities in a, b, and c little by little irradiate into l, m, and n, and as *all* these processes are somehow connected with Z, their combined irradiations upon Z, repre-

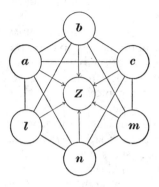

FIG. 61.

sented by the centripetal arrows, succeed in rousing Z also to full activity.

Turn now to the case of finding the unknown means to a distinctly conceived end. The end here stands in the place of *a*, *b*, *c*, in the diagram. It is the starting-point of the irradiations of suggestion; and here, as in that case, what the voluntary attention does is only to dismiss some of the suggestions as irrelevant, and hold fast to others which are felt to be more pertinent—let these be symbolized by *l*, *m*, *n*. These latter at last accumulate sufficiently to discharge all together into Z, the excitement of which process is, in the mental sphere, equivalent to the solution of our problem. The only difference between this and the previous case is that in this one there need be no original sub-excitement in Z, coöperating from the very first. In the solving of a problem, all that we are aware of in advance seems to be its *relations*. It must be a cause, or it must be an effect, or it must contain an attribute, or it must be a means, or what not. We know, in short, a lot *about* it, whilst as yet we have no *acquaintance* with it. Our perception that one of the objects which turn up is, at last, our *quæsitum*, is due to our recognition that its relations are identical with those we had in mind, and this may be a rather slow act of judgment. Everyone knows that an object may be for some time present to his mind before its relations to other matters are perceived. Just so the relations may be there before the object is.

From the guessing of newspaper enigmas to the plotting of the policy of an empire there is no other process than this. We must trust to the laws of cerebral nature to present us spontaneously with the appropriate idea, but we must know it for the right one when it comes.

It is foreign to my purpose here to enter into any detailed analysis of the different classes of mental pursuit. In a scientific research we get perhaps as rich an example as can be found. The inquirer starts with a fact of which he seeks the reason, or with an hypothesis of which he seeks the proof. In either case he keeps turning the matter incessantly in his mind until, by the arousal of associate upon associate, some habitual, some similar, one arises which he recognizes to suit his need. This, however, may take years. No rules can be given by which the investigator may proceed straight to his result; but both here and in the case of reminiscence the accumulation of helps in the way of associations may advance more rapidly by the use of certain routine methods. In striving to recall a thought, for example, we may of set purpose run through the successive classes of circumstance with which it may possibly have been connected, trusting that when the right member of the class has turned up it will help the thought's revival. Thus we may run through all the *places* in which we may have had it. We may run through the *persons* whom we remember to have conversed with, or we may call up successively all the *books* we have lately been reading. If we are trying to remember a person we may run through a list of streets or of professions. Some item out of the lists thus methodically gone over will very likely be associated with the fact we are in need of, and may suggest it or help to do so. And yet the item might never have arisen without such systematic procedure. In scientific research this accumulation of associates has been methodized by Mill under the title of "The Four Methods of Experimental Inquiry." By the 'method of agreement,' by that of 'difference,' by those of 'residues' and 'concomitant variations' (which cannot here be more nearly defined), we make certain lists of cases; and by ruminating these lists in our minds the cause we seek will be more likely to emerge. But the final stroke of discovery is only prepared, not effected, by them. The brain-tracts must, of their own accord, shoot the right way at last, or we shall still grope in darkness. That in some brains the tracts *do* shoot the right way much oftener than in others, and that we cannot tell why,—these are ultimate facts to which we must never close our eyes. Even in forming our lists of instances according to Mill's methods, we are at the mercy of the spontaneous workings of Similarity in our brain. How are a number of facts, resembling the one whose cause we seek, to be brought together in a list unless one will rapidly suggest another through association by similarity?

Similarity no Elementary Law.—Such is the analysis I propose, first of the three main types of spontaneous, and then of voluntary, trains of thought. It will be observed that the *object called up may bear any logical relation whatever to the one which suggested it*. The law requires only that one condition should be fulfilled. The fading object must be due to a brain-process some of whose elements awaken through habit some of the elements of the brain-process of the object which comes to view. This awakening is the causal agency in the kind of association called Similarity, as in any other sort. The similarity *itself* between the objects has no causal agency in carrying us from one to the other. It is but a result—the effect of the usual causal agent when this happens to work in a certain way. Ordinary writers talk as if the similarity of the objects were itself an agent, coördinate with habit, and independent of it, and like it able to push objects before the mind. This is quite unintelligible. The similarity of two things does not exist till both things are there—it is meaningless to talk of it as an *agent of production* of anything, whether in the physical or the psychical realms. It is a relation which the mind perceives after the fact, just as it may perceive the relations of superiority, of distance, of causality, of container and content, of substance and accident, or of contrast, between an object and some second object which the associative machinery calls up.

Conclusion.—To sum up, then, we see that *the difference between the three kinds of association reduces itself to a simple difference in the amount of that portion of the nerve-tract supporting* *the going thought which is operative in calling up the thought which comes.* But the *modus operandi* of this active part is the same, be it large or be it small. The items constituting the coming object waken in every instance because their nerve-tracts once were excited continuously with those of the going object or its operative part. This ultimate physiological law of habit among the neural elements is what *runs* the train. The direction of its course and the form of its transitions are due to the unknown conditions by which in some brains action tends to focalize itself in small spots, while in others it fills patiently its broad bed. What these differing conditions are, it seems impossible to guess. Whatever they are, they are what separate the man of genius from the prosaic creature of habit and routine thinking. In the chapter on Reasoning we shall need to recur again to this point. I trust that the student will now feel that the way to a deeper understanding of the order of our ideas lies in the direction of cerebral physiology. The *elementary* process of revival can be nothing but the law of habit. Truly the day is distant when physiologists shall actually trace from cell-group to cell-group the irradiations which we have hypothetically invoked. Probably it will never arrive. The schematism we have used is, moreover, taken immediately from the analysis of objects into their elementary parts, and only extended by analogy to the brain. And yet it is only as incorporated in the brain that such a schematism can represent anything *causal*. This is, to my mind, the conclusive reason for saying that the order of *presentation of the mind's materials* is due to cerebral physiology alone.

The law of accidental prepotency of certain processes over others falls also within the sphere of cerebral probabilities. Granting such instability as the brain-tissue requires, certain points must always discharge more quickly and strongly than others; and this prepotency would shift its place from moment to moment by accidental causes, giving us a perfect mechanical diagram of the capricious play of similar association in the most gifted mind. A study of dreams confirms this view. The usual abundance of paths of irradiation seems, in the dormant brain, reduced. A few only are pervious, and the most fantastic sequences occur because the currents run—

'like sparks in burnt-up paper'—wherever the nutrition of the moment creates an opening, but nowhere else.

The *effects of interested attention and volition* remain. These activities seem to hold fast to certain elements and, by emphasizing them and dwelling on them, to make their associates the only ones which are evoked. *This* is the point at which an anti-mechanical psychology must, if anywhere, make its stand in dealing with association. Everything else is pretty certainly due to cerebral laws. My own opinion on the question of active attention and spiritual spontaneity is expressed elsewhere (see p. 227). But even though there be a mental spontaneity, it can certainly not create ideas or summon them *ex abrupto*. Its power is limited to *selecting* amongst those which the associative machinery introduces. If it can emphasize, reinforce, or protract for half a second either one of these, it can do all that the most eager advocate of free-will need demand; for it then decides the direction of the *next* associations by making them hinge upon the emphasized term; and determining in this wise the course of the man's thinking, it also determines his acts.

CHAPTER XVII

THE SENSE OF TIME

The sensible present has duration. Let anyone try, I will not say to arrest, but to notice or attend to, the *present* moment of time. One of the most baffling experiences occurs. Where is it, this present? It has melted in our grasp, fled ere we could touch it, gone in the instant of becoming. As a poet, quoted by Mr. Hodgson, says,

"Le moment où je parle est déjà loin de moi,"

and it is only as entering into the living and moving organization of a much wider tract of time that the strict present is apprehended at all. It is, in fact, an altogether ideal abstraction, not only never realized in sense, but probably never even conceived of by those unaccustomed to philosophic meditation. Reflection leads us to the conclusion that it *must* exist, but that it *does* exist can never be a fact of our immediate experience. The only fact of our immediate experience is what has been well called 'the specious' present, a sort of saddleback of time with a certain length of its own, on which we sit perched, and from which we look in two directions into time. The unit of composition of our perception of time is a *duration*, with a bow and a stern, as it were—a rearward- and a forward-looking end. It is only as parts of this *duration-block* that the relation of *succession* of one end to the other is perceived. We do not first feel one end and then feel the other after it, and from the perception of the succession infer an interval of time between, but we seem to feel the interval of time as a whole, with its two ends embedded in it. The experience is from the outset a synthetic datum, not a simple one; and to sensible perception its elements are inseparable, although attention looking back may easily decompose the experience, and distinguish its beginning from its end.

The moment we pass beyond a very few seconds our consciousness of duration ceases to be an immediate perception and becomes a construction more or less symbolic. To realize even an hour, we must count 'now! now! now! now!' indefinitely. Each 'now' is the feeling of a separate *bit* of time, and the exact sum of the bits never makes a clear impression on our mind. The *longest bit of duration* which we can apprehend at once so as to discriminate it from longer and shorter bits of time would seem (from experiments made for another purpose in Wundt's laboratory) to be about 12 seconds. *The shortest interval* which we can feel as time at all would seem to be ⅟₅₀₀ of a second. That is, Exner recognized two electric sparks to be successive when the second followed the first at that interval.

We have no sense for empty time. Let one sit with closed eyes and, abstracting entirely from the outer world, attend exclusively to the passage of time, like one who wakes, as the poet says, "to hear time flowing in the middle of the night, and all things creeping to a day of doom." There seems under such circumstances as these no variety in the material content of our thought, and what we notice appears, if anything, to be the pure series of durations budding, as it were, and growing beneath our indrawn gaze. Is this really so or not? The question is important; for, if the experience be what it roughly seems, we have a sort of special sense for pure time — a sense to which empty duration is an adequate stimulus; while if it be an illusion, it must be that our perception of time's flight, in the experiences quoted, is due to the *filling* of the time, and to our *memory* of a content which it had a moment previous, and which we feel to agree or disagree with its content now.

It takes but a small exertion of introspection to show that the latter alternative is the true one, and that *we can no more perceive a duration than we can perceive an extension, devoid of all sensible content*. Just as with closed eyes we see a dark visual field in which a curdling play of obscurest luminosity is always going on; so, be we never so abstracted from distinct outward impressions, we are always inwardly immersed in what Wundt has somewhere called the twilight of our general consciousness. Our heart-beats, our breathing, the pulses of our attention, fragments of words or sentences that pass through our imagination, are what people this dim habitat. Now, all these processes are rhythmical, and are apprehended by us, as they occur, in their totality; the breathing and pulses of attention, as coherent successions, each with its rise and fall; the heart-beats similarly, only relatively far more brief; the words not separately, but in connected groups. In short, empty our minds as we may, some form of *changing process* remains for us to feel, and cannot be expelled. And along with the sense of the process and its rhythm goes the sense of the length of time it lasts. Awareness of *change* is thus the condition on which our perception of time's flow depends; but there exists no reason to suppose that empty time's own changes are sufficient for the awareness of change to be aroused. The change must be of some concrete sort.

Appreciation of Longer Durations. — In the experience of watching empty time flow — 'empty' to be taken hereafter in the relative sense just set forth — we tell it off in pulses. We say 'now! now! now!' or we count 'more! more! more!' as we feel it bud. This composition out of units of duration is called the law of time's *discrete flow*. The discreteness is, however, merely due to the fact that our successive acts of *recognition* or *apperception* of *what* it is are discrete. The sensation is as continuous as any sensation can be. All continuous sensations are *named* in beats. We notice that a certain finite 'more' of them is passing or already past. To adopt Hodgson's image, the sensation is the measuring-tape, the perception the dividing-engine which stamps its length. As we listen to a steady sound, we *take it in* in discrete pulses of recognition, calling it successively 'the same! the same! the same!' The case stands no otherwise with time.

After a small number of beats our impression of the amount we have told off becomes quite vague. Our only way of knowing it accurately is by counting, or noticing the clock, or through some other symbolic conception. When the times exceed hours or days, the conception is absolutely symbolic. We think of the amount we mean either solely as a *name*, or by running over a few salient *dates* therein, with no pretence of imagining the full durations that lie between them. No one has anything like a *perception* of the greater length of the time between now and the first century than of that between now and the tenth. To an historian, it is true, the longer interval will suggest a host of additional dates and events, and so appear a more *multitudinous* thing. And for the same reason most people will think they directly perceive the length of the past fortnight to exceed that of the past week. But there is properly no comparative time-*intuition* in these cases at all. It is but dates and events representing time, their abundance symbolizing its length. I am sure that this is so, even where the times compared are no more than an hour or so in length. It is the same with spaces of many miles, which we always compare with each other by the numbers that measure them.

From this we pass naturally to speak of certain familiar variations in our estimation of lengths of time. *In general, a time filled with varied and interesting experiences seems short in passing, but long as we look back. On the other hand, a tract of time empty of experiences seems long in passing, but in retrospect short.* A week of travel and sight-seeing may subtend an angle more like three weeks in the memory; and a month of sickness yields hardly more memories than a day. The length in retrospect depends obviously on the multitudinousness of the memories which the time affords. Many objects, events, changes, many subdivisions, immediately widen the view as we look back. Emptiness, monotony, familiarity, make it shrivel up.

The same space of time seems shorter as we grow older—that is, the days, the months, and the years do so; whether the hours do so is doubtful, and the minutes and seconds to all appearance remain about the same. An old man probably does not *feel* his past life to be any longer than he did when he was a boy, though it may be a dozen times as long. In most men all the events of manhood's years are of such familiar *sorts* that the individual impressions do not last. At the same time more and more of the earlier events get forgotten, the result being that no greater multitude of distinct objects remains in the memory.

So much for the apparent shortening of tracts of time in *retrospect*. They shorten *in passing* whenever we are so fully occupied with their content as not to note the actual time itself. A day full of excitement, with no pause, is said to pass 'ere we know it.' On the contrary, a day full of waiting, of unsatisfied desire for change, will seem a small eternity. *Tædium, ennui, Langweile, boredom*, are words for which, probably, every language known to man has its equivalent. It comes about whenever, from the relative emptiness of content of a tract of time, we grow attentive to the passage of the time itself. Expecting, and being ready for, a new impression to succeed; when it fails to come, we get an empty time instead of it; and such experiences, ceaselessly renewed, make us most formidably aware of the extent of the mere time itself. Close your eyes and simply wait to hear somebody tell you that a minute has elapsed, and the full length of your leisure with it seems incredible. You engulf yourself into its bowels as into those of that interminable first week of an ocean voyage, and find yourself wondering that history can have overcome many such periods in its course. All because you attend so closely to the mere feeling of the time *per se*, and because your attention to that is susceptible of such fine-grained successive subdivision. The *odiousness* of the whole experience comes from its insipidity; for *stimulation* is the indispensable requisite for pleasure in an experience, and the feeling of bare time is the least stimulating experience we can have. The sensation of tedium is a *protest*, says Volkmann, against the entire present.

The feeling of past time is a present feeling. In reflecting on the *modus operandi* of our consciousness of time, we are at first tempted to suppose it the easiest thing in the world to understand. Our inner states succeed each other. They know themselves as they are; then of course, we say, they must know their own succession. But this philosophy is too crude; for between the mind's own changes *being* successive, and *knowing their own succession*, lies as broad a chasm as between the object and subject of any case of cognition in the world. *A succession of feelings, in and of itself, is not a feeling of succession. And since, to our successive feelings, a feeling of their succession is added, that must be treated as an additional fact requiring its own special elucidation*, which this talk about the feelings knowing their time-relations as a matter of course leaves all untouched.

If we represent the actual time-stream of our thinking by an horizontal line, the thought *of* the stream or of any segment of its length, past, present, or to come, might be figured in a perpendicular raised upon the horizontal at a certain point. The length of this perpendicular stands for a certain object or content, which in this case is the time thought of at the actual moment of the stream upon which the perpendicular is raised.

There is thus a sort of *perspective projection* of past objects upon present consciousness, similar to that of wide landscapes upon a camera-screen.

And since we saw a while ago that our maximum distinct *perception* of duration hardly covers more than a dozen seconds (while our maximum vague perception is probably not more than that of a minute or so), we must suppose that *this amount of duration is pictured fairly steadily in each passing instant of consciousness* by virtue of some fairly constant feature in the brain-process to which the consciousness is tied. *This feature of the brain-process, whatever it be, must be the cause of our perceiving the fact of time at all.* The duration thus steadily perceived is hardly more than the 'specious present,' as it was called a few pages back. Its *content* is in a constant flux, events dawning into its forward end as fast as they fade out of its rearward one, and each of them changing its time-coefficient from 'not yet,' or 'not quite yet,' to 'just gone,' or 'gone,' as it passes by. Meanwhile, the specious present, the intuited duration, stands permanent, like the rainbow on the waterfall, with its own quality unchanged by the events that stream through it. Each of these, as it slips out, retains the power of being reproduced; and when reproduced, is reproduced with the duration and neighbors which it originally had. Please observe, however, that the reproduction of an event, *after* it has once completely dropped out of the rearward end of the specious present, is an entirely different psychic fact from its direct perception in the specious present as a thing immediately past. A creature might be entirely devoid of *reproductive* memory, and yet have the time-sense; but the latter would be limited, in his case, to the few seconds immediately passing by. In the next chapter, assuming the sense of time as given, we will turn to the analysis of what happens in reproductive memory, the recall of *dated* things.

CHAPTER XVIII

MEMORY

Analysis of the Phenomenon of Memory.—Memory proper, or secondary memory as it might be styled, is the knowledge of a former state of mind after it has already once dropped from consciousness; or rather *it is the knowledge of an event, or fact,* of which meantime we have not been thinking, *with the additional consciousness that we have thought or experienced it before.*

The first element which such a knowledge involves would seem to be the revival in the mind of an image or copy of the original event. And it is an assumption made by many writers that such revival of an image is all that is needed to constitute the memory of the original occurrence. But such a revival is obviously not a *memory*, whatever else it may be; it is simply a duplicate, a second event, having absolutely no connection with the first event except that it happens to resemble it. The clock strikes to-day; it struck yesterday; and may strike a million times ere it wears out. The rain pours through the gutter this week; it did so last week; and will do so *in sæcula sæculorum.* But does the present clock-stroke become aware of the past ones, or the present stream recollect the past stream, because they repeat and resemble them? Assuredly not. And let it not be said that this is because clock-strokes and gutters are physical and not psychical objects; for psychical objects (sensations, for example) simply recurring in successive editions will remember each other *on that account* no more than clock-strokes do. No memory is involved in the mere fact of recurrence. The successive editions of a feeling are so many independent events, each snug in its own skin. Yesterday's feeling is dead and buried; and the presence of to-day's is no reason why it should resuscitate along with to-day's. A farther condition is required before the present image can be held to stand for a *past original.*

That condition is that the fact imagined be *expressly referred to the past,* thought as *in the past.* But how can we think a thing as in the past, except by thinking of the past together with the thing, and of the relation of the two? And how can we think of the past? In the chapter on Time-perception we have seen that our intuitive or immediate consciousness of pastness hardly carries us more than a few seconds backwards of the present instant of time. Remoter dates are conceived, not perceived; known symbolically by names, such as 'last week,' '1850'; or thought of by events which happened in them, as the year in which we attended such a school, or met with such a loss. So that if we wish to think of a particular past epoch, we must think of a name or other symbol, or else of certain concrete events, associated therewithal. Both must be thought of, to think the past epoch adequately. And to 'refer' any special fact to the past epoch is to think that fact *with* the names and events which characterize its date, to think it, in short, with a lot of contiguous associates.

But even this would not be memory. Memory requires more than mere dating of a fact in the past. It must be dated in *my* past. In other words, I must think that I directly experienced its occurrence. It must have that 'warmth and intimacy' which were so often spoken of in the chapter on the Self, as characterizing all experiences 'appropriated' by the thinker as his own.

A general feeling of the past direction in time, then, a particular date conceived as lying along that direction, and defined by its name or phenomenal contents, an event imagined as located therein, and owned as part of my experience,— such are the elements of every object of memory.

Retention and Recall.—Such being the phenomenon of memory, or the analysis of its object, can we see how it comes to pass? can we lay bare its causes?

Its complete exercise presupposes two things:

1) The *retention* of the remembered fact; and

2) Its *reminiscence, recollection, reproduction*, or *recall*.

Now *the cause both of retention and of recollection is the law of habit in the nervous system, working as it does in the 'association of ideas.'*

Association explains Recall.—Associationists have long explained *recollection* by association. James Mill gives an account of it which I am unable to improve upon, unless it might be by translating his word 'idea' into 'thing thought of,' or 'object.'

"There is," he says, "a state of mind familiar to all men, in which we are said to try to remember. In this state, it is certain that we have not in the mind the idea which we are trying to have in it. How then is it, that we proceed in the course of our endeavour, to procure its introduction into the mind? If we have not the idea itself, we have certain ideas connected with it. We run over those ideas, one after another, in hopes that some one of them will suggest the idea we are in quest of; and if any one of them does, it is always one so connected with it, as to call it up in the way of association. I meet an old acquaintance, whose name I do not remember, and wish to recollect. I run over a number of names, in hopes that some of them may be associated with the idea of the individual. I think of all the circumstances in which I have seen him engaged; the time when I knew him, the persons along with whom I knew him, the things he did, or the things he suffered; and, if I chance upon any idea with which the name is associated, then immediately I have the recollection; if not, my pursuit of it is in vain. There is another set of cases, very familiar, but affording very important evidence on the subject. It frequently happens, that there are matters which we desire not to forget. What is the contrivance to which we have recourse for preserving the memory; that is, for making sure that it will be called into existence, when it is our wish that it should. All men, invariably employ the same expedient. They endeavour to form an association between the idea of the thing to be remembered, and some sensation, or some idea, which they know beforehand will occur at or near the time when they wish the remembrance to be in their minds. If this association is formed, and the sensation or the idea, with which it has been formed, occurs; the sensation, or idea, calls up the remembrance; and the object of him who formed the association is attained. To use a vulgar instance: a man receives a commission from his friend, and, that he may not forget it, ties a knot on his handkerchief. How is this fact to be explained? First of all, the idea of the commission is associated with the making of the knot. Next, the handker-

chief is a thing which it is known beforehand will be frequently seen, and of course at no great distance of time from
the occasion on which the memory is desired. The handkerchief being seen, the knot is seen, and this sensation recalls
the idea of the commission, between which and itself, the association had been purposely formed."

In short, we make search in our memory for a forgotten
idea, just as we rummage our house for a lost object. In both
cases we visit what seems to us the probable *neighborhood* of
that which we miss. We turn over the things under which, or
within which, or alongside of which, it may possibly be; and
if it lies near them, it soon comes to view. But these matters,
in the case of a mental object sought, are nothing but its *associates*. The machinery of recall is thus the same as the machinery of association, and the machinery of association, as we
know, is nothing but the elementary law of habit in the nerve-
centres.

It also explains retention. And this same law of habit is
the machinery of retention also. Retention means *liability* to
recall, and it means nothing more than such liability. The only
proof of there being retention is that recall actually takes
place. The retention of an experience is, in short, but another
name for the *possibility* of thinking it again, or the *tendency* to
think it again, with its past surroundings. Whatever accidental
cue may turn this tendency into an actuality, the permanent
ground of the tendency itself lies in the organized neural paths
by which the cue calls up the memorable experience, the past
associates, the sense that the self was there, the belief that it
all really happened, etc., as previously described. When the
recollection is of the 'ready' sort, the resuscitation takes place
the instant the cue arises; when it is slow, resuscitation comes
after delay. But be the recall prompt or slow, the condition
which makes it possible at all (or, in other words, the 'retention' of the experience) is neither more nor less than the
brain-paths which *associate* the experience with the occasion
and cue of the recall. *When slumbering, these paths are the condition of retention; when active, they are the condition of recall.*

Brain-scheme.—A simple scheme will now make the
whole cause of memory plain. Let *n* be a past event, *o* its 'setting' (concomitants, date, self present, warmth and intimacy,

etc., etc., as already set forth), and *m* some present thought or fact which may appropriately become the occasion of its recall. Let the nerve-centres, active in the thought of *m*, *n*, and *o*, be represented by *M*, *N*, and *O*, respectively; then the *existence* of the *paths* symbolized by the lines between *M* and *N* and *N* and *O* will be the fact indicated by the phrase 'retention of the event *n* in the memory,' and the *excitement* of the brain along these paths will be the condition of the event *n*'s actual recall. The *retention* of *n*, it will be observed, is no mysterious storing up of an 'idea' in an unconscious state. It is not a fact of the mental order at all. It is a purely physical phenomenon, a morphological feature, the presence of these 'paths,' namely, in the finest recesses of the brain's tissue. The recall or recollection, on the other hand, is a *psycho-physical* phenomenon, with both a bodily and a mental side. The bodily side is the excitement of the paths in question; the mental side is the conscious representation of the past occurrence, and the belief that we experienced it before.

The only hypothesis, in short, to which the facts of inward experience give countenance is that *the brain-tracts excited by the event proper, and those excited in its recall, are in part* DIF-FERENT *from each other.* If we could revive the past event without any associates we should exclude the possibility of memory, and simply dream that we were undergoing the experience as if for the first time. Wherever, in fact, the recalled event does appear without a definite setting, it is hard to distinguish it from a mere creation of fancy. But in proportion as its image lingers and recalls associates which gradually become more definite, it grows more and more distinctly into a

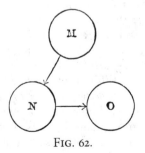

FIG. 62.

remembered thing. For example, I enter a friend's room and see on the wall a painting. At first I have the strange, wondering consciousness, 'Surely I have seen that before,' but when or how does not become clear. There only clings to the picture a sort of penumbra of familiarity,—when suddenly I exclaim: "I have it! It is a copy of part of one of the Fra Angelicos in the Florentine Academy—I recollect it there." Only when the image of the Academy arises does the picture become remembered, as well as seen.

The Conditions of Goodness in Memory.—The remembered fact being *n*, then, the path N—O is what arouses for *n* its setting when it *is* recalled, and makes it other than a mere imagination. The path M—N, on the other hand, gives the cue or occasion of its being recalled at all. *Memory being thus altogether conditioned on brain-paths, its excellence in a given individual will depend partly on the* NUMBER *and partly on the* PERSISTENCE *of these paths.*

The persistence or permanence of the paths is a physiological property of the brain-tissue of the individual, whilst their number is altogether due to the facts of his mental experience. Let the quality of permanence in the paths be called the native tenacity, or physiological retentiveness. This tenacity differs enormously from infancy to old age, and from one person to another. Some minds are like wax under a seal—no impression, however disconnected with others, is wiped out. Others, like a jelly, vibrate to every touch, but under usual conditions retain no permanent mark. These latter minds, before they can recollect a fact, must weave it into their permanent stores of knowledge. They have no *desultory* memory. Those persons, on the contrary, who retain names, dates and addresses, anecdotes, gossip, poetry, quotations, and all sorts of miscellaneous facts, without an effort, have desultory memory in a high degree, and certainly owe it to the unusual tenacity of their brain-substance for any path once formed therein. No one probably was ever effective on a voluminous scale without a high degree of this physiological retentiveness. In the practical as in the theoretic life, the man whose acquisitions *stick* is the man who is always achieving and advancing, whilst his neighbors, spending most of their time in relearning what they once knew but have forgotten, simply hold their own. A

Charlemagne, a Luther, a Leibnitz, a Walter Scott, any example, in short, of your quarto or folio editions of mankind, must needs have amazing retentiveness of the purely physiological sort. Men without this retentiveness may excel in the *quality* of their work at this point or at that, but will never do such mighty sums of it, or be influential contemporaneously on such a scale.

But there comes a time of life for all of us when we can do no more than hold our own in the way of acquisitions, when the old paths fade as fast as the new ones form in our brain, and when we forget in a week quite as much as we can learn in the same space of time. This equilibrium may last many, many years. In extreme old age it is upset in the reverse direction, and forgetting prevails over acquisition, or rather there is no acquisition. Brain-paths are so transient that in the course of a few minutes of conversation the same question is asked and its answer forgotten half a dozen times. Then the superior tenacity of the paths formed in childhood becomes manifest: the dotard will retrace the facts of his earlier years after he has lost all those of later date.

So much for the permanence of the paths. Now for their number.

It is obvious that the more there are of such paths as M—N in the brain, and the more of such possible cues or occasions for the recall of *n* in the mind, the prompter and surer, on the whole, the memory of *n* will be, the more frequently one will be reminded of it, the more avenues of approach to it one will possess. In mental terms, *the more other facts a fact is associated with in the mind, the better possession of it our memory retains*. Each of its associates becomes a hook to which it hangs, a means to fish it up by when sunk beneath the surface. Together, they form a network of attachments by which it is woven into the entire tissue of our thought. The 'secret of a good memory' is thus the secret of forming diverse and multiple associations with every fact we care to retain. But this forming of associations with a fact, what is it but *thinking about* the fact as much as possible? Briefly, then, of two men with the same outward experiences and the same amount of mere native tenacity, *the one who* THINKS *over his experiences most, and weaves them into systematic relations with each other, will be the one with the best memory.* We see examples of this on every hand. Most men have a good memory for facts connected with their own pursuits. The college athlete who remains a dunce at his books will astonish you by his knowledge of men's 'records' in various feats and games, and will be a walking dictionary of sporting statistics. The reason is that he is constantly going over these things in his mind, and comparing and making series of them. They form for him not so many odd facts, but a concept-system—so they stick. So the merchant remembers prices, the politician other politicians' speeches and votes, with a copiousness which amazes outsiders, but which the amount of thinking they bestow on these subjects easily explains. The great memory for facts which a Darwin and a Spencer reveal in their books is not incompatible with the possession on their part of a brain with only a middling degree of physiological retentiveness. Let a man early in life set himself the task of verifying such a theory as that of evolution, and facts will soon cluster and cling to him like grapes to their stem. Their relations to the theory will hold them fast; and the more of these the mind is able to discern, the greater the erudition will become. Meanwhile the theorist may have little, if any, desultory memory. Unutilizable facts may be unnoted by him and forgotten as soon as heard. An ignorance almost as encyclopædic as his erudition may coexist with the latter, and hide, as it were, in the interstices of its web. Those who have had much to do with scholars and *savants* will readily think of examples of the class of mind I mean.

In a system, every fact is connected with every other by some thought-relation. The consequence is that every fact is retained by the combined suggestive power of all the other facts in the system, and forgetfulness is well-nigh impossible.

The reason why cramming is such a bad mode of study is now made clear. I mean by cramming that way of preparing for examinations by committing 'points' to memory during a few hours or days of intense application immediately preceding the final ordeal, little or no work having been performed during the previous course of the term. Things learned thus in a few hours, on one occasion, for one purpose, cannot possibly have formed many associations with other things in the mind. Their brain-processes are led into by few paths, and are relatively little liable to be awakened again. Speedy oblivion is the almost inevitable fate of all that is committed to memory in this simple way. Whereas, on the contrary, the same materials taken in gradually, day after day, recurring in different contexts, considered in various relations, associated with other external incidents, and repeatedly reflected on, grow into such a system, form such connections with the rest of the mind's fabric, lie open to so many paths of approach, that they remain permanent possessions. This is the *intellectual* reason why habits of continuous application should be enforced in educational establishments. Of course there is no moral turpitude in cramming. Did it lead to the desired end of secure learning, it were infinitely the best method of study. But it does not; and students themselves should understand the reason why.

One's native retentiveness is unchangeable. It will now appear clear that *all improvement of the memory lies in the line of* ELABORATING THE ASSOCIATES of each of the several things to be remembered. *No amount of culture would seem capable of modifying a man's* GENERAL *retentiveness*. This is a physiological quality, given once for all with his organization, and which he can never hope to change. It differs no doubt in disease and health; and it is a fact of observation that it is better in fresh and vigorous hours than when we are fagged or ill. We may say, then, that a man's native tenacity will fluctuate somewhat with his hygiene, and that whatever is good for his tone of health will also be good for his memory. We may even say that whatever amount of intellectual exercise is bracing to the general tone and nutrition of the brain will also be profitable to the general retentiveness. But more than this we cannot say; and this, it is obvious, is far less than most people believe.

It is, in fact, commonly thought that certain exercises, systematically repeated, will strengthen, not only a man's remembrance of the particular facts used in the exercises, but his faculty for remembering facts at large. And a plausible case is always made out by saying that practice in learning words by heart makes it easier to learn new words in the same way. If this be true, then what I have just said is false, and the whole doctrine of memory as due to 'paths' must be revised. But I am disposed to think the alleged fact untrue. I have carefully questioned several mature actors on the point, and all have denied that the practice of learning parts has made any such difference as is alleged. What it has done for them is to improve their power of *studying* a part systematically. Their mind is now full of precedents in the way of intonation, emphasis, gesticulation; the new words awaken distinct suggestions and decisions; are caught up, in fact, into a preëxisting network, like the merchant's prices, or the athlete's store of 'records,' and are recollected easier, although the mere native tenacity is not a whit improved, and is usually, in fact, impaired by age. It is a case of better remembering by better *thinking*. Similarly when schoolboys improve by practice in ease of learning by heart, the improvement will, I am sure, be always found to reside in the *mode of study of the particular piece* (due to the greater interest, the greater suggestiveness, the generic similarity with other pieces, the more sustained attention, etc., etc.), and not at all to any enhancement of the brute retentive power.

The error I speak of pervades an otherwise useful and judicious book, *How to Strengthen the Memory*, by Dr. M. L. Holbrook of New York. The author fails to distinguish between the general physiological retentiveness and the retention of particular things, and talks as if both must be benefited by the same means.

"I am now treating," he says, "a case of loss of memory in a person advanced in years, who did not know that his memory had failed most remarkably till I told him of it. He is making vigorous effort to bring it back again, and with partial success. The method pursued is to spend two hours daily, one in the morning and one in the evening, in exercising this faculty. The patient is instructed to give the closest attention to all that he learns, so that it shall be impressed on his mind clearly. He is asked to recall every evening all the facts and experiences of the day, and again the next morning. Every name heard is written down and impressed on his mind clearly, and an effort made to recall it at intervals. Ten names from among public men are ordered to be committed to memory every week. A verse of poetry is to be learned, also a verse from the Bible, daily. He is asked to remember the number of the page in any book where any interesting fact is recorded. These and other methods are slowly resuscitating a failing memory."

I find it very hard to believe that the memory of the poor old gentleman is a bit the better for all this torture except in respect of the particular facts thus wrought into it, and other matters that may have been connected therewithal.

Improving the Memory.—All improvement of memory consists, then, in the improvement of one's *habitual methods of recording facts*. Methods have been divided into the mechanical, the ingenious, and the judicious.

The *mechanical methods* consist in the intensification, prolongation, and *repetition* of the impression to be remembered. The modern method of teaching children to read by blackboard work, in which each word is impressed by the fourfold channel of eye, ear, voice, and hand, is an example of an improved mechanical method of memorizing.

Judicious methods of remembering things are nothing but logical ways of conceiving them and working them into rational systems, classifying them, analyzing them into parts, etc., etc. All the sciences are such methods.

Of *ingenious methods* many have been invented, under the name of technical memories. By means of these systems it is often possible to retain entirely disconnected facts, lists of names, numbers, and so forth, so multitudinous as to be entirely unrememberable in a natural way. The method consists usually in a framework learned mechanically, of which the mind is supposed to remain in secure and permanent possession. Then, whatever is to be remembered is deliberately associated by some fanciful analogy or connection with some part of this framework, and this connection thenceforward helps its recall. The best known and most used of these devices is the figure-alphabet. To remember numbers, e.g., a figure-alphabet is first formed, in which each numerical digit is represented by one or more letters. The number is then translated into such letters as will best make a word, if possible a word suggestive of the object to which the number belongs. The word will then be remembered when the numbers alone might be forgotten.[1] The recent system of Loisette is a method, much less mechanical, of weaving the thing into associations which may aid its recall.

Recognition.—If, however, a phenomenon be met with too often, and with too great a variety of contexts, although its image is retained and reproduced with correspondingly great facility, it fails to come up with any one particular setting, and the projection of it backwards to a particular past date consequently does not come about. We *recognize* but do not *remember* it—its associates form too confused a cloud. A similar result comes about when a definite setting is only nascently aroused. We then feel that we have seen the object already, but when or where we cannot say, though we may seem to ourselves to be on the brink of saying it. That nascent cerebral excitations can thus affect consciousness is obvious from what happens when we seek to remember a name. It tingles, it trembles on the verge, but does not come. Just such a tingling and trembling of unrecovered associates is the penumbra of recognition that may surround any experience and make it seem familiar, though we know not why.

There is a curious experience which everyone seems to have had—the feeling that the present moment in its completeness has been experienced before—we were saying just this thing, in just this place, to just these people, etc. This 'sense of preëxistence' has been treated as a great mystery and occasioned much speculation. Dr. Wigan considered it due to a dissociation of the action of the two hemispheres, one of them becoming conscious a little later than the other, but both of the same fact. I must confess that the quality of mystery seems to me here a little strained. I have over and over again in my own case succeeded in resolving the phenomenon into a case of memory, so indistinct that whilst some past circumstances are presented again, the others are not. The dissimilar por-

---

[1] A common figure-alphabet is this:

1	2	3	4	5	6	7	8	9	0
t	n	m	r	l	sh	g	f	b	s
d					j	k	v	p	c
					ch	c			z
					g	qu			

tions of the past do not arise completely enough at first for the date to be identified. All we get is the present scene with a general suggestion of pastness about it. That faithful observer, Prof. Lazarus, interprets the phenomenon in the same way; and it is noteworthy that just as soon as the past context grows complete and distinct the emotion of weirdness fades from the experience.

Forgetting.—In the practical use of our intellect, forgetting is as important a function as remembering. 'Total recall' (see p. 249) we saw to be comparatively rare in association. If we remembered everything, we should on most occasions be as ill off as if we remembered nothing. It would take as long for us to recall a space of time as it took the original time to elapse, and we should never get ahead with our thinking. All recollected times undergo, accordingly, what M. Ribot calls foreshortening; and this foreshortening is due to the omission of an enormous number of the facts which filled them. "We thus reach the paradoxical result," says M. Ribot, "that one condition of remembering is that we should forget. Without totally forgetting a prodigious number of states of consciousness, and momentarily forgetting a large number, we could not remember at all. Oblivion, except in certain cases, is thus no malady of memory, but a condition of its health and its life."

Pathological Conditions.—Hypnotic subjects as a rule forget all that has happened in their trance. But in a succeeding trance they will often remember the events of a past one. This is like what happens in those cases of 'double personality' in which no recollection of one of the lives is to be found in the other. The sensibility in these cases often differs from one of the alternate personalities to another, the patient being often anæsthetic in certain respects in one of the secondary states. Now the memory may come and go with the sensibility. M. Pierre Janet proved in various ways that what his patients forgot when anæsthetic they remembered when the sensibility returned. For instance, he restored their tactile sense temporarily by means of electric currents, passes, etc., and then made them handle various objects, such as keys and pencils, or make particular movements, like the sign of the cross. The moment the anæsthesia returned they found it impossible to recollect the objects or the acts. "They had had nothing in their hands, they had done nothing," etc. The next day, however, sensibility being again restored by similar processes, they remembered perfectly the circumstance, and told what they had handled or done.

All these pathological facts are showing us that the sphere of possible recollection may be wider than we think, and that in certain matters apparent oblivion is no proof against possible recall under other conditions. They give no countenance, however, to the extravagant opinion that absolutely no part of our experience can be forgotten.

CHAPTER XIX

IMAGINATION

What it is.—*Sensations, once experienced, modify the nervous organism, so that copies of them arise again in the mind after the original outward stimulus is gone.* No mental copy, however, can arise in the mind, of any kind of sensation which has never been directly excited from without.

The blind may dream of sights, the deaf of sounds, for years after they have lost their vision or hearing; but the man *born* deaf can never be made to imagine what sound is like, nor can the man *born* blind ever have a mental vision. In Locke's words, already quoted, "the mind can frame unto itself no one new simple idea." The originals of them all must have been given from without. Fantasy, or Imagination, are the names given to the faculty of reproducing copies of originals once felt. The imagination is called 'reproductive' when the copies are literal; 'productive' when elements from different originals are recombined so as to make new wholes.

When represented with surroundings concrete enough to constitute a *date*, these pictures, when they revive, form *recollections*. We have just studied the machinery of recollection. When the mental pictures are of data freely combined, and reproducing no past combination exactly, we have acts of imagination properly so called.

Men differ in visual imagination. Our ideas or images of past sensible experiences may be either distinct and adequate or dim, blurred, and incomplete. It is likely that the different degrees in which different men are able to make them sharp and complete has had something to do with keeping up such philosophic disputes as that of Berkeley with Locke over abstract ideas. Locke had spoken of our possessing 'the general idea of a triangle' which "must be neither oblique, nor rectangle, neither equilateral, equicrural, nor scalenon; but all and none of these at once." Berkeley says: "If any man has the faculty of framing in his mind such an idea of a triangle as is here described, it is in vain to pretend to dispute him out of it, nor would I go about it. All I desire is that the reader

286

would fully and certainly inform himself whether *he* has such an idea or no."

Until very recent years it was supposed by philosophers that there was a typical human mind which all individual minds were like, and that propositions of universal validity could be laid down about such faculties as 'the Imagination.' Lately, however, a mass of revelations have poured in which make us see how false a view this is. There are imaginations, not 'the Imagination,' and they must be studied in detail.

Mr. Galton in 1880 began a statistical inquiry which may be said to have made an era in descriptive psychology. He addressed a circular to large numbers of persons asking them to describe the image in their mind's eye of their breakfast-table on a given morning. The variations were found to be enormous; and, strange to say, it appeared that eminent scientific men on the average had less visualizing power than younger and more insignificant persons.

The reader will find details in Mr. Galton's *Inquiries into Human Faculty*, pp. 83–114. I have myself for many years collected from each and all of my psychology-students descriptions of their own visual imagination; and found (together with some curious idiosyncrasies) corroboration of all the variations which Mr. Galton reports. As examples, I subjoin extracts from two cases near the ends of the scale. The writers are first cousins, grandsons of a distinguished man of science. The one who is a good visualizer says:

"This morning's breakfast-table is both dim and bright; it is dim if I try to think of it when my eyes are open upon any object; it is perfectly clear and bright if I think of it with my eyes closed.—All the objects are clear at once, yet when I confine my attention to any one object it becomes far more distinct.—I have more power to recall color than any other one thing: if, for example, I were to recall a plate decorated with flowers I could reproduce in a drawing the exact tone, etc. The color of anything that was on the table is perfectly vivid.—There is very little limitation to the extent of my images: I can see all four sides of a room, I can see all four sides of two, three, four, even more rooms with such distinctness that if you should ask me what was in any particular place in any one, or ask me to count the chairs, etc., I could do it without the least hesitation.—The more I learn by heart the more clearly do I see images of my pages. Even before I can recite the lines I see them so that I could give them very slowly word for word, but my mind is so occupied in looking at my printed image that I have no idea of what I am saying, of the sense of it, etc. When I first found myself doing this I used to think it was merely because I knew the lines imperfectly; but I have quite convinced myself that I really do see an image. The strongest proof that such is really the fact is, I think, the following:

"I can look down the mentally seen page and see the words that *commence* all the lines, and from any one of these words I can continue the line. I find this much easier to do if the words begin in a straight line than if there are breaks. Example:

> *Étant fait* . . . . .
> *Tous* . . . . .
> *A des* . . . . .
> *Que fit* . . . . .
> *Céres* . . . . .
>   *Avec* . . . . .
> *Un fleuve* . . . . .
>   *Comme* . . . . .
> (La Fontaine 8, iv.)"

The poor visualizer says:

"My ability to form mental images seems, from what I have studied of other people's images, to be defective and somewhat peculiar. The process by which I seem to remember any particular event is not by a series of distinct images, but a sort of panorama, the faintest impressions of which are perceptible through a thick fog.—I cannot shut my eyes and get a distinct image of anyone, although I used to be able to a few years ago, and the faculty seems to have gradually slipped away.—In my most vivid dreams, where the events appear like the most real facts, I am often troubled with a dimness of sight which causes the images to appear indistinct.—To come to the question of the breakfast-table, there is nothing definite about it. Everything is vague. I cannot say *what* I see. I could not possibly count the chairs, but I happen to know that there are ten. I see nothing in detail.—The chief thing is a general impression that I cannot tell exactly what I do see. The coloring is about the same, as far as I can recall it, only very much washed out. Perhaps the only color I can see at all distinctly is that of the table-cloth, and I could probably see the color of the wall-paper if I could remember what color it was."

A person whose visual imagination is strong finds it hard to understand how those who are without the faculty can think at all. *Some people undoubtedly have no visual images at all worthy of the name*, and instead of *seeing* their breakfast-table, they tell you that they *remember* it or *know* what was on it. The 'mind-stuff' of which this 'knowing' is made seems to be verbal images exclusively. But if the words 'coffee,' 'bacon,' 'muffins,' and 'eggs' lead a man to speak to his cook, to pay his bills, and to take measures for the morrow's meal exactly as visual and gustatory memories would, why are they not, for all practical intents and purposes, as good a kind of material in which to think? In fact, we may suspect them to be for most purposes better than terms with a richer imaginative coloring. The scheme of relationship and the conclusion being the essential things in thinking, that kind of mind-stuff which is handiest will be the best for the purpose. Now words, uttered or unexpressed, are the handiest mental elements we have. Not only are they very *rapidly* revivable, but they are revivable as actual sensations more easily than any other items of our experience. Did they not possess some such advantage as this, it would hardly be the case that the older men are and the more effective as thinkers, the more, as a rule, they have lost their visualizing power, as Mr. Galton found to be the case with members of the Royal Society.

Images of Sounds.—These also differ in individuals. Those who think by preference in auditory images are called *audiles* by Mr. Galton. *This type*, says M. Binet, "*appears to be rarer than the visual.* Persons of this type imagine what they think of in the language of sound. In order to remember a lesson they impress upon their mind, not the look of the page, but the sound of the words. They reason, as well as remember, by ear. In performing a mental addition they repeat verbally the names of the figures, and add, as it were, the sounds, without any thought of the graphic signs. Imagination also takes the auditory form. 'When I write a scene,' said Legouvé to Scribe, 'I *hear*; but you *see*. In each phrase which I write, the voice of the personage who speaks strikes my ear. *Vous, qui êtes le théâtre même*, your actors walk, gesticulate before your eyes; I am a *listener*, you a *spectator*.'—'Nothing more true,' said Scribe; 'do you know where I am when I write a piece? In the middle of the parterre.' It is clear that the *pure audile*, seeking to develop only a single one of his faculties, may, like the pure visualizer, perform astounding feats of memory—Mozart, for example, noting from memory the *Miserere* of the Sistine Chapel after two hearings; the deaf Beethoven, composing and inwardly repeating his enormous symphonies. On the other hand, the man of auditory type, like the visual, is exposed to serious dangers; for if he lose his auditory images, he is without resource and breaks down completely."

Images of Muscular Sensations.—Professor Stricker of Vienna, who seems to be a 'motile' or to have this form of imagination developed in unusual strength, has given a careful analysis of his own case. His recollections both of his own movements and of those of other things are accompanied invariably by distinct muscular feelings in those parts of his body which would naturally be used in effecting or in following the movement. In thinking of a soldier marching, for example, it is as if he were helping the image to march by marching himself in his rear. And if he suppresses this sympathetic feeling in his own legs and concentrates all his attention on the imagined soldier, the latter becomes, as it were, paralyzed. In general his imagined movements, of whatsoever objects, seem paralyzed, the moment no feelings of movement either in his own eyes or in his own limbs accompany them. The movements of articulate speech play a predominant part in his mental life. "When after my experimental work," he says, "I proceed to its description, as a rule I reproduce in the first instance only words which I had already associated with the perception of the various details of the observation whilst the latter was going on. For speech plays in all my observing so important a part that I ordinarily clothe phenomena in words as fast as I observe them."

Most persons, on being asked *in what sort of terms they imagine words*, will say, 'In terms of hearing.' It is not until their attention is expressly drawn to the point that they find it difficult to say whether auditory images or motor images connected with the organs of articulation predominate. A good way of bringing the difficulty to consciousness is that proposed by Stricker: Partly open your mouth and then imagine any word with labials or dentals in it, such as 'bubble,' 'toddle.' Is your image under these conditions distinct? To most people the image is at first 'thick,' as the sound of the word would be if they tried to pronounce it with the lips parted. Many can never imagine the words clearly with the mouth open; others succeed after a few preliminary trials. The experiment proves how dependent our verbal imagination is on actual feelings in lips, tongue, throat, larynx, etc. Prof. Bain says that "a *suppressed articulation is in fact the material of our recollection*, the intellectual manifestation, the *idea* of speech." In persons whose auditory imagination is weak, the articulatory image does indeed seem to constitute the whole material for verbal thought. Professor Stricker says that in his own case no auditory image enters into the words of which he thinks.

Images of Touch.—These are very strong in some people. The most vivid touch-images come when we ourselves barely escape local injury, or when we see another injured. The place may then actually tingle with the imaginary sensation—perhaps not altogether imaginary, since goose-flesh, paling or reddening, and other evidences of actual muscular contraction in the spot, may result.

"An educated man," says Herr G. H. Meyer, "told me once that on entering his house one day he received a shock from crushing the finger of one of his little children in the door. At the moment of his fright he felt a violent pain in the corresponding finger of his own body, and this pain abode with him three days."

The imagination of a blind deaf-mute like Laura Bridgman must be confined entirely to tactile and motor material. *All blind persons must belong to the 'tactile' and 'motile' types* of the French authors. When the young man whose cataracts were removed by Dr. Franz was shown different geometric figures, he said he "had not been able to form from them the idea of a square and a disc, until he perceived a sensation of what he saw in the points of his fingers, as if he really touched the objects."

Pathological Differences.—The study of Aphasia (see p. 118) has of late years shown how unexpectedly individuals differ in the use of their imagination. In some the habitual 'thought-stuff,' if one may so call it, is visual; in others it is auditory, articulatory, or motor; in most, perhaps, it is evenly mixed. These are the "indifferents" of Charcot. The same local cerebral injury must needs work different practical results in persons who differ in this way. In one what is thrown out of gear is a much-used brain-tract; in the other an unimportant region is affected. A particularly instructive case was published by Charcot in 1883. The patient was a merchant, an exceedingly accomplished man, but a visualizer of the most exclusive type. Owing to some intra-cerebral accident he suddenly lost all his visual images, and with them much of his intellectual power, without any other perversion of faculty. He soon discovered that he could carry on his affairs by using his memory in an altogether new way, and described clearly the difference between his two conditions. "Every time he returns to A., from which place business often calls him, he seems to himself as if entering a strange city. He views the monuments, houses, and streets with the same surprise as if he saw them for the first time. When asked to describe the principal public place of the town, he answered, 'I know that it is there, but it is impossible to imagine it, and I can tell you nothing about it.'

"He can no more remember his wife's and children's faces than he can remember A. Even after being with them some time they seem unusual to him. He forgets his own face, and once spoke to his image in a mirror, taking it for a stranger. He complains of his loss of feeling for colors. 'My wife has black hair, this I know; but I can no more recall its color than I can her person and features.' This visual amnesia extends to objects dating from his childhood's years—paternal mansion, etc., forgotten. No other disturbances but this loss of visual images. Now when he seeks something in his correspondence, he must rummage among the letters like other men, until he meets the passage. He can recall only the first few verses of the *Iliad*, and must *grope* to recite Homer, Virgil, and Horace. Figures which he adds he must now whisper to himself. He realizes clearly that he must help his memory out with auditory images, which he does with effort. *The words and expressions which he recalls seem now to echo in his ear, an altogether novel sensation for him.* If he wishes to learn by heart anything, a series of phrases for example, he must *read them several times aloud,* so as to impress his ear. When later he repeats the thing in question, the sensation of inward hearing which precedes articulation rises up in his mind. This feeling was formerly unknown to him."

Such a man would have suffered relatively little inconvenience if his images for hearing had been those suddenly destroyed.

The Neural Process in Imagination.—Most medical writers assume that the cerebral activity on which imagination depends occupies a different *seat* from that subserving sensation. It is, however, a simpler interpretation of the facts to suppose that *the same nerve-tracts are concerned in the two processes.* Our mental images are aroused always by way of association; some previous idea or sensation must have 'suggested' them. Association is surely due to currents from one cortical centre to another. Now all we need suppose is that these intra-cortical currents are unable to produce in the cells the strong explosions which currents from the sense-organs occasion, to account for the subjective difference between images and sensations, without supposing any difference in their local seat. To the strong degree of explosion corresponds the character of 'vividness' or sensible presence, in the object of thought; to the weak degree, that of 'faintness' or outward unreality.

If we admit that sensation and imagination are due to the activity of the same parts of the cortex, we can see a very good teleological reason why they should correspond to discrete kinds of process in these centres, and why the process which gives the sense that the object is really there ought normally to be arousable only by currents entering from the periphery and not by currents from the neighboring cortical parts. We can see, in short, why *the sensational process* OUGHT

TO *be discontinuous with all normal ideational processes, however intense*. For, as Dr. Münsterberg justly observes, "Were there not this peculiar arrangement we should not distinguish reality and fantasy, our conduct would not be accommodated to the facts about us, but would be inappropriate and senseless, and we could not keep ourselves alive."

Sometimes, by exception, the deeper sort of explosion may take place from intra-cortical excitement alone. In the sense of hearing, sensation and imagination *are* hard to discriminate where the sensation is so weak as to be just perceptible. At night, hearing a very faint striking of the hour by a far-off clock, our imagination reproduces both rhythm and sound, and it is often difficult to tell which was the last real stroke. So of a baby crying in a distant part of the house, we are uncertain whether we still hear it, or only imagine the sound. Certain violin-players take advantage of this in diminuendo terminations. After the pianissimo has been reached they continue to bow as if still playing, but are careful not to touch the strings. The listener hears in imagination a degree of sound fainter than the pianissimo. *Hallucinations*, whether of sight or hearing, are another case in point, to be touched on in the next chapter. I may mention as a fact still unexplained that several observers (Herr G. H. Meyer, M. Charles Féré, Professor Scott of Ann Arbor, and Mr. T. C. Smith, one of my students) have noticed negative after-images of objects which they had been imagining with the mind's eye. It is as if the retina itself were locally fatigued by the act.

CHAPTER XX

PERCEPTION

Perception and Sensation compared.—A pure sensation we saw above, p. 20, to be an abstraction never realized in adult life. Anything which affects our sense-organs does also more than that: it arouses processes in the hemispheres which are partly due to the organization of that organ by past experiences, and the results of which in consciousness are described as ideas which the sensation suggests. The first of these ideas is that of the *thing* to which the sensible quality belongs. *The consciousness of particular material things present to sense* is nowadays called *perception*. The consciousness of such things may be more or less complete; it may be of the mere name of the thing and its other essential attributes, or it may be of the thing's various remoter relations. It is impossible to draw any sharp line of distinction between the barer and the richer consciousness, because the moment we get beyond the first crude sensation all our consciousness is of what is *suggested*, and the various suggestions shade gradually into each other, being one and all products of the same psychological machinery of association. In the directer consciousness fewer, in the remoter more, associative processes are brought into play.

Sensational and reproductive brain-processes combined, then, are what give us the content of our perceptions. Every concrete particular material thing is a conflux of sensible qualities, with which we have become acquainted at various times. Some of these qualities, since they are more constant, interesting, or practically important, we regard as essential constituents of the thing. In a general way, such are the tangible shape, size, mass, etc. Other properties, being more fluctuating, we regard as more or less accidental or inessential. We call the former qualities the reality, the latter its appearances. Thus, I hear a sound, and say 'a horse-car'; but the sound is not the horse-car, it is one of the horse-car's least important manifestations. The real horse-car is a feelable, or at most a feelable and visible, thing which in my imagination the sound calls up. So when I get, as now, a brown eye-picture with lines not parallel, and with angles unlike, and call it my big solid rectangular walnut library-table, that picture is not the table. It is not even like the table as the table is for vision, when rightly seen. It is a distorted perspective view of three of the sides of what I mentally *perceive* (more or less) in its totality and undistorted shape. The back of the table, its square corners, its size, its heaviness, are features of which I am conscious when I look, almost as I am conscious of its name. The suggestion of the name is of course due to mere custom. But no less is that of the back, the size, weight, squareness, etc.

Nature, as Reid says, is frugal in her operations, and will not be at the expense of a particular instinct to give us that knowledge which experience and habit will soon produce. Reproduced attributes tied together with presently felt attributes in the unity of a *thing* with a name, these are the materials out of which my actually perceived table is made. Infants must go through a long education of the eye and ear before they can perceive the realities which adults perceive. *Every perception is an acquired perception.*

The Perceptive State of Mind is not a Compound.— There is no reason, however, for supposing that this involves a 'fusion' of separate sensations and ideas. The thing perceived is the object of a unique state of thought; due no doubt in part to sensational, and in part to ideational currents, but in no wise 'containing' psychically the identical 'sensations' and images which these currents would severally have aroused if the others were not simultaneously there. We can often directly notice a sensible difference in the consciousness, between the latter case and the former. The sensible quality changes under our very eye. Take the already-quoted catch, *Pas de lieu Rhône que nous*: one may read this over and over again without recognizing the sounds to be identical with those of the words *paddle your own canoe*. As the English associations arise, the sound itself appears to change. Verbal sounds are usually perceived with their meaning at the moment of being heard. Sometimes, however, the associative irradiations are inhibited for a few moments (the mind being preoccupied with other thoughts) whilst the words linger on the ear as mere echoes of acoustic sensation. Then, usually, their interpretation suddenly occurs. But at that moment one may often surprise a change in the very *feel* of the word. Our own language would sound very different to us if we heard it without understanding, as we hear a foreign tongue. Rises and falls of voice, odd sibilants and other consonants, would fall on our ear in a way of which we can now form no notion. Frenchmen say that English sounds to them like the *gazouille-ment des oiseaux*—an impression which it certainly makes on no native ear. Many of us English would describe the sound of Russian in similar terms. All of us are conscious of the strong inflections of voice and explosives and gutturals of German speech in a way in which no German can be conscious of them.

This is probably the reason why, if we look at an isolated printed word and repeat it long enough, it ends by assuming an entirely unnatural aspect. Let the reader try this with any word on this page. He will soon begin to wonder if it can possibly be the word he has been using all his life with that meaning. It stares at him from the paper like a glass eye, with no speculation in it. Its body is indeed there, but its soul is fled. It is reduced, by this new way of attending to it, to its sensational nudity. We never before attended to it in this way, but habitually got it clad with its meaning the moment we caught sight of it, and rapidly passed from it to the other words of the phrase. We apprehended it, in short, with a cloud of associates, and thus perceiving it, we felt it quite otherwise than as we feel it now divested and alone.

Another well-known change is when we look at a landscape with our head upside-down. Perception is to a certain extent baffled by this manœuvre; gradations of distance and other space-determinations are made uncertain; the reproductive or associative processes, in short, decline; and, simultaneously with their diminution, the colors grow richer and more var-ied, and the contrasts of light and shade more marked. The same thing occurs when we turn a painting bottom-upward. We lose much of its meaning, but, to compensate for the loss, we feel more freshly the value of the mere tints and shadings, and become aware of any lack of purely sensible harmony or balance which they may show. Just so, if we lie on the floor and look up at the mouth of a person talking behind us. His lower lip here takes the habitual place of the upper one upon our retina, and seems animated by the most extraordinary and unnatural mobility, a mobility which now strikes us because (the associative processes being disturbed by the unaccustomed point of view) we get it as a naked sensation and not as part of a familiar object perceived.

Once more, then, we find ourselves driven to admit that when qualities of an object impress our sense and we thereupon perceive the object, the pure sensation as such of those qualities does not still exist inside of the perception and form a constituent thereof. The pure sensation is one thing and the perception another, and neither can take place at the same time with the other, because their cerebral conditions are not the same. They may *resemble* each other, but in no respect are they identical states of mind.

Perception is of Definite and Probable Things.—The chief cerebral conditions of perception are old paths of association radiating from the sense-impression. If a certain impression be strongly associated with the attributes of a certain thing, that thing is almost sure to be perceived when we get the impression. Examples of such things would be familiar people, places, etc., which we recognize and name at a glance. But *where the impression is associated with more than one reality*, so that either of two discrepant sets of residual properties may arise, the perception is doubtful and vacillating, and *the most that can then be said of it is that it will be of a* PROBABLE *thing*, of the thing which would most usually have given us that sensation.

In these ambiguous cases it is interesting to note that perception is rarely abortive; *some* perception takes place. The two discrepant sets of associates do not neutralize each other or mix and make a blur. What we more commonly get is first one object in its completeness, and then the other in its completeness. In other words, *all brain-processes are such as give rise to what we may call* FIGURED *consciousness*. If paths are shot-through at all, they are shot-through in consistent systems, and occasion thoughts of definite objects, not mere hodge-podges of elements. Even where the brain's functions are half thrown out of gear, as in aphasia or dropping asleep, this law of figured consciousness holds good. A person who suddenly

gets sleepy whilst reading aloud will read wrong; but instead
of emitting a mere broth of syllables, he will make such
mistakes as to read 'supper-time' instead of 'sovereign,'
'overthrow' instead of 'opposite,' or indeed utter entirely
imaginary phrases, composed of several definite words, instead of phrases of the book. So in aphasia: where the disease
is mild the patient's mistakes consist in using entire wrong
words instead of right ones. It is only in the gravest lesions
that he becomes quite inarticulate. These facts show how subtle is the associative link; how delicate yet how strong that
connection among brain-paths which makes any number of
them, once excited together, thereafter tend to vibrate as a
systematic whole. A small group of elements, 'this,' common
to two systems, A and B, may touch off A or B according as
accident decides the next step (see Fig. 63). If it happen that a
single point leading from 'this' to B is momentarily a little
more pervious than any leading from 'this' to A, then that
little advantage will upset the equilibrium in favor of the entire system B. The currents will sweep first through that point
and thence into all the paths of B, each increment of advance
making A more and more impossible. The thoughts correlated with A and B, in such a case, will have objects different,
though similar. The similarity will, however, consist in some
very limited feature if the 'this' be small. *Thus the faintest sensations will give rise to the perception of definite things if only they
resemble sensations which the things are wont to arouse.*

Illusions.—Let us now, for brevity's sake, treat A and B in
Fig. 63 as if they stood for objects instead of brain-processes.
And let us furthermore suppose that A and B are, both of

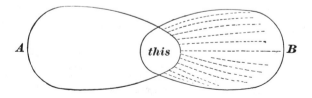

FIG. 63.

them, objects which might probably excite the sensation which I have called '*this*,' but that on the present occasion *A* and not *B* is the one which actually does so. If, then, on this occasion '*this*' suggests *A* and not *B*, the result is a *correct perception*. But if, on the contrary, '*this*' suggests *B* and not *A*, the result is a *false perception*, or, as it is technically called, an *illusion*. But the *process* is the same, whether the perception be true or false.

Note that in every illusion what is false is what is inferred, not what is immediately given. The '*this*,' if it were felt by itself alone, would be all right; it only becomes misleading by what it suggests. If it is a sensation of sight, it may suggest a tactile object, for example, which later tactile experiences prove to be not there. *The so-called 'fallacy of the senses,' of which the ancient sceptics made so much account, is not fallacy of the senses proper, but rather of the intellect, which interprets wrongly what the senses give.*[1]

So much premised, let us look a little closer at these illusions. They are due to two main causes. *The wrong object is perceived either because*

1) *Although not on this occasion the real cause, it is yet the habitual, inveterate, or most probable cause of 'this'*; or because

2) *The mind is temporarily full of the thought of that object, and therefore 'this' is peculiarly prone to suggest it at this moment.*

I will give briefly a number of examples under each head. The first head is the more important, because it includes a number of constant illusions to which all men are subject, and which can only be dispelled by much experience.

Illusions of the First Type.—One of the oldest instances dates from Aristotle. Cross two fingers and roll a pea, penholder, or other small object between them. It will seem double. Professor Croom Robertson has given the clearest analysis of this illusion. He observes that if the object be brought into contact first with the forefinger and next with

---

[1]In *Mind*, IX, 206, M. Binet points out the fact that what is fallaciously inferred is always an object of some other sense than the 'this.' 'Optical illusions' are generally errors of touch and muscular sensibility, and the fallaciously perceived object and the experiences which correct it are both tactile in these cases.

FIG. 64.

the second finger, the two contacts seem to come in at different points of space. The forefinger-touch seems higher,
though the finger is really lower; the second-finger-touch
seems lower, though the finger is really higher. "We perceive
the contacts as double because we refer them to two distinct
parts of space." The touched sides of the two fingers are normally not together in space, and customarily never do touch
one thing; the one thing which now touches them, therefore,
seems in two places, i.e., seems two things.

There is a whole batch of illusions which come from optical
sensations interpreted by us in accordance with our usual rule,
although they are now produced by an unusual object. The
stereoscope is an example. The eyes see a picture apiece, and the
two pictures are a little disparate, the one seen by the right
eye being a view of the object taken from a point slightly to
the right of that from which the left eye's picture is taken.
Pictures thrown on the two eyes by solid objects present this
sort of disparity, so that we react on the sensation in our
usual way, and perceive a solid. If the pictures be exchanged
we perceive a hollow mould of the object, for a hollow mould
would cast just such disparate pictures as these. Wheatstone's
instrument, the *pseudoscope*, allows us to look at solid objects
and see with each eye the other eye's picture. We then perceive the solid object hollow, *if it be an object which might
probably be hollow*, but not otherwise. Thus the perceptive process is true to its law, which is *always to react on the sensation in
a determinate and figured fashion if possible, and in as probable a
fashion as the case admits*. A human face, e.g., never appears
hollow to the pseudoscope, for to couple faces and hollowness violates all our habits. For the same reason it is very

easy to make an intaglio cast of a face, or the painted inside of a pasteboard mask, look convex, instead of concave as they are.

Curious illusions of movement in objects occur whenever the eyeballs move without our intending it. We have learned in an earlier chapter (p. 78) that the original visual feeling of movement is produced by any image passing over the retina. Originally, however, this sensation is definitely referred neither to the object nor to the eyes. Such definite reference grows up later, and obeys certain simple laws. For one thing, we believe *objects* to move whenever we get the retinal movement-feeling, but think our *eyes* are still. This gives rise to an illusion when, after whirling on our heel, we stand still; for then objects appear to continue whirling in the same direction in which, a moment previous, our body actually whirled. The reason is that our *eyes* are animated, under these conditions, by an involuntary *nystagmus* or oscillation in their orbits, which may easily be observed in anyone with vertigo after whirling. As these movements are unconscious, the retinal movement-feelings which they occasion are naturally referred to the objects seen. The whole phenomenon fades out after a few seconds. And it ceases if we voluntarily fix our eyes upon a given point.

There is an illusion of movement of the opposite sort, with which everyone is familiar at *railway stations*. Habitually, when we ourselves move forwards, our entire field of view glides backwards over our retina. When our movement is due to that of the windowed carriage, car, or boat in which we sit, all stationary objects visible through the window give us a sensation of gliding in the opposite direction. Hence, whenever we get this sensation, of a window with *all* objects visible through it moving in one direction, we react upon it in our customary way, and perceive a stationary field of view, over which the window, and we ourselves inside of it, are passing by a motion of our own. Consequently when another train comes alongside of ours in a station, and fills the entire window, and, after standing still awhile, begins to glide away, we judge that it is *our* train which is moving, and that the other train is still. If, however, we catch a glimpse of any part of the station through the windows, or between the cars, of the other train, the illusion of our own movement instantly disappears, and we perceive the other train to be the one in motion. This, again, is but making the usual and probable inference from our sensation.

Another illusion due to movement is explained by Helmholtz. Most wayside objects, houses, trees, etc., look small when seen from the windows of a swift train. This is because we perceive them in the first instance unduly near. And we perceive them unduly near because of their extraordinarily rapid parallactic flight backwards. When we ourselves move forwards all objects glide backwards, as aforesaid; but the nearer they are, the more rapid is this apparent translocation. Relative rapidity of passage backwards is thus so familiarly associated with nearness that when we feel it we perceive nearness. But with a given size of retinal image the nearer an object is, the smaller do we judge its actual size to be. Hence in the train, the faster we go, the nearer do the trees and houses seem; and the nearer they seem, the smaller (with that size of retinal image) must they look.

The feelings of our eyes' convergence, of their accommodation, the size of the retinal image, etc., may give rise to illusions about the size and distance of objects, which also belong to this first type.

Illusions of the Second Type.—In this type we perceive a wrong object because our mind is full of the thought of it at the time, and any sensation which is in the least degree connected with it touches off, as it were, a train already laid, and gives us a sense that the object is really before us. Here is a familiar example:

"If a sportsman while shooting woodcock in cover sees a bird about the size and colour of a woodcock get up and fly through the foliage, not having time to see more than that it is a bird of such a size and colour, he immediately supplies by inference the other qualities of a woodcock, and is afterwards disgusted to find that he has shot a thrush. I have done so myself, and could hardly believe that the thrush was the bird I had fired at, so complete was my mental supplement to my visual perception."[2]

---

[2]Romanes: *Mental Evolution in Animals*, p. 324.

As with game, so with enemies, ghosts, and the like. Any-one waiting in a dark place and expecting or fearing strongly a certain object will interpret any abrupt sensation to mean that object's presence. The boy playing 'I spy,' the criminal skulking from his pursuers, the superstitious person hurrying through the woods or past the churchyard at midnight, the man lost in the woods, the girl who tremulously has made an evening appointment with her swain, all are subject to illu-sions of sight and sound which make their hearts beat till they are dispelled. Twenty times a day the lover, perambulating the streets with his preoccupied fancy, will think he perceives his idol's bonnet before him.

The Proof-reader's Illusion.—I remember one night in Bos-ton, whilst waiting for a 'Mount Auburn' car to bring me to Cambridge, reading most distinctly that name upon the sign-board of a car on which (as I afterwards learned) 'North Ave-nue' was painted. The illusion was so vivid that I could hardly believe my eyes had deceived me. All reading is more or less performed in this way.

"Practised novel- or newspaper-readers could not possibly get on so fast if they had to see accurately every single letter of every word in order to perceive the words. More than half of the words come out of their mind, and hardly half from the printed page. Were this not so, did we perceive each letter by itself, typographic errors in well-known words would never be overlooked. Children, whose ideas are not yet ready enough to perceive words at a glance, read them wrong if they are printed wrong, that is, right according to the way of printing. In a foreign language, although it may be printed with the same letters, we read by so much the more slowly as we do not understand, or are unable promptly to perceive, the words. But we notice misprints all the more readily. For this reason Latin and Greek, and still better Hebrew, works are more correctly printed, because the proofs are better cor-rected, than in German works. Of two friends of mine, one knew much Hebrew, the other little; the latter, however, gave instruction in Hebrew in a gymnasium; and when he called the other to help correct his pupils' exercises, it turned out that he could find out all sorts of little errors better than his friend, because the latter's perception of the words as totals was too swift."[3]

Testimony to personal identity is proverbially fallacious for similar reasons. A man has witnessed a rapid crime or accident, and carries away his mental image. Later he is confronted by a prisoner whom he forthwith perceives in the light of that image, and recognizes or 'identifies' as the criminal, although he may never have been near the spot. Similarly at the so-called 'materializing séances' which fraudulent mediums give: in a dark room a man sees a gauze-robed figure who in a whisper tells him she is the spirit of his sister, mother, wife, or child, and falls upon his neck. The darkness, the previous forms, and the expectancy have so filled his mind with premonitory images that it is no wonder he perceives what is suggested. These fraudulent 'séances' would furnish most precious documents to the psychology of perception, if they could only be satisfactorily inquired into. In the hypnotic trance any suggested object is sensibly perceived. In certain subjects this happens more or less completely after waking from the trance. It would seem that under favorable conditions a somewhat similar susceptibility to suggestion may exist in certain persons who are not otherwise entranced at all.

This suggestibility obtains in all the senses, although high authorities have doubted this power of imagination to falsify present impressions of sense. Everyone must be able to give instances from the smell-sense. When we have paid the faithless plumber for pretending to mend our drains, the intellect inhibits the nose from perceiving the same unaltered odor, until perhaps several days go by. As regards the ventilation or heating of rooms, we are apt to feel for some time as we think we ought to feel. If we believe the ventilator is shut, we feel

---

[3]M. Lazarus: *Das Leben der Seele* (1857), II, p. 32. In the ordinary hearing of speech half the words we seem to hear are supplied out of our own head. A language with which we are familiar is understood even when spoken in low tones and far off. An unfamiliar language is unintelligible under these conditions. The 'ideas' for interpreting the sounds by not being ready-made in our minds, as they are in our familiar mother-tongue, do not start up at so faint a cue.

the room close. On discovering it open, the oppression disappears.

It is the same with touch. Everyone must have felt the sensible quality change under his hand, as sudden contact with something moist or hairy, in the dark, awoke a shock of disgust or fear which faded into calm recognition of some familiar object. Even so small a thing as a crumb of potato on the table-cloth, which we pick up, thinking it a crumb of bread, feels horrible for a few moments to our fancy, and different from what it is.

In the sense of hearing, similar mistakes abound. Everyone must recall some experience in which sounds have altered their character as soon as the intellect referred them to a different source. The other day a friend was sitting in my room, when the clock, which has a rich low chime, began to strike. "Hollo!" said he, "hear that hand-organ in the garden," and was surprised at finding the real source of the sound. I have had myself a striking illusion of the sort. Sitting reading, late one night, I suddenly heard a most formidable noise proceeding from the upper part of the house, which it seemed to fill. It ceased, and in a moment renewed itself. I went into the hall to listen, but it came no more. Resuming my seat in the room, however, there it was again, low, mighty, alarming, like a rising flood or the *avant-courier* of an awful gale. It came from all space. Quite startled, I again went into the hall, but it had already ceased once more. On returning a second time to the room, I discovered that it was nothing but the breathing of a little Scotch terrier which lay asleep on the floor. The noteworthy thing is that as soon as I recognized what it was, I was compelled to think it a different sound, and could not then hear it as I had heard it a moment before.

The sense of sight is pregnant with illusions of both the types considered. No sense gives such fluctuating impressions of the same object as sight does. With no sense are we so apt to treat the sensations immediately given as mere signs; with none is the invocation from memory of a *thing*, and the consequent perception of the latter, so immediate. The 'thing' which we perceive always resembles, as we shall hereafter see, the object of some absent sensation, usually another optical figure which in our mind has come to be a standard bit of reality; and it is this incessant reduction of our immediately given optical objects to more standard and 'real' forms which has led some authors into the mistake of thinking that our optical sensations are originally and natively of no particular form at all.

Of accidental and occasional illusions of sight many amusing examples might be given. One will suffice. It is a reminiscence of my own. I was lying in my berth in a steamer listening to the sailors 'at their devotions with the holystones' outside; when, on turning my eyes to the window, I perceived with perfect distinctness that the chief-engineer of the vessel had entered my state-room, and was standing looking through the window at the men at work upon the guards. Surprised at his intrusion, and also at his intentness and immobility, I remained watching him and wondering how long he would stand thus. At last I spoke; but getting no reply, sat up in my berth, and then saw that what I had taken for the engineer was my own cap and coat hanging on a peg beside the window. The illusion was complete; the engineer was a peculiar-looking man; and I saw him unmistakably; but after the illusion had vanished I found it hard voluntarily to make the cap and coat look like him at all.

'**Apperception.**'—In Germany since Herbart's time psychology has always had a great deal to say about a process called *Apperception*. The incoming ideas or sensations are said to be 'apperceived' by 'masses' of ideas already in the mind. It is plain that the process we have been describing as perception is, at this rate, an apperceptive process. So are all recognition, classing, and naming; and passing beyond these simplest suggestions, all farther thoughts about our percepts are apperceptive processes as well. I have myself not used the word apperception, because it has carried very different meanings in the history of philosophy, and 'psychic reaction,' 'interpretation,' 'conception,' 'assimilation,' 'elaboration,' or simply 'thought,' are perfect synonyms for its Herbartian meaning, widely taken. It is, moreover, hardly worth while to pretend to analyze the so-called apperceptive performances beyond the first or perceptive stage, because their variations and degrees are literally innumerable. 'Apperception' is a name for the sum-total of the effects of what we have studied as association; and it is obvious that the things which a given experience will suggest to a man depend on what Mr. Lewes calls his entire psychostatical conditions, his nature and stock of ideas, or, in other words, his character, habits, memory, education, previous experience, and momentary mood. We gain no insight into what really occurs either in the mind or in the brain by calling all these things the 'apperceiving mass,' though of course this may upon occasion be convenient. On the whole I am inclined to think Mr. Lewes's term of 'assimilation' the most fruitful one yet used.

The 'apperceiving mass' is treated by the Germans as the active factor, the apperceived sensation as the passive one; the sensation being usually modified by the ideas in the mind. Out of the interaction of the two, cognition is produced. But as Steinthal remarks, the apperceiving mass is itself often modified by the sensation. To quote him: "Although the *a priori* moment commonly shows itself to be the more powerful, apperception-processes can perfectly well occur in which the new observation transforms or enriches the apperceiving group of ideas. A child who hitherto has seen none but four-cornered tables apperceives a round one as a table; but by this the apperceiving mass ('table') is enriched. To his previous knowledge of tables comes this new feature that they need not be four-cornered, but may be round. In the history of science it has happened often enough that some discovery, at the same time that it was apperceived, i.e., brought into connection with the system of our knowledge, transformed the whole system. In principle, however, we must maintain that, although either factor is both active and passive, the *a priori* factor is almost always the more active of the two."[4]

Genius and Old-fogyism.—This account of Steinthal's brings out very clearly the *difference between our psychological conceptions and what are called concepts in logic.* In logic a concept is unalterable; but what are popularly called our 'conceptions of things' alter by being used. The aim of 'Science' is to attain conceptions so adequate and exact that we shall never need to change them. There is an everlasting struggle in every mind between the tendency to keep unchanged, and the ten-

[4]*Einleitung in die Psychologie und Sprachwissenschaft* (1881), p. 173.

dency to renovate, its ideas. Our education is a ceaseless compromise between the conservative and the progressive factors.
Every new experience must be disposed of under *some* old
head. The great point is to find the head which has to be least
altered to take it in. Certain Polynesian natives, seeing horses
for the first time, called them pigs, that being the nearest
head. My child of two played for a week with the first orange
that was given him, calling it a 'ball.' He called the first whole
eggs he saw 'potatoes,' having been accustomed to see 'eggs'
already broken in a glass, and potatoes without the skin.
A folding pocket-corkscrew he unhesitatingly called 'bad-
scissors.' Hardly any one of us can make new heads easily
when fresh experiences come. Most of us grow more and
more enslaved to the stock conceptions with which we have
once become familiar, and less and less capable of assimilating
impressions in any but the old ways. Old-fogyism, in short, is
the inevitable terminus to which life sweeps us on. Objects
which violate our established habits of 'apperception' are simply not taken account of at all; or, if on some occasion we are
forced by dint of argument to admit their existence, twenty-
four hours later the admission is as if it were not, and every
trace of the unassimilable truth has vanished from our
thought. Genius, in truth, means little more than the faculty
of perceiving in an unhabitual way.

On the other hand, nothing is more congenial, from babyhood to the end of life, than to be able to assimilate the new
to the old, to meet each threatening violator or burster of our
well-known series of concepts, as it comes in, see through its
unwontedness, and ticket it off as an old friend in disguise.
This victorious assimilation of the new is in fact the type of all
intellectual pleasure. The lust for it is scientific curiosity. The
relation of the new to the old, before the assimilation is performed, is wonder. We feel neither curiosity nor wonder concerning things so far beyond us that we have no concepts to
refer them to or standards by which to measure them.[5] The

[5]The great maxim in pedagogy is to knit every new piece of knowledge on
to a preëxisting curiosity—i.e., to assimilate its matter in some way to what
is already known. Hence the advantage of "comparing all that is far off and
foreign to something that is near home, of making the unknown plain by the
example of the known, and of connecting all the instruction with the personal

Fuegians, in Darwin's voyage, wondered at the small boats, but took the big ship as a 'matter of course.' Only what we partly know already inspires us with a desire to know more. The more elaborate textile fabrics, the vaster works in metal, to most of us are like the air, the water, and the ground, absolute existences which awaken no ideas. It is a matter of course that an engraving or a copper-plate inscription should possess that degree of beauty. But if we are shown a *pen*-drawing of equal perfection, our personal sympathy with the difficulty of the task makes us immediately wonder at the skill. The old lady admiring the Academician's picture says to him: "And is it really all done *by hand*?"

The Physiological Process in Perception.—Enough has now been said to prove the general law of perception, which is this: that *whilst part of what we perceive comes through our senses from the object before us, another part* (and it may be the larger part) *always comes out of our own mind*.

At bottom this is but a case of the general fact that our nerve-centres are organs for reacting on sense-impressions, and that our hemispheres, in particular, are given us that records of our past private experience may coöperate in the reaction. Of course such a general statement is vague. If we try to put an exact meaning into it, what we find most natural to believe is that the *brain reacts* by paths which the previous experiences have worn, *and which make us perceive the probable thing*, i.e., the thing by which on the previous occasions the reaction was most frequently aroused. The reaction of the hemispheres consists in the lighting up of a certain system of paths by the current entering from the outer world. What corresponds to this mentally is a certain special pulse of thought, the thought, namely, of that most probable object. Farther than this in the analysis we can hardly go.

---

experience of the pupil. . . . If the teacher is to explain the distance of the sun from the earth, let him ask . . . 'If anyone there in the sun fired off a cannon straight at you, what should you do?' 'Get out of the way,' would be the answer. 'No need of that,' the teacher might reply. 'You may quietly go to sleep in your room, and get up again, you may wait till your confirmation-day, you may learn a trade, and grow as old as I am,—*then* only will the cannon-ball be getting near, *then* you may jump to one side! See, so great as that is the sun's distance!' " (K. Lange: *Über Apperception*, 1879, p. 74.)

Hallucinations.—Between normal perception and illusion we have seen that there is no break, the *process* being identically the same in both. The last illusions we considered might fairly be called hallucinations. We must now consider the false perceptions more commonly called by that name. In ordinary parlance hallucination is held to differ from illusion in that, whilst there is an object really there in illusion, *in hallucination there is no objective stimulus at all*. We shall presently see that this supposed absence of objective stimulus in hallucination is a mistake, and that hallucinations are often only *extremes* of the perceptive process, in which the secondary cerebral reaction is out of all normal proportion to the peripheral stimulus which occasions the activity. Hallucinations usually appear abruptly and have the character of being forced upon the subject. But they possess various degrees of apparent *objectivity*. One mistake *in limine* must be guarded against. They are often talked of as *images* projected outwards by mistake. But where an hallucination is complete, it is much more than a mental image. *An hallucination, subjectively considered, is a sensation, as good and true a sensation as if there were a real object there.* The object happens not to be there, that is all.

The milder degrees of hallucination have been designated as *pseudo-hallucinations.* Pseudo-hallucinations and hallucinations have been sharply distinguished from each other only within a few years. From ordinary images of memory and fancy, pseudo-hallucinations differ in being much more vivid, minute, detailed, steady, abrupt, and spontaneous, in the sense that all feeling of our own activity in producing them is lacking. Dr. Kandinsky had a patient who, after taking opium or haschisch, had abundant pseudo-hallucinations and hallucinations. As he also had strong visualizing power and was an educated physician, the three sorts of phenomena could be easily compared. Although projected outwards (usually not farther than the limit of distinctest vision, a foot or so), the pseudo-hallucinations *lacked the character of objective reality* which the hallucinations possessed, but, unlike the pictures of imagination, it was almost impossible to produce them at will. Most of the 'voices' which people hear (whether they give rise to delusions or not) are pseudo-hallucinations.

They are described as '*inner*' voices, although their character is entirely unlike the inner speech of the subject with himself. I know several persons who hear such inner voices making unforeseen remarks whenever they grow quiet and listen for them. They are a very common incident of delusional insanity, and may at last grow into vivid or completely exteriorized hallucinations. The latter are comparatively frequent occurrences in sporadic form; and certain individuals are liable to have them often. From the results of the 'Census of Hallucinations,' which was begun by Edmund Gurney, it would appear that, roughly speaking, one person at least in every ten is likely to have had a vivid hallucination at some time in his life. The following case from a healthy person will give an idea of what these hallucinations are:

"When a girl of eighteen, I was one evening engaged in a very painful discussion with an elderly person. My distress was so great that I took up a thick ivory knitting-needle that was lying on the mantelpiece of the parlor and broke it into small pieces as I talked. In the midst of the discussion I was very wishful to know the opinion of a brother with whom I had an unusually close relationship. I turned round and saw him sitting at the farther side of a centre-table, with his arms folded (an unusual position with him), but, to my dismay, I perceived from the sarcastic expression of his mouth that he was not in sympathy with me, was not 'taking my side,' as I should then have expressed it. The surprise cooled me, and the discussion was dropped.

"Some minutes after, having occasion to speak to my brother, I turned towards him, but he was gone. I inquired when he left the room, and was told that he had not been in it, which I did not believe, thinking that he had come in for a minute and had gone out without being noticed. About an hour and a half afterwards he appeared, and convinced me, with some trouble, that he had never been near the house that evening. He is still alive and well."

The hallucinations of fever-delirium are a mixture of pseudo-hallucination, true hallucination, and illusion. Those of opium, haschisch, and belladonna resemble them in this respect. The commonest hallucination of all is that of hearing one's own name called aloud. Nearly one half of the sporadic cases which I have collected are of this sort.

Hallucination and Illusion.—Hallucinations are easily produced by verbal suggestion in hypnotic subjects. Thus, point to a dot on a sheet of paper, and call it 'General Grant's photograph,' and your subject will see a photograph of the General there instead of the dot. The dot gives objectivity to the appearance, and the suggested notion of the General gives it form. Then magnify the dot by a lens; double it by a prism or by nudging the eyeball; reflect it in a mirror; turn it upside-down; or wipe it out; and the subject will tell you that the 'photograph' has been enlarged, doubled, reflected, turned about, or made to disappear. In M. Binet's language, the dot is the outward *point de repère* which is needed to give objectivity to your suggestion, and without which the latter will only produce an inner image in the subject's mind. M. Binet has shown that such a peripheral *point de repère* is used in an enormous number, not only of hypnotic hallucinations, but of hallucinations of the insane. These latter are often *unilateral*; that is, the patient hears the voices always on one side of him, or sees the figure only when a certain one of his eyes is open. In many of these cases it has been distinctly proved that a morbid irritation in the internal ear, or an opacity in the humors of the eye, was the starting point of the current which the patient's diseased acoustic or optical centres clothed with their peculiar products in the way of ideas. *Hallucinations produced in this way are 'illusions'; and M. Binet's theory, that all hallucinations must start in the periphery, may be called an attempt to reduce hallucination and illusion to one physiological type*, the type, namely, to which normal perception belongs. In every case, according to M. Binet, whether of perception, of hallucination, or of illusion, we get the sensational vividness by means of a current from the peripheral nerves. It may be a mere trace of a current. But that trace is enough to kindle the maximal process of disintegration in the cells (cf. p. 293), and to give to the object perceived the character of *externality*. What the *nature* of the object shall be will depend wholly on the particular system of paths in which the process is kindled. Part of the thing in all cases comes from the sense-organ, the rest is furnished by the mind. But we cannot by introspection distinguish between these parts; and our only formula for the result is that the brain has *reacted on* the impression in the resulting way.

M. Binet's theory accounts indeed for a multitude of cases, but certainly not for all. The prism does not always double the false appearance, nor does the latter always disappear when the eyes are closed. For Binet, an abnormally or exclusively active part of the cortex gives the *nature* of what shall appear, whilst a peripheral sense-organ alone can give the *intensity* sufficient to make it appear projected into real space. But since this intensity is after all but a matter of degree, one does not see why, under rare conditions, the degree in question *might* not be attained by inner causes exclusively. In that case we should have certain hallucinations centrally initiated, as well as the peripherally initiated hallucinations which are the only sort that M. Binet's theory allows. *It seems probable on the whole, therefore, that centrally initiated hallucinations can exist.* How often they do exist is another question. The existence of hallucinations which affect more than one sense is an argument for central initiation. For, grant that the thing seen may have its starting point in the outer world, the voice which it is heard to utter must be due to an influence from the visual region, i.e., must be of central origin.

Sporadic cases of hallucination, visiting people only once in a lifetime (which seem to be a quite frequent type), are on any theory hard to understand in detail. They are often extraordinarily complete; and the fact that many of them are reported as *veridical*, that is, as coinciding with real events, such as accidents, deaths, etc., of the persons seen, is an additional complication of the phenomenon. The first really scientific study of hallucination in all its possible bearings, on the basis of a large mass of empirical material, was begun by Mr. Edmund Gurney and is continued by other members of the Society for Psychical Research; and the Census is now being applied to several countries under the auspices of the International Congress of Experimental Psychology. It is to be hoped that out of these combined labors something solid

will eventually grow. The facts shade off into the phenomena
of motor automatism, trance, etc.; and nothing but a wide
comparative study can give really instructive results.[6]

[6]The writer of the present work is Agent of the Census for America, and
will thankfully receive accounts of cases of hallucination of vision, hearing,
etc., of which the reader may have knowledge.

CHAPTER XXI

THE PERCEPTION OF SPACE

As ADULT THINKERS we have a definite and apparently instantaneous knowledge of the sizes, shapes, and distances of the things amongst which we live and move; and we have moreover a practically definite notion of the whole great infinite continuum of real space in which the world swings and in which all these things are located. Nevertheless it seems obvious that the baby's world is vague and confused in all these respects. How does our definite knowledge of space grow up? This is one of the quarrelsome problems in psychology. This chapter must be so brief that there will be no room for the polemic and historic aspects of the subject, and I will state simply and dogmatically the conclusions which seem most plausible to me.

The quality of voluminousness exists in all sensations, just as intensity does. We call the reverberations of a thunderstorm more voluminous than the squeaking of a slate-pencil; the entrance into a warm bath gives our skin a more massive feeling than the prick of a pin; a little neuralgic pain, fine as a cobweb, in the face, seems less extensive than the heavy soreness of a boil or the vast discomfort of a colic or a lumbago; and a solitary star looks smaller than the noonday sky. Muscular sensations and semicircular-canal sensations have volume. Smells and tastes are not without it; and sensations from our inward organs have it in a marked degree.

Repletion and emptiness, suffocation, palpitation, headache, are examples of this, and certainly not less spatial is the consciousness we have of our general bodily condition in nausea, fever, heavy drowsiness, and fatigue. Our entire cubic content seems then sensibly manifest to us as such, and feels much larger than any local pulsation, pressure, or discomfort. Skin and retina are, however, the organs in which the space-element plays the most active part. Not only does the maximal vastness yielded by the retina surpass that yielded by any other organ, but the intricacy with which our attention can subdivide this vastness and perceive it to be composed of lesser portions simultaneously coexisting alongside of each other is without a parallel elsewhere. The ear gives a greater vastness than the skin, but is considerably less able to subdivide it. The *vastness, moreover, is as great in one direction as in another*. Its dimensions are so vague that in it there is no question as yet of surface as opposed to depth; 'volume' being the best short name for the sensation in question.

Sensations of different orders are roughly comparable with each other as to their volumes. Persons born blind are said to be surprised at the largeness with which objects appear to them when their sight is restored. Franz says of his patient cured of cataract: "He saw everything much larger than he had supposed from the idea obtained by his sense of touch. Moving, and especially living, objects appeared very large." Loud sounds have a certain enormousness of feeling. 'Glowing' bodies, as Hering says, give us a perception "which seems *roomy (raumhaft)* in comparison with that of strictly surface-color. A glowing iron looks luminous through and through, and so does a flame." The interior of one's mouth-cavity feels larger when explored by the tongue than when looked at. The crater of a newly-extracted tooth, and the movements of a loose tooth in its socket, feel quite monstrous. A midge buzzing against the drum of the ear will often seem as big as a butterfly. The pressure of the air in the tympanic cavity upon the membrane gives an astonishingly large sensation.

The voluminousness of the feeling seems to bear very little relation to the size of the organ that yields it. The ear and eye are comparatively minute organs, yet they give us feelings of great volume. The same lack of exact proportion between size of feeling and size of organ affected obtains within the limits of particular sensory organs. An object appears smaller on the lateral portions of the retina than it does on the fovea, as may be easily verified by holding the two forefingers parallel and a couple of inches apart, and transferring the gaze of one eye from one to the other. Then the finger not directly looked at will appear to shrink. On the skin, if two points kept equidistant (blunted compass- or scissors-points, for example) be drawn along so as really to describe a pair of parallel lines, the lines will appear farther apart in some spots than in others. If, for example, we draw them across the face, the person ex-

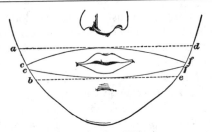

FIG. 65 (after Weber).
The dotted lines give the real course of the points, the
continuous lines the course as felt.

perimented upon will feel as if they began to diverge near the
mouth and to include it in a well-marked ellipse.

NOW MY FIRST THESIS IS THAT THIS EXTENSITY, *discernible
in each and every sensation, though more developed in some than
in others,* IS THE ORIGINAL SENSATION OF SPACE, out of
which all the exact knowledge about space that we afterwards
come to have is woven by processes of discrimination, association, and selection.

The Construction of Real Space.—To the babe who first
opens his senses upon the world, though the experience is one
of vastness or extensity, it is of an extensity within which no
definite divisions, directions, sizes, or distances are yet marked
out. Potentially, the room in which the child is born is subdi-
visible into a multitude of parts, fixed or movable, which at
any given moment of time have definite relations to each
other and to his person. Potentially, too, this room taken as a
whole can be prolonged in various directions by the addition
to it of those farther-lying spaces which constitute the outer
world. But actually the further spaces are unfelt, and the subdivisions are undiscriminated, by the babe; the chief part of
whose education during his first year of life consists in his
becoming acquainted with them and recognizing and identifying them in detail. This process may be called that of the
construction of real space, as a newly apprehended object, out of
the original chaotic experiences of vastness. It consists of several subordinate processes:

First, the total object of vision or of feeling at any time
must have smaller objects definitely discriminated within it;

Secondly, *objects seen or tasted must be identified with objects felt, heard*, etc., and *vice versa*, so that *the same 'thing'* may come to be recognized, although apprehended in such widely differing ways;

Third, the total extent felt at any time must be conceived as *definitely located in the midst of the surrounding extents of which the world consists*;

Fourth, these objects *must appear arranged in definite order* in the so-called three dimensions; and

Fifth, their relative sizes must be perceived—in other words, *they must be measured*.

Let us take these processes in regular order.

1) **Subdivision or Discrimination.**—Concerning this there is not much to be added to what was set forth in Chapter XV. Moving parts, sharp parts, brightly colored parts of the total field of perception 'catch the attention' and are then discerned as special objects surrounded by the remainder of the field of view or touch. That when such objects are discerned apart they should appear as thus surrounded, must be set down as an ultimate fact of our sensibility of which no farther account can be given. Later, as one partial object of this sort after another has become familiar and identifiable, the attention can be caught by more than one at once. We then see or feel a number of distinct objects alongside of each other in the general extended field. The 'alongsideness' is in the first instance vague—it may not carry with it the sense of definite directions or distances—and it too must be regarded as an ultimate fact of our sensibility.

2) **Coalescence of Different Sensations into the Same 'Thing.'**—When two senses are impressed simultaneously we tend to identify their objects as *one thing*. When a conductor is brought near the skin, the snap heard, the spark seen, and the sting felt, are all located together and believed to be different aspects of one entity, the 'electric discharge.' The space of the seen object fuses with the space of the heard object and with that of the felt object by an ultimate law of our consciousness, which is that we simplify, unify, and identify as much as we possibly can. *Whatever sensible data can be attended to together we locate together. Their several extents seem one extent. The place at which each appears is held to be the same*

with the place at which the others appear. This is the first and great 'act' by which our world gets spatially arranged.

In this *coalescence in a 'thing,'* one of the coalescing sensations is held to *be* the thing, the other sensations are taken for its more or less accidental *properties*, or modes of appearance. The sensation chosen to be essentially the thing is the most constant and practically important of the lot; most often it is hardness or weight. But the hardness or weight is never without tactile bulk; and as we can always see something in our hand when we feel something there, we equate the bulk felt with the bulk seen, and thenceforward this common bulk is also apt to figure as of the essence of the 'thing.' Frequently a shape so figures, sometimes a temperature, a taste, etc.; but for the most part temperature, smell, sound, color, or whatever other phenomena may vividly impress us simultaneously with the bulk felt or seen, figure among the accidents. Smell and sound impress us, it is true, when we neither see nor touch the thing; but they are strongest when we see or touch, so we locate the *source* of these properties within the touched or seen space, whilst the properties themselves we regard as overflowing in a weakened form into the spaces filled by other things. *In all this, it will be observed, the sense-data whose spaces coalesce into one are yielded by different sense-organs.* Such data have no tendency to displace each other from consciousness, but can be attended to together all at once. Often indeed they vary concomitantly and reach a maximum together. We may be sure, therefore, that the general rule of our mind is to locate IN *each other* all sensations which are associated in simultaneous experience and do not interfere with each other's perception.

3) **The Sense of the Surrounding World.**—*Different impressions on the same sense-organ* do interfere with each other's perception and cannot well be attended to at once. Hence *we do not locate them in each other's spaces, but arrange them in a serial order of exteriority, each alongside of the rest, in a space larger than that which any one sensation brings.* We can usually recover anything lost from our sight by moving our eyes back in its direction; and it is through these constant changes that every field of seen things comes at last to be thought of as always having a fringe of *other things possible to be seen*

spreading in all directions round about it. Meanwhile the movements concomitantly with which the various fields alternate are also felt and remembered; and gradually (through association) this and that movement come in our thought to suggest this or that extent of fresh objects introduced. Gradually, too, since the objects vary indefinitely in kind, we abstract from their several natures and think separately of their mere extents, of which extents the various movements remain as the only constant introducers and associates. More and more, therefore, do we think of movement and seen extent as mutually involving each other, until at last we may get to regard them as synonymous; and, empty space then meaning for us mere *room for movement*, we may, if we are psychologists, readily but erroneously assign to the 'muscular sense' the chief rôle in perceiving extensiveness at all.

4) **The Serial Order of Locations.**—The muscular sense *has* much to do with defining the *order of position* of things seen, felt, or heard. We look at a point; another point upon the retina's margin catches our attention, and in an instant we turn the fovea upon it, letting its image successively fall upon all the points of the intervening retinal line. The line thus traced so rapidly by the second point is itself a visual object, with the first and second point at its respective ends. It *separates* the points, which become *located by its length* with reference to each other. If a third point catch the attention, more peripheral still than the second point, then a still greater movement of the eyeball and a continuation of the line will result, the second point now appearing *between* the first and third. Every moment of our life, peripherally-lying objects are drawing lines like this between themselves and other objects which they displace from our attention as we bring them to the centre of our field of view. Each peripheral retinal point comes in this way to *suggest* a line at the end of which it lies, a line which a possible movement will trace; and even the motionless field of vision ends at last by signifying a system of positions brought out by possible movements between its centre and all peripheral parts.

It is the same with our skin and joints. By moving our hand over objects we trace lines of direction, and new impressions arise at their ends. The 'lines' are sometimes on the articular surfaces, sometimes on the skin as well; in either case they give a definite order of arrangement to the successive objects between which they intervene. Similarly with sounds and smells. With our heads in a certain position, a certain sound or a certain smell is most distinct. Turning our head makes this experience fainter and brings another sound, or another smell, to its maximum. The two sounds or smells are thus separated by the movement located at its ends, the movement itself being realized as a sweep through space whose value is given partly by the semicircular-canal feeling, partly by the articular cartilages of the neck, and partly by the impressions produced upon the eye.

By such general principles of action as these everything looked at, felt, smelt, or heard comes to be located in a more or less definite position relatively to other collateral things either actually presented or only imagined as possibly there. I say 'collateral' things, for I prefer not to complicate the account just yet with any special consideration of the 'third dimension,' distance, or depth, as it has been called.

5) **The Measurement of Things in Terms of Each Other.**—Here the first thing that seems evident is that we have no *immediate* power of comparing together with any accuracy the extents revealed by different sensations. Our mouth-cavity feels indeed to the tongue larger than it feels to the finger or eye, our lips feel larger than a surface equal to them on our thigh. So much comparison is immediate; but it is vague; and for anything exact we must resort to other help.

The great agent in comparing the extent felt by one sensory surface with that felt by another is superposition —superposition of one surface upon another, and superposition of one outer thing upon many surfaces.

Two surfaces of skin superposed on each other are felt simultaneously, and by the law laid down on p. 319 are judged to occupy an identical place. Similarly of our hand, when seen and felt at the same time by its resident sensibility.

In these identifications and reductions of the many to the one it must be noticed that *when the resident sensations of largeness of two opposed surfaces conflict, one of the sensations is chosen as the true standard and the other treated as illusory.* Thus an empty tooth-socket is believed to be *really smaller* than the finger-tip which it will not admit, although it may *feel* larger; and in general it may be said that the hand, as the almost exclusive organ of palpation, gives its own magnitude to the other parts, instead of having its size determined by them.

But even though exploration of one surface by another were impossible, *we could always measure our various surfaces against each other by applying the same extended object first to one and then to another.* We might of course at first suppose that the object itself waxed and waned as it glided from one place to another (cf. above, Fig. 65); but the principle of simplifying as much as possible our world would soon drive us out of that assumption into the easier one that objects as a rule keep their sizes, and that most of our sensations are affected by errors for which a constant allowance must be made.

In the retina there is no reason to suppose that the bignesses of two impressions (lines or blotches) falling on different regions are at first felt to stand in any exact mutual ratio. But if the impressions come from the *same object*, then we might judge their sizes to be just the same. This, however, only when the relation of the object to the eye is believed to be on the whole unchanged. When the object, by moving, changes its relations to the eye, the sensation excited by its image even on the same retinal region becomes so fluctuating that we end by ascribing no absolute import whatever to the retinal space-feeling which at any moment we may receive. So complete does this overlooking of retinal magnitude become that it is next to impossible to compare the visual magnitudes of objects at different distances without making the experiment of superposition. We cannot say beforehand how much of a distant house or tree our finger will cover. The various answers to the familiar question, How large is the moon?— answers which vary from a cartwheel to a wafer—illustrate this most strikingly. The hardest part of the training of a young draughtsman is his learning to feel directly the retinal (i.e., primitively sensible) magnitudes which the different objects in the field of view subtend. To do this he must recover what Ruskin calls the 'innocence of the eye'—that is, a sort of childish perception of stains of color merely as such, without consciousness of what they mean.

With the rest of us this innocence is lost. *Out of all the visual magnitudes of each known object we have selected one as the 'real' one to think of, and degraded all the others to serve as its signs.* This real magnitude is determined by æsthetic and practical interests. It is that which we get when the object is at the distance most propitious for exact visual discrimination of its details. This is the distance at which we hold anything we are examining. Farther than this we see it too small, nearer too large. And the larger and the smaller feeling vanish in the act of suggesting this one, their more important *meaning*. As I look along the dining-table I overlook the fact that the farther plates and glasses *feel* so much smaller than my own, for I *know* that they are all equal in size; and the feeling of them, which is a present sensation, is eclipsed in the glare of the knowledge, which is a merely imagined one.

It is the same with shape as with size. Almost all the visible shapes of things are what we call perspective 'distortions.' Square table-tops constantly present two acute and two obtuse angles; circles drawn on our wall-papers, our carpets, or on sheets of paper, usually show like ellipses; parallels approach as they recede; human bodies are foreshortened; and the transitions from one to another of these altering forms are infinite and continual. Out of the flux, however, one phase always stands prominent. It is the form the object has when we see it easiest and best: and that is when our eyes and the object both are in what may be called *the normal position.* In this position our head is upright and our optic axes either parallel or symmetrically convergent; the plane of the object is perpendicular to the visual plane; and if the object is one containing many lines, it is turned so as to make them, as far as possible, either parallel or perpendicular to the visual plane. In this situation it is that we compare all shapes with each other; here every exact measurement and every decision is made.

Most sensations are signs to us of other sensations whose space-value is held to be more real. *The thing as it would appear to the eye if it were in the normal position* is what we *think of* whenever we get one of the other optical views. Only as represented in the normal position do we believe we see the object as it *is*; elsewhere, only as it seems. Experience and custom soon teach us, however, that the seeming appearance passes into the real one by continuous gradations. They teach us, moreover, that seeming and being may be strangely interchanged. Now a real circle may slide into a seeming ellipse; now an ellipse may, by sliding in the same direction, become a seeming circle; now a rectangular cross grows slant-legged; now a slant-legged one grows rectangular.

Almost any form in oblique vision may be thus a derivative of almost any other in 'primary' vision; and we must learn, when we get one of the former appearances, to translate it into the appropriate one of the latter class; we must learn of what optical 'reality' it is one of the optical signs. Having learned this, we do but obey that law of economy or simplification which dominates our whole psychic life, when we think exclusively of the 'reality' and ignore as much as our consciousness will let us the 'sign' by which we came to apprehend it. The signs of each probable real thing being multiple and the thing itself one and fixed, we gain the same mental relief by abandoning the former for the latter that we do when we abandon mental images, with all their fluctuating characters, for the definite and unchangeable *names* which they suggest. The selection of the several 'normal' appearances from out of the jungle of our optical experiences, to serve as the real sights of which we shall think, has thus some analogy to the habit of thinking in words, in that by both we substitute terms few and fixed for terms manifold and vague.

If an optical sensation can thus be a mere sign to recall another sensation of the same sense, judged more real, *a fortiori* can sensations of one sense be signs of realities which are objects of another. Smells and tastes make us believe the *visible* cologne-bottle, strawberry, or cheese to be there. Sights suggest objects of touch, touches suggest objects of sight, etc. In all this substitution and suggestive recall the only law that holds good is that in general the most *interesting* of the sensations which the 'thing' can give us is held to represent its real nature most truly. It is a case of the selective activity mentioned on p. 168 ff.

The Third Dimension or Distance.—This service of sensations as mere signs, to be ignored when they have evoked the other sensations which are their significates, was noticed first by Berkeley in his new theory of vision. He dwelt particularly on the fact that the signs were not *natural* signs, but properties of the object merely *associated by experience* with the more real aspects of it which they recall. The tangible 'feel' of a thing, and the 'look' of it to the eye, have absolutely no point in common, said Berkeley; and if I think of the look of it when I get the feel, or think of the feel when I get the look, that is merely due to the fact that I have on so many previous occasions had the two sensations at once. When we open our eyes, for example, we think we see how far off the object is. But this feeling of distance, according to Berkeley, cannot possibly be a retinal sensation, for a point in outer space can only impress our retina by the single dot which it projects 'in the fund of the eye,' and this dot is the same for *all* distances. Distance from the eye, Berkeley considered not to be an optical object at all, but an object of *touch*, of which we have optical signs of various sorts, such as the image's apparent magnitude, its 'faintness' or 'confusion,' and the 'strain' of accommodation and convergence. By distance being an object of 'touch,' Berkeley meant that our notion of it consists in ideas of the amount of muscular movement of arm or legs which would be required to place our hand upon the object. Most authors have agreed with Berkeley that creatures unable to move either their eyes or limbs would have no notion whatever of distance or the third dimension.

This opinion seems to me unjustifiable. I cannot get over the fact that all our sensations are of *volume*, and that the primitive field of view (however imperfectly distance may be discriminated or measured in it) cannot be of something *flat*, as these authors unanimously maintain. Nor can I get over the fact that distance, when I see it, is a genuinely *optical feeling*, even though I be at a loss to assign any one physiological process in the organ of vision to the varying degrees of which the variations of the feeling uniformly correspond. It is awakened by all the optical signs which Berkeley mentioned, and by more besides, such as Wheatstone's binocular disparity, and by the parallax which follows on slightly moving the head. When awakened, however, it seems optical, and not heterogeneous with the other two dimensions of the visual field.

The mutual equivalencies of the distance-dimension with the up-and-down and right-to-left dimensions of the field of view can easily be settled without resorting to experiences of touch. A being reduced to a single eyeball would perceive the same tridimensional world which we do, if he had our intellectual powers. For the *same moving things*, by alternately covering different parts of his retina, would determine the mutual equivalencies of the first two dimensions of the field of view; and by exciting the physiological cause of his perception of depth in various degrees, they would establish a scale of equivalency between the first two and the third.

First of all, one of the sensations given by the object would be chosen to represent its 'real' size and shape, in accordance with the principles so lately laid down. One sensation would measure the 'thing' present, and the 'thing' would measure the other sensations—the peripheral parts of the retina would be equated with the central by receiving the image of the same object. This needs no elucidation in case the object does not change its distance or its front. But suppose, to take a more complicated case, that the object is a stick, seen first in its whole length, and then rotated round one of its ends; let this fixed end be the one near the eye. In this movement the stick's image will grow progressively shorter; its farther end will appear less and less separated laterally from its fixed near end; soon it will be screened by the latter, and then reappear on the opposite side, the image there finally resuming its original length. Suppose this movement to become a familiar experience; the mind will presumably react upon it after its usual fashion (which is that of unifying all data which it is in any way possible to unify), and consider it the movement of a constant object rather than the transformation of a fluctuating one. Now, the *sensation of depth* which it receives during the experience is awakened more by the far than by the near end of the object. But how much depth? What shall measure its amount? Why, at the moment the far end is about to be eclipsed, the difference of its distance from the near end's distance must be judged equal to the stick's whole length; but that length has already been seen and measured by a certain visual sensation of breadth. *So we find that given amounts of the visual depth-feeling become signs of given amounts of the visual breadth-feeling, depth becoming equated with breadth. The measurement of distance is, as Berkeley truly said, a result of suggestion and experience. But visual experience alone is adequate to produce it, and this he erroneously denied.*

The Part played by the Intellect in Space-perception.— But although Berkeley was wrong in his assertion that out of optical experience alone no perception of distance can be evolved, he gave a great impetus to psychology by showing how originally incoherent and incommensurable in respect of their extensiveness our different sensations are, and how our actually so rapid space-perceptions are almost altogether acquired by education. Touch-space is one world; sight-space is another world. The two worlds have no essential or intrinsic congruence, and only through the 'association of ideas' do we know what a seen object signifies in terms of touch. Persons with congenital cataracts relieved by surgical aid, whose world until the operation has been a world of tangibles exclusively, are ludicrously unable at first to name any of the objects which newly fall upon their eye. "It might very well be *a horse*," said the latest patient of this sort of whom we have an account, when a 10-litre bottle was held up a foot from his face.[1] Neither do such patients have any accurate notion in motor terms of the relative distances of things from their eyes. All such confusions very quickly disappear with practice, and the novel optical sensations translate themselves into the familiar language of touch. The facts do not prove in the least that the optical sensations are not *spatial*, but only that it needs a subtler sense for analogy than most people have, to discern the *same* spatial aspects and relations in them which previously-known tactile and motor experiences have yielded.

Conclusion.—To sum up, the whole history of space-perception is explicable if we admit on the one hand sensations with certain amounts of extensity native to them, and on

[1] Cf. Raehlmann in *Zeitschrift für Psychologie und Physiologie der Sinnesorgane*, II, 79.

the other the ordinary powers of discrimination, selection, and association in the mind's dealings with them. The fluctuating import of many of our optical sensations, the same sensation being so ambiguous as regards size, shape, locality, and the like, has led many to believe that such attributes as these could not possibly be the result of sensation at all, but must come from some higher power of intuition, synthesis, or whatever it might be called. But the fact that a present sensation can at any time become the sign of a represented one judged to be more real, sufficiently accounts for all the phenomena without the need of supposing that the quality of extensity is created out of non-extensive experiences by a super-sensational faculty of the mind.

CHAPTER XXII

REASONING

W hat Reasoning is.—We talk of man being the rational animal; and the traditional intellectualist philosophy has always made a great point of treating the brutes as wholly irrational creatures. Nevertheless, it is by no means easy to decide just what is meant by reason, or how the peculiar thinking process called reasoning differs from other thought-sequences which may lead to similar results.

Much of our thinking consists of trains of images suggested one by another, of a sort of spontaneous revery of which it seems likely enough that the higher brutes should be capable. This sort of thinking leads nevertheless to rational conclusions, both practical and theoretical. The links between the terms are either 'contiguity' or 'similarity,' and with a mixture of both these things we can hardly be very incoherent. As a rule, in this sort of irresponsible thinking, the terms which fall to be coupled together are empirical concretes, not abstractions. A sunset may call up the vessel's deck from which I saw one last summer, the companions of my voyage, my arrival into port, etc.; or it may make me think of solar myths, of Hercules' and Hector's funeral pyres, of Homer and whether he could write, of the Greek alphabet, etc. If habitual contiguities predominate, we have a prosaic mind; if rare contiguities or similarities have free play, we call the person fanciful, poetic, or witty. But the thought as a rule is of matters taken in their entirety. Having been thinking of one, we find later that we are thinking of another, to which we have been lifted along, we hardly know how. If an abstract quality figures in the procession, it arrests our attention but for a moment, and fades into something else; and is never very abstract. Thus, in thinking of the sun-myths, we may have a gleam of admiration at the gracefulness of the primitive human mind, or a moment of disgust at the narrowness of modern interpreters. But, in the main, we think less of qualities than of concrete things, real or possible, just as we may experience them.

Our thought here may be rational, but it is not *reasoned*, is not reasoning in the strict sense of the term. In reasoning, although our results may be thought of as concrete things, they are *not suggested immediately by other concrete things*, as in the trains of simply associative thought. They are linked to the concretes which precede them by intermediate steps, and these steps are formed by *abstract general characters* articulately denoted and expressly analyzed out. A thing inferred by reasoning need neither have been an habitual associate of the datum from which we infer it, nor need it be similar to it. It may be a thing entirely unknown to our previous experience, something which no simple association of concretes could ever have evoked. The great difference, in fact, between that simpler kind of rational thinking which consists in the concrete objects of past experience merely suggesting each other, and reasoning distinctively so called, is this: that whilst the empirical thinking is only reproductive, reasoning is productive. An empirical, or 'rule-of-thumb,' thinker can deduce nothing from data with whose behavior and associates in the concrete he is unfamiliar. But put a reasoner amongst a set of concrete objects which he has neither seen nor heard of before, and with a little time, if he is a good reasoner, he will make such inferences from them as will quite atone for his ignorance. Reasoning helps us out of unprecedented situations—situations for which all our common associative wisdom, all the 'education' which we share in common with the beasts, leaves us without resource.

Exact Definition of it.—*Let us make this ability to deal with novel data the technical differentia of reasoning.* This will sufficiently mark it out from common associative thinking, and will immediately enable us to say just what peculiarity it contains.

It contains analysis and abstraction. Whereas the merely empirical thinker stares at a fact in its entirety, and remains helpless, or gets 'stuck,' if it suggests no concomitant or similar, the reasoner breaks it up and notices some one of its separate attributes. This attribute he takes to be the essential part of the whole fact before him. This attribute has properties or consequences which the fact until then was not known to have, but which, now that it is noticed to contain the attribute, it must have.

Call the fact or concrete datum S;
    the essential attribute M;
    the attribute's property P.

Then the reasoned inference of P from S cannot be made without M's intermediation. The 'essence' M is thus that third or middle term in the reasoning which a moment ago was pronounced essential. *For his original concrete S the reasoner substitutes its abstract property M.* What is true of M, what is coupled with M, thereupon holds true of S, is coupled with S. As M is properly one of the *parts* of the entire S, *reasoning may then be very well defined as the substitution of parts and their implications or consequences for wholes.* And the art of the reasoner will consist of two stages:

First, *sagacity*, or the ability to discover what part, M, lies embedded in the whole S which is before him;

Second, *learning*, or the ability to recall promptly M's consequences, concomitants, or implications.

If we glance at the ordinary syllogism—

$$M \text{ is } P;$$
$$S \text{ is } M;$$
$$\therefore S \text{ is } P$$

—we see that the second or minor premise, the 'subsumption' as it is sometimes called, is the one requiring the sagacity; the first or major the one requiring the fertility, or fulness of learning. Usually the learning is more apt to be ready than the sagacity, the ability to seize fresh aspects in concrete things being rarer than the ability to learn old rules; so that, in most actual cases of reasoning, the minor premise, or the way of conceiving the subject, is the one that makes the novel step in thought. This is, to be sure, not always the case; for the fact that M carries P with it may also be unfamiliar and now formulated for the first time.

The perception that S is M is a *mode of conceiving S.* The statement that M is P is an *abstract or general proposition.* A word about both is necessary.

What is meant by a Mode of Conceiving.—When we conceive of S merely as M (of vermilion merely as a mercury-compound, for example), we neglect all the other attributes which it may have, and attend exclusively to this one. We mutilate the fulness of S's reality. Every reality has an infinity of aspects or properties. Even so simple a fact as a line which you trace in the air may be considered in respect to its form, its length, its direction, and its location. When we reach more complex facts, the number of ways in which we may regard them is literally endless. Vermilion is not only a mercury-compound, it is vividly red, heavy, and expensive, it comes from China, and so on, *ad infinitum*. All objects are well-springs of properties, which are only little by little developed to our knowledge, and it is truly said that to know one thing thoroughly would be to know the whole universe. Mediately or immediately, that one thing is related to everything else; and to know *all* about it, all its relations need be known. But each relation forms one of its attributes, one angle by which someone may conceive it, and while so conceiving it may ignore the rest of it. A man is such a complex fact. But out of the complexity all that an army commissary picks out as important for his purposes is his property of eating so many pounds a day; the general, of marching so many miles; the chair-maker, of having such a shape; the orator, of responding to such and such feelings; the theatre-manager, of being willing to pay just such a price, and no more, for an evening's amusement. Each of these persons singles out the particular side of the entire man which has a bearing on *his* concerns, and not till this side is distinctly and separately conceived can the proper practical conclusions *for that reasoner* be drawn; and when they are drawn the man's other attributes may be ignored.

All ways of conceiving a concrete fact, if they are true ways at all, are equally true ways. *There is no property* ABSOLUTELY *essential to any one thing*. The same property which figures as the essence of a thing on one occasion becomes a very inessential feature upon another. Now that I am writing, it is essential that I conceive my paper as a surface for inscription. If I failed to do that, I should have to stop my work. But if I wished to light a fire, and no other materials were by, the essential way of conceiving the paper would be as combustible material; and I need then have no thought of any of its other destinations. It is really *all* that it is: a combustible, a writing surface, a thin thing, a hydrocarbonaceous thing, a thing eight inches one way and ten another, a thing just one furlong east of a certain stone in my neighbor's field, an American thing, etc., etc., *ad infinitum*. Whichever one of these aspects of its being I temporarily class it under makes me unjust to the other aspects. But as I always am classing it under one aspect or another, I am always unjust, always partial, always exclusive. My excuse is necessity—the necessity which my finite and practical nature lays upon me. My thinking is first and last and always for the sake of my doing, and I can only do one thing at a time. A God who is supposed to drive the whole universe abreast may also be supposed, without detriment to his activity, to see all parts of it at once and without emphasis. But were our human attention so to disperse itself, we should simply stare vacantly at things at large and forfeit our opportunity of doing any particular act. Mr. Warner, in his Adirondack story, shot a bear by aiming, not at his eye or heart, but 'at him generally.' But we cannot aim 'generally' at the universe; if we do, we miss our game. Our scope is narrow, and we must attack things piecemeal, ignoring the solid fulness in which the elements of Nature exist, and stringing one after another of them together in a serial way, to suit our little interests as they change from hour to hour. In this, the partiality of one moment is partly atoned for by the different sort of partiality of the next. To me now, writing these words, emphasis and selection seem to be the essence of the human mind. In other chapters other qualities have seemed, and will again seem, more important parts of psychology.

Men are so ingrainedly partial that, for common-sense and scholasticism (which is only common-sense grown articulate), the notion that there is no one quality genuinely, absolutely, and exclusively essential to anything is almost unthinkable. "A thing's essence makes it *what* it is. Without an exclusive essence it would be nothing in particular, would be quite nameless, we could not say it was this rather than that. What you write on, for example,—why talk of its being combustible, rectangular, and the like, when you know that these are mere accidents, and that what it really is, and was made to be, is just *paper* and nothing else?" The reader is pretty sure to make some such comment as this. But he is himself merely insisting on an aspect of the thing which suits his own petty purpose, that of *naming* the thing; or else on an aspect which suits the manufacturer's purpose, that of *producing an article for which there is a vulgar demand*. Meanwhile the reality overflows these purposes at every pore. Our usual purpose with it, our commonest title for it, and the properties which this title suggests, have in reality nothing sacramental. They characterize *us* more than they characterize the thing. But we are so stuck in our prejudices, so petrified intellectually, that to our vulgarest names, with their suggestions, we ascribe an eternal and exclusive worth. The thing must be, essentially, what the vulgarest name connotes; what less usual names connote, it can be only in an 'accidental' and relatively unreal sense.[1]

Locke undermined the fallacy. But none of his successors, so far as I know, have radically escaped it, or seen that *the only meaning of essence is teleological, and that classification and conception are purely teleological weapons of the mind*. The essence of a thing is that one of its properties which is so *important for my interests* that in comparison with it I may neglect the rest. Amongst those other things which have this important property I class it, after this property I name it, as a thing endowed with this property I conceive it; and whilst so classing, naming, and conceiving it, all other truths about it become to me as naught. The properties which are important vary from man to man and from hour to hour. Hence divers appellations and conceptions for the same thing. But many objects of daily use—as paper, ink, butter, overcoat—have proerties of such constant unwavering importance, and have such stereotyped names, that we end by believing that to conceive them in those ways is to conceive them in the only true way. Those are no truer ways of conceiving them than any others; they are only more frequently serviceable ways to us.

---

[1] Readers brought up on Popular Science may think that the molecular structure of things is their real essence in an absolute sense, and that water is $H-O-H$ more deeply and truly than it is a solvent of sugar or a slaker of thirst. Not a whit! It is *all* of these things with equal reality, and the only reason why *for the chemist* it is $H-O-H$ primarily, and only secondarily the other things, is that *for his purpose* of laboratory analysis and synthesis, and inclusion in the science which treats of compositions and decompositions, the $H-O-H$ aspect of it is the more important one to bear in mind.

Reasoning is always for a subjective interest. To revert now to our symbolic representation of the reasoning process:

$$\frac{\begin{array}{l} M \text{ is } P \\ S \ \text{ is } M \end{array}}{S \ \text{ is } P}$$

M is discerned and picked out for the time being to be the essence of the concrete fact, phenomenon, or reality, S. But M in this world of ours is inevitably conjoined with P; so that P is the next thing that we may expect to find conjoined with the fact S. We may conclude or infer P, through the intermediation of the M which our sagacity began by discerning, when S came before it, to be the essence of the case.

Now note that if P have any value or importance for us, M was a very good character for our sagacity to pounce upon and abstract. If, on the contrary, P were of no importance, some other character than M would have been a better essence for us to conceive of S by. Psychologically, as a rule, P overshadows the process from the start. We are *seeking* P, or something like P. But the bare totality of S does not yield it to our gaze; and casting about for some point in S to take hold of which will lead us to P, we hit, if we are sagacious, upon M, because M happens to be just the character which is knit up with P. Had we wished Q instead of P, and were N a property of S conjoined with Q, we ought to have ignored M, noticed N, and conceived of S as a sort of N exclusively.

Reasoning is always to attain some particular conclusion, or to gratify some special curiosity. It not only breaks up the datum placed before it and conceives it abstractly; it must conceive it *rightly* too; and conceiving it rightly means conceiving it by that one particular abstract character which leads to the one sort of conclusion which it is the reasoner's temporary interest to attain.

The *results* of reasoning may be hit upon by accident. The stereoscope was actually a result of reasoning; it is conceivable, however, that a man playing with pictures and mirrors might accidentally have hit upon it. Cats have been known to open doors by pulling latches, etc. But no cat, if the latch got out of order, could open the door again, unless some new accident of random fumbling taught her to associate some new total movement with the total phenomenon of the closed door. A reasoning man, however, would open the door by first analyzing the hindrance. He would ascertain what particular feature of the door was wrong. The lever, e.g., does not raise the latch sufficiently from its slot—case of insufficient elevation: raise door bodily on hinges! Or door sticks at bottom by friction against sill: raise it bodily up! Now it is obvious that a child or an idiot might without this reasoning learn the *rule* for opening that particular door. I remember a clock which the maid-servant had discovered would not go unless it were supported so as to tilt slightly forwards. She had stumbled on this method after many weeks of groping. The reason of the stoppage was the friction of the pendulum-bob against the back of the clock-case, a reason which an educated man would have analyzed out in five minutes. I have a student's lamp of which the flame vibrates most unpleasantly unless the chimney be raised about a sixteenth of an inch. I learned the remedy after much torment by accident, and now always keep the chimney up with a small wedge. But my procedure is a mere association of two totals, diseased object and remedy. One learned in pneumatics could have abstracted the *cause* of the disease, and thence inferred the remedy immediately. By many measurements of triangles one might find their area always equal to their height multiplied by half their base, and one might formulate an empirical law to that effect. But a reasoner saves himself all this trouble by seeing that it is the essence (*pro hac vice*) of a triangle to be the half of a parallelogram whose area is the height into the entire base. To see this he must invent additional lines; and the geometer must often draw such to get at the essential property he may require in a figure. The essence consists in some *relation of the figure to the new lines*, a relation not obvious at all until they are put in. The geometer's genius lies in the imagining of the new lines, and his sagacity in the perceiving of the relation.

Thus, there are two great points in reasoning. *First, an extracted character is taken as equivalent to the entire datum from which it comes; and,*

Second, the character thus taken suggests a certain consequence more obviously than it was suggested by the total datum as it originally came. Take these points again, successively.

1) Suppose I say, when offered a piece of cloth, "I won't buy that; it looks as if it would fade," meaning merely that something about it suggests the idea of fading to my mind,—my judgment, though possibly correct, is not reasoned, but purely empirical; but if I can say that into the color there enters a certain dye which I know to be chemically unstable, and that *therefore* the color will fade, my judgment is reasoned. The notion of the dye, which is one of the parts of the cloth, is the connecting link between the latter and the notion of fading. So, again, an uneducated man will expect from past experience to see a piece of ice melt if placed near the fire, and the tip of his finger look coarse if he view it through a convex glass. In neither of these cases could the result be anticipated without full previous acquaintance with the entire phenomenon. It is not a result of reasoning.

But a man who should conceive heat as a mode of motion, and liquefaction as identical with increased motion of molecules; who should know that curved surfaces bend light-rays in special ways, and that the apparent size of anything is connected with the amount of the 'bend' of its light-rays as they enter the eye,—such a man would make the right inferences for all these objects, even though he had never in his life had any concrete experience of them: and he would do this because the ideas which we have above supposed him to possess would mediate in his mind between the phenomena he starts with and the conclusions he draws. But these ideas are all mere extracted portions or circumstances. The motions which form heat, the bending of the light-waves, are, it is true, excessively recondite ingredients; the hidden pendulum I spoke of above is less so; and the sticking of a door on its sill in the earlier example would hardly be so at all. But each and all agree in this, that they bear a *more evident relation* to the conclusion than did the facts in their immediate totality.

2) And now to prove the second point: Why are the couplings, consequences, and implications of extracts more evident and obvious than those of entire phenomena? For two reasons.

First, the extracted characters are more general than the concretes, and the connections they may have are, therefore, more familiar to us, having been more often met in our experience. Think of heat as motion, and whatever is true of motion will be true of heat; but we have had a hundred experiences of motion for every one of heat. Think of the rays passing through this lens as bending towards the perpendicular, and you substitute for the comparatively unfamiliar lens the very familiar notion of a particular change in direction of a line, of which notion every day brings us countless examples.

The other reason why the relations of the extracted characters are so evident is that their properties are so *few*, compared with the properties of the whole, from which we derived them. In every concrete fact the characters and their consequences are so inexhaustibly numerous that we may lose our way among them before noticing the particular consequence it behooves us to draw. But, if we are lucky enough to single out the proper character, we take in, as it were, by a single glance all its possible consequences. Thus the character of scraping the sill has very few suggestions, prominent among which is the suggestion that the scraping will cease if we raise the door; whilst the entire refractory door suggests an enormous number of notions to the mind. Such an example may seem trivial, but it contains the essence of the most refined and transcendental theorizing. The reason why physics grows more deductive the more the fundamental properties it assumes are of a mathematical sort, such as molecular mass or wave-length, is that the immediate consequences of these notions are so few that we can survey them all at once, and promptly pick out those which concern us.

Sagacity.—To reason, then, we must be able to extract characters,—not *any* characters, but the right characters for our conclusion. If we extract the wrong character, it will not lead to that conclusion. Here, then, is the difficulty: *How are characters extracted, and why does it require the advent of a genius in many cases before the fitting character is brought to light?* Why cannot anybody reason as well as anybody else? Why does it need a Newton to notice the law of the squares, a Darwin to notice the survival of the fittest? To answer these questions we must begin a new research, and see how our insight into facts naturally grows.

All our knowledge at first is vague. When we say that a thing is vague, we mean that it has no subdivisions *ab intra*, nor precise limitations *ab extra*; but still all the forms of thought may apply to it. It may have unity, reality, externality, extent, and what not—*thinghood*, in a word, but thinghood only as a whole. In this vague way, probably, does the room appear to the babe who first begins to be conscious of it as something other than his moving nurse. It has no subdivisions in his mind, unless, perhaps, the window is able to attract his separate notice. In this vague way, certainly, does every entirely new experience appear to the adult. A library, a museum, a machine-shop, are mere confused wholes to the uninstructed, but the machinist, the antiquary, and the bookworm perhaps hardly notice the whole at all, so eager are they to pounce upon the details. Familiarity has in them bred discrimination. Such vague terms as 'grass,' 'mould,' and 'meat' do not exist for the botanist or the anatomist. They know too much about grasses, moulds, and muscles. A certain person said to Charles Kingsley, who was showing him the dissection of a caterpillar, with its exquisite viscera, "Why, I thought it was nothing but skin and squash!" A layman present at a shipwreck, a battle, or a fire is helpless. Discrimination has been so little awakened in him by experience that his consciousness leaves no single point of the complex situation accented and standing out for him to begin to act upon. But the sailor, the fireman, and the general know directly at what corner to take up the business. They 'see into the situation'— that is, they analyze it—with their first glance. It is full of delicately differenced ingredients which their education has little by little brought to their consciousness, but of which the novice gains no clear idea.

How this power of analysis was brought about we saw in our chapters on Discrimination and Attention. We dissociate the elements of originally vague totals by attending to them or noticing them alternately, of course. But what determines which element we shall attend to first? There are two immediate and obvious answers: first, our practical or instinctive interests; and second, our æsthetic interests. The dog singles

out of any situation its smells, and the horse its sounds, because they may reveal facts of practical moment, and are
instinctively exciting to these several creatures. The infant
notices the candle-flame or the window, and ignores the rest
of the room, because those objects give him a vivid pleasure.
So, the country boy dissociates the blackberry, the chestnut,
and the wintergreen, from the vague mass of other shrubs and
trees, for their practical uses, and the savage is delighted with
the beads, the bits of looking-glass, brought by an exploring
vessel, and gives no heed to the features of the vessel itself,
which is too much beyond his sphere. These æsthetic and
practical interests, then, are the weightiest factors in making
particular ingredients stand out in high relief. What they lay
their accent on, that we notice; but what they are in themselves we cannot say. We must content ourselves here with
simply accepting them as irreducible ultimate factors in determining the way our knowledge grows.

Now, a creature which has few instinctive impulses, or interests practical or æsthetic, will dissociate few characters, and
will, at best, have limited reasoning powers; whilst one whose
interests are very varied will reason much better. Man, by his
immensely varied instincts, practical wants, and æsthetic feelings, to which every sense contributes, would, by dint of
these alone, be sure to dissociate vastly more characters than
any other animal; and accordingly we find that the lowest savages reason incomparably better than the highest brutes. The
diverse interests lead, too, to a diversification of experiences,
whose accumulation becomes a condition for the play of that
law of dissociation by varying concomitants of which I treated on
p. 240.

The Help given by Association by Similarity.—It is
probable, also, that man's *superior association by similarity* has
much to do with those discriminations of character on which
his higher flights of reasoning are based. As this latter is an
important matter, and as little or nothing was said of it in the
chapter on Discrimination, it behooves me to dwell a little
upon it here.

What does the reader do when he wishes to see in what the
precise likeness or difference of two objects lies? He transfers
his attention as rapidly as possible, backwards and forwards,

from one to the other. The rapid alteration in consciousness shakes out, as it were, the points of difference or agreement, which would have slumbered forever unnoticed if the consciousness of the objects compared had occurred at widely distant periods of time. What does the scientific man do who searches for the reason or law embedded in a phenomenon? He deliberately accumulates all the instances he can find which have any analogy to that phenomenon; and, by simultaneously filling his mind with them all, he frequently succeeds in detaching from the collection the peculiarity which he was unable to formulate in one alone; even though that one had been preceded in his former experience by all of those with which he now at once confronts it. These examples show that the mere general fact of having occurred at some time in one's experience, with varying concomitants, is not by itself a sufficient reason for a character to be dissociated now. We need something more; we need that the varying concomitants should in all their variety be brought into consciousness *at once*. Not till then will the character in question escape from its adhesion to each and all of them and stand alone. This will immediately be recognized by those who have read Mill's *Logic* as the ground of Utility in his famous 'four methods of experimental inquiry,' the methods of agreement, of difference, of residues, and of concomitant variations. Each of these gives a list of analogous instances out of the midst of which a sought-for character may roll and strike the mind.

Now it is obvious that any mind in which association by similarity is highly developed is a mind which will spontaneously form lists of instances like this. Take a present fact A, with a character m in it. The mind may fail at first to notice this character m at all. But if A calls up C, D, E, and F,— these being phenomena which resemble A in possessing m, but which may not have entered for months into the experience of the animal who now experiences A, why, plainly, such association performs the part of the reader's deliberately rapid comparison referred to above, and of the systematic consideration of like cases by the scientific investigator, and may lead to the noticing of m in an abstract way. Certainly this is obvious; and no conclusion is left to us but to assert that, after the

few most powerful practical and æsthetic interests, our chief
help towards noticing those special characters of phenomena
which, when once possessed and named, are used as reasons,
class names, essences, or middle terms, *is this association by similarity.* Without it, indeed, the deliberate procedure of the scientific man would be impossible: he could never collect his
analogous instances. But it operates of itself in highly-gifted
minds without any deliberation, spontaneously collecting
analogous instances, uniting in a moment what in nature the
whole breadth of space and time keeps separate, and so permitting a perception of identical points in the midst of different circumstances, which minds governed wholly by the law
of contiguity could never begin to attain.

Figure 66 shows this. If m, in the present representation A,
calls up B, C, D, and E, which are similar to A in possessing
it, and calls them up in rapid succession, then m, being associated almost simultaneously with such varying concomitants,
will 'roll out' and attract our separate notice.

If so much is clear to the reader, he will be willing to admit
that the mind *in which this mode of association most prevails* will,
from its better opportunity of extricating characters, be the
one most prone to reasoned thinking; whilst, on the other

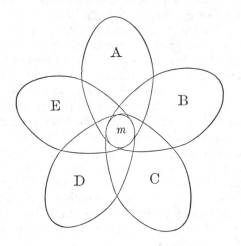

Fig. 66.

hand, a mind in which we do not detect reasoned thinking will probably be one in which association by contiguity holds almost exclusive sway.

Geniuses are, by common consent, considered to differ from ordinary minds by an unusual development of association by similarity. One of Professor Bain's best strokes of work is the exhibition of this truth. It applies to geniuses in the line of reasoning as well as in other lines.

The Reasoning Powers of Brutes.—As the genius is to the vulgarian, so the vulgar human mind is to the intelligence of a brute. Compared with men, it is probable that brutes neither attend to abstract characters, nor have associations by similarity. Their thoughts probably pass from one concrete object to its habitual concrete successor far more uniformly than is the case with us. In other words, their associations of ideas are almost exclusively by contiguity. So far, however, as any brute might think by abstract characters instead of by the association of concretes, he would have to be admitted to be a reasoner in the true human sense. How far this may take place is quite uncertain. Certain it is that the more intelligent brutes *obey* abstract characters, whether they mentally single them out as such or not. They act upon things according to their *class*. This involves some sort of emphasizing, if not abstracting, of the class-essence by the animal's mind. A concrete individual with none of his characters emphasized is one thing; a sharply conceived attribute marked off from everything else by a name is another. But between no analysis of a concrete, and complete analysis; no abstraction of an embedded character, and complete abstraction, every possible intermediary grade must lie. And some of these grades ought to have names, for they are certainly represented in the mind. Dr. Romanes has proposed the name *recept*, and Prof. Lloyd Morgan the name *construct*, for the idea of a vaguely abstracted and generalized object-class. A definite abstraction is called an *isolate* by the latter author. Neither *construct* nor *recept* seems to me a felicitous word; but poor as both are, they form a distinct addition to psychology, so I give them here. Would such a word as *influent* sound better than *recept* in the following passage from Romanes?

"Water-fowl adopt a somewhat different mode of alighting

upon land, or even upon ice, from that which they adopt when alighting upon water; and those kinds which dive from a height (such as terns and gannets) never do so upon land or upon ice. These facts prove that the animals have one recept answering to a solid substance, and another answering to a fluid. Similarly, a man will not dive from a height over hard ground or over ice, nor will he jump into water in the same way as he jumps upon dry land. In other words, like the water-fowl, he has two distinct recepts, one of which answers to solid ground, and the other to an unresisting fluid. But, unlike the water-fowl, he is able to bestow upon each of these recepts a name, and thus to raise them both to the level of concepts. So far as the practical purposes of locomotion are concerned, it is of course immaterial whether or not he thus raises his recepts into concepts; but . . . for many other purposes it is of the highest importance that he is able to do this."[2]

A certain well-bred retriever of whom I know never bit his birds. But one day having to bring two birds at once, which, though unable to fly, were 'alive and kicking,' he deliberately gave one a bite which killed it, took the other one still alive to his master, and then returned for the first. It is impossible not to believe that some such abstract thoughts as 'alive— get away—must kill,' . . . etc., passed in rapid succession through this dog's mind, whatever the sensible imagery may have been with which they were blended. Such practical obedience to the special aspects of things which may be important involves the essence of reasoning. But the characters whose presence impress brutes are very few, being only those which are directly connected with their most instinctive interests. They never extract characters for the mere fun of the thing, as men do. One is tempted to explain this as the result in them of an almost entire absence of such association by similarity as characterizes the human mind. A thing may remind a brute of its full similars, but not of things to which it is but slightly similar; and all that dissociation by varying concomitants, which in man is based so largely on association by similarity, hardly seems to take place at all in the infra-human

[2]*Mental Evolution in Man*, p. 74.

mind. One total object suggests another total object, and the lower mammals find themselves acting with propriety, they know not why. The great, the fundamental, defect of their minds seems to be the inability of their groups of ideas to break across in unaccustomed places. They are enslaved to routine, to cut-and-dried thinking; and if the most prosaic of human beings could be transported into his dog's soul, he would be appalled at the utter absence of fancy which there reigns. Thoughts would not be found to call up their similars, but only their habitual successors. Sunsets would not suggest heroes' deaths, but supper-time. This is why man is the only metaphysical animal. To wonder why the universe should be as it is presupposes the notion of its being different, and a brute, who never reduces the actual to fluidity by breaking up its literal sequences in his imagination, can never form such a notion. He takes the world simply for granted, and never wonders at it at all.

CHAPTER XXIII

CONSCIOUSNESS AND MOVEMENT

All consciousness is motor. The reader will not have forgotten, in the jungle of purely inward processes and products through which the last chapters have borne him, that the final result of them all must be some form of bodily activity due to the escape of the central excitement through outgoing nerves. The whole neural organism, it will be remembered, is, physiologically considered, but a machine for converting stimuli into reactions; and the intellectual part of our life is knit up with but the middle or 'central' part of the machine's operations. We now go on to consider the final or emergent operations, the bodily activities, and the forms of consciousness consequent thereupon.

Every impression which impinges on the incoming nerves produces some discharge down the outgoing ones, whether we be aware of it or not. Using sweeping terms and ignoring exceptions, *we might say that every possible feeling produces a movement, and that the movement is a movement of the entire organism, and of each and all its parts*. What happens patently when an explosion or a flash of lightning startles us, or when we are tickled, happens latently with every sensation which we receive. The only reason why we do not feel the startle or tickle in the case of insignificant sensations is partly its very small amount, partly our obtuseness. Professor Bain many years ago gave the name of the Law of Diffusion to this phenomenon of general discharge, and expressed it thus: "According as an impression is accompanied with Feeling, the aroused currents diffuse themselves freely over the brain, leading to a general agitation of the moving organs, as well as affecting the viscera."

There are probably no exceptions to the diffusion of every impression through the *nerve-centres*. The *effect* of a new wave through the centres may, however, often be to interfere with processes already going on there; and the outward consequence of such interference may be the checking of bodily activities in process of occurrence. When this happens it probably is like the siphoning of certain channels by currents flow-ing through others; as when, in walking, we suddenly stand still because a sound, sight, smell, or thought catches our at-tention. But there are cases of arrest of peripheral activity which depend, not on inhibition of centres, but on stimula-tion of centres which discharge outgoing currents of an inhib-itory sort. Whenever we are startled, for example, our heart momentarily stops or slows its beating, and then palpitates with accelerated speed. The brief arrest is due to an outgoing current down the pneumogastric nerve. This nerve, when stimulated, stops or slows the heart-beats, and this particular effect of startling fails to occur if the nerve be cut.

In general, however, the stimulating effects of a sense-impression preponderate over the inhibiting effects, so that we may roughly say, as we began by saying, that the wave of discharge produces an activity in all parts of the body. The task of tracing out *all* the effects of any one incoming sensa-tion has not yet been performed by physiologists. Recent years have, however, begun to enlarge our information; and we have now experimental proof that the heart-beats, the ar-terial pressure, the respiration, the sweat-glands, the pupil, the bladder, bowels, and uterus, as well as the voluntary mus-cles, may have their tone and degree of contraction altered even by the most insignificant sensorial stimuli. In short, a *process set up anywhere in the centres reverberates everywhere, and in some way or other affects the organism throughout, making its activities either greater or less*. It is as if the nerve-central mass were like a good conductor charged with electricity, of which the tension cannot be changed at all without changing it everywhere at once.

Herr Schneider has tried to show, by an ingenious zoölog-ical review, that all the *special* movements which highly evolved animals make are differentiated from the two origi-nally simple movements of contraction and expansion in which the entire body of simple organisms takes part. The tendency to contract is the source of all the self-protective impulses and reactions which are later developed, including that of flight. The tendency to expand splits up, on the con-trary, into the impulses and instincts of an aggressive kind, feeding, fighting, sexual intercourse, etc. I cite this as a sort of evolutionary reason to add to the mechanical *a priori* reason why there *ought* to be the diffusive wave which *a posteriori* instances show to exist.

I shall now proceed to a detailed study of the more important classes of movement consequent upon cerebro-mental change. They may be enumerated as—

1) Expressions of Emotion;
2) Instinctive or Impulsive Performances; and
3) Voluntary Deeds;

and each shall have a chapter to itself.

CHAPTER XXIV

EMOTION

Emotions compared with Instincts.—An emotion is a tendency to feel, and an instinct is a tendency to act, characteristically, when in presence of a certain object in the environment. But the emotions also have their bodily 'expression,' which may involve strong muscular activity (as in fear or anger, for example); and it becomes a little hard in many cases to separate the description of the 'emotional' condition from that of the 'instinctive' reaction which one and the same object may provoke. Shall *fear* be described in the chapter on Instincts or in that on Emotions? Where shall one describe *curiosity, emulation,* and the like? The answer is quite arbitrary from the scientific point of view, and practical convenience may decide. As inner mental conditions, emotions are quite indescribable. Description, moreover, would be superfluous, for the reader knows already how they feel. Their relations to the objects which prompt them and to the reactions which they provoke are all that one can put down in a book.

Every object that excites an instinct excites an emotion as well. The only distinction one may draw is that the reaction called emotional terminates in the subject's own body, whilst the reaction called instinctive is apt to go farther and enter into practical relations with the exciting object. In both instinct and emotion the mere memory or imagination of the object may suffice to liberate the excitement. One may even get angrier in thinking over one's insult than one was in receiving it; and melt more over a mother who is dead than one ever did when she was living. In the rest of the chapter I shall use the word *object* of emotion indifferently to mean one which is physically present or one which is merely thought of.

The varieties of emotion are innumerable. *Anger, fear, love, hate, joy, grief, shame, pride,* and their varieties, may be called the *coarser* emotions, being coupled as they are with relatively strong bodily reverberations. The *subtler* emotions are the moral, intellectual, and æsthetic feelings, and their bodily reaction is usually much less strong. The mere description of the objects, circumstances, and varieties of the different species of emotion may go to any length. Their internal shadings merge endlessly into each other, and have been partly commemorated in language, as, for example, by such synonyms as hatred, antipathy, animosity, resentment, dislike, aversion, malice, spite, revenge, abhorrence, etc., etc. Dictionaries of synonyms have discriminated them, as well as textbooks of psychology—in fact, many German psychological text-books *are* nothing but dictionaries of synonyms when it comes to the chapter on Emotion. But there are limits to the profitable elaboration of the obvious, and the result of all this flux is that the merely descriptive literature of the subject, from Descartes downwards, is one of the most tedious parts of psychology. And not only is it tedious, but you feel that its subdivisions are to a great extent either fictitious or unimportant, and that its pretences to accuracy are a sham. But unfortunately there is little psychological writing about the emotions which is not merely descriptive. As emotions are described in novels, they interest us, for we are made to share them. We have grown acquainted with the concrete objects and emergencies which call them forth, and any knowing touch of introspection which may grace the page meets with a quick and feeling response. Confessedly literary works of aphoristic philosophy also flash lights into our emotional life, and give us a fitful delight. But as far as the 'scientific psychology' of the emotions goes, I may have been surfeited by too much reading of classic works on the subject, but I should as lief read verbal descriptions of the shapes of the rocks on a New Hampshire farm as toil through them again. They give one nowhere a central point of view, or a deductive or generative principle. They distinguish and refine and specify *in infinitum* without ever getting on to another logical level. Whereas the beauty of all truly scientific work is to get to ever deeper levels. Is there no way out from this level of individual description in the case of the emotions? I believe there is a way out, if one will only take it.

The Cause of their Varieties.—The trouble with the emotions in psychology is that they are regarded too much as absolutely individual things. So long as they are set down as so many eternal and sacred psychic entities, like the old immutable species in natural history, so long all that *can* be done with them is reverently to catalogue their separate characters, points, and effects. But if we regard them as products of more general causes (as 'species' are now regarded as products of heredity and variation), the mere distinguishing and cataloguing becomes of subsidiary importance. Having the goose which lays the golden eggs, the description of each egg already laid is a minor matter. I will devote the next few pages to setting forth one very general cause of our emotional feeling, limiting myself in the first instance to what may be called the *coarser* emotions.

The feeling, in the coarser emotions, results from the bodily expression. Our natural way of thinking about these coarser emotions is that the mental perception of some fact excites the mental affection called the emotion, and that this latter state of mind gives rise to the bodily expression. My theory, on the contrary, is that *the bodily changes follow directly the perception of the exciting fact, and that our feeling of the same changes as they occur* IS *the emotion*. Common-sense says, we lose our fortune, are sorry and weep; we meet a bear, are frightened and run; we are insulted by a rival, are angry and strike. The hypothesis here to be defended says that this order of sequence is incorrect, that the one mental state is not immediately induced by the other, that the bodily manifestations must first be interposed between, and that the more rational statement is that we feel sorry because we cry, angry because we strike, afraid because we tremble, and not that we cry, strike, or tremble because we are sorry, angry, or fearful, as the case may be. Without the bodily states following on the perception, the latter would be purely cognitive in form, pale, colorless, destitute of emotional warmth. We might then see the bear and judge it best to run, receive the insult and deem it right to strike, but we should not actually *feel* afraid or angry.

Stated in this crude way, the hypothesis is pretty sure to meet with immediate disbelief. And yet neither many nor far-fetched considerations are required to mitigate its paradoxical character, and possibly to produce conviction of its truth.

To begin with, *particular perceptions certainly do produce wide-spread bodily effects by a sort of immediate physical influence, antecedent to the arousal of an emotion or emotional idea.* In listening to poetry, drama, or heroic narrative we are often surprised at the cutaneous shiver which like a sudden wave flows over us, and at the heart-swelling and the lachrymal effusion that unexpectedly catch us at intervals. In hearing music the same is even more strikingly true. If we abruptly see a dark moving form in the woods, our heart stops beating, and we catch our breath instantly and before any articulate idea of danger can arise. If our friend goes near to the edge of a precipice, we get the well-known feeling of 'all-overishness,' and we shrink back, although we positively *know* him to be safe, and have no distinct imagination of his fall. The writer well remembers his astonishment, when a boy of seven or eight, at fainting when he saw a horse bled. The blood was in a bucket, with a stick in it, and, if memory does not deceive him, he stirred it round and saw it drip from the stick with no feeling save that of childish curiosity. Suddenly the world grew black before his eyes, his ears began to buzz, and he knew no more. He had never heard of the sight of blood producing faintness or sickness, and he had so little repugnance to it, and so little apprehension of any other sort of danger from it, that even at that tender age, as he well remembers, he could not help wondering how the mere physical presence of a pailful of crimson fluid could occasion in him such formidable bodily effects.

The best proof that the immediate cause of emotion is a physical effect on the nerves is furnished by *those pathological cases in which the emotion is objectless.* One of the chief merits, in fact, of the view which I propose seems to be that we can so easily formulate by its means pathological cases and normal cases under a common scheme. In every asylum we find examples of absolutely unmotived fear, anger, melancholy, or conceit; and others of an equally unmotived apathy which persists in spite of the best of outward reasons why it should give way. In the former cases we must suppose the nervous machinery to be so 'labile' in some one emotional direction that almost every stimulus (however inappropriate) causes it to upset in that way, and to engender the particular complex of feelings of which the psychic body of the emotion consists. Thus, to take one special instance, if inability to draw deep breath, fluttering of the heart, and that peculiar epigastric change felt as 'precordial anxiety,' with an irresistible tendency to take a somewhat crouching attitude and to sit still, and with perhaps other visceral processes not now known, all spontaneously occur together in a certain person, his feeling of their combination *is* the emotion of dread, and he is the victim of what is known as morbid fear. A friend who has had occasional attacks of this most evil of all maladies tells me that in his case the whole drama seems to centre about the region of the heart and respiratory apparatus, that his main effort during the attacks is to get control of his inspirations and to slow his heart, and that the moment he attains to breathing deeply and to holding himself erect, the dread, *ipso facto*, seems to depart.

The emotion here is nothing but the feeling of a bodily state, and it has a purely bodily cause.

The next thing to be noticed is this, that *every one of the bodily changes, whatsoever it be, is* FELT, *acutely or obscurely, the moment it occurs*. If the reader has never paid attention to this matter, he will be both interested and astonished to learn how many different local bodily feelings he can detect in himself as characteristic of his various emotional moods. It would be perhaps too much to expect him to arrest the tide of any strong gust of passion for the sake of any such curious analysis as this; but he can observe more tranquil states, and that may be assumed here to be true of the greater which is shown to be true of the less. Our whole cubic capacity is sensibly alive; and each morsel of it contributes its pulsations of feeling, dim or sharp, pleasant, painful, or dubious, to that sense of personality that every one of us unfailingly carries with him. It is surprising what little items give accent to these complexes of sensibility. When worried by any slight trouble, one may find that the focus of one's bodily consciousness is the contraction, often quite inconsiderable, of the eyes and brows. When momentarily embarrassed, it is something in the pharynx that compels either a swallow, a clearing of the throat, or a slight cough; and so on for as many more instances as might be named. The various permutations of which these organic changes are susceptible make it abstractly possible that no shade of emotion should be without a bodily reverberation as unique, when taken in its totality, as is the mental mood itself. The immense number of parts modified is what makes it so difficult for us to reproduce in cold blood the total and integral expression of any one emotion. We may catch the trick with the voluntary muscles, but fail with the skin, glands, heart, and other viscera. Just as an artificially imitated sneeze lacks something of the reality, so the attempt to imitate grief or enthusiasm in the absence of its normal instigating cause is apt to be rather 'hollow.'

I now proceed to urge the vital point of my whole theory, which is this: *If we fancy some strong emotion, and then try to abstract from our consciousness of it all the feelings of its bodily symptoms, we find we have nothing left behind,* no 'mind-stuff' out of which the emotion can be constituted, and that a cold and neutral state of intellectual perception is all that remains. It is true that, although most people, when asked, say that their introspection verifies this statement, some persist in saying theirs does not. Many cannot be made to understand the question. When you beg them to imagine away every feeling of laughter and of tendency to laugh from their consciousness of the ludicrousness of an object, and then to tell you what the feeling of its ludicrousness would be like, whether it be anything more than the perception that the object belongs to the class 'funny,' they persist in replying that the thing proposed is a physical impossibility, and that they always *must* laugh if they see a funny object. Of course the task proposed is not the practical one of seeing a ludicrous object and annihilating one's tendency to laugh. It is the purely speculative one of subtracting certain elements of feeling from an emotional state supposed to exist in its fulness, and saying what the residual elements are. I cannot help thinking that all who rightly apprehend this problem will agree with the proposition above laid down. What kind of an emotion of fear would be left if the feeling neither of quickened heart-beats nor of shallow breathing, neither of trembling lips nor of weakened limbs, neither of goose-flesh nor of visceral stirrings, were present, it is quite impossible for me to think. Can one fancy the state of rage and picture no ebullition in the chest, no flushing of the face, no dilatation of the nostrils, no clenching of the teeth, no impulse to vigorous action, but in their stead limp muscles, calm breathing, and a placid face? The present writer, for one, certainly cannot. The rage is as completely evaporated as the sensation of its so-called manifestations, and the only thing that can possibly be supposed to take its place is some cold-blooded and dispassionate judicial sentence, confined entirely to the intellectual realm, to the effect that a certain person or persons merit chastisement for their sins. In like manner of grief: what would it be without its tears, its sobs, its suffocation of the heart, its pang in the breast-bone? A feelingless cognition that certain circumstances are deplorable, and nothing more. Every passion in turn tells the same story. A disembodied human emotion is a sheer nonentity. I do not say that it is a contradiction in the nature of things, or that pure spirits are necessarily condemned to cold intellectual lives; but I say that for *us* emotion dissociated from all bodily feeling is inconceivable. The more closely I scrutinize my states, the more persuaded I become that whatever 'coarse' affections and passions I have are in very truth constituted by, and made up of, those bodily changes which we ordinarily call their expression or consequence; and the more it seems to me that if I were to become corporeally anæsthetic, I should be excluded from the life of the affections, harsh and tender alike, and drag out an existence of merely cognitive or intellectual form. Such an existence, although it seems to have been the ideal of ancient sages, is too apathetic to be keenly sought after by those born after the revival of the worship of sensibility, a few generations ago.

Let not this view be called materialistic. It is neither more nor less materialistic than any other view which says that our emotions are conditioned by nervous processes. No reader of this book is likely to rebel against such a saying so long as it is expressed in general terms; and if anyone still finds materialism in the thesis now defended, that must be because of the special processes invoked. They are *sensational* processes, processes due to inward currents set up by physical happenings. Such processes have, it is true, always been regarded by the platonizers in psychology as having something peculiarly base about them. But our emotions must always be *inwardly* what they are, whatever be the physiological ground of their apparition. If they are deep pure worthy spiritual facts

on any conceivable theory of their physiological source, they
remain no less deep pure spiritual and worthy of regard on
this present sensational theory. They carry their own inner
measure of worth with them; and it is just as logical to use
the present theory of the emotions for proving that sensational processes need not be vile and material, as to use their
vileness and materiality as a proof that such a theory cannot
be true.

This view explains the great variability of emotion. If
such a theory is true, then each emotion is the resultant of a
sum of elements, and each element is caused by a physiological process of a sort already well known. The elements are all
organic changes, and each of them is the reflex effect of the
exciting object. Definite questions now immediately arise—
questions very different from those which were the only
possible ones without this view. Those were questions of
classification: "Which are the proper genera of emotion, and
which the species under each?"—or of description: "By what
expression is each emotion characterized?" The questions now
are *causal*: "Just what changes does this object and what
changes does that object excite?" and "How come they to excite these particular changes and not others?" We step from a
superficial to a deep order of inquiry. Classification and description are the lowest stage of science. They sink into the
background the moment questions of causation are formulated, and remain important only so far as they facilitate our
answering these. Now the moment an emotion is causally accounted for, as the arousal by an object of a lot of reflex acts
which are forthwith felt, *we immediately see why there is no limit
to the number of possible different emotions which may exist, and
why the emotions of different individuals may vary indefinitely*,
both as to their constitution and as to the objects which call
them forth. For there is nothing sacramental or eternally fixed
in reflex action. Any sort of reflex effect is possible, and reflexes actually vary indefinitely, as we know.

In short, *any classification of the emotions is seen to be as true
and as 'natural' as any other*, if it only serves some purpose;
and such a question as "What is the 'real' or 'typical' expression of anger, or fear?" is seen to have no objective meaning
at all. Instead of it we now have the question as to how any

given 'expression' of anger or fear may have come to exist; and that is a real question of physiological mechanics on the one hand, and of history on the other, which (like all real questions) is in essence answerable, although the answer may be hard to find. On a later page I shall mention the attempts to answer it which have been made.

A Corollary verified. — If our theory be true, a necessary corollary of it ought to be this: that any voluntary and cold-blooded arousal of the so-called manifestations of a special emotion should give us the emotion itself. Now within the limits in which it can be verified, experience corroborates rather than disproves this inference. Everyone knows how panic is increased by flight, and how the giving way to the symptoms of grief or anger increases those passions themselves. Each fit of sobbing makes the sorrow more acute, and calls forth another fit stronger still, until at last repose only ensues with lassitude and with the apparent exhaustion of the machinery. In rage, it is notorious how we 'work ourselves up' to a climax by repeated outbreaks of expression. Refuse to express a passion, and it dies. Count ten before venting your anger, and its occasion seems ridiculous. Whistling to keep up courage is no mere figure of speech. On the other hand, sit all day in a moping posture, sigh, and reply to everything with a dismal voice, and your melancholy lingers. There is no more valuable precept in moral education than this, as all who have experience know: if we wish to conquer undesirable emotional tendencies in ourselves, we must assiduously, and in the first instance cold-bloodedly, go through the *outward movements* of those contrary dispositions which we prefer to cultivate. The reward of persistency will infallibly come, in the fading out of the sullenness or depression, and the advent of real cheerfulness and kindliness in their stead. Smooth the brow, brighten the eye, contract the dorsal rather than the ventral aspect of the frame, and speak in a major key, pass the genial compliment, and your heart must be frigid indeed if it do not gradually thaw!

Against this it is to be said that many actors who perfectly mimic the outward appearances of emotion in face, gait, and voice declare that they feel no emotion at all. Others, however, according to Mr. William Archer, who has made a very instructive statistical inquiry among them, say that the emotion of the part masters them whenever they play it well. The explanation for the discrepancy amongst actors is probably simple. The *visceral and organic* part of the expression can be suppressed in some men, but not in others, and on this it must be that the chief part of the felt emotion depends. Those actors who feel the emotion are probably unable, those who are inwardly cold are probably able, to affect the dissociation in a complete way.

An Objection replied to.—It may be objected to the general theory which I maintain that stopping the expression of an emotion often makes it worse. The funniness becomes quite excruciating when we are forbidden by the situation to laugh, and anger pent in by fear turns into tenfold hate. Expressing either emotion freely, however, gives relief.

This objection is more specious than real. *During* the expression the emotion is always felt. *After* it, the centres having normally discharged themselves, we feel it no more. But where the facial part of the discharge is suppressed the thoracic and visceral may be all the more violent and persistent, as in suppressed laughter; or the original emotion may be changed, by the combination of the provoking object with the restraining pressure, into *another emotion altogether*, in which different and possibly profounder organic disturbance occurs. If I would kill my enemy but dare not, my emotion is surely altogether other than that which would possess me if I let my anger explode.—On the whole, therefore this objection has no weight.

The Subtler Emotions.—In the æsthetic emotions the bodily reverberation and the feeling may both be faint. A connoisseur is apt to judge a work of art dryly and intellectually, and with no bodily thrill. On the other hand, works of art may arouse intense emotion; and whenever they do so, the experience is completely covered by the terms of our theory. Our theory requires that *incoming currents* be the basis of emotion. But, whether secondary organic reverberations be or be not aroused by it, the perception of a work of art (music, decoration, etc.) is always in the first instance at any rate an affair of incoming currents. The work itself is an object of sensation; and, the perception of an object of sensation being a 'coarse' or vivid experience, what pleasure goes with it will partake of the 'coarse' or vivid form.

That there may be subtle pleasure too, I do not deny. In other words, there may be purely cerebral emotion, independent of all currents from outside. Such feelings as moral satisfaction, thankfulness, curiosity, relief at getting a problem solved, may be of this sort. But the thinness and paleness of these feelings, when unmixed with bodily effects, is in very striking contrast to the coarser emotions. In all sentimental and impressionable people the bodily effects mix in: the voice breaks and the eyes moisten when the moral truth is felt, etc. Wherever there is anything like *rapture*, however intellectual its ground, we find these secondary processes ensue. Unless we actually laugh at the neatness of the demonstration or witticism; unless we thrill at the case of justice, or tingle at the act of magnanimity, our state of mind can hardly be called emotional at all. It is in fact a mere intellectual perception of how certain things are to be called—neat, right, witty, generous, and the like. Such a judicial state of mind as this is to be classed among cognitive rather than among emotional acts.

Description of Fear.—For the reasons given on p. 351, I will append no inventory or classification of emotions or description of their symptoms. The reader has practically almost all the facts in his own hand. As an example, however, of the best sort of descriptive work on the symptoms, I will quote Darwin's account of them in fear.

"Fear is often preceded by astonishment, and is so far akin to it, that both lead to the senses of sight and hearing being instantly aroused. In both cases the eyes and mouth are widely opened, and the eyebrows raised. The frightened man at first stands like a statue motionless and breathless, or crouches down as if instinctively to escape observation. The heart beats quickly and violently, so that it palpitates or knocks against the ribs; but it is very doubtful whether it then works more efficiently than usual, so as to send a greater supply of blood to all parts of the body; for the skin instantly becomes pale, as during incipient faintness. This paleness of the surface, however, is probably in large part, or exclusively, due to the vaso-motor centre being affected in such a manner as to cause the contraction of the small arteries of the skin.

That the skin is much affected under the sense of great fear, we see in the marvellous manner in which perspiration immediately exudes from it. This exudation is all the more remarkable, as the surface is then cold, and hence the term a cold sweat; whereas, the sudorific glands are properly excited into action when the surface is heated. The hairs also on the skin stand erect; and the superficial muscles shiver. In connection with the disturbed action of the heart, the breathing is hurried. The salivary glands act imperfectly; the mouth becomes dry, and is often opened and shut. I have also noticed that under slight fear there is a strong tendency to yawn. One of the best-marked symptoms is the trembling of all the muscles of the body; and this is often first seen in the lips. From this cause, and from the dryness of the mouth, the voice becomes husky or indistinct, or may altogether fail. 'Obstupui, steteruntque comæ, et vox faucibus hæsit.' . . . As fear increases into an agony of terror, we behold, as under all violent emotions, diversified results. The heart beats wildly, or may fail to act and faintness ensue; there is a death-like pallor; the breathing is laboured; the wings of the nostrils are widely dilated; 'there is a gasping and convulsive motion of the lips, a tremor on the hollow cheek, a gulping and catching of the throat'; the uncovered and protruding eyeballs are fixed on the object of terror; or they may roll restlessly from side to side, *huc illuc volvens oculos totumque pererrat.* The pupils are said to be enormously dilated. All the muscles of the body may become rigid, or may be thrown into convulsive movements. The hands are alternately clenched and opened, often with a twitching movement. The arms may be protruded, as if to avert some dreadful danger, or may be thrown wildly over the head. The Rev. Mr. Hagenauer has seen this latter action in a terrified Australian. In other cases there is a sudden and uncontrollable tendency to headlong flight; and so strong is this, that the boldest soldiers may be seized with a sudden panic."[1]

Genesis of the Emotional Reactions.—How come the various objects which excite emotion to produce such special and different bodily effects? This question was not asked till

[1] *The Expression of the Emotions in Man and Animals* (N.Y. ed.), p. 290.

quite recently, but already some interesting suggestions towards answering it have been made.

Some movements of expression can be accounted for as *weakened repetitions of movements which formerly* (when they were stronger) *were of utility to the subject*. Others are similarly weakened repetitions of movements which under other conditions were *physiologically necessary concomitants of the useful movements*. Of the latter reactions the respiratory disturbances in anger and fear might be taken as examples—organic reminiscences, as it were, reverberations in imagination of the blowings of the man making a series of combative efforts, of the pantings of one in precipitate flight. Such at least is a suggestion made by Mr. Spencer which has found approval. And he also was the first, so far as I know, to suggest that other movements in anger and fear could be explained by the nascent excitation of formerly useful acts.

"To have in a slight degree," he says, "such psychical states as accompany the reception of wounds, and are experienced during flight, is to be in a state of what we call fear. And to have in a slight degree such psychical states as the processes of catching, killing, and eating imply, is to have the desires to catch, kill, and eat. That the propensities to the acts are nothing else than nascent excitations of the psychical state involved in the acts, is proved by the natural language of the propensities. Fear, when strong, expresses itself in cries, in efforts to escape, in palpitations, in tremblings; and these are just the manifestations that go along with an actual suffering of the evil feared. The destructive passion is shown in a general tension of the muscular system, in gnashing of teeth and protrusion of the claws, in dilated eyes and nostrils, in growls; and these are weaker forms of the actions that accompany the killing of prey. To such objective evidences, every one can add subjective evidences. Every one can testify that the psychical state called fear, consists of mental representations of certain painful results; and that the one called anger, consists of mental representations of the actions and impressions which would occur while inflicting some kind of pain."

The principle of *revival, in weakened form, of reactions useful in more violent dealings with the object inspiring the emotion*, has found many applications. So slight a symptom as the snarl or sneer, the one-sided uncovering of the upper teeth, is accounted for by Darwin as a survival from the time when our ancestors had large canines, and unfleshed them (as dogs now do) for attack. Similarly the raising of the eyebrows in outward attention, the opening of the mouth in astonishment, come, according to the same author, from the utility of these movements in extreme cases. The raising of the eyebrows goes with the opening of the eye for better vision; the opening of the mouth with the intensest listening, and with the rapid catching of the breath which precedes muscular effort. The distention of the nostrils in anger is interpreted by Spencer as an echo of the way in which our ancestors had to breathe when, during combat, their "mouth was filled up by a part of an antagonist's body that had been seized" (!). The trembling of fear is supposed by Mantegazza to be for the sake of warming the blood (!). The reddening of the face and neck is called by Wundt a compensatory arrangement for relieving the brain of the blood-pressure which the simultaneous excitement of the heart brings with it. The effusion of tears is explained both by this author and by Darwin to be a blood-withdrawing agency of a similar sort. The contraction of the muscles around the eyes, of which the primitive use is to protect those organs from being too much gorged with blood during the screaming fits of infancy, survives in adult life in the shape of the frown, which instantly comes over the brow when anything difficult or displeasing presents itself either to thought or action.

"As the habit of contracting the brows has been followed by infants during innumerable generations, at the commencement of every crying or screaming fit," says Darwin, "it has become firmly associated with the incipient sense of something distressing or disagreeable. Hence under similar circumstances it would be apt to be continued during maturity, although never then developed into a crying-fit. Screaming or weeping begins to be voluntarily restrained at an early period of life, whereas frowning is hardly ever restrained at any age."

Another principle, to which Darwin perhaps hardly does sufficient justice, may be called the principle of *reacting similarly to analogous-feeling stimuli*. There is a whole vocabulary of descriptive adjectives common to impressions belonging to different sensible spheres—experiences of all classes are *sweet*, impressions of all classes *rich* or *solid*, sensations of all classes *sharp*. Wundt and Piderit accordingly explain many of our most expressive reactions upon moral causes as symbolic gustatory movements. As soon as any experience arises which has an affinity with the feeling of sweet, or bitter, or sour, the same movements are executed which would result from the taste in point. "All the states of mind which language designates by the metaphors bitter, harsh, sweet, combine themselves, therefore, with the corresponding mimetic movements of the mouth." Certainly the emotions of disgust and satisfaction do express themselves in this mimetic way. Disgust is an incipient regurgitation or retching, limiting its expression often to the grimace of the lips and nose; satisfaction goes with a sucking smile, or tasting motion of the lips. The ordinary gesture of negation—among us, moving the head about its axis from side to side—is a reaction originally used by babies to keep disagreeables from getting into their mouth, and may be observed in perfection in any nursery. It is now evoked where the stimulus is only an unwelcome idea. Similarly the nod forwards in affirmation is after the analogy of taking food into the mouth. The connection of the expression of moral or social disdain or dislike, especially in women, with movements having a perfectly definite original olfactory function, is too obvious for comment. Winking is the effect of any threatening surprise, not only of what puts the eyes in danger; and a momentary aversion of the eyes is very apt to be one's first symptom of response to an unexpectedly unwelcome proposition.—These may suffice as examples of movements expressive from analogy.

But if certain of our emotional reactions can be explained by the two principles invoked—and the reader will himself have felt how conjectural and fallible in some of the instances the explanation is—there remain many reactions which cannot so be explained at all, and these we must write down for the present as purely idiopathic effects of the stimulus. Amongst them are the effects on the viscera and internal glands, the dryness of the mouth and diarrhœa and nausea of fear, the liver-disturbances which sometimes produce jaundice after excessive rage, the urinary secretion of sanguine excitement, and the bladder-contraction of apprehension, the gaping of expectancy, the 'lump in the throat' of grief, the tickling there and the swallowing of embarrassment, the 'precordial anxiety' of dread, the changes in the pupil, the various sweatings of the skin, cold or hot, local or general, and its flushings, together with other symptoms which probably exist but are too hidden to have been noticed or named. Trembling, which is found in many excitements besides that of terror, is, *pace* Mr. Spencer and Sig. Mantegazza, quite pathological. So are terror's other strong symptoms: they are harmful to the creature who presents them. In an organism as complex as the nervous system there must be many *incidental* reactions which would never themselves have been evolved independently, for any utility they might possess. Seasickness, ticklishness, shyness, the love of music, of the various intoxicants, nay, the entire æsthetic life of man, must be traced to this accidental origin. It would be foolish to suppose that none of the reactions called emotional could have arisen in this *quasi*-accidental way.

CHAPTER XXV

INSTINCT

*I*ts **Definition.**—*Instinct is usually defined as the faculty of acting in such a way as to produce certain ends, without foresight of the ends, and without previous education in the performance.* Instincts are the functional correlatives of structure. With the presence of a certain organ goes, one may say, almost always a native aptitude for its use.

The actions we call instinctive all conform to the general reflex type; they are called forth by determinate sensory stimuli in contact with the animal's body, or at a distance in his environment. The cat runs after the mouse, runs or shows fight before the dog, avoids falling from walls and trees, shuns fire and water, etc., not because he has any notion either of life or of death, or of self, or of preservation. He has probably attained to no one of these conceptions in such a way as to react definitely upon it. He acts in each case separately, and simply because he cannot help it; being so framed that when that particular running thing called a mouse appears in his field of vision he *must* pursue; that when that particular barking and obstreperous thing called a dog appears there he *must* retire, if at a distance, and scratch if close by; that he *must* withdraw his feet from water and his face from flame, etc. His nervous system is to a great extent a preorganized bundle of such reactions—they are as fatal as sneezing, and as exactly correlated to their special excitants as it is to its own. Although the naturalist may, for his own convenience, class these reactions under general heads, he must not forget that in the animal it is a particular sensation or perception or image which calls them forth.

At first this view astounds us by the enormous number of special adjustments it supposes animals to possess ready-made in anticipation of the outer things among which they are to dwell. *Can* mutual dependence be so intricate and go so far? Is each thing born fitted to particular other things, and to them exclusively, as locks are fitted to their keys? Undoubtedly this must be believed to be so. Each nook and cranny of creation, down to our very skin and entrails, has its living inhabitants, with organs suited to the place, to devour and digest the food it harbors and to meet the dangers it conceals; and the minuteness of adaptation thus shown in the way of *structure* knows no bounds. Even so are there no bounds to the minuteness of adaptation in the way of *conduct* which the several inhabitants display.

The older writings on instinct are ineffectual wastes of words, because their authors never came down to this definite and simple point of view, but smothered everything in vague wonder at the clairvoyant and prophetic power of the animals—so superior to anything in man—and at the beneficence of God in endowing them with such a gift. But God's beneficence endows them, first of all, with a nervous system; and, turning our attention to this, makes instinct immediately appear neither more nor less wonderful than all the other facts of life.

Every instinct is an impulse. Whether we shall call such impulses as blushing, sneezing, coughing, smiling, or dodging, or keeping time to music, instincts or not, is a mere matter of terminology. The process is the same throughout. In his delightfully fresh and interesting work, *Der thierische Wille,* Herr G. H. Schneider subdivides impulses (*Triebe*) into sensation-impulses, perception-impulses, and idea-impulses. To crouch from cold is a sensation-impulse; to turn and follow, if we see people running one way, is a perception-impulse; to cast about for cover, if it begins to blow and rain, is an imagination-impulse. A single complex instinctive action may involve successively the awakening of impulses of all three classes. Thus a hungry lion starts to *seek* prey by the awakening in him of imagination coupled with desire; he begins to *stalk* it when, on eye, ear, or nostril, he gets an impression of its presence at a certain distance; he *springs* upon it, either when the booty takes alarm and flees, or when the distance is sufficiently reduced; he proceeds to *tear* and *devour* it the moment he gets a sensation of its contact with his claws and fangs. Seeking, stalking, springing, and devouring are just so many different kinds of muscular contraction, and neither kind is called forth by the stimulus appropriate to the other.

Now, why do the various animals do what seem to us such strange things, in the presence of such outlandish stimuli? Why does the hen, for example, submit herself to the tedium of incubating such a fearfully uninteresting set of objects as a nestful of eggs, unless she have some sort of a prophetic inkling of the result? The only answer is *ad hominem.* We can only interpret the instincts of brutes by what we know of instincts in ourselves. Why do men always lie down, when they can, on soft beds rather than on hard floors? Why do they sit round the stove on a cold day? Why, in a room, do they place themselves, ninety-nine times out of a hundred, with their faces towards its middle rather than to the wall? Why do they prefer saddle of mutton and champagne to hardtack and pond-water? Why does the maiden interest the youth so that everything about her seems more important and significant than anything else in the world? Nothing more can be said than that these are human ways, and that every creature *likes* its own ways, and takes to the following them as a matter of course. Science may come and consider these ways, and find that most of them are useful. But it is not for the sake of their utility that they are followed, but because at the moment of following them we feel that that is the only appropriate and natural thing to do. Not one man in a billion, when taking his dinner, ever thinks of utility. He eats because the food tastes good and makes him want more. If you ask him *why* he should want to eat more of what tastes like that, instead of revering you as a philosopher he will probably laugh at you for a fool. The connection between the savory sensation and the act it awakens is for him absolute and *selbstverständlich,* an '*a priori* synthesis' of the most perfect sort, needing no proof but its own evidence. It takes, in short, what Berkeley calls a mind debauched by learning to carry the process of making the natural seem strange, so far as to ask for the *why* of any instinctive human act. To the metaphysician alone can such questions occur as: Why do we smile, when pleased, and not scowl? Why are we unable to talk to a crowd as we talk to a single friend? Why does a particular maiden turn our wits so upside-down? The common man can only say, "*Of course* we smile, *of course* our heart palpitates at the sight of the crowd, *of course* we love the maiden, that beautiful soul clad in that perfect form, so palpably and flagrantly made from all eternity to be loved!"

And so, probably, does each animal feel about the particular things it tends to do in presence of particular objects. They, too, are *a priori* syntheses. To the lion it is the lioness which is made to be loved; to the bear, the she-bear. To the broody hen the notion would probably seem monstrous that there should be a creature in the world to whom a nestful of eggs was not the utterly fascinating and precious and never-to-be-too-much-sat-upon object which it is to her.

Thus we may be sure that, however mysterious some animals' instincts may appear to us, our instincts will appear no less mysterious to them. And we may conclude that, to the animal which obeys it, every impulse and every step of every instinct shines with its own sufficient light, and seems at the moment the only eternally right and proper thing to do. It is done for its own sake exclusively. What voluptuous thrill may not shake a fly, when she at last discovers the one particular leaf, or carrion, or bit of dung, that out of all the world can stimulate her ovipositor to its discharge? Does not the discharge then seem to her the only fitting thing? And need she care or know anything about the future maggot and its food?

Instincts are not always blind or invariable. Nothing is commoner than the remark that man differs from lower creatures by the almost total absence of instincts, and the assumption of their work in him by 'reason.' A fruitless discussion might be waged on this point by two theorizers who were careful not to define their terms. We must of course avoid a quarrel about words, and the facts of the case are really tolerably plain. Man has a far greater variety of *impulses* than any lower animal; and any one of these impulses, taken in itself, is as 'blind' as the lowest instinct can be; but, owing to man's memory, power of reflection, and power of inference, they come each one to be felt by him, after he has once yielded to them and experienced their results, in connection with a *foresight* of those results. In this condition an impulse acted out may be said to be acted out, in part at least, *for the sake* of its results. It is obvious that *every instinctive act, in an animal with memory, must cease to be 'blind' after being once repeated*, and must be accompanied with foresight of its 'end' just so far as that end may have fallen under the animal's cognizance. An insect that lays her eggs in a place where she never sees them hatch must always do so 'blindly'; but a hen who has already hatched a brood can hardly be assumed to sit with perfect 'blindness' on her second nest. Some expectation of consequences must in every case like this be aroused; and this expectation, according as it is that of something desired or of something disliked, must necessarily either re-enforce or inhibit the mere impulse. The hen's idea of the chickens would probably encourage her to sit; a rat's memory, on the other hand, of a former escape from a trap would neutralize his impulse to take bait from anything that reminded him of that trap. If a boy sees a fat hopping-toad, he probably has incontinently an impulse (especially if with other boys) to smash the creature with a stone, which impulse we may suppose him blindly to obey. But something in the expression of the dying toad's clasped hands suggests the meanness of the act, or reminds him of sayings he has heard about the sufferings of animals being like his own; so that, when next he is tempted by a toad, an idea arises which, far from spurring him again to the torment, prompts kindly actions, and may even make him the toad's champion against less reflecting boys.

It is plain, then, that, *no matter how well endowed an animal may originally be in the way of instincts, his resultant actions will be much modified if the instincts combine with experience*, if in addition to impulses he have memories, associations, inferences, and expectations, on any considerable scale. An object O, on which he has an instinctive impulse to react in the manner A, would *directly* provoke him to that reaction. But O has meantime become for him a *sign* of the nearness of P, on which he has an equally strong impulse to react in the manner B, quite unlike A. So that when he meets O, the immediate impulse A and the remote impulse B struggle in his breast for the mastery. The fatality and uniformity said to be characteristic of instinctive actions will be so little manifest that one might be tempted to deny to him altogether the possession of any instinct about the object O. Yet how false this judgment would be! The instinct about O is there; only by the compli-

cation of the associative machinery it has come into conflict
with another instinct about P.

Here we immediately reap the good fruits of our simple
physiological conception of what an instinct is. If it be a mere
excito-motor impulse, due to the preëxistence of a certain 'reflex arc' in the nerve-centres of the creature, of course it must
follow the law of all such reflex arcs. One liability of such arcs
is to have their activity 'inhibited' by other processes going on
at the same time. It makes no difference whether the arc be
organized at birth, or ripen spontaneously later, or be due to
acquired habit; it must take its chances with all the other arcs,
and sometimes succeed, and sometimes fail, in drafting off the
currents through itself. The mystical view of an instinct would
make it invariable. The physiological view would require it to
show occasional irregularities in any animal in whom the
number of separate instincts, and the possible entrance of the
same stimulus into several of them, were great. And such irregularities are what every superior animal's instincts do show
in abundance.

Wherever the mind is elevated enough to discriminate;
wherever several distinct sensory elements must combine to
discharge the reflex arc; wherever, instead of plumping into
action instantly at the first rough intimation of what *sort* of a
thing is there, the agent waits to see which *one* of its kind it is
and what the *circumstances* are of its appearance; wherever different individuals and different circumstances can impel him
in different ways; wherever these are the conditions—we
have a masking of the elementary constitution of the instinctive life. The whole story of our dealings with the lower wild
animals is the history of our taking advantage of the way in
which they judge of everything by its mere label, as it were,
so as to ensnare or kill them. Nature, in them, has left matters
in this rough way, and made them act *always* in the manner
which would be *oftenest* right. There are more worms unat-
tached to hooks than impaled upon them; therefore, on the
whole, says Nature to her fishy children, bite at *every* worm
and take your chances. But as her children get higher, and
their lives more precious, she reduces the risks. Since what
seems to be the same object may be now a genuine food and
now a bait; since in gregarious species each individual may

prove to be either the friend or the rival, according to the circumstances, of another; since any entirely unknown object may be fraught with weal or woe, *Nature implants contrary impulses to act on many classes of things*, and leaves it to slight alterations in the conditions of the individual case to decide which impulse shall carry the day. Thus, greediness and suspicion, curiosity and timidity, coyness and desire, bashfulness and vanity, sociability and pugnacity, seem to shoot over into each other as quickly, and to remain in as unstable an equilibrium, in the higher birds and mammals as in man. All are impulses, congenital, blind at first, and productive of motor reactions of a rigorously determinate sort. *Each one of them then is an instinct*, as instincts are commonly defined. *But they contradict each other*—'experience' in each particular opportunity of application usually deciding the issue. *The animal that exhibits them loses the 'instinctive' demeanor* and appears to lead a life of hesitation and choice, an intellectual life; *not, however, because he has no instincts—rather because he has so many that they block each other's path*.

Thus we may confidently say that however uncertain man's reactions upon his environment may sometimes seem in comparison with those of lower mammals, the uncertainty is probably not due to their possession of any principles of action which he lacks. *On the contrary, man possesses all the impulses that they have, and a great many more besides.* In other words, there is no material antagonism between instinct and reason. Reason, *per se*, can inhibit no impulses; the only thing that can neutralize an impulse is an impulse the other way. Reason may, however, make an *inference which will excite the imagination so as to let loose* the impulse the other way; and thus, though the animal richest in reason is also the animal richest in instinctive impulses too, he never seems the fatal automaton which a *merely* instinctive animal must be.

Two Principles of Non-uniformity.—Instincts may be masked in the mature animal's life by two other causes. These are:

a. The *inhibition of instincts by habits*; and

b. The *transitoriness of instincts*.

a. The law of **inhibition of instincts by habits** is this: *When objects of a certain class elicit from an animal a certain sort*

of reaction, it often happens that the animal becomes partial to the
first specimen of the class on which it has reacted, and will not
afterwards react on any other specimen.

The selection of a particular hole to live in, of a particular
mate, of a particular feeding-ground, a particular variety of
diet, a particular anything, in short, out of a possible multitude, is a very wide-spread tendency among animals, even
those low down in the scale. The limpet will return to the
same sticking-place in its rock, and the lobster to its favorite
nook on the sea-bottom. The rabbit will deposit its dung in
the same corner; the bird makes its nest on the same bough.
But each of these preferences carries with it an insensibility to
other opportunities and occasions — an insensibility which can
only be described physiologically as an inhibition of new impulses by the habit of old ones already formed. The possession of homes and wives of our own makes us strangely
insensible to the charms of those of other people. Few of us
are adventurous in the matter of food; in fact, most of us
think there is something disgusting in a bill of fare to which
we are unused. Strangers, we are apt to think, cannot be
worth knowing, especially if they come from distant cities,
etc. The original impulse which got us homes, wives, dietar-
ies, and friends at all, seems to exhaust itself in its first
achievements and to leave no surplus energy for reacting on
new cases. And so it comes about that, witnessing this torpor,
an observer of mankind might say that no *instinctive* propensity towards certain objects existed at all. It existed, but it
existed *miscellaneously*, or as an instinct pure and simple, only
before habit was formed. A habit, once grafted on an instinctive tendency, restricts the range of the tendency itself, and
keeps us from reacting on any but the habitual object, although other objects might just as well have been chosen had
they been the first-comers.

Another sort of arrest of instinct by habit is where the same
class of objects awakens contrary instinctive impulses. Here
the impulse first followed towards a given individual of the
class is apt to keep him from ever awakening the opposite
impulse in us. In fact, the whole class may be protected by
this individual specimen from the application to it of the
other impulse. Animals, for example, awaken in a child the

opposite impulses of fearing and fondling. But if a child, in his first attempts to pat a dog, gets snapped at or bitten, so that the impulse of fear is strongly aroused, it may be that for years to come no dog will excite in him the impulse to fondle again. On the other hand, the greatest natural enemies, if carefully introduced to each other when young and guided at the outset by superior authority, settle down into those 'happy families' of friends which we see in our menageries. Young animals, immediately after birth, have no instinct of fear, but show their dependence by allowing themselves to be freely handled. Later, however, they grow 'wild,' and, if left to themselves, will not let man approach them. I am told by farmers in the Adirondack wilderness that it is a very serious matter if a cow wanders off and calves in the woods and is not found for a week or more. The calf, by that time, is as wild and almost as fleet as a deer, and hard to capture without violence. But calves rarely show any wildness to the men who have been in contact with them during the first days of their life, when the instinct to attach themselves is uppermost, nor do they dread strangers as they would if brought up wild.

Chickens give a curious illustration of the same law. Mr. Spalding's wonderful article on instinct shall supply us with the facts. These little creatures show opposite instincts of attachment and fear, either of which may be aroused by the same object, man. If a chick is born in the absence of the hen, it "will follow any moving object. And, when guided by sight alone, they seem to have no more disposition to follow a hen than to follow a duck, or a human being. Unreflecting onlookers, when they saw chickens a day old running after me," says Mr. Spalding, "and older ones following me miles and answering to my whistle, imagined that I must have some occult power over the creatures, whereas I simply allowed them to follow me from the first. There is the instinct to follow; and . . . their ear prior to experience attaches them to the right object."[1]

But if a man presents himself for the first time when the instinct of *fear* is strong, the phenomena are altogether re-

[1]Spalding: *Macmillan's Magazine*, Feb. 1873, p. 287.

versed. Mr. Spalding kept three chickens hooded until they were nearly four days old, and thus describes their behavior:

"Each of these on being unhooded evinced the greatest terror of me, dashing off in the opposite direction whenever I sought to approach it. The table on which they were unhooded stood before a window, and each in its turn beat against the glass like a wild bird. One of them darted behind some books, and squeezing itself into a corner, remained cowering for a length of time. We might guess at the meaning of this strange and exceptional wildness; but the odd fact is enough for my present purpose. Whatever might have been the meaning of this marked change in their mental constitution—had they been unhooded on the previous day they would have run to me instead of from me—it could not have been the effect of experience; it must have resulted wholly from changes in their own organization."[2]

Their case was precisely analogous to that of the Adirondack calves. The two opposite instincts relative to the same object ripen in succession. If the first one engenders a habit, that habit will inhibit the application of the second instinct to that object. All animals are tame during the earliest phase of their infancy. Habits formed then limit the effects of whatever instincts of wildness may later be evolved.

b. This leads us to the **law of transitoriness**, which is this: *Many instincts ripen at a certain age and then fade away.* A consequence of this law is that if, during the time of such an instinct's vivacity, objects adequate to arouse it are met with, a *habit* of acting on them is formed, which remains when the original instinct has passed away; but that if no such objects are met with, then no habit will be formed; and, later on in life, when the animal meets the objects, he will altogether fail to react, as at the earlier epoch he would instinctively have done.

No doubt such a law is restricted. Some instincts are far less transient than others—those connected with feeding and 'self-preservation' may hardly be transient at all—and some, after fading out for a time, recur as strong as ever; e.g., the

[2]*Ibid.*, p. 289.

instincts of pairing and rearing young. The law, however, though not absolute, is certainly very widespread, and a few examples will illustrate just what it means.

In the chickens and calves above mentioned it is obvious that the instinct to follow and become attached fades out after a few days, and that the instinct of flight then takes its place, the conduct of the creature towards man being decided by the formation or non-formation of a certain habit during those days. The transiency of the chicken's instinct to follow is also proved by its conduct towards the hen. Mr. Spalding kept some chickens shut up till they were comparatively old, and, speaking of these, he says:

"A chicken that has not heard the call of the mother until eight or ten days old then hears it as if it heard it not. I regret to find that on this point my notes are not so full as I could wish, or as they might have been. There is, however, an account of one chicken that could not be returned to the mother when ten days old. The hen followed it, and tried to entice it in every way; still it continually left her and ran to the house or to any person of whom it caught sight. This it persisted in doing, though beaten back with a small branch dozens of times, and indeed cruelly maltreated. It was also placed under the mother at night, but it again left her in the morning."

The instinct of sucking is ripe in all mammals at birth, and leads to that habit of taking the breast which, in the human infant, may be prolonged by daily exercise long beyond its usual term of a year or a year and a half. But the instinct itself is transient, in the sense that if, for any reason, the child be fed by spoon during the first few days of its life and not put to the breast, it may be no easy matter after that to make it suck at all. So of calves. If their mother die, or be dry, or refuse to let them suck for a day or two, so that they are fed by hand, it becomes hard to get them to suck at all when a new nurse is provided. The ease with which sucking creatures are weaned, by simply breaking the habit and giving them food in a new way, shows that the instinct, purely as such, must be entirely extinct.

Assuredly the simple fact that instincts are transient, and that the effect of later ones may be altered by the habits which earlier ones have left behind, is a far more philosophical explanation than the notion of an instinctive constitution vaguely 'deranged' or 'thrown out of gear.'

I have observed a Scotch terrier, born on the floor of a stable in December, and transferred six weeks later to a carpeted house, make, when he was less than four months old, a very elaborate pretence of burying things, such as gloves, etc., with which he had played till he was tired. He scratched the carpet with his fore-feet, dropped the object from his mouth upon the spot, then scratched all about it, and finally went away and let it lie. Of course, the act was entirely useless. I saw him perform it at that age some four or five times, and never again in his life. The conditions were not present to fix a habit which should last when the prompting instinct died away. But suppose meat instead of a glove, earth instead of a carpet, hunger-pangs instead of a fresh supper a few hours later, and it is easy to see how this dog might have got into a habit of burying superfluous food, which might have lasted all his life. Who can swear that the strictly instinctive part of the food-burying propensity in the wild *Canidæ* may not be as short-lived as it was in this terrier?

Leaving lower animals aside, and turning to human instincts, we see the law of transiency corroborated on the widest scale by the alternation of different interests and passions as human life goes on. With the child, life is all play and fairy-tales and learning the external properties of 'things'; with the youth, it is bodily exercises of a more systematic sort, novels of the real world, boon-fellowship and song, friendship and love, nature, travel and adventure, science and philosophy; with the man, ambition and policy, acquisitiveness, responsibility to others, and the selfish zest of the battle of life. If a boy grows up alone at the age of games and sports, and learns neither to play ball, nor row, nor sail, nor ride, nor skate, nor fish, nor shoot, probably he will be sedentary to the end of his days; and, though the best of opportunities be afforded him for learning these things later, it is a hundred to one but he will pass them by and shrink back from the effort of taking those necessary first steps the prospect of which, at an earlier age, would have filled him with eager delight. The sexual passion expires after a protracted reign; but it is well known that

its peculiar manifestations in a given individual depend almost
entirely on the habits he may form during the early period of
its activity. Exposure to bad company then makes him a loose
liver all his days; chastity kept at first makes the same easy
later on. In all pedagogy the great thing is to strike the iron
while hot, and to seize the wave of the pupil's interest in each
successive subject before its ebb has come, so that knowledge
may be got and a habit of skill acquired—a headway of interest, in short, secured, on which afterwards the individual may
float. There is a happy moment for fixing skill in drawing, for
making boys collectors in natural history, and presently dis-
sectors and botanists; then for initiating them into the harmonies of mechanics and the wonders of physical and chemical
law. Later, introspective psychology and the metaphysical and
religious mysteries take their turn; and, last of all, the drama
of human affairs and worldly wisdom in the widest sense of
the term. In each of us a saturation-point is soon reached in
all these things; the impetus of our purely intellectual zeal
expires, and unless the topic be one associated with some urgent personal need that keeps our wits constantly whetted
about it, we settle into an equilibrium, and live on what we
learned when our interest was fresh and instinctive, without
adding to the store. Outside of their own business, the ideas
gained by men before they are twenty-five are practically the
only ideas they shall have in their lives. They *cannot* get anything new. Disinterested curiosity is past, the mental grooves
and channels set, the power of assimilation gone. If by chance
we ever do learn anything about some entirely new topic, we
are afflicted with a strange sense of insecurity, and we fear to
advance a resolute opinion. But with things learned in the
plastic days of instinctive curiosity we never lose entirely our
sense of being at home. There remains a kinship, a sentiment
of intimate acquaintance, which, even when we know we have
failed to keep abreast of the subject, flatters us with a sense of
power over it, and makes us feel not altogether out of the
pale.

Whatever individual exceptions to this might be cited are of
the sort that 'prove the rule.'

To detect the moment of the instinctive readiness for the
subject is, then, the first duty of every educator. As for the

pupils, it would probably lead to a more earnest temper on the part of college students if they had less belief in their un- limited future intellectual potentialities, and could be brought to realize that whatever physics and political economy and philosophy they are now acquiring are, for better or worse, the physics and political economy and philosophy that will have to serve them to the end.

Enumeration of Instincts in Man.—Professor Preyer, in his careful little work, *Die Seele des Kindes*, says "instinctive acts are in man few in number, and, apart from those con- nected with the sexual passion, difficult to recognize after early youth is past." And he adds, "so much the more atten- tion should we pay to the instinctive movements of new-born babies, sucklings, and small children." That instinctive acts should be easiest *recognized* in childhood would be a very nat- ural effect of our principles of transitoriness, and of the re- strictive influence of habits once acquired; but they are far indeed from being 'few in number' in man. Professor Preyer divides the movements of infants into *impulsive*, *reflex*, and *instinctive*. By impulsive movements he means *random* move- ments of limbs, body, and voice, with no aim, and before perception is aroused. Among the first reflex movements are crying on contact with the air, *sneezing, snuffling, snoring, coughing, sighing, sobbing, gagging, vomiting, hiccuping, start- ing, moving the limbs when touched*, and *sucking*. To these may now be added *hanging by the hands* (see *Nineteenth Century*, Nov. 1891). Later on come *biting, clasping objects*, and *carrying them to the mouth, sitting up, standing, creeping*, and *walking*. It is probable that the centres for executing these three latter acts ripen spontaneously, just as those for flight have been proved to do in birds, and that the appearance of *learning* to stand and walk, by trial and failure, is due to the exercise beginning in most children before the centres are ripe. Chil- dren vary enormously in the rate and manner in which they learn to walk. With the first impulses to *imitation*, those to significant *vocalization* are born. *Emulation* rapidly ensues, with *pugnacity* in its train. *Fear* of definite objects comes in early, *sympathy* much later, though on the instinct (or emo- tion?—see p. 350) of sympathy so much in human life de- pends. *Shyness* and *sociability*, *play*, *curiosity*, *acquisitiveness*, all begin very early in life. The *hunting instinct*, *modesty*, *love*, the *parental instinct*, etc., come later. By the age of 15 or 16 the whole array of human instincts is complete. It will be observed that *no other mammal, not even the monkey, shows so large a list*. In a perfectly-rounded development every one of these instincts would start a habit towards certain objects and inhibit a habit towards certain others. Usually this is the case; but, in the one-sided development of civilized life, it happens that the timely age goes by in a sort of starvation of objects, and the individual then grows up with gaps in his psychic constitution which future experiences can never fill. Compare the accomplished gentleman with the poor artisan or tradesman of a city: during the adolescence of the former, objects appropriate to his growing interests, bodily and mental, were offered as fast as the interests awoke, and, as a consequence, he is armed and equipped at every angle to meet the world. Sport came to the rescue and completed his education where real things were lacking. He has tasted of the essence of every side of human life, being sailor, hunter, athlete, scholar, fighter, talker, dandy, man of affairs, etc., all in one. Over the city poor boy's youth no such golden opportunities were hung, and in his manhood no desires for most of them exist. Fortunate it is for him if gaps are the only anomalies his instinctive life presents; perversions are too often the fruit of his unnatural bringing-up.

Description of Fear.—In order to treat at least one instinct at greater length, I will take the instance of *fear*.

Fear is a reaction aroused by the same objects that arouse ferocity. The antagonism of the two is an interesting study in instinctive dynamics. We both fear, and wish to kill, anything that may kill us; and the question which of the two impulses we shall follow is usually decided by some one of those collateral circumstances of the particular case, to be moved by which is the mark of superior mental natures. Of course this introduces uncertainty into the reaction; but it is an uncertainty found in the higher brutes as well as in men, and ought not to be taken as proof that we are less instinctive than they. Fear has bodily expressions of an extremely energetic kind, and stands, beside lust and anger, as one of the three most exciting emotions of which our nature is susceptible. The progress from brute to man is characterized by nothing so much as by the decrease in frequency of proper occasions for fear. In civilized life, in particular, it has at last become possible for large numbers of people to pass from the cradle to the grave without ever having had a pang of genuine fear. Many of us need an attack of mental disease to teach us the meaning of the word. Hence the possibility of so much blindly optimistic philosophy and religion. The atrocities of life become 'like a tale of little meaning tho' the words are strong'; we doubt if anything like *us* ever really was within the tiger's jaws, and conclude that the horrors we hear of are but a sort of painted tapestry for the chambers in which we lie so comfortably at peace with ourselves and with the world.

Be this as it may, fear is a genuine instinct, and one of the earliest shown by the human child. *Noises* seem especially to call it forth. Most noises from the outer world, to a child bred in the house, have no exact significance. They are simply startling. To quote a good observer, M. Perez:

"Children between three and ten months are less often alarmed by visual than by auditory impressions. In cats, from the fifteenth day, the contrary is the case. A child, three and a half months old, in the midst of the turmoil of a conflagration, in presence of the devouring flames and ruined walls, showed neither astonishment nor fear, but smiled at the woman who was taking care of him, while his parents were busy. The noise, however, of the trumpet of the firemen, who were approaching, and that of the wheels of the engine, made him start and cry. At this age I have never yet seen an infant startled at a flash of lightning, even when intense; but I have seen many of them alarmed at the voice of the thunder. . . . Thus fear comes rather by the ears than by the eyes, to the child without experience."[3]

The effect of noise in heightening any terror we may feel in adult years is very marked. The *howling* of the storm, whether on sea or land, is a principal cause of our anxiety when exposed to it. The writer has been interested in noticing in his own person, while lying in bed, and kept awake by the wind outside, how invariably each loud gust of it arrested momen-

[3]*Psychologie de l'enfant*, p. 72.

tarily his heart. A dog attacking us is much more dreadful by reason of the noises he makes.

Strange men, and *strange animals*, either large or small, excite fear, but especially men or animals advancing towards us in a threatening way. This is entirely instinctive and antecedent to experience. Some children will cry with terror at their very first sight of a cat or dog, and it will often be impossible for weeks to make them touch it. Others will wish to fondle it almost immediately. Certain kinds of 'vermin,' especially spiders and snakes, seem to excite a fear unusually difficult to overcome. It is impossible to say how much of this difference is instinctive and how much the result of stories heard about these creatures. That the fear of 'vermin' ripens gradually seemed to me to be proved in a child of my own to whom I gave a live frog once, at the age of six to eight months, and again when he was a year and a half old. The first time, he seized it promptly, and holding it in spite of its struggling, at last got its head into his mouth. He then let it crawl up his breast, and get upon his face, without showing alarm. But the second time, although he had seen no frog and heard no story about a frog between-whiles, it was almost impossible to induce him to touch it. Another child, a year old, eagerly took some very large spiders into his hand. At present he is afraid, but has been exposed meanwhile to the teachings of the nursery. One of my children from her birth upwards saw daily the pet pug-dog of the house, and never betrayed the slightest fear until she was (if I recollect rightly) about eight months old. Then the instinct suddenly seemed to develop, and with such intensity that familiarity had no mitigating effect. She screamed whenever the dog entered the room, and for many months remained afraid to touch him. It is needless to say that no change in the pug's unfailingly friendly conduct had anything to do with this change of feeling in the child. Two of my children were afraid, when babies, of *fur*: Richet reports a similar observation.

Preyer tells of a young child screaming with fear on being carried near to the *sea*. The great source of terror to infancy is solitude. The teleology of this is obvious, as is also that of the infant's expression of dismay—the never-failing cry—on waking up and finding himself alone.

Black things, and especially *dark places*, holes, caverns, etc., arouse a peculiarly gruesome fear. This fear, as well as that of solitude, of being 'lost,' are explained after a fashion by ancestral experience. Says Schneider:

"It is a fact that men, especially in childhood, fear to go into a dark cavern or a gloomy wood. This feeling of fear arises, to be sure, partly from the fact that we easily suspect that dangerous beasts may lurk in these localities—a suspicion due to stories we have heard and read. But, on the other hand, it is quite sure that this fear at a certain perception is also directly inherited. Children who have been carefully guarded from all ghost-stories are nevertheless terrified and cry if led into a dark place, especially if sounds are made there. Even an adult can easily observe that an uncomfortable timidity steals over him in a lonely wood at night, although he may have the fixed conviction that not the slightest danger is near.

"This feeling of fear occurs in many men even in their own house after dark, although it is much stronger in a dark cavern or forest. The fact of such instinctive fear is easily explicable when we consider that our savage ancestors through innumerable generations were accustomed to meet with dangerous beasts in caverns, especially bears, and were for the most part attacked by such beasts during the night and in the woods, and that thus an inseparable association between the perceptions of darkness, caverns, woods, and fear took place, and was inherited."[4]

High places cause fear of a peculiarly sickening sort, though here, again, individuals differ enormously. The utterly blind instinctive character of the motor impulses here is shown by the fact that they are almost always entirely unreasonable, but that reason is powerless to suppress them. That they are a mere incidental peculiarity of the nervous system, like liability to sea-sickness, or love of music, with no teleological significance, seems more than probable. The fear in question varies so much from one person to another, and its detrimental effects are so much more obvious than its uses, that it is hard to see how it could be a selected instinct. Man is anatomically one of the best fitted of animals for climbing about high

[4]*Der menschliche Wille*, p. 224.

places. The best psychical complement to this equipment would seem to be a 'level head' when there, not a dread of going there at all. In fact, the teleology of fear, beyond a certain point, is more than dubious. A certain amount of timidity obviously adapts us to the world we live in, but the *fear-paroxysm* is surely altogether harmful to him who is its prey.

Fear of the supernatural is one variety of fear. It is difficult to assign any normal object for this fear, unless it were a genuine ghost. But, in spite of psychical-research societies, science has not yet adopted ghosts; so we can only say that certain *ideas* of supernatural agency, associated with real circumstances, produce a peculiar kind of horror. This horror is probably explicable as the result of a combination of simpler horrors. To bring the ghostly terror to its maximum, many usual elements of the dreadful must combine, such as loneliness, darkness, inexplicable sounds, especially of a dismal character, moving figures half discerned (or, if discerned, of dreadful aspect), and a vertiginous baffling of the expectation. This last element, which is *intellectual*, is very important. It produces a strange emotional 'curdle' in our blood to see a process with which we are familiar deliberately taking an unwonted course. Anyone's heart would stop beating if he perceived his chair sliding unassisted across the floor. The lower animals appear to be sensitive to the mysteriously exceptional as well as ourselves. My friend Professor W. K. Brooks told me of his large and noble dog being frightened into a sort of epileptic fit by a bone being drawn across the floor by a thread which the dog did not see. Darwin and Romanes have given similar experiences. The idea of the supernatural involves that the usual should be set at naught. In the witch and hobgoblin supernatural, other elements still of fear are brought in—caverns, slime and ooze, vermin, corpses, and the like. A human corpse seems normally to produce an instinctive dread, which is no doubt somewhat due to its mysteriousness, and which familiarity rapidly dispels. But, in view of the fact that cadaveric, reptilian, and underground horrors play so specific and constant a part in many nightmares and forms of delirium, it seems not altogether unwise to ask whether these forms of dreadful circumstance may not at a former period have been more normal objects of the environment than now. The ordinary cock-sure evolutionist ought to have no difficulty in explaining these terrors, and the scenery that provokes them, as relapses into the consciousness of the cave-men, a consciousness usually overlaid in us by experiences of more recent date.

There are certain other pathological fears, and certain peculiarities in the expression of ordinary fear, which might receive an explanatory light from ancestral conditions, even infra-human ones. In ordinary fear, one may either run, or remain semi-paralyzed. The latter condition reminds us of the so-called death-shamming instinct shown by many animals. Dr. Lindsay, in his work *Mind in Animals*, says this must require great self-command in those that practise it. But it is really no feigning of death at all, and requires no self-command. It is simply a terror-paralysis which has been so useful as to become hereditary. The beast of prey does not think the motionless bird, insect, or crustacean dead. He simply fails to notice them at all; because his senses, like ours, are much more strongly excited by a moving object than by a still one. It is the same instinct which leads a boy playing 'I spy' to hold his very breath when the seeker is near, and which makes the beast of prey himself in many cases motionlessly lie in wait for his victim or silently 'stalk' it, by stealthy advances alternated with periods of immobility. It is the opposite of the instinct which makes us jump up and down and move our arms when we wish to attract the notice of someone passing far away, and makes the shipwrecked sailor upon the raft where he is floating frantically wave a cloth when a distant sail appears. Now, may not the statue-like, crouching immobility of some melancholiacs, insane with general anxiety and fear of everything, be in some way connected with this old instinct? They can give no *reason* for their fear to move; but immobility makes them feel safer and more comfortable. Is not this the mental state of the 'feigning' animal?

Again, take the strange symptom which has been described of late years by the rather absurd name of *agoraphobia*. The patient is seized with palpitation and terror at the sight of any open place or broad street which he has to cross alone. He trembles, his knees bend, he may even faint at the idea. Where he has sufficient self-command he sometimes accomplishes the object by keeping safe under the lee of a vehicle going across, or joining himself to a knot of other people. But usually he slinks round the sides of the square, hugging the houses as closely as he can. This emotion has no utility in a civilized man, but when we notice the chronic agoraphobia of our domestic cats, and see the tenacious way in which many wild animals, especially rodents, cling to cover, and only venture on a dash across the open as a desperate measure—even then making for every stone or bunch of weeds which may give a momentary shelter—when we see this we are strongly tempted to ask whether such an odd kind of fear in us be not due to the accidental resurrection, through disease, of a sort of instinct which may in some of our remote ancestors have had a permanent and on the whole a useful part to play?

CHAPTER XXVI

WILL

Voluntary Acts.—Desire, wish, will, are states of mind which everyone knows, and which no definition can make plainer. We desire to feel, to have, to do, all sorts of things which at the moment are not felt, had, or done. If with the desire there goes a sense that attainment is not possible, we simply *wish*; but if we believe that the end is in our power, we *will* that the desired feeling, having, or doing shall be real; and real it presently becomes, either immediately upon the willing or after certain preliminaries have been fulfilled.

The only ends which follow *immediately* upon our willing seem to be movements of our own bodies. Whatever *feelings* and *havings* we may will to get come in as results of preliminary movements which we make for the purpose. This fact is too familiar to need illustration; so that we may start with the proposition that the only *direct* outward effects of our will are bodily movements. The mechanism of production of these voluntary movements is what befalls us to study now.

They are secondary performances. The movements we have studied hitherto have been automatic and reflex, and (on the first occasion of their performance, at any rate) unforeseen by the agent. The movements to the study of which we now address ourselves, being desired and intended beforehand, are of course done with full prevision of what they are to be. It follows from this that *voluntary movements must be secondary, not primary, functions of our organism.* This is the first point to understand in the psychology of Volition. Reflex, instinctive, and emotional movements are all primary performances. The nerve-centres are so organized that certain stimuli pull the trigger of certain explosive parts; and a creature going through one of these explosions for the first time undergoes an entirely novel experience. The other day I was standing at a railroad station with a little child, when an express-train went thundering by. The child, who was near the edge of the platform, started, winked, had his breathing convulsed, turned pale, burst out crying, and ran frantically towards me and hid his face. I have no doubt that this youngster was almost as much astonished by his own behavior as he was by the train, and more than I was, who stood by. Of course if such a reaction has many times occurred we learn what to expect of ourselves, and can then foresee our conduct, even though it remain as involuntary and uncontrollable as it was before. But if, in voluntary action properly so called, the act must be foreseen, it follows that no creature not endowed with prophetic power can perform an act voluntarily for the first time. Well, we are no more endowed with prophetic vision of what movements lie in our power than we are endowed with prophetic vision of what sensations we are capable of receiving. As we must wait for the sensations to be given us, so we must wait for the movements to be performed involuntarily, before we can frame ideas of what either of these things are. We learn all our possibilities by the way of experience. When a particular movement, having once occurred in a random, reflex, or involuntary way, has left an image of itself in the memory, then the movement can be desired again, and deliberately willed. But it is impossible to see how it could be willed before.

A supply of ideas of the various movements that are possible, left in the memory by experiences of their involuntary performance, is thus the first prerequisite of the voluntary life.

Two Kinds of Ideas of Movement.—Now these ideas may be either *resident* or *remote*. That is, they may be of the movement as it feels, when taking place, in the moving parts; or they may be of the movement as it feels in some other part of the body which it affects (strokes, presses, scratches, etc.), or as it sounds, or as it looks. The resident sensations in the parts that move have been called *kinæsthetic* feelings, the memories of them are kinæsthetic ideas. It is by these kinæsthetic sensations that we are made conscious of *passive movements*—movements communicated to our limbs by others. If you lie with closed eyes, and another person noiselessly places your arm or leg in any arbitrarily chosen attitude, you receive a feeling of what attitude it is, and can reproduce it yourself in the arm or leg of the opposite side. Similarly a man waked suddenly from sleep in the dark is aware of how he finds himself lying. At least this is what happens in normal cases. But when the feelings of passive movement as well as all the other feelings of a limb are lost, we get such results as are given in the following account by Prof. A. Strümpell of his wonderful anæsthetic boy, whose only sources of feeling were the right eye and the left ear:[1]

"Passive movements could be imprinted on all the extremities to the greatest extent, without attracting the patient's notice. Only in violent forced hyperextension of the joints, especially of the knees, there arose a dull vague feeling of strain, but this was seldom precisely localized. We have often, after bandaging the eyes of the patient, carried him about the room, laid him on a table, given to his arms and legs the most fantastic and apparently the most inconvenient attitudes, without his having a suspicion of it. The expression of astonishment in his face, when all at once the removal of the handkerchief revealed his situation, is indescribable in words. Only when his head was made to hang away down he immediately spoke of dizziness, but could not assign its ground. Later he sometimes inferred from the sounds connected with the manipulation that something special was being done with him. . . . He had no feelings of muscular fatigue. If, with his eyes shut, we told him to raise his arm and to keep it up, he did so without trouble. After one or two minutes, however, the arm began to tremble and sink without his being aware of it. He asserted still his ability to keep it up. . . . Passively holding still his fingers did not affect him. He thought constantly that he opened and shut his hand, whereas it was really fixed."

No third kind of idea is called for. We need, then, when we perform a movement, either a kinæsthetic or a remote idea of which special movement it is to be. In addition to this it has often been supposed that we need an *idea of the amount of innervation* required for the muscular contraction. The discharge from the motor centre into the motor nerve is supposed to give a sensation *sui generis*, opposed to all our other sensations. These accompany incoming currents, whilst that, it is said, accompanies an outgoing current, and no movement is supposed to be totally defined in our mind, unless an

[1] *Deutsches Archiv für klinische Medicin*, xxii, 321.

anticipation of this feeling enter into our idea. The movement's degree of strength, and the effort required to perform it, are supposed to be specially revealed by the feeling of innervation. Many authors deny that this feeling exists, and the proofs given of its existence are certainly insufficient.

The various degrees of 'effort' actually felt in making the same movement against different resistances are all accounted for by the incoming feelings from our chest, jaws, abdomen, and other parts sympathetically contracted whenever the effort is great. There is no need of a consciousness of the amount of outgoing current required. If anything be obvious to introspection, it is that the degree of strength put forth is completely revealed to us by incoming feelings from the muscles themselves and their insertions, from the vicinity of the joints, and from the general fixation of the larynx, chest, face, and body. When a certain degree of energy of contraction rather than another is thought of by us, this complex aggregate of afferent feelings, forming the material of our thought, renders absolutely precise and distinctive our mental image of the exact strength of movement to be made, and the exact amount of resistance to be overcome.

Let the reader try to direct his will towards a particular movement, and then notice what *constituted* the direction of the will. Was it anything over and above the notion of the different feelings to which the movement when effected would give rise? If we abstract from these feelings, will any sign, principle, or means of orientation be left by which the will may innervate the proper muscles with the right intensity, and not go astray into the wrong ones? Strip off these images anticipative of the results of the motion, and so far from leaving us with a complete assortment of directions into which our will may launch itself, you leave our consciousness in an absolute and total vacuum. If I will to write *Peter* rather than *Paul*, it is the thought of certain digital sensations, of certain alphabetic sounds, of certain appearances on the paper, and of no others, which immediately precedes the motion of my pen. If I will to utter the word *Paul* rather than *Peter*, it is the thought of my voice falling on my ear, and of certain muscular feelings in my tongue, lips, and larynx, which guide the utterance. All these are incoming feelings, and between the thought of them, by which the act is mentally specified with all possible completeness, and the act itself, there is no room for any third order of mental phenomenon.

There is indeed the *fiat*, the element of consent, or resolve that the act shall ensue. This, doubtless, to the reader's mind, as to my own, constitutes the essence of the voluntariness of the act. This *fiat* will be treated of in detail farther on. It may be entirely neglected here, for it is a constant coefficient, affecting all voluntary actions alike, and incapable of serving to distinguish them. No one will pretend that its quality varies according as the right arm, for example, or the left is used.

An anticipatory image, then, of the sensorial consequences of a movement, plus (on certain occasions) the fiat that these consequences shall become actual, is the only psychic state which introspection lets us discern as the forerunner of our voluntary acts. There is no coercive evidence of any feeling attached to the efferent discharge.

The entire content and material of our consciousness—consciousness of movement, as of all things else—seems thus to be of peripheral origin, and to come to us in the first instance through the peripheral nerves.

The Motor-cue.—Let us call the last idea which in the mind precedes the motor discharge the 'motor-cue.' Now do 'resident' images form the only motor-cue, or will 'remote' ones equally suffice?

There can be no doubt whatever that the cue may be an image either of the resident or of the remote kind. Although, at the outset of our learning a movement, it would seem that the resident feelings must come strongly before consciousness, later this need not be the case. The rule, in fact, would seem to be that they tend to lapse more and more from consciousness, and that the more practised we become in a movement, the more 'remote' do the ideas become which form its mental cue. What we are *interested* in is what sticks in our consciousness; everything else we get rid of as quickly as we can. Our resident feelings of movement have no substantive interest for us at all, as a rule. What interest us are the ends which the movement is to attain. Such an end is generally a remote sensation, an impression which the movement produces on the eye or ear, or sometimes on the skin, nose, or palate. Now let the idea of such an end associate itself definitely with the right discharge, and the thought of the innervation's *resident* effects will become as great an encumbrance as we have already concluded that the feeling of the innervation itself is. The mind does not need it; the end alone is enough.

The idea of the end, then, tends more and more to make itself all-sufficient. Or, at any rate, if the kinæsthetic ideas are called up at all, they are so swamped in the vivid kinæsthetic feelings by which they are immediately overtaken that we have no time to be aware of their separate existence. As I write, I have no anticipation, as a thing distinct from my sensation, of either the look or the digital feel of the letters which flow from my pen. The words chime on my mental *ear*, as it were, before I write them, but not on my mental eye or hand. This comes from the rapidity with which the movements follow on their mental cue. An end consented to as soon as conceived innervates directly the centre of the first movement of the chain which leads to its accomplishment, and then the whole chain rattles off *quasi*-reflexly, as was described on pp. 142–143.

The reader will certainly recognize this to be true in all fluent and unhesitating voluntary acts. The only special fiat there is at the outset of the performance. A man says to himself, "I must change my clothes," and involuntarily he has taken off his coat, and his fingers are at work in their accustomed manner on his waistcoat-buttons, etc.; or we say, "I must go downstairs," and ere we know it we have risen, walked, and turned the handle of the door;—all through the idea of an end coupled with a series of guiding sensations which successively arise. It would seem indeed that we fail of accuracy and certainty in our attainment of the end whenever we are preoccupied with the way in which the movement will feel. We walk a beam the better the less we think of the position of our feet upon it. We pitch or catch, we shoot or chop the better the less tactile and muscular (the less resident), and the more exclusively optical (the more remote), our consciousness is. Keep your *eye* on the place aimed at, and your hand will fetch it; think of your hand, and you will very likely miss your aim. Dr. Southard found that he could touch a spot with a pencil-point more accurately with a visual than with a tactile mental cue. In the former case he looked at a small object and closed his eyes before trying to touch it. In the latter case he *placed* it with closed eyes, and then after removing his hand tried to touch it again. The average error with touch (when the results were most favorable) was 17.13 mm. With sight it was only 12.37 mm.—All these are plain results of introspection and observation. By what neural machinery they are made possible we do not know.

In Chapter XIX we saw how enormously individuals differ in respect to their mental imagery. In the type of imagination called *tactile* by the French authors, it is probable that the kinæsthetic ideas are more prominent than in my account. We must not expect too great a uniformity in individual accounts, nor wrangle overmuch as to which one 'truly' represents the process.

I trust that I have now made clear what that 'idea of a movement' is which must precede it in order that it be voluntary. It is not the thought of the innervation which the movement requires. It is the anticipation of the movement's sensible effects, resident or remote, and sometimes very remote indeed. Such anticipations, to say the least, determine *what* our movements shall be. I have spoken all along as if they also might determine *that* they shall be. This, no doubt, has disconcerted many readers, for it certainly seems as if a special fiat, or consent to the movement, were required in addition to the mere conception of it, in many cases of volition; and this fiat I have altogether left out of my account. This leads us to the next point in our discussion.

Ideo-motor Action.—The question is this: *Is the bare idea of a movement's sensible effects its sufficient motor-cue, or must there be an additional mental antecedent, in the shape of a fiat, decision, consent, volitional mandate, or other synonymous phenomenon of consciousness, before the movement can follow?*

I answer: Sometimes the bare idea is sufficient, but sometimes an additional conscious element, in the shape of a fiat, mandate, or express consent, has to intervene and precede the movement. The cases without a fiat constitute the more fundamental, because the more simple, variety. The others involve a special complication, which must be fully discussed at the proper time. For the present let us turn to *ideo-motor action*, as it has been termed, or the sequence of movement upon the mere thought of it, without a special fiat, as the type of the process of volition.

Wherever a movement *unhesitatingly and immediately* follows upon the idea of it, we have ideo-motor action. We are then aware of nothing between the conception and the execution. All sorts of neuro-muscular processes come between, of course, but we know absolutely nothing of them. We think the act, and it is done; and that is all that introspection tells us of the matter. Dr. Carpenter, who first used, I believe, the name of ideo-motor action, placed it, if I mistake not, among the curiosities of our mental life. The truth is that it is no curiosity, but simply the normal process stripped of disguise. Whilst talking I become conscious of a pin on the floor, or of some dust on my sleeve. Without interrupting the conversation I brush away the dust or pick up the pin. I make no express resolve, but the mere perception of the object and the fleeting notion of the act seem of themselves to bring the latter about. Similarly, I sit at table after dinner and find myself from time to time taking nuts or raisins out of the dish and eating them. My dinner properly is over, and in the heat of the conversation I am hardly aware of what I do; but the perception of the fruit, and the fleeting notion that I may eat it, seem fatally to bring the act about. There is certainly no express fiat here; any more than there is in all those habitual goings and comings and rearrangements of ourselves which fill every hour of the day, and which incoming sensations instigate so immediately that it is often difficult to decide whether not to call them reflex rather than voluntary acts. As Lotze says:

"We see in writing or piano-playing a great number of very complicated movements following quickly one upon the other, the instigative representations of which remained scarcely a second in consciousness, certainly not long enough to awaken any other volition than the general one of resigning one's self without reserve to the passing over of representation into action. All the acts of our daily life happen in this wise: Our standing up, walking, talking, all this never demands a distinct impulse of the will, but is adequately brought about by the pure flux of thought."[2]

In all this the determining condition of the unhesitating and resistless sequence of the act seems to be *the absence of any conflicting notion in the mind*. Either there is nothing else at all in the mind, or what is there does not conflict. We know what it is to get out of bed on a freezing morning in a room without a fire, and how the very vital principle within us protests against the ordeal. Probably most persons have lain on certain mornings for an hour at a time unable to brace themselves to the resolve. We think how late we shall be, how the duties of the day will suffer; we say, "I *must* get up, this is ignominious," etc.; but still the warm couch feels too delicious, the cold outside too cruel, and resolution faints away and postpones itself again and again just as it seemed on the verge of bursting the resistance and passing over into the decisive act. Now how do we *ever* get up under such circumstances? If I may generalize from my own experience, we more often than not get up without any struggle or decision at all. We suddenly find that we *have* got up. A fortunate lapse of consciousness occurs; we forget both the warmth and the cold; we fall into some revery connected with the day's life, in the course of which the idea flashes across us, "Hollo! I must lie here no longer"—an idea which at that lucky instant awakens no contradictory or paralyzing suggestions, and consequently produces immediately its appropriate motor effects. It was our acute consciousness of both the warmth and the cold during the period of struggle, which paralyzed our activity then and kept our idea of rising in the condition of *wish* and not of *will*. The moment these inhibitory ideas ceased, the original idea exerted its effects.

This case seems to me to contain in miniature form the data for an entire psychology of volition. It was in fact through meditating on the phenomenon in my own person that I first became convinced of the truth of the doctrine which these pages present, and which I need here illustrate by no farther examples. The reason why that doctrine is not a self-evident truth is that we have so many ideas which *do not* result in

[2]*Medicinische Psychologie*, p. 293.

action. But it will be seen that in every such case, without exception, that is because other ideas simultaneously present rob them of their impulsive power. But even here, and when a movement is inhibited from *completely* taking place by contrary ideas, it will *incipiently* take place. To quote Lotze once more:

"The spectator accompanies the throwing of a billiard-ball, or the thrust of the swordsman, with slight movements of his arm; the untaught narrator tells his story with many gesticulations; the reader while absorbed in the perusal of a battle-scene feels a slight tension run through his muscular system, keeping time as it were with the actions he is reading of. These results become the more marked the more we are absorbed in thinking of the movements which suggest them; they grow fainter exactly in proportion as a complex consciousness, under the dominion of a crowd of other representations, withstands the passing over of mental contemplation into outward action."

The 'willing-game,' the exhibitions of so-called 'mind-reading,' or more properly muscle-reading, which have lately grown so fashionable, are based on this incipient obedience of muscular contraction to idea, even when the deliberate intention is that no contraction shall occur.

We may then lay it down for certain that *every representation of a movement awakens in some degree the actual movement which is its object; and awakens it in a maximum degree whenever it is not kept from so doing by an antagonistic representation present simultaneously to the mind.*

The express fiat, or act of mental consent to the movement, comes in when the neutralization of the antagonistic and inhibitory idea is required. But that there is no express fiat needed when the conditions are simple, the reader ought now to be convinced. Lest, however, he should still share the common prejudice that voluntary action without 'exertion of will-power' is *Hamlet* with the prince's part left out, I will make a few farther remarks. The first point to start from, in understanding voluntary action and the possible occurrence of it with no fiat or express resolve, is the fact that consciousness is *in its very nature impulsive*. We do not first have a sensation or thought, and then have to *add* something dynamic to it to get a movement. Every pulse of feeling which we have is the cor-relate of some neural activity that is already on its way to instigate a movement. Our sensations and thoughts are but cross-sections, as it were, of currents whose essential conse-quence is motion, and which have no sooner run in at one nerve than they are ready to run out by another. The popular notion that consciousness is not essentially a forerunner of activity, but that the latter must result from some superadded 'will-force,' is a very natural inference from those special cases in which we think of an act for an indefinite length of time without the action taking place. These cases, however, are not the norm; they are cases of inhibition by antagonistic thoughts. When the blocking is released we feel as if an in-ward spring were let loose, and this is the additional impulse or *fiat* upon which the act effectively succeeds. We shall study anon the blocking and its release. Our higher thought is full of it. But where there is no blocking, there is naturally no hiatus between the thought-process and the motor discharge. *Movement is the natural immediate effect of the process of feeling, irrespective of what the quality of the feeling may be. It is so in reflex action, it is so in emotional expression, it is so in the volun-tary life.* Ideo-motor action is thus no paradox, to be softened or explained away. It obeys the type of all conscious action, and from it one must start to explain the sort of action in which a special fiat is involved.

It may be remarked in passing, that the inhibition of a movement no more involves an express effort or command than its execution does. Either of them *may* require it. But in all simple and ordinary cases, just as the bare presence of one idea prompts a movement, so the bare presence of another idea will prevent its taking place. Try to feel as if you were crooking your finger, whilst keeping it straight. In a minute it will fairly tingle with the imaginary change of position; yet it will not sensibly move, because *its not really moving* is also a part of what you have in mind. Drop *this* idea, think purely and simply of the movement, and nothing else, and, presto! it takes place with no effort at all.

A waking man's behavior is thus at all times the resultant of two opposing neural forces. With unimaginable fineness some currents among the cells and fibres of his brain are playing on his motor nerves, whilst other currents, as unimaginably fine, are playing on the first currents, damming or helping them, altering their direction or their speed. The upshot of it all is, that whilst the currents must always end by being drained off through *some* motor nerves, they are drained off sometimes through one set and sometimes through another; and sometimes they keep each other in equilibrium so long that a superficial observer may think they are not drained off at all. Such an observer must remember, however, that from the physiological point of view a gesture, an expression of the brow, or an expulsion of the breath are movements as much as an act of locomotion is. A king's breath slays as well as an assassin's blow; and the outpouring of those currents which the magic imponderable streaming of our ideas accompanies need not always be of an explosive or otherwise physically conspicuous kind.

Action after Deliberation.—We are now in a position to describe *what happens in deliberate action*, or when the mind has many objects before it, related to each other in antagonistic or in favorable ways. One of these objects of its thought may be an act. By itself this would prompt a movement; some of the additional objects or considerations, however, block the motor discharge, whilst others, on the contrary, solicit it to take place. The result is that peculiar feeling of inward unrest known as *indecision*. Fortunately it is too familiar to need description, for to describe it would be impossible. As long as it lasts, with the various objects before the attention, we are said to *deliberate*; and when finally the original suggestion either prevails and makes the movement take place, or gets definitively quenched by its antagonists, we are said to *decide*, or to *utter our voluntary fiat*, in favor of one or the other course. The reinforcing and inhibiting objects meanwhile are termed the *reasons* or *motives* by which the decision is brought about.

The process of deliberation contains endless degrees of complication. At every moment of it our consciousness is of an extremely complex thing, namely, the whole set of motives and their conflict. Of this complicated object, the totality of which is realized more or less dimly all the while by consciousness, certain parts stand out more or less sharply at one moment in the foreground, and at another moment other parts, in consequence of the oscillations of our attention, and of the 'associative' flow of our ideas. But no matter how sharp the foreground-reasons may be, or how imminently close to bursting through the dam and carrying the motor consequences their own way, the background, however dimly felt, is always there as a fringe (p. 162); and its presence (so long as the indecision actually lasts) serves as an effective check upon the irrevocable discharge. The deliberation may last for weeks or months, occupying at intervals the mind. The motives which yesterday seemed full of urgency and blood and life to-day feel strangely weak and pale and dead. But as little to-day as to-morrow is the question finally resolved. Something tells us that all this is provisional; that the weakened reasons will wax strong again, and the stronger weaken; that equilibrium is unreached; that testing our reasons, not obeying them, is still the order of the day, and that we must wait awhile, patiently or impatiently, until our mind is made up 'for good and all.' This inclining, first to one, then to another future, both of which we represent as possible, resembles the oscillations to and fro of a material body within the limits of its elasticity. There is inward strain, but no outward rupture. And this condition, plainly enough, is susceptible of indefinite continuance, as well in the physical mass as in the mind. If the elasticity give way, however, if the dam ever do break, and the currents burst the crust, vacillation is over and decision is irrevocably there.

The decision may come in any one of many modes. I will try briefly to sketch the most characteristic types of it, merely warning the reader that this is only an introspective account of symptoms and phenomena, and that all questions of causal agency, whether neural or spiritual, are relegated to a later page.

Five Chief Types of Decision.—Turning now to the form of the decision itself, we may distinguish five chief types. *The first may be called the reasonable type.* It is that of those cases in which the arguments for and against a given course seem gradually and almost insensibly to settle themselves in the mind and to end by leaving a clear balance in favor of one alternative, which alternative we then adopt without effort or constraint. Until this rational balancing of the books is consummated we have a calm feeling that the evidence is not yet all in, and this keeps action in suspense. But some day we wake with the sense that we see the matter rightly, that no new light will be thrown on it by farther delay, and that it had better be settled *now*. In this easy transition from doubt to assurance we seem to ourselves almost passive; the 'reasons' which decide us appearing to flow in from the nature of things, and to owe nothing to our will. We have, however, a perfect sense of being *free*, in that we are devoid of any feeling of coercion. The conclusive reason for the decision in these cases usually is the discovery that we can refer the case to a *class* upon which we are accustomed to act unhesitatingly in a certain stereotyped way. It may be said in general that a great part of every deliberation consists in the turning over of all the possible modes of *conceiving* the doing or not doing of the act in point. The moment we hit upon a conception which lets us apply some principle of action which is a fixed and stable part of our Ego, our state of doubt is at an end. Persons of authority, who have to make many decisions in the day, carry with them a set of heads of classification, each bearing its volitional consequence, and under these they seek as far as possible to range each new emergency as it occurs. It is where the emergency belongs to a species without precedent, to which consequently no cut-and-dried maxim will apply, that we feel most at a loss, and are distressed at the indeterminateness of our task. As soon, however, as we see our way to a familiar classification, we are at ease again. *In action as in reasoning, then, the great thing is the quest of the right conception.* The concrete dilemmas do not come to us with labels gummed upon their backs. We may name them by many names. The wise man is he who succeeds in finding the name which suits the needs of the particular occasion best (p. 335 ff.). A 'reasonable' character is one who has a store of stable and worthy ends, and who does not decide about an action till he has calmly ascertained whether it be ministerial or detrimental to any one of these.

In the next two types of decision, the final fiat occurs before the evidence is all 'in.' It often happens that no paramount and authoritative reason for either course will come. Either seems a good, and there is no umpire to decide which should yield its place to the other. We grow tired of long hesitation and inconclusiveness, and the hour may come when we feel that even a bad decision is better than no decision at all. Under these conditions it will often happen that some accidental circumstance, supervening at a particular moment upon our mental weariness, will upset the balance in the direction of one of the alternatives, to which then we feel ourselves committed, although an opposite accident at the same time might have produced the opposite result.

In the *second type* our feeling is to a great extent that of letting ourselves drift with a certain indifferent acquiescence in a direction accidentally determined *from without*, with the conviction that, after all, we might as well stand by this course as by the other, and that things are in any event sure to turn out sufficiently right.

In the *third type* the determination seems equally accidental, but it comes from within, and not from without. It often happens, when the absence of imperative principle is perplexing and suspense distracting, that we find ourselves acting, as it were, automatically, and as if by a spontaneous discharge of our nerves, in the direction of one of the horns of the dilemma. But so exciting is this sense of motion after our intolerable pent-up state that we eagerly throw ourselves into it. 'Forward now!' we inwardly cry, 'though the heavens fall.' This reckless and exultant espousal of an energy so little premeditated by us that we feel rather like passive spectators cheering on the display of some extraneous force than like voluntary agents is a type of decision too abrupt and tumultuous to occur often in humdrum and cool-blooded natures. But it is probably frequent in persons of strong emotional endowment and unstable or vacillating character. And in men of the world-shaking type, the Napoleons, Luthers, etc., in whom tenacious passion combines with ebullient activity, when by any chance the passion's outlet has been dammed by scruples or apprehensions, the resolution is probably often of this catastrophic kind. The flood breaks quite unexpectedly through the dam. That it should so often do so is quite sufficient to account for the tendency of these characters to a fatalistic mood of mind. And the fatalistic mood itself is sure to reinforce the strength of the energy just started on its exciting path of discharge.

There is a *fourth form* of decision, which often ends deliberation as suddenly as the third form does. It comes when, in consequence of some outer experience or some inexplicable inward change, *we suddenly pass from the easy and careless to the sober and strenuous mood*, or possibly the other way. The whole scale of values of our motives and impulses then undergoes a change like that which a change of the observer's level produces on a view. The most sobering possible agents are objects of grief and fear. When one of these affects us, all 'light fantastic' notions lose their motive power, all solemn ones find theirs multiplied many-fold. The consequence is an instant abandonment of the more trivial projects with which we had been dallying, and an instant practical acceptance of the more grim and earnest alternative which till then could not extort our mind's consent. All those 'changes of heart,' 'awakenings of conscience,' etc., which make new men of so many of us may be classed under this head. The character abruptly rises to another 'level,' and deliberation comes to an immediate end.

In the *fifth and final type* of decision, the feeling that the evidence is all in, and that reason has balanced the books, may be either present or absent. But in either case we feel, in deciding, as if we ourselves by our own wilful act inclined the beam: in the former case by adding our living effort to the weight of the logical reason which, taken alone, seems powerless to make the act discharge; in the latter by a kind of creative contribution of something instead of a reason which does a reason's work. The slow dead heave of the will that is felt in these instances makes of them a class altogether different subjectively from all the four preceding classes. What the heave of the will betokens metaphysically, what the effort might lead us to infer about a will-power distinct from motives, are not matters that concern us yet. Subjectively and phenomenally, the *feeling of effort*, absent from the former decisions, accompanies these. Whether it be the dreary resignation for the sake of austere and naked duty of all sorts of rich mundane delights; or whether it be the heavy resolve that of two mutually exclusive trains of future fact, both sweet and good and with no strictly objective or imperative principle of choice between them, one shall forevermore become impossible, while the other shall become reality; it is a desolate and acrid sort of act, an entrance into a lonesome moral wilderness. If examined closely, its chief difference from the former cases appears to be that in those cases the mind at the moment of deciding on the triumphant alternative dropped the other one wholly or nearly out of sight, whereas here both alternatives are steadily held in view, and in the very act of murdering the vanquished possibility the chooser realizes how much in that instant he is making himself lose. It is deliberately driving a thorn into one's flesh; and the sense of *inward effort* with which the act is accompanied is an element which sets this fifth type of decision in strong contrast with the previous four varieties, and makes of it an altogether peculiar sort of mental phenomenon. The immense majority of human decisions are decisions without effort. In comparatively few of them, in most people, does effort accompany the final act. We are, I think, misled into supposing that effort is more frequent than it is by the fact that *during deliberation* we so often have a feeling of how great an effort it would take to make a decision *now*. Later, after the decision has made itself with ease, we recollect this and erroneously suppose the effort also to have been made then.

The existence of the effort as a phenomenal fact in our consciousness cannot of course be doubted or denied. Its significance, on the other hand, is a matter about which the gravest difference of opinion prevails. Questions as momentous as that of the very existence of spiritual causality, as vast as that of universal predestination or free-will, depend on its interpretation. It therefore becomes essential that we study with some care the conditions under which the feeling of volitional effort is found.

The Feeling of Effort.—When I said, awhile back, that *consciousness* (or the neural process which goes with it) *is in its very nature impulsive*, I should have added the proviso that *it must be sufficiently intense*. Now there are remarkable differences in the power of different sorts of consciousness to excite movement. The intensity of some feelings is practically apt to be below the discharging point, whilst that of others is apt to be above it. By practically apt, I mean apt under ordinary circumstances. These circumstances may be habitual inhibitions, like that comfortable feeling of the *dolce far niente* which gives to each and all of us a certain dose of laziness only to be overcome by the acuteness of the impulsive spur; or they may consist in the native inertia, or internal resistance, of the motor centres themselves, making explosion impossible until a certain inward tension has been reached and overpassed. These conditions may vary from one person to another, and in the same person from time to time. The neural inertia may wax or wane, and the habitual inhibitions dwindle or augment. The intensity of particular thought-processes and stimulations may also change independently, and particular paths of association grow more pervious or less so. There thus result great possibilities of alteration in the actual impulsive efficacy of particular motives compared with others. It is where the normally less efficacious motive becomes more efficacious, and the normally more efficacious one less so, that actions ordinarily effortless, or abstinences ordinarily easy, either become impossible, or are effected (if at all) by the expenditure of effort. A little more description will make it plainer what these cases are.

Healthiness of Will.—*There is a certain normal ratio in the impulsive power of different mental objects, which characterizes what may be called ordinary healthiness of will,* and which is departed from only at exceptional times or by exceptional individuals. The states of mind which normally possess the most impulsive quality are either those which represent objects of passion, appetite, or emotion—objects of instinctive reaction, in short; or they are feelings or ideas of pleasure or of pain; or ideas which for any reason we have grown accustomed to obey, so that the habit of reacting on them is ingrained; or finally, in comparison with ideas of remoter objects, they are ideas of objects present or near in space and time. Compared with these various objects, all far-off considerations, all highly abstract conceptions, unaccustomed reasons, and motives foreign to the instinctive history of the race, have little or no impulsive power. They prevail, when they ever do prevail, *with effort; and the normal,* as distinguished from the patho-logical, *sphere of effort is thus found wherever non-instinctive motives to behavior must be reinforced so as to rule the day.*

Healthiness of will moreover requires a certain amount of complication in the process which precedes the fiat or the act. Each stimulus or idea, at the same time that it wakens its own impulse, must also arouse other ideas along with *their* characteristic impulses, and action must finally follow, neither too slowly nor too rapidly, as the resultant of all the forces thus engaged. Even when the decision is pretty prompt, the normal thing is thus a sort of preliminary survey of the field and a vision of which course is best before the fiat comes. And where the will is healthy, *the vision must be right* (i.e., the motives must be on the whole in a normal or not too unusual ratio to each other), *and the action must obey the vision's lead.*

Unhealthiness of will may thus come about in many ways. The action may follow the stimulus or idea too rapidly, leaving no time for the arousal of restraining associates—*we then have a precipitate will.* Or, although the associates may come, the ratio which the impulsive and inhibitive forces normally bear to each other may be distorted, and we then have *a will which is perverse.* The perversity, in turn, may be due to either of many causes—too much intensity, or too little, here; too much or too little inertia there; or elsewhere too much or too little inhibitory power. *If we compare the outward symptoms of perversity together, they fall into two groups,* in one of which normal actions are impossible, and in the other abnormal ones are irrepressible. Briefly, *we may call them respectively the obstructed and the explosive will.*

It must be kept in mind, however, that since the resultant action is always due to the *ratio* between the obstructive and the explosive forces which are present, we never can tell by the mere outward symptoms to what *elementary* cause the perversion of a man's will may be due, whether to an increase of one component or a diminution of the other. One may grow explosive as readily by losing the usual brakes as by getting up more of the impulsive steam; and one may find things impossible as well through the enfeeblement of the original desire as through the advent of new lions in the path. As Dr. Clouston says, "The driver may be so weak that he cannot control well-broken horses, or the horses may be so hard-mouthed that no driver can pull them up."

The Explosive Will. I.) **From Defective Inhibition.**— There is a normal type of character, for example, in which impulses seem to discharge so promptly into movements that inhibitions get no time to arise. These are the 'dare-devil' and 'mercurial' temperaments, overflowing with animation and fizzling with talk, which are so common in the Slavic and Celtic races, and with which the cold-blooded and long-headed English character forms so marked a contrast. Simian these people seem to us, whilst we seem to them reptilian. It is quite impossible to judge, as between an obstructed and an explosive individual, which has the greater sum of vital energy. An explosive Italian with good perception and intellect will cut a figure as a perfectly tremendous fellow, on an inward capital that could be tucked away inside of an obstructed Yankee and hardly let you know that it was there. He will be the king of his company, sing the songs and make the speeches, lead the parties, carry out the practical jokes, kiss the girls, fight the men, and, if need be, lead the forlorn hopes and enterprises, so that an onlooker would think he has more life in his little finger than can exist in the whole body of a correct judicious fellow. But the judicious fellow all the while may have all these possibilities and more besides, ready to break out in the same or even a more violent way, if only the brakes were taken off. It is the absence of scruples, of consequences, of considerations, the extraordinary simplification of each moment's mental outlook, that gives to the explosive individual such motor energy and ease; it need not be the greater intensity of any of his passions, motives, or thoughts. As mental evolution goes on, the complexity of human consciousness grows ever greater, and with it the multiplication of the inhibitions to which every impulse is exposed. How much freedom of discourse we English folk lose because we feel obliged always to speak the truth! This predominance of inhibition has a bad as well as a good side; and if a man's impulses are in the main orderly as well as prompt, if he has courage to accept their consequences, and intellect to lead them to a successful end, he is all the better for his hair-trigger organization, and for not being 'sicklied o'er with the pale cast of thought.' Many of the most successful military and revolutionary characters in history have belonged to this simple but quick-witted impulsive type. Problems come much harder to reflective and inhibitive minds. They can, it is true, solve much vaster problems; and they can avoid many a mistake to which the men of impulse are exposed. But when the latter do not make mistakes, or when they are always able to retrieve them, theirs is one of the most engaging and indispensable of human types.

In infancy, and in certain conditions of exhaustion, as well as in peculiar pathological states, the inhibitory power may fail to arrest the explosions of the impulsive discharge. We have then an explosive temperament temporarily realized in an individual who at other times may be of a relatively obstructed type. In other persons, again, hysterics, epileptics, criminals of the neurotic class called *dégénérés* by French authors, there is such a native feebleness in the mental machinery that before the inhibitory ideas can arise the impulsive ones have already discharged into act. In persons healthy-willed by nature bad habits can bring about this condition, especially in relation to particular sorts of impulse. Ask half the common drunkards you know why it is that they fall so often a prey to temptation, and they will say that most of the time they cannot tell. It is a sort of vertigo with them. Their nervous centres have become a sluice-way pathologically unlocked by every passing conception of a bottle and a glass. They do not thirst for the beverage; the taste of it may even appear repugnant; and they perfectly foresee the morrow's remorse. But when they think of the liquor or see it, they find themselves preparing to drink, and do not stop themselves: and more than this they cannot say. Similarly a man may lead a life of incessant love-making or sexual indulgence, though what spurs him thereto seems to be trivial suggestions and notions of possibility rather than any real solid strength of passion or desire. Such characters are too flimsy even to be bad in any deep sense of the word. The paths of natural (or it may be unnatural) impulse are so pervious in them that the slightest rise in the level of innervation produces an overflow. It is the condition recognized in pathology as 'irritable weakness.' The phase known as nascency or latency is so short in the excitement of the neural tissues that there is no opportunity for strain or tension to accumulate within them; and the consequence is that with all the agitation and activity, the amount of real feeling engaged may be very small. The hysterical temperament is the playground *par excellence* of this unstable equilibrium. One of these subjects will be filled with what seems the most genuine and settled aversion to a certain line of conduct, and the very next *instant* follow the stirring of temptation and plunge in it up to the neck.

2.) **From Exaggerated Impulsion.**—Disorderly and impulsive conduct may, on the other hand, come about where the neural tissues preserve their proper inward tone, and where the inhibitory power is normal or even unusually great. In such cases *the strength of the impulsive idea is preternaturally exalted*, and what would be for most people the passing suggestion of a possibility becomes a gnawing, craving urgency to act. Works on insanity are full of examples of these morbid insistent ideas, in obstinately struggling against which the unfortunate victim's soul often sweats with agony ere at last it gets swept away.

The craving for drink in real dipsomaniacs, or for opium or chloral in those subjugated, is of a strength of which normal persons can form no conception. "Were a keg of rum in one corner of a room and were a cannon constantly discharging balls between me and it, I could not refrain from passing before that cannon in order to get at the rum"; "If a bottle of brandy stood at one hand, and the pit of hell yawned at the other, and I were convinced that I would be pushed in as sure as I took one glass, I could not refrain": such statements abound in dipsomaniacs' mouths. Dr. Mussey of Cincinnati relates this case:

"A few years ago a tippler was put into an almshouse in this State. Within a few days he had devised various expedients to procure rum, but failed. At length, however, he hit upon one which was successful. He went into the wood-yard of the establishment, placed one hand upon the block, and with an axe in the other, struck it off at a single blow. With the stump raised and streaming, he ran into the house and cried, 'Get some rum! get some rum! My hand is off.' In the confusion and bustle of the occasion a bowl of rum was brought, into which he plunged the bleeding member of his body; then raising the bowl to his mouth, drank freely, and exultingly exclaimed, 'Now I am satisfied!' Dr. J. E. Turner tells of a man, who while under treatment for inebriety, during four weeks secretly drank the alcohol from six jars containing morbid specimens. On asking him why he had committed this loathsome act, he replied, 'Sir, it is as impossible for me to control this diseased appetite as it is for me to control the pulsations of my heart.' "

Often the insistent idea is of a trivial sort, but it may wear the patient's life out. His hands feel dirty, they must be washed. He *knows* they are not dirty; yet to get rid of the teasing idea he washes them. The idea, however, returns in a moment, and the unfortunate victim, who is not in the least deluded *intellectually*, will end by spending the whole day at the wash-stand. Or his clothes are not 'rightly' put on; and to banish the thought he takes them off and puts them on again, till his toilet consumes two or three hours of time. Most people have the potentiality of this disease. To few has it not happened to conceive, after getting into bed, that they may have forgotten to lock the front door, or to turn out the entry gas. And few of us have not on some occasion got up to repeat the performance, less because we believed in the reality of its omission than because only so could we banish the worrying doubt and get to sleep.

The Obstructed Will.—In striking contrast with the cases in which inhibition is insufficient or impulsion in excess are those in which impulsion is insufficient or inhibition in excess. We all know the condition described on p. 211, in which the mind for a few moments seems to lose its focussing power and to be unable to rally its attention to any determinate thing. At such times we sit blankly staring and do nothing. The objects of consciousness fail to touch the quick or break the skin. They are there, but do not reach the level of effectiveness. This state of non-efficacious presence is the normal condition of *some* objects, in all of us. Great fatigue or exhaustion may make it the condition of almost all objects; and an apathy resembling that then brought about is recognized in asylums under the name of *abulia* as a symptom of mental disease. The healthy state of the will requires, as aforesaid, both that vision should be right, and that action should obey its lead. But in the morbid condition in question the vision may be wholly unaffected, and the intellect clear, and yet the act either fails to follow or follows in some other way.

"Video meliora proboque, deteriora sequor" is the classic expression of this latter condition of mind. The moral tragedy of human life comes almost wholly from the fact that the link is ruptured which normally should hold between vision of the truth and action, and that this pungent sense of effective reality will not attach to certain ideas. Men do not differ so much in their mere feelings and conceptions. Their notions of possibility and their ideals are not as far apart as might be argued from their differing fates. No class of them have better sentiments or feel more constantly the difference between the higher and the lower path in life than the hopeless failures, the sentimentalists, the drunkards, the schemers, the 'deadbeats,' whose life is one long contradiction between knowledge and action, and who, with full command of theory, never get to holding their limp characters erect. No one eats of the fruit of the tree of knowledge as they do; so far as moral insight goes, in comparison with them the orderly and prosperous philistines whom they scandalize are sucking babes. And yet their moral knowledge, always there grumbling and rumbling in the background,—discerning, commenting, protesting, longing, half resolving,—never wholly resolves, never gets its voice out of the minor into the major key, or its speech out of the subjunctive into the imperative mood, never breaks the spell, never takes the helm into its hands. In such characters as Rousseau and Restif it would seem as if the lower motives had all the impulsive efficacy in their hands. Like trains with the right of way, they retain exclusive possession of the track. The more ideal motives exist alongside of them in profusion, but they never get switched on, and the man's conduct is no more influenced by them than an express train is influenced by a wayfarer standing by the roadside and calling to be taken aboard. They are an inert accompaniment to the end of time; and the consciousness of inward hollowness that accrues from habitually seeing the

better only to do the worse, is one of the saddest feelings one
can bear with him through this vale of tears.

Effort feels like an original force. We now see at one view
when it is that effort complicates volition. It does so whenever a rarer and more ideal impulse is called upon to neutralize others of a more instinctive and habitual kind; it does
so whenever strongly explosive tendencies are checked, or
strongly obstructive conditions overcome. The *âme bien née*,
the child of the sunshine, at whose birth the fairies made
their gifts, does not need much of it in his life. The hero and
the neurotic subject, on the other hand, do. Now our spontaneous way of conceiving the effort, under all these circumstances, is as an active force adding its strength to that
of the motives which ultimately prevail. When outer forces
impinge upon a body, we say that the resultant motion is in
the line of least resistance, or of greatest traction. But it is a
curious fact that our spontaneous language never speaks of
volition with effort in this way. Of course if we proceed *a
priori* and define the line of least resistance as the line that is
followed, the physical law must also hold good in the mental
sphere. But we *feel*, in all hard cases of volition, as if the line
taken, when the rarer and more ideal motives prevail, were
the line of greater resistance, and as if the line of coarser
motivation were the more pervious and easy one, even at
the very moment when we refuse to follow it. He who under
the surgeon's knife represses cries of pain, or he who exposes himself to social obloquy for duty's sake, feels as if he
were following the line of greatest temporary resistance.
He speaks of conquering and overcoming his impulses and
temptations.

But the sluggard, the drunkard, the coward, never talk of
their conduct in that way, or say they resist their energy, overcome their sobriety, conquer their courage, and so forth. If in
general we class all springs of action as propensities on the
one hand and ideals on the other, the sensualist never says of
his behavior that it results from a victory over his ideals, but
the moralist always speaks of his as a victory over his propensities. The sensualist uses terms of inactivity, says he forgets
his ideals, is deaf to duty, and so forth; which terms seem to

imply that the ideal motives *per se* can be annulled without energy or effort, and that the strongest mere traction lies in the line of the propensities. The ideal impulse appears, in comparison with this, a still small voice which must be artificially reinforced to prevail. Effort is what reinforces it, making things seem as if, while the force of propensity were essentially a fixed quantity, the ideal force might be of various amount. But what determines the amount of the effort when, by its aid, an ideal motive becomes victorious over a great sensual resistance? The very greatness of the resistance itself. If the sensual propensity is small, the effort is small. The latter is *made great* by the presence of a great antagonist to overcome. And if a brief definition of ideal or moral action were required, none could be given which would better fit the appearances than this: *It is action in the line of the greatest resistance.*

The facts may be most briefly symbolized thus, P standing for the propensity, I for the ideal impulse, and E for the effort:

$$I \text{ } per \text{ } se < P.$$
$$I + E > P.$$

In other words, if E adds itself to I, P immediately offers the least resistance, and motion occurs in spite of it.

But the E does not seem to form an integral part of the I. It appears adventitious and indeterminate in advance. We can make more or less as we please, and *if* we make enough we can convert the greatest mental resistance into the least. Such, at least, is the impression which the facts spontaneously produce upon us. But we will not discuss the truth of this impression at present; let us rather continue our descriptive detail.

Pleasure and Pain as Springs of Action.—Objects and thoughts of objects start our action, but the pleasures and pains which action brings modify its course and regulate it; and later the thoughts of the pleasures and the pains acquire themselves impulsive and inhibitive power. Not that the thought of a pleasure need be itself a pleasure, usually it is the reverse—*nessun maggior dolore*—as Dante says—and not that the thought of pain need be a pain, for, as Homer says, "griefs are often afterwards an entertainment." But as present pleasures are tremendous reinforcers, and present pains tremendous inhibitors of whatever action leads to them, so the thoughts of pleasures and pains take rank amongst the thoughts which have most impulsive and inhibitive power. The precise relation which these thoughts hold to other thoughts is thus a matter demanding some attention.

If a movement feels agreeable, we repeat and repeat it as long as the pleasure lasts. If it hurts us, our muscular contractions at the instant stop. So complete is the inhibition in this latter case that it is almost impossible for a man to cut or mutilate himself slowly and deliberately—his hand invincibly refusing to bring on the pain. And there are many pleasures which, when once we have begun to taste them, make it all but obligatory to keep up the activity to which they are due. So widespread and searching is this influence of pleasures and pains upon our movements that a premature philosophy has decided that these are our only spurs to action, and that wherever they seem to be absent, it is only because they are so far on among the 'remoter' images that prompt the action that they are overlooked.

This is a great mistake, however. Important as is the influence of pleasures and pains upon our movements, they are far from being our only stimuli. With the manifestations of instinct and emotional expression, for example, they have absolutely nothing to do. Who smiles for the pleasure of the smiling, or frowns for the pleasure of the frown? Who blushes to escape the discomfort of not blushing? Or who in anger, grief, or fear is actuated to the movements which he makes by the pleasures which they yield? In all these cases the movements are discharged fatally by the *vis a tergo* which the stimulus exerts upon a nervous system framed to respond in just that way. The objects of our rage, love, or terror, the occasions of our tears and smiles, whether they be present to our senses, or whether they be merely represented in idea, have this peculiar sort of impulsive power. The *impulsive quality* of mental states is an attribute behind which we cannot go. Some states of mind have more of it than others, some have it in this direction and some in that. Feelings of pleasure and pain have it, and perceptions and imaginations of fact have it, but neither have it exclusively or peculiarly. It is of the essence of all consciousness (or of the neural process which underlies it) to instigate movement of some sort. That with one creature and object it should be of one sort, with others of another sort, is a problem for evolutionary history to explain. However the actual impulsions may have arisen, they must now be described as they exist; and those persons obey a curiously narrow teleological superstition who think themselves bound to interpret them in every instance as effects of the secret solicitancy of pleasure and repugnancy of pain. If the thought of pleasure can impel to action, surely other thoughts may. Experience only can decide which thoughts do. The chapters on Instinct and Emotion have shown us that their name is legion; and with this verdict we ought to remain contented, and not seek an illusory simplification at the cost of half the facts.

If in these our *first* acts pleasures and pains bear no part, as little do they bear in our last acts, or those artificially acquired performances which have become habitual. All the daily routine of life, our dressing and undressing, the coming and going from our work or carrying through of its various operations, is utterly without mental reference to pleasure and pain, except under rarely realized conditions. It is ideo-motor action. As I do not breathe for the pleasure of the breathing, but simply find that I *am* breathing, so I do not write for the pleasure of the writing, but simply because I have once begun, and being in a state of intellectual excitement which keeps venting itself in that way, find that I *am* writing still. Who will pretend that when he idly fingers his knife-handle at the table, it is for the sake of any pleasure which it gives him, or pain which he thereby avoids? We do all these things because at the moment we cannot help it; our nervous systems are so shaped that they overflow in just that way; and for many of our idle or purely 'nervous' and fidgety performances we can assign absolutely no *reason* at all.

Or what shall be said of a shy and unsociable man who receives point-blank an invitation to a small party? The thing is to him an abomination; but your presence exerts a compulsion on him, he can think of no excuse, and so says yes, cursing himself the while for what he does. He is unusually *sui compos* who does not every week of his life fall into some such blundering act as this. Such instances of *voluntas invita* show not only that our acts cannot all be conceived as effects of represented pleasure, but that they cannot even be classed as cases of represented *good*. The class 'goods' contains many more generally influential motives to action than the class 'pleasants.' But almost as little as under the form of pleasures do our acts invariably appear to us under the form of *goods*. All diseased impulses and pathological fixed ideas are instances to the contrary. It is the very badness of the act that gives it then its vertiginous fascination. Remove the prohibition, and the attraction stops. In my university days a student threw himself from an upper entry window of one of the college buildings and was nearly killed. Another student, a friend of my own, had to pass the window daily in coming and going from his room, and experienced a dreadful temptation to imitate the deed. Being a Catholic, he told his director, who said, 'All right! if you must, you must,' and added, 'Go ahead and do it,' thereby instantly quenching his desire. This director knew how to minister to a mind diseased. But we need not go to minds diseased for examples of the occasional tempting-power of simple badness and unpleasantness as such. Everyone who has a wound or hurt anywhere, a sore tooth, e.g., will ever and anon press it just to bring out the pain. If we are near a new sort of stink, we must sniff it again just to verify once more how bad it is. This very day I have been repeating over and over to myself a verbal jingle whose mawkish silliness was the secret of its haunting power. I loathed yet could not banish it.

What holds attention determines action. If one must have a single name for the condition upon which the impulsive and inhibitive quality of objects depends, one had better call it their *interest*. 'The interesting' is a title which covers not only the pleasant and the painful, but also the morbidly fascinating, the tediously haunting, and even the simply habitual, inasmuch as the attention usually travels on habitual lines, and what-we-attend-to and what-interests-us are synonymous terms. It seems as if we ought to look for the secret of an idea's impulsiveness, not in any peculiar relations which it may have with paths of motor discharge,—for *all* ideas have relations with some such paths,—but rather in a preliminary phenomenon, the *urgency, namely, with which it is able to compel attention and dominate in consciousness.* Let it once so dominate, let no other ideas succeed in displacing it, and whatever motor effects belong to it by nature will inevitably occur—its impulsion, in short, will be given to boot, and will manifest itself as a matter of course. This is what we have seen in instinct, in emotion, in common ideo-motor action, in hypnotic suggestion, in morbid impulsion, and in *voluntas invita*,—the impelling idea is simply the one which possesses the attention. It is the same where pleasure and pain are the motor spurs— they drive other thoughts from consciousness at the same time that they instigate their own characteristic 'volitional' effects. And this is also what happens at the moment of the *fiat*, in all the five types of 'decision' which we have described. In short, one does not see any case in which the steadfast occupancy of consciousness does not appear to be the prime condition of impulsive power. It is still more obviously the prime condition of inhibitive power. What checks our impulses is the mere thinking of reasons to the contrary—it is their bare presence to the mind which gives the veto, and makes acts, otherwise seductive, impossible to perform. If we could only *forget* our scruples, our doubts, our fears, what exultant energy we should for a while display!

Will is a relation between the mind and its 'ideas.' In closing in, therefore, after all these preliminaries, upon the more *intimate* nature of the volitional process, we find ourselves driven more and more exclusively to consider the conditions which make ideas prevail in the mind. With the prevalence, once there as a fact, of the motive idea, the *psychology* of volition properly stops. The movements which ensue are exclusively physiological phenomena, following according to physiological laws upon the neural events to which the idea corresponds. The *willing* terminates with the prevalence of the idea; and whether the act then follows or not is a matter quite immaterial, so far as the willing itself goes. I will to write, and the act follows. I will to sneeze, and it does not. I will that the distant table slide over the floor towards me; it also does not. My willing representation can no more instigate my sneezing-centre than it can instigate the table to activity. But in both cases it is as true and good willing as it was when I willed to write. In a word, volition is a psychic or moral fact pure and simple, and is absolutely completed when the stable state of the idea is there. The supervention of motion is a supernumerary phenomenon depending on executive ganglia whose function lies outside the mind. If the ganglia work duly, the act occurs perfectly. If they work, but work wrongly, we have St. Vitus's dance, locomotor ataxy, motor aphasia, or minor degrees of awkwardness. If they don't work at all, the act fails altogether, and we say the man is paralyzed. He may make a tremendous effort, and contract the other muscles of the body, but the paralyzed limb fails to move. In all these cases, however, the volition considered as a psychic process is intact.

Volitional effort is effort of attention. We thus find that *we reach the heart of our inquiry into volition when we ask by what process it is that the thought of any given action comes to prevail stably in the mind.* Where thoughts prevail without effort, we have sufficiently studied in the several chapters on Sensation, Association, and Attention, the laws of their advent before consciousness and of their stay. We shall not go over that ground again, for we know that interest and association are the words, let their worth be what it may, on which our explanations must perforce rely. Where, on the other hand, the prevalence of the thought is accompanied by the phenomenon of effort, the case is much less clear. Already in the chapter on Attention we postponed the final consideration of voluntary attention with effort to a later place. We have now brought things to a point at which we see that attention with effort is all that any case of volition implies. *The essential achievement of the will, in short, when it is most 'voluntary,' is to attend to a difficult object and hold it fast before the mind.* The so-doing *is* the *fiat*; and it is a mere physiological incident that when the object is thus attended to, immediate motor consequences should ensue.

Effort of attention is thus the essential phenomenon of will.[3]
Every reader must know by his own experience that this is
so, for every reader must have felt some fiery passion's grasp.
What constitutes the difficulty for a man laboring under an
unwise passion of acting as if the passion were wise? Certainly
there is no physical difficulty. It is as easy physically to avoid a
fight as to begin one, to pocket one's money as to squander it
on one's cupidities, to walk away from as towards a coquette's
door. The difficulty is mental: it is that of getting the idea of
the wise action to stay before our mind at all. When any
strong emotional state whatever is upon us, the tendency is
for no images but such as are congruous with it to come up.
If others by chance offer themselves, they are instantly smothered and crowded out. If we be joyous, we cannot keep thinking of those uncertainties and risks of failure which abound
upon our path; if lugubrious, we cannot think of new triumphs, travels, loves, and joys; nor if vengeful, of our oppres-
sor's community of nature with ourselves. The cooling advice
which we get from others when the fever-fit is on us is the
most jarring and exasperating thing in life. Reply we cannot,
so we get angry; for by a sort of self-preserving instinct which
our passion has, it feels that these chill objects, if they once
but gain a lodgment, will work and work until they have frozen the very vital spark from out of all our mood and brought
our airy castles in ruin to the ground. Such is the inevitable
effect of reasonable ideas over others—*if they can once get a
quiet hearing*; and passion's cue accordingly is always and

[3]This *volitional* effort pure and simple must be carefully distinguished from
the *muscular* effort with which it is usually confounded. The latter consists of
all those peripheral feelings to which a muscular 'exertion' may give rise.
These feelings, whenever they are massive and the body is not 'fresh,' are
rather disagreeable, especially when accompanied by stopped breath, con-
gested head, bruised skin of fingers, toes, or shoulders, and strained joints.
And it is only *as thus disagreeable* that the mind must make its *volitional* effort
in stably representing their reality and consequently bringing it about. That
they happen to be made real by muscular activity is a purely accidental circumstance. There are instances where the fiat demands great volitional effort
though the muscular exertion be insignificant, e.g., the getting out of bed
and bathing one's self on a cold morning. Again, a soldier standing still to be
fired at expects disagreeable sensations from his muscular passivity. The action of his will, in sustaining the expectation, is identical with that required
for a painful muscular effort. What is hard for both is *facing an idea as real.*

everywhere to prevent their still small voice from being heard at all. "Let me not think of that! Don't speak to me of that!" This is the sudden cry of all those who in a passion perceive some sobering considerations about to check them in mid-career. There is something so icy in this cold-water bath, something which seems so hostile to the movement of our life, so purely negative, in Reason, when she lays her corpse-like finger on our heart and says "Halt! give up! leave off! go back! sit down!" that it is no wonder that to most men the steadying influence seems, for the time being, a very minister of death.

The strong-willed man, however, is the man who hears the still small voice unflinchingly, and who, when the death-bringing consideration comes, looks at its face, consents to its presence, clings to it, affirms it, and holds it fast, in spite of the host of exciting mental images which rise in revolt against it and would expel it from the mind. Sustained in this way by a resolute effort of attention, the difficult object erelong begins to call up its own congeners and associates and ends by changing the disposition of the man's consciousness altogether. And with his consciousness his action changes, for the new object, once stably in possession of the field of his thoughts, infallibly produces its own motor effects. The difficulty lies in the gaining possession of that field. Though the spontaneous drift of thought is all the other way, the attention must be kept strained on that one object until at last it *grows*, so as to maintain itself before the mind with ease. This strain of the attention is the fundamental act of will. And the will's work is in most cases practically ended when the bare presence to our thought of the naturally unwelcome object has been secured. For the mysterious tie between the thought and the motor centres next comes into play, and, in a way which we cannot even guess at, the obedience of the bodily organs follows as a matter of course.

In all this one sees how the immediate point of application of the volitional effort lies exclusively within the mental world. The whole drama is a mental drama. The whole difficulty is a mental difficulty, a difficulty with an ideal object of our thought. It is, in one word, an *idea* to which our will applies itself, an idea which if we let it go would slip away, but which we will not let go. *Consent to the idea's undivided presence, this is effort's sole achievement.* Its only function is to get this feeling of consent into the mind. And for this there is but one way. The idea to be consented to must be kept from flickering and going out. It must be held steadily before the mind until it *fills* the mind. Such filling of the mind by an idea, with its congruous associates, *is* consent to the idea and to the fact which the idea represents. If the idea be that, or include that, of a bodily movement of our own, then we call the consent thus laboriously gained a motor volition. For Nature here 'backs' us instantaneously and follows up our inward willingness by outward changes on her own part. She does this in no other instance. Pity she should not have been more generous, nor made a world whose other parts were as immediately subject to our will!

On page 400, in describing the 'reasonable type' of decision, it was said that it usually came when the right conception of the case was found. Where, however, the right conception is an anti-impulsive one, the whole intellectual ingenuity of the man usually goes to work to crowd it out of sight, and to find for the emergency names by the help of which the dispositions of the moment may sound sanctified, and sloth or passion may reign unchecked. How many excuses does the drunkard find when each new temptation comes! It is a new brand of liquor which the interests of intellectual culture in such matters oblige him to test; moreover it is poured out and it is sin to waste it; also others are drinking and it would be churlishness to refuse. Or it is but to enable him to sleep, or just to get through this job of work; or it isn't drinking, it is because he feels so cold; or it is Christmas-day; or it is a means of stimulating him to make a more powerful resolution in favor of abstinence than any he has hitherto made; or it is just this once, and once doesn't count, etc., etc., *ad libitum*—it is, in fact, anything you like except *being a drunkard. That* is the conception that will not stay before the poor soul's attention. But if he once gets able to pick out that way of conceiving, from all the other possible ways of conceiving the various opportunities which occur, if through thick and thin he holds to it that this is being a drunkard and is nothing else, he is not likely to remain one long. The effort by which he succeeds in keeping the right *name* unwaveringly present to his mind proves to be his saving moral act.

Everywhere, then, the function of the effort is the same: to keep affirming and adopting a thought which, if left to itself, would slip away. It may be cold and flat when the spontaneous mental drift is towards excitement, or great and arduous when the spontaneous drift is towards repose. In the one case the effort has to inhibit an explosive, in the other to arouse an obstructed will. The exhausted sailor on a wreck has a will which is obstructed. One of his ideas is that of his sore hands, of the nameless exhaustion of his whole frame which the act of farther pumping involves, and of the deliciousness of sinking into sleep. The other is that of the hungry sea ingulfing him. "Rather the aching toil!" he says; and it becomes reality then, in spite of the inhibiting influence of the relatively luxurious sensations which he gets from lying still. Often again it may be the thought of sleep and what leads to it which is the hard one to keep before the mind. If a patient afflicted with insomnia can only control the whirling chase of his ideas so far as to think of *nothing at all* (which can be done), or so far as to imagine one letter after another of a verse of scripture or poetry spelt slowly and monotonously out, it is almost certain that here, too, specific bodily effects will follow, and that sleep will come. The trouble is to keep the mind upon a train of objects naturally so insipid. *To sustain a representation, to think*, is, in short, the only moral act, for the impulsive and the obstructed, for sane and lunatics alike. Most maniacs know their thoughts to be crazy, but find them too pressing to be withstood. Compared with them the sane truths are so deadly sober, so cadaverous, that the lunatic cannot bear to look them in the face and say, "Let these alone be my reality!" But with sufficient effort, as Dr. Wigan says, "Such a man can for a time *wind himself up*, as it were, and determine that the notions of the disordered brain shall not be manifested. Many instances are on record similar to that told by Pinel, where an inmate of the Bicêtre, having stood a long cross-examination, and given every mark of restored reason, signed his name to the paper authorizing his discharge, 'Jesus Christ,' and then went off into all the vagaries connected with that delusion. In the phraseology of the gentleman whose case is related in an early part of this [Wigan's] work, he had 'held himself tight' during the examination, in order to attain his object; this once accomplished, he 'let himself down' again, and, if even *conscious* of his delusion, could not control it. I have observed with such persons that it requires a considerable time to wind themselves up to the pitch of complete self-control, and that the effort is a painful tension of the mind. When thrown off their guard by any accidental remark, or worn out by the length of the examination, they *let themselves go*, and cannot gather themselves up again without preparation."

To sum it all up in a word, *the terminus of the psychological process in volition, the point to which the will is directly applied, is always an idea.* There are at all times *some* ideas from which we shy away like frightened horses the moment we get a glimpse of their forbidding profile upon the threshold of our thought. *The only resistance which our will can possibly experience is the resistance which such an idea offers to being attended to at all.* To attend to it is the volitional act, and the only inward volitional act which we ever perform.

The Question of 'Free-will.'—As was remarked on p. 411, in the experience of effort we feel as if we might make more or less than we actually at any moment are making.

The effort appears, in other words, not as a fixed reaction on our part which the object that resists us necessarily calls forth, but as what the mathematicians call an 'independent variable' amongst the fixed data of the case, our motives, character, etc. If it be really so, if the amount of our effort is not a determinate function of those other data, then, in common parlance, *our wills are free.* If, on the contrary, the amount of effort be a fixed function, so that whatever object at any time fills our consciousness was from eternity bound to fill it then and there, and compel from us the exact effort, neither more nor less, which we bestow upon it,—then our wills are not free, and all our acts are foreordained. *The question of fact in the free-will controversy is thus extremely simple. It relates solely to the amount of effort of attention which we can at any time put forth.* Are the duration and intensity of this effort fixed functions of the object, or are they not? Now, as I just said, it *seems* as if we might exert more or less in any given case.

When a man has let his thoughts go for days and weeks until at last they culminate in some particularly dirty or cowardly or cruel act, it is hard to persuade him, in the midst of his remorse, that he might not have reined them in; hard to make him believe that this whole goodly universe (which his act so jars upon) required and exacted it of him at that fatal moment, and from eternity made aught else impossible. But, on the other hand, there is the certainty that all his *effortless* volitions are resultants of interests and associations whose strength and sequence are mechanically determined by the structure of that physical mass, his brain; and the general continuity of things and the monistic conception of the world may lead one irresistibly to postulate that a little fact like effort can form no real exception to the overwhelming reign of deterministic law. Even in effortless volition we have the consciousness of the alternative being also possible. This is surely a delusion here; why is it not a delusion everywhere?

The fact is that the question of free-will is insoluble on strictly psychologic grounds. After a certain amount of effort of attention has been given to an idea, it is manifestly impossible to tell whether either more or less of it *might* have been given or not. To tell that, we should have to ascend to the antecedents of the effort, and defining them with mathematical exactitude, prove, by laws of which we have not at present even an inkling, that the only amount of sequent effort which could *possibly* comport with them was the precise amount that actually came. Such measurements, whether of psychic or of neural quantities, and such deductive reasonings as this method of proof implies, will surely be forever beyond human reach. No serious psychologist or physiologist will venture even to suggest a notion of how they might be practically made. Had one no motives drawn from elsewhere to make one partial to either solution, one might easily leave the matter undecided. But a psychologist cannot be expected to be thus impartial, having a great motive in favor of determinism. He wants to build a *Science*; and a Science is a system of fixed relations. Wherever there are independent variables, there Science stops. So far, then, as our volitions may be independent variables, a scientific psychology must ignore that fact, and treat of them only so far as they are fixed functions. In other words, she must deal with the *general laws* of volition exclusively; with the impulsive and inhibitory character of ideas; with the nature of their appeals to the attention; with the conditions under which effort may arise, etc.; but not with the precise amounts of effort, for these, if our wills be free, are impossible to compute. She thus abstracts from free-will, without necessarily denying its existence. Practically, however, such abstraction is not distinguished from rejection; and most actual psychologists have no hesitation in denying that free-will exists.

For ourselves, we can hand the free-will controversy over to metaphysics. Psychology will surely never grow refined enough to discover, in the case of any individual's decision, a discrepancy between her scientific calculations and the fact. Her prevision will never foretell, whether the effort be completely predestinate or not, the way in which each individual emergency is resolved. Psychology will be psychology, and Science science, as much as ever (as much and no more) in this world, whether free-will be true in it or not.

We can thus ignore the free-will question in psychology. As we said on p. 417, the operation of free effort, if it existed, could only be to hold some one ideal object, or part of an object, a little longer or a little more intensely before the mind. Amongst the alternatives which present themselves as *genuine possibles*, it would thus make one effective. And although such quickening of one idea might be morally and historically momentous, yet, if considered *dynamically*, it would be an operation amongst those physiological infinitesimals which an actual science must forever neglect.

Ethical Importance of the Phenomenon of Effort.—But whilst eliminating the question about the amount of our effort as one which psychology will never have a practical call to decide, I must say one word about the extraordinarily intimate and important character which the phenomenon of effort assumes in our own eyes as individual men. Of course we measure ourselves by many standards. Our strength and our intelligence, our wealth and even our good luck, are things which warm our heart and make us feel ourselves a match for life. But deeper than all such things, and able to suffice unto itself without them, is the sense of the amount of effort which we can put forth. Those are, after all, but effects, products, and reflections of the outer world within. But the effort seems to belong to an altogether different realm, as if it were the substantive thing which we *are*, and those were but externals which we *carry*. If the 'searching of our heart and reins' be the purpose of this human drama, then what is sought seems to be what effort we can make. He who can make none is but a shadow; he who can make much is a hero. The huge world that girdles us about puts all sorts of questions to us, and tests us in all sorts of ways. Some of the tests we meet by actions that are easy, and some of the questions we answer in articulately formulated words. But the deepest question that is ever asked admits of no reply but the dumb turning of the will and the tightening of our heart-strings as we say, *"Yes, I will even have it so!"* When a dreadful object is presented, or when life as a whole turns up its dark abysses to our view, then the worthless ones among us lose their hold on the situation altogether, and either escape from its difficulties by averting their attention, or if they cannot do that, collapse into yielding masses of plaintiveness and fear. The effort required for facing and consenting to such objects is beyond their power to make. But the heroic mind does differently. To it, too, the objects are sinister and dreadful, unwelcome, incompatible with wished-for things. But it can face them if necessary, without for that losing its hold upon the rest of life. The world thus finds in the heroic man its worthy match and mate; and the effort which he is able to put forth to hold himself erect and keep his heart unshaken is the direct measure of his worth and function in the game of human life. He can *stand* this Universe. He can meet it and keep up his faith in it in presence of those same features which lay his weaker brethren low. He can still find a zest in it, not by 'ostrich-like forgetfulness,' but by pure inward willingness to take it with those deterrent objects there. And hereby he makes himself one of the masters and the lords of life. He must be counted with henceforth; he forms a part of human destiny. Neither in the theoretic nor in the practical sphere do we care for, or go for help to, those who have no head for risks, or sense for living on the perilous edge. Our religious life lies more, our practical life lies less, than it used to, on the perilous edge.

But just as our courage is so often a reflex of another's cour- age, so our faith is apt to be a faith in someone else's faith. We draw new life from the heroic example. The prophet has drunk more deeply than anyone of the cup of bitterness, but his countenance is so unshaken and he speaks such mighty words of cheer that his will becomes our will, and our life is kindled at his own.

Thus not only our morality but our religion, so far as the latter is deliberate, depend on the effort which we can make. *"Will you or won't you have it so?"* is the most probing question we are ever asked; we are asked it every hour of the day, and about the largest as well as the smallest, the most theoretical as well as the most practical, things. We answer by *consents or non-consents* and not by words. What wonder that these dumb responses should seem our deepest organs of communication with the nature of things! What wonder if the effort de- manded by them be the measure of our worth as men! What wonder if the amount which we accord of it were the one strictly underived and original contribution which we make to the world!

EPILOGUE

PSYCHOLOGY AND PHILOSOPHY

What the Word Metaphysics means.—In the last chapter we handed the question of free-will over to 'metaphysics.' It would indeed have been hasty to settle the question absolutely, inside the limits of psychology. Let psychology frankly admit that *for her scientific purposes* determinism may be *claimed*, and no one can find fault. If, then, it turn out later that the claim has only a relative purpose, and may be crossed by counter-claims, the readjustment can be made. Now ethics makes a counter-claim; and the present writer, for one, has no hesitation in regarding her claim as the stronger, and in assuming that our wills are 'free.' For him, then, the deterministic assumption of psychology is merely provisional and methodological. This is no place to argue the ethical point; and I only mention the conflict to show that all these special sciences, marked off for convenience from the remaining body of truth (cf. p. 11), must hold their assumptions and results subject to revision in the light of each other's needs. The forum where they hold discussion is called metaphysics. Metaphysics means only an unusually obstinate attempt to think clearly and consistently. The special sciences all deal with data that are full of obscurity and contradiction; but from the point of view of their limited purposes these defects may be overlooked. Hence the disparaging use of the name metaphysics which is so common. To a man with a limited purpose any discussion that is over-subtle for that purpose is branded as 'metaphysical.' A geologist's purposes fall short of understanding Time itself. A mechanist need not know how action and reaction are possible at all. A psychologist has enough to do without asking how both he and the mind which he studies are able to take cognizance of the same outer world. But it is obvious that problems irrelevant from one standpoint may be essential from another. And as soon as one's purpose is the attainment of the maximum of possible insight into the world as a whole, the metaphysical puzzles become the most urgent ones of all. Psychology contributes to general philosophy her full share of these; and I propose in this last chapter to indicate briefly which of them seem the more important. And first, of the

Relation of Consciousness to the Brain.—When psychology is treated as a natural science (after the fashion in which it has been treated in this book), 'states of mind' are taken for granted, as data immediately given in experience; and the working hypothesis (see p. 15) is the mere empirical law that to the entire state of the brain at any moment one unique state of mind always 'corresponds.' This does very well till we begin to be metaphysical and ask ourselves just what we mean by such a word as 'corresponds.' This notion appears dark in the extreme, the moment we seek to translate it into something more intimate than mere parallel variation. Some think they make the notion of it clearer by calling the mental state and the brain the inner and outer 'aspects,' respectively, of 'One and the Same Reality.' Others consider the mental state as the 'reaction' of a unitary being, the Soul, upon the multiple activities which the brain presents. Others again comminute the mystery by supposing each brain-cell to be separately conscious, and the empirically given mental state to be the appearance of all the little consciousnesses fused into one, just as the 'brain' itself is the appearance of all the cells together, when looked at from one point of view.

We may call these three metaphysical attempts the *monistic*, the *spiritualistic*, and the *atomistic* theories respectively. Each has its difficulties, of which it seems to me that those of the spiritualistic theory are *logically* much the least grave. But the spiritualistic theory is quite out of touch with the facts of multiple consciousness, alternate personality, etc. (pp. 201–207). These lend themselves more naturally to the atomistic formulation, for it seems easier to think of a lot of minor consciousnesses now gathering together into one large mass, and now into several smaller ones, than of a Soul now reacting totally, now breaking into several disconnected simultaneous reactions. The localization of brain-functions also makes for the atomistic view. If in my experience, say of a bell, it is my occipital lobes which are the condition of its being seen, and my temporal lobes which are the condition of its being heard, what is more natural than to say that the former *see* it and the latter *hear* it, and then 'combine their information'? In view of the extreme naturalness of such a way of representing the well-established fact that the appearance of the several parts of an object to consciousness at any moment does depend on as many several parts of the brain being then active, all such objections as were urged, on pp. 30, 64, and elsewhere, to the notion that 'parts' of consciousness *can* 'combine' will be rejected as far-fetched, unreal, and 'metaphysical' by the atomistic philosopher. His 'purpose' is to gain a formula which shall unify things in a natural and easy manner, and for such a purpose the atomistic theory seems expressly made to his hand.

But the difficulty with the problem of 'correspondence' is not only that of solving it, it is that of even stating it in elementary terms.

"L'ombre en ce lieu s'amasse, et la nuit est la toute."

Before we can know just what sort of goings-on occur when thought corresponds to a change in the brain, we must know the *subjects* of the goings-on. We must know which sort of mental fact and which sort of cerebral fact are, so to speak, in immediate juxtaposition. We must find the minimal mental fact whose being reposes directly on a brain-fact; and we must similarly find the minimal brain-event which can have a mental counterpart at all. Between the mental and the physical minima thus found there will be an immediate relation, the expression of which, if we had it, would be the elementary psycho-physic law.

Our own formula has escaped the metempiric assumption of psychic atoms by *taking the entire thought* (even of a complex object) *as the minimum with which it deals on the mental* side, and the entire brain as the minimum on the physical side. But the 'entire brain' is not a physical fact at all! It is nothing but our name for the way in which a billion of molecules arranged in certain positions may affect our sense. On the principles of the corpuscular or mechanical philosophy, the only realities are the separate molecules, or at most the cells. Their aggregation into a 'brain' is a fiction of popular speech. Such a figment cannot serve as the objectively real counterpart to any psychic state whatever. Only a genuinely physical fact can so serve, and the molecular fact is the only genuine physical fact. Whereupon we seem, if we are to have an elementary psycho-physic law at all, thrust right back upon something like the mental-atom-theory, for the molecular fact, being an element of the 'brain,' would seem naturally to correspond, not to total thoughts, but to elements of thoughts. Thus the real in psychics seems to 'correspond' to the unreal in physics, and *vice versa*; and our perplexity is extreme.

The Relation of States of Mind to their 'Objects.'—The perplexity is not diminished when we reflect upon our assumption that states of consciousness can *know* (pp. 12–13). From the common-sense point of view (which is that of all the natural sciences) knowledge is an ultimate relation between two mutually external entities, the knower and the known. The world first exists, and then the states of mind; and these gain a cognizance of the world which gets gradually more and more complete. But it is hard to carry through this simple dualism, for idealistic reflections will intrude. Take the states of mind called pure sensations (so far as such may exist), that for example of *blue*, which we may get from looking into the zenith on a clear day. Is the blue a determination of the feeling itself, or of its 'object'? Shall we describe the experience as a quality of our feeling or as our feeling of a quality? Ordinary speech vacillates incessantly on this point. The ambiguous word 'content' has been recently invented instead of 'object,' to escape a decision; for 'content' suggests something not exactly out of the feeling, nor yet exactly identical with the feeling, since the latter remains suggested as the container or vessel. Yet of our feelings as vessels apart from their content we really have no clear notion whatever. The fact is that such an experience as *blue*, as it is immediately given, can only be called by some such neutral name as that of *phenomenon*. It does not *come* to us *immediately* as a relation between two realities, one mental and one physical. It is only when, still thinking of it as the *same* blue (cf. p. 229), we trace relations between it and other things, that it doubles itself, so to speak, and develops in two directions; and, taken in connection with some associates, figures as a physical quality, whilst with others it figures as a feeling in the mind.

Our non-sensational, or conceptual, states of mind, on the other hand, seem to obey a different law. They present themselves immediately as referring beyond themselves. Although they also possess an immediately given 'content,' they have a 'fringe' beyond it (p. 166), and claim to 'represent' something else than it. The 'blue' we have just spoken of, for instance, was, substantively considered, a *word*; but it was a word with a *meaning*. The quality blue was the *object* of the thought, the word was its *content*. The mental state, in short, was not self-sufficient as sensations are, but expressly pointed at something more in which it meant to terminate.

But the moment when, as in sensations, object and conscious state seem to be different ways of considering one and the same fact, it becomes hard to justify our denial that mental states consist of parts. The blue sky, considered physically, is a sum of mutually external parts; why is it not such a sum, when considered as a content of sensation?

The only result that is plain from all this is that the relations of the known and the knower are infinitely complicated, and that a genial, whole-hearted, popular-science way of formulating them will not suffice. The only possible path to understanding them lies through metaphysical subtlety; and Idealism and *Erkenntnistheorie* must say their say before the natural-science assumption that thoughts 'know' things grows clear.

The changing character of consciousness presents another puzzle. We first assumed conscious 'states' as the units with which psychology deals, and we said later that they were in constant change. Yet any state must have a certain duration to be *effective* at all—a pain which lasted but a hundredth of a second would practically be no pain—and the question comes up, how long may a state last and still be treated as *one* state? In time-perception for example, if the 'present' as known (the 'specious present,' as we called it) may be a dozen seconds long (p. 267), how long need the present as knower be? That is, what is the minimum duration of the consciousness in which those twelve seconds can be apprehended as just past, the minimum which can be called a 'state,' for such a cognitive purpose? Consciousness, as a process in time, offers the paradoxes which have been found in all continuous change. There are no 'states' in such a thing, any more than there are facets in a circle, or places where an arrow 'is' when it flies. The vertical raised upon the time-line on which (p. 270) we represented the past to be 'projected' at any given instant of memory, is only an ideal construction. Yet anything broader than that vertical *is* not, for the *actual* present is only the joint between the past and future and has no breadth of its own. Where everything is change and process, how can we talk of 'state'? Yet how can we do without 'states,' in describing what the vehicles of our knowledge seem to be?

States of consciousness themselves are not verifiable facts. But 'worse remains behind.' Neither common-sense, nor psychology so far as it has yet been written, has ever doubted that the states of consciousness which that science studies are immediate data of experience. 'Things' have been doubted, but thoughts and feelings have never been doubted. The outer world, but never the inner world, has been denied. Everyone assumes that we have direct introspective acquaintance with our thinking activity as such, with our consciousness as something inward and contrasted with the outer objects which it knows. Yet I must confess that for my part I cannot feel sure of this conclusion. Whenever I try to become sensible of my thinking activity as such, what I catch is some bodily fact, an impression coming from my brow, or head, or throat, or nose. It seems as if consciousness as an inner activity were rather a *postulate* than a sensibly given fact, the postulate, namely, of a *knower* as correlative to all this known; and as if '*scious*ness' might be a better word by which to describe it. But 'sciousness postulated as an hypothesis' is practically a very different thing from 'states of consciousness apprehended with infallible certainty by an inner sense.' For one thing, it throws the question of *who the knower really is* wide open again, and makes the answer which we gave to it at the end of Chapter XII a mere provisional statement from a popular and prejudiced point of view.

Conclusion.—When, then, we talk of 'psychology as a natural science,' we must not assume that that means a sort of psychology that stands at last on solid ground. It means just the reverse; it means a psychology particularly fragile, and into which the waters of metaphysical criticism leak at every joint, a psychology all of whose elementary assumptions and data must be reconsidered in wider connections and translated into other terms. It is, in short, a phrase of diffidence, and not of arrogance; and it is indeed strange to hear people talk triumphantly of 'the New Psychology,' and write 'Histories of Psychology,' when into the real elements and forces which the word covers not the first glimpse of clear insight exists. A string of raw facts; a little gossip and wrangle about opinions; a little classification and generalization on the mere descriptive level; a strong prejudice that we *have* states of mind, and that our brain conditions them: but not a single law in the sense in which physics shows us laws, not a single proposition from which any consequence can causally be deducted. We don't even know the terms between which the elementary laws would obtain if we had them (p. 430). This is no science, it is only the hope of a science. The matter of a science is with us. Something definite happens when to a certain brain-state a certain 'sciousness' corresponds. A genuine glimpse into what it is would be *the* scientific achievement, before which all past achievements would pale. But at present psychology is in the condition of physics before Galileo and the laws of motion, of chemistry before Lavoisier and the notion that mass is preserved in all reactions. The Galileo and the Lavoisier of psychology will be famous men indeed when they come, as come they some day surely will, or past successes are no index to the future. When they do come, however, the necessities of the case will make them 'metaphysical.' Meanwhile the best way in which we can facilitate their advent is to understand how great is the darkness in which we grope, and never to forget that the natural-science assumptions with which we started are provisional and revisable things.

THE END

Index

Abstract ideas, 230, 240; characters, 332; propositions, 332
Abstraction, 240; see *Distraction*
Accommodation, of crystalline lens, 39; of ear, 55–56
Acquaintance, 22
Acquisitiveness, 379
Action, what holds attention determines, 415–416
After-images, 51–52
AGASSIZ, 135
Alexia, 116
ALLEN, GRANT, 119
Alternating personality, 199 ff.
AMIDON, 134
Analysis, 63, 238, 239, 339
Anger, 350
Aphasia, 113, 118; loss of images in, 292
Apperception, 307–308
Aqueduct of Silvius, 85
Arachnoid membrane, 90
Arbor vitæ, 92
ARISTOTLE, 300
Articular sensibility, 80
Association, Chapter XVI; the order of our ideas, 242; determined by cerebral laws, 243–244; is not of ideas, but of things thought of, 244; the elementary principle of, 244; the ultimate cause of is habit, 244; indeterminateness of its results, 246; total recall, 247; partial recall and the law of interest, 249; frequency, recency, vividness, and emotional congruity tend to determine the object recalled, 251; focalized recall or by similarity, 255, 341; voluntary trains of thought, 257; problems, 259
Atomistic theories of consciousness, 428
Attention, Chapter XIII; its relation to interest, 168; narrowness of field of consciousness, 210; its physiological ground, 210; to how many things possible, 211–212; to simultaneous sight and sound, 213; its varieties, 213; involuntary, 213; voluntary, 216; change necessary to, 217; its relation to genius, 219; physiological conditions of, 220; the sense-organ must be adapted, 220–221; the idea of the object must be aroused, 223; pedagogic remarks, 227; attention and free-will, 227–228; what holds attention determines action, 415; volitional effort is effort of attention, 417
Auditory centre in brain, 118
Auditory type of imagination, 289–290
AUSTEN, Miss, 249
Automaton theory, 19, 107
AZAM, 204

BAHNSEN, 148
BAIN, 146, 344, 347
BERKELEY, 286, 326
BINET, 300, 313
Black, 53
Blind Spot, 37–38
BLIX, 71, 75
Blood-supply, cerebral, 133
Bodily expression, cause of emotions, 352
BRACE, JULIA, 241
Brain, the functions of, Chapter VIII, 98
Brain, its connection with mind, 14–16; its relations to outer forces, 18; relations of consciousness to, 428
Brain, structure of, Chapter VII, 84 ff.; vesicles, 84 ff.; dissection of sheep's, 87; how to preserve, 89; functions of, Chapter VIII, 98 ff.
BRIDGMAN, LAURA, 241, 291
BROCA, 113, 118, 120
Broca's convolution, 113
BRODHUN, 53
BROOKS, Prof. W. K., 384
Brutes, reasoning of, 344

Calamus scriptorius, 91
Canals, semicircular, 56
CARPENTER, 215, 216
CATTELL, 128, 129, 130
Caudate nucleus, 87, 94
Centres, nerve, 99
Cerebellum, its relation to equilibrium, 82; its anatomy, 84, 90
Cerebral laws, of association, 243–244
Cerebral process, see *Neural Process*
Cerebrum, see *Brain, Hemispheres*
Changing character of consciousness, 153, 431
CHARCOT, 118, 292
Choice, see *Interest*
Coalescence of different sensations into the same 'thing,' 319
Cochlea, 57–58, 59
Cognition, see *Reasoning*
Cold, sensations of, 71 ff.; nerves of, 71
Color, 47–49
Commissure, middle, 95 ff.; anterior, 95; posterior, 95
Commissures, 90
Comparison of magnitudes, 322
Compound objects, analysis of, 238
Compounding of sensations, 30, 49, 64
Concatenated acts, dependent on habit, 142
Conceiving, mode of, what is meant by, 332–333
Conceptions, Chapter XIV; defined, 229; their permanence, 229; different states of mind can mean the same, 229; abstract, universal, and problematic, 230; the thought of 'the same' is not the same thought over again, 232
Conceptual order different from perceptual, 232
Concomitants, law of varying, 240
Consciousness, stream of, Chapter XI, 152; four characters in, 153; personal, 153; is in constant change, 154, 431; same state of mind never occurs twice, 154; consciousness is continuous, 157; substantive and transitive states of, 159; interested in one part of its object more than another, 168–169; double consciousness, 199

ff.; narrowness of field of, 210; relations of to brain, 428
Consciousness and Movement, Chapter XXIII; all consciousness is motor, 347
Consent, in willing, 420
Continuity of object of consciousness, 157
Contrast, 33, 52
Convergence of eyeballs, 39, 40
Convolutions, motor, 111–112
Corpora fimbriata, 93
Corpora quadrigemina, 84, 92, 96
Corpus albicans, 90
Corpus callosum, 86, 90
Corpus striatum, 87, 94, 115
Cortex, 19, note
Cortex, localization in, 110; motor region of, 111–112
Corti's organ, 59
Cramming, 279
Crura of brain, 84, 90, 115
Curiosity, 379
Currents, in nerves, 18–19
CZERMAK, 77

DARWIN, 363
Deafness, mental, 119
Decision, five types, 399
DELAGE, 82–83
Deliberation, 416
Delusions of insane, 201
Dermal senses, 67 ff.
Determinism and psychology, 427
Differences, 31; directly felt, 235; not resolvable into composition, 235; inferred, 237
Diffusion of movements, the law of, 347
Dimension, third, 322, 325
Discharge, nervous, 124
Discord, 65
Discrimination, Chapter XV; hearing, 65; touch, 69; defined, 234; conditions which favor, 235; sensation of difference, 236; differences inferred, 237; analysis of compound objects, 238–239; to be easily singled out a quality should already be separately known, 239; dissociation by varying

concomitants, 240; practice improves discrimination, 241; of space, 319. See *Differences*

'Disparate' retinal points, 42

Dissection, of sheep's brain, 87

Distance, as seen, 46; between members of series, 31; in space, see *Third dimension*

Distraction, 211 ff.

Division of space, 319

DONALDSON, 71

Double consciousness, 199 ff.

Double images, 43

Double personality, 199

Duality of brain, 199

DUMONT, 138

Dura mater, 88

Duration, the primitive object in time-perception, 266; our estimation of short, 267

Ear, 54 ff.

Effort, feeling of, 403; feels like an original force, 411; volitional effort is effort of attention, 417; ethical importance of the phenomenon of effort, 424–425

Ego, see *Self*

Embryological sketch, Chapter VII, 84

Emotion, Chapter XXIV; compared with instincts, 350; varieties of, innumerable, 350; causes of varieties, 351, 357; results from bodily expression, 352; this view not materialistic, 356; the subtler emotions, 359; fear, 360; genesis of reactions, 361

Emotional congruity, determines association, 253–254

Empirical self, see *Self*

Emulation, 379

End-organs, 19; of touch, 67; of pressure, 67; of temperature, 71; of pain, 74

Environment, 13

Essence of reason, always for subjective interest, 336

Essential characters, in reason, 333

Ethical importance of effort, 424–425

Exaggerated impulsion, causes an explosive will, 408

EXNER, 127, 267

Experience, 210, 234

Explosive will, from defective inhibition, 406; from exaggerated impulsion, 408

Expression, bodily, cause of emotions, 352

Extensity, primitive to all sensation, 316

Exteriority of objects, 23

External world, 23

Extirpation of higher nerve-centres, 102 ff.

Eye, its anatomy, 35–38

Familiarity, sense of, see *Recognition*

Fear, 360, 379, 380

FECHNER, 29, 221

Feeling of effort, 403

FÉRÉ, 294

FERRIER, 135

Fissure of Rolando, seat of motor incitations, 112

Fissure of Sylvius, 114

Foramen of Monro, 94

Force, original, effort feels like, 411

Forgetting, 284

Fornix, 87, 94, 95, 96

Fovea centralis, 38–39

FRANKLIN, 125

FRANZ, Dr., 291

Free-will and attention, 227; relates solely to effort of attention, 422; insoluble on strictly psychologic grounds, 423; ethical importance of the phenomena of effort, 424–425

Freedom of the will, 227

Frequency, determines association, 252

'Fringes' of mental objects, 162 ff.

Frogs' lower centres, 102

Functions of the Brain, Chapter VIII, 98; nervous functions, general idea of, 98

Fusion of mental states, 193, 235, 319

Fusion, of sensations, 30, 49, 64

GALTON, 129, 253, 287, 289

Genius, 219, 308

GOETHE, 147, 157

GOLDSCHEIDER, 20, 71, 75

GOLTZ, 106
GUITEAU, 181
GURNEY, EDMUND, 312, 314

Habit, Chapter X, 137 ff.; has a physical basis, 137; due to plasticity, 138; due to pathways through nerve-centres, 139; effects of, 140; practical use of, 140; depends on sensations not attended to, 143; ethical and pedagogical importance of, 144 ff.; habit the ultimate cause of association, 244
HAGENAUER, 361
HALL, ROBERT, 215
Hallucinations, 311 ff.
HAMILTON, 248, 255
Harmony, 65
HARTLEY, 244
Hearing, 54 ff.; centre of, in cortex, 118
Heat-sensations, 71 ff.; nerves of, 71
HELMHOLTZ, 33, 49, 51, 62, 64, 65, 124, 217, 218, 222, 224, 225, 303
Hemispheres, general notion of, 104; chief seat of memory, 104; effects of deprivation of, on frogs, 99; on pigeons, 103
HERBART, 214, 307
HERBARTIAN SCHOOL, 157
HERING, 32, 33
HERZEN, 127, 128
Hippocampi, 94
HODGSON, 250, 251, 266, 268
HOLBROOK, 281
HORSLEY, 112, 123
HUME, 181, 234
Hunger, sensations of, 76
HUXLEY, 144
Hypnotic conditions, 284

Ideas, the theory of, 154 ff.; never come twice the same, 154; they do not permanently exist, 157; abstract ideas, 230, 240; universal, 230; order of ideas by association, 242
'Identical retinal points,' 42
Identity, personal, 195; mutations of, 199 ff.; alternating personality, 199
Ideo-motor action the type of all volition, 393

Illusions, 299 ff., 311
Images, mental, compared with sensations, 22; double, in vision, 43; 'after-images,' 51–52; visual, 286; auditory, 289; motor, 290; tactile, 291
Imagination, Chapter XIX; defined, 286; differs in individuals, 286; visual, 286; Galton's statistics of, 287; auditory, 289; motor, 290; tactile, 291; pathological differences, 292; cerebral process of, 293; not locally distinct from that of sensation, 293
Imitation, 379
Inattention, 211, 227
Increase of stimulus, 27; serial, 31
Infundibulum, 88, 90, 95
Inhibition, defective, causes an Explosive Will, 406
Inhibition of instincts by habits, 372
Insane delusions, 29
Instinct, Chapter XXV; emotions compared with, 350; definition of, 366; every instinct is an impulse, 367; not always blind or invariable, 369; modified by experience, 370; man has more than beasts, 372, 379; two principles of non-uniformity, 372; transitory, 375; of children, 379; fear, 380
Intellect, part played by, in space-perception, 328
Intensity of sensations, 24
Interest, selects certain objects and determines thoughts, 168–169; influence in association, 249–250
Introspection, 123

JACKSON, HUGHLINGS, 111, 121
JANET, 204, 205, 284
Joints, their sensibility, 80

KANDINSKY, 311
Knowledge, theory of, 12, 430, 432; two kinds of, 22
KÖNIG, 53
KRISHABER, 202

Labyrinth, 54, 56–58
LANGE, K., 310

Law, Weber's, 25; —, Fechner's, 29; —, of relativity, 31–32

Laws, cerebral, of association, 243–244

LAZARUS, 284, 305

Lenticular nucleus, 87

LEWES, 20, 223, 308

Likeness, 232, 341

LINDSAY, Dr., 385

Localization of Functions in the hemispheres, 110 ff.

Localization, Skin, 68

Locations, in environment, 320; serial order of, 321

LOCKE, 234, 286, 335

LOCKIAN SCHOOL, 157

Locomotion, instinct of, 379

LOMBARD, 134

Longitudinal fissure, 90

LOTZE, 173

Love, 380

Lower Centres, of frogs and pigeons, 102 ff.

LUDWIG, 133

MACH, 81

Mamillary bodies, 90

Man's intellectual distinction from brutes, 344

MANTEGAZZA, 363, 365

MARTIN, 47, 51, 52, 55, 58, 60, 67, 68, 72, 76

MARTINEAU, 290

Materialism and emotion, 356

MATTEUCI, 124

MAUDSLEY, 140

Measurement, of sensations, 29; of space, 322

'Mediumships,' 206

Medulla oblongata, 90, 91, 114

Memory, Chapter XVIII; hemispheres physical seat of, 104; defined, 272; analysis of the phenomenon of memory, 272 ff.; return of a mental image is not memory, 272; association explains recall and retention, 273; brain-scheme of, 275; conditions of good memory, 277; multiple associations favor, 278; effects of cramming on, 279; how to improve memory,

282; recognition, 283; forgetting, 284; hypnotics, 284

Mental blindness, 115

Mental images, 22

Mental operations, simultaneous, 212

Mental states, cannot fuse, 193; relation of, to their objects, 430

MERKEL, 65, 73

Metaphysics, what the word means, 427

MEYER, G. H., 291, 294

MEYNERT, 111, 121

MILL, J. S., 148, 157

MILL, JAMES, 192, 262, 273

Mimicry, 379

Mind depends on brain conditions, 13–16; states of, their relation to their objects, 430; see Consciousness

Modesty, 380

Monistic theories of consciousness, 428

MORGAN, LLOYD, 344

MOSSO, 133, 134

Motion, sensations of, Chapter VI, 77 ff.; feeling of motion over surfaces, 77

Motor aphasia, 113

Motor region of cortex, 111

Motor type of imagination, 290

Movement, consciousness and, Chapter XXIII; images of movement, 290; all consciousness is motor, 347

MUNK, 116

MÜNSTERBERG, 30, 394

Muscular sensation, 72 ff.; relations to space, 73, 80; muscular centre in cortex, 112

MUSSEY, Dr., 408

NAUNYN, 120

Nerve-currents, 18

Nerve-endings in the skin, 67; in muscles and tendons, 72–73; pain, 74 ff.; nerve-centres, 99

Nerves, general functions of, 98 ff.

Nervous discharge, 124

Neural activity, general conditions of, Chapter IX, 124; nervous discharge, 124

Neural functions, general idea of, 98

Neural process, in habit, 137 ff.; in

association, 243 ff.; in memory, 275; in imagination, 293; in perception, 310

Nucleus lenticularis, 87, 114; caudatus, 87, 114

Object, the, of sensation, 21–23; of thought, 155, 162; one part of, more interesting than another, 168–169; object must change to hold attention, 217; objects as signs and as realities, 325; relation of states of mind to their object, 430

Occipital lobes, seat of visual centre, 114

Old-fogyism vs. genius, 308

Olfactory lobes, 88, 90

Olivary bodies, 92

Optic nerve, 88, 96

Optic tracts, 90

Original force, effort feels like one, 411

Overtones, 62–63

Pain, 74 ff.; pain and pleasure as springs of action, 412

PASCAL, 215

Past time, known in a present feeling, 270; the immediate past is a portion of the present duration-block, 266

PAULHAN, 212

Pedagogic remarks on habit, 144; on attention, 227

Peduncles, 91, 92

Perception, Chapter XX; compared with sensation, 295; involves reproductive processes, 295; the perceptive state of mind is not a compound, 296; perception is of definite and probable things, 298; illusory perceptions, 299; physiological process of perception, 310

Perception of Space, Chapter XXI

PEREZ, M., 381

Personal Identity, 195; mutations of, 199 ff.; alternating personality, 199 ff.

Personality, alterations of, 200 ff.

Philosophy, Psychology and, Epilogue, 427

Phosphorus and thought, 135

Pia mater, 88

Pigeons' lower centres, 103

Pitch, 60–62

Pituitary body, 88, 96

Place, a series of positions, 321

Plasticity, as basis of habit, defined, 138

PLATO, 229

Play, 379

Pleasure, and pain, as springs of action, 412

Pons Varolii, 84, 90, 115

Positions, place a series of, 321

Practice, improves discrimination, 241

Present, the present moment, 266

Pressure sense, 67

PREYER, 379

Probability determines what object shall be perceived, 298, 310

Problematic conceptions, 230

Problems, solution of, 260

Projection of sensations, eccentric, 23

Psychology and Philosophy, Epilogue, 427

Psychology, defined, 11; a natural science, 11; what data it assumes, 12; Psychology and Philosophy, Epilogue

Psycho-physic law, 24, 31, 53, 65, 73, 75

Pugnacity, 379

PURKINJE, 81

Pyramids, 92

Quality, 21, 30, 32, 63

RAEHLMANN, 328

Rationality, 171

Reaction-time, 124 ff.

Real magnitude, determined by æsthetic and practical interests, 324

Real space, 318

Reason, 243

Reasoning, Chapter XXII; what it is, 330; involves use of abstract characters, 331; what is meant by an essential character, 333; the essence is always for a subjective interest, 336; two great points in reasoning, 337; sagacity, 339; help from association by similarity, 341; reasoning power of brutes, 344

Recall, 273
Recency, determines association, 253
'Recepts,' 344
Recognition, 283
Recollection, 273 ff.
Redintegration, 252
Reflex acts, defined, 98; reaction-time measures one, 126; concatenated habits are constituted by a chain of, 142
REID, 296
Relations, between objects, 161; feelings of, 161
'*Relativity* of knowledge,' 32
Reproduction in memory, 273 ff.; voluntary, 257
Resemblance, 232
Retention in memory, 273
Retentiveness, organic, 275; it is unchangeable, 280–281
Retina, peripheral parts of, act as sentinels, 80
Revival in memory, 273 ff.
RIBOT, 284
RICHET, 382
Rivalry of selves, 182
ROBERTSON, Prof. CROOM, 300
Rolando, fissure of, 112
ROMANES, 131, 303, 344
ROSENTHAL, 20
Rotation, sense of, 81
ROUSSEAU, 149

Sagacity, 339
Sameness, 196, 197
SCHÄFER, 112, 116, 123
SCHIFF, 134
SCHNEIDER, 79, 348, 367
Science, natural, 11
SCOTT, Prof., 294
Sea-sickness, accidental origin, 365
Seat of consciousness, 14
Selection, 18; a cardinal function of consciousness, 168–169
Self, The, Chapter XII; not primary, 174; the empirical self, 174; its constituents, 175; the material self, 175; the social self, 176; the spiritual self, 178; self-appreciation, 179; self-seeking, bodily, social, and spiritual, 180; rivalry of the mes, 182; their

hierarchy, 186; teleology of self-interest, 189; the I, or 'pure ego,' 191; thoughts are not compounded of 'fused' sensations, 192; the soul as a combining medium, 195; the sense of personal identity, 195; explained by identity of function in successive passing thoughts, 197; mutations of the self, 199; insane delusions, 201; alternating personalities, 203; mediumships, 206; who is the thinker? 208
Self-appreciation, 179
Self-interest, theological uses of, 189; teleological character of, 189
Selves, their rivalry, 182
Semicircular canals, 56–57
Semicircular canals, their relation to sensations of rotation, 81
Sensations, in General, Chapter II, 18; distinguished from perceptions, 20; from images, 21; *first* things in consciousness, 21; make us acquainted with qualities, 21; their exteriority, 23; intensity of sensations, 24; their measurement, 28; they are not compounds, 30
Sensations, of touch, 67; of skin, 67 ff.; of pressure, 67; of heat, 71; of cold, 71; muscular, 72; of pain, 74; of taste, 76; of smell, 76; of hunger, 76; of thirst, 76; of motion, 77; of joints, 80; of movement through space, 81; of rotation, 81; of translation, 82
Sense of time, see *Time*
Sensory centres in the cortex, 118 ff.
Septum lucidum, 94
Serial order of locations, 321
Shame, 350
Sheep's brain, dissection of, 87
Sight, 35 ff.; see *Vision*
Signs, 47; sensations are, to us of other sensations, whose space-value is held to be more real, 324 ff.
Similarity, association by, 255, 341; see *Likeness*
Size, 47
Skin—senses, 67 ff.; localizing power of, 68; discrimination of points on, 236
Smell, 76; centre of, in cortex, 121

SMITH, T. C., 294
Sociability, 379
Soul, the, as ego or thinker, 191; as a combining medium, 195, 197
Sound, 60–66; images of, 289–290
Space, Perception of, Chapter XXI; extensity in three dimensions primitive to all sensation, 316; construction of real space, 318; the processes which it involves: (1) Subdivision, 319; (2) Coalescence of different sensible data into one 'thing,' 319; (3) Location in an environment, 320; objects which are signs, and objects which are realities, 325; the third dimension, 325; Berkeley's theory of distance, 326; part played by intellect in space-perception, 328
Space, relation of muscular sense to, 73 80
SPALDING, 374 ff.
Span of consciousness, 211, 271
Specific energies, 19–20
Speech, centres of, in cortex, 113; thought possible without it, 168; see Aphasia
SPENCER, 109, 362, 365
Spinal cord, conduction of pain by, 75; centre of defensive movements, 100
Spiritual substance, see Soul
Spiritualistic theories of consciousness, 428
Spontaneous trains of thought, 246; examples, 246 ff.
STARR, 112, 119, 120
STEINTHAL, 308
Stream of Consciousness, Chapter XI, 152
STRICKER, 290
Subdivision of space, 319
Substantive states of mind, 159
Succession vs. duration, 266; not known by successive feelings, 270
Summation of stimuli, 131
Surfaces, feeling of motion over, 77

Tactile centre in cortex, 121
Tactile images, 291
TAINE, 202
Taste, 76; centre of, in cortex, 121

Teleological character of consciousness, 13; of self-interest, 189
Temperature-sense, 71 ff.
Terminal organs, 19, 36, 58
Thalami, 85, 92, 95, 115
Thermometry, cerebral, 134
'Thing,' coalescence of sensations to form the same, 319
Thinking principle, see Soul
Third dimension of space, 325
Thirst, sensations of, 76
THOMSON, Dr. ALLEN, 132
Thought, the 'Topic' of, 166; stream of, 152; can be carried on in any terms, 166; unity of, 191; spontaneous trains of, 246; the entire thought the minimum, 429
'Timbre,' 62
Time, sense of, Chapter XVII; begins with duration, 266; no sense of empty time, 267; compared with perception of space, 267; discrete flow of time, 268; long intervals conceived symbolically, 268; we measure duration by events that succeed in it, 269; variations in our estimations of its length, 269; cerebral processes of, 271
Touch, 67 ff.; centre of, in cortex, 121; images of, 291
Transcendental self or ego, 191
Transitive states of mind, 159
Translation, sense of, 82
Trapezium, 92
TURNER, Dr. J. E., 409
Tympanum, 54
Types of decision, 399

Unity of the passing thought, 191
Universal conceptions, 250
URBANTSCHITSCH, 33

Valve of Vieussens, 85, 92
Variability of the emotions, 357
Varying concomitants, law of dissociation by, 240
Ventricles, 85 ff.
VIERORDT, 78
Vision, 35 ff.; binocular, 40–47; of solidity, 44

Visual centre of cortex, 114, 120
Visual imagination, 286
Visualizing power, 286
Vividness, determines association, 253
Volition, see *Will*
VOLKMANN, 270
Voluminousness, primitive, of sensations, 316
Voluntary acts, defined, 99; voluntary attention, 216; voluntary trains of thought, 257

Weber's law, 25, 31, 53, 65
Weber's law—weight, 73; pain, 74
Weight, sensibility to, 73
WERNICKE, 116, 118, 120
WESLEY, 215
WHEATSTONE, 326
WIGAN, 283
Will, Chapter XXVI; voluntary acts, 387; they are secondary performances, 387; no third kind of idea is called for, 389; the motor-cue, 391; ideo-motor action, 393; action after deliberation, 398; five types of decision, 399; feeling of effort, 403; healthiness of will, 404; defects of, 405; the explosive will: (1) from defective inhibition, 406; (2) from exaggerated impulsion, 408; the obstructed will, 409; effort feels like an original force, 411; pleasure and pain as springs of action, 412; what holds attention determines action, 415; will is a relation between the mind and its ideas, 416; volitional effort is effort of attention, 417; free-will, 422; ethical importance of effort, 424−425
Willing terminates with the prevalence of the idea, 416
WUNDT, 20, 26, 32, 65, 126, 127, 128, 129, 130, 213, 267

THE WILL TO BELIEVE

and Other Essays in Popular Philosophy

To

My Old Friend,

CHARLES SANDERS PEIRCE,

To whose philosophic comradeship in old times
and to whose writings in more recent years
I owe more incitement and help than
I can express or repay.

Preface

At most of our American Colleges there are Clubs formed by the students devoted to particular branches of learning; and these clubs have the laudable custom of inviting once or twice a year some maturer scholar to address them, the occasion often being made a public one. I have from time to time accepted such invitations, and afterwards had my discourse printed in one or other of the Reviews. It has seemed to me that these addresses might now be worthy of collection in a volume, as they shed explanatory light upon each other, and taken together express a tolerably definite philosophic attitude in a very untechnical way.

Were I obliged to give a short name to the attitude in question, I should call it that of *radical empiricism*, in spite of the fact that such brief nicknames are nowhere more misleading than in philosophy. I say "empiricism," because it is contented to regard its most assured conclusions concerning matters of fact as hypotheses liable to modification in the course of future experience; and I say "radical," because it treats the doctrine of monism itself as an hypothesis, and, unlike so much of the half-way empiricism that is current under the name of positivism or agnosticism or scientific naturalism, it does not dogmatically affirm monism as something with which all experience has got to square. The difference between monism and pluralism is perhaps the most pregnant of all the differences in philosophy. *Primâ facie* the world is a pluralism; as we find it, its unity seems to be that of any collection; and our higher thinking consists chiefly of an effort to redeem it from that first crude form. Postulating more unity than the first experiences yield, we also discover more. But absolute unity, in spite of brilliant dashes in its direction, still remains undiscovered, still remains a *Grenzbegriff*. "Ever not quite" must be the rationalistic philosopher's last confession concerning it. After all that reason can do has been done, there still remains the opacity of the finite facts as merely given, with most of their peculiarities mutually unmediated and unexplained. To the very last, there are the various "points of view" which the philosopher must distinguish in

447

discussing the world; and what is inwardly clear from one point remains a bare externality and datum to the other. The negative, the alogical, is never wholly banished. Something—call it "fate, chance, freedom, spontaneity, the devil, what you will"—is still wrong and other and outside and unincluded, from *your* point of view, even though you be the greatest of philosophers. Something is always mere fact and *givenness*; and there may be in the whole universe no one point of view extant from which this would not be found to be the case. "Reason," as a gifted writer says, "is but one item in the mystery; and behind the proudest consciousness that ever reigned, Reason and Wonder blushed face to face. . . . The inevitable stales, while doubt and hope are sisters. Not unfortunately the universe is wild—game flavored as a hawk's wing. Nature is miracle all; the same returns not, save to bring the different. The slow round of the engraver's lathe gains but the breadth of a hair, but the difference is distributed back over the whole curve, never an instant true—ever not quite."[1]

This is pluralism, somewhat rhapsodically expressed. He who takes for his hypothesis the notion that it is the permanent form of the world is what I call a radical empiricist. For him the crudity of experience remains an eternal element thereof. There is no possible point of view from which the world can appear an absolutely single fact. Real possibilities, real indeterminations, real beginnings, real ends, real evil, real crises, catastrophes, and escapes, a real God, and a real moral life, just as common-sense conceives these things, may remain in empiricism as conceptions which that philosophy gives up the attempt either to "overcome" or to reinterpret in monistic form.

Many of my professionally trained *confrères* will smile at the irrationalism of this view, and at the artlessness of my essays in point of technical form. But they should be taken as illustrations of the radically empiricist attitude rather than as argumentations for its validity. That admits meanwhile of being argued in as technical a shape as anyone can desire, and

[1] B. P. Blood: *The Flaw in Supremacy*: Published by the Author, Amsterdam, N. Y., 1893.

possibly I may be spared to do later a share of that work. Meanwhile these essays seem to light up with a certain dramatic reality the attitude itself, and make it visible alongside of the higher and lower dogmatisms between which in the pages of philosophic history it has generally remained eclipsed from sight.

The first four essays are largely concerned with defending the legitimacy of religious faith. To some rationalizing readers such advocacy will seem a sad misuse of one's professional position. Mankind, they will say, is only too prone to follow faith unreasoningly, and needs no preaching nor encouragement in that direction. I quite agree that what mankind at large most lacks is criticism and caution, not faith. Its cardinal weakness is to let belief follow recklessly upon lively conception, especially when the conception has instinctive liking at its back. I admit, then, that were I addressing the Salvation Army or a miscellaneous popular crowd it would be a misuse of opportunity to preach the liberty of believing as I have in these pages preached it. What such audiences most need is that their faiths should be broken up and ventilated, that the northwest wind of science should get into them and blow their sickliness and barbarism away. But academic audiences, fed already on science, have a very different need. Paralysis of their native capacity for faith and timorous *abulia* in the religious field are their special forms of mental weakness, brought about by the notion, carefully instilled, that there is something called scientific evidence by waiting upon which they shall escape all danger of shipwreck in regard to truth. But there is really no scientific or other method by which men can steer safely between the opposite dangers of believing too little or of believing too much. To face such dangers is apparently our duty, and to hit the right channel between them is the measure of our wisdom as men. It does not follow, because recklessness may be a vice in soldiers, that courage ought never to be preached to them. What *should* be preached is courage weighted with responsibility—such courage as the Nelsons and Washingtons never failed to show after they had taken everything into account that might tell against their success, and made every provision to minimize disaster in case they met defeat. I do not think that anyone can accuse me of preaching reckless faith. I have preached the right of the individual to indulge his personal faith at his personal risk. I have discussed the kinds of risk; I have contended that none of us escape all of them; and I have only pleaded that it is better to face them open-eyed than to act as if we did not know them to be there.

After all, though, you will say, Why such an ado about a matter concerning which, however we may theoretically differ, we all practically agree? In this age of toleration, no scientist will ever try actively to interfere with our religious faith, provided we enjoy it quietly with our friends and do not make a public nuisance of it in the market-place. But it is just on this matter of the market-place that I think the utility of such essays as mine may turn. If religious hypotheses about the universe be in order at all, then the active faiths of individuals in them, freely expressing themselves in life, are the experimental tests by which they are verified, and the only means by which their truth or falsehood can be wrought out. The truest scientific hypothesis is that which, as we say, "works" best; and it can be no otherwise with religious hypotheses. Religious history proves that one hypothesis after another has worked ill, has crumbled at contact with a widening knowledge of the world, and has lapsed from the minds of men. Some articles of faith, however, have maintained themselves through every vicissitude, and possess even more vitality to-day than ever before: it is for the "science of religions" to tell us just which hypotheses these are. Meanwhile the freest competition of the various faiths with one another, and their openest application to life by their several champions, are the most favorable conditions under which the survival of the fittest can proceed. They ought therefore not to lie hid each under its bushel, indulged-in quietly with friends. They ought to live in publicity, vying with each other; and it seems to me that (the régime of tolerance once granted, and a fair field shown) the scientist has nothing to fear for his own interests from the liveliest possible state of fermentation in the religious world of his time. Those faiths will best stand the test which adopt also his hypotheses, and make them integral elements of their own. He should welcome therefore every species of religious agitation and discussion, so long as he is willing to allow that some religious hypothesis *may* be true. Of course there are plenty of scientists who would deny that dogmatically, maintaining that science has already ruled all possible religious hypotheses out of court. Such scientists ought, I agree, to aim at imposing privacy on religious faiths, the public manifestation of which could only be a nuisance in their eyes. With all such scientists, as well as with their allies outside of science, my quarrel openly lies; and I hope that my book may do something to persuade the reader of their crudity, and range him on my side. Religious fermentation is always a symptom of the intellectual vigor of a society; and it is only when they forget that they are hypotheses and put on rationalistic and authoritative pretensions, that our faiths do harm. The most interesting and valuable things about a man are his ideals and over-beliefs. The same is true of nations and historic epochs; and the excesses of which the particular individuals and epochs are guilty are compensated in the total, and become profitable to mankind in the long run.

The essay "On Some Hegelisms" doubtless needs an apology for the superficiality with which it treats a serious subject. It was written as a squib, to be read in a college-seminary in Hegel's logic, several of whose members, mature men, were devout champions of the dialectical method. My blows therefore were aimed almost entirely at that. I reprint the paper here (albeit with some misgivings), partly because I believe the dialectical method to be wholly abominable when worked by concepts alone, and partly because the essay casts some positive light on the pluralist-empiricist point of view.

The paper on Psychical Research is added to the volume for convenience and utility. Attracted to this study some years ago by my love of sportsmanlike fair play in science, I have seen enough to convince me of its great importance, and I wish to gain for it what interest I can. The American Branch of the Society is in need of more support, and if my article draws some new associates thereto, it will have served its turn.

Apology is also needed for the repetition of the same passage in two essays (pp. 500–501 and 528–529, 531–532). My excuse is that one cannot always express the same thought in two ways that seem equally forcible, so one has to copy one's former words.

The Crillon-quotation on page 503 is due to Mr. W. M. Salter (who employed it in a similar manner in the *Index* for August 24, 1882), and the dream-metaphor on p. 588 is a reminiscence from some novel of George Sand's—I forget which—read by me thirty years ago.

Finally, the revision of the essays has consisted almost entirely in excisions. Probably less than a page and a half in all of new matter has been added.

HARVARD UNIVERSITY,
    CAMBRIDGE, MASSACHUSETTS,
        December, 1896.

Contents

THE WILL TO BELIEVE 457
Hypotheses and options. Pascal's wager. Clifford's veto.
Psychological causes of belief. Thesis of the Essay. Empiricism
and absolutism. Objective certitude and its unattainability.
Two different sorts of risks in believing. Some risk
unavoidable. Faith may bring forth its own verification.
Logical conditions of religious belief.

IS LIFE WORTH LIVING? 480
Temperamental Optimism and Pessimism. How reconcile
with life one bent on suicide? Religious melancholy and its
cure. Decay of Natural Theology. Instinctive antidotes to
pessimism. Religion involves belief in an unseen extension of
the world. Scientific positivism. Doubt actuates conduct as
much as belief does. To deny certain faiths is logically
absurd, for they make their objects true. Conclusion.

THE SENTIMENT OF RATIONALITY 504
Rationality means fluent thinking. Simplification.
Clearness. Their antagonism. Inadequacy of the abstract.
The thought of nonentity. Mysticism. Pure theory cannot
banish wonder. The passage to practice may restore the
feeling of rationality. Familiarity and expectancy.
"Substance." A rational world must appear congruous with
our powers. But these differ from man to man. Faith is one
of them. Inseparable from doubt. May verify itself. Its rôle
in ethics. Optimism and pessimism. Is this a moral
universe?—what does the problem mean? Anæsthesia versus
energy. Active assumption necessary. Conclusion.

REFLEX ACTION AND THEISM 540
Prestige of Physiology. Plan of neural action. God the mind's
adequate object. Contrast between world as perceived and as
conceived. God. The mind's three departments. Science due

*to a subjective demand. Theism a mean between two
extremes. Gnosticism. No intellection except for practical
ends. Conclusion.*

THE DILEMMA OF DETERMINISM   566
*Philosophies seek a rational world. Determinism and
Indeterminism defined. Both are postulates of rationality.
Objections to chance considered. Determinism involves
pessimism. Escape* via *Subjectivism. Subjectivism leads to
corruption. A world with chance in it is morally the less
irrational alternative. Chance not incompatible with an
ultimate Providence.*

THE MORAL PHILOSOPHER AND THE MORAL LIFE   595
*The moral philosopher postulates a unified system. Origin of
moral judgments. Goods and ills are created by judgments.
Obligations are created by demands. The conflict of ideals.
Its solution. Impossibility of an abstract system of Ethics. The
easy-going and the strenuous mood. Connection between
Ethics and Religion.*

GREAT MEN AND THEIR ENVIRONMENT   618
*Solidarity of causes in the world. The human mind abstracts
in order to explain. Different cycles of operation in Nature.
Darwin's distinction between causes that produce and causes
that preserve a variation. Physiological causes produce, the
environment only adopts or preserves, great men. When
adopted they become social ferments. Messrs. Spencer and
Allen criticized. Messrs. Wallace and Gryzanowski quoted.
The laws of history. Mental evolution. Analogy between
original ideas and Darwin's accidental variations. Criticism
of Spencer's views.*

THE IMPORTANCE OF INDIVIDUALS   647
*Small differences may be important. Individual differences
are important because they are the causes of social change.
Hero-worship justified.*

On Some Hegelisms 653
The world appears as a pluralism. Elements of unity in the
pluralism. Hegel's excessive claims. He makes of negation a
bond of union. The principle of totality. Monism and
pluralism. The fallacy of accident in Hegel. The good and
the bad infinite. Negation. Conclusion. —Note on the
Anæsthetic Revelation.

What Psychical Research Has Accomplished 680
The unclassified residuum. The Society for Psychical
Research and its history. Thought-transference. Gurney's
work. The census of hallucinations. Mediumship. The
"subliminal self." "Science" and her counter-presumptions.
The scientific character of Mr. Myers's work. The
mechanical-impersonal view of life versus *the personal-*
romantic view.

Index 701

The Will to Believe [1]

IN THE RECENTLY published *Life* by Leslie Stephen of his brother, Fitzjames, there is an account of a school to which the latter went when he was a boy. The teacher, a certain Mr. Guest, used to converse with his pupils in this wise: "Gurney, what's the difference between justification and sanctification?—Stephen, prove the Omnipotence of God!" etc. In the midst of our Harvard freethinking and indifference we are prone to imagine that here at your good old orthodox College conversation continues to be somewhat upon this order; and to show you that we at Harvard have not lost all interest in these vital subjects, I have brought with me to-night something like a sermon on justification by faith to read to you—I mean an essay in justification *of* faith, a defence of our right to adopt a believing attitude in religious matters, in spite of the fact that our merely logical intellect may not have been coerced. "The Will to Believe," accordingly, is the title of my paper.

I have long defended to my own students the lawfulness of voluntarily adopted faith; but as soon as they have got well imbued with the logical spirit, they have as a rule refused to admit my contention to be lawful philosophically, even though in point of fact they were personally all the time chock-full of some faith or other themselves. I am all the while, however, so profoundly convinced that my own position is correct, that your invitation has seemed to me a good occasion to make my statements more clear. Perhaps your minds will be more open than those with which I have hitherto had to deal. I will be as little technical as I can, though I must begin by setting up some technical distinctions that will help us in the end.

I

Let us give the name of *hypothesis* to anything that may be proposed to our belief; and just as the electricians speak of

[1] An Address to the Philosophical Clubs of Yale and Brown Universities. Published in the *New World*, June, 1896.

live and dead wires, let us speak of any hypothesis as either *live* or *dead*. A live hypothesis is one which appeals as a real possibility to him to whom it is proposed. If I ask you to believe in the Mahdi, the notion makes no electric connection with your nature—it refuses to scintillate with any credibility at all. As an hypothesis it is completely dead. To an Arab, however (even if he be not one of the Mahdi's followers), the hypothesis is among the mind's possibilities: it is alive. This shows that deadness and liveness in an hypothesis are not intrinsic properties, but relations to the individual thinker. They are measured by his willingness to act. The maximum of liveness in an hypothesis means willingness to act irrevocably. Practically, that means belief; but there is some believing tendency wherever there is willingness to act at all.

Next, let us call the decision between two hypotheses an *option*. Options may be of several kinds. They may be—1, *living* or *dead*; 2, *forced* or *avoidable*; 3, *momentous* or *trivial*; and for our purposes we may call an option a *genuine* option when it is of the forced, living and momentous kind.

1. A living option is one in which both hypotheses are live ones. If I say to you: "Be a theosophist or be a mahomedan," it is probably a dead option, because for you neither hypothesis is likely to be alive. But if I say "Be an agnostic or be a Christian," it is otherwise: trained as you are, each hypothesis makes some appeal, however small, to your belief.

2. Next, if I say to you: "Choose between going out with your umbrella or without it," I do not offer you a genuine option, for it is not forced. You can easily avoid it by not going out at all. Similarly, if I say "Either love me or hate me," "Either call my theory true or call it false," your option is avoidable. You may remain indifferent to me, neither loving nor hating, and you may decline to offer any judgment as to my theory. But if I say "Either accept this truth or go without it," I put on you a forced option, for there is no standing place outside of the alternative. Every dilemma based on a complete logical disjunction, with no possibility of not choosing, is an option of this forced kind.

3. Finally, if I were Dr. Nansen and proposed to you to join my North Pole expedition, your option would be momentous; for this would probably be your only similar opportunity,

and your choice now would either exclude you from the North Pole sort of immortality altogether or put at least the chance of it into your hands. He who refuses to embrace a unique opportunity loses the prize as surely as if he tried and failed. *Per contra*, the option is trivial when the opportunity is not unique, when the stake is insignificant, or when the decision is reversible if it later prove unwise. Such trivial options abound in the scientific life. A chemist finds an hypothesis live enough to spend a year in its verification: he believes in it to that extent. But if his experiments prove inconclusive either way, he is quit for his loss of time, no vital harm being done.

It will facilitate our discussion if we keep all these distinctions well in mind.

II

The next matter to consider is the actual psychology of human opinion. When we look at certain facts, it seems as if our passional and volitional nature lay at the root of all our convictions. When we look at others, it seems as if they could do nothing when the intellect had once said its say. Let us take the latter facts up first.

Does it not seem preposterous on the very face of it to talk of our opinions being modifiable at will? Can our will either help or hinder our intellect in its perceptions of truth? Can we, by just willing it, believe that Abraham Lincoln's existence is a myth, and that the portraits of him in *McClure's Magazine* are all of someone else? Can we, by any effort of our will, or by any strength of wish that it were true, believe ourselves well and about when we are roaring with rheumatism in bed, or feel certain that the sum of the two one-dollar bills in our pocket must be a hundred dollars? We can *say* any of these things, but we are absolutely impotent to believe them; and of just such things is the whole fabric of the truths that we do believe in made up—matters of fact, immediate or remote, as Hume said, and relations between ideas, which are either there or not there for us if we see them so, and which if not there cannot be put there by any action of our own.

In Pascal's *Thoughts* there is a celebrated passage known

in literature as Pascal's wager. In it he tries to force us into Christianity by reasoning as if our concern with truth resembled our concern with the stakes in a game of chance. Translated freely his words are these: You must either believe or not believe that God is—which will you do? Your human reason cannot say. A game is going on between you and the nature of things which at the day of judgment will bring out either heads or tails. Weigh what your gains and your losses would be if you should stake all you have on heads, or God's existence: If you win in such case, you gain eternal beatitude; if you lose, you lose nothing at all. If there were an infinity of chances, and only one for God in this wager, still you ought to stake your all on God; for though you surely risk a finite loss by this procedure, any finite loss is reasonable, even a certain one is reasonable, if there is but the possibility of infinite gain. Go, then, and take holy water, and have masses said; belief will come and stupefy your scruples—*Cela vous fera croire et vous abêtira*. Why should you not? At bottom, what have you to lose?

You probably feel that when religious faith expresses itself thus, in the language of the gaming-table, it is put to its last trumps. Surely Pascal's own personal belief in masses and holy water had far other springs; and this celebrated page of his is but an argument for others, a last desperate snatch at a weapon against the hardness of the unbelieving heart. We feel that a faith in masses and holy water adopted wilfully after such a mechanical calculation would lack the inner soul of faith's reality; and if we were ourselves in the place of the Deity, we should probably take particular pleasure in cutting off believers of this pattern from their infinite reward. It is evident that unless there be some pre-existing tendency to believe in masses and holy water, the option offered to the will by Pascal is not a living option. Certainly no Turk ever took to masses and holy water on its account; and even to us Protestants these means of salvation seem such foregone impossibilities that Pascal's logic, invoked for them specifically, leaves us unmoved. As well might the Mahdi write to us, saying "I am the Expected One whom God has created in his effulgence. You shall be infinitely happy if you confess me; otherwise you shall be cut off from the light of the sun. Weigh, then, your infinite gain if I am genuine against your finite sacrifice if I am not!" His logic would be that of Pascal; but he would vainly use it on us, for the hypothesis he offers us is dead. No tendency to act on it exists in us to any degree.

The talk of believing by our volition seems, then, from one point of view, simply silly. From another point of view it is worse than silly, it is vile. When one turns to the magnificent edifice of the physical sciences, and sees how it was reared; what thousands of disinterested moral lives of men lie buried in its mere foundations; what patience and postponement, what choking down of preference, what submission to the icy laws of outer fact are wrought into its very stones and mortar; how absolutely impersonal it stands in its vast augustness— then how besotted and contemptible seems every little sentimentalist who comes blowing his voluntary smoke-wreaths, and pretending to decide things from out of his private dream! Can we wonder if those bred in the rugged and manly school of science should feel like spewing such subjectivism out of their mouths? The whole system of loyalties which grow up in the schools of science go dead against its toleration; so that it is only natural that those who have caught the scientific fever should pass over to the opposite extreme, and write sometimes as if the incorruptibly truthful intellect ought positively to prefer bitterness and unacceptableness to the heart in its cup.

> "It fortifies my soul to know
> That, though I perish, Truth is so—"

sings Clough, whilst Huxley exclaims: "My only consolation lies in the reflection that, however bad our posterity may become, so long as they hold by the plain rule of not pretending to believe what they have no reason to believe because it may be to their advantage so to pretend [the word 'pretend' is surely here redundant], they will not have reached the lowest depths of immorality." And that delicious *enfant terrible* Clifford writes: "Belief is desecrated when given to unproved and unquestioned statements, for the solace and private pleasure of the believer. . . . Whoso would deserve well of his fellows in this matter will guard the purity of his belief with a very fanaticism of jealous care, lest at any time it should rest on an unworthy object, and catch a stain which can never be wiped away. . . . If [a] belief has been accepted on insufficient evidence [even though the belief be true, as Clifford on the same page explains], the pleasure is a stolen one. . . . It is sinful, because it is stolen in defiance of our duty to mankind. That duty is to guard ourselves from such beliefs as from a pestilence, which may shortly master our own body and then spread to the rest of the town. . . . It is wrong always, everywhere, and for anyone, to believe anything upon insufficient evidence."

III

All this strikes one as healthy, even when expressed, as by Clifford, with somewhat too much of robustious pathos in the voice. Free-will and simple wishing do seem, in the matter of our credences, to be only fifth wheels to the coach. Yet if anyone should thereupon assume that intellectual insight is what remains after wish and will and sentimental preference have taken wing, or that pure reason is what then settles our opinions, he would fly quite as directly in the teeth of the facts.

It is only our already dead hypotheses that our willing nature is unable to bring to life again. But what has made them dead for us is for the most part a previous action of our willing nature of an antagonistic kind. When I say "willing nature," I do not mean only such deliberate volitions as may have set up habits of belief that we cannot now escape from—I mean all such factors of belief as fear and hope, prejudice and passion, imitation and partisanship, the circumpressure of our caste and set. As a matter of fact we find ourselves believing, we hardly know how or why. Mr. Balfour gives the name of "authority" to all those influences, born of the intellectual climate, that make hypotheses possible or impossible for us, alive or dead. Here in this room, we all of us believe in molecules and the conservation of energy, in democracy and necessary progress, in Protestant Christianity and the duty of fighting for "the doctrine of the immortal Monroe," all for no reasons worthy of the name. We see into these matters with no more inner clearness, and probably with much less, than any disbeliever in them might possess. His unconventionality would probably have some grounds to show for its conclusions; but for us, not insight, but the *prestige* of the opinions, is what makes the spark shoot from them and light up our sleeping magazines of faith. Our reason is quite satisfied, in nine hundred and ninety-nine cases out of every thousand of us, if it can find a few arguments that will do to recite in case our credulity is criticized by someone else. Our faith is faith in someone else's faith, and in the greatest matters this is most the case. Our belief in truth itself, for instance, that there is a truth, and that our minds and it are made for each other— what is it but a passionate affirmation of desire, in which our social system backs us up? We want to have a truth; we want to believe that our experiments and studies and discussions must put us in a continually better and better position towards it; and on this line we agree to fight out our thinking lives. But if a pyrrhonistic sceptic asks us *how we know* all this, can our logic find a reply? No! Certainly it cannot. It is just one volition against another—we willing to go in for life upon a trust or assumption which he, for his part, does not care to make.[2]

As a rule we disbelieve all facts and theories for which we have no use. Clifford's cosmic emotions find no use for Christian feelings. Huxley belabors the bishops because there is no use for sacerdotalism in his scheme of life. Newman, on the contrary, goes over to Romanism, and finds all sorts of reasons good for staying there, because a priestly system is for him an organic need and delight. Why do so few "scientists" even look at the evidence for telepathy, so called? Because they think, as a leading biologist, now dead, once said to me, that even if such a thing were true, scientists ought to band together to keep it suppressed and concealed. It would undo the uniformity of Nature and all sorts of other things without which scientists cannot carry on their pursuits. But if this very man had been shown something which as a scientist he might *do* with telepathy, he might not only have examined the evidence, but even have found it good enough. This very law

[2]Compare the admirable page 310 in S. H. Hodgson's *Time and Space*, London, 1865.

which the logicians would impose upon us—if I may give the name of logicians to those who would rule out our willing nature here—is based on nothing but their own natural wish to exclude all elements for which they, in their professional quality of logicians, can find no use.

Evidently, then, our non-intellectual nature does influence our convictions. There are passional tendencies and volitions which run before and others which come after belief, and it is only the latter that are too late for the fair; and they are not too late when the previous passional work has been already in their own direction. Pascal's argument, instead of being powerless, then seems a regular clincher, and is the last stroke needed to make our faith in masses and holy water complete. The state of things is evidently far from simple; and pure insight and logic, whatever they might do ideally, are not the only things that really do produce our creeds.

IV

Our next duty, having recognized this mixed-up state of affairs, is to ask whether it be simply reprehensible and pathological, or whether, on the contrary, we must treat it as a normal element in making up our minds. The thesis I defend is, briefly stated, this: *Our passional nature not only lawfully may, but must, decide an option between propositions, whenever it is a genuine option that cannot by its nature be decided on intellectual grounds; for to say, under such circumstances, "Do not decide, but leave the question open," is itself a passional decision — just like deciding yes or no —and is attended with the same risk of losing the truth.* The thesis thus abstractly expressed will, I trust, soon become quite clear. But I must first indulge in a bit more of preliminary work.

V

It will be observed that for the purposes of this discussion we are on "dogmatic" ground—ground, I mean, which leaves systematic philosophical scepticism altogether out of account. The postulate that there is truth, and that it is the destiny of our minds to attain it, we are deliberately resolving to make, though the sceptic will not make it. We part company with him, therefore, absolutely, at this point. But the faith that truth exists, and that our minds can find it, may be held in two ways. We may talk of the *empiricist* way and of the *absolutist* way of believing in truth. The absolutists in this matter say that we not only can attain to knowing truth, but we can *know when* we have attained to knowing it; whilst the empiricists think that although we may attain it, we cannot infallibly know when. To *know* is one thing, and to know for certain *that* we know is another. One may hold to the first being possible without the second; hence the empiricists and the absolutists, although neither of them is a sceptic in the usual philosophic sense of the term, show very different degrees of dogmatism in their lives.

If we look at the history of opinions, we see that the empiricist tendency has largely prevailed in science, whilst in philosophy the absolutist tendency has had everything its own way. The characteristic sort of happiness, indeed, which philosophies yield has mainly consisted in the conviction felt by each successive school or system that by it bottom-certitude had been attained. "Other philosophies are collections of opinions, mostly false; *my* philosophy gives standing-ground forever"—who does not recognize in this the key-note of every system worthy of the name? A system, to be a system at all, must come as a *closed* system, reversible in this or that detail, perchance, but in its essential features never!

Scholastic orthodoxy, to which one must always go when one wishes to find perfectly clear statement, has beautifully elaborated this absolutist conviction in a doctrine which it calls that of "objective evidence." If, for example, I am unable to doubt that I now exist before you, that two is less than three, or that if all men are mortal then I am mortal too, it is because these things illumine my intellect irresistibly. The final ground of this objective evidence possessed by certain propositions is the *adæquatio intellectûs nostri cum rê*. The certitude it brings involves an *aptitudinem ad extorquendum certum assensum* on the part of the truth envisaged, and on the side of the subject a *quietem in cognitione*, when once the object is mentally received, that leaves no possibility of doubt behind; and in the whole transaction nothing operates but the *entitas ipsa* of the object and the *entitas ipsa* of the mind. We slouchy modern thinkers dislike to talk in Latin—indeed, we dislike to talk in set terms at all; but at bottom our own state of mind is very much like this whenever we uncritically abandon ourselves: You believe in objective evidence, and I do. Of some things we feel that we are certain: we know, and we know that we do know. There is something that gives a click inside of us, a bell that strikes twelve, when the hands of our mental clock have swept the dial and meet over the meridian hour. The greatest empiricists among us are only empiricists on reflection: when left to their instincts, they dogmatize like infallible popes. When the Cliffords tell us how sinful it is to be Christians on such "insufficient evidence," insufficiency is really the last thing they have in mind. For them the evidence is absolutely sufficient, only it makes the other way. They believe so completely in an anti-christian order of the universe that there is no living option: Christianity is a dead hypothesis from the start.

VI

But now, since we are all such absolutists by instinct, what in our quality of students of philosophy ought we to do about the fact? Shall we espouse and indorse it? Or shall we treat it as a weakness of our nature from which we must free ourselves, if we can?

I sincerely believe that the latter course is the only one we can follow as reflective men. Objective evidence and certitude are doubtless very fine ideals to play with, but where on this moonlit and dream-visited planet are they found? I am, therefore, myself a complete empiricist so far as my theory of human knowledge goes. I live, to be sure, by the practical faith that we must go on experiencing and thinking over our experience, for only thus can our opinions grow more true; but to hold any one of them—I absolutely do not care which—as if it never could be re-interpretable or corrigible, I believe to be a tremendously mistaken attitude, and I think that the whole history of philosophy will bear me out. There is but one indefectibly certain truth, and that is the truth that pyrrhonistic scepticism itself leaves standing—the truth that the present phenomenon of consciousness exists. That, however, is the bare starting-point of knowledge, the mere admission of a stuff to be philosophized-about. The various philosophies are but so many attempts at expressing what this stuff really is. And if we repair to our libraries what disagreement do we discover! Where is a certainly true answer found? Apart from abstract propositions of comparison (such as two and two are the same as four), propositions which tell us nothing by themselves about concrete reality, we find no proposition ever regarded by anyone as evidently certain that has not either been called a falsehood, or at least had its truth sincerely questioned by someone else. The transcending of the axioms of geometry, not in play but in earnest, by certain of our contemporaries (as Zöllner and Charles H. Hinton), and the rejection of the whole aristotelian logic by the Hegelians, are striking instances in point.

No concrete test of what is really true has ever been agreed upon. Some make the criterion external to the moment of perception, putting it either in revelation, the *consensus gentium*, the instincts of the heart, or the systematized experience of the race. Others make the perceptive moment its own test—Descartes, for instance, with his clear and distinct ideas guaranteed by the veracity of God; Reid with his "common-sense"; and Kant with his forms of synthetic judgment *a priori*. The inconceivability of the opposite; the capacity to be verified by sense; the possession of complete organic unity or self-relation, realized when a thing is its own other—are standards which, in turn, have been used. The much lauded objective evidence is never triumphantly there; it is a mere aspiration or *Grenzbegriff*, marking the infinitely remote ideal of our thinking life. To claim that certain truths now possess it, is simply to say that when you think them true and they *are* true, then their evidence is objective, otherwise it is not. But practically one's conviction that the evidence one goes by is of the real objective brand, is only one more subjective opinion added to the lot. For what a contradictory array of opinions have objective evidence and absolute certitude been claimed! The world is rational through and through—its existence is an ultimate brute fact; there is a personal God—a personal God is inconceivable; there is an extra-mental physical world immediately known—the mind can only know its own ideas; a moral imperative exists—obligation is only the resultant of desires; a permanent spiritual principle is in everyone—there are only shifting states of mind; there is an endless chain of causes—there is an absolute first cause; an eternal necessity —a freedom; a purpose—no purpose; a primal One—a primal Many; a universal continuity—an essential disconti- nuity in things; an infinity—no infinity. There is this—there is that; there is indeed nothing which someone has not thought absolutely true, whilst his neighbor deemed it abso- lutely false; and not an absolutist among them seems ever to have considered that the trouble may all the time be essential, and that the intellect, even with truth directly in its grasp, may have no infallible signal for knowing whether it be truth or no. When, indeed, one remembers that the most striking practical application to life of the doctrine of objective certi- tude has been the conscientious labors of the Holy Office of the Inquisition, one feels less tempted than ever to lend the doctrine a respectful ear.

But please observe, now, that when as empiricists we give up the doctrine of objective certitude, we do not thereby give up the quest or hope of truth itself. We still pin our faith on its existence, and still believe that we gain an ever better posi- tion towards it by systematically continuing to roll up experi- ences and think. Our great difference from the scholastic lies in the way we face. The strength of his system lies in the principles, the origin, the *terminus a quo* of his thought; for us the strength is in the outcome, the upshot, the *terminus ad quem*. Not where it comes from but what it leads to is to decide. It matters not to an empiricist from what quarter an hypothesis may come to him: he may have acquired it by fair means or by foul; passion may have whispered or accident suggested it; but if the total drift of thinking continues to confirm it, that is what he means by its being true.

VII

One more point, small but important, and our prelimi- naries are done. There are two ways of looking at our duty in the matter of opinion—ways entirely different, and yet ways

about whose difference the theory of knowledge seems hitherto to have shown very little concern. *We must know the
truth*; and *we must avoid error*—these are our first and great
commandments as would-be knowers; but they are not two
ways of stating an identical commandment, they are two separable laws. Although it may indeed happen that when we
believe the truth *A*, we escape as an incidental consequence
from believing the falsehood *B*, it hardly ever happens that by
merely disbelieving *B* we necessarily believe *A*. We may in
escaping *B* fall into believing other falsehoods, *C* or *D*, just as
bad as *B*; or we may escape *B* by not believing anything at all,
not even *A*.

Believe truth! Shun error!—these, we see, are two materially different laws; and by choosing between them we may
end by colouring differently our whole intellectual life. We
may regard the chase for truth as paramount, and the avoidance of error as secondary; or we may, on the other hand,
treat the avoidance of error as more imperative, and let truth
take its chance. Clifford, in the instructive passage which I
have quoted, exhorts us to the latter course. Believe nothing,
he tells us, keep your mind in suspense forever, rather than by
closing it on insufficient evidence incur the awful risk of believing lies. You, on the other hand, may think that the risk of
being in error is a very small matter when compared with the
blessings of real knowledge, and be ready to be duped many
times in your investigation rather than postpone indefinitely
the chance of guessing true. I myself find it impossible to go
with Clifford. We must remember that these feelings of our
duty about either truth or error are in any case only expressions of our passional life. Biologically considered, our minds
are as ready to grind out falsehood as veracity, and he who
says "Better go without belief forever than believe a lie!"
merely shows his own preponderant private horror of becoming a dupe. He may be critical of many of his desires and
fears, but this fear he slavishly obeys. He cannot imagine anyone questioning its binding force. For my own part, I have
also a horror of being duped; but I can believe that worse
things than being duped may happen to a man in this world:
so Clifford's exhortation has to my ears a thoroughly fantastic
sound. It is like a general informing his soldiers that it is

better to keep out of battle forever than to risk a single wound. Not so are victories either over enemies or over nature gained. Our errors are surely not such awfully solemn things. In a world where we are so certain to incur them in spite of all our caution, a certain lightness of heart seems healthier than this excessive nervousness on their behalf. At any rate, it seems the fittest thing for the empiricist philosopher.

VIII

And now, after all this introduction, let us go straight at our question. I have said, and now repeat it, that not only as a matter of fact do we find our passional nature influencing us in our opinions, but that there are some options between opinions in which this influence must be regarded both as an inevitable and as a lawful determinant of our choice.

I fear here that some of you my hearers will begin to scent danger, and lend an inhospitable ear. Two first steps of passion you have indeed had to admit as necessary—we must think so as to avoid dupery, and we must think so as to gain truth; but the surest path to those ideal consummations, you will probably consider, is from now onwards to take no farther passional step.

Well, of course I agree as far as the facts will allow. Wherever the option between losing truth and gaining it is not momentous, we can throw the chance of *gaining truth* away, and at any rate save ourselves from any chance of *believing falsehood*, by not making up our minds at all till objective evidence has come. In scientific questions, this is almost always the case; and even in human affairs in general, the need of acting is seldom so urgent that a false belief to act on is better than no belief at all. Law courts, indeed, have to decide on the best evidence attainable for the moment, because a judge's duty is to make law as well as to ascertain it, and (as a learned judge once said to me) few cases are worth spending much time over: the great thing is to have them decided on *any* acceptable principle, and got out of the way. But in our dealings with objective nature we obviously are recorders, not makers, of the truth; and decisions for the mere sake of deciding promptly and getting on to the next business would be wholly out of place. Throughout the breadth of physical nature facts are what they are quite independently of us, and seldom is there any such hurry about them that the risks of being duped by believing a premature theory need be faced. The questions here are always trivial options, the hypotheses are hardly living (at any rate not living for us spectators), the choice between believing truth or falsehood is seldom forced. The attitude of sceptical balance is therefore the absolutely wise one if we would escape mistakes. What difference, indeed, does it make to most of us whether we have or have not a theory of the Röntgen rays, whether we believe or not in mind-stuff, or have a conviction about the causality of conscious states? It makes no difference. Such options are not forced on us. On every account it is better not to make them, but still keep weighing reasons *pro et contra* with an indifferent hand.

I speak, of course, here of the purely judging mind. For purposes of discovery such indifference is to be less highly recommended, and science would be far less advanced than she is if the passionate desires of individuals to get their own faiths confirmed had been kept out of the game. See for example the sagacity which Spencer and Weismann now display. On the other hand, if you want an absolute duffer in an investigation, you must, after all, take the man who has no interest whatever in its results: he is the warranted incapable, the positive fool. The most useful investigator, because the most sensitive observer, is always he whose eager interest in one side of the question is balanced by an equally keen nervousness lest he become deceived.[3] Science has organized this nervousness into a regular *technique*, her so-called method of verification; and she has fallen so deeply in love with the method that one may even say she has ceased to care for truth by itself at all. It is only truth as technically verified that interests her. The truth of truths might come in merely affirmative form, and she would decline to touch it. Such truth as that, she might repeat with Clifford, would be stolen in defiance of her duty to mankind. Human passions, however, are stronger

[3]Compare Wilfrid Ward's Essay, "The Wish to Believe," in his *Witnesses to the Unseen*, Macmillan & Co., 1893.

than technical rules. "Le cœur a ses raisons," as Pascal says, "que la raison ne connaît point"; and however indifferent to all but the bare rules of the game the umpire, the abstract intellect, may be, the concrete players who furnish him the materials to judge of are usually, each one of them, in love with some pet "live hypothesis" of his own. Let us agree, however, that wherever there is no forced option, the dispassionately judicial intellect with no pet hypothesis, saving us, as it does, from dupery at any rate, ought to be our ideal.

The question next arises: Are there not somewhere forced options in our speculative questions, and can we (as men who may be interested at least as much in positively gaining truth as in merely escaping dupery) always wait with impunity till the coercive evidence shall have arrived? It seems *a priori* improbable that the truth should be so nicely adjusted to our needs and powers as that. In the great boarding-house of nature, the cakes and the butter and the syrup seldom come out so even and leave the plates so clean. Indeed, we should view them with scientific suspicion if they did.

IX

Moral questions immediately present themselves as questions whose solution cannot wait for sensible proof. A moral question is a question not of what sensibly exists, but of what is good, or would be good if it did exist. Science can tell us what exists; but to compare the *worths*, both of what exists and of what does not exist, we must consult not science, but what Pascal calls our heart. Science herself consults her heart when she lays it down that the infinite ascertainment of fact and correction of false belief are the supreme goods for man. Challenge the statement and science can only repeat it oracularly, or else prove it by showing that such ascertainment and correction bring man all sorts of other goods which man's heart in turn declares. The question of having moral beliefs at all or not having them is decided by our will. Are our moral preferences true or false, or are they only odd biological phenomena, making things good or bad for *us*, but in themselves indifferent? How can your pure intellect decide? If your heart does not *want* a world of moral reality, your head will assuredly never make you believe in one. Mephistophelian scepticism, indeed, will satisfy the head's play-instincts much better than any rigorous idealism can. Some men (even at the student age) are so naturally cool-hearted that the moralistic hypothesis never has for them any pungent life, and in their supercilious presence the hot young moralist always feels strangely ill at ease. The appearance of knowingness is on their side, of *naiveté* and gullibility on his. Yet, in the inarticulate heart of him, he clings to it that he is not a dupe, and that there is a realm in which (as Emerson says) all their wit and intellectual superiority is no better than the cunning of a fox. Moral scepticism can no more be refuted or proved by logic than intellectual scepticism can. When we stick to it that there *is* truth (be it of either kind), we do so with our whole nature, and resolve to stand or fall by the results. The sceptic with his whole nature adopts the doubting attitude; but which of us is the wiser, Omniscience only knows.

Turn now from these wide questions of good to a certain class of questions of fact, questions concerning personal relations, states of mind between one man and another. *Do you like me or not?*—for example. Whether you do or not depends, in countless instances, on whether I meet you halfway, am willing to assume that you must like me, and show you trust and expectation. The previous faith on my part in your liking's existence is in such cases what makes your liking come. But if I stand aloof, and refuse to budge an inch until I have objective evidence, until you shall have done something apt, as the absolutists say, *ad extorquendum assensum meum*, ten to one your liking never comes. How many women's hearts are vanquished by the mere sanguine insistence of some man that they *must* love him! he will not consent to the hypothesis that they cannot. The desire for a certain kind of truth here brings about that special truth's existence; and so it is in innumerable cases of other sorts. Who gains promotions, boons, appointments, but the man in whose life they are seen to play the part of live hypotheses, who discounts them, sacrifices other things for their sake before they have come, and takes risks for them in advance? His faith acts on the powers above him as a claim, and creates its own verification.

A social organism of any sort whatever, large or small, is

what it is because each member proceeds to his own duty with a trust that the other members will simultaneously do theirs. Wherever a desired result is achieved by the co-operation of many independent persons, its existence as a fact is a pure consequence of the precursive faith in one another of those immediately concerned. A government, an army, a commercial system, a ship, a college, an athletic team, all exist on this condition, without which not only is nothing achieved, but nothing is even attempted. A whole train of passengers (individually brave enough) will be looted by a few highwaymen, simply because the latter can count on one another, while each passenger fears that if he makes a movement of resistance, he will be shot before anyone else backs him up. If we believed that the whole car-full would rise at once with us, we should each severally rise, and train-robbing would never even be attempted. There are, then, cases where a fact cannot come at all unless a preliminary faith exists in its coming. *And where faith in a fact can help create the fact*, that would be an insane logic which should say that faith running ahead of scientific evidence is the "lowest kind of immorality" into which a thinking being can fall. Yet such is the logic by which our scientific absolutists pretend to regulate our lives!

X

In truths dependent on our personal action, then, faith based on desire is certainly a lawful and possibly an indispensable thing.

But now, it will be said, these are all childish human cases, and have nothing to do with great cosmical matters, like the question of religious faith. Let us then pass on to that. Religions differ so much in their accidents that in discussing the religious question we must make it very generic and broad. What then do we now mean by the religious hypothesis? Science says things are; morality says some things are better than other things; and religion says essentially two things.

First, she says that the best things are the more eternal things, the overlapping things, the things in the universe that throw the last stone, so to speak, and say the final word. "Perfection is eternal"—this phrase of Charles Secrétan seems a good way of putting this first affirmation of religion, an affirmation which obviously cannot yet be verified scientifically at all.

The second affirmation of religion is that we are better off even now if we believe her first affirmation to be true.

Now let us consider what the logical elements of this situation are *in case the religious hypothesis in both its branches be really true*. (Of course, we must admit that possibility at the outset. If we are to discuss the question at all, it must involve a living option. If for any of you religion be a hypothesis that cannot, by any living possibility be true, then you need go no farther. I speak to the "saving remnant" alone.) So proceeding, we see, first, that religion offers itself as a *momentous* option. We are supposed to gain, even now, by our belief, and to lose by our non-belief, a certain vital good. Secondly, religion is a *forced* option, so far as that good goes. We cannot escape the issue by remaining sceptical and waiting for more light, because, although we do avoid error in that way *if religion be untrue*, we lose the good, *if it be true*, just as certainly as if we positively chose to disbelieve. It is as if a man should hesitate indefinitely to ask a certain woman to marry him because he was not perfectly sure that she would prove an angel after he brought her home. Would he not cut himself off from that particular angel-possibility as decisively as if he went and married someone else? Scepticism, then, is not avoidance of option; it is option of a certain particular kind of risk. *Better risk loss of truth than chance of error*—that is your faith-vetoer's exact position. He is actively playing his stake as much as the believer is; he is backing the field against the religious hypothesis, just as the believer is backing the religious hypothesis against the field. To preach scepticism to us as a duty until "sufficient evidence" for religion be found, is tantamount therefore to telling us, when in presence of the religious hypothesis, that to yield to our fear of its being error is wiser and better than to yield to our hope that it may be true. It is not intellect against all passions, then; it is only intellect with one passion laying down its law. And by what, forsooth, is the supreme wisdom of this passion warranted? Dupery for dupery, what proof is there that dupery through hope is so much worse than dupery through fear? I, for one, can see no proof; and I simply refuse obedience to the scientist's command to imitate his kind of option, in a case where my own stake is important enough to give me the right to choose my own form of risk. If religion be true and the evidence for it be still insufficient, I do not wish, by putting your extinguisher upon my nature (which feels to me as if it had after all some business in this matter), to forfeit my sole chance in life of getting upon the winning side—that chance depending, of course, on my willingness to run the risk of acting as if my passional need of taking the world religiously might be prophetic and right.

All this is on the supposition that it really may be prophetic and right, and that, even to us who are discussing the matter, religion is a live hypothesis which may be true. Now to most of us religion comes in a still farther way that makes a veto on our active faith even more illogical. The more perfect and more eternal aspect of the universe is represented in our religions as having personal form. The universe is no longer a mere *It* to us, but a *Thou*, if we are religious; and any relation that may be possible from person to person might be possible here. For instance, although in one sense we are passive portions of the universe, in another we show a curious autonomy, as if we were small active centres on our own account. We feel, too, as if the appeal of religion to us were made to our own active good-will, as if evidence might be forever withheld from us unless we met the hypothesis half-way. To take a trivial illustration: just as a man who in a company of gentlemen made no advances, asked a warrant for every concession, and believed no one's word without proof, would cut himself off by such churlishness from all the social rewards that a more trusting spirit would earn—so here, one who should shut himself up in snarling logicality and try to make the gods extort his recognition willy-nilly, or not get it at all, might cut himself off forever from his only opportunity of making the gods' acquaintance. This feeling, forced on us we know not whence, that by obstinately believing that there are gods (although not to do so would be so easy both for our logic and our life) we are doing the universe the deepest service we can, seems part of the living essence of the religious hypothesis. If the hypothesis *were* true in all its parts, including this one, then pure intellectualism, with its veto on our making willing advances, would be an absurdity; and some participation of our sympathetic nature would be logically required. I, therefore, for one, cannot see my way to accepting the agnostic rules for truth-seeking, or wilfully agree to keep my willing nature out of the game. I cannot do so for this plain reason, that *a rule of thinking which would absolutely prevent me from acknowledging certain kinds of truth if those kinds of truth were really there, would be an irrational rule.* That for me is the long and short of the formal logic of the situation, no matter what the kinds of truth might materially be.

I confess I do not see how this logic can be escaped. But sad experience makes me fear that some of you may still shrink from radically saying with me, *in abstracto*, that we have the right to believe at our own risk any hypothesis that is live enough to tempt our will. I suspect, however, that if this is so, it is because you have got away from the abstract logical point of view altogether, and are thinking (perhaps without realizing it) of some particular religious hypothesis which for you is dead. The freedom to "believe what we will" you apply to the case of some patent superstition; and the faith you think of is the faith defined by the schoolboy when he said, "Faith is when you believe something that you know ain't true." I can only repeat that this is misapprehension. *In concreto*, the freedom to believe can only cover living options which the intellect of the individual cannot by itself resolve; and living options never seem absurdities to him who has them to consider. When I look at the religious question as it really puts itself to concrete men, and when I think of all the possibilities which both practically and theoretically it involves, then this command that we shall put a stopper on our heart, instincts and courage, and *wait*—acting of course meanwhile more or less as if religion were *not* true[4]—till

---

[4]Since belief is measured by action, he who forbids us to believe religion to be true, necessarily also forbids us to act as we should if we did believe it to be true. The whole defence of religious faith hinges upon action. If the action required or inspired by the religious hypothesis is in no way different from that dictated by the naturalistic hypothesis, then religious faith is a pure superfluity, better pruned away, and controversy about its legitimacy is a piece

doomsday, or till such time as our intellect and senses working together may have raked in evidence enough—this command, I say, seems to me the queerest idol ever manufactured in the philosophic cave. Were we scholastic absolutists, there might be more excuse. If we had an infallible intellect with its objective certitudes, we might feel ourselves disloyal to such a perfect organ of knowledge in not trusting to it exclusively, in not waiting for its releasing word. But if we are empiricists, if we believe that no bell in us tolls to let us know for certain when truth is in our grasp, then it seems a piece of idle fantasticality to preach so solemnly our duty of waiting for the bell. Indeed we *may* wait if we will—I hope you do not think that I am denying that—but if we do so, we do so at our peril as much as if we believed. In either case we *act*, taking our life in our hands. No one of us ought to issue vetoes to the other, nor should we bandy words of abuse. We ought, on the contrary, delicately and profoundly to respect one another's mental freedom—then only shall we bring about the intellectual republic; then only shall we have that spirit of inner tolerance without which all our outer tolerance is soulless, and which is empiricism's glory; then only shall we live and let live, in speculative as well as in practical things.

I began by a reference to Fitzjames Stephen; let me end by a quotation from him. "What do you think of yourself? What do you think of the world? . . . These are questions with which all must deal as it seems good to them. They are riddles of the Sphinx, and in some way or other we must deal with them. . . . In all important transactions of life we have to take a leap in the dark. . . . If we decide to leave the riddles unanswered, that is a choice. If we waver in our answer, that too is a choice; but whatever choice we make, we make it at our peril. If a man chooses to turn his back altogether on God and the future, no one can prevent him. No one can show beyond reasonable doubt that he is mistaken. If a man thinks otherwise, and acts as he thinks, I do not see how any one can

---

of idle trifling, unworthy of serious minds. I myself believe, of course, that the religious hypothesis gives to the world an expression which specifically determines our reactions, and makes them in a large part unlike what they might be on a purely naturalistic scheme of belief.

prove that *he* is mistaken. Each must act as he thinks best, and if he is wrong so much the worse for him. We stand on a mountain pass in the midst of whirling snow and blinding mist, through which we get glimpses now and then of paths which may be deceptive. If we stand still, we shall be frozen to death. If we take the wrong road, we shall be dashed to pieces. We do not certainly know whether there is any right one. What must we do? 'Be strong and of a good courage.' Act for the best, hope for the best, and take what comes. . . . If death ends all, we cannot meet death better."[5]

[5]*Liberty, Equality, Fraternity*, p. 353, 2d edition. London, 1874.

Is Life Worth Living? [1]

WHEN Mr. Mallock's book with this title appeared some fifteen years ago, the jocose answer that "it depends on the *liver*" had great currency in the newspapers. The answer which I propose to give to-night cannot be jocose. In the words of one of Shakespeare's prologues,

> "I come no more to make you laugh; things now,
> That bear a weighty and a serious brow,
> Sad, high, and working, full of state and woe,"

must be my theme. In the deepest heart of all of us there is a corner in which the ultimate mystery of things works sadly; and I know not what such an association as yours intends, nor what you ask of those whom you invite to address you, unless it be to lead you from the surface-glamour of existence, and for an hour at least to make you heedless to the buzzing and jigging and vibration of small interests and excitements that form the tissue of our ordinary consciousness. Without further explanation or apology, then, I ask you to join me in turning an attention, commonly too unwilling, to the profounder bass-note of life. Let us search the lonely depths for an hour together, and see what answers in the last folds and recesses of things our question may find.

I

With many men the question of life's worth is answered by a temperamental optimism which makes them incapable of believing that anything seriously evil can exist. Our dear old Walt Whitman's works are the standing text-book of this kind of optimism. The mere joy of living is so immense in Walt Whitman's veins that it abolishes the possibility of any other kind of feeling.

[1] An Address to the Harvard Young Men's Christian Association. Published in the *International Journal of Ethics* for October, 1895, and as a pocket volume by S. B. Weston, Philadelphia, 1896.

"To breathe the air, how delicious!
To speak—to walk—to seize something by the hand! . . .
To be this incredible God I am! . . .
O amazement of things—even the least particle!
O spirituality of things! . . .
I too carol the sun, usher'd or at noon, or as now, setting,
I too throb to the brain and beauty of the earth and of all
      the growths of the earth. . . .

I sing to the last the equalities modern or old,
I sing the endless finalés of things,
I say Nature continues, glory continues,
I praise with electric voice,
For I do not see one imperfection in the universe,
And I do not see one cause or result lamentable at last."

So Rousseau, writing of the nine years he spent at Annecy, with nothing but his happiness to tell:

> "How tell what was neither said nor done nor even thought, but tasted only and felt, with no object of my felicity but the emotion of felicity itself! I rose with the sun, and I was happy; I went to walk, and I was happy; I saw 'Maman,' and I was happy; I left her, and I was happy. I rambled through the woods and over the vine-slopes, I wandered in the valleys, I read, I lounged, I worked in the garden, I gathered the fruits, I helped at the indoor work, and happiness followed me everywhere. It was in no one assignable thing; it was all within myself; it could not leave me for a single instant."

If moods like this could be made permanent, and constitutions like these universal, there would never be any occasion for such discourses as the present one. No philosopher would seek to prove articulately that life is worth living, for the fact that it absolutely is so would vouch for itself, and the problem disappear in the vanishing of the question rather than in the coming of anything like a reply. But we are not magicians to make the optimistic temperament universal; and alongside of the deliverances of temperamental optimism concerning life, those of temperamental pessimism always exist, and oppose to them a standing refutation. In what is called "circular insanity," phases of melancholy succeed phases of mania, with no outward cause that we can discover; and often enough to one and the same well person life will present incarnate radiance to-day and incarnate dreariness to-morrow, according to the fluctuations of what the older medical books used to call "the concoction of the humors." In the words of the newspaper joke, "it depends on the liver." Rousseau's ill-balanced constitution undergoes a change, and behold him in his latter evil days a prey to melancholy and black delusions of suspicion and fear. Some men seem launched upon the world even from their birth with souls as incapable of happiness as Walt Whitman's was of gloom, and they have left us their messages in even more lasting verse than his—the exquisite Leopardi, for example; or our own contemporary, James Thomson, in that pathetic book, *The City of Dreadful Night*, which I think is less well-known than it should be for its literary beauty, simply because men are afraid to quote its words—they are so gloomy, and at the same time so sincere. In one place the poet describes a congregation gathered to listen to a preacher in a great unillumined cathedral at night. The sermon is too long to quote, but it ends thus:

"O Brothers of sad lives! they are so brief;
    A few short years must bring us all relief:
        Can we not bear these years of labouring breath?
But if you would not this poor life fulfil,
Lo, you are free to end it when you will,
    Without the fear of waking after death.—

The organ-like vibrations of his voice
    Thrilled through the vaulted aisles and died away;
The yearning of the tones which bade rejoice
    Was sad and tender as a requiem lay:
Our shadowy congregation rested still
As brooding on that 'End it when you will.'
    .   .   .   .

Our shadowy congregation rested still,
    As musing on that message we had heard
And brooding on that 'End it when you will;'
    Perchance awaiting yet some other word;

When keen as lightning through a muffled sky
Sprang forth a shrill and lamentable cry: —

The man speaks sooth, alas! the man speaks sooth:
    We have no personal life beyond the grave;
There is no God; Fate knows nor wrath nor ruth:
    Can I find here the comfort which I crave?

In all eternity I had one chance,
    One few years' term of gracious human life:
The splendours of the intellect's advance,
    The sweetness of the home with babes and wife;

The social pleasures with their genial wit;
    The fascination of the worlds of art,
The glories of the worlds of nature, lit
    By large imagination's glowing heart;

The rapture of mere being, full of health;
    The careless childhood and the ardent youth,
The strenuous manhood winning various wealth,
    The reverend age serene with life's long truth:

All the sublime prerogatives of Man;
    The storied memories of the times of old,
The patient tracking of the world's great plan
    Through sequences and changes myriadfold.

This chance was never offered me before;
    For me the infinite Past is blank and dumb:
This chance recurreth never, nevermore;
    Blank, blank for me the infinite To-come.

And this sole chance was frustrate from my birth,
    A mockery, a delusion; and my breath
Of noble human life upon this earth
    So racks me that I sigh for senseless death.

My wine of life is poison mixed with gall,
    My noonday passes in a nightmare dream,
I worse than lose the years which are my all:
    What can console me for the loss supreme?

Speak not of comfort where no comfort is,
    Speak not at all: can words make foul things fair?

Our life's a cheat, our death a black abyss:
   Hush and be mute envisaging despair.—

This vehement voice came from the northern aisle
   Rapid and shrill to its abrupt harsh close;
And none gave answer for a certain while,
   For words must shrink from these most wordless woes;
At last the pulpit speaker simply said,
With humid eyes and thoughtful drooping head:—

My Brother, my poor Brothers, it is thus;
This life itself holds nothing good for us,
   But it ends soon and nevermore can be;
And we knew nothing of it ere our birth,
And shall know nothing when consigned to earth:
   I ponder these thoughts and they comfort me."

"It ends soon and nevermore can be," "Lo, you are free to end it when you will"—these verses flow truthfully from the melancholy Thomson's pen, and are in truth a consolation for all to whom, as to him, the world is far more like a steady den of fear than a continual fountain of delight. That life is *not* worth living the whole army of suicides declare—an army whose roll-call, like the famous evening gun of the British army, follows the sun round the world and never terminates. We, too, as we sit here in our comfort, must "ponder these things" also, for we are of one substance with these suicides, and their life is the life we share. The plainest intellectual integrity—nay, more, the simplest manliness and honor— forbid us to forget their case.

"If suddenly," says Mr. Ruskin, "in the midst of the enjoyments of the palate and lightnesses of heart of a London dinner party, the walls of the chamber were parted, and through their gap the nearest human beings who were famishing and in misery were borne into the midst of the company—feasting and fancy free—if, pale from death, horrible in destitution, broken by despair, body by body, they were laid upon the soft carpet, one beside the chair of every guest, would only the crumbs of the dainties be cast to them—would only a passing glance, a passing thought, be vouchsafed to them? Yet the actual facts, the real relation of each Dives and Lazarus, are not al- tered by the intervention of the house wall between the table and the sick bed—by the few feet of ground (how few!) which are indeed all that separate the merriment from the misery."

II

To come immediately to the heart of my theme, then, what I propose is to imagine ourselves reasoning with a fellow-mortal who is on such terms with life that the only comfort left him is to brood on the assurance "you may end it when you will." What reasons can we plead that may render such a brother (or sister) willing to take up the burden again? Ordinary Christians, reasoning with would-be suicides, have little to offer them beyond the usual negative "thou shalt not." God alone is master of life and death, they say, and it is a blasphemous act to anticipate his absolving hand. But can *we* find nothing richer or more positive than this, no reflections to urge whereby the suicide may actually see, and in all sad seriousness feel, that in spite of adverse appearances even for him life is still worth living? There are suicides and suicides (in the United States about three thousand of them every year), and I must frankly confess that with perhaps the majority of these my suggestions are impotent to deal. Where suicide is the result of insanity or sudden frenzied impulse, reflection is impotent to arrest its headway; and cases like these belong to the ultimate mystery of evil, concerning which I can only offer considerations tending towards religious patience at the end of this hour. My task, let me say now, is practically narrow, and my words are to deal only with that metaphysical *tedium vitæ* which is peculiar to reflecting men. Most of you are devoted, for good or ill, to the reflective life. Many of you are students of philosophy, and have already felt in your own persons the scepticism and unreality that too much grubbing in the abstract roots of things will breed. This is, indeed, one of the regular fruits of the over-studious career. Too much questioning and too little active responsibility lead, almost as often as too much sensualism does, to the edge of the slope, at the bottom of which lie pessimism and the nightmare or suicidal view of life. But to the diseases which reflection breeds, still further reflection can oppose effective remedies; and it is of the melancholy and *Weltschmerz* bred of reflection that I now proceed to speak.

Let me say, immediately, that my final appeal is to nothing more recondite than religious faith. So far as my argument is to be destructive, it will consist in nothing more than the sweeping away of certain views that often keep the springs of religious faith compressed; and so far as it is to be constructive, it will consist in holding up to the light of day certain considerations calculated to let loose these springs in a normal, natural way. Pessimism is essentially a religious disease. In the form of it to which you are most liable, it consists in nothing but a religious demand to which there comes no normal religious reply.

Now there are two stages of recovery from this disease, two different levels upon which one may emerge from the midnight view to the daylight view of things, and I must treat of them in turn. The second stage is the more complete and joyous, and it corresponds to the freer exercise of religious trust and fancy. There are, as is well known, persons who are naturally very free in this regard, others who are not at all so. There are persons, for instance, whom we find indulging to their heart's content in prospects of immortality; and there are others who experience the greatest difficulty in making such a notion seem real to themselves at all. These latter persons are tied to their senses, restricted to their natural experience; and many of them, moreover, feel a sort of intellectual loyalty to what they call "hard facts," which is positively shocked by the easy excursions into the unseen that other people make at the bare call of sentiment. Minds of either class may, however, be intensely religious. They may equally desire atonement and reconciliation, and crave acquiescence and communion with the total soul of things. But the craving, when the mind is pent in to the hard facts, especially as science now reveals them, can breed pessimism, quite as easily as it breeds optimism when it inspires religious trust and fancy to wing their way to another and a better world.

That is why I call pessimism an essentially religious disease. The nightmare view of life has plenty of organic sources; but its great reflective source has at all times been the contradiction between the phenomena of nature and the craving of the

heart to believe that behind nature there is a spirit whose expression nature is. What philosophers call "natural theology"
has been one way of appeasing this craving; that poetry of
nature in which our English literature is so rich has been another way. Now suppose a mind of the latter of our two
classes, whose imagination is pent in consequently, and who
takes its facts "hard"; suppose it, moreover, to feel strongly
the craving for communion, and yet to realize how desper-
ately difficult it is to construe the scientific order of nature
either theologically or poetically—and what result *can* there
be but inner discord and contradiction? Now this inner discord (merely as discord) can be relieved in either of two ways.
The longing to read the facts religiously may cease, and leave
the bare facts by themselves; or, supplementary facts may be
discovered or believed-in, which permit the religious reading
to go on. These two ways of relief are the two stages of recovery, the two levels of escape from pessimism, to which I made
allusion a moment ago, and which the sequel will, I trust,
make more clear.

III

Starting then with nature, we naturally tend, if we have the
religious craving, to say with Marcus Aurelius, "O Universe!
what thou wishest I wish." Our sacred books and traditions
tell us of one God who made heaven and earth, and, looking
on them, saw that they were good. Yet, on more intimate
acquaintance, the visible surfaces of heaven and earth refuse
to be brought by us into any intelligible unity at all. Every
phenomenon that we would praise there exists cheek by jowl
with some contrary phenomenon that cancels all its religious
effect upon the mind. Beauty and hideousness, love and cruelty, life and death keep house together in indissoluble partnership; and there gradually steals over us, instead of the old
warm notion of a man-loving Deity, that of an awful power
that neither hates nor loves, but rolls all things together
meaninglessly to a common doom. This is an uncanny, a sinister, a nightmare view of life, and its peculiar *unheimlichkeit*,
or poisonousness, lies expressly in our holding two things together which cannot possibly agree—in our clinging, on the

one hand, to the demand that there shall be a living spirit of the whole; and, on the other, to the belief that the course of nature must be such a spirit's adequate manifestation and expression. It is in the contradiction between the supposed being of a spirit that encompasses and owns us, and with which we ought to have some communion, and the character of such a spirit as revealed by the visible world's course, that this particular death-in-life paradox and this melancholy-breeding puzzle reside. Carlyle expresses the result in that chapter of his immortal *Sartor Resartus* entitled "The Everlasting No." "I lived," writes poor Teufelsdröckh, "in a continual, indefinite, pining fear; tremulous, pusillanimous, apprehensive of I knew not what: it seemed as if all things in the Heavens above and the Earth beneath would hurt me; as if the Heavens and the Earth were but boundless jaws of a devouring monster, wherein I, palpitating, waited to be devoured."

This is the first stage of speculative melancholy. No brute can have this sort of melancholy; no man who is irreligious can become its prey. It is the sick shudder of the frustrated religious demand, and not the mere necessary outcome of animal experience. Teufelsdröckh himself could have made shift to face the general chaos and bedevilment of this world's experiences very well, were he not the victim of an originally unlimited trust and affection towards them. If he might meet them piecemeal, with no suspicion of any whole expressing itself in them, shunning the bitter parts and husbanding the sweet ones, as the occasion served, and as the day was foul or fair, he could have zigzagged towards an easy end, and felt no obligation to make the air vocal with his lamentations. The mood of levity, of "I don't care," is for this world's ills a sovereign and practical anæsthetic. But, no! something deep down in Teufelsdröckh and in the rest of us tells us that there *is* a Spirit in things to which we owe allegiance, and for whose sake we must keep up the serious mood. And so the inner fever and discord also are kept up; for nature taken on her visible surface reveals no such Spirit, and beyond the facts of nature we are at the present stage of our inquiry not supposing ourselves to look.

Now, I do not hesitate frankly and sincerely to confess to you that this real and genuine discord seems to me to carry with it the inevitable bankruptcy of natural religion naively and simply taken. There were times when Leibnitzes with their heads buried in monstrous wigs could compose Theodicies, and when stall-fed officials of an established church could prove by the valves in the heart and the round ligament of the hip-joint the existence of a "Moral and Intelligent Contriver of the World." But those times are past; and we of the nineteenth century, with our evolutionary theories and our mechanical philosophies, already know nature too impartially and too well to worship unreservedly any God of whose character she can be an adequate expression. Truly, all we know of good and duty proceeds from nature; but none the less so all we know of evil. Visible nature is all plasticity and indifference—a moral multiverse, as one might call it, and not a moral universe. To such a harlot we owe no allegiance; with her as a whole we can establish no moral communion; and we are free in our dealings with her several parts to obey or destroy, and to follow no law but that of prudence in coming to terms with such of her particular features as will help us to our private ends. If there be a divine Spirit of the universe, nature, such as we know her, cannot possibly be its *ultimate word* to man. Either there is no Spirit revealed in nature, or else it is inadequately revealed there; and (as all the higher religions have assumed) what we call visible nature, or *this* world, must be but a veil and surface-show whose full meaning resides in a supplementary unseen or *other* world.

I cannot help, therefore, accounting it on the whole a gain (though it may seem for certain poetic constitutions a very sad loss) that the naturalistic superstition, the worship of the God of nature, simply taken as such, should have begun to loosen its hold upon the educated mind. In fact, if I am to express my personal opinion unreservedly, I should say (in spite of its sounding blasphemous at first to certain ears) that the initial step towards getting into healthy ultimate relations with the universe is the act of rebellion against the idea that such a God exists. Such rebellion essentially is that which in the chapter I have quoted from Carlyle goes on to describe:

" 'Wherefore, like a coward, dost thou forever pip and whimper, and go cowering and trembling? Despicable biped! . . . Hast thou not a heart; canst thou not suffer whatsoever it be; and, as a Child of Freedom, though outcast, trample Tophet itself under thy feet, while it consumes thee? Let it come, then; I will meet it and defy it!' And as I so thought, there rushed like a stream of fire over my whole soul; and I shook base Fear away from me forever. . . .

"Thus had the Everlasting No pealed authoritatively through all the recesses of my Being, of my Me; and then was it that my whole Me stood up, in native God-created majesty, and recorded its Protest. Such a Protest, the most important transaction in Life, may that same Indignation and Defiance, in a psychological point of view, be fitly called. The Everlasting No had said: 'Behold, thou art fatherless, outcast, and the Universe is mine;' to which my whole Me now made answer: '*I* am not thine, but Free, and forever hate thee!' From that hour," Teufelsdröckh-Carlyle adds, "I began to be a Man."

And our poor friend, James Thomson, similarly writes:

" 'Who is most wretched in this dolorous place?
    I think myself; yet I would rather be
    My miserable self than He, than He
Who formed such creatures to His own disgrace.

'The vilest thing must be less vile than Thou
    From whom it had its being, God and Lord!
    Creator of all woe and sin! abhorred,
Malignant and implacable! I vow

'That not for all Thy power furled and unfurled,
    For all the temples to Thy glory built,
    Would I assume the ignominious guilt
Of having made such men in such a world.' "

We are familiar enough in this community with the spectacle of persons exulting in their emancipation from belief in the God of their ancestral Calvinism—him who made the garden and the serpent, and pre-appointed the eternal fires of hell. Some of them have found humaner gods to worship, others are simply converts from all theology; but, both alike, they assure us that to have got rid of the sophistication of thinking they could feel any reverence or duty towards that impossible idol gave a tremendous happiness to their souls. Now, to make an idol of the spirit of nature, and worship it, also leads to sophistication; and in souls that are religious and would also be scientific the sophistication breeds a philosoph-ical melancholy, from which the first natural step of escape is the denial of the idol; and with the downfall of the idol, whatever lack of positive joyousness may remain, there comes also the downfall of the whimpering and cowering mood. With evil simply taken as such, men can make short work, for their relations with it then are only practical. It looms up no longer so spectrally, it loses all its haunting and perplexing significance, as soon as the mind attacks the instances of it singly, and ceases to worry about their derivation from the "one and only Power."

Here, then, on this stage of mere emancipation from mo-nistic superstition, the would-be suicide may already get en-couraging answers to his question about the worth of life. There are in most men instinctive springs of vitality that re-spond healthily when the burden of metaphysical and infinite responsibility rolls off. The certainty that you now *may* step out of life whenever you please, and that to do so is not blasphemous or monstrous, is itself an immense relief. The thought of suicide is now no longer a guilty challenge and obsession.

> "This little life is all we must endure,
>   The grave's most holy peace is ever sure,"

says Thomson; adding, "I ponder these thoughts and they comfort me." Meanwhile we can always stand it for twenty-four hours longer, if only to see what to-morrow's newspaper will contain, or what the next postman will bring.

But far deeper forces than this mere vital curiosity are arousable, even in the pessimistically-tending mind; for where the loving and admiring impulses are dead, the hating and fighting impulses will still respond to fit appeals. This evil which we feel so deeply is something that we can also help to overthrow; for its sources, now that no "Substance" or "Spirit" is behind them, are finite, and we can deal with each of them in turn. It is, indeed, a remarkable fact that sufferings and hardships do not, as a rule, abate the love of life; they seem, on the contrary, usually to give it a keener zest. The sovereign source of melancholy is repletion. Need and strug-gle are what excite and inspire us; our hour of triumph is what brings the void. Not the Jews of the captivity, but those of the days of Solomon's glory are those from whom the pessimistic utterances in our Bible come. Germany, when she lay trampled beneath the hoofs of Bonaparte's troopers, produced perhaps the most optimistic and idealistic literature that the world has seen; and not till the French "milliards" were distributed after 1871 did pessimism overrun the country in the shape in which we see it there to-day. The history of our own race is one long commentary on the cheerfulness that comes with fighting ills. Or take the Waldenses, of whom I lately have been reading, as examples of what strong men will endure. In 1485 a papal bull of Innocent VIII. enjoined their extermination. It absolved those who should take up the crusade against them from all ecclesiastical pains and penalties, released them from any oath, legitimized their title to all property which they might have illegally acquired, and promised remission of sins to all who should kill the heretics.

"There is no town in Piedmont," says a Vaudois writer, "where some of our brethren have not been put to death. Jordan Terbano was burnt alive at Susa; Hippolite Rossiero at Turin; Michael Goneto, an octogenarian, at Sarcena; Villermin Ambrosio hanged on the Col di Meano; Hugo Chiambs, of Fenestrelle, had his entrails torn from his living body at Turin; Peter Geymarali, of Bobbio, in like manner had his entrails taken out in Luzerna, and a fierce cat thrust in their place to torture him further; Maria Romano was buried alive at Rocca-patia; Magdalena Fauno underwent the same fate at San Giovanni; Susanna Michelini was bound hand and foot, and left to perish of cold and hunger on the snow at Sarcena; Bartolomeo Fache, gashed with sabres, had the wounds filled up with quick-lime, and perished thus in agony at Fenile; Daniel Michelini had his tongue torn out at Bobbio for having praised God; James Baridari perished covered with sulphureous matches, which had been forced into his flesh under the nails, between the fingers, in the nostrils, in the lips, and all over his body, and then lighted; Daniel Revelli had his mouth filled with gunpowder, which being lighted blew his head to pieces; . . . Sara Rostignol was slit open from the legs to the bosom, and left so to perish on the road between Eyral and Luzerna; Anna Charbonnier was impaled, and carried thus on a pike from San Giovanni to La Torre."[2]

[2]Quoted by George E. Waring in his book on Tyrol. Compare A. Bérard: *Les Vaudois*, Lyon, Storck, 1892.

Und dergleichen mehr! In 1630 the plague swept away one-half of the Vaudois population, including fifteen of their seventeen pastors. The places of these were supplied from Geneva and Dauphiny, and the whole Vaudois people learned French in order to follow their services. More than once their number fell, by unremitting persecution, from the normal standard of twenty-five thousand to about four thousand. In 1686 the Duke of Savoy ordered the three thousand that remained to give up their faith or leave the country. Refusing, they fought the French and Piedmontese armies till only eighty of their fighting men remained alive or uncaptured, when they gave up, and were sent in a body to Switzerland. But in 1689, encouraged by William of Orange and led by one of their pastor-captains, between eight hundred and nine hundred of them returned to conquer their old homes again. They fought their way to Bobbio, reduced to four hundred men in the first half year, and met every force sent against them; until at last the Duke of Savoy, giving up his alliance with that abomination of desolation, Louis XIV., restored them to comparative freedom—since which time they have increased and multiplied in their barren Alpine valleys to this day.

What are our woes and sufferance compared with these? Does not the recital of such a fight so obstinately waged against such odds fill us with resolution against *our* petty powers of darkness—machine politicians, spoilsmen, and the rest? Life is worth living, no matter what it bring, if only such combats may be carried to successful terminations and one's heel set on the tyrant's throat. To the suicide, then, in his supposed world of multifarious and immoral nature, you can appeal—and appeal in the name of the very evils that make his heart sick there—to wait and see *his* part of the battle out. And the consent to live on, which you ask of him under these circumstances, is not the sophistical "resignation" which devotees of cowering religions preach: it is not resignation in the sense of licking a despotic Deity's hand. It is, on the contrary, a resignation based on manliness and pride. So long as your would-be suicide leaves an evil of his own unremedied, so long he has strictly no concern with evil in the abstract and at large. The submission which you demand of yourself to the general fact of evil in the world, your apparent acquiescence in it, is here nothing but the conviction that evil at large is *none of your business* until your business with your private particular evils is liquidated and settled up. A challenge of this sort, with proper designation of detail, is one that need only be made to be accepted by men whose normal instincts are not decayed; and your reflective, would-be suicide may easily be moved by it to face life with a certain interest again. The sentiment of honor is a very penetrating thing. When you and I, for instance, realize how many innocent beasts have had to suffer in cattle-cars and slaughter-pens and lay down their lives that we might grow up, all fattened and clad, to sit together here in comfort and carry on this discourse, it does, indeed, put our relation to the universe in a more solemn light. "Does not," as a young Amherst philosopher (Xenos Clark, now dead) once wrote, "the acceptance of a happy life on such conditions involve a point of honor?" Are we not bound to take some suffering upon ourselves, to do some self-denying service with our lives, in return for all those lives upon which ours are built? To hear this question is to answer it in but one possible way, if one have a normally constituted heart.

Thus, then, we see that mere instinctive curiosity, pugnacity, and honor may make life on a purely naturalistic basis seem worth living from day to day to men who have cast away all metaphysics in order to get rid of hypochondria, but who are resolved to owe nothing as yet to religion and its more positive gifts. A poor half-way stage, some of you may be inclined to say; but at least you must grant it to be an honest stage; and no man should dare to speak meanly of these instincts which are our nature's best equipment, and to which religion herself must in the last resort address her own peculiar appeals.

IV

And now, in turning to what religion may have to say to the question, I come to what is the soul of my discourse. Religion has meant many things in human history; but when from now onward I use the word I mean to use it in the supernaturalist sense, as declaring that the so-called order of nature, which constitutes this world's experience, is only one portion of the total universe, and that there stretches beyond this visible world an unseen world of which we now know nothing positive, but in its relation to which the true significance of our present mundane life consists. A man's religious faith (whatever more special items of doctrine it may involve) means for me essentially his faith in the existence of an unseen order of some kind in which the riddles of the natural order may be found explained. In the more developed religions the natural world has always been regarded as the mere scaffolding or vestibule of a truer, more eternal world, and affirmed to be a sphere of education, trial, or redemption. In these religions, one must in some fashion die to the natural life before one can enter into life eternal. The notion that this physical world of wind and water, where the sun rises and the moon sets, is absolutely and ultimately the divinely aimed-at and established thing, is one which we find only in very early religions, such as that of the most primitive Jews. It is this natural religion (primitive still, in spite of the fact that poets and men of science whose good-will exceeds their perspicacity keep publishing it in new editions tuned to our contemporary ears) that, as I said a while ago, has suffered definitive bankruptcy in the opinion of a circle of persons, amongst whom I must count myself, and who are growing more numerous every day. For such persons the physical order of nature, taken simply as science knows it, cannot be held to reveal any one harmonious spiritual intent. It is mere *weather*, as Chauncey Wright called it, doing and undoing without end.

Now I wish to make you feel, if I can in the short remainder of this hour, that we have a right to believe the physical order to be only a partial order; that we have a right to supplement it by an unseen spiritual order which we assume on trust, if only thereby life may seem to us better worth living again. But as such a trust will seem to some of you sadly mystical and execrably unscientific, I must first say a word or two to weaken the veto which you may consider that science opposes to our act.

There is included in human nature an ingrained naturalism and materialism of mind which can only admit facts that are actually tangible. Of this sort of mind the entity called "science" is the idol. Fondness for the word "scientist" is one of the notes by which you may know its votaries; and its short way of killing any opinion that it disbelieves in is to call it "unscientific." It must be granted that there is no slight excuse for this. Science has made such glorious leaps in the last three hundred years, and extended our knowledge of nature so enormously both in general and in detail; men of science, moreover, have as a class displayed such admirable virtues — that it is no wonder if the worshippers of science lose their head. In this very University, accordingly, I have heard more than one teacher say that all the fundamental conceptions of truth have already been found by science, and that the future has only the details of the picture to fill in. But the slightest reflection on the real conditions will suffice to show how barbaric such notions are. They show such a lack of scientific imagination, that it is hard to see how one who is actively advancing any part of science can make a mistake so crude. Think how many absolutely new scientific conceptions have arisen in our own generation, how many new problems have been formulated that were never thought of before, and then cast an eye upon the brevity of science's career. It began with Galileo, not three hundred years ago. Four thinkers since Galileo, each informing his successor of what discoveries his own lifetime had seen achieved, might have passed the torch of science into our hands as we sit here in this room. Indeed, for the matter of that, an audience much smaller than the present one, an audience of some five or six score people, if each person in it could speak for his own generation, would carry us away to the black unknown of the human species, to days without a document or monument to tell their tale. Is it credible that such a mushroom knowledge, such a growth overnight as this, *can* represent more than the minutest glimpse of what the universe will really prove to be when adequately understood? No! our science is a drop, our ignorance a sea. Whatever else be certain, this at least is certain — that the world of our present natural knowledge *is* enveloped in a larger world of *some* sort of whose residual properties we at present can frame no positive idea.

Agnostic positivism, of course, admits this principle theoretically in the most cordial terms, but insists that we must not turn it to any practical use. We have no right, this doctrine tells us, to dream dreams, or suppose anything about the unseen part of the universe, merely because to do so may be for what we are pleased to call our highest interests. We must always wait for sensible evidence for our beliefs; and where such evidence is inaccessible we must frame no hypotheses whatever. Of course this is a safe enough position *in abstracto*. If a thinker had no stake in the unknown, no vital needs, to live or languish according to what the unseen world contained, a philosophic neutrality and refusal to believe either one way or the other would be his wisest cue. But, unfortunately, neutrality is not only inwardly difficult, it is also outwardly unrealizable, where our relations to an alternative are practical and vital. This is because, as the psychologists tell us, belief and doubt are living attitudes, and involve conduct on our part. Our only way, for example, of doubting, or refusing to believe, that a certain thing *is*, is continuing to act as if it were *not*. If, for instance, I refuse to believe that the room is getting cold, I leave the windows open and light no fire just as if it still were warm. If I doubt that you are worthy of my confidence, I keep you uninformed of all my secrets just as if you were *un*worthy of the same. If I doubt the need of insuring my house, I leave it uninsured as much as if I believed there were no need. And so if I must not believe that the world is divine, I can only express that refusal by declining ever to act distinctively as if it were so, which can only mean acting on certain critical occasions as if it were *not* so, or in an irreligious way. There are, you see, inevitable occasions in life when inaction is a kind of action, and must count as action, and when not to be for is to be practically against; and in all such cases strict and consistent neutrality is an unattainable thing.

And, after all, is not this duty of neutrality where only our inner interests would lead us to believe, the most ridiculous of commands? Is it not sheer dogmatic folly to say that our inner interests can have no real connection with the forces that the hidden world may contain? In other cases divinations based on inner interests have proved prophetic enough. Take science itself! Without an imperious inner demand on our part for ideal logical and mathematical harmonies, we should never have attained to proving that such harmonies lie hidden between all the chinks and interstices of the crude natural world. Hardly a law has been established in science, hardly a fact ascertained, which was not first sought after, often with sweat and blood, to gratify an inner need. Whence such needs come from we do not know: we find them in us, and biological psychology so far only classes them with Darwin's "accidental variations." But the inner need of believing that this world of nature is a sign of something more spiritual and eternal than itself is just as strong and authoritative in those who feel it, as the inner need of uniform laws of causation ever can be in a professionally scientific head. The toil of many generations has proved the latter need prophetic. Why *may* not the former one be prophetic, too? And if needs of ours outrun the visible universe, why *may* not that be a sign that an invisible universe is there? What, in short, has authority to debar us from trusting our religious demands? Science as such assuredly has no authority, for she can only say what is, not what is not; and the agnostic "thou shalt not believe without coercive sensible evidence" is simply an expression (free to anyone to make) of private personal appetite for evidence of a certain peculiar kind.

Now, when I speak of trusting our religious demands, just what do I mean by "trusting"? Is the word to carry with it license to define in detail an invisible world, and to anathematize and excommunicate those whose trust is different? Certainly not! Our faculties of belief were not primarily given us to make orthodoxies and heresies withal; they were given us to live by. And to trust our religious demands means first of all to live in the light of them, and to act as if the invisible world which they suggest were real. It is a fact of human nature, that men can live and die by the help of a sort of faith that goes without a single dogma or definition. The bare assurance that this natural order is not ultimate but a mere sign or vision, the external staging of a many-storied universe, in which spiritual forces have the last word and are eternal—this bare assurance is to such men enough to make life seem worth living in spite of every contrary presumption suggested by its circumstances on the natural plane. Destroy this inner assurance, however, vague as it is, and all the light and radiance of existence is extinguished for these persons at a stroke. Often enough the wild-eyed look at life—the suicidal mood —will then set in.

And now the application comes directly home to you and me. Probably to almost every one of us here the most adverse life would seem well worth living, if we only could be *certain* that our bravery and patience with it were terminating and eventuating and bearing fruit somewhere in an unseen spiritual world. But granting we are not certain, does it then follow that a bare trust in such a world is a fool's paradise and lubberland, or rather that it is a living attitude in which we are free to indulge? Well, we are free to trust at our own risks anything that is not impossible, and that can bring analogies to bear in its behalf. That the world of physics is probably not absolute, all the converging multitude of arguments that make in favor of idealism tend to prove; and that our whole physical life may lie soaking in a spiritual atmosphere, a dimension of being that we at present have no organ for apprehending, is vividly suggested to us by the analogy of the life of our domestic animals. Our dogs, for example, are in our human life but not of it. They witness hourly the outward body of events whose inner meaning cannot, by any possible operation, be revealed to their intelligence—events in which they themselves often play the cardinal part. My terrier bites a teasing boy, for example, and the father demands damages. The dog may be present at every step of the negotiations, and see the money paid, without an inkling of what it all means, without a suspicion that it has anything to do with *him*; and he never *can* know in his natural dog's life. Or take another case which used greatly to impress me in my medical-student days. Consider a poor dog whom they are vivisecting in a laboratory. He lies strapped on a board and shrieking at his executioners, and to his own dark consciousness is literally in a sort of hell. He cannot see a single redeeming ray in the whole business; and yet all these diabolical-seeming events are often controlled by human intentions with which, if his poor benighted mind could only be made to catch a glimpse of them, all that is heroic in him would religiously acquiesce. Healing truth, relief to future sufferings of beast and man, are to be bought by them. It may be genuinely a process of re-demption. Lying on his back on the board there he may be performing a function incalculably higher than any that pros-perous canine life admits of; and yet, of the whole perfor-mance, this function is the one portion that must remain absolutely beyond his ken.

Now turn from this to the life of man. In the dog's life we see the world invisible to him because we live in both worlds. In human life, although we only see our world, and his within it, yet encompassing both these worlds a still wider world may be there, as unseen by us as our world is by him; and to believe in that world *may* be the most essential function that our lives in this world have to perform. But "*may* be! *may* be!" one now hears the positivist contemptuously exclaim; "what use can a scientific life have for maybes?" Well, I reply, the "scientific" life itself has much to do with maybes, and human life at large has everything to do with them. So far as man stands for anything, and is productive or originative at all, his entire vital function may be said to have to deal with maybes. Not a victory is gained, not a deed of faithfulness or courage is done, except upon a maybe; not a service, not a sally of generosity, not a scientific exploration or experiment or text-book, that may not be a mistake. It is only by risking our persons from one hour to another that we live at all. And often enough our faith beforehand in an uncertified result *is the only thing that makes the result come true.* Suppose, for in-stance, that you are climbing a mountain, and have worked yourself into a position from which the only escape is by a terrible leap. Have faith that you can successfully make it, and your feet are nerved to its accomplishment. But mistrust yourself, and think of all the sweet things you have heard the scientists say of *maybes*, and you will hesitate so long that, at last, all unstrung and trembling, and launching yourself in a moment of despair, you roll in the abyss. In such a case (and it belongs to an enormous class), the part of wisdom as well as of courage is to *believe what is in the line of your needs*, for only by such belief is the need fulfilled. Refuse to believe, and you shall indeed be right, for you shall irretrievably perish. But believe, and again you shall be right, for you shall save yourself. You make one or the other of two possible universes true by your trust or mistrust—both universes having been only *maybes*, in this particular, before you contributed your act.

Now, it appears to me that the question whether life is worth living is subject to conditions logically much like these. It does, indeed, depend on you *the liver*. If you surrender to the nightmare view and crown the evil edifice by your own suicide, you have indeed made a picture totally black. Pessimism, completed by your act, is true beyond a doubt, so far as your world goes. Your mistrust of life has removed whatever worth your own enduring existence might have given to it; and now, throughout the whole sphere of possible influence of that existence, the mistrust has proved itself to have had divining power. But suppose, on the other hand, that instead of giving way to the nightmare view you cling to it that this world is not the *ultimatum*. Suppose you find yourself a very well-spring, as Wordsworth says, of

"Zeal, and the virtue to exist by faith
As soldiers live by courage; as, by strength
Of heart, the sailor fights with roaring seas."

Suppose, however thickly evils crowd upon you, that your unconquerable subjectivity proves to be their match, and that you find a more wonderful joy than any passive pleasure can bring in trusting ever in the larger whole. Have you not now made life worth living on these terms? What sort of a thing would life really be, with your qualities ready for a tussle with it, if it only brought fair weather and gave these higher faculties of yours no scope? Please remember that optimism and pessimism are definitions of the world, and that our own reactions on the world, small as they are in bulk, are integral parts of the whole thing, and necessarily help to determine the definition. They may even be the decisive elements in determining the definition. A large mass can have its unstable equilibrium overturned by the addition of a feather's weight; a long phrase may have its sense reversed by the addition of the three letters *n-o-t*. This life *is* worth living, we can say, *since it is what we make it, from the moral point of view*; and we are determined to make it from that point of view, so far as we have anything to do with it, a success.

Now, in this description of faiths that verify themselves I have assumed that our faith in an invisible order is what inspires those efforts and that patience which make this visible order good for moral men. Our faith in the seen world's goodness (goodness now meaning fitness for successful moral and religious life) has verified itself by leaning on our faith in the unseen world. But will our faith in the unseen world similarly verify itself? Who knows?

Once more it is a case of *maybe*; and once more *maybes* are the essence of the situation. I confess that I do not see why the very existence of an invisible world may not in part depend on the personal response which any one of us may make to the religious appeal. God himself, in short, may draw vital strength and increase of very being from our fidelity. For my own part, I do not know what the sweat and blood and tragedy of this life mean, if they mean anything short of this. If this life be not a real fight, in which something is eternally gained for the universe by success, it is no better than a game of private theatricals from which one may withdraw at will. But it *feels* like a real fight—as if there were something really wild in the universe which we, with all our idealities and faithfulnesses, are needed to redeem; and first of all to redeem our own hearts from atheisms and fears. For such a half-wild, half-saved universe our nature is adapted. The deepest thing in our nature is this *Binnenleben* (as a German doctor lately has called it), this dumb region of the heart in which we dwell alone with our willingnesses and unwillingnesses, our faiths and fears. As through the cracks and crannies of caverns those waters exude from the earth's bosom which then form the fountain-heads of springs, so in these crepuscular depths of personality the sources of all our outer deeds and decisions take their rise. Here is our deepest organ of communication with the nature of things; and compared with these concrete movements of our soul all abstract statements and scientific arguments—the veto, for example, which the strict positivist pronounces upon our faith—sound to us like mere chatterings of the teeth. For here possibilities, not finished facts, are the realities with which we have actively to deal; and to quote my friend William Salter, of the Philadelphia Ethical

Society, "as the essence of courage is to stake one's life on a possibility, so the essence of faith is to believe that the possibility exists."

These, then, are my last words to you: Be not afraid of life. Believe that life *is* worth living, and your belief will help create the fact. The "scientific proof" that you are right may not be clear before the day of judgment (or some stage of being which that expression may serve to symbolize) is reached. But the faithful fighters of this hour, or the beings that then and there will represent them, may then turn to the faint-hearted, who here decline to go on, with words like those with which Henry IV. greeted the tardy Crillon after a great victory had been gained: "Hang yourself, brave Crillon! We fought at Arques, and you were not there."

The Sentiment of Rationality [1]

I

WHAT IS the task which philosophers set themselves to perform; and why do they philosophize at all? Almost everyone will immediately reply: They desire to attain a conception of the frame of things which shall on the whole be more rational than that somewhat chaotic view which everyone by nature carries about with him under his hat. But suppose this rational conception attained, how is the philosopher to recognize it for what it is, and not let it slip through ignorance? The only answer can be that he will recognize its rationality as he recognizes everything else, by certain subjective marks with which it affects him. When he gets the marks, he may know that he has got the rationality.

What, then, are the marks? A strong feeling of ease, peace, rest, is one of them. The transition from a state of puzzle and perplexity to rational comprehension is full of lively relief and pleasure.

But this relief seems to be a negative rather than a positive character. Shall we then say that the feeling of rationality is constituted merely by the absence of any feeling of irrationality? I think there are very good grounds for upholding such a view. All feeling whatever, in the light of certain recent psychological speculations, seems to depend for its physical condition not on simple discharge of nerve-currents, but on their discharge under arrest, impediment or resistance. Just as we feel no particular pleasure when we breathe freely, but a very intense feeling of distress when the respiratory motions are prevented—so any unobstructed tendency to action discharges itself without the production of much cogitative accompaniment, and any perfectly fluent course of thought awakens but little feeling; but when the movement is inhibited, or when the thought meets with difficulties, we ex-

[1] This essay as far as page 513 consists of extracts from an article printed in *Mind* for July, 1879. Thereafter it is a reprint of an address to the Harvard Philosophical Club, delivered in 1880, and published in the *Princeton Review*, July, 1882.

perience distress. It is only when the distress is upon us that we can be said to strive, to crave, or to aspire. When enjoying plenary freedom either in the way of motion or of thought, we are in a sort of anæsthetic state in which we might say with Walt Whitman, if we cared to say anything about ourselves at such times, "I am sufficient as I am." This feeling of the sufficiency of the present moment, of its absoluteness—this absence of all need to explain it, account for it, or justify it—is what I call the Sentiment of Rationality. As soon, in short, as we are enabled from any cause whatever to think with perfect fluency, the thing we think of seems to us *pro tanto* rational.

Whatever modes of conceiving the cosmos facilitate this fluency, produce the sentiment of rationality. Conceived in such modes, being vouches for itself and needs no further philosophic formulation. But this fluency may be obtained in various ways; and first I will take up the theoretic way.

The facts of the world in their sensible diversity are always before us, but our theoretic need is that they should be conceived in a way that reduces their manifoldness to simplicity. Our pleasure at finding that a chaos of facts is the expression of a single underlying fact is like the relief of the musician at resolving a confused mass of sound into melodic or harmonic order. The simplified result is handled with far less mental effort than the original data; and a philosophic conception of nature is thus in no metaphorical sense a labor-saving contrivance. The passion for parsimony, for economy of means in thought, is the philosophic passion *par excellence*; and any character or aspect of the world's phenomena which gathers up their diversity into monotony will gratify that passion, and in the philosopher's mind stand for that essence of things compared with which all their other determinations may by him be overlooked.

More universality or extensiveness is, then, one mark which the philosopher's conceptions must possess. Unless they apply to an enormous number of cases they will not bring him relief. The knowledge of things by their causes, which is often given as a definition of rational knowledge, is useless to him unless the causes converge to a minimum number, whilst still producing the maximum number of effects. The more multiple then are the instances, the more flowingly does his mind rove from fact to fact. The phenomenal transitions are no real transitions; each item is the same old friend with a slightly altered dress.

Who does not feel the charm of thinking that the moon and the apple are, as far as their relation to the earth goes, identical; of knowing respiration and combustion to be one; of understanding that the balloon rises by the same law whereby the stone sinks; of feeling that the warmth in one's palm when one rubs one's sleeve is identical with the motion which the friction checks; of recognizing the difference between beast and fish to be only a higher degree of that between human father and son; of believing our strength when we climb the mountain or fell the tree to be no other than the strength of the sun's rays which made the corn grow out of which we got our morning meal?

But alongside of this passion for simplification there exists a sister passion, which in some minds—though they perhaps form the minority—is its rival. This is the passion for distinguishing; it is the impulse to be *acquainted* with the parts rather than to comprehend the whole. Loyalty to clearness and integrity of perception, dislike of blurred outlines, of vague identifications, are its characteristics. It loves to recognize particulars in their full completeness, and the more of these it can carry the happier it is. It prefers any amount of incoherence, abruptness and fragmentariness (so long as the literal details of the separate facts are saved) to an abstract way of conceiving things that, while it simplifies them, dissolves away at the same time their concrete fulness. Clearness and simplicity thus set up rival claims, and make a real dilemma for the thinker.

A man's philosophic attitude is determined by the balance in him of these two cravings. No system of philosophy can hope to be universally accepted among men which grossly violates either need, or entirely subordinates the one to the other. The fate of Spinosa, with his barren union of all things in one substance, on the one hand; that of Hume, with his equally barren "looseness and separateness" of everything, on the other—neither philosopher owning any strict and systematic disciples to-day, each being to posterity a warning as well as a stimulus—show us that the only possible philosophy must be a compromise between an abstract monotony and a concrete heterogeneity. But the only way to mediate between diversity and unity is to class the diverse items as cases of a common essence which you discover in them. Classification of things into extensive "kinds" is thus the first step; and classification of their relations and conduct into extensive "laws" is the last step, in their philosophic unification. A completed theoretic philosophy can thus never be anything more than a completed classification of the world's ingredients; and its results must always be abstract, since the basis of every classification is the abstract essence embedded in the living fact— the rest of the living fact being for the time ignored by the classifier. This means that none of our explanations are complete. They subsume things under heads wider or more familiar; but the last heads, whether of things or of their connections, are mere abstract genera, data which we just find in things and write down.

When, for example, we think that we have rationally explained the connection of the facts A and B by classing both under their common attribute x, it is obvious that we have really explained only so much of these items as *is x*. To explain the connection of choke-damp and suffocation by the lack of oxygen is to leave untouched all the other peculiarities both of choke-damp and of suffocation—such as convulsions and agony on the one hand, density and explosibility on the other. In a word, so far as A and B contain l, m, n, and o, p, q, respectively, in addition to x, they are not explained by x. Each additional particularity makes its distinct appeal. A single explanation of a fact only explains it from a single point of view. The entire fact is not accounted for until each and all of its characters have been classed with their likes elsewhere. To apply this now to the case of the universe, we see that the explanation of the world by molecular movements explains it only so far as it actually *is* such movements. To invoke the "Unknowable" explains only so much as is unknowable, "Thought" only so much as is thought, "God" only so much as is God. *Which* thought? *Which* God?—are questions that have to be answered by bringing in again the residual data from which the general term was abstracted. All those data that cannot be analytically identified with the attribute invoked as universal principle, remain as independent kinds or natures, associated empirically with the said attribute but devoid of rational kinship with it.

Hence the unsatisfactoriness of all our speculations. On the one hand, so far as they retain any multiplicity in their terms, they fail to get us out of the empirical sand-heap world; on the other, so far as they eliminate multiplicity the practical man despises their empty barrenness. The most they can say is that the elements of the world are such and such, and that each is identical with itself wherever found; but the question Where is it found? the practical man is left to answer by his own wit. Which, of all the essences, shall here and now be held the essence of this concrete thing, the fundamental philosophy never attempts to decide. We are thus led to the conclusion that the simple classification of things is, on the one hand, the best possible theoretic philosophy, but is, on the other, a most miserable and inadequate substitute for the fulness of the truth. It is a monstrous abridgment of life, which, like all abridgments is got by the absolute loss and casting out of real matter. This is why so few human beings truly care for philosophy. The particular determinations which she ignores are the real matter exciting needs, quite as potent and authoritative as hers. What does the moral enthusiast care for philosophical ethics? Why does the *Æsthetik* of every German philosopher appear to the artist an abomination of desolation?

> "Grau, theurer Freund, ist alle Theorie
> Und grün des Lebens goldner Baum."

The entire man, who feels all needs by turns, will take nothing as an equivalent for life but the fulness of living itself. Since the essences of things are as a matter of fact disseminated through the whole extent of time and space, it is in their spread-outness and alternation that he will enjoy them. When weary of the concrete clash and dust and pettiness, he will refresh himself by a bath in the eternal springs, or fortify himself by a look at the immutable natures. But he will only be a visitor, not a dweller in the region; he will never carry the philosophic yoke upon his shoulders, and when tired of the gray monotony of her problems and insipid spaciousness of her results, will always escape gleefully into the teeming and dramatic richness of the concrete world.

So our study turns back here to its beginning. Every way of classifying a thing is but a way of handling it for some particular purpose. Conceptions, "kinds," are teleological instruments. No abstract concept can be a valid substitute for a concrete reality except with reference to a particular interest in the conceiver. The interest of theoretic rationality, the relief of identification, is but one of a thousand human purposes. When others rear their heads, it must pack up its little bundle and retire till its turn recurs. The exaggerated dignity and value that philosophers have claimed for their solutions is thus greatly reduced. The only virtue their theoretic conception need have is simplicity, and a simple conception is an equivalent for the world only so far as the world is simple— the world meanwhile, whatever simplicity it may harbor, being also a mightily complex affair. Enough simplicity remains, however, and enough urgency in our craving to reach it, to make the theoretic function one of the most invincible of human impulses. The quest of the fewest elements of things is an ideal that some will follow, as long as there are men to think at all.

But suppose the goal attained. Suppose that at last we have a system unified in the sense that has been explained. Our world can now be conceived simply, and our mind enjoys the relief. Our universal concept has made the concrete chaos rational. But now I ask, Can that which is the ground of rationality in all else be itself properly called rational? It would seem at first sight that it might. One is tempted at any rate to say that, since the craving for rationality is appeased by the identification of one thing with another, a datum which left nothing else outstanding might quench that craving definitively, or be rational *in se*. No otherness being left to annoy us, we should sit down at peace. In other words, as the theoretic tranquillity of the boor results from his spinning no further considerations about his chaotic universe, so any datum whatever (provided it were simple, clear, and ultimate) ought to banish puzzle from the universe of the philosopher and confer peace, inasmuch as there would then be for him absolutely no further considerations to spin.

This in fact is what some persons think. Professor Bain says:

"A difficulty is solved, a mystery unriddled, when it can be shown to resemble something else; to be an example of a fact already known. Mystery is isolation, exception, or it may be apparent contradiction; the resolution of the mystery is found in assimilation, identity, fraternity. When all things are assimilated, so far as assimilation can go, so far as likeness holds, there is an end to explanation; there is an end to what the mind can do, or can intelligently desire. . . . The path of science, as exhibited in modern ages, is towards generality, wider and wider, until we reach the highest, the widest laws of every department of things; there explanation is finished, mystery ends, perfect vision is gained."

But, unfortunately, this first answer will not hold. Our mind is so wedded to the process of seeing an *other* beside every item of its experience, that when the notion of an absolute datum is presented to it, it goes through its usual procedure and remains pointing at the void beyond, as if in that lay further matter for contemplation. In short, it spins for itself the further positive consideration of a nonentity enveloping the being of its datum; and as that leads nowhere, back recoils the thought towards its datum again. But there is no natural bridge between nonentity and this particular datum, and the thought stands oscillating to and fro, wondering "Why was there anything but nonentity; why just this universal datum and not another?" and finds no end, in wandering mazes lost. Indeed, Bain's words are so untrue that in reflecting men it is just when the attempt to fuse the manifold into a single totality has been most successful, when the conception of the universe as a unique fact is nearest its perfection, that the craving for further explanation, the ontological wonder-sickness, arises in its extremest form. As Schopenhauer says, "The uneasiness which keeps the never-resting clock of metaphysics in motion, is the consciousness that the non-existence of this world is just as possible as its existence."

The notion of nonentity may thus be called the parent of the philosophic craving in its subtlest and profoundest sense. Absolute existence is absolute mystery, for its relations with the nothing remain unmediated to our understanding. One philosopher only has pretended to throw a logical bridge over this chasm. Hegel, by trying to show that nonentity and concrete being are linked together by a series of identities of a synthetic kind, binds everything conceivable into a unity, with no outlying notion to disturb the free rotary circulation of the mind within its bounds. Since such unchecked movement gives the feeling of rationality, he must be held, if he has succeeded, to have eternally and absolutely quenched all rational demands.

But for those who deem Hegel's heroic effort to have failed, nought remains but to confess that when all things have been unified to the supreme degree, the notion of a possible other than the actual may still haunt our imagination and prey upon our system. The bottom of being is left logically opaque to us, as something which we simply come upon and find, and about which (if we wish to act) we should pause and wonder as little as possible. The philosopher's logical tranquillity is thus in essence no other than the boor's. They differ only as to the point at which each refuses to let further considerations upset the absoluteness of the data he assumes. The boor does so immediately, and is liable at any moment to the ravages of many kinds of doubt. The philosopher does not do so till unity has been reached, and is warranted against the inroads of those considerations, but only practically, not essentially, secure from the blighting breath of the ultimate Why? If he cannot exorcise this question, he must ignore or blink it, and, assuming the data of his system as something given, and the gift as ultimate, simply proceed to a life of contemplation or of action based on it. There is no doubt that this acting on an opaque necessity is accompanied by a certain pleasure. See the reverence of Carlyle for brute fact: "There is an infinite significance in Fact." "Necessity," says Dühring, and he means not rational but given necessity, "is the last and highest point that we can reach. . . . It is not only the interest of ultimate and definitive knowledge, but also that of the feelings, to find a last repose and an ideal equilibrium in an uttermost datum which can simply not be other than it is."

Such is the attitude of ordinary men in their theism, God's fiat being in physics and morals such an uttermost datum. Such also is the attitude of all hard-minded analysts and *Verstandesmenschen*. Lotze, Renouvier, and Hodgson promptly say that of experience as a whole no account can be given, but neither seek to soften the abruptness of the confession nor to reconcile us with our impotence.

But mediating attempts may be made by more mystical minds. The peace of rationality may be sought through ecstasy when logic fails. To religious persons of every shade of doctrine moments come when the world, as it is, seems so divinely orderly, and the acceptance of it by the heart so rapturously complete, that intellectual questions vanish; nay, the intellect itself is hushed to sleep—as Wordsworth says, "thought is not; in enjoyment it expires." Ontological emotion so fills the soul that ontological speculation can no longer overlap it and put her girdle of interrogation-marks round existence. Even the least religious of men must have felt with Walt Whitman, when loafing on the grass on some transparent summer morning, that "swiftly arose and spread around him the peace and knowledge that pass all the argument of the earth." At such moments of energetic living we feel as if there were something diseased and contemptible, yea vile, in theoretic grubbing and brooding. In the eye of healthy sense the philosopher is at best a learned fool.

Since the heart can thus wall out the ultimate irrationality which the head ascertains, the erection of its procedure into a systematized method would be a philosophic achievement of first-rate importance. But as used by mystics hitherto it has lacked universality, being available for few persons and at few times, and even in these being apt to be followed by fits of reaction and dryness; and if men should agree that the mystical method is a subterfuge without logical pertinency, a plaster but no cure, and that the idea of nonentity can never be exorcised, empiricism will be the ultimate philosophy. Existence then will be a brute fact to which as a whole the emotion of ontologic wonder shall rightfully cleave, but remain eternally unsatisfied. Then wonderfulness or mysteriousness will be an essential attribute of the nature of things, and the exhibition and emphasizing of it will continue to be an ingredient in the philosophic industry of the race. Every generation will produce its Job, its Hamlet, its Faust, or its Sartor Resartus.

With this we seem to have considered the possibilities of purely theoretic rationality. But we saw at the outset that rationality meant only unimpeded mental function. Impediments that arise in the theoretic sphere might perhaps be avoided if the stream of mental action should leave that sphere betimes and pass into the practical. Let us therefore inquire what constitutes the feeling of rationality in its *practical* aspect. If thought is not to stand forever pointing at the universe in wonder, if its movement is to be diverted from the issueless channel of purely theoretic contemplation, let us ask what conception of the universe will awaken active impulses capable of effecting this diversion. A definition of the world which will give back to the mind the free motion which has been blocked in the purely contemplative path may so far make the world seem rational again.

Well, of two conceptions equally fit to satisfy the logical demand, that one which awakens the active impulses, or satisfies other æsthetic demands better than the other, will be accounted the more rational conception, and will deservedly prevail.

There is nothing improbable in the supposition that an analysis of the world may yield a number of formulæ, all consistent with the facts. In physical science different formulæ may explain the phenomena equally well—the one-fluid and the two-fluid theories of electricity, for example. Why may it not be so with the world? Why may there not be different points of view for surveying it, within each of which all data harmonize, and which the observer may therefore either choose between, or simply cumulate one upon another? A Beethoven string-quartet is truly, as someone has said, a scraping of horses' tails on cats' bowels, and may be exhaustively described in such terms; but the application of this description in no way precludes the simultaneous applicability of an entirely different description. Just so a thorough-going interpretation of the world in terms of mechanical sequence is compatible with its being interpreted teleologically, for the mechanism itself may be designed.

If, then, there were several systems excogitated, equally satisfying to our purely logical needs, they would still have to be passed in review, and approved or rejected by our æsthetic and practical nature. Can we define the tests of rationality which these parts of our nature would use?

Philosophers long ago observed the remarkable fact that mere familiarity with things is able to produce a feeling of their rationality. The empiricist school has been so much struck by this circumstance as to have laid it down that the feeling of rationality and the feeling of familiarity are one and the same thing, and that no other kind of rationality than this exists. The daily contemplation of phenomena juxtaposed in a certain order begets an acceptance of their connection, as absolute as the repose engendered by theoretic insight into their coherence. To explain a thing is to pass easily back to its antecedents; to know it is easily to foresee its consequents. Custom, which lets us do both, is thus the source of whatever rationality the thing may gain in our thought.

In the broad sense in which rationality was defined at the outset of this essay, it is perfectly apparent that custom must be one of its factors. We said that any perfectly fluent and easy thought was devoid of the sentiment of irrationality. Inasmuch then as custom acquaints us with all the relations of a thing, it teaches us to pass fluently from that thing to others, and *pro tanto* tinges it with the rational character.

Now there is one particular relation of greater practical importance than all the rest—I mean the relation of a thing to its future consequences. So long as an object is unusual, our expectations are baffled; they are fully determined as soon as it becomes familiar. I therefore propose this as the first practical requisite which a philosophic conception must satisfy: *It must, in a general way at least, banish uncertainty from the future.* The permanent presence of the sense of futurity in the mind has been strangely ignored by most writers, but the fact is that our consciousness at a given moment is never free from the ingredient of expectancy. Everyone knows how when a painful thing has to be undergone in the near future, the vague feeling that it is impending penetrates all our thought with uneasiness and subtly vitiates our mood even when it does not control our attention; it keeps us from being at rest, at home in the given present. The same is true when a great happiness awaits us. But when the future is neutral and perfectly certain, "we do not mind it," as we say, but give an undisturbed attention to the actual. Let now this haunting sense of futurity be thrown off its bearings or left without an object, and immediately uneasiness takes possession of the mind. But in every novel or unclassified experience this is just what occurs; we do not know what will come next; and novelty *per se* becomes a mental irritant, while custom *per se* is a mental sedative, merely because the one baffles whilst the other settles our expectations.

Every reader must feel the truth of this. What is meant by coming "to feel at home" in a new place, or with new people? It is simply that, at first, when we take up our quarters in a new room, we do not know what draughts may blow in upon our back, what doors may open, what forms may enter, what interesting objects may be found in cupboards and corners. When after a few days we have learned the range of all these possibilities, the feeling of strangeness disappears. And so it does with people, when we have got past the point of expecting any essentially new manifestations from their character.

The utility of this emotional effect of expectation is perfectly obvious; "natural selection," in fact, was bound to bring it about sooner or later. It is of the utmost practical importance to an animal that he should have prevision of the qualities of the objects that surround him, and especially that he should not come to rest in presence of circumstances that might be fraught either with peril or advantage—go to sleep, for example, on the brink of precipices, in the dens of enemies, or view with indifference some new-appearing object that might, if chased, prove an important addition to the larder. Novelty *ought* to irritate him. All curiosity has thus a practical genesis. We need only look at the physiognomy of a dog or a horse when a new object comes into his view, his mingled fascination and fear, to see that the element of conscious insecurity or perplexed expectation lies at the root of his emotion. A dog's curiosity about the movements of his master or a strange object only extends as far as the point of deciding what is going to happen next. That settled, curiosity is quenched. The dog quoted by Darwin, whose behavior in presence of a newspaper moved by the wind seemed to testify to a sense "of the supernatural," was merely exhibiting the irritation of an uncertain future. A newspaper which could move spontaneously was in itself so unexpected that the poor brute could not tell what new wonders the next moment might bring forth.

To turn back now to philosophy. An ultimate datum, even though it be logically unrationalized, will, if its quality is such as to define expectancy, be peacefully accepted by the mind; whilst if it leave the least opportunity for ambiguity in the future, it will to that extent cause mental uneasiness if not distress. Now in the ultimate explanations of the universe which the craving for rationality has elicited from the human mind, the demands of expectancy to be satisfied have always played a fundamental part. The term set up by philosophers as primordial has been one which banishes the incalculable. "Substance," for example, means, as Kant says, *das Beharrliche*, which will be as it has been, because its being is essential and eternal. And although we may not be able to prophesy in detail the future phenomena to which the substance shall give rise, we may set our minds at rest in a general way, when we have called the substance God, Perfection, Love, or Reason, by the reflection that whatever is in store for us can never at bottom be inconsistent with the character of this term; so that our attitude even towards the unexpected is in a general sense defined. Take again the notion of immortality, which for common people seems to be the touchstone of every philosophic or religious creed: what is this but a way of saying that the determination of expectancy is the essential factor of rationality? The wrath of science against miracles, of certain philosophers against the doctrine of free-will, has precisely the same root—dislike to admit any ultimate factor in things which may rout our prevision or upset the stability of our outlook.

Anti-substantialist writers strangely overlook this function in the doctrine of substance: "If there be such a *substratum*," says Mill, "suppose it at this instant miraculously annihilated, and let the sensations continue to occur in the same order, and how would the *substratum* be missed? By what signs should we be able to discover that its existence had terminated? Should we not have as much reason to believe that it still existed as we now have? And if we should not then be warranted in believing it, how can we be so now?" Truly enough, if we have already securely bagged our facts in a certain order, we can dispense with any further warrant for that order. But with regard to the facts yet to come the case is far different. It does not follow that if substance may be dropped from our conception of the irrecoverably past, it need be an equally empty complication to our notions of the future. Even if it were true that, for aught we know to the contrary, the substance might develop at any moment a wholly new set of attributes, the mere logical form of referring things to a substance would still (whether rightly or wrongly) remain accompanied by a feeling of rest and future confidence. In spite of the acutest nihilistic criticism, men will therefore always have a liking for any philosophy which explains things *per substantiam*.

A very natural reaction against the theosophizing conceit and hide-bound confidence in the upshot of things, which vulgarly optimistic minds display, has formed one factor of the scepticism of empiricists, who never cease to remind us of the reservoir of possibilities alien to our habitual experience which the cosmos may contain, and which, for any warrant we have to the contrary, may turn it inside out to-morrow. Agnostic substantialism like that of Mr. Spencer, whose Unknowable is not merely the unfathomable but the absolute-irrational, on which, if consistently represented in thought, it is of course impossible to count, performs the same function of rebuking a certain stagnancy and smugness in the manner in which the ordinary philistine feels his security. But considered as anything else than as reactions against an opposite excess, these philosophies of uncertainty cannot be acceptable; the general mind will fail to come to rest in their presence, and will seek for solutions of a more reassuring kind.

We may then, I think, with perfect confidence lay down as a first point gained in our inquiry, that a prime factor in the philosophic craving is the desire to have expectancy defined; and that no philosophy will definitively triumph which in an emphatic manner denies the possibility of gratifying this need.

We pass with this to the next great division of our topic. It is not sufficient for our satisfaction merely to know the future as determined, for it may be determined in either of many ways, agreeable or disagreeable. For a philosophy to succeed on a universal scale it must define the future *congruously with our spontaneous powers*. A philosophy may be unimpeachable in other respects, but either of two defects will be fatal to its universal acceptance. First, its ultimate principle must not be one that essentially baffles and disappoints our dearest desires and most cherished powers. A pessimistic principle like Schopenhauer's incurably vicious Will-substance, or Hartmann's wicked jack-of-all-trades the Unconscious, will perpetually call forth essays at other philosophies. Incompatibility of the future with their desires and active tendencies is, in fact, to most men a source of more fixed disquietude than uncertainty itself. Witness the attempts to overcome the "problem of evil," the "mystery of pain." There is no "problem of good."

But a second and worse defect in a philosophy than that of contradicting our active propensities is to give them no object whatever to press against. A philosophy whose principle is so incommensurate with our most intimate powers as to deny them all relevancy in universal affairs, as to annihilate their motives at one blow, will be even more unpopular than pessimism. Better face the enemy than the eternal Void! This is why materialism will always fail of universal adoption, however well it may fuse things into an atomistic unity, however clearly it may prophesy the future eternity. For materialism denies reality to the objects of almost all the impulses which we most cherish. The real *meaning* of the impulses, it says, is something which has no emotional interest for us whatever. Now what is called "extradition" is quite as characteristic of our emotions as of our senses: both point to an object as the cause of the present feeling. What an intensely objective reference lies in fear! In like manner an enraptured man and a dreary-feeling man are not simply aware of their subjective states; if they were, the force of their feelings would all evaporate. Both believe there is outward cause why they should feel as they do: either "it is a glad world! how good life is!" or "what a loathsome tedium is existence!" Any philosophy which annihilates the validity of the reference by explaining away its objects or translating them into terms of no emotional pertinency, leaves the mind with little to care or act for. This is the opposite condition from that of nightmare, but when acutely brought home to consciousness it produces a kindred horror. In nightmare we have motives to act, but no power; here we have powers, but no motives. A nameless *unheimlichkeit* comes over us at the thought of there being nothing eternal in our final purposes, in the objects of those loves and aspirations which are our deepest energies. The monstrously lopsided equation of the universe and its knower, which we postulate as the ideal of cognition, is perfectly paralleled by the no less lopsided equation of the universe and the *doer*. We demand in it a character for which our emotions and active propensities shall be a match. Small as we are, minute as is the point by which the cosmos impinges upon each one of us, each one desires to feel that his reaction at that point is congruous with the demands of the vast whole — that he balances the latter, so to speak, and is able to do what it expects of him. But as his abilities to do lie wholly in the line of his natural propensities; as he enjoys reacting with such emotions as fortitude, hope, rapture, admiration, earnestness, and the like; and as he very unwillingly reacts with fear, disgust, despair, or doubt — a philosophy which should only legitimate emotions of the latter sort would be sure to leave the mind a prey to discontent and craving.

It is far too little recognized how entirely the intellect is built up of practical interests. The theory of evolution is beginning to do very good service by its reduction of all mentality to the type of reflex action. Cognition, in this view, is but a fleeting moment, a cross-section at a certain point, of what in its totality is a motor phenomenon. In the lower forms of life no one will pretend that cognition is anything more than a guide to appropriate action. The germinal question concerning things brought for the first time before consciousness is not the theoretic "What is that?" but the practical "Who goes there?" or rather, as Horwicz has admirably put it, "What is to be done?"—"Was fang' ich an?" In all our discussions about the intelligence of lower animals, the only test we use is that of their *acting* as if for a purpose. Cognition, in short, is incomplete until discharged in act; and although it is true that the later mental development, which attains its maximum through the hypertrophied cerebrum of man, gives birth to a vast amount of theoretic activity over and above that which is immediately ministerial to practice, yet the earlier claim is only postponed, not effaced, and the active nature asserts its rights to the end.

When the cosmos in its totality is the object offered to consciousness, the relation is in no whit altered. React on it we must in some congenial way. It was a deep instinct in Schopenhauer which led him to reinforce his pessimistic argumentation by a running volley of invective against the practical man and his requirements. No hope for pessimism unless he is slain!

Helmholtz's immortal works on the eye and ear are to a great extent little more than a commentary on the law that practical utility wholly determines which parts of our sensations we shall be aware of, and which parts we shall ignore. We notice or discriminate an ingredient of sense only so far as we depend upon it to modify our actions. We *comprehend* a thing when we synthetize it by identity with another thing. But the other great department of our understanding, *acquaintance* (the two departments being recognized in all languages by the antithesis of such words as *wissen* and *kennen*; *scire* and *noscere*, etc.), what is that also but a synthesis—a synthesis of a passive perception with a certain tendency to reaction? We are acquainted with a thing as soon as we have learned how to behave towards it, or how to meet the behavior which we expect from it. Up to that point it is still "strange" to us.

If there be anything at all in this view, it follows that however vaguely a philosopher may define the ultimate universal datum, he cannot be said to leave it unknown to us so long as he in the slightest degree pretends that our emotional or active attitude towards it should be of one sort rather than another. He who says "life is real, life is earnest," however much he may speak of the fundamental mysteriousness of things, gives a distinct definition to that mysteriousness by ascribing to it the right to claim from us the particular mood called seriousness—which means the willingness to live with energy, though energy bring pain. The same is true of him who says that all is vanity. For indefinable as the predicate "vanity" may be *in se*, it is clearly something that permits anæsthesia, mere escape from suffering, to be our rule of life. There can be no greater incongruity than for a disciple of Spencer to proclaim with one breath that the substance of things is unknowable, and with the next that the thought of it should inspire us with awe, reverence, and a willingness to add our co-operative push in the direction towards which its manifestations seem to be drifting. The unknowable may be unfathomed, but if it make such distinct demands upon our activity we surely are not ignorant of its essential quality.

If we survey the field of history and ask what feature all great periods of revival, of expansion of the human mind, display in common, we shall find, I think, simply this: that each and all of them have said to the human being, "The inmost nature of the reality is congenial to *powers* which you possess." In what did the emancipating message of primitive Christianity consist but in the announcement that God recognizes those weak and tender impulses which paganism had so rudely overlooked? Take repentance: the man who can do nothing rightly can at least repent of his failures. But for paganism this faculty of repentance was a pure supernumerary, a straggler too late for the fair. Christianity took it, and made it the one power within us which appealed straight to the heart of God. And after the night of the middle ages had so long branded with obloquy even the generous impulses of the flesh, and defined the reality to be such that only slavish natures could commune with it, in what did the *sursum corda* of the platonizing renaissance lie but in the proclamation that the archetype of verity in things laid claim on the widest activity of our whole æsthetic being? What were Luther's mission and Wesley's but appeals to powers which even the meanest of men might carry with them—faith and self-despair—but which were personal, requiring no priestly in-

termediation, and which brought their owner face to face
with God? What caused the wildfire influence of Rousseau
but the assurance he gave that man's nature was in harmony
with the nature of things, if only the paralyzing corruptions
of custom would stand from between? How did Kant and
Fichte, Goethe and Schiller, inspire their time with cheer, except by saying, "Use all your powers; that is the only obedience the universe exacts"? And Carlyle with his gospel of
work, of fact, of veracity, how does he move us except by
saying that the universe imposes no tasks upon us but such as
the most humble can perform? Emerson's creed that everything that ever was or will be is here in the enveloping now;
that man has but to obey himself—"He who will rest in what
he *is*, is a part of Destiny"—is in like manner nothing but an
exorcism of all scepticism as to the pertinency of one's natural
faculties.

In a word, "Son of Man, *stand upon thy feet* and I will speak
unto thee!" is the only revelation of truth to which the solving epochs have helped the disciple. But that has been enough
to satisfy the greater part of his rational need. *In se* and *per se*
the universal essence has hardly been more defined by any of
these formulas than by the agnostic x; but the mere assurance
that my powers, such as they are, are not irrelevant to it, but
pertinent; that it speaks to them and will in some way recognize their reply; that I can be a match for it if I will, and not a
footless waif—suffices to make it rational to my feeling in the
sense given above. Nothing could be more absurd than to
hope for the definitive triumph of any philosophy which
should refuse to legitimate, and to legitimate in an emphatic
manner, the more powerful of our emotional and practical
tendencies. Fatalism, whose solving word in all crises of behavior is "all striving is vain," will never reign supreme, for
the impulse to take life strivingly is indestructible in the race.
Moral creeds which speak to that impulse will be widely successful in spite of in_{consistency}, vagueness, and shadowy determination of expect ncy. Man needs a rule for his will, and
will invent one if one be not given him.

But now observe a most important consequence. Men's active impulses are so differently mixed that a philosophy fit in

this respect for Bismarck will almost certainly be unfit for a valetudinarian poet. In other words, although one can lay down in advance the rule that a philosophy which utterly denies all fundamental ground for seriousness, for effort, for hope, which says the nature of things is radically alien to human nature, can never succeed—one cannot in advance say what particular dose of hope, or of gnosticism of the nature of things, the definitively successful philosophy shall contain. In short, it is almost certain that personal temperament will here make itself felt, and that although all men will insist on being spoken to by the universe in some way, few will insist on being spoken to in just the same way. We have here, in short, the sphere of what Matthew Arnold likes to call *Aberglaube*, legitimate, inexpugnable, yet doomed to eternal variations and disputes.

Take idealism and materialism as examples of what I mean, and suppose for a moment that both give a conception of equal theoretic clearness and consistency, and that both determine our expectations equally well. Idealism will be chosen by a man of one emotional constitution, materialism by another. At this very day all sentimental natures, fond of conciliation and intimacy, tend to an idealistic faith. Why? Because idealism gives to the nature of things such kinship with our personal selves. Our own thoughts are what we are most at home with, what we are least afraid of. To say then that the universe essentially is thought, is to say that I myself, potentially at least, am all. There is no radically alien corner, but an all-pervading *intimacy*. Now in certain sensitively egotistic minds this conception of reality is sure to put on a narrow, close, sick-room air. Everything sentimental and priggish will be consecrated by it. That element in reality which every strong man of common-sense willingly feels there because it calls forth powers that he owns—the rough, harsh, sea-wave, north-wind element, the denier of persons, the democratizer—is banished because it jars too much on the desire for communion. Now it is the very enjoyment of this element that throws many men upon the materialistic or agnostic hypothesis, as a polemic reaction against the contrary extreme. They sicken at a life wholly constituted of intimacy. There is an overpowering desire at moments to escape personality, to revel in the action of forces that have no respect for our ego, to let the tides flow, even though they flow over us. The strife of these two kinds of mental temper will, I think, always be seen in philosophy. Some men will keep insisting on the reason, the atonement, that lies in the heart of things, and that we can act *with*; others, on the opacity of brute fact that we must react *against*.

Now there is one element of our active nature which the Christian religion has emphatically recognized, but which philosophers as a rule have with great insincerity tried to huddle out of sight in their pretension to found systems of absolute certainty. I mean the element of faith. Faith means belief in something concerning which doubt is still theoretically possible; and as the test of belief is willingness to act, one may say that faith is the readiness to act in a cause the prosperous issue of which is not certified to us in advance. It is in fact the same moral quality which we call courage in practical affairs; and there will be a very widespread tendency in men of vigorous nature to enjoy a certain amount of uncertainty in their philosophic creed, just as risk lends a zest to worldly activity. Absolutely certified philosophies seeking the *inconcussum* are fruits of mental natures in which the passion for identity (which we saw to be but one factor of the rational appetite) plays an abnormally exclusive part. In the average man, on the contrary, the power to trust, to risk a little beyond the literal evidence, is an essential function. Any mode of conceiving the universe which makes an appeal to this generous power, and makes the man seem as if he were individually helping to create the actuality of the truth whose metaphysical reality he is willing to assume, will be sure to be responded to by large numbers.

The necessity of faith as an ingredient in our mental attitude is strongly insisted on by the scientific philosophers of the present day; but by a singularly arbitrary caprice they say that it is only legitimate when used in the interests of one particular proposition—the proposition, namely, that the course of nature is uniform. That nature will follow to-morrow the same laws that she follows to-day is, they all admit, a truth which no man can *know*; but in the interests of cognition as well as of action we must postulate or assume it. As Helmholtz says: "Hier gilt nur der eine Rath: vertraue und handle!" And Professor Bain urges: "Our only error is in proposing to give any reason or justification of the postulate, or to treat it other wise than as begged at the very outset."

With regard to all other possible truths, however, a number of our most influential contemporaries think that an attitude of faith is not only illogical but shameful. Faith in a religious dogma for which there is no outward proof, but which we are tempted to postulate for our emotional interests, just as we postulate the uniformity of nature for our intellectual interests, is branded by Professor Huxley as "the lowest depth of immorality." Citations of this kind from leaders of the modern *Aufklärung* might be multiplied almost indefinitely. Take Professor Clifford's article on the "Ethics of Belief." He calls it "guilt" and "sin" to believe even the truth without "scientific evidence." But what is the use of being a genius, unless *with the same scientific evidence* as other men, one can reach more truth than they? Why does Clifford fearlessly proclaim his belief in the conscious-automaton theory, although the "proofs" before him are the same which make Mr. Lewes reject it? Why does he believe in primordial units of "mind-stuff" on evidence which would seem quite worthless to Professor Bain? Simply because, like every human being of the slightest mental originality, he is peculiarly sensitive to evidence that bears in some one direction. It is utterly hopeless to try to exorcise such sensitiveness by calling it the disturbing subjective factor, and branding it as the root of all evil. "Subjective" be it called! and "disturbing" to those whom it foils! But if it helps those who, as Cicero says, "vim naturæ magis sentiunt," it is good and not evil. Pretend what we may, the whole man within us is at work when we form our philosophical opinions. Intellect, will, taste, and passion co-operate just as they do in practical affairs; and lucky it is if the passion be not something as petty as a love of personal conquest over the philosopher across the way. The absurd abstraction of an intellect verbally formulating all its evidence and carefully estimating the probability thereof by a vulgar fraction by the size of whose denominator and numerator alone it is swayed, is ideally as inept as it is actually impossible.

It is almost incredible that men who are themselves working philosophers should pretend that any philosophy can be, or ever has been, constructed without the help of personal preference, belief, or divination. How have they succeeded in so stultifying their sense for the living facts of human nature as not to perceive that every philosopher, or man of science either, whose initiative counts for anything in the evolution of thought, has taken his stand on a sort of dumb conviction that the truth must lie in one direction rather than another, and a sort of preliminary assurance that his notion can be made to work; and has borne his best fruit in trying to make it work? These mental instincts in different men are the spontaneous variations upon which the intellectual struggle for existence is based. The fittest conceptions survive, and with them the names of their champions shining to all futurity.

The coil is about us, struggle as we may. The only escape from faith is mental nullity. What we enjoy most in a Huxley or a Clifford is not the professor with his learning, but the human personality ready to go in for what it feels to be right, in spite of all appearances. The concrete man has but one interest—to be right. That for him is the art of all arts, and all means are fair which help him to it. Naked he is flung into the world, and between him and nature there are no rules of civilized warfare. The rules of the scientific game, burdens of proof, presumptions, *experimenta crucis*, complete inductions, and the like, are only binding on those who enter that game. As a matter of fact we all more or less do enter it, because it helps us to our end. But if the means presume to frustrate the end and call us cheats for being right in advance of their slow aid, by guesswork or by hook or crook, what shall we say of them? Were all of Clifford's works, except the "Ethics of Belief," forgotten, he might well figure in future treatises on psychology in place of the somewhat threadbare instance of the miser who has been led by the association of ideas to prefer his gold to all the goods he might buy therewith.

In short, if I am born with such a superior general reaction to evidence that I can guess right and act accordingly, and gain all that comes of right action, while my less gifted neighbor (paralyzed by his scruples and waiting for more evidence which he dares not anticipate, much as he longs to) still stands shivering on the brink, by what law shall I be forbidden to reap the advantages of my superior native sensitiveness? Of course I yield to my belief in such a case as this or distrust it, alike at my peril, just as I do in any of the great practical decisions of life. If my inborn faculties are good, I am a prophet; if poor, I am a failure: nature spews me out of her mouth, and there is an end of me. In the total game of life we stake our persons all the while; and if in its theoretic part our persons will help us to a conclusion, surely we should also stake them there, however inarticulate they may be.[2]

But in being myself so very articulate in proving what to all readers with a sense for reality will seem a platitude, am I not wasting words? We cannot live or think at all without some degree of faith. Faith is synonymous with working hypothesis. The only difference is that while some hypotheses can be refuted in five minutes, others may defy ages. A chemist who conjectures that a certain wall-paper contains arsenic, and has faith enough to lead him to take the trouble to put some of it into a hydrogen bottle, finds out by the results of his action whether he was right or wrong. But theories like that of Darwin, or that of the kinetic constitution of matter, may exhaust the labors of generations in their corroboration, each tester of their truth proceeding in this simple way—that he acts as if it were true, and expects the result to disappoint him if his assumption is false. The longer disappointment is delayed, the stronger grows his faith in his theory.

[2]At most, the command laid upon us by science to believe nothing not yet verified by the senses is a prudential rule intended to maximize our right thinking and minimize our errors *in the long run*. In the particular instance we must frequently lose truth by obeying it; but on the whole we are safer if we follow it consistently, for we are sure to cover our losses with our gains. It is like those gambling and insurance rules based on probability, in which we secure ourselves against losses in detail by hedging on the total run. But this hedging philosophy requires that long run should be there; and this makes it inapplicable to the question of religious faith as the latter comes home to the individual man. He plays the game of life not to escape losses, for he brings nothing with him to lose; he plays it for gains; and it is now or never with him, for the long run which exists indeed for humanity, is not there for him. Let him doubt, believe, or deny, he runs his risk, and has the natural right to choose which one it shall be.

Now in such questions as God, immortality, absolute morality, and free-will, no non-papal believer at the present day
pretends his faith to be of an essentially different complexion;
he can always doubt his creed. But his intimate persuasion is
that the odds in its favor are strong enough to warrant him in
acting all along on the assumption of its truth. His corroboration or repudiation by the nature of things may be deferred
until the day of judgment. The uttermost he now means is
something like this: "I *expect* then to triumph with tenfold
glory; but if it should turn out, as indeed it may, that I have
spent my days in a fool's paradise, why, better have been the
dupe of *such* a dreamland than the cunning reader of a world
like that which then beyond all doubt unmasks itself to view."
In short, we *go in* against materialism very much as we should
go in, had we a chance, against the second French empire or
the Church of Rome, or any other system of things towards
which our repugnance is vast enough to determine energetic
action, but too vague to issue in distinct argumentation. Our
reasons are ludicrously incommensurate with the volume of
our feeling, yet on the latter we unhesitatingly act.

Now I wish to show what to my knowledge has never been
clearly pointed out, that belief (as measured by action) not
only does and must continually outstrip scientific evidence,
but that there is a certain class of truths of whose reality belief
is a factor as well as a confessor; and that as regards this class
of truths faith is not only licit and pertinent, but essential and
indispensable. The truths cannot become true till our faith has
made them so.

Suppose, for example, that I am climbing in the Alps, and
have had the ill-luck to work myself into a position from
which the only escape is by a terrible leap. Being without
similar experience, I have no evidence of my ability to perform it successfully; but hope and confidence in myself make
me sure I shall not miss my aim, and nerve my feet to execute
what without those subjective emotions would perhaps have
been impossible. But suppose that, on the contrary, the emotions of fear and mistrust preponderate; or suppose that, having just read the "Ethics of Belief," I feel it would be sinful to
act upon an assumption unverified by previous experience—

why, then I shall hesitate so long that at last, exhausted and trembling, and launching myself in a moment of despair, I miss my foothold and roll into the abyss. In this case (and it is one of an immense class) the part of wisdom clearly is to believe what one desires; for the belief is one of the indispensable preliminary conditions of the realization of its object. *There are then cases where faith creates its own verification.* Believe, and you shall be right, for you shall save yourself; doubt, and you shall again be right, for you shall perish. The only difference is that to believe is greatly to your advantage.

The future movements of the stars or the facts of past history are determined now once for all, whether I like them or not. They are given irrespective of my wishes, and in all that concerns truths like these subjective preference should have no part; it can only obscure the judgment. But in every fact into which there enters an element of personal contribution on my part, as soon as this personal contribution demands a certain degree of subjective energy which, in its turn, calls for a certain amount of faith in the result—so that, after all, the future fact is conditioned by my present faith in it—how trebly asinine would it be for me to deny myself the use of the subjective method, the method of belief based on desire!

In every proposition whose bearing is universal (and such are all the propositions of philosophy), the acts of the subject and their consequences throughout eternity should be included in the formula. If M represent the entire world *minus* the reaction of the thinker upon it, and if $M + x$ represent the absolutely total matter of philosophic propositions (x standing for the thinker's reaction and its results)—what would be a universal truth if the term x were of one complexion, might become egregious error if x altered its character. Let it not be said that x is too infinitesimal a component to change the character of the immense whole in which it lies imbedded. Everything depends on the point of view of the philosophic proposition in question. If we have to define the universe from the point of view of sensibility, the critical material for our judgment lies in the animal kingdom, insignificant as that is, quantitatively considered. The moral definition of the world may depend on phenomena more restricted still in range. In short, many a long phrase may have its sense reversed by the addition of three letters, *n-o-t*; many a monstrous mass have its unstable equilibrium discharged one way or the other by a feather weight that falls.

Let us make this clear by a few examples. The philosophy of evolution offers us to-day a new criterion to serve as an ethical test between right and wrong. Previous criteria, it says, being subjective, have left us still floundering in variations of opinion and the *status belli*. Here is a criterion which is objective and fixed: *That is to be called good which is destined to prevail or survive*. But we immediately see that this standard can only remain objective by leaving myself and my conduct out. If what prevails and survives does so by my help, and cannot do so without that help; if something else will prevail in case I alter my conduct—how can I possibly now, conscious of alternative courses of action open before me, either of which I may suppose capable of altering the path of events, decide which course to take by asking what path events will follow? If they follow my direction, evidently my direction cannot wait on them. The only possible manner in which an evolutionist can use his standard is the obsequious method of forecasting the course society would take *but for him*, and then putting an extinguisher on all personal idiosyncrasies of desire and interest, and with bated breath and tiptoe tread following as straight as may be at the tail, and bringing up the rear of everything. Some pious creatures may find a pleasure in this; but not only does it violate our general wish to lead and not to follow (a wish which is surely not immoral if we but lead aright), but if it be treated as every ethical principle must be treated—namely, as a rule good for all men alike—its general observance would lead to its practical refutation by bringing about a general deadlock. Each good man hanging back and waiting for orders from the rest, absolute stagnation would ensure. Happy, then, if a few unrighteous ones contribute an initiative which sets things moving again!

All this is no caricature. That the course of destiny may be altered by individuals no wise evolutionist ought to doubt. Everything for him has small beginnings, has a bud which may be "nipped," and nipped by a feeble force. Human races and tendencies follow the law, and have also small beginnings. The best, according to evolution, is that which has the biggest endings. Now, if a present race of men, enlightened in the evolutionary philosophy, and able to forecast the future, were able to discern in a tribe arising near them the potentiality of future supremacy; were able to see that their own race would eventually be wiped out of existence by the newcomers if the expansion of these were left unmolested—these present sages would have two courses open to them, either perfectly in harmony with the evolutionary test: Strangle the new race *now*, and ours survives; help the new race, and *it* survives. In both cases the action is right as measured by the evolutionary standard—it is action for the winning side.

Thus the evolutionist foundation of ethics is purely objective only to the herd of nullities whose votes count for zero in the march of events. But for others, leaders of opinion or potentates, and in general those to whose actions position or genius gives a far-reaching import, and to the rest of us, each in his measure—whenever we espouse a cause we contribute to the determination of the evolutionary standard of right. The truly wise disciple of this school will then admit faith as an ultimate ethical factor. Any philosophy which makes such questions as What is the ideal type of humanity? What shall be reckoned virtues? What conduct is good? depend on the question What is going to succeed?—must needs fall back on personal belief as one of the ultimate conditions of the truth. For again and again success depends on energy of act; energy again depends on faith that we shall not fail; and that faith in turn on the faith that we are right—which faith thus verifies itself.

Take as an example the question of optimism or pessimism, which makes so much noise just now in Germany. Every human being must sometime decide for himself whether life is worth living. Suppose that in looking at the world and seeing how full it is of misery, of old age, of wickedness and pain, and how unsafe is his own future, he yields to the pessimistic conclusion, cultivates disgust and dread, ceases striving, and finally commits suicide. He thus adds to the mass M of mundane phenomena, independent of his subjectivity, the subjective complement x, which makes of the whole an utterly black picture illumined by no gleam of good. Pessimism completed, verified by his moral reaction and the deed in which this ends, is true beyond a doubt. $M + x$ expresses a state of things totally bad. The man's belief supplied all that was lacking to make it so, and now that it is made so the belief was right.

But now suppose that with the same evil facts M, the man's reaction x is exactly reversed; suppose that instead of giving way to the evil he braves it, and finds a sterner, more wonderful joy than any passive pleasure can yield in triumphing over pain and defying fear; suppose he does this successfully, and however thickly evils crowd upon him proves his dauntless subjectivity to be more than their match—will not everyone confess that the bad character of the M is here the *conditio sine qua non* of the good character of the x? Will not everyone instantly declare a world fitted only for fair-weather human beings susceptible of every passive enjoyment, but without independence, courage, or fortitude, to be from a moral point of view incommensurably inferior to a world framed to elicit from the man every form of triumphant endurance and conquering moral energy? As James Hinton says:

"Little inconveniences, exertions, pains; these are the only things in which we rightly feel our life at all. If these be not there, existence becomes worthless or worse; success in putting them all away is fatal. So it is men engage in athletic sports, spend their holidays in climbing up mountains, find nothing so enjoyable as that which taxes their endurance and their energy. This is the way we are made, I say. It may or may not be a mystery or a paradox; it is a fact. Now this enjoyment in endurance is just according to the intensity of the life; the more physical vigour and balance, the more endurance can be made an element of satisfaction. A sick man cannot stand it. The line of enjoyable suffering is not a fixed one; it fluctuates with the perfectness of the life. . . . That our pains are, as they are, unendurable, awful, overwhelming, crushing, not to be borne save in misery and dumb impatience, which utter exhaustion alone makes patient,—that our pains are thus unendurable, means not that they are too great, but that *we are sick*. We have not got our proper life. . . . So you perceive pain is no more necessarily an evil, but an essential element of the highest good."[3]

But the highest good can be achieved only by our getting

[3] *Life of James Hinton*, pp. 172, 173. See also the excellent chapter on "Faith and Sight" in the *Mystery of Matter*, by J. Allanson Picton. Hinton's *Mystery of Pain* will undoubtedly always remain the classical utterance on this subject.

our proper life; and that can come about only by help of a moral energy born of the faith that in some way or other we shall succeed in getting it if we try pertinaciously enough. This world *is* good, we must say, since it is what we make it—and we shall make it good. How can we exclude from the cognition of a truth a faith which is involved in the creation of the truth? M has its character indeterminate, susceptible of forming part of a thorough-going pessimism on the one hand, or of a meliorism, a moral (as distinguished from a sensual) optimism on the other. All depends on the character of the personal contribution x. Wherever the facts to be formulated contain such a contribution, we may logically, legitimately, and inexpugnably believe what we desire. The belief creates its verification. The thought becomes literally father to the fact, as the wish was father to the thought.[4]

Let us now turn to the radical question of life—the question whether this be at bottom a moral or an unmoral universe—and see whether the method of faith may legitimately have a place there. It is really the question of materialism. Is the world a simple brute actuality, an existence *de facto* about which the deepest thing that can be said is that it happens so to be; or is the judgment of *better* or *worse*, of *ought*, as intimately pertinent to phenomena as the simple judgment *is* or *is not*? The materialistic theorists say that judgments of worth are themselves mere matters of fact; that the words "good" and "bad" have no sense apart from subjective passions and interests which we may, if we please, play fast and loose with at will, so far as any duty of ours to the non-human universe is concerned. Thus, when a materialist says it is better for him to suffer great inconvenience than to break a promise, he only means that his social interests have become so knit up with

---

[4]Observe that in all this not a word has been said of free-will. It all applies as well to a predetermined as to an indeterminate universe. If $M + x$ is fixed in advance, the belief which leads to x and the desire which prompts the belief are also fixed. But fixed or not, these subjective states form a phenomenal condition necessarily preceding the facts; necessarily constitutive, therefore, of the truth $M + x$ which we seek. If, however, free acts be possible, a faith in their possibility, by augmenting the moral energy which gives them birth, will increase their frequency in a given individual.

keeping faith that, those interests once being granted, it *is* better for him to keep the promise in spite of everything. But the interests themselves are neither right nor wrong, except possibly with reference to some ulterior order of interests which themselves again are mere subjective data without character, either good or bad.

For the absolute moralists, on the contrary, the interests are not there merely to be felt—they are to be believed in and obeyed. Not only is it best for my social interests to keep my promise, but best for me to have those interests, and best for the cosmos to have this me. Like the old woman in the story who described the world as resting on a rock, and then explained that rock to be supported by another rock, and finally when pushed with questions said it was rocks all the way down—he who believes this to be a radically moral universe must hold the moral order to rest either on an absolute and ultimate *should*, or on a series of *shoulds* all the way down.[5]

The practical difference between this objective sort of moralist and the other one is enormous. The subjectivist in morals, when his moral feelings are at war with the facts about him, is always free to seek harmony by toning down the sensitiveness of the feelings. Being mere data, neither good nor evil in themselves, he may pervert them or lull them to sleep by any means at his command. Truckling, compromise, time-serving, capitulations of conscience, are conventionally opprobrious names for what, if successfully carried out, would be on his principles by far the easiest and most praiseworthy mode of bringing about that harmony between inner and outer relations which is all that he means by good. The absolute moralist, on the other hand, when his interests clash with the world, is not free to gain harmony by sacrificing the ideal interests. According to him, these latter should be as they are and not otherwise. Resistance then, poverty, martyrdom if need be, tragedy in a word—such are the solemn feasts of his inward faith. Not that the contradiction

[5]In either case, as a later essay explains (see p. 601), the *should* which the moralist regards as binding upon *him* must be rooted in the feeling of some other thinker, or collection of thinkers, to whose demands he individually bows.

between the two men occurs every day; in commonplace matters all moral schools agree. It is only in the lonely emergencies of life that our creed is tested: then routine maxims fail, and we fall back on our gods. It cannot then be said that the question Is this a moral world? is a meaningless and unverifiable question because it deals with something non-phenomenal. Any question is full of meaning to which, as here, contrary answers lead to contrary behavior. And it seems as if in answering such a question as this we might proceed exactly as does the physical philosopher in testing an hypothesis. He deduces from the hypothesis an experimental action, x; this he adds to the facts M already existing. It fits them if the hypothesis be true; if not, there is discord. The results of the action corroborate or refute the idea from which it flowed. So here: the verification of the theory which you may hold as to the objectively moral character of the world can consist only in this—that if you proceed to act upon your theory it will be reversed by nothing that later turns up as your action's fruit; it will harmonize so well with the entire drift of experience that the latter will, as it were, adopt it, or at most give it an ampler interpretation, without obliging you in any way to change the essence of its formulation. If this be an objectively moral universe, all acts that I make on that assumption, all expectations that I ground on it, will tend more and more completely to interdigitate with the phenomena already existing. $M + x$ will be in accord; and the more I live, and the more the fruits of my activity come to light, the more satisfactory the consensus will grow. Whilst if it be not such a moral universe, and I mistakenly assume that it is, the course of experience will throw ever new impediments in the way of my belief, and become more and more difficult to express in its language. Epicycle upon epicycle of subsidiary hypothesis will have to be invoked to give to the discrepant terms a temporary appearance of squaring with each other; but at last even this resource will fail.

If, on the other hand, I rightly assume the universe to be not moral, in what does my verification consist? It is that by letting moral interests sit lightly, by disbelieving that there is any duty about *them* (since duty obtains only as *between* them and other phenomena), and so throwing them over if I find it hard to get them satisfied—it is that by refusing to take up a tragic attitude, I deal in the long-run most satisfactorily with the facts of life. "All is vanity" is here the last word of wisdom. Even though in certain limited series there may be a great appearance of seriousness, he who in the main treats things with a degree of good-natured scepticism and radical levity will find that the practical fruits of his epicurean hypothesis verify it more and more, and not only save him from pain but do honor to his sagacity. Whilst, on the other hand, he who contrary to reality stiffens himself in the notion that certain things absolutely should be, and rejects the truth that at bottom it makes no difference what is, will find himself evermore thwarted and perplexed and bemuddled by the facts of the world, and his tragic disappointment will, as experience accumulates, seem to drift farther and farther away from that final atonement or reconciliation which certain partial tragedies often get.

Anæsthesia is the watchword of the moral sceptic brought to bay and put to his trumps. *Energy* is that of the moralist. Act on my creed, cries the latter, and the results of your action will prove the creed true, and that the nature of things is earnest infinitely. Act on mine, says the epicurean, and the results will prove that seriousness is but a superficial glaze upon a world of fundamentally trivial import. You and your acts and the nature of things will be alike enveloped in a single formula, a universal *vanitas vanitatum*.

For the sake of simplicity I have written as if the verification might occur in the life of a single philosopher—which is manifestly untrue, since the theories still face each other, and the facts of the world give countenance to both. Rather should we expect, that, in a question of this scope, the experience of the entire human race must make the verification, and that all the evidence will not be "in" till the final integration of things, when the last man has had his say and contributed his share to the still unfinished x. Then the proof will be complete; then it will appear without doubt whether the moralistic x has filled up the gap which alone kept the M of the world from forming an even and harmonious unity, or whether the non-moralistic x has given the finishing touches which were alone needed to make the M appear outwardly as vain as it inwardly was.

But if this be so, is it not clear that the facts M, taken *per se*, are inadequate to justify a conclusion either way in advance of my action? My action is the complement which, by proving congruous or not, reveals the latent nature of the mass to which it is applied. The world may in fact be likened unto a lock, whose inward nature, moral or unmoral, will never reveal itself to our simply expectant gaze. The positivists, forbidding us to make any assumptions regarding it, condemn us to eternal ignorance, for the "evidence" which they wait for can never come so long as we are passive. But nature has put into our hands two keys, by which we may test the lock. If we try the moral key *and it fits*, it is a moral lock. If we try the unmoral key and *it* fits, it is an unmoral lock. I cannot possibly conceive of any other sort of "evidence" or "proof" than this. It is quite true that the co-operation of generations is needed to educe it. But in these matters the solidarity (so called) of the human race is a patent fact. The essential thing to notice is that our active preference is a legitimate part of the game—that it is our plain business as men to try one of the keys, and the one in which we most confide. If then the proof exist not till I have acted, and I must needs in acting run the risk of being wrong, how can the popular science professors be right in objurgating in me as infamous a "credulity" which the strict logic of the situation requires? If this really be a moral universe; if by my acts I be a factor of its destinies; if to believe where I may doubt be itself a moral act analogous to voting for a side not yet sure to win—by what right shall they close in upon me and steadily negate the deepest conceivable function of my being by their preposterous command that I shall stir neither hand nor foot, but remain balancing myself in eternal and insoluble doubt? Why, doubt itself is a decision of the widest practical reach, if only because we may miss by doubting what goods we might be gaining by espousing the winning side. But more than that! it is often practically impossible to distinguish doubt from dogmatic negation. If I refuse to stop a murder because I am in doubt whether it be not justifiable homicide, I am virtually abetting the crime. If I refuse to bale out a boat because I am in doubt whether my efforts will keep her afloat, I am really helping to sink her. If in the mountain precipice I doubt my right to risk a leap, I actively connive at my destruction. He who commands himself not to be credulous of God, of duty, of freedom, of immortality, may again and again be indistinguishable from him who dogmatically denies them. Scepticism in moral matters is an active ally of immorality. Who is not for is against. The universe will have no neutrals in these questions. In theory as in practice, dodge or hedge, or talk as we like about a wise scepticism, we are really doing volunteer military service for one side or the other.

Yet obvious as this necessity practically is, thousands of innocent magazine readers lie paralyzed and terrified in the network of shallow negations which the leaders of opinion have thrown over their souls. All they need to be free and hearty again in the exercise of their birthright is that these fastidious vetoes should be swept away. All that the human heart wants is its chance. It will willingly forego certainty in universal matters if only it can be allowed to feel that in them it has that same inalienable right to run risks, which no one dreams of refusing to it in the pettiest practical affairs. And if I, in these last pages, like the mouse in the fable, have gnawed a few of the strings of the sophistical net that has been binding down its lion-strength, I shall be more than rewarded for my pains.

To sum up: No philosophy will permanently be deemed rational by all men which (in addition to meeting logical demands) does not to some degree pretend to determine expectancy, and in a still greater degree make a direct appeal to all those powers of our nature which we hold in highest esteem. Faith, being one of these powers, will always remain a factor not to be banished from philosophic constructions, the more so since in many ways it brings forth its own verification. In these points, then, it is hopeless to look for literal agreement amongst mankind.

The ultimate philosophy, we may therefore conclude, must not be too strait-laced in form, must not in all its parts divide heresy from orthodoxy by too sharp a line. There must be left over and above the propositions to be subscribed *ubique, semper, et ab omnibus*, another realm into which the stifled soul may escape from pedantic scruples and indulge its own faith at its own risks; and all that can here be done will be to mark out distinctly the questions which fall within faith's sphere.

Reflex Action and Theism [1]

MEMBERS OF THE MINISTERS' INSTITUTE:

Let me confess to the diffidence with which I find myself standing here to-day. When the invitation of your committee reached me last fall, the simple truth is that I accepted it as most men accept a challenge—not because they wish to fight, but because they are ashamed to say no. Pretending in my small sphere to be a teacher, I felt it would be cowardly to shrink from the keenest ordeal to which a teacher can be exposed—the ordeal of teaching other teachers. Fortunately, the trial will last but one short hour; and I have the consolation of remembering Goethe's verses—

> "Vor den Wissenden sich stellen,
> Sicher ist's in allen Fällen!"—

for if experts are the hardest people to satisfy, they have at any rate the liveliest sense of the difficulties of one's task, and they know quickest when one hits the mark.

Since it was as a teacher of physiology that I was most unworthily officiating when your committee's invitation reached me, I must suppose it to be for the sake of bringing a puff of the latest winds of doctrine which blow over that somewhat restless sea that my presence is desired. Among all the healthy symptoms that characterize this age, I know no sounder one than the eagerness which theologians show to assimilate results of science, and to hearken to the conclusions of men of science about universal matters. One runs a better chance of being listened to to-day if one can quote Darwin and Helmholtz than if one can only quote Schleiermacher or Coleridge. I almost feel myself this moment that were I to produce a frog and put him through his physiological performances in a masterly manner before your eyes, I should gain more reverential ears for what I have to say during the remainder of the hour. I will not ask whether there be not something of mere fashion in this prestige which the words of

[1] Address delivered to the Unitarian Ministers' Institute at Princeton, Mass., 1881, and printed in the *Unitarian Review* for November of that year.

the physiologists enjoy just now. If it be a fashion, it is certainly a beneficial one upon the whole; and to challenge it would come with a poor grace from one who at the moment he speaks is so conspicuously profiting by its favors.

I will therefore only say this: that the *latest* breeze from the physiological horizon need not necessarily be the most important one. Of the immense amount of work which the laboratories of Europe and America, and one may add of Asia and Australia, are producing every year, much is destined to speedy refutation; and of more it may be said that its interest is purely technical, and not in any degree philosophical or universal.

This being the case, I know you will justify me if I fall back on a doctrine which is fundamental and well established rather than novel, and ask you whether by taking counsel together we may not trace some new consequences from it which shall interest us all alike as men. I refer to the doctrine of reflex action, especially as extended to the brain. This is, of course, so familiar to you that I hardly need define it. In a general way, all educated people know what reflex action means.

It means that the acts we perform are always the result of outward discharges from the nervous centres, and that these outward discharges are themselves the result of impressions from the external world, carried in along one or another of our sensory nerves. Applied at first to only a portion of our acts, this conception has ended by being generalized more and more, so that now most physiologists tell us that every action whatever, even the most deliberately weighed and calculated, does, so far as its organic conditions go, follow the reflex type. There is not one which cannot be remotely, if not immediately, traced to an origin in some incoming impression of sense. There is no impression of sense which, unless inhibited by some other stronger one, does not immediately or remotely express itself in action of some kind. There is no one of those complicated performances in the convolutions of the brain to which our trains of thought correspond, which is not a mere middle term interposed between an incoming sensation that arouses it and an outgoing discharge of some sort, inhibitory if not exciting, to which itself gives rise. The structural unit of the nervous system is in fact a triad, neither of whose elements has any independent existence. The sensory impression exists only for the sake of awaking the central process of reflection, and the central process of reflection exists only for the sake of calling forth the final act. All action is thus *re*-action upon the outer world; and the middle stage of consideration or contemplation or thinking is only a place of transit, the bottom of a loop, both whose ends have their point of application in the outer world. If it should ever have no roots in the outer world, if it should ever happen that it led to no active measures, it would fail of its essential function, and would have to be considered either pathological or abortive. The current of life which runs in at our eyes or ears is meant to run out at our hands, feet, or lips. The only use of the thoughts it occasions while inside is to determine its direction to whichever of these organs shall, on the whole, under the circumstances actually present, act in the way most propitious to our welfare.

The willing department of our nature, in short, dominates both the conceiving department and the feeling department; or, in plainer English, perception and thinking are only there for behavior's sake.

I am sure I am not wrong in stating this result as one of the fundamental conclusions to which the entire drift of modern physiological investigation sweeps us. If asked what great contribution physiology has made to psychology of late years, I am sure every competent authority will reply that her influence has in no way been so weighty as in the copious illustration, verification, and consolidation of this broad, general point of view.

I invite you, then, to consider what may be the possible speculative consequences involved in this great achievement of our generation. Already, it dominates all the new work done in psychology; but what I wish to ask is whether its influence may not extend far beyond the limits of psychology, even into those of theology herself. The relations of the doctrine of reflex action with no less a matter than the doctrine of theism is, in fact, the topic to which I now invite your attention.

We are not the first in the field. There have not been want-ing writers enough to say that reflex action and all that follows from it give the *coup de grâce* to the superstition of a God.

If you open, for instance, such a book on comparative psy-chology, as *Der Thierische Wille* of G. H. Schneider, you will find, sandwiched in among the admirable dealings of the author with his proper subject, and popping out upon us in unexpected places, the most delightfully *naïf* German onslaughts on the degradation of theologians, and the utter incompatibility of so many reflex adaptations to the en-vironment with the existence of a creative intelligence. There was a time, remembered by many of us here, when the exis-tence of reflex action and all the other harmonies between the organism and the world were held to prove a God. Now, they are held to disprove him. The next turn of the whirligig may bring back proof of him again.

Into this debate about his existence, I will not pretend to enter. I must take up humbler ground, and limit my am-bition to showing that a God, whether existent or not, is at all events the kind of being which, if he did exist, would form *the most adequate possible object* for minds framed like our own to conceive as lying at the root of the universe. My thesis, in other words, is this: that *some* outward reality of a nature defined as God's nature must be defined, is the only ultimate object that is at the same time rational and possible for the human mind's contemplation. *Anything short of God is not rational, anything more than God is not possible*, if the human mind be in truth the triadic structure of im-pression, reflection, and reaction which we at the outset allowed.

Theism, whatever its objective warrant, would thus be seen to have a subjective anchorage in its congruity with our na-ture as thinkers; and, however it may fare with its truth, to derive from this subjective adequacy the strongest possible guaranty of its permanence. It is and will be the classic mean of rational opinion, the centre of gravity of all attempts to solve the riddle of life—some falling below it by defect, some flying above it by excess, itself alone satisfying every mental need in strictly normal measure. Our gain will thus in the first instance be psychological. We shall merely have investigated a chapter in the natural history of the mind, and found that, as a matter of such natural history, God may be called the normal object of the mind's belief. Whether over and above this he be really the living truth is another question. If he is, it will show the structure of our mind to be in accordance with the nature of reality. Whether it be or not in such accordance is, it seems to me, one of those questions that belong to the province of personal faith to decide. I will not touch upon the question here, for I prefer to keep to the strictly natural-history point of view. I will only remind you that each one of us is entitled either to doubt or to believe in the harmony between his faculties and the truth; and that, whether he doubt or believe, he does it alike on his personal responsibility and risk.

> "Du musst glauben, du musst wagen,
>   Denn die Götter leihn kein Pfand,
>   Nur ein Wunder kann dich tragen
>   In das schöne Wunderland."

I will presently define exactly what I mean by God and by Theism, and explain what theories I referred to when I spoke just now of attempts to fly beyond the one and to outbid the other.

But, first of all, let me ask you to linger a moment longer over what I have called the reflex theory of mind, so as to be sure that we understand it absolutely before going on to consider those of its consequences of which I am more particularly to speak. I am not quite sure that its full scope is grasped even by those who have most zealously promulgated it. I am not sure, for example, that all physiologists see that it commits them to regarding the mind as an essentially teleological mechanism. I mean by this that the conceiving or theorizing faculty—the mind's middle department—functions *exclusively for the sake of ends* that do not exist at all in the world of impressions we receive by way of our senses, but are set by our emotional and practical subjectivity altogether.[2] It is a transformer of the world of our impressions into a totally different world—the world of our conception; and the transformation is effected in the interests of our volitional nature, and for no other purpose whatsoever. Destroy the volitional nature, the definite subjective purposes, preferences, fondnesses for certain effects, forms, orders, and not the slightest motive would remain for the brute order of our experience to be remodelled at all. But, as we have the elaborate volitional constitution we do have, the remodelling must be effected; there is no escape. The world's contents are *given* to each of us in an order so foreign to our subjective interests that we can hardly by an effort of the imagination picture to ourselves what it is like. We have to break that order altogether—and by picking out from it the items which concern us, and connecting them with others far away, which we say "belong" with them, we are able to make out definite threads of sequence and tendency; to foresee particular liabilities and get ready for them; and to enjoy simplicity and harmony in place of what was chaos. Is not the sum of your actual experience taken at this moment and impartially added together an utter chaos? The strains of my voice, the lights and shades inside the room and out, the murmur of the wind, the ticking of the clock, the various organic feelings you may happen individually to possess, do these make a whole at all? Is it not the only condition of your mental sanity in the midst of them that most of them should become non-existent for you, and that a few others—the sounds, I hope, which I am uttering—should evoke from places in your memory that have nothing to do with this scene associates fitted to combine with them in what we call a rational train of thought—rational, because it leads to a conclusion which we have some organ to appreciate? We have no organ or faculty to appreciate the simply given order. The real world as it is given objectively at this moment is the sum total of all its beings and events now. But can we think of such a sum? Can we realize for an instant what a cross-section of all existence at a definite point of time

[2]See some "Remarks on Spencer's Definition of Mind," in the *Journal of Speculative Philosophy* for January, 1878.

would be? While I talk and the flies buzz, a sea-gull catches a
fish at the mouth of the Amazon, a tree falls in the Adirondack wilderness, a man sneezes in Germany, a horse dies in
Tartary, and twins are born in France. What does that mean?
Does the contemporaneity of these events with one another
and with a million others as disjointed, form a rational bond
between them, and unite them into anything that means for
us a world? Yet just such a collateral contemporaneity, and
nothing else, is the real order of the world. It is an order with
which we have nothing to do but to get away from it as fast
as possible. As I said, we break it: we break it into histories,
and we break it into arts, and we break it into sciences; and
then we begin to feel at home. We make ten thousand separate serial orders of it, and on any one of these we react
as though the others did not exist. We discover among its
various parts relations that were never given to sense at all
(mathematical relations, tangents, squares, and roots and
logarithmic functions), and out of an infinite number of these
we call certain ones essential and lawgiving, and ignore the
rest. Essential these relations are, but only *for our purpose*, the
other relations being just as real and present as they; and our
purpose is to *conceive simply* and to *foresee*. Are not simple conception and prevision subjective ends pure and simple? They
are the ends of what we call science; and the miracle of miracles, a miracle not yet exhaustively cleared up by any philosophy, is that the given order lends itself to the remodelling. It
shows itself plastic to many of our scientific, to many of our
æsthetic, to many of our practical purposes and ends.

When the man of affairs, the artist, or the man of science
fails, he is not rebutted. He tries again. He says the impressions of sense *must* give way, *must* be reduced to the desiderated form.[3] They all postulate in the interests of their

---

[3]"No amount of failure in the attempt to subject the world of sensible
experience to a thorough-going system of conceptions, and to bring all happenings back to cases of immutably valid law, is able to shake our faith in the
rightness of our principles. We hold fast to our demand that even the greatest
apparent confusion must sooner or later solve itself in transparent formulas.
We begin the work ever afresh; and, refusing to believe that nature will permanently withhold the reward of our exertions, think rather that we have
hitherto only failed to push them in the right direction. And all this perti-

volitional nature a harmony between the latter and the nature of things. The theologian does no more. And the reflex doctrine of the mind's structure, though all theology should as yet have failed of its endeavor, could but confess that the endeavor itself at least obeyed in form the mind's most necessary law.[4]

Now for the question I asked above: What kind of a being would God be if he did exist? The word "God" has come to mean many things in the history of human thought, from Venus and Jupiter to the "Idee" which figures in the pages of Hegel. Even the laws of physical nature have, in these positivistic times, been held worthy of divine honor and presented as the only fitting object of our reverence.[5] Of course, if our discussion is to bear any fruit, we must mean something more definite than this. We must not call any object of our loyalty a "God" without more ado, simply because to awaken our loyalty happens to be one of God's functions. He must have some intrinsic characteristics of his own besides; and theism must mean the faith of that man who believes that the object of *his* loyalty has those other attributes, negative or positive, as the case may be.

Now, as regards a great many of the attributes of God, and their amounts and mutual relations, the world has been delivered over to disputes. All such may for our present purpose be considered as quite inessential. Not only such matters as his mode of revealing himself, the precise extent of his providence and power and their connection with our free-will, the

---

nacity flows from a conviction that we *have no right* to renounce the fulfilment of our task. What, in short, sustains the courage of investigators is the force of obligation of an ethical idea." (Sigwart: *Logik*, ii, 23.)

This is a true account of the spirit of science. Does it essentially differ from the spirit of religion? And is anyone entitled to say in advance, that, while the one form of faith shall be crowned with success, the other is certainly doomed to fail?

[4]Concerning the transformation of the given order into the order of conception, see S. H. Hodgson, *The Philosophy of Reflection*, chap. v.; H. Lotze, *Logik*, sects. 342–351; C. Sigwart, *Logik*, sects. 60–63, 105.

[5]Haeckel has recently (*Der Monismus*, 1893, p. 37) proposed the Cosmic Ether as a divinity fitted to reconcile science with theistic faith.

proportion of his mercy to his justice, and the amount of his responsibility for evil; but also his metaphysical relation to the phenomenal world, whether causal, substantial, ideal, or what not—are affairs of purely sectarian opinion that need not concern us at all. Whoso debates them presupposes the essential features of theism to be granted already; and it is with these essential features, the bare poles of the subject, that our business exclusively lies.

Now, what are these essential features? First, it is essential that God be conceived as the deepest power in the universe; and, second, he must be conceived under the form of a mental personality. The personality need not be determined intrinsically any further than is involved in the holding of certain things dear, and in the recognition of our dispositions towards those things, the things themselves being all good and righteous things. But, extrinsically considered, so to speak, God's personality is to be regarded, like any other personality, as something lying outside of my own and other than me, and whose existence I simply come upon and find. A power not ourselves, then, which not only makes for righteousness, but means it, and which recognizes us—such is the definition which I think nobody will be inclined to dispute. Various are the attempts to shadow forth the other lineaments of so supreme a personality to our human imagination; various the ways of conceiving in what mode the recognition, the hearkening to our cry, can come. Some are gross and idolatrous; some are the most sustained efforts man's intellect has ever made to keep still living on that subtle edge of things where speech and thought expire. But, with all these differences, the essence remains unchanged. In whatever other respects the divine personality may differ from ours or may resemble it, the two are consanguineous at least in this—that both have purposes for which they care, and each can hear the other's call.

Meanwhile, we can already see one consequence and one point of connection with the reflex-action theory of mind. Any mind, constructed on the triadic-reflex pattern, must first get its impression from the object which it confronts; then define what that object is, and decide what active measures its presence demands; and finally react. The stage of reaction depends on the stage of definition, and these, of course, on the nature of the impressing object. When the objects are concrete, particular, and familiar, our reactions are firm and certain enough—often instinctive. I see the desk, and lean on it; I see your quiet faces, and I continue to talk. But the objects will not stay concrete and particular: they fuse themselves into general essences, and they sum themselves into a whole—the universe. And then the object that confronts us, that knocks on our mental door and asks to be let in, and fixed and decided upon and actively met, is just this whole universe itself and its essence.

What are *they*, and how shall I meet *them*?

The whole flood of faiths and systems here rush in. Philosophies and denials of philosophy, religions and atheisms, scepticisms and mysticisms, confirmed emotional moods and habitual practical biases, jostle one another; for all are alike trials, hasty, prolix, or of seemly length, to answer this momentous question. And the function of them all, long or short, that which the moods and the systems alike subserve and pass into, is the third stage—the stage of action. For no one of them itself is final. They form but the middle segment of the mental curve, and not its termination. As the last theoretic pulse dies away, it does not leave the mental process complete: it is but the forerunner of the practical moment, in which alone the cycle of mentality finds its rhythmic pause.

We easily delude ourselves about this middle stage. Sometimes we think it final, and sometimes we fail to see, amid the monstrous diversity in the length and complication of the cogitations which may fill it, that it can have but one essential function, and that the one we have pointed out—the function of defining the direction which our activity, immediate or remote, shall take.

If I simply say, "Vanitas vanitatum, omnia vanitas!" I am defining the total nature of things in a way that carries practical consequences with it as decidedly as if I write a treatise *De Natura Rerum* in twenty volumes. The treatise may trace its consequences more minutely than the saying; but the only worth of either treatise or saying is that the consequences are there. The long definition can do no more than draw them;

the short definition does no less. Indeed, it may be said that if two apparently different definitions of the reality before us should have identical consequences, those two definitions would really be identical definitions, made delusively to appear different merely by the different verbiage in which they are expressed.[6]

My time is unfortunately too short to stay and give to this truth the development it deserves; but I will assume that you grant it without further parley, and pass to the next step in my argument. And here, too, I shall have to bespeak your close attention for a moment, while I pass over the subject far more rapidly than it deserves. Whether true or false, any view of the universe which shall completely satisfy the mind must obey conditions of the mind's own imposing, must at least let the mind be the umpire to decide whether it be fit to be called a rational universe or not. Not any nature of things which may seem to *be* will also seem to be *ipso facto* rational; and if it do not seem rational, it will afflict the mind with a ceaseless uneasiness, till it be formulated or interpreted in some other and more congenial way. The study of what the mind's criteria of rationality are, the definition of its exactions in this respect, form an intensely interesting subject into which I cannot enter now with any detail.[7] But so much I think you will grant me without argument—that all three departments of the mind alike have a vote in the matter, and that no conception will pass muster which violates any of their essential modes of activity, or which leaves them without a chance to work. By what title is it that every would-be universal formula, every system of philosophy which rears its head, receives the inevitable critical volley from one-half of mankind, and falls to the rear, to become at the very best the creed of some partial sect? Either it has dropped out of its net some of our impressions of sense—what we call the facts of nature—or it has left the theoretic and defining department

---

[6]See the admirably original "Illustrations of the Logic of Science," by C. S. Peirce, especially the second paper, "How to Make Our Ideas Clear," in the *Popular Science Monthly* for January, 1878.

[7]On this subject, see the preceding Essay.

with a lot of inconsistencies and unmediated transitions on its hands; or else, finally, it has left some one or more of our fundamental active and emotional powers with no object outside of themselves to react-on or to live for. Any one of these defects is fatal to its complete success. Someone will be sure to discover the flaw, to scout the system, and to seek another in its stead.

I need not go far to collect examples to illustrate to an audience of theologians what I mean. Nor will you in particular, as champions of the Unitarianism of New England, be slow to furnish, from the motives which led to your departure from our orthodox ancestral Calvinism, instances enough under the third or practical head. A God who gives so little scope to love, a predestination which takes from endeavor all its zest with all its fruit, are irrational conceptions, because they say to our most cherished powers, There is no object for you.

Well, just as within the limits of theism some kinds are surviving others by reason of their greater practical rationality, so theism itself, by reason of its practical rationality, is certain to survive all lower creeds. Materialism and agnosticism, even were they true, could never gain universal and popular acceptance; for they both, alike, give a solution of things which is irrational to the practical third of our nature, and in which we can never volitionally feel at home. Each comes out of the second or theoretic stage of mental functioning, with its definition of the essential nature of things, its formula of formulas prepared. The whole array of active forces of our nature stands waiting, impatient for the word which shall tell them how to discharge themselves most deeply and worthily upon life. "Well!" cry they, "what shall we do?" "Ignoramus, ignorabimus!" says agnosticism. "React upon atoms and their concussions!" says materialism. What a collapse! The mental train misses fire, the middle fails to ignite the end, the cycle breaks down half-way to its conclusion; and the active powers left alone, with no proper object on which to vent their energy, must either atrophy, sicken, and die, or else by their pent-up convulsions and excitement keep the whole machinery in a fever until some less incommensurable solution, some more practically rational formula, shall provide a normal issue for the currents of the soul.

Now theism always stands ready with the most practically rational solution it is possible to conceive. Not an energy of our active nature to which it does not authoritatively appeal, not an emotion of which it does not normally and naturally release the springs. At a single stroke, it changes the dead blank *it* of the world into a living *thou*, with whom the whole man may have dealings. To you, at any rate, I need waste no words in trying to prove its supreme commensurateness with all the demands that department Number Three of the mind has the power to impose on department Number Two.

Our volitional nature must then, until the end of time, exert a constant pressure upon the other departments of the mind to induce them to function to theistic conclusions. No contrary formulas can be more than provisionally held. Infra-theistic theories must be always in unstable equilibrium; for department Number Three ever lurks in ambush, ready to assert its rights; and on the slightest show of justification it makes its fatal spring, and converts them into the other form in which alone mental peace and order can permanently reign.

The question is, then, *Can* departments One and Two, *can* the facts of nature and the theoretic elaboration of them, always lead to theistic conclusions?

The future history of philosophy is the only authority capable of answering that question. I, at all events, must not enter into it to-day, as that would be to abandon the purely natural-history point of view I mean to keep.

This only is certain, that the theoretic faculty lives between two fires which never give her rest, and make her incessantly revise her formulations. If she sink into a premature, short-sighted, and idolatrous theism, in comes department Number One with its battery of facts of sense, and dislodges her from her dogmatic repose. If she lazily subside into equilibrium with the same facts of sense viewed in their simple mechanical outwardness, up starts the practical reason with its demands, and makes *that* couch a bed of thorns. From generation to generation thus it goes—now a movement of reception from without, now one of expansion from within; department Number Two always worked to death, yet never excused from taking the most responsible part in the arrangements. To-day, a crop of new facts; to-morrow, a flowering of new motives—the theoretic faculty always having to effect the transition, and life growing withal so complex and subtle and immense that her powers of conceiving are almost ruptured with the strain. See how, in France, the mummy-cloths of the academic and official theistic philosophy are rent by the facts of evolution, and how the young thinkers are at work! See, in Great Britain, how the dryness of the strict associationist school, which under the ministration of Mill, Bain, and Spencer dominated us but yesterday, gives way to more generous idealisms, born of more urgent emotional needs and wrapping the same facts in far more massive intellectual harmonies! These are but tackings to the common port, to that ultimate *Weltanschauung* of maximum subjective as well as objective richness, which, whatever its other properties may be, will at any rate wear the theistic form.

Here let me say one word about a remark we often hear coming from the anti-theistic wing: It is base, it is vile, it is the lowest depth of immorality, to allow department Number Three to interpose its demands, and have any vote in the question of what is true and what is false; the mind must be a passive, reactionless sheet of white paper, on which reality will simply come and register its own philosophic definition, as the pen registers the curve on the sheet of a chronograph. "Of all the cants that are canted in this canting age" this has always seemed to me the most wretched, especially when it comes from professed psychologists. As if the mind could, consistently with its definition, be a reactionless sheet at all! As if conception could possibly occur except for a teleological purpose, except to show us the way from a state of things our senses cognize to another state of things our will desires! As if "science" itself were anything else than such an end of desire, and a most peculiar one at that! And as if the "truths" of bare physics in particular, which these sticklers for intellectual purity contend to be the only uncontaminated form, were not as great an alteration and falsification of the simply "given" order of the world, into an order conceived solely for the mind's convenience and delight, as any theistic doctrine possibly can be!

Physics is but one chapter in the great jugglery which our

conceiving faculty is forever playing with the order of being as it presents itself to our reception. It transforms the unutterable dead level and continuum of the "given" world into an utterly unlike world of sharp differences and hierarchic subordinations for no other reason than to satisfy certain subjective passions we possess.[8]

And, so far as we can see, the given world is there only for the sake of the operation. At any rate, to operate upon it is our only chance of approaching it; for never can we get a glimpse of it in the unimaginable insipidity of its virgin estate. To bid the man's subjective interests be passive till truth express itself from out the environment, is to bid the sculptor's chisel be passive till the statue express itself from out the stone. Operate we must! and the only choice left us is that between operating to poor or to rich results. The only possible duty there can be in the matter is the duty of getting the richest results that the material given will allow. The richness lies, of course, in the energy of all three departments of the mental cycle. Not a sensible "fact" of department One must be left in the cold, not a faculty of department Three be paralyzed; and department Two must form an indestructible bridge. It is natural that the habitual neglect of department One by theologians should arouse indignation; but it is most *un*natural that the indignation should take the form of a wholesale denunciation of department Three. It is the story of Kant's dove over again, denouncing the pressure of the air. Certain of our positivists keep chiming to us, that, amid the wreck of every other god and idol, one divinity still stands upright—that his name is Scientific Truth, and that he has but one commandment, but that one supreme, saying, *Thou shalt not be a theist*, for that would be to satisfy thy subjective propensities, and the satisfaction of those is intellectual damnation. These most conscientious gentlemen think they have jumped off their own feet—emancipated their mental operations from the control of their subjective propensities at large

---

[8]"As soon as it is recognized that our thought, as logic deals with it, reposes on our *will to think*, the primacy of the will, even in the theoretical sphere, must be conceded; and the last of presuppositions is not merely [Kant's] that 'I think' must accompany all my representations, but also that 'I will' must dominate all my thinking." (Sigwart: *Logik*, ii, 25.)

and *in toto*. But they are deluded. They have simply chosen from among the entire set of propensities at their command those that were certain to construct, out of the materials given, the leanest, lowest, aridest result—namely, the bare molecular world—and they have sacrificed all the rest.[9]

Man's chief difference from the brutes lies in the exuberant excess of his subjective propensities—his pre-eminence over them simply and solely in the number and in the fantastic and unnecessary character of his wants, physical, moral, æsthetic, and intellectual. Had his whole life not been a quest for the superfluous, he would never have established himself as inexpugnably as he has done in the necessary. And from the consciousness of this he should draw the lesson that his wants are to be trusted; that even when their gratification seems farthest off, the uneasiness they occasion is still the best guide of his life, and will lead him to issues entirely beyond his present powers of reckoning. Prune down his extravagance, sober him, and you undo him. The appetite for immediate consistency at any cost, or what the logicians call the "law of parsimony"—which is nothing but the passion for conceiving the universe in the most labor-saving way—will, if made the exclusive law of the mind, end by blighting the development of the intellect itself quite as much as that of the feelings or the will. The scientific conception of the world as an army of molecules gratifies this appetite after its fashion most exquisitely. But if the religion of exclusive scientificism should ever succeed in suffocating all other appetites out of a nation's mind, and imbuing a whole race with the persuasion that simplicity and consistency demand a *tabula rasa* to be made of every notion that does not form part of the *soi-disant* scientific synthesis, that nation, that race, will just as surely go to ruin, and fall a prey to their more richly constituted neighbors, as the beasts of the field, as a whole, have fallen a prey to man.

[9]As our ancestors said, *Fiat justitia, pereat mundus*, so we, who do not believe in justice or any absolute good, must, according to these prophets, be willing to see the world perish, in order that *scientia fiat*. Was there ever a more exquisite idol of the den, or rather of the *shop*? In the clean sweep to be made of superstitions, let the idol of stern obligation to be scientific go with the rest, and people will have a fair chance to understand one another. But this blowing of hot and of cold makes nothing but confusion.

I have myself little fear for our Anglo-Saxon race. Its moral, æsthetic, and practical wants form too dense a stubble to be mown by any scientific Occam's razor that has yet been forged. The knights of the razor will never form among us more than a sect; but when I see their fraternity increasing in numbers, and, what is worse, when I see their negations acquiring almost as much prestige and authority as their affirmations legitimately claim over the minds of the docile public, I feel as if the influences working in the direction of our mental barbarization were beginning to be rather strong, and needed some positive counteraction. And when I ask myself from what quarter the invasion may best be checked, I can find no answer as good as the one suggested by casting my eyes around this room. For this needful task, no fitter body of men than the Unitarian clergy exists. Who can uphold the rights of department Three of the mind with better grace than those who long since showed how they could fight and suffer for department One? As, then, you burst the bonds of a narrow ecclesiastical tradition, by insisting that no fact of sense or result of science must be left out of account in the religious synthesis, so may you still be the champions of mental completeness and all-sidedness. May you, with equal success, avert the formation of a narrow scientific tradition, and burst the bonds of any synthesis which would pretend to leave out of account those forms of being, those relations of reality, to which at present our active and emotional tendencies are our only avenues of approach. I hear it said that Unitarianism is not growing in these days. I know nothing of the truth of the statement; but if it be true, it is surely because the great ship of Orthodoxy is nearing the port and the pilot is being taken on board. If you will only lead in a theistic science, as successfully as you have led in a scientific theology, your separate name as Unitarians may perish from the mouths of men; for your task will have been done, and your function at an end. Until that distant day, you have work enough in both directions awaiting you.

Meanwhile, let me pass to the next division of our subject. I said that we are forced to regard God as the normal object of the mind's belief, inasmuch as any conception that falls short of God is irrational, if the word "rational" be taken in its fullest sense; while any conception that goes beyond God is impossible, if the human mind be constructed after the triadic-reflex pattern we have discussed at such length. The first half of the thesis has been disposed of. Infra-theistic conceptions, materialisms and agnosticisms, are irrational because they are inadequate stimuli to man's practical nature. I have now to justify the latter half of the thesis.

I dare say it may for an instant have perplexed some of you that I should speak of conceptions that aimed at going beyond God, and of attempts to fly above him or outbid him; so I will now explain exactly what I mean. In defining the essential attributes of God, I said he was a personality lying outside our own and other than us—a power not ourselves. Now, the attempts to fly beyond theism, of which I speak, are attempts to get over this ultimate duality of God and his believer, and to transform it into some sort or other of identity. If infra-theistic ways of looking on the world leave it in the third person, a mere *it*; and if theism turns the *it* into a *thou*—so we may say that these other theories try to cover it with the mantle of the first person, and to make it a part of *me*.

I am well aware that I begin here to tread on ground in which trenchant distinctions may easily seem to mutilate the facts.

That sense of emotional reconciliation with God which characterizes the highest moments of the theistic consciousness may be described as "oneness" with him, and so from the very bosom of theism a monistic doctrine seems to arise. But this consciousness of self-surrender, of absolute practical union between one's self and the divine object of one's contemplation, is a totally different thing from any sort of substantial identity. Still the object God and the subject I are two. Still I simply come upon him, and find his existence given to me; and the climax of my practical union with what is given, forms at the same time the climax of my perception that as a numerical fact of existence I am something radically other than the Divinity with whose effulgence I am filled.

Now, it seems to me that the only sort of union of creature with creator with which theism, properly so called, comports,

is of this emotional and practical kind; and it is based un-
changeably on the empirical fact that the thinking subject and
the object thought are numerically two. How my mind and
will, which are not God, can yet cognize and leap to meet
him, how I ever came to be so separate from him, and how
God himself came to be at all, are problems that for the theist
can remain unsolved and insoluble forever. It is sufficient for
him to know that he himself simply is, and needs God; and
that behind this universe God simply is and will be forever,
and will in some way hear his call. In the practical assurance
of these empirical facts, without "Erkenntnistheorie" or philosophical ontology, without metaphysics of emanation or
creation to justify or make them more intelligible, in the
blessedness of their mere acknowledgment as given, lie all the
peace and power he craves. The floodgates of the religious life
are opened, and the full currents can pour through.

It is this empirical and practical side of the theistic position,
its theoretic chastity and modesty, which I wish to accentuate
here. The highest flights of theistic mysticism, far from
pretending to penetrate the secrets of the *me* and the *thou* in
worship, and to transcend the dualism by an act of intelligence, simply turn their backs on such attempts. The problem
for them has simply vanished—vanished from the sight of an
attitude which refuses to notice such futile theoretic difficulties. Get but that "peace of God which passeth understanding," and the questions of the understanding will cease from
puzzling and pedantic scruples be at rest. In other words, theistic mysticism, that form of theism which at first sight seems
most to have transcended the fundamental otherness of God
from man, has done it least of all in the theoretic way. The
pattern of its procedure is precisely that of the simplest man
dealing with the simplest fact of his environment. Both he
and the theist tarry in department Two of their minds only so
long as is necessary to define what is the presence that confronts them. The theist decides that its character is such as to
be fitly responded to on his part by a religious reaction; and
into that reaction he forthwith pours his soul. His insight
into the *what* of life leads to results so immediately and intimately rational that the *why*, the *how*, and the *whence* of it are
questions that lose all urgency. "Gefühl ist Alles," Faust says.

The channels of department Three have drained those of department Two of their contents; and happiness over the fact that being has made itself what it is, evacuates all speculation as to how it could make itself at all.

But now, although to most human minds such a position as this will be the position of rational equilibrium, it is not difficult to bring forward certain considerations, in the light of which so simple and practical a mental movement begins to seem rather short-winded and second-rate and devoid of intellectual style. This easy acceptance of an opaque limit to our speculative insight; this satisfaction with a Being whose character we simply apprehend without comprehending anything more about him, and with whom after a certain point our dealings can be only of a volitional and emotional sort; above all, this sitting down contented with a blank unmediated dualism—are they not the very picture of unfaithfulness to the rights and duties of our theoretic reason?

Surely, if the universe is reasonable (and we must believe that it is so), it must be susceptible, potentially at least, of being reasoned *out* to the last drop without residuum. Is it not rather an insult to the very word "rational" to say that the rational character of the universe and its creator means no more than that we practically feel at home in their presence, and that our powers are a match for their demands? Do they not in fact demand to be *understood* by us still more than to be reacted on? Is not the unparalleled development of department Two of the mind in man his crowning glory and his very essence; and may not the *knowing of the truth* be his absolute vocation? And if it is, ought he flatly to acquiesce in a spiritual life of "reflex type," whose form is no higher than that of the life that animates his spinal cord—nay, indeed, that animates the writhing segments of any mutilated worm?

It is easy to see how such arguments and queries may result in the erection of an ideal of our mental destiny, far different from the simple and practical religious one we have described. We may well begin to ask whether such things as practical reactions can be the final upshot and purpose of all our cognitive energy. Mere outward acts, changes in the position of parts of matter (for they are nothing else), can they possibly be the culmination and consummation of our relations with the nature of things? Can they possibly form a result to which our godlike powers of insight shall be judged merely subservient? Such an idea, if we scan it closely, soon begins to seem rather absurd. Whence this piece of matter comes and whither that one goes, what difference ought that to make to the nature of things, except so far as with the comings and the goings our wonderful inward conscious harvest may be reaped?

And so, very naturally and gradually, one may be led from the theistic and practical point of view to what I shall call the *gnostical* one. We may think that department Three of the mind, with its doings of right and its doings of wrong, must be there only to serve department Two; and we may suspect that the sphere of our activity exists for no other purpose than to illumine our cognitive consciousness by the experience of its results. Are not all sense and all emotion at bottom but turbid and perplexed modes of what in its clarified shape is intelligent cognition? Is not all experience just the eating of the fruit of the tree of *knowledge* of good and evil, and nothing more?

These questions fan the fire of an unassuageable gnostic thirst, which is as far removed from theism in one direction as agnosticism was removed from it in the other; and which aspires to nothing less than an absolute unity of knowledge with its object, and refuses to be satisfied short of a fusion and solution and saturation of both impression and action with reason, and an absorption of all three departments of the mind into one. Time would fail us to-day (even had I the learning, which I have not) to speak of gnostic systems in detail. The aim of all of them is to shadow forth a sort of process by which spirit, emerging from its beginnings and exhausting the whole circle of finite experience in its sweep, shall at last return and possess itself as its own object at the climax of its career. This climax is the religious consciousness. At the giddy height of this conception, whose latest and best known form is the hegelian philosophy, definite words fail to serve their purpose; and the ultimate goal—where object and subject, worshipped and worshipper, facts and the knowledge of them, fall into one, and where no other is left outstanding beyond this one that alone is, and that we may call indifferently act or fact, reality or idea, God or creation—this goal, I say, has to be adumbrated to our halting and gasping intelligence by coarse physical metaphors, "positings" and "self-returnings" and "removals" and "settings free," which hardly help to make the matter clear.

But from the midst of the curdling and the circling of it all we seem dimly to catch a glimpse of a state in which the reality to be known and the power of knowing shall have become so mutually adequate that each exhaustively is absorbed by the other and the twain become one flesh, and in which the light shall somehow have soaked up all the outer darkness into its own ubiquitous beams. Like all headlong ideals, this apotheosis of the bare conceiving faculty has its depth and wildness, its pang and its charm. To many it sings a truly siren strain; and so long as it is held only as a postulate, as a mere vanishing point to give perspective to our intellectual aim, it is hard to see any empirical title by which we may deny the legitimacy of gnosticism's claims. That we are not as yet near the goal it prefigures can never be a reason why we might not continue indefinitely to approach it; and to all sceptical arguments, drawn from our reason's actual finiteness, gnosticism can still oppose its indomitable faith in the infinite character of its potential destiny.

Now here it is that the physiologist's generalization, as it seems to me, may fairly come in, and by ruling any such extravagant faith out of court help to legitimate our personal mistrust of its pretensions. I confess that I myself have always had a great mistrust of the pretensions of the gnostic faith. Not only do I utterly fail to understand what a cognitive faculty erected into the absolute of being, with itself as its object, can mean; but even if we grant it a being other than itself for object, I cannot reason myself out of the belief that however familiar and at home we might become with the character of that being, the bare being of it, the fact that it is there at all, must always be something blankly given and presupposed in order that conception may begin its work; must in short lie beyond speculation, and not be enveloped in its sphere.

Accordingly, it is with no small pleasure that as a student of physiology and psychology I find the only lesson I can learn from these sciences to be one that corroborates these convictions. From its first dawn to its highest actual attainment, we find that the cognitive faculty, where it appears to exist at all, appears but as one element in an organic mental whole, and as a minister to higher mental powers—the powers of will. Such a thing as its emancipation and absolution from these organic relations receives no faintest color of plausibility from any fact we can discern. Arising as a part, in a mental and objective world which are both larger than itself, it must, whatever its powers of growth may be (and I am far from wishing to disparage them), remain a part to the end. This is the character of the cognitive element in all the mental life we know, and we have no reason to suppose that that character will ever change. On the contrary, it is more than probable that to the end of time our power of moral and volitional response to the nature of things will be the deepest organ of communication therewith we shall ever possess. In every being that is real there is something external to, and sacred from, the grasp of every other. God's being is sacred from ours. To co-operate with his creation by the best and rightest response seems all he wants of us. In such co-operation with his purposes, not in any chimerical speculative conquest of him, not in any theoretic drinking of him up, must lie the real meaning of our destiny.

This is nothing new. All men know it at those rare moments when the soul sobers herself, and leaves off her chattering and protesting and insisting about this formula or that. In the silence of our theories we then seem to listen, and to hear something like the pulse of Being beat; and it is borne in upon us that the mere turning of the character, the dumb willingness to suffer and to serve this universe, is more than all theories about it put together. The most any theory about it can do is to bring us to that. Certain it is that the acutest theories, the greatest intellectual power, the most elaborate education, are a sheer mockery when, as too often happens, they feed mean motives and a nerveless will. And it is equally certain that a resolute moral energy, no matter how inarticulate or unequipped with learning its owner may be, extorts from us a respect we should never pay were we not satisfied that the essential root of human personality lay there.

I have sketched my subject in the briefest outlines; but still I hope you will agree that I have established my point, and that the physiological view of mentality, so far from invalidating, can but give aid and comfort to the theistic attitude of mind. Between agnosticism and gnosticism, theism stands midway, and holds to what is true in each. With agnosticism, it goes so far as to confess that we cannot know how Being made itself or us. With gnosticism, it goes so far as to insist that we can know Being's character when made, and how it asks us to behave.

If anyone fear that in insisting so strongly that behavior is the aim and end of every sound philosophy I have curtailed the dignity and scope of the speculative function in us, I can only reply that in this ascertainment of the *character* of Being lies an almost infinite speculative task. Let the voluminous considerations by which all modern thought converges towards idealistic or pan-psychic conclusions speak for me. Let the pages of a Hodgson, of a Lotze, of a Renouvier, reply whether within the limits drawn by purely empirical theism the speculative faculty finds not, and shall not always find, enough to do. But do it little or much, its *place* in a philosophy is always the same, and is set by the structural form of the mind. Philosophies, whether expressed in sonnets or systems, all must wear this form. The thinker starts from some experience of the practical world, and asks its meaning. He launches himself upon the speculative sea, and makes a voyage long or short. He ascends into the empyrean, and communes with the eternal essences. But whatever his achievements and discoveries be while gone, the utmost result they can issue in is some new practical maxim or resolve, or the denial of some old one, with which inevitably he is sooner or later washed ashore on the *terra firma* of concrete life again.

Whatever thought takes this voyage is a philosophy. We have seen how theism takes it. And in the philosophy of a thinker who, though long neglected, is doing much to renovate the spiritual life of his native France to-day (I mean Charles Renouvier, whose writings ought to be better known among us than they are), we have an instructive example of the way in which this very empirical element in theism, its confession of an ultimate opacity in things, of a dimension of being which escapes our theoretic control, may suggest a most definite practical conclusion—this one, namely, that "our wills are free." I will say nothing of Renouvier's line of reasoning; it is contained in many volumes which I earnestly recommend to your attention.[10] But to enforce my doctrine that the number of volumes is not what makes the philosophy, let me conclude by recalling to you the little poem of Tennyson, published last year, in which the speculative voyage is made, and the same conclusion reached in a few lines:

> "Out of the deep, my child, out of the deep,
>   From that great deep before our world begins
>   Whereon the Spirit of God moves as he will—
>   Out of the deep, my child, out of the deep,
>   From that true world within the world we see,
>   Whereof our world is but the bounding shore—
>   Out of the deep, Spirit, out of the deep,
>   With this ninth moon that sends the hidden sun
>   Down yon dark sea, thou comest, darling boy.
>   For in the world which is not ours, They said,
>   'Let us make man' and that which should be man,
>   From that one light no man can look upon,
>   Drew to this shore lit by the suns and moons
>   And all the shadows. O dear Spirit, half-lost
>   In thine own shadow and this fleshly sign
>   That thou art thou—who wailest being born
>   And banish'd into mystery, . . .
> 　　　　　　　　　. . . our mortal veil
>   And shatter'd phantom of that infinite One,
>   Who made thee unconceivably thyself

[10]Especially the *Essais de critique générale*, 2me Édition, 6 vols., 12mo, Paris, 1875; and the *Esquisse d'une classification systématique des doctrines philosophiques*, 2 vols., 8vo, Paris, 1885.

Out of His whole World-self and all in all—
Live thou, and of the grain and husk, the grape
And ivyberry, choose; and still depart
From death to death thro' life and life, and find
Nearer and ever nearer Him who wrought
Not Matter, nor the finite-infinite,
But this main miracle, that thou art thou,
With power on thine own act and on the world."

The Dilemma of Determinism [1]

A COMMON OPINION prevails that the juice has ages ago been pressed out of the free-will controversy, and that no new champion can do more than warm up stale arguments which everyone has heard. This is a radical mistake. I know of no subject less worn out, or in which inventive genius has a better chance of breaking open new ground—not, perhaps, of forcing a conclusion or of coercing assent, but of deepening our sense of what the issue between the two parties really is, of what the ideas of fate and of free-will imply. At our very side almost, in the past few years, we have seen falling in rapid succession from the press works that present the alternative in entirely novel lights. Not to speak of the English disciples of Hegel, such as Green and Bradley; not to speak of Hinton and Hodgson, nor of Hazard here—we see in the writings of Renouvier, Fouillée, and Delbœuf [2] how completely changed and refreshed is the form of all the old disputes. I cannot pretend to vie in originality with any of the masters I have named, and my ambition limits itself to just one little point. If I can make two of the necessarily implied corollaries of determinism clearer to you than they have been made before, I shall have made it possible for you to decide for or against that doctrine with a better understanding of what you are about. And if you prefer not to decide at all, but to remain doubters, you will at least see more plainly what the subject of your hesitation is. I thus disclaim openly on the threshold all pretension to prove to you that the freedom of the will is true. The most I hope is to induce some of you to follow my own example in assuming it true, and acting as if it were true. If it be true, it seems to me that this is involved in the strict logic of the case. Its truth ought not to be forced willy-nilly down our indifferent throats. It ought to be freely espoused by men who can equally well turn their backs upon it. In other words, our first act of freedom, if we are free,

[1] An Address to the Harvard Divinity Students, published in the *Unitarian Review* for September, 1884.
[2] And I may now say Charles S. Peirce—see the *Monist*, for 1892–93.

ought in all inward propriety to be to affirm that we are free. This should exclude, it seems to me, from the free-will side of the question all hope of a coercive demonstration—a demonstration which I, for one, am perfectly contented to go without.

With thus much understood at the outset, we can advance. But not without one more point understood as well. The arguments I am about to urge all proceed on two suppositions: first, when we make theories about the world and discuss them with one another, we do so in order to attain a conception of things which shall give us subjective satisfaction; and, second, if there be two conceptions, and the one seems to us, on the whole, more rational than the other, we are entitled to suppose that the more rational one is the truer of the two. I hope that you are all willing to make these suppositions with me; for I am afraid that if there be any of you here who are not, they will find little edification in the rest of what I have to say. I cannot stop to argue the point; but I myself believe that all the magnificent achievements of mathematical and physical science—our doctrines of evolution, of uniformity of law, and the rest—proceed from our indomitable desire to cast the world into a more rational shape in our minds than the shape into which it is thrown there by the crude order of our experience. The world has shown itself, to a great extent, plastic to this demand of ours for rationality. How much farther it will show itself plastic no one can say. Our only means of finding out is to try; and I, for one, feel as free to try conceptions of moral as of mechanical or of logical rationality. If a certain formula for expressing the nature of the world violates my moral demand, I shall feel as free to throw it overboard, or at least to doubt it, as if it disappointed my demand for uniformity of sequence, for example; the one demand being, so far as I can see, quite as subjective and emotional as the other is. The principle of causality, for example—what is it but a postulate, an empty name covering simply a demand that the sequence of events shall some day manifest a deeper kind of belonging of one thing with another than the mere arbitrary juxtaposition which now phenomenally appears? It is as much an altar to an unknown god as the one that Saint

Paul found at Athens. All our scientific and philosophic ideals
are altars to unknown gods. Uniformity is as much so as is
free-will. If this be admitted, we can debate on even terms.
But if anyone pretends that while freedom and variety are, in
the first instance, subjective demands, necessity and uniformity are something altogether different, I do not see how we
can debate at all.[3]

To begin, then, I must suppose you acquainted with all the
usual arguments on the subject. I cannot stop to take up the
old proofs from causation, from statistics, from the certainty
with which we can foretell one another's conduct, from the
fixity of character, and all the rest. But there are two *words*
which usually encumber these classical arguments, and which
we must immediately dispose of if we are to make any
progress. One is the eulogistic word *freedom*, and the other is
the opprobrious word *chance*. The word "chance" I wish to

---

[3]"The whole history of popular beliefs about Nature refutes the notion
that the thought of a universal physical order can possibly have arisen from
the purely passive reception and association of particular perceptions. Indubitable as it is that men infer from known cases to unknown, it is equally
certain that this procedure, if restricted to the phenomenal materials that
spontaneously offer themselves, would never have led to the belief in a general uniformity, but only to the belief that law and lawlessness rule the world
in motley alternation. From the point of view of strict experience, nothing
exists but the sum of particular perceptions, with their coincidences on the
one hand, their contradictions on the other.

"That there is more order in the world than appears at first sight is not
discovered *till the order is looked for*. The first impulse to look for it proceeds
from practical needs: where ends must be attained, we must know trustwor-
thy means which infallibly possess a property, or produce a result. But the
practical need is only the first occasion for our reflection on the conditions of
true knowledge; and even were there no such need, motives would still be
present for carrying us beyond the stage of mere association. For not with an
equal interest, or rather with an equal lack of interest, does man contemplate
those natural processes in which a thing is linked with its former mate, and
those in which it is linked to something else. *The former processes harmonize
with the conditions of his own thinking:* the latter do not. In the former, his
concepts, general judgments, and *inferences* apply to reality: in the latter, they
have no such application. And thus the intellectual satisfaction which at first
comes to him without reflection, at last excites in him the conscious wish to
find realized throughout the entire phenomenal world those rational continuities, uniformities, and necessities which are the fundamental element and
guiding principle of his own thought." (Sigwart, *Logik*, bd. 2, s. 382.)

keep, but I wish to get rid of the word "freedom." Its eulogistic associations have so far overshadowed all the rest of its meaning that both parties claim the sole right to use it, and determinists to-day insist that they alone are freedom's champions. Old-fashioned determinism was what we may call *hard* determinism. It did not shrink from such words as fatality, bondage of the will, necessitation, and the like. Nowadays, we have a *soft* determinism which abhors harsh words, and, repudiating fatality, necessity, and even predetermination, says that its real name is freedom; for freedom is only necessity understood, and bondage to the highest is identical with true freedom. Even a writer as little used to making capital out of soft words as Mr. Hodgson hesitates not to call himself a "free-will determinist."

Now, all this is a quagmire of evasion under which the real issue of fact has been entirely smothered. Freedom in all these senses presents simply no problem at all. No matter what the soft determinist mean by it—whether he mean the acting without external constraint, whether he mean the acting rightly, or whether he mean the acquiescing in the law of the whole—who cannot answer him that sometimes we are free and sometimes we are not? But there *is* a problem, an issue of fact and not of words, an issue of the most momentous importance, which is often decided without discussion in one sentence—nay, in one clause of a sentence—by those very writers who spin out whole chapters in their efforts to show what "true" freedom is; and that is the question of determinism, about which we are to talk to-night.

Fortunately, no ambiguities hang about this word or about its opposite, indeterminism. Both designate an outward way in which things may happen, and their cold and mathematical sound has no sentimental associations that can bribe our partiality either way in advance. Now, evidence of an external kind to decide between determinism and indeterminism is, as I intimated a while back, strictly impossible to find. Let us look at the difference between them and see for ourselves. What does determinism profess?

It professes that those parts of the universe already laid down absolutely appoint and decree what the other parts shall be. The future has no ambiguous possibilities hidden in its womb: the part we call the present is compatible with only one totality. Any other future complement than the one fixed from eternity is impossible. The whole is in each and every part, and welds it with the rest into an absolute unity, an iron block, in which there can be no equivocation or shadow of turning.

> "With Earth's first Clay They did the Last Man knead,
>   And there of the Last Harvest sow'd the Seed;
>   And the first Morning of Creation wrote
>   What the Last Dawn of Reckoning shall read."

Indeterminism, on the contrary, says that the parts have a certain amount of loose play on one another, so that the laying down of one of them does not necessarily determine what the others shall be. It admits that possibilities may be in excess of actualities, and that things not yet revealed to our knowledge may really in themselves be ambiguous. Of two alternative futures which we conceive, both may now be really possible; and the one become impossible only at the very moment when the other excludes it by becoming real itself. Indeterminism thus denies the world to be one unbending unit of fact. It says there is a certain ultimate pluralism in it; and, so saying, it corroborates our ordinary unsophisticated view of things. To that view, actualities seem to float in a wider sea of possibilities from out of which they are chosen; and, *somewhere*, indeterminism says, such possibilities exist, and form a part of truth.

Determinism, on the contrary, says they exist *nowhere*, and that necessity on the one hand and impossibility on the other are the sole categories of the real. Possibilities that fail to get realized are, for determinism, pure illusions: they never were possibilities at all. There is nothing inchoate, it says, about this universe of ours, all that was or is or shall be actual in it having been from eternity virtually there. The cloud of alternatives our minds escort this mass of actuality withal is a cloud of sheer deceptions, to which "impossibilities" is the only name that rightfully belongs.

The issue, it will be seen, is a perfectly sharp one, which no eulogistic terminology can smear over or wipe out. The truth *must* lie with one side or the other, and its lying with one side makes the other false.

The question relates solely to the existence of possibilities, in the strict sense of the term, as things that may, but need not, be. Both sides admit that a volition, for instance, has occurred. The indeterminists say another volition might have occurred in its place: the determinists swear that nothing could possibly have occurred in its place. Now can science be called in to tell us which of these two point-blank contradicters of each other is right? Science professes to draw no conclusions but such as are based on matters of fact, things that have actually happened; but how can any amount of assurance that something actually happened give us the least grain of information as to whether another thing might or might not have happened in its place? Only facts can be proved by other facts. With things that are possibilities and not facts, facts have no concern. If we have no other evidence than the evidence of existing facts, the possibility-question must remain a mystery never to be cleared up.

And the truth is that facts practically have hardly anything to do with making us either determinists or indeterminists. Sure enough, we make a flourish of quoting facts this way or that; and if we are determinists, we talk about the infallibility with which we can predict one another's conduct; while if we are indeterminists, we lay great stress on the fact that it is just because we cannot foretell one another's conduct, either in war or statecraft or in any of the great and small intrigues and businesses of men, that life is so intensely anxious and hazardous a game. But who does not see the wretched insufficiency of this so-called objective testimony on both sides? What fills up the gaps in our minds is something not objective, not external. What divides us into possibility men and anti-possibility men is different faiths or postulates—postulates of rationality. To this man the world seems more rational with possibilities in it—to that man more rational with possibilities excluded; and talk as we will about having to yield to evidence, what makes us monists or pluralists, determinists or indeterminists, is at bottom always some sentiment like this.

*   *   *

The stronghold of the deterministic sentiment is the antipathy to the idea of chance. As soon as we begin to talk indeterminism to our friends, we find a number of them shaking their heads. This notion of alternative possibility, they say, this admission that any one of several things may come to pass, is, after all, only a roundabout name for chance; and chance is something the notion of which no sane mind can for an instant tolerate in the world. What is it, they ask, but barefaced crazy unreason, the negation of intelligibility and law? And if the slightest particle of it exist anywhere, what is to prevent the whole fabric from falling together, the stars from going out, and chaos from recommencing her topsyturvy reign?

Remarks of this sort about chance will put an end to discussion as quickly as anything one can find. I have already told you that "chance" was a word I wished to keep and use. Let us then examine exactly what it means, and see whether it ought to be such a terrible bugbear to us. I fancy that squeezing the thistle boldly will rob it of its sting.

The sting of the word "chance" seems to lie in the assumption that it means something positive, and that if anything happens by chance, it must needs be something of an intrinsically irrational and preposterous sort. Now chance means nothing of the kind. It is a purely negative and relative term,[4] giving us no information about that of which it is predicated, except that it happens to be disconnected with something else—not controlled, secured, or necessitated by other things in advance of its own actual presence. As this point is the most subtle one of the whole lecture, and at the same time the point on which all the rest hinges, I beg you to pay particular attention to it. What I say is that it tells us nothing about what a thing may be in itself to call it "chance." It may be a bad thing, it may be a good thing. It may be lucidity, transparency, fitness incarnate, matching the whole system of other things, when it has once befallen, in an unimaginably perfect way. All you mean by calling it "chance" is that this is not guaranteed, that it may also fall out otherwise. For the system

[4]Speaking technically, it is a word with a positive denotation, but a connotation that is negative. Other things must be silent about *what* it is: it alone can decide that point at the moment in which it reveals itself.

of other things has no positive hold on the chance-thing. Its origin is in a certain fashion negative: it escapes, and says, Hands off! coming, when it comes, as a free gift, or not at all.

This negativeness, however, and this opacity of the chance-thing when thus considered *ab extra*, or from the point of view of previous things or distant things, do not preclude its having any amount of positiveness and luminosity from within, and at its own place and moment. All that its chance-character asserts about it is that there is something in it really of its own, something that is not the unconditional property of the whole. If the whole wants this property, the whole must wait till it can get it, if it be a matter of chance. That the universe may actually be a sort of joint-stock society of this sort, in which the sharers have both limited liabilities and limited powers, is of course a simple and conceivable notion.

Nevertheless, many persons talk as if the minutest dose of disconnectedness of one part with another, the smallest modicum of independence, the faintest tremor of ambiguity about the future, for example, would ruin everything, and turn this goodly universe into a sort of insane sand-heap or nulliverse, no universe at all. Since future human volitions are as a matter of fact the only ambiguous things we are tempted to believe in, let us stop for a moment to make ourselves sure whether their independent and accidental character need be fraught with such direful consequences to the universe as these.

What is meant by saying that my choice of which way to walk home after the lecture is ambiguous and matter of chance as far as the present moment is concerned? It means that both Divinity Avenue and Oxford Street are called; but that only one, and that one *either* one, shall be chosen. Now, I ask you seriously to suppose that this ambiguity of my choice is real; and then to make the impossible hypothesis that the choice is made twice over, and each time falls on a different street. In other words, imagine that I first walk through Divinity Avenue, and then imagine that the powers governing the universe annihilate ten minutes of time with all that it contained, and set me back at the door of this hall just as I was before the choice was made. Imagine then that, everything else being the same, I now make a different choice and traverse Oxford Street. You, as passive spectators, look on and see the two alternative universes—one of them with me walking through Divinity Avenue in it, the other with the same me walking through Oxford Street. Now, if you are determinists you believe one of these universes to have been from eternity impossible: you believe it to have been impossible because of the intrinsic irrationality or accidentality somewhere involved in it. But looking outwardly at these universes, can you say which is the impossible and accidental one, and which the rational and necessary one? I doubt if the most iron-clad determinist among you could have the slightest glimmer of light on this point. In other words, either universe *after the fact* and once there would, to our means of observation and understanding, appear just as rational as the other. There would be absolutely no criterion by which we might judge one necessary and the other matter of chance. Suppose now we relieve the gods of their hypothetical task and assume my choice, once made, to be made forever. I go through Divinity Avenue for good and all. If, as good determinists, you now begin to affirm, what all good determinists punctually do affirm, that in the nature of things I *couldn't* have gone through Oxford Street—had I done so it would have been chance, irrationality, insanity, a horrid gap in nature—I simply call your attention to this, that your affirmation is what the Germans call a *Machtspruch*, a mere conception fulminated as a dogma and based on no insight into details. Before my choice, either street seemed as natural to you as to me. Had I happened to take Oxford Street, Divinity Avenue would have figured in your philosophy as the gap in nature; and you would have so proclaimed it with the best deterministic conscience in the world.

But what a hollow outcry, then, is this against a chance which, if it were present to us, we could by no character whatever distinguish from a rational necessity! I have taken the most trivial of examples, but no possible example could lead to any different result. For what are the alternatives which, in point of fact, offer themselves to human volition? What are those futures that now seem matters of chance? Are they not one and all like the Divinity Avenue and Oxford Street of our example? Are they not all of them *kinds* of things already here and based in the existing frame of nature? Is anyone ever tempted to produce an *absolute* accident, something utterly irrelevant to the rest of the world? Do not all the motives that assail us, all the futures that offer themselves to our choice, spring equally from the soil of the past; and would not either one of them, whether realized through chance or through necessity, the moment it was realized, seem to us to fit that past, and in the completest and most continuous manner to interdigitate with the phenomena already there?[5]

The more one thinks of the matter, the more one wonders that so empty and gratuitous a hubbub as this outcry against chance should have found so great an echo in the hearts of men. It is a word which tells us absolutely nothing about what chances, or about the *modus operandi* of the chancing; and the use of it as a war-cry shows only a temper of intellectual absolutism, a demand that the world shall be a solid block, subject to one control—which temper, which demand, the world may not be bound to gratify at all. In every outwardly verifiable and practical respect, a world in which the alternatives that now actually distract *your* choice were decided by pure chance would be by *me* absolutely undistinguished from the world in which I now live. I am, therefore, entirely willing to call it, so far as your choices go, a world of chance for me. To *yourselves*, it is true, those very acts of choice, which to me are so blind, opaque, and external, are the opposites of this, for you are within them and effect them. To you they appear as decisions; and decisions, for him who makes them, are altogether peculiar psychic facts. Self-luminous and self-justifying at the living moment at which they occur, they appeal to no outside moment to put its stamp upon them or make them continuous with the rest of

---

[5]A favorite argument against free-will is that if it be true, a man's murderer may as probably be his best friend as his worst enemy, a mother be as likely to strangle as to suckle her first-born, and all of us be as ready to jump from fourth-story windows as to go out of front doors, etc. Users of this argument should properly be excluded from debate till they learn what the real question is. "Free-will" does not say that everything that is physically conceivable is also morally possible. It merely says that of alternatives that really *tempt* our will more than one is really possible. Of course, the alternatives that do thus tempt our will are vastly fewer than the physical possibilities we can coldly fancy. Persons really tempted often do murder their best friends, mothers do strangle their first-born, people do jump out of fourth-story windows, etc.

nature. Themselves it is rather who seem to make nature continuous; and in their strange and intense function of granting consent to one possibility and withholding it from another, to transform an equivocal and double future into an inalterable and simple past.

But with the psychology of the matter we have no concern this evening. The quarrel which determinism has with chance fortunately has nothing to do with this or that psychological detail. It is a quarrel altogether metaphysical. Determinism denies the ambiguity of future volitions, because it affirms that nothing future can be ambiguous. But we have said enough to meet the issue. Indeterminate future volitions *do* mean chance. Let us not fear to shout it from the house-tops if need be; for we now know that the idea of chance is, at bottom, exactly the same thing as the idea of gift—the one simply being a disparaging, and the other a eulogistic, name for anything on which we have no effective *claim*. And whether the world be the better or the worse for having either chances or gifts in it will depend altogether on *what* these uncertain and unclaimable things turn out to be.

And this at last brings us within sight of our subject. We have seen what determinism means: we have seen that indeterminism is rightly described as meaning chance; and we have seen that chance, the very name of which we are urged to shrink from as from a metaphysical pestilence, means only the negative fact that no part of the world, however big, can claim to control absolutely the destinies of the whole. But although, in discussing the word "chance," I may at moments have seemed to be arguing for its real existence, I have not meant to do so yet. We have not yet ascertained whether this be a world of chance or no; at most, we have agreed that it seems so. And I now repeat what I said at the outset, that, from any strict theoretical point of view, the question is insoluble. To deepen our theoretic sense of the *difference* between a world with chances in it and a deterministic world is the most I can hope to do; and this I may now at last begin upon, after all our tedious clearing of the way.

I wish first of all to show you just what the notion that this is a deterministic world implies. The implications I call your attention to are all bound up with the fact that it is a world in which we constantly have to make what I shall, with your permission, call judgments of regret. Hardly an hour passes in which we do not wish that something might be otherwise; and happy indeed are those of us whose hearts have never echoed the wish of Omar Khayyam,

> "That we might catch ere closed the Book of Fate,
>   And make The Writer on a fairer leaf
> Inscribe our names, or quite obliterate!

> "Ah Love! could you and I with Fate conspire
> To grasp this sorry Scheme of Things entire,
>   Would not we shatter it to bits — and then
> Re-mould it nearer to the Heart's Desire!"

Now, it is undeniable that most of these regrets are foolish, and quite on a par in point of philosophic value with the criticisms on the universe of that friend of our infancy, the hero of the fable "The Atheist and the Acorn,"

> "Fool! had that bough a pumpkin bore,
> Thy whimsies would have worked no more," etc.

Even from the point of view of our own ends, we should probably make a botch of remodelling the universe. How much more then from the point of view of ends we cannot see! Wise men therefore regret as little as they can. But still some regrets are pretty obstinate and hard to stifle — regrets for acts of wanton cruelty or treachery, for example, whether performed by others or by ourselves. Hardly anyone can remain *entirely* optimistic after reading the confession of the murderer at Brockton the other day: how, to get rid of the wife whose continued existence bored him, he inveigled her into a desert spot, shot her four times, and then, as she lay on the ground and said to him, "You didn't do it on purpose, did you, dear?" replied, "No, I didn't do it on purpose," as he raised a rock and smashed her skull. Such an occurrence, with the mild sentence and self-satisfaction of the prisoner, is a field for a crop of regrets, which one need not take up in detail. We feel that, although a perfect mechanical fit to the rest of the universe, it is a bad moral fit, and that something else would really have been better in its place.

But for the deterministic philosophy the murder, the sentence, and the prisoner's optimism were all necessary from eternity; and nothing else for a moment had a ghost of a chance of being put into their place. To admit such a chance, the determinists tell us, would be to make a suicide of reason; so we must steel our hearts against the thought. And here our plot thickens, for we see the first of those difficult implications of determinism and monism which it is my purpose to make you feel. If this Brockton murder was called for by the rest of the universe, if it had to come at its preappointed hour, and if nothing else would have been consistent with the sense of the whole, what are we to think of the universe? Are we stubbornly to stick to our judgment of regret, and say, though it *couldn't* be, yet it *would* have been a better universe with something different from this Brockton murder in it? That, of course, seems the natural and spontaneous thing for us to do; and yet it is nothing short of deliberately espousing a kind of pessimism. The judgment of regret calls the murder bad. Calling a thing bad means, if it means anything at all, that the thing ought not to be, that something else ought to be in its stead. Determinism, in denying that anything else can be in its stead, virtually defines the universe as a place in which what ought to be is impossible—in other words, as an organism whose constitution is afflicted with an incurable taint, an irremediable flaw. The pessimism of a Schopenhauer says no more than this—that the murder is a symptom; and that it is a vicious symptom because it belongs to a vicious whole, which can express its nature no otherwise than by bringing forth just such a symptom as that at this particular spot. Regret for the murder must transform itself, if we are determinists and wise, into a larger regret. It is absurd to regret the murder alone. Other things being what they are, *it* could not be different. What we should regret is that whole frame of things of which the murder is one member. I see no escape whatever from this pessimistic conclusion, if, being determinists, our judgment of regret is to be allowed to stand at all.

The only deterministic escape from pessimism is everywhere to abandon the judgment of regret. That this can be done, history shows to be not impossible. The devil, *quoad existentiam*, may be good. That is, although he be a *principle* of evil, yet the universe, with such a principle in it, may practically be a better universe than it could have been without. On every hand, in a small way, we find that a certain amount of evil is a condition by which a higher form of good is bought. There is nothing to prevent anybody from generalizing this view, and trusting that if we could but see things in the largest of all ways, even such matters as this Brockton murder would appear to be paid for by the uses that follow in their train. An optimism *quand même*, a systematic and infatuated optimism like that ridiculed by Voltaire in his *Candide*, is one of the possible ideal ways in which a man may train himself to look on life. Bereft of dogmatic hardness and lit up with the expression of a tender and pathetic hope, such an optimism has been the grace of some of the most religious characters that ever lived.

> "Throb thine with Nature's throbbing breast,
> And all is clear from east to west."

Even cruelty and treachery may be among the absolutely blessed fruits of time, and to quarrel with any of their details may be blasphemy. The only real blasphemy, in short, may be that pessimistic temper of the soul which lets it give way to such things as regrets, remorse, and grief.

Thus, our deterministic pessimism may become a deterministic optimism at the price of extinguishing our judgments of regret.

But does not this immediately bring us into a curious logical predicament? Our determinism leads us to call our judgments of regret wrong, because they are pessimistic in implying that what is impossible yet ought to be. But how then about the judgments of regret themselves? If they are wrong, other judgments, judgments of approval presumably, ought to be in their place. But as they are necessitated, nothing else *can* be in their place; and the universe is just what it was before—namely, a place in which what ought to be appears impossible. We have got one foot out of the pessimistic bog, but the other one sinks all the deeper. We have rescued our actions from the bonds of evil, but our judgments are now held fast. When murders and treacheries cease to be sins, regrets are theoretic absurdities and errors. The theoretic and the active life thus play a kind of see-saw with each other on the ground of evil. The rise of either sends the other down. Murder and treachery cannot be good without regret being bad: regret cannot be good without treachery and murder being bad. Both, however, are supposed to have been foredoomed; so something must be fatally unreasonable, absurd, and wrong in the world. It must be a place of which either sin or error forms a necessary part. From this dilemma there seems at first sight no escape. Are we then so soon to fall back into the pessimism from which we thought we had emerged? And is there no possible way by which we may, with good intellectual consciences, call the cruelties and the treacheries, the reluctances and the regrets, *all* good together?

Certainly there is such a way, and you are probably most of you ready to formulate it yourselves. But, before doing so, remark how inevitably the question of determinism and indeterminism slides us into the question of optimism and pessimism, or, as our fathers called it, "the question of evil." The theological form of all these disputes is the simplest and the deepest, the form from which there is the least escape—not because, as some have sarcastically said, remorse and regret are clung to with a morbid fondness by the theologians as spiritual luxuries, but because they are existing facts of the world, and as such must be taken into account in the deterministic interpretation of all that is fated to be. If they are fated to be error, does not the bat's wing of irrationality still cast its shadow over the world?

The refuge from the quandary lies, as I said, not far off. The necessary acts we erroneously regret may be good, and yet our error in so regretting them may be also good, on one simple condition; and that condition is this: The world must not be regarded as a machine whose final purpose is the making real of any outward good, but rather as a contrivance for deepening the theoretic consciousness of what goodness and evil in their intrinsic natures are. Not the doing either of good or of evil is what nature cares for, but the knowing of them. Life is one long eating of the fruit of the tree of *knowledge*. I am in the habit, in thinking to myself, of calling this point of view the *gnostical* point of view. According to it, the world is neither an optimism nor a pessimism, but a *gnosticism*. But as this term may perhaps lead to some misunderstandings, I will use it as little as possible here, and speak rather of *subjectivism*, and the *subjectivistic* point of view.

Subjectivism has three great branches—we may call them scientificism, sentimentalism, and sensualism, respectively. They all agree essentially about the universe, in deeming that what happens there is subsidiary to what we think or feel about it. Crime justifies its criminality by awakening our intelligence of that criminality, and eventually our remorses and regrets; and the error included in remorses and regrets, the error of supposing that the past could have been different, justifies itself by its use. Its use is to quicken our sense of *what* the irretrievably lost is. When we think of it as that which might have been ("the saddest words of tongue or pen"), the quality of its worth speaks to us with a wilder sweetness; and, conversely, the dissatisfaction wherewith we think of what seems to have driven it from its natural place gives us the severer pang. Admirable artifice of nature! we might be tempted to exclaim—deceiving us in order the better to enlighten us, and leaving nothing undone to accentuate to our consciousness the yawning distance of those opposite poles of good and evil between which creation swings.

We have thus clearly revealed to our view what may be called the dilemma of determinism, so far as determinism pretends to think things out at all. A merely mechanical determinism, it is true, rather rejoices in not thinking them out. It is very sure that the universe must satisfy its postulate of a physical continuity and coherence, but it smiles at anyone who comes forward with a postulate of moral coherence as well. I may suppose, however, that the number of purely mechanical or hard determinists among you this evening is small.

The determinism to whose seductions you are most exposed is what I have called soft determinism—the determinism which allows considerations of good and bad to mingle with those of cause and effect in deciding what sort of a universe this may rationally be held to be. The dilemma of this determinism is one whose left horn is pessimism and whose right horn is subjectivism. In other words, if determinism is to escape pessimism, it must leave off looking at the goods and ills of life in a simple objective way, and regard them as materials, indifferent in themselves, for the production of consciousness, scientific and ethical, in us.

To escape pessimism is, as we all know, no easy task. Your own studies have sufficiently shown you the almost desperate difficulty of making the notion that there is a single principle of things, and that principle absolute perfection, rhyme together with our daily vision of the facts of life. If perfection be the principle, how comes there any imperfection here? If God be good, how came he to create—or, if he did not create, how comes he to permit—the devil? The evil facts must be explained as seeming: the devil must be whitewashed, the universe must be disinfected, if neither God's goodness nor his unity and power are to remain impugned. And of all the various ways of operating the disinfection, and making bad seem less bad, the way of subjectivism appears by far the best.[6]

For, after all, is there not something rather absurd in our ordinary notion of external things being good or bad in themselves? Can murders and treacheries, considered as mere outward happenings, or motions of matter, be bad without anyone to feel their badness? And could paradise properly be good in the absence of a sentient principle by which the goodness was perceived? Outward goods and evils seem prac-

---

[6]To a reader who says he is satisfied with a pessimism, and has no objection to thinking the whole bad, I have no more to say: he makes fewer demands on the world than I, who, making them, wish to look a little farther before I give up all hope of having them satisfied. If, however, all he means is that the badness of some parts does not prevent his acceptance of a universe whose *other* parts give him satisfaction, I welcome him as an ally. He has abandoned the notion of the *Whole*, which is the essence of deterministic monism, and views things as a pluralism, just as I do in this paper.

tically indistinguishable except in so far as they result in getting moral judgments made about them. But then the moral
judgments seem the main thing, and the outward facts mere
perishing instruments for their production. This is subjectivism. Everyone must at some time have wondered at that
strange paradox of our moral nature, that, though the pursuit
of outward good is the breath of its nostrils, the attainment of
outward good would seem to be its suffocation and death.
Why does the painting of any paradise or utopia, in heaven or
on earth, awaken such yawnings for nirvana and escape? The
white-robed harp-playing heaven of our sabbath-schools, and
the ladylike tea-table elysium represented in Mr. Spencer's
Data of Ethics, as the final consummation of progress, are exactly on a par in this respect—lubberlands, pure and simple,
one and all.[7] We look upon them from this delicious mess of
insanities and realities, strivings and deadnesses, hopes and
fears, agonies and exultations, which forms our present state,
and *tedium vitæ* is the only sentiment they awaken in our
breasts. To our crepuscular natures, born for the conflict, the
Rembrandtesque moral chiaroscuro, the shifting struggle of
the sunbeam in the gloom, such pictures of light upon light
are vacuous and expressionless, and neither to be enjoyed nor
understood. If *this* be the whole fruit of the victory, we say; if
the generations of mankind suffered and laid down their lives;
if prophets confessed and martyrs sang in the fire, and all the
sacred tears were shed for no other end than that a race of
creatures of such unexampled insipidity should succeed, and
protract in *sæcula sæculorum* their contented and inoffensive
lives—why, at such a rate, better lose than win the battle, or
at all events better ring down the curtain before the last act of
the play, so that a business that began so importantly may be
saved from so singularly flat a winding-up.

All this is what I should instantly say, were I called on to
plead for gnosticism; and its real friends, of whom you will
presently perceive I am not one, would say without difficulty
a great deal more. Regarded as a stable finality, every outward good becomes a mere weariness to the flesh. It must be

---

[7]Compare Sir James Stephen's *Essays* by a Barrister, London, 1862, pp. 138,
318.

menaced, be occasionally lost, for its goodness to be fully felt as such. Nay, more than occasionally lost. No one knows the worth of innocence till he knows it is gone forever, and that money cannot buy it back. Not the saint, but the sinner that repenteth, is he to whom the full length and breadth, and height and depth, of life's meaning is revealed. Not the absence of vice, but vice there, and virtue holding her by the throat, seems the ideal human state. And there seems no reason to suppose it not a permanent human state. There is a deep truth in what the school of Schopenhauer insists on— the illusoriness of the notion of moral progress. The more brutal forms of evil that go are replaced by others more subtle and more poisonous. Our moral horizon moves with us as we move, and never do we draw nearer to the far-off line where the black waves and the azure meet. The final purpose of our creation seems most plausibly to be the greatest possible enrichment of our ethical consciousness, through the intensest play of contrasts and the widest diversity of characters. This of course obliges some of us to be vessels of wrath, whilst it calls others to be vessels of honor. But the subjectivist point of view reduces all these outward distinctions to a common denominator. The wretch languishing in the felon's cell may be drinking draughts of the wine of truth that will never pass the lips of the so-called favorite of fortune. And the peculiar consciousness of each of them is an indispensable note in the great ethical concert which the centuries as they roll are grinding out of the living heart of man.

So much for subjectivism! If the dilemma of determinism be to choose between it and pessimism, I see little room for hesitation from the strictly theoretical point of view. Subjectivism seems the more rational scheme. And the world may, possibly, for aught I know, be nothing else. When the healthy love of life is on one, and all its forms and its appetites seem so unutterably real; when the most brutal and the most spiritual things are lit by the same sun, and each is an integral part of the total richness—why, then it seems a grudging and sickly way of meeting so robust a universe to shrink from any of its facts and wish them not to be. Rather take the strictly dramatic point of view, and treat the whole thing as a great unending romance which the spirit of the universe, striving to realize its own content, is eternally thinking out and representing to itself.[8]

No one, I hope, will accuse me, after I have said all this, of underrating the reasons in favor of subjectivism. And now that I proceed to say why those reasons, strong as they are, fail to convince my own mind, I trust the presumption may be that my objections are stronger still.

I frankly confess that they are of a practical order. If we practically take up subjectivism in a sincere and radical manner and follow its consequences, we meet with some that make us pause. Let a subjectivism begin in never so severe and intellectual a way, it is forced by the law of its nature to develop another side of itself and end with the corruptest curiosity. Once dismiss the notion that certain duties are good in themselves, and that we are here to do them, no matter how we feel about them; once consecrate the opposite notion that our performances and our violations of duty are for a common purpose, the attainment of subjective knowledge and feeling, and that the deepening of these is the chief end of our lives—and at what point on the downward slope are we to stop? In theology, subjectivism develops as its "left wing" antinomianism. In literature, its left wing is romanticism. And in practical life it is either a nerveless sentimentality or a sensualism without bounds.

Everywhere it fosters the fatalistic mood of mind. It makes those who are already too inert more passive still; it renders wholly reckless those whose energy is already in excess. All through history we find how subjectivism, as soon as it has a free career, exhausts itself in every sort of spiritual, moral, and practical license. Its optimism turns to an ethical indifference, which infallibly brings dissolution in its train. It is perfectly safe to say now that if the hegelian gnosticism, which has begun to show itself here and in Great Britain, were to become a popular philosophy, as it once was in Germany, it

[8]"Cet univers est un spectacle que Dieu se donne à lui-même. Servons les intentions du grand chorège en contribuant à rendre le spectacle aussi brillant, aussi varié que possible."—RENAN.

would certainly develop its left wing here as there, and produce a reaction of disgust. Already I have heard a graduate of
this very school express in the pulpit his willingness to sin like
David, if only he might repent like David. You may tell me
he was only sowing his wild, or rather his tame, oats; and
perhaps he was. But the point is that in the subjectivistic or
gnostical philosophy oat-sowing, wild or tame, becomes a
systematic necessity and the chief function of life. After the
pure and classic truths, the exciting and rancid ones must be
experienced; and if the stupid virtues of the philistine herd do
not then come in and save society from the influence of the
children of light, a sort of inward putrefaction becomes its
inevitable doom.

Look at the last runnings of the romantic school, as we see
them in that strange contemporary Parisian literature, with
which we of the less clever countries are so often driven to
rinse out our minds after they have become clogged with the
dulness and heaviness of our native pursuits. The romantic
school began with the worship of subjective sensibility and
the revolt against legality of which Rousseau was the first
great prophet; and through various fluxes and refluxes, right
wings and left wings, it stands to-day with two men of genius, M. Renan and M. Zola, as its principal exponents—one
speaking with its masculine, and the other with what might
be called its feminine, voice. I prefer not to think now of less
noble members of the school, and the Renan I have in mind
is of course the Renan of latest dates. As I have used the term
gnostic, both he and Zola are gnostics of the most pronounced sort. Both are athirst for the facts of life, and both
think the facts of human sensibility to be of all facts the most
worthy of attention. Both agree, moreover, that sensibility
seems to be there for no higher purpose—certainly not, as
the Philistines say, for the sake of bringing mere outward
rights to pass and frustrating outward wrongs. One dwells on
the sensibilities for their energy, the other for their sweetness;
one speaks with a voice of bronze, the other with that of an
Æolian harp; one ruggedly ignores the distinction of good
and evil, the other plays the coquette between the craven un-
manliness of his Philosophic Dialogues and the butterfly optimism of his *Souvenirs de jeunesse*. But under the pages of

both there sounds incessantly the hoarse bass of *vanitas vani-tatum, omnia vanitas*, which the reader may hear, whenever he will, between the lines. No writer of this French romantic school has a word of rescue from the hour of satiety with the things of life—the hour in which we say, "I take no pleasure in them"—or from the hour of terror at the world's vast meaningless grinding, if perchance such hours should come. For terror and satiety are facts of sensibility like any others; and at their own hour they reign in their own right. The heart of the romantic utterances, whether poetical, critical, or his-torical, is this inward remedilessness, what Carlyle calls this far-off whimpering of wail and woe. And from this romantic state of mind there is absolutely no possible *theoretic* escape. Whether, like Renan, we look upon life in a more refined way, as a romance of the spirit; or whether, like the friends of M. Zola, we pique ourselves on our "scientific" and "analytic" character, and prefer to be cynical, and call the world a "roman experimental" on an infinite scale—in either case the world appears to us potentially as what the same Carlyle once called it, a vast, gloomy, solitary Golgotha and mill of death.

The only escape is by the practical way. And since I have mentioned the nowadays much-reviled name of Carlyle, let me mention it once more, and say it is the way of his teach-ing. No matter for Carlyle's life, no matter for a great deal of his writing. What was the most important thing he said to us? He said: "Hang your sensibilities! Stop your snivelling com-plaints, and your equally snivelling raptures! Leave off your general emotional tomfoolery, and get to WORK like men!" But this means a complete rupture with the subjectivist phi-losophy of things. It says conduct, and not sensibility, is the ultimate fact for our recognition. With the vision of certain works to be done, of certain outward changes to be wrought or resisted, it says our intellectual horizon terminates. No matter how we succeed in doing these outward duties, whether gladly and spontaneously, or heavily and unwillingly, do them we somehow must; for the leaving of them undone is perdition. No matter how we feel; if we are only faithful in the outward act and refuse to do wrong, the world will in so far be safe, and we quit of our debt towards it. Take, then, the yoke upon our shoulders; bend our neck beneath the heavy legality of its weight; regard something else than our feeling as our limit, our master, and our law; be willing to live and die in its service—and, at a stroke, we have passed from the subjective into the objective philosophy of things, much as one awakens from some feverish dream, full of bad lights and noises, to find one's self bathed in the sacred coolness and quiet of the air of the night.

But what is the essence of this philosophy of objective conduct, so old-fashioned and finite, but so chaste and sane and strong, when compared with its romantic rival? It is the recognition of limits, foreign and opaque to our understanding. It is the willingness, after bringing about some external good, to feel at peace; for our responsibility ends with the performance of that duty, and the burden of the rest we may lay on higher powers.[9]

> "Look to thyself, O Universe!
> Thou art better, and not worse,"

we may say in that philosophy, the moment we have done our stroke of conduct, however small. For in the view of that philosophy the universe belongs to a plurality of semi-independent forces, each one of which may help or hinder, and be helped or hindered by, the operations of the rest.

But this brings us right back, after such a long détour, to the question of indeterminism and to the conclusion of all I came here to say to-night. For the only consistent way of representing a pluralism and a world whose parts may affect one another through their conduct being either good or bad is the indeterministic way. What interest, zest, or excitement can there be in achieving the right way, unless we are enabled to feel that the wrong way is also a possible and a natural way— nay, more, a menacing and an imminent way? And what sense can there be in condemning ourselves for taking the wrong way, unless we need have done nothing of the sort, unless the right way was open to us as well? I cannot understand the

[9]The burden, for example, of seeing to it that the *end* of all our righteousness be some positive universal gain.

willingness to act, no matter how we feel, without the belief that acts are really good and bad. I cannot understand the belief that an act is bad, without regret at its happening. I cannot understand regret without the admission of real, genuine possibilities in the world. Only *then* is it other than a mockery to feel, after we have failed to do our best, that an irreparable opportunity is gone from the universe, the loss of which it must forever after mourn.

If you insist that this is all superstition, that possibility is in the eye of science and reason impossibility, and that if I act badly 'tis that the universe was foredoomed to suffer this defect, you fall right back into the dilemma, the labyrinth, of pessimism and subjectivism, from out of whose toils we have just wound our way.

Now, we are of course free to fall back, if we please. For my own part, though, whatever difficulties may beset the philosophy of objective right and wrong, and the indeterminism it seems to imply, determinism, with its alternative of pessimism or romanticism, contains difficulties that are greater still. But you will remember that I expressly repudiated awhile ago the pretension to offer any arguments which could be coercive in a so-called scientific fashion in this matter. And I consequently find myself, at the end of this long talk, obliged to state my conclusions in an altogether personal way. This personal method of appeal seems to be among the very conditions of the problem; and the most anyone can do is to confess as candidly as he can the grounds for the faith that is in him, and leave his example to work on others as it may.

Let me, then, without circumlocution say just this. The world is enigmatical enough in all conscience, whatever theory we may take up towards it. The indeterminism I defend, the free-will theory of popular sense based on the judgment of regret, represents that world as vulnerable, and liable to be injured by certain of its parts if they act wrong. And it represents their acting wrong as a matter of possibility or accident, neither inevitable nor yet to be infallibly warded off. In all this, it is a theory devoid either of transparency or of stability. It gives us a pluralistic, restless universe, in which no single point of view can ever take in the whole scene; and to a mind possessed of the love of unity at any cost, it will, no doubt, remain forever inacceptable. A friend with such a mind once told me that the thought of my universe made him sick, like the sight of the horrible motion of a mass of maggots in their carrion bed.

But whilst I freely admit that the pluralism and the restlessness are repugnant and irrational in a certain way, I find that every alternative to them is irrational in a deeper way. The indeterminism with its maggots, if you please to speak so about it, offends only the native absolutism of my intellect—an absolutism which, after all, perhaps, deserves to be snubbed and kept in check. But the determinism with its necessary carrion, to continue the figure of speech, and with no possible maggots to eat the latter up, violates my sense of moral reality through and through. When, for example, I imagine such carrion as the Brockton murder, I cannot conceive it as an act by which the universe, as a whole, logically and necessarily expresses its nature without shrinking from complicity with such a whole. And I deliberately refuse to keep on terms of loyalty with the universe by saying blankly that the murder, since it does flow from the nature of the whole, is not carrion. There are *some* instinctive reactions which I, for one, will not tamper with. The only remaining alternative, the attitude of gnostical romanticism, wrenches my personal instincts in quite as violent a way. It falsifies the simple objectivity of their deliverance. It makes the gooseflesh the murder excites in me a sufficient reason for the perpetration of the crime. It transforms life from a tragic reality into an insincere melodramatic exhibition, as foul or as tawdry as anyone's diseased curiosity pleases to carry it out. And with its consecration of the "roman naturaliste" state of mind, and its enthronement of the baser crew of Parisian *littérateurs* among the eternally indispensable organs by which the infinite spirit of things attains to that subjective illumination which is the task of its life, it leaves me in presence of a sort of subjective carrion considerably more noisome than the objective carrion I called it in to take away.

No! better a thousand times, than such systematic corruption of our moral sanity, the plainest pessimism, so that it be straightforward; but better far than that the world of chance.

Make as great an uproar about chance as you please, I know that chance means pluralism and nothing more. If some of the members of the pluralism are bad, the philosophy of pluralism, whatever broad views it may deny me, permits me, at least, to turn to the other members with a clean breast of affection and an unsophisticated moral sense. And if I still wish to think of the world as a totality, it lets me feel that a world with a *chance* in it of being altogether good, even if the chance never come to pass, is better than a world with no such chance at all. That "chance" whose very notion I am exhorted and conjured to banish from my view of the future as the suicide of reason concerning it, that "chance" is—what? Just this—the chance that in moral respects the future may be other and better than the past has been. This is the only chance we have any motive for supposing to exist. Shame, rather, on its repudiation and its denial! For its presence is the vital air which lets the world live, the salt which keeps it sweet.

And here I might legitimately stop, having expressed all I care to see admitted by others to-night. But I know that if I do stop here, misapprehensions will remain in the minds of some of you, and keep all I have said from having its effect; so I judge it best to add a few more words.

In the first place, in spite of all my explanations, the word "chance" will still be giving trouble. Though you may yourselves be adverse to the deterministic doctrine, you wish a pleasanter word than "chance" to name the opposite doctrine by; and you very likely consider my preference for such a word a perverse sort of a partiality on my part. It certainly *is* a bad word to make converts with; and you wish I had not thrust it so butt-foremost at you—you wish to use a milder term.

Well, I admit there may be just a dash of perversity in its choice. The spectacle of the mere word-grabbing game played by the soft determinists has perhaps driven me too violently the other way; and, rather than be found wrangling with them for the good words, I am willing to take the first bad one which comes along, provided it be unequivocal. The question is of things, not of eulogistic names for them; and the best word is the one that enables men to know the quick-est whether they disagree or not about the things. But the word "chance," with its singular negativity, is just the word for this purpose. Whoever uses it instead of "freedom," squarely and resolutely gives up all pretence to control the things he says are free. For *him*, he confesses that they are no better than mere chance would be. It is a word of *impotence*, and is therefore the only sincere word we can use, if, in grant-ing freedom to certain things, we grant it honestly, and really risk the game. "Who chooses me must give and forfeit all he hath." Any other word permits of quibbling, and lets us, after the fashion of the soft determinists, make a pretence of restor-ing the caged bird to liberty with one hand, whilst with the other we anxiously tie a string to its leg to make sure it does not get beyond our sight.

But now you will bring up your final doubt. Does not the admission of such an unguaranteed chance or freedom pre-clude utterly the notion of a Providence governing the world? Does it not leave the fate of the universe at the mercy of the chance-possibilities, and so far insecure? Does it not, in short, deny the craving of our nature for an ultimate peace behind all tempests, for a blue zenith above all clouds?

To this my answer must be very brief. The belief in free-will is not in the least incompatible with the belief in Providence, provided you do not restrict the Providence to fulminating nothing but *fatal* decrees. If you allow him to provide possi-bilities as well as actualities to the universe, and to carry on his own thinking in those two categories just as we do ours, chances may be there, uncontrolled even by him, and the course of the universe be really ambiguous; and yet the end of all things may be just what he intended it to be from all eternity.

An analogy will make the meaning of this clear. Suppose two men before a chessboard—the one a novice, the other an expert player of the game. The expert intends to beat. But he cannot foresee exactly what any one actual move of his adver-sary may be. He knows, however, all the *possible* moves of the latter; and he knows in advance how to meet each of them by a move of his own which leads in the direction of victory.

And the victory infallibly arrives, after no matter how devious a course, in the one predestined form of check-mate to the novice's king.

Let now the novice stand for us finite free agents, and the expert for the infinite mind in which the universe lies. Suppose the latter to be thinking out his universe before he actually creates it. Suppose him to say, I will lead things to a certain end, but I will not *now*[10] decide on all the steps thereto. At various points, ambiguous possibilities shall be left open, *either* of which, at a given instant, may become actual. But whichever branch of these bifurcations become real, I know what I shall do at the *next* bifurcation to keep things from drifting away from the final result I intend.[11]

The creator's plan of the universe would thus be left blank as to many of its actual details, but all possibilities would be marked down. The realization of some of these would be left absolutely to chance; that is, would only be determined when the moment of realization came. Other possibilities would be

[10] This of course leaves the creative mind subject to the law of time. And to anyone who insists on the timelessness of that mind I have no reply to make. A mind to whom all time is simultaneously present must see all things under the form of actuality, or under some form to us unknown. If he thinks certain moments as ambiguous in their content whilst future, he must simultaneously know how the ambiguity will have been decided when they are past. So that none of his mental judgments can possibly be called hypothetical, and his world is one from which chance is excluded. Is not, however, the timeless mind rather a gratuitous fiction? And is not the notion of eternity being given at a stroke to omniscience only just another way of whacking upon us the block-universe, and of denying that possibilities exist?—just the point to be proved. To say that time is an illusory appearance is only a round-about manner of saying there is no real plurality, and that the frame of things is an absolute unit. Admit plurality, and time may be its form.

[11] And this of course means "miraculous" interposition, but not necessarily of the gross sort our fathers took such delight in representing, and which has so lost its magic for us. Emerson quotes some Eastern sage as saying that if evil were really done under the sun, the sky would incontinently shrivel to a snakeskin and cast it out in spasms. But, says Emerson, the spasms of Nature are years and centuries; and it will tax man's patience to wait so long. We may think of the reserved possibilities God keeps in his own hand, under as invisible and molecular and slowly self-summating a form as we please. We may think of them as counteracting human agencies which he inspires *ad hoc*. In short, signs and wonders and convulsions of the earth and sky are not the only neutralizers of obstruction to a god's plans of which it is possible to think.

contingently determined; that is, their decision would have to wait till it was seen how the matters of absolute chance fell out. But the rest of the plan, including its final upshot, would be rigorously determined once for all. So the creator himself would not need to know *all* the details of actuality until they came; and at any time his own view of the world would be a view partly of facts and partly of possibilities, exactly as ours is now. Of one thing, however, he might be certain; and that is that his world was safe, and that no matter how much it might zigzag he could surely bring it home at last.

Now, it is entirely immaterial, in this scheme, whether the creator leave the absolute chance-possibilities to be decided by himself, each when its proper moment arrives, or whether, on the contrary, he alienate this power from himself, and leave the decision out and out to finite creatures such as we men are. The great point is that the possibilities are really *here*. Whether it be we who solve them, or he working through us, at those soul-trying moments when fate's scales seem to quiver, and good snatches the victory from evil or shrinks nerveless from the fight, is of small account, so long as we admit that the issue is decided nowhere else than *here* and *now*. *That* is what gives the palpitating reality to our moral life and makes it tingle, as Mr. Mallock says, with so strange and elaborate an excitement. This reality, this excitement, are what the determinisms, hard and soft alike, suppress by their denial that *anything* is decided here and now, and their dogma that all things were foredoomed and settled long ago. If it be so, may you and I then have been foredoomed to the error of continuing to believe in liberty.[12] It is fortunate for the winding up of controversy that in every discussion with determinism this *argumentum ad hominem* can be its adversary's last word.

[12]As long as languages contain a future perfect tense, determinists, following the bent of laziness or passion, the lines of least resistance, can reply in that tense, saying, "It will have been fated," to the still small voice which urges an opposite course; and thus excuse themselves from effort in a quite unanswerable way.

The Moral Philosopher and the Moral Life [1]

THE MAIN PURPOSE of this paper is to show that there is no such thing possible as an ethical philosophy dogmatically made up in advance. We all help to determine the content of ethical philosophy so far as we contribute to the race's moral life. In other words, there can be no final truth in ethics any more than in physics, until the last man has had his experience and said his say. In the one case as in the other, however, the hypotheses which we now make while waiting, and the acts to which they prompt us, are among the indispensable conditions which determine what that "say" shall be.

First of all, what is the position of him who seeks an ethical philosophy? To begin with, he must be distinguished from all those who are satisfied to be ethical sceptics. He *will* not be a sceptic; therefore so far from ethical scepticism being one possible fruit of ethical philosophizing, it can only be regarded as that residual alternative to all philosophy which from the outset menaces every would-be philosopher who may give up the quest discouraged, and renounce his original aim. That aim is to find an account of the moral relations that obtain among things, which will weave them into the unity of a stable system, and make of the world what one may call a genuine universe from the ethical point of view. So far as the world resists reduction to the form of unity, so far as ethical propositions seem unstable, so far does the philosopher fail of his ideal. The subject-matter of his study is the ideals he finds existing in the world; the purpose which guides him is this ideal of his own, of getting them into a certain form. This ideal is thus a factor in ethical philosophy whose legitimate presence must never be overlooked; it is a positive contribution which the philosopher himself necessarily makes to the problem. But it is his only positive contribution. At the outset of his inquiry he ought to have no other

[1]An Address to the Yale Philosophical Club, published in the *International Journal of Ethics*, April, 1891.

ideals. Were he interested peculiarly in the triumph of any one kind of good, he would *pro tanto* cease to be a judicial investigator, and become an advocate for some limited element of the case.

There are three questions in ethics which must be kept apart. Let them be called respectively the *psychological* question, the *metaphysical* question, and the *casuistic* question. The psychological question asks after the historical *origin* of our moral ideas and judgments; the metaphysical question asks what the very *meaning* of the words "good," "ill," and "obligation" are; the casuistic question asks what is the *measure* of the various goods and ills which men recognize, so that the philosopher may settle the true order of human obligations.

I

The psychological question is for most disputants the only question. When your ordinary doctor of divinity has proved to his own satisfaction that an altogether unique faculty called "conscience" must be postulated to tell us what is right and what is wrong; or when your popular-science enthusiast has proclaimed that "apriorism" is an exploded superstition, and that our moral judgments have gradually resulted from the teaching of the environment, each of these persons thinks that ethics is settled and nothing more is to be said. The familiar pair of names, Intuitionist and Evolutionist, so commonly used now to connote all possible differences in ethical opinion, really refer to the psychological question alone. The discussion of this question hinges so much upon particular details that it is impossible to enter upon it at all within the limits of this paper. I will therefore only express dogmatically my own belief, which is this—that the Benthams, the Mills, and the Bains have done a lasting service in taking so many of our human ideals and showing how they must have arisen from the association with acts of simple bodily pleasures and reliefs from pain. Association with many remote pleasures will unquestionably make a thing significant of goodness in our minds; and the more vaguely the goodness is conceived of, the more mysterious will its source appear to be. But it is surely impossible to explain all our sentiments and preferences in this simple way. The more minutely psychology studies human nature, the more clearly it finds there traces of secondary affections, relating the impressions of the environment with one another and with our impulses in quite different ways from those mere associations of coexistence and succession which are practically all that pure empiricism can admit. Take the love of drunkenness; take bashfulness, the terror of high places, the tendency to sea-sickness, to faint at the sight of blood, the susceptibility to musical sounds; take the emotion of the comical, the passion for poetry, for mathematics, or for metaphysics—no one of these things can be wholly explained by either association or utility. They *go with* other things that can be so explained, no doubt; and some of them are prophetic of future utilities, since there is nothing in us for which some use may not be found. But their origin is in incidental complications to our cerebral structure, a structure whose original features arose with no reference to the perception of such discords and harmonies as these.

Well, a vast number of our moral perceptions also are certainly of this secondary and brain-born kind. They deal with directly felt fitnesses between things, and often fly in the teeth of all the prepossessions of habit and presumptions of utility. The moment you get beyond the coarser and more commonplace moral maxims, the Decalogues and Poor Richard's Almanacs, you fall into schemes and positions which to the eye of common-sense are fantastic and over-strained. The sense for abstract justice which some persons have is as excentric a variation, from the natural-history point of view, as is the passion for music or for the higher philosophical consistencies which consumes the soul of others. The feeling of the inward dignity of certain spiritual attitudes, as peace, serenity, simplicity, veracity; and of the essential vulgarity of others, as querulousness, anxiety, egoistic fussiness, etc.—are quite inexplicable except by an innate preference of the more ideal attitude for its own pure sake. The nobler thing *tastes* better, and that is all that we can say. "Experience" of consequences may truly teach us what things are *wicked*, but what have consequences to do with what is *mean* and *vulgar*? If a man has shot his wife's paramour, by reason of what subtle repug-

nancy in things is it that we are so disgusted when we hear
that the wife and the husband have made it up and are living
comfortably together again? Or if the hypothesis were offered
us of a world in which Messrs. Fourier's and Bellamy's and
Morris's utopias should all be outdone, and millions kept
permanently happy on the one simple condition that a certain
lost soul on the far-off edge of things should lead a life of
lonely torture, what except a specifical and independent sort
of emotion can it be which would make us immediately feel,
even though an impulse arose within us to clutch at the
happiness so offered, how hideous a thing would be its enjoyment when deliberately accepted as the fruit of such a
bargain? To what, once more, but subtle brain-born feelings
of discord can be due all these recent protests against the
entire race-tradition of retributive justice?—I refer to Tolstoï
with his ideas of non-resistance, to Mr. Bellamy with his substitution of oblivion for repentance (in his novel of Dr.
Heidenhain's Process), to M. Guyau with his radical condemnation of the punitive ideal. All these subtleties of the moral
sensibility go as much beyond what can be ciphered out from
the "laws of association" as the delicacies of sentiment possible between a pair of young lovers go beyond such precepts
of the "etiquette to be observed during engagement" as are
printed in manuals of social form.

No! Purely inward forces are certainly at work here. All the
higher, more penetrating ideals are revolutionary. They
present themselves far less in the guise of effects of past experience than in that of probable causes of future experience,
factors to which the environment and the lessons it has so far
taught us must learn to bend.

This is all I can say of the psychological question now.
In the last chapter of a recent work[2] I have sought to prove
in a general way the existence, in our thought, of relations
which do not merely repeat the couplings of experience. Our
ideals have certainly many sources. They are not all explicable as signifying corporeal pleasures to be gained, and pains
to be escaped. And for having so constantly perceived this
psychological fact, we must applaud the intuitionist school.

[2]*The Principles of Psychology*, New York, H. Holt & Co., 1890.

Whether or not such applause must be extended to that school's other characteristics will appear as we take up the following questions.

The next one in order is the metaphysical question, of what we mean by the words "obligation," "good," and "ill."

II

First of all, it appears that such words can have no application or relevancy in a world in which no sentient life exists. Imagine an absolutely material world, containing only physical and chemical facts, and existing from eternity without a God, without even an interested spectator: would there be any sense in saying of that world that one of its states is better than another? Or if there were two such worlds possible, would there be any rhyme or reason in calling one good and the other bad—good or bad positively, I mean, and apart from the fact that one might relate itself better than the other to the philosopher's private interests? But we must leave these private interests out of the account, for the philosopher is a mental fact, and we are asking whether goods and evils and obligations exist in physical facts *per se*. Surely there is no *status* for good and evil to exist in, in a purely insentient world. How can one physical fact, considered simply as a physical fact, be "better" than another? Betterness is not a physical relation. In its mere material capacity, a thing can no more be good or bad than it can be pleasant or painful. Good for what? Good for the production of another physical fact, do you say? But what in a purely physical universe demands the production of that other fact? Physical facts simply *are* or are *not*; and neither when present or absent, can they be supposed to make demands. If they do, they can only do so by having desires; and then they have ceased to be purely physical facts, and have become facts of conscious sensibility. Goodness, badness, and obligation must be *realized* somewhere in order really to exist; and the first step in ethical philosophy is to see that no merely inorganic "nature of things" can realize them. Neither moral relations nor the moral law can swing *in vacuo*. Their only habitat can be a mind which feels them; and no world composed of merely physical facts can possibly be a world to which ethical propositions apply.

The moment one sentient being, however, is made a part of the universe, there is a chance for goods and evils really to exist. Moral relations now have their *status*, in that being's consciousness. So far as he feels anything to be good, he *makes* it good. It *is* good, for him; and being good for him, is absolutely good, for he is the sole creator of values in that universe, and outside of his opinion things have no moral character at all.

In such a universe as that it would of course be absurd to raise the question of whether the solitary thinker's judgments of good and ill are true or not. Truth supposes a standard outside of the thinker to which he must conform; but here the thinker is a sort of divinity, subject to no higher judge. Let us call the supposed universe which he inhabits a *moral solitude*. In such a moral solitude it is clear that there can be no outward obligation, and that the only trouble the god-like thinker is liable to have will be over the consistency of his own several ideals with one another. Some of these will no doubt be more pungent and appealing than the rest, their goodness will have a profounder, more penetrating taste; they will return to haunt him with more obstinate regrets if violated. So the thinker will have to order his life with them as its chief determinants, or else remain inwardly discordant and unhappy. Into whatever equilibrium he may settle, though, and however he may straighten out his system, it will be a right system; for beyond the facts of his own subjectivity there is nothing moral in the world.

If now we introduce a second thinker with his likes and dislikes into the universe, the ethical situation becomes much more complex, and several possibilities are immediately seen to obtain.

One of these is that the thinkers may ignore each other's attitude about good and evil altogether, and each continue to indulge his own preferences, indifferent to what the other may feel or do. In such a case we have a world with twice as much of the ethical quality in it as our moral solitude, only it is without ethical unity. The same object is good or bad there, according as you measure it by the view which this one or that one of the thinkers takes. Nor can you find any possible ground in such a world for saying that one thinker's opinion is more correct than the other's, or that either has the truer moral sense. Such a world, in short, is not a moral universe but a moral dualism. Not only is there no single point of view within it from which the values of things can be unequivocally judged, but there is not even a demand for such a point of view, since the two thinkers are supposed to be indifferent to each other's thoughts and acts. Multiply the thinkers into a pluralism, and we find realized for us in the ethical sphere something like that world which the antique sceptics conceived of—in which individual minds are the measures of all things, and in which no one "objective" truth, but only a multitude of "subjective" opinions, can be found.

But this is the kind of world with which the philosopher, so long as he holds to the hope of a philosophy, will not put up. Among the various ideals represented, there must be, he thinks, some which have the more truth or authority; and to these the others *ought* to yield, so that system and subordination may reign. Here in the word "ought" the notion of *obligation* comes emphatically into view, and the next thing in order must be to make its meaning clear.

Since the outcome of the discussion so far has been to show us that nothing can be good or right except so far as some consciousness feels it to be good or thinks it to be right, we perceive on the very threshold that the real superiority and authority which are postulated by the philosopher to reside in some of the opinions, and the really inferior character which he supposes must belong to others, cannot be explained by any abstract moral "nature of things" existing antecedently to the concrete thinkers themselves with their ideals. Like the positive attributes good and bad, the comparative ones better and worse must be *realized* in order to be real. If one ideal judgment be objectively better than another, that betterness must be made flesh by being lodged concretely in someone's actual perception. It cannot float in the atmosphere, for it is not a sort of meteorological phenomenon, like the aurora borealis or the zodiacal light. Its *esse* is *percipi*, like the *esse* of the ideals themselves between which it obtains. The philosopher, therefore, who seeks to know which ideal ought to have supreme weight and which one ought to be subordinated, must trace the *ought* itself to the *de facto* constitution of some existing consciousness, behind which, as one of the data of the universe, he as a purely ethical philosopher is unable to go. This consciousness must make the one ideal right by feeling it to be right, the other wrong by feeling it to be wrong. But now what particular consciousness in the universe *can* enjoy this prerogative of obliging others to conform to a rule which it lays down?

If one of the thinkers were obviously divine, while all the rest were human, there would probably be no practical dispute about the matter. The divine thought would be the model, to which the others should conform. But still the theoretic question would remain, What is the ground of the obligation, even here?

In our first essays at answering this question, there is an inevitable tendency to slip into an assumption which ordinary men follow when they are disputing with one another about questions of good and bad. They imagine an abstract moral order in which the objective truth resides; and each tries to prove that this pre-existing order is more accurately reflected in his own ideas than in those of his adversary. It is because one disputant is backed by this overarching abstract order that we think the other should submit. Even so, when it is a question no longer of two finite thinkers, but of God and ourselves—we follow our usual habit, and imagine a sort of *de jure* relation, which antedates and overarches the mere facts, and would make it right that we should conform our thoughts to God's thoughts, even though he made no claim to that effect, and though we preferred *de facto* to go on thinking for ourselves.

But the moment we take a steady look at the question, *we see not only that without a claim actually made by some concrete person there can be no obligation, but that there is some obligation wherever there is a claim.* Claim and obligation are, in fact, coextensive terms; they cover each other exactly. Our ordinary attitude of regarding ourselves as subject to an overarching system of moral relations, true "in themselves," is therefore either an out-and-out superstition, or else it must be treated as a merely provisional abstraction from that real Thinker in whose actual demand upon us to think as he does our obligation must be ultimately based. In a theistic-ethical philosophy that thinker in question is, of course, the Deity to whom the existence of the universe is due.

I know well how hard it is for those who are accustomed to what I have called the superstitious view, to realize that every *de facto* claim creates in so far forth an obligation. We inveterately think that something which we call the "validity" of the claim is what gives to it its obligatory character, and that this validity is something outside of the claim's mere existence as a matter of fact. It rains down upon the claim, we think, from some sublime dimension of being, which the moral law inhabits, much as upon the steel of the compass-needle the influence of the Pole rains down from out of the starry heavens. But again, how can such an inorganic abstract character of imperativeness, additional to the imperativeness which is in the concrete claim itself, *exist*? Take any demand, however slight, which any creature, however weak, may make. Ought it not, for its own sole sake, to be satisfied? If not, prove why not. The only possible kind of proof you could adduce would be the exhibition of another creature who should make a demand that ran the other way. The only possible reason there can be why any phenomenon ought to exist is that such a phenomenon actually is desired. Any desire is imperative to the extent of its amount; it *makes* itself valid by the fact that it exists at all. Some desires, truly enough, are small desires; they are put forward by insignificant persons, and we customarily make light of the obligations which they bring. But the fact that such personal demands as these impose small obligations does not keep the largest obligations from being personal demands.

If we must talk impersonally, to be sure we can say that "the universe" requires, exacts, or makes obligatory such or such an action, whenever it expresses itself through the desires of such or such a creature. But it is better not to talk about the universe in this personified way, unless we believe in a universal or divine consciousness which actually exists. If there be such a consciousness, then its demands carry the most of obligation simply because they are the greatest in amount. But it is even then not *abstractly* right that we should respect them. It is only *concretely* right—or right after the fact, and by virtue of the fact, that they are actually made. Suppose we do not respect them, as seems largely to be the case in this queer world. That ought not to be, we say; that is wrong. But in what way is this fact of wrongness made more acceptable or intelligible when we imagine it to consist rather in the laceration of an *à priori* ideal order than in the disappointment of a living personal God? Do we, perhaps, think that we cover God and protect him and make his impotence over us less ultimate, when we back him up with this *à priori* blanket from which he may draw some warmth of further appeal? But the only force of appeal to *us,* which either a living God or an abstract ideal order can wield, is found in the "everlasting ruby vaults" of our own human hearts, as they happen to beat responsive and not irresponsive to the claim. So far as they do feel it when made by a living consciousness, it is life answering to life. A claim thus livingly acknowledged is acknowledged with a solidity and fulness which no thought of an "ideal" backing can render more complete; while if, on the other hand, the heart's response is withheld, the stubborn phenomenon is there of an impotence in the claims which the universe embodies, which no talk about an eternal nature of things can gloze over or dispel. An ineffective *à priori* order is as impotent a thing as an ineffective God; and in the eye of philosophy, it is as hard a thing to explain.

We may now consider that what we distinguished as the metaphysical question in ethical philosophy is sufficiently answered, and that we have learned what the words "good," "bad," and "obligation" severally mean. They mean no absolute natures, independent of personal support. They are objects of feeling and desire, which have no foothold or anchorage in Being, apart from the existence of actually living minds.

Wherever such minds exist, with judgments of good and ill, and demands upon one another, there is an ethical world in its essential features. Were all other things, gods and men and starry heavens, blotted out from this universe, and were there left but one rock with two loving souls upon it, that rock would have as thoroughly moral a constitution as any possible world which the eternities and immensities could harbor. It would be a tragic constitution, because the rock's inhabitants would die. But while they lived, there would be real good things and real bad things in the universe; there would be obligations, claims, and expectations; obediences, refusals, and disappointments; compunctions and longings for harmony to come again, and inward peace of conscience when it was restored; there would, in short, be a moral life, whose active energy would have no limit but the intensity of interest in each other with which the hero and heroine might be endowed.

We, on this terrestrial globe, so far as the visible facts go, are just like the inhabitants of such a rock. Whether a God exist, or whether no God exist, in yon blue heaven above us bent, we form at any rate an ethical republic here below. And the first reflection which this leads to is that ethics have as genuine and real a foothold in a universe where the highest consciousness is human, as in a universe where there is a God as well. "The religion of humanity" affords a basis for ethics as well as theism does. Whether the purely human system can gratify the philosopher's demand as well as the other is a different question, which we ourselves must answer ere we close.

III

The last fundamental question in Ethics was, it will be remembered, the *casuistic* question. Here we are, in a world where the existence of a divine thinker has been and perhaps always will be doubted by some of the lookers-on, and where, in spite of the presence of a large number of ideals in which human beings agree, there are a mass of others about which no general consensus obtains. It is hardly necessary to present a literary picture of this, for the facts are too well known. The wars of the flesh and the spirit in each man, the concupiscences of different individuals pursuing the same unshareable material or social prizes, the ideals which contrast so according to races, circumstances, temperaments, philosophical beliefs, etc.—all form a maze of apparently inextricable confusion with no obvious Ariadne's thread to lead one out. Yet the philosopher, just because he is a philosopher, adds his own peculiar ideal to the confusion (with which if he were willing to be a sceptic he would be passably content), and insists that over all these individual opinions there is a *system of truth* which he can discover if he only takes sufficient pains.

We stand ourselves at present in the place of that philosopher, and must not fail to realize all the features that the situation comports. In the first place we will not be sceptics; we hold to it that there is a truth to be ascertained. But in the second place we have just gained the insight that that truth cannot be a self-proclaiming set of laws, or an abstract "moral reason," but can only exist in act, or in the shape of an opinion held by some thinker really to be found. There is, however, no visible thinker invested with authority. Shall we then simply proclaim our own ideals as the lawgiving ones? No; for if we are true philosophers we must throw our own spontaneous ideals, even the dearest, impartially in with that total mass of ideals which are fairly to be judged. But how then can we as philosophers ever find a test; how avoid complete moral scepticism on the one hand, and on the other escape bringing a wayward personal standard of our own along with us, on which we simply pin our faith?

The dilemma is a hard one, nor does it grow a bit more easy as we revolve it in our minds. The entire undertaking of the philosopher obliges him to seek an impartial test. That test, however, must be incarnated in the demand of some actually existent person; and how can he pick out the person save by an act in which his own sympathies and prepossessions are implied?

One method indeed presents itself, and has as a matter of history been taken by the more serious ethical schools. If the heap of things demanded proved on inspection less chaotic than at first they seemed, if they furnished their own relative test and measure, then the casuistic problem would be solved. If it were found that all goods *quâ* goods contained a common essence, then the amount of this essence involved in any one good would show its rank in the scale of goodness, and order could be quickly made; for this essence would be *the* good upon which all thinkers were agreed, the relatively objective and universal good that the philosopher seeks. Even his own private ideals would be measured by their share of it, and find their rightful place among the rest.

Various essences of good have thus been found and proposed as bases of the ethical system. Thus, to be a mean between two extremes; to be recognized by a special intuitive faculty; to make the agent happy for the moment; to make others as well as him happy in the long run; to add to his perfection or dignity; to harm no one; to follow from reason or flow from universal law; to be in accordance with the will of God; to promote the survival of the human species on this planet — are so many tests, each of which has been maintained by somebody to constitute the essence of all good things or actions so far as they are good.

No one of the measures that have been actually proposed has, however, given general satisfaction. Some are obviously not universally present in all cases — *e.g.*, the character of harming no one, or that of following a universal law; for the best course is often cruel; and many acts are reckoned good on the sole condition that they be exceptions, and serve not as examples of a universal law. Other characters, such as following the will of God, are unascertainable and vague. Others again, like survival, are quite indeterminate in their consequences, and leave us in the lurch where we most need their help: a philosopher of the Sioux Nation, for example, will be certain to use the survival-criterion in a very different way from ourselves. The best, on the whole, of these marks and measures of goodness seems to be the capacity to bring happiness. But in order not to break down fatally, this test must be taken to cover innumerable acts and impulses that never *aim* at happiness; so that, after all, in seeking for a universal principle we inevitably are carried onward to the *most* universal principle — that *the essence of good is simply to satisfy demand.* The demand may be for anything under the sun. There is really no more ground for supposing that all our demands can be accounted for by one universal underlying kind of motive than there is ground for supposing that all physical phenomena are cases of a single law. The elementary forces in ethics are probably as plural as those of physics are. The various ideals have no common character apart from the fact that they are ideals. No single abstract principle can be so used as to yield to the philosopher anything like a scientifically accurate and genuinely useful casuistic scale.

A look at another peculiarity of the ethical universe, as we find it, will still farther show us the philosopher's perplexities. As a purely theoretic problem, namely, the casuistic question would hardly ever come up at all. If the ethical philosopher were only asking after the best *imaginable* system of goods he would indeed have an easy task; for all demands as such are *primâ facie* respectable, and the best simply imaginary world would be one in which *every* demand was gratified as soon as made. Such a world would, however, have to have a physical constitution entirely different from that of the one which we inhabit. It would need not only a space, but a time, "of *n*–dimensions," to include all the acts and experiences incompatible with one another here below, which would then go on in conjunction—such as spending our money, yet growing rich; taking our holiday, yet getting ahead with our work; shooting and fishing, yet doing no hurt to the beasts; gaining no end of experience, yet keeping our youthful freshness of heart; and the like. There can be no question that such a system of things, however brought about, would be the absolutely ideal system; and that if a philosopher could create universes *à priori*, and provide all the mechanical conditions, that is the sort of universe which he should unhesitatingly create.

But this world of ours is made on an entirely different pattern, and the casuistic question here is most tragically practical. The actually possible in this world is vastly narrower than all that is demanded; and there is always a *pinch* between the ideal and the actual which can only be got through by leaving part of the ideal behind. There is hardly a good which we can imagine except as competing for the possession of the same bit of space and time with some other imagined good. Every end of desire that presents itself appears exclusive of some other end of desire. Shall a man drink and smoke, *or* keep his nerves in condition?—he cannot do both. Shall he follow his fancy for Amelia, *or* for Henrietta?—both cannot be the choice of his heart. Shall he have the dear old Republican party, *or* a spirit of unsophistication in public affairs?—he cannot have both, etc. So that the ethical philosopher's demand for the right scale of subordination in ideals is the fruit of an altogether practical need. Some part of the ideal must be butchered, and he needs to know which part. It is a tragic situation, and no mere speculative conundrum, with which he has to deal.

Now *we* are blinded to the real difficulty of the philosopher's task by the fact that we are born into a society whose ideals are largely ordered already. If we follow the ideal which is conventionally highest, the others which we butcher either die and do not return to haunt us; or if they come back and accuse us of murder, everyone applauds us for turning to them a deaf ear. In other words, our environment encourages us not to be philosophers but partisans. The philosopher, however, cannot, so long as he clings to his own ideal of objectivity, rule out any ideal from being heard. He is confident, and rightly confident, that the simple taking counsel of his own intuitive preferences would be certain to end in a mutilation of the fulness of the truth. The poet Heine is said to have written "Bunsen" in the place of "Gott" in his copy of that author's work entitled "God in History," so as to make it read "Bunsen in der Geschichte." Now, with no disrespect to the good and learned Baron, is it not safe to say that any single philosopher, however wide his sympathies, must be just such a Bunsen in der Geschichte of the moral world, so soon as he attempts to put his own ideas of order into that howling mob of desires, each struggling to get breathing-room for the ideal to which it clings? The very best of men must not only be insensible, but be ludicrously and peculiarly insensible, to many goods. As a militant, fighting free-handed that the goods to which he *is* sensible may not be submerged and lost from out of life, the philosopher, like every other human being, is in a natural position. But think of Zeno and of Epicurus, think of Calvin and of Paley, think of Kant and Schopenhauer, of Herbert Spencer and John Henry Newman, no longer as one-sided champions of special ideals, but as schoolmasters deciding what all must think—and what more grotesque topic could a satirist wish for on which to exercise his pen? The fabled attempt of Mrs. Partington to arrest the

rising tide of the North Atlantic with her broom was a reasonable spectacle compared with their effort to substitute the
content of their clean-shaven systems for that exuberant
mass of goods with which all human nature is in travail, and
groaning to bring to the light of day. Think, furthermore, of
such individual moralists, no longer as mere schoolmasters,
but as pontiffs armed with the temporal power, and having
authority in every concrete case of conflict to order which
good shall be butchered and which shall be suffered to survive—and the notion really turns one pale. All one's slumbering revolutionary instincts waken at the thought of any single
moralist wielding such powers of life and death. Better chaos
forever than an order based on any closet-philosopher's rule,
even though he were the most enlightened possible member
of his tribe. No! if the philosopher is to keep his judicial position, he must never become one of the parties to the fray.

What can he do, then, it will now be asked, except to fall
back on scepticism and give up the notion of being a philosopher at all?

But do we not already see a perfectly definite path of escape
which is open to him just because he is a philosopher, and not
the champion of one particular ideal? Since everything which
is demanded is by that fact a good, must not the guiding
principle for ethical philosophy (since all demands conjointly
cannot be satisfied in this poor world) be simply to satisfy at
all times *as many demands as we can*? That act must be the best
act, accordingly, which makes for the *best whole*, in the sense
of awakening the least sum of dissatisfactions. In the casuistic
scale, therefore, those ideals must be written highest which
prevail at the least cost, or by whose realization the least possible number of other ideals are destroyed. Since victory and
defeat there must be, the victory to be philosophically prayed
for is that of the more inclusive side—of the side which even
in the hour of triumph will to some degree do justice to the
ideals in which the vanquished party's interests lay. The
course of history is nothing but the story of men's struggles
from generation to generation to find the more and more inclusive order. *Invent some manner* of realizing your own ideals
which will also satisfy the alien demands—that and that only

is the path of peace! Following this path, society has shaken itself into one sort of relative equilibrium after another by a series of social discoveries quite analogous to those of science. Polyandry and polygamy and slavery, private warfare and liberty to kill, judicial torture and arbitrary royal power have slowly succumbed to actually aroused complaints; and though someone's ideals are unquestionably the worse off for each improvement, yet a vastly greater total number of them find shelter in our civilized society than in the older savage ways. So far then, and up to date, the casuistic scale is made for the philosopher already far better than he can ever make it for himself. An experiment of the most searching kind has proved that the laws and usages of the land are what yield the maximum of satisfaction to the thinkers taken all together. The presumption in cases of conflict must always be in favor of the conventionally recognized good. The philosopher must be a conservative, and in the construction of his casuistic scale must put the things most in accordance with the customs of the community on top.

And yet if he be a true philosopher he must see that there is nothing final in any actually given equilibrium of human ideals, but that, as our present laws and customs have fought and conquered other past ones, so they will in their turn be overthrown by any newly discovered order which will hush up the complaints that they still give rise to, without producing others louder still. "Rules are made for man, not man for rules"—that one sentence is enough to immortalize Green's *Prolegomena to Ethics*. And although a man always risks much when he breaks away from established rules and strives to realize a larger ideal whole than they permit, yet the philosopher must allow that it is at all times open to anyone to make the experiment, provided he fear not to stake his life and character upon the throw. The pinch is always here. Pent in under every system of moral rules are innumerable persons whom it weighs upon, and goods which it represses; and these are always rumbling and grumbling in the background, and ready for any issue by which they may get free. See the abuses which the institution of private property covers, so that even to-day it is shamelessly asserted among us that one of the prime functions of the national government is to help the

adroiter citizens to grow rich. See the unnamed and unnam-
able sorrows which the tyranny, on the whole so beneficient,
of the marriage-institution brings to so many, both of the
married and the unwed. See the wholesale loss of opportunity
under our *régime* of so-called equality and industrialism, with
the drummer and the counter-jumper in the saddle, for so
many faculties and graces which could flourish in the feudal
world. See our kindliness for the humble and the outcast,
how it wars with that stern weeding-out which until now has
been the condition of every perfection in the breed. See everywhere the struggle and the squeeze; and everlastingly the
problem how to make them less. The anarchists, nihilists, and
free-lovers; the free-silverites, socialists, and single-tax men;
the free-traders and civil-service reformers; the prohibitionists
and anti-vivisectionists; the radical darwinians with their idea
of the suppression of the weak—these and all the conservative sentiments of society arrayed against them, are simply deciding through actual experiment by what sort of conduct the
maximum amount of good can be gained and kept in this
world. These experiments are to be judged, not *à priori*, but
by actually finding, after the fact of their making, how much
more outcry or how much appeasement comes about. What
closet-solutions can possibly anticipate the result of trials
made on such a scale? Or what can any superficial theorist's
judgment be worth, in a world where every one of hundreds
of ideals has its special champion already provided in the
shape of some genius expressly born to feel it, and to fight to
death in its behalf? The pure philosopher can only follow the
windings of the spectacle, confident that the line of least resistance will always be towards the richer and the more inclusive
arrangement, and that by one tack after another some approach to the kingdom of heaven is incessantly made.

IV

All this amounts to saying that, so far as the casuistic question goes, ethical science is just like physical science, and instead of being deducible all at once from abstract principles,
must simply bide its time, and be ready to revise its conclusions from day to day. The presumption of course, in both

sciences, always is that the vulgarly accepted opinions are true, and the right casuistic order that which public opinion believes in; and surely it would be folly quite as great, in most of us, to strike out independently and to aim at originality in ethics as in physics. Every now and then, however, someone is born with the right to be original, and his revolutionary thought or action may bear prosperous fruit. He may replace old "laws of nature" by better ones; he may, by breaking old moral rules in a certain place, bring in a total condition of things more ideal than would have followed had the rules been kept.

On the whole, then, we must conclude that no philosophy of ethics is possible in the old-fashioned absolute sense of the term. Everywhere the ethical philosopher must wait on facts. The thinkers who create the ideals come he knows not whence, their sensibilities are evolved he knows not how; and the question as to which of two conflicting ideals will give the best universe then and there, can be answered by him only through the aid of the experience of other men. I said some time ago, in treating of the "first" question, that the intuitional moralists deserve credit for keeping most clearly to the psychological facts. They do much to spoil this merit on the whole, however, by mixing with it that dogmatic temper which, by absolute distinctions and unconditional "thou shalt nots," changes a growing, elastic, and continuous life into a superstitious system of relics and dead bones. In point of fact, there are no absolute evils, and there are no non-moral goods; and the *highest* ethical life—however few may be called to bear its burdens—consists at all times in the breaking of rules which have grown too narrow for the actual case. There is but one unconditional commandment, which is that we should seek incessantly, with fear and trembling, so to vote and to act as to bring about the very largest total universe of good which we can see. Abstract rules indeed can help; but they help the less in proportion as our intuitions are more piercing, and our vocation is the stronger for the moral life. For every real dilemma is in literal strictness a unique situation; and the exact combination of ideals realized and ideals disappointed which each decision creates is always a universe without a precedent, and for which no adequate previous rule exists. The philosopher, then, *quâ* philosopher, is no better able to determine the best universe in the concrete emergency than other men. He sees, indeed, somewhat better than most men what the question always is—not a question of this good or that good simply taken, but of the two total universes with which these goods respectively belong. He knows that he must vote always for the richer universe, for the good which seems most organizable, most fit to enter into complex combinations, most apt to be a member of a more inclusive whole. But which particular universe this is he cannot know for certain in advance; he only knows that if he makes a bad mistake the cries of the wounded will soon inform him of the fact. In all this the philosopher is just like the rest of us non-philosophers, so far as we are just and sympathetic instinctively, and so far as we are open to the voice of complaint. His function is in fact indistinguishable from that of the best kind of statesman at the present day. His books upon ethics, therefore, so far as they truly touch the moral life, must more and more ally themselves with a literature which is confessedly tentative and suggestive rather than dogmatic—I mean with novels and dramas of the deeper sort, with sermons, with books on statecraft and philanthropy and social and economical reform. Treated in this way ethical treatises may be voluminous and luminous as well; but they never can be *final*, except in their abstractest and vaguest features; and they must more and more abandon the old-fashioned, clear-cut, and would-be "scientific" form.

V

The chief of all the reasons why concrete ethics cannot be final is that they have to wait on metaphysical and theological beliefs. I said some time back that real ethical relations existed in a purely human world. They would exist even in what we called a moral solitude if the thinker had various ideals which took hold of him in turn. His self of one day would make demands on his self of another; and some of the demands might be urgent and tyrannical, while others were gentle and easily put aside. We call the tyrannical demands *imperatives*. If we ignore these we do not hear the last of it. The good which we have wounded returns to plague us with interminable crops of consequential damages, compunctions, and regrets. Obligation can thus exist inside a single thinker's consciousness; and perfect peace can abide with him only so far as he lives according to some sort of a casuistic scale which keeps his more imperative goods on top. It is the nature of these goods to be cruel to their rivals. Nothing shall avail when weighed in the balance against them. They call out all the mercilessness in our disposition, and do not easily forgive us if we are so soft-hearted as to shrink from sacrifice in their behalf.

The deepest difference, practically, in the moral life of man is the difference between the easy-going and the strenuous mood. When in the easy-going mood the shrinking from present ill is our ruling consideration. The strenuous mood, on the contrary, makes us quite indifferent to present ill, if only the greater ideal be attained. The capacity for the strenuous mood probably lies slumbering in every man, but it has more difficulty in some than in others in waking up. It needs the wilder passions to arouse it, the big fears, loves, and indignations; or else the deeply penetrating appeal of some one of the higher fidelities, like justice, truth or freedom. Strong relief is a necessity of its vision; and a world where all the mountains are brought down and all the valleys are exalted is no congenial place for its habitation. This is why in a solitary thinker this mood might slumber on forever without waking. His various ideals, known to him to be mere preferences of his own, are too nearly of the same denominational value: he can play fast or loose with them at will. This too is why, in a merely human world without a God, the appeal to our moral energy falls short of its maximal stimulating power. Life, to be sure, is even in such a world a genuinely ethical symphony; but it is played in the compass of a couple of poor octaves, and the infinite scale of values fails to open up. Many of us, indeed—like Sir James Stephen in those eloquent *Essays by a Barrister*—would openly laugh at the very idea of the strenuous mood being awakened in us by those claims of remote posterity which constitute the last appeal of the religion of humanity. We do not love these men of the future keenly enough; and we love them perhaps the less the more we hear of their evolutionized perfection, their high average longevity and education, their freedom from war and crime, their relative immunity from pain and zymotic disease, and all their other negative superiorities. This is all too finite, we say; we see too well the vacuum beyond. It lacks the note of infinitude and mystery, and may all be dealt with in the don't-care mood. No need of agonizing ourselves or making others agonize for these good creatures just at present.

When, however, we believe that a God is there, and that he is one of the claimants, the infinite perspective opens out. The scale of the symphony is incalculably prolonged. The more imperative ideals now begin to speak with an altogether new objectivity and significance, and to utter the penetrating, shattering, tragically challenging note of appeal. They ring out like the call of Victor Hugo's alpine eagle, "qui parle au précipice et que le gouffre entend," and the strenuous mood awakens at the sound. It saith among the trumpets, ha, ha! it smelleth the battle afar off, the thunder of the captains and the shouting. Its blood is up; and cruelty to the lesser claims, so far from being a deterrent element, does but add to the stern joy with which it leaps to answer to the greater. All through history, in the periodical conflicts of puritanism with the don't-care temper, we see the antagonism of the strenuous and genial moods, and the contrast between the ethics of infinite and mysterious obligation from on high, and those of prudence and the satisfaction of merely finite need.

The capacity of the strenuous mood lies so deep down among our natural human possibilities that even if there were no metaphysical or traditional grounds for believing in a God, men would postulate one simply as a pretext for living hard, and getting out of the game of existence its keenest possibilities of zest. Our attitude towards concrete evils is entirely different in a world where we believe there are none but finite demanders, from what it is in one where we joyously face tragedy for an infinite demander's sake. Every sort of energy and endurance, of courage and capacity for handling life's evils, is set free in those who have religious faith. For this reason the strenuous type of character will on the battlefield of human history always outwear the easy-going type, and religion will drive irreligion to the wall.

It would seem, too—and this is my final conclusion—that the stable and systematic moral universe for which the ethical philosopher asks is fully possible only in a world where there is a divine thinker with all-enveloping demands. If such a thinker existed, his way of subordinating the demands to one another would be the finally valid casuistic scale; his claims would be the most appealing; his ideal universe would be the most inclusive realizable whole. If he now exist, then actualized in his thought already must be that ethical philosophy which we seek as the pattern which our own must evermore approach.[3] In the interests of our own ideal of systematically unified moral truth, therefore, we, as would-be philosophers, must postulate a divine thinker, and pray for the victory of the religious cause. Meanwhile, exactly what the thought of the infinite thinker may be is hidden from us even were we sure of his existence; so that our postulation of him after all serves only to let loose in us the strenuous mood. But this is what it does in all men, even those who have no interest in philosophy. The ethical philosopher, therefore, whenever he ventures to say which course of action is the best, is on no essentially different level from the common man. "See, I have set before thee this day life and good, and death and evil; therefore, choose life that thou and thy seed may live"— when this challenge comes to us, it is simply our total character and personal genius that are on trial; and if we invoke any so-called philosophy, our choice and use of that also are but revelations of our personal aptitude or incapacity for moral life. From this unsparing practical ordeal no professor's lectures and no array of books can save us. The solving word, for the learned and the unlearned man alike, lies in the last resort in the dumb willingnesses and unwillingnesses of their interior characters, and nowhere else. It is not in heaven, neither is it beyond the sea; but the word is very nigh unto thee, in thy mouth and in thy heart, that thou mayest do it.

[3]All this is set forth with great freshness and force in the work of my colleague, Professor Josiah Royce: *The Religious Aspect of Philosophy*, Boston, 1885.

Great Men and Their Environment [1]

A REMARKABLE PARALLEL, which I think has never been noticed, obtains between the facts of social evolution on the one hand, and of zoölogical evolution as expounded by Mr. Darwin on the other.

It will be best to prepare the ground for my thesis by a few very general remarks on the method of getting at scientific truth. It is a common platitude that a complete acquaintance with any one thing, however small, would require a knowledge of the entire universe. Not a sparrow falls to the ground but some of the remote conditions of his fall are to be found in the milky way, in our federal constitution, or in the early history of Europe. That is to say, alter the milky way, alter the federal constitution, alter the facts of our barbarian ancestry, and the universe would so far be a different universe from what it now is. One fact involved in the difference might be that the particular little street-boy who threw the stone which brought down the sparrow might not find himself opposite the sparrow at that particular moment; or, finding himself there, he might not be in that particular serene and disengaged mood of mind which expressed itself in throwing the stone. But, true as all this is, it would be very foolish for anyone who was inquiring the cause of the sparrow's fall to overlook the boy as too personal, proximate, and so to speak anthropomorphic an agent, and to say that the true cause is the federal constitution, the westward migration of the Celtic race, or the structure of the milky way. If we proceeded on that method, we might say with perfect legitimacy that a friend of ours, who had slipped on the ice upon his door-step and cracked his skull, some months after dining with thirteen at the table, died because of that ominous feast. I know, in fact, one such instance; and I might, if I chose, contend with perfect logical propriety that the slip on the ice was no real accident. "There are no accidents," I might say, "for science. The whole history of the world converged to produce that

[1] A lecture before the Harvard Natural History Society; published in the *Atlantic Monthly*, October, 1880.

slip. If anything had been left out, the slip would not have occurred just there and then. To say it would is to deny the relations of cause and effect throughout the universe. The real cause of the death was not the slip, *but the conditions which engendered the slip*—and among them his having sat at a table, six months previous, one among thirteen. *That* is truly the reason why he died within the year."

It will soon be seen whose arguments I am, in form, reproducing here. I would fain lay down the truth without polemics or recrimination. But unfortunately we never fully grasp the import of any true statement until we have a clear notion of what the opposite untrue statement would be. The error is needed to set off the truth, much as a dark background is required for exhibiting the brightness of a picture. And the error which I am going to use as a foil to set off what seems to me the truth of my own statements is contained in the philosophy of Mr. Herbert Spencer and his disciples. Our problem is, What are the causes that make communities change from generation to generation—that make the England of Queen Anne so different from the England of Elizabeth, the Harvard College of to-day so different from that of thirty years ago?

I shall reply to this problem, The difference is due to the accumulated influences of individuals, of their examples, their initiatives, and their decisions. The spencerian school replies, The changes are irrespective of persons, and independent of individual control. They are due to the environment, to the circumstances, the physical geography, the ancestral conditions, the increasing experience of outer relations; to everything, in fact, except the Grants and the Bismarcks, the Joneses and the Smiths.

Now I say that these theorizers are guilty of precisely the same fallacy as he who should ascribe the death of his friend to the dinner with thirteen, or the fall of the sparrow to the milky way. Like the dog in the fable, who drops his real bone to snatch at its image, they drop the real causes to snatch at others, which from no possible human point of view are available or attainable. Their fallacy is a practical one. Let us see where it lies. Although I believe in free-will myself, I will waive that belief in this discussion, and assume with the Spencerians the predestination of all human actions. On that assumption I gladly allow that were the intelligence investigating the man's or the sparrow's death omniscient and omnipresent, able to take in the whole of time and space at a single glance, there would not be the slightest objection to the milky way or the fatal feast being invoked among the sought-for causes. Such a divine intelligence would see instantaneously all the infinite lines of convergence towards a given result, and it would, moreover, see impartially: it would see the fatal feast to be as much a condition of the sparrow's death as of the man's; it would see the boy with the stone to be as much a condition of the man's fall as of the sparrow's.

The human mind, however, is constituted on an entirely different plan. It has no such power of universal intuition. Its finiteness obliges it to see but two or three things at a time. If it wishes to take wider sweeps it has to use "general ideas," as they are called, and in so doing to drop all concrete truths. Thus, in the present case, if we as men wish to feel the connection between the milky way and the boy and the dinner and the sparrow and the man's death, we can do so only by falling back on the enormous emptiness of what is called an abstract proposition. We must say, All things in the world are fatally predetermined, and hang together in the adamantine fixity of a system of natural law. But in the vagueness of this vast proposition we have lost all the concrete facts and links; and in all practical matters the concrete links are the only things of importance. The human mind is essentially partial. It can be efficient at all only by *picking out* what to attend to, and ignoring everything else—by narrowing its point of view. Otherwise, what little strength it has is dispersed, and it loses its way altogether. Man always wants his curiosity gratified for a particular purpose. If, in the case of the sparrow, the purpose is punishment, it would be idiotic to wander off from the cats, boys, and other possible agencies close by in the street, to survey the early Celts and the milky way: the boy would meanwhile escape. And if, in the case of the unfortunate man, we lose ourselves in contemplation of the thirteen-at-table mystery, and fail to notice the ice on the step and cover it with ashes, some other poor fellow, who never dined out in his life, may slip on it in coming to the door, and fall and break his head too.

It is, then, a necessity laid upon us as human beings to limit our view. In mathematics we know how this method of ignoring and neglecting quantities lying outside of a certain range has been adopted in the differential calculus. The calculator throws out all the "infinitesimals" of the quantities he is considering. He treats them (under certain rules) as if they did not exist. In themselves they exist perfectly all the while; but they are as if they did not exist for the purposes of his calculation. Just so an astronomer, in dealing with the tidal movements of the ocean, takes no account of the waves made by the wind, or by the pressure of all the steamers which day and night are moving their thousands of tons upon its surface. Just so the marksman, in sighting his rifle, allows for the motion of the wind, but not for the equally real motion of the earth and solar system. Just so a business man's punctuality may overlook an error of five minutes, whilst a physicist, measuring the velocity of light, must count each thousandth of a second.

There are, in short, *different cycles of operation* in nature; different departments, so to speak, relatively independent of one another, so that what goes on at any moment in one may be compatible with almost any condition of things at the same time in the next. The mould on the biscuit in the store-room of a man-of-war vegetates in absolute indifference to the nationality of the flag, the direction of the voyage, the weather, and the human dramas that may go on on board; and a mycologist may study it in complete abstraction from all these larger details. Only by so studying it, in fact, is there any chance of the mental concentration by which alone he may hope to learn something of its nature. On the other hand, the captain who in manœuvering the vessel through a naval fight should think it necessary to bring the mouldy biscuit into his calculations would very likely lose the battle by reason of the excessive "thoroughness" of his mind.

The causes which operate in these incommensurable cycles are connected with one another only *if we take the whole universe into account*. For all lesser points of view it is lawful—

nay, more, it is for human wisdom necessary—to regard them as disconnected and irrelevant to one another.

And this brings us nearer to our special topic. If we look at an animal or a human being, distinguished from the rest of his kind by the possession of some extraordinary peculiarity, good or bad, we shall be able to discriminate between the causes which originally *produced* the peculiarity in him and the causes that *maintain* it after it is produced; and we shall see, if the peculiarity be one that he was born with, that these two sets of causes belong to two such irrelevant cycles. It was the triumphant originality of Darwin to see this, and to act accordingly. Separating the causes of production under the title of "tendencies to spontaneous variation," and relegating them to a physiological cycle which he forthwith agreed to ignore altogether,[2] he confined his attention to the causes of preservation, and under the names of natural selection and sexual selection studied them exclusively as functions of the cycle of the environment.

Pre-darwinian philosophers had also tried to establish the doctrine of descent with modification; but they all committed the blunder of clumping the two cycles of causation into one. What preserves an animal with his peculiarity, if it be a useful one, they saw to be the nature of the environment to which the peculiarity was adjusted. The giraffe with his peculiar neck is preserved by the fact that there are in his environment tall trees whose leaves he can digest. But these philosophers went further, and said that the presence of the trees not only maintained an animal with a long neck to browse upon their branches, but also produced him. They *made* his neck long by the constant striving they aroused in him to reach up to them. The environment, in short, was supposed by these writers to mould the animal by a kind of direct pressure, very much as a seal presses the wax into harmony with itself. Numerous instances were given of the way in which this goes on under our

[2]Darwin's theory of pangenesis is, it is true, an attempt to account (among other things) for variation. But it occupies its own separate place, and its author no more invokes the environment when he talks of the adhesions of gemmules than he invokes these adhesions when he talks of the relations of the whole animal to the environment. *Divide et impera!*

eyes. The exercise of the forge makes the right arm strong, the palm grows callous to the oar, the mountain air distends the chest, the chased fox grows cunning and the chased bird shy, the arctic cold stimulates the animal combustion, and so forth. Now these changes, of which many more examples might be adduced, are at present distinguished by the special name of *adaptive* changes. Their peculiarity is that that very feature in the environment to which the animal's nature grows adjusted, itself produces the adjustment. The "inner relation," to use Mr. Spencer's phrase, "corresponds" with its own efficient cause.

Darwin's first achievement was to show the utter insignificance in amount of these changes produced by direct adaptation, the immensely greater mass of changes being produced by internal molecular accidents, of which we know nothing. His next achievement was to define the true problem with which we have to deal when we study the effects of the visible environment on the animal. That problem is simply this: Is the environment more likely to *preserve or to destroy him*, on account of this or that peculiarity with which he may be born? In giving the name of "accidental variations" to those peculiarities with which an animal is born, Darwin does not for a moment mean to suggest that they are not the fixed outcome of natural law. If the total system of the universe be taken into account, the causes of these variations and the visible environment which preserves or destroys them, undoubtedly do, in some remote and roundabout way, hang together. What Darwin means is, that, since that environment is a perfectly known thing, and its relations to the organism in the way of destruction or preservation are tangible and distinct, it would utterly confuse our finite understandings and frustrate our hopes of science to mix in with it facts from such a disparate and incommensurable cycle as that in which the variations are produced. This last cycle is that of occurrences before the animal is born. It is the cycle of influences upon ova and embryos; in which lie the causes that tip them and tilt them towards masculinity or feminity, towards strength or weakness, towards health or disease, and towards divergence from the parent type. What are the causes there?

In the first place, they are molecular and invisible—inaccessible, therefore, to direct observation of any kind. Secondly, their operations are compatible with any social, political, and physical conditions of environment. The same parents, living in the same environing conditions, may at one birth produce a genius, at the next an idiot or a monster. The visible external conditions are therefore not direct determinants of this cycle; and the more we consider the matter, the more we are forced to believe that two children of the same parents are made to differ from each other by causes as disproportionate to their ultimate effects as is the famous pebble on the Rocky Mountain crest, which separates two raindrops, to the Gulf of St. Lawrence and the Pacific Ocean towards which it makes them severally flow.

The great mechanical distinction between transitive forces and discharging forces is nowhere illustrated on such a scale as in physiology. Almost all causes there are forces of *detent*, which operate by simply unlocking energy already stored up. They are upsetters of unstable equilibria, and the resultant effect depends infinitely more on the nature of the materials upset than on that of the particular stimulus which joggles them down. Galvanic work, equal to unity, done on a frog's nerve will discharge from the muscle to which the nerve belongs mechanical work equal to seventy thousand; and exactly the same muscular effect will emerge if other irritants than galvanism are employed. The irritant has merely started or provoked something which then went on of itself—as a match may start a fire which consumes a whole town. And qualitatively as well as quantitatively the effect may be absolutely incommensurable with the cause. We find this condition of things in all organic matter. Chemists are distracted by the difficulties which the instability of albuminoid compounds opposes to their study. Two specimens, treated in what outwardly seem scrupulously identical conditions, behave in quite different ways. You know about the invisible factors of fermentation, and how the fate of a jar of milk—whether it turn into a sour clot or a mass of koumiss—depends on whether the lactic acid ferment or the alcoholic is introduced first, and gets ahead of the other in starting the process. Now, when the result is the tendency of an ovum, itself invisible to the naked eye, to tip towards this direction or that in its further evolution—to bring forth a genius or a dunce, even as the rain-drop passes east or west of the pebble—is it not obvious that the deflecting cause must lie in a region so recondite and minute, must be such a ferment of a ferment, an infinitesimal of so high an order, that surmise itself may never succeed even in attempting to frame an image of it?

Such being the case, was not Darwin right to turn his back upon that region altogether, and to keep his own problem carefully free from all entanglement with matters such as these? The success of his work is a sufficiently affirmative reply.

And this brings us at last to the heart of our subject. The causes of production of great men lie in a sphere wholly inaccessible to the social philosopher. He must simply accept geniuses as data, just as Darwin accepts his spontaneous variations. For him, as for Darwin, the only problem is, these data being given, How does the environment affect them, and how do they affect the environment? Now I affirm that the relation of the visible environment to the great man is in the main exactly what it is to the "variation" in the darwinian philosophy. It chiefly adopts or rejects, preserves or destroys, in short *selects* him.[3] And whenever it adopts and preserves the great man, it becomes modified by his influence in an entirely original and peculiar way. He acts as a ferment, and changes its constitution, just as the advent of a new zoölogical species changes the faunal and floral equilibrium of the region in which it appears. We all recollect Mr. Darwin's famous statement of the influence of cats on the growth of clover in their neighborhood. We all have read of the effects of the European rabbit in New Zealand, and we have many of us taken part in the controversy about the English sparrow here—whether he kills most canker-worms, or drives away most native birds. Just so the great man, whether he be an

[3]It is true that it remodels him, also, to some degree, by its educative influence, and that this constitutes a considerable difference between the social case and the zoölogical case. I neglect this aspect of the relation here, for the other is the more important. At the end of the article I will return to it incidentally.

importation from without like Clive in India or Agassiz here, or whether he spring from the soil like Mahomet or Franklin, brings about a rearrangement, on a large or a small scale, of the pre-existing social relations.

The mutations of societies, then, from generation to generation, are in the main due directly or indirectly to the acts or the example of individuals whose genius was so adapted to the receptivities of the moment, or whose accidental position of authority was so critical that they became ferments, initiators of movement, setters of precedent or fashion, centres of corruption, or destroyers of other persons, whose gifts, had they had free play, would have led society in another direction.

We see this power of individual initiative exemplified on a small scale all about us, and on a large scale in the case of the leaders of history. It is only following the common-sense method of a Lyell, a Darwin, and a Whitney to interpret the unknown by the known, and reckon up cumulatively the only causes of social change we can directly observe. Societies of men are just like individuals, in that both at any given moment offer ambiguous potentialities of development. Whether a young man enters business or the ministry may depend on a decision which has to be made before a certain day. He takes the place offered in the counting-house, and is *committed*. Little by little, the habits, the knowledges, of the other career, which once lay so near, cease to be reckoned even among his possibilities. At first, he may sometimes doubt whether the self he murdered in that decisive hour might not have been the better of the two; but with the years such questions themselves expire, and the old alternative *ego*, once so vivid, fades into something less substantial than a dream. It is no otherwise with nations. They may be committed by kings and ministers to peace or war, by generals to victory or defeat, by prophets to this religion or to that, by various geniuses to fame in art, science, or industry. A war is a true point of bifurcation of future possibilities. Whether it fail or succeed, its declaration must be the starting-point of new policies. Just so does a revolution, or any great civic precedent, become a deflecting influence, whose operations widen with the course of time. Communities obey their ideals; and an accidental success fixes an ideal, as an accidental failure blights it.

Would England have to-day the "imperial" ideal which she now has, if a certain boy named Bob Clive had shot himself, as he tried to do, at Madras? Would she be the drifting raft she is now in European affairs[4] if a Frederic the Great had inherited her throne instead of a Victoria, and if Messrs. Bentham, Mill, Cobden, and Bright had all been born in Prussia? England has, no doubt, to-day precisely the same intrinsic value relatively to the other nations that she ever had. There is no such fine accumulation of human material upon the globe. But in England the material has lost effective form, whilst in Germany it has found it. Leaders give the form. Would England be crying forward and backward at once, as she does now, "letting I will not wait upon I would," wishing to conquer but not to fight, if her ideal had in all these years been fixed by a succession of statesmen of supremely commanding personality, working in one direction? Certainly not. She would have espoused, for better or worse, either one course or another. Had Bismarck died in his cradle, the Germans would still be satisfied with appearing to themselves as a race of spectacled *Gelehrten* and political herbivora, and to the French as *ces bons*, or *ces naïfs, Allemands*. Bismarck's will showed them, to their own great astonishment, that they could play a far livelier game. The lesson will not be forgotten. Germany may have many vicissitudes, but they—

"will never do away, I ween,
The marks of that which once hath been,"—

of Bismarck's initiative, namely, from 1860 to 1873.

The fermentative influence of geniuses must be admitted as, at any rate, one factor in the changes that constitute social evolution. The community *may* evolve in many ways. The accidental presence of this or that ferment decides in which way it *shall* evolve. Why, the very birds of the forest, the parrot, the mino, have the power of human speech, but never develop it of themselves; someone must be there to teach them.

[4]The reader will remember when this was written.

So with us individuals. Rembrandt must teach us to enjoy the struggle of light with darkness, Wagner to enjoy peculiar musical effects; Dickens gives a twist to our sentimentality, Artemus Ward to our humor; Emerson kindles a new moral light within us. But it is like Columbus's egg. "All can raise the flowers now, for all have got the seed." But if this be true of the individuals in the community, how can it be false of the community as a whole? If shown a certain way, a community may take it; if not, it will never find it. And the ways are to a large extent indeterminate in advance. A nation may obey either of many alternative impulses given by different men of genius, and still live and be prosperous, just as a man may enter either of many businesses. Only, the prosperities may differ in their type.

But the indeterminism is not absolute. Not every "man" fits every "hour." Some incompatibilities there are. A given genius may come either too early or too late. Peter the Hermit would now be sent to a lunatic asylum. John Mill in the tenth century would have lived and died unknown. Cromwell and Napoleon need their revolutions, Grant his civil war. An Ajax gets no fame in the day of telescopic-sighted rifles; and, to express differently an instance which Spencer uses, what could a Watt have effected in a tribe which no precursive genius had taught to smelt iron or to turn a lathe?

Now the important thing to notice is that what makes a certain genius now incompatible with his surroundings is usually the fact that some previous genius of a different strain has warped the community away from the sphere of his possible effectiveness. After Voltaire, no Peter the Hermit; after Charles IX. and Louis XIV., no general protestantization of France; after a Manchester school, a Beaconsfield's success is transient; after a Philip II., a Castelar makes little headway; and so on. Each bifurcation cuts off certain sides of the field altogether, and limits the future possible angles of deflection. A community is a living thing, and in words which I can do no better than quote from Professor Clifford,[5] "it is the peculiarity of living things not merely that they change under the influence of surrounding circumstances, but that any change

[5]*Lectures and Essays*, i, 82.

which takes place in them is not lost but retained, and, as it were, built into the organism to serve as the foundation for future actions. If you cause any distortion in the growth of a tree and make it crooked, whatever you may do afterwards to make the tree straight, the mark of your distortion is there; it is absolutely indelible; it has become part of the tree's nature . . . . Suppose, however, that you take a lump of gold, melt it, and let it cool . . . . No one can tell by examining a piece of gold how often it has been melted and cooled in geologic ages, or even in the last year by the hand of man. Anyone who cuts down an oak can tell by the rings in its trunk how many times winter has frozen it into widowhood, and how many times summer has warmed it into life. A living being must always contain within itself the history not merely of its own existence but of all its ancestors."

Every painter can tell us how each added line deflects his picture in a certain sense. Whatever lines follow must be built on those first laid down. Every author who starts to rewrite a piece of work knows how impossible it becomes to use any of the first-written pages again. The new beginning has already excluded the possibility of those earlier phrases and transitions, whilst it has at the same time created the possibility of an indefinite set of new ones, no one of which, however, is completely determined in advance. Just so the social surroundings of the past and present hour exclude the possibility of accepting certain contributions from individuals; but they do not positively define what contributions shall be accepted, for in themselves they are powerless to fix what the nature of the individual offerings shall be.[6]

Thus social evolution is a resultant of the interaction of two wholly distinct factors—the individual, deriving his peculiar gifts from the play of physiological and infra-social forces, but bearing all the power of initiative and origination in his hands; and, second, the social environment, with its power of adopting or rejecting both him and his gifts. Both factors are

[6]Mr. Grant Allen himself, in an article from which I shall presently quote, admits that a set of people who, if they had been exposed ages ago to the geographical agencies of Timbuctoo, would have developed into negroes might now, after a protracted exposure to the conditions of Hamburg, never become negroes if transplanted to Timbuctoo.

essential to change. The community stagnates without the impulse of the individual. The impulse dies away without the sympathy of the community.

All this seems nothing more than common-sense. All who wish to see it developed by a man of genius should read that golden little work, Bagehot's *Physics and Politics*, in which (it seems to me) the complete sense of the way in which concrete things grow and change is as livingly present as the straining after a pseudo-philosophy of evolution is livingly absent. But there are never wanting minds to whom such views seem personal and contracted, and allied to an anthropomorphism long exploded in other fields of knowledge. "The individual withers, and the world is more and more," to these writers; and in a Buckle, a Draper, and a Taine we all know how much the "world" has come to be almost synonymous with the *climate*. We all know, too, how the controversy has been kept up between the partisans of a "science of history" and those who deny the existence of anything like necessary "laws" where human societies are concerned. Mr. Spencer, at the opening of his *Study of Sociology*, makes an onslaught on the "great-man theory" of history, from which a few passages may be quoted:—

"The genesis of societies by the actions of great men may be comfortably believed so long as, resting in general notions, you do not ask for particulars. But now, if, dissatisfied with vagueness, we demand that our ideas shall be brought into focus and exactly defined, we discover the hypothesis to be utterly incoherent. If, not stopping at the explanation of social progress as due to the great man, we go back a step and ask whence comes the great man, we find that the theory breaks down completely. The question has two conceivable answers: his origin is supernatural, or it is natural. Is his origin supernatural? Then he is a deputy-god, and we have Theocracy once removed—or, rather, not removed at all . . . . Is this an unacceptable solution? Then the origin of the great man is natural; and immediately this is recognized he must be classed with all other phenomena in the society that gave him birth, as a product of its antecedents. Along with the whole generation of which he forms a minute part—along with its institutions, language, knowledge, manners, and its multitudinous arts and appliances, he is a *resultant* . . . . You must admit that the genesis of the great man depends on the long series of complex influences which has produced the race in which he appears, and the social state into which that race has slowly grown. . . . Before he can re-make his society, his society must make him. All those changes of which he is the proximate initiator have their chief causes in the generations he descended from. If there is to be anything like a real explanation of these changes, it must be sought in that aggregate of conditions out of which both he and they have arisen."[7]

Now it seems to me that there is something which one might almost call impudent in the attempt which Mr. Spencer makes, in the first sentence of this extract, to pin the reproach of vagueness upon those who believe in the power of initiative of the great man.

Suppose I say that the singular moderation which now distinguishes social, political, and religious discussion in England, and contrasts so strongly with the bigotry and dogmatism of sixty years ago, is largely due to J. S. Mill's example. I may possibly be wrong about the facts; but I am, at any rate, "asking for particulars," and not "resting in general notions." And if Mr. Spencer should tell me it started from no personal influence whatever, but from the "aggregate of conditions," the "generations," Mill and all his contemporaries "descended from," the whole past order of nature in short, surely he, not I, would be the person "satisfied with vagueness."

The fact is that Mr. Spencer's sociological method is identical with that of one who would invoke the zodiac to account for the fall of the sparrow, and the thirteen at table to explain the gentleman's death. It is of little more scientific value than the oriental method of replying to whatever question arises by the unimpeachable truism, "God is great." *Not* to fall back on the gods, where a proximate principle may be found, has with us Westerners long since become the sign of an efficient as distinguished from an inefficient intellect.

To believe that the cause of everything is to be found in its antecedents is the starting-point, the initial postulate, not the goal and consummation, of science. If she is simply to lead us out of the labyrinth by the same hole we went in by three or four thousand years ago, it seems hardly worth while to have

[7] *Study of Sociology*, pp. 33–35.

followed her through the darkness at all. If anything is humanly certain it is that the great man's society, properly so called, does *not* make him before he can remake it. Physiological forces, with which the social, political, geographical, and to a great extent anthropological conditions have just as much and just as little to do as the condition of the crater of Vesuvius has to do with the flickering of this gas by which I write, are what make him. Can it be that Mr. Spencer holds the convergence of sociological pressures to have so impinged on Stratford-upon-Avon about the 26th of April, 1564, that a W. Shakespeare, with all his mental peculiarities, had to be born there—as the pressure of water outside a certain boat will cause a stream of a certain form to ooze into a particular leak? And does he mean to say that if the aforesaid W. Shakespeare had died of cholera infantum, another mother at Stratford-upon-Avon would needs have engendered a duplicate copy of him, to restore the sociologic equilibrium—just as the same stream of water will reappear, no matter how often you pass a sponge over the leak, so long as the outside level remains unchanged? Or might the substitute arise at "Stratford-atte-Bowe"? Here, as elsewhere, it is very hard, in the midst of Mr. Spencer's vagueness, to tell what he does mean at all.

We have, however, in his disciple, Mr. Grant Allen, one who leaves us in no doubt whatever of his precise meaning. This widely informed, suggestive, and brilliant writer published last year a couple of articles in the *Gentleman's Magazine*, in which he maintained that individuals have no initiative in determining social change.

"The differences between one nation and another, whether in intellect, commerce, art, morals, or general temperament, ultimately depend, not upon any mysterious properties of race, nationality, or other unknown and unintelligible abstractions, but simply and solely upon the physical circumstances to which they are exposed. If it be a fact, as we know it to be, that the French nation differs recognizably from the Chinese, and the people of Hamburg differ recognizably from the people of Timbuctoo, then the notorious and conspicuous differences between them are wholly due to the geographical position of the various races. If the people who went to Hamburg had gone to Timbuctoo, they would now be indistinguishable from the semi-barbarous negroes who inhabit that Central African metropolis:[8] and if the people who went to Timbuctoo had gone to Hamburg, they would now have been white-skinned merchants driving a roaring trade in imitation sherry and indigestible port. . . . The differentiating agency must be sought in the great permanent geographical features of land and sea; . . . these have necessarily and inevitably moulded the characters and the histories of every nation upon earth. . . . We cannot regard any nation as an active agent in differentiating itself. Only the surrounding circumstances can have any effect in such a direction. [These two sentences dogmatically deny the existence of the relatively independent physiological cycle of causation.] To suppose otherwise is to suppose that the mind of man is exempt from the universal law of causation. There is no caprice, no spontaneous impulse in human endeavors. Even taste and inclinations *must* themselves be the result of surrounding causes."[9]

Elsewhere Mr. Allen, writing of the Greek culture, says:

"It was absolutely and unreservedly the product of the geographical Hellas, acting upon the given factor of the undifferentiated Aryan brain. . . . To me it seems a self-evident proposition that nothing whatsoever can differentiate one body of men from another except the physical conditions in which they are set, including, of course, under the term *physical conditions*, the relations of place and time in which they stand with regard to other bodies of men. To suppose otherwise is to deny the primordial law of causation. To imagine that the mind can differentiate itself is to imagine that it can be differentiated without a cause."[10]

This outcry about the law of universal causation being undone, the moment we refuse to invest in the kind of causation which is peddled round by a particular school, makes one im-

[8]No! not even though they were bodily brothers! The geographical factor utterly vanishes before the ancestral factor. The difference between Hamburg and Timbuctoo as a cause of ultimate divergence of two races is as nothing to the difference of constitution of the ancestors of the two races, even though as in twin brothers, this difference might be invisible to the naked eye. No two couples of the most homogeneous race could possibly be found so identical as, if set in identical environments, to give rise to two identical lineages. The minute divergence at the start grows broader with each generation, and ends with entirely dissimilar breeds.

[9]Article "Nation-Making," in *Gentleman's Magazine*, 1878. I quote from the reprint in the *Popular Science Monthly Supplement*, December, 1878, pp. 121, 123, 126.

[10]Article "Hellas," in *Gentleman's Magazine*, 1878. Reprint in *Popular Science Monthly Supplement*, September, 1878.

patient. These writers have no imagination of alternatives. With them there is no *tertium quid* between outward environment and miracle. *Aut Cæsar, aut nullus! Aut* Spencerism, *aut* catechism!

If by "physical conditions" Mr. Allen means what he does mean, the outward cycle of visible nature and man, his assertion is simply physiologically false. For a national mind differentiates "itself" whenever a genius is born in its midst by causes acting in the invisible and molecular cycle. But if Mr. Allen means by "physical conditions" the whole of nature, his assertion, though true, forms but the vague Asiatic profession of belief in an all-enveloping fate, which certainly need not plume itself on any specially advanced or scientific character.

And how can a thinker so clever as Mr. Allen fail to have distinguished in these matters between *necessary* conditions and *sufficient* conditions of a given result? The French say that to have an omelet we must break our eggs; that is, the breaking of eggs is a necessary condition of the omelet. But is it a sufficient condition? Does an omelet appear whenever three eggs are broken? So of the Greek mind. To get such versatile intelligence it may be that such commercial dealings with the world as the geographical Hellas afforded are a necessary condition. But if they are a sufficient condition, why did not the Phœnicians outstrip the Greeks in intelligence? No geographical environment can produce a given type of mind. It can only foster and further certain types fortuitously produced, and thwart and frustrate others. Once again, its function is simply selective, and determines what shall actually be only by destroying what is positively incompatible. An arctic environment is incompatible with improvident habits in its denizens; but whether the inhabitants of such a region shall unite with their thrift the peacefulness of the Eskimo or the pugnacity of the Norseman is, so far as the climate is concerned, an accident. Evolutionists should not forget that we all have five fingers not because four or six would not do just as well, but merely because the first vertebrate above the fishes *happened* to have that number. He owed his prodigious success in founding a line of descent to some entirely other quality—we know not which—but the inessential five fingers were taken in tow

and preserved to the present day. So of most social peculiarities. Which of them shall be taken in tow by the few qualities
which the environment necessarily exacts is a matter of what
physiological accidents shall happen among individuals. Mr.
Allen promises to prove his thesis in detail by the examples of
China, India, England, Rome, etc. I have not the smallest
hesitation in predicting that he will do no more with these
examples than he has done with Hellas. He will appear upon
the scene after the fact, and show that the quality developed
by each race was, naturally enough, not incompatible with its
habitat. But he will utterly fail to show that the particular
form of compatibility fallen into in each case was the one necessary and only possible form.

Naturalists know well enough how indeterminate the harmonies between a fauna and its environment are. An animal
may better his chances of existence in either of many ways—
growing aquatic, arboreal, or subterranean; small and swift,
or massive and bulky; spiny, horny, slimy, or venomous;
more timid or more pugnacious; more cunning or more fertile of offspring; more gregarious or more solitary; or in other
ways besides—and any one of these ways may suit him to
many widely different environments.

Readers of Mr. A. R. Wallace will well remember the striking illustrations of this in his *Malay Archipelago*:

"Borneo closely resembles New Guinea not only in its vast size
and its freedom from volcanoes, but in its variety of geological structure, its uniformity of climate, and the general aspect of the forest
vegetation that clothes its surface. The Moluccas are the counterpart
of the Philippines in their volcanic structure, their extreme fertility,
their luxuriant forests, and their frequent earthquakes; and Bali with
the east end of Java has a climate almost as dry and a soil almost as
arid as that of Timor. Yet between these corresponding groups of
islands, constructed as it were after the same pattern, subjected to the
same climate, and bathed by the same oceans, there exists the greatest possible contrast when we compare their animal productions.
Nowhere does the ancient doctrine—that differences or similarities
in the various forms of life that inhabit different countries are due to
corresponding physical differences or similarities in the countries
themselves—meet with so direct and palpable a contradiction. Borneo and New Guinea, as alike physically as two distinct countries can
be, are zoologically wide as the poles asunder; while Australia, with

its dry winds, its open plains, its stony deserts, and its temperate climate, yet produces birds and quadrupeds which are closely related to those inhabiting the hot damp luxuriant forests which everywhere clothe the plains and mountains of New Guinea."

Here we have similar physical-geography environments harmonizing with widely differing animal lives, and similar animal lives harmonizing with widely differing geographical environments. A singularly accomplished writer, E. Gryzanowski, in the *North American Review*,[11] uses the instances of Sardinia and Corsica in support of this thesis with great effect. He says:

"These sister islands, lying in the very centre of the Mediterranean, at almost equal distances from the three centres of Latin and Neolatin civilization, within easy reach of the Phœnician, the Greek, and the Saracen, with a coast-line of more than one thousand miles, endowed with obvious and tempting advantages, and hiding untold sources of agricultural and mineral wealth, have nevertheless remained unknown, unheeded, and certainly uncared for during the thirty centuries of European history. . . . These islands have dialects, but no language, records of battles, but no history. They have customs, but no laws, the *vendetta,* but no justice; they have wants and wealth, but no commerce, timber and ports, but no shipping; they have legends, but no poetry, beauty, but no art, and twenty years ago it could still be said they had universities, but no students. . . . That Sardinia, with all her emotional and picturesque barbarism, has never produced a single artist, is almost as strange as her barbarism itself. . . . Near the focus of European civilization, in the very spot which an *a priori* geographer would point out as the most favorable place for material and intellectual, commercial and political development, these strange sister islands have slept their secular sleep, like *nodes* on the sounding-board of history."

This writer then goes on to compare Sardinia and Sicily with some detail. All the material advantages are in favor of Sardinia, "and the Sardinian population, being of an ancestry more mixed than that of the English race, would justify far higher expectations than that of Sicily." Yet Sicily's past history has been brilliant in the extreme, and her commerce to-day is great. Dr. Gryzanowski has his own theory of the

[11]Vol. cxiii, p. 318 (October, 1871).

historic torpor of these favored isles. He thinks they stagnated because they never gained political autonomy, being always owned by some Continental power. I will not dispute the theory; but I will ask, Why did they not gain it? and answer immediately: Simply because no individuals were born there with patriotism and ability enough to inflame their country-men with national pride, ambition, and thirst for independent life. Corsicans and Sardinians are probably as good stuff as any of their neighbors. But the best wood-pile will not blaze till a torch is applied, and the appropriate torches seem to have been wanting.[12]

Sporadic great men come everywhere. But for a community to get vibrating through and through with intensely active life, many geniuses coming together and in rapid succession are required. This is why great epochs are so rare—why the sudden bloom of a Greece, an early Rome, a Renaissance, is

[12]I am well aware that in much that follows (though in nothing that precedes) I seem to be crossing the heavily shotted bows of Mr. Galton, for whose laborious investigations into the heredity of genius I have the greatest respect. Mr. Galton inclines to think that genius of intellect and passion is bound to express itself, whatever the outward opportunity, and that within any given race an equal number of geniuses of each grade must needs be born in every equal period of time; a subordinate race cannot possibly engender a large number of high-class geniuses, etc. He would, I suspect, infer the suppositions I go on to make—of great men fortuitously assembling around a given epoch and making it great, and of their being fortuitously absent from certain places and times (from Sardinia, from Boston now, etc.)—to be radically vicious. I hardly think, however, that he does justice to the great complexity of the conditions of *effective* greatness, and to the way in which the physiological averages of production may be masked entirely during long periods, either by the accidental mortality of geniuses in infancy, or by the fact that the particular geniuses born happened not to find tasks. I doubt the truth of his assertion that *intellectual* genius, like murder, "will out." It is true that certain types are irrepressible. Voltaire, Shelley, Carlyle, can hardly be conceived leading a dumb and vegetative life in any epoch. But take Mr. Galton himself, take his cousin Mr. Darwin, and take Mr. Spencer: nothing is to me more conceivable than that at another epoch all three of these men might have died "with all their music in them," known only to their friends as persons of strong and original character and judgment. What has started them on their career of effective greatness is simply the accident of each stumbling upon a task vast, brilliant, and congenial enough to call out the convergence of all his passions and powers. I see no more reason why, in case they had not fallen in with their several hobbies at propitious periods in their life, they need necessarily have hit upon other hobbies, and made themselves

such a mystery. Blow must follow blow so fast that no cooling can occur in the intervals. Then the mass of the nation grows incandescent, and may continue to glow by pure inertia long after the originators of its internal movement have passed away. We often hear surprise expressed that in these high tides of human affairs not only the people should be filled with stronger life, but that individual geniuses should seem so exceptionally abundant. This mystery is just about as deep as the time-honored conundrum as to why great rivers flow by great towns. It is true that great public fermentations awaken and adopt many geniuses, who in more torpid times would have had no chance to work. But over and above this there must be an exceptional concourse of genius about a time, to make the fermentation begin at all. The unlikeliness of the concourse is far greater than the unlikeliness of any particular genius; hence the rarity of these periods and the exceptional aspect which they always wear.

It is folly, then, to speak of the "laws of history" as of something inevitable, which science has only to discover, and whose consequences anyone can then foretell but do nothing to alter or avert. Why, the very laws of physics are conditional, and deal with *ifs*. The physicist does not say, "The water will boil anyhow"; he only says it will boil if a fire be kindled beneath it. And so the utmost the student of sociology can ever predict is that *if* a genius of a certain sort show the way, society will be sure to follow. It might long ago have been predicted with great confidence that both Italy and Germany would reach a stable unity if someone could but succeed in starting the process. It could not have been predicted, however, that the *modus operandi* in each case would be subordination to a paramount state rather than federation, because no historian could have calculated the freaks of birth and

equally great. Their case seems similar to that of the Washingtons, Cromwells, and Grants, who simply rose to their occasions. But apart from these causes of fallacy, I am strongly disposed to think that where transcendent geniuses are concerned the numbers anyhow are so small that their appearance will not fit into any scheme of averages. That is, two or three might appear together, just as the two or three balls nearest the target centre might be fired consecutively. Take longer epochs and more firing, and the great geniuses and near balls would on the whole be more spread out.

fortune which gave at the same moment such positions of authority to three such peculiar individuals as Napoleon III., Bismarck, and Cavour. So of our own politics. It is certain now that the movement of the independents, reformers, or whatever one please to call them, will triumph. But whether it do so by converting the republican party to its ends, or by rearing a new party on the ruins of both our present factions, the historian cannot say. There can be no doubt that the reform movement would make more progress in one year with an adequate personal leader than as now in ten without one. Were there a great citizen, splendid with every civic gift, to be its candidate, who can doubt that he would lead us to victory? But at present, we, his environment, who sigh for him and would so gladly preserve and adopt him if he came, can neither move without him, nor yet do anything to bring him forth.[13]

To conclude: The evolutionary view of history, when it denies the vital importance of individual initiative, is, then, an utterly vague and unscientific conception, a lapse from modern scientific determinism into the most ancient oriental fatalism. The lesson of the analysis that we have made (even on the completely deterministic hypothesis with which we started) forms an appeal of the most stimulating sort to the energy of the individual. Even the dogged resistance of the reactionary conservative to changes which he cannot hope entirely to defeat is justified and shown to be effective. He retards the movement; deflects it a little by the concessions he extracts; gives it a resultant momentum, compounded of his inertia and his adversaries' speed; and keeps up, in short, a constant lateral pressure, which, to be sure, never heads it round about, but brings it up at last at a goal far to the right or left of that to which it would have drifted had he allowed it to drift alone.

I now pass to the last division of my subject, the function of the environment in *mental* evolution. After what I have already said, I may be quite concise. Here, if anywhere, it

[13]Since this paper was written, President Cleveland has to a certain extent met the need. But who can doubt that if he had certain other qualities which he has not yet shown, his influence would have been still more decisive? (1896.)

would seem at first sight as if that school must be right which makes the mind passively plastic, and the environment actively productive of the form and order of its conceptions; which, in a word, thinks that all mental progress must result from a series of adaptive changes, in the sense already defined of that word. We know what a vast part of our mental furniture consists of purely remembered, not reasoned, experience. The entire field of our habits and associations by contiguity belongs here. The entire field of those abstract conceptions which were taught us with the language into which we were born belongs here also. And, more than this, there is reason to think that the order of "outer relations" experienced by the individual may itself determine the order in which the general characters imbedded therein shall be noticed and extracted by his mind.[14] The pleasures and benefits, moreover, which certain parts of the environment yield, and the pains and hurts which other parts inflict, determine the direction of our interest and our attention, and so decide at which points the accumulation of mental experiences shall begin. It might, accordingly, seem as if there were no room for any other agency than this; as if the distinction we have found so useful between "spontaneous variation," as the producer of changed forms, and the environment, as their preserver and destroyer, did not hold in the case of mental progress; as if, in a word, the parallel with darwinism might no longer obtain, and Spencer might be quite right with his fundamental law of intelligence, which says, "The cohesion between psychical states is proportionate to the frequency with which the relation between the answering external phenomena has been repeated in experience."[15]

But, in spite of all these facts, I have no hesitation whatever in holding firm to the darwinian distinction even here. I

[14]That is, if a certain general character be rapidly repeated in our outer experience with a number of strongly contrasted concomitants, it will be sooner abstracted than if its associates are invariable or monotonous.

[15]*Principles of Psychology*, i, 460. See also pp. 463, 464, 500. On page 408 the law is formulated thus: The *persistence* of the connection in consciousness is proportionate to the *persistence* of the outer connection. Mr. Spencer works most with the law of frequency. Either law, from my point of view, is false; but Mr. Spencer ought not to think them synonymous.

maintain that the facts in question are all drawn from the lower strata of the mind, so to speak—from the sphere of its least evolved functions, from the region of intelligence which man possesses in common with the brutes. And I can easily show that throughout the whole extent of those mental departments which are highest, which are most characteristically human, Spencer's law is violated at every step; and that as a matter of fact the new conceptions, emotions, and active tendencies which evolve are originally produced in the shape of random images, fancies, accidental out-births of spontaneous variation in the functional activity of the excessively instable human brain, which the outer environment simply confirms or refutes, adopts or rejects, preserves or destroys—selects, in short, just as it selects morphological and social variations due to molecular accidents of an analogous sort.

It is one of the tritest of truisms that human intelligences of a simple order are very literal. They are slaves of habit, doing what they have been taught without variation; dry, prosaic, and matter-of-fact in their remarks; devoid of humor, except of the coarse physical kind which rejoices in a practical joke; taking the world for granted; and possessing in their faithfulness and honesty the single gift by which they are sometimes able to warm us into admiration. But even this faithfulness seems to have a sort of inorganic ring, and to remind us more of the immutable properties of a piece of inanimate matter than of the steadfastness of a human will capable of alternative choice. When we descend to the brutes, all these peculiarities are intensified. No reader of Schopenhauer can forget his frequent allusions to the *trockener ernst* of dogs and horses, nor to their *ehrlichkeit*. And every noticer of their ways must receive a deep impression of the fatally literal character of the few, simple, and treadmill-like operations of their minds.

But turn to the highest order of minds, and what a change! Instead of thoughts of concrete things patiently following one another in a beaten track of habitual suggestion, we have the most abrupt cross-cuts and transitions from one idea to another, the most rarefied abstractions and discriminations, the most unheard-of combinations of elements, the subtlest associations of analogy; in a word, we seem suddenly introduced into a seething caldron of ideas, where everything is fizzling and bobbing about in a state of bewildering activity, where partnerships can be joined or loosened in an instant, tread-mill routine is unknown, and the unexpected seems the only law. According to the idiosyncrasy of the individual, the scintillations will have one character or another. They will be sallies of wit and humor; they will be flashes of poetry and eloquence; they will be constructions of dramatic fiction or of mechanical device, logical or philosophic abstractions, business projects, or scientific hypotheses, with trains of experimental consequences based thereon; they will be musical sounds, or images of plastic beauty or picturesqueness, or visions of moral harmony. But, whatever their differences may be, they will all agree in this—that their genesis is sudden and, as it were, spontaneous. That is to say, the same premises would not, in the mind of another individual, have engendered just that conclusion; although, when the conclusion is offered to the other individual, he may thoroughly accept and enjoy it, and envy the brilliancy of him to whom it first occurred.

To Professor Jevons is due the great credit of having emphatically pointed out[16] how the genius of discovery depends altogether on the number of these random notions and guesses which visit the investigator's mind. To be fertile in hypotheses is the first requisite, and to be willing to throw them away the moment experience contradicts them is the next. The baconian method of collating tables of instances may be a useful aid at certain times. But one might as well expect a chemist's note-book to write down the name of the body analyzed, or a weather table to sum itself up into a prediction of probabilities of its own accord, as to hope that the mere fact of mental confrontation with a certain series of facts will be sufficient to make *any* brain conceive their law. The conceiving of the law is a spontaneous variation in the strictest sense of the term. It flashes out of one brain, and no other, because the instability of that brain is such as to tip and upset itself in just that particular direction. But the important thing to notice is that the good flashes and the bad flashes, the tri-

---

[16]In his *Principles of Science*, chapters xi, xii, xxvi.

umphant hypotheses and the absurd conceits, are on an exact equality in respect of their origin. Aristotle's absurd *Physics* and his immortal *Logic* flow from one source: the forces that produce the one produce the other. When walking along the street, thinking of the blue sky or the fine spring weather, I may either smile at some grotesque whim which occurs to me, or I may suddenly catch an intuition of the solution of a long-unsolved problem, which at that moment was far from my thoughts. Both notions are shaken out of the same reservoir—the reservoir of a brain in which the reproduction of images in the relations of their outward persistence or frequency has long ceased to be the dominant law. But to the thought, when it is once engendered, the consecration of agreement with outward relations may come. The conceit perishes in a moment, and is forgotten. The scientific hypothesis arouses in me a fever of desire for verification. I read, write, experiment, consult experts. Everything corroborates my notion, which being then published in a book spreads from review to review and from mouth to mouth, till at last there is no doubt I am enshrined in the Pantheon of the great diviners of nature's ways. The environment *preserves* the conception which it was unable to *produce* in any brain less idiosyncratic than my own.

Now the spontaneous upsettings of brains this way and that at particular moments into particular ideas and combinations are matched by their equally spontaneous permanent tiltings or saggings towards determinate directions. The humorous bent is quite characteristic; the sentimental one equally so. And the personal tone of each mind, which makes it more alive to certain classes of experience than others, more attentive to certain impressions, more open to certain reasons, is equally the result of that invisible and unimaginable play of the forces of growth within the nervous system which, irresponsibly to the environment, makes the brain peculiarly apt to function in a certain way. Here again the selection goes on. The products of the mind with the determined æsthetic bent please or displease the community. We adopt Wordsworth, and grow unsentimental and serene. We are fascinated by Schopenhauer, and learn from him the true luxury of woe. The adopted bent becomes a ferment in the community, and alters its tone. The alteration may be a benefit or a misfortune, for it is (*pace* Mr. Allen) a differentiation from within, which has to run the gauntlet of the larger environment's selective power. Civilized Languedoc, taking the tone of its scholars, poets, princes, and theologians, fell a prey to its rude Catholic environment in the Albigensian crusade. France in 1792, taking the tone of its St. Justs and Marats, plunged into its long career of unstable outward relations. Prussia in 1806, taking the tone of its Humboldts and its Steins, proved itself in the most signal way "adjusted" to its environment in 1872.

Mr. Spencer, in one of the strangest chapters of his *Psychology*,[17] tries to show the necessary order in which the development of conceptions in the human race occurs. No abstract conception can be developed, according to him, until the outward experiences have reached a certain degree of heterogeneity, definiteness, coherence, and so forth.

"Thus the belief in an unchanging order—the belief in *law*, . . . is a belief of which the primitive man is absolutely incapable. . . . Experiences such as he receives furnish but few data for the conception of uniformity, whether as displayed in things or in relations. . . . The daily impressions which the savage gets, yield the notion very imperfectly and in but few cases. Of all the objects around—trees, stones, hills, pieces of water, clouds, and so forth— most differ widely, . . . and few approach complete likeness so nearly as to make discrimination difficult. Even between animals of the same species . . . it rarely happens that, whether alive or dead, they are presented in just the same attitudes. . . . It is only along with a gradual development of the arts . . . that there come frequent experiences of perfectly straight lines admitting of complete apposition; bringing the perceptions of equality and inequality. Still more devoid is savage life of the experiences which generate the conception of uniformity of succession. The sequences observed from hour to hour and day to day, seem anything but uniform: difference is a far more conspicuous trait among them. . . . So that if we contemplate primitive human life as a whole, we see that multiformity of sequence rather than uniformity is the notion which it tends to generate. . . . Only as fast as the practice of the arts develops the idea of *measure,* can the consciousness of uniformity become clear. . . . Those conditions furnished by advancing civilization which make possible the notion of uniformity, simultaneously make possible the

[17]Part viii, chap. iii.

notion of *exactness*. . . . Hence the primitive man has little experience which cultivates the consciousness of what we call *truth*. How closely allied this is to the consciousness which the practice of the arts cultivates, is implied even in language. We speak of a true surface as well as of a true statement. Exactness describes perfection in a mechanical fit, as well as perfect agreement between the results of calculations."

The whole burden of Mr. Spencer's book is to show the fatal way in which the mind, supposed passive, is moulded by its experiences of "outer relations." In this chapter the yard-stick, the balance, the chronometer, and other machines and instruments come to figure among the "relations" external to the mind. Surely they are so, after they have been manufactured; but only because of the preservative power of the social environment. Originally all these things and all other institutions were flashes of genius in an individual head, of which the outer environment showed no sign. Adopted by the race and become its heritage, they then supply instigations to new geniuses whom they environ to make new inventions and discoveries; and so the ball of progress rolls. But take out the geniuses, or alter their idiosyncrasies, and what increasing uniformities will the environment show? We defy Mr. Spencer or anyone else to reply.

The plain truth is that the "philosophy" of evolution (as distinguished from our special information about particular cases of change) is a metaphysical creed, and nothing else. It is a mood of contemplation, an emotional attitude, rather than a system of thought—a mood which is old as the world, and which no refutation of any one incarnation of it (such as the spencerian philosophy) will dispel; the mood of fatalistic pantheism, with its intuition of the One and All, which was, and is, and ever shall be, and from whose womb each single thing proceeds. Far be it from us to speak slightingly here of so hoary and mighty a style of looking on the world as this. What we at present call scientific discoveries had nothing to do with bringing it to birth, nor can one easily conceive that they should ever give it its *quietus*, no matter how logically incompatible with its spirit the ultimate phenomenal distinctions which science accumulates should turn out to be. It can laugh at the phenomenal distinctions on which science is based, for it draws its vital breath from a region which—whether above or below—is at least altogether different from that in which science dwells. A critic, however, who cannot disprove the truth of the metaphysic creed, can at least raise his voice in protest against its disguising itself in "scientific" plumes. I think that all who have had the patience to follow me thus far will agree that the spencerian "philosophy" of social and intellectual progress is an obsolete anachronism, reverting to a pre-darwinian type of thought, just as the spencerian philosophy of "Force," effacing all the previous distinctions between actual and potential energy, momentum, work, force, mass, etc., which physicists have with so much agony achieved, carries us back to a pre-galilean age.

The Importance of Individuals

THE PREVIOUS ESSAY, on Great Men, etc., called forth two replies—one by Mr. Grant Allen, entitled the "Genesis of Genius," in the *Atlantic Monthly*, vol. xlvii. p. 371; the other entitled "Sociology and Hero-Worship," by Mr. John Fiske, *ibidem*, p. 75. The article which follows is a rejoinder to Mr. Allen's article. It was refused at the time by the *Atlantic*, but saw the day later in the *Open Court* for August, 1890. It appears here as a natural supplement to the foregoing article, on which it casts some explanatory light.

Mr. Allen's contempt for hero-worship is based on very simple considerations. A nation's great men, he says, are but slight deviations from the general level. The hero is merely a special complex of the ordinary qualities of his race. The petty differences impressed upon ordinary Greek minds by Plato or Aristotle or Zeno, are nothing at all compared with the vast differences between every Greek mind and every Egyptian or Chinese mind. We may neglect them in a philosophy of history, just as in calculating the impetus of a locomotive we neglect the extra impetus given by a single piece of better coal. What each man adds is but an infinitesimal fraction compared with what he derives from his parents, or indirectly from his earlier ancestry. And if what the past gives to the hero is so much bulkier than what the future receives from him, it is what really calls for philosophical treatment. The problem for the sociologist is as to what produces the average man; the extraordinary men and what they produce may by the philosophers be taken for granted, as too trivial variations to merit deep inquiry.

Now as I wish to vie with Mr. Allen's unrivalled polemic amiability and be as conciliatory as possible, I will not cavil at his facts or try to magnify the chasm between an Aristotle, a Goethe, or a Napoleon and the average level of their respective tribes. Let it be as small as Mr. Allen thinks. All that I object to is that he should think the mere *size* of a difference is capable of deciding whether that difference be or be not a fit

647

subject for philosophic study. Truly enough, the details vanish
in the bird's-eye view; but so does the bird's-eye view vanish
in the details. Which is the right point of view for philosophic
vision? Nature gives no reply, for both points of view, being
equally real, are equally natural; and no one natural reality *per
se* is any more emphatic than any other. Accentuation, foreground, and background are created solely by the interested
attention of the looker-on; and if the small difference between
the genius and his tribe interests me most, while the large one
between that tribe and another tribe interests Mr. Allen, our
controversy cannot be ended until a complete philosophy, accounting for all differences impartially, shall justify us both.

An unlearned carpenter of my acquaintance once said in my
hearing: "There is very little difference between one man and
another; but what little there is, *is very important.*" This distinction seems to me to go to the root of the matter. It is not
only the size of the difference which concerns the philosopher, but also its place and its kind. An inch is a small thing,
but we know the proverb about an inch on a man's nose.
Messrs. Allen and Spencer, in inveighing against hero-
worship, are thinking exclusively of the size of the inch; I, as a
hero-worshipper, attend to its seat and function.

Now there is a striking law over which few people seem to
have pondered. It is this: That among all the differences
which exist, the only ones that interest us strongly are those
we do not take for granted. We are not a bit elated that our
friend should have two hands and the power of speech, and
should practice the matter-of-course human virtues; and quite
as little are we vexed that our dog goes on all fours and fails
to understand our conversation. Expecting no more from the
latter companion, and no less from the former, we get what
we expect and are satisfied. We never think of communing
with the dog by discourse of philosophy, or with the friend
by head-scratching or the throwing of crusts to be snapped
at. But if either dog or friend fall above or below the expected standard, they arouse the most lively emotion. On our
brother's vices or genius we never weary of descanting; to his
bipedism or his hairless skin we do not consecrate a thought.
What he says may transport us; that he is able to speak at all
leaves us stone cold. The reason of all this is that his virtues

and vices and utterances might, compatibly with the current range of variation in our tribe, be just the opposites of what they are, whilst his zoölogically human attributes cannot possibly go astray. There is thus a zone of insecurity in human affairs in which all the dramatic interest lies; the rest belongs to the dead machinery of the stage. This is the formative zone, the part not yet ingrained into the race's average, not yet a typical, hereditary, and constant factor of the social community in which it occurs. It is like the soft layer beneath the bark of the tree in which all the year's growth is going on. Life has abandoned the mighty trunk inside, which stands inert and belongs almost to the inorganic world. Layer after layer of human perfection separates me from the central Africans who pursued Stanley with cries of "meat, meat!" This vast difference ought, on Mr. Allen's principles, to rivet my attention far more than the petty one which obtains between two such birds of a feather as Mr. Allen and myself. Yet whilst I never feel proud that the sight of a passer-by awakens in me no cannibalistic waterings of the mouth, I am free to confess that I shall feel very proud if I do not publicly appear inferior to Mr. Allen in the conduct of this momentous debate. To me as a teacher the intellectual gap between my ablest and my dullest student counts for infinitely more than that between the latter and the amphioxus: indeed, I never thought of the latter chasm till this moment. Will Mr. Allen seriously say that this is all human folly, and tweedledum and tweedledee?

To a Veddah's eyes the differences between two white literary men seem slight indeed—same clothes, same spectacles, same harmless disposition, same habit of scribbling on paper and poring over books, etc. "Just two white fellows," the Veddah will say, "with no perceptible difference." But what a difference to the literary men themselves! Think, Mr. Allen, of confounding our philosophies together merely because both are printed in the same magazines and are indistinguishable to the eye of a Veddah! Our flesh creeps at the thought.

But in judging of history Mr. Allen deliberately prefers to place himself at the Veddah's point of view, and to see things *en gros* and out of focus, rather than minutely. It is quite true that there are things and differences enough to be seen either way. But which are the humanly important ones, those most worthy to arouse our interest—the large distinctions or the small? In the answer to this question lies the whole divergence of the hero-worshippers from the sociologists. As I said at the outset, it is merely a quarrel of emphasis; and the only thing I can do is to state my personal reasons for the emphasis I prefer.

The zone of the individual differences, and of the social "twists" which by common confession they initiate, is the zone of formative processes, the dynamic belt of quivering uncertainty, the line where past and future meet. It is the theatre of all we do not take for granted, the stage of the living drama of life; and however narrow its scope, it is roomy enough to lodge the whole range of human passions. The sphere of the race's average, on the contrary, no matter how large it may be, is a dead and stagnant thing, an achieved possession, from which all insecurity has vanished. Like the trunk of a tree, it has been built up by successive concretions of successive active zones. The moving present in which we live with its problems and passions, its individual rivalries, victories, and defeats, will soon pass over to the majority and leave its small deposit on this static mass, to make room for fresh actors and a newer play. And though it may be true, as Mr. Spencer predicts, that each later zone shall fatally be narrower than its forerunners; and that when the ultimate lady-like tea-table elysium of the *Data of Ethics* shall prevail, such questions as the breaking of eggs at the large or the small end will span the whole scope of possible human warfare—still even in this shrunken and enfeebled generation, *spatio aetatis defessa vetusto*, what eagerness there will be! Battles and defeats will occur, the victors will be glorified and the vanquished dishonored just as in the brave days of yore, the human heart still withdrawing itself from the much it has in safe possession, and concentrating all its passion upon those evanescent possibilities of fact which still quiver in fate's scale.

And is not its instinct right? Do not we here grasp the race-differences *in the making*, and catch the only glimpse it is allotted to us to attain of the working units themselves, of whose differentiating action the race-gaps form but the stagnant sum? What strange inversion of scientific procedure does Mr. Allen practice when he teaches us to neglect elements and attend only to aggregate resultants? On the contrary, simply because the active ring, whatever its bulk, *is elementary*, I hold that the study of its conditions (be these never so "proximate") is the highest of topics for the social philosopher. If individual variations determine its ups and downs and hairbreadth escapes and twists and turns, as Mr. Allen and Mr. Fiske both admit, Heaven forbid us from tabooing the study of these in favor of the average! On the contrary, let us emphasize these, and the importance of these; and in picking out from history our heroes, and communing with their kindred spirits—in imagining as strongly as possible what differences their individualities brought about in this world, whilst its surface was still plastic in their hands, and what whilom feasibilities they made impossible—each one of us may best fortify and inspire what creative energy may lie in his own soul.[1]

This is the lasting justification of hero-worship, and the pooh-poohing of it by "sociologists" is the everlasting excuse for popular indifference to their general laws and averages. The difference between an America rescued by a Washington or by a "Jenkins" may, as Mr. Allen says, be "little," but it is, in the words of my carpenter friend, "important." Some organizing genius must in the nature of things have emerged from the French revolution; but what Frenchman will affirm it to have been an accident of no consequence that he should have had the supernumerary idiosyncrasies of a Bonaparte? What animal, domestic or wild, will call it a matter of no moment that scarce a word of sympathy with brutes should have survived from the teachings of Jesus of Nazareth?

The preferences of sentient creatures are what *create* the importance of topics. They are the absolute and ultimate lawgiver here. And I for my part cannot but consider the talk of the contemporary sociological school about averages and general laws and predetermined tendencies, with its obligatory undervaluing of the importance of individual differences, as the most pernicious and immoral of fatalisms. Suppose

[1] J. G. Tarde's book (itself a work of genius), *Les Lois de l'imitation, étude sociologique* (2me Édition, Paris, Alcan, 1895), is the best possible commentary on this text—"invention" on the one hand, and "imitation" on the other, being for this author the two sole factors of social change.

there is a social equilibrium fated to be, whose is it to be—
that of your preference, or mine? There lies the question
of questions, and it is one which no study of averages can
decide.

On Some Hegelisms [1]

W E ARE just now witnessing a singular phenomenon in British and American philosophy. Hegelism, so defunct on its native soil that I believe but a single youthful disciple of the school is to be counted among the privatdocenten and younger professors of Germany, and whose older champions are all passing off the stage, has found among us so zealous and able a set of propagandists that today it may really be reckoned one of the most powerful influences of the time in the higher walks of thought. And there is no doubt that, as a movement of reaction against the traditional British empiricism, the hegelian influence represents expansion and freedom, and is doing service of a certain kind. Such service, however, ought not to make us blindly indulgent. Hegel's philosophy mingles mountain-loads of corruption with its scanty merits, and must, now that it has become quasi-official, make ready to defend itself as well as to attack others. It is with no hope of converting independent thinkers, but rather with the sole aspiration of showing some chance youthful disciple that there *is* another point of view in philosophy that I fire this skirmisher's shot, which may, I hope, soon be followed by somebody else's heavier musketry.

The point of view I have in mind will become clearer if I begin with a few preparatory remarks on the motives and difficulties of philosophizing in general.

To show that the real is identical with the ideal may roughly be set down as the mainspring of philosophic activity. The atomic and mechanical conception of the world is as ideal from the point of view of some of our faculties as the teleological one is from the point of view of others. In the realm of every ideal we can begin anywhere and roam over the field, each term passing us to its neighbor, each member calling for the next, and our reason rejoicing in its glad activity. Where the parts of a conception seem thus to belong together by inward kinship, where the whole is defined in a way

[1] Reprinted from *Mind*, April, 1882.

congruous with our powers of reaction, to see is to approve
and to understand.

Much of the real seems at the first blush to follow a different law. The parts seem, as Hegel has said, to be shot out of a
pistol at us. Each asserts itself as a simple brute fact, uncalled
for by the rest, which, so far as we can see, might even make a
better system without it. Arbitrary, foreign, jolting, discontinuous—are the adjectives by which we are tempted to describe
it. And yet from out the bosom of it a partial ideality constantly arises which keeps alive our aspiration that the whole
may some day be construed in ideal form. Not only do the
materials lend themselves under certain circumstances to æsthetic manipulation, but underlying their worst disjointedness
are three great continua in which for each of us reason's ideal
is actually reached. I mean the continua of memory or personal consciousness, of time and of space. In these great ma-
trices of all we know, we are absolutely at home. The things
we meet are many, and yet are one; each is itself, and yet all
belong together; continuity reigns, yet individuality is not
lost.

Consider, for example, space. It is a unit. No force can in
any way break, wound, or tear it. It has no joints between
which you can pass your amputating knife, for it penetrates
the knife and is not split. Try to make a hole in space by
annihilating an inch of it. To make a hole you must drive
something else through. But what can you drive through
space except what is itself spatial?

But notwithstanding it is this very paragon of unity, space
in its parts contains an infinite variety, and the unity and the
variety do not contradict each other, for they obtain in different respects. The one is the whole, the many are the parts.
Each part is one again, but only one fraction; and part lies
beside part in absolute nextness, the very picture of peace and
non-contradiction. It is true that the space between two
points both unites and divides them, just as the bar of a
dumb-bell both unites and divides the two balls. But the
union and the division are not *secundum idem*: it divides them
by keeping them out of the space between, it unites them by
keeping them out of the space beyond; so the double function
presents no inconsistency. Self-contradiction in space could

only ensue if one part tried to oust another from its position; but the notion of such an absurdity vanishes in the framing, and cannot stay to vex the mind.[2] Beyond the parts we see or think at any given time extend farther parts; but the beyond is homogeneous with what is embraced, and follows the same law; so that no surprises, no foreignness, can ever emerge from space's womb.

Thus with space our intelligence is absolutely intimate; it is rationality and transparency incarnate. The same may be said of the ego and of time. But if for simplicity's sake we ignore them, we may truly say that when we desiderate rational knowledge of the world the standard set by our knowledge of space is what governs our desire.[3] Cannot the breaks, the jolts, the margin of foreignness, be exorcised from other things and leave them unitary like the space they fill? Could this be done, the philosophic kingdom of heaven would be at hand.

But the moment we turn to the material qualities of being, we find the continuity ruptured on every side. A fearful jolting begins. Even if we simplify the world by reducing it to its mechanical bare poles—atoms and their motions—the dis-

---

[2]The seeming contradiction between the infinitude of space and the fact that it is all finished and given and there, can be got over in more than one way. The simplest way is by idealism, which distinguishes between space as actual and space as potential. For idealism, space only exists so far as it is represented; but all actually represented spaces are finite; it is only possibly representable spaces that are infinite.

[3]Not only for simplicity's sake do we select space as the paragon of a rationalizing continuum. Space determines the relations of the items that enter it in a far more intricate way than does time; in a far more fixed way than does the ego. By this last clause I mean that if things are in space at all, they must conform to geometry; whilst the being in an ego at all need not make them conform to logic or any other manner of rationality. Under the sheltering wings of a self the matter of unreason can lodge itself as safely as any other kind of content. One cannot but respect the devoutness of the ego-worship of some of our English-writing Hegelians. But at the same time one cannot help fearing lest the monotonous contemplation of so barren a principle as that of the pure formal self (which, be it never so essential a condition of the existence of a world of organized experience at all, must notwithstanding take its own *character* from, not give the character to, the separate empirical data over which its mantle is cast), one cannot but fear, I say, lest the religion of the transcendental ego should, like all religions of the "one thing needful," end by sterilizing and occluding the minds of its believers.

continuity is bad enough. The laws of clash, the effects of distance upon attraction and repulsion, all seem arbitrary collocations of data. The atoms themselves are so many independent facts, the existence of any one of which in no wise seems to involve the existence of the rest. We have not banished discontinuity, we have only made it finer-grained. And to get even that degree of rationality into the universe we have had to butcher a great part of its contents. The secondary qualities we stripped off from the reality and swept into the dust-bin labelled "subjective illusion," still *as such* are facts, and must themselves be rationalized in some way.

But when we deal with facts believed to be purely subjective, we are farther than ever from the goal. We have not now the refuge of distinguishing between the "reality" and its appearances. Facts of thought being the only facts, differences of thought become the only differences, and identities of thought the only identities there are. Two thoughts that seem different are different to all eternity. We can no longer speak of heat and light being reconciled in any *tertium quid* like wave-motion. For motion is motion, and light is light, and heat heat forever, and their discontinuity is as absolute as their existence. Together with the other attributes and things we conceive, they make up Plato's realm of immutable ideas. Neither *per se* calls for the other, hatches it out, is its "truth," creates it, or has any sort of inward community with it except that of being comparable in an ego and found more or less differing, or more or less resembling, as the case may be. The world of qualities is a world of things almost wholly discontinuous *inter se*. Each only says, "I am that I am," and each says it on its own account and with absolute monotony. The continuities of which they *partake*, in Plato's phrase, the ego, space, and time, are for most of them the only grounds of union they possess.

It might seem as if in the mere "partaking" there lay a contradiction of the discontinuity. If the white must partake of space, the heat of time, and so forth—do not whiteness and space, heat and time, mutually call for or help to create each other?

Yes; a few such *a priori* couplings must be admitted. They

are the axioms: no feeling except as occupying some space and time, or as a moment in some ego; no motion but of something moved; no thought but of an object; no time without a previous time—and the like. But they are limited in number, and they obtain only between excessively broad genera of concepts, and leave quite undetermined what the specifications of those genera shall be. What feeling shall fill *this* time, what substance execute *this* motion, what qualities combine in *this* being, are as much unanswered questions as if the metaphysical axioms never existed at all.

The existence of such syntheses as they are does then but slightly mitigate the jolt, jolt, jolt we get when we pass over the facts of the world. Everywhere indeterminate variables, subject only to these few vague enveloping laws, independent in all besides—such seems the truth.

In yet another way, too, ideal and real are so far apart that their conjunction seems quite hopeless. To eat our cake and have it, to lose our soul and save it, to enjoy the physical privileges of selfishness and the moral luxury of altruism at the same time, would be the ideal. But the real offers us these terms in the shape of mutually exclusive alternatives of which only one can be true at once; so that we must choose, and in choosing murder one possibility. The wrench is absolute: "Either—or!" Just as whenever I bet a hundred dollars on an event, there comes an instant when I am a hundred dollars richer or poorer without any intermediate degrees passed over; just as my wavering between a journey to Portland or to New York does not carry me from Cambridge in a resultant direction in which both motions are compounded, say to Albany, but at a given moment results in the conjunction of reality in all its fulness for one alternative and impossibility in all its fulness for the other—so the bachelor joys are utterly lost from the face of being for the married man, who must henceforward find his account in something that is not them but is good enough to make him forget them; so the careless and irresponsible living in the sunshine, the "unbuttoning after supper and sleeping upon benches in the afternoon," are stars that have set upon the path of him who in good earnest makes himself a moralist. The transitions are abrupt, absolute,

truly shot out of a pistol; for while many possibilities are
called, the few that are chosen are chosen in all their sudden
completeness.

Must we then think that the world that fills space and time
can yield us no acquaintance of that high and perfect type
yielded by empty space and time themselves? Is what unity
there is in the world mainly derived from the fact that the
world is *in* space and time and "partakes" of them? Can no
vision of it forestall the facts of it, or know from some fractions the others before the others have arrived? Are there real
logically indeterminate possibilities which forbid there being
any equivalent for the happening of it all but the happening
itself? Can we gain no anticipatory assurance that what is to
come will have no strangeness? Is there no substitute, in
short, for life but the living itself in all its long-drawn weary
length and breadth and thickness?

In the negative reply to all these questions, a modest
common-sense finds no difficulty in acquiescing. To such a
way of thinking the notion of "partaking" has a deep and real
significance. Whoso partakes of a thing enjoys his share, and
comes into contact with the thing and its other partakers. But
he claims no more. His share in no wise negates the thing or
their share; nor does it preclude his possession of reserved
and private powers with which they have nothing to do, and
which are not all absorbed in the mere function of sharing.
Why may not the world be a sort of republican banquet of
this sort, where all the qualities of being respect one another's
personal sacredness, yet sit at the common table of space and
time?

To me this view seems deeply probable. Things cohere, but
the act of cohesion itself implies but few conditions, and
leaves the rest of their qualifications indeterminate. As the
first three notes of a tune comport many endings, all melo-
dious, but the tune is not named till a particular ending has
actually come—so the parts actually known of the universe
may comport many ideally possible complements. But as the
facts are not the complements, so the knowledge of the one is
not the knowledge of the other in anything but the few necessary elements of which all must partake in order to be together at all. Why, if one act of knowledge could from one

point take in the total perspective, with all mere possibilities abolished, should there ever have been anything more than that act? Why duplicate it by the tedious unrolling, inch by inch, of the foredone reality? No answer seems possible. On the other hand, if we stipulate only a partial community of partially independent powers, we see perfectly why no one part controls the whole view, but each detail must come and be actually given, before, in any special sense, it can be said to be determined at all. This is the moral view, the view that gives to other powers the same freedom it would have itself— not the ridiculous "freedom to do right," which in my mouth can only mean the freedom to do as *I* think right, but the freedom to do as *they* think right, or wrong either. After all, what accounts do the nethermost bounds of the universe owe to me? By what insatiate conceit and lust of intellectual despotism do I arrogate the right to know their secrets, and from my philosophic throne to play the only airs they shall march to, as if I were the Lord's anointed? Is not my knowing them at all a gift and not a right? And shall it be given before they are given? *Data! gifts!* something to be thankful for! It is a gift that we can approach things at all, and, by means of the time and space of which our minds and they partake, alter our actions so as to meet them.

There are "bounds of ord'nance" set for all things, where they must pause or rue it. "Facts" are the bounds of human knowledge, set for it, not by it.

Now to a mind like Hegel's such pusillanimous twaddle sounds simply loathsome. Bounds that we can't overpass! data! facts that say "Hands off, till we are given"! possibilities we can't control! a banquet of which we merely share! Heavens, this is intolerable; such a world is no world for a philosopher to have to do with. He must have all or nothing. If the world cannot be rational in my sense, in the sense of unconditional surrender, I refuse to grant that it is rational at all. It is pure incoherence, a chaos, a nulliverse, to whose haphazard sway I will not truckle. But, no! this is not the world. The world is philosophy's own—a single block, of which, if she once get her teeth on any part, the whole shall inevitably become her prey and feed her all-devouring theoretic maw.

Naught shall be but the necessities she creates and impossibilities; freedom shall mean freedom to obey her will; ideal and
actual shall be one: she, and I as her champion, will be satisfied on no lower terms.

The insolence of sway, the ὕβρις on which gods take ven-
geance, is in temporal and spiritual matters usually admitted
to be a vice. A Bonaparte and a Philip II. are called monsters.
But when an *intellect* is found insatiate enough to declare that
all existence must bend the knee to its requirements, we do
not call its owner a monster, but a philosophic prophet. May
not this be all wrong? Is there any one of our functions ex-
empted from the common lot of liability to excess? And
where everything else must be contented with its part in the
universe, shall the theorizing faculty ride rough-shod over the
whole?

I confess I can see no *a priori* reason for the exception. He
who claims it must be judged by the consequences of his acts,
and by them alone. Let Hegel then confront the universe with
his claim, and see how he can make the two match.

The universe absolutely refuses to let him travel without
jolt. Time, space, and his ego are continuous; so are degrees
of heat, shades of light and colour, and a few other serial
things; so too do potatoes call for salt, and cranberries for
sugar, in the taste of one who knows what salt and sugar are.
But on the whole there is naught to soften the shock of surprise to his intelligence, as it passes from one quality of being
to another. Light is not heat, heat is not light; and to him
who holds the one the other is not given till it give itself. Real
being comes moreover and goes from any concept at its own
sweet will, with no permission asked of the conceiver. In despair must Hegel lift vain hands of imprecation; and since he
will take nothing but the whole, he must throw away even the
part he might retain, and call the nature of things an *absolute*
muddle and incoherence.

But, hark! What wondrous strain is this that steals upon his
ear? Incoherence itself, may it not be the very sort of coherence I require? Muddle! is it anything but a peculiar sort of
transparency? Is not jolt passage? Is friction other than a kind
of lubrication? Is not a chasm a filling?—a queer kind of

filling, but a filling still. Why seek for a glue to hold things together when their very falling apart is the only glue you need? Let all that negation which seemed to disintegrate the universe be the mortar that combines it, and the problem stands solved. The paradoxical character of the notion could not fail to please a mind monstrous even in its native Germany, where mental excess is endemic. Richard, for a moment brought to bay, is himself again. He vaults into the saddle, and from that time his career is that of a philosophic desperado—one series of outrages upon the chastity of thought.

And can we not ourselves sympathize with his mood in some degree? The old receipts of squeezing the thistle and taking the bull by the horns have many applications. An evil frankly accepted loses half its sting and all its terror. The Stoics had their cheap and easy way of dealing with evil. *Call* your woes goods, they said; refuse to *call* your lost blessings by that name—and you are happy. So of the unintelligibilities: call them means of intelligibility, and what farther do you require? There is even a more legitimate excuse than that. In the exceedingness of the facts of life over our formulas lies a standing temptation at certain times to give up trying to say anything adequate about them, and to take refuge in wild and whirling words which but confess our impotence before their ineffability. Thus Baron Bunsen writes to his wife: "Nothing is near but the far; nothing true but the highest; nothing credible but the inconceivable; nothing so real as the impossible; nothing clear but the deepest; nothing so visible as the invisible; and no life is there but through death." Of these ecstatic moments the *credo quia impossibile* is the classical expression. Hegel's originality lies in his making their mood permanent and sacramental, and authorized to supersede all others—not as a mystical bath and refuge for feeling when tired reason sickens of her intellectual responsibilities (thank Heaven! that bath is always ready), but as the very form of intellectual responsibility itself.

And now after this long introduction, let me trace some of Hegel's ways of applying his discovery. His system resembles a mouse-trap, in which if you once pass the door you may

be lost forever. Safety lies in not entering. Hegelians have
anointed, so to speak, the entrance with various considerations which, stated in an abstract form, are so plausible as to
slide us unresistingly and almost unwittingly through the fatal
arch. It is not necessary to drink the ocean to know that it is
salt; nor need a critic dissect a whole system after proving that
its premises are rotten. I shall accordingly confine myself to a
few of the points that captivate beginners most; and assume
that if they break down, so must the system which they prop.

First of all, Hegel has to do utterly away with the sharing
and partaking business he so much loathes. He will not call
contradiction the glue in one place and identity in another;
that is too half-hearted. Contradiction must be a glue universal, and must derive its credit from being shown to be latently
involved in cases that we hitherto supposed to embody pure
continuity. Thus, the relations of an ego with its objects, of
one time with another time, of one place with another place,
of a cause with its effect, of a thing with its properties, and
especially of parts with wholes, must be shown to involve
contradiction. Contradiction, shown to lurk in the very heart
of coherence and continuity, cannot after that be held to defeat them, and must be taken as the universal solvent—or,
rather, there is no longer any need of a solvent. To "dissolve"
things in identity was the dream of earlier cruder schools.
Hegel will show that their very difference is their identity,
and that in the act of detachment the detachment is undone,
and they fall into each other's arms.

Now at the very outset it seems rather odd that a philosopher who pretends that the world is absolutely rational, or in
other words that it can be completely understood, should fall
back on a principle (the identity of contradictories) which utterly defies understanding, and obliges him in fact to use the
word "understanding," whenever it occurs in his pages, as a
term of contempt. Take the case of space we used above. The
common man who looks at space believes there is nothing in
it to be acquainted with beyond what he sees; no hidden machinery, no secrets, nothing but the parts as they lie side by
side and make the static whole. His intellect is satisfied with
accepting space as an ultimate genus of the given. But Hegel
cries to him: "Dupe! dost thou not see it to be one nest of

incompatibilities? Do not the unity of its wholeness and the diversity of its parts stand in patent contradiction? Does it not both unite and divide things; and but for this strange and irreconcilable activity, would it be at all? The hidden dynamism of self-contradiction is what incessantly produces the static appearance by which your sense is fooled."

But if the man ask how self-contradiction *can* do all this, and how its dynamism may be seen to work, Hegel can only reply by showing him the space itself and saying: "Lo, *thus.*" In other words, instead of the principle of explanation being more intelligible than the thing to be explained, it is absolutely unintelligible if taken by itself, and must appeal to its pretended product to prove its existence. Surely such a system of explaining *notum per ignotum*, of making the *explicans* borrow credentials from the *explicand*, and of creating paradoxes and impossibilities where none were suspected, is a strange candidate for the honor of being a complete rationalizer of the world.

The principle of the contradictoriness of identity and the identity of contradictories is the essence of the hegelian system. But what probably washes this principle down most with beginners is the combination in which its author works it with another principle which is by no means characteristic of his system, and which, for want of a better name, might be called the "principle of totality." This principle says that you cannot adequately know even a part until you know of what whole it forms a part. As Aristotle writes and Hegel loves to quote, an amputated hand is not even a hand. And as Tennyson says,

> "Little flower—but if I could understand
> What you are, root and all, and all in all,
> I should know what God and man is."

Obviously until we have taken in all the relations, immediate or remote, into which the thing actually enters or potentially may enter, we do not know all *about* the thing.

And obviously for such an exhaustive acquaintance with the thing, an acquaintance with every other thing, actual and potential, near and remote, is needed; so that it is quite fair to say that omniscience alone can completely know any one thing as it stands. Standing in a world of relations, that world must be known before the thing is fully known. This doctrine is of course an integral part of empiricism, an integral part of common-sense. Since when could good men not apprehend the passing hour in the light of life's larger sweep—not grow dispassionate the more they stretched their view? Did the "law of sharing" so little legitimate their procedure that a law of identity of contradictories, forsooth, must be trumped up to give it scope? Out upon the idea!

Hume's account of causation is a good illustration of the way in which empiricism may use the principle of totality. We call something a cause; but we at the same time deny its effect to be in any latent way contained in or substantially identical with it. We thus cannot tell what its causality amounts to until its effect has actually supervened. The effect, then, or something beyond the thing is what makes the thing to be so far as it is a cause. Humism thus says that its causality is something adventitious and not necessarily given when its other attributes are there. Generalizing this, empiricism contends that we must everywhere distinguish between the intrinsic being of a thing and its relations, and, among these, between those that are essential to our knowing it at all and those that may be called adventitious. The thing as actually present in a given world is there with *all* its relations; for it to be known as it *there* exists, they must be known too, and it and they form a single fact for any consciousness large enough to embrace that world as a unity. But what constitutes this singleness of fact, this unity? Empiricism says, Nothing but the relation-yielding matrix in which the several items of the world find themselves embedded—time, namely, and space, and the mind of the knower. And it says that were some of the items quite different from what they are and others the same, still, for aught we can see, an equally unitary world might be, provided each item were an object for consciousness and occupied a determinate point in space and time. All the adventitious relations would in such a world be changed, along with the intrinsic natures and places of the beings between which they obtained; but the "principle of totality" in knowledge would in no wise be affected.

But Hegelism dogmatically denies all this to be possible. In the first place it says there are no intrinsic natures that may change; in the second it says there are no adventitious relations. When the relations of what we call a thing are told, no *caput mortuum* of intrinsicality, no "nature," is left. The relations soak up all there is of the thing; the "items" of the world are but *foci* of relation with other *foci* of relation; and all the relations are necessary. The unity of the world has nothing to do with any "matrix." The matrix and the items, each with all, make a unity, simply because each in truth *is* all the rest. The proof lies in the *hegelian* principle of totality, which demands that if any one part be posited alone all the others shall forthwith *emanate* from it and infallibly reproduce the whole. In the *modus operandi* of the emanation comes in, as I said, that partnership of the principle of totality with that of the identity of contradictories which so recommends the latter to beginners in Hegel's philosophy. To posit one item *alone* is to deny the rest; to deny them is to refer to them; to refer to them is to begin, at least, to bring them on the scene; and to begin is in the fulness of time to end.

If we call this a monism, Hegel is quick to cry, Not so! To say simply that the one item is the rest of the universe is as false and one-sided as to say that it is simply itself. It is both and neither; and the only condition on which we gain the right to affirm that it is, is that we fail not to keep affirming all the while that it is not, as well. Thus the truth refuses to be expressed in any single act of judgment or sentence. The world appears as a monism *and* a pluralism, just as it appeared in our own introductory exposition.

But the trouble that keeps us and Hegel from ever joining hands over this apparent formula of brotherhood is that we distinguish, or try to distinguish, the respects in which the world is one from those in which it is many, while all such stable distinctions are what he most abominates. The reader may decide which procedure helps his reason most. For my own part, the time-honored formula of empiricist pluralism, that the world cannot be set down in any single proposition, grows less instead of more intelligible when I add, "And yet the different propositions that express it are one!" The unity of the propositions is that of the mind that harbors them. Anyone who insists that their diversity is in any way itself their unity, can only do so because he loves obscurity and mystification for their own pure sakes.

Where you meet with a contradiction among realities, Herbart used to say, it shows you have failed to make a real distinction. Hegel's sovereign method of going to work and saving all possible contradictions, lies in pertinaciously refusing to distinguish. He takes what is true of a term *secundum quid*, treats it as true of the same term *simpliciter*, and then, of course, applies it to the term *secundum aliud*. A good example of this is found in the first triad. This triad shows that the mutability of the real world is due to the fact that being constantly negates itself; that whatever *is* by the same act *is not*, and gets undone and swept away; and that thus the irremediable torrent of life about which so much rhetoric has been written has its roots in an ineluctable necessity which lies revealed to our logical reason. This notion of a being which forever stumbles over its own feet, and has to change in order to exist at all, is a very picturesque symbol of the reality, and is probably one of the points that make young readers feel as if a deep core of truth lay in the system.

But how is the reasoning done? Pure being is assumed, without determinations, being *secundum quid*. In this respect it agrees with nothing. Therefore *simpliciter* it is nothing; wherever we find it, it is nothing; crowned with complete determinations then, or *secundum aliud*, it is nothing still, and *hebt sich auf*.

It is as if we said, Man without his clothes may be named "the naked." Therefore man *simpliciter* is the naked; and finally man with his hat, shoes, and overcoat on is the naked still.

Of course we may in this instance or any other repeat that the conclusion is strictly true, however comical it seems. Man within the clothes is naked, just as he is without them. Man would never have invented the clothes had he not been naked. The fact of his being clad at all does prove his essential nudity. And so in general—the form of any judgment, being the addition of a predicate to a subject, shows that the subject has been conceived without the predicate, and thus by a strained metaphor may be called the predicate's negation. Well and good! let the expression pass. But we must notice this. The judgment has now created a new subject, the naked-clad, and all propositions regarding this must be judged on their own merits; for those true of the old subject, "the naked," are no longer true of this one. For instance, we cannot say because the naked pure and simple must not enter the drawing-room or is in danger of taking cold, that the naked with his clothes on will also take cold or must stay in his bedroom. Hold to it eternally that the clad man *is* still naked if it amuse you—'tis designated in the bond; but the so-called contradiction is a sterile boon. Like Shylock's pound of flesh, it leads to no consequences. It does not entitle you to one drop of his christian blood either in the way of catarrh, social exclusion, or what further results pure nakedness may involve.

In a version of the first step given by our foremost American Hegelian,[4] we find this playing with the necessary form of judgment. Pure being, he says, has no determinations. But the having none is itself a determination. Wherefore pure being contradicts its own self, and so on. Why not take heed to the *meaning* of what is said? When we make the predication concerning pure being, our meaning is merely the denial of all other determinations than the particular one we make. The showman who advertised his elephant as "larger than any elephant in the world except himself" must have been in an hegelian country where he was afraid that if he were less explicit the audience would dialectically proceed to say: "This elephant, larger than any in the world, involves a contradiction; for he himself is in the world, and so stands endowed with the virtue of being both larger and smaller than himself—a perfect hegelian elephant, whose immanent self-contradictoriness can only be removed in a higher synthesis. Show us the higher synthesis! We don't care to see such a mere abstract creature as your elephant." It may be (and it was indeed suggested in antiquity) that all things are of their own size by being both larger and smaller than themselves. But in the case of this elephant the scrupulous showman

[4]*Journal of Speculative Philosophy*, viii, 37.

nipped such philosophizing and all its inconvenient consequences in the bud, by explicitly intimating that larger than
any *other* elephant was all he meant.

Hegel's quibble with this word *other* exemplifies the same
fallacy. All "others," as such, are according to him identical.
That is, "otherness," which can only be predicated of a given
thing *A*, *secundum quid* (as other than *B*, etc.), is predicated
simpliciter, and made to identify the *A* in question with *B*,
which is other only *secundum aliud*—namely other than *A*.

Another maxim that Hegelism is never tired of repeating is
that "to know a limit is already to be beyond it." "Stone walls
do not a prison make, nor iron bars a cage." The inmate of
the penitentiary shows by his grumbling that he is still in the
stage of abstraction and of separative thought. The more
keenly he thinks of the fun he might be having outside, the
more deeply he ought to feel that the walls identify him with
it. They set him beyond them *secundum quid*, in imagination,
in longing, in despair; *argal* they take him there *simpliciter* and
in every way—in flesh, in power, in deed. Foolish convict, to
ignore his blessings!

Another mode of stating his principle is this: "To know the
finite as such, is also to know the infinite." Expressed in this
abstract shape, the formula is as insignificant as it is unobjec-
tionable. We can cap every word with a negative particle, and
the word *finished* immediately suggests the word *unfinished*,
and we know the two words together.

But it is an entirely different thing to take the knowledge of
a concrete case of ending, and to say that it virtually makes us
acquainted with other concrete facts *in infinitum*. For, in the
first place, the end may be an absolute one. The *matter* of the
universe, for instance, is according to all appearances in finite
amount; and if we knew that we had counted the last bit of it,
infinite knowledge in that respect, so far from being given,
would be impossible. With regard to *space*, it is true that in
drawing a bound we are aware of more. But to treat this little
fringe as the equal of infinite space is ridiculous. It resembles
infinite space *secundum quid*, or in but one respect—its spatial
quality. We believe it homogeneous with whatever spaces may

remain; but it would be fatuous to say, because one dollar in my pocket is homogeneous with all the dollars in the country, that to have it is to have them. The further points of space are as numerically distinct from the fringe as the dollars from the dollar, and not until we have actually intuited them can we be said to "know" them *simpliciter*. The hegelian reply is that the *quality* of space constitutes its only *worth*; and that there is nothing true, good, or beautiful to be known in the spaces beyond which is not already known in the fringe. This introduction of a eulogistic term into a mathematical question is original. The "true" and the "false" infinite are about as appropriate distinctions in a discussion of cognition as the good and the naughty rain would be in a treatise on meteorology. But when we grant that all the worth of the knowledge of distant spaces is due to the knowledge of what they may carry in them, it then appears more than ever absurd to say that the knowledge of the fringe is an equivalent for the infinitude of the distant knowledge. The distant spaces even *simpliciter* are not yet yielded to our thinking; and if they were yielded *simpliciter*, would not be yielded *secundum aliud*, or in respect to their material filling out.

Shylock's bond was an omnipotent instrument compared with this knowledge of the finite, which remains the ignorance it always was, till the infinite by its own act has piece by piece placed itself in our hands.

Here Hegelism cries out: "By the identity of the knowledges of infinite and finite I never meant that one could be a *substitute* for the other; nor does true philosophy ever mean by identity capacity for substitution." This sounds suspiciously like the good and the naughty infinite, or rather like the mysteries of the Trinity and the Eucharist. To the unsentimental mind there are but two sorts of identity—total identity and partial identity. Where the identity is total, the things can be substituted wholly for one another. Where substitution is impossible, it must be that the identity is incomplete. It is the duty of the student then to ascertain the exact *quid, secundum* which it obtains, as we have tried to do above. Even the Catholic will tell you that when he believes in the identity of the wafer with Christ's body, he does not mean in all respects—so that he might use it to exhibit muscular fibre, or a cook make it smell like baked meat in the oven. He means that in the one sole respect of nourishing his being in a certain way, it is identical with and *can* be substituted for the very body of his Redeemer.

"The knowledge of opposites is one," is one of the hegelian first principles, of which the preceding are perhaps only derivatives. Here again Hegelism takes "knowledge" *simpliciter*, and substituting it for knowledge in a particular respect, avails itself of the confusion to cover other respects never originally implied. When the knowledge of a thing is given us, we no doubt think that the thing may or must have an opposite. This postulate of something opposite we may call a "knowledge of the opposite" if we like; but it is a knowledge of it in only that one single respect, that it is something opposite. No number of opposites to a quality we have never directly experienced could ever lead us positively to infer what that quality is. There is a jolt between the negation of them and the actual positing of it in its proper shape, that twenty logics of Hegel harnessed abreast cannot drive us smoothly over.

The use of the maxim "All determination is negation" is the fattest and most full-blown application of the method of refusing to distinguish. Taken in its vague confusion, it probably does more than anything else to produce the sort of flicker and dazzle which are the first mental conditions for the reception of Hegel's system. The word "negation" taken *simpliciter* is treated as if it covered an indefinite number of *secundums*, culminating in the very peculiar one of self-negation. Whence finally the conclusion is drawn that assertions are universally self-contradictory. As this is an important matter, it seems worth while to treat it a little minutely.

When I measure out a pint, say of milk, and so determine it, what do I do? I virtually make two assertions regarding it—it *is* this pint; it is *not* those other gallons. One of these is an affirmation, the other a negation. Both have a common subject; but the predicates being mutually exclusive, the two assertions lie beside each other in endless peace.

I may with propriety be said to make assertions more remote still—assertions of which those other gallons are the subject. As it is not they, so are they not the pint which it is.

The determination "this is the pint" carries with it the negation—"those are not the pints." Here we have the same predicate; but the subjects are exclusive of each other, so there is again endless peace. In both couples of propositions negation and affirmation are *secundum aliud*: this is *a*; this isn't not-*a*. This kind of negation involved in determination cannot possibly be what Hegel wants for his purposes. The table is not the chair, the fireplace is not the cupboard—these are literal expressions of the law of identity and contradiction, those principles of the abstracting and separating understanding for which Hegel has so sovereign a contempt, and which his logic is meant to supersede.

And accordingly Hegelians pursue the subject farther, saying there is in every determination an element of real conflict. Do you not in determining the milk to be this pint exclude it forever from the chance of being those gallons, frustrate it from expansion? And so do you not equally exclude them from the being which it now maintains as its own?

Assuredly if you had been hearing of a land flowing with milk and honey, and had gone there with unlimited expectations of the rivers the milk would fill; and if you found there was but this single pint in the whole country—the determination of the pint would exclude another determination which your mind had previously made of the milk. There would be a real conflict resulting in the victory of one side. The rivers would be negated by the single pint being affirmed; and as rivers and pint are affirmed of the same milk (first as supposed and then as found), the contradiction would be complete.

But it is a contradiction that can never by any chance occur in real nature or being. It can only occur between a false representation of a being and the true idea of the being when actually cognized. The first got into a place where it had no rights and had to be ousted. But in *rerum naturâ* things do not get into one another's logical places. The gallons first spoken of never say "We are the pint"; the pint never says "I am the gallons." It never tries to expand; and so there is no chance for anything to exclude or negate it. It thus remains affirmed absolutely.

Can it be believed in the teeth of these elementary truths

that the principle *determinatio negatio* is held throughout Hegel to imply an active contradiction, conflict, and exclusion? Do the horse-cars jingling outside negate me writing in this room? Do I, reader, negate you? Of course, if I say, "Reader, we are two, and therefore I am two," I negate you, for I am actually thrusting a part into the seat of the whole. The orthodox logic expresses the fallacy by saying the *we* is taken by me distributively instead of collectively; but as long as I do not make this blunder, and am content with my part, we all are safe. In *rerum naturâ*, parts remain parts. Can you imagine one position in space trying to get into the place of another position and having to be "contradicted" by that other? Can you imagine your thought of an object trying to dispossess the real object from its being, and so being negated by it? The great, the sacred law of partaking, the noiseless step of continuity, seems something that Hegel cannot possibly understand. All or nothing is his one idea. For him each point of space, of time, each feeling in the ego, each quality of being, is clamoring, "I am the all—there is naught else but me." This clamor is its essence, which has to be negated in another act which gives it its true determination. What there is of affirmative in this determination is thus the mere residuum left from the negation by others of the negation it originally applied to them.

But why talk of residuum? The Kilkenny cats of fable could leave a residuum in the shape of their undevoured tails. But the Kilkenny cats of existence as it appears in the pages of Hegel are all-devouring, and leave no residuum. Such is the unexampled fury of their onslaught that they get clean out of themselves and into each other, nay more, pass right through each other, and then "return into themselves" ready for another round, as insatiate, but as inconclusive, as the one that went before.

If I characterized Hegel's own mood as ὕβρις, the insolence of excess, what shall I say of the mood he ascribes to being? Man makes the gods in his image; and Hegel, in daring to insult the spotless σωφροσύνη of space and time, the bound-respecters, in branding as strife that law of sharing under whose sacred keeping, like a strain of music, like an odor of incense (as Emerson says), the dance of the atoms goes forward still, seems to me but to manifest his own deformity.

This leads me to animadvert on an erroneous inference which hegelian idealism makes from the form of the negative judgment. Every negation, it says, must be an intellectual act. Even the most *naïf* realism will hardly pretend that the non-table as such exists *in se* after the same fashion as the table does. But table and non-table, since they are given to our thought together, must be consubstantial. Try to make the position or affirmation of the table as simple as you can, it is also the negation of the non-table; and thus positive being itself seems after all but a function of intelligence, like negation. Idealism is proved, realism is unthinkable. Now I have not myself the least objection to idealism—an hypothesis which voluminous considerations make plausible, and whose difficulties may be cleared away any day by new discriminations or discoveries. But I object to proving by these patent ready-made *a priori* methods that which can only be the fruit of a wide and patient induction. For the truth is that our affirmations and negations do not stand on the same footing at all, and are anything but consubstantial. An affirmation says something about an objective existence. A negation says something *about an affirmation*—namely, that it is false. There are no negative predicates or falsities in nature. Being makes no false hypotheses that have to be contradicted. The only denials she can be in any way construed to perform are denials of our errors. This shows plainly enough that denial must be of something mental, since the thing denied is always a fiction. "The table is not the chair" supposes the speaker to have been playing with the false notion that it may have been the chair. But affirmation may perfectly well be of something having no such necessary and constitutive relation to thought. Whether it really is of such a thing is for harder considerations to decide.

If idealism be true, the great question that presents itself is whether its truth involve the necessity of an infinite, unitary, and omniscient consciousness, or whether a republic of semi-detached consciousness will do—consciousnesses united by a certain common fund of representations, but each possessing a private store which the others do not share. Either hypothesis is to me conceivable. But whether the egos be one or many, the *nextness* of representations to one another within them is the principle of unification of the universe. To be thus consciously next to some other representation is the condition to which each representation must submit, under penalty of being excluded from this universe, and like Lord Dundreary's bird "flocking all alone," and forming a separate universe by itself. But this is only a condition of which the representations *partake*; it leaves all their other determinations undecided. To say, because representation *b* cannot be in the same universe with *a* without being *a's neighbor*; that therefore *a* possesses, involves or necessitates *b*, hide and hair, flesh and fell, all appurtenances and belongings—is only the silly hegelian all-or-nothing insatiateness once more.

Hegel's own logic, with all the senseless hocus-pocus of its triads, utterly fails to prove his position. The only evident compulsion which representations exert upon one another is compulsion to submit to the conditions of entrance into the same universe with them—the conditions of continuity, of selfhood, space and time—under penalty of being excluded. But what this universe shall be is a matter of fact which we cannot decide till we know what representations *have* submitted to these its sole conditions. The conditions themselves impose no further requirements. In short, the notion that real contingency and ambiguity may be features of the real world is a perfectly unimpeachable hypothesis. Only in such a world can moral judgments have a claim to be. For the bad is that which takes the place of something else which possibly might have been where *it* now is, and the better is that which absolutely might be where it absolutely is not. In the universe of Hegel—the absolute block whose parts have no loose play, the pure plethora of necessary being with the oxygen of possibility all suffocated out of its lungs—there can be neither good nor bad, but one dead level of mere fate.

But I have tired the reader out. The worst of criticizing Hegel is that the very arguments we use against him give forth strange and hollow sounds that make them seem almost as fantastic as the errors to which they are addressed. The sense of a universal mirage, of a ghostly unreality, steals over us, which is the very moonlit atmosphere of Hegelism itself. What wonder then if, instead of converting, our words do but rejoice and delight, those already baptized in the faith of confusion? To their charmed senses we all seem children of Hegel together, only some of us have not the wit to know our own father. Just as Romanists are sure to inform us that our reasons against Papal Christianity unconsciously breathe the purest spirit of Catholicism, so Hegelism benignantly smiles at our exertions, and murmurs, "If the red slayer think he slays"; "When me they fly, I am the wings," etc.

To forefend this unwelcome adoption, let me recapitulate in a few propositions the reasons why I am *not* an Hegelian.

1. We cannot eat our cake and have it; that is, the only real contradiction there can be between thoughts is where one is true, the other false. When this happens, one must go forever; nor is there any "higher synthesis" in which both can wholly revive.

2. A chasm is not a bridge in any utilizable sense; that is, no mere negation can be the instrument of a positive advance in thought.

3. The continua, time, space, and the ego, are bridges, because they are without chasm.

4. But they bridge over the chasms between represented qualities only partially.

5. This partial bridging, however, makes the qualities share in a common world.

6. The other characteristics of the qualities are separate facts.

7. But the same quality appears in many times and spaces. Generic sameness of the quality wherever found becomes thus a further means by which the jolts are reduced.

8. But between different qualities jolts remain. Each, as far as the other is concerned, is an absolutely separate and contingent being.

9. The moral judgment may lead us to postulate as irreducible the contingencies of the world.

10. Elements mutually contingent are not in conflict so long as they partake of the continua of time, space, etc.—partaking being the exact opposite of strife. They conflict only

when, as mutually exclusive possibilities, they strive to possess themselves of the same parts of time, space, and ego.

II. That there are such real conflicts, irreducible to any intelligence, and giving rise to an excess of possibility over actuality, is an hypothesis, but a credible one. No philosophy should pretend to be anything more.

NOTE.—Since the preceding article was written, some observations on the effects of nitrous-oxide-gas-intoxication which I was prompted to make by reading the pamphlet called *The Anæsthetic Revelation and the Gist of Philosophy*, by Benjamin Paul Blood, Amsterdam, N. Y., 1874, have made me understand better than ever before both the strength and the weakness of Hegel's philosophy. I strongly urge others to repeat the experiment, which with pure gas is short and harmless enough. The effects will of course vary with the individual, just as they vary in the same individual from time to time; but it is probable that in the former case, as in the latter, a generic resemblance will obtain. With me, as with every other person of whom I have heard, the keynote of the experience is the tremendously exciting sense of an intense metaphysical illumination. Truth lies open to the view in depth beneath depth of almost blinding evidence. The mind sees all the logical relations of being with an apparent subtlety and instantaneity to which its normal consciousness offers no parallel; only as sobriety returns, the feeling of insight fades, and one is left staring vacantly at a few disjointed words and phrases, as one stares at a cadaverous-looking snow-peak from which the sunset glow has just fled, or at the black cinder left by an extinguished brand.

The immense emotional sense of *reconciliation* which characterizes the "maudlin" stage of alcoholic drunkenness—a stage which seems silly to lookers-on, but the subjective rapture of which probably constitutes a chief part of the temptation to the vice—is well known. The centre and periphery of things seem to come together. The ego and its objects, the *meum* and the *tuum*, are one. Now this, only a thousandfold enhanced, was the effect upon me of the gas: and its first result was to make peal through me with unutterable power the conviction that Hegelism was true after all, and that the deepest convictions of my intellect hitherto were wrong. Whatever idea or representation occurred to the mind was seized by the same logical forceps, and served to illustrate the same truth; and that truth was that every opposition, among whatsoever things, vanishes in a higher unity in which it is based; that all contradictions, so called, are but differences; that all differences are of degree; that all degrees are of a common kind; that unbroken continuity is of the essence of being; and that we are literally in the midst of *an infinite*, to perceive the existence of which is the utmost we can attain. Without the *same* as a basis, how could strife occur? Strife presupposes something to be striven about; and in this common topic, the same for both parties, the differences merge. From the hardest contradiction to the tenderest diversity of verbiage differences evaporate; *yes* and *no* agree at least in being assertions; a denial of a statement is but another mode of stating the same, contradiction can only occur of the same thing—all opinions are thus synonyms, are synonymous, are the same. But the same phrase by difference of emphasis is two; and here again difference and no-difference merge in one.

It is impossible to convey an idea of the torrential character of the identification of opposites as it streams through the mind in this experience. I have sheet after sheet of phrases dictated or written during the intoxication, which to the sober reader seem meaningless drivel, but which at the moment of transcribing were fused in the fire of infinite rationality. God and devil, good and evil, life and death, I and thou, sober and drunk, matter and form, black and white, quantity and quality, shiver of ecstasy and shudder of horror, vomiting and swallowing, inspiration and expiration, fate and reason, great and small, extent and intent, joke and earnest, tragic and comic, and fifty other contrasts figure in these pages in the same monotonous way. The mind saw how each term *belonged* to its contrast through a knife-edge moment of transition which *it* effected, and which, perennial and eternal, was the *nunc stans* of life. The thought of mutual implication of the parts in the bare form of a judgment of opposition, as "nothing—but," "no more—than," "only—if," etc., produced a perfect delirium of theoretic rapture. And at last, when definite ideas to work on came slowly, the mind went through the mere *form* of recognizing sameness in identity by contrasting the same word with itself, differently emphasized, or shorn of its initial letter. Let me transcribe a few sentences:

"What's mistake but a kind of take?
What's nausea but a kind of -ausea?
Sober, drunk, -*unk*, astonishment.
Everything can become the subject of criticism—how criticize without something *to* criticize?
Agreement—disagreement!!
Emotion—motion!!!
Die away from, *from*, die away (without the *from*).

Reconciliation of opposites; sober, drunk, all the same!
Good and evil reconciled in a laugh!
It escapes, it escapes!
But———
What escapes, WHAT escapes?
Emphasis, EMphasis; there must be some emphasis in order for
there to be a phasis.
No verbiage can give it, because the verbiage is *other*.
*In*coherent, coherent—same.
And it fades! And it's infinite! AND it's infinite!
If it wasn't *going*, why should you hold on to it?
Don't you see the difference, don't you see the identity?
Constantly opposites united!
The same me telling you to write and not to write!
Extreme—extreme, extreme! Within the *ex*tensity that "extreme"
contains is contained the *"extreme"* of *in*tensity.
Something, and *other* than that thing!
Intoxication, and *otherness* than intoxication.
Every attempt at betterment—every attempt at otherment—is
a———.
It fades forever and forever as we move.
There *is* a reconciliation!
Reconciliation—*e*conciliation!
By God, how that hurts! By God, how it *doesn't* hurt! Reconcilia-
tion of two extremes.
By George, nothing but *oth*ing!
That sounds like nonsense, but it is pure *on*sense!
Thought deeper than speech———!
Medical school; divinity school, *school*! SCHOOL! Oh my God, oh
God, oh God!"

The most coherent and articulate sentence which came was this:—
"There are no differences but differences of degree between different degrees of difference and no difference."

This phrase has the true hegelian ring, being in fact a regular *sich
als sich auf sich selbst beziehende Negativität*. And true Hegelians will
überhaupt be able to read between the lines and feel, at any rate,
what *possible* ecstasies of cognitive emotion might have bathed these
tattered fragments of thought when they were alive. But for the assurance of a certain amount of respect from them, I should hardly
have ventured to print what must be such caviare to the general.

But now comes the reverse of the medal. What is the principle of
unity in all this monotonous rain of instances? Although I did not
see it at first, I soon found that it was in each case nothing but the

abstract *genus* of which the conflicting terms were opposite species. In other words, although the flood of ontologic *emotion* was hegelian through and through, the *ground* for it was nothing but the world-old principle that things are the same only so far and no farther than they *are* the same, or partake of a common nature—the principle that Hegel most tramples under foot. At the same time the rapture of beholding a process that was infinite, changed (as the nature of the infinitude was realized by the mind) into the sense of a dreadful and ineluctable fate, with whose magnitude every finite effort is incommensurable and in the light of which whatever happens is indifferent. This instantaneous revulsion of mood from rapture to horror is, perhaps, the strongest emotion I have ever experienced. I got it repeatedly when the inhalation was continued long enough to produce incipient nausea; and I cannot but regard it as the normal and inevitable outcome of the intoxication, if sufficiently prolonged. A pessimistic fatalism, depth within depth of impotence and indifference, reason and silliness united, not in a higher synthesis, but in the fact that whichever you choose it is all one—this is the upshot of a revelation that began so rosy bright.

Even when the process stops short of this ultimatum, the reader will have noticed from the phrases quoted how often it ends by losing the clue. Something "fades," "escapes"; and the feeling of insight is changed into an intense one of bewilderment, puzzle, confusion, astonishment. I know no more singular sensation than this intense bewilderment, with nothing particular left to be bewildered at save the bewilderment itself. It seems, indeed, a *causa sui*, or "spirit become its own object."

My conclusion is that the togetherness of things in a common world, the law of sharing, of which I have said so much, may, when perceived, engender a very powerful emotion; that Hegel was so unusually susceptible to this emotion throughout his life that its gratification became his supreme end, and made him tolerably unscrupulous as to the means he employed; that *indifferentism* is the true outcome of every view of the world which makes infinity and continuity to be its essence, and that pessimistic or optimistic attitudes pertain to the mere accidental subjectivity of the moment; finally, that the identification of contradictories, so far from being the self-developing process which Hegel supposes, is really a self-consuming process, passing from the less to the more abstract, and terminating either in a laugh at the ultimate nothingness, or in a mood of vertiginous amazement at a meaningless infinity.

What Psychical Research Has Accomplished [1]

"THE GREAT FIELD for new discoveries," said a scientific friend to me the other day, "is always the unclassified residuum." Round about the accredited and orderly facts of every science there ever floats a sort of dust-cloud of exceptional observations, of occurrences minute and irregular and seldom met with, which it always proves more easy to ignore than to attend to. The ideal of every science is that of a closed and completed system of truth. The charm of most sciences to their more passive disciples consists in their appearing, in fact, to wear just this ideal form. Each one of our various *ologies* seems to offer a definite head of classification for every possible phenomenon of the sort which it professes to cover; and so far from free is most men's fancy, that, when a consistent and organized scheme of this sort has once been comprehended and assimilated, a different scheme is unimaginable. No alternative, whether to whole or parts, can any longer be conceived as possible. Phenomena unclassifiable within the system are therefore paradoxical absurdities, and must be held untrue. When, moreover, as so often happens, the reports of them are vague and indirect; when they come as mere marvels and oddities rather than as things of serious moment—one neglects or denies them with the best of scientific consciences. Only the born geniuses let themselves be worried and fascinated by these outstanding exceptions, and get no peace till they are brought within the fold. Your Galileos, Galvanis, Fresnels, Purkinjes, and Darwins are always getting confounded and troubled by insignificant things. Anyone will renovate his science who will steadily look after the irregular phenomena. And when the science is renewed, its new formulas often have more of the voice of the exceptions in them than of what were supposed to be the rules.

No part of the unclassified residuum has usually been

[1]This Essay is formed of portions of an article in *Scribner's Magazine* for March, 1890, of an article in the *Forum* for July, 1892, and of the President's Address before the Society for Psychical Research, published in the *Proceedings* for June, 1896, and in *Science*.

treated with a more contemptuous scientific disregard than the mass of phenomena generally called *mystical*. Physiology will have nothing to do with them. Orthodox psychology turns its back upon them. Medicine sweeps them out; or, at most, when in an anecdotal vein, records a few of them as "effects of the imagination"—a phrase of mere dismissal, whose meaning, in this connection, it is impossible to make precise. All the while, however, the phenomena are there, lying broadcast over the surface of history. No matter where you open its pages, you find things recorded under the name of divinations, inspirations, demoniacal possessions, apparitions, trances, ecstasies, miraculous healings and productions of disease, and occult powers possessed by peculiar individuals over persons and things in their neighborhood. We suppose that "mediumship" originated in Rochester, N. Y., and animal magnetism with Mesmer; but once look behind the pages of official history, in personal memoirs, legal documents, and popular narratives and books of anecdote, and you will find that there never was a time when these things were not reported just as abundantly as now. We college-bred gentry, who follow the stream of cosmopolitan culture exclusively, not infrequently stumble upon some old-established journal, or some voluminous native author, whose names are never heard of in *our* circle, but who number their readers by the quarter-million. It always gives us a little shock to find this mass of human beings not only living and ignoring us and all our gods, but actually reading and writing and cogitating without ever a thought of our canons and authorities. Well, a public no less large keeps and transmits from generation to generation the traditions and practices of the occult; but academic science cares as little for its beliefs and opinions as you, gentle reader, care for those of the readers of the *Waverley* and the *Fireside Companion*. To no one type of mind is it given to discern the totality of truth. Something escapes the best of us—not accidentally, but systematically, and because we have a twist. The scientific-academic mind and the feminine-mystical mind shy from each other's facts, just as they fly from each other's temper and spirit. Facts are there only for those who have a mental affinity with them. When once they are indisputably ascertained and admitted, the academic and critical minds are by far the best fitted ones to interpret and discuss them—for surely to pass from mystical to scientific speculations is like passing from lunacy to sanity; but on the other hand if there is anything which human history demonstrates, it is the extreme slowness with which the ordinary academic and critical mind acknowledges facts to exist which present themselves as wild facts, with no stall or pigeon-hole, or as facts which threaten to break up the accepted system. In psychology, physiology, and medicine, wherever a debate between the mystics and the scientifics has been once for all decided, it is the mystics who have usually proved to be right about the *facts*, while the scientifics had the better of it in respect to the theories. The most recent and flagrant example of this is "animal magnetism," whose facts were stoutly dismissed as a pack of lies by academic medical science the world over, until the non-mystical theory of "hypnotic suggestion" was found for them—when they were admitted to be so excessively and dangerously common that special penal laws, forsooth, must be passed to keep all persons unequipped with medical diplomas from taking part in their production. Just so stigmatizations, invulnerabilities, instantaneous cures, inspired discourses, and demoniacal possessions, the records of which were shelved in our libraries but yesterday in the alcove headed "superstitions," now, under the brand-new title of "cases of hystero-epilepsy," are republished, reobserved, and reported with an even too credulous avidity.

Repugnant as the mystical style of philosophizing may be (especially when self-complacent), there is no sort of doubt that it goes with a gift for meeting with certain kinds of phenomenal experience. The writer of these pages has been forced in the past few years to this admission; and he now believes that he who will pay attention to facts of the sort dear to mystics, while reflecting upon them in academic-scientific ways, will be in the best possible position to help philosophy. It is a circumstance of good augury that certain scientifically trained minds in all countries seem drifting to the same conclusion. The Society for Psychical Research has been one means of bringing science and the occult together in England and America; and believing that this Society fulfils a function which, though limited, is destined to be not unimportant in the organization of human knowledge, I am glad to give a brief account of it to the uninstructed reader.

According to the newspaper and drawing-room myth, softheadedness and idiotic credulity are the bond of sympathy in this Society, and general wonder-sickness its dynamic principle. A glance at the membership fails, however, to corroborate this view. The president is Prof. Henry Sidgwick,[2] known by his other deeds as the most incorrigibly and exasperatingly critical and sceptical mind in England. The hard-headed Arthur Balfour is one vice-president, and the hard-headed Prof. J. P. Langley, secretary of the Smithsonian Institution, is another. Such men as Professor Lodge, the eminent English physicist, and Professor Richet, the eminent French physiologist, are amongst the most active contributors to the Society's *Proceedings*; and through the catalogue of membership are sprinkled names honored throughout the world for their scientific capacity. In fact, were I asked to point to a scientific journal where hard-headedness and never-sleeping suspicion of sources of error might be seen in their full bloom, I think I should have to fall back on the *Proceedings of the Society for Psychical Research*. The common run of papers, say on physiological subjects, which one finds in other professional organs, are apt to show a far lower level of critical consciousness. Indeed, the rigorous canons of evidence applied a few years ago to testimony in the case of certain "mediums" led to the secession from the Society of a number of spiritualists. Messrs. Stainton Moses and A. R. Wallace, amongst others, thought that no experiences based on mere eyesight could ever have a chance to be admitted as true, if such an impossibly exacting standard of proof were insisted on in every case.

The S. P. R., as I shall call it for convenience, was founded in 1882 by a number of gentlemen, foremost amongst whom seem to have been Professors Sidgwick, W. F. Barrett, and Balfour Stewart, and Messrs. R. H. Hutton, Hensleigh Wedgwood, Edmund Gurney, and F. W. H. Myers. Their purpose was twofold—first, to carry on systematic experimentation

---

[2]Written in 1891. Since then, Mr. Balfour, the present writer, and Professor William Crookes have held the presidential office.

with hypnotic subjects, mediums, clairvoyants, and others; and, secondly, to collect evidence concerning apparitions, haunted houses, and similar phenomena which are incidentally reported, but which, from their fugitive character, admit of no deliberate control. Professor Sidgwick, in his introductory address, insisted that the divided state of public opinion on all these matters was a scandal to science—absolute disdain on *a priori* grounds characterizing what may be called professional opinion, whilst indiscriminate credulity was too often found amongst those who pretended to have a first-hand acquaintance with the facts.

As a sort of weather-bureau for accumulating reports of such meteoric phenomena as apparitions, the S. P. R. has done an immense amount of work. As an experimenting body, it cannot be said to have completely fulfilled the hopes of its founders. The reasons for this lie in two circumstances: first, the clairvoyant and other subjects who will allow themselves to be experimented upon are few and far between; and, secondly, work with them takes an immense amount of time, and has had to be carried on at odd intervals by members engaged in other pursuits. The Society has not yet been rich enough to control the undivided services of skilled experimenters in this difficult field. The loss of the lamented Edmund Gurney, who more than anyone else had leisure to devote, has been so far irreparable. But were there no experimental work at all, and were the S. P. R. nothing but a weather-bureau for catching sporadic apparitions, etc., in their freshness, I am disposed to think its function indispensable in the scientific organism. If any one of my readers, spurred by the thought that so much smoke must needs betoken fire, has ever looked into the existing literature of the supernatural for proof, he will know what I mean. This literature is enormous, but it is practically worthless for evidential purposes. Facts enough are cited, indeed; but the records of them are so fallible and imperfect that at most they lead to the opinion that it may be well to keep a window open upon that quarter in one's mind.

In the S. P. R.'s *Proceedings*, on the contrary, a different law prevails. Quality, and not mere quantity, is what has been mainly kept in mind. The witnesses, where possible, have in

every reported case been cross-examined personally, the collateral facts have been looked up, and the story appears with
its precise coefficient of evidential worth stamped on it, so
that all may know just what its weight as proof may be. Outside of these *Proceedings*, I know of no systematic attempt to
weigh the evidence for the supernatural. This makes the value
of the volumes already published unique; and I firmly believe
that as the years go on and the ground covered grows still
wider, the *Proceedings* will more and more tend to supersede
all other sources of information concerning phenomena traditionally deemed occult. Collections of this sort are usually
best appreciated by the rising generation. The young anthropologists and psychologists who will soon have full occupancy of the stage will feel how great a scientific scandal it has
been to leave a great mass of human experience to take its
chances between vague tradition and credulity on the one
hand and dogmatic denial at long range on the other, with no
body of persons extant who are willing and competent to
study the matter with both patience and rigor. If the Society
lives long enough for the public to become familiar with its
presence, so that any apparition, or house or person infested
with unaccountable noises or disturbances of material objects,
will as a matter of course be reported to its officers, we shall
doubtless end by having a mass of facts concrete enough to
theorize upon. Its sustainers, therefore, should accustom
themselves to the idea that its first duty is simply to exist from
year to year and perform this recording function well, though
no conclusive results of any sort emerge at first. All our
learned societies have begun in some such modest way.

But one cannot by mere outward organization make much
progress in matters scientific. Societies can back men of genius, but can never take their place. The contrast between the
parent Society and the American Branch illustrates this. In
England, a little group of men with enthusiasm and genius
for the work supplied the nucleus; in this country, Mr. Hodgson had to be imported from Europe before any tangible
progress was made. What perhaps more than anything else
has held the Society together in England is Professor Sidgwick's extraordinary gift of inspiring confidence in diverse
sorts of people. Such tenacity of interest in the result and such

absolute impartiality in discussing the evidence are not once in a century found in an individual. His obstinate belief that there is something yet to be brought to light communicates patience to the discouraged; his constitutional inability to draw any precipitate conclusion reassures those who are afraid of being dupes. Mrs. Sidgwick—a sister, by the way, of the great Arthur Balfour—is a worthy ally of her husband in this matter, showing a similarly rare power of holding her judgment in suspense, and a keenness of observation and capacity for experimenting with human subjects which are rare in either sex.

The *worker* of the Society, as originally constituted, was Edmund Gurney. Gurney was a man of the rarest sympathies and gifts. Although, like Carlyle, he used to groan under the burden of his labors, he yet exhibited a colossal power of dispatching business and getting through drudgery of the most repulsive kind. His two thick volumes on *Phantasms of the Living*, collected and published in three years, are a proof of this. Besides this, he had exquisite artistic instincts, and his massive volume on *The Power of Sound* was, when it appeared, the most important work on æsthetics in the English language. He had also the tenderest heart and a mind of rare metaphysical power, as his volumes of essays, *Tertium Quid*, will prove to any reader. Mr. Frederic Myers, already well known as one of the most brilliant of English essayists, is the *ingenium præfervidum* of the S. P. R. Of the value of Mr. Myers' theoretic writings I will say a word later. Dr. Hodgson, the American secretary, is distinguished by a balance of mind almost as rare in its way as Sidgwick's. He is persuaded of the reality of many of the phenomena called spiritualistic, but he also has uncommon keenness in detecting error; and it is impossible to say in advance whether it will give him more satisfaction to confirm or to smash a given case offered to his examination.

It is now time to cast a brief look upon the actual contents of these *Proceedings*. The first two years were largely taken up with experiments in thought-transference. The earliest lot of these were made with the daughters of a clergyman named Creery, and convinced Messrs. Balfour Stewart, Barrett,

Myers, and Gurney that the girls had an inexplicable power of guessing names and objects thought of by other persons. Two years later, Mrs. Sidgwick and Mr. Gurney, recommencing experiments with the same girls, detected them signalling to each other. It is true that for the most part the conditions of the earlier series had excluded signalling, and it is also possible that the cheating may have grafted itself on what was originally a genuine phenomenon. Yet Gurney was wise in abandoning the entire series to the scepticism of the reader. Many critics of the S. P. R. seem out of all its labors to have heard only of this case. But there are experiments recorded with upwards of thirty other subjects. Three were experimented upon at great length during the first two years: one was Mr. G. A. Smith; the other two were young ladies in Liverpool in the employment of Mr. Malcolm Guthrie.

It is the opinion of all who took part in these latter experiments that sources of conscious and unconscious deception were sufficiently excluded, and that the large percentage of correct reproductions by the subjects of words, diagrams, and sensations occupying other persons' consciousness were entirely inexplicable as results of chance. The witnesses of these performances were in fact all so satisfied of the genuineness of the phenomena, that "telepathy" has figured freely in the papers of the *Proceedings* and in Gurney's book on *Phantasms* as a *vera causa* on which additional hypotheses might be built. No mere reader can be blamed, however, if he demand, for so revolutionary a belief, a more overwhelming bulk of testimony than has yet been supplied. Any day, of course, may bring in fresh experiments in successful picture-guessing. But meanwhile, and lacking that, we can only point out that the present data are strengthened in the flank, so to speak, by all observations that tend to corroborate the possibility of other kindred phenomena, such as telepathic impression, clairvoyance, or what is called "test-mediumship." The wider genus will naturally cover the narrower species with its credit.

Gurney's papers on hypnotism must be mentioned next. Some of them are less concerned with establishing new facts than with analyzing old ones. But omitting these, we find that in the line of pure observation Gurney claims to have ascertained in more than one subject the following phenomenon:

The subject's hands are thrust through a blanket, which screens the operator from his eyes, and his mind is absorbed in conversation with a third person. The operator meanwhile points with his finger to one of the fingers of the subject, which finger alone responds to this silent selection by becoming stiff or anæsthetic, as the case may be. The interpretation is difficult, but the phenomenon, which I have myself witnessed, seems authentic.

Another observation made by Gurney seems to prove the possibility of the subject's mind being directly influenced by the operator's. The hypnotized subject responds, or fails to respond, to questions asked by a third party according to the operator's silent permission or refusal. Of course, in these experiments all obvious sources of deception were excluded. But Gurney's most important contribution to our knowledge of hypnotism was his series of experiments on the automatic writing of subjects who had received post-hypnotic suggestions. For example, a subject during trance is told that he will poke the fire in six minutes after waking. On being waked he has no memory of the order, but while he is engaged in conversation his hand is placed on a *planchette*, which immediately writes the sentence, "P., you will poke the fire in six minutes." Experiments like this, which were repeated in great variety, seem to prove that below the upper consciousness the hypnotic consciousness persists, engrossed with the suggestion and able to express itself through the involuntarily moving hand.

Gurney shares, therefore, with Janet and Binet, the credit of demonstrating the simultaneous existence of two different strata of consciousness, ignorant of each other, in the same person. The "extra-consciousness," as one may call it, can be kept on tap, as it were, by the method of automatic writing. This discovery marks a new era in experimental psychology, and it is impossible to overrate its importance. But Gurney's greatest piece of work is his laborious *Phantasms of the Living*. As an example of the drudgery stowed away in the volumes, it may suffice to say that in looking up the proofs for the alleged physical phenomena of witchcraft, Gurney reports a careful search through two hundred and sixty books on the subject, with the result of finding no first-hand evidence recorded in the trials except the confessions of the victims themselves; and these, of course, are presumptively due to either torture or hallucination. This statement, made in an unobtrusive note, is only one instance of the care displayed throughout the volumes. In the course of these, Gurney discusses about seven hundred cases of apparitions which he collected. A large number of these were "veridical," in the sense of coinciding with some calamity happening to the person who appeared. Gurney's explanation is that the mind of the person undergoing the calamity was at that moment able to impress the mind of the percipient with an hallucination.

Apparitions, on this "telepathic" theory, may be called "objective" facts, although they are not "material" facts. In order to test the likelihood of such veridical hallucinations being due to mere chance, Gurney instituted the "census of hallucinations," which has been continued with the result of obtaining answers from over twenty-five thousand persons, asked at random in different countries whether, when in good health and awake, they had ever heard a voice, seen a form, or felt a touch which no material presence could account for. The result seems to be, roughly speaking, that in England about one adult in ten has had such an experience at least once in his life, and that of the experiences themselves a large number coincide with some distant event. The question is, Is the frequency of these latter cases too great to be deemed fortuitous, and must we suppose an occult connection between the two events? Mr. and Mrs. Sidgwick have worked out this problem on the basis of the English returns, seventeen thousand in number, with a care and thoroughness that leave nothing to be desired. Their conclusion is that the cases where the apparition of a person is seen on the day of his death are four hundred and forty times too numerous to be ascribed to chance. The reasoning employed to calculate this number is simple enough. If there be only a fortuitous connection between the death of an individual and the occurrence of his apparition to some one at a distance, the death is no more likely to fall on the same day as the apparition than it is to occur on the same day with any other event in nature. But the chance-probability that any individual's death will fall on any given day marked in advance by some other event is just equal to the chance-probability that the individual will die at all on any specified day; and the national death-rate gives that probability as one in nineteen thousand. If, then, when the death of a person coincides with an apparition of the same person, the coincidence be merely fortuitous, it ought not to occur oftener than once in nineteen thousand cases. As a matter of fact, however, it does occur (according to the census) once in forty-three cases, a number (as aforesaid) four hundred and forty times too great. The American census, of some seven thousand answers, gives a remarkably similar result. Against this conclusion the only rational answer that I can see is that the data are still too few; that the net was not cast wide enough; and that we need, to get fair averages, far more than twenty-four thousand answers to the census question. This may, of course, be true, though it seems exceedingly unlikely; and in our own twenty-four thousand answers veridical cases may possibly have heaped themselves unduly.

The next topic worth mentioning in the *Proceedings* is the discussion of the physical phenomena of mediumship (slate-writing, furniture-moving, and so forth) by Mrs. Sidgwick, Mr. Hodgson, and "Mr. Davey." This, so far as it goes, is destructive of the claims of all the mediums examined. "Mr. Davey" himself produced fraudulent slate-writing of the highest order, while Mr. Hodgson, a "sitter" in his confidence, reviewed the written reports of the series of his other sitters—all of them intelligent persons—and showed that in every case they failed to see the essential features of what was done before their eyes. This Davey-Hodgson contribution is probably the most damaging document concerning eye-witnesses' evidence that has ever been produced. Another substantial bit of work based on personal observation is Mr. Hodgson's report on Madame Blavatsky's claims to physical mediumship. This is adverse to the lady's pretensions; and although some of Madame Blavatsky's friends make light of it, it is a stroke from which her reputation will not recover.

Physical mediumship in all its phases has fared hard in the *Proceedings*. The latest case reported on is that of the famous Eusapia Paladino, who being detected in fraud at Cambridge, after a brilliant career of success on the continent, has, according to the draconian rules of method which govern the

Society, been ruled out from a further hearing. The case of Stainton Moses, on the other hand, concerning which Mr. Myers has brought out a mass of unpublished testimony, seems to escape from the universal condemnation, and appears to force upon us what Mr. Andrew Lang calls the choice between a moral and a physical miracle.

In the case of Mrs. Piper, not a physical but a trance medium, we seem to have no choice offered at all. Mr. Hodgson and others have made prolonged study of this lady's trances, and are all convinced that supernormal powers of cognition are displayed therein. These are *primâ facie* due to "spirit-control." But the conditions are so complex that a dogmatic decision either for or against the spirit-hypothesis must as yet be postponed.

One of the most important experimental contributions to the *Proceedings* is the article of Miss X. on "Crystal Vision." Many persons who look fixedly into a crystal or other vaguely luminous surface fall into a kind of daze, and see visions. Miss X. has this susceptibility in a remarkable degree, and is, moreover, an unusually intelligent critic. She reports many visions which can only be described as apparently clairvoyant, and others which beautifully fill a vacant niche in our knowledge of subconscious mental operations. For example, looking into the crystal before breakfast one morning she reads in printed characters of the death of a lady of her acquaintance, the date and other circumstances all duly appearing in type. Startled by this, she looks at the *Times* of the previous day for verification, and there amongst the deaths are the identical words which she has seen. On the same page of the *Times* are other items which she remembers reading the day before; and the only explanation seems to be that her eyes then inattentively observed, so to speak, the death-item, which forthwith fell into a special corner of her memory, and came out as a visual hallucination when the peculiar modification of consciousness induced by the crystal-gazing set in.

Passing from papers based on observation to papers based on narrative, we have a number of ghost stories, etc., sifted by Mrs. Sidgwick and discussed by Messrs. Myers and Podmore. They form the best ghost literature I know of from the point of view of emotional interest. As to the conclusions drawn,

Mrs. Sidgwick is rigorously non-committal, while Mr. Myers and Mr. Podmore show themselves respectively hospitable and inhospitable to the notion that such stories have a basis of objectivity dependent on the continued existence of the dead.

I must close my gossip about the *Proceedings* by naming what, after all, seems to me the most important part of its contents. This is the long series of articles by Mr. Myers on what he now calls the "subliminal self," or what one might designate as ultra-marginal consciousness. The result of Myers' learned and ingenious studies in hypnotism, hallucinations, automatic writing, mediumship, and the whole series of allied phenomena is a conviction which he expresses in the following terms:

"Each of us is in reality an abiding psychical entity far more extensive than he knows—an individuality which can never express itself completely through any corporeal manifestation. The Self manifests itself through the organism; but there is always some part of the Self unmanifested; and always, as it seems, some power of organic expression in abeyance or in reserve."

The ordinary consciousness Mr. Myers likens to the visible part of the solar spectrum; the total consciousness is like that spectrum prolonged by the inclusion of the ultra-red and ultra-violet rays. In the psychic spectrum the "ultra" parts may embrace a far wider range, both of physiological and of psychical activity, than is open to our ordinary consciousness and memory. At the lower end we have the *physiological* extension, mind-cures, "stigmatization" of ecstatics, etc.; in the upper, the hyper-normal cognitions of the medium-trance. Whatever the judgment of the future may be on Mr. Myers' speculations, the credit will always remain to them of being the first attempt in any language to consider the phenomena of hallucination, hypnotism, automatism, double personality, and mediumship as connected parts of one whole subject. All constructions in this field must be provisional, and it is as something provisional that Mr. Myers offers us his formulations. But, thanks to him, we begin to see for the first time what a vast interlocked and graded system these phenomena, from the rudest motor-automatisms to the most startling sensory-apparition, form. Quite apart from Mr. Myers' conclusions, his methodical treatment of them by classes and series is the first great step towards overcoming the distaste of orthodox science to look at them at all.

One's reaction on hearsay testimony is always determined by one's own experience. Most men who have once convinced themselves, by what seems to them a careful examination, that any one species of the supernatural exists, begin to relax their vigilance as to evidence, and throw the doors of their minds more or less wide open to the supernatural along its whole extent. To a mind that has thus made its *salto mortale*, the minute work over insignificant cases and quiddling discussion of "evidential values," of which the Society's reports are full, seems insufferably tedious. And it is so; few species of literature are more truly dull than reports of phantasms. Taken simply by themselves, as separate facts to stare at, they appear so devoid of meaning and sweep, that, even were they certainly true, one would be tempted to leave them out of one's universe for being so idiotic. Every other sort of fact has some context and continuity with the rest of nature. These alone are contextless and discontinuous.

Hence I think that the sort of loathing—no milder word will do—which the very words "psychical research" and "psychical researcher" awaken in so many honest scientific breasts is not only natural, but in a sense praiseworthy. A man who is unable himself to conceive of any *orbit* for these mental meteors can only suppose that Messrs. Gurney, Myers & Co.'s mood in dealing with them must be that of silly marvelling at so many detached prodigies. And such prodigies! So science simply falls back on her general *non-possumus*; and most of the would-be critics of the *Proceedings* have been contented to oppose to the phenomena recorded the simple presumption that in some way or other the reports *must* be fallacious—for so far as the order of nature has been subjected to really scientific scrutiny, it always has been proved to run the other way. But the oftener one is forced to reject an alleged sort of fact by the use of this mere presumption, the weaker does the presumption itself get to be; and one might in course of time use up one's presumptive privileges in this way, even though one started (as our anti-telepathists do) with as good a case as the great induction of psychology that all our knowledge comes by the use of our eyes and ears and other senses. And we must remember also that this undermining of the strength of a presumption by reiterated report of facts to the contrary does not logically require that the facts in question should all be well proved. A lot of rumors in the air against a business man's credit, though they might all be vague, and no one of them amount to proof that he is unsound, would certainly weaken the *presumption* of his soundness. And all the more would they have this effect if they formed what Gurney called a fagot and not a chain—that is, if they were independent of one another, and came from different quarters. Now the evidence for telepathy, weak and strong, taken just as it comes, forms a fagot and not a chain. No one item cites the content of another item as part of its own proof. But taken together the items have a certain general consistency; there is a method in their madness, so to speak. So each of them adds presumptive value to the lot; and cumulatively, as no candid mind can fail to see, they subtract presumptive force from the orthodox belief that there can be nothing in anyone's intellect that has not come in through ordinary experiences of sense.

But it is a miserable thing for a question of truth to be confined to mere presumption and counter-presumption, with no decisive thunderbolt of fact to clear the baffling darkness. And, sooth to say, in talking so much of the merely presumption-weakening value of our records, I have myself been wilfully taking the point of view of the so-called "rigorously scientific" disbeliever, and making an *ad hominem* plea. My own point of view is different. For me the thunderbolt *has* fallen, and the orthodox belief has not merely had its presumption weakened, but the truth itself of the belief is decisively overthrown. If I may employ the language of the professional logic-shop, a universal proposition can be made untrue by a particular instance. If you wish to upset the law that all crows are black, you must not seek to show that no crows are; it is enough if you prove one single crow to be white. My own white crow is Mrs. Piper. In the trances of this medium, I cannot resist the conviction that knowledge appears which she has never gained by the ordinary waking use of her eyes and ears and wits. What the source of this knowledge may be I know not, and have not the glimmer of an explanatory suggestion to make; but from admitting the fact of such knowledge I can see no escape. So when I turn to the rest of the evidence, ghosts and all, I cannot carry with me the irreversibly negative bias of the "rigorously scientific" mind, with its presumption as to what the true order of nature ought to be. I feel as if, though the evidence be flimsy in spots, it may nevertheless collectively carry heavy weight. The rigorously scientific mind may, in truth, easily overshoot the mark. Science means, first of all, a certain dispassionate method. To suppose that it means a certain set of results that one should pin one's faith upon and hug forever is sadly to mistake its genius, and degrades the scientific body to the status of a sect.

We all, scientists and non-scientists, live on some inclined plane of credulity. The plane tips one way in one man, another way in another; and may he whose plane tips in no way be the first to cast a stone! As a matter of fact, the trances I speak of have broken down for my own mind the limits of the admitted order of nature. Science, so far as science denies such exceptional occurrences, lies prostrate in the dust for me; and the most urgent intellectual need which I feel at present is that science be built up again in a form in which such things may have a positive place. Science, like life, feeds on its own decay. New facts burst old rules; then newly divined conceptions bind old and new together into a reconciling law.

And here is the real instructiveness of Messrs. Myers and Gurney's work. They are trying with the utmost conscientiousness to find a reconciling conception which shall subject the old laws of nature to the smallest possible strain. Mr. Myers uses that method of gradual approach which has performed such wonders in Darwin's hands. When Darwin met a fact which seemed a poser to his theory, his regular custom, as I have heard an able colleague say, was to fill in all round it with smaller facts, as a wagoner might heap dirt round a big rock in the road, and thus get his team over without upsetting. So Mr. Myers, starting from the most ordinary facts of inattentive consciousness, follows this clue through a long series which terminates in ghosts, and seeks to show that these are but extreme manifestations of a common truth—the truth that the invisible segments of our minds are susceptible, under rarely realized conditions, of acting and being acted upon by the invisible segments of other conscious lives. This may not be ultimately true (for the theosophists, with their astral bodies and the like, may, for aught I now know, prove to be on the correcter trail), but no one can deny that it is in good scientific form—for science always takes a known kind of phenomenon, and tries to extend its range.

I have myself, as American agent for the census, collected hundreds of cases of hallucination in healthy persons. The result is to make me feel that we all have potentially a "subliminal" self, which may make at any time irruption into our ordinary lives. At its lowest, it is only the depository of our forgotten memories; at its highest, we do not know what it is at all. Take, for instance, a series of cases. During sleep, many persons have something in them which measures the flight of time better than the waking self does. It wakes them at a preappointed hour; it acquaints them with the moment when they first awake. It may produce an hallucination—as in a lady who informs me that at the instant of waking she has a vision of her watch-face with the hands pointing (as she has often verified) to the exact time. It may be the feeling that some physiological period has elapsed; but, whatever it is, it is subconscious.

A subconscious something may also preserve experiences to which we do not openly attend. A lady taking her lunch in town finds herself without her purse. Instantly a sense comes over her of rising from the breakfast-table and hearing her purse drop upon the floor. On reaching home she finds nothing under the table, but summons the servant to say where she has put the purse. The servant produces it, saying: "How did you know where it was? You rose and left the room as if you didn't know you'd dropped it." The same subconscious something may recollect what we have forgotten. A lady accustomed to taking salicylate of soda for muscular rheumatism wakes one early winter morning with an aching neck. In the twilight she takes what she supposes to be her customary powder from a drawer, dissolves it in a glass of water, and is about to drink it down, when she feels a sharp slap on her shoulder and hears a voice in her ear saying, "Taste it!" On examination, she finds she has got a morphine powder by mistake. The natural interpretation is that a sleeping memory of the morphine powders awoke in this quasi-explosive way. A like explanation offers itself as most plausible for the following case: A lady, with little time to catch the train, and the expressman about to call, is excitedly looking for the lost key of a packed trunk. Hurrying upstairs with a bunch of keys, proved useless, in her hand, she hears an "objective" voice distinctly say, "Try the key of the cake-box." Being tried, it fits. This also may well have been the effect of forgotten experience.

Now, the effect is doubtless due to the same hallucinatory mechanism; but the source is less easily assigned as we ascend the scale of cases. A lady, for instance, goes after breakfast to see about one of her servants who has become ill over night. She is startled at distinctly reading over the bedroom door in gilt letters the word "small-pox." The doctor is sent for, and ere long pronounces small-pox to be the disease, although the lady says, "The thought of the girl's having small-pox never entered my mind till I saw the apparent inscription." Then come other cases of warning; for example, that of a youth sitting in a wagon under a shed, who suddenly hears his dead mother's voice say, "Stephen, get away from here quick!" and jumps out just in time to see the shed-roof fall.

After this come the experiences of persons appearing to distant friends at or near the hour of death. Then, too, we have the trance-visions and utterances, which may appear astonishingly profuse and continuous, and maintain a fairly high intellectual level. For all these higher phenomena, it seems to me that whilst the proximate mechanism is that of "hallucination," it is straining an hypothesis unduly to name any ordinary subconscious mental operation—such as expectation, recollection, or inference from inattentive perception—as the ultimate cause that starts it up. It is far better tactics, if you wish to get rid of mystery, to brand the narratives themselves as unworthy of trust. The trustworthiness of most of them is to my own mind far from proved. And yet in the light of the medium-trance, which *is* proved, it seems as if they might well all be members of a natural kind of fact of which we do not yet know the full extent.

Thousands of sensitive organizations in the United States

to-day live as steadily in the light of these experiences, and are as indifferent to modern science, as if they lived in Bohemia in the twelfth century. They are indifferent to science, because science is so callously indifferent to their experiences. Although in its essence science only stands for a method and for no fixed belief, yet as habitually taken, both by its votaries and outsiders, it is identified with a certain fixed belief—the belief that the hidden order of nature is mechanical exclusively, and that non-mechanical categories are irrational ways of conceiving and explaining even such things as human life. Now this mechanical rationalism, as one may call it, makes, if it becomes one's only way of thinking, a violent breach with the ways of thinking that have played the greatest part in human history. Religious thinking, ethical thinking, poetical thinking, teleological, emotional, sentimental thinking, what one might call the personal view of life to distinguish it from the impersonal and mechanical, and the romantic view of life to distinguish it from the rationalistic view, have been, and even still are, outside of well-drilled scientific circles, the dominant forms of thought. But for mechanical rationalism, personality is an insubstantial illusion. The chronic belief of mankind, that events may happen for the sake of their personal significance, is an abomination; and the notions of our grandfathers about oracles and omens, divinations and apparitions, miraculous changes of heart and wonders worked by inspired persons, answers to prayer and providential leadings, are a fabric absolutely baseless, a mass of sheer *un*truth.

Now, of course, we must all admit that the excesses to which the romantic and personal view of nature may lead, if wholly unchecked by impersonal rationalism, are direful. Central African Mumbo-jumboism is one of unchecked romanticism's fruits. One ought accordingly to sympathize with that abhorrence of romanticism as a sufficient world-theory; one ought to understand that lively intolerance of the least grain of romanticism in the views of life of other people, which are such characteristic marks of those who follow the scientific professions to-day. Our debt to science is literally boundless, and our gratitude for what is positive in her teachings must be correspondingly immense. But the S. P. R.'s *Proceedings* have, it seems to me, conclusively proved one thing to the candid reader; and that is that the verdict of pure insanity, of gratuitous preference for error, of superstition without an excuse, which the scientists of our day are led by their intellectual training to pronounce upon the entire thought of the past, is a most shallow verdict. The personal and romantic view of life has other roots besides wanton exuberance of imagination and perversity of heart. It is perennially fed by *facts of experience*, whatever the ulterior interpretation of those facts may prove to be; and at no time in human history would it have been less easy than now—at most times it would have been much more easy—for advocates with a little industry to collect in its favor an array of contemporary documents as good as those which our publications present. These documents all relate to real experiences of persons. These experiences have three characters in common: They are capricious, discontinuous, and not easily controlled; they require peculiar persons for their production; their significance seems to be wholly for personal life. Those who preferentially attend to them, and still more those who are individually subject to them, not only easily may find, but are logically bound to find, in them valid arguments for their romantic and personal conception of the world's course. Through my slight participation in the investigations of the S. P. R. I have become acquainted with numbers of persons of this sort, for whom the very word "science" has become a name of reproach, for reasons that I now both understand and respect. It is the intolerance of science for such phenomena as we are studying, her peremptory denial either of their existence or of their significance (except as proofs of man's absolute innate folly), that has set science so apart from the common sympathies of the race. I confess that it is on this, its humanizing mission, that the Society's best claim to the gratitude of our generation seems to me to depend. It has restored continuity to history. It has shown some reasonable basis for the most superstitious aberrations of the foretime. It has bridged the chasm, healed the hideous rift that science, taken in a certain narrow way, has shot into the human world.

I will even go one step farther. When from our present advanced standpoint we look back upon the past stages of human thought, whether it be scientific thought or theological thought, we are amazed that a universe which appears to us of so vast and mysterious a complication should ever have seemed to anyone so little and plain a thing. Whether it be Descartes' world or Newton's, whether it be that of the materialists of the last century or that of the Bridgewater treatises of our own, it always looks the same to us—incredibly perspectiveless and short. Even Lyell's, Faraday's, Mill's, and Darwin's consciousness of their respective subjects are already beginning to put on an infantile and innocent look. Is it then likely that the science of our own day will escape the common doom; that the minds of its votaries will never look old-fashioned to the grandchildren of the latter? It would be folly to suppose so. Yet if we are to judge by the analogy of the past, when our science once becomes old-fashioned, it will be more for its omissions of fact, for its ignorance of whole ranges and orders of complexity in the phenomena to be explained, than for any fatal lack in its spirit and principles. The spirit and principles of science are mere affairs of method; there is nothing in them that need hinder science from dealing successfully with a world in which personal forces are the starting-point of new effects. The only form of thing that we directly encounter, the only experience that we concretely have, is our own personal life. The only complete category of our thinking, our professors of philosophy tell us, is the category of personality, every other category being one of the abstract elements of that. And this systematic denial on science's part of personality as a condition of events, this rigorous belief that in its own essential and innermost nature our world is a strictly impersonal world, may, conceivably, as the whirligig of time goes round, prove to be the very defect that our descendants will be most surprised at in our own boasted science, the omission that to their eyes will most tend to make *it* look perspectiveless and short.

Index

ABSOLUTISM, 465–466, 477–478.

Abstract conceptions, 620.

Action, as a measure of belief, 458, 477–479.

Actual world narrower than ideal, 608–609.

Agnosticism, 496–497, 517, 551.

Allen, G., 629, 632, 647.

Alps, leap in the, 500, 528–529.

Alternatives, 573–574, 578, 608–609, 657–658.

Ambiguity of choice, 573–574; of being, 674.

Anæsthetic revelation, 676.

Apparitions, 689–690.

A priori truths, 656.

Aristotle, 643.

Associationism, in Ethics, 696–697.

Atheist and acorn, 577.

Authorities in Ethics, 609–610; *versus* champions, 611–612.

Axioms, 656–657.

BAGEHOT, 630.

Bain, 510, 525.

Balfour, 462.

Being, its character, 563; in Hegel, 666.

Belief, 500–501. See 'Faith.'

Bellamy, 598.

Bismarck, 627.

Block-universe, 674.

Blood, B. P., 448, 676.

Brockton murderer, 577, 590.

Bunsen, 609, 661.

CALVINISM, 490.

Carlyle, 488, 489, 490, 511, 522, 587.

'Casuistic question' in Ethics, 605.

Causality, 568.

Causation, Hume's doctrine of, 664.

Census of hallucinations, 689–690.

Certitude, 465, 477–479.

Chance, 568, 572–576, 591–594.

Choice, 573–574.

Christianity, 460, 466.

Cicero, 525.

City of dreadful night, 482–484.

Clark, X., 494.

Classifications, 507.

Clifford, 461–462, 463, 466, 469, 471, 525, 526, 628.

Clive, 627.

Clough, 461.

Common-sense, 658.

Conceptual order of world, 544–545.

Conscience, 596–598.

Contradiction, as used by Hegel, 662–664.

Contradictions of philosophers, 467.

Crillon, 503.

Criterion of truth, 466, 468; in Ethics, 610–611.

Crude order of experience, 645.

Crystal vision, 691.

Cycles in Nature, 621, 624.

DARWIN, 622, 623, 625, 695.

Data, 659.

Davey, 690.

Demands, as creators of value, 607.

'Determination is negation,' 670–673.

Determinism, 569–570; the Dilemma of, 566–594, 579, 581–582; hard and soft, 569.

Dogmatism, 464.

Dogs, 499.

Doubt, 497, 537–538.

Dupery, 475.

EASY-GOING mood, 615, 616.

Elephant, 667–668.

Emerson, 473, 588.

Empiricism, 447, 465–466, 467, 468, 664.

England, 627.

Environment, its relation to great men, 623, 625; to great thoughts, 642.

Error, 580; duty of avoiding, 469–470.

Essence of good and bad, 607.

Ethical ideals, 607–608.

Ethical philosophy, 612, 614, 617.

Ethical standards, 610; diversity of, 606.

Ethics, its three questions, 596.

Evidence, objective, 465, 467, 468.

Evil, 490–491, 493, 577, 599.

Evolution, social, 629, 633; mental, 639.

Evolutionism, its test of right, 530–531.

Expectancy, 514–516.

Experience, crude, *versus* rationalized, 545; tests our faiths, 535.

FACTS, 659.

Faith, that truth exists, 463, 473; in our fellows, 473–474; school boys' definition of, 477; a remedy for pessimism, 501, 531; religious, 498; defined, 524; defended against 'scientific' objections, 424–427, 524–527; may create its own verification, 500, 528–533.

Familiarity confers rationality, 514.

Fatalism, 522.

Fiske, 647, 651.

Fitzgerald, 577.

Freedom, 533, 659.

Free-will, 533, 566, 575.

GALTON, 637.

Geniuses, 625, 627.

Ghosts, 691.

Gnosticism, 560, 581, 583.

God, 502, 507; of Nature, 488–489; the most adequate object for our mind, 543–544, 547–548; our relations to him, 556–558; his providence, 593–594; his demands create obligation, 601–603; his function in Ethics, 616–617.

Goethe, 540.

Good, 582, 606, 607.

Goodness, 599.

Great-man theory of history, 630.

Great men and their environment, 618–646.

Green, 611.

Gryzanowski, 636–637.

Gurney, 686–689.

Guthrie, 687.

Guyau, 598.

HALLUCINATIONS, Census of, 689–690.

Happiness, 480.

Harris, 667.

Hegel, 511, 653; his excessive claims, 659; his use of negation, 661, 673; of contradiction, 662, 663; on being, 666; on otherness, 668; on infinity, 668–669; on identity, 669; on determination, 672; his ontological emotion, 679.

Hegelisms, on some, 653–679.

Heine, 609.

Helmholtz, 520, 525.

Henry IV., 503.

Herbart, 666.

Hero-worship, 651.

Hinton, C. H., 467.

Hinton, J., 532.

Hodgson, R., 686.

Hodgson, S. H., 463.

Honor, 494.

Hugo, 619.

Human mind, its habit of abstracting, 620.

Hume on causation, 664.

Huxley, 461, 463, 525.

Hypnotism, 682, 687.

Hypotheses, live or dead, 457–458; their verification, 535; of genius, 641–643.

IDEALISM, 523, 673.

Ideals, 606; their conflict, 608.

Identity, 669.

Imperatives, 614.

Importance of individuals, the, 647–652; of things, its ground, 647–648.

Indeterminism, 570.

Individual differences, 650.

Individuals, the importance of, 647–652.

Infinite, 668–669.

Intuitionism, in Ethics, 596, 598–599.

JEVONS, 642.

Judgments of regret, 577.

KNOWING, 464–465.

Knowledge, 519.

LEAP on precipice, 500, 528.

Leibnitz, 489.

Life, is it worth living, 480–503.

MAGGOTS, 590.
Mahdi, the, 458, 460.
Mallock, 480, 594.
Marcus Aurelius, 487.
Materialism, 551.
'Maybes,' 501.
Measure of good, 610.
Mediumship, physical, 690, 691.
Melancholy, 481, 485, 488.
Mental evolution, 639–641; structure, 541, 544.
Mill, 631.
Mind, its triadic structure, 541, 544; its evolution, 639; its three departments, 542, 548, 552–553.
Monism, 665.
Moods, the strenuous and the easy, 615, 616–617.
Moralists, objective and subjective, 533–537.
Moral judgments, their origin, 596–598; obligation, 601–605; order, 602; philosophy, 595–596.
Moral philosopher and the moral life, the, 595–615.
Murder, 590.
Murderer, 577, 590.
Myers, 687, 691, 695.
Mystical phenomena, 680.
Mysticism, 512–513.

NAKED, the, 666.
Natural theology, 487–491.
Nature, 470, 486, 498.
Negation, as used by Hegel, 661.
Newman, 463.
Nitrous oxide, 676–679.
Nonentity, 510.

OBJECTIVE evidence, 465, 466, 467.
Obligation, 601–605.
Occult phenomena, 681; examples of, 697.
Omar Khayyam, 577.
Optimism, 501, 532, 580.
Options offered to belief, 458, 464, 475–476.
Origin of moral judgments, 596–598.
'Other,' in Hegel, 668.

PARSIMONY, law of, 555.
Partaking, 656, 658, 662, 674.
Pascal's wager, 459, 464.
Personality, 698, 700.
Pessimism, 486, 491, 501, 531, 578, 582.
Philosophy, 505; depends on personal demands, 525–526; makes world unreal, 485; seeks unification, 507–509; the ultimate, 538; its contradictions, 464.
Physiology, its *prestige*, 540.
Piper, Mrs., 691, 694.
Plato, 656.
Pluralism, 447–448, 570, 590, 601, 654, 656.
Positivism, 496, 537.
Possibilities, 570, 592–594, 674, 675.
Postulates, 525.
Powers, our powers as congruous with the world, 521.
Providence, 592.
Psychical research, what it has accomplished, 680–700; Society for, 682, 696, 698–699.
Pugnacity, 492, 494.

QUESTIONS, three, in Ethics, 566.

RATIONALISM, 464, 477.
Rationality, the sentiment of, 504–539; limits of theoretic, 505–513; mystical, 512–513; practical, 518–520; postulates of, 571.
Rational order of world, 545, 550–551, 567.
Reflex action and theism, 540–565.
Reflex action defined, 541–542; it refutes gnosticism, 561–562.
Regret, judgments of, 577.
Religion, natural, 495; of humanity, 605.
Religious hypothesis, 474, 478, 495.
Religious minds, 486.
Renan, 585, 586.
Renouvier, 563–564.
Risks of belief or disbelief, 449–450, 475; rules for minimizing, 527.
Romantic view of world, 698.
Romanticism, 585–588.
Rousseau, 481, 482, 522.
Ruskin, 489.

SALTER, 503.
Scepticism, 464, 473, 537–538.
Scholasticism, 465.
Schopenhauer, 510, 584.
Science, 463, 471; its recency, 496; due to peculiar desire, 553–556, 567; its disbelief of the occult, 693–695; its negation of personality, 698–699; cannot decide question of determinism, 571.
Science of Ethics, 612–614.
Selection of great men, 625.
Sentiment of rationality, 504.
Seriousness, 521.
Shakespeare, 480, 632.
Sidgwick, 683, 685.
Sigwart, 547, 568.
Society for psychical research, 682; its 'Proceedings,' 684, 699.
Sociology, 650.
Solitude, moral, 600.
Space, 654.
Spencer, 683, 619, 630–632, 640, 644, 650.
Stephen, L., 457.
Stephen, Sir J., 457, 478, 615.
Stoics, 661.
Strenuous mood, 615–616, 617.
Subjectivism, 581, 584.
'Subliminal self,' 692, 696.
Substance, 516–517.
Suicide, 485, 493, 501.
System in philosophy, 465, 595–596, 606.

TELEPATHY, 463, 487.
Theism, 551, 557–559. See 'God.'
Theism, and reflex action, 540–565.

Theology, natural, 487; Calvinistic, 490.
Theoretic faculty, 552.
Thomson, 482–484, 490, 491.
Thought-transference, 687.
Toleration, 478.
Tolstoï, 598.
'Totality,' the principle of, 664.
Triadic structure of mind, 548.
Truth, criteria of, 466–467, and error, 469; moral, 599–601.

UNITARIANS, 551, 556.
Universe = M + x, 531; its rationality, 550–552, 559.
Unknowable, the, 507, 517.
Unseen world, 495, 497, 498, 502.
Utopias, 583.

VALUE, judgments of, 534.
Variations, in heredity, etc., 624, 643.
Vaudois, 493.
Veddah, 649.
Verification of theories, 527, 535–537.
Vivisection, 499.

WALDENSES, 492–493.
Wallace, 635, 683.
Whitman, 480, 505, 512.
Wordsworth, 501.
World, its ambiguity, 513; the invisible, 495, 497, 498; two orders of, 545.
Worth, judgments of, 534.
Wright, 495.

X., Miss, 691.

ZOLA, 586.
Zöllner, 467.

TALKS TO TEACHERS
ON PSYCHOLOGY

and to Students on
Some of Life's Ideals

Preface

IN 1892 I was asked by the Harvard Corporation to give a few public lectures on psychology to the Cambridge teachers. The talks now printed form the substance of that course, which has since then been delivered at various places to various teacher-audiences. I have found by experience that what my hearers seem least to relish is analytical technicality, and what they most care for is concrete practical application. So I have gradually weeded out the former, and left the latter unreduced; and now that I have at last written out the lectures, they contain a minimum of what is deemed 'scientific' in psychology, and are practical and popular in the extreme.

Some of my colleagues may possibly shake their heads at this; but in taking my cue from what has seemed to me to be the feeling of the audiences I believe that I am shaping my book so as to satisfy the more genuine public need.

Teachers, of course, will miss the minute divisions, subdivisions, and definitions, the lettered and numbered headings, the variations of type, and all the other mechanical artifices on which they are accustomed to prop their minds. But my main desire has been to make them conceive, and, if possible, reproduce sympathetically in their imagination, the mental life of their pupil as the sort of active unity which he himself feels it to be. *He* doesn't chop himself into distinct processes and compartments; and it would have frustrated this deeper purpose of my book to make it look, when printed, like a Baedeker's handbook of travel or a text-book of arithmetic. So far as books printed like this book force the fluidity of the facts upon the young teacher's attention, so far I am sure they tend to do his intellect a service, even though they may leave unsatisfied a craving (not altogether without its legitimate grounds) for more nomenclature, head-lines, and subdivisions.

Readers acquainted with my larger books on Psychology will meet much familiar phraseology. In the chapters on habit and memory I have even copied several pages verbatim, but I do not know that apology is needed for such plagiarism as this.

The talks to students, which conclude the volume, were written in response to invitations to deliver 'addresses' to students at women's colleges. The first one was to the graduating class of the Boston Normal School of Gymnastics. Properly, it continues the series of talks to teachers. The second and the third address belong together, and continue another line of thought.

I wish I were able to make the second, "On a Certain Blindness in Human Beings," more impressive. It is more than the mere piece of sentimentalism which it may seem to some readers. It connects itself with a definite view of the world and of our moral relations to the same. Those who have done me the honor of reading my volume of philosophic essays will recognize that I mean the pluralistic or individualistic philosophy. According to that philosophy, the truth is too great for any one actual mind, even though that mind be dubbed 'the Absolute,' to know the whole of it. The facts and worths of life need many cognizers to take them in. There is no point of view absolutely public and universal. Private and uncommunicable perceptions always remain over, and the worst of it is that those who look for them from the outside never know *where*.

The practical consequence of such a philosophy is the well-known democratic respect for the sacredness of individuality—is, at any rate, the outward tolerance of whatever is not itself intolerant. These phrases are so familiar that they sound now rather dead in our ears. Once they had a passionate inner meaning. Such a passionate inner meaning they may easily acquire again if the pretension of our nation to inflict its own inner ideals and institutions *vi et armis* upon Orientals should meet with a resistance as obdurate as so far it has been gallant and spirited. Religiously and philosophically, our ancient national doctrine of live and let live may prove to have a far deeper meaning than our people now seem to imagine it to possess.

CAMBRIDGE, MASS., March, 1899.

Contents

TALKS TO TEACHERS

CHAPTER I

PSYCHOLOGY AND THE TEACHING ART 715
*The American educational organization—What teachers
may expect from psychology—Teaching methods must agree
with psychology, but cannot be immediately deduced
therefrom—The science of teaching and the science of
war—The educational uses of psychology defined—The
teacher's duty towards child-study.*

CHAPTER II

THE STREAM OF CONSCIOUSNESS 722
*Our mental life is a succession of conscious 'fields'—They
have a focus and a margin—This description contrasted
with the theory of 'ideas'—Wundt's conclusions, note.*

CHAPTER III

THE CHILD AS A BEHAVING ORGANISM 726
*Mind as pure reason and mind as practical guide—The
latter view the more fashionable one to-day—It will be
adopted in this work—Why so?—The teacher's function is
to train pupils to behavior.*

CHAPTER IV

EDUCATION AND BEHAVIOR. 730
*Education defined—Conduct is always its outcome—
Different national ideals: Germany and England.*

CHAPTER V

THE NECESSITY OF REACTIONS 733
*No impression without expression—Verbal reproduction—
Manual training—Pupils should know their 'marks.'*

CHAPTER VI

NATIVE REACTIONS AND ACQUIRED REACTIONS 736

The acquired reactions must be preceded by native ones —
Illustration: teaching child to ask instead of snatching —
Man has more instincts than other mammals.

CHAPTER VII

WHAT THE NATIVE REACTIONS ARE 740

Fear and love —Curiosity —Imitation —Emulation —
Forbidden by Rousseau —His error —Ambition, pugnacity,
and pride. Soft pædagogics and the fighting impulse —
Ownership —Its educational uses —Constructiveness —
Manual teaching —Transitoriness in instincts —Their order
of succession.

CHAPTER VIII

THE LAWS OF HABIT 750

Good and bad habits —Habit due to plasticity of organic
tissues —The aim of education is to make useful habits
automatic —Maxims relative to habit-forming: 1. Strong
initiative —2. No exception —3. Seize first opportunity
to act —4. Don't preach —Darwin and poetry: without
exercise our capacities decay —The habit of mental
and muscular relaxation —Fifth maxim, keep the
faculty of effort trained —Sudden conversions compatible
with laws of habit —Momentous influence of habits on
character.

CHAPTER IX

THE ASSOCIATION OF IDEAS. 759

A case of habit —The two laws, contiguity and similarity —
The teacher has to build up useful systems of association —
Habitual associations determine character —
Indeterminateness of our trains of association —We can
trace them backward, but not foretell them —Interest
deflects —Prepotent parts of the field —In teaching,
multiply cues.

CHAPTER X

INTEREST 766
*The child's native interests —How uninteresting things
acquire an interest —Rules for the teacher —'Preparation'
of the mind for the lesson: the pupil must have something to
attend with —All latter interests are borrowed from original
ones.*

CHAPTER XI

ATTENTION 771
*Interest and attention are two aspects of one
fact —Voluntary attention comes in beats —Genius and
attention —The subject must change to win attention —
Mechanical aids —The physiological process —The new in
the old is what excites interest —Interest and effort are
compatible —Mind-wandering —Not fatal to mental
efficiency.*

CHAPTER XII

MEMORY 779
*Due to association —No recall without a cue —Memory is
due to brain-plasticity —Native retentiveness —Number of
associations may practically be its equivalent —Retentiveness
is a fixed property of the individual —Memory versus
memories —Scientific system as help to memory —Technical
memories —Cramming —Elementary memory
unimprovable —Utility of verbal memorizing —
Measurements of immediate memory —They throw little
light —Passion is the important factor in human
efficiency —Eye-memory, ear-memory, etc. —The rate of
forgetting, Ebbinghaus's results —Influence of the
unreproducible —To remember, one must think and connect.*

CHAPTER XIII

THE ACQUISITION OF IDEAS. 794
*Education gives a stock of conceptions —The order of their
acquisition —Value of verbal material —Abstractions of
different orders: when are they assimilable —False
conceptions of children.*

CHAPTER XIV

APPERCEPTION 800

Often a mystifying idea —The process defined —The law of economy —Old-fogyism —How many types of apperception? —New heads of classification must continually be invented —Alteration of the apperceiving mass —Class-names are what we work by —Few new fundamental conceptions acquired after twenty-five.

CHAPTER XV

THE WILL 808

The word defined —All consciousness tends to action —Ideo-motor action —Inhibition —The process of deliberation — Why so few of our ideas result in acts —The associationist account of the will —A balance of impulses and inhibitions —The over-impulsive and the over-obstructed type —The perfect type —The balky will —What character-building consists in —Right action depends on right apperception of the case —Effort of will is effort of attention: the drunkard's dilemma —Vital importance of voluntary attention —Its amount may be indeterminate — Affirmation of free will —Two types of inhibition —Spinoza on inhibition by a higher good —Conclusion.

TALKS TO STUDENTS

I

THE GOSPEL OF RELAXATION 825

II

ON A CERTAIN BLINDNESS IN HUMAN BEINGS 841

III

WHAT MAKES A LIFE SIGNIFICANT 861

INDEX 881

Talks to Teachers

CHAPTER I

PSYCHOLOGY AND THE TEACHING ART

IN THE GENERAL ACTIVITY and uprising of ideal interests which everyone with an eye for fact can discern all about us in American life, there is perhaps no more promising feature than the fermentation which for a dozen years or more has been going on amongst the teachers. In whatever sphere of education their functions may lie, there is to be seen amongst them a really inspiring amount of searching of the heart about the highest concerns of their profession. The renovation of nations begins always at the top, amongst the reflective members of the State, and spreads slowly outward and downward. The teachers of this country, one may say, have its future in their hands. The earnestness which they at present show in striving to enlighten and strengthen themselves is an index of the nation's probabilities of advance in all ideal directions. The outward organization of education which we have in our United States is perhaps, on the whole, the best organization that exists in any country. The State school systems give a diversity and flexibility, an opportunity for experiment and keenness of competition, nowhere else to be found on such an important scale. The independence of so many of the colleges and universities; the give and take of students and instructors between them all; their emulation, and their happy organic relations to the lower schools; the traditions of instruction in them, evolved from the older American recitation-method (and so avoiding on the one hand the pure lecture-system prevalent in Germany and Scotland, which considers too little the individual student, and yet not involving the sacrifice of the instructor to the individual student, which the English tutorial system would seem too often to entail)—all these things (to say nothing of that coeducation of the sexes in whose benefit so many of us heartily believe), all these things, I say, are most happy features of our scholastic life, and from them the most sanguine auguries may be drawn.

Having so favorable an organization, all we need is to impregnate it with geniuses, to get superior men and women working more and more abundantly in it and for it and at it, and in a generation or two America may well lead the education of the world. I must say that I look forward with no little confidence to the day when that shall be an accomplished fact.

No one has profited more by the fermentation of which I speak, in pædagogical circles, than we psychologists. The desire of the schoolteachers for a completer professional training, and their aspiration towards the 'professional' spirit in their work, have led them more and more to turn to us for light on fundamental principles. And in these few hours which we are to spend together you look to me, I am sure, for information concerning the mind's operations, which may enable you to labor more easily and effectively in the several school-rooms over which you preside.

Far be it from me to disclaim for psychology all title to such hopes. Psychology ought certainly to give the teacher radical help. And yet I confess that, acquainted as I am with the height of some of your expectations, I feel a little anxious lest, at the end of these simple talks of mine, not a few of you may experience some disappointment at the net results. In other words, I am not sure that you may not be indulging fancies that are just a shade exaggerated. That would not be altogether astonishing, for we have been having something like a 'boom' in psychology in this country. Laboratories and professorships have been founded, and reviews established. The air has been full of rumors. The editors of educational journals and the arrangers of conventions have had to show themselves enterprising and on a level with the novelties of the day. Some of the professors have not been unwilling to co-operate, and I am not sure even that the publishers have been entirely inert. 'The new psychology' has thus become a term to conjure up portentous ideas withal; and you teachers, docile and receptive and aspiring as many of you are, have been plunged in an atmosphere of vague talk about our science, which to a great extent has been more mystifying than enlightening. Altogether it does seem as if there were a certain fatality of mystification laid upon the teachers of our day. The matter of their profession, compact enough in itself, has to be frothed up for them in journals and institutes, till its outlines often threaten to be lost in a kind of vast uncertainty. Where the disciples are not independent and critical-minded enough (and I think that if you teachers in the earlier grades have any defect—the slightest touch of a defect in the world—it is that you are a mite too docile), we are pretty sure to miss accuracy and balance and measure in those who get a license to lay down the law to them from above.

As regards this subject of psychology, now, I wish at the very threshold to do what I can to dispel the mystification. So I say at once that in my humble opinion there *is* no 'new psychology' worthy of the name. There is nothing but the old psychology which began in Locke's time, plus a little physiology of the brain and senses and theory of evolution, and a few refinements of introspective detail, for the most part without adaptation to the teacher's use. It is only the fundamental conceptions of psychology which are of real value to the teacher; and they, apart from the aforesaid theory of evolution, are very far from being new.—I trust that you will see better what I mean by this at the end of all these talks.

I say moreover that you make a great, a very great mistake, if you think that psychology, being the science of the mind's laws, is something from which you can deduce definite programmes and schemes and methods of instruction for immediate school-room use. Psychology is a science, and teaching is an art; and sciences never generate arts directly out of themselves. An intermediary inventive mind must make the application, by using its originality.

The science of logic never made a man reason rightly, and the science of ethics (if there be such a thing) never made a man behave rightly. The most such sciences can do is to help us to catch ourselves up and check ourselves, if we start to reason or to behave wrongly; and to criticise ourselves more articulately after we have made mistakes. A science only lays down lines within which the rules of the art must fall, laws which the follower of the art must not transgress; but what particular thing he shall positively do within those lines is left exclusively to his own genius. One genius will do his work well and succeed in one way, whilst another succeeds as well quite differently; yet neither will transgress the lines.

The art of teaching grew up in the school-room, out of inventiveness and sympathetic concrete observation. Even where (as in the case of Herbart) the advancer of the art was also a psychologist, the pædagogics and the psychology ran side by side, and the former was not derived in any sense from the latter. The two were congruent, but neither was subordinate. And so everywhere the teaching must *agree* with the psychology, but need not necessarily be the only kind of teaching that would so agree; for many diverse methods of teaching may equally well agree with psychological laws.

To know psychology, therefore, is absolutely no guarantee that we shall be good teachers. To advance to that result we must have an additional endowment altogether, a happy tact and ingenuity to tell us what definite things to say and do when the pupil is before us. That ingenuity in meeting and pursuing the pupil, that tact for the concrete situation, though they are the alpha and omega of the teacher's art, are things to which psychology cannot help us in the least.

The science of psychology, and whatever science of general pædagogics may be based on it, are in fact much like the science of war. Nothing is simpler or more definite than the principles of either. In war, all you have to do is to work your enemy into a position from which the natural obstacles prevent him from escaping if he tries to; then to fall on him in numbers superior to his own, at a moment when you have led him to think you far away; and so, with a minimum of exposure of your own troops, to hack his force to pieces, and take the remainder prisoners. Just so, in teaching, you must simply work your pupil into such a state of interest in what you are going to teach him that every other object of attention is banished from his mind; then reveal it to him so impressively that he will remember the occasion to his dying day; and finally fill him with devouring curiosity to know what the next steps in connection with the subject are. The principles being so plain, there would be nothing but victories for the masters of the science, either on the battlefield or in the school-room, if they did not both have to make their application to an incalculable quantity in the shape of the mind of their opponent. The mind of your own enemy, the pupil, is working away from you as keenly and eagerly as is the mind of the commander on the other side from the scientific general. Just what the respective enemies want and think, and what they know and do not know, are as hard things for the teachers as for the general to find out. Divination and perception, not psychological pædagogics or theoretic strategy, are the only helpers here.

But if the use of psychological principles thus be negative rather than positive, it does not follow that it may not be a great use, all the same. It certainly narrows the path for experiments and trials: we know in advance, if we are psychologists, that certain methods will be wrong, so our psychology saves us from mistakes. It makes us, moreover, more clear as to what we are about. We gain confidence in respect to any method which we are using as soon as we believe that it has theory as well as practice at its back. Most of all, it fructifies our independence, and it reanimates our interest, to see our subject at two different angles—to get a stereoscopic view, so to speak, of the youthful organism who is our enemy; and whilst handling him with all our concrete tact and divination, to be able, at the same time, to represent to ourselves the curious inner elements of his mental machine. Such a complete knowledge as this of the pupil, at once intuitive and analytic, is surely the knowledge at which every teacher ought to aim.

Fortunately for you teachers, the elements of the mental machine can be clearly apprehended, and their workings easily grasped. And as the most general elements and workings are just those parts of psychology which the teacher finds most directly useful, it follows that the amount of this science which is necessary to all teachers need not be very great. Those who find themselves loving the subject may go as far as they please, and become possibly none the worse teachers for the fact, even though in some of them one might apprehend a little loss of balance from the tendency observable in all of us to overemphasize certain special parts of a subject when we are studying it intensely and abstractly. But for the great majority of you a general view is enough, provided it be a true one; and such a general view, one may say, might almost be written on the palm of one's hand.

Least of all need you, merely *as teachers*, deem it part of your duty to become contributors to psychological science or to make psychological observations in a methodical or responsible manner. I fear that some of the enthusiasts for child-study have thrown a certain burden on you in this way. By all means let child-study go on—it is refreshing all our sense of the child's life. There are teachers who take a spontaneous delight in filling syllabuses, inscribing observations, compiling statistics, and computing the per cent. Child-study will certainly enrich their lives. And if its results, as treated statistically, would seem on the whole to have but trifling value, yet the anecdotes and observations of which it in part consists do certainly acquaint us more intimately with our pupils. Our eyes and ears grow quickened to discern in the child before us processes similar to those we have read of as noted in the children—processes of which we might otherwise have remained inobservant. But, for Heaven's sake, let the rank and file of teachers be passive readers if they so prefer, and feel free not to contribute to the accumulation. Let not the prosecution of it be preached as an imperative duty or imposed by regulation on those to whom it proves an exterminating bore, or who in any way whatever miss in themselves the appropriate vocation for it. I cannot too strongly agree with my colleague, Professor Münsterberg, when he says that the teacher's attitude towards the child, being concrete and ethical, is positively opposed to the psychological observer's, which is abstract and analytic. Although some of us may conjoin the attitudes successfully, in most of us they must conflict.

The worst thing that can happen to a good teacher is to get a bad conscience about her profession because she feels herself hopeless as a psychologist. Our teachers are overworked already. Everyone who adds a jot or tittle of unnecessary weight to their burden is a foe of education. A bad conscience increases the weight of every other burden; yet I know that child-study, and other pieces of psychology as well, have been productive of bad conscience in many a really innocent pædagogic breast. I should indeed be glad if this passing word from me might tend to dispel such a bad conscience, if any of you have it; for it is certainly one of those fruits of more or less systematic mystification of which I have already complained. The best teacher may be the poorest contributor of child-study material, and the best contributor may be the poorest teacher. No fact is more palpable than this.

So much for what seems the most reasonable general attitude of the teacher towards the subject which is to occupy our attention.

CHAPTER II

THE STREAM OF CONSCIOUSNESS

I SAID a few minutes ago that the most general elements and workings of the mind are all that the teacher absolutely needs to be acquainted with for his purposes.

Now the *immediate* fact which psychology, the science of mind, has to study is also the most general fact. It is the fact that in each of us, when awake (and often when asleep), *some kind of consciousness is always going on*. There is a stream, a succession of states, or waves, or fields (or of whatever you please to call them), of knowledge, of feeling, of desire, of deliberation, etc., that constantly pass and repass, and that constitute our inner life. The existence of this stream is the primal fact, the nature and origin of it form the essential problem, of our science. So far as we class the states or fields of consciousness, write down their several natures, analyze their contents into elements, or trace their habits of succession, we are on the descriptive or analytic level. So far as we ask where they come from or why they are just what they are, we are on the explanatory level.

In these talks with you, I shall entirely neglect the questions that come up on the explanatory level. It must be frankly confessed that in no fundamental sense do we know where our successive fields of consciousness come from, or why they have the precise inner constitution which they do have. They certainly follow or accompany our brain states, and of course their special forms are determined by our past experiences and education. But if we ask just *how* the brain conditions them, we have not the remotest inkling of an answer to give; and if we ask just how the education moulds the brain, we can speak but in the most abstract, general, and conjectural terms. On the other hand, if we should say that they are due to a spiritual being called our Soul, which reacts on our brain states by these peculiar forms of spiritual energy, our words would be familiar enough, it is true; but I think you will agree that they would offer little genuine explanatory meaning. The truth is that we really *do not know* the answers to the problems on the explanatory level, even though in some directions of inquiry there may be promising speculations to be found. For our present purposes I shall therefore dismiss them entirely, and turn to mere description. This state of things was what I had in mind when, a moment ago, I said there was no 'new psychology' worthy of the name.

We have thus fields of consciousness—that is the first general fact; and the second general fact is that the concrete fields are always complex. They contain sensations of our bodies and of the objects around us, memories of past experiences and thoughts of distant things, feelings of satisfaction and dissatisfaction, desires and aversions, and other emotional conditions, together with determinations of the will, in every variety of permutation and combination.

In most of our concrete states of consciousness all these different classes of ingredients are found simultaneously present to some degree, though the relative proportion they bear to one another is very shifting. One state will seem to be composed of hardly anything but sensations, another of hardly anything but memories, etc. But around the sensation, if one consider carefully, there will always be some fringe of thought or will, and around the memory some margin or penumbra of emotion or sensation.

In most of our fields of consciousness there is a core of sensation that is very pronounced. You, for example, now, although you are also thinking and feeling, are getting through your eyes sensations of my face and figure, and through your ears sensations of my voice. The sensations are the *centre* or *focus*, the thoughts and feelings the *margin*, of your actually present conscious field.

On the other hand, some object of thought, some distant image, may have become the focus of your mental attention even whilst I am speaking—your mind, in short, may have wandered from the lecture; and in that case, the sensations of my face and voice, although not absolutely vanishing from your conscious field, may have taken up there a very faint and marginal place.

Again, to take another sort of variation, some feeling connected with your own body may have passed from a marginal to a focal place, even whilst I speak.

The expressions 'focal object' and 'marginal object,' which we owe to Mr. Lloyd Morgan, require, I think, no farther explanation. The distinction they embody is a very important one, and they are the first technical terms which I shall ask you to remember.

In the successive mutations of our fields of consciousness, the process by which one dissolves into another is often very gradual, and all sorts of inner rearrangements of contents occur. Sometimes the focus remains but little changed, whilst the margin alters rapidly. Sometimes the focus alters, and the margin stays. Sometimes focus and margin change places. Sometimes, again, abrupt alterations of the whole field occur. There can seldom be a sharp description. All we know is that, for the most part, each field has a sort of practical unity for its possessor, and that from this practical point of view we can class a field with other fields similar to it, by calling it a state of emotion, of perplexity, of sensation, of abstract thought, of volition, and the like.

Vague and hazy as such an account of our stream of consciousness may be, it is at least secure from positive error and free from admixture of conjecture or hypothesis. An influential school of psychology, seeking to avoid haziness of outline, has tried to make things appear more exact and scientific by making the analysis more sharp. The various fields of consciousness, according to this school, result from a definite number of perfectly definite elementary mental states, mechanically associated into a mosaic or chemically combined. According to some thinkers—Spencer, for example, or Taine—these resolve themselves at last into little elementary psychic particles or atoms of 'mind-stuff,' out of which all the more immediately known mental states are said to be built up. Locke introduced this theory in a somewhat vague form. Simple 'ideas' of sensation and reflection, as he called them, were for him the bricks of which our mental architecture is built up. If I ever have to refer to this theory again, I shall refer to it as the theory of 'ideas.' But I shall try to steer clear of it altogether. Whether it be true or false, it is at any rate only conjectural; and for your practical purposes as teachers, the more unpretending conception of the stream of consciousness, with its total waves or fields incessantly changing, will amply suffice.[1]

[1]In the light of some of the expectations that are abroad concerning the 'new psychology,' it is instructive to read the unusually candid confession of its founder Wundt, after his thirty years of laboratory-experience:

"The service which it [the experimental method] can yield consists essentially in perfecting our inner observation, or rather, as I believe, in making this really possible, in any exact sense. Well, has our experimental self-observation, so understood, already accomplished aught of importance? No general answer to this question can be given, because in the unfinished state of our science, there is, even inside of the experimental lines of inquiry, no universally accepted body of psychologic doctrine. . . .

"In such a discord of opinions (comprehensible enough at a time of uncertain and groping development), the individual inquirer can only tell for what views and insights he himself has to thank the newer methods. And if I were asked in what for me the worth of experimental observation in psychology has consisted, and still consists, I should say that it has given me an entirely new idea of the nature and connection of our inner processes. I learned in the achievements of the sense of sight to apprehend the fact of creative mental synthesis. . . . From my inquiry into time-relations, etc., . . . I attained an insight into the close union of all those psychic functions usually separated by artificial abstractions and names, such as ideation, feeling, will; and I saw the indivisibility and inner homogeneity, in all its phases, of the mental life. The chronometric study of association-processes finally showed me that the notion of distinct mental 'images' [*reproducirten Vorstellungen*] was one of those numerous self-deceptions which are no sooner stamped in a verbal term than they forthwith thrust non-existent fictions into the place of the reality. I learned to understand an 'idea' as a process no less melting and fleeting than an act of feeling or of will, and I comprehended the older doctrine of association of 'ideas' to be no longer tenable. . . . Besides all this, experimental observation yielded much other information about the span of consciousness, the rapidity of certain processes, the exact numerical value of certain psychophysical data, and the like. But I hold all these more special results to be relatively insignificant by-products, and by no means the important thing."—
"Über psychische Causalität und das Princip des psychophysischen Parallelismus," *Philosophische Studien*, x [1894], 122–124. The whole passage should be read. As I interpret it, it amounts to a complete espousal of the vaguer conception of the stream of thought, and a complete renunciation of the whole business, still so industriously carried on in text-books, of chopping up 'the mind' into distinct units of composition or function, numbering these off, and labelling them by technical names.

CHAPTER III

THE CHILD AS A BEHAVING ORGANISM

I WISH NOW to continue the description of the peculiarities of the stream of consciousness by asking whether we can in any intelligible way assign its *functions*.

It has two functions that are obvious: it leads to knowledge, and it leads to action.

Can we say which of these functions is the more essential?

An old historic divergence of opinion comes in here. Popular belief has always tended to estimate the worth of a man's mental processes by their effects upon his practical life. But philosophers have usually cherished a different view. "Man's supreme glory," they have said, "is to be a *rational* being, to know absolute and eternal and universal truth. The uses of his intellect for practical affairs are therefore subordinate matters. 'The theoretic life' is his soul's genuine concern." Nothing can be more different in its results for our personal attitude than to take sides with one or the other of these views, and emphasize the practical or the theoretical ideal. In the latter case, abstraction from the emotions and passions and withdrawal from the strife of human affairs would be not only pardonable, but praiseworthy; and all that makes for quiet and contemplation should be regarded as conducive to the highest human perfection. In the former, the man of contemplation would be treated as only half a human being, passion and practical resource would become once more glories of our race, a concrete victory over this earth's outward powers of darkness would appear an equivalent for any amount of passive spiritual culture, and conduct would remain as the test of every education worthy of the name.

It is impossible to disguise the fact that in the psychology of our own day the emphasis is transferred from the mind's purely rational function, where Plato and Aristotle, and what one may call the whole classic tradition in philosophy had placed it, to the so long neglected practical side. The theory of evolution is mainly responsible for this. Man, we now have reason to believe, has been evolved from infra-human ancestors, in whom pure reason hardly existed, if at all, and whose mind, so far as it can have had any function, would appear to have been an organ for adapting their movements to the impressions received from the environment, so as to escape the better from destruction. Consciousness would thus seem in the first instance to be nothing but a sort of super-added biological perfection—useless unless it prompted to useful conduct, and inexplicable apart from that consideration.

Deep in our own nature the biological foundations of our consciousness persist, undisguised and undiminished. Our sensations are here to attract us or to deter us, our memories to warn or encourage us, our feelings to impel and our thoughts to restrain our behavior, so that on the whole we may prosper and our days be long in the land. Whatever of transmundane metaphysical insight or of practically inapplicable æsthetic perception or ethical sentiment we may carry in our interiors might at this rate be regarded as only part of the incidental excess of function that necessarily accompanies the working of every complex machine.

I shall ask you now—not meaning at all thereby to close the theoretic question, but merely because it seems to me the point of view likely to be of greatest practical use to you as teachers—to adopt with me, in this course of lectures, the biological conception, as thus expressed, and to lay your own emphasis on the fact that man, whatever else he may be, is primarily a practical being, whose mind is given him to aid in adapting him to this world's life.

In the learning of all matters, we have to start with some one deep aspect of the question, abstracting it as if it were the only aspect; and then we gradually correct ourselves by adding those neglected other features which complete the case. No one believes more strongly than I do that what our senses know as 'this world' is only one portion of our mind's total environment and object. Yet, because it is the primal portion, it is the *sine qua non* of all the rest. If you grasp the facts about it firmly, you may proceed to higher regions undisturbed. As our time must be so short together, I prefer being elementary and fundamental to being complete, so I propose to you to hold fast to the ultra-simple point of view.

The reasons why I call it so fundamental can be easily told.

First, human and animal psychology thereby become less discontinuous. I know that to some of you this will hardly seem an attractive reason, but there are others whom it will affect.

Second, mental action is conditioned by brain action, and runs parallel therewith. But the brain, so far as we understand it, is given us for practical behavior. Every current that runs into it from skin or eye or ear runs out again into muscles, glands, or viscera, and helps to adapt the animal to the environment from which the current came. It therefore generalizes and simplifies our view to treat the brain life and the mental life as having one fundamental kind of purpose.

Third, those very functions of the mind that do not refer directly to this world's environment, the ethical utopias, æsthetic visions, insights into eternal truth, and fanciful logical combinations, could never be carried on at all by a human individual, unless the mind that produced them in him were also able to produce more practically useful products. The latter are thus the more essential, or at least the more primordial results.

Fourth, the inessential 'unpractical' activities are themselves far more connected with our behavior and our adaptation to the environment than at first sight might appear. No truth, however abstract, is ever perceived, that will not probably at some time influence our earthly action. You must remember that when I talk of action here, I mean action in the widest sense. I mean speech, I mean writing, I mean yeses and noes, and tendencies 'from' things and tendencies 'towards' things, and emotional determinations; and I mean them in the future as well as in the immediate present. As I talk here, and you listen, it might seem as if no action followed. You might call it a purely theoretic process, with no practical result. But it *must* have a practical result. It cannot take place at all and leave your conduct unaffected. If not to-day, then on some far future day, you will answer some question differently by reason of what you are thinking now. Some of you will be led by my words into new veins of inquiry, into reading special books. These will develop your opinion, whether for or against. That opinion will in turn be expressed, will receive criticism from others in your environment, and will affect your standing in their eyes. We cannot escape our destiny, which is practical; and even our most theoretic faculties contribute to its working out.

These few reasons will perhaps smooth the way for you to acquiescence in my proposal. As teachers, I sincerely think it will be a sufficient conception for you to adopt of the youthful psychological phenomena handed over to your inspection if you consider them from the point of view of their relation to the future conduct of their possessor. Sufficient at any rate as a first conception and as a main conception. You should regard your professional task as if it consisted chiefly and essentially in *training the pupil to behavior*; taking behavior, not in the narrow sense of his manners, but in the very widest possible sense, as including every possible sort of fit reaction on the circumstances into which he may find himself brought by the vicissitudes of life.

The reaction may, indeed, often be a negative reaction. *Not* to speak, *not* to move, is one of the most important of our duties, in certain practical emergencies. "Thou shalt refrain, renounce, abstain!" This often requires a great effort of will power, and, physiologically considered, is just as positive a nerve function as is motor discharge.

CHAPTER IV

EDUCATION AND BEHAVIOR

I N OUR FOREGOING TALK we were led to frame a very simple conception of what an education means. In the last analysis it consists in the organizing of *resources* in the human being, of powers of conduct which shall fit him to his social and physical world. An 'uneducated' person is one who is nonplused by all but the most habitual situations. On the contrary, one who is educated is able practically to extricate himself, by means of the examples with which his memory is stored and of the abstract conceptions which he has acquired, from circumstances in which he never was placed before. Education, in short, cannot be better described than by calling it *the organization of acquired habits of conduct and tendencies to behavior.*

To illustrate. You and I are each and all of us educated, in our several ways; and we show our education at this present moment by different conduct. It would be quite impossible for me, with my mind technically and professionally organized as it is, and with the optical stimulus which your presence affords, to remain sitting here entirely silent and inactive. Something tells me that I am expected to speak, and must speak; something forces me to keep on speaking. My organs of articulation are continuously innervated by outgoing currents, which the currents passing inward at my eyes and through my educated brain have set in motion; and the particular movements which they make have their form and order determined altogether by the training of all my past years of lecturing and reading. Your conduct, on the other hand, might seem at first sight purely receptive and inactive— leaving out those amongst you who happen to be taking notes. But the very listening which you are carrying on is itself a determinate kind of conduct. All the muscular tensions of your body are distributed in a peculiar way as you listen. Your head, your eyes, are fixed characteristically. And when the lecture is over, it will inevitably eventuate in some stroke of behavior, as I said on the previous occasion: you may be guided differently in some special emergency in the school-room by words which I now let fall.—So it is with the impressions you will make there on your pupil. You should get into the habit of regarding them all as leading to the acquisition by him of capacities for behavior—emotional, social, bodily, vocal, technical, or what not. And this being the case, you ought to feel willing, in a general way, and without hair-splitting or farther ado, to take up for the purposes of these lectures with the biological conception of the mind, as of something given us for practical use. That conception will certainly cover the greater part of your own educational work.

If we reflect upon the various ideals of education that are prevalent in the different countries, we see that what they all aim at is to organize capacities for conduct. This is most immediately obvious in Germany, where the explicitly avowed aim of the higher education is to turn the student into an instrument for advancing scientific discovery. The German universities are proud of the number of young specialists whom they turn out every year—not necessarily men of any original force of intellect, but men so trained to research that when their professor gives them an historical or philological thesis to prepare, or a bit of laboratory work to do, with a general indication as to the best method, they can go off by themselves and use apparatus and consult sources in such a way as to grind out in the requisite number of months some little pepper-corn of new truth worthy of being added to the store of extant human information on that subject. Little else is recognized in Germany as a man's title to academic advancement than his ability thus to show himself an efficient instrument of research.

In England, it might seem at first sight as if the higher education of the universities aimed at the production of certain static types of character rather than at the development of what one may call this dynamic scientific efficiency. Professor Jowett, when asked what Oxford could do for its students, is said to have replied, "Oxford can teach an English gentleman how to *be* an English gentleman." But if you ask what it means to 'be' an English gentleman, the only reply is in terms of conduct and behavior. An English gentleman is a bundle of specifically qualified reactions, a creature who for all the emergencies of life has his line of behavior distinctly marked out for him in advance. Here, as elsewhere, England expects every man to do his duty.

CHAPTER V

THE NECESSITY OF REACTIONS

If all this be true, then immediately one general aphorism emerges which ought by logical right to dominate the entire conduct of the teacher in the class-room.

No reception without reaction, no impression without correlative expression—this is the great maxim which the teacher ought never to forget.

An impression which simply flows in at the pupil's eyes or ears, and in no way modifies his active life, is an impression gone to waste. It is physiologically incomplete. It leaves no fruits behind it in the way of capacity acquired. Even as mere impression, it fails to produce its proper effect upon the memory; for, to remain fully amongst the acquisitions of this latter faculty, it must be wrought into the whole cycle of our operations. Its *motor consequences* are what clench it. Some effect due to it in the way of an activity must return to the mind in the form of the *sensation of having acted*, and connect itself with the impression. The most durable impressions are those on account of which we speak or act, or else are inwardly convulsed.

The older pædagogic method of learning things by rote, and reciting them parrot-like in the school-room, rested on the truth that a thing merely read or heard, and never verbally reproduced, contracts the weakest possible adhesion in the mind. Verbal recitation or reproduction is thus a highly important kind of reactive behavior on our impressions; and it is to be feared that, in the reaction against the old parrot-recitations as the beginning and end of instruction, the extreme value of verbal recitation as an element of complete training may nowadays be too much forgotten.

When we turn to modern pædagogics, we see how enormously the field of reactive conduct has been extended by the introduction of all those methods of concrete object teaching which are the glory of our contemporary schools. Verbal reactions, useful as they are, are insufficient. The pupil's words may be right, but the conceptions corresponding to them are often direfully wrong. In a modern school, therefore, they form only a small part of what the pupil is required to do. He must keep notebooks, make drawings, plans, and maps, take measurements, enter the laboratory and perform experiments, consult authorities, and write essays. He must do in his fashion what is often laughed at by outsiders when it appears in prospectuses under the title of 'original work,' but what is really the only possible training for the doing of original work thereafter. The most colossal improvement which recent years have seen in secondary education lies in the introduction of the manual-training schools; not because they will give us a people more handy and practical for domestic life and better skilled in trades, but because they will give us citizens with an entirely different intellectual fibre. Laboratory work and shop work engender a habit of observation, a knowledge of the difference between accuracy and vagueness, and an insight into nature's complexity and into the inadequacy of all abstract verbal accounts of real phenomena, which, once wrought into the mind, remain there as lifelong possessions. They confer precision; because if you are *doing* a thing, you must do it definitely right or definitely wrong. They give honesty; for when you express yourself by making things, and not by using words, it becomes impossible to dissimulate your vagueness or ignorance by ambiguity. They beget a habit of self-reliance; they keep the interest and attention always cheerfully engaged, and reduce the teacher's disciplinary functions to a minimum.

Of the various systems of manual training, so far as wood-work is concerned, the Swedish Sloyd system, if I may have an opinion on such matters, seems to me by far the best, psychologically considered. Manual-training methods, fortunately, are being slowly but surely introduced into all our large cities; but there is still an immense distance to traverse before they shall have gained the extension which they are destined ultimately to possess.

No impression without expression, then—that is the first pædagogic fruit of our evolutionary conception of the mind as something instrumental to adaptive behavior. But a word may be said in continuation. The expression itself comes back to us, as I intimated a moment ago, in the form of a still farther impression—the impression, namely, of what we have done. We thus receive sensible news of our behavior and its results. We hear the words we have spoken, feel our own blow as we give it, or read in the bystander's eyes the success or failure of our conduct. Now this return wave of impression pertains to the completeness of the whole experience, and a word about its importance in the school-room may not be out of place.

It would seem only natural to say that since after acting we normally get some return impression of result, it must be well to let the pupil get such a return impression in every possible case. Nevertheless, in schools where examination marks and 'standing' and other returns of result are concealed, the pupil is frustrated of this natural termination of the cycle of his activities, and often suffers from the sense of incompleteness and uncertainty; and there are persons who defend this system as encouraging the pupil to work for the work's sake, and not for extraneous reward. Of course, here as elsewhere, concrete experience must prevail over psychological deduction. But so far as our psychological deduction goes, it would suggest that the pupil's eagerness to know how well he does is in the line of his normal completeness of function, and should never be balked except for very definite reasons indeed.

Acquaint them, therefore, with their marks and standing and prospects, unless in the individual case you have some special practical reason for not so doing.

CHAPTER VI

WE ARE by this time fully launched upon the biological conception. Man is an organism for reacting on impressions; his mind is there to help determine his reactions, and the purpose of his education is to make them numerous and perfect. *Our education means, in short, little more than a mass of possibilities of reaction,* acquired at home, at school, or in the training of affairs. The teacher's task is that of supervising the acquiring process.

This being the case, I will immediately state a principle which underlies the whole process of acquisition and governs the entire activity of the teacher. It is this:

Every acquired reaction is, as a rule, either a complication grafted on a native reaction, or a substitute for a native reaction which the same object originally tended to provoke.

The teacher's art consists in bringing about the substitution or complication; and success in the art presupposes a sympathetic acquaintance with the reactive tendencies natively there.

Without an equipment of native reactions on the child's part, the teacher would have no hold whatever upon the child's attention or conduct. You may take a horse to the water, but you cannot make him drink; and so you may take a child to the school-room, but you cannot make him learn the new things you wish to impart, except by soliciting him in the first instance by something which natively makes him react. He must take the first step himself. He must *do* something before you can get your purchase on him. That something may be something good or something bad. A bad reaction is better than no reaction at all; for if bad, you can couple it with consequences which awake him to its badness. But imagine a child so lifeless as to react in *no* way to the teacher's first appeals, and how can you possibly take the first step in his education?

To make this abstract conception more concrete, assume the case of a young child's training in good manners. The child has a native tendency to snatch with his hands at anything that attracts his curiosity; also to draw back his hands when slapped, to cry under these latter conditions, to smile when gently spoken to, and to imitate one's gestures.

Suppose now you appear before the child with a new toy intended as a present for him. No sooner does he see the toy than he seeks to snatch it. You slap the hand; it is withdrawn, and the child cries. You then hold up the toy, smiling and saying, "Beg for it nicely—so!" The child stops crying, imitates you, receives the toy, and crows with pleasure; and that little cycle of training is complete. You have substituted the new reaction of 'begging' for the native reaction of snatching, when that kind of impression comes.

Now, if the child had no memory, the process would not be educative. No matter how often you came in with a toy, the same series of reactions would fatally occur, each called forth by its own impression: see, snatch; slap, cry; hear, ask; receive, smile. But with memory there, the child, at the very instant of snatching, recalls the rest of the earlier experience, thinks of the slap and the frustration, recollects the begging and the reward, inhibits the snatching impulse, substitutes the 'nice' reaction for it, and gets the toy immediately by eliminating all the intermediary steps. If a child's first snatching impulse be excessive or his memory poor, many repetitions of the discipline may be needed before the acquired reaction comes to be an ingrained habit; but in an eminently educable child a single experience will suffice.

One can easily represent the whole process by a brain-diagram. Such a diagram can be little more than a symbolic translation of the immediate experience into spatial terms; yet it may be useful, so I subjoin it.

Figure 1 shows the paths of the four successive reflexes executed by the lower or instinctive centres. The dotted lines that lead from them to the higher centres and connect the latter together, represent the processes of memory and association which the reactions impress upon the higher centres as they take place.

In Figure 2 we have the final result. The impression *see* awakens the chain of memories, and the only reactions that take place are the *beg* and *smile*. The thought of the *slap*, connected with the activity of Centre 2, inhibits the *snatch*, and

CENTRES OF MEMORY AND WILL.

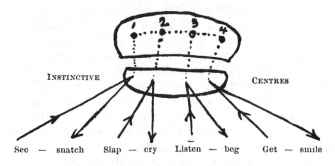

FIGURE 1. THE BRAIN-PROCESSES BEFORE EDUCATION.

CENTRES OF MEMORY AND WILL.

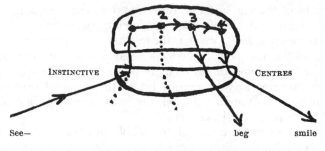

FIGURE 2. THE BRAIN-PROCESS AFTER EDUCATION.

makes it abortive, so it is represented only by a dotted line of discharge not reaching the terminus. Ditto of the *cry* reaction. These are, as it were, short-circuited by the current sweeping through the higher centres from *see* to *smile*. *Beg* and *smile*, thus substituted for the original reaction *snatch*, become at last the immediate responses when the child sees a snatchable object in someone's hands.

The first thing, then, for the teacher to understand is the

native reactive tendencies—the impulses and instincts of childhood—so as to be able to substitute one for another, and turn them on to artificial objects.

It is often said that man is distinguished from the lower animals by having a much smaller assortment of native instincts and impulses than they; but this is a great mistake. Man, of course, has not the marvellous egg-laying instincts which some articulates have; but if we compare him with the mammalia, we are forced to confess that he is appealed to by a much larger array of objects than any other mammal, that his reactions on these objects are characteristic and determinate in a very high degree. The monkeys, and especially the anthropoids, are the only beings that approach him in their analytic curiosity and width of imitativeness. His instinctive impulses, it is true, get overlaid by the secondary reactions due to his superior reasoning power; and thus man loses the *simply* instinctive demeanor. But the life of instinct is only disguised in him, not lost; and when the higher brain-functions are in abeyance, as happens in imbecility or dementia, his instincts sometimes show their presence in truly brutish ways.

I will therefore say a few words about those instinctive tendencies which are the most important from the teacher's point of view.

CHAPTER VII

WHAT THE NATIVE REACTIONS ARE

FIRST OF ALL, *Fear*. Fear of punishment has always been the great weapon of the teacher, and will always, of course, retain some place in the conditions of the school-room. The subject is so familiar that nothing more need be said about it.

The same is true of *Love*, and the instinctive desire to please those whom we love. The teacher who succeeds in getting herself loved by the pupils will obtain results which one of a more forbidding temperament finds it impossible to secure.

Next, a word might be said about *Curiosity*. This is perhaps a rather poor term by which to designate the *impulse towards better cognition* in its full extent; but you will readily understand what I mean. Novelties in the way of sensible objects, especially if their sensational quality is bright, vivid, startling, invariably arrest the attention of the young and hold it until the desire to know more about the object is assuaged. In its higher, more intellectual form, the impulse towards completer knowledge takes the character of scientific or philosophic curiosity. In both its sensational and its intellectual form the instinct is more vivacious during childhood and youth than in after life. Young children are possessed by curiosity about every new impression that assails them. It would be quite impossible for a young child to listen to a lecture for more than a few minutes, as you are now listening to me. The outside sights and sounds would inevitably carry his attention off. And for most people in middle life, the sort of intellectual effort required of the average schoolboy in mastering his greek or latin lesson, his algebra or physics, would be out of the question. The middle-aged citizen attends exclusively to the routine details of his business; and new truths, especially when they require involved trains of close reasoning, are no longer within the scope of his capacity.

The sensational curiosity of childhood is appealed to more particularly by certain determinate kinds of objects. Material things, things that move, living things, human actions and accounts of human action, will win the attention better than anything that is more abstract. Here again comes in the advantage of the object-teaching and manual-training methods. The pupil's attention is spontaneously held by any problem that involves the presentation of a new material object or of an activity on anyone's part. The teacher's earliest appeals, therefore, must be through objects shown or acts performed or described. Theoretic curiosity, curiosity about the rational relations between things, can hardly be said to awake at all until adolescence is reached. The sporadic metaphysical inquiries of children as to who made God, and why they have five fingers, need hardly be counted here. But when the theoretic instinct is once alive in the pupil, an entirely new order of pædagogic relations begins for him. Reasons, causes, abstract conceptions, suddenly grow full of zest, a fact with which all teachers are familiar. And both in its sensible and in its rational developments, disinterested curiosity may be successfully appealed to in the child with much more certainty than in the adult, in whom this intellectual instinct has grown so torpid as usually never to awake unless it enters into association with some selfish personal interest. Of this latter point I will say more anon.

Imitation. Man has always been recognized as the imitative animal *par excellence*; and there is hardly a book on psychology, however old, which has not devoted at least one paragraph to this fact. It is strange, however, that the full scope and pregnancy of the imitative impulse in man has had to wait till the last dozen years to become adequately recognized. M. Tarde led the way in his admirably original work, *Les Lois de l'imitation*; and in our own country Professors Royce and Baldwin have kept the ball rolling with all the energy that could be desired. Each of us is in fact what he is almost exclusively by virtue of his imitativeness. We become conscious of what we ourselves are by imitating others—the consciousness of what the others are precedes—the sense of self grows by the sense of pattern. The entire accumulated wealth of mankind—languages, arts, institutions, and sciences—is passed on from one generation to another by what Baldwin has called social heredity, each generation simply imitating the last. Into the particulars of this most fascinating chapter of psychology I have no time to go. The moment one hears Tarde's proposition uttered, however, one feels how supremely true it is. Invention, using the term most broadly, and imitation, are the two legs, so to call them, on which the human race historically has walked.

Imitation shades imperceptibly into *Emulation*. Emulation is the impulse to imitate what you see another doing, in order not to appear inferior; and it is hard to draw a sharp line between the manifestations of the two impulses, so inextricably do they mix their effects. Emulation is the very nerve of human society. Why are you, my hearers, sitting here before me? If no one whom you ever heard of had attended a 'summer school' or teachers' institute, would it have occurred to any one of you to break out independently and do a thing so unprescribed by fashion? Probably not. Nor would your pupils come to you unless the children of their parents' neighbors were all simultaneously being sent to school. We wish not to be lonely or eccentric, and we wish not to be cut off from our share in things which to our neighbors seem desirable privileges.

In the school-room, imitation and emulation play absolutely vital parts. Every teacher knows the advantage of having certain things performed by whole bands of children at a time. The teacher who meets with most success is the teacher whose own ways are the most imitable. A teacher should never try to make the pupils do a thing which she cannot do herself. "Come and let me show you how" is an incomparably better stimulus than "Go and do it as the book directs." Children admire a teacher who has skill. What he does seems easy, and they wish to emulate it. It is useless for a dull and devitalized teacher to exhort her pupils to wake up and take an interest. She must first take one herself; then her example is effective as no exhortation can possibly be.

Every school has its tone, moral and intellectual. And this tone is a mere tradition kept up by imitation, due in the first instance to the example set by teachers and by previous pupils of an aggressive and dominating type, copied by the others, and passed on from year to year, so that the new pupils take the cue almost immediately. Such a tone changes very slowly, if at all; and then always under the modifying influence of new personalities aggressive enough in character to set new patterns and not merely to copy the old. The classic example of this sort of tone is the often quoted case of Rugby under Dr. Arnold's administration. He impressed his own character as a model on the imagination of the oldest boys, who in turn were expected and required to impress theirs upon the younger set. The contagiousness of Arnold's genius was such that a Rugby man was said to be recognizable all through life by a peculiar turn of character which he acquired at school. It is obvious that psychology as such can give in this field no precepts of detail. As in so many other fields of teaching, success depends mainly on the native genius of the teacher, the sympathy, tact, and perception which enable him to seize the right moment and to set the right example.

Amongst the recent modern reforms of teaching methods, a certain disparagement of emulation, as a laudable spring of action in the school-room, has often made itself heard. More than a century ago, Rousseau, in his *Émile*, branded rivalry between one pupil and another as too base a passion to play a part in an ideal education. "Let Émile," he said, "never be led to compare himself to other children. No rivalries, not even in running, as soon as he begins to have the power of reason. It were a hundred times better that he should not learn at all what he could only learn through jealousy or vanity. But I would mark out every year the progress he may have made, and I would compare it with the progress of the following years. I would say to him: 'You are now grown so many inches taller; there is the ditch which you jumped over, there is the burden which you raised. There is the distance to which you could throw a pebble, there the distance you could run over without losing breath. See how much more you can do now!' Thus I should excite him without making him jealous of anyone. He would wish to surpass himself. I can see no inconvenience in this emulation with his former self."

Unquestionably, emulation with one's former self is a noble form of the passion of rivalry, and has a wide scope in the training of the young. But to veto and taboo all possible rivalry of one youth with another, because such rivalry may degenerate into greedy and selfish excess, does seem to savor somewhat of sentimentality, or even of fanaticism. The feeling of rivalry lies at the very basis of our being, all social improvement being largely due to it. There is a noble and generous kind of rivalry, as well as a spiteful and greedy kind; and the noble and generous form is particularly common in childhood. All games owe the zest which they bring with them to the fact that they are rooted in the emulous passion; yet they are the chief means of training in fairness and magnanimity. Can the teacher afford to throw such an ally away? Ought we seriously to hope that marks, distinctions, prizes, and other goals of effort, based on the pursuit of recognized superiority, should be forever banished from our schools? As a psychologist, obliged to notice the deep and pervasive character of the emulous passion, I must confess my doubts.

The wise teacher will use this instinct as he uses others, reaping its advantages, and appealing to it in such a way as to reap a maximum of benefit with a minimum of harm; for, after all, we must confess, with a French critic of Rousseau's doctrine, that the deepest spring of action in us is the sight of action in another. The spectacle of effort is what awakens and sustains our own effort. No runner running all alone on a race-track will find in his own will the power of stimulation which his rivalry with other runners incites, when he feels them at his heels about to pass. When a trotting horse is 'speeded,' a running horse must go beside him to keep him to the pace.

As imitation slides into emulation, so emulation slides into *Ambition*; and ambition connects itself closely with *Pugnacity* and *Pride*. Consequently, these five instinctive tendencies form an interconnected group of factors, hard to separate in the determination of a great deal of our conduct. The *Ambitious Impulses* would perhaps be the best name for the whole group.

Pride and pugnacity have often been considered unworthy passions to appeal to in the young; but in their more refined and noble forms they play a great part in the school-room and in education generally, being in some characters most potent spurs to effort. Pugnacity need not be thought of merely in the form of physical combativeness. It can be taken in the sense of a general unwillingness to be beaten by any kind of difficulty. It is what makes us feel 'stumped' and challenged by arduous achievements, and is essential to a spirited and enterprising character. We have of late been hearing much of the philosophy of tenderness in education; 'interest' must be assiduously awakened in everything, difficulties must be smoothed away. *Soft* pædagogics have taken the place of the old steep and rocky path to learning. But from this lukewarm air the bracing oxygen of effort is left out. It is nonsense to suppose that every step in education *can* be interesting. The fighting impulse must often be appealed to. Make the pupil feel ashamed of being scared at fractions, of being 'downed' by the law of falling bodies; rouse his pugnacity and pride, and he will rush at the difficult places with a sort of inner wrath at himself that is one of his best moral faculties. A victory scored under such conditions becomes a turning-point and crisis of his character. It represents the high-water mark of his powers, and serves thereafter as an ideal pattern for his self-imitation. The teacher who never rouses this sort of pugnacious excitement in his pupils falls short of one of his best forms of usefulness.

The next instinct which I shall mention is that of *Ownership*, also one of the radical endowments of the race. It often is the antagonist of imitation. Whether social progress is due more to the passion for keeping old things and habits or to the passion of imitating and acquiring new ones may in some cases be a difficult thing to decide. The sense of ownership begins in the second year of life; amongst the first words which an infant learns to utter are the words 'my' and 'mine,' and woe to the parents of twins who fail to provide their gifts in duplicate. The depth and primitiveness of this instinct would seem to cast a sort of psychological discredit in advance upon all radical forms of communistic utopia. Private proprietorship cannot be practically abolished until human nature is changed. It seems essential to mental health that the individual should have something beyond the bare clothes on his back to which he can assert exclusive possession, and which he may defend adversely against the world. Even those religious orders who make the most stringent vows of poverty have found it necessary to relax the rule a little in favor of the human heart made unhappy by reduction to too disinterested terms. The monk must have his books; the nun must have her little garden, and the images and pictures in her room.

In education, the instinct of ownership is fundamental, and can be appealed to in many ways. In the house, training in order and neatness begins with the arrangement of the child's own personal possessions. In the school, ownership is particularly important in connection with one of its special forms of activity, the collecting impulse. An object possibly not very interesting in itself, like a shell, a postage stamp, or a single map or drawing, will acquire an interest if it fills a gap in a collection or helps to complete a series. Much of the scholarly work of the world, so far as it is mere bibliography, memory, and erudition (and this lies at the basis of all our human scholarship), would seem to owe its interest rather to the way in which it gratifies the accumulating and collecting instinct than to any special appeal which it makes to our cravings after rationality. A man wishes a complete collection of information, wishes to know more about a subject than anybody else, much as another may wish to own more dollars or more early editions or more engravings before the letter than anybody else.

The teacher who can work this impulse into the school tasks is fortunate. Almost all children collect something. A tactful teacher may get them to take pleasure in collecting books; in keeping a neat and orderly collection of notes; in starting, when they are mature enough, a card catalogue; in preserving every drawing or map which they may make. Neatness, order, and method are thus instinctively gained, along with the other benefits which the possession of the collection entails. Even such a noisome thing as a collection of postage stamps may be used by the teacher as an inciter of interest in the geographical and historical information which she desires to impart. Sloyd successfully avails itself of this instinct in causing the pupil to make a collection of wooden implements fit for his own private use at home. Collecting is, of course, the basis of all natural history study; and probably nobody ever became a good naturalist who was not an unusually active collector when a boy.

Constructiveness is another great instinctive tendency with which the school-room has to contract an alliance. Up to the eighth or ninth year of childhood one may say that the child does hardly anything else than handle objects, explore things with his hands, doing and undoing, setting up and knocking down, putting together and pulling apart; for, from the psychological point of view, construction and destruction are two names for the same manual activity. Both signify the production of change, and the working of effects, in outward things. The result of all this is that intimate familiarity with the physical environment, that acquaintance with the properties of material things, which is really the foundation of human consciousness. To the very last, in most of us, the conceptions of objects and their properties are limited to the notion of what we can *do with them*. A 'stick' means something we can lean upon or strike with; 'fire,' something to cook, or warm ourselves, or burn things up withal; 'string,' something with which to tie things together. For most people these objects have no other meaning. In geometry, the cylinder, circle, sphere, are defined as what you get by going through certain processes of construction, revolving a parallelogram upon one of its sides, etc. The more different kinds of things a child thus gets to know by treating and handling them, the more confident grows his sense of kinship with the world in which he lives. An unsympathetic adult will wonder at the fascinated hours which a child will spend in putting his blocks together and rearranging them. But the wise education takes the tide at the flood, and from the kindergarten upward devotes the first years of education to training in construction and to object-teaching. I need not recapitulate here what I said awhile back about the superiority of the objective and experimental methods. They occupy the pupil in a way most congruous with the spontaneous interests of his age. They absorb him, and leave impressions durable and profound. Compared with the youth taught by these methods, one brought up exclusively by books carries through life a certain remoteness from reality; he stands, as it were, out of the pale, and feels that he stands so; and often suffers a kind of melancholy from which he might have been rescued by a more real education.

There are other impulses, such as love of approbation or vanity, shyness and secretiveness, of which a word might be said; but they are too familiar to need it. You can easily pursue the subject by your own reflection. There is one general law, however, that relates to many of our instinctive tendencies, and that has no little importance in education; and I must refer to it briefly before I leave the subject. It has been called the law of transitoriness in instincts. Many of our impulsive tendencies ripen at a certain period; and if the appropriate objects be then and there provided, habits of conduct towards them are acquired which last. But if the objects be not forthcoming then, the impulse may die out before a habit is formed; and later it may be hard to teach the creature to react appropriately in those directions. The sucking instincts in mammals, the following instinct in certain birds and quadrupeds, are examples of this; they fade away shortly after birth.

In children we observe a ripening of impulses and interests in a certain determinate order. Creeping, walking, climbing, imitating vocal sounds, constructing, drawing, calculating, possess the child in succession; and in some children the possession, while it lasts, may be of a semi-frantic and exclusive sort. Later, the interest in any one of these things may wholly fade away. Of course, the proper pædagogic moment to work skill in, and to clench the useful habit, is when the native impulse is most acutely present. Crowd on the athletic opportunities, the mental arithmetic, the verse-learning, the drawing, the botany, or what not, the moment you have reason to think the hour is ripe. The hour may not last long; and whilst it continues you may safely let all the child's other occupations take a second place. In this way you economize time and deepen skill; for many an infant prodigy, artistic or mathematical, has a flowering epoch of but a few months.

One can draw no specific rules for all this. It depends on close observation in the particular case, and parents here have a great advantage over teachers. In fact, the law of transitoriness has little chance of individualized application in the schools.

Such is the little interested and impulsive psychophysical organism whose springs of action the teacher must divine, and to whose ways he must become accustomed. He must start with the native tendencies, and enlarge the pupil's entire passive and active experience. He must ply him with new objects and stimuli, and make him taste the fruits of his behavior, so that now that whole context of remembered experience is what shall determine his conduct when he gets the stimulus, and not the bare immediate impression. As the pupil's life thus enlarges, it gets fuller and fuller of all sorts of memories and associations and substitutions; but the eye accustomed to psychological analysis will discern, underneath it all, the outlines of our simple psychophysical scheme.

Respect then, I beg you, always the original reactions, even when you are seeking to overcome their connection with certain objects, and to supplant them with others that you wish to make the rule. Bad behavior, from the point of view of the teacher's art, is as good a starting-point as good behavior; in fact, paradoxical as it may sound to say so, it is often a better starting-point than good behavior would be.

The acquired reactions must be made habitual whenever they are appropriate. Therefore Habit is the next subject to which your attention is invited.

CHAPTER VIII

THE LAWS OF HABIT

IT IS VERY IMPORTANT that teachers should realize the importance of habit, and psychology helps us greatly at this point. We speak, it is true, of good habits and of bad habits; but when people use the word 'habit,' in the majority of instances it is a bad habit which they have in mind. They talk of the smoking-habit and the swearing-habit and the drinking-habit, but not of the abstention-habit or the moderation-habit or the courage-habit. But the fact is that our virtues are habits as much as our vices. All our life, so far as it has definite form, is but a mass of habits—practical, emotional, and intellectual—systematically organized for our weal or woe, and bearing us irresistibly towards our destiny, whatever the latter may be.

Since pupils can understand this at a comparatively early age, and since to understand it contributes in no small measure to their feeling of responsibility, it would be well if the teacher were able himself to talk to them of the philosophy of habit in some such abstract terms as I am now about to talk of it to you.

I believe that we are subject to the law of habit in consequence of the fact that we have bodies. The plasticity of the living matter of our nervous system, in short, is the reason why we do a thing with difficulty the first time, but soon do it more and more easily, and finally, with sufficient practice, do it semi-mechanically, or with hardly any consciousness at all. Our nervous systems have (in Dr. Carpenter's words) *grown* to the way in which they have been exercised, just as a sheet of paper or a coat, once creased or folded, tends to fall forever afterwards into the same identical folds.

Habit is thus a second nature, or rather, as the Duke of Wellington said, it is 'ten times nature'—at any rate as regards its importance in adult life; for the acquired habits of our training have by that time inhibited or strangled most of the natural impulsive tendencies which were originally there.

Ninety-nine hundredths or, possibly, nine hundred and ninety-nine thousandths of our activity is purely automatic and habitual, from our rising in the morning to our lying down each night. Our dressing and undressing, our eating and drinking, our greetings and partings, our hat-raisings and giving way for ladies to precede, nay, even most of the forms of our common speech, are things of a type so fixed by repetition as almost to be classed as reflex actions. To each sort of impression we have an automatic, ready-made response. My very words to you now are an example of what I mean; for having already lectured upon habit and printed a chapter about it in a book, and read the latter when in print, I find my tongue inevitably falling into its old phrases and repeating almost literally what I said before.

So far as we are thus mere bundles of habit, we are stereotyped creatures, imitators and copiers of our past selves. And since this, under any circumstances, is what we always tend to become, it follows first of all that the teacher's prime concern should be to ingrain into the pupil that assortment of habits that shall be most useful to him throughout life. Education is for behavior, and habits are the stuff of which behavior consists.

To quote my earlier book directly, the great thing in all education is to *make our nervous system our ally instead of our enemy*. It is to fund and capitalize our acquisitions, and live at ease upon the interest of the fund. *For this we must make automatic and habitual, as early as possible, as many useful actions as we can*, and as carefully guard against the growing into ways that are likely to be disadvantageous. The more of the details of our daily life we can hand over to the effortless custody of automatism, the more our higher powers of mind will be set free for their own proper work. There is no more miserable human being than one in whom nothing is habitual but indecision, and for whom the lighting of every cigar, the drinking of every cup, the time of rising and going to bed every day, and the beginning of every bit of work are subjects of express volitional deliberation. Full half the time of such a man goes to the deciding or regretting of matters which ought to be so ingrained in him as practically not to exist for his consciousness at all. If there be such daily duties not yet ingrained in any one of my hearers, let him begin this very hour to set the matter right.

In Professor Bain's chapter on "The Moral Habits" there are some admirable practical remarks laid down. Two great maxims emerge from the treatment. The first is that in the acquisition of a new habit, or the leaving off of an old one, we must take care to *launch ourselves with as strong and decided an initiative as possible*. Accumulate all the possible circumstances which shall reinforce the right motives; put yourself assiduously in conditions that encourage the new way; make engagements incompatible with the old; take a public pledge, if the case allows; in short, envelope your resolution with every aid you know. This will give your new beginning such a momentum that the temptation to break down will not occur as soon as it otherwise might; and every day during which a breakdown is postponed adds to the chances of its not occurring at all.

I remember long ago reading in an Austrian paper the advertisement of a certain Rudolph Somebody, who promised fifty gulden reward to anyone who after that date should find him at the wine-shop of Ambrosius So-and-so. "This I do," the advertisement continued, "in consequence of a promise which I have made my wife." With such a wife, and such an understanding of the way in which to start new habits, it would be safe to stake one's money on Rudolph's ultimate success.

The second maxim is, *Never suffer an exception to occur till the new habit is securely rooted in your life*. Each lapse is like the letting fall of a ball of string which one is carefully winding up; a single slip undoes more than a great many turns will wind again. Continuity of training is the great means of making the nervous system act infallibly right. As Professor Bain says:

"The peculiarity of the moral habits, contra-distinguishing them from the intellectual acquisitions, is the presence of two hostile powers, one to be gradually raised into the ascendant over the other. It is necessary, above all things, in such a situation, never to lose a battle. Every gain on the wrong side undoes the effect of many conquests on the right. The essential precaution, therefore, is, so to regulate the two opposing powers that the one may have a series of uninterrupted successes, until repetition has fortified it to such a degree as to enable it to cope with the opposition, under any circumstances. This is the theoretically best career of mental progress."

A third maxim may be added to the preceding pair: *Seize the very first possible opportunity to act on every resolution you make, and on every emotional prompting you may experience in the direction of the habits you aspire to gain*. It is not in the moment of their forming, but in the moment of their producing motor effects, that resolves and aspirations communicate the new 'set' to the brain.

No matter how full a reservoir of maxims one may possess, and no matter how good one's sentiments may be, if one have not taken advantage of every concrete opportunity to act, one's character may remain entirely unaffected for the better. With good intentions, hell proverbially is paved. This is an obvious consequence of the principles I have laid down. A "character," as J. S. Mill says, "is a completely fashioned will"; and a will, in the sense in which he means it, is an aggregate of tendencies to act in a firm and prompt and definite way upon all the principal emergencies of life. A tendency to act only becomes effectively ingrained in us in proportion to the uninterrupted frequency with which the actions actually occur, and the brain 'grows' to their use. When a resolve or a fine glow of feeling is allowed to evaporate without bearing practical fruit, it is worse than a chance lost; it works so as positively to hinder future resolutions and emotions from taking the normal path of discharge. There is no more contemptible type of human character than that of the nerveless sentimentalist and dreamer, who spends his life in a weltering sea of sensibility, but never does a concrete manly deed.

This leads to a fourth maxim. *Don't preach too much to your pupils or abound in good talk in the abstract*. Lie in wait rather for the practical opportunities, be prompt to seize those as they pass, and thus at one operation get your pupils both to think, to feel, and to do. The strokes of *behavior* are what give the new set to the character, and work the good habits into its organic tissue. Preaching and talking too soon become an ineffectual bore.

There is a passage in Darwin's short autobiography which has been often quoted, and which, for the sake of its bearing on our subject of habit, I must now quote again. Darwin says: "Up to the age of thirty, or beyond it, poetry of many kinds . . . gave me great pleasure, and even as a schoolboy I took intense delight in Shakespeare, especially in the historical plays. I have also said that formerly pictures gave me considerable, and music very great delight. But now for many years I cannot endure to read a line of poetry: I have tried lately to read Shakespeare, and found it so intolerably dull that it nauseated me. I have also almost lost my taste for pictures or music. . . . My mind seems to have become a kind of machine for grinding general laws out of large collections of facts, but why this should have caused the atrophy of that part of the brain alone, on which the higher tastes depend, I cannot conceive. . . . If I had to live my life again, I would have made a rule to read some poetry and listen to some music at least once every week; for perhaps the parts of my brain now atrophied would thus have been kept active through use. The loss of these tastes is a loss of happiness, and may possibly be injurious to the intellect, and more probably to the moral character, by enfeebling the emotional part of our nature."

We all intend when young to be all that may become a man, before the destroyer cuts us down. We wish and expect to enjoy poetry always, to grow more and more intelligent about pictures and music, to keep in touch with spiritual and religious ideas, and even not to let the greater philosophic thoughts of our time develop quite beyond our view. We mean all this in youth, I say; and yet in how many middle-aged men and women is such an honest and sanguine expectation fulfilled? Surely, in comparatively few; and the laws of habit show us why. Some interest in each of these things arises in everybody at the proper age; but if not persistently fed with the appropriate matter, instead of growing into a powerful and necessary habit, it atrophies and dies, choked by the rival interests to which the daily food is given. We make ourselves into Darwins in this negative respect by persistently ignoring the essential practical conditions of our case. We say abstractly: "I mean to enjoy poetry, and to absorb a lot of it, of course. I fully intend to keep up my love of music, to read the books that shall give new turns to the thought of my time, to keep my higher spiritual side alive, etc." But we do not attack these things concretely, and we do not begin *to-day*. We forget that every good that is worth possessing must be paid for in strokes of daily effort. We postpone and postpone, until those smiling possibilities are dead. Whereas ten minutes a day of poetry, of spiritual reading or meditation, and an hour or two a week at music, pictures, or philosophy, provided we began *now* and suffered no remission, would infallibly give us in due time the fulness of all we desire. By neglecting the necessary concrete labor, by sparing ourselves the little daily tax, we are positively digging the graves of our higher possibilities. This is a point concerning which you teachers might well give a little timely information to your older and more aspiring pupils.

According as a function receives daily exercise or not, the man becomes a different kind of being in later life. We have lately had a number of accomplished Hindoo visitors at Cambridge, who talked freely of life and philosophy. More than one of them has confided to me that the sight of our faces, all contracted as they are with the habitual American over-intensity and anxiety of expression, and our ungraceful and distorted attitudes when sitting, made on him a very painful impression. "I do not see," said one, "how it is possible for you to live as you do, without a single minute in your day deliberately given to tranquillity and meditation. It is an invariable part of our Hindoo life to retire for at least half an hour daily into silence, to relax our muscles, govern our breathing, and meditate on eternal things. Every Hindoo child is trained to this from a very early age." The good fruits of such a discipline were obvious in the physical repose and lack of tension, and the wonderful smoothness and calmness of facial expression, and imperturbability of manner of these Orientals. I felt that my countrymen were depriving themselves of an essential grace of character. How many American children ever hear it said, by parent or teacher, that they should moderate their piercing voices, that they should relax their unused muscles, and as far as possible, when sitting, sit quite still? Not one in a thousand, not one in five thousand! Yet, from its reflex influence on the inner mental states, this ceaseless over-tension, over-motion, and over-expression are working on us grievous national harm.

I beg you teachers to think a little seriously of this matter. Perhaps you can help our rising generation of Americans towards the beginning of a better set of personal ideals.[1]

To go back now to our general maxims, I may at last, as a fifth and final practical maxim about habits, offer something like this: *Keep the faculty of effort alive in you by a little gratuitous exercise every day*. That is, be systematically heroic in little unnecessary points, do every day or two something for no other reason than its difficulty, so that, when the hour of dire need draws nigh, it may find you not unnerved and untrained to stand the test. Asceticism of this sort is like the insurance which a man pays on his house and goods. The tax does him no good at the time, and possibly may never bring him a return. But if the fire *does* come, his having paid it will be his salvation from ruin. So with the man who has daily inured himself to habits of concentrated attention, energetic volition, and self-denial in unnecessary things. He will stand like a tower when everything rocks around him, and his softer fellow-mortals are winnowed like chaff in the blast.

I have been accused, when talking of the subject of habit, of making old habits appear so strong that the acquiring of new ones, and particularly anything like a sudden reform or conversion, would be made impossible by my doctrine. Of course, this would suffice to condemn the latter; for sudden conversions, however infrequent they may be, unquestionably do occur. But there is no incompatibility between the general laws I have laid down and the most startling sudden alterations in the way of character. New habits *can* be launched, I have expressly said, on condition of there being new stimuli

[1] See the Address on the Gospel of Relaxation, later in this volume.

and new excitements. Now life abounds in these, and sometimes they are such critical and revolutionary experiences that
they change a man's whole scale of values and system of ideas.
In such cases, the old order of his habits will be ruptured; and
if the new motives are lasting, new habits will be formed, and
build up in him a new or regenerate 'nature.'

All this kind of fact I fully allow. But the general laws of
habit are no wise altered thereby, and the physiological study
of mental conditions still remains on the whole the most
powerful ally of hortatory ethics. The hell to be endured hereafter, of which theology tells, is no worse than the hell we
make for ourselves in this world by habitually fashioning our
characters in the wrong way. Could the young but realize
how soon they will become mere walking bundles of habits,
they would give more heed to their conduct while in the plastic state. We are spinning our own fates, good or evil, and
never to be undone. Every smallest stroke of virtue or of vice
leaves its never-so-little scar. The drunken Rip Van Winkle, in
Jefferson's play, excuses himself for every fresh dereliction by
saying, "I won't count this time!" Well, he may not count it,
and a kind Heaven may not count it; but it is being counted
none the less. Down amongst his nerve-cells and fibres the
molecules are counting it, registering and storing it up to be
used against him when the next temptation comes. Nothing
we ever do is, in strict scientific literalness, wiped out.

Of course, this has its good side as well as its bad one. As
we become permanent drunkards by so many separate drinks,
so we become saints in the moral, and authorities and experts
in the practical and scientific spheres, by so many separate acts
and hours of work. Let no youth have any anxiety about the
upshot of his education, whatever the line of it may be. If he
keep faithfully busy each hour of the working day, he may
safely leave the final result to itself. He can with perfect certainty count on waking up some fine morning to find himself
one of the competent ones of his generation, in whatever pursuit he may have singled out. Silently, between all the details
of his business, the *power of judging* in all that class of matter
will have built itself up within him as a possession that will
never pass away. Young people should know this truth in

advance. The ignorance of it has probably engendered more discouragement and faint-heartedness in youths embarking on arduous careers than all other causes put together.

CHAPTER IX

THE ASSOCIATION OF IDEAS

IN MY LAST TALK, in treating of Habit, I chiefly had in mind our *motor* habits—habits of external conduct. But our thinking and feeling processes are also largely subject to the law of habit, and one result of this is a phenomenon which you all know under the name of 'the association of ideas.' To that phenomenon I ask you now to turn.

You remember that consciousness is an ever-flowing stream of objects, feelings, and impulsive tendencies. We saw already that its phases or pulses are like so many fields or waves, each field or wave having usually its central point of liveliest attention, in the shape of the most prominent object in our thought, whilst all around this lies a margin of other objects more dimly realized, together with the margin of emotional and active tendencies which the whole entails. Describing the mind thus in fluid terms, we cling as close as possible to nature. At first sight, it might seem as if, in the fluidity of these successive waves, everything is indeterminate. But inspection shows that each wave has a constitution which can be to some degree explained by the constitution of the waves just passed away. And this relation of the wave to its predecessors is expressed by the two fundamental 'laws of association,' so called, of which the first is named the Law of Contiguity, the second that of Similarity.

The *Law of Contiguity* tells us that objects thought of in the coming wave are such as in some previous experience were *next* to the objects represented in the wave that is passing away. The vanishing objects were once formerly their neighbors in the mind. When you recite the alphabet or your prayers, or when the sight of an object reminds you of its name, or the name reminds you of the object, it is through the law of contiguity that the terms are suggested to the mind.

The *Law of Similarity* says that, when contiguity fails to describe what happens, the coming objects will prove to *resemble* the going objects, even though the two were never experienced together before. In our 'flights of fancy,' this is frequently the case.

If, arresting ourselves in the flow of reverie, we ask the question, "How came we to be thinking of just this object now?" we can almost always trace its presence to some previous object which has introduced it to the mind, according to one or the other of these laws. The entire routine of our memorized acquisitions, for example, is a consequence of nothing but the Law of Contiguity. The words of a poem, the formulas of trigonometry, the facts of history, the properties of material things, are all known to us as definite systems or groups of objects which cohere in an order fixed by innumerable iterations, and of which any one part reminds us of the others. In dry and prosaic minds, almost all the mental sequences flow along these lines of habitual routine repetition and suggestion.

In witty, imaginative minds, on the other hand, the routine is broken through with ease at any moment; and one field of mental objects will suggest another with which perhaps in the whole history of human thinking it had never once before been coupled. The link here is usually some *analogy* between the objects successively thought of—an analogy often so subtle that, although we feel it, we can with difficulty analyze its ground; as where, for example, we find something masculine in the colour red and something feminine in the colour pale blue, or where, of three human beings' characters, one will remind us of a cat, another of a dog, the third perhaps of a cow.

Psychologists have of course gone very deeply into the question of what the causes of association may be; and some of them have tried to show that contiguity and similarity are not two radically diverse laws, but that either presupposes the presence of the other. I myself am disposed to think that the phenomena of association depend on our cerebral constitution, and are not immediate consequences of our being rational beings. In other words, when we shall have become disembodied spirits, it may be that our trains of consciousness will follow different laws. These questions are discussed in the books on psychology, and I hope that some of you will be interested in following them there. But I will, on the present occasion, ignore them entirely; for, as teachers, it is the *fact* of association that practically concerns you, let its grounds be spiritual or cerebral or what they may, and let its laws be reducible, or non-reducible, to one. Your pupils, whatever else they are, are at any rate little pieces of associating machinery. Their education consists in the organizing within them of determinate tendencies to associate one thing with another— impressions with consequences, these with reactions, those with results, and so on indefinitely. The more copious the associative systems, the completer the individual's adaptations to the world.

The teacher can formulate his function to himself therefore in terms of 'association' as well as in terms of 'native and acquired reaction.' It is mainly that of *building up useful systems of association* in the pupil's mind. This description sounds wider than the one I began by giving. But when one thinks that our trains of association, whatever they may be, normally issue in acquired reactions or behavior, one sees that in a general way the same mass of facts is covered by both formulas.

It is astonishing how many mental operations we can explain when we have once grasped the principles of association. The great problem which association undertakes to solve is, *Why does just this particular field of consciousness, constituted in this particular way, now appear before my mind?* It may be a field of objects imagined; it may be of objects remembered or of objects perceived; it may include an action resolved on. In either case, when the field is analyzed into its parts, those parts can be shown to have proceeded from parts of fields previously before consciousness, in consequence of one or other of the laws of association just laid down. Those laws *run* the mind; interest, shifting hither and thither, deflects it; and attention, as we shall later see, steers it and keeps it from too zigzag a course.

To grasp these factors clearly gives one a solid and simple understanding of the psychological machinery. The 'nature,' the 'character,' of an individual means really nothing but the habitual form of his associations. To break up bad associations or wrong ones, to build others in, to guide the associative tendencies into the most fruitful channels, is the educator's principal task. But here, as with all other simple principles, the difficulty lies in the application. Psychology can state the laws; concrete tact and talent alone can work them to useful results.

Meanwhile it is a matter of the commonest experience that our minds may pass from one object to another by various intermediary fields of consciousness. The indeterminateness of our paths of association *in concreto* is thus almost as striking a feature of them as the uniformity of their abstract form. Start from any idea whatever, and the entire range of your ideas is potentially at your disposal. If we take as the associative starting-point, or cue, some simple word which I pronounce before you, there is no limit to the possible diversity of suggestions which it may set up in your minds. Suppose I say 'blue,' for example: some of you may think of the blue sky and hot weather from which we now are suffering, then go off on thoughts of summer clothing, or possibly of meteorology at large; others may think of the spectrum and the physiology of colour-vision, and glide into X-rays and recent physical speculations; others may think of blue ribbons, or of the blue flowers on a friend's hat, and proceed on lines of personal reminiscence. To others, again, etymology and linguistic thoughts may be suggested; or blue may be 'apperceived' as a synonym for melancholy, and a train of associates connected with morbid psychology may proceed to unroll themselves.

In the same person, the same word heard at different times will provoke, in consequence of the varying marginal preoccupations, either one of a number of diverse possible associative sequences. Professor Münsterberg performed this experiment methodically, using the same words four times over, at three-month intervals, as 'cues' for four different persons who were the subjects of observation. He found almost no constancy in their associations taken at these different times. In short, the entire potential content of one's consciousness is accessible from any one of its points. This is why we can never work the laws of association forward; starting from the present field as a cue, we can never cipher out in advance just what the person will be thinking of five minutes later. The elements which may become prepotent in the process, the parts of each successive field round which the associations shall chiefly turn, the possible bifurcations of suggestion are so numerous and ambiguous as to be indeterminable before the fact. But although we cannot work the laws of association forward, we can always work them backward. We cannot say now what we shall find ourselves thinking of five minutes hence; but whatever it may be, we shall then be able to trace it through intermediary links of contiguity or similarity to what we are thinking now. What so baffles our prevision is the shifting part played by the margin and focus—in fact, by each element by itself of the margin or focus—in calling up the next ideas.

For example, I am reciting "Locksley Hall," in order to divert my mind from a state of suspense that I am in concerning the will of a relative that is dead. The will still remains in the mental background as an extremely marginal or ultra-marginal portion of my field of consciousness; but the poem fairly keeps my attention from it, until I come to the line, "I the heir of all the ages, in the foremost files of time." The words 'I the heir,' immediately make an electric connection with the marginal thought of the will; that, in turn, makes my heart beat with anticipation of my possible legacy, so that I throw down the book and pace the floor excitedly with visions of my future fortune pouring through my mind. Any portion of the field of consciousness that has more potentialities of emotional excitement than another may thus be roused to predominant activity; and the shifting play of interest now in one portion, now in another, deflects the currents in all sorts of zigzag ways, the mental activity running hither and thither as the sparks run in burnt-up paper.

One more point, and I shall have said as much to you as seems necessary about the process of association.

You just saw how a single exciting word may call up its own associates prepotently, and deflect our whole train of thinking from the previous track. The fact is that every portion of the field *tends* to call up its own associates; but if these associates be severally different, there is rivalry, and as soon as one or a few begin to be effective the others seem to get siphoned out, as it were, and left behind. Seldom, however, as in our example, does the process seem to turn round a single item in the mental field, or even round the entire field that is immediately in the act of passing. It is a matter of *constellation*, into which portions of fields that are already past especially seem to enter and have their say. Thus, to go back to "Locksley Hall," each word as I recite it in its due order is suggested not solely by the previous word now expiring on my lips, but it is rather the effect of all the previous words, taken together, of the verse. "Ages," for example, calls up "in the foremost files of time," when preceded by "I the heir of all the"—; but when preceded by "yet I doubt not through the"—it calls up "one increasing purpose runs." Similarly, if I write on the blackboard the letters A B C D E F, . . . they probably suggest to you G H I . . . . But if I write A B A D D E F, if they suggest anything, they suggest as their complement E C T or E F I C I E N C Y. The result depending on the total constellation, even though most of the single items be the same.

My practical reason for mentioning this law is this, that it follows from it that, in working associations into your pupils' minds, you must not rely on single cues, but multiply the cues as much as possible. Couple the desired reaction with numerous constellations of antecedents—don't always ask the question, for example, in the same way; don't use the same kind of data in numerical problems; vary your illustrations, etc., as much as you can. When we come to the subject of memory, we shall learn still more about this.

So much, then, for the general subject of association. In leaving it for other topics (in which, however, we shall abundantly find it involved again), I cannot too strongly urge you to acquire a habit of thinking of your pupils in associative terms. All governors of mankind, from doctors and jail-wardens to demagogues and statesmen, instinctively come so to conceive their charges. If you do the same, thinking of them (however else you may think of them besides) as so many little systems of associating machinery, you will be astonished at the intimacy of insight into their operations and at the practicality of the results which you will gain. We think of our acquaintances, for example, as characterized by certain 'tendencies.' These tendencies will in almost every instance prove to be tendencies to association. Certain ideas in them are always followed by certain other ideas, these by certain feelings and impulses to approve or disapprove, assent or decline. If the topic arouse one of those first ideas, the practical outcome can be pretty well foreseen. 'Types of character' in short are largely types of association.

CHAPTER X

INTEREST

AT OUR LAST MEETING I treated of the native tendencies of the pupil to react in characteristically definite ways upon different stimuli or exciting circumstances; in fact, I treated of the pupil's instincts. Now some situations appeal to special instincts from the very outset, and others fail to do so until the proper connections have been organized in the course of the person's training. We say of the former set of objects or situations that they are *interesting* in themselves and originally; of the latter we say that they are natively uninteresting, and that interest in them has first to be acquired.

No topic has received more attention from pædagogical writers than that of interest. It is the natural sequel to the instincts we so lately discussed, and it is therefore well fitted to be the next subject which we take up.

Since some objects are natively interesting and in others interest is artificially acquired, the teacher must know which the natively interesting ones are; for, as we shall see immediately, other objects can artificially acquire an interest only through first becoming associated with some of these natively interesting things.

The native interests of children lie altogether in the sphere of sensation. Novel things to look at or novel sounds to hear, especially when they involve the spectacle of action of a violent sort, will always divert the attention from abstract conceptions of objects verbally taken in. The grimace that Johnny is making, the spitballs that Tommy is ready to throw, the dog-fight in the street, or the distant firebells ringing—these are the rivals with which the teacher's powers of being interesting have incessantly to cope. The child will always attend more to what a teacher does than to what the same teacher says: during the performance of experiments or whilst the teacher is drawing on the blackboard, the children are tranquil and absorbed. I have seen a roomful of college students suddenly become perfectly still, to look at their professor of physics tie a piece of string around a stick which he was going to use in an experiment, but immediately grow restless when he began to explain the experiment. A lady told me that one day, during a lesson, she was delighted at having captured so completely the attention of one of her young charges. He did not remove his eyes from her face; but he said to her after the lesson was over, "I looked at you all the time, and your upper jaw did not move once!" That was the only fact that he had taken in.

Living things, then, moving things, or things that savor of danger or of blood, that have a dramatic quality—these are the objects natively interesting to childhood, to the exclusion of almost everything else; and the teacher of young children, until more artificial interests have grown up, will keep in touch with her pupils by constant appeal to such matters as these. Instruction must be carried on objectively, experimentally, anecdotally. The blackboard-drawing and story-telling must constantly come in. But of course these methods cover only the first steps, and carry one but a little way.

Can we now formulate any general principle by which the later and more artificial interests connect themselves with these early ones that the child brings with him to the school?

Fortunately, we can; there is a very simple law that relates the acquired and the native interests with each other.

Any object not interesting in itself may become interesting through becoming associated with an object in which an interest already exists. The two associated objects grow, as it were, together; the interesting portion sheds its quality over the whole; and thus things not interesting in their own right borrow an interest which becomes as real and as strong as that of any natively interesting thing. The odd circumstance is that the borrowing does not impoverish the source, the objects taken together being more interesting, perhaps, than the originally interesting portion was by itself.

This is one of the most striking proofs of the range of application of the principle of association of ideas in psychology. An idea will infect another with its own emotional interest when they have become both associated together into any sort of a mental total. As there is no limit to the various associations into which an interesting idea may enter, one sees in how many ways an interest may be derived.

You will understand this abstract statement easily if I take the most frequent of concrete examples—the interest which things borrow from their connection with our own personal welfare. The most natively interesting object to a man is his own personal self and its fortunes. We accordingly see that the moment a thing becomes connected with the fortunes of the self, it forthwith becomes an interesting thing. Lend the child his books, pencils, and other apparatus; then give them to him, make them his own, and notice the new light with which they instantly shine in his eyes. He takes a new kind of care of them altogether. In mature life, all the drudgery of a man's business or profession, intolerable in itself, is shot through with engrossing significance because he knows it to be associated with his personal fortunes. What more deadly uninteresting object can there be than a railroad time-table? Yet where will you find a more interesting object if you are going on a journey, and by its means can find your train? At such times the time-table will absorb a man's entire attention, its interest being borrowed solely from its relation to his personal life. *From all these facts there emerges a very simple abstract programme for the teacher to follow in keeping the attention of the child: Begin with the line of his native interests, and offer him objects that have some immediate connection with these.* The kindergarten methods, the object-teaching routine, the blackboard and manual-training work—all recognize this feature. Schools in which these methods preponderate are schools where discipline is easy, and where the voice of the master claiming order and attention in threatening tones need never be heard.

Next, step by step, connect with these first objects and experiences the later objects and ideas which you wish to instill. Associate the new with the old in some natural and telling way, so that the interest, being shed along from point to point, finally suffuses the entire system of objects of thought.

This is the abstract statement; and, abstractly, nothing can be easier to understand. It is in the fulfilment of the rule that the difficulty lies; for the difference between an interesting and a tedious teacher consists in little more than the inventiveness by which the one is able to mediate these associations and connections, and in the dulness in discovering such transitions which the other shows. One teacher's mind will fairly coruscate with points of connection between the new lesson and the circumstances of the children's other experience. Anecdotes and reminiscences will abound in her talk; and the shuttle of interest will shoot backward and forward, weaving the new and the old together in a lively and entertaining way. Another teacher has no such inventive fertility, and his lesson will always be a dead and heavy thing. This is the psychological meaning of the Herbartian principle of 'preparation' for each lesson, and of correlating the new with the old. It is the psychological meaning of that whole method of concentration in studies of which you have been recently hearing so much. When the geography and English and history and arithmetic simultaneously make cross-references to one another, you get an interesting set of processes all along the line.

If, then, you wish to insure the interest of your pupils, there is only one way to do it; and that is to make certain that they have something in their minds *to attend with*, when you begin to talk. That something can consist in nothing but a previous lot of ideas already interesting in themselves, and of such a nature that the incoming novel objects which you present can dovetail into them and form with them some kind of a logically associated or systematic whole. Fortunately, almost any kind of a connection is sufficient to carry the interest along. What a help is our Philippine war at present in teaching geography! But before the war you could ask the children if they ate pepper with their eggs, and where they supposed the pepper came from. Or ask them if glass is a stone, and if not, why not; and then let them know how stones are formed and glass manufactured. External links will serve as well as those that are deeper and more logical. But interest once shed upon a subject is liable to remain always with that subject. Our acquisitions become in a measure portions of our personal self; and little by little, as cross-associations multiply and habits of familiarity and practice grow, the entire system of our objects of thought consolidates, most of it becoming interesting for some purposes and in some degree.

An adult man's interests are almost every one of them intensely artificial; they have slowly been built up. The objects of professional interest are most of them, in their original nature, repulsive; but by their connection with such natively exciting objects as one's personal fortune, one's social responsibilities, and especially by the force of inveterate habit, they grow to be the only things for which in middle life a man profoundly cares. But in all these the spread and consolidation have followed nothing but the principles first laid down. If we could recall for a moment our whole individual history, we should see that our professional ideals and the zeal they inspire are due to nothing but the slow accretion of one mental object to another, traceable backward from point to point till we reach the moment when, in the nursery or in the school-room, some little story told, some little object shown, some little operation witnessed, brought the first new object and new interest within our ken by associating it with some one of those primitively there. The interest now suffusing the whole system took its rise in that little event, so insignificant to us now as to be entirely forgotten. As the bees in swarming cling to one another in layers till the few are reached whose feet grapple the bough from which the swarm depends; so with the objects of our thinking—they hang to each other by associated links, but the *original* source of interest in all of them is the native interest which the earliest one once possessed.

CHAPTER XI

ATTENTION

WHOEVER TREATS of interest inevitably treats of attention; for to say that an object is interesting is only another way of saying that it excites attention. But in addition to the attention which any object already interesting or just becoming interesting claims—passive attention or spontaneous attention, we may call it—there is a more deliberate attention—voluntary attention or attention with effort, as it is called—which we can give to objects less interesting or uninteresting in themselves. The distinction between active and passive attention is made in all books on psychology, and connects itself with the deeper aspects of the topic. From our present purely practical point of view, however, it is not necessary to be intricate; and passive attention to natively interesting material requires no farther elucidation on this occasion. All that we need explicitly to note is that the more the passive attention is relied on, by keeping the material interesting; and the less the kind of attention requiring effort is appealed to; the more smoothly and pleasantly the class-room work goes on. I must say a few more words, however, about this latter process of voluntary and deliberate attention.

One often hears it said that genius is nothing but a power of sustained attention; and the popular impression probably prevails that men of genius are remarkable for their voluntary powers in this direction. *But a little introspective observation will show anyone that voluntary attention cannot be continuously sustained—that it comes in beats.* When we are studying an uninteresting subject, if our mind tends to wander, we have to bring back our attention every now and then by using distinct pulses of effort which revivify the topic for a moment, the mind then running on for a certain number of seconds or minutes with spontaneous interest, until again some intercurrent idea captures it and takes it off. Then the processes of volitional recall must be repeated once more. Voluntary attention, in short, is only a momentary affair. The process, whatever it is, exhausts itself in the single act; and unless the matter is then taken in hand by some trace of interest inherent in the subject, the mind fails to follow it at all. The sustained attention of the genius, sticking to his subject for hours together, is for the most part of the passive sort. The minds of geniuses are full of copious and original associations. The subject of thought, once started, develops all sorts of fascinating consequences; the attention is led along one of these to another in the most interesting manner, and the attention never once tends to stray away.

In a commonplace mind, on the other hand, a subject develops much less numerous associates; it dies out then quickly; and if the man is to keep up thinking of it at all, he must bring his attention back to it by a violent wrench. In him, therefore, the faculty of voluntary attention receives abundant opportunity for cultivation in daily life. It is your despised business man, your common man of affairs (so looked down on by the literary awarders of fame), whose virtue in this regard is likely to be most developed; for he has to listen to the concerns of so many uninteresting people, and to transact so much drudging detail, that the faculty in question is always kept in training. A genius, on the contrary, is the man in whom you are least likely to find the power of attending to anything insipid or distasteful in itself; he breaks his engagements, leaves his letters unanswered, neglects his family duties incorrigibly, because he is powerless to turn his attention down and back from those more interesting trains of imagery with which his genius constantly occupies his mind.

Voluntary attention is thus an essentially instantaneous affair. You can claim it, for your purposes in the school-room, by commanding it in loud, imperious tones; and you can easily get it in this way. But unless the subject to which you thus recall their attention has inherent power to interest the pupils, you will have got it for only a brief moment; and their minds will soon be wandering again. To keep them where you have called them, you must make the subject too interesting for them to wander again. And for that there is one prescription; but the prescription, like all our prescriptions, is abstract, and to get practical results from it you must couple it with mother-wit.

The prescription is that *the subject must be made to show new aspects of itself; to prompt new questions; in a word, to change.* From an unchanging subject the attention inevitably wanders away. You can test this by the simplest possible case of sensorial attention. Try to attend steadfastly to a dot on the paper or on the wall. You presently find that one or the other of two things has happened: either your field of vision has become blurred, so that you now see nothing distinct at all; or else you have involuntarily ceased to look at the dot in question, and are looking at something else. But if you ask yourself successive questions about the dot—how big it is, how far, of what shape, what shade of color, etc.; in other words, if you turn it over, if you think of it in various ways, and along with various kinds of associates—you can keep your mind on it for a comparatively long time. This is what the genius does, in whose hands a given topic coruscates and grows. And this is what the teacher must do for every topic if he wishes to avoid too frequent appeals to voluntary attention of the coerced sort. In all respects, reliance upon such attention as this is a wasteful method, bringing bad temper and nervous wear and tear as well as imperfect results. The teacher who can get along by keeping spontaneous interest excited must be regarded as the teacher with the greatest skill.

There is, however, in all school-room work a large mass of material that must be dull and unexciting, and to which it is impossible in any continuous way to contribute an interest associatively derived. There are, therefore, certain external methods, which every teacher knows, of voluntarily arousing the attention from time to time and keeping it upon the subject. Mr. Fitch has a lecture on the art of securing attention, and he briefly passes these methods in review: the posture must be changed; places can be changed. Questions, after being answered singly, may occasionally be answered in concert; elliptical questions may be asked, the pupil supplying the missing word. The teacher must pounce upon the most listless child, and wake him up. The habit of prompt and ready response must be kept up; recapitulations, illustrations, examples, novelty of order, and ruptures of routine—all these are means for keeping the attention alive and contributing a little interest to a dull subject. Above all, the teacher must himself be alive and ready, and must use the contagion of his own example.

But when all is said and done, the fact remains that some teachers have a naturally inspiring presence and can make their exercises interesting, whilst others simply cannot. And psychology and general pædagogy here confess their failure, and hand things over to the deeper springs of human personality to conduct the task.

A brief reference to the physiological theory of the attentive process may serve still farther to elucidate these practical remarks, and confirm them by showing them from a slightly different point of view.

What is the attentive process, psychologically considered? Attention to an object is what takes place whenever that object most completely occupies the mind. For simplicity's sake suppose the object to be an object of sensation—a figure approaching us at a distance on the road. It is far off, barely perceptible, and hardly moving; we do not know with certainty whether it is a man or not. Such an object as this, if carelessly looked at, may hardly catch our attention at all; the optical impression may affect solely the marginal consciousness, whilst the mental focus keeps engaged with rival things. We may indeed not 'see' it till someone points it out. But if so, how does he point it out? By his finger, and by describing its appearance—by creating a premonitory image of *where* to look and of *what* to expect to see. This premonitory image is already an excitement of the same nerve-centres that are to be concerned with the impression. The impression comes, and excites them still farther; and now the object enters the focus of the field, consciousness being sustained both by impression and by preliminary idea. But the maximum of attention to it is not yet reached. Although we see it, we may not care for it; it may suggest nothing important to us; and a rival stream of objects or of thoughts may quickly take our mind away. If, however, our companion defines it in a significant way, arouses in the mind a set of experiences to be apprehended from it—names it an enemy or as a messenger of important tidings—the residual and marginal ideas now aroused, so far from being its rivals, become its associates and allies; they shoot together into one system with it; they converge upon it; they keep it steadily in focus; the mind attends to it with maximum power.

The attentive process, therefore, at its maximum may be physiologically symbolized by a brain-cell played on in two ways, from without and from within. Incoming currents from the periphery arouse it, and collateral currents from the centres of memory and imagination reinforce these.

In this process the incoming impression is the newer element; the ideas which reinforce and sustain it are amongst the older possessions of the mind. And the maximum of attention may then be said to be found whenever we have a systematic harmony or unification between the novel and the old. It is an odd circumstance that neither the old nor the new, by itself, is interesting: the absolutely old is insipid; the absolutely new makes no appeal at all. The old *in* the new is what claims the attention—the old with a slightly new turn. No one wants to hear a lecture on a subject completely disconnected with his previous knowledge, but we all like lectures on subjects of which we know a little already; just as, in the fashions, every year must bring its slight modification of last year's suit, but an abrupt jump from the fashion of one decade into another would be distasteful to the eye.

The genius of the interesting teacher consists in sympathetic divination of the sort of material with which the pupil's mind is likely to be already spontaneously engaged, and in the ingenuity which discovers paths of connection from that material to the matters to be newly learned. The principle is easy to grasp, but the accomplishment is difficult in the extreme. And a knowledge of such psychology as this which I am recalling can no more make a good teacher than a knowledge of the laws of perspective can make a landscape painter of effective skill.

A certain doubt may now occur to some of you. Awhile ago, apropos of the pugnacious instinct, I spoke of our modern pædagogy as being possibly too 'soft.' You may perhaps here face me with my own words, and ask whether the exclusive effort on the teacher's part to keep the pupil's spontaneous interest going, and to avoid the more strenuous path of voluntary attention to repulsive work, does not savor also of sentimentalism. The greater part of school-room work, you say, must, in the nature of things, always be repulsive. To face uninteresting drudgery is a good part of life's work; why seek to eliminate it from the school-room or minimize the sterner law?

A word or two will obviate what might perhaps become a serious misunderstanding here.

It is certain that most school-room work, till it has become habitual and automatic, is repulsive, and cannot be done without voluntarily jerking back the attention to it every now and then. This is inevitable, let the teacher do what he will. It flows from the inherent nature of the subjects and of the learning mind. The repulsive processes of verbal memorizing, of discovering steps of mathematical identity, and the like, must borrow their interest at first from purely external sources, mainly from the personal interests with which success in mastering them is associated, such as gaining of rank, avoiding punishment, not being beaten by a difficulty, and the like. Without such borrowed interest, the child could not attend to them at all. But in these processes what becomes interesting enough to be attended to is not thereby attended to *without effort*. Effort always has to go on, derived interest, for the most part, not awakening attention that is *easy*, however spontaneous it may now have to be called. The interest which the teacher, by his utmost skill, can lend to the subject, proves over and over again to be only an interest sufficient *to let loose the effort*. The teacher, therefore, need never concern himself about *inventing* occasions where effort must be called into play. Let him still awaken whatever sources of interest in the subject he can by stirring up connections between it and the pupil's nature, whether in the line of theoretic curiosity, of personal interest, or of pugnacious impulse. The laws of mind will then bring enough pulses of effort into play to keep the pupil exercised in the direction of the subject. There is, in fact, no greater school of effort than the steady struggle to attend to immediately repulsive or difficult objects of thought which have grown to interest us through their association, as means, with some remote ideal end.

The Herbartian doctrine of interest ought not, therefore, in principle to be reproached with making pædagogy soft. If it do so, it is because it is unintelligently carried on. Do not, then, for the mere sake of discipline, command attention from your pupils in thundering tones; do not too often beg it from them as a favor, nor claim it as a right, nor try habitually to excite it by preaching the importance of the subject. Sometimes, indeed, you must do these things; but the more you have to do them, the less skilful teacher you will show yourself to be. Elicit interest from within, by the warmth with which you care for the topic yourself, and by following the laws I have laid down.

If the topic be highly abstract, show its nature by concrete examples; if it be unfamiliar, trace some point of analogy in it with the known; if it be inhuman, make it figure as part of a story; if it be difficult, couple its acquisition with some prospect of personal gain. Above all things, make sure that it shall run through certain inner changes, since no unvarying object can possibly hold the mental field for long. Let your pupil wander from one aspect to another of your subject, if you do not wish him to wander from it altogether to something else, variety in unity being the secret of all interesting talk and thought. The relation of all these things to the native genius of the instructor is too obvious to need comment again.

One more point, and I am done with the subject of attention. There is unquestionably a great native variety amongst individuals in the type of their attention. Some of us are naturally scatter-brained, and others follow easily a train of connected thoughts without temptation to swerve aside to other subjects. This seems to depend on a difference between individuals in the type of their field of consciousness. In some persons this is highly focalized and concentrated, and the focal ideas predominate in determining association. In others we must suppose the margin to be brighter, and to be filled with something like meteoric showers of images, which strike into it at random, displacing the focal ideas, and carrying association in their own direction. Persons of the latter type find their attention wandering every minute, and must bring it back by a voluntary pull. The others sink into a subject of meditation deeply, and when interrupted are 'lost' for a moment before they come back to the outer world.

The possession of such a steady faculty of attention is unquestionably a great boon. Those who have it can work more rapidly, and with less nervous wear and tear. I am inclined to think that no one who is without it naturally can by any amount of drill or discipline attain it in a very high degree. Its amount is probably a fixed characteristic of the individual. But I wish to make a remark here which I shall have occasion to make again in other connections. It is that no one need deplore unduly the inferiority in himself of any one elementary faculty. This concentrated type of attention is an elementary faculty; it is one of the things that might be ascertained and measured by exercises in the laboratory. But having ascertained it in a number of persons, we could never rank them in a scale of actual and practical mental efficiency based on its degrees. The total mental efficiency of a man is the resultant of the working together of all his faculties; he is too complex a being for any one of them to have the casting vote. If any one of them do have the casting vote, it is more likely to be the strength of his desire and passion, the strength of the interest he takes in what is proposed. Concentration, memory, reasoning power, inventiveness, excellence of the senses—all are subsidiary to this. No matter how scatter-brained the type of a man's successive fields of consciousness may be, if he really *care* for a subject, he will return to it incessantly from his incessant wanderings, and first and last do more with it, and get more results from it, than another person whose attention may be more continuous during a given interval, but whose passion for the subject is of a more languid and less permanent sort. Some of the most efficient workers I know are of the ultra-scatter-brained type. One friend, who does a prodigious quantity of work, has in fact confessed to me that, if he wants to get ideas on any subject, he sits down to work at something else, his best results coming through his mind-wanderings. This is perhaps an epigrammatic exaggeration on his part; but I seriously think that no one of us need be too much distressed at his own shortcomings in this regard. Our mind may enjoy but little comfort, may be restless and feel confused; but it may be extremely efficient all the same.

CHAPTER XII

MEMORY

WE ARE FOLLOWING a somewhat arbitrary order. Since each and every faculty we possess is either in whole or in part a resultant of the play of our associations, it would have been as natural, after treating of association, to treat of memory as to treat of interest and attention next. But since we did take the latter operations first, we must take memory now without farther delay; for the phenomena of memory are amongst the simplest and most immediate consequences of the fact that our mind is essentially an associating machine. There is no more pre-eminent example for exhibiting the fertility of the laws of association as principles of psychological analysis. Memory, moreover, is so important a faculty in the school-room that you are probably waiting with some eagerness to know what psychology has to say about it for your help.

In old times, if you asked a person to explain why he came to be remembering at that moment some particular incident in his previous life, the only reply he could make was that his soul is endowed with a faculty called memory; that it is the inalienable function of this faculty to recollect; and that, therefore, he necessarily at that moment must have a cognition of that portion of the past. This explanation by a 'faculty' is one thing which explanation by association has superseded altogether. If by saying we have a faculty of memory, you mean nothing more than the fact that we can remember, nothing more than an abstract name for our power inwardly to recall the past, there is no harm done; we do have the faculty; for we unquestionably have such a power. But if, by faculty, you mean a principle of *explanation of our general power to recall*, your psychology is empty. The associationist psychology, on the other hand, gives an explanation of each particular fact of recollection; and in so doing, it also gives an explanation of the general faculty. The 'faculty' of memory is thus no real or ultimate explanation; for it is itself explained as a result of the association of ideas.

Nothing is easier than to show you just what I mean by this. Suppose I am silent for a moment, and then say, in commanding accents: "Remember! Recollect!" Does your faculty of memory obey the order, and reproduce any definite image from your past? Certainly not. It stands staring into vacancy, and asking, "What kind of a thing do you wish me to remember?" It needs, in short, a *cue*. But if I say, remember the date of your birth, or remember what you had for breakfast, or remember the succession of notes in the musical scale; then your faculty of memory immediately produces the required result: the 'cue' determines its vast set of potentialities towards a particular point. And if you now look to see how this happens, you immediately perceive that the cue is something *contiguously associated* with the thing recalled. The words, 'date of my birth,' have an ingrained association with a particular number, month, and year; the words, 'breakfast this morning,' cut off all other lines of recall except those which lead to coffee and bacon and eggs; the words, 'musical scale,' are inveterate mental neighbors of do, ré, mi, fa, sol, la, etc. The laws of association govern, in fact, all the trains of our thinking which are not interrupted by sensations breaking on us from without. Whatever appears in the mind must be *introduced*; and, when introduced, it is as the associate of something already there. This is as true of what you are recollecting as it is of everything else you think of.

Reflection will show you that there are peculiarities in your memory which would be quite whimsical and unaccountable if we were forced to regard them as the product of a purely spiritual faculty. Were memory such a faculty, granted to us solely for its practical use, we ought to remember easiest whatever we most *needed* to remember; and frequency of repetition, recency, and the like, would play no part in the matter. That we should best remember frequent things and recent things, and forget things that are ancient or were experienced only once, could only be regarded as an incomprehensible anomaly on such a view. But if we remember because of our associations, and if these are (as the physiological psychologists believe) due to our organized brain-paths, we easily see how the law of recency and repetition should prevail. Paths frequently and recently ploughed are those that lie most open, those which may be expected most easily to lead to results. The laws of our memory, as we find them, therefore, are incidents of our associational constitution; and when we are emancipated from the flesh, it is conceivable that they may no longer continue to obtain.

We may assume, then, that recollection is a resultant of our associative processes, these themselves in the last analysis being most probably due to the workings of our brain.

Descending more particularly into the faculty of memory, we have to distinguish between its potential aspect as a magazine or storehouse and its actual aspect as recollection now of a particular event. Our memory contains all sorts of items which we do not now recall, but which we may recall, provided a sufficient cue be offered. Both the general retention and the special recall are explained by association. An educated memory depends on an organized system of associations; and its goodness depends on two of their peculiarities: first, on the persistency of the associations; and, second, on their number.

Let us consider each of these points in turn.

First, the persistency of the associations.—This gives what may be called the *quality of native retentiveness* to the individual. If, as I think we are forced to, we consider the brain to be the organic condition by which the vestiges of our experience are associated with each other, we may suppose that some brains are 'wax to receive and marble to retain.' The slightest impressions made on them abide. Names, dates, prices, anecdotes, quotations, are indelibly retained, their several elements fixedly cohering together, so that the individual soon becomes a walking cyclopædia of information. All this may occur with no philosophic tendency in the mind, no impulse to weave the materials acquired into anything like a logical system. In the books of anecdotes, and, more recently, in the psychology-books, we find recorded instances of monstrosities, as we may call them, of this desultory memory; and they are often otherwise very stupid men. It is, of course, by no means incompatible with a philosophic mind; for mental characteristics have infinite capacities for permutation. And when both memory and philosophy combine together in one person, then indeed we have the highest sort of intellectual efficiency. Your Walter Scotts, your Leibnitzes, your Gladstones, and your Goethes, all your folio copies of mankind, belong to this type. Efficiency on a colossal scale would indeed seem to require it. For although your philosophic or systematic mind without good desultory memory may know how to work out results and recollect where in the books to find them, the time lost in the searching process handicaps the thinker, and gives to the more ready type of individual the economical advantage.

The extreme of the contrasted type, the type with associations of small persistency, is found in those who have almost no desultory memory at all. If they are also deficient in logical and systematizing power, we call them simply feeble intellects; and no more need to be said about them here. Their brain-matter, we may imagine, is like a fluid jelly, in which impressions may be easily made, but are soon closed over again, so that the brain reverts to its original indifferent state.

But it may occur here, just as in other gelatinous substances, that an impression will vibrate throughout the brain, and send waves into other parts of it. In cases of this sort, although the immediate impression may fade out quickly, it does modify the cerebral mass; for the paths it makes there may remain, and become so many avenues through which the impression may be reproduced if they ever get excited again. And its liability to reproduction will depend of course upon the variety of these paths and upon the frequency with which they are used. Each path is in fact an associated process, the number of these associates becoming thus to a great degree a substitute for the independent tenacity of the original impression. As I have elsewhere written: Each of the associates is a hook to which it hangs, a means to fish it up when sunk below the surface. Together they form a network of attachments by which it is woven into the entire tissue of our thought. The 'secret of a good memory' is thus the secret of forming diverse and multiple associations with every fact we care to retain. But this forming of associations with a fact— what is it but thinking *about* the fact as much as possible?

Briefly, then, of two men with the same outward experiences, *the one who thinks over his experiences most*, and weaves them into the most systematic relations with each other, will be the one with the best memory.

But if our ability to recollect a thing be so largely a matter of its associations with other things which thus become its cues, an important pædagogic consequence follows. *There can be no improvement of the general or elementary faculty of memory; there can only be improvement of our memory for special systems of associated things*; and this latter improvement is due to the way in which the things in question are woven into association with each other in the mind. Intricately or profoundly woven, they are held; disconnected, they tend to drop out just in proportion as the native brain retentiveness is poor. And no amount of training, drilling, repeating, and reciting employed upon the matter of one system of objects, the history-system, for example, will in the least improve either the facility or the durability with which objects belonging to a wholly disparate system—the system of facts of chemistry, for instance—tend to be retained. That system must be separately worked into the mind by itself—a chemical fact which is thought about in connection with the other chemical facts, tending then to stay, but otherwise easily dropping out.

We have, then, not so much a faculty of memory as many faculties of memory. We have as many as we have systems of objects habitually thought of in connection with each other. A given object is held in the memory by the associates it has acquired within its own system exclusively. Learning the facts of another system will in no wise help it to stay in the mind, for the simple reason that it has no 'cues' within that other system.

We see examples of this on every hand. Most men have a good memory for facts connected with their own pursuits. A college athlete, who remains a dunce at his books, may amaze you by his knowledge of the 'records' at various feats and games, and prove himself a walking dictionary of sporting statistics. The reason is that he is constantly going over these things in his mind, and comparing and making series of them. They form for him, not so many odd facts, but a concept-system, so they stick. So the merchant remembers prices, the politician other politicians' speeches and votes, with a copiousness which astonishes outsiders, but which the amount of thinking they bestow on these subjects easily explains.

The great memory for facts which a Darwin or a Spencer reveal in their books is not incompatible with the possession on their part of a mind with only a middling degree of physiological retentiveness. Let a man early in life set himself the task of verifying such a theory as that of evolution, and facts will soon cluster and cling to him like grapes to their stem. Their relations to the theory will hold them fast; and the more of these the mind is able to discern, the greater the erudition will become. Meanwhile the theorist may have little, if any, desultory memory. Unutilizable facts may be unnoted by him, and forgotten as soon as heard. An ignorance almost as encyclopædic as his erudition may coexist with the latter, and hide, as it were, within the interstices of its web. Those of you who have had much to do with scholars and *savants* will readily think of examples of the class of mind I mean.

The best possible sort of system into which to weave an object, mentally, is a *rational* system, or what is called a 'science.' Place the thing in its pigeon-hole in a classificatory series; explain it logically by its causes, and deduce from it its necessary effects; find out of what natural law it is an instance—and you then know it in the best of all possible ways. A 'science' is thus the greatest of labor-saving contrivances. It relieves the memory of an immense number of details, replacing, as it does, merely contiguous associations by the logical ones of identity, similarity, or analogy. If you know a 'law,' you may discharge your memory of masses of particular instances, for the law will reproduce them for you whenever you require them. The law of refraction, for example: If you know that, you can with a pencil and a bit of paper immediately discern how a convex lens, a concave lens, or a prism, must severally alter the appearance of an object. But if you don't know the general law, you must charge your memory separately with each of the three kinds of effect.

A 'philosophic' system, in which all things found their rational explanation and were connected together as causes and effects, would be the perfect mnemonic system, in which the greatest economy of means would bring about the greatest richness of results. So that, if we have poor desultory memories, we can save ourselves by cultivating the philosophic turn of mind.

There are many artificial systems of mnemonics, some public, some sold as secrets. They are all so many devices for training us into certain methodical and stereotyped *ways of thinking* about the facts we seek to retain. Even were I competent, I could not here go into these systems in any detail. But a single example, from a popular system, will show what I mean. I take the number-alphabet, the great mnemonic device for recollecting numbers and dates. In this system each digit is represented by a consonant, thus: 1 is *t* or *d*; 2, *n*; 3, *m*; 4, *r*; 5, *l*; 6, *sh*, *j*, *ch*, or *g*; 7, *c*, *k*, *g*, or *qu*; 8, *f* or *v*; 9, *b* or *p*; 0, *s*, *c*, or *z*. Suppose, now, you wish to remember the velocity of sound, 1,142 feet a second: *t*, *t*, *r*, *n*, are the letters you must use. They make the consonants of *tight run*, and it would be a 'tight run' for you to keep up such a speed. So 1649, the date of the execution of Charles I, may be remembered by the word *sharp*, which recalls the headsman's axe.

Apart from the extreme difficulty of finding words that are appropriate in this exercise, it is clearly an excessively poor, trivial, and silly way of 'thinking' about dates; and the way of the historian is much better. He has a lot of landmark-dates already in his mind. He knows the historic concatenation of events, and can usually place an event at its right date in the chronology-table, by thinking of it in a rational way, referring to its antecedents, tracing its concomitants and consequences, and thus ciphering out its date by connecting it with theirs. The artificial memory-systems, recommending, as they do, such irrational methods of thinking, are only to be recommended for the first landmarks in a system, or for such purely detached facts as enjoy no rational connection with the rest of our ideas. Thus the student of physics may remember the order of the spectral colours by the word *vibgyor* which their initial letters make. The student of anatomy may remember the position of the Mitral valve on the Left side of the heart by thinking that L. M. stands also for 'long meter' in the hymn-books.

You now see why 'cramming' must be so poor a mode of study. Cramming seeks to stamp things in by intense application immediately before the ordeal. But a thing thus learned can form but few associations. On the other hand, the same thing recurring on different days, in different contexts, read, recited on, referred to again and again, related to other things and reviewed, gets well wrought into the mental structure. This is the reason why you should enforce on your pupils habits of continuous application. There is no moral turpitude in cramming. It would be the best, because the most economical, mode of study if it led to the results desired. But it does not, and your older pupils can readily be made to see the reason why.

It follows also, from what has been said, that *the popular idea that 'the Memory,' in the sense of a general elementary faculty, can be improved by training, is a great mistake*. Your memory for facts of a certain class can be improved very much by training in that class of facts, because the incoming new fact will then find all sorts of analogues and associates already there, and these will keep it liable to recall. But other kinds of fact will reap none of that benefit, and unless one have been also trained and versed in *their* class, will be at the mercy of the mere crude retentiveness of the individual, which, as we have seen, is practically a fixed quantity. Nevertheless, one often hears people say: "A great sin was committed against me in my youth: my teachers entirely failed to exercise my memory. If they had only made me learn a lot of things by heart at school, I should not be, as I am now, forgetful of everything I read and hear." This is a great mistake: learning poetry by heart will make it easier to learn and remember other poetry, but nothing else; and so of dates; and so of chemistry and geography.

But after what I have said, I am sure you will need no farther argument on this point; and I therefore pass it by.

But since it has brought me to speak of learning things by heart, I think that a general practical remark about verbal memorizing may now not be out of place. The excesses of old-fashioned verbal memorizing, and the immense advantages of object-teaching in the earlier stages of culture, have perhaps led those who philosophize about teaching to an unduly strong reaction; and learning things by heart is now probably somewhat too much despised. For when all is said and done, the fact remains that verbal material is, on the whole, the handiest and most useful material in which thinking can be carried on. Abstract conceptions are far and away the most economical instruments of thought, and abstract conceptions are fixed and incarnated for us in words. Statistical inquiry would seem to show that, as men advance in life, they tend to make less and less use of visual images, and more and more use of words. One of the first things that Mr. Galton discovered was that this appeared to be the case with the members of the Royal Society whom he questioned as to their mental images. I should say, therefore, that constant exercise in verbal memorizing must still be an indispensable feature in all sound education. Nothing is more deplorable than that inarticulate and helpless sort of mind that is reminded by everything of some quotation, case, or anecdote, which it cannot now exactly recollect. Nothing, on the other hand, is more convenient to its possessor, or more delightful to his comrades, than a mind able, in telling a story, to give the exact words of the dialogue or to furnish a quotation accurate and complete. In every branch of study there are happily turned, concise, and handy formulas which in an incomparable way sum up results. The mind that can retain such formulas is in so far a superior mind, and the communication of them to the pupil ought always to be one of the teacher's favorite tasks.

In learning 'by heart,' there are, however, efficient and inefficient methods; and by making the pupil skilful in the best method, the teacher can both interest him and abridge the task. The best method is of course not to 'hammer in' the sentences, by mere reiteration, but to analyze them, and think. For example, if the pupil should have to learn this last sentence, let him first strip out its grammatical core, and learn, "The best method is not to hammer in, but to analyze," and then add the amplificative and restrictive clauses, bit by bit, thus: "The best method is of course not to hammer in *the sentences*, but to analyze *them and think*." Then finally insert the words '*by mere reiteration*,' and the sentence is complete, and both better understood and quicker remembered than by a more purely mechanical method.

In conclusion, I must say a word about the contributions to our knowledge of memory which have recently come from the laboratory-psychologists. Many of the enthusiasts for scientific or brass-instrument child-study are taking accurate measurements of children's elementary faculties, and amongst these what we may call *immediate memory* admits of easy measurement. All we need do is to exhibit to the child a series of letters, syllables, figures, pictures, or what-not, at intervals of one, two, three, or more seconds, or to sound a similar series of names at the same intervals, within his hearing, and then see how completely he can reproduce the list, either directly, or after an interval of ten, twenty, or sixty seconds, or some longer space of time. According to the results of this exercise, the pupils may be rated in a memory-scale; and some persons go so far as to think that the teacher should modify her treatment of the child according to the strength or feebleness of its faculty as thus made known.

Now I can only repeat here what I said to you when treating of attention: man is too complex a being for light to be thrown on his real efficiency by measuring any one mental faculty taken apart from its consensus in the working whole. Such an exercise as this, dealing with incoherent and insipid objects, with no logical connection with each other, or practical significance outside of the 'test,' is an exercise the like of which in real life we are hardly ever called upon to perform. In real life, our memory is always used in the service of some interest: we remember things which we care for or which are associated with things we care for; and the child who stands at the bottom of the scale thus experimentally established might, by dint of the strength of his passion for a subject, and in consequence of the logical association into which he weaves the actual materials of his experience, be a very effective memorizer indeed, and do his school-tasks on the whole much better than an immediate parrot who might stand at the top of the 'scientifically accurate' list.

This preponderance of interest, of passion, in determining the results of a human being's working life, obtains throughout. No elementary measurement, capable of being performed in a laboratory, can throw any light on the actual efficiency of the subject; for the vital thing about him, his emotional and moral energy and doggedness, can be measured by no single experiment, and becomes known only by the total results in the long run. A blind man like Huber, with his passion for bees and ants, can observe them through other people's eyes better than these can through their own. A man born with neither arms nor legs, like the late Kavanagh, M. P.—and what an icy heart his mother must have had about him in his babyhood, and how 'negative' would the laboratory-measurements of his motor-functions have been!—can be an adventurous traveller, an equestrian and sportsman, and lead an athletic outdoor life. Mr. Romanes studied the elementary rate of apperception in a large number of persons by making them read a paragraph as fast as they could take it in, and then immediately write down all they could reproduce of its contents. He found astonishing differences in the rapidity, some taking four times as long as others to absorb the paragraph, and the swiftest readers being, as a rule, the best immediate recollectors, too. But not—and this is my point—*not* the most *intellectually capable subjects*, as tested by the results of what Mr. Romanes rightly names 'genuine' intellectual work; for he tried the experiment with several highly distinguished men in science and literature, and most of them turned out to be slow readers.

In the light of all such facts one may well believe that the total impression which a perceptive teacher will get of the pupil's condition, as indicated by his general temper and manner, by the listlessness or alertness, by the ease or painfulness with which his school work is done, will be of much more value than those unreal experimental tests, those pedantic elementary measurements of fatigue, memory, association, and attention, etc., which are urged upon us as the only basis of a genuinely scientific pædagogy. Such measurements can give us useful information only when we combine them with observations made without brass instruments, upon the total demeanor of the measured individual, by teachers with eyes in

their heads and common sense, and some feeling for the concrete facts of human nature in their hearts.

Depend upon it, no one need be too much cast down by
the discovery of his deficiency in any elementary faculty of the
mind. What tells in life is the whole mind working together,
and the deficiencies of any one faculty can be compensated by
the efforts of the rest. You can be an artist without visual
images, a reader without eyes, a mass of erudition with a bad
elementary memory. In almost any subject your passion for
the subject will save you. If you only care enough for a result,
you will almost certainly attain it. If you wish to be rich, you
will be rich; if you wish to be learned, you will be learned; if
you wish to be good, you will be good. Only you must, then,
really wish these things, and wish them with exclusiveness,
and not wish at the same time a hundred other incompatible
things just as strongly.

One of the most important discoveries of the 'scientific' sort
that have recently been made in psychology is that of Mr.
Galton and others concerning the great variations amongst
individuals in the type of their imagination. Everyone is now
familiar with the fact that human beings vary enormously in
the brilliancy, completeness, definiteness, and extent of their
visual images. These are singularly perfect in a large number
of individuals, and in a few are so rudimentary as hardly to
exist. The same is true of the auditory and motor images, and
probably of those of every kind; and the recent discovery of
distinct brain-areas for the various orders of sensation would
seem to provide a physical basis for such variations and discrepancies. The facts, as I said, are nowadays so popularly
known that I need only remind you of their existence. They
might seem at first sight of practical importance to the
teacher; and, indeed, teachers have been recommended to sort
their pupils in this way, and treat them as the result falls out.
You should interrogate them as to their imagery, it is said, or
exhibit lists of written words to their eyes, and then sound
similar lists in their ears, and see by which channel a child
retains most words. Then, in dealing with that child, make
your appeals predominantly through that channel. If the class
were very small, results of some distinctness might doubtless
thus be obtained by a painstaking teacher. But it is obvious

that in the usual school-room no such differentiation of appeal is possible; and the only really useful practical lesson that emerges from this analytic psychology in the conduct of large schools is the lesson already reached in a purely empirical way, that the teacher ought always to impress the class through as many sensible channels as he can. Talk and write and draw on blackboard, permit the pupils to talk, and make them write and draw, exhibit pictures, plans, and curves, have your diagrams coloured differently in their different parts, etc.; and out of the whole variety of impressions the individual child will find the most lasting ones for himself. In all primary school work this principle of multiple impressions is well recognized, so I need say no more about it here.

This principle of multiplying channels and varying associations and appeals is important, not only for teaching pupils to remember, but for teaching them to understand. It runs, in fact, through the whole teaching art.

One word about the unconscious and unreproducible part of our acquisitions, and I shall have done with the topic of memory.

Professor Ebbinghaus, in a heroic little investigation into the laws of memory which he performed a dozen or more years ago by the method of learning lists of nonsense syllables, devised a method of measuring the rate of our forgetfulness, which lays bare an important law of the mind.

His method was to read over his list until he could repeat it once by heart unhesitatingly. The number of repetitions required for this was a measure of the difficulty of the learning in each particular case. Now, after having once learned a piece in this way, if we wait five minutes, we find it impossible to repeat it again in the same unhesitating manner. We must read it over again to revive some of the syllables, which have already dropped out or got transposed. Ebbinghaus now systematically studied the number of readings-over which were necessary to revive the unhesitating recollection of the piece after five minutes, half an hour, an hour, a day, a week, a month, had elapsed. The number of rereadings required he took to be a measure of the *amount of forgetting* that had occurred in the elapsed interval. And he found some remarkable facts. The process of forgetting, namely, is vastly more rapid at first than later on. Thus full half of the piece seems to be forgotten within the first half-hour, two-thirds of it are forgotten at the end of eight hours, but only four-fifths at the end of a month. He made no trials beyond one month of interval; but if we ourselves prolong ideally the curve of remembrance, whose beginning his experiments thus obtain, it is natural to suppose that, no matter how long a time might elapse, the curve would never descend quite so low as to touch the zero-line. In other words, no matter how long ago we may have learned a poem, and no matter how complete our inability to reproduce it now may be, yet the first learning will still show its lingering effects in the abridgment of the time required for learning it again. In short, Professor Ebbinghaus's experiments show that things which we are quite unable definitely to recall have nevertheless impressed themselves, in some way, upon the structure of the mind. We are different for having once learned them. The resistances in our systems of brain-paths are altered. Our apprehensions are quickened. Our conclusions from certain premises are probably not just what they would be if those modifications were not there. The latter influence the whole margin of our consciousness, even though their products, not being distinctly reproducible, do not directly figure at the focus of the field.

The teacher should draw a lesson from these facts. We are all too apt to measure the gains of our pupils by their proficiency in directly reproducing in a recitation or an examination such matters as they may have learned, and inarticulate power in them is something of which we always underestimate the value. The boy who tells us, "I know the answer, but I can't say what it is," we treat as practically identical with him who knows absolutely nothing about the answer at all. But this is a great mistake. It is but a small part of our experience in life that we are ever able articulately to recall. And yet the whole of it has had its influence in shaping our character and defining our tendencies to judge and act. Although the ready memory is a great blessing to its possessor, the vaguer memory of a subject, of having once had to do with it, of its neighborhood, and of where we may go to recover it again, constitutes in most men and women the chief fruit of their education. This is true even in professional education. The doctor, the lawyer, are seldom able to decide upon a case off-hand. They differ from other men only through the fact that they know how to get at the materials for decision in five minutes or half an hour; whereas the layman is unable to get at the materials at all, not knowing in what books and indexes to look or not understanding the technical terms.

Be patient, then, and sympathetic with the type of mind that cuts a poor figure in examinations. It may, in the long examination which life sets us, come out in the end in better shape than the glib and ready reproducer, its passions being deeper, its purposes more worthy, its combining power less commonplace, and its total mental output consequently more important.

Such are the chief points which it has seemed worth while for me to call to your notice under the head of memory. We can sum them up for practical purposes by saying that the art of remembering is the art of *thinking*; and by adding, with Dr. Pick, that, when we wish to fix a new thing in either our own mind or a pupil's, our conscious effort should not be so much to *impress* and *retain* it as to *connect* it with something else already there. The connecting *is* the thinking; and if we attend clearly to the connection, the connected thing will certainly be likely to remain within recall.

I shall next ask you to consider the process by which we acquire new knowledge—the process of 'Apperception,' as it is called, by which we receive and deal with new experiences, and revise our stock of ideas so as to form new or improved conceptions.

CHAPTER XIII

THE ACQUISITION OF IDEAS

THE IMAGES of our past experiences, of whatever nature they may be, visual or verbal, blurred and dim, vivid and distinct, abstract or concrete, need not be memory images, in the strict sense of the word. That is, they need not rise before the mind in a marginal fringe or context of concomitant circumstances, which mean for us their *date*. They may be mere conceptions, floating pictures of an object, or of its type or class. In this undated condition, we call them products of 'imagination' or 'conception.' Imagination is the term commonly used where the object represented is thought of as an individual thing. Conception is the term where we think of it as a type or class. For our present purpose the distinction is not important; and I will permit myself to use either the word 'conception,' or the still vaguer word 'idea,' to designate the inner objects of contemplation, whether these be individual things, like 'the sun' or 'Julius Cæsar,' or classes of things, like 'animal kingdom,' or, finally, entirely abstract attributes, like 'rationality' or 'rectitude.'

The result of our education is to fill the mind little by little, as experiences accrete, with a stock of such ideas. In the illustration I used at our first meeting, of the child snatching the toy and getting slapped, the vestiges left by the first experience answered to so many ideas which he acquired thereby—ideas that remained with him associated in a certain order, and from the last one of which the child eventually proceeded to act. The sciences of grammar and of logic are little more than attempts methodically to classify all such acquired ideas and to trace certain laws of relationship amongst them. The forms of relation between them, becoming themselves in turn noticed by the mind, are treated as conceptions of a higher and more abstract order, as when we speak of a 'syllogistic relation' between propositions, or of four quantities making a 'proportion,' or of the 'inconsistency' of two conceptions, or the 'implication' of one in the other.

So you see that the process of education, taken in a large

way, may be described as nothing but the process of acquiring ideas or conceptions, the best educated mind being the mind which has the largest stock of them, ready to meet the largest possible variety of the emergencies of life. The lack of education means only the failure to have acquired them, and the consequent liability to be 'floored' and 'rattled' in the vicissitudes of experience.

In all this process of acquiring conceptions, a certain instinctive order is followed. There is a native tendency to assimilate certain kinds of conception at one age, and other kinds of conception at a later age. During the first seven or eight years of childhood the mind is most interested in the sensible properties of material things. *Constructiveness* is the instinct most active; and by the incessant hammering and sawing, and dressing and undressing dolls, putting of things together and taking them apart, the child not only trains the muscles to co-ordinate action, but accumulates a store of physical conceptions which are the basis of his knowledge of the material world through life. Object-teaching and manual training wisely extend the sphere of this order of acquisition. Clay, wood, metals, and the various kinds of tools are made to contribute to the store. A youth brought up with a sufficiently broad basis of this kind is always at home in the world. He stands within the pale. He is acquainted with Nature, and Nature in a certain sense is acquainted with him. Whereas the youth brought up alone at home, with no acquaintance with anything but the printed page, is always afflicted with a certain remoteness from the material facts of life, and a correlative insecurity of consciousness which make of him a kind of alien on the earth in which he ought to feel himself perfectly at home.

I already said something of this in speaking of the constructive impulse, and I must not repeat myself. Moreover, you fully realize, I am sure, how important for life—for the moral tone of life, quite apart from definite practical pursuits—is this sense of readiness for emergencies which a man gains through early familiarity and acquaintance with the world of material things. To have grown up on a farm, to have haunted a carpenter's and blacksmith's shop, to have handled horses and cows and boats and guns, and to have ideas and abilities

connected with such objects are an inestimable part of youthful acquisition. After adolescence it is rare to be able to get
into familiar touch with any of these primitive things. The
instinctive propensions have faded, and the habits are hard to
acquire.

Accordingly, one of the best fruits of the 'child-study'
movement has been to reinstate all these activities to their
proper place in a sound system of education. *Feed* the growing human being, feed him with the sort of experience for
which from year to year he shows a natural craving, and he
will develop in adult life a sounder sort of mental tissue, even
though he may seem to be 'wasting' a great deal of his growing time, in the eyes of those for whom the only channels of
learning are books and verbally communicated information.

It is not till adolescence is reached that the mind grows able
to take in the more abstract aspects of experience, the hidden
similarities and distinctions between things, and especially
their causal sequences. Rational knowledge of such things as
mathematics, mechanics, chemistry, and biology, is now possible; and the acquisition of conceptions of this order form
the next phase of education. Later still, not till adolescence is
well advanced, does the mind awaken to a systematic interest
in abstract human relations—moral relations, properly so
called—to sociological ideas and to metaphysical abstractions.

This general order of sequence is followed traditionally of
course in the school-room. It is foreign to my purpose to do
more than indicate that general psychological principle of the
successive order of awakening of the faculties on which the
whole thing rests. I have spoken of it already, apropos of the
transitoriness of instincts. Just as many a youth has to go permanently without an adequate stock of conceptions of a certain order, because experiences of that order were not yielded
at the time when new curiosity was most acute, so it will
conversely happen that many another youth is spoiled for a
certain subject of study (although he would have enjoyed it
well if led into it at a later age) through having had it thrust
upon him so prematurely that disgust was created, and the
bloom quite taken off from future trials. I think I have seen
college students unfitted forever for 'philosophy' from having
taken that study up a year too soon.

In all these later studies, verbal material is the vehicle by which the mind thinks. The abstract conceptions of physics and sociology may, it is true, be embodied in visual or other images of phenomena, but they need not be so; and the truth remains that, after adolescence has begun, "words, words, words," must constitute a large part, and an always larger part as life advances, of what the human being has to learn. This is so even in the natural sciences, so far as these are causal and rational, and not merely confined to description. So I go back to what I said awhile ago apropos of verbal memorizing. The more accurately words are learned, the better, if only the teacher make sure that what they signify is also understood. It is the failure of this latter condition, in so much of the old-fashioned recitation, that has caused that reaction against 'parrot-like reproduction' that we are so familiar with to-day. A friend of mine, visiting a school, was asked to examine a young class in geography. Glancing at the book, she said: "Suppose you should dig a hole in the ground, hundreds of feet deep, how should you find it at the bottom—warmer or colder than on top?" None of the class replying, the teacher said: "I'm sure they know, but I think you don't ask the question quite rightly. Let me try." So, taking the book, she asked: "In what condition is the interior of the globe?" and received the immediate answer from half the class at once: "The interior of the globe is in a condition of *igneous fusion*." Better exclusive object-teaching than such verbal recitations as that; and yet verbal reproduction, intelligently connected with more objective work, must always play a leading, and surely *the* leading, part in education. Our modern reformers, in their books, write too exclusively of the earliest years of the pupil. These lend themselves better to explicit treatment; and I myself, in dwelling so much upon the native impulses, and object-teaching, and anecdotes, and all that, have paid my tribute to the line of least resistance in describing. Yet away back in childhood we find the beginnings of purely intellectual curiosity, and the intelligence of abstract terms. The object-teaching is mainly to *launch* the pupils, with some concrete conceptions of the facts concerned, upon the more abstract ideas.

To hear some authorities on teaching, however, you would suppose that geography not only began, but ended with the school-yard and neighboring hill, that physics was one endless round of repeating the same sort of tedious weighing and measuring operation; whereas a very few examples are usually sufficient to set the imagination free on genuine lines, and then what the mind craves is more rapid, general, and abstract treatment. I heard a lady say that she had taken her child to the kindergarten, "but he is so bright that he saw through it immediately." Too many school children 'see' as immediately 'through' the namby-pamby attempts of the softer pædagogy to lubricate things for them, and make them interesting. Even they can enjoy abstractions, provided they be of the proper order; and it is a poor compliment to their rational appetite to think that anecdotes about little Tommies and little Jennies are the only kind of things their minds can digest.

But here, as elsewhere, it is a matter of more or less; and, in the last resort, the teacher's own tact is the only thing that can bring out the right effect. The great difficulty with abstractions is that of knowing just what meaning the pupil attaches to the terms he uses. The words may sound all right, but the meaning remains the child's own secret. So varied forms of words must be insisted on, to bring the secret out. And a strange secret does it often prove. A relative of mine was trying to explain to a little girl what was meant by 'the passive voice': "Suppose that you kill me: you who do the killing are in the active voice, and I, who am killed, am in the passive voice." "But how can you speak if you're killed?" said the child. "Oh, well, you may suppose that I am not yet quite dead!" The next day the child was asked, in class, to explain the passive voice, and said, "It's the kind of voice you speak with when you ain't quite dead."

In such a case as this the illustration ought to have been more varied. Everyone's memory will probably furnish examples of the fantastic meaning which their childhood attached to certain verbal statements (in poetry often), and which their elders, not having any reason to suspect, never corrected. I remember being greatly moved emotionally at the age of eight by the ballad of Lord Ullin's Daughter. Yet I thought that the staining of the heather by the blood was the evil chiefly dreaded, and that, when the boatman said,

> "I'll row you o'er the ferry.
> It is not for your silver bright,
> But for your winsome lady,"

he was to receive the lady for his pay. Similarly, I recently found that one of my own children was reading (and accepting) a verse of Tennyson's *In Memoriam* as

> "Ring out the *food* of rich and poor,
> Ring in *redness* to all mankind,"

and finding no inward difficulty.

The only safeguard against this sort of misconceiving is to insist on varied statement, and to bring the child's conceptions, wherever it be possible, to some sort of practical test.

Let us next pass to the subject of Apperception.

CHAPTER XIV

APPERCEPTION

'APPERCEPTION' is a word which cuts a great figure in the pædagogics of the present day. Read, for example, this advertisement of a certain text-book, which I take from an educational journal:

WHAT IS APPERCEPTION?

For an explanation of Apperception see Blank's PSYCHOLOGY, Vol. —— of the —— Education Series, just published.

The difference between Perception and Apperception is explained for the teacher in the preface to Blank's PSYCHOLOGY.

Many teachers are inquiring, "What is the meaning of Apperception in educational psychology?" Just the book for them is Blank's PSYCHOLOGY in which the idea was first expounded.

The most important idea in educational psychology is Apperception. The teacher may find this expounded in Blank's PSYCHOLOGY. The idea of Apperception is making a revolution in educational methods in Germany. It is explained in Blank's PSYCHOLOGY, Vol. —— of the —— Education Series, just published.

Blank's PSYCHOLOGY will be mailed prepaid to any address on receipt of $1.00.

Such an advertisement is in sober earnest a disgrace to all concerned; and such talk as it indulges-in is the sort of thing I had in view when I said at our first meeting that the teachers were suffering at the present day from a certain industrious mystification on the part of editors and publishers. Perhaps the word 'apperception,' flourished in their eyes and ears as it nowadays often is, embodies as much of this mystification as any other single thing. The conscientious young teacher is led to believe that it contains a recondite and portentous secret, by losing the true inwardness of which her whole career may be shattered. And yet, when she turns to the books and reads about it, it seems so trivial and commonplace a matter— meaning nothing more than the manner in which we receive a thing into our minds—that she fears she must have missed the point through the shallowness of her intelligence, and goes about thereafter afflicted with a sense either of uncertainty or of stupidity, and in each case remaining mortified at being so inadequate to her mission.

Now apperception is an extremely useful word in pædagogics, and offers a convenient name for a process to which every teacher must frequently refer. But it verily means nothing more than the act of taking a thing into the mind. It corresponds to nothing peculiar or elementary in psychology, being only one of the innumerable results of the psychological process of association of ideas; and psychology itself can easily dispense with the word, useful as it may be in pædagogics.

The gist of the matter is this: Every impression that comes in from without, be it a sentence which we hear, an object of vision, or an effluvium which assails our nose, no sooner enters our consciousness than it is drafted off in some determinate direction or other, making connection with the other materials already there, and finally producing what we call our reaction. The particular connections it strikes into are determined by our past experiences and the 'associations' of the present sort of impression with them. If, for instance, you hear me call out A, B, C, it is ten to one that you will react on the impression by inwardly or outwardly articulating D, E, F. The impression arouses its old associates; they go out to meet it; it is received by them, recognized by the mind as 'the beginning of the alphabet.' It is the fate of every impression thus to fall into a mind preoccupied with memories, ideas, and interests, and by these it is taken in. Educated as we already are, we never get an experience that remains for us completely nondescript; it always *reminds* of something similar in quality, or of some context that might have surrounded it before, and which it now in some way suggests. This mental escort which the mind supplies is drawn, of course, from the mind's ready-made stock. We *conceive* the impression in some definite way. We dispose of it according to our acquired possibilities, be they few or many, in the way of 'ideas.' This way of taking in the object is the process of apperception. The conceptions which meet and assimilate it are called by Herbart the 'apperceiving mass.' The apperceived impression is engulfed in this, and the result is a new field of consciousness, of which one part (and often a very small part) comes from the outer world, and another part (sometimes by far the largest) comes from the previous contents of the mind.

I think that you see plainly enough now that the process of apperception is what I called it a moment ago, a resultant of the association of ideas. The product is a sort of fusion of the new with the old, in which it is often impossible to distinguish the share of the two factors. For example, when we listen to a person speaking or read a page of print, much of what we think we see or hear is supplied from our memory. We overlook misprints, imagining the right letters, though we see the wrong ones; and how little we actually hear, when we listen to speech, we realize when we go to a foreign theatre; for there what troubles us is not so much that we cannot understand what the actors say as that we cannot hear their words. The fact is that we hear quite as little under similar conditions at home, only our mind, being fuller of English verbal associations, supplies the requisite material for comprehension upon a much slighter auditory hint.

In all the apperceptive operations of the mind, a certain general law makes itself felt—the law of economy. In admitting a new body of experience, we instinctively seek to disturb as little as possible our pre-existing stock of ideas. We always try to name a new experience in some way which will assimilate it to what we already know. We hate anything *absolutely* new, anything without any name, and for which a new name must be forged. So we take the nearest name, even though it be inappropriate. A child will call snow, when he sees it for the first time, sugar or white butterflies. The sail of a boat he calls a curtain; an egg in its shell, seen for the first time, he calls a pretty potato; an orange, a ball; a folding corkscrew, a pair of bad scissors. Caspar Hauser called the first geese he saw horses, and the Polynesians called Captain Cook's horses pigs. Mr. Rooper has written a little book on apperception, to which he gives the title of "*A Pot of Green Feathers*," that being the name applied to a pot of ferns by a child who had never seen ferns before.

In later life this economical tendency to leave the old undisturbed leads to what we know as 'old fogyism.' A new idea or a fact which would entail extensive rearrangement of the previous system of beliefs is always ignored or extruded from the mind in case it cannot be sophistically reinterpreted so as to tally harmoniously with the system. We have all conducted discussions with middle-aged people, overpowered them with our reasons, forced them to admit our contention, and a week later found them back as secure and constant in their old opinion as if they had never conversed with us at all. We call them old fogies; but there are young fogies, too. Old fogyism begins at a younger age than we think. I am almost afraid to say so, but I believe that in the majority of human beings it begins at about twenty-five.

In some of the books we find the various forms of apperception codified, and their subdivisions numbered and ticketed in tabular form in the way so delightful to the pædagogic eye. In one book which I remember reading there were sixteen different types of apperception discriminated from each other. There was associative apperception, subsumptive apperception, assimilative apperception, and others up to sixteen. It is needless to say that this is nothing but an exhibition of the crass artificiality which has always haunted psychology, and which perpetuates itself by lingering along, especially in these works which are advertised as 'written for the use of teachers.' The flowing life of the mind is sorted into parcels suitable for presentation in the recitation-room, and chopped up into supposed 'processes' with long greek and latin names, which in real life have no distinct existence.

There is no reason, if we are classing the different types of apperception, why we should stop at sixteen rather than sixteen hundred. There are as many types of apperception as there are possible ways in which an incoming experience may be reacted on by an individual mind. A little while ago, at Buffalo, I was the guest of a lady who, a fortnight before, had taken her seven-year-old boy for the first time to Niagara Falls.

The child silently glared at the phenomenon until his mother, supposing him struck speechless by its sublimity, said, "Well, my boy, what do you think of it?" to which, "Is that the kind of spray I spray my nose with?" was the boy's only reply. That was his mode of apperceiving the spectacle. You may claim this as a particular type, and call it by the greek name of rhinotherapeutical apperception, if you like; and if you do, you will hardly be more trivial or artificial than are some of the authors of the books.

M. Perez, in one of his books on childhood, gives a good example of the different modes of apperception of the same phenomenon which are possible at different stages of individual experience. A dwelling-house took fire, and an infant in the family, witnessing the conflagration from the arms of his nurse, standing outside, expressed nothing but the liveliest delight at its brilliancy. But when the bell of the fire-engine was heard approaching, the child was thrown by the sound into a paroxysm of fear, strange sounds being, as you know, very alarming to young children. In what opposite ways must the child's parents have apperceived the burning house and the engine respectively!

The self-same person, according to the line of thought he may be in or to his emotional mood, will apperceive the same impression quite differently on different occasions. A medical or engineering expert retained on one side of a case will not apperceive the facts in the same way as if the other side had retained him. When people are at loggerheads about the interpretation of a fact, it usually shows that they have too few heads of classification to apperceive by; for, as a general thing, the fact of such a dispute is enough to show that neither one of their rival interpretations is a perfect fit. Both sides deal with the matter by approximation, squeezing it under the handiest or least disturbing conception; whereas it would, nine times out of ten, be better to enlarge their stock of ideas or invent some altogether new title for the phenomenon.

Thus, in biology, we used to have interminable discussion as to whether certain single-celled organisms were animals or vegetables, until Haeckel introduced the new apperceptive name of Protista, which ended the disputes. In law courts no *tertium quid* is recognized between insanity and sanity. If

sane, a man is punished; if insane, acquitted; and it is seldom
hard to find two experts who will take opposite views of his
case. All the while, nature is more subtle than our doctors.
Just as a room is neither dark nor light absolutely, but might
be dark for a watchmaker's uses, and yet light enough to eat
in or play in, so a man may be sane for some purposes and
insane for others—sane enough to be left at large, yet not
sane enough to take care of his financial affairs. The word
'crank,' which became familiar at the time of Guiteau's trial,
fulfilled the need of a *tertium quid*. The foreign terms 'déséquilibré,' 'hereditary degenerate,' and 'psychopathic subject,'
have arisen in response to the same need.

The whole progress of our sciences goes on by the invention of newly forged technical names whereby to designate the newly remarked aspects of phenomena—phenomena
which could only be squeezed with violence into the pigeon-
holes of the earlier stock of conceptions. As time goes on, our
vocabulary becomes thus ever more and more voluminous,
having to keep up with the ever-growing multitude of our
stock of apperceiving ideas.

In this gradual process of interaction between the new and
the old, not only is the new modified and determined by the
particular sort of old which apperceives it, but the apperceiving mass, the old itself, is modified by the particular kind of
new which it assimilates. Thus, to take the stock German example of the child brought up in a house where there are no
tables but square ones, 'table' means for him a thing in which
square corners are essential. But if he goes to a house where
there are round tables and still calls them tables, his apperceiving notion 'table' acquires immediately a wider inward
content. In this way, our conceptions are constantly dropping
characters once supposed essential, and including others once
supposed inadmissible. The extension of the notion 'beast' to
porpoises and whales, of the notion 'organism' to society, are
familiar examples of what I mean.

But be our conceptions adequate or inadequate, and be our
stock of them large or small, they are all we have to work
with. If an educated man is, as I said, a group of organized
tendencies to conduct, what prompts the conduct is in every
case the man's conception of the way in which to name and

classify the actual emergency. The more adequate the stock of
ideas, the more 'able' is the man, the more uniformly appropriate is his behavior likely to be. When later we take up the
subject of the will, we shall see that the essential preliminary
to every decision is the finding of the right *names* under
which to class the proposed alternatives of conduct. He who
has few names is in so far forth an incompetent deliberator.
The names—and each name stands for a conception or
idea—are our instruments for handling our problems and
solving our dilemmas. Now, when we think of this, we are
too apt to forget an important fact, which is that in most
human beings the stock of names and concepts is mostly acquired during the years of adolescence and the earliest years
of adult life. I probably shocked you a moment ago by saying
that most men begin to be old fogies at the age of twenty-
five. It is true that a grown-up adult keeps gaining well into
middle age a great knowledge of details, and a great acquaintance with individual cases connected with his profession or
business life. In this sense, his conceptions increase during a
very long period; for his knowledge grows more extensive
and minute. But the larger categories of conception, the sorts
of thing, and wider classes of relation between things, of
which we take cognizance, are all got into the mind at a comparatively youthful date. Few men ever do acquaint themselves with the principles of a new science after even twenty-
five. If you do not study political economy in college, it is a
thousand to one that its main conceptions will remain unknown to you through life. Similarly with biology, similarly
with electricity. What percentage of persons now fifty years
old have any definite conception whatever of a dynamo, or
how the trolley-cars are made to run? Surely, a small fraction
of one per cent. But the boys in colleges are all acquiring
these conceptions.

There is a sense of infinite potentiality in us all, when
young, which makes some of us draw up lists of books we
intend to read hereafter, and makes most of us think that we
can easily acquaint ourselves with all sorts of things which
we are now neglecting by studying them out hereafter in the
intervals of leisure of our business lives. Such good intentions
are hardly ever carried out. The conceptions acquired before

thirty remain usually the only ones we ever gain. Such exceptional cases of perpetually self-renovating youth as Mr. Gladstone's only prove, by the admiration they awaken, the universality of the rule. And it may well solemnize a teacher, and confirm in him a healthy sense of the importance of his mission, to feel how exclusively dependent upon his present ministrations in the way of imparting conceptions the pupil's future life is probably bound to be.

CHAPTER XV

THE WILL

SINCE MENTALITY terminates naturally in outward conduct, the final chapter in psychology has to be the chapter on the will. But the word 'will' can be used in a broader and in a narrower sense. In the broader sense, it designates our entire capacity for impulsive and active life, including our instinctive reactions and those forms of behavior that have become secondarily automatic and semi-unconscious through frequent repetition. In the narrower sense, acts of will are such acts only as cannot be inattentively performed. A distinct idea of what they are, and a deliberate *fiat* on the mind's part, must precede their execution.

Such acts are often characterized by hesitation, and accompanied by a feeling, altogether peculiar, of resolve, a feeling which may or may not carry with it a farther feeling of effort. In my earlier talks, I said so much of our impulsive tendencies that I will restrict myself in what follows to volition in this narrower sense of the term.

All our deeds were considered by the early psychologists to be due to a peculiar faculty called the will, without whose fiat action could not occur. Thoughts and impressions, being intrinsically inactive, were supposed to produce conduct only through the intermediation of this superior agent. Until they twitched its coat-tails, so to speak, no outward behavior could occur. This doctrine was long ago exploded by the discovery of the phenomena of reflex action, in which sensible impressions, as you know, produce movement immediately and of themselves. The doctrine may also be considered exploded as far as ideas go.

The fact is that there is no sort of consciousness whatever, be it sensation, feeling, or idea, which does not directly and of itself tend to discharge into some motor effect. The motor effect need not always be an outward stroke of behavior. It may be only an alteration of the heart-beats or breathing, or a modification in the distribution of blood, such as blushing or turning pale; or else a secretion of tears, or what not. But in any case, it is there in some shape when any consciousness is there; and a belief as fundamental as any in modern psychology is the belief at last attained that conscious processes of any sort, conscious processes merely as such, *must* pass over into motion, open or concealed.

The least complicated case of this tendency is the case of a mind possessed by only a single idea. If that idea be of an object connected with a native impulse, the impulse will immediately proceed to discharge. If it be the idea of a movement, the movement will occur. Such a case of action from a single idea has been distinguished from more complex cases by the name of 'ideo-motor' action, meaning action without express decision or effort. Most of the habitual actions to which we are trained are of this ideo-motor sort. We perceive, for instance, that the door is open, and we rise and shut it; we perceive some raisins in a dish before us, and extend our hand and carry one of them to our mouth without interrupting the conversation; or, when lying in bed, we suddenly think that we shall be late for breakfast, and instantly we get up with no particular exertion or resolve. All the ingrained procedures by which life is carried on—the manners and customs, dressing and undressing, acts of salutation, etc.—are executed in this semi-automatic way unhesitatingly and efficiently, the very outermost margin of consciousness seeming to be concerned in them, whilst the focus may be occupied with widely different things.

But now turn to a more complicated case. Suppose two thoughts to be in the mind together, of which one, A, taken alone, would discharge itself in a certain action; but of which the other, B, suggests an action of a different sort, or a consequence of the first action calculated to make us shrink. The psychologists now say that the second idea, B, will probably arrest or *inhibit* the motor effects of the first idea, A. One word, then, about 'inhibition' in general, to make this particular case more clear.

One of the most interesting discoveries of physiology was the discovery, made simultaneously in France and Germany fifty years ago, that nerve currents do not only start muscles into action, but may check action already going on or keep it from occurring as it otherwise might. *Nerves of arrest* were thus distinguished alongside of motor nerves. The pneumogastric nerve, for example, if stimulated, arrests the movements of the heart; the splanchnic nerve arrests those of the intestines, if already begun. But it soon appeared that this was too narrow a way of looking at the matter, and that arrest is not so much the specific function of certain nerves as a general function which any part of the nervous system may exert upon other parts under the appropriate conditions. The higher centres, for example, seem to exert a constant inhibitive influence on the excitability of those below. The reflexes of an animal with its hemispheres wholly or in part removed become exaggerated. You all know that common reflex in dogs whereby, if you scratch the animal's side, the corresponding hind leg will begin to make scratching movements, usually in the air. Now in dogs with mutilated hemispheres this scratching reflex is so incessant that, as Goltz first described them, the hair gets all worn off their sides. In idiots, the functions of the hemispheres being largely in abeyance, the lower impulses, not inhibited, as they would be in normal human beings, often express themselves in most odious ways. You know also how any higher emotional tendency will quench a lower one. Fear arrests appetite, maternal love annuls fear, respect checks sensuality, and the like; and in the more subtle manifestations of the moral life, whenever an ideal stirring is suddenly quickened into intensity, it is as if the whole scale of values of our motives changed its equilibrium. The force of old temptations vanishes, and what a moment ago was impossible is now not only possible, but easy, because of their inhibition. This has been well called the 'expulsive power of the higher emotion.'

It is easy to apply this notion of inhibition to the case of our ideational processes. I am lying in bed, for example, and think it is time to get up; but alongside of this thought there is present to my mind a realization of the extreme coldness of the morning and the pleasantness of the warm bed. In such a situation the motor consequences of the first idea are blocked; and I may remain for half an hour or more with the two ideas oscillating before me in a kind of deadlock, which is what we call the state of hesitation or deliberation. In a case like this the deliberation can be resolved and the decision reached in either of two ways:

(1) I may forget for a moment the thermometric conditions, and then the idea of getting up will immediately discharge into act: I shall suddenly find that I have got up—or

(2) Still mindful of the freezing temperature, the thought of the duty of rising may become so pungent that it determines action in spite of inhibition. In the latter case, I have a sense of energetic moral effort, and consider that I have done a virtuous act.

All cases of wilful action properly so called, of choice after hesitation and deliberation, may be conceived after one of these latter patterns. So you see that volition, in the narrower sense, takes place only when there are a number of conflicting systems of ideas, and depends on our having a complex field of consciousness. The interesting thing to note is the extreme delicacy of the inhibitive machinery. A strong and urgent motor idea in the focus may be neutralized and made inoperative by the presence of the very faintest contradictory idea in the margin. For instance, I hold out my forefinger, and with closed eyes try to realize as vividly as possible that I hold a revolver in my hand and am pulling the trigger. I can even now fairly feel my finger quivering with the tendency to contract; and if it were hitched to a recording apparatus, it would certainly betray its state of tension by registering incipient movements. Yet it does not actually crook, and the movement of pulling the trigger is not performed. Why not? Simply because, all concentrated though I am upon the idea of the movement, I nevertheless also realize the total conditions of the experiment, and in the back of my mind, so to speak, or in its fringe and margin, have the simultaneous idea that the movement is not to take place. The mere presence of that marginal intention, without effort, urgency, or emphasis, or any special reinforcement from my attention, suffices to the inhibitive effect.

And this is why so few of the ideas that flit through our minds do, in point of fact, produce their motor consequences. Life would be a curse and a care for us if every fleeting fancy were to do so. Abstractly, the law of ideo-motor action is true; but in the concrete our fields of consciousness are always so complex that the inhibiting margin keeps the centre inoperative most of the time. In all this, you see, I speak as if ideas by their mere presence or absence determined behavior, and as if between the ideas themselves on the one hand and the conduct on the other there were no room for any third intermediate principle of activity, like that called 'the will.'

If you are struck by the materialistic or fatalistic doctrines which seem to follow this conception, I beg you to suspend your judgment for a moment, as I shall soon have something more to say about the matter. But, meanwhile yielding one's self to the mechanical conception of the psychophysical organism, nothing is easier than to indulge in a picture of the fatalistic character of human life. Man's conduct appears as the mere resultant of all his various impulsions and inhibitions. One object, by its presence, makes us act; another object checks our action. Feelings aroused and ideas suggested by objects sway us one way and another; emotions complicate the game by their mutual inhibitive effects, the higher abolishing the lower or perhaps being itself swept away. The life in all this becomes prudential and moral; but the psychological agents in the drama may be described, you see, as nothing but the 'ideas' themselves—ideas for the whole system of which what we call the 'soul' or 'character' or 'will' of the person is nothing but a collective name. As Hume said, the ideas are themselves the actors, the stage, the theatre, the spectators, and the play. This is the so-called 'associationist' psychology, brought down to its radical expression: it is useless to ignore its power as a conception. Like all conceptions, when they become clear and lively enough, this conception has a strong tendency to impose itself upon belief; and psychologists trained on biological lines usually adopt it as the last word of science on the subject. No one can have an adequate notion of modern psychological theory unless he has at some time apprehended this view in the full force of its simplicity.

Let us humor it for a while, for it has advantages in the way of exposition.

Voluntary action, then, is at all times a resultant of the compounding of our impulsions with our inhibitions.

From this it immediately follows that there will be two types of will, in one of which impulsions will predominate, in the other inhibitions. We may speak of them, if you like, as the precipitate and the obstructed will, respectively. When fully pronounced, they are familiar to everybody. The extreme example of the precipitate will is the maniac; his ideas discharge into action so rapidly, his associative processes are so extravagantly lively, that inhibitions have no time to arrive, and he says and does whatever pops into his head without a moment of hesitation.

Certain melancholiacs furnish the extreme example of the over-inhibited type. Their minds are cramped in a fixed emotion of fear or helplessness, their ideas confined to the one thought that for them life is impossible. So they show a condition of perfect 'abulia,' or inability to will or act. They cannot change their posture or speech or execute the simplest command.

The different races of men show different temperaments in this regard. The Southern races are commonly accounted the more impulsive and precipitate; the English race, especially our New England branch of it, is supposed to be all sicklied over with repressive forms of self-consciousness, and condemned to express itself through a jungle of scruples and checks.

The highest form of character, however, abstractly considered, must be full of scruples and inhibitions. But action, in such a character, far from being paralyzed, will succeed in energetically keeping on its way, sometimes overpowering the resistances, sometimes steering along the line where they lie thinnest.

Just as our extensor muscles act most firmly when a simultaneous contraction of the flexors guides and steadies them; so the mind of him whose fields of consciousness are complex, and who, with the reasons for the action, sees the reasons against it, and yet, instead of being palsied, acts in the way that takes the whole field into consideration—so, I say, is such a mind the ideal sort of mind that we should seek to reproduce in our pupils. Purely impulsive action, or action that proceeds to extremities regardless of consequences, on the other hand, is the easiest action in the world, and the lowest in type. Anyone can show energy when made quite reckless. An oriental despot requires but little ability: as long as he lives he succeeds, for he has absolutely his own way; and when the world can no longer endure the horror of him, he is assassinated. But not to proceed immediately to extremities, to be still able to act energetically under an array of inhibitions—that indeed is rare and difficult. Cavour, when urged to proclaim martial law in 1859, refused to do so, saying: "Anyone can govern in that way. I will be constitutional." Your parliamentary rulers, your Lincoln, your Gladstone, are the strongest type of man, because they accomplish results under the most intricate possible conditions. We think of Napoleon Bonaparte as a colossal monster of will-power, and truly enough he was so. But from the point of view of the psychological machinery, it would be hard to say whether he or Gladstone was the larger volitional quantity; for Napoleon disregarded all the usual inhibitions, and Gladstone, passionate as he was, scrupulously considered them in his statesmanship.

A familiar example of the paralyzing power of scruples is the inhibitive effect of conscientiousness upon conversation. Nowhere does conversation seem to have flourished as brilliantly as in France during the last century. But if we read old French memoirs, we see how many brakes of scrupulosity which tie our tongues to-day were then removed. Where mendacity, treachery, obscenity, and malignity find unhampered expression, talk can be brilliant indeed; but its flame waxes dim where the mind is stitched all over with conscientious fear of violating the moral and social proprieties.

The teacher often is confronted in the school-room with an abnormal type of will, which we may call the 'balky will.' Certain children, if they do not succeed in doing a thing immediately, remain completely inhibited in regard to it; it becomes literally impossible for them to understand it if it be an intellectual problem, or to do it if it be an outward operation, as long as this particular inhibited condition lasts. Such children are usually treated as sinful, and are punished; or else the teacher pits his or her will against the child's will, considering that the latter must be 'broken.' "Break your child's will, in order that it may not perish," wrote John Wesley. "Break its will as soon as it can speak plainly—or even before it can speak at all. It should be forced to do as it is told, even if you have to whip it ten times running. Break its will, in order that its soul may live." Such will-breaking is always a scene with a great deal of nervous wear and tear on both sides, a bad state of feeling left behind it, and the victory not always with the would-be will-breaker.

When a situation of the kind is once fairly developed, and the child is all tense and excited inwardly, nineteen times out of twenty it is best for the teacher to apperceive the case as one of neural pathology rather than as one of moral culpability. So long as the inhibiting sense of impossibility remains in the child's mind, he will continue unable to get beyond the obstacle. The aim of the teacher should then be to make him simply forget. Drop the subject for the time, divert the mind to something else; then, leading the pupil back by some circuitous line of association, spring it on him again before he has time to recognize it, and as likely as not he will go over it now without any difficulty. It is in no other way that we overcome balkiness in a horse: we divert his attention, do something to his nose or ear, lead him round in a circle, and thus get him over a place where flogging would only have made him more invincible. A tactful teacher will never let these strained situations come up at all.

You perceive now, my friends, what your general or abstract duty is as teachers. Although you have to generate in your pupils a large stock of ideas, any one of which may be inhibitory, yet you must also see to it that no habitual hesitancy or paralysis of the will ensues, and that the pupil still retains his power of vigorous action. Psychology can state your problem in these terms, but you see how impotent she is to furnish the elements of its practical solution. When all is said and done, and your best efforts are made, it will probably remain true that the result will depend more on a certain native tone or temper in the pupil's psychological constitution than on anything else. Some persons appear to have a naturally poor focalization of the field of consciousness; and in such persons actions hang slack, and inhibitions seem to exert peculiarly easy sway.

But let us now close in a little more closely on this matter of the education of the will. Your task is to build up a *character* in your pupils; and a character, as I have so often said, consists in an organized set of habits of reaction. Now of what do such habits of reaction themselves consist? They consist of tendencies to act characteristically when certain ideas possess us, and to refrain characteristically when possessed by other ideas.

Our volitional habits depend, then, first, on what the stock of ideas is which we have; and second, on the habitual coupling of the several ideas with action or inaction respectively. How is it when an alternative is presented to you for choice, and you are uncertain what you ought to do? You first hesitate, and then you deliberate. And in what does your deliberation consist? It consists in trying to apperceive the case successively by a number of different ideas, which seem to fit it more or less, until at last you hit on one which seems to fit it exactly. If that be an idea which is a customary forerunner of action in you, which enters into one of your maxims of positive behavior, your hesitation ceases, and you act immediately. If, on the other hand, it be an idea which carries inaction as its habitual result, if it ally itself with *prohibition*, then you unhesitatingly refrain. The problem is, you see, to find the right idea or conception for the case. This search for the right conception may take days or weeks.

I spoke as if the action were easy when the conception once is found. Often it is so, but it may be otherwise; and when it is otherwise, we find ourselves at the very centre of a moral situation, into which I should now like you to look with me a little nearer.

The proper conception, the true head of classification, may be hard to attain; or it may be one with which we have contracted no settled habits of action. Or again, the action to which it would prompt may be dangerous and difficult; or else inaction may appear deadly cold and negative when our impulsive feeling is hot. In either of these latter cases it is hard to hold the right idea steadily enough before the attention to let it exert its adequate effects. Whether it be stimulative or inhibitive, it is *too reasonable* for us; and the more instinctive passional propensity then tends to extrude it from our consideration. We shy away from the thought of it; it twinkles and goes out the moment it appears in the margin of our consciousness; and we need a resolute effort of voluntary attention to drag it into the focus of the field, and to keep it there long enough for its associative and motor effects to be exerted. Everyone knows only too well how the mind flinches from looking at considerations hostile to the reigning mood of feeling.

Once brought, however, in this way to the centre of the field of consciousness, and held there, the reasonable idea will exert these effects inevitably; for the laws of connection between our consciousness and our nervous system provide for the action then taking place. Our moral effort, properly so called, terminates in our holding fast to the appropriate idea.

If, then, you are asked, "*In what does a moral act consist* when reduced to its simplest and most elementary form?" you can make only one reply. You can say that *it consists in the effort of attention by which we hold fast to an idea* which but for that effort of attention would be driven out of the mind by the other psychological tendencies that are there. *To think*, in short, is the secret of will, just as it is the secret of memory.

This comes out very clearly in the kind of excuse which we most frequently hear from persons who find themselves confronted by the sinfulness or harmfulness of some part of their behavior. "I never *thought*," they say. "I never *thought* how mean the action was, I never *thought* of these abominable consequences." And what do we retort when they say this? We say: "Why *didn't* you think? What were you there for but to think?" And we read them a moral lecture on their irreflectiveness.

The hackneyed example of moral deliberation is the case of an habitual drunkard under temptation. He has made a resolve to reform, but he is now solicited again by the bottle. His moral triumph or failure literally consists in his finding the right *name* for the case. If he says that it is a case of not wasting good liquor already poured out, or a case of not being churlish and unsociable when in the midst of friends, or a case of learning something at last about a brand of whiskey which he never met before, or a case of celebrating a public holiday, or a case of stimulating himself to a more energetic resolve in favor of abstinence than any he has ever yet made, then he is lost; his choice of the wrong name seals his doom. But if, in spite of all the plausible good names with which his thirsty fancy so copiously furnishes him, he unwaveringly clings to the truer bad name, and apperceives the case as that of "being a drunkard, being a drunkard, being a drunkard," his feet are planted on the road to salvation; he saves himself by thinking rightly.

Thus are your pupils to be saved: first, by the stock of ideas with which you furnish them; second, by the amount of voluntary attention that they can exert in holding to the right ones, however unpalatable; and third, by the several habits of acting definitely on these latter to which they have been successfully trained.

In all this the power of voluntarily attending is the point of the whole procedure. Just as a balance turns on its knife-edges, so on it our moral destiny turns. You remember that, when we were talking of the subject of attention, we discovered how much more intermittent and brief our acts of voluntary attention are than is commonly supposed. If they were all summed together, the time that they occupy would cover an almost incredibly small portion of our lives. But I also said, you will remember, that their brevity was not in proportion to their significance, and that I should return to the subject again. So I return to it now. It is not the mere size of a thing which constitutes its importance; it is its position in the organism to which it belongs. Our acts of voluntary attention, brief and fitful as they are, are nevertheless momentous and critical, determining us, as they do, to higher or lower destinies. The exercise of voluntary attention in the school-room must therefore be counted one of the most important points of training that take place there; and the first-rate teacher, by the keenness of the remoter interests which he is able to awaken, will provide abundant opportunities for its occurrence. I hope that you appreciate this now without any farther explanation.

*   *   *

I have been accused of holding up before you, in the course of these talks, a mechanical and even a materialistic view of the mind. I have called it an organism and a machine; I have spoken of its reaction on the environment as the essential thing about it; and I have referred this, either openly or implicitly, to the construction of the nervous system. I have, in consequence, received notes from some of you, begging me to be more explicit on this point; and to let you know frankly whether I am a complete materialist, or not.

Now in these lectures I wish to be strictly practical and useful, and to keep free from all speculative complications. Nevertheless, I do not wish to leave any ambiguity about my own position; and I will therefore say, in order to avoid all misunderstanding, that in no sense do I count myself a materialist. I cannot see how such a thing as our consciousness can possibly be *produced* by a nervous machinery, though I can perfectly well see how, if 'ideas' do accompany the workings of the machinery, the *order* of the ideas might very well follow exactly the *order* of the machine's operations. Our habitual associations of ideas, trains of thought, and sequences of action might thus be consequences of the succession of currents in our nervous systems. And the possible stock of ideas which a man's free spirit would have to choose from might depend exclusively on the native and acquired powers of his brain. If this were all, we might indeed adopt the fatalist conception which I sketched for you but a short while ago. Our ideas would be determined by brain currents, and these by purely mechanical laws.

But after what we have just seen—namely, the part played by voluntary attention in volition—a belief in free will and purely spiritual causation is still open to us. The duration and amount of this attention *seem* within certain limits indeterminate. We *feel* as if we could make it really more or less, and as if our free action in this regard were a genuine critical point in nature, a point on which our destiny and that of others might hinge. The whole question of free will concentrates itself, then, at this same small point: "Is or is not the appearance of indetermination at this point an illusion?"

It is plain that such a question can be decided only by general analogies, and not by accurate observations. The freewillist believes the appearance to be a reality; the determinist believes that it is an illusion. I myself hold with the freewillists—not because I cannot conceive the fatalist theory clearly, or because I fail to understand its plausibility, but simply because, if free will *were* true, it would be absurd to have the belief in it fatally forced on our acceptance. Considering the inner fitness of things, one would rather think that the very first act of a will endowed with freedom should be to sustain the belief in the freedom itself. I accordingly believe freely in my freedom; I do so with the best of scientific consciences, knowing that the predetermination of the amount of my effort of attention can never receive objective proof, and hoping that, whether you follow my example in this respect or not, it will at least make you see that such psychological and psychophysical theories as I hold do not necessarily force a man to become a fatalist or a materialist.

Let me say one more final word now about the will, and therewith conclude both that important subject and these lectures.

There are two types of will; there are also two types of inhibition. We may call them inhibition by repression or by negation, and inhibition by substitution, respectively. The difference between them is that, in the case of inhibition by repression, both the inhibited idea and the inhibiting idea, the impulsive idea and the idea that negates it, remain along with each other in consciousness, producing a certain inward strain or tension there; whereas, in inhibition by substitution, the inhibiting idea supersedes altogether the idea which it inhibits, and the latter quickly vanishes from the field.

For instance, your pupils are wandering in mind, are listening to a sound outside the window, which presently grows interesting enough to claim all their attention. You can call the latter back again by bellowing at them not to listen to those sounds, but to keep their minds on their books or on what you are saying. And by thus keeping them conscious that your eye is sternly on them, you may produce a good effect. But it will be a wasteful effect and an inferior effect; for the moment you relax your supervision the attractive disturbance, always there soliciting their curiosity, will overpower them, and they will be just as they were before; whereas if, without saying anything about the street disturbances, you open a counter-attraction by starting some very interesting talk or demonstration yourself, they will altogether forget the distracting incident, and without any effort follow you along. There are many interests that can never be inhibited by the way of negation. To a man in love, for example, it is literally impossible, by any effort of will, to annul his passion; but let 'some new planet swim into his ken,' and the former idol will immediately cease to engross his mind.

It is clear that in general we ought, whenever we can, to employ the method of inhibition by substitution. He whose life is based upon the word 'no,' who tells the truth because a lie is wicked, and who has constantly to grapple with his envious and cowardly and mean propensities, is in an inferior situation in every respect to what he would be if the love of truth and magnanimity positively possessed him from the outset, and he felt no inferior temptations. Your born gentleman is certainly, for this world's purposes, a more valuable being than your "Crump, with his grunting resistance to his native devils," even though in God's sight the latter may, as the Catholic theologians say, be rolling up great stores of 'merit.'

Spinoza long ago wrote in his *Ethics* that anything that a man can avoid under the notion that it is bad he may also avoid under the notion that something else is good. He who habitually acts *sub specie mali*, under the negative notion, the notion of the bad, is called a slave by Spinoza. To him who acts habitually under the notion of good he gives the name of freeman. See to it now, I beg you, that you make freemen of your pupils by habituating them to act, whenever possible, under the notion of a good. Get them habitually to tell the truth, not so much through showing them the wickedness of lying as by arousing their enthusiasm for honor and veracity. Wean them from their native cruelty by imparting to them some of your own positive sympathy with an animal's inner springs of joy. And in the lessons which you may be legally obliged to conduct upon the bad effects of alcohol, lay less stress than the books do on the drunkard's stomach, kidneys, nerves, and social miseries, and more on the blessings of having an organism kept in lifelong possession of its full youthful elasticity by a sweet, sound blood, to which stimulants and narcotics are unknown, and to which the morning sun and air and dew will daily come as sufficiently powerful intoxicants.

CONCLUSION

I have now ended these talks. If to some of you the things I have said seem obvious or trivial, it is possible that they may appear less so when, in the course of a year or two, you find yourselves noticing and apperceiving events in the schoolroom a little differently, in consequence of some of the conceptions I have tried to make more clear. I cannot but think that to apperceive your pupil as a little sensitive, impulsive, associative, and reactive organism, partly fated and partly free, will lead to a better intelligence of all his ways. Understand him, then, as such a subtle little piece of machinery. And if, in addition, you can also see him *sub specie boni*, and love him as well, you will be in the best possible position for becoming perfect teachers.

Talks to Students

I

I WISH in the following hour to take certain psychological doctrines and show their practical applications to mental hygiene—to the hygiene of our American life more particularly. Our people, especially in academic circles, are turning towards psychology nowadays with great expectations; and if psychology is to justify them, it must be by showing fruits in the pædagogic and therapeutic lines.

The reader may possibly have heard of a peculiar theory of the emotions, commonly referred to in psychological literature as the Lange-James theory. According to this theory, our emotions are mainly due to those organic stirrings that are aroused in us in a reflex way by the stimulus of the exciting object or situation. An emotion of fear, for example, or surprise, is not a direct effect of the object's presence on the mind, but an effect of that still earlier effect, the bodily commotion which the object suddenly excites; so that, were this bodily commotion suppressed, we should not so much *feel* fear as call the situation fearful; we should not feel surprise, but coldly recognize that the object was indeed astonishing. One enthusiast has even gone so far as to say that when we feel sorry it is because we weep, when we feel afraid it is because we run away, and not conversely. Some of you may perhaps be acquainted with the paradoxical formula. Now, whatever exaggeration may possibly lurk in this account of our emotions (and I doubt myself whether the exaggeration be very great), it is certain that the main core of it is true, and that the mere giving way to tears, for example, or to the outward expression of an anger-fit, will result for the moment in making the inner grief or anger more acutely felt. There is, accordingly, no better known or more generally useful precept in the moral training of youth, or in one's personal self-discipline, than that which bids us pay primary attention to what we do and express, and not to care too much for what we feel. If we only check a cowardly impulse in time, for example; or if we only *don't* strike the blow or rip out with the complaining or insulting word that we shall regret as long as we live, our feelings themselves will presently be the calmer and better, with no particular guidance from us on their own account. Action seems to follow feeling, but really action and feeling go together; and by regulating the action, which is under the more direct control of the will, we can indirectly regulate the feeling, which is not.

Thus the sovereign voluntary path to cheerfulness, if our spontaneous cheerfulness be lost, is to sit up cheerfully, to look round cheerfully, and to act and speak as if cheerfulness were already there. If such conduct does not make you soon feel cheerful, nothing else on that occasion can. So to feel brave, act as if we *were* brave, use all our will to that end, and a courage-fit will very likely replace the fit of fear. Again, in order to feel kindly towards a person to whom we have been inimical, the only way is more or less deliberately to smile, to make sympathetic inquiries, and to force ourselves to say genial things. One hearty laugh together will bring enemies into a closer communion of heart than hours spent on both sides in inward wrestling with the mental demon of uncharitable feeling. To wrestle with a bad feeling only pins our attention on it, and keeps it still fastened in the mind; whereas if we act as if from some better feeling, the old bad feeling soon folds its tent like an Arab and silently steals away.

The best manuals of religious devotion accordingly reiterate the maxim that we must let our feelings go and pay no regard to them whatever. In an admirable and widely successful little book called *The Christian's Secret of a Happy Life*, by Mrs. Hannah Whitall Smith, I find this lesson on almost every page. *Act* faithfully, and you really have faith, no matter how cold and even how dubious you may feel. "It is your purpose God looks at," writes Mrs. Smith, "not your feelings about that purpose; and your purpose, or will, is therefore the only thing you need attend to. . . . Let your emotions come or let them go, just as God pleases, and make no account of them either way. . . . They really have nothing to do with the matter. They are not the indicators of your spiritual state, but are merely the indicators of your temperament or of your present physical condition."

But you all know these facts already, so I need no longer

press them on your attention. From our acts and from our attitudes ceaseless inpouring currents of sensation come, which help to determine from moment to moment what our inner states shall be—that is a fundamental law of psychology which I will therefore proceed to assume.

A Viennese neurologist of considerable reputation has recently written about the *Binnenleben*, as he terms it, or buried life of human beings. No doctor, this writer says, can get into really profitable relations with a nervous patient until he gets some sense of what the patient's *Binnenleben* is, of the sort of unuttered inner atmosphere in which his consciousness dwells alone with the secrets of its prison-house. This inner personal tone is what we can't communicate or describe articulately to others; but the wraith and ghost of it, so to speak, are often what our friends and intimates feel as our most characteristic quality. In the unhealthy-minded, apart from all sorts of old regrets, ambitions checked by shames and aspirations obstructed by timidities, it consists mainly of bodily discomforts not distinctly localized by the sufferer, but breeding a general self-mistrust and sense that things are not as they should be with him. Half the thirst for alcohol that exists in the world exists simply because alcohol acts as a temporary anæsthetic and effacer to all these morbid feelings that never ought to be in a human being at all. In the healthy-minded, on the contrary, there are no fears or shames to discover; and the sensations that pour in from the organism only help to swell the general vital sense of security and readiness for anything that may turn up.

Consider, for example, the effects of a well-toned *motor-apparatus*, nervous and muscular, on our general personal self-consciousness, the sense of elasticity and efficiency that results. They tell us that in Norway the life of the women has lately been entirely revolutionized by the new order of muscular feelings with which the use of the *ski*, or long snow-shoes, as a sport for both sexes, has made the women acquainted. Fifteen years ago the Norwegian women were even more than the women of other lands votaries of the old-fashioned ideal of femininity, the 'domestic angel,' the 'gentle and refining influence' sort of thing. Now these sedentary fireside tabby-cats of Norway have been trained, they say, by the snow-shoes into lithe and audacious creatures for whom no night is too dark or height too giddy; and who are not only saying good-bye to the traditional feminine pallor and delicacy of constitution, but actually taking the lead in every educational and social reform. I cannot but think that the tennis and tramping and skating habits and the bicycle-craze which are so rapidly extending among our dear sisters and daughters in this country are going also to lead to a sounder and heartier moral tone, which will send its tonic breath through all our American life.

I hope that here in America more and more the ideal of the well-trained and vigorous body will be maintained neck by neck with that of the well-trained and vigorous mind as the two coequal halves of the higher education for men and women alike. The strength of the British Empire lies in the strength of character of the individual Englishman, taken all alone by himself; and that strength, I am persuaded, is perennially nourished and kept up by nothing so much as by the national worship, in which all classes meet, of athletic outdoor life and sport.

I recollect, years ago, reading a certain work by an American doctor on hygiene and the laws of life and the type of future humanity. I have forgotten its author's name and its title, but I remember well an awful prophecy that it contained about the future of our muscular system. Human perfection, the writer said, means ability to cope with the environment; but the environment will more and more require mental power from us, and less and less will ask for bare brute strength. Wars will cease, machines will do all our heavy work, man will become more and more a mere director of nature's energies, and less and less an exerter of energy on his own account. So that if the *homo sapiens* of the future can only digest his food and think, what need will he have of well-developed muscles at all? And why, pursued this writer, should we not even now be satisfied with a more delicate and intellectual type of beauty than that which pleased our ancestors? Nay, I have heard a fanciful friend make a still farther advance in this 'new-man' direction. With our future food, he says, itself prepared in liquid form from the chemical elements of the atmosphere, pepsinated or half-digested in advance, and sucked up through a glass tube from a tin can, what need shall we have of teeth, or stomachs even? They may go, along with our muscles and our physical courage, whilst, challenging ever more and more our proper admiration, will grow the gigantic domes of our crania, arching over our spectacled eyes, and animating our flexible little lips to those floods of learned and ingenious talk which will constitute our most congenial occupation.

I am sure that your flesh creeps at this apocalyptic vision. Mine certainly did so; and I cannot believe that our muscular vigor will ever be a superfluity. Even if the day ever dawns in which it will not be needed for fighting the old heavy battles against Nature, it will still always be needed to furnish the background of sanity, serenity, and cheerfulness to life, to give moral elasticity to our disposition, to round off the wiry edge of our fretfulness, and make us good-humored and easy of approach. Weakness is too apt to be what the doctors call irritable weakness. And that blessed internal peace and confidence, that *acquiescentia in seipso*, as Spinoza used to call it, that wells up from every part of the body of a muscularly well-trained human being, and soaks the indwelling soul of him with satisfaction, is, quite apart from every consideration of its mechanical utility, an element of spiritual hygiene of supreme significance.

And now let me go a step deeper into mental hygiene, and try to enlist your insight and sympathy in a cause which I believe is one of paramount patriotic importance to us Yankees. Many years ago a Scottish medical man, Dr. Clouston, a mad-doctor as they call him there, or what we should call an asylum physician (the most eminent one in Scotland), visited this country and said something that has remained in my memory ever since. "You Americans," he said, "wear too much expression on your faces. You are living like an army with all its reserves engaged in action. The duller countenances of the British population betoken a better scheme of life. They suggest stores of reserved nervous force to fall back upon, if any occasion should arise that requires it. This inexcitability, this presence at all times of power not used, I regard," continued Dr. Clouston, "as the great safeguard of our British people. The other thing in you gives me a sense of insecurity, and you ought somehow to tone yourselves down. You really do carry too much expression, you take too intensely the trivial moments of life."

Now Dr. Clouston is a trained reader of the secrets of the soul as expressed upon the countenance, and the observation of his which I quote seems to me to mean a great deal. And all Americans who stay in Europe long enough to get accustomed to the spirit that reigns and expresses itself there, so unexcitable as compared with ours, make a similar observation when they return to their native shores. They find a wild-eyed look upon their compatriots' faces, either of too desperate eagerness and anxiety or of too intense responsiveness and good-will. It is hard to say whether the men or the women show it most. It is true that we do not all feel about it as Dr. Clouston felt. Many of us, far from deploring it, admire it. We say: "What intelligence it shows! How different from the stolid cheeks, the codfish eyes, the slow, inanimate demeanor we have been seeing in the British Isles!" Intensity, rapidity, vivacity of appearance, are indeed with us something of a nationally accepted ideal; and the medical notion of 'irritable weakness' is not the first thing suggested by them to our mind, as it was to Dr. Clouston's. In a weekly paper not very long ago I remember reading a story in which, after describing the beauty and interest of the heroine's personality, the author summed up her charms by saying that to all who looked upon her an impression as of 'bottled lightning' was irresistibly conveyed.

Bottled lightning, in truth, is one of our American ideals, even of a young girl's character! Now it is most ungracious, and it may seem to some persons unpatriotic, to criticise in public the physical peculiarities of one's own people, of one's own family, so to speak. Besides, it may be said, and said with justice, that there are plenty of bottled-lightning temperaments in other countries, and plenty of phlegmatic temperaments here; and that when all is said and done the more or less of tension about which I am making such a fuss is a very small item in the sum total of a nation's life, and not worth solemn treatment at a time when agreeable rather than disagreeable things should be talked about. Well, in one sense the more or less of tension in our faces and in our unused muscles *is* a small thing; not much mechanical work is done by these contractions. But it is not always the material size of a thing that measures its importance; often it is its place and function. One of the most philosophical remarks I ever heard made was by an unlettered workman who was doing some repairs at my house many years ago. "There is very little difference between one man and another," he said, "when you go to the bottom of it. But what little there is, is very important." And the remark certainly applies to this case. The general over-contraction may be small when estimated in foot-pounds, but its importance is immense on account of its *effects on the over-contracted person's spiritual life*. This follows as a necessary consequence from the theory of our emotions to which I made reference at the beginning of this article. For by the sensations that so incessantly pour in from the over-tense excited body the over-tense and excited habit of mind is kept up; and the sultry, threatening, exhausting, thunderous inner atmosphere never quite clears away. If you never wholly give yourself up to the chair you sit in, but always keep your leg- and body-muscles half contracted for a rise; if you breathe eighteen or nineteen instead of sixteen times a minute, and never quite breathe out at that—what mental mood *can* you be in but one of inner panting and expectancy, and how can the future and its worries possibly forsake your mind? On the other hand, how can they gain admission to your mind if your brow be unruffled, your respiration calm and complete, and your muscles all relaxed?

Now what is the cause of this absence of repose, this bottled-lightning quality in us Americans? The explanation of it that is usually given is that it comes from the extreme dryness of our climate and the acrobatic performances of our thermometer, coupled with the extraordinary progressiveness of our life, the hard work, the railroad speed, the rapid success, and all the other things we know so well by heart. Well, our climate is certainly exciting, but hardly more so than that of many parts of Europe, where nevertheless no bottled-lightning girls are found. And the work done and the pace of life are as extreme in every great capital of Europe as they are here. To me both of these pretended causes are utterly insufficient to explain the facts.

To explain them, we must go not to physical geography, but to psychology and sociology. The latest chapter both in sociology and in psychology to be developed in a manner that approaches adequacy is the chapter on the imitative impulse. First Bagehot, then Tarde, then Royce and Baldwin here, have shown that invention and imitation, taken together, form, one may say, the entire warp and woof of human life, in so far as it is social. The American over-tension and jerkiness and breathlessness and intensity and agony of expression are primarily social, and only secondarily physiological, phenomena. They are *bad habits*, nothing more or less, bred of custom and example, born of the imitation of bad models and the cultivation of false personal ideals. How are idioms acquired, how do local peculiarities of phrase and accent come about? Through an accidental example set by someone, which struck the ears of others, and was quoted and copied till at last everyone in the locality chimed in. Just so it is with national tricks of vocalization or intonation, with national manners, fashions of movement and gesture, and habitual expressions of face. We, here in America, through following a succession of pattern-setters whom it is now impossible to trace, and through influencing each other in a bad direction, have at last settled down collectively into what, for better or worse, is our own characteristic national type—a type with the production of which, so far as these habits go, the climate and conditions have had practically nothing at all to do.

This type, which we have thus reached by our imitativeness, we now have fixed upon us, for better or worse. Now no type can be *wholly* disadvantageous; but so far as our type follows the bottled-lightning fashion, it cannot be wholly good. Dr. Clouston was certainly right in thinking that eagerness, breathlessness, and anxiety are not signs of strength; they are signs of weakness and of bad co-ordination. The even forehead, the slab-like cheek, the codfish eye, may be less interesting for the moment; but they are more promising signs than intense expression is of what we may expect of their possessor in the long run. Your dull, unhurried worker gets over a great deal of ground, because he never goes backward or breaks down. Your intense, convulsive worker breaks down and has bad moods so often that you never know where he may be when you most need his help—he may be having one of his 'bad days.' We say that so many of our fellow-countrymen collapse, and have to be sent abroad to rest their nerves, because they work so hard. I suspect that this is an immense mistake. I suspect that neither the nature nor the amount of our work is accountable for the frequency and severity of our breakdowns, but that their cause lies rather in those absurd feelings of hurry and having no time, in that breathlessness and tension, that anxiety of feature and that solicitude for results, that lack of inner harmony and ease, in short, by which with us the work is so apt to be accompanied, and from which a European who should do the same work would nine times out of ten be free. These perfectly wanton and unnecessary tricks of inner attitude and outer manner in us, caught from the social atmosphere, kept up by tradition, and idealized by many as the admirable way of life, are the last straws that break the American camel's back, the final over-flowers of our measure of wear and tear and fatigue.

The voice, for example, in a surprisingly large number of us has a tired and plaintive sound. Some of us are really tired (for I do not mean absolutely to deny that our climate has a tiring quality); but far more of us are not tired at all, or would not be tired at all unless we had got into a wretched trick of feeling tired by following the prevalent habits of vocalization and expression. And if talking high and tired, and living excit-edly and hurriedly, would only enable us to *do* more by the way, even whilst breaking us down in the end, it would be different. There would be some compensation, some excuse, for going on so. But the exact reverse is the case: It is your relaxed and easy worker, who is in no hurry, and quite thoughtless most of the while of consequences, who is your efficient worker; and tension and anxiety, and present and fu-ture, all mixed up together in our mind at once, are the surest drags upon steady progress and hindrances to our success. My colleague, Professor Münsterberg, an excellent observer, who came here recently, has written some notes on America to German papers. He says in substance that the appearance of unusual energy in America is superficial and illusory, being really due to nothing but the habits of jerkiness and bad co-ordination for which we have to thank the defective training of our people. I think myself that it is high time for old legends and traditional opinions to be changed; and that if anyone should begin to write about Yankee inefficiency and feebleness, and inability to do anything with time except to waste it, he would have a very pretty paradoxical little thesis to sustain, with a great many facts to quote, and a great deal of experience to appeal to in its proof.

Well, my friends, if our dear American character is weak-ened by all this over-tension—and I think, whatever reserves you may make, that you will agree as to the main facts—where does the remedy lie? It lies, of course, where lay the origins of the disease. If a vicious fashion and taste are to blame for the thing, the fashion and taste must be changed. And though it is no small thing to inoculate seventy millions of people with new standards, yet, if there is to be any relief, that will have to be done. We must change ourselves from a race that admires jerk and snap for their own sakes, and looks down upon low voices and quiet ways as dull, to one that, on the contrary, has calm for its ideal, and for their own sakes loves harmony, dignity, and ease.

So we go back to the psychology of imitation again. There is only one way to improve ourselves, and that is by some of us setting an example which the others may pick up and imi-tate till the new fashion spreads from east to west. Some of us are in more favorable positions than others to set new fash-ions. Some are much more striking personally and imitable, so to speak. But no living person is sunk so low as not to be imitated by somebody. Thackeray somewhere says of the Irish nation that there never was an Irishman so poor that he didn't have a still poorer Irishman living at his expense; and surely there is no human being whose example doesn't work conta-giously in *some* particular. The very idiots at our public insti-tutions imitate each other's peculiarities. And if you should individually achieve calmness and harmony in your own per-son, you may depend upon it that a wave of imitation will spread from you, as surely as the circles spread outward when a stone is dropped into a lake.

Fortunately, we shall not have to be absolute pioneers. Even now in New York they have formed a society for the improvement of our national vocalization, and one perceives its machinations already in the shape of various newspaper paragraphs intended to stir up dissatisfaction with the awful thing that it is. And better still than that, because more radical and general, is the gospel of relaxation, as one may call it, preached by Miss Annie Payson Call, of Boston, in her admirable little volume called *Power through Repose*, a book that ought to be in the hands of every teacher and student in America of either sex. You need only be followers, then, on a path already opened up by others. But of one thing be confident—others still will follow you.

And this brings me to one more application of psychology to practical life, to which I will call attention briefly, and then close. If one's example of easy and calm ways is to be effectively contagious, one feels by instinct that the less voluntarily one aims at getting imitated, the more unconscious one keeps in the matter, the more likely one is to succeed. *Become the imitable thing*, and you may then discharge your minds of all responsibility for the imitation. The laws of social nature will take care of that result. Now the psychological principle on which this precept reposes is a law of very deep and widespread importance in the conduct of our lives, and at the same time a law which we Americans most grievously neglect. Stated technically, the law is this, that *strong feeling about one's self tends to arrest the free association of one's objective ideas and motor processes*. We get the extreme example of this in the mental disease called melancholia.

A melancholic patient is filled through and through with intensely painful emotion about himself. He is threatened, he is guilty, he is doomed, he is annihilated, he is lost. His mind is fixed as if in a cramp on these feelings of his own situation; and in all the books on insanity you may read that the usual varied flow of his thoughts has ceased. His associative processes, to use the technical phrase, are inhibited; and his ideas stand stock-still, shut up to their one monotonous function of reiterating inwardly the fact of the man's desperate estate. And this inhibitive influence is not due to the mere fact that his emotion is *painful*. Joyous emotions about the self also

stop the association of our ideas. A saint in ecstasy is as motionless and irresponsive and one-idea'd as a melancholiac.
And without going as far as ecstatic saints, we know how in
everyone a great or sudden pleasure may paralyze the flow of
thought. Ask young people returning from a party or a spectacle, and all excited about it, what it was. "Oh, it was *fine*! it
was *fine*! it was *fine*!" is all the information you are likely to
receive until the excitement has calmed down. Probably every
one of my hearers has been made temporarily half-idiotic by
some great success or piece of good fortune. "*Good!* GOOD!
GOOD!" is all we can at such times say to ourselves until we
smile at our own very foolishness.

Now from all this we can draw an extremely practical conclusion. If, namely, we wish our trains of ideation and volition to be copious and varied and effective, we must form the
habit of freeing them from the inhibitive influence of reflection upon them, of egoistic preoccupation about their results.
Such a habit, like other habits, can be formed. Prudence and
duty and self-regard, emotions of ambition and emotions of
anxiety, have, of course, a needful part to play in our lives.
But confine them as far as possible to the occasions when you
are making your general resolutions and deciding on your
plans of campaign, and keep them out of the details. When
once a decision is reached and execution is the order of the
day, dismiss absolutely all responsibility and care about the
outcome. *Unclamp*, in a word, your intellectual and practical
machinery, and let it run free; and the service it will do you
will be twice as good. Who are the scholars who get 'rattled'
in the recitation-room? Those who think of the possibilities of
failure and feel the great importance of the act. Who are those
who do recite well? Often those who are most indifferent.
Their ideas reel themselves out of their memory of their own
accord. Why do we hear the complaint so often that social life
in New England is either less rich and expressive or more
fatiguing than it is in some other parts of the world? To what
is the fact, if fact it be, due unless to the over-active conscience
of the people, afraid of either saying something too trivial and
obvious, or something insincere, or something unworthy of
one's interlocutor, or something in some way or other not
adequate to the occasion? How can conversation possibly

steer itself through such a sea of responsibilities and inhibitions as this? On the other hand, conversation does flourish and society is refreshing, and neither dull on the one hand nor exhausting from its effort on the other, wherever people forget their scruples and take the brakes off their hearts, and let their tongues wag as automatically and irresponsibly as they will.

They talk much in pædagogic circles to-day about the duty of the teacher to prepare for every lesson in advance. To some extent this is useful. But we Yankees are assuredly not those to whom such a general doctrine should be preached. We are only too careful as it is. The advice I should give to most teachers would be in the words of one who is herself an admirable teacher. Prepare yourself in the *subject so well that it shall be always on tap*; then in the class-room trust your spontaneity and fling away all farther care.

My advice to students, especially to girl-students, would be somewhat similar. Just as a bicycle-chain may be too tight, so may one's carefulness and conscientiousness be so tense as to hinder the running of one's mind. Take, for example, periods when there are many successive days of examination impending. One ounce of good nervous tone in an examination is worth many pounds of anxious study for it in advance. If you want really to do your best at an examination, fling away the book the day before, say to yourself, "I won't waste another minute on this miserable thing, and I don't care an iota whether I succeed or not." Say this sincerely, and feel it; and go out and play, or go to bed and sleep, and I am sure the results next day will encourage you to use the method permanently. I have heard this advice given to a student by Miss Call, whose book on muscular relaxation I quoted a moment ago. In her later book, entitled *As a Matter of Course*, the gospel of moral relaxation, of dropping things from the mind, and not 'caring,' is preached with equal success. Not only our preachers, but our friends the theosophists and mind-curers of various religious sects are also harping on this string. And with the doctors, the Delsarteans, the various mind-curing sects, and such writers as Mr. Dresser, Prentice Mulford, Mr. Horace Fletcher, and Mr. Trine to help, and the whole band of schoolteachers and magazine-readers chiming in, it really looks as if a good start might be made in the direction of changing our American mental habit into something more in-different and strong.

Worry means always and invariably inhibition of associa-tions and loss of effective power. Of course, the sovereign cure for worry is religious faith; and this, of course, you also know. The turbulent billows of the fretful surface leave the deep parts of the ocean undisturbed, and to him who has a hold on vaster and more permanent realities the hourly vicis-situdes of his personal destiny seem relatively insignificant things. The really religious person is accordingly unshakable and full of equanimity, and calmly ready for any duty that the day may bring forth. This is charmingly illustrated by a little work with which I recently became acquainted: *The Practice of the Presence of God, the Best Rule of a Holy Life, by Brother Lawrence, Being Conversations and Letters of Nicholas Herman of Lorraine, Translated from the French.*[1] I extract a few passages, the conversations being given in indirect discourse. Brother Lawrence was a Carmelite friar, converted at Paris in 1666. He said "that he had been footman to M. Fieubert, the treasurer, and that he was a great awkward fellow who broke every-thing. That he had desired to be received into a monastery, thinking that he would there be made to smart for his awk-wardness and the faults he should commit, and so he should sacrifice to GOD his life, with its pleasures; but that GOD had disappointed him, he having met with nothing but satisfac-tion in that state. . . .

"That he had been long troubled in mind from a certain belief that he should be damned; that all the men in the world could not have persuaded him to the contrary; but that he had thus reasoned with himself about it: *I engaged in a reli-gious life only for the love of* GOD, *and I have endeavored to act only for Him; whatever becomes of me, whether I be lost or saved, I will always continue to act purely for the love of* GOD. *I shall have this good at least, that till death I shall have done all that is in me to love Him.* . . . That since then he had passed his life in perfect liberty and continual joy. . . .

"That when an occasion of practising some virtue offered,

[1]Fleming H. Revell Company, New York [1895].

he addressed himself to GOD, saying, LORD, *I cannot do this unless Thou enablest me*; and that then he received strength more than sufficient. That when he had failed in his duty, he only confessed his fault, saying to GOD, *I shall never do otherwise if You leave me to myself; it is You who must hinder my falling, and mend what is amiss*. That after this he gave himself no further uneasiness about it. . . .

"That he had been lately sent into Burgundy, to buy the provision of wine for the society, which was a very unwelcome task for him, because he had no turn for business, and because he was lame and could not go about the boat but by rolling himself over the casks. That, however, he gave himself no uneasiness about it, nor about the purchase of the wine. That he said to GOD, *It was His business he was about*, and that he afterward found it very well performed. That he had been sent into Auvergne, the year before, upon the same account; that he could not tell how the matter passed, but that it proved very well.

"So, likewise, in his business in the kitchen (to which he had naturally a great aversion), having accustomed himself to do everything there for the love of GOD, and with prayer, upon all occasions, for His grace to do his work well, he had found everything easy, during fifteen years that he had been employed there.

"That he was very well pleased with the post he was now in; but that he was as ready to quit that as the former, since he was always pleasing himself in every condition by doing little things for the love of GOD. . . .

"That the goodness of GOD assured him He would not forsake him utterly, and that He would give him strength to bear whatever evil He permitted to happen to him; and therefore that he feared nothing, and had no occasion to consult with anybody about his state. That when he had attempted to do it, he had always come away more perplexed."

The simple-heartedness of the good Brother Lawrence, and the relaxation of all unnecessary solicitudes and anxieties in him, is a refreshing spectacle.

The need of feeling responsible all the livelong day has been preached long enough in our New England. Long enough exclusively, at any rate—and long enough to the female sex. What our girl-students and woman-teachers most need nowadays is not the exacerbation, but rather the toning-down of their moral tensions. Even now I fear that some one of my fair hearers may be making an undying resolve to become strenuously relaxed, cost what it will, for the remainder of her life. It is needless to say that that is not the way to do it. The way to do it, paradoxical as it may seem, is genuinely not to care whether you are doing it or not. Then, possibly, by the grace of God, you may all at once find that you *are* doing it; and, having learned what the trick feels like, you may (again by the grace of God) be enabled to go on.

And that something like this may be the happy experience of all my hearers is, in closing, my most earnest wish.

II

OUR JUDGMENTS concerning the worth of things, big or little, depend on the *feelings* the things arouse in us. Where we judge a thing to be precious in consequence of the *idea* we frame of it, this is only because the idea is itself associated already with a feeling. If we were radically feelingless, and if ideas were the only things our mind could entertain, we should lose all our likes and dislikes at a stroke, and be unable to point to any one situation or experience in life more valuable or significant than any other.

Now the blindness in human beings of which this discourse will treat is the blindness with which we all are afflicted in regard to the feelings of creatures and people different from ourselves.

We are practical beings, each of us with limited functions and duties to perform. Each is bound to feel intensely the importance of his own duties and the significance of the situations that call these forth. But this feeling is in each of us a vital secret, for sympathy with which we vainly look to others—the others are too much absorbed in their own vital secrets to take an interest in ours. Hence the stupidity and injustice of our opinions, so far as they deal with the significance of alien lives. Hence the falsity of our judgments, so far as they presume to decide in an absolute way on the value of other persons' conditions or ideals.

Take our dogs and ourselves, connected as we are by a tie more intimate than most ties in this world; and yet, outside of that tie of friendly fondness, how insensible, each of us, to all that makes life significant for the other!—we to the rapture of bones under hedges, or smells of trees and lamp-posts, they to the delights of literature and art. As you sit reading the most moving romance you ever fell upon, what sort of a judge is your fox-terrier of your behavior? With all his good will towards you, the nature of your conduct is absolutely excluded from his comprehension. To sit there like a senseless statue, when you might be taking him to walk and throwing sticks for him to catch! What queer disease is this that comes over you every day, of holding things and staring at them like that for hours together, paralyzed of motion and vacant of all conscious life? The african savages came nearer the truth; but they, too, missed it, when they gathered wonderingly round one of our american travellers who in the interior had just come into possession of a stray copy of the New York *Commercial Advertiser*, and was devouring it column by column. When he got through, they offered him a high price for the mysterious object; and being asked for what they wanted it, they said: "For an eye-medicine"—that being the only reason they could conceive of for the protracted bath which he had given his eyes upon its surface.

The spectator's judgment is sure to miss the root of the matter and to possess no truth. The subject judged knows a part of the world of reality which the judging spectator fails to see, knows more whilst the spectator knows less; and wherever there is conflict of opinion and difference of vision, we are bound to believe that the truer side is the side that feels the more and not the side that feels the less.

Let me take a personal example of the kind that befals each one of us daily.

Some years ago, whilst journeying in the mountains of North Carolina, I passed by a large number of 'coves,' as they call them there, or heads of small valleys between the hills, which had been newly cleared and planted. The impression on my mind was one of unmitigated squalor. The settler had in every case cut down the more manageable trees, and left their charred stumps standing. The larger trees he had girdled and killed, in order that their foliage should not cast a shade. He had then built a log cabin, plastering its chinks with clay, and had set up a tall zigzag rail fence around the scene of his havoc, to keep the pigs and cattle out. Finally, he had irregularly planted the intervals between the stumps and trees with Indian corn, which grew among the chips; and there he dwelt with his wife and babes—an axe, a gun, a few utensils, and some pigs and chickens feeding in the woods, being the sum total of his possessions.

The forest had been destroyed; and what had 'improved' it out of existence was hideous, a sort of ulcer, without a single element of artificial grace to make up for the loss of Nature's beauty. Ugly indeed seemed the life of the squatter, scudding, as the sailors say, under bare poles, beginning again away back where our first ancestors started, and by hardly a single item the better off for all the achievements of the intervening generations.

Talk about going back to Nature! I said to myself, oppressed by the dreariness, as I drove by. Talk of a country life for one's old age and for one's children! Never thus, with nothing but the bare ground and one's bare hands to fight the battle! Never, without the best spoils of culture woven in! The beauties and commodities gained by the centuries are sacred. They are our heritage and birthright. No modern person ought to be willing to live a day in such a state of rudimentariness and denudation.

Then I said to the mountaineer who was driving me: "What sort of people are they who have to make these new clearings?" "All of us," he replied; "why, we ain't happy here unless we are getting one of these coves under cultivation." I instantly felt that I had been losing the whole inward significance of the situation. Because to me the clearings spoke of naught but denudation, I thought that to those whose sturdy arms and obedient axes had made them they could tell no other story. But when *they* looked on the hideous stumps, what they thought of was personal victory. The chips, the girdled trees and the vile split rails spoke of honest sweat, persistent toil and final reward. The cabin was a warrant of safety for self and wife and babes. In short, the clearing, which to me was a mere ugly picture on the retina, was to them a symbol redolent with moral memories and sang a very pæan of duty, struggle, and success.

I had been as blind to the peculiar ideality of their conditions as they certainly would also have been to the ideality of mine, had they had a peep at my strange indoor academic ways of life at Cambridge.

Wherever a process of life communicates an eagerness to him who lives it, there the life becomes genuinely significant. Sometimes the eagerness is more knit up with the motor activities, sometimes with the perceptions, sometimes with the imagination, sometimes with reflective thought. But wherever it is found, there is the zest, the tingle, the excitement, of reality; and there *is* 'importance' in the only real and positive sense in which importance ever anywhere can be.

Robert Louis Stevenson has illustrated this by a case drawn from the sphere of the imagination, in an essay which I really think deserves to become immortal, both for the truth of its matter and the excellence of its form.

"Toward the end of September," Stevenson writes, "when school-time was drawing near and the nights were already black, we would begin to sally from our respective villas, each equipped with a tin bull's-eye lantern. The thing was so well known that it had worn a rut in the commerce of Great Britain; and the grocers, about the due time, began to garnish their windows with our particular brand of luminary. We wore them buckled to the waist upon a cricket belt, and over them, such was the rigour of the game, a buttoned top-coat. They smelled noisomely of blistered tin; they never burned aright, though they would always burn our fingers; their use was naught; the pleasure of them merely fanciful; and yet a boy with a bull's-eye under his top-coat asked for nothing more. The fishermen used lanterns about their boats, and it was from them, I suppose, that we had got the hint; but theirs were not bull's-eyes, nor did we ever play at being fishermen. The police carried them at their belts, and we had plainly copied them in that; yet we did not pretend to be policemen. Burglars, indeed, we may have had some haunting thoughts of; and we had certainly an eye to past ages when lanterns were more common, and to certain story-books in which we had found them to figure very largely. But take it for all in all, the pleasure of the thing was substantive; and to be a boy with a bull's-eye under his top-coat was good enough for us.

"When two of these asses met, there would be an anxious 'Have you got your lantern?' and a gratified 'Yes!' That was the shibboleth, and very needful too; for, as it was the rule to keep our glory contained, none could recognise a lantern-bearer, unless (like the polecat) by the smell. Four or five would sometimes climb into the belly of a ten-man lugger, with nothing but the thwarts above them—for the cabin was usually locked, or choose out some hollow of the links where the wind might whistle overhead. There the coats would be unbuttoned and the bull's-eyes discovered; and in the chequering glimmer, under the huge windy hall of the night, and cheered by a rich steam of toasting tinware, these fortunate young gentlemen would crouch together in the cold sand of the links or on the scaly bilges of the fishing-boat, and delight themselves with inappropriate talk. Woe is me that I may not give some specimens . . . . But the talk was but a condiment; and these gatherings themselves only accidents in the career of the lantern-bearer. The essence of this bliss was to walk by yourself in the black night; the slide shut, the top-coat buttoned; not a ray escaping, whether to conduct your footsteps or to make your glory public: a mere pillar of darkness in the dark; and all the while, deep down in the privacy of your fool's heart, to know you had a bull's-eye at your belt, and to exult and sing over the knowledge.

"It is said that a poet has died young in the breast of the most stolid. It may be contended, rather, that this (somewhat minor) bard in almost every case survives, and is the spice of life to his possessor. Justice is not done to the versatility and the unplumbed childishness of man's imagination. His life from without may seem but a rude mound of mud; there will be some golden chamber at the heart of it, in which he dwells delighted; and for as dark as his pathway seems to the observer, he will have some kind of a bull's-eye at his belt.

". . . There is one fable that touches very near the quick of life: the fable of the monk who passed into the woods, heard a bird break into song, hearkened for a trill or two, and found himself on his return a stranger at his convent gates; for he had been absent fifty years, and of all his comrades there survived but one to recognise him. It is not only in the woods that this enchanter carols, though perhaps he is native there. He sings in the most doleful places. The miser hears him and chuckles, and the days are moments. With no more apparatus than an ill-smelling lantern I have evoked him on the naked links. All life that is not merely mechanical is spun out of two strands: seeking for that bird and hearing him. And it is just this that makes life so hard to value, and the delight of each so incommunicable. And just a knowledge of this, and a remembrance of those fortunate hours in which the bird *has* sung to *us*, that fills us with such wonder when we turn the pages of the realist. There, to be sure, we find a picture of life in so far as it consists of mud and of old iron, cheap desires and cheap fears, that which we are ashamed to remember and that which we are careless whether we forget; but of the note of that time-devouring nightingale we hear no news.

". . . Say that I came [in such a realistic romance] on some such business as that of my lantern-bearers on the links; and described the boys as very cold, spat upon by flurries of rain, and drearily surrounded, all of which they were; and their talk as silly and indecent, which it certainly was. . . . To the eye of the observer they *are* wet and cold and drearily surrounded; but ask themselves, and they are in the heaven of a recondite pleasure, the ground of which is an ill-smelling lantern.

"For, to repeat, the ground of a man's joy is often hard to hit. It may hinge at times upon a mere accessory, like the lantern, it may reside in the mysterious inwards of psychology. . . . It has so little bond with externals . . . that it may even touch them not; and the man's true life, for which he consents to live, lie altogether in the field of fancy. . . . In such a case the poetry runs underground. The observer (poor soul, with his documents!) is all abroad. For to look at the man is but to court deception. We shall see the trunk from which he draws his nourishment; but he himself is above and abroad in the green dome of foliage, hummed through by winds and nested in by nightingales. And the true realism were that of the poets, to climb up after him like a squirrel, and catch some glimpse of the heaven for which he lives. And the true realism, always and everywhere, is that of the poets: to find out where joy resides, and give it a voice far beyond singing.

"For to miss the joy is to miss all. In the joy of the actors lies the sense of any action. That is the explanation, that the excuse. To one who has not the secret of the lanterns, the scene upon the links is meaningless. And hence the haunting and truly spectral unreality of realistic books. . . . In each, we miss the personal poetry, the enchanted atmosphere, that rainbow work of fancy that clothes what is naked and seems to ennoble what is base; in each, life falls dead like dough, instead of soaring away like a balloon into the colours of the sunset; each is true, each inconceivable; for no man lives in the external truth, among salts and acids, but in the warm, phantasmagoric chamber of his brain, with the painted windows and the storied walls."[1]

These paragraphs are the best thing I know in all Stevenson. "To miss the joy is to miss all." Indeed, it is. Yet we are but finite, and each one of us has some single specialized vocation of his own. And it seems as if energy in the service of its particular duties might be got only by hardening the heart towards everything unlike them. Our deadness towards all but one particular kind of joy would thus be the price we inevitably have to pay for being practical creatures. Only in some pitiful dreamer, some philosopher, poet, or romancer, or when the common practical man becomes a lover, does the hard externality give way, and a gleam of insight into the ejective world, as Clifford called it, the vast world of inner life beyond us, so different from that of outer seeming, illuminate our mind. Then the whole scheme of our customary values gets confounded, then our self is riven and its narrow interests fly to pieces, then a new centre and a new perspective must be found.

The change is well described by my colleague, Josiah Royce:

"What then is thy neighbor? Thou hast regarded his thought, his feeling, as somehow different from thine. Thou hast said: 'A pain in him is not like a pain in me, but something far easier to bear.' He seems to thee a little less living than thou. His life is dim, it is cold, it is a pale fire beside thy own burning desires. . . . So, dimly and by instinct, thou hast lived with thy neighbor, and hast known him not, being blind. Thou hast made [of him] a thing, no Self at all. Have done with this illusion and simply try to know the truth. Pain is pain, joy is joy, everywhere even as in thee. In all the songs of the forest birds; in all the cries of the wounded and dying, struggling in the captor's power; in the boundless sea, where

---

[1] "The Lantern-Bearers," in the volume entitled *Across the Plains*. Abridged in the quotation.

the myriads of water-creatures strive and die; amid all the countless hordes of savage men; in all sickness and sorrow; in all exultation and hope; everywhere from the lowest to the noblest, the same conscious, burning, willful life is found, endlessly manifold as the forms of the living creatures, unquenchable as the fires of the sun, real as these impulses that even now throb in thy own little selfish heart. Lift up thy eyes, behold that life, and then turn away and forget it as thou canst; but if thou hast *known* that, thou hast begun to know thy duty."[2]

This higher vision of an inner significance in what, until then, we had realized only in the dead external way, often comes over a person suddenly; and when it does so, it makes an epoch in his history. As Emerson says, there is a depth in those moments that constrains us to ascribe more reality to them than to all other experiences. The passion of love will shake one like an explosion, or some act will awaken a remorseful compunction that hangs like a cloud over all one's later day.

This mystic sense of hidden meaning starts upon us often from non-human natural things. I take this passage from *Obermann*, a french novel that had some vogue in its day: "Paris, March 7. — It was dark and rather cold. I was gloomy, and walked because I had nothing to do. I passed by some flowers placed breast-high upon a wall. A jonquil in bloom was there. It is the strongest expression of desire: it was the first perfume of the year. I felt all the happiness destined for man. This unutterable harmony of souls, the phantom of the ideal world, arose in me complete. I never felt anything so great or so instantaneous. I know not what shape, what analogy, what secret of relation it was that made me see in this flower a limitless beauty. . . . I shall never enclose in a conception this power, this immensity that nothing will express; this form that nothing will contain; this ideal of a better world which one feels, but which it would seem that nature has not made."[3]

[2]*The Religious Aspect of Philosophy* [1885], pp. 157–162 (abridged).
[3]De Sénancour: *Obermann* [Brussels, 1837], Lettre XXX.

Wordsworth and Shelley are similarly full of this sense of a limitless significance in natural things. In Wordsworth it was a somewhat austere and moral significance, a 'lonely cheer.'

> "To every natural form, rock, fruit or flower,
>   Even the loose stones that cover the high-way,
>   I gave a moral life: I saw them feel,
>   Or linked them to some feeling: the great mass
>   Lay bedded in a quickening soul, and all
>   That I beheld respired with inward meaning."[4]

"Authentic tidings of invisible things!" Just what this hidden presence in Nature was, which Wordsworth so rapturously felt, and in the light of which he lived, tramping the hills for days together, the poet never could explain logically or in articulate conceptions. Yet to the reader who may himself have had gleaming moments of a similar sort the verses in which Wordsworth simply proclaims the fact of them come with a heart-satisfying authority:

> "Magnificent
> The morning rose, in memorable pomp,
> Glorious as e'er I had beheld—in front,
> The sea lay laughing at a distance; near,
> The solid mountains shone, bright as the clouds,
> Grain-tinctured, drenched in empyrean light;
> And in the meadows and the lower grounds
> Was all the sweetness of a common dawn—
> Dews, vapours, and the melody of birds,
> And labourers going forth to till the fields."

> "Ah! need I say, dear Friend! that to the brim
> My heart was full; I made no vows, but vows
> Were then made for me; bond unknown to me
> Was given, that I should be, else sinning greatly,
> A dedicated Spirit.   On I walked
> In thankful blessedness, which yet survives."[5]

As Wordsworth walked, filled with his strange inner joy, responsive thus to the secret life of Nature roundabout him,

[4] *The Prelude*, Book III.
[5] *The Prelude*, Book IV.

his rural neighbors, tightly and narrowly intent upon their own affairs, their crops and lambs and fences, must have thought him a very insignificant and foolish personage. It surely never occurred to any one of them to wonder what was going on inside of *him* or what it might be worth. And yet that inner life of his carried the burden of a significance that has fed the souls of others, and fills them to this day with inner joy.

Richard Jefferies has written a remarkable autobiographic document entitled *The Story of My Heart*. It tells, in many pages, of the rapture with which in youth the sense of the life of nature filled him. On a certain hill-top, he says:

"I was utterly alone with the sun and the earth. Lying down on the grass, I spoke in my soul to the earth, the sun, the air, and the distant sea far beyond sight. . . . With all the intensity of feeling which exalted me, all the intense communion I held with the earth, the sun and sky, the stars hidden by the light, with the ocean—in no manner can the thrilling depth of these feelings be written—with these I prayed, as if they were the keys of an instrument . . . . The great sun burning with light; the strong earth, dear earth; the warm sky; the pure air; the thought of ocean; the inexpressible beauty of all filled me with a rapture, an ecstasy, an inflatus. With this inflatus, too, I prayed. . . . The prayer, this soul-emotion, was in itself, not for an object; it was a passion. I hid my face in the grass, I was wholly prostrated, I lost myself in the wrestle, I was rapt and carried away. . . . Had any shepherd accidentally seen me lying on the turf, he would only have thought that I was resting a few minutes. I made no outward show. Who could have imagined the whirlwind of passion that was going on within me as I reclined there!"[6]

Surely a worthless hour of life when measured by the usual standards of commercial value. Yet in what other *kind* of value can the preciousness of any hour, made precious by any standard, consist, if it consist not in feelings of excited significance like these, engendered in someone by what the hour contains?

[6]*Op. cit.* (Boston: Roberts, 1883), pp. 3, 4, 5, 6.

Yet so blind and dead does the clamor of our own practical interests make us to all other things, that it seems almost as if it were necessary to become worthless as a practical being, if one is to hope to attain to any breadth of insight into the impersonal world of worths as such, to have any perception of life's meaning on a large objective scale. Only your mystic, your dreamer, or your insolvent tramp or loafer, can afford so sympathetic an occupation, an occupation which will change the usual standards of human values in the twinkling of an eye, giving to foolishness a place ahead of power, and laying low in a minute the distinctions which it takes a hard-working conventional man a lifetime to build up. You may be a prophet at this rate; but you cannot be a worldly success.

Walt Whitman, for instance, is accounted by many of us a contemporary prophet. He abolishes the usual human distinctions, brings all conventionalisms into solution, and loves and celebrates hardly any human attributes save those elementary ones common to all members of the race. For this he becomes a sort of ideal tramp, a rider on omnibus-tops and ferry-boats, and, considered either practically or academically, a worthless unproductive being. His verses are but ejaculations—things mostly without subject or verb, a succession of interjections on an immense scale. He felt the human crowd as rapturously as Wordsworth felt the mountains, felt it as an overpoweringly significant presence, simply to absorb one's mind in which should be business sufficient and worthy to fill the days of a serious man. As he crosses Brooklyn ferry, this is what he feels:

Flood-tide below me! I watch you face to face;
Clouds of the west! sun there half an hour high! I see you also face to face.
Crowds of men and women attired in the usual costumes! how curious you are to me!
On the ferry-boats, the hundreds and hundreds that cross, returning home, are more curious to me than you suppose;
And you that shall cross from shore to shore years hence, are more to me, and more in my meditations, than you might suppose.

Others will enter the gates of the ferry, and cross from
    shore to shore;
Others will watch the run of the flood-tide;
Others will see the shipping of Manhattan north and west,
    and the heights of Brooklyn to the south and east;
Others will see the islands large and small;
Fifty years hence, others will see them as they cross, the sun
    half an hour high;
A hundred years hence, or ever so many hundred years
    hence, others will see them,
Will enjoy the sunset, the pouring in of the flood-tide, the
    falling back to the sea of the ebb-tide.
It avails not, neither time or place—distance avails not;
Just as you feel when you look on the river and sky, so I
    felt;
Just as any of you is one of a living crowd, I was one of a
    crowd;
Just as you are refresh'd by the gladness of the river and the
    bright flow, I was refresh'd;
Just as you stand and lean on the rail, yet hurry with the
    swift current, I stood, yet was hurried;
Just as you look on the numberless masts of ships, and the
    thick-stem'd pipes of steamboats, I look'd.
I too many and many a time cross'd the river, the sun half
    an hour high;
I watched the Twelfth-month sea-gulls—I saw them high
    in the air, floating with motionless wings, oscillating
    their bodies,
I saw how the glistening yellow lit up parts of their bodies,
    and left the rest in strong shadow,
I saw the slow-wheeling circles, and the gradual edging
    toward the south.
Saw the white sails of schooners and sloops—saw the ships
    at anchor,
The sailors at work in the rigging, or out astride the
    spars,
The scallop-edged waves in the twilight, the ladled cups,
    the frolicsome crests and glistening,
The stretch afar growing dimmer and dimmer, the gray
    walls of the granite store-houses by the docks,

On the neighboring shore, the fires from the foundry
    chimneys burning high . . . into the night,
Casting their flicker of black . . . into the clefts of streets.
These, and all else, were to me the same as they are to you.[7]

And so on, through the rest of a divinely beautiful poem.
And if you wish to see what this hoary loafer considered the
most worthy way of profiting by life's heaven-sent opportunities, read the delicious volume of his letters to a young car-
conductor who had become his friend:

                      "*New York, Oct.* 9, 1868.

   "DEAR PETE. It is splendid here this forenoon—bright and
cool. I was out early taking a short walk by the river only two
squares from where I live. . . . Shall I tell you about [my life]
just to fill up? I generally spend the forenoon in my room
writing, etc., then take a bath fix up and go out about 12 and
loafe somewhere or call on someone down town or on business, or perhaps if it is very pleasant and I feel like it ride a
trip with some driver friend on Broadway from 23rd Street to
Bowling Green, three miles each way. (Every day I find I have
plenty to do, every hour is occupied with something.) You
know it is a never ending amusement and study and recre-
ation for me to ride a couple of hours of a pleasant afternoon
on a Broadway stage in this way. You see everything as you
pass, a sort of living, endless panorama—shops and splendid
buildings and great windows: and on the broad sidewalks
crowds of women richly dressed continually passing altogether different, superior in style and looks from any to be
seen anywhere else—in fact a perfect stream of people—men
too dressed in high style, and plenty of foreigners—and then
in the streets the thick crowd of carriages, stages, carts, hotel
and private coaches, and in fact all sorts of vehicles and many
first class teams, mile after mile, and the splendor of such a
great street and so many tall, ornamental, noble buildings
many of them of white marble, and the gayety and motion on
every side: you will not wonder how much attraction all this
is on a fine day, to a great loafer like me, who enjoys so much
seeing the busy world move by him, and exhibiting itself for

[7]"Crossing Brooklyn Ferry" (abridged).

his amusement, while he takes it easy and just looks on and observes."[8]

Truly a futile way of passing the time, some of you may say, and not altogether creditable to a grown-up man. And yet, from the deepest point of view, who knows the more of truth, and who knows the less—Whitman on his omnibus-top, full of the inner joy with which the spectacle inspires him, or you, full of the disdain which the futility of his occupation excites?

When your ordinary Brooklynite or New Yorker, leading a life replete with too much luxury, or tired and careworn about his personal affairs, crosses the ferry or goes up Broadway, *his* fancy does not thus 'soar away into the colors of the sunset' as did Whitman's, nor does he inwardly realize at all the indisputable fact that this world never did anywhere or at any time contain more of essential divinity, or of eternal meaning, than is embodied in the fields of vision over which his eyes so carelessly pass. There is life; and there, a step away, is death. There is the only kind of beauty there ever was. There is the old human struggle and its fruits together. There is the text and the sermon, the real and the ideal in one. But to the jaded and unquickened eye it is all dead and common, pure vulgarism, flatness and disgust. "Hech! it is a sad sight!" says Carlyle, walking at night with someone who appeals to him to note the splendor of the stars. And that very repetition of the scene to new generations of men *in secula seculorum*, that eternal recurrence of the common order, which so fills a Whitman with mystic satisfaction, is to a Schopenhauer, with the emotional anæsthesia, the feeling of 'awful inner emptiness' from out of which he views it all, the chief ingredient of the tedium it instils. What is life on the largest scale, he asks, but the same recurrent inanities, the same dog barking, the same fly buzzing, forevermore? Yet of the kind of fibre of which such inanities consist is the material woven of all the excitements, joys and meanings that ever were, or ever shall be, in this world.

To be rapt with satisfied attention, like Whitman, to the mere spectacle of the world's presence, is one way, and the

[8]*Calamus* (Boston, 1897), pp. 41, 42.

most fundamental way, of confessing one's sense of its unfathomable significance and importance. But how can one attain to the feeling of the vital significance of an experience, if one have it not to begin with? There is no receipt which one can follow. Being a secret and a mystery, it often comes in mysteriously unexpected ways. It blossoms sometimes from out of the very grave wherein we imagined that our happiness was buried. Benvenuto Cellini, after a life all in the outer sunshine, made of adventures and artistic excitements, suddenly finds himself cast into a dungeon in the Castle of San Angelo. The place is horrible. Rats and wet and mould possess it. His leg is broken; and his teeth fall out, apparently with scurvy. But his thoughts turn to God as they have never turned before. He gets a bible, which he reads during the one hour in the twenty-four in which a wandering ray of daylight penetrates his cavern; he has religious visions; he sings psalms to himself and composes hymns; and thinking, on the last day of July, of the festivities customary on the morrow in Rome, he says to himself: "All these past years I celebrated this holiday with the vanities of the world; from this year henceforward I will do it with the divinity of God. And then I said to myself, 'Oh, how much more happy I am for this present life of mine than for all those things remembered!' "[9]

But the great understander of these mysterious ebbs and flows is Tolstoi. They throb all through his novels. In his *War and Peace*, the hero, Peter, is supposed to be the richest man in the russian empire. During the french invasion he is taken prisoner, and dragged through much of the retreat. Cold, vermin, hunger, and every form of misery assail him, the result being a revelation to him of the real scale of life's values. "Here only, and for the first time, he appreciated, because he was deprived of it, the happiness of eating when he was hungry, of drinking when he was thirsty, of sleeping when he was sleepy, and of talking when he felt the desire to exchange some words. . . . Later in life he always recurred with joy to this month of captivity, and never failed to speak with enthusiasm of the powerful and ineffaceable sensations, and especially of the moral calm, which he had experienced at this

[9]*Vita*, lib. 2, chap. iv.

epoch. When at daybreak, on the morrow of his imprison-
ment, he saw [I abridge here Tolstoi's description] the mountains with their wooded slopes disappearing in the grayish
mist; when he felt the cool breeze caress him; when he saw
the light drive away the vapors, and the sun rise majestically
behind the clouds and cupolas, and the crosses, the dew, the
distance, the river, sparkle in the splendid, cheerful rays; his
heart overflowed with emotion. This emotion kept continually with him, and increased a hundred-fold as the difficulties
of his situation grew graver. . . . He learnt that man is
meant for happiness, and that this happiness is in him, in the
satisfaction of the daily needs of existence, and that unhappiness is the fatal result, not of our need, but of our abundance. . . . When calm reigned in the camp, and the embers
paled and little by little went out, the full moon had reached
the zenith. The woods and the fields roundabout lay clearly
visible; and beyond the inundation of light which filled them,
the view plunged into the limitless horizon. Then Peter cast
his eyes upon the firmament, filled at that hour with myriads
of stars. 'All that is mine,' he thought. 'All that is in me, is
me! And that is what they think they have taken prisoner!
That is what they have shut up in a cabin!'—So he smiled,
and turned in to sleep among his comrades."[10]

The occasion and the experience, then, are nothing. It all
depends on the capacity of the soul to be grasped, to have its
life-currents absorbed by what is given. "Crossing a bare common," says Emerson, "in snow puddles, at twilight, under a
clouded sky, without having in my thoughts any occurrence
of special good fortune, I have enjoyed a perfect exhilaration.
I am glad to the brink of fear."

Life is always worth living if one have such responsive sensibilities. But we of the highly educated classes (so called)
have most of us got far, far away from Nature. We are trained
to seek the choice, the rare, the exquisite, exclusively, and to
overlook the common. We are stuffed with abstract conceptions, and glib with verbalities and verbosities; and in the culture of these higher functions the peculiar sources of joy
connected with our simpler functions often dry up, and we

[10]*La Guerre et la paix* (Paris, 1884), vol. iii, pp. 268, 275, 316.

grow stone-blind and insensible to life's more elementary and general goods and joys.

The remedy under such conditions is to descend to a more profound and primitive level. To be imprisoned or ship-wrecked or forced into the army would permanently show the good of life to many an over-educated pessimist. Living in the open air and on the ground, the lop-sided beam of the balance slowly rises to the level line; and the over-sensibilities and insensibilities even themselves out. The good of all the artificial schemes and fevers fades and pales; and that of seeing, smelling, tasting, sleeping, and daring and doing with one's body, grows and grows. The savages and children of nature to whom we deem ourselves so much superior, certainly are alive where we are often dead, along these lines; and could they write as glibly as we do, they would read us impressive lectures on our impatience for improvement and on our blindness to the fundamental static goods of life. "Ah, my brother," said a chieftain to his white guest, "thou wilt never know the happiness of both thinking of nothing and doing nothing; this, next to sleep, is the most enchanting of all things. Thus we were before our birth, and thus we shall be after death. Thy people, . . . when they have finished reaping one field, they begin to plough another, and as if the day were not enough, I have seen them plough by moonlight. What is their life to ours—their life that is as nought to them? Blind that they are, they lose it all! But we live in the present."[11]

The intense interest that life can assume when brought down to the non-thinking level, the level of pure sensorial perception, has been beautifully described by a man who *can* write, Mr. W. H. Hudson, in his volume, *Idle Days in Patagonia.*

"I spent the greater part of one winter," says this admirable author, "at a point on the Rio Negro, seventy or eighty miles from the sea . . . . It was my custom to go out every morning on horseback with my gun, and, followed by one dog, to ride away from the valley; and no sooner would I climb the terrace and plunge into the grey universal thicket, than I would find myself as completely alone as if five hundred instead of only

---

[11]Quoted by Lotze, *Microcosmus*, English translation, vol. ii, p. 240.

five miles separated me from the valley and river. So wild and solitary and remote seemed that grey waste, stretching away into infinitude, a waste untrodden by man, and where the wild animals are so few that they have made no discoverable path in the wilderness of thorns. . . . Not once, nor twice, nor thrice, but day after day I returned to this solitude, going to it in the morning as if to attend a festival, and leaving it only when hunger and thirst and the westering sun compelled me. And yet I had no object in going—no motive which could be put into words; for although I carried a gun, there was nothing to shoot—the shooting was all left behind in the valley. . . . Sometimes I would pass an entire day without seeing one mammal, and perhaps not more than a dozen birds of any size. The weather at that time was cheerless, generally with a grey film of cloud spread over the sky, and a bleak wind, often cold enough to make my bridle hand quite numb. . . . At a slow pace, which would have seemed intolerable in other circumstances, I would ride about for hours at a stretch. On arriving at a hill, I would slowly ride to its summit, and stand there to survey the prospect. On every side it stretched away in great undulations, wild and irregular. How grey it all was! hardly less so near at hand than on the haze-wrapped horizon, where the hills were dim and the outline blurred by distance. Descending from my look-out, I would take up my aimless wanderings again, and visit other elevations to gaze on the same landscape from another point; and so on for hours, and at noon I would dismount and sit or lie on my folded poncho for an hour or longer. One day, in these rambles, I discovered a small grove composed of twenty to thirty trees, growing at a convenient distance apart, that had evidently been resorted to by a herd of deer or other wild animals. This grove was on a hill differing in shape from other hills in its neighbourhood; and after a time I made a point of finding and using it as a resting-place every day at noon. I did not ask myself why I made choice of that one spot, sometimes going miles out of my way to sit there, instead of sitting down under any one of the millions of trees and bushes on any other hillside. I thought nothing about it, but acted unconsciously; only afterwards it seemed to me that after having rested there once, each time I wished to rest again the wish came associated with the image of that particular clump of trees, with polished stems and clean bed of sand beneath; and in a short time I formed a habit of returning, animal-like, to repose at that same spot.

"It was perhaps a mistake to say that I would sit down and rest, since I was never tired: and yet without being tired, that noon-day pause, during which I sat for an hour without moving, was strangely grateful. All day there would be no sound, not even the rustle of a leaf. One day while *listening* to the silence, it occurred to my mind to wonder what the effect would be if I were to shout aloud. This seemed at the time a horrible suggestion, which almost made me shudder. But during those solitary days it was a rare thing for any thought to cross my mind. In the state of mind I was in, thought had become impossible. My state was one of *suspense* and *watchfulness*: yet I had no expectation of meeting with an adventure, and felt as free from apprehension as I feel now when sitting in a room in London. The state seemed familiar rather than strange, and accompanied by a strong feeling of elation; and I did not know that something had come between me and my intellect until I returned to my former self—to thinking, and the old insipid existence [again].

"I had undoubtedly *gone back*; and that state of intense watchfulness, or alertness rather, with suspension of the higher intellectual faculties, represented the mental state of the pure savage. He thinks little, reasons little, having a surer guide in his [mere sensory perceptions]; he is in perfect harmony with nature, and is nearly on a level, mentally, with the wild animals he preys on, and which in their turn sometimes prey on him."[12]

For the spectator, such hours as Mr. Hudson writes of form a mere tale of emptiness, in which nothing happens, nothing is gained, and there is nothing to describe. They are meaningless and vacant tracts of time. To him who feels their inner secret, they tingle with an importance that unutterably vouches for itself. I am sorry for the boy or girl, or man or woman, who has never been touched by the spell of this mysterious sensorial life, with its irrationality, if so you like to call

[12]*Op. cit.,* pp. 210–222 (abridged).

it, but its vigilance and its supreme felicity. The holidays of life are its most vitally significant portions, because they are, or at least should be, covered with just this kind of magically irresponsible spell.

And now what is the result of all these considerations and quotations? It is negative in one sense, but positive in another. It absolutely forbids us to be forward in pronouncing on the meaninglessness of forms of existence other than our own; and it commands us to tolerate, respect, and indulge those whom we see harmlessly interested and happy in their own ways, however unintelligible these may be to us. Hands off: neither the whole of truth, nor the whole of good, is revealed to any single observer, although each observer gains a partial superiority of insight from the peculiar position in which he stands. Even prisons and sick-rooms have their special revelations. It is enough to ask of each of us that he should be faithful to his own opportunities and make the most of his own blessings, without presuming to regulate the rest of the vast field.

III

WHAT MAKES A LIFE SIGNIFICANT

In my previous talk, "On a Certain Blindness," I tried to make you feel how soaked and shot-through life is with values and meanings which we fail to realize because of our external and insensible point of view. The meanings are there for the others, but they are not there for us. There lies more than a mere interest of curious speculation in understanding this. It has the most tremendous practical importance. I wish that I could convince you of it as I feel it myself. It is the basis of all our tolerance, social, religious, and political. The forgetting of it lies at the root of every stupid and sanguinary mistake that rulers over subject-peoples make. The first thing to learn in intercourse with others is non-interference with their own peculiar ways of being happy, provided those ways do not assume to interfere by violence with ours. No one has insight into all the ideals. No one should presume to judge them off-hand. The pretension to dogmatize about them in each other is the root of most human injustices and cruelties, and the trait in human character most likely to make the angels weep.

Every Jack sees in his own particular Jill charms and perfections to the enchantment of which we stolid onlookers are stone-cold. And which has the superior view of the absolute truth, he or we? Which has the more vital insight into the nature of Jill's existence, as a fact? Is he in excess, being in this matter a maniac? or are we in defect, being victims of a pathological anæsthesia as regards Jill's magical importance? Surely the latter; surely to Jack are the profounder truths revealed; surely poor Jill's palpitating little life-throbs *are* among the wonders of creation, *are* worthy of this sympathetic interest; and it is to our shame that the rest of us cannot feel like Jack. For Jack realizes Jill concretely, and we do not. He struggles towards a union with her inner life, divining her feelings, anticipating her desires, understanding her limits as manfully as he can, and yet inadequately, too; for he also is afflicted with some blindness, even here. Whilst we, dead clods that we are, do not even seek after these things, but are contented that that portion of eternal fact named Jill should be for us as if it were not. Jill, who knows her inner life, knows that Jack's way of taking it—so importantly—is the true and serious way; and she responds to the truth in him by taking him truly and seriously, too. May the ancient blindness never wrap its clouds about either of them again! Where would any of *us* be, were there no one willing to know us as we really are or ready to repay us for *our* insight by making recognizant return? We ought, all of us, to realize each other in this intense, pathetic, and important way.

If you say that this is absurd, and that we cannot be in love with everyone at once, I merely point out to you that, as a matter of fact, certain persons do exist with an enormous capacity for friendship and for taking delight in other people's lives; and that such persons know more of truth than if their hearts were not so big. The vice of ordinary Jack and Jill affection is not its intensity, but its exclusions and its jealousies. Leave those out, and you see that the ideal I am holding up before you, however impracticable to-day, yet contains nothing intrinsically absurd.

We have unquestionably a great cloud-bank of ancestral blindness weighing down upon us, only transiently riven here and there by fitful revelations of the truth. It is vain to hope for this state of things to alter much. Our inner secrets must remain for the most part impenetrable by others, for beings as essentially practical as we are are necessarily short of sight. But if we cannot gain much positive insight into one another, cannot we at least use our sense of our own blindness to make us more cautious in going over the dark places? Cannot we escape some of those hideous ancestral intolerances and cruelties, and positive reversals of the truth?

For the remainder of this hour I invite you to seek with me some principle to make our tolerance less chaotic. And as I began my previous lecture by a personal reminiscence, I am going to ask your indulgence for a similar bit of egotism now.

A few summers ago I spent a happy week at the famous Assembly Grounds on the borders of Chautauqua Lake. The moment one treads that sacred enclosure, one feels one's self in an atmosphere of success. Sobriety and industry, intelligence and goodness, orderliness and ideality, prosperity and cheerfulness, pervade the air. It is a serious and studious picnic on a gigantic scale. Here you have a town of many thousands of inhabitants, beautifully laid out in the forest and drained, and equipped with means for satisfying all the necessary lower and most of the superfluous higher wants of man. You have a first-class college in full blast. You have magnificent music—a chorus of seven hundred voices, with possibly the most perfect open-air auditorium in the world. You have every sort of athletic exercise from sailing, rowing, swimming, bicycling, to the ball-field and the more artificial doings which the gymnasium affords. You have kindergartens and model secondary schools. You have general religious services and special club-houses for the several sects. You have perpetually running soda-water fountains, and daily popular lectures by distinguished men. You have the best of company, and yet no effort. You have no zymotic diseases, no poverty, no drunkenness, no crime, no police. You have culture, you have kindness, you have cheapness, you have equality, you have the best fruits of what mankind has fought and bled and striven for under the name of civilization for centuries. You have, in short, a foretaste of what human society might be, were it all in the light, with no suffering and no dark corners.

I went in curiosity for a day. I stayed for a week, held spellbound by the charm and ease of everything, by the middleclass paradise, without a sin, without a victim, without a blot, without a tear.

And yet what was my own astonishment, on emerging into the dark and wicked world again, to catch myself quite unexpectedly and involuntarily saying: "Ouf! what a relief! Now for something primordial and savage, even though it were as bad as an Armenian massacre, to set the balance straight again. This order is too tame, this culture too second-rate, this goodness too uninspiring. This human drama without a villain or a pang; this community so refined that ice-cream soda-water is the utmost offering it can make to the brute animal in man; this city simmering in the tepid lakeside sun; this atrocious harmlessness of all things—I cannot abide with them. Let me take my chances again in the big outside worldly wilderness with all its sins and sufferings. There are the heights and depths, the precipices and the steep ideals, the gleams of the awful and the infinite; and there is more hope and help a thousand times than in this dead level and quintessence of every mediocrity."

Such was the sudden right-about-face performed for me by my lawless fancy! There had been spread before me the realization—on a small, sample scale of course—of all the ideals for which our civilization has been striving: security, intelligence, humanity, and order; and here was the instinctive hostile reaction, not of the natural man, but of a so-called cultivated man upon such a Utopia. There seemed thus to be a self-contradiction and paradox somewhere, which I, as a professor drawing a full salary, was in duty bound to unravel and explain, if I could.

So I meditated. And, first of all, I asked myself what the thing was that was so lacking in this Sabbatical city, and the lack of which kept one forever falling short of the higher sort of contentment. And I soon recognized that it was the element that gives to the wicked outer world all its moral style, expressiveness and picturesqueness—the element of precipitousness, so to call it, of strength and strenuousness, intensity and danger. What excites and interests the looker-on at life, what the romances and the statues celebrate and the grim civic monuments remind us of, is the everlasting battle of the powers of light with those of darkness; with heroism, reduced to its bare chance, yet ever and anon snatching victory from the jaws of death. But in this unspeakable Chautauqua there was no potentiality of death in sight anywhere, and no point of the compass visible from which danger might possibly appear. The ideal was so completely victorious already that no sign of any previous battle remained, the place just resting on its oars. But what our human emotions seem to require is the sight of the struggle going on. The moment the fruits are being merely eaten, things become ignoble. Sweat and effort, human nature strained to its uttermost and on the rack, yet getting through alive, and then turning its back on its success to pursue another more rare and arduous still—this is the sort of thing the presence of which inspires us, and the reality of which it seems to be the function of all the higher forms of literature and fine art to bring home to us and suggest. At

Chautauqua there were no racks, even in the place's historical museum; and no sweat, except possibly the gentle moisture on the brow of some lecturer, or on the sides of some player in the ball-field.

Such absence of human nature *in extremis* anywhere seemed, then, a sufficient explanation for Chautauqua's flatness and lack of zest.

But was not this a paradox well calculated to fill one with dismay? It looks indeed, thought I, as if the romantic idealists with their pessimism about our civilization were, after all, quite right. An irremediable flatness is coming over the world. Bourgeoisie and mediocrity, church sociables and teachers' conventions, are taking the place of the old heights and depths and romantic chiaroscuro. And to get human life in its wild intensity, we must in future turn more and more away from the actual, and forget it, if we can, in the romancer's or the poet's pages. The whole world, delightful and sinful as it may still appear for a moment to one just escaped from the Chautauquan enclosure, is nevertheless obeying more and more just those ideals that are sure to make of it in the end a mere Chautauqua Assembly on an enormous scale. *Was im Gesang soll leben muss im Leben untergehn.* Even now, in our own country, correctness, fairness, and compromise for every small advantage are crowding out all other qualities. The higher heroisms and the old rare flavors are passing out of life.[1]

With these thoughts in my mind, I was speeding with the train towards Buffalo, when, near that city, the sight of a workman doing something on the dizzy edge of a sky-scaling iron construction brought me to my senses very suddenly. And now I perceived, by a flash of insight, that I had been steeping myself in pure ancestral blindness, and looking at life with the eyes of a remote spectator. Wishing for heroism and the spectacle of human nature on the rack, I had never noticed the great fields of heroism lying roundabout me, I had failed to see it present and alive. I could only think of it as

[1]This address was composed before the Cuban and Philippine wars. Such outbursts of the passion of mastery are, however, only episodes in a social process which in the long run seems everywhere tending towards the Chautauquan ideals.

dead and embalmed, labelled and costumed, as it is in the pages of romance. And yet there it was before me in the daily lives of the laboring classes. Not in clanging fights and desperate marches only is heroism to be looked for, but on every railway bridge and fire-proof building that is going up to-day. On freight-trains, on the decks of vessels, in cattle-yards and mines, on lumber-rafts, among the firemen and the policemen, the demand for courage is incessant; and the supply never fails. There, every day of the year somewhere, is human nature *in extremis* for you. And wherever a scythe, an axe, a pick, or a shovel is wielded, you have it sweating and aching and with its powers of patient endurance racked to the utmost under the length of hours of the strain.

As I awoke to all this unidealized heroic life around me, the scales seemed to fall from my eyes; and a wave of sympathy greater than anything I had ever before felt with the common life of common men began to fill my soul. It began to seem as if virtue with horny hands and dirty skin were the only virtue genuine and vital enough to take account of. Every other virtue poses; none is absolutely unconscious and simple, and unexpectant of decoration or recognition, like this. These are our soldiers, thought I, these our sustainers, these the very parents of our life.

Many years ago, when in Vienna, I had had a similar feeling of awe and reverence in looking at the peasant-women, in from the country on their business at the market for the day. Old hags many of them were, dried and brown and wrinkled, kerchiefed and short-petticoated, with thick wool stockings on their bony shanks, stumping through the glittering thoroughfares, looking neither to the right nor the left, bent on duty, envying nothing, humble-hearted, remote;—and yet at bottom, when you came to think of it, bearing the whole fabric of the splendors and corruptions of that city on their laborious backs. For where would any of it have been without their unremitting, unrewarded labor in the fields? And so with us: not to our generals and poets, I thought, but to the Italian and Hungarian laborers in the Subway, rather, ought the monuments of gratitude and reverence of a city like Boston to be reared.

* * *

If any of you have been readers of Tolstoi, you will see that I passed into a vein of feeling similar to his, with its abhorrence of all that conventionally passes for distinguished, and its exclusive deification of the bravery, patience, kindliness, and dumbness of the unconscious natural man.

Where now is *our* Tolstoi, I said, to bring the truth of all this home to our American bosoms, fill us with a better insight, and wean us away from that spurious literary romanticism on which our wretched culture—as it calls itself—is fed? Divinity lies all about us, and culture is too hidebound to even suspect the fact. Could a Howells or a Kipling be enlisted in this mission? or are they still too deep in the ancestral blindness, and not humane enough for the inner joy and meaning of the laborer's existence to be really revealed? Must we wait for someone born and bred and living as a laborer himself, but who, by grace of Heaven, shall also find a literary voice?

And there I rested on that day, with a sense of widening of vision, and with what it is surely fair to call an increase of religious insight into life. In God's eyes, the differences of social position, of intellect, of culture, of cleanliness, of dress, which different men exhibit, and all the other rarities and exceptions on which they so fantastically pin their pride, must be so small as, practically, quite to vanish; and all that should remain is the common fact that here we are, a countless multitude of vessels of life, each of us pent in to peculiar difficulties, with which we must severally struggle by using whatever of fortitude and goodness we can summon up. The exercise of the courage, patience, and kindness, must be the significant portion of the whole business; and the distinctions of position can only be a manner of diversifying the phenomenal surface upon which these underground virtues may manifest their effects. At this rate, the deepest human life is everywhere, is eternal. And if any human attributes exist only in particular individuals, they must belong to the mere trapping and decoration of the surface-show.

Thus are men's lives levelled up as well as levelled down—levelled up in their common inner meaning, levelled down in their outer gloriousness and show. Yet always, we must confess, this levelling insight tends to be obscured again; and

always the ancestral blindness returns and wraps us up, so
that we end once more by thinking that creation can be for
no other purpose than to develop remarkable situations and
conventional distinctions and merits. And then always some
new leveller in the shape of a religious prophet has to arise—
the Buddha, the Christ, or some Saint Francis, some Rousseau or Tolstoi—to redispel our blindness. Yet, little by little,
there comes some stable gain; for the world does get more
humane, and the religion of democracy tends towards permanent increase.

   This, as I said, became for a time my conviction, and gave
me great content. I have put the matter into the form of a
personal reminiscence, so that I might lead you into it more
directly and completely, and so save time. But now I am going
to discuss the rest of it with you in a more impersonal way.
   Tolstoi's levelling philosophy began long before he had the
crisis of melancholy commemorated in that wonderful document of his entitled *My Confession*, which led the way to his
more specifically religious works. In his masterpiece *War and
Peace*—assuredly the greatest of human novels—the rôle of
the spiritual hero is given to a poor little soldier named Karataieff, so helpful, so cheerful, and so devout that, in spite of
his ignorance and filthiness, the sight of him opens the heavens, which have been closed, to the mind of the principal
character of the book; and his example evidently is meant by
Tolstoi to let God into the world again for the reader. Poor
little Karataieff is taken prisoner by the French; and when too
exhausted by hardship and fever to march, is shot as other
prisoners were in the famous retreat from Moscow. The last
view one gets of him is his little figure leaning against a white
birch-tree, and uncomplainingly awaiting the end.
   "The more," writes Tolstoi in the work *My Confession*, "the
more I examined the life of these laboring folks, the more
persuaded I became that they veritably have faith, and get
from it alone the sense and the possibility of life. . . . Con-
trariwise to those of our own class, who protest against destiny and grow indignant at its rigor, these people receive
maladies and misfortunes without revolt, without opposition,
and with a firm and tranquil confidence that all had to be like

that, could not be otherwise, and that it is all right so. . . . The more we live by our intellect, the less we understand the meaning of life. We see only a cruel jest in suffering and death, whereas these people live, suffer, and draw near to death with tranquillity, and oftener than not with joy. . . . There are enormous multitudes of them happy with the most perfect happiness, although deprived of what for us is the sole good of life. Those who understand life's meaning, and know how to live and die thus, are to be counted not by twos, threes, tens, but by hundreds, thousands, millions. They labor quietly, endure privations and pains, live and die, and throughout everything see the good without seeing the vanity. I had to love these people. The more I entered into their life, the more I loved them; and the more it became possible for me to live, too. It came about not only that the life of our society, of the learned and of the rich, disgusted me—more than that, it lost all semblance of meaning in my eyes. All our actions, our deliberations, our sciences, our arts, all appeared to me with a new significance. I understood that these things might be charming pastimes, but that one need seek in them no depth, whereas the life of the hard-working populace, of that multitude of human beings who really contribute to existence, appeared to me in its true light. I understood that there veritably is life, that the meaning which life there receives is the truth; and I accepted it."[2]

In a similar way does Stevenson appeal to our piety towards the elemental virtue of mankind.

"What a wonderful thing," he writes,[3] "is this Man! How surprising are his attributes! Poor soul, here for so little, cast among so many hardships, savagely surrounded, savagely descended, irremediably condemned to prey upon his fellow lives: who should have blamed him had he been of a piece with his destiny and a being merely barbarous? . . . [Yet] it matters not where we look, under what climate we observe him, in what stage of society, in what depth of ignorance, burthened with what erroneous morality; in ships at sea, a man inured to hardship and vile pleasures, his brightest hope

[2]*Ma confession* [Paris, 1887], X (condensed).
[3]*Across the Plains*: "Pulvis et Umbra" (abridged).

a fiddle in a tavern and a bedizened trull who sells herself to
rob him, and he for all that simple, innocent, cheerful, kindly
like a child, constant to toil, brave to drown, for others; in the
slums of cities, moving among indifferent millions to mechanical employments, without hope of change in the future, with
scarce a pleasure in the present, and yet true to his virtues,
honest up to his lights, kind to his neighbours, tempted perhaps in vain by the bright gin-palace, . . . often repaying the
world's scorn with service, often standing firm upon a scruple,
. . . everywhere some virtue cherished or affected, everywhere some decency of thought and courage, everywhere the
ensign of man's ineffectual goodness:—ah! if I could show
you this! if I could show you these men and women, all the
world over, in every stage of history, under every abuse of
error, under every circumstance of failure, without hope,
without help, without thanks, still obscurely fighting the lost
fight of virtue, still clinging to some rag of honour, the poor
jewel of their souls!"

All this is as true as it is splendid, and terribly do we need
our Tolstois and Stevensons to keep our sense for it alive. Yet
you remember the Irishman who, when asked, "Is not one
man as good as another?" replied: "Yes; and a great deal better, too!" Similarly (it seems to me) does Tolstoi overcorrect
our social prejudices, when he makes his love of the peasant
so exclusive, and hardens his heart towards the educated man
as absolutely as he does. Grant that at Chautauqua there was
little moral effort, little sweat or muscular strain in view. Still,
deep down in the souls of the participants we may be sure
that something of the sort was hid, some inner stress, some
vital virtue not found wanting when required. And, after all,
the question recurs, and forces itself upon us, Is it so certain
that the surroundings and circumstances of the virtue do
make so little difference in the importance of the result? Is the
functional utility, the worth to the universe of a certain definite amount of courage, kindliness, and patience, no greater if
the possessor of these virtues is in an educated situation,
working out far-reaching tasks, than if he be an illiterate nobody, hewing wood and drawing water, just to keep himself
alive? Tolstoi's philosophy, deeply enlightening though it certainly is, remains a false abstraction. It savors too much of

that oriental pessimism and nihilism of his, which declares the whole phenomenal world and its facts and their distinctions to be a cunning fraud.

A mere bare fraud is just what our Western common sense will never believe the phenomenal world to be. It admits fully that the inner joys and virtues are the *essential* part of life's business, but it is sure that *some* positive part is also played by the adjuncts of the show. If it is idiotic in romanticism to recognize the heroic only when it sees it labelled and dressed-up in books, it is really just as idiotic to see it only in the dirty boots and sweaty shirt of someone in the fields. It is with us really under every disguise: at Chautauqua; here in your college; in the stock-yards and on the freight-trains; and in the czar of Russia's court. But, instinctively, we make a combination of two things in judging the total significance of a human being. We feel it to be some sort of a product (if such a product only could be calculated) of his inner virtue *and* his outer place—neither singly taken, but both conjoined. If the outer differences had no meaning for life, why indeed should all this immense variety of them exist? They *must* be significant elements of the world as well.

Just test Tolstoi's deification of the mere manual laborer by the facts. This is what Mr. Walter Wyckoff, after working as an unskilled laborer in the demolition of some buildings at West Point, writes of the spiritual condition of the class of men to which he temporarily chose to belong:

"The salient features of our condition are plain enough. We are grown men, and are without a trade. In the labor market we stand ready to sell to the highest bidder our mere muscular strength for so many hours each day. We are thus in the lowest grade of labor. And selling our muscular strength in the open market for what it will bring, we sell it under peculiar conditions. It is all the capital that we have. We have no reserve means of subsistence, and cannot, therefore, stand off for a 'reserve price.' We sell under the necessity of satisfying imminent hunger. Broadly speaking, we must sell our labor or starve; and as hunger is a matter of a few hours, and we have no other way of meeting this need, we must sell at once for what the market offers for our labor.

"Our employer is buying labor in a dear market, and he will certainly get from us as much work as he can at the price. The gang-boss is secured for this purpose, and thoroughly does he know his business. He has sole command of us. He never saw us before, and he will discharge us all when the débris is cleared away. In the meantime he must get from us, if he can, the utmost of physical labor which we, individually and collectively, are capable of. If he should drive some of us to exhaustion, and we should not be able to continue at work, he would not be the loser, for the market would soon supply him with others to take our places.

"We are ignorant men, but so much we clearly see: that we have sold our labor where we could sell it dearest, and our employer has bought it where he could buy it cheapest. He has paid high, and he must get all the labor that he can; and, by a strong instinct which possesses us, we shall part with as little as we can. From work like ours there seems to us to have been eliminated every element which constitutes the nobility of labor. We feel no personal pride in its progress, and no community of interest with our employer. There is none of the joy of responsibility, none of the sense of achievement, only the dull monotony of grinding toil, with the longing for the signal to quit work, and for our wages at the end.

"And being what we are, the dregs of the labor market, and having no certainty of permanent employment, and no organization among ourselves, we must expect to work under the watchful eye of a gang-boss, and be driven, like the wage-slaves that we are, through our tasks.

"All this is to tell us, in effect, that our lives are hard, barren, hopeless lives" [abridged].

And such hard, barren, hopeless lives, surely, are not lives in which one ought to be willing permanently to remain. And why is this so? Is it because they are so dirty? Well, Nansen grew a great deal dirtier on his polar expedition; and we think none the worse of his life for that. Is it the insensibility? Our soldiers have to grow vastly more insensible, and we extol them to the skies. Is it the poverty? Poverty has been reckoned the crowning beauty of many a heroic career. Is it the slavery to a task, the loss of finer pleasures? Such slavery and loss are of the very essence of the higher fortitude, and are always counted to its credit—read the records of missionary devotion all over the world. It is not any one of these things, then, taken by itself—no, nor all of them together—that make such a life undesirable. A man might in truth live like an unskilled laborer, and do the work of one, and yet count as one of the noblest of God's creatures. Quite possibly there were some such persons in the gang that our author describes; but the current of their souls ran underground; and he was too steeped in the ancestral blindness to discern it.

If there *were* any such morally exceptional individuals, however, what made them different from the rest? It can only have been this—that their souls worked and endured in obedience to some inner *ideal*, whilst their comrades were not actuated by anything worthy of that name. These ideals of other lives are among those secrets that we can almost never penetrate, although something about the man may often tell us when they are there. In Mr. Wyckoff's own case we know exactly what the self-imposed ideal was. Partly he had stumped himself, as the boys say, to carry through a strenuous achievement; but mainly he wished to enlarge his sympathetic insight into fellow-lives. For this his sweat and toil acquire a certain heroic significance, and make us accord to him exceptional esteem. But it is easy to imagine his fellows with various other ideals. To say nothing of wives and babies, one may have been a convert of the Salvation Army, and had a nightingale singing of expiation and forgiveness in his heart all the while he labored. Or there might have been an apostle like Tolstoi himself, or his compatriot Bondareff, in the gang, voluntarily embracing labor as their religious mission. Class-loyalty was undoubtedly an ideal with many. And who knows how much of that higher manliness of poverty, of which Phillips Brooks has spoken so penetratingly, was or was not present in that gang?

"A rugged, barren land," says Phillips Brooks, "is poverty to live in,—a land where I am thankful very often if I can get a berry or a root to eat; but living in it really, letting it bear witness to me of itself, not dishonoring it all the time by judging it after the standards of the other lands, gradually there come out its qualities. Behold! no land like this barren and naked land of poverty could show the moral geology of

the world. See how the hard ribs . . . stand out strong and
solid. No life like poverty could so get one to the heart of
things and make men know their meaning, could so let us feel
life and the world with all the soft cushions stripped off and
thrown away. . . . Poverty makes men come very near each
other, and recognize each other's human hearts; and poverty,
highest and best of all, demands and cries out for faith in
God. . . . I know how superficial and unfeeling, how like
mere mockery, words in praise of poverty may seem. . . .
But I am sure that the poor man's dignity and freedom, his
self-respect and energy, depend upon his cordial knowledge
that his poverty is a true region and kind of life with its own
chances of character, its own springs of happiness, and revelations of God. Let him resist the characterlessness which often
comes with being poor. Let him insist on respecting the condition where he lives. Let him learn to love it so that by and
by [if] he grows rich he shall go out of the low door of the
old familiar poverty with a true pang of regret, and with a
true honor for the narrow home where he has lived so long."[4]

The barrenness and ignobleness of the more usual laborer's
life consist in the fact that it is moved by no such ideal inner
springs. The backache, the long hours, the danger, are patiently endured—for what? To gain a quid of tobacco, a glass
of beer, a cup of coffee, a meal, and a bed, and to begin again
the next day and shirk as much as one can. This really is why
we raise no monument to the laborers in the Subway, even
though they be our conscripts, and even though after a fashion our city is indeed based upon their patient hearts and
enduring backs and shoulders. And this is why we do raise
monuments to our soldiers, whose outward conditions were
even brutaller still. The soldiers are supposed to have followed
an ideal, and the laborers are supposed to have followed none.

You see, my friends, how the plot now thickens; and how
strangely the complexities of this wonderful human nature of
ours begin to develop under our hands. We have seen the
blindness and deadness to each other which are our natural
inheritance; and in spite of them, we have been led to ac-

[4]*The Light of the World and Other Sermons*, 5th Series (New York: E. P.
Dutton, 1891), pp. 166, 167.

knowledge an inner meaning which passeth show, and which may be present in the lives of others where we least descry it. And now we are led to say that such inner meaning can be *complete*, and *valid for us also*, only when the inner joy, courage, and endurance are joined with an ideal.

But what, exactly, do we mean by an ideal? Can we give no definite account of such a word?

To a certain extent we can. An ideal, for instance, must be something intellectually conceived, something of which we are not unconscious, if we have it; and it must carry with it that sort of outlook, uplift, and brightness that go with all intellectual facts. Secondly, there must be *novelty* in an ideal—novelty at least for him whom the ideal grasps. Sodden routine is incompatible with ideality, although what is sodden routine for one person may be ideal novelty for another. This shows that there is nothing absolutely ideal: ideals are relative to the lives that entertain them. To keep out of the gutter is for us here no part of consciousness at all, yet for many of our brethren it is the most legitimately engrossing of ideals.

Now, taken nakedly, abstractly, and immediately, you see that mere ideals are the cheapest things in life. Everybody has them in some shape or other, personal or general, sound or mistaken, low or high; and the most worthless sentimentalists and dreamers, drunkards, shirks and verse-makers, who never show a grain of effort, courage, or endurance, possibly have them on the most copious scale. Education, enlarging as it does our horizon and perspective, is a means of multiplying our ideals, of bringing new ones into view. And your college professor, with a starched shirt and spectacles, would, if a stock of ideals were all alone by itself enough to render a life significant, be the most absolutely and deeply significant of men. Tolstoi would be completely blind in despising him for a prig, a pedant and a parody; and all our new insight into the divinity of muscular labor would be altogether off the track of truth.

But such consequences as this, you instinctively feel, are erroneous. The more ideals a man has, the more contemptible, on the whole, do you continue to deem him, if the matter ends there for him, and if none of the laboring man's virtues are called into action on his part—no courage shown, no privations undergone, no dirt or scars contracted in the attempt to get them realized. It is quite obvious that something more than the mere possession of ideals is required to make a life significant in any sense that claims the spectator's admiration. Inner joy, to be sure, it may *have*, with its ideals; but that is its own private sentimental matter. To extort from us, outsiders as we are, with our own ideals to look after, the tribute of our grudging recognition, it must back its ideal visions with what the laborers have, the sterner stuff of manly virtue; it must multiply their sentimental surface by the dimension of the active will, if we are to have *depth*, if we are to have anything cubical and solid in the way of character.

The significance of a human life for communicable and publicly recognizable purposes is thus the offspring of a marriage of two different parents, either of whom alone is barren. The ideals taken by themselves give no reality, the virtues by themselves no novelty. And let the orientalists and pessimists say what they will, the thing of deepest—or, at any rate, of comparatively deepest—significance in life does seem to be its character of *progress*, or that strange union of reality with ideal novelty which it continues from one moment to another to present. To recognize ideal novelty is the task of what we call intelligence. Not everyone's intelligence can tell which novelties are ideal. For many the ideal thing will always seem to cling still to the older more familiar good. In this case character, though not significant totally, may be still significant pathetically. So if we are to choose which is the more essential factor of human character, the fighting virtue or the intellectual breadth, we must side with Tolstoi, and choose that simple faithfulness to his light or darkness which any common unintellectual man can show.

But with all this beating and tacking on my part, I fear you take me to be reaching a confused result. I seem to be just taking things up and dropping them again. First I took up Chautauqua, and dropped that; then Tolstoi and the heroism of common toil, and dropped them; finally, I took up ideals, and seem now almost dropping those. But please observe in what sense it is that I drop them. It is when they pretend *singly* to redeem life from insignificance. Culture and refinement all alone are not enough to do so. Ideal aspirations are not enough, when uncombined with pluck and will. But neither are pluck and will, dogged endurance and insensibility to danger enough, when taken all alone. There must be some sort of fusion, some chemical combination among these principles, for a life objectively and thoroughly significant to result.

Of course, this is a somewhat vague conclusion. But in a question of significance, of worth, like this, conclusions can never be precise. The answer of appreciation, of sentiment, is always a more or a less, a balance struck by sympathy, insight, and good will. But it is an answer, all the same, a real conclusion. And in the course of getting it, it seems to me that our eyes have been opened to many important things. Some of you are, perhaps, more livingly aware than you were an hour ago of the depths of worth that lie around you, hid in alien lives. And when you ask how much sympathy you ought to bestow, although the amount is, truly enough, a matter of ideal on your own part, yet in this notion of the combination of ideals with active virtues you have a rough standard for shaping your decision. In any case, your imagination is extended. You divine in the world about you matter for a little more humility on your own part, and tolerance, reverence, and love for others; and you gain a certain inner joyfulness at the increased importance of our common life. Such joyfulness is a religious inspiration and an element of spiritual health, and worth more than large amounts of that sort of technical and accurate information which we professors are supposed to be able to impart.

To show the sort of thing I mean by these words, I will just make one brief practical illustration, and then close.

We are suffering to-day in America from what is called the labor-question; and when you go out into the world, you will each and all of you be caught up in its perplexities. I use the brief term labor-question to cover all sorts of anarchistic discontents and socialistic projects, and the conservative resistances which they provoke. So far as this conflict is unhealthy and regrettable—and I think it is so only to a limited extent—the unhealthiness consists solely in the fact that one-half of our fellow-countrymen remain entirely blind to the internal significance of the lives of the other half. They miss the joys and sorrows, they fail to feel the moral virtue, and they do not guess the presence of the intellectual ideals. They are at cross-purposes all along the line, regarding each other as they might regard a set of dangerously gesticulating automata, or if they seek to get at the inner motivation, making the most horrible mistakes. Often all that the poor man can think of in the rich man is a cowardly greediness for safety, luxury, and effeminacy, and a boundless affectation. What he is, is not a human being, but a pocket-book, a bank-account. And a similar greediness, turned by disappointment into envy, is all that many rich men can see in the state of mind of the dissatisfied poor. And if the rich man begins to do the sentimental act over the poor man, what senseless blunders does he make, pitying him for just those very duties and those very immunities which, rightly taken, are the condition of his most abiding and characteristic joys! Each, in short, ignores the fact that happiness and unhappiness and significance are a vital mystery; each pins them absolutely on some ridiculous feature of the external situation; and everybody remains outside of everybody else's sight.

Society has, with all this, undoubtedly got to pass towards some newer and better equilibrium, and the distribution of wealth has doubtless slowly got to change; such changes have always happened, and will happen to the end of time. But if, after all that I have said, any of you expect that they will make any *genuine vital difference*, on a large scale, to the lives of our descendants, you will have missed the significance of my entire lecture. The solid meaning of life is always the same eternal thing—the marriage, namely, of some unhabitual ideal, however special, with some fidelity, courage, and endurance; with some man's or woman's pains.—And whatever or wherever life may be, there will always be the chance for that marriage to take place.

Fitzjames Stephen wrote many years ago words to this effect more eloquent than any I can speak: "The *Great Eastern*, or some of her successors," he said, "will perhaps defy the roll of the Atlantic, and cross the seas without allowing their passengers to feel that they have left the firm land. The voyage from the cradle to the grave may come to be performed with similar facility. Progress and science may, perhaps, enable untold millions to live and die without a care, without a pang, without an anxiety. They will have a pleasant passage, and plenty of brilliant conversation. They will wonder that men ever believed at all in clanging fights, and blazing towns, and sinking ships, and praying hands; and, when they come to the end of their course, they will go their way, and the place thereof will know them no more. But it seems unlikely that they will have such a knowledge of the great ocean on which they sail, with its storms and wrecks, its currents and icebergs, its huge waves and mighty winds, as those who battled with it for years together in the little craft, which, if they had few other merits, brought those who navigated them full into the presence of time and eternity, their Maker and themselves, and forced them to have some definite views of their relations to them and to each other."[5]

In this solid and tridimensional sense, so to call it, those philosophers are right who contend that the world is a standing thing, with no progress, no real history. The changing conditions of history touch only the surface of the show. The altered equilibriums and redistributions only diversify our opportunities and open chances to us for new ideals. But with each new ideal that comes into life, the chance for a life based on some old ideal will vanish; and he would needs be a presumptuous calculator who should with confidence say that the total sum of significances is positively and absolutely greater at any one epoch than at any other of the world.

I am speaking broadly, I know, and omitting to consider certain qualifications in which I myself believe. But one can only make one point in one lecture, and I shall be well content if I have brought my point home to you this evening in even a slight degree. *There are compensations*; and no outward changes of condition in life can keep the nightingale of its eternal meaning from singing in all sorts of different men's

[5]Sir James Fitzjames Stephen, *Essays by a Barrister* (London, 1862), p. 318.

hearts. That is the main fact to remember. If we could not only admit it with our lips, but really and truly believe it, how our convulsive insistences, how our antipathies and dreads of each other, would soften down! If the poor and the rich could look at each other in this way, *sub specie æternitatis*, how gentle would grow their disputes! what tolerance and good humor, what willingness to live and let live, would come into the world!

Index

Absolute, 708

Abstractions, 733, 796, 797–798

Across the Plains (R. L. Stevenson), 847, 869

Action: and consciousness, 726–729; and training, 730–731; and learning, 733–735; and emulation, 742–744; and habits, 750, 759; and will, 753; and association, 760; and mind, 808–809; and inhibition, 809–813; voluntary, 812; types of, 813–814; and attention, 815–819; and goodness, 821; and feeling, 825–826; and ideals, 877. *See also* Behavior

Adaptation, 727–728

Adolescence, 796, 797

Aesthetics, 727, 728

Africans, 842

Alcohol, 827

Ambition, 744–745

America, 708, 715. *See also* United States

American character, 755, 829–834, 837

Analogy, 760

Animals, 739

Anxiety, 755

Apperceiving mass, 802, 805

Apperception: measurement, 788; and novelty, 793; and education, 799, 800–801; described, 802; and economy, 802–803; types, 803–805; and behavior, 806; and deliberation, 816

Aristotle, 726

Armenia, 863

Arnold, Thomas, 743

Art of teaching, 717–718

As a Matter of Course (A. P. Call), 837

Association: and habits, 759; laws of, 759–760; causes, 760; and education, 761, 764; and prediction, 762–763; and constellation, 764; and interest, 767–768, 770; and memory, 779–783, 784–785, 793; and science, 784; and apperception, 801–802

Associationism, 812

Attention: and manual training, 734; and instincts, 736–737; and novelty, 740; and sensation, 740; and interest, 766, 767, 768, 769; voluntary,

771–773, 776, 818; and change, 773; physiology of, 774–775; varieties of, 777–778; and action, 815–817; and moral effort, 817

Bagehot, Walter, 832

Bain, Alexander, 752–753

Baldwin, James Mark, 741, 832

Beauty, 854

Behavior: and theory, 727; and teaching, 729, 730–731; and association, 761; and apperception, 805–806; and mind, 808–809; and inhibition, 809–813; and impulse, 812. *See also* Action

Binnenleben, 827

Biology, 796, 804

Blindness: and other lives, 841–848, 865; and nature, 848–854; and tolerance, 861–862; and the labor-question, 878

Bondarev, Timofei Mikhailovich, 873

Boston, Mass., 866

Boston Normal School of Gymnastics, 708

Bottled-lightning quality, 830–831, 832

Brain: and psychology, 717; and mind, 722, 728, 819; and reflexes, 737–738; and attention, 775; and memory, 780, 782; and forgetting, 791; and inhibition, 809

Brooks, Phillips, 873–874

Buddha, 868

Buffalo, N.Y., 803, 865

Calamus (W. Whitman), 853–854

Call, Annie Payson, 835, 837

Cambridge, Mass., 707, 755, 843

Campbell, Thomas, 799

Carlyle, Thomas, 854

Carpenter, William Benjamin, 750

Causation, spiritual, 819

Cavour, Camillo Benso, Conte di, 814

Cellini, Benvenuto, 855

Change, 773, 879–880

Character: and habit, 753; and association, 761–762, 764; and inhibition,

813; development, 816–818; American, 829–834, 838
Charles I, 785
Chautauqua Assembly, 862–865, 870, 876
Chemistry, 796
Children: and instincts, 738; and curiosity, 740–741, 796; and ownership, 745–746; and constructiveness, 747; and habits, 748–749; and relaxation, 755; and interest, 767; and learning, 794–796; and will-breaking, 814–815; and cruelty, 821; general view of, 822
Child-study, 720–721, 796
Choice, 811, 816
Christ, 868
Christian's Secret, The (H. W. Smith), 826
Civilization, 863, 867
Clifford, William Kingdon, 847
Climate, 831
Clouston, Thomas Smith, 829, 830, 832
Collecting, 746
Commercial Advertiser (New York), 842
Communism, 745
Conception, 794, 816
Conduct, 730
Conscience, 720, 836
Consciousness: nature of, 722–725, 759; functions, 726–729; and imitation, 741; foundation of, 747; and association, 760, 801; fields, 777; and action, 808, 815; and inhibition, 810–813; and organisms, 818–819; of self, 827, 835–836
Constellation, 764
Constructiveness, 747, 795
Contemplation, 726
Contiguity, 759–760
Conversation, 814, 836
Conversion, 756
Cook, James, 802
Cramming, 786
Crump (literary character), 821
Cuba, 865n
Culture, 843, 856, 863, 867, 877
Curiosity, 740–741, 796

Danger, 863–866
Darwin, Charles: quoted, 754; mentioned, 784

Degenerate, hereditary, 805
Deliberation, 810–811, 816, 817–818
Delsarteans, 837
Democracy, 708, 868
Déséquilibré, 805
Destruction, 747
Determinism, 819
Discipline, 734, 768
Dogs, 841–842
Dresser, Horatio Willis, 837
Drunkard, habitual, 817–818

Ebbinghaus, Hermann, 791–792
Economy, law of, 802–803
Educability, 736
Education: organization of, 715; and psychology, 716–721, 774; and behavior, 729, 730–732; and expression, 733–735; meaning of, 736; and instincts, 736–739; and curiosity, 740–741; and imitation, 741–744; and interest, 745–746, 775–777; and habits, 749, 750, 751–753, 757; and association, 760–763; and mental powers, 777–778; and memory, 783–785; and memorization, 786–788; and measurement, 788–789; and learning, 794–798; and apperception, 799, 800–801, 805–807; of will, 815–818; and heroism, 871; and ideals, 875. *See also* Teaching
Effort: and habits, 755; training, 756; and attention, 771, 772, 776; and will, 808; moral, 816–818
Ejects, 847
Emerson, Ralph Waldo, 848, 856
Émile (J. J. Rousseau), 743
Emotion: and inhibition, 812, 835; theory of, 825; control of, 825–826; and value, 841
Emotions and the Will, The (A. Bain), 752
Emulation, 742–743
Energy, American, 833
England: education in, 715, 731–732; character in, 828, 829
Essays (J. F. Stephen), 879
Ethics: and conduct, 717; and the nervous system, 727, 728, 757; and stages of learning, 796; and inhibition, 810
Ethics (Spinoza), 821

Europe, 830–832
Evolution, 717, 726, 734, 784
Examinations, 837
Experimentation, 715, 719, 747
Explanation, 722–723, 779
Expression, 733–735

Faculties, in psychology, 779
Fatalism, 812
Fear, 740, 810, 825
Feeling, 723, 825, 841, 842
Feminity, 827
Fiat, 808
Fitch, Joshua Girling, 773
Fletcher, Horace, 837
Focus, 723–724, 777
Fogyism, 803, 806
Forgetting, 791–792
France, 809, 814
Francis of Assisi, Saint, 868
Freeman, 821
Free will, 812, 819–820
Fringe, the, 723

Galton, Francis, 787, 790
Genius: and teaching, 717; and associa-
  tion, 760; and attention, 771–772;
  and novelty, 773
Gentlemen, 731
Geography, 769, 797, 798
Geometry, 747
Germany: education in, 715, 731; physi-
  ology in, 809
Gladstone, William Ewart, 782, 807, 814
Goethe, Johann Wolfgang von, 782
Goltz, Friedrich Leopold, 810
Goodness, 821–822
"Gospel of Relaxation, The" (W.
  James): history of, 708; mentioned,
  756n
Grading, 735
Grammar, 794
Great Britain, 829, 830
Guerre et la paix, La (L. Tolstoi), 856
Guiteau, Charles, 805

Habit: and education, 730, 749,
  757–758; and instinct, 748; and plasticity, 750; acquisition, 750–757; and
  anxiety, 755; and effort, 756; and association, 759; and character, 761,

815–816; and ideo-motor action, 809;
  volitional, 816; and tension, 831–834;
  and relaxation, 834
Haeckel, Ernst Heinrich, 804
Harmony, 775
Harvard Corporation, 707
Hauser, Caspar, 802
Health, 827–828
Healthy-mindedness, 827
Herbart, Johann Friedrich: and teach-
  ing, 718; on apperception, 802
Herbartians, 769, 777
Heredity, social, 741
Herman, Nicolas, 838, 839
Heroism, 865–868, 871
Hindoos, 755
Honesty, 734
Howells, William Dean, 867
Huber, François, 789
Hudson, William Henry, 857–859
Hume, David, 812
Hygiene, 829

Ideals, 873–878, 879
Ideas: simple, 724; acquisition, 794,
  806–807; and action, 810–813,
  816–818; and worth, 841
Ideo-motor action, 809, 811
Idle Days in Patagonia (W. H. Hud-
  son), 857
Images, 794
Imagination, 790, 794
Imitation: and education, 741–744;
  and tension, 832–834; and relaxation,
  835
Impression, 801–802
Impulses, 738, 812–815
Individualism, 708
Inhibition: and will, 809–813, 814–816;
  and character, 813–814; kinds of,
  820–821; and emotion, 835
Injustice, 861
Insanity, 835
Insight: and other lives, 841–848, 865;
  moments of, 848–849; and nature,
  848–854; and tolerance, 861–862;
  and the labor-question, 878
Instincts: human, 739; listed, 740–748;
  transitoriness of, 748, 795–796; and
  education, 748–749; and interests,
  766

Intelligence, 876

Intensity, 862–866

Interest: and manual training, 734; and education, 745, 775–777; atrophy of, 753–755; native, 766–767, 768; acquired, 766, 767–770; and attention, 771–773; and memory, 788–789

Introspection, 717

Invention, 742, 832

Ireland, 834

Jefferies, Richard, 850

Jefferson, Joseph, 757

Jowett, Benjamin, 731

Joy, 847, 875–877

Kavanagh, Arthur Macmorough, 789

Kipling, Rudyard, 867

Knowledge: and consciousness, 726–729; and curiosity, 740–741; and apperception, 793

Laboratory work, 734

Labor-question, 878

Lange, Carl Georg, 825

Lange-James theory, 825

Language, 797, 805–806

Lawrence, Brother. See Herman, Nicolas

Learning: and forgetting, 791–792; stages, 795–797, 806

Lecturing, 715–716

Leibniz, Gottfried Wilhelm von, 782

Life: meaning of, 708, 851, 861, 869, 876–877, 878; and habits, 750–751, 809; quality of, 795; and inhibition, 810–813; and psychology, 835; reality of, 843–844; appreciation, 853–860; and intensity, 862–866; and work, 866–868; and education, 870; and ideals, 873–875; and progress, 876

Light of the World, The (P. Brooks), 874

Lincoln, Abraham, 814

Locke, John, 717, 724

Logic, 717, 794

Lois de l'imitation, Les (G. Tarde), 741

Longfellow, Henry Wadsworth, 826

Lord Ullin's Daughter (literary character), 798

Lotze, Rudolph Hermann, 857

Love, 740

Ma confession (L. Tolstoi), 868–869

Man: nature of, 726–729, 736, 841; and instincts, 739; and imitation, 741; and habits, 750–751; and association, 764–765; and interest, 770; and attention, 777–778; energies of, 789; and imagery, 790; and free will, 812–813; and mental health, 827–829; future of, 828–829; and insight, 841–854; and nature, 848–854; and injustice, 861; and progress, 868, 876; Stevenson on, 869–870; and education, 870; and ideals, 875–876

Maniacs, 813

Manual training: and education, 734; and constructiveness, 795

Margin, 723–724, 777

Materialism, 819

Mathematics, 776, 796

Measurement, 788–789

Mechanics, 796

Melancholia, 813, 835–836

Memorization, 776, 786–787

Memory: and consciousness, 722; and educability, 736; and mental power, 778; and association, 779–781, 793; kinds of, 781; and retentiveness, 781–783; training, 783–785, 786–787; and science, 784; and mnemonics, 785; immediate, 788; and forgetting, 791–792; and words, 797; and thought, 817

Metaphysics, 727, 796

Microcosmus (H. Lotze), 857

Mill, John Stuart, 753

Mind: study of, 718; and brain, 722, 728; functions, 726–729, 736; and evolution, 734; nature of, 759, 819; and association, 760–761, 770; efficiency, 778; types, 781, 813; and economy, 802–803; and action, 808–809; and inhibition, 809–812; hygiene, 825; and health, 827–828; and progress, 828–829; breakdowns, 833

Mind-cure, 837

Mind-stuff, 724

Mnemonics, 785

Monkeys, 739

Monks, 746
Moral action, 816–818
Moral life, 810
Moral relations, 796
Morgan, Conwy Lloyd, 724
Movement, 766–767
Mulford, Prentice, 837
Münsterberg, Hugo: on teaching, 720; on association, 762; on America, 833
Muscles, 827–829
Mystics, 851

Names, 805–806
Nansen, Fridtjof, 872
Napoleon Bonaparte, 814
Natural history, 746
Nature, 848–854, 856–859
Nerves of arrest, 810
Nervous system, 750–751, 810, 827
New England, 836, 839
New psychology, the, 716–717, 723, 725
New York, 835, 853–854
Niagara Falls, 803
North Carolina, 842
Norway, 827–828
Novelty: and attention, 740, 766, 773, 775; and apperception, 802–803; and learning, 806; and ideals, 875, 876
Nuns, 746

Obermann (É. P. de Sénancour), 848
"On a Certain Blindness in Human Beings" (W. James), 708, 861
Ownership, 745–746
Oxford University, 731

Peace, 829
Pedagogy, soft, 745, 775–777
Perception, 708
Perez, Bernard, 804
Pessimism, 871
Philippines, 769, 865
Philosophy: pluralistic, 708; and theory, 726; method of, 727–728; study, 796; Tolstoi's, 868–869, 871; and change, 879
Physics, 797, 798
Physiology, 757, 809
Pick, Edward, 793
Plato, 726
Pluralism, 708

Politics, 715, 861
"Pot of Green Feathers, A" (T. G. Rooper), 803
Poverty, 745, 872, 873–874, 878
Power through Repose (A. P. Call), 835
Practical, the, 851
Practice of the Presence of God, The (N. Herman), 838
Prediction, 761–764
Prelude, The (W. Wordsworth), 849
Preparation, 769
Pride, 744–745
Principles of Psychology, The (W. James), 707
Progress, 868, 876
Property, private, 745–746
Psychology: and education, 716–720, 734, 761, 773, 815; history of, 717; data, 722; explanation in, 722–723, 779; and simple ideas, 724; Wundt on, 725; and action, 726; comparative, 728; and imitation, 741–742; and association, 779–780; measurements in, 788; and apperception, 800–801; and will, 809; agents in, 812; and free will, 819; and mental hygiene, 825; law of, 827; and tension, 832; and life, 835
Psychopathic subject, 805
Pugnacity, 744–745
Punishment, 740, 776

Reaction, 736–739, 766
Reading, 789
Reality, 844
Reasoning, 778
Recitation, 733
Reflex action, 737, 751, 808, 810
Reform, 715
Relaxation: and habits, 755; and work, 833; and imitation, 834; Call on, 835; and self-consciousness, 835–837; and religion, 837–839
Religion, 837–839, 861
Religious Aspect of Philosophy, The (J. Royce), 848
Repression, 820–821
Resolve, 808
Retentiveness, 781
Rip Van Winkle, 757
Rivalry, 743–744

Romanes, George John, 789
Rooper, Thomas Godolphin, 803
Rousseau, Jean Jacques, 743–744, 868
Royal Society, 787
Royce, Josiah: on imitation, 741, 832; quoted, 847–848
Rudolph Somebody anecdote, 752
Rugby School, 743
Russia, 871

Sanctity, 757, 836
Sanity, 829
Savages, 842, 857
Schiller, Friedrich, 865
Scholarship, 746
Schools, 715–716, 733, 741–744, 767
Schopenhauer, Arthur, 854
Science, 716–718, 731, 784, 805
Scotland, 715
Scott, Walter, 782
Scrupulosity, 814
Self, 768
Self-consciousness, 827, 835–836
Self-reliance, 734
Sénancour, Étienne Pivert de, 848
Sensation: and consciousness, 722–724; function of, 726; and novelty, 740; and attention, 740; and interest, 766–767
Senses, 717
Sentimentality, 753
Shakespeare, William, 754
Shelley, Percy Bysshe, 849
Shyness, 748
Similarity, 759–760
Sloyd system, 734, 746
Smith, Hannah Whitall, 826
Sociology, 796, 797, 832
Soldiers, 874
Soul, 722, 779–781
Spectator, 842, 859, 865
Spencer, Herbert: and mind-stuff, 724; mentioned, 784
Spinoza, Baruch, 821, 829
Spirits, 760
States, 715
Stephen, James Fitzjames, 879
Stevenson, Robert Louis, 844–847, 869–870
Story of My Heart, The (R. Jefferies), 850

Stream of consciousness, 722–725, 759
Substitution, 820–822

Taine, Hippolyte Adolphe, 724
Tarde, Jean Gabriel: on imitation, 741, 742, 832
Tassi, Francesco, 855
Teaching: interest in, 715–716; art of, 717–718; and child-study, 720–721; and psychology, 722, 761; aim of, 729, 730, 761–762, 815–816, 818; and fear, 740; and emulation, 742–744; and ambition, 744–745; and ownership, 745–746; and constructiveness, 747; and impulses, 748–749; and habits, 756; and association, 764; and interest, 766–770; and attention, 771–774, 775, 815; and drudgery, 776; and cramming, 786; and memory, 787–789; and imagination, 790–791; and forgetting, 791–792; and stages of learning, 795–797; and abstractions, 798–799; importance of, 806; and balky wills, 814–815; and inhibition, 820–821; and goodness, 821–822; improvement, 822; and preparation, 837. See also Education
Tedium, 854
Temperament, 813, 830
Tenderness, 745
Tennyson, Alfred, Lord, 799
Tension, 830–834, 835–837, 837–840
Testing, 788
Thackeray, William Makepeace, 834
Theory, 726–727, 728, 740, 783–785
Theosophy, 837
Thought: and sensation, 723; and habits, 759; and words, 797; and will, 808, 817
Tolerance, 708, 860, 861–862, 880
Tolstoi, Lev Nikolayevich: quoted, 855–856, 868–869; mentioned, 867, 868, 870, 873, 875, 876, 877
Trine, Ralph Waldo, 837
Truth, 728, 842

United States: education in, 715; character in, 755; and mental hygiene, 825, 828, 838; and tension, 829–834; and the labor-question, 878

Universities, 715, 731
Utopia, 728, 745, 864

Vagueness, 734
Values, 841, 850
Vanity, 748
Vices, 750
Vienna, 866
Virtues, 750, 876
Vita di Benvenuto Cellini, 855
Volition, 777, 811

War, 718–719
War and Peace (L. Tolstoi), 855, 868
Weakness, 829, 832
Wealth, 878
Wellington, Arthur Wellesley, Duke of, 750
Wesley, John, 815
Whitman, Walt, 851–853, 854

Will: and sensation, 723; described, 753, 808; and attention, 771, 818–820; and naming, 805–806; and inhibition, 809–813; freedom of, 812; kinds of, 813–814, 819; breaking, 815; education, 816–818; and thought, 817; and emotion, 825
Will to Believe, The (W. James), 707–708
Women, 827–828, 840
Words, 797
Wordsworth, William, 849, 851
Work: and tension, 832–834; value of, 870–871; Tolstoi on, 868–869, 870; Wyckoff on, 871–873; and ideals, 873–875; and the labor-question, 878
World, 726–728, 870, 879
Worry, 838
Worth, 841
Wundt, Wilhelm, 725
Wyckoff, Walter Augustus, 871–873

SELECTED ESSAYS

Contents

Remarks on Spencer's Definition of Mind as
   Correspondence 893

Brute and Human Intellect 910

The Sentiment of Rationality 950

On Some Omissions of Introspective Psychology 986

Absolutism and Empiricism 1014

The Psychology of Belief 1021

The Knowing of Things Together 1057

Philosophical Conceptions and Practical Results 1077

Human Immortality: Two Supposed Objections to the
   Doctrine 1098

Index 1129

Remarks on Spencer's Definition of Mind as Correspondence

As a rule it may be said that, at a time when readers are so overwhelmed with work as they are at the present day, all purely critical and destructive writing ought to be reprobated. The half-gods generally refuse to go, in spite of the ablest criticism, until the gods actually *have* arrived; but then, too, criticism is hardly needed. But there are cases in which every rule may be broken. "What!" exclaimed Voltaire, when accused of offering no substitute for the Christianity he attacked, *"je vous délivre d'une bête féroce, et vous me demandez par quoi je la remplace!"* Without comparing Mr. Spencer's definition of Mind either to Christianity or to a *"bête féroce,"* it may certainly be said to be very far-reaching in its consequences, and, according to certain standards, noxious; whilst probably a large proportion of those hard-headed readers who subscribe to the *Popular Science Monthly* and *Nature*, and whose sole philosopher Mr. Spencer is, are fascinated by it without being in the least aware what its consequences are.

The defects of the formula are so glaring that I am surprised it should not long ago have been critically overhauled. The reader will readily recollect what it is. In part III of his *Principles of Psychology*, Mr. Spencer, starting from the supposition that the most essential truth concerning mental evolution will be that which allies it to the evolution nearest akin to it, namely, that of Life, finds that the formula *"adjustment of inner to outer relations,"* which was the definition of life, comprehends also "the entire process of mental evolution." In a series of chapters of great apparent thoroughness and minuteness he shows how all the different grades of mental perfection are expressed by the degree of extension of this adjustment, or, as he here calls it, "correspondence," in space, time, speciality, generality, and integration. The polyp's tentacles contract only to immediately present stimuli, and to almost all alike. The mammal will store up food for a day, or even for a season; the bird will start on its migration for a goal hundreds of miles away; the savage will sharpen his arrows to hunt next year's game; while the astronomer will proceed, equipped with all his instruments, to a point thousands of miles distant, there to watch, at a fixed day, hour, and minute, a transit of Venus or an eclipse of the Sun.

The picture drawn is so vast and simple, it includes such a multitude of details in its monotonous frame-work, that it is no wonder that readers of a passive turn of mind are, usually, more impressed by it than by any portion of the book. But on the slightest scrutiny its solidity begins to disappear. In the first place, one asks, what right has one, in a formula embracing professedly the "entire process of mental evolution," to mention only phenomena of cognition, and to omit all sentiments, all æsthetic impulses, all religious emotions and personal affections? The ascertainment of outward fact constitutes only one species of mental activity. The genus contains, in addition to purely cognitive judgments, or judgments of the actual—judgments that things do, as a matter of fact, exist so or so—an immense number of emotional judgments: judgments of the ideal, judgments that things *should* exist thus and not so. How much of our mental life is occupied with this matter of a better or a worse? How much of it involves preferences or repugnances on our part? We cannot laugh at a joke, we cannot go to one theater rather than another, take more trouble for the sake of our own child than our neighbor's; we cannot long for vacation, show our best manners to a foreigner, or pay our pew rent, without involving in the premises of our action some element which has nothing whatever to do with simply cognizing the actual, but which, out of alternative possible actuals, selects one and cognizes that as the ideal. In a word, "Mind," as we actually find it, contains all sorts of laws—those of logic, of fancy, of wit, of taste, decorum, beauty, morals, and so forth, as well as of perception of fact. Common sense estimates mental excellence by a combination of all these standards, and yet how few of them correspond to anything that actually *is*—they are laws of the Ideal, dictated by subjective *interests* pure and simple. Thus the greater part of Mind, quantitatively considered, refuses to have anything to do with Mr. Spencer's definition. It is quite true that these ideal judgments are treated by him with great ingenuity and felicity at the close of his work—

indeed, his treatment of them there seems to me to be its most admirable portion. But they are there handled as separate items having no connection with that extension of the "correspondence" which is maintained elsewhere to be the all-sufficing law of mental growth.

Most readers would dislike to admit without coercion that a law was adequate which obliged them to erase from literature (if by literature were meant anything worthy of the title of "mental product") all works except treatises on natural science, history, and statistics. Let us examine the reason that Mr. Spencer appears to consider coercive.

It is this: That, since every process grows more and more complicated as it develops, more swarmed over by incidental and derivative conditions which disguise and adulterate its original simplicity, the only way to discover its true and essential form is to trace it back to its earliest beginning. There it will appear in its genuine character pure and undefiled. Religious, æsthetic, and ethical judgments, having grown up in the course of evolution, by means that we can very plausibly divine, of course may be stripped off from the main stem of intelligence and leave that undisturbed. With a similar intent Mr. Tylor says: "Whatever throws light on the origin of a conception throws light on its validity." Thus, then, there is no resource but to appeal to the polyp, or whatever shows us the form of evolution just *before* intelligence, and what that, and only what that, contains will be the root and heart of the matter.

But no sooner is the reason for the law thus enunciated than many objections occur to the reader. In the first place, the general principle seems to lead to absurd conclusions. If the embryologic line of appeal can alone teach us the genuine essences of things, if the polyp is to dictate our law of mind to us because he came first, where are we to stop? He must himself be treated in the same way. Back of him lay the not-yet-polyp, and, back of all, the universal mother, fire-mist. To seek there for the reality, of course would reduce all thinking to nonentity, and, although Mr. Spencer would probably not regard this conclusion as a *reductio ad absurdum* of his principle, since it would only be another path to his theory of the Unknowable, less systematic thinkers may hesitate. But, waiving for the moment the question of principle, let us admit that relatively to *our* thought, at any rate, the polyp's thought is pure and undefiled. Does the study of the polyp lead us distinctly to Mr. Spencer's formula of correspondence? To begin with, if that formula be meant to include disinterested scientific curiosity, or "correspondence" in the sense of cognition, with no ulterior selfish end, the polyp gives it no countenance whatever. He is as innocent of scientific as of moral and æsthetic enthusiasm; he is the most narrowly teleological of organisms; reacting, so far as he reacts at all, only for self-preservation.

This leads us to ask what Mr. Spencer exactly means by the word correspondence. Without explanation, the word is wholly indeterminate. Everything corresponds in some way with everything else that co-exists in the same world with it. But, as the formula of correspondence was originally derived from biology, we shall possibly find in our author's treatise on that science an exact definition of what he means by it. On seeking there, we find nowhere a definition, but numbers of synonyms. The inner relations are "adjusted," "conformed," "fitted," "related," to the outer. They must "meet" or "balance" them. There must be "concord" or "harmony" between them. Or, again, the organism must "counteract" the changes in the environment. But these words, too, are wholly indeterminate. The fox is most beautifully "adjusted" to the hounds and huntsmen who pursue him; the limestone "meets" molecule by molecule the acid which corrodes it; the man is exquisitely "conformed" to the *trichina* which invades him, or to the typhus poison which consumes him; and the forests "harmonize" incomparably with the fires that lay them low. Clearly, a further specification is required; and, although Mr. Spencer shrinks strangely from enunciating this specification, he everywhere works his formula so as to imply it in the clearest manner.

Influence on physical well-being or survival is his implied criterion of the rank of mental action. The moth which flies into the candle, instead of away from it, "fails," in Spencer's words (vol. I, p. 409), to "correspond" with its environment; but clearly, in this sense, pure cognitive inference of the existence of heat after a perception of light would not suffice to constitute correspondence; while a moth which, on feeling the light, should merely vaguely fear to approach it, but have no proper image of the heat, would "correspond." So that the Spencerian formula, to mean anything definite at all, must, at least, be re-written as follows: "Right or intelligent mental action consists in the establishment, corresponding to outward relations, of such inward relations and reactions as will favor the survival of the thinker, or, at least, his physical well-being."

Such a definition as this is precise, but at the same time it is frankly teleological. It explicitly postulates a distinction between mental action pure and simple, and *right* mental action; and, furthermore, it proposes, as criteria of this latter, certain ideal ends—those of physical prosperity or survival, which are pure *subjective interests* on the animal's part, brought with it upon the scene and corresponding to no relation already there.[1] No mental action is right or intelligent which fails to fit this standard. No correspondence can pass muster till it shows its subservience to these ends. Corresponding itself to no actual outward thing; referring merely to a future which *may* be, but which these interests now say *shall* be; purely ideal, in a word, they judge, dominate, determine all correspondences between the inner and the outer. Which is as much as to say that *mere* correspondence with the outer world is a notion on which it is wholly impossible to base a defini-

[1] These interests are the real *a priori* element in cognition. By saying that their pleasures and pains have nothing to do with correspondence, I mean simply this: To a large number of terms in the environment there may be inward correlatives of a neutral sort as regards feeling. The "correspondence" is already there. But, now, suppose some to be accented with pleasure, others with pain; that is a fact additional to the correspondence, a fact with no outward correlative. But it immediately orders the correspondences in this way: that the pleasant or interesting items are singled out, dwelt upon, developed into their farther connections, whilst the unpleasant or insipid ones are ignored or suppressed. The future of the Mind's development is thus mapped out in advance by the way in which the lines of pleasure and pain run. The interests precede the outer relations noticed. Take the utter absence of response of a dog or a savage to the greater mass of environing relations. How can you alter it unless you previously *awaken an interest*—*i.e.*, produce a susceptibility to intellectual pleasure in certain modes of cognitive exercise? Interests, then, are an all-essential factor which no writer pretending to give an account of mental evolution has a right to neglect.

tion of mental action. Mr. Spencer's occult reason for leaving unexpressed the most important part of the definition he works with probably lies in its apparent implication of subjective spontaneity. The mind, according to his philosophy, should be pure product, absolute derivative from the nonmental. To make it dictate conditions, bring independent interests into the game which may determine what we shall call correspondence, and what not, might, at first sight, appear contrary to the notion of evolution which forbids the introduction at any point of an absolutely new factor. In what sense the existence of survival interest does postulate such a factor we shall hereafter see. I think myself that it is possible to express all its outward results in non-mental terms. But the unedifying look of the thing, its simulation of an independent mental teleology, seems to have frightened Mr. Spencer here, as elsewhere, away from a serious scrutiny of the facts. But let us be indulgent to his timidity, and assume that survival was all the while a "mental reservation" with him, only excluded from his formula by reason of the comforting sound it might have to Philistine ears.

We should then have, as the embodiment of the highest ideal perfection of mental development, a creature of superb cognitive endowments, from whose piercing perceptions no fact was too minute or too remote to escape; whose all-embracing foresight no contingency could find unprepared; whose invincible flexibility of resource no array of outward onslaught could overpower; but in whom all these gifts were swayed by the single passion of love of life, of survival at any price. This determination filling his whole energetic being, consciously realized, intensified by meditation, becomes a fixed idea, would use all the other faculties as its means, and, if they ever flagged, would by its imperious intensity spur them and hound them on to ever fresh exertions and achievements. There can be no doubt that, if such an incarnation of earthly prudence existed, a race of beings in whom this monotonously narrow passion for tribal self-preservation were aided by every cognitive gift, they would soon be kings of all the earth. All known human races would wither before their breath, and be as dust beneath their conquering feet.

But whether any Spencerian would hail with hearty joy

their advent is another matter. Certainly Mr. Spencer would not; while the common sense of mankind would stand aghast at the thought of them. Why does common opinion abhor such a being? Why does it crave greater "richness" of nature in its mental ideal? Simply because, to common sense, survival is only one out of many interests—*primus inter pares*, perhaps, but still in the midst of peers. What are these interests? Most men would reply that they are all that makes survival worth securing. The social affections, all the various forms of play, the thrilling intimations of art, the delights of philosophic contemplation, the rest of religious emotion, the joy of moral self-approbation, the charm of fancy and of wit—some or all of these are absolutely required to make the notion of mere existence tolerable; and individuals who, by their special powers, satisfy these desires are protected by their fellows and enabled to survive, though their mental constitution should in other respects be lamentably ill-"adjusted" to the outward world. The story-teller, the musician, the theologian, the actor, or even the mere charming fellow, have never lacked means of support, however helpless they might individually have been to conform with those outward relations which we know as the powers of nature. The reason is very plain. To the individual man, as a social being, the interests of his fellow are a part of his environment. If his powers correspond to the wants of this social environment, he may survive, even though he be ill-adapted to the natural or "outer" environment. But these wants are pure subjective ideals, with nothing outward to correspond to them. So that, as far as the individual is concerned, it becomes necessary to modify Spencer's survival formula still further, by introducing into the term environment a reference, not only to existent things, but also to ideal wants. It would have to run in some such way as this: "Excellence of the individual mind consists in the establishment of inner relations more and more extensively conformed to the outward facts of nature, and to the ideal wants of the individual's fellows, but all of such a character as will promote survival or physical prosperity."

But here, again, common sense will meet us with an objection. Mankind desiderate certain qualities in the individual which are incompatible with his chance of survival being a maximum. Why do we all so eulogize and love the heroic, recklessly generous, and disinterested type of character? These qualities certainly imperil the survival of their possessor. The reason is very plain. Even if headlong courage, pride, and martyr-spirit do ruin the individual, they benefit the community as a whole whenever they are displayed by one of its members against a competing tribe. "It is death to you, but fun for us." Our interest in having the hero as he is, plays indirectly into the hands of our survival, though not of his.

This explicit acknowledgment of the survival interests of the tribe, as accounting for many interests in the individual which seem at first sight either unrelated to survival or at war with it, seems, after all, to bring back unity and simplicity into the Spencerian formula. Why, the Spencerian may ask, may not all the luxuriant foliage of ideal interests—æsthetic, philosophic, theologic, and the rest—which co-exist along with that of survival, be present in the tribe and so form part of the individual's environment, merely by virtue of the fact that they minister in an indirect way to the survival of the tribe as a whole? The disinterested scientific appetite of cognition, the sacred philosophic love of consistency, the craving for luxury and beauty, the passion for amusement, may all find their proper significance as processes of mind, strictly so-called, in the incidental utilitarian discoveries which flow from the energy they set in motion. Conscience, thoroughness, purity, love of truth, susceptibility to discipline, eager delight in fresh impressions, although none of them are traits of Intelligence *in se*, may thus be marks of a general mental energy, without which victory over nature and over other human competitors would be impossible. And, as victory means survival, and survival is the criterion of Intelligent "Correspondence," these qualities, though not expressed in the fundamental law of mind, may yet have been all the while understood by Mr. Spencer to form so many secondary consequences and corollaries of that law.

But here it is decidedly time to take our stand and refuse our aid in propping up Mr. Spencer's definition by any further good-natured translations and supplementary contributions of our own. It is palpable at a glance that a mind whose survival interest could only be adequately secured by such a wasteful array of energy squandered on side issues would be immeasurably inferior to one like that which we supposed a few pages back, in which the monomania of tribal preservation should be the one all-devouring passion.

Surely there is nothing in the essence of intelligence which should oblige it forever to delude itself as to its own ends, and to strive towards a goal successfully only at the cost of consciously appearing to have far other aspirations in view.

A furnace which should produce along with its metal fifty different varieties of ash and slag, a planing-mill whose daily yield in shavings far exceeded that in boards, would rightly be pronounced inferior to one of the usual sort, even though more energy should be displayed in its working, and at moments some of that energy be directly effective. If ministry to survival be the sole criterion of mental excellence, then luxury and amusement, Shakespeare, Beethoven, Plato, and Marcus Aurelius, stellar spectroscopy, diatom markings, and nebular hypotheses are by-products on too wasteful a scale. The slag-heap is too big—it abstracts more energy than it contributes to the ends of the machine; and every serious evolutionist ought resolutely to bend his attention henceforward to the reduction in number and amount of these outlying interests, and the diversion of the energy they absorb into purely prudential channels.

Here, then, is our dilemma: One man may say that the law of mental development is dominated solely by the principle of conservation; another, that richness is the criterion of mental evolution; a third, that pure cognition of the actual is the essence of worthy thinking—but who shall pretend to decide which is right? The umpire would have to bring a standard of his own upon the scene, which would be just as subjective and personal as the standards used by the contestants. And yet some standard there must be, if we are to attempt to define in any way the worth of different mental manifestations.

Is it not already clear to the reader's mind that the whole difficulty in making Mr. Spencer's law work lies in the fact that it is not really a constitutive, but a regulative, law of thought which he is erecting, and that he does not frankly say so? Every law of Mind must be either a law of the *cogitatum* or a law of the *cogitandum*. If it be a law in the sense of an analysis of what we *do* think, then it will include error, non-sense, the worthless as well as the worthy, metaphysics, and mythologies as well as scientific truths which mirror the actual environment. But such a law of the *cogitatum* is already well known. It is no other than the association of ideas according to their several modes; or, rather, it is this association defini-tively perfected by the inclusion of the teleological factor of interest by Mr. Hodgson in the fifth chapter of his masterly *Time and Space*.

That Mr. Spencer, in the part of his work which we are considering, has no such law as this in view is evident from the fact that he has striven to give an original formulation to such a law in another part of his book, in that chapter, namely, on the associability of relations, in the first volume, where the apperception of times and places, and the suppres-sion of association by similarity, are made to explain the facts in a way whose artificiality has puzzled many a simple reader.

Now, every living man would instantly define right think-ing as thinking in correspondence with reality. But Spencer, in saying that right thought is that which conforms to exis-tent outward relations, and this exclusively, undertakes to de-cide what the reality *is*. In other words, under cover of an apparently formal definition he really smuggles in a material definition of the most far-reaching import. For the Stoic, to whom *vivere convenienter naturæ* was also the law of mind, the reality was an archetypal Nature; for the Christian, whose mental law is to discover the will of God, and make one's actions correspond thereto, *that* is the reality. In fact, the philosophic problem which all the ages have been trying to solve in order to make thought in some way correspond with it, and which disbelievers in philosophy call insoluble, is just that: What is the reality? All the thinking, all the conflict of ideals, going on in the world at the present moment is in some way tributary to this quest. To attempt, therefore, with Mr. Spencer, to decide the matter merely incidentally, to fore-stall discussion by a definition—to carry the position by sur-prise, in a word—is a proceeding savoring more of piracy than philosophy. No, Spencer's definition of what we ought to think cannot be suffered to lurk in ambush; it must stand out explicitly with the rest, and expect to be challenged and give an account of itself like any other ideal norm of thought.

We have seen how he seems to vacillate in his determination of it. At one time, "scientific" thought, mere passive mirroring of outward nature, purely registrative cognition; at another time, thought in the exclusive service of survival, would seem to be his ideal. Let us consider the latter ideal first, since it has the polyp's authority in its favor: "We must survive—that end must regulate all our thought." The poor man who said to Talleyrand, *"Il faut bien que je vive!"* expressed it very well. But criticise this ideal, or transcend it as Talleyrand did by his cool reply, *"Je n'en vois pas la necessité,"* and it can say nothing more for itself. *A priori* it is a mere brute teleological affirmation on a par with all others. Vainly you should hope to prove it to a person bent on suicide, who has but the one longing—to escape, to cease. Vainly you would argue with a Buddhist or a German pessimist, for they feel the full imperious strength of the desire, but have an equally profound persuasion of its essential wrongness and mendacity. Vainly, too, would you talk to a Christian, or even to any believer in the simple creed that the deepest meaning of the world is moral. For they hold that mere conformity with the outward—worldly success and survival—is not the absolute and exclusive end. In the *failures* to "adjust"—in the rubbish-heap, according to Spencer—lies, for them, the real key to the truth—the sole mission of life being to teach that the outward actual is not the whole of being.

And, now—if, falling back on the scientific ideal, you say that to *know* is the one τέλος of intelligence—not only will the inimitable Turkish cadi in Layard's Nineveh praise God in your face that he seeks not that which he requires not, and ask, "Will much knowledge create thee a double belly?"—not only may I, if it please me, legitimately refuse to stir from my fool's paradise of theosophy and mysticism, in spite of all your calling (since, after all, your true knowledge and my pious feeling have alike nothing to back them save their seeming good to our respective personalities)—not only this, but to the average sense of mankind, whose ideal of mental nature is best expressed by the word "richness," your statistical and cognitive intelligence will seem insufferably narrow, dry, tedious, and unacceptable.

The truth appears to be that every individual man may, if it please him, set up his private categorical imperative of what rightness or excellence in thought shall consist in, and these different ideals, instead of entering upon the scene armed with a warrant—whether derived from the polyp or from a transcendental source—appear only as so many brute affirmations left to fight it out upon the chess-board among themselves. They are, at best, postulates, each of which must depend on the general consensus of experience as a whole to bear out its validity. The formula which proves to have the most massive destiny will be the true one. But this is a point which can only be solved *ambulando*, and not by any *a priori* definition. The attempt to forestall the decision is free to all to make, but all make it at their risk. Our respective hypotheses and postulates help to shape the course of thought, but the only thing which we all agree in assuming is, that thought will be coerced away from them if they are wrong. If Spencer to-day says, "Bow to the actual," whilst Swinburne spurns "compromise with the nature of things," I exclaim, *"Fiat justitia, pereat mundus,"* and Mill says, "To hell I will go, rather than 'adjust' myself to an evil God," what umpire can there be between us but the future? The idealists and the empiricists confront each other like Guelphs and Ghibellines, but each alike waits for adoption, as it were, by the course of events.

In other words, we are all fated to be, *a priori*, teleologists whether we will or no. Interests which we bring with us, and simply posit or take our stand upon, are the very flour out of which our mental dough is kneaded. The organism of thought, from the vague dawn of discomfort or ease in the polyp to the intellectual joy of Laplace among his formulas, is teleological through and through. Not a cognition occurs but feeling is there to comment on it, to stamp it as of greater or less worth. Spencer and Plato are *ejusdem farinæ*. To attempt to hoodwink teleology out of sight by saying nothing about it, is the vainest of procedures. Spencer merely takes sides with the τέλος he happens to prefer, whether it be that of physical well-being or that of cognitive registration. He represents a particular teleology. Well might teleology (had she a voice) exclaim with Emerson's Brahma:

> "If the red slayer think he slays,
>   Or if the slain think he is slain,
> They know not well the subtle ways
>   I keep, and pass, and turn again.
>
> *   *   *   *   *   *   *   *   *   *
>
> "They reckon ill who leave me out;
>   When me they fly, I am the wings;
> I am the doubter and the doubt," etc.

But now a scientific man, feeling something uncanny in this omnipresence of a teleological factor dictating *how* the mind shall correspond—an interest seemingly tributary to nothing non-mental—may ask us what we meant by saying sometime back that in one sense it is perfectly possible to express the existence of interests in non-mental terms. We meant simply this: That the reactions or outward consequences of the interests could be so expressed. The interest of survival which has hitherto been treated as an ideal *should-be*, presiding from the start and marking out the way in which an animal must react, is, from an outward and physical point of view, nothing more than an objective future implication of the reaction (if it occurs) as an actual fact. If the animal's brain acts fortuitously in the right way, he survives. His young do the same. The reference to survival in noway preceded or conditioned the intelligent act; but the fact of survival was merely bound up with it as an incidental consequence, and may, therefore, be called accidental, rather than instrumental, to the production of intelligence. It is the same with all other interests. They are pleasures and pains incidentally implied in the workings of the nervous mechanism, and, therefore, in their ultimate origin, non-mental; for the idiosyncrasies of our nervous centers are mere "spontaneous variations," like any of those which form the ultimate *data* for Darwin's theory. A brain which functions so as to insure survival may, therefore, be called intelligent in no other sense than a tooth, a limb, or a stomach, which should serve the same end—the sense, namely, of appropriate; as when we say "that is an intelligent device,"

meaning a device fitted to secure a certain end which we assume. If *nirvana* were the end, instead of survival, then it is
true the means would be different, but in both cases alike the
end would not precede the means, or even be coeval with
them, but depend utterly upon them, and follow them in
point of time. The fox's cunning and the hare's speed are thus
alike creations of the non-mental. The τέλος they entail is no
more an agent in one case than another, since in both alike it
is a resultant. Spencer, then, seems justified in not admitting
it to appear as an irreducible ultimate factor of Mind, any
more than of Body.

This position is perfectly unassailable so long as one describes the phenomena in this manner from without. The
τέλος in that case can only be hypothetically, not impera-
tively, stated: *if* such and such be the end, then such brain
functions are the most intelligent, just as such and such diges-
tive functions are the most appropriate. But such and such
cannot be declared *as* the end, except by the commenting mind of an outside spectator. The organs themselves, in
their working at any instant, cannot but be supposed indifferent as to what product they are destined fatally to bring
forth, cannot be imagined whilst fatally producing one result
to have at the same time a notion of a different result which
should be their truer end, but which they are unable to
secure.

Nothing can more strikingly show, it seems to me, the essential difference between the point of view of consciousness
and that of outward existence. We can describe the latter only
in teleological terms, hypothetically, or else by the addition of
a supposed contemplating mind which measures what it sees
going on by its private teleological standard, and judges it
intelligent. But consciousness itself is not merely intelligent in
this sense. It is *intelligent intelligence*. It seems both to supply
the means and the standard by which they are measured. It
not only *serves* a final purpose, but *brings* a final purpose—
posits, declares it. This purpose is not a mere hypothesis—"*if*
survival is to occur, then brain must so perform," etc.—but
an imperative decree: "Survival *shall* occur, and, therefore,
brain *must* so perform!" It seems hopelessly impossible to formulate anything of this sort in non-mental terms, and this is

why I must still contend that the phenomena of subjective "interest," as soon as the animal consciously realizes the latter, appears upon the scene as an absolutely new factor, which we can only suppose to be latent thitherto in the physical environment by crediting the physical atoms, etc., each with a consciousness of its own, approving or condemning its motions.

This, then, must be our conclusion: That no law of the *cogitandum*, no norm-ative receipt for excellence in thinking, can be authoritatively promulgated. The only formal canon that we can apply to mind which is unassailable is the barren truism that it must think rightly. We can express this in terms of correspondence by saying that thought must correspond with truth; but whether that truth be actual or ideal is left undecided.

We have seen that the invocation of the polyp to decide for us that it is actual (apart from the fact that he does not decide in that way) is based on a principle which refutes itself if consistently carried out. Spencer's formula has crumbled into utter worthlessness in our hands, and we have nothing to replace it by except our several individual hypotheses, convictions, and beliefs. Far from being vouched for by the past, these are verified only by the future. They are all of them, in some sense, laws of the ideal. They have to keep house together, and the weakest goes to the wall. The survivors constitute the right way of thinking. While the issue is still undecided, we can only call them our prepossessions. But, decided or not, "go in" we each must for one set of interests or another. The question for each of us in the battle of life is, "Can we *come out* with it?" Some of these interests admit to-day of little dispute. Survival, physical well-being, and undistorted cognition of what is, will hold their ground. But it is truly strange to see writers like Messrs. Huxley and Clifford, who show themselves able to call most things in question, unable, when it comes to the interest of cognition, to touch it with their solvent doubt. They assume some mysterious imperative laid upon the mind, declaring that the infinite ascertainment of facts is its supreme duty, which he who evades is a blasphemer and child of shame. And yet these authors can hardly have failed to reflect, at some moment or other, that the disinterested love of information, and still more the love of consistency in thought (that true scientific *œstrus*), and the ideal fealty to Truth (with a capital T), are all so many particular forms of æsthetic interest, late in their evolution, arising in conjunction with a vast number of similar æsthetic interests, and bearing with them no *a priori* mark of being worthier than these. If we may doubt one, we may doubt all. How shall I say that knowing fact with Messrs. Huxley and Clifford is a better use to put my mind to than feeling good with Messrs. Moody and Sankey, unless by slowly and painfully finding out that in the long run it works best?

I, for my part, cannot escape the consideration, forced upon me at every turn, that the knower is not simply a mirror floating with no foot-hold anywhere, and passively reflecting an order that he comes upon and finds simply existing. The knower is an actor, and co-efficient of the truth on one side, whilst on the other he registers the truth which he helps to create. Mental interests, hypotheses, postulates, so far as they are bases for human action—action which to a great extent transforms the world—help to *make* the truth which they declare. In other words, there belongs to mind, from its birth upward, a spontaneity, a vote. It is in the game, and not a mere looker-on; and its judgments of the *should-be*, its ideals, cannot be peeled off from the body of the *cogitandum* as if they were excrescences, or meant, at most, survival. We know so little about the ultimate nature of things, or of ourselves, that it would be sheer folly dogmatically to say that an ideal rational order may not be real. The only objective criterion of reality is coerciveness, in the long run, over thought. Objective facts, Spencer's outward relations, are real only because they coerce sensation. Any interest which should be coercive on the same massive scale would be *eodem jure* real. By its very essence, the reality of a thought is proportionate to the way it grasps us. Its intensity, its seriousness—its interest, in a word—taking these qualities, not at any given instant, but as shown by the total upshot of experience. If judgments of the *should-be* are fated to grasp us in this way, they are what "correspond." The ancients placed the conception of Fate at the bottom of things—deeper than the gods themselves. "The fate of thought," utterly barren and indeterminate as such a formula is, is the only unimpeachable regulative Law of Mind.

Brute and Human Intellect

EVERYONE who has owned a dog must, over and over again, have felt a strange sense of wonder that the animal, being as intelligent as he is, should not be vastly more so. His conditions would be easier to understand if he were either more universally stupid or more generally rational. The quickness with which he learns the signs which indicate that his master is going out, such as putting off slippers and putting on overcoat, seems incompatible with his utter inability to learn that dropping more coal into the grate will make a hotter fire. Accordingly, quite apart from theological and metaphysical prejudice, it is not surprising that men's opinions regarding the mental state of brutes should have oscillated between the two extremes of claiming for them, on the one hand, reasoning powers in no essential respect other than those of man, and, on the other, of denying to them all properly intellectual attributes whatever, and calling their powers of appropriate action the result of "instinct," or, still worse, of mere blind mechanism. Most of us adopt a medium course, and feel as if our domestic pets had real, though peculiarly limited, intellectual powers, and at various times attempts have been made to define exactly what this limitation consists in. It has been said that they were like men dreaming; that they could not form abstract ideas; that they had no proper self-consciousness; that they were incapable of apprehending the notion of a sign as such; that they were incapable of language; and that these incapacities, severally or all together, were sufficient to explain the observed differences. All these statements are, no doubt, true in the main. Everyone in fact feels them to be true when he goes into the midst of his quadrupedal relatives, and yet these formulas hardly clear up the matters much, for they themselves express results, rather than elementary factors in the case. *Why* does not a dog frame abstract ideas? *Why* does he not reflect on his self, or *ego*? And the rest. If we could find the elementary point of divergence in his mental constitution which leads to all these peculiar shortcomings, we should be much better off.

Now, it seems to the writer that to a certain extent we can reduce all the above differences, and others too, to one simpler difference; and, although this last is itself by no means ultimate, still, to have ascertained it will be a real progress as far as it goes, and may put us, moreover, on the track of further definite inquiries. A new question distinctly formulated is always a philosophic gain.

To make clear if possible what this common root is which makes our dog's thoughts seem so different from our own is the object of the present essay. If it dwells chiefly on his thoughts, and little on his passions, emotions, and so forth, it is for obvious reasons: first, the lack of space; and, second, the relative plainness of the latter phenomena. But, to find what difference there is between brute thinking and human thinking, we must begin by forming a clear idea of what human thinking is.

To say that all human thinking is essentially of two kinds — reasoning on the one hand, and narrative, descriptive, contemplative thinking on the other — is to say only what every reader's experience will corroborate. If, further, it be asked what the latter kind of thinking is, everyone will reply that in the main it consists of a procession through the mind of groups of images of concrete things, persons, places, and events, together with the feelings which they awaken, and in an order which, if our attention is guided by some dominant interest, such as recollecting an actual set of facts, or inventing a coherent story, is in the main derived from our actual experience of the order of things in the real outward world. If, on the contrary, there be no presiding interest, but our thoughts merely bud one out of the other according to the caprice of our revery, there may occur very abrupt transitions between one set of images and the next, so that we may juxtapose thoughts whose *things* were never juxtaposed since the world stood. In the case where there is a presiding interest the link by which one thought is made to succeed another is in the main that known to psychologists by the name of "association by contiguity." We are apt to go over the circumstances as they happened or were likely to happen. The thought of a last summer's sunset will call up the vessel's deck from which I saw it, the companions of my voyage, and the arrival into port.

In revery, on the other hand, "association by similarity" is more prominent. A sunset may lead me to think of the letters of the Greek alphabet, and I may at first be quite unable to give the steps by which so incongruous a consequence was suggested to me. When ascertained, however, I may see that I was reminded in succession of the recent attempts to explain nearly all mythology by solar myths, of Hercules' history as such a myth, of Hector's funeral pyre, of Homer, and whether he could write, and then of the Greek alphabet.

Where contiguity predominates we have a dry, prosaic, literal sort of mind; and, on the contrary, where similarity has free play, we are apt to call the person fanciful, poetic, or witty. But both cases agree, the reader will notice, in this: that the thinker passes along from one concrete whole of representation to another. His thought is always of matters taken in their entirety. Having been thinking of one, he finds later that he is thinking of another, to which, as it were, he has been naturally lifted along, he hardly knows how. If an abstract quality figures for a moment in the procession, it arrests the attention but for a moment, and fades into something else; and it is never very abstract. Thus, in thinking of the sun-myths, I may have a gleam of admiration at the *gracefulness* of the primitive human mind, or a moment of disgust at the *narrowness* of modern interpreters. But, in the main, I think less of qualities than of whole things, real or possible, just as I may experience them.

Having mentioned the two kinds of association, let us now pause for a moment before proceeding further, and form a somewhat more distinct notion of the way in which they differ from each other. The law of association by contiguity has been thus stated: "Actions, Sensations, and States of Feeling, occurring together, or in close succession, tend to grow together, or cohere, in such a way that when any of them is afterwards presented to the mind, the others are apt to be brought up in idea."[1]

The same writer has expressed the law of Similarity as follows: "Present Actions, Sensations, Thoughts, or Emotions tend to revive their LIKE among previously occurring

[1]Alexander Bain's *Mental and Moral Science*, London, 1868, p. 85.

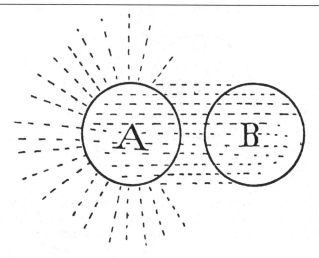

F𝐈𝐆. 𝐈.

states."[2] Let us make schematic diagrams of these two modes of association. Since all logical processes are to-day hypothetically explained as brain processes, by translating ideas into cells and their connections into fibers, the same figures will do for an imaginary representation of what goes on in the brain—each circle being supposed to represent a group of cells united by fibers, whilst the dotted lines are fibers alone.

Fig. 1 represents association by contiguity; all the elements of the whole A are operative together, and call up all the elements of B together, B having been previously experienced in company with A. In Fig. 2, on the contrary, where association by similarity is represented, most of the elements of A are inactive. The single element, *m*, breaks out from its concert with them—a concert which would naturally have resulted in their combining in the only *united* action possible to them, viz., the arousal of B—and calls up a whole with which *it* alone has contiguous associations, the whole Z. But, now, does not a mere glance at the figure show us that A and Z are

[2]*Ibid.*, p. 127.

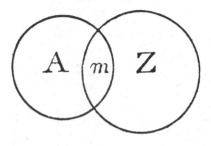

Fig. 2.

called similar only because they are in part identical? identical in the character *m*, which vibrates throughout both? This *m*, it is true, may be larger or smaller; but, whichever it is, it cannot, as it exists in Z, fitly be said to be associated with itself as it exists in A. On the contrary, it is one and the same *m* in both. Association properly so called obtains between the residual ingredients of A and Z respectively. Each set of these is associated with the common *m*, and, moreover, associated with it by contiguity pure and simple. All association, therefore, is at bottom association by contiguity—that alone binds two ideas together. What in ordinary parlance is called contiguous association is only the particular case of it in which all the items of a cluster of ideas operate *together* to call up another cluster with which in its totality they were each and all once experienced. What we call "similarity" is only the other special case, in which a *part* of a cluster acts, as we say, on its own hook, and revives another cluster with whose totality *it* alone has been experienced. The two clusters cohere together by respectively cohering by their *residual* characters with *it*. But this cohesion is contiguous. The *m*—the character by which the clusters are identical in the fullest sense of the term—is the common heart of both, and indirectly keeps them together by its contiguity with their several other parts. Contiguity is, then, the only operative bond of association. Identity is no association at all. What is called similarity is a resultant, compounded of both identity and contiguity.

Having thus parenthetically defined our notions of association, let us pass on to reasoned thinking. Wherein does it differ from the contemplative—or, as we may now call it, empirical—thinking, which we have alone considered hitherto? Reason may be, and often is, defined in two ways: Either as the power to understand things by their causes, or as the power, if the notion of an end is given, to find the means of attaining it. That is, reason has a theoretic and a practical sphere. But in their essence the two spheres are one; they involve the same form of process, which is simply that of finding an intermediate representation, m, which will, in a peculiarly evident manner, link together two *data*, A and Z. In the theoretic sphere m is the "reason" for "inferring" Z; in the sphere of action it is the "means" (or the instrument) for "attaining" Z. The immensely superior utility of reasoned to merely habitual thinking lies in this: that by reason we may infer or attain Z, even though Z and A may never have been conjoined in our actual experience. In empirical thinking this would be impossible. To get at Z at all in empirical thought we must already have passed, in some concrete case, from A to it. If in the theoretic sphere that has happened, then when A next recurs it will suggest Z—pass us on to it by a law which we blindly obey, we know not why. Whilst, if the previous experience was in the realm of practice, the notion of the end, Z, coinciding with our actual circumstances, A, will together resuscitate a representation of the manner, x, in which we formerly passed from one to the other.

In reasoned thought, on the other hand, no previous experience is needed of the concrete case we have to deal with. We pass over the bridge, m, whose relations to the terms A and Z we may never have been aware of before. What is m? It is always a partial character (or a combination of such, with their suggestions) embedded in the totality of one or both of our items of thought, which we dissect out and fix our attention upon. Particular cases of reasoning vary enormously in complication. Thus, in theoretic reasoning, Z may from the first be an abstract attribute, and then, probably, the extraction of the partial characters will be performed solely upon A. Vermilion is heavy, for example. Why? Because it contains mercury, and that is heavy. Sometimes, again, A and Z are both concretes, and m unites them by our noticing that it is a common, identical, partial character in both. Thus I may per-

ceive five francs to be equal to four shillings as soon as, in the
mass of different suggestions of each, I discern the common
character of being equal to a dollar. Equivalence to a dollar is
the *m* here, as mercury was in the previous case. Or, I may be
in an inclosure, over the north wall of which someone is calling to me; but I may see no way of getting to him till I
observe that in the south wall there is a passage to the street,
and that the street will lead me to my friend. Here the *m* is
double; first, the inclosure yields the character of a southern
exit to the street, and the street, among its other included
characters, contains that of leading to the spot I wish to
reach.

The accompanying diagrams will symbolize the process in
these simple cases. In Fig. 3 the mercury, or the dollar value,
involved as an ingredient in A calls up the Z, with which it is
equally congruent, and binds it and the A together. In Fig. 4

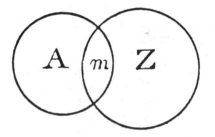

FIG. 3.

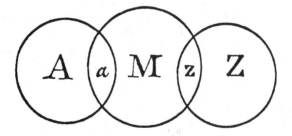

FIG. 4.

the southern exit, a, is part of the larger whole, M, the street, one of whose other parts is z, which is also congruent with Z, the place of my friend.[3]

The most complicated cases may be symbolized by a mere extension of the last diagram, such as Fig. 5 shows us.

Here the reason or process for passing from A to Z consists of a long series of links, each of which is constructed in the same fashion. A partial character, a, embedded in A, will red-integrate (that is, recall) its associates, and among them b, which in like manner recalls c, and so forth until Z is reached. Or the analysis of Z into z, which calls up y, and so on, may be simultaneously begun. In that case the two ends of the chain advancing towards each other will meet somewhere in the middle, m being a term resulting from both analyses—consequently identical in each. The result is, of course, the same. The whole chain of steps may in a large way be called the "reason," M, why A and B are related to each other as they are; or any partial number of them taken together may become the "means" by which we reach Z from A, if the junction of these terms be a practical problem.

The large bracket, uniting directly A to Z, symbolizes their junction when we know it merely empirically, as when we simply learn that alkalies will cure some cases of dyspepsia, or oxalic acid remove ink-spots. The small brackets represent that in almost every case in which the partial characters, a and b, b and c, and so on, suggest each other, it is equally by virtue of an empirical connection of the same sort that they do so. Even when they form two features of the same phe-

---

[3]The reader will, of course, observe the difference between these and the ordinary syllogism diagrams of logical treatises. Fig. 3, for example, if taken to symbolize a syllogism, would yield no valid conclusion. The syllogisms of logical treatises differ, however, from the living acts of reasoning, which I am here describing, by this very point: that they are ideally perfect, while our concrete acts of reasoning are almost always liable to error, and to the partic-ular form of error which Fig. 3 makes manifest. Only *so far as we are right* in identifying in our thought the total A and the total Z, with their ingredient, m, and in ignoring the outlying portions of the circles, can we reason from one to the other. If either identification be inapt, we have made a blunder. And it is just in this that the difficulty of going right lies. *Which* part of a phenomenon—*which m*—shall we consider its essence in any given case? What concept shall subsume it?

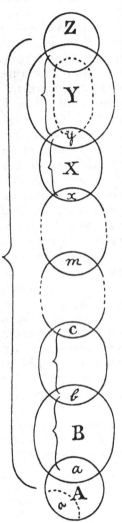

FIG. 5.

nomenon, we are seldom able to say *why* they do so. For instance, we may go on to learn that sodic carbonate calls forth in a dog's stomach a flow of gastric juice, on the one hand, and that some cases of human dyspepsia, on the other hand, seem due to a defect of this flow. Z here, the cured dyspepsia, involves the flow, as a partial character contained in its phenomenal totality. A, the alkaline application, contains it in like manner. It is a character identically in A and Z. But why it exists in A—why soda involves among its innumerable properties that of making gastric juice flow—no one can yet say. It is empirically known, and that is all. Just so if we take the cured dyspepsia. It involves among its other attributes the notion of the food being dissolved. This solution, Z, redintegrates the total notion of a normal digestion, Y, which, among its other partial characters, contains that of an abundance of gastric juice, *y*. Why *y*, in the phenomenon Y, should produce Z, we cannot rationally state; or, at least, we can make but a single approximation to a rational statement. Pepsin and acid will dissolve meat, and gastric juice contains both these ingredients. The smaller dotted circle may be taken to represent this additional reason—which, however, itself is merely a new empirical statement. Such empirical laws as these are called "proximate" reasons. The terms which are coupled in them might, for aught we can understand to the contrary, have been coupled in other ways. But in some rare cases we can carry our dissection of characters so far that we find a link or more in the chain formed of a couple of characters whose disjunction we cannot even conceive. Such a couple as this is an axiom, or "ultimate" reason for the phenomenal *data* it binds together. The nature of such ultimate reasons has long been a bone of contention among philosophers. The *a priori* school has asserted that the two characters thus evidently joined—*e.g.*, the characters of straightness and shortness in a line—are at bottom but two aspects of the same character, a primordial synthesis; whilst the empiricists have contended that they are distinct in essence, and that their bond owes its illusory appearance of necessity and evidence merely to the familiarity which great generality has produced in our minds. Into this quarrel we, of course, cannot enter. The *a priorists* would have to modify our diagram, in case the bond c—x were such an axiom, by making these two segments coalesce into one, as at *m*. These two letters would then merely represent the two manners in which the fundamental fact, *m*, looks towards the terms of the main proposition. Action and reaction, having a sensation and knowing it (J. Mill), swiftness and mechanical effectiveness, would be examples of terms united in this way.

This will no doubt have been found by the reader a pretty dry description. We may sum it up by a simple definition: Reasoning is the substitution of parts and their couplings for wholes and their couplings. The utility of the process lies wholly in the fact, that when we have got the parts clearly in our minds, *their* couplings become more obvious, more evident, than were the couplings of the wholes. Later we shall ask why the parts are more obviously connected than the wholes; but here the reader must pause to notice one fact, and that is the absolute necessity that the partial character taken as a reason should be the right one. If in the total called sodic carbonate we do not light upon the ingredient "makes gastric juice flow," but on some other ingredient, such as "effervesces with acids," it will be worse than useless to lead us to the anti-dyspeptic conclusion. In Fig. 5, *a* is the only partial character of A which leads to Z, and *n*, for example, has no connection with it. But if it were required to find the reason for another Z—for instance, why a man who has just taken a spoonful of the carbonate for "acidity" should feel a pressure at the epigastrum—a (if it stood for the effervescence) would be the right character to choose. In a word, we may say that the particular part which may be substituted for the whole, and considered its equivalent in an act of reasoning, wholly depends on our purpose, interest, or point of view at the time. No rules can be given for choosing it except that it *must lead to the result*, and to follow this rule is an affair of *genius*. This, which is a matter of the deepest philosophic importance, must merely be noticed here in passing, and not further discussed.

Before leaving the diagrams it may be well again parenthetically to call attention to their resemblance to the diagram by which association by similarity was represented (Fig. 2). There, also, partial characters redintegrated their circumstances, and so passed us on to ideas of new wholes. But there, as a rule, we were not aware of the partial characters *in se*. They operated without separately attracting our notice. In reasoning proper they only operate by attracting our attention; but it is obvious that a man starting from the fact A might evolve the truth Z in either way, by consciously using the right successively embedded characters to deduce Z, or, on the other hand, by merely obeying their influence and at last finding Z suggested to him, he knows not how. Later on we shall see how similar association and reasoning do often coincide in this way in their results.

Let us now, by a few concrete examples, clear up whatever obscurity our abstract account may have left upon the reader's mind. We have to illustrate two points: first, that in every reasoning an extracted character is taken as equivalent to the entire *datum* from which it comes; and, second, that the couplings of the characters thus taken have an extreme degree of evidence. Take the first point first.

Suppose I say, when offered a piece of cloth, "I won't buy that; it looks as if it would fade," meaning merely that something about it suggests the idea of fading to my mind, my judgment, though possibly quite correct, is purely empirical; but, if I can say that into the color enters a certain dye which I know to be chemically unstable, and that *therefore* the color will not last, my judgment is reasoned. The notion of the dye which is one of the ingredients of the cloth is the connecting link between the latter and the notion of fading. So, again, an uneducated man will expect from past experience to see a piece of ice melt if placed near the fire, and the tip of his finger look coarse if he views it through a convex glass. A child may open a refractory door by lifting it bodily on its hinges; or he may know enough to tip sideways a stopped mantel-clock, to make it tick again after winding it up—in each case, because the process "always" has the desired effect—and in none of these cases could the result be anticipated without full previous acquaintance with the entire phenomenon.

It is not reasoned; but a man who should conceive heat as a mode of motion, and liquefaction as identical with increased motion of molecules; who should know that curved surfaces bend light-rays in special ways, and that the apparent size of anything is connected with the amount of the "bend" of its light-rays as they enter the eye; who should perceive that this particular door sags on its *sill*, or should reflect that no clock can tick until its pendulum swing, and that tipping may start the oscillations of a hidden pendulum—such a man would handle all these objects intelligently, even though he had never in his life had any concrete experience of them; and he would do this because the ideas which we have above supposed him to possess mediate in his mind between the phenomena he starts with and the conclusions he draws. But these ideas or reasons for his conclusions are all mere extracted portions or circumstances singled out from the mass of characters which make up the entire phenomena. The motions which form heat, the bending of the light-waves, are, it is true, excessively recondite ingredients; the hidden pendulum is less so; and the sticking of the door on its sill is hardly so at all. But each and all bear a more evident relation to the consequent idea than did the antecedent in its full totality.

The difficulty is, in each case, to extract from the antecedent phenomenon that particular ingredient which shall have this very evident relation to the consequent. Every phenomenon or so-called "fact" has an infinity of aspects or properties. Even so simple a fact as a line which you trace in the air may be considered in respect to its form, its length, its direction, and its location. When we reach more complex facts, the number of ways in which we may regard them is literally countless. They are perfect well-springs of properties, which are only little by little developed to our knowledge; but each of which may in turn come to be regarded as the essence of the phenomenon or fact in question, while the rest can be for that occasion ignored. Thus a Man is a complex fact. But out of the complexity all that an army commissary need pick out as important for his purposes is his property of eating so many pounds a day; the general, of marching so many miles; the chair-maker, of having such a shape; the orator, of responding to such and such feeling; the theater-manager, of being willing to pay just such a price, and no more, for an evening's amusement. Each of these persons singles out the particular side of the entire man which has a bearing on *his* concerns, and not till this side is distinctly and separately conceived can the proper practical conclusions be drawn. The existence of the separate side or partial aspect which each of these several persons may substitute for the whole complex man in laying his plans is the *reason* for those plans.

These simple examples show sufficiently that our first point is true. Each case of reasoning involves the extraction of a particular partial aspect of the phenomena thought about. Whilst Empirical Thought simply associates the phenomena in their entirety, Reasoned Thought couples them by the conscious use of this extract.

And, now, to prove the second point: Why are the couplings of extracts more evident and obvious than those of entire phenomena? For two reasons: First, the extracted characters are more general than the concretes, and the connections they may have are, therefore, more familiar to us, as having been more often met in our experience. Think of heat as motion, and whatever is true of motion will be true of heat; but we have had a hundred experiences of motion for every one of heat. Think of the rays passing through this lens as bending towards the perpendicular, and you substitute for the unfamiliar lens the very familiar notion of a particular change in direction of a line, of which notion every day brings us countless examples. The other reason why the relations of the extracted characters are so evident is that their properties are so *few*, compared with the properties of the whole, from which we derived them. In every concrete total the characters and their consequences are so inexhaustibly numerous that we may lose our way among them before noticing the particular consequence it behooves us to draw. But, if we are lucky enough to single out the proper character, we take in, as it were, by a single glance all of its possible consequences. Thus the character of scraping the sill has very few suggestions, prominent among which is the suggestion that the scraping will cease if we raise the door; whilst the entire refractory door suggests an enormous number of notions to the mind.

Take another example. I am sitting in a railroad car, waiting for the train to start. It is winter, and the stove fills the car with pungent smoke. The brakeman enters, and my neighbor asks him to "stop that stove smoking." He replies that it will stop entirely as soon as the car begins to move. "Why so," asks the passenger. "It *always* does," replies the brakeman. It is evident from this "always" that the connection between car moving and smoke stopping was a purely empirical one in the brakeman's mind, bred of habit. But, if the passenger had been an acute reasoner, he, with no experience of what that stove always did, might have anticipated the brakeman's reply, and spared his own question. Had he singled out of all the numerous points involved in a stove's not smoking the one special point of smoke pouring freely out of the stove-pipe's mouth, he would, probably, owing to the few associations of that idea, have been immediately reminded of the law that a fluid passes more rapidly out of a pipe's mouth if another fluid be at the same time streaming over that mouth; and then the rapid draught of air over the stove-pipe's mouth, which is one of the points involved in the car's motion, would immediately have occurred to him.

Thus a couple of extracted characters, with a couple of their few and obvious connections, would have formed the reasoned link in the passenger's mind between the concrete phenomena, smoke stopping and car moving, which were only linked as wholes in the brakeman's mind. Such examples may seem trivial, but they contain the essence of the most refined and transcendental theorizing. The reason why physics grows more deductive the more the fundamental properties it assumes are of a mathematical sort, such as molecular mass or wave length, is that the immediate consequences of such a mathematical notion are so few that we can survey them all at once, and promptly pick out the one which concerns us.

To reason, then, we must be able to extract characters, and not *any* characters, but the right characters for our conclusion. If we extract the wrong character, it will not lead to that conclusion. Here, then, is the difficulty: How are characters extracted, and why does it require the advent of a genius in many cases before the fitting character is brought to light? Why does it need a Newton to notice the law of the squares, a Darwin, to notice the survival of the fittest? To answer these questions we must begin a new research, and see how our insight into facts naturally grows.

All our knowledge at first is vague. When we say that a thing is vague, we mean that it has no subdivisions *ab intra*, nor precise limitations *ab extra*, but, still, all the forms of thought may apply to it. It may have unity, reality, externality, extent, and what not—*thinghood*, in a word, but thinghood only as a whole. In this vague way, probably, does the room appear to the babe who first begins to be conscious of it as something other than his moving nurse. It has no subdivisions in his mind, unless, perhaps, the window is able to attract his separate notice. In this vague way, certainly, does every entirely new experience appear to the adult. A library, a museum, a machine-shop, are mere confused wholes to the uninstructed, but the machinist, the antiquary, and the bookworm perhaps hardly notice the whole at all, so eager are they to pounce upon the details. Familiarity has in them bred discrimination. Such vague terms as "grass," "mould," and "meat" do not exist for the botanist or the anatomist. They know too much about grasses, moulds, and muscles. A certain person said to Mr. Kingsley, who was showing him the dissection of a caterpillar, with its exquisite viscera, "Why, I thought it was nothing but skin and squash!" A layman present at a shipwreck, a battle, or a fire is helpless. Discrimination has been so little awakened in him by experience that his consciousness leaves no single point of the complex situation accented and standing out for him to begin to act upon.

But the sailor, the fireman, and the general know directly at what point to take up the business. They "see into the situation"—that is, analyze it—with their first glance. Knowledge, then, if it begins thus with vague confusion, is not, as some philosophers say, purely and simply the result of association. To quote Mr. Martineau, in an admirable passage, "It is an utter falsification of the order of nature to speak of sensations grouping themselves to aggregates, and so composing for us the objects of which we think; and the whole language of the theory [of association], in regard to the field of synchronous existences, is a direct inversion of the truth. Experience proceeds and intellect is trained, not by Association, but by *Dissociation*, not by reduction of pluralities of impression to one, but by the opening out of one into many; and a true psychological history must expound itself in analytic rather than synthetic terms."[4]

According to this, any original Whole of experience is an eternal well of ever new and more delicately differenced ingredients, which little by little come to light. A man's reasoning powers may, then, if our previous account of reasoning is correct, be said to be in direct proportion to his ability to break up these wholes and dissociate their ingredients.

How, then, do we come to dissociate the elements of the originally vague syncretism of consciousness? By noticing or attending to them, of course. But what determines which element we shall attend to first? There are two immediate and obvious answers: first, our practical interests; and, second, our æsthetic interests. The dog singles out of any situation it smells, and the horse its sounds, because they may reveal facts of practical moment. The child notices the candle-flame or the window, and ignores the rest of the room, because these objects give him a vivid pleasure. So, the country boy dissociates the blackberry, the chestnut, and the wintergreen, from the vague mass of other shrubs and trees, for their practical uses, and the savage is delighted with the beads, the bits of looking-glass, brought by an exploring vessel, and gives no heed to the features of the vessel itself, which is too much beyond his sphere. These æsthetic and practical interests,

[4]James Martineau: *Essays, Philosophical and Theological*, Boston, 1866, p. 273.

then, are the weightiest factors in making particular ingredients stand out in high relief. What they lay their accent on, that we notice; but what they are in themselves, we cannot say. We must content ourselves here with simply accepting them as irreducible ultimate factors in determining the way our knowledge grows.

Now, a creature which has few interests, practical or æsthetic, will dissociate few characters, and will, at best, have limited reasoning powers; whilst one whose interests are very varied will reason much better. Man, by his immensely varied practical wants, and his æsthetic feelings, to which every sense contributes, would, by dint of these alone, be sure to dissociate vastly more characters than any other animal, and, accordingly, we find that the lowest savages reason incomparably better than the highest brutes. But if these were the only operators of dissociation, man's superiority would rest here, and he would remain a savage. We must have recourse to another cause to explain dissociation of characters to which the spur of acute practical or æsthetic interest is lacking, and which we attend to, as we say, merely out of disinterested curiosity. Why are such characters not left slumbering forever? how do we single them out at all? They are singled out by a process which many psychologists have recognized; but none, perhaps, as emphatically as it deserves. This process is so important that we shall perhaps do well to baptize it by a special name, and call it the *Law of dissociation by varying concomitants*. This law would run as follows: "In order that a character, possessing no vivid practical or æsthetic interest be dissociated from a group, it must have been previously experienced in connection with *other* characters than those of that group." As Spencer says, "If the property A occurs here along with the properties B, C, D; there along with C, F, H; and again with E, G, B; . . . it must happen that by multiplication of experiences, the impressions produced by these properties on the organism will be disconnected, and rendered so far independent in the organism as the properties are in the environment. Whence must eventually result a power to recognize attributes in themselves, apart from particular bodies."[5] As ex-

[5]Herbert Spencer: *Psychology*, vol. I, p. 345.

pressed still better by Mr. Martineau, "When a red ivory-ball, seen for the first time, has been withdrawn, it will leave a mental representation of itself, in which all that it simultaneously gave us will indistinguishably co-exist. Let a white ball succeed to it; now, and not before, will an attribute detach itself, and the *color*, by force of contrast, be shaken out into the foreground. Let the white ball be replaced by an egg: and this new difference will bring the *form* into notice from its previous slumber. And thus, that which began by being simply an object, cut out from the surrounding scene, becomes for us first a *red* object, and then a *red round* object; and so on. Instead, therefore, of the qualities, as separately given, subscribing together and adding themselves up to present us with the object as their aggregate, the object is beforehand with them, and from its integrity delivers them out to our knowledge, one by one."[6]

In other words, an absolutely unchanging group of attributes could never be analyzed. If all liquids were transparent, and no non-liquid was transparent, it would be long before we had separate names for liquidity and transparency. If the color blue, for example, were a function of position above the earth's surface, so that the higher a thing was, the bluer it became, one word would serve for blue and high. We have, in truth, a number of sensations whose concomitants are invariably the same. When, for example, we look at a near object, we have two sets of sensations: one, that produced by converging the eye-balls; the other, that which results from accommodating the focus. For every distance of the object these sensations are, in common life, immutably linked. The consequence is that we are wholly unable to separate them from each other in our consciousness, or to separate them as a whole from the particular distance on the part of the object to which they testify. The genius of Helmholtz has shown what a vast number of such unseparated sensations underlie our perceptions. We never think of them except as embedded in the totality of the perception to which they belong. Helmholtz calls them its "unconscious premises." We may, how-

[6]James Martineau: *Essays, Philosophical and Theological*, Boston, 1866, pp. 271–272.

ever, bring them separately to our consciousness by an artificial device which consists in nothing but varying their concomitants. I may, for example, by prisms cause my eyes to change their convergence when looking at a near object, and I may succeed, at least, in accommodating my focus for the nearness of the object, in spite of the very unusual convergence of the eye-balls. In this case I shall end by becoming aware of the accommodation in itself, and afterwards succeed in reproducing it at will without the prisms.

Why the repetition of the character in combination with different wholes will cause it thus to break up its adhesion with any one of them, and roll out, as it were, alone upon the table of consciousness, must here be left a mystery. Mr. Spencer appears to think that the mere fact of its being repeated more often than any one of its associates will, of itself, give it a degree of intensity equivalent to the accent derived from interest.

This, at first sight, has a plausible sound, but breaks down when examined closely. It is not always the often-repeated character which is first noticed when its concomitants have varied a certain number of times; it is even more likely to be the most novel of all the concomitants which will succeed in arresting our attention. If a boy has seen nothing all his life but sloops and schooners, he will probably never distinctly have singled out in his notion of "sail" the character of being hung lengthwise. When for the first time he sees a square-rigged ship, the opportunity of extracting the lengthwise mode of hanging as a special accident, and of dissociating it from the general notion of sail, is offered. But there are twenty chances to one that that will not be the form of the boy's consciousness. What he *notices* will be the new and exceptional character of being hung crosswise. He will go home and speak of that, and perhaps never consciously formulate what the often-repeated peculiarity consists in. Leaving, then, the question of *how* and *why* the law operates as one of the most interesting questions of psychology, we may content ourselves with simply registering it as empirically true.

So far, then, we have found out two things: *First*, a reasoning animal must easily dissociate and extract characters; *second*, in order to do so, characters must have some peculiar æsthetic or practical interest for him; *third*, or, failing in that, must form variable connections in his experience.

The English writer who has professed to give the most thorough account of the evolution of the mind is Mr. Herbert Spencer, in his *Principles of Psychology*. Perhaps a brief criticism of his theory will be the easiest manner in which fully to clear up what may still seem obscure in our own. Spencer, throughout his work, ignores entirely the reactive spontaneity, both emotional and practical, of the animal. Devoted to his great task of proving that mind from its lowest to its highest forms is a mere product of the environment, he is unwilling, even cursorily, to allude to such notorious facts (which, nevertheless, in *principle* are perfectly consistent with his fundamental idea) as the existence of peculiar idiosyncrasies of interest or selective attention on the part of every sentient being. He regards the creature as absolutely passive clay, upon which "experience" rains down. The clay will be impressed most deeply where the drops fall thickest, and so the final shape of the mind is moulded. Give time enough, and all sentient things must end by assuming an identical mental constitution—for "experience," the sole shaper, is a constant fact, and the order of its items must end by being exactly reflected by the passive mirror which we call the sentient organism. The law of dissociation would work, on this theory, only for the first reason suggested above. That is, in the varied shufflings and rearrangements of characters which natural groups of objects and events afford, the character which objectively recurred the oftenest would be the first one noticed by us; the rest would passively follow in the order of their frequency, as experience presented them; and "experience" here would mean the mere presence of the outward fact to the animal's senses.

How Mr. Spencer came to give so inadequate an account, we shall not here inquire. But every reader will already cry out against his interpretation of the word "experience" as being equivalent to the mere presence of a certain outward order. Millions of items of the outward order are present to my senses which never properly enter into my experience. Why? Because they have no interest for me. My experience is what I agree to attend to. Only those items which I notice shape my mind—without selective interest, experience is an utter chaos. Interest alone gives accent and emphasis, light and shade, background and foreground—intelligible perspective, in a word. It varies in every creature, but without it the consciousness of every creature would be a gray chaotic uniformity, impossible for us even to conceive. If Spencer's account were true, a race of dogs bred for generations, say in the Vatican, would have characters of visual shape, sculptured in marble, presented to their eyes, in every variety of form and combination. The result of this reiterated "experience" would be to make them dissociate and discriminate before long the finest shades of these peculiar characters. In a word, they would infallibly become, if time were given, accomplished *connoisseurs* of sculpture. The reader may judge of the probability of this consummation. Surely an eternity of experience of the statues would leave the dog as inartistic as he was at first, for the lack of an original interest to knit his discriminations onto. Meanwhile the odors at the bases of the pedestals would have organized themselves in the consciousness of this breed of dogs into a system of "correspondences" to which the most hereditary caste of *custodi* would never approximate, merely because to them, as human beings, the dog's interest in those odors would forever be an inscrutable mystery. Mr. Spencer has, then, utterly ignored the glaring fact that subjective interest may, by laying its weighty index-finger on particular items of experience, so accent them as to give to the least frequent associations far more power to shape our forms of thought than the most frequent ones possess.

But, if Mr. Spencer is at fault in his account of those cases where powerful interests do the analytic work, we think he is hardly less so in the cases where powerful interest is absent, and "where the law of dissociation by varying concomitants" has all alone to play into the hands of disinterested curiosity. Mr. Spencer writes as if, under these circumstances, man, before he could single out a character, would have merely to wait until such time as nature should sufficiently have varied the concomitants of that character for him. He would single out the notion quadruped, for example, earlier than the notion vertebrate, because vertebrate coexisted more uniformly than quadruped with the other animal attributes. On page

464 of his first volume he writes as if any character frequently repeated in the outer world will, *ipso facto*, tend to stand out prominently in the mind. An "accumulation of experiences" is by itself sufficient to shake out the embedded character. If this were true, man, to dissociate characters, would be wholly at the mercy of the order of frequency in which they outwardly had been present to him. But the fact is that man is, even in the absence of the stronger interests, in the highest degree independent of this outward order, and has within himself a means of abridging in the most striking manner the slow work of nature. This means is nothing else than our familiar friend, *association by similarity*. But here the plot begins to thicken, and as we are approaching the elementary difference we sought between the mind of man and the mind of brutes we will pause an instant, and, by going back a few steps, advance with all the greater impetus.

What does the reader do who wishes to see in what the precise likeness or difference of two objects lies? He transfers his attention as rapidly as possible, backwards and forwards, from one to the other. The rapid alteration in consciousness shakes out, as it were, the points of difference or agreement, which would have slumbered forever unnoticed if the consciousness of the objects compared had occurred at widely distant periods of time. What does the scientific man do who searches for the reason or law embedded in a phenomenon? He deliberately accumulates all the instances he can find which have an analogy to that phenomenon, and, by simultaneously filling his mind with them all, he frequently succeeds in detaching from the collection the peculiarity which he was unable to formulate in one alone; even though that one had been preceded in his former experience by all of those with which he now at once confronts it. These examples show that the mere general fact of having occurred at some time in one's experience, with varying concomitants, is not by itself a sufficient reason for a character to be dissociated now. We need something more; we need that the varying concomitants should in all their variety be brought into consciousness *at once*. Not till then will the character in question escape from its adhesion to each and all of them, and stand revealed alone. Spencer's account omits this last condition, which will immediately be recognized by the reader as the ground of utility in Mill's famous methods of induction, the "method of Agreement," that of "Difference," of "concomitant variations," etc.

But, now, is it not immediately obvious that this condition is supplied in the organization of every mind in which similar association is largely developed? If the character m in the midst of A will call up C, D, E, and F immediately—these being phenomena which resemble A in possessing m, but which may not have entered for months into the experience of the animal who now experiences A, why, plainly, such association performs the part of the deliberately rapid comparison referred to above, and of the systematic simultaneous consideration of like cases by the scientific investigator. Certainly this is obvious, and no conclusion is left to us but to assert that, after the few most powerful practical and æsthetic interests, our only instrument for dissecting out those special characters of phenomena, which, when once possessed and named, are used as reasons, *is this association by similarity*. Without it, indeed, the deliberate procedure of the scientific man would be impossible; he could never collect his analogous instances. But it operates of itself in highly-gifted minds without any deliberation, spontaneously collecting analogous instances, uniting in a moment what in nature the whole breadth of space and time keeps separate, and so permitting a perception of identical points in the midst of different circumstances, which minds governed wholly by the law of contiguity could never begin to attain.

Diagram 6 shows this. If m, in the present representation A, calls up B, C, D, and E, which are similar to A in possessing it, and calls them up in rapid succession, then m, being associated almost simultaneously with such varying concomitants, will "roll out" and attract our separate notice.

If so much is clear to the reader, he will be willing to admit that the mind *in which this mode of association most prevails* will, from its better opportunity of extricating characters, be one most prone to reasoned thinking; whilst, on the other hand, a mind in which we do not detect reasoned thinking will probably be one in which association by contiguity holds almost exclusive sway.

I will try now to show, by taking the best stories I can find

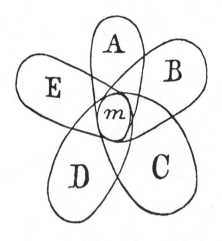

Fig. 6.

of animal sagacity, that the mental process involved may as a rule be perfectly accounted for by mere contiguous association, based on experience. Mr. Darwin, in his *Descent of Man*, instances the Arctic dogs, described by Dr. Hayes, as scattering, when drawing a sledge, as soon as the ice begins to crack. This might be called by some an exercise of reason. The test would be, Would the most intelligent Esquimau dogs that ever lived act so when placed upon ice for the first time together? A band of men from the tropics might do so easily. Recognizing cracking to be a sign of breaking, and seizing immediately the partial character that the point of rupture is the point of greatest strain, and that the massing of weight at a given point concentrates there the strain, a Hindoo might quickly infer that scattering would stop the cracking, and by crying out to his comrades to disperse save the party from immersion. But in the dog's case we need only suppose that they have individually experienced wet skins after cracking, that they have often noticed cracking to begin when they were huddled together, and that they have observed it to cease when they scattered. Naturally, therefore, the sound would redintegrate all these former experiences, including that of scattering, which latter they would promptly renew.

A friend of the writer gave as a proof of the almost human intelligence of his dog that he took him one day down to his boat on the shore, but found the boat full of dirt and water. He remembered that the sponge was up at the house, a third of a mile distant; but, disliking to go back himself, he made various gestures of wiping out the boat and so forth, saying to his terrier, "Sponge, sponge; go fetch the sponge." But he had little expectation of a result, since the dog had never received the slightest training with the boat or the sponge. Nevertheless, off trotted the latter to the house, and, to his owner's great surprise and admiration, brought the sponge in his jaws. Sagacious as this was, it required nothing but ordinary contiguous association of ideas. The terrier was only exceptional in the minuteness of his spontaneous observation. Most terriers would have taken no interest in the boat-cleaning operation, nor noticed what the sponge was for. This terrier, in having picked those details out of the crude mass of boat experience distinctly enough to be reminded of them, was truly enough ahead of his peers on the line which leads to human reason. But his act was not yet an act of reasoning proper. It might fairly have been called so if, unable to find the sponge at the house, he had brought back a dipper or a mop instead. Such a substitution would have shown that, embedded in the very different appearances of these articles, he had been able to discriminate the identical partial attribute of capacity to take up water, and had reflected, "For the present purpose they are identical." This, which the dog did not do, any man but the very stupidest could not fail to do.

If the reader will take the trouble to analyze the best dog and elephant stories he knows, he will find that, in most cases, this simple contiguous calling up of one whole by another is quite sufficient to explain the phenomena. Sometimes, it is true, we have to suppose the recognition of a property or character as such, but it is then a character which the mere practical interest of the animal may have singled out. A dog, noticing his master's hat on its peg, may possibly infer that he has not gone out. Intelligent dogs recognize by the tone of the master's voice whether the latter is angry or not. A dog will perceive whether you have kicked him by accident or by design, and behave accordingly. The character inferred by him, the particular mental state in you, whether represented in his mind by images of further hostile or friendly acts, or in whatever other way, is still a partial character extracted from the totality of your phenomenal being, and is his reason for crouching and skulking, or the reverse. Dogs, moreover, seem to have the feeling of the value of their master's personal property, or at least a particular *interest* in objects their master uses. A dog left with his master's coat will defend it, though never taught to do so. We know of a dog accustomed to swim after sticks in the water, but who always refused to dive for stones. Nevertheless, when a fish-basket, which he had never been trained to carry, but merely knew as his master's, fell overboard from a boat, he immediately dove after it and brought it up. Dogs thus discern, at any rate so far as to be able to act, this partial character of *being valuable*, which lies hidden in certain things. Stories are told of dogs carrying coppers to pastry-cooks to get buns, and it is said that a certain dog, if he gave two coppers, would never leave without two buns. This may have been mere contiguous association, but it is possible that the animal noticed the character of duality, and identified it as the same in the coin and the cake. If so, it is probably the maximum of canine abstract thinking. Another story told to the writer is this: A dog was sent to a lumber-camp to fetch a wedge, with which he was known to be acquainted. After half an hour, not returning, he was sought and found biting and tugging at the handle of an axe which was driven deeply into a stump. The wedge could not be found. The teller of the story thought that the dog must have had a clear perception of the common character of serving to split which was involved in both the instruments, and, from their identity in this respect, inferred their identity for the purposes required.

It cannot be denied that this interpretation is a possible one, but it seems to us to far transcend the limits of ordinary canine abstraction. The property in question was not one which had direct personal interest for the dog, such as that of mere belonging to his master is in the case of the coat or the basket. If the dog in the sponge story had returned to the boat with a dipper, it would have hardly been more remarkable. It seems more probable, therefore, that this wood-

cutter's dog had also been accustomed to carry the axe, and
now, excited by the vain hunt for the wedge, had discharged
his carrying powers upon the former instrument in a sort of
confusion—just as a man may pick up a sieve to carry water
in, in the excitement of putting out a fire.[7]

Thus, then, the characters extracted by animals are very
few, and always related to their immediate interests or emotions. That dissociation by varying concomitants, which in
man is based so largely on association by similarity, hardly
seems to take place at all in the mind of brutes. One total
thought suggests to them another total thought, and they find
themselves acting with propriety, they know not why. The
great, the fundamental, defect of their minds seems to be the
inability of their groups of ideas to break across in unaccustomed places. They are enslaved to routine, to cut and dried
thinking, and if the most prosaic of human beings could be
transported into his dog's sensorium, he would be appalled at
the utter absence of fancy which reigns there. Thoughts will
not call up their similars, but only their habitual successors.
Sunsets will not suggest heroes' deaths, but only supper-time.
This is why man is the only metaphysical animal. To wonder
why the universe should be as it is presupposes the notion of
its being different, and a brute which never reduces the actual
to fluidity by breaking up its literal sequences in his imagination can never form such a notion. He takes the world simply
for granted, and never wonders at it at all.

Another well-known *differentia* of man is that he is the only
laughing animal. But humor has been defined as the recognition of certain identities in things different. When the man in
Coriolanus says of that hero that "there is no more mercy in
him than there is milk in a male tiger," both the invention of
the phrase and its enjoyment by the hearer depend on a peculiarly perplexing power to associate ideas by similarity.

Language is certainly a capital distinction between man and

---

[7]This matter of confusion is important and interesting. Since confusion is
mistaking the wrong part of the phenomenon for the whole, whilst reasoning
is, according to our definition, based on the substitution of the right part for
the whole, it might be said that confusion and reasoning were generically the
same process. There are, however, other and more subtle considerations
which intervene and prevent us from treating the matter further in this place.

brute. But it may readily be shown how this distinction merely flows from those we have pointed out, easy dissociation of a representation into its ingredients, and association by similarity.

Language is a system of *signs*, different from the things signified, but able to suggest them.

No doubt brutes have a number of such signs. When a dog yelps in front of a door, and his master, understanding his desire, opens it, the dog may, after a certain number of repetitions, get to repeat in cold blood a yelp which was at first the involuntary interjectional expression of strong emotion. The same dog may be taught to "beg" for food, and afterwards come to do so deliberately when hungry. The dog also learns to understand the signs of men, and the word "rat" uttered to a terrier suggests exciting thoughts of the rat-hunt. If the dog had the varied impulse to vocal utterance which some other animals have, he would probably repeat the word "rat" whenever he spontaneously happened to think of a rat-hunt—he no doubt does have it as an auditory image, just as a parrot calls out different words spontaneously from its repertory, and having learned the name of a given dog will utter it on the sight of a different dog. In each of these separate cases the particular sign *may* be consciously noticed by the animal, as distinct from the particular thing signified, and will thus, so far as it goes, be a true manifestation of language. But when we come to man we find a great difference. He has a deliberate intention to apply a sign to everything. The linguistic impulse is with him generalized and systematic. For things hitherto unnoticed or unfelt, he *desires* a sign before he has one. Even though the dog should possess his "yelp" for this thing, his "beg" for that, and his auditory image "rat" for a third, the matter with him rests there. If a fourth thing interests him for which no sign happens already to have been learned, he remains tranquilly without it and goes no further. But the man *postulates* it, its absence irritates him, and he ends by inventing it. This *general purpose* constitutes, I take it, the peculiarity of human speech, and explains its prodigious development.

How, then, does the general purpose arise? As soon as the notion of the sign *as such*, apart from any particular import, is born; and it is born by dissociation from the outstanding portions of a number of concrete cases of signification. The "yelp," the "beg," the "rat," differ as to their import—and as to their own physical constitution. They agree only in so far as they have the same *use*—to be signs, to stand for something more important than themselves. The dog whom this similarity could strike would have grasped the sign *per se* as such, and would have become a speaker in the human sense. But how can the similarity strike him? Not without the juxtaposition of the similars (in virtue of the law we have so often repeated, that in order to be segregated an experience must be repeated with varying concomitants)—not unless the "yelp" of the dog at the moment it occurs *recalls* to him his "beg," by the delicate bond of their subtle similarity of use—not till then can this thought flash through his mind: "Why, yelp and beg, in spite of all their unlikeness, are yet alike in this: that they are actions, signs, which lead to important boons. Other boons, *any* boons, may then be got by other signs!" This reflection made, the gulf is passed. Animals probably never make it, because the bond of similarity is not delicate enough. Each sign is drowned in *its* import, and never awakens other signs and other imports in juxtaposition. The rat-hunt idea is too absorbingly interesting in itself to be interrupted by anything so uncontiguous to it as the "beg for food," or "the door-open yelp," nor in their turn do they awaken the rat-hunt.

In the human child, however, these ruptures of contiguous association are very soon made; far off cases of sign-using arise when we make a sign now; and soon language is launched. The child in each case makes the discovery for himself. No one can help him except by furnishing him with the conditions. But as he is constituted, the conditions will sooner or later shoot together into the result.[8]

---

[8]There are two other conditions of language in the human being, additional to association by similarity, that assist its action, or rather pave the way for it. These are: first, the great natural loquacity; and, second, the great imitativeness of man. The first produces the original reflex interjectional sign; the second (as Bleek has well shown) fixes it, stamps it, and ends by multiplying the number of determinate specific signs which are a requisite preliminary to the general conscious purpose of sign-making, which I have called the

The exceedingly interesting account which Dr. Howe gives of the education of his various blind-deaf mutes illustrates this point admirably. He began to teach Laura Bridgman by gumming raised letters on various familiar articles. The child was taught by mere contiguity to pick out a certain number of particular articles when made to feel the letters. But this was merely a collection of particular signs out of the mass of which the general purpose of *signification* had not yet been extracted by the child's mind. Dr. Howe compares his situation at this moment to that of one lowering a line to the bottom of the deep sea in which Laura's soul lay, and waiting until she should spontaneously take hold of it and be raised into the light. The moment came, "accompanied by a radiant flash of intelligence and glow of joy"; she seemed suddenly to become aware of the general purpose embedded in the different details of all these signs, and from that moment her education went on with extreme rapidity.

Another of the great capacities in which man has been said to differ fundamentally from the animal is that of possessing self-consciousness or reflective knowledge of himself as a thinker. But this capacity also flows from our criterion— without going into the matter very deeply, we may say that the brute never reflects on himself as a thinker, because he has never clearly dissociated, in the full concrete act of thought,

characteristic human element in language. The way in which imitativeness fixes the meaning of signs is this: When a primeval man has a given emotion, he utters his natural interjection; or when (to avoid supposing that the reflex sounds are exceedingly determinate by nature) a group of such men experience a common emotion, and one takes the lead in the cry, the others cry like him from sympathy or imitativeness. Now, let one of the group hear another, who is in presence of the experience, utter the cry; he, even without the experience, will repeat the cry from pure imitativeness. But, as he repeats the sign, he will be reminded by it of his own former experience. Thus, first, he has the sign with the emotion; then, without it; then, with it again. It is "dissociated by change of concomitants"; he feels it as a separate entity and yet as having a connection with the emotion. Immediately it becomes possible for him to couple it deliberately with the emotion, in cases where the latter would either have provoked no interjectional cry or not the same one. In a word, his mental procedure tends to *fix* this cry on *that* emotion; and when this occurs, in many instances, he is provided with a stock of signs, like the yelp, beg, rat of the dog, each of which suggests a determinate image. On this stock, then, similarity works in the way above explained.

the element of the thing thought of and the operation by which he thinks it. They remain always fused, conglomerated—just as the interjectional vocal sign of the brute almost invariably merges in his mind with the thing signified, and is not independently attended to *in se*.[9]

Now, the dissociation of these two elements probably occurs first in the child's mind on the occasion of some error or false expectation which would make him experience the shock of difference between merely imagining a thing and getting it. The thought experienced once with the concomitant reality, and then without it or with opposite concomitants, reminds the child of other cases in which the same provoking phenomenon occurred. Thus the general ingredient of error may be dissociated and noticed *per se*, and from the notion of error or wrong thought to that of thought in general, the transition is easy. The brute, no doubt, has plenty of instances of error and disappointment in his life, but the similar shock is in him most likely always swallowed up in the accidents of the actual case. An expectation disappointed may breed dubiety as to the realization of that particular thing when the dog next expects it. But that disappointment, that dubiety, while they are present in the mind, will not call up other cases in which the material details were different, but this feature of possible error was the same. The brute will, therefore, stop short of dissociating the general notion of error *per se*, and *a fortiori* will never attain the conception of Thought itself as such.

We may then, we think, consider it proven that the most characteristic single difference between the human mind and that of brutes lies in this deficiency on the brute's part to associate ideas by similarity—characters, the abstraction of which depends on this sort of association, must in the brute always remain drowned, swamped in the total phenomenon which they help constitute, and never used to reason from. But *other* characters (few and far between) may be singled out by practical interests.

But, now, since nature never makes a jump, it is evident that we should find the lowest men occupying in this respect

[9]See an interesting article on the "Evolution of Self-Consciousness" in *Philosophical Discussions*, by Chauncey Wright. New York: Holt & Co., 1877.

an intermediate position between the brutes and the highest men, and so we do. Beyond the analogies which their own minds suggest by breaking up the literal sequence of their experience, there is a whole world of analogies which they can appreciate when imparted to them by their betters, but which they could never excogitate alone. This answers the question we asked some time back, why Darwin and Newton had to be waited for so long. The flash of similarity between an apple and the moon, between the rivalry for food in nature and the rivalry for man's approbation, was too recondite to have occurred to any but exceptional minds. Genius, then, is identical with the possession of Similar Association to an extreme degree. Professor Bain, in his admirable work on the *Study of Character*, says: "This I count the leading fact of genius . . . I consider it quite impossible to afford any explanation of intellectual originality, except on the supposition of an unusual energy on this point" (p. 327). He proceeds to show how alike in the arts, in literature, in practical affairs, and in science, association by similarity is the prime condition of success. But as, according to our view, there are two stages in reasoned thought, one where similarity merely *operates* to call up cognate thoughts, and another farther stage, where the bond of identity between the cognate thoughts is *noticed*, so minds of genius may be divided into two main sorts, those who notice the bond and those who merely obey it. The first are the abstract reasoners, the men of science, and philosophers—the analysts, in a word; the latter are the poets, the critics—the artists, in a word, the men of intuitions. These judge rightly, classify cases, characterize them by the most striking analogic epithets, but go no further. At first sight it might seem that the analytic mind represented simply a higher intellectual stage, and that the intuitive mind represented an arrested stage of intellectual development; but the difference is not so simple as this. Professor Bain has said that a man's advance to the scientific stage (the stage of noticing and abstracting the bond of association) may often be due to an *absence* of certain emotional sensibilities. The sense of color, he says, may no less determine a mind away from science than it determines it towards painting. There must be a penury in one's interest in the details of particular forms in order to permit the forces of the intellect to be concentrated on what is common to many forms.[10] In other words, supposing a mind fertile in the suggestions of analogies, but, at the same time, keenly interested in the particulars of each suggested image, that mind would be far less apt to single out the particular character which called up the analogy than one whose interests were less generally lively. A certain richness of the æsthetic nature may, therefore, easily keep one in the intuitive stage. All the poets are examples of this. Take Homer: "Ulysses, too, spied round the house to see if any man were still alive and hiding, trying to get away from gloomy death. He found them all fallen in the blood and dirt, and in such number as the fish which the fishermen to the low shore, out of the foaming sea, drag with their meshy nets. These all, sick for the ocean water, are strewn around the sands, while the blazing sun takes their life from them. So there the suitors lay strewn round on one another." Or again: "And as when a Mæonian or a Carian woman stains ivory with purple to be a cheek-piece for horses, and it is kept in the chamber, and many horsemen have prayed to bear it off; but it is kept a treasure for a king, both a trapping for his horse and a glory to the driver—in such wise were thy stout thighs, Menelaos, and legs and fair ankles stained with blood."

A man in whom all the accidents of an analogy rise up as vividly as this, may be excused for not attending to the ground of the analogy. But he need not on that account be deemed intellectually the inferior of a man of drier mind, in whom the ground should not be eclipsed by the general splendor. Rarely are both sorts of intellect, the splendid and the analytic, found in conjunction. Plato among philosophers, and M. Taine, who cannot quote a child's saying without describing the *"voix chantante, étonnée, heureuse"* in which it is uttered, are only exceptions, whose strangeness proves the rule.

An often-quoted writer has said that Shakespeare possessed more *intellectual power* than anyone else that ever lived. If by this he meant the power to pass from given premises to right or congruous conclusions, it is no doubt true. The abrupt

[10]Bain: *On the Study of Character*, p. 317.

transitions in Shakespeare's thought astonish the reader by their unexpectedness no less than they delight him by their fitness. Why, for instance, does the death of Othello so stir the spectator's blood and leave him with a sense of reconcilement? Shakespeare himself could very likely not say why; for his invention, though rational, was not ratiocinative. Wishing the curtain to fall upon a reinstated Othello, that speech about the turbaned Turk suddenly simply flashed across him as the right end of all that went before. The dry critic who comes after can, however, point out the subtle bonds of identity that guided Shakespeare's pen through that speech to the death of the Moor. Othello is sunk in ignominy, lapsed from his height at the beginning of the play. What better way to rescue him at last from this abasement than to make him for an instant identify himself in memory with the old Othello of better days, and then execute justice on his present disowned body, as he used then to smite all enemies of the State? But Shakespeare, whose mind supplied these means, could probably not have told why they were so effective.

But though this is true, and though it would be absurd in an absolute way to say that a given analytic mind was superior to any intuitional one, yet it is none the less true that the former *represents* the higher stage. Men, taken historically, reason by analogy long before they have learned to reason by abstract characters. We saw some time back how association by similarity and true reasoning were identical in their results. If a philosopher wishes to prove to you why you should do a certain thing, he may do so by using abstract considerations exclusively; a savage will prove the same by reminding you of a similar case in which you notoriously do as he now proposes, and this with no ability to state the *point* in which the cases are similar. In all primitive literature, in all savage oratory, we find persuasion carried on exclusively by parables and similes, and travelers in savage countries readily adopt the native custom. Take, for example, Dr. Livingstone's argument with the negro conjurer. The missionary was trying to dissuade the savage from his fetichistic ways of invoking rain. You see, said he, that, after all your operations, sometimes it rains and sometimes it doesn't, exactly as when you have not operated at all. But, replied the sorcerer, it is just the same with you doctors; you give your remedies, and sometimes the patient gets well and sometimes he dies, just as when you do nothing at all. To that the pious missionary replied, the doctor does his duty, after which God performs the cure if it pleases Him. Well, rejoined the savage, it is just so with me. I do what is necessary to procure rain, after which God sends it or withholds it according to His pleasure.[11]

This is the stage in which proverbial philosophy reigns supreme. "An empty sack can't stand straight" will stand for the reason why a man with debts may lose his honesty; and "a bird in the hand is worth two in the bush" will serve to back up one's exhortations to prudence. Or we answer the question: "Why is snow white?" by saying, "For the same reason that soap-suds or whipped eggs are white"—in other words, instead of giving the *reason* for a fact, we give another *example* of the same fact. This offering a similar instance, instead of a reason, has often been criticised as one of the forms of logical depravity in men. But manifestly it is not a perverse act of thought, but only an incomplete one. Furnishing parallel cases is the necessary first step towards abstracting the reason embedded in them all.

As it is with reasons, so it is with words. The first words are probably always names of entire things and entire actions— extensive, coherent groups. A new experience in the primitive man can only be talked about by him in terms of the old experiences which have received names. It reminds him of certain ones from among them, but the *points* in which it agrees with them are neither named nor dissociated. Pure similarity must work before the abstraction which is based upon it. The first words are probably names of entire things and entire actions—extensive, coherent groups. Similarity working before abstraction, which as a rule we have seen to be based upon it, the first adjectives will be total nouns embodying the striking character. The primeval man will say not "the bread is hard," but "the bread is stone"; not "the face is round," but "the face is moon"; not "the fruit is sweet," but "the fruit is sugar-cane." The first words are thus neither particular nor general, but *vaguely* concrete. Just as we speak of an "oval" face, a

[11]Quoted by Renouvier: *Critique Philosophique*, October 19, 1876.

"velvet" skin, or an "iron" will, without meaning to connote any other attributes of the adjective-noun than those in which it *does* resemble the noun it is used to qualify. After a while certain of these adjectively-used nouns come only to signify the particular quality for whose sake they are oftenest used; the *entire thing* which they originally meant receives another name, and they become true abstract and general terms. Oval, for example, with us suggests *only* shape. The first abstract qualities thus formed are, no doubt, qualities of the same sense, found in different objects—as big, sweet; next, analogies between different senses, as "sharp" of taste, "high" of sound, etc.; then, analogies of motor combinations, or form of relation, as simple, confused, difficult, reciprocal, relative, spontaneous, etc. The extreme degree of subtlety in analogy is reached in such cases, as when we say certain English art critics' writing reminds us of a close room in which pastilles have been burning, or that the mind of certain Frenchmen is like old Roquefort cheese. Here language utterly fails to hit upon the bases of resemblance.

Over an immense department of our thought we are still, all of us, in the savage state. Similarity operates in us, but abstraction has not taken place. We know what the present case is like, we know what it reminds us of, we have an intuition of the right course to take, if it be a practical matter. But analytic thought has made no tracks, and we cannot justify ourselves to others. In ethical, psychological, and æsthetic matters, to give a clear reason for one's judgment is universally recognized as a mark of rare genius. The helplessness of uneducated people to account for their likes and dislikes is often ludicrous. Ask the first Irish girl why she likes this country better or worse than her home, and see how much she can tell you. But if you ask your most educated friend why he prefers Titian to Paul Veronese, you will hardly get more of a reply; and you will probably get absolutely none if you inquire why Beethoven reminds him of Michael Angelo, or how it comes that a mere reclining figure by the latter can suggest all the moral tragedy of life. His thought obeys a *nexus*, but can't name it. And so it is with all those judgments of *experts*, which even though unmotivated are so valuable. Saturated with experience of a particular class of materials, an

expert intuitively feels whether a newly-reported fact is probable or not, whether a proposed hypothesis is worthless or
the reverse. He instinctively knows that, in a novel case, this
and not that will be the promising course of action. The well-
known story of the old judge advising the new one never to
give reasons for his decisions, "the decisions will probably be
right, the reasons will surely be wrong," illustrates this. The
doctor will feel that the patient is doomed, the dentist will
have a premonition that the tooth will break, though neither
can articulate a reason for his foreboding. The reason lies embedded, but not yet laid bare, in all the countless previous
cases dimly suggested by the actual one, all calling up the
same conclusion, which the adept thus finds himself swept on
to, he knows not how or why.

A final conclusion remains to be drawn. If the theory be
true which assigns to the cerebral hemispheres definite localities in which the various images, motor and sensible, which
constitute our thoughts are stored up, then it follows that the
great cerebral difference between habitual and reasoned thinking is this: that in the former an entire system of cells vibrating at any one moment discharges in its totality into another
entire system, and that the order of the discharges tends to be
a constant one in time; whilst in the latter a part of the prior
system still keeps vibrating in the midst of the subsequent
system, and the order—which part this shall be, and what
shall be its concomitants in the subsequent system—has little
tendency to fixedness in time. But this physical selection, so
to call it, of one part to vibrate persistently whilst the others
rise and subside, which is the basis of similar association,
seems but a minor degree of that still more urgent and impor-
tunate localize-vibration which we can easiest conceive to underlie the mental fact of interest, attention, or dissociation. In
terms of the brain-process, then, all these mental facts resolve
themselves into a single peculiarity: that of indeterminateness
of connection between the different tracts, and tendency of
action to focalize itself, so to speak, in small localities which
vary infinitely at different times, and from which irradiation
may proceed in countless shifting ways. (Compare Diagram
6.) To discover, or (what more befits the present stage of
nerve physiology) to adumbrate by some at least possible

guess, on what chemical or molecular-mechanical fact this in-stable equilibrium of the human brain may depend, should be the next task of the physiologist who ponders over the pas-sage from brute to man. Whatever the physical peculiarity in question may be, *it* is the cause why a man, whose brain has it, reasons so much, whilst his horse, whose brain lacks it, reasons so little. We have ourselves tried our best to form some hypothesis, but wholly without success. We bequeath, therefore, the problem to abler hands.

But, meanwhile, this mode of stating the matter suggests a couple of other inferences, with which we may conclude. The first is brief. If *focalization* of brain activity be the fundamental fact of reasonable thought, we see why intense interest or concentrated passion makes us think so much more truly and profoundly. The persistent *focalization* of motion in certain tracts is the cerebral fact corresponding to the persistent dom-ination in consciousness of the important feature of the sub-ject. When not "focalized," we are scatter-brained; but, when thoroughly impassioned, we never wander from the point. None but congruous and relevant images arise. When roused by indignation or moral enthusiasm, how trenchant are our reflections, how smiting are our words. The whole net-work of petty scruples and bye-considerations which, at ordinary languid times, surrounded the matter like a cobweb, holding back our thought, as Gulliver was pinned to the earth by the myriad Liliputian threads, are dashed through at a blow, and the subject stands with its essential and vital lines revealed.

The last point is relative to Spencer's theory that what was acquired habit in the ancestor may become congenital ten-dency in the offspring. So vast a superstructure is raised upon this principle, both by Mr. Spencer and by others, that the paucity of empirical evidence for it has alike been matter of regret to its adherents, and of triumph to its opponents. The pointer pup, the birds on desert islands, the young of the tame rabbit, and Brown-Séquard's epileptic guinea-pigs con-stitute the whole beggarly array of proof. In the human race, where our opportunities for observation are the most com-plete, we seem to have no evidence whatever which would support the hypothesis, unless it be the probable law that city-bred children are more apt to be near-sighted than country children, and that is not a *mental* law. In the mental world we do not observe that the children of great travelers get their geography lessons with unusual ease, or that a baby whose ancestors have spoken German for thirty generations will, on that account, learn Italian any the less easily from its Italian nurse. But, if the considerations we have been led to are true, they explain perfectly well why this law of Spencer's *should not* be verified in the human race, and why, therefore, in looking for evidence on the subject, we should confine ourselves exclusively to lower animals. In them fixed habit is the essential and characteristic law of nervous action. The brain grows to the exact modes in which it has been exercised, and the inheritance of these modes—than called instincts—would have in it nothing surprising. But in man the negation of all fixed modes is the essential characteristic. He owes his whole preëminence as a reasoner, his whole human quality, we may say, to the facility with which a given mode of thought in him may suddenly be broken up into elements, which re-combine anew. Only at the price of inheriting no settled instinctive tendencies, is he able to settle every novel case by the fresh discovery by his reason of novel principles. He is, *par excellence*, the *educable* animal. If, then, Spencer's law were found exemplified in him, he would, in so far forth, fall short of his human perfections, and, when we survey the human races, we actually do find that those which are most instinctive at the outset are those which, on the whole, are least educated in the end. An untutored Italian is, to a great extent, a man of the world; he has instinctive perceptions, tendencies to behavior, reactions, in a word, upon his environment, which the untutored German wholly lacks. If the latter be not drilled, he is apt to be a thoroughly loutish personage; but, on the other hand, the mere absence in his brain of definite innate tendencies enables him to advance by the development, through education, of his purely reasoned thinking, into complex regions of consciousness that the Italian probably could never approach.

We observe an identical difference between men as a whole, and women as a whole. A young woman of twenty reacts with intuitive promptitude and security in all the usual circumstances in which she may be placed. Her likes and dislikes are formed; her opinions, to a great extent, the same that they will be through life. Her character is, in fact, finished in its essentials. How inferior to her is a boy of twenty in all these respects. His character is still gelatinous, uncertain what shape to assume, "trying it on" in every direction. Feeling his power, yet ignorant of the manner in which he shall express it, he is, when compared with his sister, a being of no definite contour. But this absence of prompt tendency in his brain to set into particular modes is the very condition which insures that it shall ultimately become so much more efficient than the woman's. The very lack of pre-appointed trains of thought is the condition by which general principles and heads of classification are formed; and the masculine brain deals with new and complex matter indirectly by means of these, in a manner which the feminine method of direct intuition, admirably and rapidly as it performs within its limits, can vainly hope to cope with.

The Sentiment of Rationality

I

WHAT IS the task which philosophers set themselves to perform? And why do they philosophize at all? Almost everyone will immediately reply: They desire to attain a conception of the frame of things which shall on the whole be more rational than the rather fragmentary and chaotic one which everyone by gift of nature carries about with him under his hat. But suppose this rational conception attained by the philosopher, how is he to recognize it for what it is, and not let it slip through ignorance? The only answer can be that he will recognize its rationality as he recognizes everything else, by certain subjective marks with which it affects him. When he gets the marks he may know that he has got the rationality.

What then are the marks? A strong feeling of ease, peace, rest, is one of them. The transition from a state of puzzle and perplexity to rational comprehension is full of lively relief and pleasure.

But this relief seems to be a negative rather than a positive character. Shall we then say that the feeling of rationality is constituted merely by the absence of any feeling of irrationality? I think there are very good grounds for upholding such a view. All feeling whatever, in the light of certain recent psychological speculations, seems to depend for its physical condition not on simply discharge of nerve-currents, but on their discharge under arrest, impediment or resistance. Just as we feel no particular pleasure when we breathe freely, but a very intense feeling of distress when the respiratory motions are prevented; so any unobstructed tendency to action discharges itself without the production of much cogitative accompaniment, and any perfectly fluent course of thought awakens but little feeling. But when the movement is inhibited or when the thought meets with difficulties, we experience a distress which yields to an opposite feeling of pleasure as fast as the obstacle is overcome. It is only when the distress is upon us that we can be said to strive, to crave, or to aspire. When enjoying plenary freedom to energize either in the way of motion or of thought, we are in a sort of anæsthetic state in which we might say with Walt Whitman, if we cared to say anything about ourselves at such times, "I am sufficient as I am." This feeling of the sufficiency of the present moment, of its absoluteness—this absence of all need to explain it, account for it or justify it—is what I call the Sentiment of Rationality. As soon, in short, as we are enabled from any cause whatever to think of a thing with perfect fluency, that things seems to us rational.

Why we should constantly gravitate towards the attainment of such fluency cannot here be said. As this is not an ethical but a psychological essay, it is quite sufficient for our purposes to lay it down as an empirical fact that we strive to formulate rationally a tangled mass of fact by a propensity as natural and invincible as that which makes us exchange a hard high stool for an arm-chair or prefer travelling by railroad to riding in a springless cart.

Whatever modes of conceiving the cosmos facilitate this fluency of our thought, produce the sentiment of rationality. Conceived in such modes Being vouches for itself and needs no further philosophic formulation. But so long as mutually obstructive elements are involved in the conception, the pent-up irritated mind recoiling on its present consciousness will criticize it, worry over it, and never cease in its attempts to discover some new mode of formulation which may give it escape from the irrationality of its actual ideas.

Now mental ease and freedom may be obtained in various ways. Nothing is more familiar than the way in which mere custom makes us at home with ideas or circumstances which, when new, filled the mind with curiosity and the need of explanation. There is no more common sight than that of men's mental worry about things incongruous with personal desire, and their thoughtless incurious acceptance of whatever happens to harmonize with their subjective ends. The existence of evil forms a "mystery"—a "problem": there is no "problem of happiness." But, on the other hand, purely theoretic processes may produce the same mental peace which custom and congruity with our native impulses in other cases give; and we have forthwith to discover how it is that so many processes can produce the same result, and how Philosophy, by emulating or using the means of all, may attain to a conception of the world which shall be rational in the maximum degree, or be warranted in the most composite manner against the inroads of mental unrest or discontent. Discarding for the present both custom and congruity, the present essay will deal with the theoretic way alone.

II

The facts of the world in their sensible diversity are always before us, but the philosophic need craves that they should be conceived in such a way as to satisfy the sentiment of rationality. The philosophic quest then is the quest of a conception. What now is a *conception*? It is a *teleological instrument*. It is a partial aspect of a thing which *for our purpose* we regard as its essential aspect, as the representative of the entire thing. In comparison with this aspect, whatever other properties and qualities the thing may have, are unimportant accidents which we may without blame ignore. But the essence, the ground of conception, varies with the end we have in view. A substance like oil has as many different essences as it has uses to different individuals. One man conceives it as a combustible, another as a lubricator, another as a food; the chemist thinks of it as a hydro-carbon; the furniture-maker as a darkener of wood; the speculator as a commodity whose market price to-day is this and to-morrow that. The soap-boiler, the physicist, the clothes-scourer severally ascribe to it other essences in relation to their needs. Ueberweg's doctrine[1] that the essential quality of a thing is the quality of most *worth*, is strictly true; but Ueberweg has failed to note that the worth is wholly relative to the temporary interests of the conceiver. And, even, when his interest is distinctly defined in his own mind, the discrimination of the quality in the object which has the closest connexion with it, is a thing which no rules can teach. The only *à priori* advice that can be given to a man embarking on life with a certain purpose is the somewhat barren counsel: Be sure that in the circumstances

[1] *Logic*, English tr., p. 139.

that meet you, you attend to the *right* ones for your purpose. To pick out the right ones is the measure of the man.
"Millions," says Hartmann, "stare at the phenomenon before
a *genialer Kopf* pounces on the concept."[2] The genius is simply
he to whom, when he opens his eyes upon the world, the
"right" characters are the prominent ones. The fool is he
who, with the same purposes as the genius, infallibly gets his
attention tangled amid the accidents.

Schopenhauer expresses well this ultimate truth when he
says that Intuition (by which in this passage he means the
power to distinguish at a glance the essence amid the accidents) "is not only the source of all knowledge, but is knowledge κατ' ἐξοχήν . . . is real *insight* . . . . *Wisdom*, the true
view of life, the right look at things, and the judgment that
hits the mark, proceed from the mode in which the man conceives the world which lies before him . . . . He who excels
in this talent knows the (Platonic) ideas of the world and of
life. Every case he looks at stands for countless cases; more
and more he goes on to conceive of each thing in accordance
with its true nature, and his acts like his judgments bear the
stamp of his insight. Gradually his face too acquires the
straight and piercing look, the expression of reason, and at
last of wisdom. For the direct sight of essences alone can set
its mark upon the face. Abstract knowledge about them has
no such effect."[3]

The right conception for the philosopher depends then on
his interests. Now the interest which he has above other men
is that of reducing the manifold in thought to simple form.
We can no more say why the philosopher is more peculiarly
sensitive to this delight, than we can explain the passion some
persons have for matching colours or for arranging cards in a
game of solitaire. All these passions resemble each other in
one point; they are all illustrations of what may be called the
æsthetic Principle of Ease. Our pleasure at finding that a
chaos of facts is at bottom the expression of a single underlying fact is like the relief of the musician at resolving a confused mass of sound into melodic or harmonic order. The
simplified result is handled with far less mental effort than the

[2]*Philosophie des Unbewussten*, 2te Auflage, p. 249.
[3]*Welt als Wille u. Vorstellung*, II., p. 83.

original data; and a philosophic conception of nature is thus
in no metaphorical sense a labor-saving contrivance. The passion for parsimony, for economy of means in thought, is thus
the philosophic passion *par excellence*, and any character or
aspect of the world's phenomena which gathers up their diversity into simplicity will gratify that passion, and in the philosopher's mind stand for that essence of things compared
with which all their other determinations may by him be
overlooked.

More universality or extensiveness is then the one mark the
philosopher's conceptions must possess. Unless they appear in
an enormous number of cases they will not bring the relief
which is his main theoretic need. The knowledge of things by
their causes, which is often given as a definition of rational
knowledge, is useless to him unless the causes converge to a
minimum number whilst still producing the maximum number of effects. The more multiple are the instances he can see
to be cases of his fundamental concept, the more flowingly
does his mind rove from fact to fact in the world. The phenomenal transitions are no real transitions; each item is the
same old friend with a slightly altered dress. This passion for
unifying things may gratify itself, as we all know, at truth's
expense. Everyone has friends bent on system and everyone
has observed how, when their system has once taken definite
shape, they become absolutely blind and insensible to the
most flagrant facts which cannot be made to fit into it. The
ignoring of data is, in fact, the easiest and most popular mode
of obtaining unity in one's thought.

But leaving these vulgar excesses let us glance briefly at
some more dignified contemporary examples of the hyper-
trophy of the unifying passion.

Its ideal goal gets permanent expression in the great notion
of Substance, the underlying One in which all differences are
reconciled. D'Alembert's often quoted lines express the postulate in its most abstract shape: "L'univers, pour qui sauroit
l'embrasser d'un seul point de vue, ne seroit, s'il est permis de
le dire, qu'un fait unique et une grande vérité." Accordingly
Mr. Spencer, after saying on page 158 of the first volume of his
Psychology, that no effort enables us to assimilate Feeling and
Motion, they have nothing in common, cannot refrain on

page 162 from invoking abruptly an "Unconditioned Being common to the two."

The craving for Monism at any cost is the parent of the entire evolutionist movement of our day, so far as it pretends to be more than history. The Philosophy of Evolution tries to show how the world at any given time may be conceived as absolutely identical, except in appearance, with itself at all past times. What it most abhors is the admission of anything which, appearing at a given point, should be judged essentially other than what went before. Notwithstanding the *lacunae* in Mr. Spencer's system; notwithstanding the vagueness of his terms; in spite of the sort of jugglery by which his use of the word "nascent" is made to veil the introduction of new primordial factors like consciousness, as if, like the girl in *Midshipman Easy*, he could excuse the illegitimacy of an infant, by saying it was a very little one — in spite of all this, I say, Mr. Spencer is, and is bound to be, the most popular of all philosophers, because more than any other he seeks to appease our strongest theoretic craving. To undiscriminating minds his system will be a sop; to acute ones a program full of suggestiveness.

When Lewes asserts in one place that the nerve-process and the feeling which accompanies it are not two things but only two "aspects" of one and the same thing, whilst in other passages he seems to imply that the cognitive feeling and the outward thing cognized (which is always other than the nerve-process accompanying the cognitive act) are again one thing in two aspects (giving us thereby as the ultimate truth One Thing in Three Aspects, very much as Trinitarian Christians affirm it to be One God in Three Persons),—the vagueness of his mode only testifies to the imperiousness of his need of unity.

The crowning feat of unification at any cost is seen in the Hegelian denial of the Principle of Contradiction. One who is willing to allow that A and not-A are one, can be checked by few farther difficulties in Philosophy.

III

But alongside of the passion for simplification, there exists a sister passion which in some minds—though they perhaps form the minority—is its rival. This is the passion for distinguishing; it is the impulse to be *acquainted* with the parts rather than to comprehend the whole. Loyalty to clearness and integrity of perception, dislike of blurred outlines, of vague identifications, are its characteristics. It loves to recognize particulars in their full completeness, and the more of these it can carry the happier it is. It is the mind of Cuvier *versus* St. Hilaire, of Hume *versus* Spinoza. It prefers any amount of incoherence, abruptness and fragmentariness (so long as the literal details of the separate facts are saved) to a fallacious unity which swamps things rather than explains them.

Clearness *versus* Simplicity is then the theoretic dilemma, and a man's philosophic attitude is determined by the balance in him of these two cravings. When John Mill insists that the ultimate laws of nature cannot possibly be less numerous than the distinguishable qualities of sensation which we possess, he speaks in the name of this æsthetic demand for clearness. When Prof. Bain says[4]:—"There is surely nothing to be dissatisfied with, to complain of, in the circumstance that the elements of our experience are, in the last resort, two, and not one. . . . Instead of our being 'unfortunate' in not being able to know the essence of either matter or mind—in not comprehending their union; our misfortune would rather be to have to know anything different from what we do know,"—he is animated by a like motive. All makers of architectonic systems like that of Kant, all multipliers of original principles, all dislikers of vague monotony, whether it bear the character of Eleatic stagnancy or of Heraclitic change, obey this tendency. *Ultimate kinds* of feeling bound together in harmony by laws, which themselves are *ultimate kinds* of relation, form the theoretic resting-place of such philosophers.

The unconditional demand which this need makes of a philosophy is that its fundamental terms should be representable. Phenomena are analyzable into feelings and relations. Causality is a relation between two feelings. To abstract the relation from the feelings, to unify all things by referring them to a first cause, and to leave this latter relation with no term of feeling before it, is to violate the fundamental habits of our thinking, to baffle the imagination, and to exasperate the minds of certain people much as everyone's eye is exasperated by a magic-lantern picture or a microscopic object out of focus. Sharpen it, we say, or for heaven's sake remove it altogether.

The matter is not at all helped when the word Substance is brought forward and the primordial causality said to obtain between this and the phenomena; for Substance *in se* cannot be directly imaged by feeling, and seems in fact but to be a peculiar form of relation between feelings—the relation of organic union between a group of them and time. Such relations, represented as non-phenomenal entities, become thus the *bête noire* and pet aversion of many thinkers. By being posited as existent they challenge our acquaintance but at the same instant defy it by being defined as noumenal. So far is this reaction against the treatment of relational terms as met-empirical entities carried, that the reigning British school seems to deny their function even in their legitimate sphere, namely as phenomenal elements or "laws" cementing the mosaic of our feelings into coherent form. Time, likeness, and unlikeness are the only phenomenal relations our English empiricists can tolerate. One of the earliest and perhaps the most famous expression of the dislike to relations considered abstractedly is the well-known passage from Hume: "When we run over libraries, persuaded of these principles, what havoc must we make? If we take in our hand any volume; of divinity or school metaphysics, for instance; let us ask, *Does it contain any abstract reasoning concerning quantity or number?* No. *Does it contain any experimental reasoning concerning matter of fact and existence?* No. Commit it then to the flames: For it can contain nothing but sophistry and illusion."[5]

Many are the variations which succeeding writers have played on this tune. As we spoke of the excesses of the unifying passion, so we may now say of the craving for clear representability that it leads often to an unwillingness to treat any abstractions whatever as if they were intelligible. Even to

[5]*Essays*, ed. Green and Grose, II., p. 135.

talk of space, time, feeling, power, &c., oppresses them with a strange sense of uncanniness. Anything to be real for them must be representable in the form of a *lump*. Its other concrete determinations may be abstracted from, but its *tangible* thinghood must remain. Minds of this order, if they can be brought to psychologize at all, abound in such phrases as "tracts" of consciousness, "areas" of emotion, "molecules" of feeling, "agglutinated portions" of thought, "gangs" of ideas &c., &c.

Those who wish an amusing example of this style of thought should read *Le Cerveau* by the anatomist Luys, surely the very worst book ever written on the much-abused subject of mental physiology. In another work, *Psychologie réaliste*, by P. Sièrebois (Paris 1876), it is maintained that "our ideas exist in us in a molecular condition, and are subject to continual movements. . . . Their mobility is as great as that of the molecules of air or any gas." When we fail to recall a word it is because our ideas are hid in some distant corner of the brain whence they cannot come to the muscles of articulation, or else "they have lost their ordinary fluidity." . . . "These ideal molecules are material portions of the brain which differs from all other matter precisely in this property which it possesses of subdividing itself into very attenuated portions which easily take on the likeness in form and quality of all external objects." In other words, when I utter the word "rhinoceros" an actual little microscopic rhinoceros gallops towards my mouth.

A work of considerable acuteness, far above the vulgar materialistic level, is that of Czolbe, *Grundzüge einer extensionalen Erkenntnisstheorie* (1875). This author explains our ideas to be extended substances endowed with mutual penetrability. The matter of which they are composed is "elastic like india-rubber." When "concentrated" by "magnetic self-attraction" into the middle of the brain, its "intensity" is such that it becomes conscious. When the attraction ceases, the idea-substance expands and diffuses itself into infinite space and so sinks from consciousness.

Again passing over these *quasi*-pathological excesses, we come to a permanent and, for our purpose, most important fact—the fact that many minds of the highest analytic power will tolerate in Philosophy no unifying terms but elements immanent in phenomena, and taken in their phenomenal and representable sense. Entities whose attributes are not directly given in feeling, phenomenal relations functioning as entities, are alike rejected. Spinozistic Substance, Spencerian Unknowable, are abhorred as unrepresentable things, numerically additional to the representable world. The substance of things for these clear minds can be no more than their common measure. The phenomena bear to it the same relation that the different numbers bear to unity. These contain no other matter than the repeated unit, but they may be classed as prime numbers, odd numbers, even numbers, square numbers, cube numbers, &c., just as truly and naturally as we class concrete things. The molecular motions, of which physicists hope that some day all events and properties will be seen to consist, form such an immanent unity of colossal simplifying power. The "infinitesimal event" of various modern writers, Taine for example, with its two "aspects," inner and outer, reaches still farther in the same direction. Writers of this class, if they deal with Psychology, repudiate the "soul" as a scholastic entity. The phenomenal unity of consciousness must flow from some element immutably present in each and every representation of the individual and binding the whole into one. To unearth and accurately define this phenomenal self becomes one of the fundamental tasks of Psychology.

But the greatest living insister on the principle that unity in our account of things shall not overwhelm clearness, is Charles Renouvier. His masterly exposition of the irreducible categories of thought in his *Essais de critique générale* ought to be far better known among us than it is. The onslaughts which this eminently clear-headed writer has made and still makes in his weekly journal, the *Critique philosophique*, on the vanity of the evolutionary principle of simplification, which supposes that you have explained away all distinctions by simply saying "they arise" instead of "they are," form the ablest criticism which the school of Evolution has received. Difference "thus displaced, transported from the *esse* to the *fieri*, is it any the less postulated? And does the *fieri* itself receive the least commencement of explanation when we suppose that everything which occurs, occurs little by little, by insensible degrees, so that, if we look at any one of these degrees, what happens does so as easily and clearly as if it did not happen at all? . . . If we want a continuous production *ex nihilo*, why not say so frankly, and abandon the idea of a 'transition without break' which explains really nothing?"[6]

IV

Our first conclusion may then be this: No system of philosophy can hope to be universally accepted among men which grossly violates either of the two great æsthetic needs of our logical nature, the need of unity and the need of clearness, or entirely subordinates the one to the other. Doctrines of mere disintegration like that of Hume and his successors, will be as widely unacceptable on the one hand as doctrines of merely engulphing substantialism like those of Schopenhauer, Hartmann and Spencer on the other. Can we for our own guidance briefly sketch out here some of the conditions of most favorable compromise?

In surveying the connexions between data we are immediately struck by the fact that some are more intimate than others. Propositions which express those we call necessary truths; and with them we contrast the laxer collocations and sequences which are known as empirical, habitual or merely fortuitous. The former seem to have an *inward* reasonableness which the latter are deprived of. The link, whatever it be, which binds the two phenomena together, seems to extend from the heart of one into the heart of the next, and to be an essential reason why the facts should always and indefeasibly be as we now know them. "Within the pale we stand." As Lotze says[7]: — "The intellect is not satisfied with merely associated representations. In its constant critical activity thought seeks to refer each representation to the rational ground which conditions the alliance of what is associated and proves that what is grouped *belongs* together. So it separates from each other those impressions which merely coalesce without inward connexions, and it renews (while corroborating them)

---

[6]*Critique philosophique*, 12 Juillet, 1877, p. 383.
[7]*Mikrokosmus*, 2nd ed., I., p. 261.

the bonds of those which, by the inward kinship of their content, have a right to permanent companionship."

On the other hand many writers seem to deny the existence
of any such inward kinship or rational bond between things.
Hume says: "All our distinct perceptions are distinct existences, and the mind never perceives any real connexion
among distinct existences."[8]

Hume's followers are less bold in their utterances than their
master, but throughout all recent British Nominalism we find
the tendency to enthrone mere juxtaposition as lord of all and
to make of the Universe what has well been styled a Nulliverse. "For my part," says Prof. Huxley, "I utterly repudiate
and anathematise the intruder [Necessity]. Fact I know; and
Law I know; but what is this Necessity, save an empty
shadow of the mind's own throwing?"

And similarly J. S. Mill writes: "What is called explaining
one law by another is but substituting one mystery for another, and does nothing to render the course of nature less
mysterious. We can no more assign a *why* for the more extensive laws than for the partial ones. The explanation may substitute a mystery which has become familiar and has grown to
seem not mysterious for one which is still strange. And this is
the meaning of explanation in common parlance. . . . The
laws thus explained or resolved are said to be *accounted for*;
but the expression is incorrect if taken to mean anything more
than what has been stated."[9]

And yet the very pertinacity with which such writers remind us that our explanations are in a strict sense of the word
no explanations at all; that our causes never unfold the essential nature of their effects; that we never seize the inward reason why attributes cluster as they do to form things, seems to
prove that they possess in their minds some ideal or pattern of
what a genuine explanation would be like in case they should
meet it. How could they brand our current explanations as
spurious, if they had no positive notion whatever of the real
thing?

Now have we the real thing? And yet may they be partly

[8]*Treatise on Human Nature*, ed. T. H. Green, I., p. 559.
[9]*Logic*, 8th ed., I., p. 549.

right in their denials? Surely both; and I think that the shares
of truth may be easily assigned. Our "laws" *are* to a great
extent but facts of larger growth, and yet things *are* inwardly
and necessarily connected notwithstanding. The entire process of philosophic simplification of the chaos of sense consists of two acts, Identification and Association. Both are
principles of union and therefore of theoretic rationality; but
the rationality between things associated is outward and
custom-bred. Only when things are identified do we pass inwardly and necessarily from one to the other.

The first step towards unifying the chaos is to classify its
items. "Every concrete thing," says Prof. Bain, "falls into as
many classes as it has attributes."[10] When we pick out a certain attribute to conceive it by, we literally and strictly identify it *in that respect* with the other concretes of the class
having that attribute for its essence, concretes which the attribute recalls. When we conceive of sugar as a white thing it
is *pro tanto* identical with snow; as a sweet thing it is the same
as liquorice; *quâ* hydro-carbon, as starch. The attribute picked
out may be *per se* most uninteresting and familiar, but if
things superficially very diverse can be found to possess it
buried within them and so be assimilated with each other,
"the mind feels a peculiar and genuine satisfaction. . . . The
intellect, oppressed with the variety and multiplicity of facts,
is joyfully relieved by the simplification and the unity of a
great principle."[11]

Who does not feel the charm of thinking that the moon
and the apple are, as far as their relation to the earth goes,
identical? of knowing respiration and combustion to be one?
of understanding that the balloon rises by the same law
whereby the stone sinks? of feeling that the warmth in one's
palm when one rubs one's sleeve is identical with the motion
which the friction checks? of recognizing the difference between beast and fish to be only a higher degree of that between human father and son? of believing our strength when
we climb or chop to be no other than the strength of the

[10]*Ment. and Mor. Science*, p. 177.
[11]Bain, *Logic*, II., p. 120.

THE SENTIMENT OF RATIONALITY 963

sun's rays which made the oats grow out of which we got our morning meal?

We shall presently see how the attribute performing this unifying function, becomes associated with some other attribute to form what is called a general law. But at present we must note that many sciences remain in this first and simplest classificatory stage. A classificatory science is merely one the fundamental concepts of which have few associations or none with other concepts. When I say a man, a lizard, and a frog are one in being vertebrates, the identification, delightful as it is in itself, leads me hardly any farther. "The idea that all the parts of a flower are modified leaves, reveals a connecting law, which surprises us into acquiescence. But now try and define the leaf, determine its essential characteristics, so as to include all the forms that we have named. You will find yourself in a difficulty, for all distinctive marks vanish, and you have nothing left, except that a leaf in the wider sense of the term is a lateral appendage of the axis of a plant. Try then to express the proposition 'the parts of the flower are modified leaves' in the language of scientific definition, and it reads, 'the parts of the flower are lateral appendages of the axis.' "[12] Truly a bald result! Yet a dozen years ago there hardly lived a naturalist who was not thrilled with rapture at identifications in "philosophic" anatomy and botany exactly on a par with this. Nothing could more clearly show that the gratification of the sentiment of rationality depends hardly at all on the worth of the attribute which strings things together but almost exclusively on the mere fact of their being strung at all. Theological implications were the utmost which the attributes of archetypal zoology carried with them, but the wretched poverty of these proves how little they had to do with the enthusiasm engendered by archetypal identifications. Take Agassiz's conception of class-characters, order-characters &c., as "thoughts of God." What meager thoughts! Take Owen's archetype of the vertebrate skeleton as revealing the artistic temperament of the Creator. It is a grotesque figure with neither beauty nor ethical suggestiveness, fitted rather to discredit than honor the

[12]Helmholtz, *Popular Scientific Lectures*, p. 47.

Divine Mind. In short the conceptions led no farther than the identification pure and simple. The transformation which Darwin has effected in the classificatory sciences is simply this—that in his theory the class-essence is not a unifying attribute pure and simple, but an attribute with wide associations. When a frog, a man and a lizard are recognized as one, not simply in having the same back-bone, &c., but in being all offspring of one parent, our thought instead of coming to a standstill, is immediately confronted with further problems and, we hope, solutions. Who were that parent's ancestors and cousins? Why was he chosen out of all to found such an enormous line? Why did he himself perish in the struggle to survive? &c.

Association of class-attributes *inter se*, is thus the next great step in the mind's simplifying industry. By it Empirical Laws are founded and sciences, from classificatory, become explanatory. Without it we should be in the position of a judge who could only decide that the cases in his court belonged each to a certain class, but who should be inhibited from passing sentence, or attaching to the class-name any further notion of duty, liability, or penalty. This *coupling* of the class-concept with certain determinate *consequences* associated therewithal, is what is practically important in the laws of nature as in those of society.

When, for example, we have identified prisms, bowls of water, lenses and strata of air as distorting media, the next step is to learn that all distorting media refract light rays towards the perpendicular. Such additional determination makes a law. But this law itself may be as inscrutable as the concrete fact we started from. The entrance of a ray and its swerving towards the perpendicular, may be simply *associated* properties, with, for aught we see, no inwardly necessary bond, coupled together as empirically as the colour of a man's eyes with the shape of his nose.

But such an empirical law may have its terms again classified. The essence of the medium may be to retard the light-wave's speed. The essence (in an obliquely-striking wave) of deflection towards the perpendicular may be earlier retardation of that part of the wave-front which enters first, so that the remaining portion swings round it before getting in.

Medium and bending towards perpendicular thus coalesce into the one identical fact of retardation. This being granted gives an inward explanation of all above it. But retardation itself remains an empirical coupling of medium and light-movement until we have classified both under a single concept. The explanation reached by the insight that two phenomena are at bottom one and the same phenomenon, is rational in the ideal and ultimate sense of the word. The ultimate identification of the subject and predicate of a mathematical theorem, an identification which we can always reach in our reasonings, is the source of the inward necessity of mathematical demonstration. We see that the top and bottom of a parallelogram must be equal as soon as we have unearthed in the parallelogram the attribute that it consists of two equal, juxtaposed triangles of which its top and bottom form homologous sides—that is, as soon as we have seen that top and bottom have an identical essence, their length, as being such sides, and that their position is an accident. This criterion of identity is that which we all unconsciously use when we discriminate between brute fact and explained fact. There is no other test.

In the contemporary striving of physicists to interpret every event as a case of motion concealed or visible, we have an adumbration of the way in which a common essence may make the sensible heterogeneity of things inwardly rational. The cause is one motion, the effect the same motion transferred to other molecules; in other words, physics aims at the same kind of rationality as mathematics. In the second volume of Lewes's *Problems* we find this anti-Humean view that the effect is the "procession" of the cause, or that they are one thing in two aspects brought prominently forward.[13]

And why, on the other hand, do all our contemporary physical philosophers so view with each other in the zeal with which they reiterate that in reality nerve-processes and brain-tremors "explain" nothing of our feelings? Why does "the

---

[13]This view is in growing favor with thinkers fed from empirical sources. See Wundt's *Physikalischen Axiome* and the important article by A. Riehl, "Causalität und Identität," in *Vierteljahrssch. f. wiss. Philos.* Bd. I., p. 365. The Humean view is ably urged by Chauncey Wright, *Philosophical Discussions*, N.Y. 1877, p. 406.

chasm between the two classes of phenomena still remain intellectually impassable"?[14] Simply because, in the words of Spencer which we quoted a few pages back, feeling and motion have nothing whatever in common, no identical essence by which we can conceive both, and so, as Tyndall says, "pass by a process of reasoning from one to the other." The "double-aspect" school postulate the blank form of "One and the Same Fact," appeal to the image of the circle which is both convex and concave, and think that they have by this symbolic identification made the matter seem more rational.

Thus then the connexions of things become strictly rational only when, by successive substitutions of essences for things, and higher for lower essences, we succeed in reaching a point of view from which we can view the things as one. A and B are concretes; *a* and *b* are partial attributes with which for the present case we conceive them to be respectively identical (classify them) and which are coupled by a general law. M is a further attribute which rationally explains the general law as soon as we perceive it to form the essence of both *a* and *b*, as soon as we identify them with each other through it. The softening of asphalt pavements in August is explained first by the empirical law that heat, which is the essence of August, produces melting, which is the essence of the pavement's change, and secondly this law is inwardly rationalized by the conception of both heat and melting being at bottom one and the same fact, namely, increased molecular mobility.

Proximate and ultimate explanations are then essentially the same thing. Classification involves all that is inward in any explanation, and a perfected rationalization of things means only a *completed* classification of them. Everyone feels that all explanation whatever, even by reference to the most proximate empirical law, does involve something of the essence of inward rationalization. How else can we understand such words as these from Prof. Huxley? "The fact that it is impossible to comprehend how it is that a physical state gives rise to a mental state, no more lessens the value of our [empirical] explanation in the latter case, than the fact that it is utterly

[14]Tyndall, *Fragments of Science*, 2nd ed., p. 121.

impossible to comprehend how motion is communicated from one body to another, weakens the force of the explanation of the motion of one billiard ball by showing that another has hit it."[15]

To return now to the philosophic problem. It is evident that our idea of the universe cannot assume an inwardly rational shape until each separate phenomenon is conceived as fundamentally identical with every other. But the important fact to notice is that in the steps by which this end is reached the really rationalizing, pregnant moments are the successive steps of conception, the moments of picking out essences. The association of these essences into laws, the empirical coupling, is done by nature for us and is hardly worthy to be called an intellectual act; and on the other hand the coalescence-into-one of all items in which the same essence is discerned, in other words the perception that an essence whether ultimate, simple and universal, or proximate and specific, is identical with itself wherever found, is a barren truism. The living question always is, Where *is* it found? To stand before a phenomenon and say *what* it is; in other words to pick out from it the embedded character (or characters) also embedded in the maximum number of *other* phenomena, and so identify it with them—here lie the stress and strain, here the test of the philosopher. So we revert to what we said far back: the genius can do no more than this; in Butler's words—

> "He knows *what's what*, and that's as high
> As metaphysic wit can fly."[16]

[15]"Modern 'Symposium,'" *Nineteenth Century*, Vol. I., 1877.

[16]This doctrine is perfectly congruous with the conclusion that identities are the only propositions necessary *à priori*, though of course it does not necessarily lead to that conclusion, since there may be in things elements which are not simple but bilateral or synthetic, like straightness and shortness in a line, convexity and concavity in a curve. Should the empiricists succeed in their attempt to resolve such Siamese-twin elements into habitual juxtapositions, the Principle of Identity would become the only *à priori* truth, and the philosophic problem like all our ordinary problems would become a question as to facts: *What* are these facts which we perceive to exist? Are there any existing facts corresponding to this or that conceived class? Lewes, in the interesting discussion on necessary and contingent truth in the Prolegomena to his *History* and in Chap. XIII. of his first *Problem*, seems at first sight to take up an opposite position, in that he maintains our commonly

V

We have now to ask ourselves how far this identification may be legitimately carried and what, when perfected, its real worth is. But before passing to these further questions we had best secure our ground by defending our fundamental notion itself from nominalistic attacks. The reigning British school has always denied that the same attribute *is* identical with it-self in different individuals. I started above with the assumption that when we look at a subject with a certain purpose, regard it from a certain point of view, some one attribute becomes its essence and identifies it, *pro hac vice*, with a class. To this James Mill replies: "But what is meant by a mode of regarding things? This is mysterious; and is as mysteriously explained, when it is said to be the taking into view the particulars in which individuals agree. For what is there, which it is possible for the mind to take into view, in that in which individuals agree? Every colour is an individual colour, every size is an individual size, every shape is an individual shape. But things have no individual colour in common, no individual shape in common, no individual size in common; that is to say, they have neither shape, colour, nor size in common. What, then, is it which they have in common, which the mind can take into view? Those who affirmed that it was some-

---

so-called contingent truths to be really necessary. But his treatment of the question most beautifully confirms the doctrine I have advanced in the text. If the proposition "A is B" is ever true, he says it is so necessarily. But he proves the necessity by showing that what we mean by A is its essential attribute x, and what we mean by B is again x. Only *in so far* as A and B are identical is the proposition true. But he admits that a fact sensibly just like A may lack x, and a fact sensibly unlike B may have it. In either case the proposition, to be true, must change. The contingency which he banishes from propositions, he thus houses in their terms; making as I do the act of conception, subsumption, classification, intuition, naming, or whatever else one may prefer to call it, the pivot on which thought turns. Before this act there is infinite indeterminateness—A and B may be anything. After the act there is the absolute certainty of truism—all x's are the same. *In* the act—is A, x? is B, x? or not?—we have the sphere of truth and error, of living experience, in short, of Fact. As Lewes himself says: "The only necessity is that a thing is what it is; the only contingency is that our proposition may not state what the thing is" (*Problems*, Vol. I., p. 395).

thing, could by no means tell. They substituted words for things; using vague and mystical phrases, which, when examined, meant nothing";[17] the truth being according to this heroic author, that the only thing that can be possessed in common is a name. Black in the coat and black in the shoe agree only in that both are named black—the fact that on this view the *name* is never the same when used twice being quite overlooked. But the blood of the giants has grown weak in these days, and the nominalistic utterances of our contemporaries are like sweet-bells jangled, sadly out of tune. If they begin with a clear nominalistic note, they are sure to end with a grating rattle which sounds very like *universalia in re*, if not *ante rem*. In M. Taine,[18] who may fairly be included in the British School, they are almost *ante rem*. This *bruit de cloche fêlée*, as the doctors say, is pathognomonic of the condition of Ockham's entire modern progeny.

But still we may find expressions like this: "When I say that the sight of any object gives me the *same* sensation or emotion to-day that it did yesterday, or the *same* which it gives to some other person, this is evidently an incorrect application of the word *same*; for the feeling which I had yesterday is gone never to return. . . . Great confusion of ideas is often produced, and many fallacies engendered, in otherwise enlightened understandings, by not being sufficiently alive to the fact (in itself not always to be avoided), that they use the same name to express ideas so different as those of identity and undistinguishable resemblance."[19]

What are the exact facts? Take the sensation I got from a cloud yesterday and from the snow to-day. The white of the

[17]*Analysis*, Vol. I., p. 249.

[18]How can M. Taine fail to have perceived that the entire doctrine of "Substitution" so clearly set forth in the nominalistic beginning of his brilliant book is utterly senseless except on the supposition of realistic principles like those which he so admirably expounds at its close? How *can* the image be a useful substitute for the sensation, the tendency for the image, the name for the tendency, unless sensation, image, tendency and name be *identical* in some respect, in respect namely of function, of the relations they enter into? Were this realistic basis laid at the outset of Taine's *De l'Intelligence*, it would be one of the most consistent instead of one of the most self-contradictory works of our day.

[19]J. S. Mill, *Logic*, 8th ed., I., p. 77.

snow and that of the cloud differ in place, time and associates; they agree in quality, and we may say in origin, being in all probability both produced by the activity of the same brain tract. Nevertheless, John Mill denies our right to call the quality the same. He says that *it* essentially differs in every different occasion of its appearance, and that no two phenomena of which it forms part are really identical even as far as *it* goes. Is it not obvious that to maintain this view he must abandon the phenomenal plane altogether? Phenomenally considered, the white *per se is* identical with itself wherever found in snow or in cloud, to-day or to-morrow. If any nominalist deny the identity I ask him to point out the difference. *Ex hypothesi* the qualities are sensibly indistinguishable, and the only difference he can indicate is that of time and place; but these are not differences in the quality. If our quality be not the same with itself, what meaning has the word "same"? Our adversary though silenced may still grudge assent, but if he analyze carefully the grounds of this reluctance he will, I think, find that it proceeds from a difficulty in believing that the *cause* of the quality can be just the same at different times. In other words he abandons altogether the platform of the sensible phenomenon and ascends into the empyrean, postulating some inner noumenal principle of *quality + time + place + concomitants*. The entire group being never twice alike, of course this ground, or being *in se*, of the quality must each time be distinct and, so to speak, personal. This transcendental view is frankly avowed by Mr. Spencer in his *Psychology*, II., p. 63— (the passage is too complex to quote); but all nominalists must start from it, if they think clearly at all.[20]

We, who are phenomenists, may leave all metaphysical entities which have the power of producing whiteness to their fate, and content ourselves with the irreversible *datum* of

[20]I fear that even after this some persons will remain unconvinced, but then it seems to me the matter has become a dispute about words. If my supposed adversary, when he says that different times and places prevent a quality which appears in them from ever being twice the same, will admit that they do not make it in any conceivable way *different*, I will willingly abandon the words "same" and "identical" to his fury; though I confess it becomes rather inconvenient to have no single positive word left by which to indicate complete absence of difference.

perception that the whiteness after it *is* manifested is the same, be it here or be it there. Of all abstractions such entities are the emptiest, being ontological hypostatizations of the mere susceptibility of being distinguished, whilst this susceptibility has its real, nameable, phenomenal ground all the while, in the time, place, and relations affected by the attribute considered.

The truly wise man will take the phenomenon in its entirety and permanently sacrifice no one aspect to another. Time, place, and relations differ, he will freely say; but let him just as freely admit that the quality is identical with itself through all these differences. Then if, *to satisfy the philosophic interest*, it becomes needful to conceive this identical part as the essence of the several entire phenomena, he will gladly call them one; whilst if some other interest be paramount, the points of difference will become essential and the identity an accident. Realism is eternal and invincible in this phenomenal sense.

We have thus vindicated against all assailants our title to consider the world as a matter susceptible of rational formulation in the deepest, most inward sense, and not as a disintegrated sand-heap; and we are consequently at liberty to ask: (1) Whether the mutual identification of its items meet with any necessary limit; and (2) What, supposing the operation completed, its real worth and import amount to.

VI

In the first place, when we have rationally explained the connexion of the items A and B by identifying both with their common attribute x, it is obvious that we have really explained only so much of these items as *is* x. To explain the connexion of choke-damp and suffocation by the lack of oxygen is to leave untouched all the other peculiarities both of choke-damp and of suffocation, such as convulsions and agony on the one hand, density and explosibility on the other. In a word, so far as A and B contain l, m, n and o, p, q, respectively in addition to x, they are not explained by x. Each additional particularity makes its distinct appeal to our rational craving. A single explanation of a fact only explains it from a single point of view.[21] The entire fact is not accounted for until each and all of its characters have been identified with their likes elsewhere. To apply this now to universal formulas we see that the explanation of the world by molecular movements explains it only so far as it actually *is* such movements. To invoke the "Unknowable" explains only so much as is unknowable; "Love" only so much as is love; "Thought" so much as is thought; "Strife" so much as is strife. All data whose actual phenomenal quality cannot be identified with the attribute invoked as Universal Principle, remain outside as ultimate, independent *kinds* or *natures*, associated by empirical laws with the fundamental attribute but devoid of truly rational kinship with it. If A and B are to be *thoroughly* rationalized together, *l*, *m*, *n* and *o*, *p*, *q*, must each and all turn out to be so many cases of *x* in disguise. This kind of wholesale identification is being now attempted by physicists when they conceive of all the ancient, separate Forces as so many determinations of one and the same essence, molecular mass, position and velocity.

Suppose for a moment that this idea were carried out for the physical world,—the subjective sensations produced by the different molecular energies, colour, sound, taste, &c., &c., the relations of likeness and contrast, of time and position, of ease and effort, the emotions of pain and delight, in short, all the mutually irreducible categories of mental life, would still remain over. Certain writers strive in turn to reduce all these to a common measure, the primordial unit of feeling, or infinitesimal mental event which builds them up as bricks build houses. But this case is wholly different from the last. The physical molecule is conceived not only as having a being *in se* apart from representation, but as being essentially of representable kind. With magnified perceptions we should

[21]In the number of the *Journal of Speculative Philosophy* for April 1879, Prof. John Watson most admirably asserts and expresses the truth which constitutes the back-bone of this article, namely that every manner of conceiving a fact is relative to some interest, and that there are no absolutely essential attributes—every attribute having the right to call itself essential in turn, and the truth consisting of nothing less than all of them together. I avow myself unable to comprehend as yet this author's Hegelian point of view, but his pages 164 to 172 are a most welcome corroboration of what I have striven to advance in the text.

actually see it. The mental molecule, on the other hand, has by its very definition no existence except in being felt, and yet by the same definition never is felt. It is neither a fact in consciousness nor a fact out of consciousness, and falls to the ground as a transcendental absurdity. Nothing could be more inconclusive than the empirical arguments for the existence of this noumenal feeling which Taine and Spencer draw from the sense of hearing.

But let us for an instant waive all this and suppose our feelings reduced to one. We should then have two primordial natures, the molecule of matter and the molecule of mind, coupled by an empirical law. Phenomenally incommensurable, the attempt to reduce them to unity by calling them two "aspects" is vain so long as it is not pointed out who is there *adspicere*; and the *Machtspruch* that they are expressions of one underlying Reality has no rationalizing function so long as that reality is confessed unknowable. Nevertheless the absolute necessity of an identical substratum for the different species of feeling on the one hand, and the genera feeling and motion on the other, if we are to have any evolutionary *explanation* of things, will lead to ever renewed attempts at an atomistic hylozoism. Already Clifford and Taine, Spencer, Fechner, Zöllner, G. S. Hall, and more besides, have given themselves up to this ideal.

But again let us waive this criticism and admit that even the chasm between feeling and motion may be rationally bridged by the conception of the bilateral atom of being. Let us grant that this atom by successive compoundings with its fellows builds up the universe; is it not still clear that each item in the universe would still be explained only as to its general *quality* and not as to its other particular determinations? The particulars depend on the exact number of primordial atoms existing at the outset and their exact distances from each other. The "universal formula" of Laplace which Du Bois-Reymond has made such striking use of in his lecture *Ueber die Grenzen des Naturerkennens*, cannot possibly get along with fewer than this almost infinite number of data. Their homogeneity does not abate their infinity—each is a separate empirical fact.

And when we now retract our provisional admissions, and

deny that feelings incommensurable *inter se* and with motion can be possibly unified, we see at once that the reduction of the phenomenal Chaos to rational form must stop at a certain point. It is a limited process,—bounded by the number of elementary attributes which cannot be mutually identified, the specific *qualia* of representation, on the one hand, and, on the other, by the number of entities (atoms or monads or what not) with their complete mathematical determinations, requisite for deducing the fulness of the concrete world. All these irreducible data form a system, no longer phenomenally rational, *inter se*, but bound together by what are for us empirical laws. We merely find the system existing as a matter of fact, and write it down. In short, a plurality of categories and an immense number of primordial entities, determined according to these categories, is the minimum of philosophic baggage, the only possible compromise between the need of clearness and the need of unity. All simplification, beyond this point, is reached either by throwing away the particular concrete determinations of the fact to be explained, or else it is illusory simplification. In the latter case it is made by invoking some sham term, some pseudo-principle, and conglomerating it and the data into one. The principle may be an immanent element but no true universal: Sensation, Thought, Will are principles of this kind; or it may be a transcendent entity like Matter, Spirit, Substance, the Unknowable, the Unconscious, &c.[22] Such attempts as these latter do but postulate unification, not effect it; and if taken avowedly to represent a mere claim, may be allowed to stand. But if offered as actual explanations, though they may serve as a sop to the rabble, they can but nauseate those whose philosophic appetite is genuine and entire. If we choose the former mode of simplification and are willing to abstract from the particulars of time, place and combination in the concrete world, we may simplify our elements very much by neglecting the numbers and collocations of our primordial elements and attending to their qualitative categories alone. The system formed by these will then really

[22]The idea of "God" in its popular function is open to neither of these objections, being conceived as a phenomenon standing in causal relation to other phenomena. As such, however, it has no unifying function of a properly *explanatory* kind.

rationalize the universe so far as its qualities go. Nothing can happen in it incommensurable with these data, and practically this abstract treatment of the world as quality is all that philosophers aim at. They are satisfied when they can see it to be a place in which none but these qualities appear, and in which the same quality appears not only once but identically repeats itself. They are willing to ignore, or leave to special sciences the knowledge of what times, places and concomitants the recurring quality is likely to affect. The *Essais de critique générale* of Renouvier form, to my mind, by far the ablest answer to the philosophic need thus understood, clearness and unity being there carried each to the farthest point compatible with the other's existence.

VII

And now comes the question as to the worth of such an achievement. How much better off is the philosopher when he has got his system than he was before it? As a mere phenomenal system it stands between two fires. On the one hand the unbridled craver of unity scorns it, as being incompletely rational, still to a great extent an empirical sand-heap; whilst on the other the practical man despises its empty and abstract barrenness. All it says is that the elements of the world are such and such and that each is identical with itself wherever found; but the question: Where is it found? (which is for the practical man the all-important question about each element) he is left to answer by his own wit. Which, of all the essences, shall here and now be held the essence of this concrete thing, the fundamental philosophy never attempts to decide. We seem thus led to the conclusion that a system of categories is, on the one hand, the only possible philosophy, but is, on the other, a most miserable and inadequate substitute for the fulness of the truth. It is a monstrous abridgment of things which like all abridgments is got by the absolute loss and casting out of real matter. This is why so few human beings truly care for Philosophy. The particular determinations which she ignores are the real matter exciting other æsthetic and practical needs, quite as potent and authoritative as hers. What does the moral enthusiast care for philosophical ethics? Why does the *Æsthetik* of every German philosopher appear to the artist like the abomination of desolation? What these men need every moment is a particular counsel, and no barren, universal truism.

> "Grau, theurer Freund, ist alle Theorie
> Und grün des Lebens goldner Baum."

The entire man, who feels all needs by turns, will take nothing as an equivalent for Life but the fulness of living itself. Since the essences of things are as a matter of fact spread out and disseminated through the whole extent of time and space, it is in their spread-outness and alternation that he will enjoy them. When weary of the concrete clash and dust and pettiness, he will refresh himself by an occasional bath in the eternal spring, or fortify himself by a daily look at the immutable Natures. But he will only be a visitor, not a dweller in the region; he will never carry the philosophic yoke upon his shoulders, and when tired of the gray monotony of her problems and insipid spaciousness of her results, will always escape gleefully into the teeming and dramatic richness of the concrete world.

So our study turns back here to its beginning. We started by calling every concept a teleological instrument (*supra* p. 952). No concept can be a valid substitute for a concrete reality except with reference to a particular interest in the conceiver. The interest of theoretic rationality, the relief of identification, is but one of a thousand human purposes. When others rear their heads it must pack up its little bundle and retire till its turn recurs. The exaggerated dignity and value that philosophers have claimed for their solutions is thus greatly reduced. The only virtue their theoretic conception need have is simplicity, and a simple conception is an equivalent for the world only so far as the world is simple; the world meanwhile, whatever simplicity it may harbor, being also a mightily complex affair. Enough simplicity remains, however, and enough urgency in our craving to reach it, to make the theoretic function one of the most invincible and authoritative of human impulses. All ages have their intellectual populace. That of our own day prides itself particularly on its love of Science and Facts and its contempt for all metaphysics. Just weaned from the Sunday-school nurture of its early years, with the taste of the catechism still in its mouth, it is perhaps not surprising that its palate should lack discrimination and fail to recognize how much of ontology is contained in the "Nature," "Force" and "Necessary Law," how much mysticism in the "Awe," "Progress" and "Loyalty to Truth" or whatever the other phrases may be with which it sweetens its rather meager fare of fragmentary physiology and physics. But its own inconsistency should teach it that the eradication of music, painting and poetry, games of chance and skill, manly sports and all other æsthetic energies from human life, would be an easy task compared with that suppression of Metaphysics which it aspires to accomplish. Metaphysics of some sort there must be. The only alternative is between the good Metaphysics of clear-headed Philosophy and the trashy Metaphysics of vulgar Positivism. Metaphysics, the quest of the last clear elements of things, is but another name for thought which seeks thorough self-consistency; and so long as men must think at all, some will be found willing to forsake all else to follow that ideal.

VIII

Suppose then the goal attained. Suppose we have at last a Metaphysics in which clearness and unity join friendly hands. Whether it be over a system of interlocked elements, or over a substance, or over such a simple fact as "phenomenon" or "representation," need not trouble us now. For the discussion which follows we will call the result the metaphysical Datum and leave its composite or simple nature uncertain. Whichever it be, and however limited as we have seen be the sphere of its utility, it satisfies, if no other need, at least the need of rationality. But now I ask: Can that which is the ground of rationality in all else be itself properly called rational? It would seem at first sight that in the sense of the word we have hitherto alone considered, it might. One is tempted at any rate to say that, since the craving for rationality in a theoretic or logical sense consists in the identification of one thing with all other outstanding things, a unique datum which left nothing else outstanding would leave no play for further rational demand, and might thus be said to quench that demand or to be rational *in se*. No *otherness* being left to annoy the mind we should sit down at peace.

In other words, just as the theoretic tranquillity of the boor results from his spinning no further considerations about his chaotic universe which may prevent him from going about his practical affairs; so any brute datum whatever (provided it were simple and clear) ought to banish mystery from the Universe of the philosopher and confer perfect theoretic peace, inasmuch as there would then be for him absolutely no further considerations to spin.

This in fact is what some persons think. Prof. Bain says: "A difficulty is solved, a mystery unriddled, when it can be shown to resemble something else; to be an example of a fact already known. Mystery is isolation, exception, or it may be apparent contradiction; the resolution of the mystery is found in assimilation, identity, fraternity. When all things are assimilated, so far as assimilation can go, so far as likeness holds, there is an end to explanation; there is an end to what the mind can do, or can intelligently desire. . . . The path of science, as exhibited in modern ages, is towards generality, wider and wider, until we reach the highest, the widest laws of every department of things; there explanation is finished, mystery ends, perfect vision is gained."

But unfortunately this first answer will not hold. Whether for good or evil, it is an empirical fact that the mind is so wedded to the process of seeing an *other* beside every item of its experience, that when the notion of an absolute datum which is all is presented to it, it goes through its usual procedure and remains *pointing* at the void beyond, as if in that lay further matter for contemplation. In short, it spins for itself the further positive consideration of a Nonentity enveloping the Being of its datum; and as that leads to no issue on the further side, back recoils the thought in a circle towards its datum again. But there is no logical identity, no natural bridge between nonentity and this particular datum, and the thought stands oscillating to and fro, wondering "Why was there anything but nonentity? Why just this universal datum and not another? Why anything at all?" and finds no end, in wandering mazes lost. Indeed, Prof. Bain's words are so un-

true that in reflecting men it is just when the attempt to fuse
the manifold into a single totality has been most successful,
when the conception of the universe as a *fait unique* (in
D'Alembert's words) is nearest its perfection, that the craving
for further explanation, the ontological θαυμάζειν arises in its
extremest pungency.

As Schopenhauer says, "The uneasiness which keeps the
never-resting clock of metaphysics in motion, is the consciousness that the non-existence of this world is just as possible as its existence."[23]

The notion of Nonentity may thus be called the parent of
the philosophic craving in its subtlest and profoundest sense.
Absolute existence is absolute mystery. Although *selbstständig*, it is not *selbstverständlich*; for its relations with the Nothing remain unmediated to our understanding. One philosopher only, so far as I know, has pretended to throw a logical
bridge over this chasm. Hegel, by trying to show that Nonentity and Being as actually determined are linked together
by a series of successive identities, binds the whole of possible thought into an adamantine unity with no conceivable
outlying notion to disturb the free rotary circulation of the
mind within its bounds. Since such unchecked motion constitutes the feeling of rationality, he must be held, if he has succeeded, to have eternally and absolutely quenched all its
logical demands.

But for those who, like most of us, deem Hegel's heroic
effort to have failed, nought remains but to confess that
when all has been unified to its supreme degree, (Prof. Bain
to the contrary notwithstanding), the notions of a Nonentity,
or of a possible Other than the actual, may still haunt our
imagination and prey upon the ultimate data of our system.
The bottom of Being is left logically opaque to us, a *datum*
in the strict sense of the word, something which we simply
come upon and find, and about which, (if we wish to act),
we should pause and wonder as little as possible. In this
confession lies the lasting truth of Empiricism, and in it
Empiricism and imaginative Faith join hands. The logical attitude of both is identical, they both say there is a *plus ultra*

---

[23] *Welt als Wille &c.*, 3 Auflage, I., p. 189.

beyond all we know, a womb of unimagined other possibility. They only differ in their sentimental temper: Empiricism says, "Into the *plus ultra* you have no right to carry your anthropomorphic affirmations"; Faith says, "You have no right to extend to it your denials." The mere ontologic emotion of wonder, of mystery, has in some minds such a tinge of the rapture of sublimity, that for this æsthetic reason alone, it will be difficult for any philosophic system completely to exorcise it.

In truth, the philosopher's logical tranquillity is after all in essence no other than the boor's. Their difference regards only the point at which each refuses to let further considerations upset the absoluteness of the data he assumes. The boor does so immediately, and is therefore liable at any moment to the ravages of many kinds of confusion and doubt. The philosopher does not do so till unity has been reached, and is therefore warranted against the inroads of *those* considerations—but only practically not essentially secure from the blighting breath of the *ultimate* "Why?" Positivism takes a middle ground, and with a certain consciousness of the beyond abruptly refuses by an inhibitory action of the will to think any further, stamps the ground and says "Physics, I espouse thee! for better or worse, be thou my absolute!"

The Absolute is what has not yet been transcended, criticized or made relative. So far from being something quintessential and unattainable as is so often pretended, it is practically the most familiar thing in life. Every thought is absolute to us at the moment of conceiving it or acting upon it. It only becomes relative in the light of further reflection. This may make it flicker and grow pale—the notion of nonentity may blow in from the infinite and extinguish the theoretic rationality of a universal datum. As regards this latter, absoluteness and rationality are in fact convertible terms. And the chief effort of the rationalizing philosopher must be to gain an absoluteness for his datum which shall be *stable* in the maximum degree, or as far as possible removed from exposure to those further considerations by which we saw that the vulgar *Weltanschauung* may so promptly be upset. I shall henceforward call the further considerations which may supervene and make relative or derationalize a mass of thought, the *reductive* of that thought. The reductive of absolute being is thus nonentity, or the notion of an *aliter possibile* which it involves. The reductive of an absolute physics is the thought that all material facts are representations in a mind. The reductive of absolute time, space, causality, atoms, &c., are the so-called antinomies which arise as soon as we think fully out the thoughts we have begun. The reductive of absolute knowledge is the constant potentiality of doubt, the notion that the next thought may always correct the present one—resulting in the notion that a noumenal world is there mocking the one we think we know. Whatever we think, some reductive seems in strict theoretic legitimacy always imminently hovering over our thought ready to blight it. Doubleness dismissed at the front door re-enters in the rear and spoils the rationality of the simple datum we flattered ourselves we had attained. Theoretically the task of the philosopher, if he cannot reconcile the datum with the reductive by the way of identification *à la* Hegel, is to exorcise the reductive so that the datum may hold up its head again and know no fear. Prof. Bain would no doubt say that nonentity was a pseud-idea not derived from experience and therefore meaningless, and so exorcise that reductive.[24] The antinomies may be exorcised by the distinction between potentiality and actuality.[25] The ordinary half educated materialist comforts himself against idealists by the notion that, after all, thought is such an obscure mystical form of existence that it is almost as bad as no existence at all, and need not be seriously taken into account by a sensible man.

If nothing else could be conceived than thoughts or fancies, these would be credited with the maximum of reality. Their reductive is the belief in an objective reality of which they are but copies. When this belief takes the form of the affirmation

[24]The author of *A Candid Examination of Theism* (Trübner, 1878) exorcises Nonentity by the notion of the all-excluding infinitude of Existence,—whether reasonably or not I refrain from deciding. The last chapter of this work (published a year after the present text was written), is on "the final Mystery of Things," and expresses in striking language much that I have said.

[25]See Renouvier: *Premier Essai.*

of a noumenal world contrasted with all possible thought, and therefore playing no other part than that of reductive pure and simple,—to discover the formula of exorcism becomes, and has been recognized ever since Kant to be, one of the principal tasks of philosophy rationally understood.

The reductive used by nominalists to discredit the self-identity of the same attribute in different phenomena is the notion of a still higher degree of identity. We easily exorcise this reductive by challenging them to show what the higher degree of sameness can possibly contain which is not already in the lower.

The notion of Nonentity is not only a reductive; it can assume upon occasion an exorcising function. If, for example, a man's ordinary mundane consciousness feels staggered at the improbability of an immaterial thinking-principle being the source of all things, Nonentity comes in and says, "Contrasted with me, (that is, considered simply as *existent*) one principle is as probable as another." If the same mundane consciousness recoils at the notion of providence towards individuals or individual immortality as involving, the one too infinite a subdivision of the divine attention, the other a too infinite accumulation of population in the heavens, Nonentity says, "As compared with me all quantities are one: the wonder is all there when God has found it worth His while to guard or save a single soul."

But if the philosopher fails to find a satisfactory formula of exorcism for his datum, the only thing he can do is to "blink" the reductive at a certain point, assume the Given as his necessary ultimate, and proceed to a life whether of contemplation or of action based on that. There is no doubt that this half wilful act of arrest, this acting on an opaque necessity, is accompanied by a certain pleasure. See the reverence of Carlyle for brute fact: "There is an infinite significance in Fact." "Necessity," says a German philosopher,[26] and he means not rational but simply given necessity, "is the last and highest point that we can reach in a rational conception of the world. . . . It is not only the interest of ultimate and

[26]Dühring: *Cursus der Philosophie*, Leipzig 1875, p. 35.

definitive knowledge, but also that of the feelings, to find a last repose and an ideal equilibrium, in an uttermost datum which can simply not be other than it is."

Such is the attitude of ordinary men in their theism, God's fiat being in physics and morals such an uttermost datum. Such also is the attitude of all hard-minded analysts and *Verstandesmenschen*. Renouvier and Hodgson, the two foremost contemporary philosophers, promptly say that of experience as a whole no account can be given, but do not seek to soften the abruptness of the confession or reconcile us with our impotence.

Such mediating attempts may be made by more mystical minds. The peace of rationality may be sought through ecstasy when logic fails. To religious persons of every shade of doctrine moments come when the world as it is seems so divinely orderly, and the acceptance of it by the heart so rapturously complete, that intellectual questions vanish, nay the intellect itself is hushed to sleep—as Wordsworth says, "Thought is not, in enjoyment it expires." Ontological emotion so fills the soul that ontological speculation can no longer overlap it and put her girdle of interrogation-marks around existence. Even the least religious of men must have felt with our national ontologic poet, Walt Whitman, when loafing on the grass on some transparent summer morning, that "Swiftly arose and spread around him the peace and knowledge that pass all the argument of the earth." At such moments of energetic living we feel as if there were something diseased and contemptible, yea vile, in theoretic grubbing and brooding. To feel "I *am* the truth" is to abolish the opposition between knowing and being.

Since the heart can thus wall out the ultimate irrationality which the head ascertains, the erection of its procedure into a systematized method would be a philosophic achievement of first-rate importance. As used by mystics hitherto it has lacked universality, being available for few persons and at few times, and even in these being apt to be followed by fits of "reaction" and "dryness"; but it may nevertheless be the forerunner of what will ultimately prove a true method. If all men could permanently say with Jacobi, "In my heart there is light," though they should for ever fail to give an articulate account of it, existence would really be rationalized.[27]

But if men should ever all agree that the mystical method is a subterfuge without logical pertinency, a plaster, but no cure, that the Hegelian method is fallacious, that the idea of Non-entity can therefore neither be exorcised nor identified, Empiricism will be the ultimate philosophy. Existence will be a brute Fact to which as a whole the emotion of ontologic wonder shall rightfully cleave, but remain eternally unsatisfied. This wonderfulness or mysteriousness will then be an essential attribute of the nature of things, and the exhibition and emphasizing of it will always continue to be an ingredient in the philosophic industry of the race. Every generation will produce its Job, its Hamlet, its Faust or its Sartor Resartus.

With this we seem to have exhausted all the possibilities of purely theoretic rationality. But we saw at the outset that when subjectively considered rationality can only be defined as perfectly unimpeded mental function. Impediments which arise in the purely theoretic sphere might perhaps be avoided

[27]A curious recent contribution to the construction of a universal mystical method is contained in the *Anæsthetic Revelation* by Benj. P. Blood (Amsterdam, N.Y., 1874). The author, who is a writer abounding in verbal felicities, thinks we may all grasp the secret of Being if we only intoxicate ourselves often enough with laughing-gas. "There is in the instant of recall from the anæsthetic stupor a moment in which the genius of being is revealed. . . . Patients try to speak of it but invariably fail in a lost mood of introspection. . . . But most will accept this as the central point of the illumination that sanity is not the basic quality of intelligence, . . . but that only in sanity is formal or contrasting thought, while the naked life is realized outside of sanity altogether. It is the instant contrast of this tasteless water of souls with formal thought as we *come to* that leaves the patient in an astonishment that the awful mystery of life is at last but a homely and common thing. . . . To minds of sanguine imagination there will be a sadness in the tenor of the mystery, as if the key-note of the universe were low—for no poetry, no emotion known to the normal sanity of man, can furnish a hint of its primeval prestige, and its all-but appalling solemnity; but for such as have felt sadly the instability of temporal things there is a comfort of serenity and ancient peace; while for the resolved and imperious spirit there are majesty and supremacy unspeakable." The logical characteristic of this state is said to be "an apodal sufficiency—to which sufficiency a wonder or fear of why it is sufficient cannot pertain and could be attributed only as an impossible disease or lack. . . . The disease of Metaphysics vanishes in the fading of the question and not in the coming of an answer."

if the stream of mental action should leave that sphere betimes and pass into the practical. The structural unit of mind is in these days, deemed to be a triad, beginning with a sensible impression, ending with a motion, and having a feeling of greater or less length in the middle. Perhaps the whole difficulty of attaining theoretic rationality is due to the fact that the very quest violates the nature of our intelligence, and that a passage of the mental function into the third stage before the second has come to an end in the *cul de sac* of its contemplation, would revive the energy of motion and keep alive the sense of ease and freedom which is its psychic counterpart. We must therefore inquire what constitutes the feeling of rationality in its *practical* aspect; but that must be done at another time and in another place.

NOTE:—This article is the first chapter of a psychological work on the motives which lead men to philosophize. It deals with the purely theoretic or logical impulse. Other chapters treat of practical and emotional motives and in the conclusion an attempt is made to use the motives as tests of the soundness of different philosophies.

On Some Omissions of
Introspective Psychology

As is well known, contradictory opinions about the value of introspection prevail. Comte and Maudsley, for example, call it worthless; Ueberweg and Brentano come near calling it infallible. Both opinions are extravagances; the first for reasons too obvious to be given, the second because it fails to discriminate between the immediate *feltness* of a mental state and its perception by a subsequent act of reflection. The *esse* of a mental state, the advocates of infallibility say, is its *sentiri*; it has no recondite mode of being "in-itself." It must therefore be felt as it really is, without chance of error. But the feltness which is its essence is its own immanent and intrinsic feltness at the moment of being experienced, and has nothing to do with the way in which future conscious acts may feel about it. Such *sentiri* in future acts is not what is meant by its *esse*. And yet such *postmortem sentiri* is the only way in which the introspective psychologist can grasp it. In its bare immediacy it is of no use to him. For his purposes it must be more than experienced; it must be remembered, reflected on, named, classed, known, related to other facts of the same order. And as in the naming, classing, and knowing of things in general we are notoriously fallible, why not also here? Comte is quite right in laying stress on the fact that a feeling, to be named, judged, or perceived, must be already past. No subjective state, whilst present, is its own object; its object is always something else. There are, it is true, cases in which we appear to be naming our present feeling, and so to be experiencing and observing the same inner fact at a single stroke, as when we say "I feel tired," "I am angry," etc. But these are illusory, and a little attention unmasks the illusion. The present conscious state, when I say "I feel tired," is not the direct feeling of tire; when I say "I feel angry," it is not the direct feeling of anger. It is the feeling of *saying-I-feel-tired*, of *saying-I-feel-angry*—entirely different matters, so different that the fatigue and anger apparently included in them are considerable modifications of the fatigue and anger directly felt the previous instant. The act of naming them has momentarily detracted from their force.

The only sound grounds on which the infallible veracity of the introspective judgment might be maintained, are empirical. If we have reason to think it has never yet deceived us, we may continue to trust it. This is the ground actually maintained by Herr Mohr in a recent little work.[1] "The illusions of our senses," says this author, "have undermined our belief in the reality of the outer world; but in the sphere of inner observation our confidence is intact, for we have never found ourselves to be in error about the reality of an act of thought or feeling. We have never been misled into thinking we were *not* in doubt or in anger when these conditions were really states of our consciousness."

But, sound as the reasoning here is, I fear the premises are not correct; and I propose in this article to supplement Mr. Sully's chapter on the Illusions of Introspection, by showing what immense tracts of our inner life are habitually overlooked and falsified by our most approved psychological authorities.

When we take a rapid general view of the wonderful stream of our consciousness, what strikes us first is the different *pace* of its different portions. Our mental life, like a bird's life, seems to be made of an alternation of flights and perchings. The rhythm of language expresses this, where every thought is expressed in a sentence, and every sentence closed by a period. The resting-places are usually occupied by sensorial imaginations of some sort, whose pecularity is that they can be held before the mind for an indefinite time, and contemplated without changing; the places of flight are filled with thoughts of relations, static or dynamic, that for the most part obtain between the matters contemplated in the periods of comparative rest.

Let us call the resting-places the "substantive parts," and the places of flight the "transitive parts," of the stream of thought. We may then say that the main end of our thinking is at all times the attainment of some other "substantive" part than the one from which we have just been dislodged. And we may say that the main use of the transitive parts is to lead

[1]*Grundlage der empirischen Psychologie*, Leipzig, 1882, p. 47.

us from one substantive conclusion to another. Of this perhaps more hereafter.

Now the first difficulty of introspection is that of seeing the
transitive parts for what they really are. If they are but flights
to a conclusion, stopping them to look at them before the
conclusion is reached is really annihilating them. Whilst if we
wait till the conclusion *be* reached, it so exceeds them in vigor
and stability that it quite eclipses and swallows them up in its
glare. Let anyone try to cut a thought across in the middle
and get a look at its section, and he will see how difficult the
introspective observation of the transitive tract is. The rush of
the thought is so headlong that it almost always brings us up
at the conclusion before we can arrest it. Or if our purpose is
nimble enough and we do arrest it, it ceases forthwith to be
itself. As a snowflake caught in the warm hand is no longer a
flake but a drop, so, instead of catching the feeling of relation
moving to its term, we find we have caught some substantive
thing, usually the last word we were pronouncing, statically
taken, and with its function, tendency and particular meaning
in the sentence quite evaporated. The attempt at introspective
analysis in these cases is in fact like seizing a spinning top to
catch its motion, or trying to turn up the gas quickly enough
to see how the darkness looks. And the challenge to *produce*
these psychoses, which is sure to be thrown by doubting psychologists at anyone who contends for their existence, is as
unfair as Zeno's treatment of the advocates of motion, when,
asking them to point out in what place an arrow *is* when it
moves, he argues the falsity of their thesis from their inability
to make to so preposterous a question an immediate reply.

If holding fast the transitive parts of thought's stream, so as
to observe them, be the first great difficulty of introspection,
then its first great fallacy must necessarily be a failure to register them and give them their due, and a far too great emphasis laid on the more substantive parts of the stream.
Accordingly we find that the orthodox empirical psychologists, whether of England, Germany, or France, record under
the name of images, *Vorstellungen*, or ideas, only such representations as have objects that can be brought to the distinct
focus of attention and there stably held in view. Hume's
fantastical assertion that we can form no idea of a thing

with either quality or quantity without representing its exact degrees of each, has remained an undisputed dogma in nominalistic minds, until Mr. Galton and Prof. Huxley, or perhaps M. Taine, first called it in question. Strange that so patent an inward fact as the existence of "blended" images could be overlooked! Strange that the assertion could virtually be made that we cannot imagine a printed page without at the same time imagining every letter on it—and made too by a school that prided itself particularly on its powers of observation! However, of such blunders is the history of psychology composed.

But if blurred and indistinct substantive states could be systematically denied, *a fortiori* was it easy to deny that *transitive* states, considered as segments of the stream of sentiency, have any existence at all. The principal effort of the Humian school has been to abrogate relations, not only from the sphere of reality, but from the sphere of consciousness; most of them being explained as words, to which no definite meanings, inner or outer, attach. The principal effort of the Platonizing schools has been to prove that, since relations are unquestionably perceived to obtain between realities, but as unquestionably cannot be perceived through any modifications of the stream of subjective sentiency comparable in nature with those through which the substantive qualities of things are perceived, they must needs be perceived by the immediate agency of a supersensible Reason, the omission to do homage to which is for the Platonists the vital defect in the psychological performances of the opposite school.

The second great fallacy of introspection, then, is the ignoring of the fact that a peculiar modification of our subjective feeling corresponds to our awareness of each objective relation, and is the condition of its being known. To Mr. Spencer belongs the honor of having exploded this fallacy, in a few pages that seem to have made but small impression on his contemporaries, but which I cannot help regarding as by far the most important portion of his *Principles of Psychology*. In §65 of that work it is distinctly laid down that, subjectively considered, "a relation proves to be itself a kind of feeling—the momentary feeling accompanying the transition from one conspicuous feeling to another conspicuous feeling"; and that, "notwithstanding its extreme brevity, its qualitative character is appreciable." The phrase "feeling of relation" will be sure to shock certain fastidious ears, but I nevertheless think we had better use it. Surely if any objective truth whatever can come to be known during, and through the instrumentality of, a feeling, there seems no *a priori* reason why a relation should not be that truth; or why, since the feeling has no proper subjective name of its own, we should hesitate to psychologize about it as "the feeling of that relation." There is no other way of talking about it at all.

But, though I have praised Mr. Spencer for being the first to use the phrase, I cannot praise him for having seen very deeply into the doctrine. Like most English psychologists, he tries to reduce the number of relations among things to a minimum; and in other passages says they are limited to likeness and unlikeness, coexistence in space and sequence in time. Whether this be true of *real* relations, does not here concern us. But it is certainly false to say that our *feelings* of relation are of only these four kinds. On the contrary, there is not a conjunction or a preposition, and hardly an adverbial phrase, syntactic form, or inflection of voice, in human speech, that does not express some shading or other of relation which we at some moment actually feel to exist between the larger objects of our thought. If we speak objectively, it is the real relations that appear revealed; if we speak subjectively, it is the stream of consciousness that matches each of them by an inward coloring of its own. In either case the relations are numberless, and no existing language is capable of doing justice to all their shades.

We ought to say a feeling of *and*, a feeling of *if*, a feeling of *but*, and a feeling of *by*, quite as readily as we say a feeling of *blue* or a feeling of *cold*. Yet we do not: so inveterate has our habit become of recognizing the existence of the substantive parts alone, that language almost refuses to lend itself to any other use. In a later place we shall see how the analogy of speech misleads us in still other ways. The Empiricists have always dwelt on its influence in making us suppose that where we have a separate name, a separate thing must needs be there to correspond with it; and they have rightly denied the existence of the mob of abstract entities, principles and forces, in whose favor no other evidence than this could be brought up. But they have said nothing of the obverse error, which in psychology is just as bad, the error, namely, of supposing that where there is *no* name no entity can exist. All *dumb* psychic states have, owing to this error, been coolly suppressed; or, if recognized at all, have been named after the substantive perception they led to, as thoughts "about" this object or "about" that, the stolid word *about* engulfing all their delicate idiosyncrasies in its monotonous sound. Thus the greater and greater accentuation and isolation of the substantive parts have continually gone on.

But the worst consequence of this vicious mode of mangling thought's stream is yet to come. From the continuously flowing thing it is, it is changed into a "manifold," broken into bits, called discrete; and in this condition, approved as its authentic and natural shape by the most opposite schools, it becomes the topic of one of the most tedious and interminable quarrels that philosophy has to show. I do not mean to say that the "Associationist" manner of representing the life of the mind as an agglutination in various shapes of separate entities called ideas, and the Herbartian way of representing it as resulting from the mutual repugnancies of separate entities called *Vorstellungen*, are not convenient formulas for roughly symbolizing the facts. So are the fluid-theories of electricity, the emission-theory of light, the archetype-theory of the skeleton, and the theory that curves are composed of small straight lines. But, if taken as literal truth, I say that any one of these theories is just as false as any other, and leads to as pernicious results. The Associationist and the Herbartian psychologies are both false and for one and the same reason, that what God has joined together they resolutely and wantonly put asunder. It would be calamitous for us, *à propos* of this matter, to get embogged in a metaphysical discussion about what real unity and continuity are. So I hasten to say that, by the continuity of the mental stream, all I here contend for is the absence of *separate* parts in it. It is for the assertors of separate parts to tell us what they mean by their separateness—a thing which (so far as I know) they have never done, except when the Kantians say it is something that nothing short of the agency of categories working under a transcendental Ego can overcome. But, be the definition of the separateness of the parts what it may, the burden of proving its existence lies with its friends. For the stream of our feeling is sensibly continuous, like time's stream.[2] This is surely the natural way of viewing it in the first instance, and as an empirical fact. It presents itself as a continuum. It is true that by it are revealed to us a multiplicity of what we are pleased to consider separate *objects*; but it ought to be proved, not simply assumed, that the proper way of describing this fact is to say we have *a cluster of feelings* as numerous as the objects, and not to say that we have a *feeling of the cluster* of objects, however numerous these may be. The whole cluster is, if apprehended at all, apprehended in one *something*. Why not as well in one subjective modification or pulse of feeling, as in one Ego? Of course this *naive* and natural way of describing the stream of knowledge ought not to prejudge the results of analysis made later on, and such analysis might show an Ego, and ever so much besides. But the ordinary plan of talking of a plurality of separate feelings from the first does prejudge the question, and abandon altogether the empirical and natural-history point of view.

And see the fruits of prejudging a matter like this, see the two schools at work!

The Empiricists, whether English or German, start with their pluralism of psychic entities, ideas or *Vorstellungen*; show their order and connection with each other; and then treat this order—which in the first instance appears as an object visible only to the psychologist, and recorded by him as a sort of physical fact—as equivalent to a mental fact apprehensible from within the series, and resulting in a modification of the manner in which the entities feel *themselves*.

The Rationalists immediately protest that the conclusions in this account are not warranted by the premises, that the ideas or *Vorstellungen*, assumed as distinct psychic factors out of which mind is to be built up, must be kept *pure* during all the processes through which the psychologist leads them; and, that if kept pure, the reciprocal order or relation in

[2]Of course I speak only of tracts of it uninterrupted by sleep or other unconsciousness.

which they may happen objectively to exist, will in no degree affect their manner of *being felt*. If the idea red is the idea red, it will be just that idea and nothing farther, whether the idea green has preceded it or not. The bald external fact of its sequence to green and its contrast to green will not make it aware of itself *as a fact* so sequent and so contrasted. Such awareness, if realized at all, could only be realized by a third psychic entity, to which the green and the red in their purity should be alike external and yet alike present; be known as separate and contrasted, and yet have the separateness overcome and the contrast removed by the way in which they lie together in the synthetic unity of the relation in which they are perceived. Such a third psychic entity cannot be a compound of the ideas themselves; for ideas cannot compound themselves, and if they could the result would be a merging into a "mean" and not, as here, a preservation of individuality intact; it cannot be a link or hyphen[3] or any sort of *intermediary* to make the ideas *continuous*, for that, though between, would be really external to, both ideas, and be merely a third feeling on its own account, as ignorant of the other two as they are ignorant of each other. Not any of these things can it be; not any fact of sensibility whatever, but a fact of an altogether higher order, to which all facts of sensibility are as the dust it treads on, an *act*, unnameable but by its own name, which is *intelligence*, inimitable in its function, which is *relating*, unique in its agent, which is the *Ego*, *self*, or *me*.

Both schools make then the same baseless hypothesis at the outset—the hypothesis that feeling is discontinuous by nature. The Kantians, Platonizers, or whatever one may please to call them, make another hypothesis to neutralize it, and so save the appearances.[4] The Sensationalists, unwilling to admit

---

[3] Such "hyphens," it may be said in passing, seem to be the feelings of relation Mr. Spencer has in mind in the section of his *Psychology* to which reference was made a short time back.

[4] Our hegelian Platonizers will of course protest that *their* withers are unwrung by this indictment, and that the Ego they contend for is no quasi-mechanical power working from without on detached materials, but only a name for the fact that what we have called the segments of the stream are consciously *for* each other. The question is a delicate one to decide. My own impression is that practically they are often tempted; and that the form the temptation takes is that of dropping into the old-fashioned psychic dualism.

the supernatural principle, end with the philosophical melancholy of a Hume at the conclusion of his treatise, or with
Mill's dismal confession of failure at the close of his chapter
on the Psychological Theory of Mind.

But if we descend to the root of the trouble and deny the
initial hypothesis, all difficulties and all need of discussion disappear at a stroke. And in truth there is no evidence whatever
for supposing the pure atomic ideas of red and yellow, and
the other elements of mental structure, to exist at all. They are
abstractions, mere fictitious psychic counterparts to those elementary qualities of which we come to believe the real world
is made up, but no one of them is an actual psychic fact.
Whenever an elementary quality of the outer world is thought
by us, the vehicle of the thinking is a feeling representing a
highly complex object, that quality in relation with something
else. Let us consider the mental stream and try to see what its
constituents are like. Everyone will admit that, as he thinks, a
procession of varying objects, now simple, now complex in
the extreme, passes before his attention, and that each one of
these objects, whatever be its character, is accompanied by
some sort of modification of his mental condition, of his subjective feeling, of the *wie ihm zu Muthe ist*, as Lotze would
say. Even the advocates of an eternally identical Ego will confess that it must know its objects, *quâ* changing, in and by

---

The Platonizing mood is essentially dualistic, for it is essentially worshipful;
and every object of worship needs the foil of a principle of evil to set off its
lustre. Sentiency as a detached principal is therefore almost indispensable to
this habit of philosophizing. Every church needs its devil, and sense and its
works are the devil of the Platonic congregation. The most amusing proof of
the Platonic demand for a dualistic psychology is given by the always delicious Ferrier, who, in Proposition 10 of his *Institutes*, affirms Plato to have
meant nothing more by his intelligible world than ordinary men mean by
their sensible world; but who, instead of remaining satisfied with this promising reduction, immediately adds: "but then his sensible world must be
moved a peg downwards. It must be thrust down into the regions of nonsense. It must be called, as we have properly called it, . . . the nonsensical
world, the world of pure infatuation, of downright contradiction, of unalloyed absurdity." Why? Not for any evidence he gives that such a world as
this *exists*, any more *intra* than *extra mentem*; but apparently for the sole
reason that an evil principle may never fail to be at hand, on which our
higher nature may, when occasion requires, exert its powers of disdain.

and through changing states, affections, acts, or attitudes, which are modifications, however superficial, of its identity. We can then represent, if not the whole, at least the changing part of the subjective stream by a continuous line, and if, as psychologists, we wish to isolate any portion of it for examination, we can symbolize that isolation by making cross-strokes. But, as Mr. Hodgson has so admirably shown, the cross-strokes do not pre-exist. They are *"artefacta"*; and the natural function of every segment of the line is to lead continuously into the next segment and carry consciousness along unbroken.

Now what differences obtain between the segments of the subjective stream—between the intervals scored off upon the line? Their differences of character must at least be as great as the differences of the objects they severally are aware of, or help to make known—whichever form of expression one prefer; otherwise there would be a difference of perception without any subjective sign or symptom, which is absurd.

If then the fact known be the-sequence-of-green-to-red-and-the-contrast-of-these-two-colors, the state of mind in which that fact comes to knowledge must be quite other than the state of mind in which either pure red or pure green comes to knowledge. In other words, if we start the stream with a feeling of pure red as its first segment, we must follow that up with a second segment which is a feeling of green-as-sequent-upon-the-red-and-contrasted-with-it; or, if we insist on having a "pure" feeling of green, we may let it come in the second segment, and then follow with a third in which the complex relation of the objects of the first two segments is perceived. In either case, the stream must contain segments that are not "pure" elementary feelings. It must contain feelings of qualities-in-relation as well as of qualities absolute. But these feelings do not cease for that to be consubstantial with the rest of the stream. They can all be figured in the same straight line. They involve no new psychic dimension, as when the transcendentalists, after letting a number of "pure" feelings successively go "bang," bring their *deus ex machinâ* of an Ego swooping down upon them from his Olympian heights to *make* a cluster of them with his wonderful "relating thought."

The only thing that can see the pure feelings as a cluster (if pure feelings there be) is a later segment of the stream, to which the "pure" segments and their content appear as objects. It is a peculiarity of the stream that its several parts are susceptible of becoming objects for each other. We cannot explain this peculiarity any more than we can explain any other cognition. As a matter of fact, *every* segment of the stream is cognitive, and seems to look at an object other than itself; and when this object turns out to be a past segment, we say the present one remembers it. The present one in our supposed case is the remembrance of something complex, but that does not keep it from being a single segment. All the arguments used by the transcendentalists to prove the real unity of the Ego, the oneness of the relating principle, apply perfectly to the case before us, and forbid us for an instant to suppose that the segment in which a complex fact is remembered is not just one feeling and no more. Whatever is known *together* is and must be known through a single modification of thought's stream. When I think the seven colors of the rainbow, I do not have seven thoughts of a color, and then a thought of a bow; that would be eight thoughts. What I have is just one thought of the whole object. And the first reasonable word has yet to be said to prove that such a "thought" as this is not, when considered in its subjective constitution, and apart from its cognitive function, also a "feeling," as specific and unique as the simplest affection of consciousness.

The demand for atoms of feeling, which shall be real units, seems a sheer vagary, an illegitimate metaphor. Rationally, we see what perplexities it brings in its train; and empirically, no fact suggests it, for the actual contents of our minds are always representations of some kind of an *ensemble*. From the dawn of an individual consciousness to its close, we find each successive pulse of it capable of mirroring a more and more complex object, into which all the previous pulses may themselves enter as ingredients, and be known. There is no reason to suppose that the same feeling ever does or can recur again. The same *thing* may recur and be known in an indefinite number of successive feelings; but does the least proof exist that in any two of them it is represented in an identical subjective state? All analogy points the other way. For when the identical thing recurs, it is always thought of in a fresh manner, seen under a somewhat different angle, apprehended in different relations from those in which it last appeared. And the feeling cognizant of it is the unitary feeling of it-in-those-relations, not a feeling of it-pure *plus* a second feeling, or a supernatural "thought," of the relations. We are so befogged by the suggestions of speech that we think a constant thing, known under a constant name, ought to be known by means of a constant mental affection. The ancient languages, with their elaborate declensions, are better guides. In them no substantive appears "pure," but varies its inflection to suit the way it is known. However it may be of the stream of real life, of the mental river the saying of Herakleitos is probably literally true: we never bathe twice in the same water there.

How could we, when the structure of our brain itself is continually growing different under the pressure of experience? For an identical feeling to recur, it would have to recur in an unmodified brain, which is an impossibility. The organ, after intervening states, cannot react as it did before they came.

If we are ever to be entitled to make psychological inferences from brain-processes, we should make them here in favor of the view I defend. The whole drift of recent brain-inquiry sets towards the notion that the brain always acts as a whole, and that no part of it can be discharging without altering the tensions of all the other parts. The best symbol for it seems to be an electric conductor, the amount of whose charge at any one point is a function of the total charge elsewhere. Some tracts are always waning in tension, some waxing, whilst others actively discharge. The states of tension, however, have as positive an influence as the discharges in determining the total condition, and consequently in deciding what the *psychosis* shall be to which the complex *neurosis* corresponds. All we know of submaximal nerve-irritations, and of the summation of apparently ineffective stimuli, tends to show that *no* changes in the brain are really physiologically ineffective, and that presumably none are bare of psychological result. But as the distribution of brain-tension shifts from one relative state of equilibrium to another, like the aurora borealis or the gyrations of a kaleidoscope, now rapid and now slow, is it likely that the brain's faithful psychic concomitant is heavier-footed than itself, that its rate of change is coarser-grained, that it cannot match each one of the organ's irradiations by a shifting inward iridescence of its own? But if it can do this, its inward iridescences must be infinite, for the brain-redistributions are in infinite variety. If so coarse a thing as a telephone-plate can be made to thrill for years and never reduplicate its inward condition, how much more must this be the case with the infinitely delicate brain?

As, in the senses, an impression feels very differently according to what has preceded it; as one color succeeding another is modified by the contrast, silence sounds delicious after noise, and a note, when the scale is sung up, sounds unlike itself when the scale is sung down; as the presence of certain lines in a figure changes the apparent form of the other lines, and as in music the whole æsthetic effect comes from the manner in which one set of sounds alters our feeling of another; so, in thought, we must admit that those portions of the brain that have just been maximally excited retain a kind of soreness which is a condition of our present consciousness, a co-determinant of how and what we now shall feel.

I am sure that this concrete and total manner of regarding the mind's changes is the only true manner, difficult as it may be to carry it out in detail. Associationism and Herbartianism are only schematisms which, the moment they are literally taken, become mythologies, and had much better be dropped than retained.[5]

Let me, by a few examples, bring the fact home for which I contend; let me show how a state of mind may be quite specific and at the same time quite inarticulate; let me exhibit some of the modifications that are probably due to nascent and waning excitements of the brain.

Suppose three successive persons say to us: "Wait!" "Hark!" "Look!" Our consciousness is thrown into three quite different attitudes of expectancy, although no definite

[5]In an article on the "Association of Ideas" published in the *Popular Science Monthly* of New York for March, 1880, I have myself tried to reinterpret the various varieties of association as due to quantitative alterations in what is always an integral action of the brain.

object is before it in any one of the three cases. Counting out different actual bodily attitudes, and counting out the reverberating images of the three words, which are of course diverse, probably no one will deny the existence of a residual conscious affection, a sense of the direction from which an impression is about to come, although no positive impression is yet there. Meanwhile we have no names for the psychoses in question but the names hark, look, and wait.

Suppose we try to recall a forgotten name. The state of our consciousness is peculiar. There is a gap therein; but no mere gap. It is a gap that is intensely active. A sort of wraith of the name is in it, beckoning us in a given direction, making us at moments tingle with the sense of our closeness, and then letting us sink back without the longed-for term. If wrong names are proposed, this singularly definite gap acts immediately so as to negate them. They do not fit into its mould. And the gap of one word does not feel like the gap of another, all empty of content as both might seem necessarily to be when described as gaps. When I vainly try to recall the name of Spalding, my consciousness is far removed from what it is when I vainly try to recall the name of Bowles. Here some ingenious persons will say: "How *can* the two consciousnesses be different when the terms which might make them different are not there? All that is there, so long as the effort to recall is vain, is the bare effort itself. How should that differ in the two cases? You are making it seem to differ by prematurely filling it out with the different names, although these, by the hypothesis, have not yet come. Stick to the two efforts as they are, without naming them after facts not yet existent, and you'll be quite unable to designate any point in which they differ." Designate, truly enough. We can only designate the difference by borrowing the names of objects not yet in the mind. Which is to say that our psychological vocabulary is wholly inadequate to name the differences that exist, even such strong differences as these. But namelessness is compatible with existence. There are innumerable consciousnesses of emptiness, no one of which taken in itself has a name, but all different from each other. The ordinary way is to assume that they are all emptinesses of consciousness, and so the same state. But the feeling of an absence is *toto cælo* other than the absence of a feeling. It is an intense feeling. The rhythm of a lost word may be there without a sound to clothe it; or the evanescent sense of something which is the initial vowel or consonant may mock us fitfully, without growing more distinct. Everyone must know the tantalizing effect of the blank rhythm of some forgotten verse, restlessly dancing in one's mind, striving to be filled out with words.

Again, what is the strange difference between an experience tasted for the first time and the same experience recognized as familiar, as having been enjoyed before, though we cannot name it or say where or when? A tune, an odor, a flavor sometimes carry this inarticulate feeling of their familiarity so deep into our consciousness that we are fairly shaken by its mysterious emotional power. But strong and characteristic as this psychosis is—it probably is due to the submaximal excitement of wide-spreading associational brain-tracts—the only name we have for all its shadings is "sense of familiarity."

When we read such phrases as "naught but," "either one or the other," "*a* is *b*, but," "although it is, nevertheless," "it is an excluded middle, there is no *tertium quid*," and a host of other verbal skeletons of logical relation, is it true that there is nothing more in our minds than the words themselves as they pass? What then is the meaning of the words which we think we understand as we read? What makes that meaning different in one phrase from what it is in the other? "Who?" "What?" "When?" "Where?" Is the difference of felt meaning in these interrogatives nothing more than their difference of sound? And is it not (just like the difference of sound itself) known and understood in an affection of consciousness correlative to it, though so impalpable to direct examination? Is not the same true of such negatives as "no," "never," "not yet"?

The truth is that large tracts of human speech are nothing but signs of direction in thought, of which direction we nevertheless have an acutely discriminative sense, though no definite sensorial image plays any part in it whatsoever. Sensorial images are stable psychic facts; we can hold them still and look at them as long as we like. These bare images of logical movement on the contrary are psychic transitions, always on the wing, so to speak, and not to be glimpsed except in flight. Their function is to lead from one set of images to another. As they pass, we feel both the waxing and the waning images in a way altogether peculiar and a way quite different from the way of their full presence. If we try to hold fast the feeling of direction, the full presence comes and the feeling of direction is lost. The blank verbal scheme of the logical movement gives us the fleeting sense of the movement as we read it, quite as well as does a rational sentence awakening definite imaginations by its words.

What is that first instantaneous glimpse of someone's meaning which we have, when in vulgar phrase we say we "twig" it? Surely an altogether specific affection of our mind. And has the reader never asked himself what kind of a mental fact is his *intention of saying a thing* before he has said it? It is an entirely definite intention, distinct from all other intentions, an absolutely distinct state of consciousness therefore; and yet how much of it consists of definite sensorial images, either of words or of things? Hardly anything! Linger, and the words and things come into the mind; the anticipatory intention, the divination is there no more. But as the words that replace it arrive, it welcomes them successively and calls them right if they agree with it, it rejects them and calls them wrong if they do not. It has therefore a nature of its own of the most positive sort, and yet what can we say about it without using words that belong to the later mental facts that replace it? The *intention-to-say-so-and-so* is the only name it can receive. One may say that a good third of our psychic life consists in these rapid premonitory perspective views of schemes of thought not yet articulate. How comes it about that a man reading something aloud for the first time is able immediately to emphasize all his words aright, unless from the very first he have a sense of at least the form of the sentence yet to come, which sense is fused with his consciousness of the present word, and modifies its emphasis in his mind so as to make him give it the proper accent as he utters it? Emphasis of this kind is almost altogether a matter of grammatical construction. If we read "no more" we expect presently to come upon a "than"; if we read "however" at the outset of a sentence it is a "yet," a "still," or a "nevertheless," that we expect. A noun in a certain position demands a verb in a certain mood and number, in another position it expects a relative pronoun. Adjectives call for nouns, verbs for adverbs, etc., etc. And this foreboding of the coming grammatical scheme combined with each successive uttered word is so practically accurate, that a reader incapable of understanding four ideas of the book he is reading aloud can nevertheless read it with the most delicately modulated expression of intelligence.

Some will interpret these facts by calling them all cases in which certain images, by laws of association, awaken others so very rapidly that we think afterwards we felt the very *tendencies* of the nascent images to arise before they were actually there. For this school the only possible materials of consciousness are images of a perfectly definite nature. Tendencies exist, but they are facts for the outside psychologist rather than for the subject of the observation. The tendency is thus a *psychical* zero; only its *results* are felt.

Now what I contend for, and accumulate examples to show, is that "tendencies" are not only descriptions from without, but that they are among the *objects* of the stream, which is thus aware of them from within, and must be described as in very large measure constituted of *feelings of tendency*, often so vague that we are unable to name them at all. It is in short the re-instatement of the vague to its proper place in our mental life which I am so anxious to press on the reader's attention. Mr. Galton and Prof. Huxley have made one step in advance in exploding the ridiculous theory of Hume and Berkeley that we can have no images but of perfectly definite things. Mr. Spencer has made another in overthrowing the equally ridiculous notion that, whilst simple objective qualities are revealed to our knowledge in feelings, relations are not. But these reforms are not half sweeping and radical enough. What must be admitted is that the definite images of traditional psychology form but the very smallest part of our minds as they actually live. The traditional psychology talks like one who should say a river consists of nothing but pailsful, spoonsful, quartpotsful, barrelsful, and other moulded forms of water. Even were the pails and the pots all actually standing in the stream, still between them the free water would continue to flow. It is just this free water of consciousness that psychologists resolutely overlook. Every definite image in the mind is steeped and dyed in the free water that flows round it. With it goes the sense of its relations, near and remote, the dying echo of whence it came to us, the dawning sense of whither it is to lead. The significance, the value, of the image is all in this halo or penumbra, that surrounds and escorts it—or rather that is fused into one with it and has become bone of its bone and flesh of its flesh; leaving it, it is true, an image of the same *thing* it was before, but making it an image of that thing newly taken and freshly understood.

What is that shadowy scheme of the "form" of an opera, play, or book, which remains in our mind and on which we pass judgment when the actual thing is done? What is our notion of a scientific or philosophical system? Great thinkers have vast premonitory glimpses of schemes of relation between terms, which hardly even as verbal images enter the mind, so rapid is the whole process. We all of us have this permanent consciousness of whither our thought is going. It is a feeling like any other, a feeling of what thoughts are next to arise, before they have arisen. This field of view of consciousness varies very much in extent, depending largely on the degree of mental freshness or fatigue. When very fresh, our minds carry an immense horizon with them. The present image shoots its perspective far before it, irradiating in advance the regions in which lie the thoughts as yet unborn. Under ordinary conditions the halo of felt relations is much more circumscribed. And in states of extreme brain-fag the horizon is narrowed almost to the passing word—the associative machinery, however, providing for the next word turning up in orderly sequence, until at last the tired thinker is led to some kind of a conclusion. At certain moments he may find himself doubting whether his thoughts have not come to a full stop; but the vague sense of a *plus ultra* makes him ever struggle on towards a more definite expression of what it may be; whilst the slowness of his utterance shows how difficult, under such conditions, the labor of thinking must be.

In the light of such considerations as these, the old dispute between Nominalism and Conceptualism seems to receive the simplest of solutions. The Nominalists say that, when we use the word *man*, meaning *mankind*, there is in the mind nothing more than either a sound or a particular image, *plus* certain tendencies which those elements have to awaken an indefinite number of images of particular men, or of other images (verbal or not) which "make sense" with *mankind*, but not with any individual. These "tendencies" are, however, for them mere physical facts, and not modes of feeling the word as it is uttered. The Conceptualists, on the other hand, see perfectly well that at the very moment of uttering the word, or even before uttering it, we know whether it is to be taken in a universal or a particular sense; and they see that there is some actual present modification of the mind which is equivalent to an *understanding* of the sense. But they call this modification, or conceptual character of the word, an act of pure intelligence, ascribe it to a higher region, and deem it not only other than, but even opposite to, all "facts of feeling" whatsoever.

Now why may we not side with the Conceptualists in saying that the universal sense of the word does correspond to a mental fact of *some* kind, but at the same time, agreeing with the Nominalists that all mental facts are modifications of subjective sensibility, why may we not call that fact a "feeling"? *Man* meant for *mankind* is in short a different feeling from *man* as a mere noise, or from *man* meant for *that* man, to wit, John Smith alone. Not that the difference consists simply in the fact that, when taken universally, the word has one of Mr. Galton's "blended" images of man associated with it. Many persons have seemed to think that these blended, or, as Prof. Huxley calls them, "generic," images are equivalent to concepts. But, in itself, a blurred thing is just as particular as a sharp thing; and the generic character of either sharp image or blurred image depends on its being felt *with its representative function*. This function is the mysterious *plus*, the understood meaning. But it is nothing applied to the image from above, no pure act of reason inhabiting a supersensible and semi-supernatural plane. It can be diagrammatized as continuous with all the other segments of the subjective stream. It is just that staining, fringe or halo of obscurely felt relation to masses of other imagery about to come, but not yet distinctly in focus, which we have so abundantly set forth.

If the image come unfringed it reveals but a simple quality, thing, or event; if it come fringed it reveals something expressly taken universally or in a scheme of relations. The difference between thought and feeling thus reduces itself, in the last subjective analysis, to the presence or absence of "fringe." And this in turn reduces itself, with much probability, in the last physiological analysis, to the absence or presence of sub-excitements of an effective degree of strength in other convolutions of the brain than those whose discharges underlie the more definite nucleus, the substantive ingredient, of the thought—in this instance, the word or image it may happen to arouse.[6]

[6]The contrast is not, as the Platonists would have it, between certain subjective facts called images and sensations, and others called acts of relating intelligence; the former being blind perishing things, knowing not even their own existence as such, whilst the latter combine past and future, the north pole and the south, in the mysterious synthesis of their cognitive sweep. The contrast is really between two *aspects*, in which all mental facts without exception may be taken; their structural aspect, as being subjective, and their functional aspect, as being cognitions. In the former aspect, the highest as well as the lowest is a feeling, a peculiarly tinged segment of the stream. This tingeing is its sensitive body, the *wie ihm zu Muthe ist*, the way it feels whilst passing. In the latter aspect, the lowest mental fact as well as the highest grasps some bit of universal truth as its content, even though that truth were as relationless a matter as a bare unlocalized and undated quality of pain. From the cognitive point of view, all mental facts are intellections. From the subjective point of view all are feelings. Once admit that the passing and evanescent are as real parts of the stream as the distinct and comparatively abiding; once allow that fringes and haloes, inarticulate perceptions, whereof the objects are as yet unnamed, mere nascencies of cognition, premonitions, awarenesses of direction, are thoughts *sui generis*, as much as articulate imaginings and propositions are; once restore, I say, the *vague* to its psychological rights, and the matter presents no further difficulty.

And then we see that the current opposition of Feeling to Knowledge is quite a false issue. If every feeling is at the same time a bit of knowledge, we ought no longer to talk of mental states differing by having more or less of the cognitive quality; they only differ in knowing more or less, in having much fact or little fact for their object. The feeling of a broad scheme of relations is a feeling that knows much; the feeling of a simple quality is a feeling that knows little. But the knowing itself, whether of much or of little, has the same essence, and is as good knowing in the one case as in the other. Concept and image, thus discriminated through their objects, are consubstantial in their inward nature, as modes of feeling. The one, as particular, will no longer be held to be a relatively base sort of an entity, to be taken for granted, whilst the other, as universal, is celebrated as a sort of standing

I wish that space were here afforded to show what, in most cases of rapid thinking, the fringe or halo is with which each successive image is enveloped. Often it cannot be more than a sense of the mutual affinity or belonging together of the successive images, and of their continuity with the main topic. This is the minimal perception of rational sequence, and can obtain between pure series of words, as well as between pictorial images, or between these and words. It gives us a lulling sense that we are "all right"; and when we have it, we let the image before us "pass" without demur. We feel that the topic is gradually being enriched, and that we are making towards the right conclusion. When we listen with relaxed attention, this vague perception that all the words we hear belong to the same language and to the same special vocabulary in that language, and that the grammatical sequence is familiar, is practically equivalent to an admission that what we hear is sense. But if an unusual foreign word be introduced, if the grammar trip, or if a term from an incongruous vocabulary suddenly appear, such as "rat-trap" or "plumber's bill" in a philosophical discourse, the sentence detonates, as it were, we receive a shock from the incongruity, and the drowsy assent is gone. The feeling of rationality in these cases seems rather a negative than a positive thing, being the mere absence of shock, or sense of discord, between the terms of thought. Provided only the right substantive conclusion be reached, the train of images that lead us to it is comparatively indifferent. They may be purely verbal, they may be mixed verbal and pictorial, or they may not be verbal at all, as in the interesting account by Mr. Ballard of his deaf-mute

---

miracle, to be adored but not explained. Both concept and image, *quâ* subjective, are singular and particular. Both are moments of the stream which come, and in an instant are no more. The word universality has no meaning as applied to their psychic body or structure, which is always finite. It only has a meaning when applied to their use, import, or reference to the kind of object they may reveal. The representation, as such, of the universal object is as particular as that of an object about which we know so little that the interjection "Ha!" is all it can evoke from us in the way of speech. Both should be weighed in the same scales, and have the same measure meted out to them, whether of worship or of contempt.

philosophizing. They may be what they please;—but if they only bring us out right, they are rational operations of thinking.[7]

Let us now pass to another introspective difficulty and source of fallacy, different from the one hitherto considered, but quite as baleful to psychology. I mean the *confusion between the psychologist's standpoint and the standpoint of the feeling* upon which he is supposed to be making his report.

The standpoint of the psychologist is external to that of the consciousness he is studying. Both itself and its own object are objects for him. They form a couple which he sees in relation, and compares together, and it follows from this that he alone can verify the cognitive character of any mental act, through his own assumed *true* knowledge of its object. Now he may err either by foisting his own knowledge of the object into the feeling, and representing the latter as aware of it just as he is. Or he may err by representing the feeling as if it felt *itself* to be what he knows it to be. Thus the psychologist may misrepresent the feeling in either of two ways, or in both.

I may mention immediately that the doctrine of the post-Kantians, that all knowledge is also self-knowledge, seems to flow from this confusion. Empirically, of course, an awareness of self accompanies most of our thinking. But that it should be needed to *make* that thinking "objective" is quite another matter. "Green-after-red-and-other-than-it" is an absolutely complete object of thought, ideally considered, and needs no added element. The fallacy seems to arise from some such reflection as this, that since the feeling *is* what it feels itself to be, so it must feel itself to be what it *is*, namely, related to each of its objects. That the last *is* covers much more ground than the first, the philosopher here does not notice. The first *is* signifies only the feeling's inward quality; the last *is* covers

---

[7]Hegel's celebrated dictum that pure being is identical with pure nothing, results from his taking the words statically, or without the fringe they wear when in a context. Taken in isolation, they agree in the single point of awakening no sensorial images. But taken dynamically, or as significant—as *thought*—their fringes of relation, their affinities and repugnances, their function and meaning, are felt and understood to be absolutely opposed.

all possible facts *about* the feeling, relational facts, which can only be known from outside points of view like that of the philosopher himself.[8]

But the great *Tummelplatz* of the confusion of the standpoints is the question of perception, and the whole problem of the manner in which the object is present to the mind in cognition. Distinguishing the standpoints explicitly leads us here to a very simple solution; and at the same time it clears up the subjective constitution of great tracts of our thinking, on which introspection hitherto has thrown but the most insufficient of lights.

The psychologist, studying this question, stands, as aforesaid, outside of the cognitive state-of-consciousness he is analyzing, and compares it with its supposed object, which he thinks he *really* knows. Let us call the object as known to him "the reality." Then the question is: Is the reality directly present to the feeling under observation, or is it represented by a mental substitute? And, if the latter: Is the representative *like* the reality, a copy of it, or is it not?

A word about the back-bone of the human mind, the psychological principle of identity, will help us here. Logic and ontology both have their principles of identity, but the psychological principle is different from either, being a highly synthetic proposition, which affirms that different mental acts can contemplate, mean to contemplate, and know that they mean to contemplate, the same objective matter, quality, thing or truth. The notion of sameness-with-something-else is in fact one of the "fringes" in which a substantive mental kernel-of-content can appear enveloped. The same reality, as we call the kernel, can, then, by virtue of this principle, be thought in widely differing ways. Some of these ways are complete ways, the others are relatively incomplete ways. As a rule, the more substantive and sensational a way is, the more complete we usually suppose it to be.

When now, as psychologists, we undertake to describe any one of these ways of thinking, we call them all "thoughts *about* that reality," ticketing them with its substantive name.

---

[8]The criticisms of the late Professor T. H. Green on empiricist writers seem to me to be so saturated with this confusion of the two standpoints, that their in many respects excellent teaching sadly loses its effectiveness.

For instance, whether I say "I write with steel pens," having such a pen in my hand, and seeing it move over the paper; or whether I say "I write with them," in a conversation whose general topic is steel-pens; or whether I say "Quills are better"; or whether I simply *intend* to say any one of these things, but no image verbal or other arises, because my attention is suddenly diverted;—whichever of these facts occur, most people would describe my mental state as "thought about steel-pens." They would name a substantive kernel, and call that the "object" of each of the several thoughts. And the professed psychologists would agree with them. But the psychologists would then begin, as the laymen do not, to wonder how thought *can* be "about" an "object," which may be present to the thought neither in its own sensible shape, nor by its name, nor even by a pronoun, or any sort of an articulate representative whatever—for these seem to be the predicaments of the last three thoughts about the pen. And the psychologists would then after their several fashions spin ingenious theories as to the typical and normal mode of "presence" to the mind of the "object" of its thoughts; each one finding in some *one* of the cases observed a warrant for his own peculiar views.

The whole puzzle arises from the wrong mode of describing the several cases, by which the layman and the psychologist alike substitute the "reality," which is their own object, and which happens to be also the substantive kernel of the object of the first thought instanced, for the several objects of the other three thoughts. Clearing up our ideas of "the object" brings us out of the wood.

The object of any thought is its entire content or deliverance, neither more or less. It is a vicious use of speech to take out a substantive kernel from its content and call that its object; and it is an equally vicious use of speech to add a substantive kernel not articulately included in its content, and to call that its object. Yet either one of these two sins we commit, whenever we content ourselves with saying that a given thought is simply "about" a certain topic, or that that topic is its "object." The object of my thought in the previous sentence, for example, is not simply "the sins we commit," nor "the sins we commit as psychologists," nor "the sins we

commit as psychologists naming the objects of thoughts." Its
object is nothing short of the entire sentence; and if we wish
to speak of it substantively, we must make a substantive of it
by writing it out in full with hyphens between all its words.
Nothing short of this can possibly name its delicate idiosyncrasy. And if we wish to *feel* that idiosyncrasy we must reproduce the thought as it was uttered, with every word fringed
and the whole sentence bathed in that original halo of obscure relations, which, like an horizon, then spread about its
meaning.

In this "fringing" may be included a feeling of *continuity
with the previous thoughts*, of there having been no breach of
topic, but of the main interest and problem being unchanged.
This would justify us psychologists in saying that the "topic"
of the successive thoughts was still steel-pins, even although
steel-pens as substantive images had long ceased to be present, and were not represented verbally even in pronominal
form.

But can anyone pretend, in strict psychology, that the
"topic" these incomplete thoughts are said to be "of" or
"about," stands in the same relation to the thoughts themselves as that in which the "reality," steel-pens, stood to the
complete thought we began with? Does it hold the same relation to them that the steel-pen holds to me, as I now take it in
my hand and watch it write? Most assuredly not: the so-called
topic is the *immediate object* of the complete thought, and of
my thought. Each of the incomplete thoughts, whilst we say
it is "of" that same topic, has all the time its *own* immediate
object, which stands in the place the topic stands in in the
complete thought and in mine. Exactly what that object is, is
a question very hard to answer introspectively, when the
thought is incomplete and transitive, and it has sped, and its
light is out. We may safely say, however, that *continuity-with-
the-complete-thought*, or with whatever previous thought first
brought the topic on the *tapis*, enters *into* the object of each
of the incomplete thoughts, so far as they can be truly said to
be "about" that topic. They do not envelop the topic in a
substantive manner, they are thrown *at* it merely. Their relation to it is that of a sense of the direction in which it lies.
That directions unmarked by explicit and substantive termini

are among the most frequently discriminated objects of our thinking, is a point that needs no proof. When a child, asked for the reason of something, says simply *"Because . . . ,"* and is satisfied; or when a man, after hearing a long plan, says "No! we cannot do it *so*, . . ."; each of them draws a line of definite relation between some substantive thing and a term not realized in the thought, but hidden out of sight and towards which the thinker merely points or looks.

Let us continue to use the name "topic" to designate the substantive reality *towards* which each of the incomplete thoughts looks, and to some conclusion from or about which the whole procession of them will probably lead. We, as outside observers of the thoughts, knowing them in this their function of being connected with it, have a perfect right to say that they are "thoughts concerning this topic." But we are absolutely wrong if we say that their *object* is the topic, or that the topic is *present* to them, or that they are in any *direct* way "of" or "about" it. We then not only thrust into them *our* object, and the object of another thought with which they are only remotely connected; but we by the same act excuse ourselves from seeking—and if we chance to seek, prevent ourselves from finding—what their own immediate objects really are.

Every thought has its *own* object immediately present to it; and the only question in each particular case is as to *what* that object is. For the traditional psychologists, however, who say that many differing thoughts may have the same object, the great question is, *how* is that object present to them all, since they seem to resemble each other as little as they do. And the difficulties of answering that question are such that we find as clear-headed writers on the whole as Reid and Stewart throwing up the sponge. Even in sense-perception, they say, the reality is no more represented by our feeling than it is in our most remotely and indirectly referential thought. There is never the least resemblance or consanguinity between the thing we know and the feeling's content. The latter is merely a signal to awaken the *knowledge* of the thing, which knowledge is an act of pure intelligence, of which absolutely nothing can be said, and whose connection with the signal is for us an arbitrary and unintelligible fact.

Now the truth is that in certain selected cases the signal *is* the reality. In complete sense-perception, for example, we normally believe that we see the latter face to face. Of what we have called the incomplete thoughts, however, this reality is only the "topic"; that is, a whole procession of them may occur without the reality's features being once directly present therein; but yet be a procession that takes note of its existence after a fashion, and is aware of itself *as* a procession leading to or from it as a terminus.

That there is a semblance of paradox here cannot be denied. Grant the procession to know its own existence as a procession; still how can it know itself as a procession to or from *that* reality—or even in the direction of that reality—without also knowing that reality itself immediately and face to face? But this apparent paradox comes from the confusion of the incomplete thought's standpoint with our own. We think the reality must be known in the procession as it is known to us, when—naming the procession—we call it a procession to or from that reality—also explicitly naming and imagining the latter too. *We* cannot *name* the topic without the reality becoming a direct present object to *us*. But the procession can and does feel its topic in an entirely different way. To substitute our way for this way is a complete falsification of the data into which, as psychologists, we are supposed to inquire. What the actual way is, is excessively difficult to make out, on account of the elusive character of those transitive and relational elements of subjectivity on which we commented at the outset of our essay, and of which the procession is mainly composed. Considering our feeling of a tune may make the matter a little clearer. A tune is a processional feeling, in which the idea of the whole is present to each note, so far as to tinge or "fringe" that note differently from the way in which it finds itself tinged or fringed in any other tune. Now the "topic" is to each incomplete thought in the procession what the "tune" is to each note. *We* have to name the topic and the tune explicitly whenever we speak of them; but as we do not pretend that each note in the tune names and hums the entire tune on its own account, at the same time that it hears itself; so we ought not to pretend that each thought in the procession names and knows the topic of the procession in the same articulate and explicit way that we do, when we try to define just which procession it is.

What *sort* of a feeling each thought in the procession has of which procession it is, is as much a mystery for us to-day as what sort of a sense each note has of the tune it is in. These are the problems for the introspection of the future. I have said enough to show, I hope, their difficulty, and some of the causes on which that difficulty depends—the main one being that our thought is a teleological organism, of which large tracts exist only for the attainment of others; and that our perception of these others, which were called its substantive parts, tends to spread itself everywhere in our reflective memory and obscure and replace the perception of the more evanescent parts that intervened. I hope I have made the reader feel how crude a thing that is which even our best text-books seek to pass off as "analysis of the human mind," and how deeply our current opinions on the subject demand revision.[9]

[9]One word on my attitude towards the Ego may avert misconception. All I have urged against it in this article, is against it in its alleged exclusive capacity of "relating" agent. I have said there is no need of an agent to relate together what never was separate, and that it is an unnecessary hypothesis for explaining *cognition*. That feelings can be "for" each other when they do not belong to the same Ego, is proved whenever one person knows what another person thinks. That their being "for" each other when they do belong to the same Ego, is not *a consequence* of such belonging—but may be more simply formulated by saying that each segment of the stream has its objects, and that the earlier segments become objects for the later—is what I have sought to show. If this "solidarity" of the stream of feelings is all that is meant by the Ego—if the Ego is merely a name for that fact—well and good—we seem agreed! For myself, however, there are certain material peculiarities about the way in which segments of the stream are *for* each other when they belong to the *same* Ego, that call for a deeper study of the question, and rather lead us to reserve the word Ego until they are quite cleared up. What is the difference between *your* feeling cognized by me, and a feeling expressly cognized by me as *mine*? A difference of intimacy, of warmth, of continuity, similar to the difference between a sense-perception and something merely imagined—which seems to point to a special *content* in each several stream of consciousness, for which Ego is perhaps the best specific name.

Absolutism and Empiricism

N O SEEKER of truth can fail to rejoice at the *terre-à-terre* sort of discussion of the issues between Empiricism and Transcendentalism (or, as the champions of the latter would probably prefer to say, between Irrationalism and Rationalism) that seems to have begun in MIND. It would seem as if, over concrete examples like Mr. J. S. Haldane's, both parties ought inevitably to come to a better understanding. As a reader with a strong bias towards Irrationalism, I have studied his article in No. XXXIII with the liveliest admiration of its temper and its painstaking effort to be clear. But the cases discussed failed to satisfy me, and I was at first tempted to write a Note animadverting upon them in detail. The growth of the limb, the sea's contour, the vicarious functioning of the nerve-centre, the digitalis curing the heart, are unfortunately *not* cases where we can *see* any *through-and-through* conditioning of the parts by the whole. They are all cases of reciprocity where subjects, supposed independently to exist, acquire certain attributes through their relations to other subjects. That they also *exist* through similar relations is only an ideal supposition, not verified to our understanding in these or any other concrete cases whatsoever.

If, however, one were to urge this solemnly, Mr. Haldane's friends could easily reply that he only gave us such examples on account of the hardness of our hearts. He knew full well their imperfection, but he hoped that to those who would not spontaneously ascend to the Notion of the Totality, these cases might prove a spur and suggest and symbolize something better than themselves. No particular case that can be brought forward is a real concrete. They are all abstractions from the Whole, and of course the 'through-and-through' character cannot be found in them. Each of them still contains among its elements what we call *things*, grammatical subjects, forming a sort of residual *caput mortuum* of Existence after all the relations that figure in the examples, have been told off. On this 'existence,' thinks popular philosophy, things may live on, like the winter bears on their own fat, never entering relations at all or, if entering them, entering an entirely different set of them from those treated of in Mr. Haldane's examples. Thus *if* the digitalis were to weaken instead of strengthening the heart, and to produce death (as sometimes happens), it would determine itself, through determining the organism, to the function of 'kill' instead of that of 'cure.' The function and relation seem adventitious, depending on what kind of a heart the digitalis gets hold of, the digitalis and the heart being facts external and, so to speak, accidental to each other. But this popular view, Mr. Haldane's friends will continue, is an illusion. What seems to us the 'existence' of digitalis and heart outside of the relations of killing or curing, is but a function in a wider system of relations, of which, *pro hac vice*, we take no account. The larger system determines the *existence* just as absolutely as the system 'kill,' or the system 'cure,' determined the *function* of the digitalis. Ascend to the absolute system, instead of biding with these relative and partial ones, and you shall see that the law of through-and-throughness must and does obtain.

Of course, this argument is entirely reasonable, and debars us completely from chopping logic about the concrete examples Mr. Haldane has chosen. It is not his fault if his categories are so fine an instrument that nothing but the sum total of things can be taken to show us the manner of their use. It is simply our misfortune that he has not the sum total of things to show it by. So let us fall back from all concrete attempts and see what we can do with his notion of through-and-throughness, avowedly taken *in abstracto*. In abstract systems the 'through-and-through' Ideal is realized on every hand. In any system, as such, the members are only *members* in the system. Abolish the system and you abolish its members, for you have conceived them through no other property than the abstract one of membership. Neither rightness nor leftness, except through bilaterality. Neither mortgager nor mortgagee, except through mortgage. The logic of all these cases is this:—*If* A, then B; but *if* B, then A: wherefore *if* either, Both; and if not Both, Nothing.

It costs nothing, not even a mental effort, to admit that the absolute totality of things *may* be organized exactly after the pattern of one of these 'through-and-through' abstractions. In fact, it is the pleasantest and freest of mental movements. Husband makes, and is made by, wife, through marriage; one makes other, by being itself other; everything self-created through its opposite—you go round like a squirrel in a cage. But if you stop and reflect upon what you are about, you lay bare the exact point at issue between common-sense and the 'through-and-through' school.

What, in fact, is the logic of these abstract systems? It is, as we said above: If any Member, then the Whole System; if not the Whole System, then Nothing. But how can Logic possibly do anything more with these two hypotheses than combine them into the single disjunctive proposition—"Either this Whole System, just as it stands, or Nothing at all." Is not that disjunction the ultimate word of Logic in the matter, and can any disjunction, as such, resolve *itself*? It may be that Mr. Haldane sees how one horn, the concept of the Whole System, carries real existence with it. But if he has been as unsuccessful as I in assimilating the Hegelian re-editings of the Anselmian proof, he will have to say that though Logic may determine *what* the system must be, *if* it is, something else than Logic must tell us *that* it is. Mr. Haldane in this case would probably consciously, or unconsciously, make an appeal to Fact: the disjunction is decided, since nobody can dispute that now, as a matter of fact, *something*, and not nothing, *is*. We must *therefore*, he would probably say, go on to admit the Whole System in the desiderated sense. Is not then the validity of the Anselmian proof the nucleus of the whole question between Logic and Fact? Ought not the efforts of Mr. Haldane and his friends to be principally devoted to its elucidation? Is it not the real door of separation between Empiricism and Rationalism? And if the Rationalists leave that door for a moment off its hinges, can any power keep that abstract, opaque, unmediated, external, irrational, and irresponsible monster, known to the vulgar as bare Fact, from getting in and contaminating the whole sanctuary with his presence? Can anything prevent Faust from changing "Im Anfang war das Wort" into "Im Anfang war die That"?

Nothing in earth or heaven. Only the Anselmian proof can keep Fact out of philosophy. The question, "Shall Fact be recognized as an ultimate principle?" is the whole issue between the Rationalists and the Empiricism of vulgar thought.

Of course, if so recognized, Fact sets a limit to the 'through-and-through' character of the world's rationality. That rationality might then mediate between all the members of our conception of the world, but not between the conception itself and reality. Reality would have to be given, not by Reason, but by Fact. Fact holds out blankly, brutally and blindly, against that universal deliquescence of everything into logical relations which the Absolutist Logic demands, and it is the only thing that does hold out. Hence the ire of the Absolutist Logic—hence its non-recognition, its 'cutting' of Fact.

The reasons it gives for the 'cutting' are that Fact is speechless, a mere word for the negation of thought, a vacuous unknowability, a dog-in-the-manger, in truth, which, having no rights of its own, can find nothing else to do than to keep its betters out of theirs.

There are two points involved here: first the claim that certain things have rights that are absolute, ubiquitous and all pervasive, and in regard to which nothing else can possibly exist in its *own* right; and second that anything that denies *this* assertion is *pure* negativity with no positive content whatsoever.

Take the latter point first. Is it true that what is negative in one way is thereby convicted of incapacity to be positive in any other way? The word 'Fact' is like the word 'Accident,' like the word 'Absolute' itself. They all have their negative connotation. In truth their whole connotation is negative and relative. All it says is that, whatever the thing may be that is denoted by the words, *other* things do not control it. Where fact, where accident is, they must be silent, it alone can speak. But that does not prevent its speaking as loudly as you please, in its own tongue. It may have an inward life, self-transparent and active in the maximum degree. An indeterminate future volition on my part, for example, would be a strict accident as far as my present self is concerned. But that could not prevent it, *in the moment in which it occurred*, from being possibly the most intensely living and luminous experience I ever had. Its quality of being a brute fact *ab extra* says nothing whatever as to its inwardness. It simply says *to outsiders*: "Hands off!"

And this brings us back to the first point of the Absolutist indictment of Fact. Is that point really anything more than a fantastic dislike to letting *anything* say "Hands off"? What else explains the contempt the Absolutist authors exhibit for a freedom defined simply on its 'negative' side, as freedom 'from,' &c.? What else prompts them to deride such freedom? But, dislike for dislike, who shall decide? Why is not their dislike at having me 'from' them, entirely on a par with mine at having them 'through' me?

I know very well that in talking of dislikes to those who never mention them, I am doing a very coarse thing, and making a sort of intellectual Orson of myself. But, for the life of me, I cannot help it, because I feel sure that likes and dislikes *must* be among the ultimate factors of their philosophy as well as of mine. Would they but admit it! How sweetly we then could hold converse together! There is *something* finite about us both, as we now stand. We do not know the Absolute Whole *yet*. *Part* of it is still negative to us. Among the *whats* of it still stalks a mob of opaque *thats*, without which we cannot think. But just as I admit that this is all possibly provisional, that even the Anselmian proof may come out all right, and creation *may* be a rational system through-and-through, why might they not also admit that it may all be otherwise, and that the shadow, the opacity, the negativity, the 'from'-ness, the plurality that is ultimate, *may* never be wholly driven from the scene. We should both then be avowedly making hypotheses, playing with Ideals. Ah! Why is the notion of hypothesis so abhorrent to the Hegelian mind?

And once down on our common level of hypothesis, we might then admit scepticism, since the Whole is not yet revealed, to be the soundest *logical* position. But since we are in the main not sceptics, we might go on and frankly confess to each other the motives for our several faiths. I frankly confess mine—I cannot but think that at bottom they are of an æsthetic and not of a logical sort. The 'through-and-through' universe seems to suffocate me with its infallible impeccable all-pervasiveness. Its necessity, with no possibilities; its relations, with no subjects, make me feel as if I had entered into a contract with no reserved rights, or rather as if I had to live in a large seaside boarding-house with no private bed-room in which I might take refuge from the society of the place. I am distinctly aware, moreover, that the old quarrel of sinner and pharisee has something to do with the matter. Certainly, to my personal knowledge, all Hegelians are not prigs, but I somehow feel as if all prigs ought to end, if developed, by becoming Hegelians. There is a story of two clergymen asked by mistake to conduct the same funeral. One came first and had got no farther than "I am the Resurrection and the Life," when the other entered. "*I* am the Resurrection and the Life," cried the latter. The 'through-and-through' philosophy, as it actually exists, reminds many of us of that clergyman. It seems too buttoned-up and white-chokered and clean-shaven a thing to speak in the name of the vast slow-breathing unconscious Kosmos with its dread abysses and its unknown tides. The 'freedom' *we* want to see there is not the freedom, with a string tied to its leg and warranted not to fly away, of that philosophy. "Let it fly away," we say, "from *us*! What then?"

Again I know I am exhibiting my mental grossness. But again, *Ich kann nicht anders*. I show my feelings; why *will* they not show theirs? I know they *have* a personal feeling about the through-and-through universe, which is entirely different from mine, and which I should very likely be much the better for gaining if they would only show me how. Their persistence in telling me that feeling has nothing to do with the question, that it is a pure matter of absolute reason, keeps me forever out of the pale. Still seeing a *that* in things which Logic does not expel, the most I can do is to *aspire* to the expulsion. At present I do not even aspire. Aspiration is a feeling. What can kindle feeling but the example of feeling? And if the Hegelians *will* refuse to set an example, what can they expect the rest of us to do? To speak more seriously, the one *fundamental* quarrel Empiricism has with Absolutism is over this repudiation by Absolutism of the personal and æsthetic factor in the construction of philosophy. That we all of us have feelings, Empiricism feels quite sure. That they may be as prophetic and anticipatory of truth as anything else we have, and some of them more so than others, cannot possibly be denied. But what hope is there of squaring and settling opinions unless Absolutism will hold parley on this common ground; and will admit that all philosophies are hypotheses, to which all our faculties, emotional as well as logical, help us, and the truest of which will at the final integration of things be found in possession of the men whose faculties on the whole had the best divining power?

The Psychology of Belief

"Mein Jetzt und Hier ist der letzte Angelpunkt für alle Wirklichkeit, also alle Erkenntniss."—THEODOR LIPPS.

EVERYONE KNOWS the difference between imagining a thing and believing in its existence, between supposing a proposition and acquiescing in its truth. In the case of acquiescence or belief, the object is not only apprehended by the mind, but is held to have reality. Belief is thus the mental state or function of cognising reality—I might, indeed, have called this paper 'The Perception of Reality'. As used in the following pages, 'Belief' will mean every degree of assurance, including the highest possible certainty and conviction.

There are, as we know, two ways of studying every psychic state. First, the way of analysis: What does it consist in? What is its inner nature? Of what sort of mind-stuff is it composed? Second, the way of history: What are its conditions of production, and its connexion with other facts?

Into the first way we cannot go very far. In its inner nature belief, or the sense of reality, is a sort of feeling more allied to the emotions than to anything else. Mr. Bagehot distinctly calls it the 'emotion' of conviction. I just now spoke of it as acquiescence. It resembles more than anything what in the psychology of volition we know as consent. Consent is recognised by all to be a manifestation of our active nature. It would naturally be described by such terms as 'willingness' or the 'turning of our disposition'. What characterises both consent and belief is the cessation of theoretic agitation, through the advent of an idea which is inwardly stable, and fills the mind solidly to the exclusion of contradictory ideas. When this is the case, motor effects are apt to follow. Hence the states of consent and belief, characterised by repose on the purely intellectual side, are both intimately connected with subsequent practical activity. This inward stability of the mind's content is as characteristic of disbelief as of belief. We shall presently see that we never disbelieve anything except for the reason that we believe something else which contradicts the first thing.[1] Disbelief is thus an incidental complication to belief, and need not be considered by itself.

The true opposites of belief, psychologically considered, are doubt and inquiry, not disbelief. In both these states the content of our mind is in unrest, and the emotion engendered thereby is, like the emotion of belief itself, perfectly distinct, but perfectly indescribable in words. Both sorts of emotion may be pathologically exalted. One of the charms of drunkenness unquestionably lies in the deepening of the sense of reality and truth which is gained therein. In whatever light things may then appear to us, they seem more utterly what they are, more 'utterly utter' than when we are sober. This goes to a fully unutterable extreme in the nitrous oxide intoxication, in which a man's very soul will sweat with conviction, and he be all the while unable to tell what he is convinced of at all.[2] The pathological state opposed to this solidity and deepening has been called the questioning mania (*Grübelsucht* by the Germans). It is sometimes found as a substantive affection, paroxysmal or chronic, and consists in the inability to rest in any conception, and the need of having it confirmed and explained. 'Why do I stand here where I stand?' 'Why is a glass a glass, a chair a chair?' 'How is it that men are only of the size they are? Why not as big as houses?' &c., &c.[3] There is, it

---

[1]Compare this psychological fact with the corresponding logical truth that all negation rests on covert assertion of something else than the thing denied. (See Bradley's *Principles of Logic*, bk. i., ch. 3.)

[2]See that very remarkable little work, *The Anæsthetic Revelation and the Gist of Philosophy*, by Benj. P. Blood (Amsterdam, N.Y., 1874). Compare also MIND vii. 206.

[3]"To one whose mind is healthy thoughts come and go unnoticed; with me they have to be faced, thought about in a peculiar fashion, and then disposed of as finished, and this often when I am utterly wearied and would be at peace; but the call is imperative. This goes on to the hindrance of all natural action. If I were told that the staircase was on fire and I had only a minute to escape, and the thought arose—'Have they sent for fire-engines? Is it probable that the man who has the key is on hand? Is the man a careful sort of person? Will the key be hanging on a peg? Am I thinking rightly? Perhaps they don't lock the depot'—my foot would be lifted to go down; I should be conscious to excitement that I was losing my chance; but I should be unable to stir until all these absurdities were entertained and disposed of. In the most critical moments of my life, when I ought to have been so *engrossed as to leave no room for any secondary thoughts*, I have been oppressed by the inability

is true, another pathological state which is as far removed from doubt as from belief, and which some may prefer to consider the proper contrary of the latter state of mind. I refer to the feeling that everything is hollow, unreal, dead. I shall speak of this state again upon a later page. The point I wish to notice here is simply that belief and disbelief are but two aspects of one psychic state.

John Mill, reviewing various opinions about belief, comes to the conclusion that no account of it can be given:

"What," he says, "is the difference *to our minds* between thinking of a reality and representing to ourselves an imaginary picture? I confess I can see no escape from the opinion that the distinction is ultimate and primordial. There is no more difficulty in holding it to be so than in holding the difference between a sensation and an idea to be primordial. It seems almost another aspect of the same difference. . . . I cannot help thinking, therefore, that there is in the remembrance of a real fact, as distinguished from that of a thought, an element which does not consist . . . in a difference between the mere ideas which are present to the mind in the two cases. This element, howsoever we define it, constitutes belief, and is the difference between Memory and Imagination. From whatever direction we approach, this difference seems to close our path. When we arrive at it, we seem to have reached, as it were, the central point of our intellectual nature, presupposed and built upon in every attempt we make to explain the more recondite phenomena of our mental being."[4]

If the words of Mill be taken to apply to the mere subjective analysis of belief—to the question, What does it feel like when we have it? they must be held, on the whole, to be correct. Belief, the sense of reality, feels like itself—that is about as much as we can say.

---

to be at peace. And in the most ordinary circumstances it is all the same. Let me instance the other morning I went to walk. The day was biting cold, but I was unable to proceed except by jerks. Once I got arrested, my feet in a muddy pool. One foot was lifted to go, knowing that it was not good to be standing in water, but there I was fast, the cause of detention being the discussing with myself the reasons why I should not stand in that pool." (T. S. Clouston, *Clinical Lectures on Mental Diseases*, 1883, p. 43. See also Berger, in *Archiv f. Psychiatrie*, vi. 217.)

[4]Note to Jas. Mill's *Analysis*, i. 412–423.

Prof. Brentano, in an admirable chapter of his *Psychologie*, expresses this by saying that conception and belief (which he names *judgment*) are two different fundamental psychic phenomena. What I myself in a former article, MIND ix. 22, called the 'object' of thought may be comparatively simple, like 'Ha! what a pain,' or 'It thunders'; or it may be complex, like 'Columbus discovered America in 1492,' or 'There exists an all-wise Creator of the world'. In either case, however, the mere thought of the object may exist as something quite distinct from the belief in its reality. The belief, as Brentano says, presupposes the mere thought:

"Every object comes into consciousness in a twofold way, as simply thought of [*vorgestellt*] and as admitted [*anerkannt*] or denied. The relation is analogous to that which is assumed by most philosophers (by Kant no less than by Aristotle) to obtain between mere thought and desire. Nothing is ever desired without being thought of; but the desiring is nevertheless a second quite new and peculiar form of relation to the object, a second quite new way of receiving it into consciousness. No more is anything judged (*i.e.*, believed or disbelieved) which is not thought of too. But we must insist that, so soon as the object of a thought becomes the object of an assenting or rejecting judgment, our consciousness steps into an entirely new relation towards it. It is then twice present in consciousness, as thought of, and as held for real or denied; just as when desire awakens for it, it is both thought and simultaneously desired" (p. 266).

The commonplace doctrine of 'judgment' is that it consists in the combination of 'ideas' by a 'copula' into a 'proposition,' which may be of various sorts, as affirmative, negative, hypothetical, &c. But who does not see that in a disbelieved or doubted or interrogative or conditional proposition, the ideas are combined in the same identical way in which they are in a proposition which is solidly believed? The way in which the ideas are combined is a part of the inner constitution of the thought's object or content. That object is sometimes an articulated whole with relations between its parts, amongst which relations that of predicate to subject may be one. But when we have got our object with its inner constitution thus defined in a proposition, then the question comes up regarding the object as a whole: 'Is it a real object, and is this proposition about it a true proposition or not?' And in the answer

Yes to *this* question lies that new psychic act which Brentano calls 'judgment,' but which I prefer to call 'belief'.

In every proposition, then, so far as it is believed, questioned or disbelieved, four elements are to be distinguished, the subject, the predicate, and their relation (of whatever sort it be), and finally the psychic attitude in which our mind stands towards the proposition taken as a whole.[5]

Admitting, then, that this attitude is a state of consciousness *sui generis*, about which nothing more can be said in the way of internal analysis, let us proceed to the second way of studying the subject of belief: *Under what circumstances does this peculiar attitude of mind arise?* We shall soon see how much matter this gives us to discuss.

Suppose a new-born mind, entirely blank and waiting for experience to begin. Suppose that it begins in the form of a visual impression (whether faint or vivid is immaterial) of a lighted candle against a dark background, and nothing else, so that whilst this image lasts it constitutes the entire universe known to the mind in question. Suppose, moreover (to simplify the hypothesis), that the candle is only imaginary, and that no 'original' of it is recognised by us psychologists outside. Will this hallucinatory candle be believed in, will it have a real existence for the mind?

What possible sense (for that mind) would a suspicion have that the candle was not real? What would doubt or disbelief of it imply? When *we*, the onlooking psychologists, say the candle is unreal, we mean something quite definite, *viz.*, that there is a world known to *us* which *is* real, and to which we perceive that the candle does not belong; it belongs exclusively to that individual mind, has no *status* anywhere else, &c. It exists, to be sure, in a fashion, for it forms the content of that mind's hallucination; but the hallucination itself, though unquestionably it is a sort of existing fact, has no knowledge of *other* facts; and since those *other* facts are the realities *par excellence* for us, and the only things we believe in, the candle is simply outside of our reality and belief altogether.

---

[5]For an excellent account of the history of opinion on this subject see A. Marty, in *Vierteljahrssch. f. wiss. Phil.*, vii. 161 ff. (1884).

By the hypothesis, however, the *mind which sees the candle* can spin no such considerations as these about it, for of other facts, actual or possible, it has no inkling whatever. That candle is its all, its absolute. Its entire faculty of attention is absorbed by it. It *is*, it is *that*; it is *there*; no other possible candle, or quality of this candle, no other possible place, or possible object in the place, no alternative, in short, suggests itself as even conceivable; so how can the mind help believing the candle real? The supposition that it might possibly not do so is, under the supposed conditions, unintelligible.

This is what Spinoza long ago announced:—

"Let us conceive a boy," he said, "imagining to himself a horse, and taking note of nothing else. As this imagination involves the existence of the horse, *and the boy has no perception which annuls its existence*, he will necessarily contemplate the horse as present, nor will he be able to doubt of its existence, however little certain of it he may be. I deny that a man in so far as he imagines [*percipit*] affirms nothing. For what is it to imagine a winged horse but to affirm that the horse [that horse, namely] has wings? For if the mind had nothing before it but the winged horse it would contemplate the same as present, would have no cause to doubt of its existence, nor any power of dissenting from its existence, unless the imagination of the winged horse were joined to an idea which contradicted [*tollit*] its existence" (*Ethics*, ii. 49, Scholium).

The sense that anything we think of is unreal can only come, then, when that thing is contradicted by some other thing of which we think. The contradicting thing may then itself be held for real, till it in turn is contradicted by some farther object of our thought. Any object which remains uncontradicted is *ipso facto* believed and posited as absolute reality.

Now, how comes it that one thing thought of can be contradicted by another? It can't unless it begins the quarrel by saying something inadmissible about that other. Take the mind with the candle or the boy with the horse. If either of them say, 'That candle or that horse, even when I don't see it, exists in real extra-mental space,' he pushes into real extra-mental space an object which may be incompatible with everything which he otherwise knows of that space. If so, he must take his choice of which to hold by, the present perceptions or the other knowledge of space. If he holds to the other knowledge, the present perceptions are annulled, so far as their relation to that extra-mental space goes. Candle and horse, whatever they may be, are not existents in *outward* space. They are existents of course; they are mental objects; mental objects have existence as mental objects. But they are situated in their own spaces, the space in which they severally appear, and neither of those spaces is space in which outer realities exist.

Take again the horse with wings. If I merely dream of a horse with wings, my horse interferes with nothing else and has not to be contradicted. That horse, its wings and its place, are all equally real. That horse exists no otherwise than as winged, and is moreover really there, for that place exists no otherwise than as the place of that horse, and claims as yet no connexion with the other places of the world. But if with this horse I make an inroad into the *world otherwise known*, and say, for example, 'That is my old mare Maggie, having grown a pair of wings where she stands in her stall,' the whole case is altered. Now the horse and place are identified with a horse and place otherwise known, and *what* is known of the latter objects is incompatible with what is perceived with the former. 'Maggie in her stall with wings! Never!' The wings are unreal, then, visionary. I have dreamed a lie about Maggie in her stall.

The reader will recognise in these two cases the two sorts of judgment called in the logic-books existential and attributive respectively. 'The candle exists as an outer reality' is an existential, 'My Maggie has got a pair of wings' is an attributive, proposition;[6] and it follows from what was first said, that

---

[6] In both existential and attributive judgments a synthesis is represented. The syllable *ex* in the word Existence, *da* in the word *Dasein*, express it. 'The candle exists' is equivalent to 'The candle is *over there*'. And the 'over there' means real space, space related to other reals. The proposition amounts to saying: 'The candle is in the same space with other reals'. It affirms of the candle a very concrete predicate—namely, this relation to other particular concrete things. *Their* real existence, as we shall later see, resolves itself into their peculiar relation to *ourselves*. Existence is thus no substantive quality when we predicate it of any object; it is a relation, ultimately terminating in ourselves, and at the moment when it terminates, becoming a practical relation. But of this more anon. I only wish now to indicate the superficial nature of the distinction between the existential and the attributive proposition.

all propositions, whether attributive or existential, are *believed through the very fact of being conceived*, unless they clash with other propositions believed at the same time, by affirming that their terms are the *same* with the terms of these other propositions. A dream-candle has existence, true enough; but not the same existence (existence for itself, namely, or *extra mentem meam*) which the candles of waking perception have. A dream-horse has wings; but then neither horse nor wings are the same with any horses or wings known to memory. That we can at any moment think of the same thing which at any former moment we thought of is the ultimate law of our intellectual constitution. But when we now think of it incompatibly with our other ways of thinking it, then we must choose which way to stand by, for we cannot continue to think in two contradictory ways at once. *The whole distinction of real and unreal, the whole psychology of belief, disbelief and doubt, is thus grounded on two mental facts, first, that we are liable to think differently of the same, and second, that when we have done so, we can choose which way of thinking to adhere to and which to disregard.*

The subjects adhered to become real subjects, the attributes adhered to real attributes, the existence adhered to real existence; whilst the subjects disregarded become imaginary subjects, the attributes disregarded erroneous attributes, and the existence disregarded an existence in no man's land, in the limbo "where footless fancies dwell".

Habitually and practically we do not *count* these disregarded things as existents at all, neither the times and spaces represented in our fancy, nor the subjects and attributes appearing located therein. The only times, places, subjects, relations, which popular thought *recognises* are those which we 'adhere to' in the way described. For the erroneous things *Vae victis* is the law; they are not even treated as appearances, in the popular philosophy; they are treated as if they were mere waste, equivalent to nothing at all. To the genuinely philosophic mind, however, they still have existence. They are not the same, nor have they the same existence, as the real things. But *as* objects of fancy, *as* errors, *as* occupants of dreamland, &c., they are in their way as indefeasible parts of life, as un-

deniable features of the Universe, as the realities are in their
way. The total world of which the philosophers must take
account is thus composed of the realities *plus* the fancies and
illusions.

Two sub-universes, at least, connected by relations which
philosophy tries to ascertain! Really there are more than two
sub-universes of which we take account, some of us of this
one, and others of that. For there are various categories both
of illusion and of reality, and alongside of the world of absolute error (*i.e.*, error confined to single individuals) but still
within the world of absolute reality (*i.e.*, reality believed by
the complete philosopher) there is the world of collective error, there are the worlds of abstract reality, of relative or practical reality, of ideal relations, and there is the supernatural
world. The popular mind conceives of all these sub-worlds
more or less disconnectedly; and, when dealing with one of
them, forgets for the time being its relations to the rest. The
complete philosopher is he who seeks not only to assign to
every given object of his thought its right place in one or
other of these sub-worlds, but he also seeks to determine the
relation of each sub-world to the others in the total world
which is.

The most important sub-universes commonly discriminated
from each other and recognised by most of us as existing,
each with its own special and separate style of existence, are
the following: —

(1) The world of sense, or of physical 'things' as we instinctively apprehend them, with such qualities as heat, colour and
sound, and such 'forces' as life, chemical affinity, gravity, electricity, all existing as such within or on the surface of the
things.

(2) The world of science, or of physical things as the
learned conceive them, with secondary qualities and 'forces'
(in the popular sense) excluded, and nothing real but solids
and fluids and their 'laws' (*i.e.*, customs) of motion.[7]

(3) The world of ideal relations, or abstract truths believed

[7]I define the scientific universe here in the radical mechanical way. Practically, it is oftener thought of in a mongrel way and resembles in more points
the popular physical world.

or believable by all, and expressed in logical, mathematical, metaphysical, ethical or æsthetic propositions.

(4) The world of 'idols of the tribe,' illusions or prejudices common to the race. All educated people recognise these as forming one sub-universe. The motion of the sky round the earth, for example, belongs to this world. That motion is not a recognised item of any of the other worlds; but as an 'idol of the tribe' it really exists. For certain philosophers 'matter' exists only as an idol of the tribe. For science, the 'secondary qualities' of matter are but 'idols of the tribe'.

(5) The various supernatural worlds, the Christian heaven and hell, the world of the Hindoo mythology, the world of things seen and heard by Swedenborg, &c. Each of these is a consistent system, with definite relations among its own parts. Neptune's trident, *e.g.*, has no status of reality whatever in the Christian heaven; but within the classic Olympus certain definite things are true of it, whether one believe in the reality of the classic mythology as a whole or not. The various worlds of deliberate fable may be ranked with these worlds of faith— the world of the *Iliad*, that of *King Lear*, of the *Pickwick Papers, &c.*[8]

(6) The various worlds of individual opinion, as numerous as men are.

(7) The worlds of sheer madness and vagary, also indefinitely numerous.

Every object we think of gets at last referred to one world or another of this or of some similar list. It settles into our belief as a common-sense object, a scientific object, an abstract object, a mythological object, an object of some one's mistaken conception, or a madman's object; and it reaches this state sometimes immediately, but often only after being hus-

[8]It thus comes about that we can say such things as that Ivanhoe did not *really* marry Rebecca, as Thackeray *falsely* makes him do. The real Ivanhoe-world is the one which Scott wrote down for us. *In that world* Ivanhoe does *not* marry Rebecca. The objects within that world are knit together by perfectly definite relations, which can be affirmed or denied. Whilst absorbed in the novel, we turn our backs on all other worlds, and, for the time, the Ivanhoe-world remains our absolute reality. When we wake from the spell, however, we find a still more real world, which reduces Ivanhoe, and all things connected with him, to the fictive status, and relegates them to one of the sub-universes grouped under No. 5.

THE PSYCHOLOGY OF BELIEF 1031

tled and bandied about amongst other objects until it finds some which will tolerate its presence and stand in relations to it which nothing contradicts. The molecules and ether-waves of the scientific world, for example, simply kick the object's warmth and colour out. But the world of 'idols of the tribe' stands ready to take them in. Just so the world of classic myth takes up the winged horse; the world of individual hallucination, the vision of the candle; the world of abstract truth, the proposition that justice is kingly, though no actual king be just. The various worlds themselves, however, appear (as aforesaid) to most men's minds in no very definitely conceived relation to each other, and our attention, when it turns to one, is apt to drop the others for the time being out of its account. Propositions concerning the different worlds are made from 'different points of view'; and in this more or less chaotic state the consciousness of most thinkers remains to the end.

Every thinker, however, practically elects from among the various worlds some one to be for him the world of *ultimate* realities. From this world's objects there is no appeal. Whatever contradicts what is believed of them must get into another world or die. The horse, *e.g.*, may have wings to its heart's content, so long as it does not pretend to be the real world's horse. The real world's horse is the horse which is absolutely wingless. For most men, as we shall immediately see, the 'things of sense' hold this prerogative position and are the absolutely real world's nucleus. Other things, to be sure, may be real for this man or for that—things of science, abstract moral relations, things of the Christian theology, or what not. But even for the special man, these things are usually real with a less real reality than that of the things of sense. They are taken less seriously; and the very utmost that can be said for anyone's belief in them is that it is as strong as his 'belief in his own senses'.

In all this the everlasting partiality of our nature shows itself, our inveterate propensity to choice. For, in the strict and ultimate sense of the word existence, everything which can be thought of at all exists as *some* sort of object, whether mythical object, individual thinker's object, or object in outer space and for intelligence at large. Errors, fictions, tribal beliefs, are

parts of the whole great Universe which God has made, and
He must have meant all these things to be in it, each in its
respective place. But for us finite creatures, " 'tis to consider
too curiously to consider so". The mere fact of appearing as
an object at all is not enough to constitute reality. That may
be metaphysical reality, reality for God; but what we need is
practical reality, reality for ourselves; and, to have that, an
object must not only appear, but it must appear both *interesting* and *important*. The worlds whose objects are neither interesting nor important we treat simply negatively, we brand
them as *un*real.

In the relative sense, then, the sense in which we contrast
reality with simple *un*reality, and in which one thing is said
to have *more* reality than another, and to be more believed,
reality means simply relation to our emotional and active life.
This is the only sense which the word ever has in the mouths
of practical men. In this sense, *whatever excites and stimulates
our interest* is real; whenever an object so appeals to us that
we turn to it, accept it, fill our mind with it, or practically
take account of it, so far it is real for us, and we believe it.
Whenever, on the contrary, we ignore it, fail to consider it or
act upon it, despise it, reject it, forget it, so far it is unreal
for us and disbelieved. Hume's account of the matter was
then essentially correct, when he said that belief in anything
was simply the having the idea of it in a lively and active
manner:—

"I say, then, that belief is nothing but a more vivid, lively, forcible,
firm, steady conception of an object, than the imagination alone is
ever able to attain. . . . It consists not in the peculiar nature or
order of the ideas, but in the *manner* of their conception and in their
feeling to the mind. I confess that it is impossible perfectly to explain
this feeling or manner of conception . . . Its true and proper name
. . . is *belief*, which is a term that everyone sufficiently understands
in common life. And in philosophy we can go no farther than assert
that belief is something felt by the mind, which distinguishes the
idea of the judgment from the fictions of the imagination.[9] It gives
them more weight and influence; makes them appear of greater importance; enforces them in the mind; gives them a superior influence

[9]Distinguishes realities from unrealities, the essential from the rubbishy
and neglectable.

on the passions; and renders them the governing principle in our actions."[10]

Or as Prof. Bain puts it: "In its essential character, belief is a phase of our active nature—otherwise called the Will".[11]

The object of belief, then, reality or real existence, is something quite different from all the other predicates which a subject may possess. Those are properties intellectually or sensibly intuited. When we add any one of them to the subject, we increase the intrinsic content of the latter, we enrich its picture in our mind. But adding reality does not enrich the picture in any such inward way; it leaves it inwardly as it finds it, and only fixes it and stamps it in to *us*. "The real," as Kant says, "contains no more than the possible. A hundred real dollars do not contain a penny more than a hundred possible dollars. . . . By whatever, and by however many, predicates I may think a thing, nothing is added to it if I add that the thing exists. . . . Whatever, therefore, our concept of an object may contain, we must always step outside of it in order to attribute to it existence."[12]

The 'stepping outside' of it is the establishment either of immediate practical relations between it and ourselves, or of relations between it and other objects with which we have immediate practical relations. Relations of this sort, which are as yet not transcended or superseded by others, are *ipso facto* real relations, and confer reality upon their objective term.

[10]*Inquiry concerning Hum. Understanding*, sec. v., pt. 2 (slightly transposed in my quotation).

[11]Note to Jas. Mill's *Analysis*, i. 394.

[12]*Critique of Pure Reason*, trans. Müller, ii. 515–17. Hume also: "When, after the simple conception of anything, we would conceive it as existent, we in reality make no addition to, or alteration on, our first idea. Thus, when we affirm that God is existent, we simply form the idea of such a being as He is represented to us; nor is the existence which we attribute to Him conceived by a particular idea, which we join to His other qualities, and can again separate and distinguish from them. . . . The belief of the existence joins no new idea to those which compose the ideas of the object. When I think of God, when I think of Him as existent, and when I believe Him to be existent, my idea of Him neither increases nor diminishes. But as 'tis certain there is a great difference betwixt the simple conception of the existence of an object and the belief of it, and as this difference lies not in the facts or compositions of the idea which we conceive, it follows that it must lie in the manner in which we conceive it" (*Treatise of Human Nature*, pt. iii., sec. 7).

The *fons et origo* of all reality, whether from the absolute or the practical point of view, is thus subjective, is *ourselves*. As bare logical thinkers, without emotional reaction, we give reality to whatever objects we think of, for they are really phenomena, or objects of our passing thought, if nothing more. But, as thinkers with emotional reaction, we give what seems to us a still higher degree of reality to whatever things we select and emphasise and turn to *with a will*. These are our *living* realities; and not only these, but all the other things which are intimately connected with these. Reality, starting from our Ego, thus sheds itself from point to point—first, upon all objects which have an immediate sting of interest for our Ego in them, and next, upon the objects most continuously related with these. It only fades when the connecting thread is lost. A whole system may be real, if it only hang to our Ego by one immediately *stinging* term. But what contradicts any such stinging term, even though it be another stinging term itself, is either not believed, or only believed after settlement of the dispute.

We reach thus the important conclusion that *our own reality, that sense of our own life which we at every moment possess, is the ultimate of ultimates for our belief.* 'As sure as I exist!'—this is our uttermost warrant for the being of all other things. As Descartes made the indubitable reality of the *cogito* go bail for the reality of all that the *cogito* involved, so we all of us, feeling our own present reality with absolutely coercive force, ascribe an all but equal degree of reality, first to whatever things we lay hold on with a sense of personal need, and second, to whatever farther things continuously belong with these.

The world of living realities as contrasted with unrealities is thus anchored in the Ego, considered as an active and emotional term.[13] That is the hook from which the rest dangles, the absolute ποῦ στῶ. And as from a painted hook it has been said that one can only hang a painted chain, so conversely, from a real hook only a real chain can properly be hung. Whatever things have intimate and continuous connexion with my life are things of whose reality I cannot doubt. What-

[13]I use the notion of the Ego here, as common-sense uses it. Nothing is prejudged as to the results (or absence of results) of ulterior attempts to analyse the notion.

ever things fail to establish this connexion are things which are practically no better for me than if they existed not at all.

In certain forms of melancholic perversion of the sensibilities and reactive powers, nothing touches us intimately, rouses us or wakens natural feeling. The consequence is the complaint so often heard from melancholic patients, that nothing is believed in by them as it used to be, and that all sense of reality is fled from life. They are sheathed in india-rubber, nothing penetrates to the quick or draws blood, as it were. According to Griesinger, 'I see, I hear!' such patients say, 'but the objects do not reach me, it is as if there were a wall between me and the outer world!'

"In such patients there often is an alteration of the cutaneous sensibility, such that things feel indistinct or sometimes rough and woolly. But even were this change always present, it would not completely explain the psychic phenomenon . . . which reminds us more of the alteration in our psychic relations to the outer world which advancing age on the one hand, and on the other emotions and passions, may bring about. In childhood we feel ourselves to be closer to the world of sensible phenomena, we live immediately with them and in them; an intimately vital tie binds us and them together. But with the ripening of reflection this tie is loosened, the warmth of our interest cools, things look differently to us, and we act more as foreigners to the outer world, even though we know it a great deal better. Joy and expansive emotions in general draw it nearer to us again. Everything makes a more lively impression, and with the quick immediate return of this warm receptivity for sense-impressions, joy makes us feel young again. In depressing emotions it is the other way. Outer things, whether living or inorganic, suddenly grow cold and foreign to us, and even our favourite objects of interest feel as if they belonged to us no more. Under these circumstances, receiving no longer from anything a lively impression, we cease to turn towards outer things, and the sense of inward loneliness grows upon us. . . . Where there is no strong intelligence to control this *blasé* condition, this psychic coldness and lack of interest, the issue of these states in which all seems so cold and hollow, the heart dried up, the world grown dead and empty, is often suicide or the deeper forms of insanity."[14]

[14]Griesinger, *Mental Diseases*, §§ 50, 98. The neologism we so often hear, that an experience 'gives us a *realising sense*' of the truth of some proposition or other, illustrates the dependence of the sense of reality upon *excitement*. Only what stirs us is realised.

But now we are met by questions of detail. What does this stirring, this exciting power, this interest, consist in, which some objects have? which *are* those 'intimate relations' with our life which give reality? And what things stand in these relations immediately, and what others are so closely connected with the former that (in Hume's language) we "carry our disposition" also on to them?

In a simple and direct way these questions cannot be answered at all. The whole history of human thought is but an unfinished attempt to answer them. For what have men been trying to find out, since men were men, but just those things: 'Where do our true interests lie—which relations shall we call the intimate and real ones—which things shall we call living realities and which not?' A few psychological points can, however, be made clear.

Any relation to our mind at all, *in the absence of a stronger relation*, suffices to make an object real. The barest appeal to our attention is enough for that. Revert to the beginning of the chapter, and take the candle entering the vacant mind. The mind was waiting for just some such object to make its spring upon. It makes its spring and the candle is believed. But when the candle appears at the same time with other objects, it must run the gauntlet of their rivalry, and then it becomes a question which of the various candidates for attention shall compel belief. As a rule we believe as much as we can. We would believe everything if we only could. When objects are represented by us quite unsystematically they conflict but little with each other, and the number of them which in this chaotic manner we can believe is limitless. The primitive savage's mind is a jungle in which hallucinations, dreams, superstitions, conceptions and sensible objects all flourish alongside of each other, unregulated except by the attention turning in this way or in that. The child's mind is the same. It is only as objects become permanent and their relations fixed that discrepancies and contradictions are felt and must be settled in some stable way. As a rule, the success with which a contradicted object maintains itself in our belief is proportional to several qualities which it must possess. Of these the one which would be put first by most people, because it characterises objects of sensation, is its—

(1) Coerciveness over attention, or the mere power to possess consciousness: then follow—

(2) Liveliness, or sensible pungency, especially in the way of exciting pleasure or pain;

(3) Stimulating effect upon the will, *i.e.*, capacity to arouse active impulses, the more instinctive the better;

(4) Emotional interest, as object of love, dread, admiration, desire, &c.;

(5) Congruity with certain favourite forms of contemplation—unity, simplicity, permanence, and the like;

(6) Independence of other causes, and its own causal importance.

These characters run into each other. Coerciveness is the result of liveliness or emotional interest. What is lively and interesting stimulates *eo ipso* the will; congruity holds of active impulses as well as of contemplative forms; causal independence and importance suit a certain contemplative demand, &c. I will therefore abandon all attempt at a formal treatment, and simply proceed to make remarks in the most convenient order of exposition.

As a whole, sensations are more lively and are judged more real than conceptions; things met with every hour more real than things seen once; attributes perceived when awake, more real than attributes perceived in a dream. But, owing to the *diverse relations contracted by the various objects with each other*, the simple rule that the lively and permanent is the real is often enough disguised. A conceived thing may be deemed more real than a certain sensible thing, if it only be intimately related to other sensible things more vivid, permanent or interesting than the first one. Conceived molecular vibrations, *e.g.*, are by the physicist judged more real than felt warmth, because so intimately related to all those other facts of motion in the world which he has made his special study. Similarly, a rare thing may be deemed more real than a permanent thing if it be more widely related to other permanent things. All the occasional crucial observations of science are examples of this. A rare experience, too, is likely to be judged more real than a permanent one, if it be more interesting and exciting. Such is the sight of Saturn through a telescope; such are the occasional insights and illuminations which upset our habitual ways of thought.

But no mere floating conception, no mere disconnected rarity, ever displaces vivid things or permanent things from our belief. A conception, to prevail, must *terminate* in the world of orderly sensible experience. A rare phenomenon, to displace frequent ones, must belong with others more frequent still. The history of science is strewn with wrecks and ruins of theory, essences and principles, fluids and forces, once fondly clung to, but found to hang together with no facts of sense. And exceptional phenomena solicit our belief in vain until such time as we chance to conceive them as of kinds already admitted to exist. What science means by 'verification' is no more than this, that no object of conception shall be believed which sooner or later has not some permanent and vivid object of sensation for its *term*.

Sensible objects are thus either our realities or the tests of our realities. Conceived objects must show sensible *effects* or else be disbelieved. And the effects, even though reduced to relative unreality when their causes come to view (as heat, which molecular vibrations make unreal), are yet the things on which our knowledge of the causes rests. Strange mutual dependence this, in which the appearance needs the reality in order to exist, but the reality needs the appearance in order to be known!

Sensible vividness or pungency is then the vital factor in reality when once the conflict between objects and the connecting of them together in the mind has begun. No object which neither possesses this vividness in its own right nor is able to borrow it from anything else has a chance of making headway against vivid rivals, or of rousing in us that reaction in which belief consists. On the vivid objects we *pin*, as the saying is, our faith in all the rest; and our belief returns instinctively even to those of them from which reflection has led it away. Witness the obduracy with which the popular world of colours, sounds and smells holds its own against that of molecules and vibrations. Let the physicist himself but nod, like Homer, and the world of sense becomes his absolute reality again.[15]

That things originally devoid of this stimulating power should be enabled, by association with other things which have it, to compel our belief as if they had it themselves, is a remarkable psychological fact, which since Hume's time it has been impossible to overlook.

"The vividness of the first conception," he writes, "diffuses itself along the relations and is conveyed, as by so many pipes or channels, to every idea that has any communication with the primary one. . . . Superstitious people are fond of the relics of saints and holy men, for the same reason that they seek after types and images, in order to enliven their devotion and give them a more intimate and strong conception of those exemplary lives. . . . Now, 'tis evident one of the best relics a devotee could procure would be the handi-work of a saint, and if his clothes and furniture are ever to be con-sidered in this light, 'tis because they were once at his disposal, and were moved and affected by him; in which respect they are . . . connected with him by a shorter train of consequences than any of those from which we learn the reality of his existence. This phenom-enon clearly proves that a present impression, with a relation of cau-sation, may enliven any idea, and consequently produce belief or assent, according to the precedent definition of it. . . . It has been

---

[15]The way in which sensations are pitted against systematised conceptions, and in which the one or the other then prevails according as the sensations are felt by ourselves or merely known by report, is interestingly illustrated at the present day by the state of public belief about 'spiritualistic' phenomena. There exist numerous narratives of movement without contact on the part of articles of furniture and other material objects, in the presence of certain privileged individuals called mediums. Such movement violates our memo-ries, and the whole system of accepted physical 'science'. Consequently those who have not seen it either brand the narratives immediately as lies or call the phenomena 'illusions' of sense, produced by fraud or due to hallucination. But one who has actually seen such a phenomenon, under what seems to him sufficiently 'test-conditions,' will hold to his sensible experience through thick and thin, even though the whole fabric of 'science' should be rent in twain. That man would be a weak-spirited creature indeed who should allow any fly-blown generalities about 'the liability of the senses to be deceived' to bully him out of his adhesion to what for him was an indubitable experience of sight. A man may err in this obstinacy, sure enough, in any particular case. But the spirit that animates him is that on which ultimately the very life and health of Science rest.

remarked among the Mahometans as well as Christians, that those pilgrims who have seen Mecca or the Holy Land are ever after more faithful and zealous believers than those who have not had that advantage. A man whose memory presents him with a lively image of the Red Sea and the Desert and Jerusalem and Galilee can never doubt of any miraculous events which are related either by Moses or the Evangelists. The lively idea of the places passes by an easy transition to the facts which are supposed to have been related to them by contiguity, and increases the belief by increasing the vivacity of the conception. The remembrance of those fields and rivers has the same influence as a new argument. . . . The ceremonies of the Catholic religion may be considered as instances of the same nature. The devotees of that strange superstition usually plead in excuse for the mummeries with which they are upbraided that they feel the good effect of external motions and postures and actions in enlivening their devotion and quickening their fervour, which otherwise would decay, if directed entirely to distant and immaterial objects. We shadow out the objects of our faith, say they, in sensible types and images, and render them more present to us by the immediate presence of these types than it is possible for us to do merely by an intellectual view and contemplation."[16]

Hume's cases are rather trivial; and the things which associated sensible objects make us believe in are supposed by him to be unreal. But all the more manifest for that is the fact of their psychological influence. Who does not 'realise' more the fact of a dead or distant friend's existence, at the moment when a portrait, letter, garment or other material reminder of him is found? The whole notion of him then grows pungent and speaks to us and shakes us, in a manner unknown at other times. In children's minds, fancies and realities live side by side. But however lively their fancies may be, they still gain help from association with reality. The imaginative child identifies its *dramatis personæ* with some doll or other material object, and this evidently solidifies belief, little as it may resemble what it is held to stand for. A thing not too interesting by its own real qualities generally does the best service here. The most useful doll I ever saw was a large cucumber in the hands of a little Amazonian-Indian girl; she nursed it and washed it and rocked it to sleep in a hammock, and talked to

[16]*Treatise of Human Nature*, bk. i., pt. iii., sec. 7.

it all day long—there was no part in life which the cucumber did not play. Says Mr. Tylor:—

"An imaginative child will make a dog do duty for a horse, or a soldier for a shepherd, till at last the objective resemblance almost disappears, and a bit of wood may be dragged about, resembling a ship on the sea or a coach on the road. Here the likeness of the bit of wood to a ship or coach is very slight indeed; but it is a thing, and can be moved about . . . and is an evident assistance to the child in enabling it to arrange and develop its ideas. . . . Of how much use . . . may be seen by taking it away, and leaving the child nothing to play with. . . . In later years and among highly educated people the mental process which goes on in a child's playing with wooden soldiers and horses, though it never disappears, must be sought for in more complex phenomena. Perhaps nothing in after-life more closely resembles the effect of a doll upon a child than the effect of the illustrations of a tale upon a grown reader. Here the objective resemblance is very indefinite . . . yet what reality is given to the scene by a good picture. . . . Mr. Backhouse one day noticed in Van Diemen's Land a woman arranging several stones that were flat, oval and about two inches wide, and marked in various directions with black and red lines. These, he learned, represented absent friends, and one larger than the rest stood for a fat native woman on Flinder's Island, known by the name of Mother Brown. Similar practices are found among far higher races than the ill-fated Tasmanians. Among some North American tribes a mother who has lost a child keeps its memory ever present to her by filling its cradle with black feathers and quills and carrying it about with her for a year or more. When she stops anywhere, she sets up the cradle and talks to it as she goes about her work, just as she would have done if the dead body had been still alive within it. Here we have an image; but in Africa we find a rude doll representing the child, kept as a memorial. . . . Bastian saw Indian women in Peru who had lost an infant carrying about on their backs a wooden doll to represent it."[17]

To many persons among us, photographs of lost ones seem to be fetishes. They, it is true, resemble; but the fact that the mere materiality of the reminder is almost as important as its resemblance is shown by the popularity a hundred years ago of the black taffeta 'silhouettes' which are still found among family relics, and of one of which Fichte could write to his affianced: "*Die Farbe fehlt, das Auge fehlt, es fehlt der himm-*

[17]*Early Hist. of Mankind*, p. 108.

lische Ausdruck deiner lieblichen Züge"—and yet go on worshipping it all the same. The opinion so stoutly professed by
many, that language is essential to thought, seems to have this
much of truth in it, that all our inward images tend invincibly
to attach themselves to something sensible so as to gain in
corporeity and life. Words serve this purpose, gestures serve
it, stones, straws, chalk-marks, anything will do. As soon as
any one of these things stands for the idea, the latter seems to
be more real. Some persons, the present writer among the
number, can hardly lecture without a black-board: the abstract conceptions must be symbolised by letters, squares or
circles, and the relations between them by lines. All this sym-
bolism, linguistic, graphic and dramatic, has other uses too,
for it abridges thought and fixes terms. But one of its uses is
surely to rouse the believing reaction and give to the ideas a
more living reality. As, when we are told a story, and shown
the very knife that did the murder, the very ring whose hiding-
place the clairvoyant revealed, the whole thing passes from
fairy-land to mother-earth, so here we believe all the more, if
only we see that "the bricks are alive to tell the tale".[18]

So much for the prerogative position of sensations in regard to our belief. But among the sensations themselves all
are not deemed equally real. The more practically important
ones, the more permanent ones, and the more æsthetically apprehensible ones are selected from the mass, to be believed in
most of all; the others are degraded to the position of mere
signs and suggesters of these. This fact has already been ad-
verted to in a former essay in MIND (vol. xii.). The real colour
of a thing is that one colour-sensation which it gives us when
most favourably lighted for vision. So of its real size, its real
shape, &c.—these are but optical sensations selected out of
thousands of others, because they have æsthetic characteristics
which appeal to our convenience or delight. But I will not
repeat what I have already written about this matter, but pass

---

[18]The reader will be reminded of the part which real sensations play in a
very large number of hallucinations or even, according to M. Binet, in all.
Some sensorial process seems requisite in order that the illusory object shall
appear *outwardly there*, though the *nature* of the object thus appearing may be
determined by inward cerebral processes with which under normal conditions
the outer *point de repère* had nothing to do.

on to our treatment of tactile and muscular sensations, as 'primary qualities,' more real than those 'secondary' qualities which eye and ear and nose reveal. Why do we thus so markedly select the *tangible* to be the real? Our motives are not far to seek. The tangible qualities are the least fluctuating. When we get them at all we get them the same. The other qualities fluctuate enormously as our relative position to the object changes. Then, more decisive still, the tactile properties are those most intimately connected with our weal or woe. A dagger hurts us only when in contact with our skin, a poison only when we take it into our mouths, and we can only use an object for our advantage when we have it in our muscular control. It is as tangibles, then, that things concern us most; and the other senses, so far as their practical use goes, do but warn us of what tangible things to expect. They are but organs of anticipatory touch, as Berkeley has with perfect clearness explained.[19]

Among all sensations, the *most* belief-compelling are those productive of pleasure or of pain. Locke expressly makes the *pleasure-* or *pain*-giving quality to be the ultimate human criterion of anything's reality. Discussing (with a supposed Berkeleyan before Berkeley) the notion that all our perceptions may be but a dream, he says:

"He may please to dream that I make him this answer . . . that I believe he will allow a very manifest difference between dreaming of being in the fire and being actually in it. But yet if he be resolved to appear so sceptical as to maintain that what I call being actually in the fire is nothing but a dream, and that we cannot thereby certainly know that any such thing as fire actually exists without us, I answer that we, certainly finding that pleasure or pain [or emotion of any sort] follows upon the application of certain objects to us, whose existence we perceive, or dream that we perceive by our senses, *this certainly is as great as our happiness or misery*, beyond which we have no concernment to know or to be."[20]

[19]See *Theory of Vision*, § 59.
[20]*Essay*, bk. iv., ch. 2, § 14. In another place: "He that sees a candle burning and hath experimented the force of its flame by putting his finger into it, will little doubt that this is something existing without him, which does him harm and puts him to great pain. . . . And if our dreamer pleases to try whether the glowing heat of a glass furnace be barely a wandering imagination in a drowsy man's fancy by putting his hand into it, he may, perhaps, be

The quality of arousing emotion, of shaking, moving us or inciting us to action, has as much to do with our belief in an object's reality as the quality of giving pleasure or pain. In MIND ix. 188, I have sought to show that our emotions probably owe their pungent quality to the bodily sensations which they involve. Our tendency to believe in emotionally exciting objects (objects of fear, desire, &c.) more than in indifferent ones is thus explained without resorting to any fundamentally new principle of choice. Speaking generally, and other things being equal, the more a conceived object *excites* us, the more reality it has. The same object excites us differently at different times. Moral and religious truths come 'home' to us far more on some occasions than on others. As Emerson says, "there is a difference between one and another hour of life in their authority and subsequent effect. Our faith comes in moments . . . yet there is a depth in those brief moments which constrains us to ascribe more reality to them than to all other experiences." The "depth" is partly, no doubt, the insight into wider systems of unified relation, but far more often than that it is the emotional thrill. Thus, to descend to more trivial examples, a man who has no belief in ghosts by daylight will temporarily believe in them when, alone at midnight, he feels his blood curdle at a mysterious sound or vision, his heart thumping, and his legs impelled to flee. The thought of falling when we walk along a kerbstone awakens no emotion of dread, so no sense of reality attaches to it, and we are sure we shall not fall. On a precipice's edge, however, the sickening emotion which the notion of a possible fall engenders makes us believe in the latter's imminent reality, and quite unfits us to proceed.

The greatest proof that a man is *sui compos* is his ability to suspend belief in presence of an emotionally exciting idea. To

---

awakened into a certainty greater than he could wish, that it is something more than bare imagination. So that the evidence is as great as we can desire, being as certain to us as our pleasure or pain, *i.e.,* happiness or misery; beyond which we have no concernment, either of knowledge or being. Such an assurance of the existence of things without us is sufficient to direct us in the attaining the good and avoiding the evil which is caused by them, which is the important concernment we have of being made acquainted with them." *Ibid.*, bk. iv., ch. ii, § 8.

give this power is the highest result of education. In untutored minds the power does not exist. Every exciting thought carries credence with it. To conceive with passion is *eo ipso* to affirm. As Bagehot says: —

"The Caliph Omar burnt the Alexandrian Library, saying: 'All books which contain what is not in the Koran are dangerous. All which contain what is in it are useless'! Probably no one ever had an intenser belief in anything than Omar had in this. Yet it is impossible to imagine it preceded by an argument. His belief in Mahomet, in the Koran, and in the sufficiency of the Koran, probably came to him in spontaneous rushes of emotion; there may have been little vestiges of argument floating here and there, but they did not justify the strength of the emotion, still less did they create it, and they hardly even excused it. . . . Probably, when the subject is thoroughly examined, conviction will be found to be one of the intensest of human emotions, and one most closely connected with the bodily state . . . accompanied or preceded by the sensation that Scott makes his seer describe as the prelude of a prophecy: —

> 'At length the fatal answer came,
> In characters of living flame —
> Not spoke in words, nor blazed in scroll,
> But borne and branded on my soul'.

A hot flash seems to burn across the brain. Men in these intense states of mind have altered all history, changed for better or worse the creed of myriads, and desolated or redeemed provinces or ages. Nor is this intensity a sign of truth, for it is precisely strongest in those points in which men differ most from each other. John Knox felt it in his anti-Catholicism; Ignatius Loyola in his anti-Protestantism; and both, I suppose, felt it as much as it is possible to feel it."[21]

The reason of the belief is undoubtedly the bodily commotion which the exciting idea sets up. 'Nothing which I can feel like *that* can be false.' All our religious and supernatural beliefs are of this order. The surest warrant for immortality is the yearning of our bowels for our dear ones; for God, the sinking sense it gives us to imagine no such Providence or help. So of our political or pecuniary hopes and fears, and things and persons dreaded and desired. "A grocer has a full

[21]W. Bagehot, "The Emotion of Conviction," *Literary Studies* i. 412–17.

creed as to foreign policy, a young lady a complete theory of the sacraments, as to which neither has any doubt. . . . A girl in a country parsonage will be sure that Paris never can be taken, or that Bismarck is a wretch"—all because they have either conceived these things at some moment with passion, or associated them with other things which they have conceived with passion.

M. Renouvier calls this belief of a thing for no other reason than that we conceive it with passion, by the name of mental vertigo.[22] Other objects whisper doubt or disbelief; but the object of passion makes us deaf to all but itself, and we affirm it unhesitatingly. Such objects are the delusions of insanity, which the insane person can at odd moments steady himself against, but which again return to sweep him off his feet. Such are the revelations of mysticism. Such, particularly, are the sudden beliefs which animate mobs of men when frenzied impulse to action is involved. Whatever be the action in point—whether the stoning of a prophet, the hailing of a conqueror, the burning of a witch, the baiting of a heretic or Jew, the starting of a forlorn hope, or the flying from a foe— the fact that to believe a certain object will cause that action to explode convulsively is a sufficient reason for that belief to come. The motor impulse sweeps it unresisting in its train.

The whole history of witchcraft and early medicine is a commentary on the facility with which anything which chances to be conceived is believed the moment the belief chimes in with an emotional mood. The cause of sickness! When a savage asks the cause of anything he means to ask exclusively 'What is to blame?' The theoretic curiosity starts from the practical life's demands. Let some one then accuse a necromancer, suggest a charm or spell which has been cast, and no more 'evidence' is asked for. What evidence is required beyond this intimate sense of the culprit's responsibility, to which our very viscera and limbs reply?[23]

[22]*Psychologie Rationelle*, ch. 12.

[23]Two examples out of a thousand:—

Reid, *Inquiry*, ch. ii., § 9:—"I remember, many years ago, a white ox was brought into the country, of so enormous size, that people came many miles to see him. There happened, some months after, an uncommon fatality among women in child-bearing. Two such uncommon events, following one

Human credulity in the way of therapeutics has similar psychological roots. If there is anything intolerable (especially to the heart of woman), it is to do nothing when a loved one is sick or in pain. To do anything is a relief. Accordingly, what-

---

another, gave a suspicion of their connexion, and occasioned a common opinion among the country people that the white ox was the cause of this fatality."

H. M. Stanley, *Through the Dark Continent*, ii. 388: — "On the third day of our stay at Mowa, feeling quite comfortable amongst the people, on account of their friendly bearing, I began to write in my note-book the terms for articles, in order to improve my already copious vocabulary of native words. I had proceeded only a few minutes when I observed a strange commotion amongst the people who had been flocking about me, and presently they ran away. In a short time we heard war-cries ringing loudly and shrilly over the table-land. Two hours afterwards, a long line of warriors were seen descending the table-land and advancing towards our camp. There may have been between five and six hundred of them. We, on the other hand, had made but few preparations except such as would justify us replying to them in the event of the actual commencement of hostilities. But I had made many firm friends among them, and I firmly believed that I should be able to avert an open rupture. When they had assembled at about a hundred yards in front of our camp, Safeni and I walked up towards them and sat down midway. Some half-dozen of the Mowa people came near, and the shauri began.

" 'What is the matter, my friends?' I asked. 'Why do you come with guns in your hands, in such numbers, as though you were coming to fight? Fight? fight us, your friends! Tut! this is some great mistake, surely.'

" 'Mundelé,' replied one of them . . . 'our people saw you yesterday make marks on some tara-tara [paper]. This is very bad. Our country will waste, our goats will die, our bananas will rot, and our women will dry up. What have we done to you that you should wish to kill us? We have sold you food and we have brought you wine each day. Your people are allowed to wander where they please without trouble. Why is the Mundelé so wicked? We have gathered together to fight you if you do not burn that tara-tara now before our eyes. If you burn it we go away, and shall be your friends as heretofore.'

"I told them to rest there, and left Safeni in their hands as a pledge that I should return. My tent was not fifty yards from the spot, but while going towards it my brain was busy in devising some plan to foil this superstitious madness. My note-book contained a vast number of valuable notes. . . . I could not sacrifice it to the childish caprice of savages. As I was rummaging my book-box, I came across a volume of *Shakespeare* [Chandos edition] much worn, and well thumbed, and which was of the same size as my field-book; its cover was similar also, and it might be passed for the field-book, provided that no one remembered its appearance too well. I took it to them. 'Is this the tara-tara, friends, that you wish burnt?'

" 'Yes, yes, that is it.'

" 'Well, take it, and burn it, or keep it.'

ever remedy may be suggested is a spark on inflammable soil. The mind makes its spring towards action on that cue, sends for that remedy, and for a day at least believes the danger past. Blame, dread and hope are thus the great belief-inspiring passions, and cover among them the future, the present and the past.

These remarks illustrate the earlier heads of the list on page 1037. Whichever represented objects give us sensations, especially interesting ones, or incite our motor impulses, or arouse our hate, desire or fear, are real enough for us. Our requirements in the way of reality terminate in our own acts and emotions, our own pleasures and pains. These are the ultimate fixities from which, as we formerly observed, the whole chain of our beliefs depends, object hanging to object, as the bees, in swarming, hang to each other until, *de proche en proche*, the supporting branch, the Self, is reached and held.

Now the merely conceived or imagined objects which our mind represents as hanging to the sensations (causing them, &c.), filling the gaps between them, and weaving their interrupted chaos into order are innumerable. Whole systems of them conflict with other systems, and our choice of which system shall carry our belief is governed by principles which are simple enough, however subtle and difficult may be their application to details. The conceived system, to pass for true, must at least include the reality of the sensible objects in it, by explaining them as *effects on us*, if nothing more. The system which includes the most of them, and definitely explains or pretends to explain the most of them, will, *ceteris paribus*,

---

" 'M—m. No, no, no. We will not touch it. It is fetish. You must burn it.'

" 'I! Well, let it be so. I will do anything to please my good friends of Mowa.'

"We walked to the nearest fire. I breathed a regretful farewell to my genial companion, which, during my many weary hours of night, had assisted to relieve my mind when oppressed by almost intolerable woes, and then gravely consigned the innocent *Shakespeare* to the flames, heaping the brush fuel over it with ceremonious care.

" 'Ah-h-h,' breathed the poor deluded natives sighing their relief. . . . 'There is no trouble now.' . . . And something approaching to a cheer was shouted among them, which terminated the episode of the burning of *Shakespeare*."

prevail. It is needless to say how far mankind still is from
having excogitated such a system. But the various materialisms, idealisms and hylozoisms show with what industry the
attempt is for ever made. It is conceivable that several rival
theories should equally well include the actual order of our
sensations in their scheme, much as the one-fluid and two-
fluid theories of electricity formulated all the common electrical phenomena equally well. The sciences are full of these
alternatives. Which theory is then to be believed? That will be
most generally believed which, besides offering us objects able
to account satisfactorily for our sensible experience, also offers
those which are most interesting, those which appeal most
urgently to our æsthetic, emotional and active needs. So here
in the higher intellectual life, the same selection among general conceptions goes on which went on among the sensations
themselves. First, a word of their relation to our emotional
and active needs—and here I can do no better than quote
from an article published some years ago.[24]

"A philosophy may be unimpeachable in other respects, but
either of two defects will be fatal to its universal acceptance.
First, its ultimate principle must not be one that essentially
baffles and disappoints our dearest desires and most cherished
powers. A pessimistic principle like Schopenhauer's incurably
vicious Will-substance, or Hartmann's wicked jack-at-all-
trades, the Unconscious, will perpetually call forth essays at
other philosophies. Incompatibility of the future with their
desires and active tendencies is, in fact, to most men a source
of more fixed disquietude than uncertainty itself. Witness the
attempts to overcome the 'problem of evil,' the 'mystery of
pain'. There is no problem of 'good'.

"But a second and worse defect in a philosophy than that of
contradicting our active propensities is to give them no Object whatever to press against. A philosophy whose principle
is so incommensurate with our most intimate powers as to
deny them all relevancy in universal affairs, as to annihilate
their motives at one blow, will be even more unpopular than
pessimism. Better face the enemy than the eternal Void! This
is why materialism will always fail of universal adoption, how-

[24]"Rationality, Activity and Faith" (*Princeton Review*, July, 1882, pp. 64–9).

ever well it may fuse things into an atomistic unity, however clearly it may prophesy the future eternity. For materialism denies reality to the objects of almost all the impulses which we most cherish. The real *meaning* of the impulses, it says, is something which has no emotional interest for us whatever. But what is called extradition is quite as characteristic of our emotions as of our sense. Both point to an Object as the cause of the present feeling. What an intensely objective reference lies in fear! In like manner an enraptured man, a dreary-feeling man, are not simply aware of their subjective states; if they were, the force of their feelings would evaporate. Both believe there is outward cause *why* they should feel as they do: either 'It is a glad world! how good is life!' or 'What a loathsome tedium is existence!' Any philosophy which annihilates the validity of the reference by explaining away its objects or translating them into terms of no emotional pertinency leaves the mind with little to care or act for. This is the opposite condition from that of nightmare, but when acutely brought home to consciousness it produces a kindred horror. In nightmare we have motives to act but no power; here we have powers but no motives. A nameless *Unheimlichkeit* comes over us at the thought of there being nothing eternal in our final purposes, in the objects of those loves and aspirations which are our deepest energies. The monstrously lopsided equation of the universe and its knower, which we postulate as the ideal of cognition, is perfectly paralleled by the no less lopsided equation of the universe and the *doer*. We demand in it a *character* for which our emotions and active propensities shall be a match. Small as we are, minute as is the point by which the Cosmos impinges upon each one of us, each one desires to feel that his reaction at that point is congruous with the demands of the vast whole, that he balances the latter, so to speak, and is able to do what it expects of him. But as his abilities to 'do' lie wholly in the line of his natural propensities; as he enjoys reaction with such emotions as fortitude, hope, rapture, admiration, earnestness and the like; and as he very unwillingly reacts with fear, disgust, despair or doubt, —a philosophy which should legitimate only emotions of the latter sort would be sure to leave the mind a prey to discontent and craving.

"It is far too little recognised how entirely the intellect is built up of practical interests. The theory of Evolution is beginning to do very good service by its reduction of all mentality to the type of reflex action. Cognition, in this view, is but a fleeting moment, a cross-section at a certain point of what in its totality is a motor phenomenon. In the lower forms of life no one will pretend that cognition is anything more than a guide to appropriate action. The germinal question concerning things brought for the first time before consciousness is not the theoretic 'What is that?' but the practical 'Who goes there?' or rather, as Horwicz has admirably put it, 'What is to be done?'—'*Was fang' ich an?*' In all our discussions about the intelligence of lower animals the only test we use is that of their *acting* as if for a purpose. Cognition, in short, is incomplete until discharged in act. And although it is true that the later mental development, which attains its maximum through the hypertrophied cerebrum of man, gives birth to a vast amount of theoretic activity over and above that which is immediately ministerial to practice, yet the earlier claim is only postponed, not effaced, and the active nature asserts its rights to the end.

"If there be any truth at all in this view, it follows, that however vaguely a philosopher may define the ultimate universal datum, he cannot be said to leave it unknown to us so long as he in the slightest degree pretends that our emotional or active attitude towards it should be of one sort rather than another. He who says, 'Life is real, life is earnest,' however much he may speak of the fundamental mysteriousness of things, gives a distinct definition to that mysteriousness by ascribing to it the right to claim from us the particular mood called seriousness, which means the willingness to live with energy, though energy bring pain. The same is true of him who says that all is vanity. Indefinable as the predicate vanity may be *in se*, it is clearly enough something which permits anæsthesia, mere escape from suffering, to be our rule of life. There is no more ludicrous incongruity than for agnostics to proclaim with one breath that the substance of things is unknowable, and with the next that the thought of it should inspire us with admiration of its glory, reverence and a willingness to add our co-operative push in the direction towards which its manifestations seem to be drifting. The unknowable may be unfathomed, but if it make such distinct demands upon our activity, we surely are not ignorant of its essential quality.

"If we survey the field of history and ask what feature all great periods of revival, of expansion of the human mind, display in common, we shall find, I think, simply this: that each and all of them have said to the human being, 'The inmost nature of the reality is congenial to *powers* which you possess'. In what did the emancipating message of primitive Christianity consist, but in the announcement that God recognises those weak and tender impulses which paganism had so rudely overlooked? Take repentance: the man who can do nothing rightly can at least repent of his failures. But for paganism this faculty of repentance was a pure supernumerary, a straggler too late for the fair. Christianity took it and made it the one power within us which appealed straight to the heart of God. And after the night of the Middle Ages had so long branded with obloquy even the generous impulses of the flesh, and defined the Reality to be such that only slavish natures could commune with it, in what did the *Sursum corda!* of the Renaissance lie but in the proclamation that the archetype of verity in things laid claim on the widest activity of our whole æsthetic being? What were Luther's mission and Wesley's but appeals to powers which even the meanest of men might carry with them, faith and self-despair, but which were personal, requiring no priestly intermediation, and which brought their owner face to face with God? What caused the wild-fire influence of Rousseau but the assurance he gave that man's nature was in harmony with the nature of things, if only the paralysing corruptions of custom would stand from between? How did Kant and Fichte, Goethe and Schiller, inspire their time with cheer, except by saying, 'Use all your powers; that is the only obedience which the universe exacts'? And Carlyle with his gospel of Work, of Fact, of Veracity, how does he move us except by saying that the universe imposes no tasks upon us but such as the most humble can perform? Emerson's creed that everything that ever was or will be is here in the developing Now; that man has but to obey himself—'He who will rest in what he *is*, is a part of

Destiny'—is in like manner nothing but an exorcism of all scepticism as to the pertinency of one's natural faculties.

"In a word, 'Son of Man, *stand upon thy feet* and I will speak unto thee!' is the only revelation of truth to which the solving epochs have helped the disciple. But that has been enough to satisfy the greater part of his rational need. *In se* and *per se* the universal essence has hardly been more defined by any of these formulæ than by the agnostic *x*; but the mere assurance that my powers, such as they are, are not irrelevant to it, but pertinent, that it speaks to them and will in some way recognise their reply, that I can be a match for it if I will, and not a footless waif, suffices to make it rational to my feeling in the sense given above. Nothing could be more absurd than to hope for the definitive triumph of any philosophy which should refuse to legitimate, and to legitimate in an emphatic manner, the more powerful of our emotional and practical tendencies. Fatalism, whose solving word in all crises of behaviour is 'All striving is vain,' will never reign supreme, for the impulse to take life strivingly is indestructible in the race. Moral creeds which speak to that impulse will be widely successful in spite of inconsistency, vagueness and shadowy determination of expectancy. Man needs a rule for his will, and will invent one if one be not given him."

After the emotional and active needs come the intellectual and æsthetic ones. The two great æsthetic principles, of richness and of ease, dominate our intellectual as well as our sensuous life. And, *ceteris paribus*, no system which should not be rich, simple and harmonious would have a chance of being chosen for belief if rich, simple and harmonious systems were there. Into the latter we should unhesitatingly settle, with that welcoming attitude of the will in which belief consists. To quote from a remarkable book:—

"This law that our consciousness constantly tends to the minimum of complexity and to the maximum of definiteness, is of great importance for all our knowledge. . . . Our own activity of attention will thus determine what we are to know and what we are to believe. If things have more than a certain complexity, not only will our limited powers of attention forbid us to unravel this complexity, but we shall strongly desire to believe the things much simpler than they are. For our thoughts about them will have a constant tendency to become as simple and definite as possible. Put a man into a perfect chaos of phenomena—sounds, sights, feelings—and if the man continued to exist, and to be rational at all, his attention would doubtless soon find for him a way to make up some kind of rhythmic regularity, which he would impute to the things about him, so as to imagine that he had discovered some laws of sequence in this mad new world. And thus, in every case where we fancy ourselves sure of a simple law of Nature, we must remember that a great deal of the fancied simplicity may be due, in the given case, not to Nature, but to the ineradicable prejudice of our own minds in favour of regularity and simplicity. All our thoughts are determined, in great measure, by this law of least effort, as it is found exemplified in our activity of attention. . . . The aim of the whole process seems to be to reach as complete and united a conception of reality as possible, a conception wherein the greatest fulness of data shall be combined with the greatest simplicity of conception. The effort of consciousness seems to be to combine the greatest richness of content with the greatest definiteness of organisation."[25]

The richness is got by including all the facts of sense in the scheme; the simplicity, by deducing them out of the smallest possible number of permanent and independent primordial entities; the definite organisation, by assimilating these latter to ideal objects between which relations of an inwardly rational sort obtain. What these ideal objects and rational relations are would require a separate article to show. Meanwhile, enough has surely been said to justify the assertion made above that no general offhand answer can be given as to which objects mankind shall choose as its realities. The fight is still under way. Our minds are yet chaotic; and at best we make a mixture and a compromise, as we yield to the claim of this interest or that, and follow first one and then another principle in turn. It is undeniably true that materialistic, or so-called 'scientific,' conceptions of the universe have so far gratified the purely intellectual interests more than the more sentimental conceptions have. But, on the other hand, as already remarked, they leave the emotional and active interests cold. The perfect object of belief would be a God or 'Soul of the World,' represented both optimistically and moralistically (if such a combination could be), and withal so definitely con-

[25]J. Royce, *The Religious Aspect of Philosophy* (Boston, 1885), pp. 317–57.

ceived as to show us *why* our phenomenal experiences should be sent to us by Him in just the very way in which they come. All Science and all History would thus be accounted for in the deepest and simplest fashion. The very room in which I sit, its sensible walls and floor, and the feeling the air and fire within it give me, no less than the 'scientific' conceptions which I am urged to frame concerning the mode of existence of all these phenomena when my back is turned, would then all be corroborated, not de-realised, by the ultimate principle of my belief. The World-soul sends me just those phenomena in order that I may react upon them; and among the reactions is the intellectual one of spinning these conceptions. What is beyond the crude experiences is not an *alternative* to them, but something that *means* them for me here and now. It is safe to say that, if ever such a system is satisfactorily excogitated, mankind will drop all other systems and cling to that one alone as real. Meanwhile the other systems co-exist with the attempts at that one, and, all being alike fragmentary, each has its little audience and day.

I have now, I trust, shown sufficiently what the psychological sources of the sense of reality are. Hume declared that its source was the idea's liveliness; Hartley and James Mill maintained that it was its association with other ideas; Prof. Bain has said that it was its connexion with our motor nature. Each is right in part; so that my completer account is less simple than any of its classic predecessors. I have not aspired in it to the slightest originality; I only hope to have woven the traditional doctrines into a less vulnerable whole than I have yet met in print. The absolute, uncriticised reality of the Self is the root of the whole matter, concerning which there is much more to be said, but not at this time and place. There is also much to be said about the connexion of the sense of reality with the Will. The will can change the relative power which objects have of compelling our attention. The will can increase or diminish our emotional and impulsive reactions upon them. The will can end by making us believe things through making us *act* as if they were real, although at first without belief. Belief and will are thus inseparable functions. But space is lacking to treat of their connexion, which I leave willingly untouched, since the masterly treatment of the subject by Renouvier is so readily accessible to every reader.[26]

[26]*Psychologie Rationelle* (1875), ii.

The Knowing of Things Together [1]

THE NATURE of the synthetic unity of consciousness is one of those great underlying problems that divide the psychological schools. We know, say, a dozen things singly through a dozen different mental states. But on another occasion we may know the same dozen things together through a single mental state. The problem is as to the relation of the previous many states to the later one state. In physical nature, it is universally agreed, a multitude of facts always remain the multitude they were and appear as one fact only when a mind comes upon the scene and so views them, as when $H-O-H$ appear as 'water' to a human spectator. But when, instead of extramental 'things,' the mind combines its own 'contents' into a unity, what happens is much less plain.

The matters of fact that give the trouble are among our most familiar experiences. We know a lot of friends and can think of each one singly. But we can also think of them together, as composing a 'party' at our house. We can see single stars appearing in succession between the clouds on a stormy night, but we can also see whole constellations of those stars at once when the wind has blown the clouds away. In a glass of lemonade we can taste both the lemon and the sugar at once. In a major chord our ear can single out the c, e, g, and c', if it has once become acquainted with these notes apart. And so on through the whole field of our experience, whether conceptual or sensible. Neither common sense nor commonplace psychology finds anything special to explain in these facts. Common sense simply says the mind 'brings the things together,' and common psychology says the 'ideas' of the various things 'combine,' and at most will admit that the occasions on which ideas combine may be made the subject of inquiry. But to formulate the phenomenon of knowing things together thus simply as a combining of ideas, is already to foist in a theory about the phenomenon. Not so should a

[1]Read as the President's Address before the American Psychological Association at Princeton, December, 1894, and reprinted with some unimportant omissions, a few slight revisions, and the addition of some explanatory notes.

question be approached. The phenomenon offers itself, in the first instance, as that of *knowing things together*; and it is in those terms that its solution must, in the first instance at least, be sought.

'Things,' then; to 'know' things; and to know the 'same' things 'together' which elsewhere we knew singly—here, indeed, are terms concerning each of which we must put the question, 'What do we *mean* by it when we use it?'—that question that Shadworth Hodgson lays so much stress on, and that is so well taught to students, as the beginning of all sound method, by our colleague Fullerton. And in exactly ascertaining what we do mean by such terms there might lie a lifetime of occupation.

For we do mean something; and we mean something true. Our terms, whatever confusion they may connote, denote at least a fundamental fact of our experience, whose existence no one here present will deny.

II

What, then, do we mean by 'things'? To this question I can only make the answer of the idealistic philosophy. For the philosophy that began with Berkeley, and has led up in our tongue to Shadworth Hodgson, things have no other nature than thoughts have, and we know of no things that are not given to somebody's experience. When I see the thing white paper before my eyes, the nature of the thing and the nature of my sensations are one. Even if with science we supposed a molecular architecture beneath the smooth whiteness of the paper, that architecture itself could only be defined as the stuff of a farther possible experience, a vision, say, of certain vibrating particles with which our acquaintance with the paper would terminate if it were prolonged by magnifying artifices not yet known. A thing may be my phenomenon or some one else's; it may be frequently or infrequently experienced; it may be shared by all of us; one of our copies of it may be regarded as the original, and the other copies as representatives of that original; it may appear very differently at different times; but whatever it be, the stuff of which it is made is thought-stuff, and whenever we speak of a thing that is out of our own mind, we either mean nothing; or we mean a thing that was or will be in our own mind on another occasion; or, finally, we mean a thing in the mind of some other possible receiver of experiences like ours.

Such being 'things,' what do we mean by saying that we 'know' them?

There are two ways of knowing things, knowing them immediately or intuitively, and knowing them conceptually or representatively. Although such things as the white paper before our eyes can be known intuitively, most of the things we know, the tigers now in India, for example, or the scholastic system of philosophy, are known only representatively or symbolically.

Suppose, to fix our ideas, that we take first a case of conceptual knowledge; and let it be our knowledge of the tigers in India, as we sit here. Exactly what do we *mean* by saying that we here know the tigers? What is the precise fact that the cognition so confidently claimed is *known-as*, to use Shadworth Hodgson's inelegant but valuable form of words?

Most men would answer that what we mean by knowing the tigers is having them, however absent in body, become in some way present to our thought; or that our knowledge of them is known as presence of our thought to them. A great mystery is usually made of this peculiar presence in absence; and the scholastic philosophy, which is only common sense grown pedantic, would explain it as a peculiar kind of existence, called *intentional inexistence*, of the tigers in our mind. At the very least, people would say that what we mean by knowing the tigers is mentally *pointing* towards them as we sit here.

But now what do we mean by *pointing*, in such a case as this? What is the pointing known-as, here?

To this question I shall have to give a very prosaic answer—one that traverses the prepossessions not only of common sense and scholasticism, but also those of nearly all the epistemological writers whom I have ever read. The answer, made brief, is this: The pointing of our thought to the tigers is known simply and solely as a procession of mental associates and motor consequences that follow on the thought, and that would lead harmoniously, if followed out, into some ideal or real context, or even into the immediate presence, of the tigers. It is known as our rejection of a jaguar, if that beast were shown us as a tiger; as our assent to a genuine tiger if so shown. It is known as our ability to utter all sorts of propositions which don't contradict other propositions that are true of the real tigers. It is even known, if we take the tigers very seriously, as actions of ours which may terminate in directly intuited tigers, as they would if we took a voyage to India for the purpose of tiger-hunting and brought back a lot of skins of the striped rascals which we had laid low. In all this there is no self-transcendency in our mental images taken by themselves. They are one physical fact; the tigers are another; and their pointing to the tigers is a perfectly commonplace physical relation, if you once grant a connecting world to be there. In short, the ideas and the tigers are in themselves as loose and separate, to use Hume's language, as any two things can be; and pointing means here an operation as external and adventitious as any that nature yields.[2]

I hope you may agree with me now that in representative knowledge there is no special inner mystery, but only an outer chain of physical or mental intermediaries connecting thought and thing. *To know an object is here to lead to it through a context which the world supplies.* All this was most instructively set forth by our colleague Miller, of Bryn Mawr, at our meeting in New York last Christmas, and for re-confirming my sometime wavering opinion, I owe him this acknowledgment.[3]

Let us next pass on to the case of immediate or intuitive acquaintance with an object, and let the object be the white paper before our eyes. The thought-stuff and the thing-stuff

[2] A stone in one field may 'fit,' we say, a hole in another field. But the relation of 'fitting,' so long as no one carries the stone to the hole and drops it in, is only one name for the fact that such an act may happen. Similarly with the knowing of the tigers here and now. It is only an anticipatory name for a further associative and terminative process that may occur.

[3] See also Dr. Miller's article on Truth and Error, in the *Philosophical Review*, July, 1893.

are here indistinguishably the same in nature, as we saw a moment since, and there is no context of intermediaries or associates to stand between and separate the thought and thing. There is no 'presence in absence' here, and no 'pointing,' but rather an allround embracing of the paper by the thought; and it is clear that the knowing cannot now be explained exactly as it was when the tigers were its object. Dotted all through our experience are states of immediate acquaintance just like this. Somewhere our belief always does rest on ultimate data like the whiteness, smoothness, or squareness of this paper. Whether such qualities be truly ultimate aspects of being or only provisional suppositions of ours, held-to till we get better informed, is quite immaterial for our present inquiry. So long as it is believed in, we see our object face to face. What now do we mean by 'knowing' such a sort of object as this? For this is also the way in which we should know the tiger if our conceptual idea of him were to terminate by having led us to his lair?

This address must not become too long, so I must give my answer in the fewest words. And let me first say this: So far as the white paper or other ultimate datum of our experience may be considered to enter also into some one else's experience, and we, in knowing it, are held to know it there as well as here; so far again as it may be considered to be a mere mask for hidden molecules that other now impossible experiences of our own might some day lay bare to view; so far it is a case of tigers in India again, for, the things known being absent experiences, the knowing can only consist in passing smoothly towards them through the intermediary context that the world supplies. But if our own private vision of the paper be considered in abstraction from every other event, as if it constituted by itself the universe (and it might perfectly well do so, for aught we can understand to the contrary), then the paper seen and the seeing of it are only two names for one indivisible fact which, properly named, is *the datum, the phenomenon, or the experience*. The paper is in the mind and the mind is around the paper, because paper and mind are only two names that are given later to the one experience, when, taken in a larger world of which it forms a part, its connections are traced in different directions.[4] *To know immediately, then, or intuitively, is for mental content and object to be identical.* This is a very different definition from that which we gave of representative knowledge; but neither definition involves those mysterious notions of self-transcendency and presence in absence which are such essential parts of the ideas of knowledge, both of common men and of philosophers. Is there no experience that can justify these notions, and show us somewhere their original?

I think the mystery of presence in absence (though we fail to find it between one experience and another remote experience to which it points, or between the 'content' and 'object' of any one experience falsely rent asunder by the application to it of these two separate names) may yet be found, and found between the parts of a single experience. Let us look for it, accordingly, in its simplest possible form. What is the smallest experience in which the mystery remains? If we seek, we find that there is no datum so small as not to show the mystery. The smallest effective pulse of consciousness, whatever else it may be consciousness of, is also consciousness of passing time. The tiniest feeling that we can possibly have

---

[4]What is meant by this is that 'the experience' can be referred to either of two great associative systems, that of the experiencer's mental history, or that of the experienced facts of the world. Of both of these systems it forms part, and may be regarded, indeed, as one of their points of intersection. One might let a vertical line

stand for the mental history; but the same object, O, appears also in the mental history of different persons, represented by the other vertical lines. It thus ceases to be the private property of one experience, and becomes, so to speak, a shared or public thing. We can track its outer history in this way, and represent it by the horizontal line. [It is also known representatively at other points of the vertical lines, or intuitively there again, so that the line of its outer history would have to be looped and wandering, but I make it straight for simplicity's sake.] In any case, however, it is the same *stuff* that figures in all the sets of lines.

involves for future reflection two sub-feelings, one earlier and the other later, and a sense of their continuous procession. All this has been admirably set forth by Mr. Shadworth Hodgson,[5] who shows that there is literally no such datum as that of the present moment, and no such content, and no such object, except as an unreal postulate of abstract thought. The *passing* moment is the only thing that ever concretely was or is or shall be; and in the phenomenon of elementary memory, whose function is to apprehend it, earlier and later are present to each other in an experience that feels either only on condition of feeling both together.

We have the same knowing together in the matter that fills the time. The rush of our thought forward through its fringes is the everlasting peculiarity of its life. We realize this life as something always off its balance, something in transition, something that shoots out of a darkness through a dawn into a brightness that we know to be the dawn fulfilled. In the very midst of the alteration our experience comes as one continuous fact. 'Yes,' we say at the moment of full brightness, *this* is what I meant. No, we feel at the moment of the dawning, this is not yet the meaning, there is more to come. In every crescendo of sensation, in every effort to recall, in every progress towards the satisfaction of desire, this succession of an emptiness and fulness that have reference to each other and are one flesh is the essence of the phenomenon. In every hindrance of desire the sense of an absent, which the only function of the present is to *mean*, is even more notoriously there. And in the movement of thoughts not ordinarily classed as involving desire, we have the same phenomenon. When I say *Socrates is mortal*, the moment *Socrates* is incomplete; it falls forward through the *is* which is pure movement, into the *mortal*, which is indeed bare mortal on the tongue, but for the mind, is *that mortal*, the *mortal Socrates*, at last satisfactorily disposed of and told off.

Here, then, inside of the minimal pulse of experience which, taken as object, is change of feeling, and, taken as content, is feeling of change, is realized that absolute and essential self-transcendency which we swept away as an illusion when we sought it between a content taken as a whole and a supposed objective thing outside. *Here in the elementary datum of which both our physical and our mental worlds are built, we find included both the original of presence in absence and the prototype of that operation of knowing many things together which it is our business to discuss.*[6] For the fact that past and future are already parts of the least experience that can really be, is just like what we find in any other case of an experience whose parts are many. Most of these experiences are of objects perceived to be simultaneous and not to be immediately successive as in the heretofore considered case. The field of view, the chord of music, the glass of lemonade are examples. But the gist of the matter is the same—it is always knowing-together. You cannot separate the consciousness of one part from that of all the rest. What is given is pooled and mutual; there is no dark spot, no point of ignorance; no one fraction is eclipsed from any other's point of view. Can we account for such a being-known-together of complex facts like these?

The general *nature* of it we can probably never account for, or tell how such a unity in manyness can be, for it seems to be the ultimate essence of all experience, and anything less than

[6]It seems to me that we have here something like what comes before us in the psychology of space and time. Our original intuition of space is the single field of view; our original intuition of time covers but a few seconds; yet by an ideal piecing together and construction we frame the notions of immensity and eternity, and suppose dated events and located things therein, of whose actual intervals we grasp no distinct idea. So in the case before us. The way in which the constituents of one undivided datum drag each other in and run into one, saying *this* is what *that* means, gives us our original intuition of what knowing is. That intuition we extend and constructively build up into the notion of a vast tissue of knowledge, shed along from experience to experience until, dropping the intermediary data from our thought, we assume that terms the most remote still know each other, just after the fashion of the parts of the prototypal fact. Cognition here is only constructive, as we have already seen. But he who should say, arguing from its nature here, that it nowhere is direct, and seek to construct it without an originally given pattern, would be like those psychologists who profess to develop our idea of space out of the association of data that possess no original extensity. Grant the *sort* of thing that is meant by presence in absence, by self-transcendency, by reference to another, by pointing forward or back, by knowledge in short, somewhere in our experience, be it in ever so small a corner, and the construction of pseudo-cases elsewhere follows as a matter of course. But to get along without the real thing *anywhere* seems difficult indeed.

it apparently cannot be at all. But the particular *conditions* whereby we know particular things together might conceivably be traced, and to that humble task I beg leave to devote the time that remains.

III

Let me say forthwith that I have no pretension to give any positive solution. My sole ambition now is, by a little classification, to smooth the ground somewhat so that some of you, more able than I, may be helped to advance, before our next meeting perhaps, to results that I cannot obtain.

Now, the first thing that strikes us in these complex cases is that the condition by which one thing may come to be known together with other things is an *event*. It is often an event of the purely physical order. A man walks suddenly into my field of view, and forthwith becomes part of it. I put a drop of cologne-water on my tongue, and, holding my nostrils, get the taste of it alone, but when I open my nostrils I get the smell together with the taste in mutual suffusion. Here it would seem as if a sufficient condition of the knowing of (say) three things together were the fact that the three several physical conditions of the knowing of each of them were realized at once. But in many other cases we find on the contrary that the physical conditions are realized without the things being known together at all. When absorbed in experiments with the cologne-water, for example, the clock may strike, and I not know that it has struck. But again, some seconds after the striking has elapsed, I may, by a certain shifting of what we call my attention, hark back to it and resuscitate the sound, and even count the strokes in memory. The condition of knowing the clock's striking is here an event of the mental order which must be added to the physical event of the striking before I can know it and the cologne-water at once. Just so in the field of view I may entirely overlook and fail to notice even so important an object as a man, until the inward event of altering my attention makes me suddenly see him with the other objects there. In those curious phenomena of dissociation of consciousness with which recent studies of hypnotic, hysteric and trance-states have made us familiar (phenomena which surely throw more new light on human nature than the work of all the psycho-physical laboratories put together), the event of hearing a 'suggestion,' or the event of passing into trance or out of it, is what decides whether a human figure shall appear in the field of view or disappear, and whether a whole set of memories shall come before the mind together, along with its other objects, or be excluded from their company. There is in fact no possible object, however completely fulfilled may be the outer condition of its perception, whose entrance into a given field of consciousness does not depend on the additional inner event called attention.

Now, it seems to me that this need of a final inner event, over and above the mere sensorial conditions, quite refutes and disposes of the associationist theory of the unity of consciousness. By associationist theory, I mean any theory that says, either implicitly or explicitly, that for a lot of objects to be known together, it suffices that a lot of conscious states, each with one of them as its content, should exist, as James Mill says, 'synchronically.' Synchronical existence of the ideas does not suffice, as the facts we now have abundantly show. Gurney's, Binet's and Janet's proofs of several dissociated consciousnesses existing synchronically, and dividing the subject's field of knowledge between them, is the best possible refutation of any such view.

Union in consciousness must be *made* by something, must be brought about; and to have perceived this truth is the great merit of the anti-associationist psychologists.[7] The form of unity, they have obstinately said, must be specially accounted for; and the form of unity the radical associationists have as obstinately shied away from and ignored, though their accounts of those preliminary conditions that supply the

[7]In this rapid paper I content myself with arguing from the experimental fact that something *happens* over and above the realization of sensorial conditions, wherever an object adds itself to others already 'before the mind.' I say nothing of the logical self-contradiction involved in the associationist doctrine that the two facts, 'A is known,' and 'B is known,' *are* the third fact. 'A + B are known together.' Those whom the criticisms already extant in print of this strange belief have failed to convince, would not be persuaded, even though one rose from the dead. The appeal to the actual facts of dissociation may make impression, however, even on such hardened hearts as theirs.

matters to be united have never been surpassed. As far as these go, we are all, I trust, associationists, and reverers of the names of Hartley, Mill, and Bain.

Let us now rapidly review the chief attempts of the anti-associationists to fill the gap they discern so well in the associationist tale.

1. *Attention.*—Attention, we say, by turning to an object, includes it with the rest; and the naming of this faculty in action has by some writers been considered a sufficient account of the decisive 'event.'[8] But it is plain that the act of Attention itself needs a farther account to be given, and such an account is what other theories of the event implicitly give.

We find four main types[9] of other theory of how particular things get known together, a physiological, a psychological, an animistic, and a transcendentalist type. Of the physiological or 'psycho-physical' type many varieties are possible, but it must be observed that none of them pretends to assign anything more than an empirical law. A psycho-physical theory can couple certain antecedent conditions with their result; but an explanation, in the sense of an inner reason why the result should have the nature of one content with many parts instead of some entirely different nature, is what a psycho-physical theory cannot give.[10]

---

[8]It might seem natural to mention Wundt's doctrine of 'Apperception' here. But I must confess my inability to say anything about it that would not resolve itself into a tedious comparison of texts. Being alternately described as intellection, will, feeling, synthesis, analysis, principle and result, it is too 'protean' a function to lend itself to any simplified account at second hand.

[9]It is only for the sake of completeness that we need mention such notions of a sort of mechanical and chemical activity between the ideas as we find in Herbart, Steinthal and others. These authors see clearly that mere synchronical existence is not combination, and attribute to the ideas dynamic influences upon each other; pressures and resistances according to Herbart, and according to Steinthal 'psychic attractions.' But the philosophical foundations of such physical theories have been so slightly discussed by their authors that it is better to treat them only as rhetorical metaphors and pass on. Herbart, moreover, must also be mentioned later, along with the animistic writers.

[10]We find this impotence already when we seek the conditions of the passing pulse of consciousness, which, as we saw, always involves time and change. We account for the passing pulse, physiologically, by the overlapping of dying and dawning brain-processes; and at first sight the elements time and change, involved in both the brain-processes and their mental result, give

2. *Reminiscence.* — Now, empirically, we have learned that things must be known in succession and singly before they can be known together.[11] If A, B, and C, for example, were outer things that came for the first time and affected our senses all at once, we should get one content from the lot of them and make no discriminations. The content would symbolically point to the objects A, B, C, and eventually terminate there, but would contain no parts that were immediately apprehended as standing for A, B, and C severally. Let A, B, and C stand for pigments, or for a tone and its overtones, and you will see what I mean when I say that the first result on consciousness of their falling together on the eye or ear would be a single new kind of feeling rather than a feeling with three kinds of inner part. Such a result has been ascribed to a 'fusion' of the three feelings of A, B, and C; but there seems no ground for supposing that, under the conditions assumed, these distinct feelings have ever been aroused at all. I should call the phenomenon one of *indiscriminate knowing together*, for the most we can say under the circumstances is that the content resembles somewhat each of the objects A, B, and C, and knows them each potentially, knows them, that is, by possibly leading to each smoothly hereafter, as we know Indian tigers even whilst sitting in this room.

But if our memory possess stored-up images of former A-s, B-s, and C-s, experienced in isolation, we get an altogether different content, namely, one through which we know A, B, and C together, and yet know each of them in discrimination through one of the content's own parts. This has been called a 'colligation' or *Verknüpfung* of the 'ideas' of A, B, and C, to distinguish it from the aforesaid fusion. Whatever we may call it, we see that its physiological condition is more complex than in the previous case. In both cases the outer objects, A,

---

a similarity that, we feel, might be the real reason for the psycho-physic coupling. But the moment we ask 'metaphysical' questions—"Why not each brain-process felt apart?—Why just this amount of time, neither more nor less?" etc., etc.—we find ourselves falling back on the empirical view as the only safe one to defend.

[11]The latest empirical contribution to this subject, with which I am acquainted, is Dr. Herbert Nichols' excellent little monograph, *Our Notions of Number and Space*, Boston, Ginn & Co., 1894.

B, and C, exert their effects on the sensorium. But in this case there is a coöperation of higher tracts of memory which in the former case was absent. *Discriminative knowing-together, in short, involves higher processes of reminiscence.* Do these give the element of manyness, whilst the lower sensorial processes that by themselves would result in mere 'fusion,' give the unity to the experience? The suggestion is one that might repay investigation, although it has against it two pretty solid objections: first, that in man the consciousness attached to infra-cortical centres is altogether subliminal, if it exist; and, second, that in the cortex itself we have not yet discriminated sensorial from ideational processes. Possibly the frontal lobes, in which Wundt has supposed an *Apperceptionsorgan*, might serve a turn here. In any case it is certain that, into our present rough notions of the cortical functions, the future will have to weave distinctions at present unknown.

3. *Synergy.*—The theory that, physiologically, the oneness precedes the manyness, may be contrasted with a theory that our colleagues Baldwin and Münsterberg are at present working out, and which places the condition of union of many data into one datum, in the fact that the many pour themselves into one motor discharge. The motor discharge being the last thing to happen, the condition of manyness would physiologically here precede and that of oneness follow. A printed word is apprehended as one object, at the same time that each letter in it is apprehended as one of its parts. Our secretary, Cattell, long ago discovered that we recognize words of four or five letters by the eye as quickly, or even more quickly, than we recognize single letters. Recognition means here the motor process of articulation; and the quickness comes from the fact that all the letters in the particular combination unhesitatingly coöperate in the one articulatory act. I suppose such facts as these to lie at the base of our colleagues' theories, which probably differ in detail, and which it would be manifestly unjust to discuss or guess about in advance of their completer publication. Let me only say that I hope the latter may not be long delayed.

These are the only types of physiological theory worthy of mention. I may next pass to what, for brevity's sake, may be called *psychological accounts* of the event that lets an object into consciousness, or, by not occurring, leaves it out. These accounts start from the fact that what figures as part of a larger object is often perceived to have relations to the other parts. Accordingly the event in question is described as an *act of relating thought*. It takes two forms.

4. *Relating to Self.*—Some authors say that nothing can enter consciousness except on condition that it be related to the self. Not *object*, but *object-plus-me*, is the minimum knowable.

5. *Relating to other Objects.*—Others think it enough if the incoming object be related to the other objects already there. To fail to appear related is to fail to be known at all. To appear related is to appear with other objects. If relations were correlates of special cerebral processes, the addition of these to the sensorial processes would be the wished-for event. But brain physiology as yet knows nothing of such special processes, so I have called this explanation purely psychological. There seem to be fatal objections to it as a universal statement, for the reference to self, if it exist, must in a host of cases be altogether subconscious; and introspection assures us that in many half-waking and half-drunken states the relations between things that we perceive together may be of the dimmest and most indefinable kind.

6. *The Individual Soul.*—So we next proceed to *the animistic account*. By this term I mean to cover every sort of individualistic soul-theory. I will say nothing of older opinions; but in modern times we have two views of the way in which the union of a many by a soul occurs. For Herbart, for example, it occurs because the soul itself *is* unity, and all its *Selbsterhaltungen* are obliged to necessarily share this form. For our colleague Ladd, on the other hand, to take the best recent example, it occurs because the soul, which *is* a real unity indeed, furthermore performs a unifying *act* on the naturally separate data of sense—an act, moreover, for which no psycho-physical analogon can be found. It must be admitted that much of the reigning bias against the soul in so-called scientific circles is an unintelligent prejudice, traceable far more to a vague impression that it is a theological superstition than to exact logical grounds. The soul is an 'entity,' and, indeed, that worst sort of entity, a 'scholastic entity'; and, moreover, it is something to be damned or saved; so let's

have no more of it! I am free to confess that in my own case the antipathy to the Soul with which I find myself burdened is an ancient hardness of heart of which I can frame no fully satisfactory account even to myself. I passively agree that if there were Souls that we could use as principles of explanation, the *formal* settlement of the questions now before us could run far more smoothly towards its end. I admit that a soul is a medium of union, and that brain-processes and ideas, be they never so 'synchronical,' leave all mediating agency out. Yet, in spite of these concessions, I never find myself actively talking up the soul, so to speak, and making it do work in my psychologizing. I speak of myself here because I am one amongst many, and probably few of us can give adequate reasons for our dislike. The more honor to our colleague from Yale, then, that he remains so unequivocally faithful to this unpopular principle! And let us hope that his forthcoming book may sweep what is blind in our hostility away.[12]

But all is not blind in our hostility. When, for example, you say that A, B, and C, which are distinct contents on other occasions, are now on this occasion joined into the compound content ABC by a unifying act of the soul, you say little more than that now they *are* united, unless you give some hint as to *how* the soul unites them. When, for example, the hysteric women whom Pierre Janet has studied with such loving care, go to pieces mentally, and their souls are unable any longer to connect the data of their experience together, though these data remain severally conscious in dissociation, what is the condition on which this inability of the soul de-

---

[12]I ought, perhaps, to apologize for not expunging from my printed text these references to Professor Ladd, which were based on the impression left on my mind by the termination of his *Physiological Psychology*. It would now appear from the paper read by him at the Princeton meeting, and his *Philosophy of Mind*, just published, that he disbelieves in the Soul of old-fashioned ontology; and on looking again at the *P. P.*, I see that I may well have misinterpreted his deeper meaning there. I incline to suspect, however, that he had himself not fully disentangled it when that work was written; and that between now and then his thought has been evolving somewhat as Lotze's did between his *Medical Psychology* and his *Metaphysic*. It is gratifying to note these converging tendencies in different philosophers; but I leave the text as I read it at Princeton, as a mark of what one could say not so very unnaturally at that date.

pends? Is it an impotence in the soul itself? or is it an impotence in the physiological conditions, which fail to stimulate
the soul sufficiently to its synthetic task? The *how* supposes on
the Soul's part a constitution adequate to the act. An hypothesis, we are told in the logic-books, ought to propose a being
that has some other constitution and definition than that of
barely performing the phenomenon it is evoked to explain.
When physicists propose the 'ether,' for example, they propose it with a lot of incidental properties. But the soul proposed to us has no special properties or constitution of which
we are informed. Nevertheless, since particular conditions do
determine its activity, it must have a constitution of some
sort. In either case, we ought to know the facts. But the soul-
doctrine, as hitherto professed, not only doesn't answer such
questions, it doesn't even ask them; and it must be radically
rejuvenated if it expects to be greeted again as a useful principle in psychological philosophy. Here is work for our spiritualist colleagues, not only for the coming year, but for the rest
of their lives.[13]

7. *The World-soul.* — The second spiritualist theory may be
named as that of *transcendentalism.* I take it typically and not
as set forth by any single author. Transcendentalism explains
things by an over-soul of which all separate souls, sensations,
thoughts, and data generally are parts. To be, as it would be
known together with everything else in the world by this
over-soul, is for transcendentalism the *true* condition of each
single thing, and to pass into this condition is for things to

---

[13]The soul can be taken in three ways as a unifying principle. An already
existing lot of animated sensations (or other psychic data) may be simply
woven into one by it; in which case the form of unity is the soul's only contribution, and the original stuff of the Many remains in the One as its stuff
also. Or, secondly, the resultant synthetic One may be regarded as an immanent *reaction* of the Soul on the preëxisting psychic Many; and in this case the
Soul, in addition to creating the new form, reproduces in itself the old stuff
of the Many, superseding it for our use, and making it for us become subliminal, but not suppressing its existence. Or, thirdly, the One may again be the
Soul's immanent reaction on a physiological, not on a mental, Many. In this
case preëxisting *sensations or ideas* would not be there at all, to be either woven together or superseded. The synthetic One would be a primal psychic
datum with parts, either of which might know the same object that a possible
sensation, realized under other physiological conditions, could also know.

fulfill their vocation. Such being known together, since it is the innermost reality of life, cannot on transcendentalist principles be explained or accounted for as a work wrought on a previous sort of reality. The monadic soul-theory starts with separate sensational data, and must show how they are *made* one. The transcendentalist theory has rather for its task to show how, being one, they can illusorily be made to appear separate. The problem for the monadic soul, in short, is that of unification, and the problem for the over-soul is that of insulation. The removal of insulating obstructions would sufficiently account for things reverting to their natural place in the over-soul and being known together. The most natural insulating or individualizing principle to invoke is the bodily organism. As the pipes of an organ let the pressing mass of air escape only in single notes, so do our brains, the organ pipes of the infinite, keep back everything but the slender threads of truth to which they may be pervious. As they obstruct more, the insulation increases, as they obstruct less it disappears. Now transcendental philosophers have as a rule not done much dabbling in psychology. But one sees no abstract reason why they might not go into psychology as fully as any one, and erect a psycho-physical science of the conditions of more separate and less separate cognition which would include all the facts that psycho-physicists in general might discover. And they would have the advantage over other psycho-physicists of not needing to explain the nature of the resultant knowing-together when it should occur, for they could say that they simply begged it as the ultimate nature of the world.

This is as broad a disjunction as I can make of the different ways in which men have considered the conditions of our knowing things together. You will agree with me that I have brought no new insight to the subject, and that I have only gossiped to while away this unlucky presidential hour to which the constellations doomed me at my birth. But since gossip we have had to have, let me make the hour more gossipy still by saying a final word about the position taken up in my own *Principles of Psychology* on the general question before us, a position which, as you doubtless remember, was so vigorously attacked by our colleague from the University of

Pennsylvania at our meeting in New York a year ago.[14] That position consisted in this, that I proposed to simply eliminate from psychology 'considered as a natural science' the whole business of ascertaining *how* we come to know things together or to know them at all. Such considerations, I said, should fall to metaphysics. That we do know things, sometimes singly and sometimes together, is a fact. That states of consciousness are the vehicle of the knowledge, and depend on brain states, are two other facts. And I thought that a natural science of psychology might legitimately confine itself to tracing the functional variations of these three sorts of fact, and to ascertaining what determinate bodily states are the condition when the states of mind know determinate things and groups of things. Most states of mind can be designated only by naming what objects they are 'thoughts-of,' *i.e.*, what things they know.

Most of those which know compound things are utterly unique and solitary mental entities demonstrably different from any collection of simpler states to which the same objects might be singly known.[15] Treat them all as unique in

[14]Printed as an article entitled 'The Psychological Standpoint,' in this REVIEW, Vol. I, p. 113. (March, 1894.)

[15]When they know conceptually they don't even remotely resemble the simpler states. When they know intuitively they resemble, sometimes closely, sometimes distantly, the simpler states. The sour and sweet in lemonade are extremely unlike the sour and sweet of lemon juice and sugar, singly taken, yet like enough for us to 'recognize' these 'objects' in the compound taste. The several objective 'notes' recognized in the chord sound differently and peculiarly there. In a motley field of view successive and simultaneous contrast give to each several tint a different hue and luminosity from that of the 'real' color into which it turns when viewed without its neighbors by a rested eye. The difference is sometimes so slight, however, that we overlook the 'representative' character of each of the parts of a complex content, and speak as if the latter were a cluster of the original 'intuitive' states of mind that, occurring singly, know the 'object's' several parts in separation. Prof. Meinong, for example, even after the true state of things had been admirably set forth by Herr H. Cornelius (in the *Vierteljahrschrift f. wiss. Phil.*, XVI, 404; XVII, 30), returns to the defence of the radical associationist view (in the *Zeitschrift f. Psychologie*, VI, 340, 417). According to him, the single sensations of the several notes lie unaltered in the chord-sensations; but his analysis of the phenomenon is vitiated by his non-recognition of the fact that the *same objects* (*i.e.*, the notes) *can be known* representatively through one compound state of mind, and directly in several simple ones, without the simple and the

entity, I said then; let their complexity reside in their plural cognitive function; and you have a psychology which, if it doesn't ultimately explain the facts, also does not, in describing them, make them self-contradictory (as the associationist psychology does when it calls them many ideas fused into one idea) or pretend to explain them (as the soul-theory so often does) by a barren verbal principle.

My intention was a good one, and a natural science infinitely more complete than the psychologies we now possess could be written without abandoning its terms. Like all authors, I have, therefore, been surprised that this child of my genius should not be more admired by others—should, in fact, have been generally either misunderstood or despised. But do not fear that on this occasion I am either going to defend or to re-explain the bantling. I am going to make things more harmonious by simply *giving it up*. I have become convinced since publishing that book that no conventional restrictions *can* keep metaphysical and so-called epistemological inquiries out of the psychology-books. I see, moreover, better now than then, that my proposal to designate mental states merely by their cognitive function leads to a somewhat strained way of talking of dreams and reveries, and to quite an unnatural way of talking of some emotional states. I am willing, consequently, henceforward that mental contents should be called complex, just as their objects are, and this even in psychology. Not because their parts are separable, as the parts of objects are; not because they have an eternal or quasi-eternal individual existence, like the parts of objects; for the various 'fields' of which they are parts are in-

---

compound states having strictly anything in common with each other. In Meinong's earlier work, 'Ueber Begriff und Eigenschaften der Empfindung' (*Vierteljahrschrift*, Vol. XII), he seems to me to have hit the truth much better, when he says that the aspect *color*, *e.g.*, in a concrete sensation of *red*, is not an abstractable *part* of the sensation, but an *external relation of resemblance* between that sensation and other sensations to the whole lot of which we give the name of colors. Such, I should say, are the aspects of c, e, g and c' in the chord. We may call them *parts* of the chord if we like, but they are not *bits* of it, identical with c's, e's, g's and c''s elsewhere. They simply resemble the c's, e's, g's and c''s elsewhere, and know these contents or objects representatively.

tegers, existentially, and their parts only live as long as *they* live. Still, *in* them, we can call parts, parts. — But when, without circumlocution or disguise, I thus come over to your views, I insist that those of you who applaud me (if any such there be) should recognize the obligations which the new agreement imposes on yourselves. Not till you have dropped the old phrases, so absurd or so empty, of ideas 'self-compounding' or 'united by a spiritual principle'; not till you have in your turn succeeded in some such long inquiry into conditions as the one I have just failed in; not till you have laid bare more of the nature of that altogether unique kind of complexity in unity which mental states involve; not till then, I say, will psychology reach any real benefit from the conciliatory spirit of which I have done what I can to set an example.

Philosophical Conceptions and Practical Results [1]

A<small>N OCCASION</small> like the present would seem to call for an absolutely untechnical discourse. I ought to speak of something connected with life rather than with logic. I ought to give a message with a practical outcome and an emotional musical accompaniment, so to speak, fitted to interest men as men, and yet also not altogether to disappoint philosophers—since philosophers, let them be as queer as they will, still are men in the secret recesses of their hearts, even here at Berkeley. I ought, I say, to produce something simple enough to catch and inspire the rest of you, and yet with just enough of ingenuity and oddity about it to keep the members of the Philosophical Union from yawning and letting their attention wander away.

I confess that I have something of this kind in my mind, a perfectly ideal discourse for the present occasion. Were I to set it down on paper, I verily believe it would be regarded by everyone as the final word of philosophy. It would bring theory down to a single point, at which every human being's practical life would begin. It would solve all the antinomies and contradictions, it would let loose all the right impulses and emotions; and everyone, on hearing it, would say, "Why, that *is* the truth!—*that* is what I have been believing, that is what I have really been living on all this time, but I never could find the words for it before. All that eludes, all that flickers and twinkles, all that invites and vanishes even whilst inviting, is here made a solidity and a possession. Here is the end of unsatisfactoriness, here the beginning of unimpeded clearness, joy, and power." Yes, my friends, I have such a discourse within me! But, do not judge me harshly, I cannot produce it on the present occasion. I humbly apologize; I have come across the continent to this wondrous Pacific Coast—to this Eden, not of the mythical antiquity, but of the

[1]An address delivered before the Philosophical Union at Berkeley, August 26, 1898, by William James, M.D., LL.D., Professor of Psychology in Harvard University.

solid future of mankind—I ought to give you something worthy of your hospitality, and not altogether unworthy of your great destiny, to help cement our rugged East and your wondrous West together in a spiritual bond,—and yet, and yet, and yet, I simply cannot. I have tried to articulate it, but it will not come. Philosophers are after all like poets. They are path-finders. What everyone can feel, what everyone can know in the bone and marrow of him, they sometimes can find words for and express. The words and thoughts of the philosophers are not exactly the words and thoughts of the poets—worse luck. But both alike have the same function. They are, if I may use a simile, so many spots, or blazes,—blazes made by the axe of the human intellect on the trees of the otherwise trackless forest of human experience. They give you somewhere to go from. They give you a direction and a place to reach. They do not give you the integral forest with all its sunlit glories and its moonlit witcheries and wonders. Ferny dells, and mossy waterfalls, and secret magic nooks escape you, owned only by the wild things to whom the region is a home. Happy they without the need of blazes! But to us the blazes give a sort of ownership. We can now use the forest, wend across it with companions, and enjoy its quality. It is no longer a place merely to get lost in and never return. The poet's words and the philosopher's phrases thus are helps of the most genuine sort, giving to all of us hereafter the freedom of the trails they made. Though they create nothing, yet for this marking and fixing function of theirs we bless their names and keep them on our lips, even whilst the thin and spotty and half-casual character of their operations is most evident.

No one like the path-finder himself feels the immensity of the forest, or knows the accidentality of his own trails. Columbus, dreaming of the ancient East, is stopped by poor pristine simple America, and gets no farther on that day; and the poets and philosophers themselves know as no one else knows that what their formulas express leaves unexpressed almost everything that they organically divine and feel. So I feel that there is a center in truth's forest where I have never been: to track it out and get there is the secret spring of all my poor life's philosophic efforts; at moments I almost strike into the final valley, there is a gleam of the end, a sense of certainty, but always there comes still another ridge, so my blazes merely circle towards the true direction; and although now, if ever, would be the fit occasion, yet I cannot take you to the wondrous hidden spot to-day. To-morrow it must be, or to-morrow, or to-morrow; and pretty surely death will overtake me ere the promise is fulfilled.

Of such postponed achievements do the lives of all philosophers consist. Truth's fulness is elusive; ever not quite, not quite! So we fall back on the preliminary blazes—a few formulas, a few technical conceptions, a few verbal pointers—which at least define the initial direction of the trail. And that, to my sorrow, is all that I can do here at Berkeley to-day. Inconclusive I must be, and merely suggestive, though I will try to be as little technical as I can.

I will seek to define with you merely what seems to be the most likely direction in which to start upon the trail of truth. Years ago this direction was given to me by an American philosopher whose home is in the East, and whose published works, few as they are and scattered in periodicals, are no fit expression of his powers. I refer to Mr. Charles S. Peirce, with whose very existence as a philosopher I dare say many of you are unacquainted. He is one of the most original of contemporary thinkers; and the principle of practicalism—or pragmatism, as he called it, when I first heard him enunciate it at Cambridge in the early '70's—is the clue or compass by following which I find myself more and more confirmed in believing we may keep our feet upon the proper trail.

Peirce's principle, as we may call it, may be expressed in a variety of ways, all of them very simple. In the *Popular Science Monthly* for January, 1878, he introduces it as follows: The soul and meaning of thought, he says, can never be made to direct itself towards anything but the production of belief, belief being the demicadence which closes a musical phrase in the symphony of our intellectual life. Thought in movement has thus for its only possible motive the attainment of thought at rest. But when our thought about an object has found its rest in belief, then our action on the subject can firmly and safely begin. Beliefs, in short, are really rules for action; and the whole function of thinking is but one step in the production of habits of action. If there were any part of a thought that made no difference in the thought's practical consequences, then that part would be no proper element of the thought's significance. Thus the same thought may be clad in different words; but if the different words suggest no different conduct, they are mere outer accretions, and have no part in the thought's meaning. If, however, they determine conduct differently, they are essential elements of the significance. "Please open the door," and, "*Veuillez ouvrir la porte,*" in French, mean just the same thing; but "D—n you, open the door," although in English, *means* something very different. Thus to develope a thought's meaning we need only determine what conduct it is fitted to produce: that conduct is for us its sole significance. And the tangible fact at the root of all our thought-distinctions, however subtle, is that there is no one of them so fine as to consist in anything but a possible difference of practice. To attain perfect clearness in our thoughts of an object, then, we need only consider what effects of a conceivably practical kind the object may involve—what sensations we are to expect from it, and what reactions we must prepare. Our conception of these effects, then, is for us the whole of our conception of the object, so far as that conception has positive significance at all.

This is the principle of Peirce, the principle of pragmatism. I think myself that it should be expressed more broadly than Mr. Peirce expresses it. The ultimate test for us of what a truth means is indeed the conduct it dictates or inspires. But it inspires that conduct because it first foretells some particular turn to our experience which shall call for just that conduct from us. And I should prefer for our purposes this evening to express Peirce's principle by saying that the effective meaning of any philosophic proposition can always be brought down to some particular consequence, in our future practical experience, whether active or passive; the point lying rather in the fact that the experience must be particular, than in the fact that it must be active.

To take in the importance of this principle, one must get accustomed to applying it to concrete cases. Such use as I am able to make of it convinces me that to be mindful of it in philosophical disputations tends wonderfully to smooth out misunderstandings and to bring in peace. If it did nothing else, then, it would yield a sovereignly valuable rule of method for discussion. So I shall devote the rest of this precious hour with you to its elucidation, because I sincerely think that if you once grasp it, it will shut your steps out from many an old false opening, and head you in the true direction for the trail.

One of its first consequences is this: Suppose there are two different philosophical definitions, or propositions, or maxims, or what not, which seem to contradict each other, and about which men dispute. If, by supposing the truth of the one, you can foresee no conceivable practical consequence to anybody at any time or place, which is different from what you would foresee if you supposed the truth of the other, why then the difference between the two propositions is no difference,—it is only a specious and verbal difference, unworthy of further contention. Both formulas mean radically the same thing, although they may say it in such different words. It is astonishing to see how many philosophical disputes collapse into insignificance the moment you subject them to this simple test. There can *be* no difference which doesn't *make* a difference—no difference in abstract truth which does not express itself in a difference of concrete fact, and of conduct consequent upon the fact, imposed on somebody, somehow, somewhere, and somewhen. It is true that a certain shrinkage of values often seems to occur in our general formulas when we measure their meaning in this prosaic and practical way. They diminish. But the vastness that is merely based on vagueness is a false appearance of importance, and not a vastness worth retaining. The x's, y's, and z's always do shrivel, as I have heard a learned friend say, whenever at the end of your algebraic computation they change into so many plain a's, b's, and c's:—but the whole function of algebra is, after all, to get them into that more definite shape; and the whole function of philosophy ought to be to find out what definite difference it will make to you and me, at definite instants of our life, if this world-formula or that world-formula be the one which is true.

If we start off with an impossible case, we shall perhaps all the more clearly see the use and scope of our principle. Let us therefore put ourselves, in imagination, in a position from which no forecasts of consequence, no dictates of conduct, can possibly be made, so that the principle of pragmatism finds no field of application. Let us, I mean, assume that the present moment is the absolutely last moment of the world, with bare nonentity beyond it, and no hereafter for either experience or conduct.

Now I say that in that case there would be no sense whatever in some of our most urgent and envenomed philosophical and religious debates. The question, "Is matter the producer of all things, or is a God there too?" would, for example, offer a perfectly idle and insignificant alternative if the world were finished and no more of it to come. Many of us, most of us I think, now feel as if a terrible coldness and deadness would come over the world were we forced to believe that no informing spirit or purpose had to do with it, but it merely accidentally had come. The actually experienced details of fact might be the same on either hypothesis, some sad, some joyous; some rational, some odd and grotesque; but without a God behind them, we think they would have something ghastly, they would tell no genuine story, there would be no speculation in those eyes that they do glare with. With the God, on the other hand, they would grow solid, warm, and altogether full of real significance.

But I say that such an alteration of feelings, reasonable enough in a consciousness that is prospective, as ours now is, and whose world is partly yet to come, would be absolutely senseless and irrational in a purely retrospective consciousness summing up a world already past. For such a consciousness, no emotional interest could attach to the alternative. The problem would be purely intellectual; and if unaided matter could, with any scientific plausibility, be shown to cipher out the actual facts, then not the faintest shadow ought to cloud the mind, of regret for the God that by the same ciphering would prove needless and disappear from our belief.

For just consider the case sincerely, and say what would be the *worth* of such a God if he *were* there, with his work accomplished and his world run down. He would be worth no more than just that world was worth. To that amount of result, with its mixed merits and defects, his creative power could attain, but go no farther. And since there is to be no future; since the whole value and meaning of the world has been already paid in and actualized in the feelings that went with it in the passing, and now go with it in the ending; since it draws no supplemental significance (such as our real world draws) from its function of preparing something yet to come; why then, by it we take God's measure, as it were. He is the Being who could once for all do *that*; and for that much we are thankful to him, but for nothing more. But now, on the contrary hypothesis, namely, that the bits of matter following their 'laws' could make that world and do no less, should we not be just as thankful to them? Wherein should we suffer loss, then, if we dropped God as an hypothesis and made the matter alone responsible? Where would the special deadness, 'crassness,' and ghastliness come in? And how, experience being what it is once for all, would God's presence in it make it any more 'living,' any richer in our sight?

Candidly, it is impossible to give any answer to this question. The actually experienced world is supposed to be the same in its details on either hypothesis, "the same, for our praise or blame," as Browning says. It stands there indefeasibly; a gift which can't be taken back. Calling matter the cause of it retracts no single one of the items that have made it up, nor does calling God the cause augment them. They are the God or the atoms, respectively, of just that and no other world. The God, if there, has been doing just what atoms could do—appearing in the character of atoms, so to speak—and earning such gratitude as is due to atoms, and no more. If his presence lends no different turn or issue to the performance, it surely can lend it no increase of dignity. Nor would indignity come to it were he absent, and did the atoms remain the only actors on the stage. When a play is once over, and the curtain down, you really make it no better by claiming an illustrious genius for its author, just as you make it no worse by calling him a common hack.

Thus if no future detail of experience or conduct is to be deduced from our hypothesis, the debate between materialism and theism becomes quite idle and insignificant. Matter and God in that event mean exactly the same thing—the power, namely, neither more nor less, that can make just this mixed, imperfect, yet completed world—and the wise man is he who in such a case would turn his back on such a supererogatory discussion. Accordingly most men instinctively, and a large class of men, the so-called positivists or scientists, deliberately, do turn their backs on philosophical disputes from which nothing in the line of definite future consequences can be seen to follow. The verbal and empty character of our studies is surely a reproach with which you of the Philosophical Union are but too sadly familiar. An escaped Berkeley student said to me at Harvard the other day—he had never been in the philosophical department here—"Words, words, words, are all that you philosophers care for." We philosophers think it all unjust; and yet, if the principle of pragmatism be true, it is a perfectly sound reproach unless the metaphysical alternatives under investigation can be shown to have alternative practical outcomes, however delicate and distant these may be. The common man and the scientist can discover no such outcomes. And if the metaphysician can discern none either, the common man and scientist certainly are in the right of it, as against him. His science is then but pompous trifling; and the endowment of a professorship for such a being would be something really absurd.

Accordingly, in every genuine metaphysical debate some practical issue, however remote, is really involved. To realize this, revert with me to the question of materialism or theism; and place yourselves this time in the real world we live in, the world that has a future, that is yet uncompleted whilst we speak. In this unfinished world the alternative of 'materialism or theism?' is intensely practical; and it is worth while for us to spend some minutes of our hour in seeing how truly this is the case.

How, indeed, does the programme differ for us, according as we consider that the facts of experience up to date are purposeless configurations of atoms moving according to eternal elementary laws, or that on the other hand they are due to the providence of God? As far as the past facts go, indeed there is no difference. These facts are in, are bagged, are captured; and the good that's in them is gained, be the atoms or be the God their cause. There are accordingly many materialists about us to-day who, ignoring altogether the future and prac-

tical aspects of the question, seek to eliminate the odium attaching to the word materialism, and even to eliminate the
word itself, by showing that, if matter could give birth to all
these gains, why then matter, functionally considered, is just
as divine an entity as God, in fact coalesces with God, is what
you mean by God. Cease, these persons advise us, to use either of these terms, with their outgrown opposition. Use
terms free of the clerical connotations on the one hand; of the
suggestion of grossness, coarseness, ignobility, on the other.
Talk of the primal mystery, of the unknowable energy, of the
one and only power, instead of saying either God or matter.
This is the course to which Mr. Spencer urges us at the end of
the first volume of his Psychology. In some well-written pages
he there shows us that a 'matter' so infinitely subtile, and
performing motions as inconceivably quick and fine as modern science postulates in her explanations, has no trace of
grossness left. He shows that the conception of spirit, as we
mortals hitherto have framed it, is itself too gross to cover the
exquisite complexity of Nature's facts. Both terms, he says, are
but symbols, pointing to that one unknowable reality in
which their oppositions cease.

Throughout these remarks of Mr. Spencer, eloquent, and
even noble in a certain sense, as they are, he seems to think
that the dislike of the ordinary man to materialism comes
from a purely æsthetic disdain of matter, as something gross
in itself, and vile and despicable. Undoubtedly such an æsthetic disdain of matter has played a part in philosophic history. But it forms no part whatever of an intelligent modern
man's dislikes. Give him a matter bound forever by its laws to
lead our world nearer and nearer to perfection, and any rational man will worship that matter as readily as Mr. Spencer
worships his own so-called unknowable power. It not only
has made for righteousness up to date, but it will make for
righteousness forever; and that is all we need. Doing practically all that a God can do, it is equivalent to God, its function is a God's function, and is exerted in a world in which a
God would be superfluous; from such a world a God could
never lawfully be missed.

But *is* the matter by which Mr. Spencer's process of cosmic
evolution is carried on any such principle of never-ending

perfection as this? Indeed it is not, for the future end of every
cosmically evolved thing or system of things is tragedy; and
Mr. Spencer, in confining himself to the æsthetic and ignoring the practical side of the controversy, has really contributed
nothing serious to its relief. But apply now our principle of
practical results, and see what a vital significance the question
of materialism or theism immediately acquires.

Theism and materialism, so indifferent when taken retro-
spectively, point, when we take them prospectively, to wholly
different practical consequences, to opposite outlooks of experience. For, according to the theory of mechanical evolution,
the laws of redistribution of matter and motion, though they
are certainly to thank for all the good hours which our organisms have ever yielded us and for all the ideals which our
minds now frame, are yet fatally certain to undo their work
again, and to redissolve everything that they have once
evolved. You all know the picture of the last foreseeable state
of the dead universe, as evolutionary science gives it forth. I
cannot state it better than in Mr. Balfour's words: "The energies of our system will decay, the glory of the sun will be
dimmed, and the earth, tideless and inert, will no longer tolerate the race which has for a moment disturbed its solitude.
Man will go down into the pit, and all his thoughts will perish. The uneasy consciousness which in this obscure corner
has for a brief space broken the contented silence of the universe, will be at rest. Matter will know itself no longer. 'Im-
perishable monuments' and 'immortal deeds,' death itself, and
love stronger than death, will be as if they had not been. Nor
will anything that *is*, be better or worse for all that the labour,
genius, devotion, and suffering of man have striven through
countless ages to effect."[2]

That is the sting of it, that in the vast driftings of the
cosmic weather, though many a jewelled shore appears, and
many an enchanted cloud-bank floats away, long lingering ere
it be dissolved—even as our world now lingers, for our joy—
yet when these transient products are gone, nothing, absolutely *nothing* remains, to represent those particular qualities,
those elements of preciousness which they may have en-

[2]The Foundations of Belief, p. 30.

shrined. Dead and gone are they, gone utterly from the very sphere and room of being. Without an echo; without a memory; without an influence on aught that may come after, to make it care for similar ideals. This utter final wreck and tragedy is of the essence of scientific materialism as at present understood. The lower and not the higher forces are the eternal forces, or the last surviving forces within the only cycle of evolution which we can definitely see. Mr. Spencer believes this as much as anyone; so why should he argue with us as if we were making silly æsthetic objections to the 'grossness' of 'matter and motion,'—the principles of his philosophy,—when what really dismays us in it is the disconsolateness of its ulterior practical results?

No, the true objection to materialism is not positive but negative. It would be farcical at this day to make complaint of it for what it *is*, for 'grossness.' Grossness is what grossness *does*—we now know *that*. We make complaint of it, on the contrary, for what it is *not*—not a permanent warrant for our more ideal interests, not a fulfiller of our remotest hopes.

The notion of God, on the other hand, however inferior it may be in clearness to those mathematical notions so current in mechanical philosophy, has at least this practical superiority over them, that it guarantees an ideal order that shall be permanently preserved. A world with a God in it to say the last word, may indeed burn up or freeze, but we then think of him as still mindful of the old ideals and sure to bring them elsewhere to fruition; so that, where he is, tragedy is only provisional and partial, and shipwreck and dissolution not the absolutely final things. This need of an eternal moral order is one of the deepest needs of our breast. And those poets, like Dante and Wordsworth, who live on the conviction of such an order, owe to that fact the extraordinary tonic and consoling power of their verse. Here then, in these different emotional and practical appeals, in these adjustments of our concrete attitudes of hope and expectation, and all the delicate consequences which their differences entail, lie the real meanings of materialism and theism—not in hair-splitting abstractions about matter's inner essence, or about the metaphysical attributes of God. Materialism means simply the denial that the moral order is eternal, and the cutting off of ultimate hopes; theism means the affirmation of an eternal moral order and the letting loose of hope. Surely here is an issue genuine enough, for anyone who feels it; and, as long as men are men, it will yield matter for serious philosophic debate. Concerning this question at any rate, the positivists and pooh-pooh-ers of metaphysics are in the wrong.

But possibly some of you may still rally to their defense. Even whilst admitting that theism and materialism make different prophecies of the world's future, you may yourselves pooh-pooh the difference as something so infinitely remote as to mean nothing for a sane mind. The essence of a sane mind, you may say, is to take shorter views, and to feel no concern about such chimæras as the latter end of the world. Well, I can only say that if you say this, you do injustice to human nature. Religious melancholy is not disposed of by a simple flourish of the word insanity. The absolute things, the last things, the overlapping things, are the truly philosophic concern; all superior minds feel seriously about them, and the mind with the shortest views is simply the mind of the more shallow man.

However, I am willing to pass over these very distant outlooks on the ultimate if any of you so insist. The theistic controversy can still serve to illustrate the principle of pragmatism for us well enough, without driving us so far afield. If there be a God, it is not likely that he is confined solely to making differences in the world's latter end; he probably makes differences all along its course. Now the principle of practicalism says that the very meaning of the conception of God lies in those differences which must be made in our experience if the conception be true. God's famous inventory of perfections, as elaborated by dogmatic theology, either means nothing, says our principle, or it implies certain definite things that we can feel and do at particular moments of our lives, things which we could not feel and should not do were no God present and were the business of the universe carried on by material atoms instead. So far as our conceptions of the Deity involve no such experiences, so far they are meaningless and verbal,—scholastic entities and abstractions, as the positivists say, and fit objects for their scorn. But so far as they do involve such definite experiences, God means something for us, and may be real.

Now if we look at the definitions of God made by dogmatic theology, we see immediately that some stand and some fall when treated by this test. God, for example, as any orthodox text-book will tell us, is a being existing not only *per se*, or by himself, as created beings exist, but *a se*, or from himself; and out of this 'aseity' flow most of his perfections. He is, for example, necessary; absolute; infinite in all respects; and single. He is simple, not compounded of essence and existence, substance and accident, actuality and potentiality, or subject and attributes, as are other things. He belongs to no genus; he is inwardly and outwardly unalterable; he knows and wills all things, and first of all his own infinite self, in one indivisible eternal act. And he is absolutely self-sufficing, and infinitely happy.—Now in which one of us practical Americans here assembled does this conglomeration of attributes awaken any sense of reality? And if in no one, then why not? Surely because such attributes awaken no responsive active feelings and call for no particular conduct of our own. How does God's 'aseity' come home to *you*? What specific thing can I do to adapt myself to his 'simplicity'? Or how determine our behavior henceforward if his 'felicity' is anyhow absolutely complete? In the '50's and '60's Captain Mayne Reid was the great writer of boys' books of out-of-door adventure. He was forever extolling the hunters and field-observers of living animals' habits, and keeping up a fire of invective against the 'closet-naturalists,' as he called them, the collectors and classifiers, and handlers of skeletons and skins. When I was a boy I used to think that a closet-naturalist must be the vilest type of wretch under the sun. But surely the systematic theologians are the closet-naturalists of the Deity, even in Captain Mayne Reid's sense. Their orthodox deduction of God's attributes is nothing but a shuffling and matching of pedantic dictionary-adjectives, aloof from morals, aloof from human needs, something that might be worked out from the mere word 'God' by a logical machine of wood and brass as well as by a man of flesh and blood. The attributes which I have quoted have absolutely nothing to do with religion, for religion is a living practical affair. Other parts, indeed, of God's traditional description do have practical connection with life, and have owed all their historic importance to that fact. His omniscience, for example, and his justice. With the one he sees us in the dark, with the other he rewards and punishes what he sees. So do his ubiquity and eternity and unalterability appeal to our confidence, and his goodness banish our fears. Even attributes of less meaning to this present audience have in past times so appealed. One of the chief attributes of God, according to the orthodox theology, is his infinite love of himself, proved by asking the question, "By what but an infinite object can an infinite affection be appeased?" An immediate consequence of this primary self-love of God is the orthodox dogma that the manifestation of his own glory is God's primal purpose in creation; and that dogma has certainly made very efficient practical connection with life. It is true that we ourselves are tending to outgrow this old monarchical conception of a Deity with his 'court' and pomp—"his state is kingly, thousands at his bidding speed," etc.—but there is no denying the enormous influence it has had over ecclesiastical history, nor, by repercussion, over the history of European states. And yet even these more real and significant attributes have the trail of the serpent over them as the books on theology have actually worked them out. One feels that, in the theologians' hands, they are only a set of dictionary-adjectives, mechanically deduced; logic has stepped into the place of vision, professionalism into that of life. Instead of bread we get a stone; instead of a fish, a serpent. Did such a conglomeration of abstract general terms give really the gist of our knowledge of the Deity, divinity-schools might indeed continue to flourish, but religion, vital religion, would have taken its flight from this world. What keeps religion going is something else than abstract definitions and systems of logically concatenated adjectives, and something different from faculties of theology and their professors. All these things are after-effects, secondary accretions upon a mass of concrete religious experiences, connecting themselves with feeling and conduct, that renew themselves *in sæcula sæculorum* in the lives of humble private men. If you ask what these experiences are, they are conversations with the unseen, voices and visions, responses to prayer, changes of heart, deliverances from fear, inflowings of help, assurances of support, whenever certain persons set their own internal attitude in certain appropriate ways. The power comes and goes and is lost, and can be found only in a certain definite direction, just as if it were a concrete material thing. These direct experiences of a wider spiritual life with which our superficial consciousness is continuous, and with which it keeps up an intense commerce, form the primary mass of direct religious experience on which all hearsay religion rests, and which furnishes that notion of an ever-present God, out of which systematic theology thereupon proceeds to make capital in its own unreal pedantic way. What the word 'God' means is just those passive and active experiences of your life. Now, my friends, it is quite immaterial to my purpose whether you yourselves enjoy and venerate these experiences, or whether you stand aloof and, viewing them in others, suspect them of being illusory and vain. Like all other human experiences, they too certainly share in the general liability to illusion and mistake. They need not be infallible. But they are certainly the originals of the God-idea, and theology is the translation; and you remember that I am now using the God-idea merely as an example, not to discuss as to its truth or error, but only to show how well the principle of pragmatism works. That the God of systematic theology should exist or not exist is a matter of small practical moment. At most it means that you may continue uttering certain abstract words and that you must stop using others. But if the God of these particular experiences be false, it is an awful thing for you, if you are one of those whose lives are stayed on such experiences. The theistic controversy, trivial enough if we take it merely academically and theologically, is of tremendous significance if we test it by its results for actual life.

I can best continue to recommend the principle of practicalism to you by keeping in the neighborhood of this theological idea. I reminded you a few minutes ago that the old monarchical notion of the Deity as a sort of Louis the Fourteenth of the Heavens is losing nowadays much of its ancient prestige. Religious philosophy, like all philosophy, is growing more and more idealistic. And in the philosophy of the Absolute, so called, that post-Kantian form of idealism which is carrying so many of our higher minds before it, we have the triumph of what in old times was summarily disposed of as the pantheistic heresy—I mean the conception of God, not as the extraneous creator, but as the indwelling spirit and substance of the world. I know not where one can find a more candid, more clear, or, on the whole, more persuasive statement of this theology of Absolute Idealism than in the addresses made before this very Union three years ago by your own great Californian philosopher (whose colleague at Harvard I am proud to be), Josiah Royce. His contributions to the resulting volume, *The Conception of God*, form a very masterpiece of popularization. Now you will remember, many of you, that in the discussion that followed Professor Royce's first address, the debate turned largely on the ideas of unity and plurality, and on the question whether, if God be One in All and All in All, "One with the unity of a single instant," as Royce calls it, "forming in His wholeness one luminously transparent moment," any room is left for real morality or freedom. Professor Howison, in particular, was earnest in urging that morality and freedom are relations between a manifold of selves, and that under the régime of Royce's monistic Absolute Thought "no true manifold of selves is or can be provided for." I will not go into any of the details of that particular discussion, but just ask you to consider for a moment whether, in general, any discussion about monism or pluralism, any argument over the unity of the universe, would not necessarily be brought into a shape where it tends to straighten itself out, by bringing our principle of practical results to bear.

The question whether the world is at bottom One or Many is a typical metaphysical question. Long has it raged! In its crudest form it is an exquisite example of the *loggerheads* of metaphysics. 'I say it is one great fact,' Parmenides and Spinoza exclaim. 'I say it is many little facts,' reply the atomists and associationists. 'I say it is both one and many, many in one,' say the Hegelians; and in the ordinary popular discussions we rarely get beyond this barren reiteration by the disputants of their pet adjectives of number. But is it not first

PHILOSOPHICAL CONCEPTIONS, ETC.

of all clear that when we take such an adjective as 'One' absolutely and abstractly, its meaning is so vague and empty that it makes no difference whether we affirm or deny it? Certainly this universe is not the mere number One; and yet you can number it 'one,' if you like, in talking about it as contrasted with other possible worlds numbered 'two' and 'three' for the occasion. What exact thing do you *practically* mean by 'One,' when you call the universe One, is the first question you must ask. In what ways does the oneness come home to your own personal life? By what difference does it express itself in your experience? How can you act differently towards a universe which is one? Inquired into in this way, the unity might grow clear and be affirmed in some ways and denied in others, and so cleared up, even though a certain vague and worshipful portentousness might disappear from the notion of it in the process.

For instance, one practical result that follows when we have one thing to handle, is that we can pass from one part of it to another without letting go of the thing. In this sense oneness must be partly denied and partly affirmed of our universe. Physically we can pass continuously in various manners from one part of it to another part. But logically and psychically the passage seems less easy, for there is no obvious transition from one mind to another, or from minds to physical things. You have to step off and get on again; so that in these ways the world is not one, as measured by that practical test.

Another practical meaning of oneness is susceptibility of collection. A collection is one, though the things that compose it be many. Now, can we practically 'collect' the universe? Physically, of course we cannot. And mentally we cannot, if we take it concretely in its details. But if we take it summarily and abstractly, then we collect it mentally whenever we refer to it, even as I do now when I fling the term 'universe' at it, and so seem to leave a mental ring around it. It is plain, however, that such abstract noetic unity (as one might call it) is practically an extremely insignificant thing.

Again, oneness may mean generic sameness, so that you can treat all parts of the collection by one rule and get the same results. It is evident that in this sense the oneness of our world is incomplete, for in spite of much generic sameness in its elements and items, they still remain of many irreducible kinds. You can't pass by mere logic all over the field of it.

Its elements have, however, an affinity or commensurability with each other, are not wholly irrelevant, but can be compared, and fit together after certain fashions. This again might practically mean that they were one *in origin*, and that, tracing them backwards, we should find them arising in a single primal causal fact. Such unity of origin would have definite practical consequences, would have them for our scientific life at least.

I can give only these hasty superficial indications of what I mean when I say that it tends to clear up the quarrel between monism and pluralism to subject the notion of unity to such practical tests. On the other hand it does but perpetuate strife and misunderstanding to continue talking of it in an absolute and mystical way. I have little doubt myself that this old quarrel might be completely smoothed out to the satisfaction of all claimants, if only the maxim of Peirce were methodically followed here. The current monism on the whole still keeps talking in too abstract a way. It says the world must be either pure disconnectedness, no universe at all, or absolute unity. It insists that there is no stopping-place half way. Any connection whatever, says this monism, is only possible if there be still more connection, until at last we are driven to admit the absolutely total connection required. But this absolutely total connection either means nothing, is the mere word 'one' spelt long; or else it means the sum of all the partial connections that can possibly be conceived. I believe that when we thus attack the question, and set ourselves to search for these possible connections, and conceive each in a definite practical way, the dispute is already in a fair way to be settled beyond the chance of misunderstanding, by a compromise in which the Many and the One both get their lawful rights.

But I am in danger of becoming technical; so I must stop right here, and let you go.

I am happy to say that it is the English-speaking philosophers who first introduced the custom of interpreting the meaning of conceptions by asking what difference they make for life. Mr. Peirce has only expressed in the form of an explicit maxim what their sense for reality led them all instinctively to do. The great English way of investigating a conception is to ask yourself right off, "What is it *known as*? In what facts does it result? What is its *cash-value*, in terms of particular experience? and what special difference would come into the world according as it were true or false?" Thus does Locke treat the conception of personal identity. What you mean by it is just your chain of memories, says he. That is the only concretely verifiable part of its significance. All further ideas about it, such as the oneness or manyness of the spiritual substance on which it is based, are therefore void of intelligible meaning; and propositions touching such ideas may be indifferently affirmed or denied. So Berkeley with his 'matter.' The cash-value of matter is our physical sensations. That is what it is known as, all that we concretely verify of its conception. That therefore is the whole meaning of the word 'matter'—any other pretended meaning is mere wind of words. Hume does the same thing with causation. It is known as habitual antecedence, and tendency on our part to look for something definite to come. Apart from this practical meaning it has no significance whatever, and books about it may be committed to the flames, says Hume. Stewart and Brown, James Mill, John Mill, and Bain, have followed more or less consistently the same method; and Shadworth Hodgson has used it almost as explicitly as Mr. Peirce. These writers have many of them no doubt been too sweeping in their negations; Hume, in particular, and James Mill, and Bain. But when all is said and done, it was they, not Kant, who introduced 'the critical method' into philosophy, the one method fitted to make philosophy a study worthy of serious men. For what seriousness can possibly remain in debating philosophic propositions that will never make an appreciable difference to us in action? And what matters it, when all propositions are practically meaningless, which of them be called true or false?

The shortcomings and the negations and baldnesses of the English philosophers in question come not from their eye to merely practical results, but solely from their failure to track the practical results completely enough to see how far they extend. Hume can be corrected and built out, and his beliefs enriched, by using Humian principles exclusively, and without making any use of the circuitous and ponderous artificialities of Kant. It is indeed a somewhat pathetic matter, as it seems to me, that this is not the course which the actual history of philosophy has followed. Hume had no English successors of adequate ability to complete him and correct his negations; so it happened, as a matter of fact, that the building out of critical philosophy has mainly been left to thinkers who were under the influence of Kant. Even in England and this country it is with Kantian catch-words and categories that the fuller view of life is pursued, and in our universities it is the courses in transcendentalism that kindle the enthusiasm of the more ardent students, whilst the courses in English philosophy are committed to a secondary place. I cannot think that this is exactly as it should be. And I say this not out of national jingoism, for jingoism has no place in philosophy; or out of excitement over the great Anglo-American alliance against the world, of which we nowadays hear so much— though heaven knows that to that alliance I wish a Godspeed. I say it because I sincerely believe that the English spirit in philosophy is intellectually, as well as practically and morally, on the saner, sounder, and truer path. Kant's mind is the rarest and most intricate of all possible antique bric-a-brac museums, and connoisseurs and dilettanti will always wish to visit it and see the wondrous and racy contents. The temper of the dear old man about his work is perfectly delectable. And yet he is really—although I shrink with some terror from saying such a thing before some of you here present—at bottom a mere curio, a 'specimen.' I mean by this a perfectly definite thing: I believe that Kant bequeathes to us not one single conception which is both indispensable to philosophy and which philosophy either did not possess before him, or was not destined inevitably to acquire after him through the growth of men's reflection upon the hypotheses by which science interprets nature. The true line of philosophic progress lies, in short, it seems to me, not so much *through* Kant as *round* him to the point where now we stand. Philosophy can perfectly well outflank him, and build herself up into adequate fulness by prolonging more directly the older English lines.

May I hope, as I now conclude, and release your attention from the strain to which you have so kindly put it on my behalf, that on this wonderful Pacific Coast, of which our race is taking possession, the principle of practicalism, in which I have tried so hard to interest you, and with it the whole English tradition in philosophy, will come to its rights, and in your hands help the rest of us in our struggle towards the light.

Human Immortality: Two Supposed Objections to the Doctrine

PREFACE TO SECOND EDITION

S O MANY CRITICS have made one and the same objection to the doorway to immortality which my lecture claims to be left open by the 'transmission-theory' of cerebral action, that I feel tempted, as the book is again going to press, to add a word of explanation.

If our finite personality here below, the objectors say, be due to the transmission through the brain of portions of a preëxisting larger consciousness, all that can remain after the brain expires is the larger consciousness itself as such, with which we should thenceforth be perforce reconfounded, the only means of our existence in finite personal form having ceased.

But this, the critics continue, is the pantheistic idea of immortality, survival, namely, in the soul of the world; not the Christian idea of immortality, which means survival in strictly personal form.

In showing the possibility of a mental life after the brain's death, they conclude, the lecture has thus at the same time shown the impossibility of its identity with the personal life, which is the brain's function.

Now I am myself anything but a pantheist of the monistic pattern; yet for simplicity's sake I did in the lecture speak of the 'mother-sea' in terms that must have sounded pantheistic, and suggested that I thought of it myself as a unit. On page 1121, I even added that future lecturers might prove the loss of some of our personal limitations after death not to be matter for absolute regret. The interpretation of my critics was therefore not unnatural; and I ought to have been more careful to guard against its being made.

In note 5 on pages 1113–1114 I partially guarded against it by saying that the 'mother-sea' from which the finite mind is supposed to be strained by the brain, need not be conceived of in pantheistic terms exclusively. There might be, I said, many minds behind the scenes as well as one. The plain truth is that *one may conceive the mental world behind the veil in as individualistic a form as one pleases, without any detriment to the general scheme by which the brain is represented as a transmissive organ.*

If the extreme individualistic view were taken, one's finite mundane consciousness would be an extract from one's larger, truer personality, the latter having even now some sort of reality behind the scenes. And in transmitting it—to keep to our extremely mechanical metaphor, which confessedly throws no light on the actual *modus operandi*—one's brain would also leave effects upon the part remaining behind the veil; for when a thing is torn, both fragments feel the operation.

And just as (to use a very coarse figure) the stubs remain in a check-book whenever a check is used, to register the transaction, so these impressions on the transcendent self might constitute so many vouchers of the finite experiences of which the brain had been the mediator; and ultimately they might form that collection within the larger self of memories of our earthly passage, which is all that, since Locke's day, the continuance of our personal identity beyond the grave has by psychology been recognized to mean.

It is true that all this would seem to have affinities rather with preëxistence and with possible re-incarnations than with the Christian notion of immortality. But my concern in the lecture was not to discuss immortality in general. It was confined to showing it to be *not incompatible* with the brain-function theory of our present mundane consciousness. I hold that it is so compatible, and compatible moreover in fully individualized form. The reader would be in accord with everything that the text of my lecture intended to say, were he to assert that every memory and affection of his present life is to be preserved, and that he shall never *in sæcula sæculorum* cease to be able to say to himself: "I am the same personal being who in old times upon the earth had those experiences."

Human Immortality

IT IS A MATTER unfortunately too often seen in history to call for much remark, that when a living want of mankind has got itself officially protected and organized in an institution, one of the things which the institution most surely tends to do is to stand in the way of the natural gratification of the want itself. We see this in laws and courts of justice; we see it in ecclesiasticisms; we see it in academies of the fine arts, in the medical and other professions, and we even see it in the universities themselves.

Too often do the place-holders of such institutions frustrate the spiritual purpose to which they were appointed to minister, by the technical light which soon becomes the only light in which they seem able to see the purpose, and the narrow way which is the only way in which they can work in its service.

I confess that I thought of this for a moment when the Corporation of our University invited me last spring to give this Ingersoll lecture. Immortality is one of the great spiritual needs of man. The churches have constituted themselves the official guardians of the need, with the result that some of them actually pretend to accord or to withhold it from the individual by their conventional sacraments,—withhold it at least in the only shape in which it can be an object of desire. And now comes the Ingersoll lectureship. Its high-minded founder evidently thought that our University might serve the cause he had at heart more liberally than the churches do, because a university is a body so much less trammeled by traditions and by impossibilities in regard to choice of persons. And yet one of the first things which the university does is to appoint a man like him who stands before you, certainly not because he is known as an enthusiastic messenger of the future life, burning to publish the good tidings to his fellowmen, but apparently because he is a university official.

Thinking in this way, I felt at first as if I ought to decline the appointment. The whole subject of immortal life has its prime roots in personal feeling. I have to confess that my own personal feeling about immortality has never been of the keenest order, and that, among the problems that give my mind solicitude, this one does not take the very foremost place. Yet there are individuals with a real passion for the matter, men and women for whom a life hereafter is a pungent craving, and the thought of it an obsession; and in whom keenness of interest has bred an insight into the relations of the subject that no one less penetrated with the mystery of it can attain. Some of these people are known to me. They are not official personages; they do not speak as the scribes, but as having direct authority. And surely, if anywhere a prophet clad in goatskins, and not a uniformed official, should be called to give inspiration, assurance, and instruction, it would seem to be here, on such a theme. Office, at any rate, ought not to displace spiritual calling.

And yet, in spite of these reflections, which I could not avoid making, I am here to-night, all uninspired and official as I am. I am sure that prophets clad in goatskins, or, to speak less figuratively, laymen inspired with emotional messages on the subject, will often enough be invited by our Corporation to give the Ingersoll lecture hereafter. Meanwhile, all negative and deadening as the remarks of a mere professional psychologist like myself may be in comparison with the vital lessons they will give, I am sure, upon mature reflection, that those who have the responsibility of administering the Ingersoll foundation are in duty bound to let the most various kinds of official personages take their turn as well. The subject is really an enormous subject. At the back of Mr. Alger's *Critical History of the Doctrine of a Future Life*, there is a bibliography of more than five thousand titles of books in which it is treated. Our Corporation cannot think only of the single lecture: it must think of the whole series of lectures *in futuro*. Single lectures, however emotionally inspired and inspiring they may be, will not be enough. The lectures must remedy each other, so that out of the series there shall emerge a collective literature worthy of the importance of the theme. This unquestionably was what the founder had in mind. He wished the subject to be turned over in all possible aspects, so that at last results might ponderate harmoniously in the true direction. Seen in this long perspective, the Ingersoll foundation calls for nothing so much as for minute division of labor. Orators must take their turn, and prophets; but narrow specialists as well. Theologians of every creed, metaphysicians, anthropologists, and psychologists must alternate with biologists and physicists and psychical researchers,—even with mathematicians. If any one of them presents a grain of truth, seen from his point of view, that will remain and accrete with truths brought by the others, his will have been a good appointment.

In the hour that lies before us, then, I shall seek to justify my appointment by offering what seem to me two such grains of truth, two points well fitted, if I am not mistaken, to combine with anything that other lecturers may bring.

These points are both of them in the nature of replies to objections, to difficulties which our modern culture finds in the old notion of a life hereafter,—difficulties that I am sure rob the notion of much of its old power to draw belief, in the scientifically cultivated circles to which this audience belong.

The first of these difficulties is relative to the absolute dependence of our spiritual life, as we know it here, upon the brain. One hears not only physiologists, but numbers of laymen who read the popular science books and magazines, saying all about us, How can we believe in life hereafter when Science has once for all attained to proving, beyond possibility of escape, that our inner life is a function of that famous material, the so-called 'gray matter' of our cerebral convolutions? How can the function possibly persist after its organ has undergone decay?

Thus physiological psychology is what is supposed to bar the way to the old faith. And it is now as a physiological psychologist that I ask you to look at the question with me a little more closely.

It is indeed true that physiological science has come to the conclusion cited; and we must confess that in so doing she has only carried out a little farther the common belief of mankind. Every one knows that arrests of brain development occasion imbecility, that blows on the head abolish memory or consciousness, and that brain-stimulants and poisons change the quality of our ideas. The anatomists, physiologists, and pathologists have only shown this generally admitted fact of a dependence to be detailed and minute. What the laboratories and hospitals have lately been teaching us is not only that thought in general is one of the brain's functions, but that the various special forms of thinking are functions of special portions of the brain. When we are thinking of things seen, it is our occipital convolutions that are active; when of things heard, it is a certain portion of our temporal lobes; when of things to be spoken, it is one of our frontal convolutions. Professor Flechsig of Leipzig (who perhaps more than any one may claim to have made the subject his own) considers that in other special convolutions those processes of association go on, which permit the more abstract processes of thought, to take place. I could easily show you these regions if I had here a picture of the brain.[1] Moreover, the diminished

[1] The gaps between the centres first recognized as motor and sensory—gaps which form in man two thirds of the surface of the hemispheres—are thus positively interpreted by Flechsig as intellectual centres strictly so called. [Compare his *Gehirn und Seele*, 2te Ausgabe, 1896, p. 23.] They have, he considers, a common type of microscopic structure; and the fibres connected with them are a month later in gaining their medullary sheath than are the fibres connected with the other centres. When disordered, they are the starting-point of the insanities, properly so called. Already Wernicke had defined insanity as disease of the organ of association, without so definitely pretending to circumscribe the latter—compare his *Grundriss der Psychiatrie*, 1894, p. 7. Flechsig goes so far as to say that he finds a difference of symptoms in general paralytics according as their frontal or their more posterior association-centres are diseased. Where it is the frontal centres, the patient's consciousness of self is more deranged than is his perception of purely objective relations. Where the posterior associative regions suffer, it is rather the patient's system of objective ideas that undergoes disintegration (*loc. cit.* pp. 89–91). In rodents Flechsig thinks there is a complete absence of association-centres,—the sensory centres touch each other. In carnivora and the lower monkeys the latter centres still exceed the association-centres in volume. Only in the katarhinal apes do we begin to find anything like the human type (p. 84).

In his little pamphlet, *Die Grenzen geistiger Gesundheit und Krankheit*, Leipzig, 1896, Flechsig ascribes the moral insensibility which is found in certain criminals to a diminution of internal pain-feeling due to degeneration of the 'Körperfühlsphäre,' that extensive anterior region first so named by Munk, in which he lays the seat of all the emotions and of the consciousness of self [*Gehirn und Seele*, pp. 62–68; *Die Grenzen*, etc., pp. 31–39, 48].—I give these references to Flechsig for concreteness' sake, not because his views are irreversibly made out.

or exaggerated associations of what this author calls the *Körperfühlsphäre* with the other regions, accounts, according to him, for the complexion of our emotional life, and eventually decides whether one shall be a callous brute or criminal, an unbalanced sentimentalist, or a character accessible to feeling, and yet well poised. Such special opinions may have to be corrected; yet so firmly established do the main positions worked out by the anatomists, physiologists, and pathologists of the brain appear, that the youth of our medical schools are everywhere taught unhesitatingly to believe them. The assurance that observation will go on to establish them ever more and more minutely is the inspirer of all contemporary research. And almost any of our young psychologists will tell you that only a few belated scholastics, or possibly some crack-brained theosophist or psychical researcher, can be found holding back, and still talking as if mental phenomena might exist as independent variables in the world.

For the purposes of my argument, now, I wish to adopt this general doctrine as if it were established absolutely, with no possibility of restriction. During this hour I wish you also to accept it as a postulate, whether you think it incontrovertibly established or not; so I beg you to agree with me to-day in subscribing to the great psycho-physiological formula: *Thought is a function of the brain.*

The question is, then, Does this doctrine logically compel us to disbelieve in immortality? Ought it to force every truly consistent thinker to sacrifice his hopes of an hereafter to what he takes to be his duty of accepting all the consequences of a scientific truth?

Most persons imbued with what one may call the puritanism of science would feel themselves bound to answer this question with a yes. If any medically or psychologically bred young scientists feel otherwise, it is probably in consequence of that incoherency of mind of which the majority of mankind happily enjoy the privilege. At one hour scientists, at another they are Christians or common men, with the will to live burning hot in their breasts; and, holding thus the two ends of the chain, they are careless of the intermediate connection. But the more radical and uncompromising disciple of science makes the sacrifice, and, sorrowfully or not, according to his temperament, submits to giving up his hopes of heaven.[2]

This, then, is the objection to immortality; and the next thing in order for me is to try to make plain to you why I believe that it has in strict logic no deterrent power. I must show you that the fatal consequence is not coercive, as is commonly imagined; and that, even though our soul's life (as here below it is revealed to us) may be in literal strictness the function of a brain that perishes, yet it is not at all impossible,

[2]So widespread is this conclusion in positivistic circles, so abundantly is it expressed in conversation, and so frequently implied in things that are written, that I confess that my surprise was great when I came to look into books for a passage explicitly denying immortality on physiological grounds, which I might quote to make my text more concrete. I was unable to find anything blunt and distinct enough to serve. I looked through all the books that would naturally suggest themselves, with no effect; and I vainly asked various psychological colleagues. And yet I should almost have been ready to take oath that I had read several such passages of the most categoric sort within the last decade. Very likely this is a false impression, and it may be with this opinion as with many others. The atmosphere is full of them; many a writer's pages logically presuppose and involve them; yet, if you wish to refer a student to an express and radical statement that he may employ as a text to comment on, you find almost nothing that will do. In the present case there are plenty of passages in which, in a general way, mind is said to be conterminous with brain-function, but hardly one in which the author thereupon explicitly denies the possibility of immortality. The best one I have found is perhaps this: "Not only consciousness, but every stirring of life, depends on functions that go out like a flame when nourishment is cut off. . . . The phenomena of consciousness correspond, element for element, to the operations of special parts of the brain. . . . The destruction of any piece of the apparatus involves the loss of some one or other of the vital operations; and the consequence is that, as far as life extends, we have before us only an organic function, not a *Ding-an-sich*, or an expression of that imaginary entity the Soul. This fundamental proposition . . . carries with it the denial of the immortality of the soul, since, where no soul exists, its mortality or immortality cannot be raised as a question. . . . The function fills its time,—the flame illuminates and therein gives out its whole being. That is all; and verily that is enough. . . . Sensation has its definite organic conditions, and, as these decay with the natural decay of life, it is quite impossible for a mind accustomed to deal with realities to suppose any capacity of sensation as surviving when the machinery of our natural existence has stopped." [E. Dühring: *Der Werth des Lebens*, 3d edition, pp. 48, 169.]

but on the contrary quite possible, that the life may still continue when the brain itself is dead.

The supposed impossibility of its continuing comes from too superficial a look at the admitted fact of functional dependence. The moment we inquire more closely into the notion of functional dependence, and ask ourselves, for example, how many kinds of functional dependence there may be, we immediately perceive that there is one kind at least that does not exclude a life hereafter at all. The fatal conclusion of the physiologist flows from his assuming offhand another kind of functional dependence, and treating it as the only imaginable kind.[3]

---

[3]The philosophically instructed reader will notice that I have all along been placing myself at the ordinary dualistic point of view of natural science and of common sense. From this point of view mental facts like feelings are made of one kind of stuff or substance, physical facts of another. An absolute phenomenism, not believing such a dualism to be ultimate, may possibly end by solving some of the problems that are insoluble when propounded in dualistic terms. Meanwhile, since the physiological objection to immortality has arisen on the ordinary dualistic plane of thought, and since absolute phenomenism has as yet said nothing articulate enough to count about the matter, it is proper that my reply to the objection should be expressed in dualistic terms—leaving me free, of course, on any later occasion to make an attempt, if I wish, to transcend them and use different categories.

Now, on the dualistic assumption, one cannot see more than two really different sorts of dependence of our mind on our brain: Either

(1) The brain brings into being the very stuff of consciousness of which our mind consists; or else

(2) Consciousness pre-exists as an entity, and the various brains give to it its various special forms.

If supposition 2 be the true one, and the stuff of mind pre-exists, there are, again, only two ways of conceiving that our brain confers upon it the specifically human form. It may exist

(a) In disseminated particles; and then our brains are organs of concentration, organs for combining and massing these into resultant minds of personal form. Or it may exist

(b) In vaster unities (absolute 'world-soul,' or something less); and then our brains are organs for separating it into parts and giving them finite form.

There are thus three possible theories of the brain's function, and no more. We may name them, severally,—

1. The theory of production;
2a. The theory of combination;
2b. The theory of separation.

In the text of the lecture, theory number 2b (specified more particularly as the transmission-theory) is defended against theory number 1. Theory 2a,

When the physiologist who thinks that his science cuts off all hope of immortality pronounces the phrase, "Thought is a function of the brain," he thinks of the matter just as he thinks when he says, "Steam is a function of the tea-kettle," "Light is a function of the electric circuit," "Power is a function of the moving waterfall." In these latter cases the several material objects have the function of inwardly creating or engendering their effects, and their function must be called *productive* function. Just so, he thinks, it must be with the brain. Engendering consciousness in its interior, much as it engenders cholesterin and creatin and carbonic acid, its relation to our soul's life must also be called productive function. Of course, if such production be the function, then when the organ perishes, since the production can no longer continue,

---

otherwise known as the mind-dust or mind-stuff theory, is left entirely unnoticed for lack of time. I also leave it uncriticised in these notes, having already considered it, as fully as the so-far published forms of it may seem to call for, in my work, *The Principles of Psychology*, New York, Holt & Co., 1892, chapter VI. I may say here, however, that Professor W. K. Clifford, one of the ablest champions of the combination-theory, and originator of the useful term 'mind-stuff,' considers that theory incompatible with individual immortality, and in his review of Stewart's and Tait's book, *The Unseen Universe*, thus expresses his conviction: —

"The laws connecting consciousness with changes in the brain are very definite and precise, and their necessary consequences are not to be evaded . . . . Consciousness is a complex thing made up of elements, a stream of feelings. The action of the brain is also a complex thing made up of elements, a stream of nerve-messages. For every feeling in consciousness there is at the same time a nerve-message in the brain. . . . Consciousness is not a simple thing, but a complex; it is the combination of feelings into a stream. It exists at the same time with the combination of nerve-messages into a stream. If individual feeling always goes with individual nerve-message, if combination or stream of feelings always goes with stream of nerve-messages, does it not follow that when the stream of nerve-messages is broken up, the stream of feelings will be broken up also, will no longer form a consciousness? does it not follow that when the messages themselves are broken up, the individual feelings will be resolved into still simpler elements? The force of this evidence is not to be weakened by any number of spiritual bodies. Inexorable facts connect our consciousness with this body that we know; and that not merely as a whole, but the parts of it are connected severally with parts of our brain-action. If there is any similar connexion with a spiritual body, it only follows that the spiritual body must die at the same time with the natural one." [*Lectures and Essays*, vol. i. pp. 247–249. Compare also passages of similar purport in vol. ii. pp. 65–70.]

the soul must surely die. Such a conclusion as this is indeed inevitable from that particular conception of the facts.[4]

But in the world of physical nature productive function of this sort is not the only kind of function with which we are

[4]The theory of production, or materialistic theory, seldom ventures to formulate itself very distinctly. Perhaps the following passage from Cabanis is as explicit as anything one can find: —

"To acquire a just idea of the operations from which thought results, we must consider the brain as a particular organ specially destined to produce it; just as the stomach and intestines are destined to operate digestion, the liver to filter bile, the parotid and maxillary glands to prepare the salivary juices. The impressions, arriving in the brain, force it to enter into activity; just as the alimentary materials, falling into the stomach, excite it to a more abundant secretion of gastric juice, and to the movements which result in their own solution. The function proper to the first organ is that of receiving [*percevoir*] each particular impression, of attaching signs to it, of combining the different impressions, of comparing them with each other, of drawing from them judgments and resolves; just as the function of the other organ is to act upon the nutritive substances whose presence excites it, to dissolve them, and to assimilate their juices to our nature.

"Do you say that the organic movements by which the brain exercises these functions are unknown? I reply that the action by which the nerves of the stomach determine the different operations which constitute digestion, and the manner in which they confer so active a solvent power upon the gastric juice, are equally hidden from our scrutiny. We see the food-materials fall into this viscus with their own proper qualities; we see them emerge with new qualities, and we infer that the stomach is really the author of this alteration. Similarly we see the impressions reaching the brain by the intermediation of the nerves; they then are isolated and without coherence. The viscus enters into action; it acts upon them, and soon it emits [*renvoie*] them metamorphosed into ideas, to which the language of physiognomy or gesture, or the signs of speech and writing, give an outward expression. We conclude, then, with an equal certitude, that the brain digests, as it were, the impressions; that it performs organically the secretion of thought." [*Rapports du physique et du moral*, 8th edition, 1844, p. 137.]

It is to the ambiguity of the word 'impression' that such an account owes whatever plausibility it may seem to have. More recent forms of the production-theory have shown a tendency to liken thought to a 'force' which the brain exerts, or to a 'state' into which it passes. Herbert Spencer, for instance, writes: —

"The law of metamorphosis, which holds among the physical forces, holds equally between them and the mental forces. . . . How this metamorphosis takes place—how a force existing as motion, heat, or light, can become a mode of consciousness—how it is possible for aerial vibrations to generate the sensation we call sound, or for the forces liberated by chemical changes in familiar. We have also releasing or permissive function; and we have transmissive function.

The trigger of a crossbow has a releasing function: it removes the obstacle that holds the string, and lets the bow fly back to its natural shape. So when the hammer falls upon a detonating compound. By knocking out the inner molecular obstructions, it lets the constituent gases resume their normal bulk, and so permits the explosion to take place.

In the case of a colored glass, a prism, or a refracting lens, we have transmissive function. The energy of light, no matter how produced, is by the glass sifted and limited in color, and

---

the brain to give rise to emotion—these are mysteries which it is impossible to fathom. But they are not profounder mysteries than the transformations of the physical forces into each other." [*First Principles*, 2nd Edition, p. 217.]

So Büchner says: "Thinking must be regarded as a special mode of general natural motion, which is as characteristic of the substance of the central nervous elements as the motion of contraction is of the muscle-substance, or the motion of light is of the universal ether. . . . That thinking is and must be a mode of motion is not merely a postulate of logic, but a proposition which has of late been demonstrated experimentally. . . . Various ingenious experiments have proved that the swiftest thought that we are able to evolve occupies at least the eighth or tenth part of a second." [*Force and Matter*, New York, 1891, p. 242.]

Heat and light, being modes of motion, 'phosphorescence' and 'incandescence' are phenomena to which consciousness has been likened by the production-theory: "As one sees a metallic rod, placed in a glowing furnace, gradually heat itself, and—as the undulations of the caloric grow more and more frequent—pass successively from the shades of bright red to dark red (*sic*), to red-white, and develope, as its temperature rises, heat and light,—so the living sensitive cells, in presence of the incitations that solicit them, exalt themselves progressively as to their most interior sensibility, enter into a phase of erethism, and at a certain number of vibrations, set free (*dégagent*) pain as a physiological expression of this same sensibility superheated to a red-white." [J. Luys: *Le Cerveau*, p. 91.]

In a similar vein Mr. Percival Lowell writes: "When we have, as we say, an idea, what happens inside us is probably something like this: the neural current of molecular change passes up the nerves, and through the ganglia reaches at last the cortical cells . . . . When it reaches the cortical cells, it finds a set of molecules which are not so accustomed to this special change. The current encounters resistance, and in overcoming this resistance it causes the cells to glow. This white-heating of the cells we call consciousness. Consciousness, in short, is probably nerve-glow." [*Occult Japan*, Boston, 1895, p. 311.]

by the lens or prism determined to a certain path and shape. Similarly, the keys of an organ have only a transmissive function. They open successively the various pipes and let the wind in the air-chest escape in various ways. The voices of the various pipes are constituted by the columns of air trembling as they emerge. But the air is not engendered in the organ. The organ proper, as distinguished from its air-chest, is only an apparatus for letting portions of it loose upon the world in these peculiarly limited shapes.

My thesis now is this: that, when we think of the law that thought is a function of the brain, we are not required to think of productive function only; *we are entitled also to consider permissive or transmissive function.* And this the ordinary psycho-physiologist leaves out of his account.

Suppose, for example, that the whole universe of material things—the furniture of earth and choir of heaven—should turn out to be a mere surface-veil of phenomena, hiding and keeping back the world of genuine realities. Such a supposition is foreign neither to common sense nor to philosophy. Common sense believes in realities behind the veil even too superstitiously; and idealistic philosophy declares the whole world of natural experience, as we get it, to be but a time-mask, shattering or refracting the one infinite Thought which is the sole reality into those millions of finite streams of consciousness known to us as our private selves.

> "Life, like a dome of many-colored glass,
>   Stains the white radiance of Eternity."

Suppose, now, that this were really so, and suppose, moreover, that the dome, opaque enough at all times to the full super-solar blaze, could at certain times and places grow less so, and let certain beams pierce through into this sublunary world. These beams would be so many finite rays, so to speak, of consciousness, and they would vary in quantity and quality as the opacity varied in degree. Only at particular times and places would it seem that, as a matter of fact, the veil of nature can grow thin and rupturable enough for such effects to occur. But in those places gleams, however finite and un-satisfying, of the absolute life of the universe, are from time to time vouchsafed. Glows of feeling, glimpses of insight, and streams of knowledge and perception float into our finite world.

Admit now that *our brains* are such thin and half-transparent places in the veil. What will happen? Why, as the white radiance comes through the dome, with all sorts of staining and distortion imprinted on it by the glass, or as the air now comes through my glottis determined and limited in its force and quality of its vibrations by the peculiarities of those vocal chords which form its gate of egress and shape it into my personal voice, even so the genuine matter of reality, the life of souls as it is in its fullness, will break through our several brains into this world in all sorts of restricted forms, and with all the imperfections and queernesses that characterize our finite individualities here below.

According to the state in which the brain finds itself, the barrier of its obstructiveness may also be supposed to rise or fall. It sinks so low, when the brain is in full activity, that a comparative flood of spiritual energy pours over. At other times, only such occasional waves of thought as heavy sleep permits get by. And when finally a brain stops acting altogether, or decays, that special stream of consciousness which it subserved will vanish entirely from this natural world. But the sphere of being that supplied the consciousness would still be intact; and in that more real world with which, even whilst here, it was continuous, the consciousness might, in ways unknown to us, continue still.

You see that, on all these suppositions, our soul's life, as we here know it, would none the less in literal strictness be the function of the brain. The brain would be the independent variable, the mind would vary dependently on it. But such dependence on the brain for this natural life would in no wise make immortal life impossible, — it might be quite compatible with supernatural life behind the veil hereafter.

As I said, then, the fatal consequence is not coercive, the conclusion which materialism draws being due solely to its one-sided way of taking the word 'function.' And, whether we care or not for immortality in itself, we ought, as mere critics doing police duty among the vagaries of mankind, to insist on the illogicality of a denial based on the flat ignoring of a palpable alternative. How much more ought we to insist, as lovers of truth, when the denial is that of such a vital hope of mankind!

In strict logic, then, the fangs of cerebralistic materialism are drawn. My words ought consequently already to exert a releasing function on your hopes. You *may* believe henceforward, whether you care to profit by the permission or not. But, as this is a very abstract argument, I think it will help its effect to say a word or two about the more concrete conditions of the case.

All abstract hypotheses sound unreal; and the abstract notion that our brains are colored lenses in the wall of nature, admitting light from the super-solar source, but at the same time tingeing and restricting it, has a thoroughly fantastic sound. What is it, you may ask, but a foolish metaphor? And how can such a function be imagined? Isn't the common materialistic notion vastly simpler? Is not consciousness really more comparable to a sort of steam, or perfume, or electricity, or nerve-glow, generated on the spot in its own peculiar vessel? Is it not more rigorously scientific to treat the brain's function as function of production?

The immediate reply is, that, if we are talking of science positively understood, function can mean nothing more than bare concomitant variation. When the brain-activities change in one way, consciousness changes in another; when the currents pour through the occipital lobes, consciousness *sees* things; when through the lower frontal region, consciousness *says* things to itself; when they stop, she goes to sleep, etc. In strict science, we can only write down the bare fact of concomitance; and all talk about either production or transmission, as the mode of taking place, is pure superadded hypothesis, and metaphysical hypothesis at that, for we can frame no more notion of the details on the one alternative than on the other. Ask for any indication of the exact process either of transmission or of production, and Science confesses her imagination to be bankrupt. She has, so far, not the least glimmer of a conjecture or suggestion,—not even a bad verbal metaphor or pun to offer. *Ignoramus, ignorabimus,* is what most physiologists, in the words of one of their number, will say here. The production of such a thing as consciousness in the brain, they will reply with the late Berlin professor of physiology, is the absolute world-enigma,—something so paradoxical and abnormal as to be a stumbling block to Nature, and almost a self-contradiction. Into the mode of production of steam in a tea-kettle we have conjectural insight, for the terms that change are physically homogeneous one with another, and we can easily imagine the case to consist of nothing but alterations of molecular motion. But in the production of consciousness by the brain, the terms are heterogeneous natures altogether; and as far as our understanding goes, it is as great a miracle as if we said, Thought is 'spontaneously generated,' or 'created out of nothing.'

The theory of production is therefore not a jot more simple or credible in itself than any other conceivable theory. It is only a little more popular. All that one need do, therefore, if the ordinary materialist should challenge one to explain how the brain *can* be an organ for limiting and determining to a certain form a consciousness elsewhere produced, is to retort with a *tu quoque*, asking him in turn to explain how it can be an organ for producing consciousness out of whole cloth. For polemic purposes, the two theories are thus exactly on a par.

But if we consider the theory of transmission in a wider way, we see that it has certain positive superiorities, quite apart from its connection with the immortality question.

Just how the process of transmission may be carried on, is indeed unimaginable; but the outer relations, so to speak, of the process, encourage our belief. Consciousness in this process does not have to be generated *de novo* in a vast number of places. It exists already, behind the scenes, coeval with the world. The transmission-theory not only avoids in this way multiplying miracles, but it puts itself in touch with general idealistic philosophy better than the production-theory does. It should always be reckoned a good thing when science and philosophy thus meet.[5]

---

[5]The transmission-theory connects itself very naturally with that whole tendency of thought known as transcendentalism. Emerson, for example, writes: "We lie in the lap of immense intelligence, which makes us receivers of its truth and organs of its activity. When we discern justice, when we discern truth, we do nothing of ourselves, but allow a passage to its beams." [*Self-Reliance*, p. 56.] But it is not necessary to identify the consciousness postulated

It puts itself also in touch with the conception of a 'threshold,'—a word with which, since Fechner wrote his book called *Psychophysik*, the so-called 'new Psychology' has rung. Fechner imagines as the condition of consciousness a certain kind of psycho-physical movement, as he terms it. Before consciousness can come, a certain degree of activity in the movement must be reached. This requisite degree is called the 'threshold'; but the height of the threshold varies under different circumstances: it may rise or fall. When it falls, as in states of great lucidity, we grow conscious of things of which we should be unconscious at other times; when it rises, as in drowsiness, consciousness sinks in amount. This rising and lowering of a psycho-physical threshold exactly conforms to our notion of a permanent obstruction to the transmission of consciousness, which obstruction may, in our brains, grow alternately greater or less.[6]

---

in the lecture, as pre-existing behind the scenes, with the Absolute Mind of transcendental Idealism, although, indeed, the notion of it might lead in that direction. The absolute Mind of transcendental Idealism is one integral Unit, one single World-mind. For the purposes of my lecture, however, there might be many minds behind the scenes as well as one. All that the transmission-theory absolutely requires is that they should transcend *our* minds,—which thus come from *something* mental that pre-exists, and is larger than themselves.

[6]Fechner's conception of a 'psycho-physical threshold' as connected with his 'wave-scheme' is little known to English readers. I accordingly subjoin it, in his own words, abridged:—

"The psychically one is connected with a physically many; the physically many contract psychically into a one, a simple, or at least a more simple. Otherwise expressed: the psychically unified and simple are resultants of physical multiplicity; the physically manifold gives unified or simple results. . . .

"The facts which are grouped together under these expressions, and which give them their meaning, are as follows: . . . With our two hemispheres we think singly; with the identical parts of our two retinæ we see singly. . . . The simplest sensation of light or sound in us is connected with processes which, since they are started and kept up by outer oscillations, must themselves be somehow of an oscillatory nature, although we are wholly unaware of the separate phases and oscillations. . . .

"It is certain, then, that some unified or simple psychic resultants depend on physical multiplicity. But, on the other hand, it is equally certain that the multiplicities of the physical world do not always combine into a simple psychical resultant,—no, not even when they are compounded in a single bodily system. Whether they may not nevertheless combine into a *unified* resultant is a matter for opinion, since one is always free to ask whether the entire world,

The transmission-theory also puts itself in touch with a whole class of experiences that are with difficulty explained by

---

as such, may not have some unified psychic resultant. But of any such resultant we at least have no consciousness. . . .

"For brevity's sake, let us distinguish *psycho-physical continuity* and *discontinuity* from each other. Continuity, let us say, takes place so far as a physical manifold gives a unified or simple psychic resultant; discontinuity, so far as it gives a distinguishable multiplicity of such resultants. Inasmuch, however, as, within the unity of a more general consciousness or phenomenon of consciousness, there still may be a multiplicity distinguished, the continuity of a more general consciousness does not exclude the discontinuity of particular phenomena.

"One of the most important problems and tasks of Psycho-physics now is this: to determine the conditions (*Gesichtspunkte*) under which the cases of continuity and of discontinuity occur.

"Whence comes it that different organisms have separate consciousnesses, although their bodies are just as much connected by general Nature as the parts of a single organism are with each other, and these latter give a single conscious resultant? Of course we can say that the connection is more intimate between the parts of an organism than between the organisms of Nature. But what do we mean by a more intimate connection? Can an absolute difference of result depend on anything so relative? And does not Nature as a whole show as strict a connection as any organism does,—yea, one even more indissoluble? And the same questions come up within each organism. How comes it that, with different nerve-fibres of touch and sight, we distinguish different space-points, but with one fibre distinguish nothing, although the different fibres are connected in the brain just as much as the parts are in the single fibre? We may again call the latter connection the more *intimate*, but then the same sort of question will arise again.

"Unquestionably the problem which here lies before Psycho-physics cannot be *sharply* answered; but we may establish a general point of view for its treatment, consistently with what we laid down in a former chapter on the relations of more general with more particular phenomena of consciousness."

[The earlier passage is here inserted:] "The essential principle is this: That human psycho-physical activity must exceed a certain intensity for any waking consciousness at all to occur, and that during the waking state any particular specification of the said activity (whether spontaneous or due to stimulation), which is capable of occasioning a particular specification of consciousness, must exceed in its turn a certain further degree of intensity for the consciousness actually to arise. . . .

"This state of things (in itself a mere fact needing no picture) may be made clearer by an image or scheme, and also more concisely spoken of. Imagine the whole psycho-physical activity of man to be a wave, and the degree of this activity to be symbolized by the height of the wave above a horizontal basal line or surface, to which every psycho-physically active point contributes an ordinate. . . . The whole form and evolution of the consciousness

the production-theory. I refer to those obscure and exceptional phenomena reported at all times throughout human
history, which the 'psychical-researchers,' with Mr. Frederic

---

will then depend on the rising and falling of this wave; the intensity of the
consciousness at any time on the wave's height at that time; and the height
must always *somewhere* exceed a certain limit, which we will call a *threshold*, if
waking consciousness is to exist at all.

"Let us call this wave the *total wave*, and the threshold in question the
principal threshold."

[Since our various states of consciousness recur, some in long, some in
short periods], "we may represent such a long period as that of the slowly
fluctuating condition of our general wakefulness and the general direction of
our attention as a wave that slowly changes the place of its summit. If we call
this the *under-wave*, then the movements of shorter period, on which the
more special conscious states depend, can be symbolized by wavelets superposed upon the under-wave, and we can call these *over-waves*. They will cause
all sorts of modifications of the under-wave's surface, and the total wave will
be the resultant of both sets of waves.

"The greater, now, the strength of the movements of short period, the
amplitude of the oscillations of the psycho-physical activity, the higher will
the crests of the wavelets that represent them rise above, and the lower will
their valleys sink below the surface of the under-wave that bears them. And
these heights and depressions must exceed a certain limit of quantity which
we may call the *upper threshold*, before the special mental state which is correlated with them can appear in consciousness" [pp. 454–456].

"So far now as we symbolize any system of psycho-physical activity, to
which a generally unified or principal consciousness corresponds, by the image of a total wave rising with its crest above a certain 'threshold,' we have a
means of schematizing in a single diagram the physical solidarity of all these
psycho-physical systems throughout Nature, together with their psycho-
physical discontinuity. For we need only draw all the waves so that they run
into each other below the threshold, whilst above it they appear distinct, as in
the figure below.

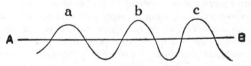

"In this figure *a*, *b*, *c* stand for three organisms, or rather for the total
waves of psycho-physical activity of three organisms, whilst A B represents
the threshold. In each wave the part that rises above the threshold is an
integrated thing, and is connected with a single consciousness. Whatever lies
below the threshold, being unconscious, separates the conscious crests, although it is still the means of physical connection.

"In general terms: wherever a psycho-physical total wave is continuous

Myers at their head, are doing so much to rehabilitate;[7] such
phenomena, namely, as religious conversions, providential
leadings in answer to prayer, instantaneous healings, premonitions, apparitions at time of death, clairvoyant visions or
impressions, and the whole range of mediumistic capacities,
to say nothing of still more exceptional and incomprehensible
things. If all our human thought be a function of the brain,
then of course, if any of these things are facts,—and to my
own mind some of them are facts,—we may not suppose that
they can occur without preliminary brain-action. But the ordinary production-theory of consciousness is knit up with a

with itself above the threshold, there we find the unity or identity of a consciousness, inasmuch as the connection of the psychical phenomena which
correspond to the parts of the wave also appears in consciousness. Whenever,
on the contrary, total waves are disconnected, or connected only underneath
the threshold, the corresponding consciousness is broken, and no connection
between its several parts appears. More briefly: consciousness is continuous
or discontinuous, unified or discrete, according as the psycho-physical total
waves that subserve it are themselves continuous or discontinuous above the
threshold. . . .

"If, in the diagram, we should raise the entire line of waves so that not only
the crests but the valleys appeared above the threshold, then these latter would
appear only as depressions in one great continuous wave above the threshold,
and the discontinuity of the consciousness would be converted into continuity. We of course cannot bring this about. We might also squeeze the wave
together so that the valleys should be pressed up, and the crests above the
threshold flow into a line; then the discretely-feeling organisms would have
become a singly-feeling organism. This, again, Man cannot voluntarily bring
about, but it is brought about in Man's nature. His two halves, the right one
and the left one, are thus united; and the number of segments of radiates and
articulates show that more than two parts can be thus psycho-physically conjoined. One need only cut them asunder, i. e. interpolate another part of
nature between them under the threshold, and they break into two separately
conscious beings." . . . [*Elemente der Psychophysik*, 1860, vol. ii. pp. 526–530.]

One sees easily how on Fechner's wave-scheme, a world-soul may be expressed. All psycho-physical activity being continuous 'below the threshold,'
the consciousness might also become continuous if the threshold sank low
enough to uncover all the waves. The threshold throughout nature in general
is, however, very high, so the consciousness that gets over it is of the discontinuous form.

[7]See the long series of articles by Mr. Myers in the *Proceedings of the Society
for Psychical Research*, beginning in the third volume with automatic writing,
and ending in the latest volumes with the higher manifestations of knowledge
by mediums. Mr. Myers's theory of the whole range of phenomena is, that
our normal consciousness is in continuous connection with a greater con-

peculiar notion of how brain-action *can* occur,—that notion being that all brain-action, without exception, is due to a prior action, immediate or remote, of the bodily sense-organs *on* the brain. Such action makes the brain produce sensations and mental images, and out of the sensations and images the higher forms of thought and knowledge in their turn are framed. As transmissionists, we also must admit this to be the condition of all our usual thought. Sense-action is what lowers the brain-barrier. My voice and aspect, for instance, strike upon your ears and eyes; your brain thereupon becomes more pervious, and an awareness on your part of what I say and who I am slips into this world from the world behind the veil. But, in the mysterious phenomena to which I allude, it is often hard to see where the sense-organs can come in. A medium, for example, will show knowledge of his sitter's private affairs which it seems impossible he should have acquired through sight or hearing, or inference therefrom. Or you will have an apparition of some one who is now dying hundreds of miles away. On the production-theory one does not see from what sensations such odd bits of knowledge are produced. On the transmission-theory, they don't have to be 'produced,'—they exist ready-made in the transcendental world, and all that is needed is an abnormal lowering of the brain-threshold to let them through. In cases of conversion, in providential leadings, sudden mental healings, etc., it seems to the subjects themselves of the experience as if a power from without, quite different from the ordinary action of the senses or of the sense-led mind, came into their life, as if the latter suddenly opened into that greater life in which it has its source. The word 'influx,' used in Swedenborgian circles, well describes this impression of new insight, or new willingness, sweeping over us like a tide. All such experiences, quite paradoxical and meaningless on the production-theory, fall very naturally into place on the other theory. We need only suppose the continuity of our consciousness with a mother-sea, to allow for exceptional waves

---

sciousness of which we do not know the extent, and to which he gives, in its relation to the particular person, the not very felicitous name—though no better one has been proposed—of his or her 'subliminal' self.

occasionally pouring over the dam. Of course the causes of these odd lowerings of the brain's threshold still remain a mystery on any terms.

Add, then, this advantage to the transmission-theory,—an advantage which I am well aware that some of you will not rate very high,—and also add the advantage of not conflicting with a life hereafter, and I hope you will agree with me that it has many points of superiority to the more familiar theory. It is a theory which, in the history of opinion on such matters, has never been wholly left out of account, though never developed at any great length. In the great orthodox philosophic tradition, the body is treated as an essential condition to the soul's life in this world of sense; but after death, it is said, the soul is set free, and becomes a purely intellectual and non-appetitive being. Kant expresses this idea in terms that come singularly close to those of our transmission-theory. The death of the body, he says, may indeed be the end of the sensational use of our mind, but only the beginning of the intellectual use. "The body," he continues, "would thus be, not the cause of our thinking, but merely a condition restrictive thereof, and, although essential to our sensuous and animal consciousness, it may be regarded as an impeder of our pure spiritual life."[8] And in a recent book of great suggestiveness and power, less well-known as yet than it deserves,—I mean *Riddles of the Sphinx*, by Mr. F. C. S. Schiller of Oxford, late of Cornell University,—the transmission-theory is defended at some length.[9]

[8] See *Kritik der reinen Vernunft*, second edition, p. 809.

[9] I subjoin a few extracts from Mr. Schiller's work: "Matter is an admirably calculated machinery for regulating, limiting, and restraining the consciousness which it encases. . . . If the material encasement be coarse and simple, as in the lower organisms, it permits only a little intelligence to permeate through it; if it is delicate and complex, it leaves more pores and exits, as it were, for the manifestations of consciousness. . . . On this analogy, then, we may say that the lower animals are still entranced in the lower stage of brute *lethargy*, while we have passed into the higher phase of *somnambulism*, which already permits us strange glimpses of a lucidity that divines the realities of a transcendent world. And this gives the final answer to Materialism: it consists in showing in detail . . . that Materialism is a hysteron proteron, a putting of the cart before the horse, which may be rectified by just inverting the connection between Matter and Consciousness. Matter is not that which *produces* Consciousness, but that which *limits* it and confines its intensity within certain

But still, you will ask, in what positive way does this theory help us to realize our immortality in imagination? What we all wish to keep is just these individual restrictions, these self-same tendencies and peculiarities that define us to ourselves and others, and constitute our identity, so called. Our finite-nesses and limitations seem to be our personal essence; and when the finiting organ drops away, and our several spirits revert to their original source and resume their unrestricted condition, will they then be anything like those sweet streams of feeling which we know, and which even now our brains

---

limits: material organization does not construct consciousness out of arrange-ments of atoms, but contracts its manifestation within the sphere which it permits. This explanation . . . admits the connection of Matter and Con-sciousness, but contends that the course of interpretation must proceed in the contrary direction. Thus it will fit the facts alleged in favour of Materialism equally well, besides enabling us to understand facts which Materialism re-jected as 'supernatural.' It explains the lower by the higher, Matter by Spirit, instead of *vice versa*, and thereby attains to an explanation which is ultimately tenable instead of one which is ultimately absurd. And it is an explanation the possibility of which no evidence in favour of Materialism can possibly affect. For if, *e. g.*, a man loses consciousness as soon as his brain is injured, it is clearly as good an explanation to say the injury to the brain destroyed the mechanism by which the manifestation of consciousness was rendered possi-ble, as to say that it destroyed the seat of consciousness. On the other hand, there are facts which the former theory suits far better. If, *e. g.*, as sometimes happens, the man after a time more or less recovers the faculties of which the injury to his brain had deprived him, and that not in consequence of a re-newal of the injured part, but in consequence of the inhibited functions being performed by the vicarious action of other parts, the easiest explanation cer-tainly is that after a time consciousness constitutes the remaining parts into a mechanism capable of acting as a substitute for the lost parts. And again, if the body is a mechanism for inhibiting consciousness, for preventing the full powers of the Ego from being prematurely actualized, it will be necessary to invert also our ordinary ideas on the subject of memory, and to account for forgetfulness instead of for memory. It will be during life that we drink the bitter cup of Lethe, it will be with our brain that we are enabled to forget. And this will serve to explain not only the extraordinary memories of the drowning and the dying generally, but also the curious hints which experi-mental psychology occasionally affords us that nothing is ever forgotten wholly and beyond recall." [*Riddles of the Sphinx*, London, Swan Sonnen-schein, 1891, p. 293 ff.]

Mr. Schiller's conception is much more complex in its relations than the simple 'theory of transmission' postulated in my lecture, and to do justice to it the reader should consult the original work.

are sifting out from the great reservoir for our enjoyment here below? Such questions are truly living questions, and surely they must be seriously discussed by future lecturers upon this Ingersoll foundation. I hope, for my part, that more than one such lecturer will penetratingly discuss the conditions of our immortality, and tell us how much we may lose, and how much we may possibly gain, if its finiting outlines should be changed? If all determination is negation, as the philosophers say, it might well prove that the loss of some of the particular determinations which the brain imposes would not appear a matter of such absolute regret.

But into these higher and more transcendental matters I refuse to enter upon this occasion; and I proceed, during the remainder of the hour, to treat of my second point. Fragmentary and negative it is, as my first one has been. Yet, between them, they do give to our belief in immortality a freer wing.

My second point is relative to the incredible and intolerable number of beings which, with our modern imagination, we must believe to be immortal, if immortality be true. I cannot but suspect that this, too, is a stumbling-block to many of my present audience. And it is a stumbling-block which I should thoroughly like to clear away.

It is, I fancy, a stumbling-block of altogether modern origin, due to the strain upon the quantitative imagination which recent scientific theories, and the moral feelings consequent upon them, have brought in their train.

For our ancestors the world was a small, and—compared with our modern sense of it—a comparatively snug affair. Six thousand years at most it had lasted. In its history a few particular human heroes, kings, ecclesiarchs, and saints stood forth very prominent, overshadowing the imagination with their claims and merits, so that not only they, but all who were associated familiarly with them, shone with a glamour which even the Almighty, it was supposed, must recognize and respect. These prominent personages and their associates were the nucleus of the immortal group; the minor heroes and saints of minor sects came next, and people without distinction formed a sort of background and filling in. The whole scene of eternity (so far, at least, as Heaven and not the

nether place was concerned in it) never struck to the believer's fancy as an overwhelmingly large or inconveniently
crowded stage. One might call this an aristocratic view of immortality; the immortals—I speak of Heaven exclusively, for
an immortality of torment need not now concern us—were
always an élite, a select and manageable number.

But, with our own generation, an entirely new quantitative
imagination has swept over our western world. The theory of
evolution now requires us to suppose a far vaster scale of
times, spaces, and numbers than our forefathers ever dreamed
the cosmic process to involve. Human history grows continuously out of animal history, and goes back possibly even to
the tertiary epoch. From this there has emerged insensibly a
democratic view, instead of the old aristocratic view, of immortality. For our minds, though in one sense they may have
grown a little cynical, in another they have been made sympathetic by the evolutionary perspective. Bone of our bone and
flesh of our flesh are these half-brutish prehistoric brothers.
Girdled about with the immense darkness of this mysterious
universe even as we are, they were born and died, suffered
and struggled. Given over to fearful crime and passion,
plunged in the blackest ignorance, preyed upon by hideous
and grotesque delusions, yet steadfastly serving the profoundest of ideals in their fixed faith that existence in any form is
better than non-existence, they ever rescued triumphantly
from the jaws of ever-imminent destruction the torch of life,
which, thanks to them, now lights the world for us. How
small indeed seem individual distinctions when we look back
on these overwhelming numbers of human beings panting
and straining under the pressure of that vital want! And how
inessential in the eyes of God must be the small surplus of the
individual's merit, swamped as it is in the vast ocean of the
common merit of mankind, dumbly and undauntedly doing
the fundamental duty and living the heroic life! We grow
humble and reverent as we contemplate the prodigious spectacle. Not our differences and distinctions,—we feel—no,
but our common animal essence of patience under suffering
and enduring effort must be what redeems us in the Deity's
sight. An immense compassion and kinship fill the heart. An
immortality from which these inconceivable billions of fellow-

strivers should be excluded becomes an irrational idea for us. That our superiority in personal refinement or in religious creed should constitute a difference between ourselves and our messmates at life's banquet, fit to entail such a consequential difference of destiny as eternal life for us, and for them torment hereafter, or death with the beasts that perish, is a notion too absurd to be considered serious. Nay, more, the very beasts themselves—the wild ones at any rate—are leading the heroic life at all times. And a modern mind, expanded as some minds are by cosmic emotion, by the great evolutionist vision of universal continuity, hesitates to draw the line even at man. If any creature lives forever, why not all?—why not the patient brutes? So that a faith in immortality, if we are to indulge it, demands of us nowadays a scale of representation so stupendous that our imagination faints before it, and our personal feelings refuse to rise up and face the task. The supposition we are swept along to is too vast, and rather than face the conclusion, we abandon the premise from which it starts. We give up our own immortality sooner than believe that all the hosts of Hottentots and Australians that have been, and shall ever be, should share it with us *in sæcula sæculorum*. Life is a good thing on a reasonably copious scale; but the very heavens themselves, and the cosmic times and spaces, would stand aghast, we think, at the notion of preserving eternally such an ever-swelling plethora and glut of it.

Having myself, as a recipient of modern scientific culture, gone through a subjective experience like this, I feel sure that it must also have been the experience of many, perhaps of most, of you who listen to my words. But I have also come to see that it harbors a tremendous fallacy; and, since the noting of the fallacy has set my own mind free again, I have felt that one service I might render to my listeners to-night would be to point out where it lies.

It is the most obvious fallacy in the world, and the only wonder is that all the world should not see through it. It is the result of nothing but an invincible blindness from which we suffer, an insensibility to the inner significance of alien lives, and a conceit that would project our own incapacity into the vast cosmos, and measure the wants of the Absolute by our own puny needs. Our christian ancestors dealt with the problem more easily than we do. We, indeed, lack sympathy; but they had a positive antipathy for these alien human creatures, and they naïvely supposed the Deity to have the antipathy, too. Being, as they were, 'heathen,' our forefathers felt a certain sort of joy in thinking that their Creator made them as so much mere fuel for the fires of hell. Our culture has humanized us beyond that point, but we cannot yet conceive them as our comrades in the fields of heaven. We have, as the phrase goes, *no use for them*, and it oppresses us to think of their survival. Take, for instance, all the Chinamen. Which of you here, my friends, sees any fitness in their eternal perpetuation unreduced in numbers? Surely not one of you. At most, you might deem it well to keep a few chosen specimens alive to represent an interesting and peculiar variety of humanity; but as for the rest, what comes in such surpassing numbers, and what you can only imagine in this abstract summary collective manner, must be something of which the units, you are sure, can have no individual preciousness. God himself, you think, can have no use for them. An immortality of every separate specimen must be to him and to the universe as indigestible a load to carry as it is to you. So, engulfing the whole subject in a sort of mental giddiness and nausea, you drift along, first doubting that the mass can be immortal, then losing all assurance in the immortality of your own particular person, precious as you all the while feel and realize the latter to be. This, I am sure, is the attitude of mind of some of you before me.

But is not such an attitude due to the veriest lack and dearth of your imagination? You take these swarms of alien kinsmen as they are *for you*: an external picture painted on your retina, representing a crowd oppressive by its vastness and confusion. As they are for you, so you think they positively and absolutely are. *I* feel no call for them, you say; therefore there *is* no call for them. But all the while, beyond this externality which is your way of realizing them, they realize themselves with the acutest internality, with the most violent thrills of life. 'Tis you who are dead, stone-dead and blind and senseless, in your way of looking on. You open your eyes upon a scene of which you miss the whole significance. Each of these grotesque or even repulsive aliens is animated by an inner joy of living as hot or hotter than that which you feel beating in your private breast. The sun rises and beauty beams to light his path. To miss the inner joy of him, as Stevenson says, is to miss the whole of him.[10] Not a being of the countless throng is there whose continued life is not called for, and called for intensely, by the consciousness that animates the being's form. That *you* neither realize nor understand nor call for it, that you have no use for it, is an absolutely irrelevant circumstance. That you have a saturation-point of interest tells us nothing of the interests that absolutely are. The Universe, with every living entity which her resources create, creates at the same time a call for that entity, and an appetite for its continuance,—creates it, if nowhere else, at least within the heart of the entity itself. It is absurd to suppose, simply because our private power of sympathetic vibration with other lives gives out so soon, that in the heart of infinite being itself there can be such a thing as plethora, or glut, or supersaturation. It is not as if there were a bounded room where the minds in possession had to move up or make place and crowd together to accommodate new occupants. Each new mind brings its own edition of the universe of space along with it, its own room to inhabit; and these spaces never crowd each other,—the space of my imagination, for example, in no way interferes with yours. The amount of possible consciousness seems to be governed by no law analogous to that of the so-called conservation of energy in the material world. When one man wakes up, or one is born, another does not have to go to sleep, or die, in order to keep the consciousness of the universe a constant quantity. Professor Wundt, in fact, in his *System of Philosophy*, has formulated a law of the universe which he calls the law of increase of spiritual energy, and which he expressly opposes to

---

[10]I beg the reader to peruse R. L. Stevenson's magnificent little essay entitled 'The Lantern Bearers,' reprinted in the collection entitled *Across the Plains*. The truth is that we are doomed, by the fact that we are practical beings with very limited tasks to attend to, and special ideals to look after, to be absolutely blind and insensible to the inner feelings, and to the whole inner significance of lives that are different from our own. Our opinion of the worth of such lives is absolutely wide of the mark, and unfit to be counted at all.

the law of conservation of energy in physical things.[11] There seems no formal limit to the positive increase of being in spiritual respects; and since spiritual being, whenever it comes, affirms itself, expands and craves continuance, we may justly and literally say, regardless of the defects of our own private sympathy, that the supply of individual life in the universe can never possibly, however immeasurable it may become, exceed the demand. The demand for that supply is there the moment the supply itself comes into being, for the beings supplied demand their own continuance.

I speak, you see, from the point of view of all the other individual beings, realizing and enjoying inwardly their own existence. If we are pantheists, we can stop there. We need, then, only say that through them, as through so many diversified channels of expression, the eternal Spirit of the Universe affirms and realizes its own infinite life. But if we are theists, we can go farther without altering the result. God, we can then say, has so inexhaustible a capacity for love that his call and need is for a literally endless accumulation of created lives. He can never faint or grow weary, as we should, under the increasing supply. His scale is infinite in all things. His sympathy can never know satiety or glut.

I hope now that you agree with me that the tiresomeness of an over-peopled Heaven is a purely subjective and illusory notion, a sign of human incapacity, a remnant of the old narrow-hearted aristocratic creed. "Revere the Maker, lift thine eye up to his style and manners of the sky," and you will believe that this is indeed a democratic universe, in which your paltry exclusions play no regulative part. Was your taste consulted in the peopling of this globe? How, then, should it be consulted as to the peopling of the vast City of God? Let us put our hand over our mouth, like Job, and be thankful that in our personal littleness we ourselves are here at all. The Deity that suffers us, we may be sure, can suffer many another queer and wondrous and only half-delightful thing.

For my own part, then, so far as logic goes, I am willing that every leaf that ever grew in this world's forests and rustled in the breeze should become immortal. It is purely a

[11]W. Wundt: *System der Philosophie*, Leipzig, Engelmann, 1889, p. 315.

question of fact: are the leaves so, or not? Abstract quantity, and the abstract needlessness in our eyes of so much reduplication of things so much alike, have no connection with the subject. For bigness and number and generic similarity are only manners of our finite way of thinking; and, considered in itself and apart from our imagination, one scale of dimensions and of numbers for the Universe is no more miraculous or inconceivable than another, the moment you grant to a universe the liberty to be at all, in place of the Non-entity that might conceivably have reigned.

The heart of being can have no exclusions akin to those which our poor little hearts set up. The inner significance of other lives exceeds all our powers of sympathy and insight. If we feel a significance in our own life which would lead us spontaneously to claim its perpetuity, let us be at least tolerant of like claims made by other lives, however numerous, however unideal they may seem to us to be. Let us at any rate not decide adversely on our own claim, whose grounds we feel directly, because we cannot decide favorably on the alien claims, whose grounds we cannot feel at all. That would be letting blindness lay down the law to sight.

Index

Absence, 999–1000

Absolute, the: meaning of, 980; pragmatic view of, 1092–1095

Abstraction, 944, 945, 957

Accommodation, 928

Acquaintance, knowledge as, 956, 1060–1062

Action: mental, 894, 896–898; and knowing, 908; and belief, 1079–1080

Adjectives, 944–945

Adjustment, in mental evolution, 893

Aesthetics: Spencer on, 895; and interest, 925, 928–929, 932; and intuition, 942; reasons in, 946

Alembert, Jean le Rond d': quoted, 954; mentioned, 979

Anæsthetic Revelation, The (B. P. Blood), 984n

Analogy, 941–945

Analysis, 927

Analysis of the Phenomena of the Human Mind (James Mill), 969n

Analysts, 941, 943

Animals: intelligence, 910, 933–936; and dissociation, 925–926; and experience, 929–930; and man, 936–937, 939–940; and language, 937–938; brains of, 946–947; and acquired traits, 948; and immortality, 1123

Animism, 1070–1072

Anselmian proof, 1016, 1018

Apperception, 1067n, 1069

A priorists, 919

Artists, 941–942

Association: of ideas, 902; and interest, 911–912; laws of, 912–914; and identity, 914; and reasoning, 914–915, 919–922; and experience, 915, 931; and knowledge, 924–925; and dissociation, 932; and animal intelligence, 933–936, 940; and humor, 936; and language, 937; and genius, 941; and simplification, 962; and explanation, 964–966; of essences, 967; and brain, 998n, 1103; and tendency, 1002; and horizon, 1003

Associationism: and continuity, 991–

992; and mind, 997; and synchronism, 1066, 1074n

Atomism, 1092

Atoms, 973

Attention: and interest, 911; and dissociation, 925; and novelty, 928; and experience, 929; and brain, 946; and association, 1067

Attraction, 1067n

Attributes: and classification, 962; identity of, 968–970; God's 1090

Axioms, 919; God's, 1090

Bagehot, W., 1021, 1045

Bain, Alexander: on association, 912–913, 1033; on genius, 941; on nonentity, 981; and pragmatism, 1095; quoted, 956, 962, 978; mentioned, 979, 1067

Baldwin, James Mark, 1069

Balfour, Arthur James, quoted, 1086

Beethoven, Ludwig van, 901, 945

Being: rationality of, 951; and nonexistence, 978–979

Belief: in sensations, 1036; in objects of emotion, 1043–1045; in theories, 1048; Peirce's view of, 1079–1081

Berkeley, Cal., 1043, 1077

Berkeley, George, 1058, 1094

Binet, Alfred, 1042, 1066

Birds, 947

Blindness, human, 1124

Blood, Benjamin Paul, on anesthetics, 984n

Body, 1106n, 1119

Boissière, Prudence, quoted, 958

"Brahma" (R. W. Emerson), 905

Brain: and thought, 912; localization, 946; and habits, 947–948; masculine and feminine, 948–949; and consciousness, 1098, 1106n, 1112–1113; and thought, 1102–1106, 1108–1110; and transmission, 1111; and abnormal mental states, 1117

Brentano, Franz, 986, 1024

Brown, Thomas, 1095

Browning, Robert, 1083

Brown-Séquard, Charles Edouard, 947
Bryn Mawr College, 1060
Büchner, Ludwig, 1109
Buddhism, 903
Butler, Samuel, quoted, 967

Cabanis, Pierre Jean Georges, 1108n
California, 1092
Candid Examination of Theism, A (G. J. Romanes), 981n
Carlyle, Thomas, 982
Cash-value, 1095
Cattell, James McKeen, 1069
"Causalität und Identität" (A. Riehl), 965n
Causality, 956–957
Causation, 1095
Cerveau et ses fonctions, Le (J. Luys), 958
Change, 994–995
Chaos, 962, 974, 1094
Character, 949, 1104
Children, 925, 940
Christianity, 893, 903, 955
Clairvoyance, 1117
Classification, 962–964
Clearness, 956
Clifford, William Kingdon, 907–908, 973, 1107n
Closet-naturalists, 1089
Clouston, Thomas Smith, 1022–1023
Cogitandum, law of the, 901–902, 907
Cogitatum, law of the, 901
Cognition, 893, 1064n
Collection, 1093
Common-sense: on mental excellence, 894, 899; on unity of consciousness, 1057; and pointing, 1059; on philosophical disputes, 1084; dualistic view of, 1106n; and realities, 1110
Compounding, 993
Comprehension, 955
Comte, Auguste, 986
Conception: and teleology, 952–953, 976; and knowledge, 1059
Conception of God, The (J. Royce), 1092
Conceptual experience, 1057–1058
Conceptualism, 1003–1004
Concomitants, law of, 926–928, 930, 931, 932
Concretes, 912, 923, 924

Conduct, 1080
Consciousness: and teleology, 904; of self, 939–940; and focalization, 947; unity of, 960, 1057, 1066; stream of, 987; and introspection, 988; and relations, 988–991; and continuity, 991–992; and unity, 992–995; and objects, 995, 996–997; and tendencies, 999–1003; study of, 1007–1013; minimum of, 1062–1065, 1067n; and attention, 1067; and reminiscence, 1068; and synergy, 1069; and relating, 1070; spiritualism on, 1070–1072; compounding of, 1075–1076; and brain, 1090, 1106n, 1112–1113; and transmission, 1110–1111; nature of, 1112; and threshold, 1114–1117
Consequences, 1060, 1080
Contiguity, 912, 913, 932–933
Continuity, 940, 991, 993, 1010
Contradiction, 955
Contrast, 927
Coriolanus (W. Shakespeare), 936
Cornelius, Hans, 1074n
Correspondence: in mental evolution, 894, 895; Spencer's view of, 895–896, 902; and survival, 900
Cosmic weather, 1086
Creator, 963–964, 1091–1092
Critical History of the Doctrine of a Future Life, A (W. R. Alger), 1101
Criticism, 893
Critics, 941, 942–943
Critique philosophique, 959–960
Curiosity, 926
Custom, 951
Cuvier, Georges, 956
Czolbe, Heinrich, 958

Dante, 1087
Darwin, Charles, 905, 964
Data, 1060, 1063–1064
Datum, the, 977, 979
Deaf-mutes: education of, 939, and thinking, 1006–1007
De l'Intelligence (H. Taine), 969n
Dependence, 1106
Descartes, René, 1034
Descent of Man, The (C. Darwin), 923
Difference, 932

Digitalis, 1014, 1015
Disbelief, 1022–1023
Discharge, 1069
Discoveries Among the Ruins of Nineveh and Babylon (A. H. Layard), 903
Discrimination, and experience, 924–925
Disputes, philosophical, 1080–1081, 1084
Dissociation: and interest, 925; and varying concomitants, 926–928; and experience, 929, 930; and similarity, 932; and animal intelligence, 936; and language, 936–937; and self-consciousness, 939–940; and brain, 947
Distinctions, 955–958, 959
Dogs: intelligence of, 910–911, 934–936; and dissociation, 925; and experience, 930; and language, 937
Doubt, 1023
Dualism, 1106
Du Bois-Reymond, Emil, 973
Dühring, Eugen Karl, 982, 1105n

Ecclesiasticism, 1100
Ego, 1034
Eleatics, 956
Elemente der Psychophysik (G. T. Fechner), 1114, 1115n–1117n
Elements of Physiological Psychology (G. T. Ladd), 1071n
Emerson, Ralph Waldo, 905, 1044
Emotion: and cognition, 894; ontologic, 980; Flechsig's view of, 1103–1104
Empirical truths, 960
Empiricism: and ideals, 905; on relations, 957; truth of 979; ultimacy of, 983
England, philosophy in, 1094–1096
Epistemology, 1075
Error, 940
Essais de critique générale (C. Renouvier), 959, 975, 981n
Essays Moral, Political, and Literary (D. Hume), 957n
Essences, 967
Ether, 1072
Ethics, 895
Event, 1065
Evil, 951–952

Evolution: mental, 893, 895, 901; and subjective interests, 897n; and monism, 955; and simplification, 959; and perfection, 1086; and immortality, 1122–1123
Excellence, 898, 907
Existence, 984, 1066
Experience: and association, 915, 921; and reason, 918, 923; and discrimination, 924; Spencer on, 929; and interest, 930–932; and language, 944; and intuitions, 946; and familiarity, 1000; and things, 1058–1059; immediate, 1061–1062; and associative systems, 1062n; minimum of, 1062–1065; in religion, 1091
Experts, 945
Explanation: J. S. Mill on, 961; nature of, 962; and association, 961–966; conditions of, 972–975

Fact: properties of, 921; Carlyle on, 982
Faith, 979
Familiarity, 1000
Fate, 908–909
Faust (literary character), 984
Fechner, Gustav Theodor: on threshold, 1114n–1117n; mentioned, 973
Feeling: and relations, 989–991; and continuity, 993; and qualities, 994; and thought, 995–996, 1004–1005; and brain, 997–1000; and tendencies, 999–1004; and universals, 1004; and rationality, 1006; and psychology, 1006; and object, 1007–1013; knowledge of, 1013n; smallest, 1062–1063; and immortality, 1100–1101
Ferrier, James Frederick, 994n
Fichte, Immanuel Hermann, 1041–1042
Finiteness, 1120
First Principles (H. Spencer), 1109n
Fitting, 1060n
Flechsig, Paul Emil, 1103
Fluency, 950–951
Focalization, 947
Force and Matter (L. Büchner), 1109n
Foundations of Belief, The (A. J. Balfour), 1086
Fragments of Science (J. Tyndall), 966n
France, 988

Freedom, 1018, 1092
Fringe, the, 1003, 1004–1007, 1008, 1010, 1063
Fullerton, George Stuart, 1058, 1073–1074
Function: kinds of, 1106n, 1107, 1109, 1111; in science, 1112

Galton, Francis, 989, 1002, 1004
Genius: and reasoning, 920, 924; nature of, 932, 953, 967; and analogy, 941; types, 941; and reasons 946
Geoffroy Saint-Hilaire, Étienne, 956
Germany, 948, 988, 992
Ghibellines, 904
God: pragmatism on, 1082–1083, 1084–1085, 1087–1092; idealism on, 1092–1093
Goethe, Johann Wolfgang von, 976
Green, Thomas Hill, 957n, 1008n
Griesinger, W, 1035
Grose, Thomas Hodge, 957n
Grübelsucht, 1022
Grundlage der empirischen Psychologie (J. Mohr), 987n
Grundzüge einer extensionalen Erkenntnistheorie (H. Czolbe), 958
Guelphs, 904
Guinea pigs, 947
Gulliver, 947
Gurney, Edmund, 1066

Habit: and experience, 923; inheritance of, 948; Peirce's principle, 1079–1080
Haldane, John Scott, 1014, 1015, 1016
Hall, Granville Stanley, 973
Hamlet (literary character), 984
Happiness, 951
Harris, William Torrey, 1067
Hartmann, Eduard von, 953, 960
Harvard University, 1092
Hayes, Isaac Israel, 933
Hector, 912
Hegel, Georg Wilhelm Friedrich: and contradiction, 955; on nonentity, 979, 981, 984; and Anselmian proof, 1016
Helmholtz, Hermann Ludwig Ferdinand von, 963
Heraclitus, 956, 997

Herbart, Johann Friedrich, 1067n, 1070
Herbartians, 991, 998
Hercules, 912
Heredity, 948
Hindoos, 933
History of Philosophy, The (G. H. Lewis), 967n–968n
Hodgson, Shadworth Hollway: on interest, 902; on experience, 983; on things, 1058; on minimum of consciousness, 1063; and pragmatism, 1095; mentioned, 1059
Homer, 912, 942
Howison, George Holmes, 1092
Hume, David: on belief, 1032–1033, 1039–1040; and pragmatism, 1095–1096; quoted, 957, 961; mentioned, 956, 960, 965, 1060
Humians, 988–989
Humor, 936
Huxley, Thomas Henry: and doubt, 907–908; on ideas, 989; on images, 1002, 1004; quoted, 961, 966
Hypothesis, 1072, 1112
Hysterics, 1071

Idealism: and ideals, 905; on things, 1058–1059; absolute, 1092; and religious philosophy, 1092
Ideals, 894, 899, 905
Ideas: Czolbe on, 958; and self-transcendence, 1060; activity of, 1067n
Identification, 962, 971–972, 977
Identities, 967n–968n
Identity: and association, 914; and purpose, 934–935; criterion of, 965; and rationality, 967; of attributes, 968–970; and immediate knowledge, 1062; personal, 1094
Images: blended, 989, 1004; sensorial, 1000–1001; and vagueness, 1002–1005; and fringe, 1004–1006; and concepts, 1005n; and rationality, 1006–1007
Imitation, 938n–939n
Immediacy, 986
Immortality: and the transmission theory, 1098–1099; and organized religion, 1100; James's view, 1101; studies, 1101–1102; physiological

objection, 1102–1106; and brain functions, 1106n, 1111–1112; and mind-stuff, 1106n–1107n, 1108n; and soul, 1119; and the self, 1120–1121; and size of population, 1121–1127
Imperative, 904
Individualism, 1099
Ingersoll, George Goldthwait, 1100, 1101
Insanity, 1103n
Intelligence, 895–896, 900, 906
Interests: subjective, 894, 897; and survival, 898–900, 903; listed, 899–900; and association, 911–912; and reasoning, 919; and essence, 922; and dissociation, 925–926, 928; and experience, 929–931; and brain, 946; and conception, 952, 972n; theoretic, 976
Intimacy, 960–961
Introspection: and psychology, 986; and stream of thought, 988–989; and knowledge, 1007–1013
Intuition: and art, 941–943, 945; Schopenhauer on, 953; and knowledge, 1059; of knowing, 1064n; and knowing things together, 1074n–1075n
Irrationalism, 1014
Irrationality, 950–951
Italy, 948

Jacobi, Friedrich Heinrich, 983–984
Janet, Pierre, 1066, 1071
Job (Biblical figure), 984, 1126
Journal of Speculative Philosophy, 972n
Judgment: kinds of, 894; veracity of, 986–987; existential, 1027

Kant, Immanuel: on the real, 1033; and critical method, 1095–1096; mentioned, 956
Kantians: on the self, 991; on experience, 993; on knowledge, 1007
Kingsley, Charles, 924
Knower, the, 908
Knowledge: and sentiments, 894; and activity, 908; and vagueness, 924; and psychology, 1007; and objects, 1008–1013; and self, 1008n; representative, 1059–1060; immediate, 1060–1062; of things together, 1063–1064,

1066, 1068, 1073–1074; and attention, 1067; and reminiscence, 1068; and synergy, 1069; minimum of, 1070; and relating, 1070; spiritualistic theories of, 1070–1073; in *The Principles of Psychology*, 1073–1074
Known-as, 1059

Ladd, George Trumball, 1071
Language: and dissociation, 938; and meaning, 937–939, 1000–1002, 1003–1004; origin of, 938n–939n; development of, 944–945; stream of thought, 987; and relations, 990; and declension, 997
Laplace, Pierre Simon, Marquis de, 904, 973
Laughter, 936
Law, 1100
Laws: mental, 894–895; nature of, 962; empirical, 964, 966; and nature, 967
Layard, Austen Henry, 903
Leading, 1001, 1012
Lewes, George Henry: and unity, 955; on causality, 965; on necessity, 967n–968n
Life: and mental evolution, 893; and philosophy, 976
Likeness, 931
Liliputians, 947
Literature, 895, 942–943
Livingstone, David, 943
Localization, 946
Locke, John: and pragmatism, 1095; quoted, 1043
Logic, 1008, 1016, 1017
Logic (A. Bain), 961n
Lotze, Hermann Rudolph: on the soul, 1071n; quoted, 960
Louis XIV, 1091
Love, 1090
Luys, Jules, 958, 1109n

Man: nature of, 922; and dissociation, 926; intelligence of, 936; and animals, 936, 939–940; and language, 936–937, 944–945; and mental evolution, 943–944; and acquired traits, 948

Marcus Aurelius, 901
Martineau, James, 925, 927
Materialism, 1082–1088, 1108n, 1111–1112, 1113
Mathematics, 924
Matter, 1082–1084, 1085, 1086, 1095
Maudsley, Henry, 986
Meaning, 1080
"Meaning of Truth and Error, The" (D. S. Miller), 1060n
Mediumship, 1117
Meinong, Alexius, 1075n
Memory, 1068
Menelaus, 942
Merit, 1122
Metaphysic (H. Lotze), 1071n
Metaphysics: phenomenists on, 970; need for, 976–977; and non-existence, 979; and psychology, 1074–1075; disputes in, 1084
Method, 1095–1096
Michaelangelo, 945
Microcosmus (H. Lotze), 960n
Mill, James: and pragmatism, 968, 1095; mentioned, 1067
Mill, James or John Stuart, 919
Mill, John Stuart: on evil, 904; on induction, 932; on laws of nature, 956; on explanation, 961; quoted, 969; his failure, 994; on belief, 1023; and pragmatism, 1095
Miller, Dickinson Sergeant, 1060
Mind-stuff, 1106n–1107n
Mind: Spencer on, 893, 895–898, 929; qualities of, 894; evolution of, 895–896, 897n, 901, 994, 995; laws of, 902, 988; and teleology, 905–907; types, 912, 932, 941, 943, 945; and brain, 913, 947; and acquired traits, 948; and objects, 986–987, 995; and stream of thought, 988–989; and continuity, 991; and tendencies, 998–999; and identity, 1008; study of, 1013; and experience, 1061; and associative systems, 1062n; elementary data of, 1064; and body, 1106n; and abnormal states, 1117
"Modern 'Symposium,' A," 967n
Mohr, Jakob, 987
Monism: and philosophy, 955; and pluralism, 1092–1095

Moody, Dwight Lyman, 908
Morality, 1092
Moral order, 1087
Moth, 896–897
Motion, 965, 988
Motor discharge, 1069
Mr Midshipman Easy (F. Marryat), 955
Munk, Hermann, 1103n
Münsterberg, Hugo, 1069
Myers, Frederic William Henry, 1117
Mystery, 978, 1060, 1062
"Mystery, and Other Violations of Relativity" (A. Bain), 956n
Mysticism, 983

Naming, 969, 986–987, 1009–1010, 1012
Narrative thinking, 911
Naturalists, 963, 1089
Nature, 940–941, 967
Nature, 893
Necessary truths, 960, 967n–968n
Necessity, 961
Newton, Isaac, 924
New York City, 1060, 1074
Nichols, Herbert, 1065n
Nineveh, 903
Nirvana, 904
Nitrous oxide intoxication, 1022
Nominalism: and necessity, 961; and rationality, 968–971; and Hume, 989; and conceptualism, 1003–1004
Nonentity, 978–979, 982, 984
Nouns, 944–945
Novelty, 928, 949
Nulliverse, 961

Objects: and feeling, 986; and stream of thought, 994; knowledge of, 996; and tendencies, 1002; and thought, 1007–1013, 1060
Occult Japan (P. Lowell), 1109n
Ockham, William of, 969
Ontological argument, 1016–1017
Otherness, 977, 978, 979
Our Notions of Number and Space (H. Nichols), 1068n
Owen, Richard, 963

Pantheism, 1091–1092, 1098–1099
Parmenides, 1092

Parts, and wholes, 919, 1014–1015
Passion, 947
Peace, 950–951, 977
Peirce, Charles Sanders: on pragmatism, 1079–1080, 1094, 1095
Perception, conditions of, 927
Perfection, 1085–1086
Perfections, God's, 1088
Perplexity, and rationality, 950
Personality: disassociated, 1066; Howison on, 1092; identity of, 1095
Pessimism, 903
Phenomena, 956–957, 959
Phenomenism, 970, 1106n
Philosophers, 1078
Philosophical Discussions (C. Wright), 965n
Philosophical Union, of the University of California, 1077, 1084
Philosophie des Unbewussten (E. von Hartmann), 953n
Philosophy: problems of, 902, 950; rationality in, 952, 953–954; and simplicity, 953–954, 962; and unity, 954–955, 959–960; and representation, 956; adequacy of, 960, 975–977; limits of explanation in, 977–982; and non-existence, 979; and empiricism, 984; motives of, 985n; meaning in, 1080; disputes in, 1080–1081, 1084; on matter, 1085; religious, 1091; critical method in, 1095–1096; progress of, 1096–1097
Philosophy of Mind (G. T. Ladd), 1071n
Philosophy of Reflection, The (S. Hodgson), 1063n
Physics, 923–924, 965
Physiology, 957, 1069, 1102–1106
Plato, 901, 904, 942
Platonism, 989, 993n–994n, 1007n
Pluralism, and monism, 1092–1093
Poetry, 912, 942–943
Pointing, 1059–1060, 1061, 1064n
Polyp, 893, 895, 903, 907
Popular Lectures on Scientific Subjects (H. Helmholtz), 963n
Popular Science Monthly, 893, 1079
Positivism, 1105n
Possible experience, 1058
Practical, the, 925, 928, 932; and religion, 1089
Practicalism, 1091

Practical man, the, and philosophy, 975–976
Practice, 915
Pragmatism: Peirce on, 1079–1080; applications of, 1080–1081; and a completed world, 1081–1083; and philosophy, 1083; and an unfinished world, 1083–1088; on the absolute, 1092–1094; and English philosophy, 1094–1095
Prayer, 1117
Preferences, 894
Premonitions, 1117
Present moment, 1063
Princeton, N.J., 1057n, 1071n
Principles of Psychology, The (W. James), 1073–1075
Principles of Psychology, The (H. Spencer), 893, 954, 970, 926n, 930
Problems of Life and Mind (G. H. Lewes), 965, 968n
Progress, 1096
Proverbs, 944
Psychical research, 1104, 1117
"Psychological Standpoint, The" (G. S. Fullerton), 1074n
Psychologie réaliste (P. Boissière), 958
Psychology: reasons in, 946; and introspection, 986; and stream of thought, 988; on relations, 989; and the brain, 997; language of, 998–999; and images, 1002–1003; fallacies in, 1007; and knowledge, 1008–1013; on unity of consciousness, 1057; on space and time, 1064n; as a natural science, 1075
Psychophysics, 1114
Purpose, 937–938

Questioning mania, 1022

Rabbits, 947
Rapports du physique et du moral (P. J. G. Cabanis), 1108n
Ratiocination, 946
Rationalism, 919, 992–993
Rationality: marks of, 950–951; theoretic, 952, 976, 977; and simplification, 953–955; and distinction, 955–960; and classification, 962–964; and

explanation, 964–966, 971–975; and identity, 967; and nominalism, 968–971; limits of, 977–985; and mysticism, 983–984; practical, 985

Realism, 971

Reality: meaning of, 902; criterion of, 908–909; and thought, 911–912; and relations, 989; and consciousness, 1008–1013; not a distinct content of consciousness, 1025; various orders of, 1026–1027; the choice of, 1028–1029; every object has some kind of reality, 1028–1030; practical, 1032–1033; means relation to the self, 1033–1035; relation of sensations to, 1035; of emotions, 1043–1044

Reason: and association, 914–915; described, 915–920, 934; and logic, 917n; and substitution, 920; examples of, 920–924; and dissociation, 926–928; and similarity, 932; stages of, 941, 945; and ratiocination, 943; and abstraction, 946

Reasoning, 911–912, 920–922

Recognition, 1069

Redintegration, 917, 918

Reductive, 980–981

Reid, Mayne, 1089

Reid, Thomas, 1011, 1046–1047

Reincarnation, 1099

Relating, 1070

Relation: and stream of thought, 988–991; and feeling, 995; and fringe, 1003; and knowledge, 1005n; and self, 1013n

Relations, 957

Religion: evolution of, 895; and practice, 1089–1090; and experience, 1091; and idealism, 1092

Reminiscence, 1068–1069

Renouvier, Charles: on unity, 959; on wholeness, 983; on belief, 1046

Representation, 956, 1004, 1007–1009, 1011–1012

Resemblance, 1075n

Revery, 911–912

Riehl, Alois, 965n

Royce, Josiah, on unity, 1092

Sameness, 968–971, 1093

Sankey, Ira David, 908

Sartor Resartus (T. Carlyle), 984

Savages, 925

Schiller, Ferdinand Canning Scott, 1119n–1120n

Scholasticism, 1060

Schopenhauer, Arthur: quoted, 953, 979; mentioned, 960

Science: passivity of, 903; and teleology, 905–906; induction in, 931–932; and mental types, 941; and classification, 963–964; and things, 1058; and psychology, 1075; and immortality, 1102, 1104; and dualism, 1105n, described, 1112; and philosophy, 1113

Self: and compounding, 993; and objects, 994–995; and awareness, 1007, and relations, 1013n

Self-consciousness, 939–940

Sensation: and reality, 908, 1035–1036; and experience, 929; and introspection, 986; and stream of thought, 987; and unity of, 993; and sameness, 997; and brain, 998–1000, 1118; and knowledge, 1005n; and things, 1058

Sensationalism, 993

Sentiments, 894

Shakespeare, William, 901, 942, 943

Shelley, Percy Bysshe, 1110

Sign, and language, 937–939

Similarity: and revery, 912; law of, 912–913; and contiguity, 913; association by, 931; and dissociation, 932; and reason, 936; and humor, 936; and language, 936–937; and animal intelligence, 940; and genius, 940–941; and abstraction, 944, 945

Simplicity, 953–955, 956

Simplification, 959, 962, 974

Socrates, 1063

Soul, the, 959, 1070–1072, 1072–1073, 1105, 1111, 1119

Space, 1064n, 1067n, 1120

Spencer, Herbert: on mind, 893, 894–895, 898, 901, 907, 908; on correspondence, 894, 896–898, 902–903; and survival, 898, 899–902, 905, 906; and teleology, 898, 964; on right thinking, 902, 904; on association, 926; on mind, 929–931; on the Unknowable, 959; on feeling, 966; his nominalism, 970; on mind-stuff, 973;

on relations, 989–990, 993n, 1002; on matter, 1084, 1087; on cosmic evolution, 1085–1086, quoted 1108n
Spinoza, Baruch, 956, 959, 1026, 1092
Spirit, 1085
Stanley, Henry, 1047–1048
Steinthal, Heymann, 1067n
Stevenson, Robert Louis, 1125
Stewart, Balfour, 1107n
Stewart, Dugald, 1011, 1095
Stream of thought: described, 987; and relations, 988–991; and objects, 994–995; and simple ideas, 996; and tendency, 1002; and knowledge, 1005n; and continuity, 1008–1013
Substance, 957, 959
Substantialism, 960
Substitution, 966
Sully, James, 987
Survival: Spencer on, 896–897; and interests, 898–900, 902–903; accidental, 904–906
Swedenborgians, 1118
Swinburne, Algernon Charles, 904
Syllogism, 917n
Symbols as substitutes for reality, 1041
Sympathy, 1124–1127
Synchronical existence, 1066
Synergy, 1069–1070
System of Logic, (F. Ueberweg), 952n
System of Logic, A (J. S. Mill), 961n, 969n
Systems, associative, 1062n

Taine, Hippolyte Adolphe: on the soul, 959; his nominalism, 969; on mind-stuff, 973
Tait, Peter Guthrie, 1107n
Talleyrand-Périgord, Charles Maurice de, 903
Teleology: and correspondence, 897–905; and Spencer, 898, 904; and consciousness, 906; and conception, 952, 976
Theism, 982–983, 1082–1089
Theology, 963, 1088–1092
Theory, 915
Thinghood, 924
Things, 1058, 1064n
Thought: standards of, 902; reality of, 908; kinds of, 911; and brain, 913, 945–946, 1102–1104, 1107–1110; and focalization, 947; life of, 1063; Peirce's view of, 1079–1080
Thought-stuff, 1060
Threshold, psychophysical, 1114
Tigers, 1060, 1061
Time: empiricism on, 957; and experience, 1062; psychology of, 1068n; knowledge of, 1067n–1068n; and evolution, 1122
Time and Space (S. Hodgson), 902
Titian, 945
Totality, 1014–1016
Transcendence, 1060, 1064n
Transcendentalism, 995, 1072–1073, 1113n–1114n
Transmission theory: critics of, 1098–1099; described, 1106n; and consciousness, 1110–1111; and threshold, 1113; and psychical research, 1117; and abnormal states, 1117–1118; and immortality, 1119–1120
Treatise of Human Nature, A (D. Hume), 961n
Trinitarianism, 955
Truth, and action, 1081
Tylor, Edward Burnett, 895, 1041

Über die Grenzen des Naturerkennens (E. Du Bois-Reymond), 973
"Ueber Begriff und Eigenschaften der Empfindung" (A. Meinong), 1075n
Ueberweg, Friedrich, 952, 986
Ulysses, 942
Unconscious premises, 927
Unity: and philosophy, 954–955, 959; principles of, 962; and classification, 962–964; and consciousness, 992–995; mental, 994–995; of experience, 996; of consciousness, 1057, 1066; associationism on, 1066; and attention, 1067; and reminiscence, 1068; and synergy, 1069; and relating, 1070; spiritualism on, 1070–1073; and compounding, 1075–1076; pragmatism on, 1093–1095
Universals, 1004, 1005n–1006n
Universe, the: mystery of, 978; unity in, 1093–1096

Unknowable, the, Spencer on, 895–896, 1085–1086
Unreality, the feeling of, 1034–1035

Vagueness, 924, 1003
Variation, spontaneous, 905
Vatican, 930
Venus (planet), 894
Veronese, Paolo, 945
Vertigo, mental, 1046
Voltaire, 893

Welt als Wille und Vorstellung, Die (A. Schopenhauer), 953n, 979n
Werth des Lebens, Der (E. K. Dühring), 1105n

Wholes, and parts, 919, 925, 1014–1018
Witchcraft, 1046
Women, 948–949
Words, and philosophy, 1084
Wordsworth, William, quoted, 983, 1087
World: connecting, 1060, 1061; and associative systems, 1062n, elementary data of, 1063–1064, completed, 1082; unfinished, 1084–1088
World-soul, 1072–1073, 1106n
Wright, Chauncey, 965n
Wundt, Wilhelm, 1067n, 1069, 965n, 1125

Zöllner, Johann Carl Friedrich, 973
Zoology, 963

Chronology

1842   Born January 11 at Astor House, New York City hotel, first child of Henry James and Mary Walsh James, and named William after paternal grandfather. (Grandfather William James emigrated from northern Ireland in 1789 at age seventeen, settled in Albany, New York, and became a merchant, banker, and landowner, leaving an estate valued at three million dollars at his death in 1832. Father, Henry, born 1811, received $1,250 annuity under terms of grandfather's will, which placed all capital in trust for twenty-one years and forbade eventual distribution to any heir leading a "grossly immoral, idle or dishonorable life." Father joined several of the eleven heirs in contesting the will and received a major distribution of the estate's capital while studying at Princeton Theological Seminary in 1837. After visiting England and Ireland, he abandoned the seminary, began to devote himself to the independent study of theology, and in 1840 married Mary Robertson Walsh, thirty-year-old daughter of a prosperous New York family of Scots-Irish descent.) Family moves to house on Washington Place, New York City, shortly after James's birth. Father meets Ralph Waldo Emerson in March (beginning long friendship), and Emerson "blesses" James during visit to their home.

1843   Brother Henry born April 15. Father's litigation results in second major distribution of estate's capital, providing annual income of $10,000 and enabling family to go abroad. They sail from New York to Liverpool in October, accompanied by mother's sister Catherine Walsh (Aunt Kate), and settle in London. Father meets J. J. Garth Wilkinson, leading English exponent and translator of Emanuel Swedenborg.

1844   Family moves to Paris and then to cottage in Windsor, England. Father has breakdown ("a perfectly insane and abject terror . . . an ever growing tempest of doubt, anxiety, and despair, with absolutely no relief from any truth I had ever encountered save a most pale and distant glimmer of the divine existence") in May and finds consolation in writings of Swedenborg.

1139

1845   Family returns to America and lives alternately in New York and at 50 North Pearl Street, Albany, a few doors from grandmother Catherine Barber James, uncle Augustus James, and numerous cousins. Brother Garth Wilkinson (Wilky) born July 21 in New York City.

1846   Brother Robertson (Bob or Rob) born August 29 in Albany. James attends kindergarten on North Pearl Street.

1847   Family moves to apartment at 11 Fifth Avenue, New York City, two blocks from maternal grandmother, Elizabeth Robertson Walsh.

1848–54   Spring, father buys and family moves into brownstone at 58 West 14th Street. Sister Alice born August 7, 1848. Father's *Moralism and Christianity* published in 1850, first of many books, influenced by Swedenborg, on religious, moral, and social questions (father also lectures). Relatives and father's friends and acquaintances, including Horace Greeley, George Ripley, Charles Anderson Dana, William Cullen Bryant, Bronson Alcott, and Emerson, are frequent guests. James explores neighborhood with friends and sometimes Henry (though James once rejects Henry's company saying, "*I* play with boys who curse and swear!"). Receives instruction from tutors and three private schools in Lower Broadway and Greenwich Village. Attends theatrical performances, Barnum's American Museum, and numerous art shows, including Thorwaldsen's sculptures of Christ and disciples at 1853 Crystal Palace exhibition. Enjoys art lessons with Benjamin Coe and begins to draw in his spare time. (Henry later describes him sitting and "drawing and drawing, always drawing, . . . and not at all with a plodding patience . . . but easily, freely, and, as who should say, infallibly.")

1855   Family, with Aunt Kate, sails for England on June 27 because father believes children will receive better education in Europe, and travels through London, Paris, and Lyons to Geneva. Attends multilingual (English, French, and German) boarding school near Geneva with Wilky, Bob, and orphaned cousins Robert and William Temple, while Henry recuperates from malarial fever and receives instruction at home in Geneva. October, family leaves for London, where Robert Thomson (later Robert Louis Stevenson's tutor) is engaged.

1856   Family returns to Paris in June, where another tutor is
            hired and children briefly attend an experimental, coedu-
            cational, international school influenced by theories of
            Fourier. Frequently visits the Louvre and Luxembourg
            Palace and is fascinated by work of Delacroix; reproduces
            his *Barque de Dante* with aid of lithograph.

1857   Family summers in Boulogne-sur-Mer on the English
            Channel. James attends Collège Impérial, local public
            school, and does well at science. Family returns to Paris in
            fall, where James is admitted to studio of painter Léon
            Cogniet, but financial effects of American depression of
            1857 force them to return to Boulogne-sur-Mer, where
            they can live more cheaply. Receives microscope as Christ-
            mas gift from father.

1858   James continues science studies at the Collège Impérial
            while taking and developing photographs, collecting and
            studying marine animals, administering mild electrical
            shocks to family and friends, mixing and heating chemi-
            cals, and occasionally trying out effects of drugs on him-
            self. June, family returns to America, stopping in New
            York and Albany before settling in Newport, Rhode Is-
            land. James becomes friends with future actor, playwright,
            and director James Steele MacKaye and future literary
            scholar and translator Thomas Sergeant Perry, grandson
            of naval hero Oliver Hazard Perry. Swims, rows, goes
            fishing, and is taught to box by MacKaye. Becomes close
            to orphaned Temple cousins, now living in Newport, es-
            pecially Katharine (Kitty) and Mary (Minny). Begins
            sketching at painter William Hunt's studio in early fall.
            Studies at Berkeley Institute, school run by local curate,
            and reads Arthur Schopenhauer and Joseph Renan.

1859   Interest in art deepens. Meets painter John La Farge, who
            comes to Newport to study with Hunt. Father decides to
            return to Europe; writes to a friend that he dreads "those
            inevitable habits of extravagance and insubordination,
            which appear to be characteristic of American youth." Oc-
            tober, family sails to France and settles in Geneva. James
            studies science at the Geneva Academy (now University of
            Geneva); takes anatomy course, attends dissections, and
            sketches cadavers (later writes that he "never had any"
            early education).

1860   July, takes walking tour of Mont Blanc region with
            Henry, then goes to Bonn, where he lives with local fam-
            ily and studies German. Tells father that he wants to re-
            turn to United States so that he can resume painting with
            Hunt; father reluctantly agrees. James writes to a friend,
            "I have fully decided to try the career of a painter. In a
            year or two I shall know definitely whether I am suited to
            it or not. If not, it will be easy to withdraw. There is
            nothing on earth more deplorable than a bad artist." Fam-
            ily returns to Newport in October and rents house at 13
            Kay Street. James and La Farge study under Hunt six days
            a week, occasionally joined in class by Henry. Wilky and
            Bob attend experimental school in Concord, run by mili-
            tant abolitionist Franklin Sanborn, with children of Emer-
            son, Nathaniel Hawthorne, and John Brown. Father
            suffers from mysterious fainting spells during winter.

1861   Decides in early summer to abandon painting and enters
            Lawrence Scientific School at Harvard in September.
            Studies chemistry under Charles William Eliot (who later
            recalls that while James was "not wholly devoted" to his
            work and suffered from "a delicacy of nervous constitu-
            tion," his "excursions into other sciences and realms of
            thought were not infrequent; his mind was excursive, and
            he liked experimenting, particularly novel experiment-
            ing"). Impressed by Lowell Lectures of naturalist Louis
            Agassiz. Meets law student Oliver Wendell Holmes, Jr.
            (who soon enlists in the Union Army), and becomes
            friends with Charles Sanders Peirce, fellow student at the
            Lawrence School, and Thomas Ward, distant cousin and
            student at Harvard College.

1862   Spends summer in Newport. Returns to Cambridge in
            the fall with Henry, who enters Harvard Law School.
            Brothers live in separate boarding houses but regularly
            dine together. September, Wilky enlists in the 44th Mas-
            sachusetts Regiment and is sent to North Carolina. James
            continues study of chemistry under Eliot, eating special
            breads to test effects of different yeasts on his urine.

1863   Withdraws from school and lives at home in Newport
            during spring and summer, reading widely in literature,
            science, history, and philosophy, including German mate-
            rialist philosopher Ludwig Büchner's *Kraft und Stoff*

(*Force and Matter*), philologist Max Müller's *History of Ancient Sanskrit Literature*, and Jonathan Edwards's *Original Sin*. Applies with Henry for position working with free blacks in the South, but plan is never carried out. Wilky becomes adjutant to Robert Gould Shaw, commander of the 54th Massachusetts, one of the first black regiments in the Union Army. Bob enlists and soon joins the 55th Massachusetts, another black regiment. Henry withdraws from law school. July 18, Wilky badly wounded during attack on Fort Wagner in which Shaw and many of his men are killed. Near death, he is brought to Newport, where James helps care for him and sketches him as he lies unconscious. James returns to Lawrence Scientific School in the fall and studies comparative anatomy and physiology under Jeffries Wyman. (Later praises Wyman as "the paragon . . . of goodness, disinterestedness, and single-minded love of the truth.")

1864   Enters Harvard School of Medicine at beginning of year. Writes to a friend, "I embraced the medical profession a couple of months ago. My first impressions are that there is much humbug therein, and that, with the exception of surgery . . . a doctor does more by the moral effect of his presence on the patient and family, than by anything else. He also extracts money from them." Continues study of anatomy under Wyman. Moves in May into new family residence at 13 Ashburton Place, Boston. Becomes friend of Oliver Wendell Holmes, Jr., who is at Harvard Law School after three years in the Union Army. Wilky, partially recovered, returns to his regiment in December.

1865   Joins expedition to Brazil organized by Agassiz to collect specimens for his zoological museum (now Harvard Museum of Comparative Zoology); expenses are paid by father and Aunt Kate. April 1, leaves New York with Agassiz and his wife, Elizabeth, four naturalists, and five other student assistants, including Thomas Ward. James is severely seasick during voyage. Contracts varioloid (mild form of smallpox) shortly after arrival in Rio de Janeiro. Suffers temporary blindness and is quarantined for four weeks (after recovery eyes remain sensitive to strain). Despondent from illness and tedium of collecting and packing specimens, resolves to return home, writing family in early June that he is "cut out for a speculative rather than an

active life," but decides to remain with expedition after
health improves. Goes up Amazon in August and makes
three collecting trips along river and its Tapajós, Içá, and
Jutaí tributaries. Expedition nears Peruvian frontier in
September, but does not cross due to rumors of impending war. James is impressed by Agassiz's energy and determination, but disagrees with some of his scientific views.
Returns to coast in December and sails for the United
States soon after Christmas.

1866   Returns to Boston in February and resumes medical stud-
            ies in March. Enjoys company of Oliver Wendell Holmes,
            Jr., and Holmes's future wife, Fanny Dixwell. Works as
            summer intern at Massachusetts General Hospital. Mid-
            July to early September, joins parents, Henry, and Alice at
            shore house in Swampscott, Massachusetts. Father begins
            to invest heavily in Florida cotton plantation run by Wilky
            and Bob, which uses paid black labor and has an inte-
            grated school on its grounds. James continues studies at
            Harvard Medical School in the fall, where his friends in-
            clude future social reformer Charles Putnam, his brother
            James Putnam, later a leading neurologist, and future
            physiologist Henry Bowditch. Engages in philosophical
            discussions with Peirce (beginning of lifelong intellectual
            dialogue), Holmes, Ward, and Chauncey Wright (meet-
            ings evolve by early 1870s into informal "metaphysical
            club," with all but Ward as members). Becomes friends
            with William Dean Howells (will read and praise many of
            Howells's novels). Moves into new family residence at 20
            Quincy Street, across from Harvard Yard, in November.
            Suffers from back pain, eyestrain, insomnia, digestive
            problems, and profound depression throughout winter;
            finds his home "loathsome" and contemplates suicide.
            Alice goes to New York for treatment of her persistent
            nervous symptoms.

1867   April, sails for Europe hoping to improve health and to
            study German and physiology. Visits Paris and spends
            summer in Dresden, reading German (including Goethe's
            Faust, essays by art historian Herman Grimm, and Ger-
            man translation of George Henry Lewes's *Aristotle*) and
            touring art galleries, and at nearby Bad Teplitz (now Te-
            plice, Czechoslovakia), drinking mineral water and taking
            thermal baths. September, goes to Berlin to enter its uni-

versity, and is joined in October by Thomas Sergeant Perry, who shares his rooms at 12 Mittelstrasse. James takes five courses and attends three lectures on physiology during the fall and is especially interested in teaching of pioneering electrophysiologist Emil Du Bois–Reymond. Reads German works on physiology and psychology and becomes interested in experimental neurology; writes Ward that "perhaps the time has come for psychology to begin to be a science. . . ." Unable to do laboratory work due to continuing eye and back problems. Writes review of Herman Grimm's novel *Unüberwindliche Mächte* (*Invincible Powers*) and sends it to Henry, asking him to revise it; review appears unsigned in *The Nation*, November 28. Sees historian George Bancroft, family acquaintance and American minister to Berlin, who introduces him to Grimm (son of folklorist Wilhelm Grimm) and his wife, Gisela von Arnim (daughter of Goethe's friend Bettina von Arnim). Meets philosopher Wilhelm Dilthey through Grimm.

1868   Breaks off studies in Berlin and returns to Bad Teplitz, January. Writes to Bob (who, depressed and in poor health, has left Florida plantation and taken job as railroad clerk in Iowa) that he feels "rather ashamed at my age to stand in the presence of you and Wilky without having earned a cent." Goes to Dresden in March, returning to Bad Teplitz for three weeks in late April and early May. Reads extensively (Shakespeare, Homer, Renan, Hippolyte Taine, Immanuel Kant, Paul Janet, Gotthold Lessing, Charles Darwin, and especially Goethe and Johann von Schiller), despite persistent depression. Writes sympathetically to Alice, who has suffered serious nervous collapse, including comic descriptions of his boarding house residents. Sends Henry criticism of his recently published stories "Poor Richard," "The Story of a Masterpiece," and "The Romance of Certain Old Clothes." Goes to Heidelberg in late June to study experimental psychology under Wilhelm Wundt and Hermann von Helmholtz but returns to Berlin six days later "under the influence of a blue despair." Visits Geneva and takes baths at Divonne in French Savoy without effect; writes to Thomas Ward of episodes of suicidal depression: "sometimes when I despair of ever doing anything, say: 'Why not step out into the green darkness?' " Reads French philosopher Charles

Renouvier and is impressed by his "vigor of style and compression . . . unequaled by anyone." Spends two weeks in Paris with Henry Bowditch. Returns to Cambridge in November. Writes five unsigned book reviews during year for *The Nation*, *Atlantic Monthly*, and *North American Review*, including two of Darwin's *The Variation of Animals and Plants under Domestication*.

1869   January, begins to review for medical school final examination. February, Henry leaves for year-long European tour. March, reviews E. Sargent's *Planchette*, book on spiritualism, for the *Boston Daily Advertiser*. Submits thesis on effects of cold on the human body, based on published sources, May 21, and passes ninety-minute oral examination given by nine professors, June 21, completing requirements for M.D. (Despite degree, never practices.) Vacations at farmhouse in Pomfret, Connecticut, with parents and Alice, where he enjoys "the life of an absolute caterpillar" and the company of twenty-two-year-old Elizabeth (Lizzie) Boott. Sketches and reads (or skims) widely in science, literature, and philosophy (including works by Johann Fichte, Ivan Turgenev, Herbert Spencer, George Henry Lewes, George Sand, Schopenhauer, Auguste Comte's *Cours de philosophie positive*, John Stuart Mill's *The Subjection of Women*, and Robert Browning's *The Ring and the Book*), recording quotations, reactions, and philosophical and psychological speculations in notebooks. Becomes severely depressed after return to Cambridge in the fall; writes Bob in November that he has resolved never to marry for fear of passing nervous disabilities on to his children.

1870   January, outlines plan of reading in neurophysiology and pathology for the coming year, and resolves to finish reading his father's works. Temporarily inflames eyelids with overdose of chloral hydrate, new hypnotic drug taken "for the fun of it as an experiment. . . ." Suffers from back pains, severe depression, and deep philosophic uncertainty. March 9, learns that beloved cousin Minny Temple has died of tuberculosis; writes in diary, March 22, "Minny, your death makes me feel the nothingness of all our egotistic fury." Encouraged by further reading of Renouvier, writes in diary on April 30, "My first act of free will shall be to believe in free will." Resolves to avoid "speculation" for the remainder of the year and to devote himself to "action" and belief in "my individual reality and creative power." Nervous symptoms and poor health persist. Henry returns to Quincy Street from Europe in May. James spends summer on Mount Desert Island, Maine, returning to Cambridge in the fall. Restricts his reading, limited to four hours a day due to eyestrain, to newspapers, novels, and biographies; writes to Bowditch in December of his "morbid shrinking" from intellectual conversation and that he is "long since dead and buried in that respect."

1871   April, enrolls in Harvard-sponsored lecture series on "Optical Phenomena and the Eye," given by B. Joy Jeffries. Wilky leaves Florida plantation, which has failed due to bad weather, falling prices, poor management, and racist harassment, and joins brother Bob, now in Milwaukee.

1872   Henry, Alice, and Aunt Kate leave for European tour in May. James vacations in Maine during summer. Accepts offer from Charles William Eliot, now president of Harvard, to teach undergraduate course in comparative physiology in spring of 1873. Writes Henry, "The appointment to teach physiology is a perfect God-send to me just now . . . a dealing with men instead of my own mind, and a diversion from those introspective studies which had bred a sort of philosophical hypochondria in me of late. . . ." Can read only three or four hours a day, and is afflicted by insomnia and general nervousness. Fall, review of Taine's *On Intelligence* published in *The Nation*. Begins to correspond with Renouvier on philosophical problems. Attends Bowditch's Harvard Medical School lectures and works in physiology laboratory. Undergoes "crisis" in late autumn (possibly the event James later disguised in *The Varieties of Religious Experience* as that of a French correspondent of his: "Whilst in this state of philosophical pessimism and general depression of spirits . . . suddenly there fell upon me without any warning, just as if it came out of the darkness, a horrible fear of my own existence. . . . I became a mass of quivering fear. After this the universe was changed for me altogether. . . ."). Bob marries Mary Holton in Milwaukee, November 18, and visits Cambridge with her later in month.

1873   Enjoys teaching and reads Wordsworth with pleasure dur-
            ing spring. After period of uncertainty, accepts appoint-
            ment from Harvard president Eliot to teach full year of
            comparative anatomy and physiology at salary of $600,
            despite reluctance to move into anatomy and away from
            "mental science." Travels along New England coast during
            summer. Decides to postpone teaching for a year due to
            continuing poor health (back pain, insomnia, and ner-
            vousness). Borrows $1,000 from Aunt Kate and sails to
            Liverpool in October, stopping in London and Paris be-
            fore joining Henry (who has stayed in Europe) in Flor-
            ence. Writes Wilky, "My old love of art returns, but not in
            full force. The years have weakened it, I am afraid." Goes
            to Rome with Henry in late November; visits Coliseum
            by night and finds it "inhuman and horrible." Returns to
            Florence in late December, sick with fever.

1874   Recovers and leaves Florence in February, visiting Venice,
            Munich, and Dresden. Returns to Cambridge in March.
            June, visits brothers in Milwaukee and meets Wilky's new
            wife, Caroline Cary James. Teaches comparative vertebrate
            anatomy and physiology in fall (gives course through
            1878–79) and becomes director of the Museum of Compar-
            ative Anatomy and the anatomy laboratory after death of
            Jeffries Wyman in September. Helps found new
            "metaphysical club," primarily devoted to the study of
            Hegel; members include George Howison, professor of
            logic at the Massachusetts Institute of Technology, W. T.
            Harris, editor of *The Journal of Speculative Philosophy* and
            a leading American exponent of Hegel, and George
            Herbert Palmer, assistant professor of philosophy at
            Harvard (soon joined by Scottish philosopher Thomas
            Davidson, who becomes friend of James). Writes seven
            unsigned reviews for general and professional journals of
            works on physiology, psychology, and philosophy (con-
            tinues to write reviews and notices regularly over the
            next twenty-five years).

1875   Writes article on vivisection, defending it in principle
            while attacking its abuses, for *The Nation*. Fall, gives grad-
            uate course on the relationship between physiology and
            psychology (teaches it through 1877–78), which includes
            first laboratory work in psychology in the United States.
            Writes tribute to Chauncey Wright for *The Nation* after

his death in September. Inhales amyl nitrate during visit to Harvard chemistry laboratory to satisfy curiosity about its effects.

1876   Introduced by Thomas Davidson to Alice Howe Gibbens (born 1849), teacher at Miss Sanger's School for Girls in Boston, after father mentions her to James, beginning long and sometimes troubled courtship. Appointed assistant professor of physiology at annual salary of $2,000, February. June, writes article on Scottish philosopher Alexander Bain and Renouvier for *The Nation*. September, submits anonymous letter to *The Nation* criticizing neglect of philosophy in American universities. Has G. Stanley Hall as graduate student (in 1878 Hall receives first Harvard Ph.D. in psychology). Teaches undergraduate course on physiological psychology, using Herbert Spencer's *Principles of Psychology* as text while criticizing it thoroughly during lectures.

1877   Summer, visited in Cambridge by Josiah Royce, graduate student at Johns Hopkins University, seeking advice on whether he should continue career in philosophy; James encourages him to persist. Again teaches undergraduate and graduate psychology courses, now under the auspices of the philosophy department. Considers offer of psychology professorship from Daniel Gilman, first president of Johns Hopkins.

1878   Delivers ten lectures on "The Brain and the Mind" at Johns Hopkins in February. April, Alice James has severe attack of hysteria. James and Alice Gibbens become engaged in May. June, signs contract with Henry Holt and Company for a text on psychology, proposing to finish by fall of 1880. Marries Alice Gibbens in Boston, July 10, and spends honeymoon at Keene Valley, New York, in the Adirondack Mountains, where he owns farmhouse with Bowditch and Charles and James Putnam. Works on book during honeymoon, to the amusement of his friends. Shortly after marriage, "Brute and Human Intellect" (first of nineteen articles that will be drawn from work on psychology text) and "Remarks on Spencer's Definition of Mind as Correspondence" appear in *Journal of Speculative Philosophy* and "Quelques Considérations sur la méthode subjective" in Renouvier's journal *Critique Philosophique*.

Fall, Jameses rent furnished rooms at 387 Harvard Street, Cambridge. Lectures on psychology at Lowell Institute in Boston. Continuing eye trouble prevents reading or writing at night. Writes, "I have found in marriage a calm and repose I never knew before."

1879   First son, Henry (Harry), born May 18. Family spends summer on Maine coast. Teaches psychology course and two philosophy courses (on Renouvier and on the philosophy of evolution) at Harvard, and gives one lecture a week on physiology and hygiene. Decides to stay at Harvard, but writes Henry complaining of scientific isolation and need for contact with German experimental psychologists. Publishes essays "Are We Automata?" and "The Sentiment of Rationality" in British journal *Mind*.

1880   Travels in Europe during summer while wife and son stay at mother-in-law's Cambridge home at 18 Garden Street. Visits Henry in London in June and meets British philosopher Shadworth Hodgson before leaving for Amsterdam in July. Sees G. Stanley Hall in Heidelberg (where Hall is studying psychology) and travels in Switzerland before going to France, where he visits Renouvier near Grenoble on August 15. Returns to Cambridge in the fall. Appointed assistant professor of philosophy. Replaces Renouvier course with psychology course using Bain's *Mental Science*. Family moves from Harvard Street to rooms on Louisburg Square in Boston. "The Association of Ideas" appears in *Popular Science Monthly*, containing first use of term "stream of consciousness." Writes Renouvier that his "principal amusement this winter has been resisting the inroads of Hegelism in our University."

1881   Goes to Milwaukee when Bob, deeply depressed and drinking heavily, decides to leave his family. Accompanies him back to Boston, where Bob stays alternately with parents and James before collapsing completely (returns to Milwaukee after short stay in asylum). Continues physiology lectures, teaches classes on "The Human Intellect" and contemporary philosophy, and gives graduate course in advanced psychology. November, Henry visits, meeting Alice and Harry for first time; Henry and Alice like each other immediately. James, father, mother, Henry, sister

Alice, and Wilky (now bankrupt and unable to work because of severe rheumatism) reunited for Christmas.

1882   Mother dies of bronchial asthma after brief illness, January
            30. Funeral brings five siblings together for last time.
            James buys small house at 15 Appian Way in Cambridge.
            "On Some Hegelisms" appears in *Mind*, including obser-
            vations made by James under influence of nitrous oxide.
            Applies for and is granted year's leave of absence at half
            pay in order to rest and meet with European philosophers
            and psychologists. Arranges for Josiah Royce, then teach-
            ing English at Berkeley, to take his place (leads to perma-
            nent Harvard professorship for Royce). Second son,
            William (Billy), born June 17. September, travels to Eu-
            rope while wife and sons stay with her mother. Sees
            Henry in London and then goes through Germany to Vi-
            enna. Spends three weeks in Venice in October, viewing
            art and suffering from constant insomnia. Visits Prague
            and meets physiologist Ewald Hering, psychologist Carl
            Stumpf (beginning long friendship), and physicist and
            philosopher Ernst Mach. November, discusses brain vivi-
            section during visit to Berlin veterinary school and attends
            lectures of physiologist Wilhelm Ludwig and experimental
            psychologist Wilhelm Wundt in Leipzig. Stays at home of
            Belgian philosopher and psychologist Joseph Rémy Léo-
            pold Delbœuf in Liège before going to Paris. Writes to
            Henry of his German trip: "I certainly got a most distinct
            impression of my own *information* in regard to *modern*
            philosophic matters being broader than that of any one I
            met, and our Harvard post of observation being more cos-
            mopolitan." Attends lectures of Jean Charcot at his neuro-
            logical clinic before receiving telegram from wife telling
            of father's rapidly weakening condition. Joins Henry in
            England, where they decide that Henry will sail for Amer-
            ica while James waits in London for further news. Writes
            farewell letter to father, December 14, while staying in
            Henry's rooms on Bolton Street ("All my intellectual life
            I derive from you; and though we have often seemed at
            odds in the expression thereof, I'm sure there's a harmony
            somewhere, and that our strivings will combine"). At-
            tends dinner of the "Scratch Eight," philosophy discussion
            group; members include Hodgson, George Croom Rob-
            ertson, first editor of *Mind*, and Leslie Stephen. Father

dies in Boston, December 18, before Henry arrives; Henry reads letter aloud beside father's grave, December 31.

1883   James remains in England at family's urging, trying to work on long-delayed psychology text, and continues to see the "Scratch Eight." Father leaves estate of $95,000. Will names Henry as executor, limits Bob's share, and excludes Wilky on grounds that money already given him for plantation and other unsuccessful ventures constitute his inheritance. James objects when Henry and sister Alice agree to divide estate equally, proposing more complex arrangement based on needs of his wife and children and wealth of Wilky's wife's family, but then agrees to equal division among the five siblings. Goes to Paris in February and returns to Cambridge in March. Lectures at Concord School of Philosophy in early summer. Spends latter part of summer with family at Keene Valley. Takes over as executor of father's estate when Henry leaves for England in late August. Teaches three philosophy courses (on evolution, the human intellect, and English philosophy) and course in advanced psychology. Has George Santayana as undergraduate philosophy student. Hurries to Milwaukee to see Wilky, who is critically ill with kidney and heart disease. Arrives October 1 and finds him temporarily improved but highly nervous; leaves the following day so that Wilky can rest. Wilky dies November 15.

1884   Third son, Herman, born January 31. Lectures at Harvard Divinity School on "The Dilemma of Determinism." Family goes to Keene Valley for summer, where James works on one-volume selection from father's work and writes long introduction. "On Some Omissions of Introspective Psychology" appears in *Mind*. September, contracts fever that affects eyes for weeks. Gives dictation to Bob, who has again left his family. Sister Alice sails for England with close friend Katherine Loring in November. James becomes corresponding member of English Society for Psychical Research and organizes informal Boston branch. *The Literary Remains of the Late Henry James* published by Houghton, Mifflin at end of year.

1885   March, wife ill with scarlet fever and family is quarantined. June, wife and son Herman fall sick with whooping cough; other children are sent away to country. Herman develops pneumonia and dies July 9; buried next to James's father. James writes to a cousin, "He was a broad, generous, patient little nature, with a noble head who would doubtless have done credit to his name if he had lived. . . . The great part of the experience to me has been the sight of Alice's devotion. I thought I knew her, but I didn't, nor did I fully know the meaning of that old human word *motherhood*." Spends summer on farm at Jaffrey, New Hampshire, with family, and alone in Cambridge, writing. Becomes full professor of philosophy, at salary of $4,000. Teaches two psychology courses and conducts experiments in hypnotism, enlisting students as subjects. December, family moves to mother-in-law's house on Garden Street while Mrs. Gibbens is in Italy recuperating from severe illness (they will remain there after her return).

1886   May, enjoys Henry's *The Bostonians* and praises it in letter to him. Summer, report on séances conducted by Helen Berry and by Mrs. William J. Piper appears in *Proceedings of the American Society for Psychical Research*. Family spends summer at Jaffrey, New Hampshire. Unable to make progress on psychology book, goes alone to Portsmouth, New Hampshire, Cambridge, and White Mountains. Purchases large farmhouse and ninety acres of land on Lake Chocorua, near Conway, New Hampshire, for $8,000. Teaches courses on logic and psychology, on English empirical philosophy, and on advanced psychological research. "The Perception of Time" appears in *Journal of Speculative Philosophy*.

1887   Seeking relief from insomnia, makes repeated visits to "mind-cure doctress," but problem persists. March 24, daughter Margaret Mary (Peggy) born. Works with architect on remodeling house at Chocorua, at expense of $2,000. Goes to Chocorua in early summer to begin garden and is joined by family when house is finished in mid-July. Goes mountain climbing in the Adirondacks at end of summer. Repeats previous year's courses, with shift toward Berkeley, Hume, and Reid in English philosophy course. "The Perception of Space" appears in four issues of *Mind*, "The Laws of Habit" and "Some Human Instincts" in *Popular Science Monthly*, and "What Is an Instinct?" in *Scribner's Magazine*.

1888   Winter, remains in Cambridge while wife and children go
            to Aiken, South Carolina, hoping to alleviate Billy's
            asthma. May, family returns to Cambridge and summers
            in Chocorua. September, returns to Cambridge and is
            joined by family in October. Teaches new ethics course in
            place of English empirical philosophy; extensive prepara-
            tory reading slows work on psychology book.

1889   Has new house built for family in Cambridge at 95 Irving
            Street and directs its design. Catherine Walsh (Aunt Kate)
            dies, March 6. James and wife attend funeral in New York
            and James inherits $10,000. Late June, sails alone for Ire-
            land. Visits Trinity College, Dublin, tours Scotland, and
            arrives in London in mid-July. Goes with Henry to visit
            sister Alice, now permanent invalid, at Royal Leamington
            Spa, Warwickshire. Attends International Congress of
            Physiological Psychology in Paris, early August. Meets
            Théodore Flournoy, Swiss experimental psychologist
            teaching at University of Geneva, and begins lasting
            friendship. Returns to England and sees Henry and Alice
            before sailing for America in late August. Family moves
            into new Irving Street house in fall. Teaches undergradu-
            ate course on logic and psychology and graduate course in
            experimental psychology. Becomes first Alford Professor
            of Psychology at Harvard in November. Helps Inter-
            national Congress of Experimental Psychology conduct
            census of hallucinations in the United States based on
            questionnaires sent to randomly chosen individuals.

1890   Works to complete psychology text, organizing and revis-
            ing previously published material and writing new sec-
            tions. After last of many late-night writing sessions, finally
            sends finished manuscript to Henry Holt, May 22. Writes
            brother Henry, "As 'Psychologies' go, it is a good one,
            but psychology is in such an ante-scientific condition that
            the whole present generation of them is predestined to
            become unreadable old medieval lumber, as soon as the
            first genuine tracks of insight are made." Corrects proofs
            in Cambridge during summer before joining family in
            Chocorua in August. *The Principles of Psychology*, published
            in two volumes by Henry Holt and Company in late Sep-
            tember, receives wide acclaim and is quickly adopted as a
            text at many American and British universities, though a
            few reviewers criticize its lively style and occasional

irreverence. Teaches undergraduate philosophy courses on metaphysics and on Descartes, Spinoza, and Leibniz, an undergraduate psychology course using *The Principles* as text, and graduate psychology seminar on pleasure and pain. Fourth son, Francis Tweedy (later renamed Alexander Robertson and called Aleck), born December 22.

1891   Begins correspondence with John Dewey. Spends summer abridging and rewriting *The Principles of Psychology* for one-volume version in Holt's "Briefer Course" series, designed for use as introductory text. July, learns that sister Alice has breast tumor. Writes to her, "When that which is *you* passes out of the body, I am sure that there will be an explosion of liberated force and life till then eclipsed and kept down. . . . Everyone will feel the shock, but you yourself will be more surprised than anybody else." September, goes to England for ten days to see Alice for the last time. Attends London opening of Henry's stage version of *The American* and advises Alice to try hypnotism as means of controlling her pain. Teaches introductory psychology, logic and psychology, and graduate psychology seminar.

1892   Accompanied by graduate student W.E.B. Du Bois (a student of James's in the late 1880s, soon to be the first black Harvard Ph.D.), visits twelve-year-old Helen Keller at her school in Boston and gives her an ostrich feather (later corresponds with her). *Psychology* (eventually known as *Psychology: Briefer Course*), shorter version of *The Principles*, published by Henry Holt in January. Gives series of lectures on psychology to Cambridge schoolteachers. Receives farewell telegram from sister Alice, March 5; she dies March 6. James is left $20,000 in her will. Arranges for Hugo Münsterberg, young German experimental psychologist, to take over Harvard's psychological laboratory for three-year trial period. Sails with family to Antwerp, May 25, beginning sabbatical leave. Meets Münsterberg in Freiburg to discuss Harvard appointment and then goes to Lucerne and Gryon, alpine village near Lake Geneva, in July. Enjoys Switzerland but finds travel with children exhausting. Arranges for Harry and Billy to live with local pastors, and goes to Vers-chez-les-Blanc, near Lausanne, where Théodore Flournoy and his family are staying. Henry visits in August and meets his youngest nephew and niece for first time, but sees little of James, who goes on previously arranged walking tour with F.W.H. Myers of the English Society for Psychical Research. Family moves to Florence in late September. James takes walks with former student Bernhard Berenson and meets Mark Twain. Sees Caroline James (Wilky's widow) and their children, Cary and Alice, who are traveling in Europe, but relations are strained. December, attends anniversary festival in honor of Galileo at the University of Padua, and receives honorary doctoral degree.

1893   Enrolls Harry in boarding school near Munich and sees Carl Stumpf. March, with Henry's approval, has lines from Dante's *Paradiso* ("And she from martyrdom and from exile found this peace") inscribed in Italian on urn for Alice's ashes in Cambridge family plot. Family returns to Switzerland in April. Declines editorship of *Psychological Review*, new publication of American Psychological Association, but becomes frequent contributor. Family returns to Cambridge in August. Teaches introductory psychology, philosophy course on cosmology (primarily devoted to theories of evolution and materialism), and graduate seminar on mental pathology. Writes Henry in September that "the coming back makes one feel strangely sad and hardens one in the resolution never to go away again unless one can go to end one's days. Such a divided soul is very bad." Makes eighteen visits to "mind-curer" for relief of melancholia and insomnia; condition improves, but James is unsure if treatment is responsible. December, accepts honorary appointment as president of English Society for Psychical Research and is elected president of the American Association of Psychologists.

1894   March, reads privately printed copy of sister Alice's diary. Writes Henry that it made "a unique and tragic impression of personal power venting itself on no opportunity. And such really *deep* humor." Opposes bill (eventually tabled) introduced in the Massachusetts legislature aimed at restricting practice of mental therapy to licensed medical doctors. Writes in *Boston Evening Transcript*, March 24: "I assuredly hold no brief for any of these healers . . . But their *facts* are patent and startling; and anything that interferes with the multiplication of such facts, and with our freest opportunity of observing and studying them, will, I

believe, be a public calamity." Writes favorable notice for
Psychological Review of Sigmund Freud and Josef Breuer's
first paper on hysteria. Repeats courses from previous
year, and gives cosmology course at newly founded Radcliffe College (will teach at Radcliffe until 1902). December, delivers presidential address, "The Knowing of
Things Together," to American Association of Psychologists meeting in Princeton (published in *Psychological Review* in 1895).

1895   Resumes directorship of psychology laboratory for one
            year when Münsterberg returns to Germany. Delivers ad-
            dress "Is Life Worth Living?" to Harvard Young Men's
            Christian Association (published in October *International
            Journal of Ethics*). Lectures on psychology to school-
            teachers in Boston, New York, and at summer school in
            Colorado Springs. Teaches introductory and advanced
            undergraduate psychology courses and graduate seminar
            in the psychology of feeling. December, deeply disturbed
            by widespread jingoism aroused by Anglo-American crisis
            over Venezuelan–British Guianese border dispute.

1896   January, in response to statement by Theodore Roosevelt
            (then police commissioner of New York City), defends
            right to dissent in foreign affairs in letter to the *Harvard
            Crimson*. Spring, delivers address "The Will to Believe" to
            philosophical clubs at Yale and Brown. Takes government-
            supplied peyote, obtained from Dr. S. Weir Mitchell, as
            experiment while preparing Chocorua house for tenant in
            June; becomes violently nauseated but does not experience
            expected hallucinatory effects. Worries about finances and
            supplements salary by repeating psychology lectures for
            schoolteachers in upstate New York, Vermont, and Chi-
            cago during summer before vacationing in Wisconsin.
            Reads *War and Peace* and *Anna Karenina*; writes Flour-
            noy that "now I feel as if I knew *perfection* in the repre-
            sentation of human life." Fall, delivers eight lectures at
            Lowell Institute in Boston on exceptional mental states;
            subjects include hypnotism, hysteria, multiple personality,
            demoniacal possession, and genius. Teaches introductory
            and abnormal psychology, philosophy of nature (similar
            to earlier cosmology course), and gives graduate seminar
            on Kant. Persuades Gertrude Stein, his student at Rad-

cliffe, to pursue study of psychology by going to medical school.

1897   *The Will to Believe, and Other Essays in Popular Philosophy* published by Longmans, Green & Co. in March. Declines Gifford Lectureship in Natural Theology at University of Aberdeen (hoping to be offered Gifford Lectureship at University of Edinburgh, which would allow more time for preparation and is better paying) and nominates Royce in his place. Is freed of responsibility for psychology laboratory by Münsterberg's return to Harvard and decides to concentrate increasingly on philosophy (appointment changed to professor of philosophy in August). Delivers oration at dedication of Augustus Saint-Gaudens's monument to Robert Gould Shaw, commander of the 54th Massachusetts, May 31. Family spends summer at Chocorua. Teaches philosophy of nature and advanced graduate psychology. November, gives Ingersoll Lecture on Human Immortality (published by Houghton, Mifflin in 1898 as *Human Immortality: Two Supposed Objections to the Doctrine*).

1898   January, warned by Henry that Bob is returning from England in highly unstable mental condition. James persuades him to enter Dansville Asylum, near Buffalo, and accompanies him there (Bob stays for several years). Accepts appointment as Gifford Lecturer at University of Edinburgh for 1899–1900 and 1900–01. March, argues before Massachusetts legislative committee against new medical licensing bill (measure is defeated). Becomes alarmed by growing annexationist sentiment in wake of American victories in Spanish-American War. July, goes to Keene Valley with friends and undergoes "a regular Walpurgis Nacht" while unable to sleep on hiking trip. (Writes to Alice that "it seemed as if the Gods of all the nature-mythologies were holding an indescribable meeting in my breast with the moral Gods of the inner life. The two kinds of Gods have nothing in common—the Edinburgh lectures made quite a hitch ahead. . . . It was one of the happiest lonesome nights of my existence, and I understand now what a poet is.") Overexerts himself the following day while hiking in mountains with younger companions. August, travels by train to British Columbia, goes through Washington and Oregon, and visits Yosemite. Delivers lecture "Philosophical Conceptions and Practical Results" at University of California at Berkeley, August 26; speaks for first time of "pragmatism" as a philosophic principle, attributing term to Charles Peirce. Teaches metaphysics and advanced seminar on abnormal psychology. November, severe chest pains lead to diagnosis of valvular lesion and permanent heart damage, attributed to hiking experiences of summer. Decides to rent Chocorua for following summer and take sabbatical in Europe while preparing Gifford Lectures.

1899   Becomes fervent public opponent of American policy in the Philippines and active member of Anti-Imperialist League. Accuses imperialists of treating Filipinos "as if they were a painted picture, an amount of mere matter in our way. They are too remote from us ever to be realized as they exist in their inwardness." *Talks to Teachers on Psychology: and to Students on Some of Life's Ideals*, based on oft-repeated 1892 Cambridge lectures, published by Henry Holt. June, gets lost while walking in Keene Valley until late at night, further damaging health. Sails with wife and daughter for Europe, July 15 (Aleck stays with Mrs. Gibbens; Harry and Billy, now Harvard undergraduates, are working as forest rangers in Washington). Goes to Bad Nauheim, spa near Frankfurt-am-Main, seeking treatment for heart condition and nervous exhaustion. Remains for seven weeks, takes baths, sits in park, and begins to read religious biographies in preparation for Gifford Lectures, but is unable to write. Closely follows Dreyfus Affair in *Le Figaro* and is outraged by Dreyfus's second conviction. September, goes to Switzerland and then to England. Visits Henry at Lamb House, his home in Rye, Sussex, for first time. Lives as invalid with Alice (daughter is at boarding school) in Henry's London flat at 34 De Vere Gardens from October until December. Dictates letters to Alice to save eyes from strain, makes slight progress on lectures and fears that he may die before they are completed, but is cheered when weather improves. December, goes on doctor's advice to take baths at West Malvern, Worcestershire, but condition worsens. Resigns lectureship and asks Harvard for second year of leave. Spends end of year in Rye and improves slightly.

1900   Leaves England with Alice, January 10, and goes to Cos-
tebelle, near Hyères, in Provence. After week in hotel,
moves with British psychic researcher F.W.H. Myers and
his family into nearby chateau, loaned to them by physiologist Charles Richet. Visited by Josiah Royce, who
gives James first volume of his *The World and the Individual*. James quickly reads it and writes to Royce, praising
its "ease, unfailing clearness, its sincerity and affability"
while stating that he "finds the arguments you use as in-
coercive as ever, and the Absolute still remains for me a
hypothesis to be tested by its uses, rather than a doctrine
to be submitted to for its credentials." Receives one-year
postponement of Gifford Lectureship and additional year
of leave from Harvard at half pay. Writes in bed for a few
hours in mornings; starts fourth lecture by end of April.
While visiting Flournoy family in Geneva, writes letter to
the *Springfield Republican* containing translation of French
naval officer's critical account of the American occupation
of the Philippines. Goes for six weeks to Bad Nauheim in
May, but baths do not improve condition and he is unable
to write. Spends summer in Geneva and Lucerne and resumes work on fourth lecture in July. Returns to Bad
Nauheim in late August for further treatment. Saddened
by death of philosopher Thomas Davidson in September.
Goes to Rome in October after doctor advises against
spending winter in England. Continues work on lectures,
writing for two hours in the morning, and makes encouraging progress; sends manuscripts to Henry for his typist
to copy. November, begins injecting new lymph compound (mixture of male goat lymph glands, spinal cords,
and brains and bull sperm) to treat heart and nervous
symptoms. (Pleased by results, later takes daily injections
for six weeks twice a year.) Stays in same hotel as anthro-
pologist James Frazer and discusses religious and psychological questions with him.

1901   Joined in Rome by gravely ill F.W.H. Myers, who dies in
James's hotel, January 17; James is profoundly impressed
by his courage in the face of death. Writes Henry that he
has finished eighth lecture, January 25. Leaves Rome in
March, visiting Perugia, Assisi, Lucerne, and Geneva; arrives in Rye in early April, where James, Alice, and Henry
are joined by Harry in May. Buys new clothes in London
before going to Edinburgh. Gives first lecture on May 16

to responsive audience of 250 and is encouraged as audiences grow to 300, but often has to rest in bed between lectures and take digitalis. Impressed by Scotland's beauty ("the air itself an *object*, holding watery vapor, tenuous smoke, and ancient sunshine in solution, so as to yield the most exquisite minglings and gradations . . ."). Delivers tenth and final lecture of first series, June 17. Returns to Bad Nauheim in late June, after visiting Henry in Rye; writes him in mid-July that the "baths stir up my aortic feeling and make me depressed." Goes to Vosges mountains in August to recover. Sees E. L. Godkin, former editor of *The Nation*, now crippled by stroke, in England before sailing for the United States on August 31. Teaches advanced course on the psychology of religious life one hour per week at salary of $2,000 per year. Despite fatigue and insomnia, writes two-thirds of second series of Gifford Lectures by end of year.

1902   Finishes second lecture series while preparing both sets for publication. Sails for England with Alice, April 1. Receives honorary LL.D. from University of Edinburgh and visits Godkin in Devonshire and Henry at Rye. Gives ten lectures at Edinburgh, May 13–June 9, before enthusiastic audiences of up to 400. Sails for Boston, June 10, and goes with family to Chocorua for summer. Gifford Lectures published in June as *The Varieties of Religious Experience: A Study in Human Nature* by Longmans, Green & Co., and quickly earn international praise (11,500 copies are printed in first year of publication, and sales help James's finances considerably). Delivers two lectures at Harvard Summer School of Theology, July. Teaches course on the philosophy of nature. December, begins correspondence with French philosopher Henri Bergson by praising his *Matière et mémoire* (*Matter and Memory*) as a work that "makes a sort of Copernican revolution as much as Berkeley's *Principles* or Kant's *Critique* did" and sending him a copy of *The Varieties of Religious Experience*.

1903   March, "The Ph.D. Octopus" appears in *Harvard Monthly*. Goes to Asheville, North Carolina, in April to recuperate from tonsillitis. Greatly enjoys rereading works of Emerson in preparation for address delivered at Emerson centenary celebration in Concord, May 25. June, sends Henry copy of W.E.B. Du Bois's *The Souls of Black Folk*;

describes it as "a decidedly moving book" and recommends that Henry read it for his planned American trip. Gives speech "The True Harvard" at commencement dinner, June 24, praising university's tolerance and respect for individualism (published in September *Harvard Graduates' Magazine*). Letter on lynching appears in the *Springfield Republican*, July 23, and is widely reprinted ("It is where the impulse is collective, and the murder is regarded as a punitive or protective duty, that the peril to civilization is greatest"). Goes to Chocorua in July and spends most of summer there, planning major work of philosophy. Writes friend in August: "I am convinced that the desire to formulate truths is a virulent disease. It has contracted an alliance lately in me with a feverish personal ambition, which I never had before, and which I recognize as an unholy thing in such a connexion. I actually dread to die until I have settled the Universe's hash in one more book . . . ! Childish idiot—as if formulas about the Universe could ruffle its majesty, and as if the common-sense world and its duties were not eternally the really real! . . ." Gives five talks on "Radical Empiricism as a Philosophy" at Glenmore, informal summer philosophy school in the Adirondacks founded by Thomas Davidson. Teaches graduate seminar in metaphysics. Resigns from Harvard at end of the year.

1904   Persuaded by Harvard president Eliot to continue teaching reduced course load. Writes Flournoy in June that two attacks of influenza and general fatigue have prevented him from writing more than thirty-two pages of new philosophy book. Visited by Henry at Chocorua for first time in September, at start of his extended American stay; James is pleased by his brother's appreciation of the landscape. Sees several foreign scholars and scientists, including Pierre Janet, on their way to and from St. Louis World Exposition. September, "Does 'Consciousness' Exist?" and "A World of Pure Experience" appear in *Journal of Philosophy, Psychology and Scientific Methods*, beginning series of articles elaborating doctrine of radical empiricism. Teaches first semester of course in metaphysics. November, visited by Henry in Cambridge.

1905   "How Two Minds Can Know One Thing" appears in March issue of *Journal of Philosophy, Psychology and Scien-*

tific Methods. Sails for Europe alone, March 11, and travels in southern Italy and Greece; cries at sight of Parthenon ("It sets a standard for other human things, showing that absolute rightness is not out of reach"). Attends Philosophical Congress in Rome at end of April, and is especially well-received by group of Italian pragmatic philosophers. Writes and delivers address "La Notion de Conscience" to Congress in French. Travels in Italy and France and visits Flournoy in Geneva. Meets Bergson for first time in Paris, May 28, and sees philosopher F.C.S. Schiller at Oxford before sailing for the United States at the beginning of June. "Is Radical Empiricism Solipsistic?" appears in *Journal of Philosophy, Psychology and Scientific Methods* in April and "The Place of Affectional Facts in a World of Pure Experience" in May. Visited by Henry in June before his return to England. Lectures at University of Chicago summer school in early July, vacations in Keene Valley, and gives talks at Glenmore. Ill with influenza during August and is unable to write. Teaches first four weeks of introductory philosophy course and fall semester of undergraduate metaphysics course. Writes Henry in October criticizing *The Golden Bowl* for its narration "by interminable elaboration of suggestive reference" and suggesting that he write a novel with "absolute straightness in the style. . . ." Henry replies by asking that James not read his works due to their greatly different sensibilities.

1906   Visits Grand Canyon on way to California, arriving in Palo Alto, January 8, to begin one-semester appointment at Stanford University. Teaches introductory course in philosophy with 300 enrolled students. Joined by Alice in early February. Delivers address "The Moral Equivalent of War" to university assembly, February 25. During great earthquake of April 18, experiences "glee at the vividness which such an abstract idea or verbal term as 'earthquake' could put on when translated into sensible reality and verified concretely. . . ." Goes with colleague, psychology professor Lillian Martin, into San Francisco in late morning to search for her sister (whom she finds). Sees city in flames and closely observes reactions to disaster, returning to Palo Alto in evening. Writes to Henry, "Everyone at San Francisco seemed in a good hearty frame of mind; there was work for every moment of the day and a kind of uplift in the sense of a 'common lot' that took away the sense of loneliness that (I imagine) gives the sharpest edge to the more usual kind of misfortune that may befall a man." University closes due to earthquake damage and James and Alice leave for Cambridge on April 26. "On Some Mental Effects of the Earthquake" appears in June issue of *Youth's Companion*. Considers writing textbook that will systematically express his philosophy. Spends summer in Cambridge, Keene Valley, Chocorua, and on the Maine coast. Praises former mental patient Clifford Beers's manuscript indicting mental health system (book is published as *A Mind That Found Itself* in 1908). Heart condition worsens. September, in response to magazine article by H. G. Wells, writes to Wells criticizing American "callousness to abstract justice" and "the moral flabbiness born of the exclusive worship of the bitch-goddess SUCCESS. That—with the squalid interpretation put on the word success—is our national disease." Teaches one-semester course on general problems in philosophy. Gives eight Lowell Lectures on "Pragmatism," November 14–December 8. Delivers presidential address "The Energies of Men" to the American Philosophical Association in New York, December 28 (published in January 1907 *Philosophical Review*).

1907   Resigns professorship January 11 and is presented with silver loving cup at last lecture on January 22. Repeats "Pragmatism" lectures at Columbia University, January 29–February 8, with over 1,000 attending. Begins to suffer from persistent angina. Becomes active supporter of Clifford Beers's efforts to organize National Committee for Mental Hygiene (founded in 1909, with James serving as trustee). Visits daughter Peggy, now student at Bryn Mawr. *Pragmatism: A New Name for Some Old Ways of Thinking*, based on Lowell and Columbia lectures, published in June by Longmans, Green & Co. Writes Bergson praising his *L'Évolution créatrice* (*Creative Evolution*) and compares its literary qualities to those of *Madame Bovary*. Spends summer in Chocorua, Cambridge, Lincoln, Massachusetts, and Keene Valley. Awarded $3,000 a year pension by Carnegie fund. Delivers address "The Social Value of the College-Bred" to Association of American Alumnae at Radcliffe (published in *McClure's Magazine*, February 1908). November, accepts invitation to give eight Hibbert

Lectures at Manchester College, Oxford, on "The Present Situation in Philosophy." Works on lectures in December and delivers address "The Meaning of the Word Truth" to the American Philosophical Association meeting at Cornell University at the end of the month.

1908   Ill with grippe in January. Finishes writing six Hibbert Lectures by mid-April, despite persistent vertigo and insomnia and uncertainty about continuing to write in a "picturesque and popular style." Sails for Liverpool with Alice on April 21. Delivers Hibbert Lectures to large audiences, May 4–28 and receives honorary D.Sc. degree on May 12. Travels throughout England in late spring and summer; meets Bertrand Russell and Lady Ottoline Morrell, receives honorary Litt.D. from University of Durham, and tours Lake District, though health prevents him from hiking. Spends late July and August with Henry in Rye, where they are joined by Harry, Peggy, and Aleck. Sends Beers $1,000 to help with costs of mental hygiene movement. Meets G. K. Chesterton and H. G. Wells. Visits Belgium, the Netherlands, and northern France before returning to England in September. Sees Henry again and goes to Devon coast before sailing for Boston, October 6. Has sample of lymph compound sent to Flournoy, and writes that he attributes most of his ability to work since 1901 to its effects (Flournoy tries it without significant results). Has portrait done in oils by son Billy (who is starting career as a painter). Repeats Hibbert Lectures at Harvard, November 6–30, to audiences of 600. December, works on lengthy report evaluating seventy-five alleged communications by the deceased psychical researcher Richard Hodgson through medium Mrs. Piper.

1909   Suffers from recurring "violent" heart pain triggered by exertion or "any mental hesitation, trepidation, or flurry." "Report on Mrs. Piper's Hodgson-Control" published in *Proceedings* of the English and American Societies for Psychical Research. Begins writing philosophy text in late March. April, Hibbert Lectures published as *A Pluralistic Universe* by Longmans, Green & Co. Spends summer in Chocorua reading proofs for collection of thirteen previously published and two new essays, published as *The Meaning of Truth: A Sequel to "Pragmatism"* by Longmans, Green & Co. in October. Cardiac pain interferes with work on new philosophy book. September, meets Sigmund Freud, Carl Gustav Jung, and Ernest Jones at conference organized by G. Stanley Hall at Clark University in Worcester, Massachusetts, and tells them that "the future of psychology belongs to your work." (Later writes Flournoy that although Freud impressed him as a man "obsessed by fixed ideas," he hopes that Freud and his pupils will "push their ideas to their utmost limits.") October, "The Confidences of a 'Psychical Researcher,' " expressing fundamental uncertainty on subject, published in *American Magazine*. Works on articles despite increasing pain, nervous tension, and angina-related breathing difficulties.

1910   Portrait, painted by cousin Ellen Emmet Rand, unveiled at testimonial dinner held at 95 Irving Street, January 18. "Bradley or Bergson?" appears in *The Journal of Philosophy, Psychology and Scientific Methods* in January and "A Suggestion about Mysticism" in February. "The Moral Equivalent of War," revised version of 1906 Stanford address, issued as pamphlet by the Association for International Conciliation. Continues to work on philosophy book. Learns in February that Henry is seriously ill. Asks Harry (now an attorney involved in family affairs) to go to England; his letters convince James that Henry has had a nervous breakdown. Decides in March to advance planned trip to Europe for heart treatment so that he and Alice can be with Henry. Before leaving, writes at top of faculty list in his copy of the Harvard catalogue: "Infinite compunctions cover every beloved name. Forgive me!" Sails on March 29 and reaches Rye on April 7. Stays with Henry before going to Paris alone on May 5 to receive electrical therapy for his arteries. Sees Bergson, Edith Wharton, Henry Adams, and others; treatments are ineffectual. Exhausted, leaves for Bad Nauheim May 17. Takes baths and is joined by Henry and Alice in early June, but condition does not improve (Alice writes that "William cannot walk and Henry cannot smile"). Goes to Switzerland with Alice and Henry in late June, visiting Zurich, Lucerne, and Geneva, but James finds high altitudes painful and breathing difficulties worsen. Learns in Geneva of brother Bob's death from heart attack in Concord on July 3. Returns to London on July 17 and Rye on July 23. "A Pluralistic Mystic," tribute to philosopher Benjamin Paul

Blood, published in July *Hibbert Journal*. Gives up hopes of completing philosophy book and writes instructions on July 26 for its publication: "Say that I hoped by it to round out my system, which now is too much like an arch built only on one side." (Published as *Some Problems in Philosophy* by Longmans, Green in May 1911, edited by his son Henry James, Jr., Horace Kallen, and Ralph Barton Perry.) James, Alice, and Henry sail from England, August 12, land in Quebec August 18, and reach Chocorua the following day. James, in intense pain, has Alice promise that she will "go to Henry when his time comes." Dies of heart failure, 2:30 P.M., August 26. Funeral service held at Appleton Chapel in Harvard Yard, August 30. Body is cremated and ashes are interred in Cambridge family plot.

Note on the Texts

This volume prints the texts of three books and nine essays by William James published between 1878 and 1899. With the exception of one essay, the texts are taken from *The Works of William James*, an edition sponsored by the American Council of Learned Societies and published by the Harvard University Press, with Frederick H. Burkhardt as General Editor, Fredson Bowers as Textual Editor, and Ignas K. Skrupskelis as Associate Editor. The essay "The Psychology of Belief" is represented in the Harvard edition in a revised form incorporated into *The Principles of Psychology*; it is printed here from its first periodical appearance.

The texts from the Harvard edition of *The Works of William James* were prepared according to the standards established by—and have received the approval of—the Center for Scholarly Editions of the Modern Language Association of America. In preparing the *Works*, Fredson Bowers collated all the printings of each work published during James's life and consulted the known surviving letters, papers, and other manuscript materials of James and his publishers. In general, only scattered portions and isolated leaves of manuscript and proofsheets for James's works are known to exist. James's own copies of his books, his files of journals, and offprints of his articles, however, contain many holograph annotations and revisions. These are part of the William James Collection at the Houghton Library of Harvard University, and they were collated against the published texts by the editors of the *Works*; emendations were then incorporated, following James's indicated revisions. The editors also corrected typographical errors, Americanized British spellings and punctuation in the articles published first in England, emended some of James's quotations by reference to his original sources, and corrected and adapted the original indexes to conform to the pagination of their edition. The Harvard edition represents the most detailed scholarly effort thus far made to establish the texts of William James's works.

Psychology: Briefer Course is a condensed and revised version of James's *The Principles of Psychology*. Before Henry Holt and Company published *Principles* in two volumes in September 1890 in its "American Science Series," James had suggested that an abridgment be prepared for Holt's textbook series. By February 1891, Holt was urging James to submit his condensed version for the "Briefer Course" line of Holt's "American Science Series," and James promised to deliver the one-volume version by the middle of the following winter. James finished work on *Psychology: Briefer Course* in August and sent the completed manuscript to Holt. This manuscript consisted of new material, particularly in the earlier chapters, interspersed with revised and annotated pages from *Principles*. James read and corrected proofs from October through December. The index was set from James's note-cards, which he sent to Holt on January 5, 1892. By January 11, 1892, the work had been shipped to booksellers. The first printing consisted of about 1,000 copies plus 500 sets of sheets for the English market. Holt claimed that 47,531 copies had been sold by 1902. A total of twelve printings of the work were issued during James's life.

No manuscript or proof sheets of *Psychology: Briefer Course* are known to be extant. The editors of the *Works* took as their text the first printing (Henry Holt and Company, 1892). This text was collated against all subsequent printings through 1910. Corrections and revisions appeared in the second, third, fourth (1893), seventh (1904), tenth (1908), eleventh (1909), and twelfth (1910) printings. Authorial corrections and revisions from the second, third, and fourth printings were incorporated into the *Works* edition, except for a few revisions made in the third printing that toned down the sexual language. The *Works* editors also compared the first printing with James's own marked copy of the second printing of *Briefer Course* and the corresponding portions in his annotated copy of *The Principles of Psychology*. Forty readings from James's marked-up copy of *Briefer Course* and twelve readings based on authorial annotations in the *Principles* were incorporated. The text printed here is that of *Psychology: Briefer Course* (1984) in the Harvard edition of the *Works*.

When James wrote his brother Henry on April 17, 1896, about a collection of his talks and essays he intended to publish, he had already decided on the title he would give it: "The Will to Believe and Other Essays in Popular Philosophy." On June 20, 1896, in an attempt to get the best return on his proposed book, James sent his manuscript to Scribner's, who had solicited a book from him, and asked Henry Holt to make a competitive bid. Scribner's, after a visit from Holt, returned the manuscript to James and declined to publish the book. James was offended by what he saw as Holt's efforts to head off an auction and decided to try other publishers. Houghton Mifflin's offer was unacceptable, but he liked Longmans Green and Company's offer, and by early December James had signed a contract with the firm. The manuscript, consisting of ten essays written between 1879 and 1896, was probably made up of revised clippings or offprints of the journal appearances. The book was issued in a printing of 1,000 copies in March 1897 as *The Will to Believe and Other Essays in Popular Philosophy*. By early 1898 the book was in its fourth printing of 1,000. A total of twelve printings were made during James's life. Only the fourth printing (March 1898) shows any changes in the plates: two corrections that appear to be authorial.

The editors of the *Works* took their copy-text from the first printing of *The Will to Believe*. This text was compared with draft holographs, annotated proofs, clippings, and offprints of the periodical appearances of the essays found in the William James Collection and authorial emendations were incorporated from these sources. Errors were corrected and some quotations were emended to correspond with James's original sources. The text printed here is that of *The Will to Believe and Other Essays in Popular Philosophy* (1979) in the Harvard edition of the *Works*.

Talks to Teachers on Psychology and to Students on Some of Life's Ideals consists of two groups of lectures. The first, "Talks to Teachers," was based on James's ten lectures in psychology given from notes in late 1891 and early 1892 in the new Department of Pedagogy at Harvard. James continued to deliver the lectures over the next few summers, repeating them at Harvard several times, and also delivering them in Colorado Springs, Buffalo, and Chicago. In a letter to Henry Holt on December 18, 1896, the same letter in which James had informed him of his contract with Longmans for *The Will to Believe*, James proposed preparing the lectures for book publication, and Holt agreed. During the summer of 1897, James again gave the lectures at Harvard summer school and began dictating portions of them for the book. The next summer, after giving the course at Harvard, he repeated it at the University of California, Berkeley, as well as at an institute for Alameda County, California, public school teachers.

The three pieces in the "Talks to Students" section derive from lectures given between 1895 and 1898 at various institutions. Versions of "The Gospel of Relaxation" were delivered at the Boston Normal School of Gymnastics in the spring of 1895, and at Wellesley, Bryn Mawr, and Vassar in January and February of 1896. Versions of "What Makes a Life Significant" were delivered at Bryn Mawr in April 1898 and at Stanford in September 1898. The lecture "On a Certain Blindness" was written sometime after James first read Tolstoy's *War and Peace* in June 1896. Exactly when James completed the lecture is not known, but in a letter from Cambridge to his wife, Alice, dated October 20, 1898, he told her that he had read it "at the Episcopal theologic school."

James resumed preparing the lectures for publication before leaving California in September 1898. In October, he arranged for portions of the work to be serialized in the *Atlantic Monthly*, and on November 5 he sent the manuscript of the "Talks to Teachers" section to Henry Holt and Company, asking that it be returned by the 15th so that it could be given to the *Atlantic Monthly*. James contracted with Holt to publish the book on a commission basis, with James supplying the bound finished copies, and he then arranged for the firm of George H. Ellis in Boston to do the typesetting, printing, and binding. By March 1899 page proofs were completed and plates were cast. James copyrighted the work on April 3, 1899, and it was published by Holt on or after April 22 in a printing of roughly 1,500 copies. A second impression (of perhaps 1,000 copies, in a slightly smaller leaf size) was advertised in September of the same year. James was apparently dissatisfied with the work of Ellis and the appearance of the edition, and he decided to have a new edition prepared. This second edition of 2,000 copies, reset to correspond page for page and line for line with the first edition, appeared early in 1900, and a second printing of this second edition was issued later in the year. James was traveling in Europe while this second edition was prepared.

More than half of the "Talks to Teachers" section appeared in four installments in the *Atlantic Monthly* (February–May 1899) and "The Gospel of Relaxation" from the "Talks to Students" section appeared in *Scribner's Magazine* in April 1899. These periodical texts were set from James's holograph manuscript. The manuscript for the first book edition was made up of holograph and revised magazine clippings of the articles. Comparison of the first book edition with the periodical appearances and the single known surviving holograph manuscript of one lecture ("On a Certain Blindness") indicates that Ellis's firm imposed its own house style on James's punctuation, often changing semicolons to colons or periods. They also regularly changed James's "whilst" to "while" and his spelling "pædagogic" to "pedagogic." The *Works* editors took the first printing of the book edition as their copy-text, corrected typographical errors, and sought to identify and reverse house-styling changes introduced by compositors at the Ellis firm, using the periodical texts and the manuscript of "On a Certain Blindness" as guides. Though some errors had been corrected in later printings, the *Works* editors found evidence of only one authorial correction in the second edition. The text printed here is that of *Talks to Teachers on Psychology and to Students on Some of Life's Ideals* (1983) in the Harvard edition of *Works*.

"Remarks on Spencer's Definition of Mind as Correspondence" appeared in the *Journal of Speculative Philosophy* in January 1878. James had sent the essay to William Torrey Harris, editor of the St. Louis–based *Journal*, on December 6, 1877, and five days later wrote to make three emendations, two of which appeared in the published text. He made two further emendations to his own annotated copy of an offprint and to a copy of the *Journal* he presented to the Harvard library. The essay was not reprinted during James's life. The editors of the *Works* took their copy-text from the *Journal of Speculative Philosophy* and incorporated the one emendation requested by James that was not made in the *Journal* and the two emendations made by James in annotated copies after publication. The text of "Remarks on Spencer's Definition of Mind as Correspondence" in this volume is taken from *Essays in Philosophy* (1978), pages 7–22, in the Harvard edition of the *Works*.

"Brute and Human Intellect" was published in *Journal of Speculative Philosophy* in July 1878. James had sent it to Harris in January 1878 for publication in April. When it did not appear in the April number he asked for it to be returned, but instead Harris published it in the next number. Parts of the essay were later revised by James for *The Principles of Psychology*. The William James Collection at the Houghton Library at Harvard also contains a photostat of the *Journal* publication with three annotations in an unknown hand but initialed "WJ." The *Works* editors took their text from the *Journal of Speculative Philosophy* and incorporated the emendations made in the marked photostat. They also incorporated minor corrections and revisions that James made to passages that later appeared in *The Principles of Psychology*. The text of "Brute and Human Intellect" printed in this volume is taken from *Essays in Psychology* (1983), pages 1–37, in the Harvard edition of the *Works*.

"The Sentiment of Rationality" appeared in *Mind* in July 1879. James submitted the first portion of the article to its editor, G. Croom Robertson, in early January 1878, asking that it appear in the April number. Robertson could not accommodate that request but expressed continued interest. James offered the essay to Harris for the *Journal of Speculative Philosophy* in November but withdrew the offer in December when he was assured by Robertson that the piece would appear in the January 1879 number of *Mind*. James evidently sent an additional installment some time after this, and the essay appeared in the July number. James successively made annotations and emendations in two copies of the essay now at the Houghton Library. The *Works* editors took the *Mind* printing as their copy-text and incorporated into it James's later emendations from his annotated copies, including one emendation from *The Will to Believe*. They Americanized *Mind*'s British spellings and punctuation according to James's own characteristic usage and also emended some quotations to follow James's original sources. A small portion of this essay was used in the essay bearing the same title included in *The Will to Believe*, but the two essays are substantially different. The text of "The Sentiment of Rationality" printed in this volume is taken from *Essays in Philosophy* (1978), pages 32–64, in the Harvard edition of the *Works*.

"On Some Omissions of Introspective Psychology" derived from a spontaneous talk James delivered in London on February 9, 1883, before the "Scratch Eight" philosophy discussion group and later developed at the Concord School of Philosophy in the summer of 1883. Immediately after the latter course James reworked the talks into an article for *Mind*, which he sent off in late July 1883. The article was published in January 1884. James later drew extensively on portions of the article in preparing *The Principles of Psychology*. The *Works* editors took the *Mind* printing as their copy-text and incorporated a few minor revisions and corrections made in passages contained in *The Principles of Psychology* and in annotations in James's own copy of *Principles*, and in one instance they corrected a quotation. They also Americanized *Mind*'s British spellings, placement of punctuation, and treatment of quotation marks and restored some of James's known usages in capitalization. The text of "On Some Omissions of Introspective Psychology" printed in this volume is taken from *Essays in Psychology* (1983), pages 142–167, in the Harvard edition of the *Works*.

"Absolutism and Empiricism" appeared in *Mind* in April 1884. The essay was not collected during James's life. Although it was included in *Essays in Radical Empiricism*, brought out posthumously in 1912 by his former student Ralph Barton Perry, it had not been part of James's own tentative table of contents for such a volume. James noted three changes in his own copy of *Mind*, and the *Works* editors incorporated these changes into the *Mind* copy-text. They also Americanized *Mind*'s British spellings, placement of punctuation, and treatment of quotation marks. The text of "Absolutism and Empiricism" printed in this volume is taken from *Essays in Radical Empiricism* (1976), pages 137–143, in the Harvard edition of the *Works*.

"The Psychology of Belief" first appeared in *Mind* in July 1889. James had mailed the manuscript to editor G. Croom Robertson on November 4, 1888, calling it part of a chapter from a work in progress. The essay subsequently appeared in revised form as Chapter XXI, "The Perception of Reality," in *The Principles of Psychology* in 1890. For this reason, the *Works* edition does not include the earlier text. The text of "The Psychology of Belief" printed in this volume is taken from *Mind*, volume 14, number 55 (July 1889), pages 321–352.

"The Knowing of Things Together" was delivered as the President's Address before the American Psychological Association at Princeton, New Jersey, on December 27, 1894, and was published in *Psychological Review* in March 1895. In 1896 James considered including the essay in *The Will to Believe* but eventually decided against it. A small part of the essay was included as "The Tigers in India" in *The Meaning of Truth* (1909). The *Works* editors took their text from the appearance in *Psychological Review* and incorporated into it revisions James made on his annotated copy of the *Review* article. The text of "The Knowing of Things Together" printed in this volume is taken from *Essays in Philosophy* (1978), pages 71–89, in the Harvard edition of the *Works*.

"Philosophical Conceptions and Practical Results" was delivered as an address before the Philosophical Union at the University of California at Berkeley on April 26, 1898. A surviving typescript at Berkeley appears to have been made from James's handwritten manuscript. This typescript was used to set type for the *University Chronicle*, which printed the address in the autumn of 1898. Standing type from the *University Chronicle* was used to prepare a pamphlet of 24 pages published by the University Press later that year. Four copies of this pamphlet survive in the William James Collection at Houghton Library. Two of these copies were marked by James; one, with revisions and deletions indicated by James, served as printer's copy for the *Journal of Philosophy, Psychology, and Scientific Methods*, which published a condensed version of the essay as "The Pragmatic Method" in December 1904. James, however, continued to circulate the earlier version of the essay as late as 1906, sending a copy to Giovanni Papini in Florence in February of that year. Portions of the essay were later incorporated into Lecture III of *Pragmatism* (1907). The *Works* editor, Fredson Bowers, took the text from the *University Chronicle*, incorporated corrections and revisions from the typescript, the pamphlet, and two of James's own marked copies of the pamphlet. The text of "Philosophical Conceptions and Practical Results" printed in this volume is from Appendix I of *Pragmatism* (1975), pages 257–270, in the Harvard edition of the *Works*.

"Human Immortality" was first presented as James's Ingersoll Lecture on Human Immortality at Harvard on November 10, 1897. James repeated the lecture in Chicago on December 26, 1897, before the Society for Ethical Culture. It was published by Houghton, Mifflin and Company in October 1898 as *Human Immortality: Two Supposed Objections to the Doctrine*, a volume of 70 pages. James read and corrected proof for this edition, and was responsible for changing the title from the earlier "A Future Life." Apart from a "Preface to the Second Edition" that was added to the fourth printing in April 1899, there were no changes to the text in subsequent printings. The *Works* editors took their text from the Houghton, Mifflin first printing and incorporated the "Preface to the Second Edition" that appeared in the fourth and later printings. They also corrected errors and emended some of James's quotations to conform with his sources. The text of "Human Immortality" printed in this volume is taken from *Essays in Religion and Morality* (1982), pages 75–101, in the Harvard edition of the *Works*.

This volume presents the texts of the printings chosen for inclusion here but it does not attempt to reproduce features of the typographic design (such as the display capitalization of chapter openings). Cross-references in James's notes have been changed to correspond to the appropriate page numbers in this volume. The indexes for *Psychology: Briefer Course* and *The Will to Believe* were originally prepared by James; they are reproduced here from the *Works* edition with the page numbers changed to correspond to the pages in this volume. The index for *Talks to Teachers on Psychology and to Students on Some of Life's Ideals* is adapted from the index prepared by the *Works* edition. A new index has been prepared for the remaining essays, based upon the indexes in the relevant volumes of the Harvard edition of the *Works*. The texts are printed without change except for the correction of typographical errors. The following are the errors corrected, cited by page and line number: 39.16, eyballs; 82.9, succesion; 312.19, mantlepiece; 667.18, Hegelian,[3]; 667.39, [3]*Journal*; 1049.15, conception; 1116.7, exit. These corrections (except at 1049.15) will be incorporated into future printings of the Harvard edition of the *Works*.

Notes

In the notes below, the reference numbers denote page and line of this volume (the line count includes chapter headings and captions). No note is made for material included in standard desk-reference books such as *Webster's Collegiate* and *Webster's Biographical* dictionaries. Footnotes in the text are James's own. For more detailed notes, references to other studies, and further biographical background, see *The Letters of William James*, edited by Henry James (2 vols., Boston: The Atlantic Monthly Press, 1920); Ralph Barton Perry, *The Thought and Character of William James* (2 vols., Boston: Little, Brown and Company, 1935); Gay Wilson Allen, *William James* (New York: The Viking Press, 1967); Howard M. Feinstein, *Becoming William James* (Ithaca: Cornell University Press, 1984); Gerald E. Myers, *William James: His Life and Thought* (New York: Yale University Press, 1986); and the individual volumes in *The Works of William James*, edited by Frederick H. Burkhardt, Fredson Bowers, and Ignas K. Skrupskelis (Cambridge: Harvard University Press): *Essays in Philosophy* (1978); *Essays in Psychology* (1983); *Essays in Radical Empiricism* (1976); *Essays in Religion and Morality* (1982); *Pragmatism* (1975); *The Principles of Psychology* (3 vols., 1981); *Psychology: Briefer Course* (1984); *Talks to Teachers on Psychology and to Students on Some of Life's Ideals* (1983); *The Will to Believe* (1979).

PSYCHOLOGY: BRIEFER COURSE

11.4–5   Professor Ladd . . . *such.*]   Psychologist, philosopher, and Yale University professor George Trumbull Ladd (1842–1921), *Outlines of Physiological Psychology* (1891).

13.38–40   Spencerian . . . relations.']   In Herbert Spencer (1820–1903), *The Principles of Psychology* (2nd edition, 1871–73), Vol. I, sec. 173, p. 387: " . . . from the lowest to the highest forms of life, the increasing adjustment of inner to outer relations is one indivisible progression."

20.8   Rosenthal, Goldscheider,]   German physiologists Isidor Rosenthal (1836–1915) and Alfred Goldscheider (1858–1935).

22.8   '**Knowledge** . . . **about.**']   The terms are from John Grote, *Exploratio Philosophica: Rough Notes on Modern Intellectual Science*, Part I (1865).

32.1–2   *Ad . . . sensus,*]   Our perception, when intent on too many things, is less able to grasp matters singly.

33.4–5   Urbantschitsch   . . .   sensations.] Victor Urbantschitsch (1847–1921), German psychologist, "Über den Einfluss einer Sinneserregung auf die übrigen Sinnesempfindungen," *Archiv für die gesammte Physiologie*, 42 (1888).

35.13   Golding Bird's]   Bird (1814–54) was an English physician and medical writer.

38.1   Küss]   French physiologist Émile Küss (1815–71), *A Course of Lectures on Physiology*.

44.22   haploscopic method]   The haploscope is an instrument for presenting to each eye a field invisible to the other.

47.39   H. Newell Martin]   Henry Newell Martin (1848–96), Irish biologist who later worked in the United States.

65.38–66.1   Merkel . . . scale.]   Julius Merkel (b. 1858), German psychologist and associate of Wilhelm Wundt, *Philosophische Studien* (founded by Wundt), V (1888), pp. 514–15.

71.17–18   Blix . . . Donaldson]   Magnus Blix (1849–1904), Swedish physiologist, and Henry H. Donaldson (1857–1938), American neurologist. See also note 20.8.

73.6–9   Sachs . . . muscle.]   German physician Carl Sachs (1853–78), "Physiologische und anatomische Untersuchungen über die sensiblen Nerven der Muskeln," *Archiv für Anatomie, Physiologie und wissenschaftliche Medicin*, 1874.

78.10–11   *Vierordt . . . illusions*,]   Karl von Vierordt (1818–84), German physician, "Die Bewegungsempfindung," *Zeitschrift für Biologie*, 12 (1876), 226–40.

79.13   G. H. Schneider]   German educator George Heinrich Schneider (1846–1904).

81.33–34   Purkinje and Mach]   Johannes E. Purkinje (1787–1869), Czechoslovakian physiologist, and Ernst Mach (1838–1916), Austrian philosopher and physicist. Mach's *Beiträge zur Analyse der Empfindungen* (1886; revised edition translated as *The Analysis of Sensations*, 1914) was a major source of influence upon James and other philosophers in analyzing sensation and perception.

85.27   (All after Huguenin.)]   Gustav Huguenin (1841–1920), Swiss physician, *Allgemeine Pathologie der Krankheiten des Nervensystems. Ein Lehrbuch für Aerzte und Studirende* (1873).

86.11   (after Huxley).]   Figures 32 and 33 are from Thomas Henry Huxley, *A Manual of the Anatomy of Vertebrated Animals* (1871).

89.2   (after Henle)]   Figures 34–36 are from German anatomist Jakob Henle (1809–85), *Grundriss der Anatomie des Menschen: Atlas* (1880).

96.4   (After Obersteiner.)]   German physiologist Heinrich Obersteiner (1847–1922), *The Anatomy of the Central Nervous Organs in Health and in Disease* (translated 1890).

103.28–104.12   Schrader's . . . prey."]   German physician Max E. G. Schrader, "Zur Physiologie des Vogelgehirns," *Archiv für die gesammte Physiologie*, 44 (1888), 230–31.

106.31–107.6   And Goltz . . . alone.]   German physiologist Friedrich Leopold Goltz's experiments on dogs were published in the *Archiv für die gesammte Physiologie* from 1876 to 1892, and the first four were reprinted in *Über die Verrichtungen des Grosshirns: Gesammelte Abhandlungen* (1881). This passage is restored to its original form. Later printings toned down the sexual language.

107.1–2   *per . . . nefas*,]   By right means or wrong.

110.8   Mr. Grant Allen]   Grant Blairfindie Allen (1848–99), Canadian-born naturalist, philosopher, and author.

111.14–19   "All . . . made."]   John Hughlings Jackson, "On Epilepsies and on the After Effects of Epileptic Discharges," *West Riding Lunatic Asylum Medical Reports*, 6 (1876).

111.19–21   Meynert . . . body.]   Theodor Meynert (1833–92), a psychiatrist working in Austria, *Psychiatry: A Clinical Treatise on Diseases of the Fore-Brain* (translated 1885).

112.11–14   from Schäfer . . . Starr,]   British physiologists Edward A. Schafer (Schäfer, Sharpey-Schafer) (1850–1935) and Victor A. Haden Horsley (1857–1916), "A Record of Experiments upon the Functions of the Cerebral Cortex," *Philosophical Transactions of the Royal Society*, series B, 179 (1888), pp. 6, 10. American neurologist Moses Allen Starr (1854–1932), *Familiar Forms of Nervous Disease* (2nd ed., 1891), p. 94.

116.3–7   Schäfer . . . cortex.]   Edward A. Schafer, "On Electrical Excitation of the Occipital Lobe and Adjacent Parts of the Monkey's Brain," *Proceedings of the Royal Society of London*, 43 (1888), and German physiologist Hermann Munk (1839–1912), "Of the Visual Area of the Cerebral Cortex, and Its Relation to Eye Movements," *Brain*, 13 (1890).

117.1   after Seguin.]   Edward Constant Seguin (1843–98), "A Contribution to the Pathology of Hemianopsia of Central Origin (Cortex-Hemianopsia)," *Journal of Nervous and Mental Disease*, 13 (January 1886).

119.3–4   latest statistical . . . Starr.]   "The Pathology of Sensory Aphasia, with an Analysis of Fifty Cases in which Broca's Centre Was not Diseased," *Brain*, 12 (July 1889).

120.14   *pro tanto*]   As far as that goes.

120.23–24   Naunyn,]   German physician Bernard Naunyn (1839–1925).

121.3   from Ross,]   British physician James Ross (1837–92), *On Aphasia: Being a Contribution to the Subject of the Dissolution of Speech from Cerebral Disease* (1887).

122.12   Marique, . . . Paneth]   Belgian physician Joseph M. Marique (b. 1856), and Austrian physiologists Sigmund Exner (1846–1926) and Joseph Paneth (1857–90).

124.17   Matteuci]   Italian physicist Carlo Matteuci (1811–68), who investigated the physiological effects of electricity.

125.4   *'eripuit cœlo fulmen,'*]   "He snatched the thunderbolt from heaven," epigram written by Anne-Robert-Jacques Turgot in honor of Benjamin Franklin and used on many portraits and sculptures of him, including a bust by French sculptor Jean Antoine Houdon. (It continues: *"mox sceptra tyrannis,"* which means: "then the sceptre from tyrants.")

125.36   Hipp's]   German-born inventor Matthäus Hipp (1813–93).

127.23   Herzen).]   Swiss physiologist Alexandre Herzen (1839–1906).

128.39   *einfache Wahlmethode,*]   Single-choice method.

129.25–28   "We do . . . evident."]   "The Time Taken Up by Cerebral Operations," *Mind*, II (1886), by James McKeen Cattell

130.15–131.13   "I pasted . . . name."]   "The Time it Takes to See and Name Objects," *Mind*, II (January 1886).

131.14–33   Dr. Romanes . . . readers."]   George Romanes, *Mental Evolution in Animals* (1883), pp. 136–37.

132.23–26   "Brücke . . . sound."]   George Lewes, *The Physical Basis of Mind* (1877), pp. 478–79, referring to Ernst von Brücke's *Vorlesungen über Physiologie*.

132.26–31   "Dr. Allen . . . movements."]   Scottish biologist Allen Thomson (1809–84), quoted from Romanes; see note 131.14–33; p. 163.

133.7–134.9   Mosso, . . . emotion.]   Examples are taken from Italian physiologist Angelo Mosso (1846–1910), working in the Leipzig laboratory of physiologist Carl Friedrich Ludwig (1816–95). Cf. *La Paura* (1884) and *Über den Kreislauf des Blutes im menschlichen Gehirn* (1881).

134.12   Dr. J. S. Lombard]   Josiah Stickney Lombard, an American physician.

134.32   Dr. Amidon]   Royal Wells Amidon (b. 1853), an American neurologist.

135.6   *'Ohne . . . Gedanke,'*]   "Without phosphorus, no thought," ascribed to Dutch physiologist and philosopher Jacob Moleschott (1822–93).

135.12   Wasser . . . Kochsalz,]   Water . . . salt.

135.15–16   a saying . . . Agassiz,]   Louis Agassiz was one of James's teachers at Harvard. In "Answers to Correspondents," *Sketches New and Old* (1875), Mark Twain writes: " 'Young Author' — Yes, Agassiz *does* recommend authors to eat fish, because the phosphorus in it makes brains. But I cannot help you to make a decision about the amount you need to eat — at least, not with certainty. If the specimen composition you send is about your fair usual average, I should judge that perhaps a couple of whales would be all you would want for the present. Not the largest kind, but simply good, middling-sized whales."

138.22–35   Léon . . . time."]   French writer Léon Dumont (1837–77), "De l'habitude," *Revue Philosophique*, 1 (April 1876).

138.36–37   *locus minoris resistentiæ*,]   Place of least resistance.

140.31   Dr. Maudsley]   Henry Maudsley (1835–1918), English physiologist.

143.39–144.25   "it is doubtful . . . *go on*."]   *Der menschliche Wille vom Standpunkte der neueren Entwickelungstheorien (Des "Darwinismus")* (1882), pp. 447–48, 439–40. See note 79.13.

144.34–40   "There . . . structure."]   Thomas Henry Huxley in *Lessons in Elementary Physiology* (1866), p. 286.

146.35   Professor Bain's . . . Habits"]   Alexander Bain, *The Emotions and the Will* (3rd edition, 1875).

147.32–34   Goethe . . . hands!"]   Julius Baumann relates the anecdote in *Handbuch der Moral nebst Abriss der Rechtsphilosophie* (1879), according to James in *The Principles of Psychology*.

148.36–37   A 'character,' . . . will']   *A System of Logic, Ratiocinative and Inductive* (8th edition, 1872), Vol. II, p. 429. Mill is quoting Novalis.

150.40   Jefferson's play]   *Rip Van Winkle* (1865) by Dionysius L. Boucicalt, with frequent revisions in the title role by Joseph Jefferson, who starred in it for years. (Boucicalt actually rewrote Jefferson's own version of the Washington Irving story, after its unsuccessful production in 1859.)

157.30   'pass . . . again.']   Ralph Waldo Emerson, "Brahma" (1857).

161.18   *extra mentem*,]   Outside the mind; beyond the mind or intellect or reasoning.

161.27   *actus purus*]   Pure act.

161.33   in rerum naturâ,]   In the nature of things; in the realm of actuality.

166.2   'mix . . . lights']   Tennyson, "Mixt their dim lights like life and death," *In Memoriam,* XCV, 63.

173.1–2   as Lotze . . . says,]   *Mikrokosmus* (1856–58).

181.27–30   Thackeray . . . arm.]   Cf. *The Book of Snobs* (1846–48), Ch. 3.

182.4–5   '*Ça me connaît,*']   'It knows me.'

184.9   *crede experto*]   Believe one who has had the experience.

184.19–23   Carlyle . . . begin.' "]   *Sartor Resartus: The Life and Opinions of Herr Teufelsdröckh* (1833–34).

184.38–185.10   "I must . . . die."]   *The Discourses* in *The Works of Epictetus* (translated by Thomas Wentworth Higginson, 1866).

185.33   *Nil . . . alienum.*]   Nothing human is alien to me.

186.8–9   Marcus Aurelius, . . . wishest,"]   *Thoughts*, Bk. IV, sec. 23.

187.2   Herr Horwicz]   Adolph Horwicz (1851–94), German philosopher.

188.26   *Socius*]   Sharer, comrade, companion.

189.10–11   "If gods . . . for it,"]   *Thoughts*, Bk. VII, sec. 41.

192.13–18   "There . . . idea?"]   *Analysis of the Phenomena of the Human Mind* (1869 edition, edited by John Stuart Mill, with notes by Alexander Bain, Andrew Findlater, George Grote, and J. S. Mill), Vol. I, p. 264.

201.23–36   "It is . . . contradiction."]   *Les Maladies de la mémoire* (1881), pp. 84–85.

202.16–17   quotes . . . Krishaber]   From a journal of observations by French physician Maurice Krishaber (1836–83).

204.8–9   case . . . Dr. Azam]   "Amnésie périodique, ou doublement de la vie," *Revue Scientifique* (May 20, 1876), and *Hypnotisme, double conscience et altérations de la personnalité* (1887) by Eugène Azam (1822–99).

204.30–206.7   "Léonie . . . her.' "]   *L'Automatisme psychologique: Essai de psychologie expérimentale sur les formes inférieures de l'activité humaine* (1889).

207.30   medium]   Leonora Piper (1859–1950).

211.15–16   *pensée . . . tête*]   Thought from the back of the mind (literally, from behind the head).

211.39–212.4   "The sentence . . . distinct."]   "Über die Trägheit der Netzhaut und des Sehcentrums," *Philosophische Studien*, 3 (1885).

212.19   M. Paulhan]   French physiologist Frédéric Paulhan (1856–1931). The quotations below are from "La Simultanéité des actes psychiques," *Revue Scientifique*, 39 (May 28, 1887).

214.37–215.28   "How . . . place."]   *Psychologie als Wissenschaft* (1824–25), Vol. II, sec. 128, pp. 225–26.

218.8–26   "I find . . . away."]   *Handbuch der physiologischen Optik* (1867), p. 770. Italicization is by James.

220.1 *compos sui*] In control of oneself; self-controlled.

221.8–36 "When . . . backwards."] *Elemente der Psychophysik* (1860), Vol. II, pp. 475–76.

224.10–23 "If . . . ear."] *Die Lehre von den Tonempfindungen, als physiologische Grundlage für die Theorie der Musik* (3rd edition, 1870), pp. 85–88.

224.25–225.3 "The same . . . intent."] *Grundzüge der physiologischen Psychologie* (2nd edition, 1880), Vol. II, pp. 208–09.

225.13–19 "In pictures . . . out."] See note 218.8–26; p. 741.

225.21–28 "It is . . . *appear*."] *Popular Lectures on Scientific Subjects* (translated 1873). James's italics.

225.39–40 '*pas . . . nous,*'] "No place, Rhone, but us."

227.16 Herbartian . . . '*Apperceptionsmasse*'] Group, or mass, of apperceptions. See note 214.37–215.28; Vol. II, p. 209 ff.

229.11 *entia rationis*] Rational entities; things which have existence only as an object of reason.

231.28 *quæsitum*] Object of a search, answer to a problem.

237.39–238.2 agreeing . . . time.] Cf. *The Odyssey*, Bk. XV, and *Inferno*, Canto V.

240.26–37 Dr. Martineau . . . so on."] James Martineau (1805–1900), English philosopher, *Essays, Philosophical and Theological* (1866), pp. 271–72.

246.2 "Locksley Hall"] By Tennyson (1842).

248.7 Hamilton . . . 'redintegration'] Scottish philosopher William Hamilton (1788–1856), *Lectures on Metaphysics and Logic* (posthumously published, 1859–60), Vol. II, p. 238.

250.15–25 "Two . . . object."] English philosopher Shadworth Hollway Hodgson (1832–1912), *Time and Space: A Metaphysical Essay* (1865), pp. 266–67.

251.2–9 resolution . . . Bayard] Legal-tender notes, or greenbacks, issued in 1862 and not redeemable in gold, were made redeemable by the specie resumption act of 1875 (effective January 1, 1879). On December 3, 1879, Thomas F. Bayard, a Democratic senator from Delaware and a staunch anti-inflationist, introduced a resolution in the Senate to withdraw the legal-tender power of the $346 million in greenbacks still in circulation. The proposal was defeated in early 1880.

251.35–252.12 "The interesting . . . redintegration."] See note 250.15–25; pp. 267–68.

252.27   The sight . . . book] *System der kritischen Philosophie* (1874–75) by
Carl Theodor Göring (1841–79). The suicide by drowning is mentioned by
Granville Stanley Hall in a letter dated "Leipzig, December 27."

255.7   Sir William Hamilton relates,] See note 248.7; Vol. I, pp. 352–53.

262.35–36   "The Four . . . Inquiry."] See note 148.36–37; Vol. I, Bk. III,
Ch. 8.

265.12–13   *ex abrupto*] All of a sudden; out of the blue.

266.7–9   poet . . . moi,"] Nicolas Boileau-Despréaux, "Épitre III,"
quoted in *Time and Space*: "The moment in which I speak is already far from
me."

267.14–15   "to hear . . . doom."] Tennyson, "The Mystic."

267.35–36   Wundt . . . consciousness.] See note 224.25–225.3; Vol. II,
p. 263.

270.18–20   The sensation . . . present.] Czechoslovakian psychologist
and philosopher Wilhelm Volkmann (1822–77), *Lehrbuch der Psychologie* (2nd
edition, 1875–76), Vol. II, p. 26.

274.4–275.6   "There is," . . . formed."] See note 192.13–18; Vol. I, pp.
322–24.

283.1   Loisette] Alphonse Loisette, pseudonym of lecturer and writer
Marcus Dwight Larrowe (b. 1832).

283.26–29   Dr. Wigan . . . fact.] Arthur Ladbroke Wigan, English physician, *The Duality of the Mind* (1844).

284.4–7   Prof. Lazarus . . . experience.] Moritz Lazarus (1824–1903),
German psychologist, "Zur Lehre von den Sinnestäuschungen," *Zeitschrift für
Völkerpsychologie und Sprachwissenschaft*, 5 (1868).

284.17–24   "We thus . . . life."] See note 201.23–36; pp. 45–46.

286.11–13   In Locke's . . . idea."] Cf. *An Essay Concerning Human Understanding* (1853), Bk. II, Ch. 25, sec. 9. The quotation was in *The Principles of
Psychology*, but was not included in *Psychology: Briefer Course*.

286.31–34   Locke . . . once."] See note 286.11–13; Bk. IV, Ch. 7, sec. 9.

286.34–287.2   Berkeley . . . or no."] George Berkeley, *A Treatise Concerning the Principles of Human Knowledge* (1874), Introduction, sec. 13, p. 182.

288.24   (La Fontaine . . . iv.)] *Fables*, "Le Pouvoir des fables," i.e., "The
Power of Fables," beginnings of lines 45–52.

289.34–290.17   "*appears* . . . completely."] *La Psychologie du raisonne-
ment: Recherches expérimentales par l'hypnotisme* (1886), pp. 25–26.

290.5   *Vous, . . . même,*] "You who are the theater itself."

290.18–40   Professor Stricker . . . them."]   Salomon Stricker (1834–98), Hungarian physiologist, *Studien über die Bewegungsvorstellungen* (1882), p. 6.

291.6–7   proposed by Stricker]   *Studien über die Sprachvorstellungen* (1880).

291.16–17   "a *supressed* . . . speech."]   *The Senses and the Intellect* (1855), p. 339.

291.30–35   "An educated . . . days."]   German psychologist Georg Hermann Meyer (1815–92), *Untersuchungen über die Physiologie der Nervenfaser* (1843), p. 233.

291.40–292.4   Dr. Franz . . . objects."]   German physician J. C. August Franz, "Memoir of the Case of a Gentleman Born Blind, and Successfully Operated upon in the 18th Year of His Age, with Physiological Observations and Experiments," *Philosophical Transactions of the Royal Society of London*, 131 (1841).

292.14–15   case . . . Charcot in 1883.]   In *Principles of Psychology*, "Imagination," James's footnote reads: "*Progrès Medical*, 21 juillet [July]. I abridge from the German report of the case in [Hermann] Wilbrand, *Die Seelenblindheit* (1887)."

294.2–6   "Were . . . alive."]   *Die Willenshandlung* (1888), p. 139.

294.23   M. Charles Féré]   French psychiatrist (1825–1907).

297.7–8   *gazouillement des oiseaux*—]   Chirping, or warbling, of birds.

300.30–301.7   Aristotle. . . . space."]   "Sense of Doubleness with Crossed Fingers," *Mind*, 1 (January 1876); Robertson cites Aristotle, *Metaphysics*, 1011a.

301.23   *pseudoscope*]   An optical instrument containing two reflecting prisms that can be adjusted to produce an apparant reversal of the convexity or concavity of an object.

306.24   *avant-courier*]   Forerunner, harbinger.

311.30   Dr. Kandinsky]   Russian psychiatrist Victor Kandinsky (1849–99).

312.10–11   Edmund Gurney]   See "What Psychical Research Has Accomplished," pp. 689–90 in this volume.

317.12–14   "He saw . . . large."]   See note 291.40–292.4.

317.15–19   'Glowing' . . . flame."]   "Der Raumsinn und die Bewegungen des Auges" in *Handbuch der Physiologie* (1879), ed. Ludwig Hermann.

323.38   what Ruskin . . . eye']   *The Elements of Drawing*, letter 1, sec. 5.

326.15   'in the fund of the eye,']   George Berkeley, *An Essay towards a New Theory of Vision* (1709). The fundus is the back part of the globe of the eye; the part farthest away from the opening.

334.15–16   Mr. Warner . . . Adirondack story,]   Charles Dudley Warner, "How I Killed a Bear," *In the Wilderness* (1878).

340.4–5   *ab intra . . . extra*]   From within . . . from without.

347.27–31   "According . . . viscera."]   See note 146.35; p. 4.

348.31   Herr Schneider . . . show,]   See page 79 and note 79.13.

361.15–16   'Obstupui, . . . hæsit.']   "I was astounded, my hair stood on end, and my voice stuck in my throat." (Virgil, *Aeneid*, Bk. II, l. 774.)

361.25   *huc . . . pererrat.*]   *Aeneid*, Bk. IV, l. 363: "Her eyes rolled this way and that way, wandering over all of him."

361.31   The Rev. Mr. Hagenauer]   The missionary F. A. Hagenauer was one of several people who observed the aboriginal people for Darwin.

362.17–37   "To have . . . pain."]   *The Principles of Psychology*, Vol. I, sec. 213, pp. 482–83.

363.13–14   "mouth . . . seized"]   See note 362.17–37; Vol. II, sec. 498, p. 548.

363.28–36   "As the habit . . . age."]   *The Expression of the Emotions in Man and Animals* (1873), p. 176.

364.9–12   "All . . . mouth."]   See note 224.25–225.3; Vol. II, pp. 423–24.

368.29   *selbstverständlich,*]   Self-evident.

374.22   Spalding's wonderful article]   Douglas Alexander Spalding (d. 1877), English naturalist, "Instinct. With Original Observations on Young Animals."

379.26–27   (see *Nineteenth* . . . 1891)]   "Darwinism in the Nursery," by Louis Robinson.

381.9   'like . . . strong']   Tennyson, "The Lotos-Eaters," line 168.

381.18   M. Perez]   Bernard Perez (1863–1903), French educator.

385.12   Dr. Lindsay]   William Lauder Lindsay (1829–80), Scottish physician.

389.3   Prof. A. Strümpell]   Adolph von Strümpell (1853–1925), German physician.

392.39   Dr. Southard]   American physician William Freeman Southard.

405.39–406.3   As Dr. Clouston . . . up."]   Scottish psychiatrist Thomas Smith Clouston (1840–1915), *Clinical Lectures on Mental Diseases* (1883), p. 317.

407.1–2   'sicklied . . . thought.']   Shakespeare, *Hamlet*, III.i.84.

408.31–409.10   Dr. Mussey . . . heart.' "]   The quotations from Reuben
Dimmond Mussey and J. E. Turner are from "On the Insanity of Inebriety"
by American physician George Burr (*Psychological and Medico-Legal Journal*,
(December 1874).

410.6   *"Video . . . sequor"*]   "I see and approve the better course, but I
follow the worse." Ovid, *Metamorphoses*, Bk. VII, l. 20.

411.8   *âme bien née,*]   Well-born soul, person of excellent disposition.

412.38–413.2   *nessun . . .* entertainment."]   "There is no greater sorrow."
See note 237.39–238.2.

413.32   *vis a tergo*]   Force from behind.

415.3–4   *sui compos*]   See note 220.1.

415.5   *voluntas invita*]   Will unwilling.

421.32–422.11   "Let these . . . preparation."]   See note 283.26–29; pp.
141–42.

421.36–37   Pinel, . . . Bicêtre,]   Philippe Pinel (1745–1826) was director of
the Bicêtre, an asylum for the insane on the outskirts of Paris.

425.5   'searching . . . reins']   Cf. Psalm 7:10, Revelation 2:23.

429.16   "L'ombre . . . toute."]   "Shadows gather in this place, and the
night is all."

431.23   *Erkenntnisstheorie*]   Theory of cognition.

THE WILL TO BELIEVE *and Other Essays in Popular Philosophy*

447.32   *Grenzbegriff.*]   Usually translated "limiting concept." (From
Kant's *Critique of Pure Reason*, A255=B11.) Literally an idea or concept on the
border, frontier, or at the edge, limit (of understanding).

447.32–33   "Ever not quite"]   American mystic Benjamin Paul Blood
(1832–1919), *The Flaw in Supremacy, A Sketch of the Nature, Process and Status
of Philosophy, as Inferring the Miracle of Nature, the Contingency of History, the
Equation of Reason and Unreason, &c., &c.*

451.34–35   American . . . Society]   James served on the committee that
organized the American Society for Psychical Research in late 1884; on January 14, 1890, at a meeting presided over by James, the Society was dissolved
and the American Branch of the English Society for Psychical Research was
established.

452.3–4   W. M. Salter . . . *Index*]   William Mackintire Salter (1853–1931),
writer on ethical culture and James's wife's brother-in-law, "Dr. James' Defense of Faith," *Free Religious Index*.

460.17–18   *Cela . . . abêtira.*] "That will make you believe and will stupify you."

461.26–28   "It fortifies . . . Clough] "It Fortifies My Soul to Know," also known as "With Whom Is No Variableness neither Shadow of Turning" and "Steadfast," by Arthur Hugh Clough (1819–61).

461.28–34   Huxley . . . immorality."] English biologist Thomas Henry Huxley (1825–95) in the conclusion to his essay for "A Modern 'Symposium'" on "The Influence Upon Morality of a Decline in Religious Belief" (*Nineteenth Century,* May 1877, p. 539).

461.34–462.10   Clifford . . . evidence."] William Kingdon Clifford (1845–79), English mathematician and philosopher whose views, as expressed in *Lectures and Essays* (1879) and opposed to James's, stimulated James to write "The Will to Believe." The quotation is from "The Ethics of Belief" in that volume.

462.30–31   Mr. Balfour . . . "authority"] Cf. *The Foundations of Belief* (1895), "Authority and Reason."

462.35–36   duty . . . Monroe,"] President James Monroe in 1823 stated that while the United States would not interfere with existing European colonies in the Western hemisphere, it would regard attempts by European powers to establish new colonies in the Americas, or to control or oppress newly-independent Latin American governments, as "dangerous to our peace and safety." President Grover Cleveland cited the Monroe Doctrine in his December 17, 1895, message to Congress on the long-standing dispute between Great Britain and Venezuela over the Venezuela–British Guiana border and asserted that the British refusal to have the dispute fully arbitrated compelled the United States to appoint a commission that would unilaterally determine the boundary. He concluded that it would then "be the duty of the United States to resist by every means in its power, as a wilful aggression upon its rights and interests" continued British jurisdiction over territory awarded by the commission to Venezuela. Cleveland's message caused widespread excitement in the United States; in a letter to his congressman James called it "a wanton and blustering provocation to war." The British government made a conciliatory response, however, and the dispute was resolved by arbitration in 1899.

465.35   *adæquatio . . . rê*] Perfect correspondence of our understanding with the thing; to make equal our understanding with the thing.

465.36–37   *aptitudinem . . . assensum*] The aptitude to force a certain agreement.

465.38   *quietem in cognitione*] Repose in knowledge.

466.1   *entitas ipsa*] Being itself.

467.14   Zöllner . . . Hinton] German astrophysicist Johann Zöllner (1834–82), who researched psychic phenomena and concluded that there was a "fourth dimension," and English mathematician Charles Howard Hinton (1853–1907), who published several works on the fourth dimension.

467.19–20   *consensus gentium*,] Consensus of the people.

471.12   mind-stuff,] According to William Kingdon Clifford, "Mind-stuff is the reality which we perceive as matter, that element of which . . . even the simplest feeling is a complex, I shall call *Mind-stuff*. A moving molecule of inorganic matter does not possess mind, or consciousness; but it possesses a small piece of mind-stuff." (*Mind*, III, 65.)

472.1–2   "Le cœur . . . point"] "The heart has its reasons which reason knows nothing of"; *Pensées* (1670), no. 277.

473.10–12   (as Emerson . . . fox.] Cf. Ralph Waldo Emerson, "The Sovereignty of Ethics," *Lectures and Biographical Sketches* (1884).

473.28   *ad . . . meum*,] To force my unqualified assent.

474.37–38   "Perfection is eternal"] *Discours laïques* (1877), page 5.

480.2   Mr. Mallock's] William Hurrell Mallock (1849–1923), English author of *Is Life Worth Living?* (1879).

480.6   one of Shakespeare's prologues,] *Henry VIII*.

481.1–14   "To breathe . . . last."] *Leaves of Grass*, "Songs at Sunset," lines 25–26, 29, 38–39, 42–43, 53–58. In Whitman, line 58 ends "in the universe."

481.15–26   Rousseau . . . instant."] *Les Confessions de J.J. Rousseau* (1881), beginning of Book. VI.

484.28–485.2   "If suddenly," . . . misery."] John Ruskin (1819–1900), "The Opening of the Crystal Palace."

492.18   Vaudois writer,] Alexis Muston (1810–88), *The Israel of the Alps: A History of the Persecutions of the Waldenses*, translated (1872) by William Hazlitt. In Muston (and Waring), no town "in Piedmont," reads no town "under a Vaudois pastor."

492.40   book on Tyrol.] *Tyrol and the Skirt of the Alps* (1880).

493.1   *Und dergleichen mehr!*] And so on and so forth!

494.15–17   "Does not," . . . honor?"] "The Study of Human Suffering" (*Open Court*, Nov. 24, 1887, pp. 603–04).

498.8–9   Darwin's "accidental variations."] *On the Origin of Species* (1859), p. 209: "I believe that the effects of habit are of quite subordinate importance to the effects of natural selection of what may be called accidental variations of instincts."

501.18–20   "Zeal . . . seas."] *The Excursion*, Bk. IV—"Despondency Corrected," lines 202–04.

502.25   *Binnenleben*]   Inner life. See also page 827.6–12 in this volume.

502.39–503.3   William Salter . . . exists."]   "Carlyle and the Social Question" (*Free Religious Index*, Sept. 1, 1881).

503.12–14   Henry IV . . . there."]   See page 452.3–4 and note. At Arques, France, Henri IV's force of 7,000 men defeated a Holy League army of 23,000 under the duc de Mayenne on Sept. 21, 1589. The story is recounted in a letter from Henri IV to Louis Breton de Crillon in *Lettres Missives de Henri IV, Collection des Documents Inédits de l'Histoire de France*, Vol. IV (1847).

505.5–6   Walt Whitman . . . I am."]   *Leaves of Grass*, "One Hour to Madness and Joy."

505.11–12   *pro tanto*]   As far as it goes.

506.37–38   Hume . . . separateness."]   *Enquiry Concerning Human Understanding* (1758) in Vol. II of *Essays, Moral, Political, and Literary*, ed. by T. H. Green and T. H. Grose (1875).

508.29–30   "Grau . . . Baum."]   Goethe, *Faust*, Part I, lines 2038–39: "Gray, dear friend, is all theory / And green life's golden tree."

510.5–17   Bain . . . gained."]   "Mystery and Other Violations of Relativity," *Fortnightly Review* n.s. 4 (1868), pp. 393–94.

510.36–39   Schopenhauer . . . existence."]   *Die Welt als Wille und Vorstellung* (*The World as Will and Idea*), Vol. I, p. 189 (3rd edition, 1859).

511.36–512.1   "Necessity," . . . it is."]   Karl Eugen Dühring (1833–1921), *Cursus der Philosophie* (1875), p. 35.

512.4–5   *Verstandesmenschen*.]   Reasonable people, common-sense people.

512.16   "thought . . . expires."]   Cf. *The Excursion*, Bk. I—"The Wanderer," line 213.

512.20–23   Walt . . . earth."]   Cf. *Leaves of Grass*, "Song of Myself," stanza 5.

516.4   dog . . . Darwin,]   Cf. *The Descent of Man, and Selection in Relation to Sex* (1871), Vol. I, p. 67.

516.21–22   *das Beharrliche*,]   That which endures. (*Critique of Pure Reason*, A182=B224.)

516.40–517.7   "If there . . . now?"]   *A System of Logic: Ratiocinative and Inductive* (8th ed., 1872), Vol. I, pp. 63–64.

519.11–12   *unheimlichkeit*]   See page 487.35–37 in this volume.

520.2   "Was fang' ich an?"]   "Where do I begin?" (Adolf Horwicz, *Analyse des Denkens* (1875), p. 82; Vol. II, part 1 of *Psychologische Analysen*.

520.19   Helmholtz . . . ear]   *Handbuch der physiologischen Optik* (1867) and *Die Lehre von den Tonempfindungen, als physiologische Grundlage für die Theorie der Musik* (3rd edition, 1870).

520.40   "life . . . earnest,"]   Cf. Henry Wadsworth Longfellow, "A Psalm of Life," stanza 2, line 1.

522.13–14   "He who . . . Destiny"]   Cf. "Greatness" in *Letters and Social Aims*: "They may well fear Fate who have only infirmity of habit or aim; but he who rests on what he is, has a habit of destiny above destiny, and can make mouths at Fortune."

522.17–18   "Son . . . thee!"]   Ezekial 2:1.

523.13–14   *Aberglaube*,]   Superstition. In *Literature and Dogma* (1873), "Dissent and Dogma," Arnold says that what is expressed in "the German word 'Aberglaube' " is "*extra-belief*, belief beyond what is certain and verifiable. Our word 'superstition' had by its derivation this same meaning, but it has come to be used in a merely bad sense, and to mean a childish and craven religiosity."

524.21   *inconcussum*]   Unshaken.

525.2–3   As Helmholtz . . . handle!"]   "The only valid advice here is: have confidence and take action." *Die Thatsachen in der Wahrnehmung* (1879), p. 42.

525.3–5   "Our . . . outset."]   In *Logic* (1870), Vol. I, p. 274.

525.12–13   Professor Huxley . . . immorality."]   See page 461.28–34 and note.

525.15–17   Professor Clifford's . . . evidence."]   See page 461.34–462.10 and note.

525.22–23   "mind-stuff"]   See note 471.12.

525.30–31   "vim . . . sentiunt,"]   "Are more affected by the force of nature."

526.25   *experimenta crucis*]   Experiments of the cross; decisive experiments.

530.8   *status belli*.]   State of war.

532.11–12   *conditio sine qua non*]   Indispensible condition.

539.1–2   *ubique, . . . omnibus*,]   "[What is believed] everywhere, at all times, and by all," the classic formula for traditional doctrine. It is derived from St. Vincent of Lérins (died c. 450), *Commonitorium*, ch. 2: "*Quod semper, quod ubique, quod ab omnibus creditum est*" which means "[That faith is catholic] which has been believed always, everywhere, and by all."

540.13–14   "Vor . . . Fällen!"—]   "Placing oneself before the initiated, / That is safe in any case!" from "Tefkir Nameh," *West-östlicher Divan* (*West-Eastern Divan*).

544.17–20   "Du . . . Wunderland."]   Friedrich von Schiller (1759–1805), "Sehnsucht" ("Desire"): "You must have faith, you must risk, / For the gods give no guarantee, / Only a miracle can carry you / Into the beautiful wonderland."

547.30   Sigwart]   Christoph Sigwart (1830–1904), German philosopher.

549.34   "Vanitas . . . vanitas!"]   "Vanity of vanities, all is vanity!" (Ecclesiastes 1:2, 1:14).

549.36–37   *De Natura Rerum*]   *On the Nature of Things*.

551.30–31   "Ignoramus, ignorabimus!"]   "We are ignorant, we shall be ignorant!"

553.24   "Of all . . . age"]   Cf. Laurence Sterne, *Tristram Shandy*, Book II, chapter 12: "Of all the cants that are canted in this canting world, though the cant of hypocrites may be the worst, the cant of criticism is the most tormenting!"

554.26   Kant's dove . . . air.]   *Critique of Pure Reason*, A5=B8: "The light dove, cleaving the air in her free flight, and feeling its resistance, might imagine that its flight would be still easier in empty space."

555.34–36   *Fiat . . . fiat.*]   Let justice be done, though the world perish . . . science be done.

558.11   "Erkenntnistheorie"]   See note 431.23.

558.25–26   "peace . . . understanding,"]   Philippians 4:7.

558.40   "Gefühl . . . Faust says]   "Feeling is all." (Part I, line 3456.)

564.17–565.8   "Out . . . *world*."]   Cf. "De Profundis: The Two Greetings," II, published in *Nineteenth Century* (May 1880). James added the italics.

566.15   Hazard]   Rowland Gibson Hazard (1801–88), American manufacturer and writer.

566.16   Renouvier]   James omits a footnote that appeared in the *Unitarian Review*: "I am duty bound to say that my own reasonings are almost entirely those of Renouvier, and may be found in his *Psychologie Rationelle*, as well as in the periodical *Critique Philosophique, passim*." (*Traité de psychologie rationelle* is one of the *Essais de critique générale*.)

567.39–568.1   altar . . . Athens.]   Acts 17:22.

570.7–10   "With . . . read."]   Edward FitzGerald, *The Rubáiyát of Omar Khayyám* (1872 edition), LXXIX.

574.24   *Machtspruch*,]   Authoritative decision, decree (literally, power-speech).

577.7–13   "That we . . . Desire!"]   Quatrains CVI and CVIII.

577.17   "The Atheist and the Acorn,"]   By Anne Finch (1661–1720), Countess of Winchilsea.

579.3–4   *quoad existentiam*,]   So far as he exists.

579.13   *quand même*,]   Nevertheless, all the same.

579.20–21   "Throb . . . west."]   "Threnody" (1846), lines 207–08, by Ralph Waldo Emerson.

581.23   ("the saddest . . . pen"),]   Cf. "Maud Muller" (1854), stanza 53, by John Greenleaf Whittier.

585.36–38   "Cet . . . possible."]   "The universe is a spectacle to which God devotes himself. Let us serve the intentions of the great choragus by helping to make the spectacle as brilliant, as varied, as possible."

587.11–21   Carlyle . . . death.]   See note 184.19–23.

588.17–18   "Look . . . worse,"]   Cf. Ralph Waldo Emerson, "The Rhea."

593.35–38   Emerson . . . long.]   See note 473.10–12.

597.25–26   Poor Richard's Almanacs]   Written and published by Benjamin Franklin, 1733–58.

598.16–18   Mr. Bellamy . . . Process),]   Edward Bellamy, *Dr. Heidenhoff's Process* (1880).

598.18–19   M. Guyau . . . ideal.]   French poet and philosopher Marie Jean Guyau (1854–88), *Esquisse d'une morale sans obligation ni sanction* (1885).

601.38   *esse* is *percipi*,]   "To be" is "to be perceived."

609.40–610.1   Mrs. Partington . . . broom]   An incident which occurred at Sidmouth during a storm in 1824 that was reported in the newspapers; it became a taunt against those who try to withstand progress. Sydney Smith used it after the defeat of the Reform Bill in 1831.

611.27   Green's]   Thomas Hill Green (1836–82), English philosopher and leading advocate of idealism.

616.15–16   "qui . . . entend,"]   From the epic poem "Le Régiment du baron Madruce" in *La Légende des siècles* (1859–83): "who speaks to the precipice, and the abyss apprehends."

617.21–23   "See, . . . live"]   Cf. Deuteronomy 30:15 and 19.

619.35   dog in the fable,]   Aesop (fl. 550), "The Dog and the Shadow."

622.13   "tendencies . . . variation,"]   See note 498.8–9.

622.39   *Divide et impera!*]   Divide and rule!

623.9–10   The "inner . . . "corresponds"]   Herbert Spencer, *Principles of Psychology* (2nd edition, 1871–73), Vol. I, p. 392.

625.28–30   Mr. Darwin's . . . neighborhood.]   *On the Origin of Species* (1859), pp. 73–74.

627.4–5   Bob Clive . . . Madras?]   Soldier and statesman Robert Clive (1725–74), a creator of British power in India, twice attempted suicide after being sent to Madras in 1743 as a clerk in the English East India Company's service; he finally took his own life.

627.15   "letting . . . would"]   Cf. *Macbeth*, I.vii.44. In Shakespeare, "will" reads "dare."

627.22–23   *Gelehrten . . . Allemands.*]   Learned people (or scholars) . . . the good, the naïve, Germans.

627.27–28   "will . . . been,"—]   Cf. Samuel Taylor Coleridge, "Christabel," lines 424–26. In the poem "will never" reads "Shall wholly . . ."

628.5   Columbus's egg]   According to legend, while at a banquet, Columbus was asked to concede that some other man would have discovered the New World if he had not. He thought for a moment, then took an egg, passed it to the guests, and challenged them to stand it on end. When no one succeeded, Columbus showed them the way—by crushing and flattening its tip.

628.5–6   "All . . . seed."]   Cf. Tennyson, "The Flower," lines 19–20.

628.31   Manchester . . . Beaconsfield's]   Manchester was the center of the campaign, led by Richard Cobden (1804–65) and John Bright (1811–89), which in 1846 won the repeal of high tariffs on grain imported into Britain. Benjamin Disraeli (1804–81), after 1876 Earl of Beaconsfield, led the parliamentary opposition to repeal of the Corn Law and defended protectionism in the following years against the continuing movement for free trade. In 1848 he gave the name "Manchester school" to Cobden, Bright, and their supporters. By 1874 all protective tariffs had been abolished in Britain.

630.12–13   "The . . . more,"]   Tennyson, "Locksley Hall," line 142.

630.14–16   in a Buckle . . . *climate.*]   English historian Henry Thomas Buckle emphasized the role of climate in *History of Civilization in England* (1857–61); American scientist John Draper discussed the influence of climate on civilization in *Thoughts on the Future Civil Policy of America* (1865), and Hippolyte Taine argued that social phenomena are the result of environment, race, and time in *Histoire de la littérature anglaise* (1864–65).

636.8–9   E.   Gryzanowski   . . .   *Review*]   Ernst   Georg   Gryzanowski
(1824–88), German physician and politician, "The Regeneration of Italy."

639.4–6   independents . . . republican party]   Disenchantment with corruption in the Grant administration and the growing power of machine
organizations within the party led many Republicans in the 1870s to focus on
the need for civil service reform and honest government. Many reformers
supported Horace Greeley, the Liberal Republican nominee who unsuccess-
fully opposed Grant in the 1872 election, and the reform movement helped
Rutherford B. Hayes win the Republican nomination in 1876 and contributed
to the defeat of Grant's bid for a third term at the 1880 Republican con-
vention.

639.36   President Cleveland]   Grover Cleveland, a Democrat, was elected
governor of New York in 1882 with the support of reformers of both parties.
In the 1884 presidential election he defeated the Republican nominee, James
G. Blaine, with the support of reform Republicans who considered Blaine
unscrupulous.

641.29–30   *trockener ernst . . . ehrlichkeit.*]   Dull or dry earnestness . . .
honesty or sincerity.

644.4–10   Languedoc   . . .   1872]   Much of the Languedoc region of
southern France was devastated by the Albigensian Crusade, waged from
1208 to 1244 against the dualistic Cathar sect that had spread through the
region in the 12th century. Revolutionary France declared war on Austria in
1792, beginning a series of international conflicts that continued through the
Napoleonic era until the battle of Waterloo in 1815. Among the reformers who
modernized Prussia after its defeat by Napoleon I in 1806 were Wilhelm von
Humboldt (1767–1835), who reformed the school system while serving as minister of education, 1809–10, and Karl vom und zum Stein (1757–1831), the chief
minister of state, 1807–08, who abolished serfdom, legalized the purchase and
sale of land, granted local self-government to towns, and overhauled the central administration. In 1870–71 Prussia defeated France and completed the
unification of Germany under its leadership.

649.13–14   central   . . .   meat!"]   Henry Morton Stanley, *Through the
Dark Continent* (1879), p. 201.

649.38   *en gros*]   Roughly.

650.28–29   *spatio . . . vetusto*]   Lucretius, *De Rerum Natura*, Book II, last
words: "Worn out (or exhausted) by the long span of years."

654.4   as Hegel has said,]   Preface to *The Phenomenology of Mind*.

654.37   *secundem idem*]   Accordingly the same.

656.23   Plato's . . . ideas,]   *The Dialogues of Plato*, translated by B. Jowett
(1871), *Parmenides*, Vol. III, p. 131 ff.

657.36–37   "unbuttoning . . . afternoon,"]   Cf. 1 *Henry IV*, I.II.3–4.

660.5   ὕβρις]   Hubris.

661.30   *credo quia impossibile*]   "I believe [it] because it is impossible." Called Tertullian's rule of faith, it is a rendering of "*Certum est, quia impossibile est*," which means "It is certain because it is impossible" (*De Carne Christi*, 5).

663.14   *notum per ignotum*,]   The known by the unknown.

663.14–15   *explicans . . . explicand*,]   Explaining . . . explained.

663.30–32   "Little . . . man is."]   From the untitled poem, sometimes called "Song," which begins: "Flower in the crannied wall" (1869).

664.11   Hume's . . . causation]   *An Enquiry Concerning Human Understanding*.

665.5   *caput mortuum*]   Death's head, skull; also, worthless residue.

666.5–7   Where you . . . distinction.]   German philosopher and psychologist Johann Friedrich Herbart, *Schriften zur Metaphysik* (1851).

666.9–11   *secundum quid . . . aliud*]   *Secundum quid* means "according to, i.e., qualified by, something"; *simpliciter* means "simply, unconditionally"; and *secundum aliud* means "according to, qualified by, another entity." In traditional logic, *secundum quid* is also a term for a fallacy called "converse fallacy of the accident" (and for its reverse, "the fallacy of the accident"). The converse fallacy is the mistake of arguing from a qualified case to one that is unconditional (*ad dictum secundum quid a dicto simpliciter*); for example, from the particular case "It is not wrong to kill if it is necessary to save my life," one arrives at the general principle, "It's never wrong to kill."

666.28   *hebt sich auf*.]   It sublates itself, i.e., eliminates itself, but is preserved as a partial element in a synthesis.

667.17–18   American Hegelian]   William Torrey Harris (1835–1909), "On Hegel's Philosophic Mind" (1874).

668.11–12   "Stone . . . cage."]   *Lucasta* (1649), "To Althea: From Prison," stanza 4, by Richard Lovelace.

668.18   *argal*]   *Argal* is a perversion of the Latin *ergo*, which means "therefore," hence: "by a clumsy piece of reasoning."

670.20   "All . . . negation"]   *The Logic of Hegel Translated from the Encyclopaedia of the Philosophical Sciences* (1874), William Wallace, translator, page 147 (additions to section 91).

672.1   *determinatio negatio*]   Determination negation.

672.25–26   The Kilkenny . . . tails.]   The story of two cats who fought so ferociously that at the end of the battle only their tails remained is an allegory of Kilkenny and Irishtown, neighboring towns in the county of Kilkenny, whose fierce contention over boundaries and rights to the end of the 17th century resulted in their mutual impoverishment.

672.37   σωφροσύνη] Wisdom.

674.8–9   Lord Dundreary's . . . alone,"] In *Our American Cousin* (1858) by Tom Taylor.

675.10–11   "If . . . wings,"] Ralph Waldo Emerson, "Brahma": "If the red slayer think he slays / Or if the slain think he is slain, / They know not well the subtle ways / I keep, and pass, and turn again. / . . . They reckon ill who leave me out; / When me they fly, I am the wings; / I am the doubter and the doubt, / And I the hymn the Brahmin sings."

676.33   *meum . . . tuum,*] Mine . . . yours.

678.34–35   *sich . . . Negativität*] Itself as itself referring to its own negativity.

678.36   *überhaupt*] Generally.

679.26   *causa sui,*] Cause of itself.

681.15   "mediumship" . . . N.Y.] The Canadian-born sisters Margaret (1833?–93) and Kate (1839?–92) Fox in 1848 claimed spirits had communicated with them at their home in Hydesville, New York. Another sister, Leah Fish of Rochester, began organizing public demonstrations of their mediumship, and the "Rochester rappings," considered a code by which spirits communicated with the girls, became famous in the area. When the sisters traveled through the United States, and later England, holding séances and attracting a large number of followers, spiritualism became a major subject of controversy and investigation.

681.33   *Waverley . . . Companion*] The *Waverley Magazine* (1850–1908) featured the fiction of amateur writers and the *Fireside Companion* (1866–1907), dime novels.

683.12   Prof. J. P. Langley,] American astronomer Samuel Pierpont Langley (1834–1906).

683.28   Stainton Moses] British clergy and spiritist William Stainton Moses (1839–92), who sometimes wrote under the pseudonym M. A. Oxon.

683.34   W. F. Barrett] British physicist William Fletcher Barrett (1844–1925).

683.35–36   R. H. Hutton . . . Wedgwood] Journalist Richard Holt Hutton (1826–97) and philologist Hensleigh Wedgwood (1903–91).

685.35–36   Mr. Hodgson] Australian-born psychical researcher Richard Hodgson (1855–1905).

686.26 *ingenium praefervidum*]   Burning genius.

686.38–39   daughters . . . Creery]   Mary, Alice, and Maude, daughters of Andrew M. Creery, who in 1881 and 1882 demonstrated thought transference. The experiments are discussed in *Proceedings of the Society for Psychical Research*, Vol. I (1882–83), and in Gurney's *Phantasms of the Living*.

687.14–15   Mr. G. A. Smith . . . Guthrie]   George Albert Smith (d. 1959) had a hypnotism stage-act, then served as Gurney's private secretary and as the hypnotist in his experiments; Malcolm Guthrie did experiments in thought-transference.

688.1–6   The subject's . . . may be.]   "An Account of Some Experiments in Mesmerism," *Proceedings of the Society for Psychical Research*, 2 (1884).

688.18–23   For example, . . . minutes."]   "Peculiarities of Certain Post-Hypnotic States," *Proceedings of the Society for Psychical Research*, 4 (1887).

688.28–30   Janet . . . consciousness,]   Pierre Janet, *L'Automisme psychologique: Essai de psychologie expérimentale sur les formes inférieures de l'activité humaine* (1889), and articles of Alfred Binet, in *Open Court*, 3 (1889): "Proof of Double Consciousness in Hysterical Individuals" (July 25), "The Relations between the Consciousness of Hysterical Individuals" (August 1), and "The Graphic Method and the Doubling of Consciousness": (Nov. 7); in *Revue Philosophique de la France et de l'Étranger*: "Recherches sur les altérations de la conscience chez les hystériques," 27 (Feb. 1889), "La Vision mentale," 27 (April 1889), "Recherches sur les mouvements volontaires dans l'anesthésie hystérique," 28 (Nov. 1889), "La Concurrence des états psychologiques," 29 (Feb. 1890).

690.9   American census]   James was an agent of the census in America and his address was given as one of those to which responses could be returned.

690.18–21   *Proceedings* . . . Davey."]   Eleanor Mildred (Mrs. Henry) Sidgwick, "Results of a Personal Investigation into the Physical Phenomena of Spiritualism," 4 (1886). "The Possibilities of Mal-Observation and Lapse of Memory from a Practical Point of View," 4 (1887), with the "Introduction" by Hodgson and the "Experimental Investigation" by S. J. Davey.

690.31–33   Mr. Hodgson's . . . mediumship.]   "Report on Phenomena Connected with Theosophy," 3 (1885), pp. 201–400, containing investigations by Hodgson and others. (Elena Blavatsky founded the Theosophical Society in 1875.)

690.38   Eusapia Paladino]   Italian psychical medium (1854–1918). Harry Sidgwick's account of her exposure in Cambridge, England, is "Eusapia Paladino," in the English *Journal of the Society for Psychical Research*, 7 (November 1895).

691.2–3   Stainton . . . testimony,]   Frederic William Henry Myers, "The Experiences of W. Stainton Moses," *Proceedings of the Society for Psychical Research*, 9 (1893–94), pp. 245–352, and 11 (1895), pp. 24–113.

691.7   Piper]   Leonore Piper (1859–1950), famous medium investigated by James and his colleagues.

691.16   Miss X. . . . Vision."]   Ada Goodrich-Freer, psychical researcher and collector of folklore, "Recent Experiments in Crystal-Vision," published anonymously in *Proceedings of the Society for Psychical Research*, 5 (1889), pp. 486–521.

692.7–19   series . . . reserve."]   "The Subliminal Consciousness," Vols. 7–11 (1891–95); the quotation is in Vol. 7, p. 305.

TALKS TO TEACHERS ON PSYCHOLOGY AND TO STUDENTS ON SOME OF LIFE'S IDEALS

708.4   Boston . . . Gymnastics.]   The Boston Normal School of Gymnastics, founded in 1889 to train teachers in Swedish gymnastics. (In 1909 it became the department of hygiene and physical education at Wellesley College.)

708.29–30   our nation . . . Orientals]   Spain ceded the Philippines to the United States in the peace treaty signed on December 10, 1898, concluding the Spanish-American War. The United States Senate ratified the treaty by a narrow margin on February 6, 1899, despite the proclamation by Filipino revolutionaries in 1898 of an independent Philippine republic. Fighting had meanwhile broken out between American troops and Filipinos on February 4. James denounced the annexation in a letter published in the Boston *Evening Transcript* on March 1, 1899, and became an active member of the Anti-Imperialist League. The insurrection was finally suppressed in 1902.

708.30   *vi et armis*]   By force of arms.

724.1–2   'focal . . . Morgan]   English biologist Conwy Lloyd Morgan (1852–1936), *An Introduction to Comparative Psychology* (1894), p. 15.

734.29   Swedish Sloyd system]   The Educational Sloyd system was developed by Swedish educator Otto Salomon (1849–1907).

741.30–31   Professors Royce and Baldwin]   Josiah Royce, James's colleague at Harvard, "Preliminary Report on Imitation," *Psychological Review*, 2 (May 1895), and James Mark Baldwin, then a Princeton professor, *Mental Development in the Child and Race* (1895).

750.28   (in Dr. Carpenter's words)]   Cf. William Benjamin Carpenter, *Principles of Mental Physiology, with Their Applications to the Training and Discipline of the Mind, and the Study of Its Morbid Conditions* (1874), pp. 19–20, 339–45.

750.32   Habit . . . nature,] Diogenes, the cynic (412–323 B.C.): "Habit is Second Nature."

751.23–753.34   To quote . . . deed.] Cf. *Psychology: Briefer Course*, pages 146.15–147.28, 148.30–149.12 in this volume. This also occurs in *The Principles of Psychology*, "Habit."

752.4   In Professor . . . Habits"] See note 146.35.

753.20   "character," . . . will";] See note 148.36–37.

754.3   Darwin's short autobiography] In *The Life and Letters of Charles Darwin* (1887–88), edited by his son Francis Darwin, Vol. I, pp. 100–02.

757.8–758.3   the physiological . . . together.] Cf. pages 150.30–151.23 in this volume; this also occurs in *The Principles of Psychology*, "Habit."

757.19   Jefferson's play] See note 150.40.

762.30–31   Münsterberg . . . experiment] *Beitrage zur experimentellen Psychologie*, part 4 (1892), pp. 23–32.

763.13   "Locksley Hall,"] See note 246.2.

769.25   Philippine war] See note 708.29–30.

773.30   Mr. Fitch . . . lecture] English educator Joshua Girling Fitch (1824–1903), *The Art of Securing Attention* (1880), published as a pamphlet and frequently reprinted.

781.26   'wax . . . retain.'] Byron, "Beppo: A Venetian Story" (1818), stanza 34.

782.32–783.4   As I . . . memory.] Cf. pages 278.30–279.1 in this volume. This also occurs in "Memory" in *The Principles of Psychology*.

783.32–784.20   We see . . . mean.] Cf. pages 279.1–28 in this volume. This also occurs in "Memory" in *The Principles of Psychology*.

787.13–16   Mr. Galton . . . images.] Francis Galton, *Inquiries into Human Faculty and its Development* (1883), pp. 83–114.

789.8–11   A blind . . . M. P.] After losing his sight, the Swiss naturalist François Huber (1750–1831) continued his work with the help of his wife. Irish politician Arthur Macmorough Kavanagh (1831–89), born with only the rudiments of arms and legs, taught himself to write and shoot with a rifle.

789.16–28   Mr. Romanes . . . readers.] See note 131.14–33.

791.21   heroic little investigation] *Über das Gedächtnis. Untersuchungen zur experimentellen Psychologie* (1885).

793.19–22   Dr. Pick . . . there.] Edward Pick (1824–99), *Lectures on Memory Culture* (c. 1899).

797.5–6   "words, words, words,"] *Hamlet*, II.ii.192.

798.39   Lord Ullin's Daughter] By Scottish poet Thomas Campbell (1777–1844).

799.9–10   "Ring . . . mankind,"] From stanza CVI, "In Memoriam A.H.H." (1850), where *"food"* reads "feud" and *"redness"* reads "redress."

802.5–6   Herbart . . . mass.'] See note 214.37–215.28; Vol. II, p. 209 ff.

802.39   Caspar Hauser] A German foundling, Hauser (1812?–33), who was picked up by the police in 1828, had been locked away from "all communication with the world" until the age of about 17.

803.1   Mr. Rooper] Thomas Rooper (1847–1903), English educator; his book is subtitled *A Study in Apperception* (1892).

804.10   M. Perez . . . childhood,] Bernard Perez (1863–1903), French educator, *La Psychologie de l'enfant*.

804.38–39   Haeckel . . . Protista] German biologist Ernst Haeckel, *The Wonders of Life* (1905).

810.16–17   in dogs . . . Goltz] See note 106.31–107.6.

812.24   As Hume said] Cf. David Hume, "Personal Identity," in *A Treatise of Human Nature* (1739–40).

815.1–6   "Break . . . live."] "The Duties of Husbands and Wives," *The Works of the Rev. John Wesley* (1826), Vol. VI.

821.9   'some . . . ken,'] Cf. John Keats, "On First Looking Into Chapman's Homer" (1816).

821.20–21   "Crump . . . devils,"] Cf. Ralph Waldo Emerson, *Essays: First Series* (1869), "Spiritual Laws": "When we see a soul whose acts are all regal, graceful, and pleasant as roses, we must thank God that such things can be and are, and not turn sourly on the angel, and say, 'Crump is a better man with his grunting resistance to all his native devils.' "

825.12   Lange-James theory.] A theory of emotion developed by James in "What Is An Emotion?" *Mind* (April 1884), and independently by Danish psychologist and physician Carl Lange in *Om Sindsbevaegelser* (1885), became known as the James-Lange theory. (Lange's work was translated into German as *Über Gemüthsbewegungen. Eine psycho-physiologische Studie* in 1897.)

826.23–24   folds . . . away.] Cf. Henry Wadsworth Longfellow, "The Day Is Done" (1845), stanza 11.

829.20   *acquiescentia in seipso*,] "Acquiescence in oneself." *Ethica Ordine Geometrico Demonstrasta*, (1667); *Ethics*, pt. III, definition 5, of "The Affects."

829.29   Dr. Clouston,] Thomas Smith Clouston (1840–1915).

834.31   Thackeray somewhere says,]   Cf. *The Irish Sketch Book* (1843).

837.37   Delsarteans]   The Delsart system of bodily movements, designed to develop coordination, grace, and strength, was devised by the French singing teacher François Delsarte (1811–71).

837.38–39   Mr. Dresser, . . . Trine]   Horace Willis Dresser (1866–1954), Prentice Mulford (1834–91), a mind-cure advocate, Horace Fletcher (1849–1919), who lectured on health and dietetics, and Ralph Waldo Trine (1866–1958), who wrote about mental health.

847.17–18   ejective]   In "Things in Themselves," *Lectures and Essays* (1879), William Kingdon Clifford wrote: "I propose . . . to call these inferred existences *ejects*, things thrown out of my consciousness, to distinguish them from *objects*, things presented in my consciousness, phenomena."

848.14–16   As Emerson . . . experiences.]   Cf. "The Over-Soul," in *Essays: First Series*.

849.10   "Authentic . . . things!"]   "The Excursion," Bk. IV, line 1144.

854.29–30   'awful inner emptiness']   *"Innere Leerheit,"* in the essay "Von Dem, was Einer ist," *Parerga und Paralipomena* (1851).

854.39   *Calamus*]   *Calamus: A Series of Letters Written During the Years 1868–1880 by Walt Whitman to a Young Friend (Peter Doyle)*, edited by Richard Maurice Bucke.

856.26–30   "Crossing . . . fear."]   "Nature," in *Nature; Addresses, and Lectures* (1849).

863.17   zymotic diseases,]   Epidemic, endemic, contageous diseases.

863.32   Armenian massacre,]   Thousands of Armenians were killed in a series of massacres perpetrated in the eastern Ottoman Empire and Constantinople from 1894 to 1896.

865.22   *Was. . . untergehn.*]   Cf. Friedrich Schiller, "Die Götter Griechenlandes" ("The Gods of Greece"): "What lives in song must perish in life."

865.37   Cuban and Philippine wars.]   Tensions arising from the Cuban revolution against Spain (1895–98) led to the Spanish-American War of 1898. American victories in Cuba and the Philippines resulted in Cuba becoming an American protectorate and the Philippines being ceded to the United States. See also note 708.29–30.

869.28   wonderful thing,"]   In Stevenson, this reads "monstrous spectre."

871.23–872.30   Mr. Walter . . . lives"]   Walter Augustus Wyckoff (1865–1908), American author, *The Workers: An Experiment in Reality (The East)* (1897), pp. 60–67.

873.28   Bondareff,]   Russian peasant Timofei Bondarev, author of *Labor: The Divine Command* (translated 1890), which has an introduction by Tolstoi.

SELECTED ESSAYS

893.6–7   half-gods . . . arrived]   Cf. Emerson, "Give All to Love,": "When half-gods go, / The gods arrive."

893.9–12   "What!" . . . *remplace!"*]   "I rescue you from a ferocious beast, and you ask me how I will replace it!" Cf. the conclusion of *Examen important de Milford Bolingbroke ou le tombeau du fanatisme*.

893.17   *Nature*]   *Nature: A Weekly Illustrated Journal of Science*, founded in 1869 by British astronomer Joseph Norman Lockyer (1836–1920).

895.39–40   Unknowable,]   *First Principles of a New System of Philosophy* (1877 edition), Part I.

896.17   author's treatise]   *The Principles of Biology* (1864–67 edition).

902.8   Mr. Hodgson]   English philosopher Shadworth Hollway Hodgson (1832–1912).

902.26   *vivere convenienter naturæ*]   To live in agreement with nature. Cf. Zeno of Citium (c. 344–c. 262 B.C.), founder of Stoicism, in Diogenes Laertius' *Lives of Prominent Philosophers*, Bk. VII, sec. 23: "The goal of life is to live in agreement with nature."

903.11–13   *"Il faut . . . necessité,"*]   "I must live!" . . . "I don't see the necessity."

903.30   τέλος]   Telos, an ultimate end.

903.31   cadi . . . Nineveh]   A letter from a Cadi, or civil judge, concludes English archaeologist and diplomat Austen Henry Layard's *Discoveries Among the Ruins of Nineveh and Babylon* (1853): "I praise God that I seek not that which I require not. Thou art learned in the things I care not for; and as for that which thou hast seen, I defile it. Will much knowledge create thee a double belly, or wilt thou seek Paradise with thine eyes?"

904.15   *ambulando,*]   In motion.

904.22–23   *"Fiat . . . mundus,"*]   "Let justice be done, though the world perish."

904.23   Mill]   Cf. John Stuart Mill (1806–73) in *An Examination of Sir William Hamilton's Philosophy* (4th edition, 1872), p. 129: "I will call no being good, who is not what I mean when I apply that epithet to my fellow-creatures; and if such a being can sentence me to hell for not so calling him, to hell I will go."

904.36   *ejusdem farinæ.*]   Of the same flour, i.e., kind.

908.33   *eodem jure*] By the same right, or law.

912.6–7   recent . . . myths,] For example, in *Comparative Mythology* (1856), *Introduction to the Science of Religion* (1873), and other writings, the German-born philologist Friedrich Max Müller argues on the basis of etymology that most myths originated as stories about the sun.

924.17–18   *ab intra, . . . extra,*] See note 340.4–5.

927.33–37   Helmholtz . . . premises."] Cf. *Handbuch der physiologischen Optik* (1867).

932.2–3   Mill's . . . variations,"] See note 148.36–37; Vol. I, pp. 448–71.

936.30–31   *Coriolanus . . . tiger,"*] From Shakespeare's *Coriolanus*, V.iv.30–31.

938.38   (as Bleek . . . shown)] William Heinrich Bleek (1827–75), South African linguist and folklorist, *On the Origins of Language*, transl. Thomas Davidson, (1869), pp. 48–49.

939.1   account . . . . Howe gives] In reports of the Perkins School, later Institute, for the Blind, which Samuel Gridley Howe helped to organize and directed from 1832 to 1876.

942.10–23   "Ulysses, . . . blood."] *Odyssey*, Bk. XXII, lines 381–89; *Iliad*, Bk. IV, lines 141–47.

942.31–32   M. Taine . . . *heureuse"*] Hippolyte Taine, *De L'intelligence* (1870), p. 44: "singing, astonished, happy, voice."

942.35   an oft-quoted writer] See Thomas Carlyle, *On Heroes, Hero-Worship, and the Heroic in History* (1840), "The Hero as Poet. Dante; Shakespeare": "That Shakespeare is the chief of all Poets hitherto; the greatest intellect who, in our recorded world, has left record of himself in the way of Literature. On the whole, I know not such a power of vision, such a faculty of thought, if we take all the characters of it, in any other man."

947.35   Brown-Séquard's . . . guinea-pigs] Charles Édouard Brown-Séquard, "Hereditary Transmission of an Epileptiform Affection Accidentally Produced," *Proceedings of the Royal Society*, 10 (1860).

951.3–5   Walt . . . am."] *Leaves of Grass*, "One Hour to Madness and Joy."

952.27–28   Ueberweg's doctrine] German philosopher Friedrich Ueberweg (1826–71), *System of Logic and History of Logical Doctrines*, transl. Thomas M. Lindsay (1871).

953.4   *genialer Kopf*] Genius.

953.13   κατ᾽ἐξοχήν] That stands out.

954.34–37   D'Alembert's often . . . vérité."]   Joan le Rond d'Alembert (1717–83), French mathematician, *L'Encyclopédie* (1751), Vol. I, *Discours préliminaire*: "The universe, for one who would know how to embrace it from one point of view, would only be, if one may say so, a single fact and a great truth."

955.14–15   the girl . . . *Easy*]   In *Mr Midshipman Easy* (1836) by Frederick Marryat, a potential wet-nurse for newborn Jack Easy is questioned regarding her moral fitness. Mrs Easy exclaims, " 'Not a married woman, and she has a child!' 'If you please, ma'am,' the young woman interrupted, dropping a curtsey, 'it was a very little one.' "

955.22–25   Lewes . . . passages]   George Henry Lewes, *The Physical Basis of Mind* (1877; 2nd series of *The Problems of Life and Mind*).

956.16–18   John Mill . . . possess,]   See note 148.36–37; Vol. II, p. 4 (Bk. III, ch. 14, sec. 2).

957.26–33   "When . . . illusion."]   The concluding remark in *An Enquiry Concerning Human Understanding*, which is the second volume in the Green and Grosse edition of Hume's work, *Essays, Moral, Political, and Literary* (1875).

958.11   Luys]   French anatomist and physician Jules Luys (1828–97).

958.14   P. Sièrebois]   R. P. Sièrebois was the pseudonym of French writer Prudence Boissière (1806–85).

958.29   Czolbe]   German physician and philosopher Heinrich Czolbe (1819–73).

959.37   *esse . . . fieri*]   Being, existing . . . becoming.

963.32–34   Agassiz's . . . God."]   Cf. *The Structure of Animal Life* (1866), pp. 5–6.

965.29–31   Lewes's . . . forward.]   *Problems of Life and Mind*, 1st series (1874–75), Vol. II, p. 376.

967.25–27   Butler's . . . fly."]   Samuel Butler, *Hudibras* (1662–80), Canto I.

967.40   *History*]   *The History of Philosophy from Thales to Comte* (3rd edition, 1867), Vol. I.

969.12–13   *universalia in re . . . ante rem.*]   Universals in the thing . . . before the thing.

969.14–15   *bruit de cloche fêlée,*]   Noise (i.e., grating rattle) of a cracked bell.

972.33–34   *Journal* . . . Watson] "The World as Force. [With Especial Reference to the Philosophy of Mr. Herbert Spencer]," Part 2. Scottish-born philosopher John Watson (1847–1939) taught in Canada.

973.15   *adspicere*; and the *Machtspruch*] To behold, look at, inspect . . . decree.

973.34–36   The "universal . . . *Naturerkennens*] In his book (1872) the physiologist Emil Du Bois-Reymond quotes, in German translation, from Pierre Simon, Marquis de Laplace, *Théorie analytique des probabilités* (1812), "Introduction": "An intellect that at one particular moment could know all the forces with which nature is animated, and the respective situation of the beings that compose it, if moreover it were vast enough to submit these givens to analysis, and could embrace the movements of the largest bodies of the universe and those of the slightest atom within the same formula: then nothing would be uncertain for it, and the future like the past, would be present before its eyes." James had attended Du Bois-Reymond's lectures in Berlin in December 1867.

976.5–6   "Grau . . . Baum."] See note 508.29–30.

978.12–24   Prof. Bain . . . gained."] See note 510.5–17.

979.5   θαυμάζειν] Wonder.

979.13–14   *selbstständig*, . . . *selbstverständlich*;] Self-standing, independent . . . self-evident, obvious.

981.4   *aliter possibile*] Another, or alternative, possibility.

981.35   The author] George John Romanes (1848–94), using the pseudonym "Physicus."

983.6–7   *Verstandesmenschen*] See note 512.4–5.

983.19   "Thought . . . expires."] See note 512.16.

983.24–26   "Swiftly . . . earth."] See note 512.20–23.

983.39–984.2   Jacobi, . . . rationalized."] Friedrich Heinrich Jacobi (1743–1819) in a letter to another German philosopher, Johann Georg Hamann, June 16, 1783, *Werke* (1812), Vol. I, p. 367.

984.21   Benj. P. Blood] See note 447.32–33.

985.15   chapter . . . work] In a footnote in "Reflex Action and Theism," *Unitarian Review*, 16 (Nov. 1881), which was reprinted in *The Will to Believe* without the footnote (page 540 in this volume), James describes "Reflex Action and Theism," "The Sentiment of Rationality," and "Rationality, Activity and Faith" (*Princeton Review*, 2, July 1882) as fragments of a "larger essay on 'The Sentiment of Rationality.' " A portion of the present "Sentiment of Rationality" together with "Rationality, Activity and Faith" constitutes "The Sentiment of Rationality" in *The Will to Believe* (page 504 in this volume).

986.10–11   *esse . . . sentiri*;] Existence, being . . . feeling, experience through the senses.

986.24–26   Comte . . . past.] Auguste Comte (1798–1857), French positivist, *Cours de philosophie positive* (1830–42), Vol. I, pp. 34–37.

987.16–17   Mr. Sully's chapter] In James Sully (1842–1923), English psychologist, *Illusions: A Psychological Study* (1881).

988.39–989.2   Hume's . . . each,] *A Treatise of Human Nature* (1874), Vol. I, pp. 326–27.

991.21–23   Herbartian . . . *Vorstellungen*] Johann Friedrich Herbart (1776–1841), *Psychologie als Wissenschaft* (1824).

994.3–4   Mill's . . . Mind.] "The Psychological Theory of Belief in Matter, How Far Applicable to Mind" in *An Examination of Sir William Hamilton's Philosophy* (4th edition, 1872).

994.22   *wie . . . ist*] A common idiomatic expression meaning "how he feels, what his mood is."

995.7–8   Mr. Hodgson . . . pre-exist.] Shadworth Hodgson, *The Philosophy of Reflection* (1878), Vol. I, pp. 290–96.

997.13   saying of Herakleitos] "You could not step twice into the same rivers; for other waters are ever flowing on to you." *On the Universe*, fragment 41.

1004.27   Galton's "blended" images] Reference to Francis Galton's experiments in which photographs of different people, projected on a screen, are "blended" into a single composite image; *Inquiries into Human Faculty and Its Development* (1883), pp. 340–48.

1006.29   account by Mr. Ballard] Melville Ballard, a deaf-mute instructor at the National Deaf-Mute College. His account of evolving a system of thought that involved abstract and eventually metaphysical concepts when as a young child without verbal comprehension he attempted to understand the origin of things, people, the world, and the universe, is quoted by Samuel Porter, "Is Thought Possible without Language?" *Princeton Review*, 57th year (January 1881).

1008.4   *Tummelplatz*] Playground.

1011.31   Reid and Stewart] Thomas Reid (1710–96) and Dugald Stewart (1753–1828), exponents of the "common sense" school of Scottish philosophy.

1014.2   *terre-à-terre*] Down-to-earth.

1014.6   MIND] *Mind: A Quarterly Review of Psychology and Philosophy*, founded in 1876 and edited until 1891 by G. Croom Robertson.

1014.10   his article] "Life and Mechanism," *Mind*, 9 (1884).

1014.34   *caput mortuum*] See note 665.5.

1016.19   Anselmian proof,] The ontological argument of St. Anselm (1033?–1109), Italian theologian, archbishop of Canterbury, that God's existence is proved, or necessitated, from the properly understood definition: "God is that, than which nothing greater can be conceived" (*Proslogion*).

1016.36–37   "Im . . . That"] "In the beginning was the Word" . . . "In the beginning was the Act." Goethe, *Faust*, Part I, lines 1224, 1227.

1018.1   *ab extra*] From the outside.

1018.14   Orson] In the early French romance, translated into English about 1550 as *History of two Valyantte Brethren, Valentyne and Orson*, young Orson is carried off and raised by a bear. He becomes a wild man, is finally found by his twin brother, now a knight, brought to court, and tamed.

1019.10   "I . . . Life,"] John 11:25.

1019.22   *Ich . . . anders.*] "I can do no other." (Martin Luther, speech at the Diet of Worms, April 18, 1521.)

1021.2–3   "Mein . . . Lipps] "My here and now is the final pivot for all reality, and thus all cognition." *Grundtatsachen des Seelenlebens* (1883), p. 400.

1022.17   (*Grübelsucht*] Mania for reflection, meditation, pondering.

1022.26   Bradley's] English philosopher Francis Herbert Bradley (1846–1924).

1022.29   MIND vii. 206.] See *On Some Hegelisms*, NOTE, pages 676–79 in this volume.

1023.38   Clouston] Scottish psychiatrist Thomas Smith Clouston (1840–1915).

1023.39   Berger . . . 217.)] German physician Oscar Berger, "Die Grübelsucht, ein psychopathisches Symptom."

1024.4   former article,] "On Some Omissions of Introspective Psychology," page 1009 in this volume.

1025.37–38   A. Marty, . . . *Phil.*,] Anton Marty (1847–1914), Swiss philosopher of language, "Über subjectlose Sätze und das Verhältniss der Grammatik zu Logik und Psychologie."

1027.31   *da . . . Dasein,*] *Dasein* means being, existence; *da* means here, there, or present. (*Sein* means to be, or being, existence, essence.)

1028.6–7   *extra mentem meam*)] Outside my mind.

1028.26   "where . . . dwell".] Tennyson, *Maud*, Part I: XIII.viii.8.

1030.3   'idols of the tribe']   Francis Bacon (1561–1626) *Novum Organum* (1620), Aphorism 39.

1030.33   as Thackeray . . . do.]   In *Rebecca and Rowena*, William Makepeace Thackeray's critical reevaluation and humorous sequal to Walter Scott's *Ivanhoe* (1813).

1032.3–4   " 'tis . . . so".]   Cf. *Hamlet* V.i.205.

1034.1   *fons et origo*]   Fount and origin.

1034.33   πο̂υ στω̂]   Place to stand. From Archimedes: "Give me a standing place (or, place to stand) and I will move the earth."

1035.10   Griesinger]   William Griesinger (1817–68), German psychiatrist, *Die Pathologie und Therapie der psychischen Krankheiten*, (2nd edition, 1867).

1039.1   nod, like Homer,]   Cf. Horace, *Ars Poetica*, 359: "If Homer, usually good, nods for a moment, I think it shame; and yet it may well be that over a work of great length one should grow drowsy now and then."

1041.40–1042.1   *"Die Farbe . . . Züge"*]   "It lacks your color, it lacks your eye, it lacks the heavenly expression of your lovely features."

1042.20   "the bricks . . . tale"]   Cf. *2 Henry VI*, IV.ii.160.

1042.28   essay in MIND]   James's article "The Perception of Space," *Mind* (Jan.–Oct. 1887).

1044.3–4   In MIND ix.]   "What is an Emotion?" (April 1884).

1044.13–18   As Emerson . . . experiences."]   The first sentences in "The Over-Soul" in *Essays: First Series*.

1044.31   *sui compos*]   In command, or control, of himself.

1045.19–22   'At length . . . soul'.]   *The Lady of the Lake*, Canto IV, stanza 6.

1045.38–1046.4   "A grocer . . . wretch"]   In Bagehot's "On the Emotion of Conviction."

1048.15–16   *de proche en proche*,]   Gradually nearer and nearer; by degrees.

1049.39   "Rationality . . . Faith"]   This article by James was a sequel to his 1879 "The Sentiment of Rationality"; see *The Will to Believe*, page 504 in this volume.

1050.21   *Unheimlichkeit*]   See page 487.35–37 in this volume.

1051.11–12   Horwicz . . . *an?*']   See note 520.2.

1051.27   "Life . . . earnest,"]   See note 520.40.

1052.40–1053.1   'He who . . . Destiny']   See note 522.13–14.

1053.3–4   'Son . . . thee!'] See note 522.17–18.

1058.11   Fullerton] American philosopher George Huart Fullerton (1859–1925), who developed a method of teaching that was more an adaptation of the classic Socratic questioning than the standard lecture form.

1059.18–20   *known-as* . . . words?] Cf. *Philosophy and Experience* (1885), p. 20: " . . . what Being is *known as*."

1060.17–18   loose . . . Hume's language,] *An Enquiry Concerning Human Understanding*, sec. 7, pt. 2 (in *Essays, Moral, Political, and Literary*, Vol. II, p. 61).

1060.26–27   Miller . . . meeting] Dickinson Sergeant Miller (1868–1963), a student and colleague of James's, often used R. E. Hobart as a pseudonym. Reference is to a meeting of the American Psychological Association at Columbia University, December 1893. The paper he presented there was published in the *Psychological Review* (Nov. 1895), titled "The Confusion of Function and Content in Mental Analysis."

1066.19–20   as James Mill . . . 'synchronically.'] *Analysis of the Phenomena of the Human Mind* (1829), Vol. I, p. 71: "According to this order, in the objects of sense, there is a synchronous, and a successive, order of our sensations. I have SYNCHRONICALLY, or at the same instant, the sight of a great variety of objects."

1066.22   Gurney's . . . proofs] See notes 688.18–23 and 688.28–30.

1068.39   Dr. Herbert Nichols'] Nichols (b. 1852), a psychologist and philosopher, was in charge of the Harvard psychological laboratory, 1891–92.

1069.13   Wundt . . . *Apperceptionsorgan*,] *Grundzüge der physiologischen Psychologie* (2nd edition, 1880), Vol. I, pp. 218–21.

1070.28–29   *Selbsterhaltungen*] Self-preservations.

1073.37–39   *Principles* . . . colleague] Fullerton, who was using the book as a text for his classes.

1074.22   REVIEW.] *Psychological Review*.

1079.30–31   In . . . *Monthly*] "How to Make our Ideas Clear."

1083.20–21   "the same . . . Browning says.] Cf. Robert Browning, "A Lovers' Quarrel."

1090.19–20   "his state . . . speed,"] John Milton, "Sonnet 19" (on his blindness), which begins: "When I consider how my light is spent."

1092.12–24   *The Conception* . . . provided for."] Royce's address, with comments by philosopher Sidney Edward Mezes (1863–1931), naturalist Joseph LeConte (1823–1901), and George Holmes Howison (1834–1916), philosopher of religion at the University of California at Berkeley and founder of the Philosophical Union there, was first published in 1895 as *The Conception of God*. It was reprinted with an introduction by Howison and a supplementary essay by Royce in 1897. For the quotation from Royce, cf. the 2nd edition, p. 292; for Howison, p. 104.

1098.3   PREFACE . . . EDITION]   This preface was added to the fourth printing in 1899 which was called the "second edition."

1100.18–26   Corporation . . . founder]   The Harvard Corporation voted James the Ingersoll Lecturer on February 15, 1897. The "Ingersoll Lecture on the Immortality of Man," founded according to the wishes of George Gold-thwait Ingersoll, was established in the bequest of his daughter Caroline Haskell Ingersoll (d. 1893).

1101.28–29   Mr. Alger's . . . bibliography]   William Rounseville Alger (1822–1905), American clergyman. The bibliography that appears in the 1861 edition was omitted from some later editions and published as a separate volume.

1103.10   Flechsig]   Paul Emil Flechsig (1847–1929), German physiologist and psychologist.

1103.41   Munk]   German physiologist Hermann Munk (1839–1912).

1105.34   *Ding-an-sich*,]   Thing-in-itself.

1107.22   Stewart's . . . *Universe*,]   *The Unseen Universe or Physical Specula-tions on a Future State* was published anonymously in 1875, but is attributed to Scottish physicists Balfour Stewart and Peter Guthrie Tait.

1109.34   J. Luys:]   See note 958.11.

1110.26–27   "Life . . . Eternity."]   Percy Bysshe Shelley, "Adonais," stanza LII.

1112.38   *Ignoramus, ignorabimus*,]   See note 551.30–31.

1113.1   the brain . . . Berlin professor]   Emil Du Bois-Reymond (1818–96), *Die sieben Welträthsel* (1882). See also note 973.34–36.

1113.39–40   [*Self-Reliance*, p.56.]]   *Essays: First Series*; James used the 1869 Fields, Osgood printing.

1115.14   (*Gesichtspunkte*)]   Point of view.

1119.28   *Kritik . . . Vernunft*,]   *Critique of Pure Reason*, A778–779= B806–807.

1126.26–27   "Revere . . . sky."]   From Emerson's "Threnody."

Cataloging Information

James, William, 1842–1910.
   Writings 1878–1899 / William James.
   Edited by Gerald E. Myers.

   (The Library of America ; 58)
     Contents: Psychology: briefer course — The will to believe and other
essays in popular philosophy — Talks to teachers on psychology and to
students on some of life's ideals — Selected essays.
     1. Psychology. 2. Religion 3. Philosophy.
     I. Title. II. Title: Psychology: briefer course. III. Title: The will to
believe and other essays in popular philosophy. IV. Talks to teachers on
psychology and to students on some of life's ideals. V. Series.
BF109.J28A25   1992   91–58225
150—dc20
ISBN 0–940450–72–0 (alk. paper)

*This book is set in 10 point Linotron Galliard,
a face designed for photocomposition by Matthew Carter
and based on the sixteenth-century face Granjon. The paper
is acid-free Ecusta Nyalite and meets the requirements for permanence of the American National Standards Institute. The binding
material is Brillianta, a 100% woven rayon cloth made by
Van Heek-Scholco Textielfabrieken, Holland. The composition is by Haddon Craftsmen, Inc., and The
Clarinda Company. Printing and binding
by R. R. Donnelley & Sons Company.
Designed by Bruce Campbell.*

THE LIBRARY OF AMERICA SERIES

1. Herman Melville, *Typee, Omoo, Mardi* (1982)
2. Nathaniel Hawthorne, *Tales and Sketches* (1982)
3. Walt Whitman, *Poetry and Prose* (1982)
4. Harriet Beecher Stowe, *Three Novels* (1982)
5. Mark Twain, *Mississippi Writings* (1982)
6. Jack London, *Novels and Stories* (1982)
7. Jack London, *Novels and Social Writings* (1982)
8. William Dean Howells, *Novels 1875–1886* (1982)
9. Herman Melville, *Redburn, White-Jacket, Moby-Dick* (1983)
10. Nathaniel Hawthorne, *Novels* (1983)
11. Francis Parkman, *France and England in North America* vol. I, (1983)
12. Francis Parkman, *France and England in North America* vol. II, (1983)
13. Henry James, *Novels 1871–1880* (1983)
14. Henry Adams, *Novels, Mont Saint Michel, The Education* (1983)
15. Ralph Waldo Emerson, *Essays and Lectures* (1983)
16. Washington Irving, *History, Tales and Sketches* (1983)
17. Thomas Jefferson, *Writings* (1984)
18. Stephen Crane, *Prose and Poetry* (1984)
19. Edgar Allan Poe, *Poetry and Tales* (1984)
20. Edgar Allan Poe, *Essays and Reviews* (1984)
21. Mark Twain, *The Innocents Abroad, Roughing It* (1984)
22. Henry James, *Essays, American & English Writers* (1984)
23. Henry James, *European Writers & The Prefaces* (1984)
24. Herman Melville, *Pierre, Israel Potter, The Confidence-Man, Tales & Billy Budd* (1985)
25. William Faulkner, *Novels 1930–1935* (1985)
26. James Fenimore Cooper, *The Leatherstocking Tales* vol. I, (1985)
27. James Fenimore Cooper, *The Leatherstocking Tales* vol. II, (1985)
28. Henry David Thoreau, *A Week, Walden, The Maine Woods, Cape Cod* (1985)
29. Henry James, *Novels 1881–1886* (1985)
30. Edith Wharton, *Novels* (1986)
31. Henry Adams, *History of the United States during the Administrations of Jefferson* (1986)
32. Henry Adams, *History of the United States during the Administrations of Madison* (1986)
33. Frank Norris, *Novels and Essays* (1986)
34. W. E. B. Du Bois, *Writings* (1986)
35. Willa Cather, *Early Novels and Stories* (1987)
36. Theodore Dreiser, *Sister Carrie, Jennie Gerhardt, Twelve Men* (1987)
37. Benjamin Franklin, *Writings* (1987)
38. William James, *Writings 1902–1910* (1987)
39. Flannery O'Connor, *Collected Works* (1988)
40. Eugene O'Neill, *Complete Plays 1913–1920* (1988)
41. Eugene O'Neill, *Complete Plays 1920–1931* (1988)
42. Eugene O'Neill, *Complete Plays 1932–1943* (1988)
43. Henry James, *Novels 1886–1890* (1989)
44. William Dean Howells, *Novels 1886–1888* (1989)
45. Abraham Lincoln, *Speeches and Writings 1832–1858* (1989)
46. Abraham Lincoln, *Speeches and Writings 1859–1865* (1989)
47. Edith Wharton, *Novellas and Other Writings* (1990)
48. William Faulkner, *Novels 1936–1940* (1990)
49. Willa Cather, *Later Novels* (1990)
50. Ulysses S. Grant, *Personal Memoirs and Selected Letters* (1990)
51. William Tecumseh Sherman, *Memoirs* (1990)
52. Washington Irving, *Bracebridge Hall, Tales of a Traveller, The Alhambra* (1991)
53. Francis Parkman, *The Oregon Trail, The Conspiracy of Pontiac* (1991)
54. James Fenimore Cooper, *Sea Tales: The Pilot, The Red Rover* (1991)
55. Richard Wright, *Early Works* (1991)
56. Richard Wright, *Later Works* (1991)
57. Willa Cather, *Stories, Poems, and Other Writings* (1992)
58. William James, *Writings 1878–1899* (1992)

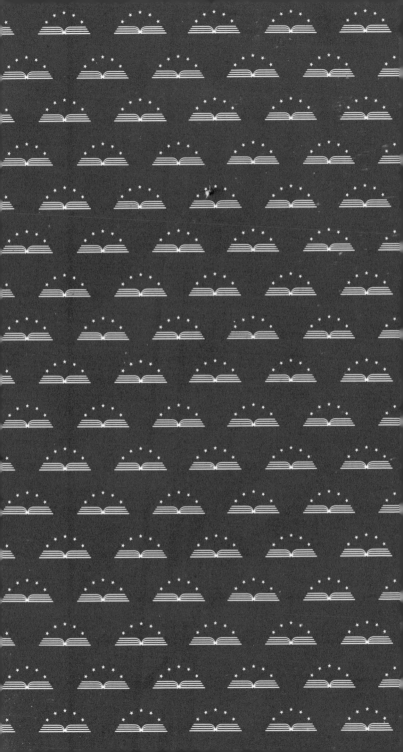